Storage Networking Protocol Fundamentals

James Long

Cisco Press

800 East 96th Street
Indianapolis, Indiana 46240 USA

Storage Networking Protocol Fundamentals

James Long

Copyright © 2006 Cisco Systems, Inc.

Published by:
Cisco Press
800 East 96th Street
Indianapolis, IN 46240 USA

Printed in the United States of America 1 2 3 4 5 6 7 8 9 0

First Printing   May 2006

Library of Congress Cataloging-in-Publication Number: 2003108300

ISBN: 1-58705-160-5

Trademark Acknowledgments

All terms mentioned in this book that are known to be trademarks or service marks have been appropriately capitalized. Cisco Press or Cisco Systems, Inc. cannot attest to the accuracy of this information. Use of a term in this book should not be regarded as affecting the validity of any trademark or service mark.

Warning and Disclaimer

This book is designed to provide information about storage networking protocols. Every effort has been made to make this book as complete and as accurate as possible, but no warranty or fitness is implied.

The information is provided on an "as is" basis. The authors, Cisco Press, and Cisco Systems, Inc. shall have neither liability nor responsibility to any person or entity with respect to any loss or damages arising from the information contained in this book or from the use of the discs or programs that may accompany it.

The opinions expressed in this book belong to the author and are not necessarily those of Cisco Systems, Inc.

Corporate and Government Sales

Cisco Press offers excellent discounts on this book when ordered in quantity for bulk purchases or special sales.

For more information please contact: **U.S. Corporate and Government Sales**   1-800-382-3419 corpsales@pearsontechgroup.com

For sales outside the U.S. please contact: **International Sales**   international@pearsoned.com

Feedback Information

At Cisco Press, our goal is to create in-depth technical books of the highest quality and value. Each book is crafted with care and precision, undergoing rigorous development that involves the unique expertise of members from the professional technical community.

Readers' feedback is a natural continuation of this process. If you have any comments regarding how we could improve the quality of this book, or otherwise alter it to better suit your needs, you can contact us through email at feedback@ciscopress.com. Please make sure to include the book title and ISBN in your message.

We greatly appreciate your assistance.

Publisher	Paul Boger
Cisco Representative	Anthony Wolfenden
Cisco Press Program Manager	Jeff Brady
Executive Editor	Mary Beth Ray
Production Manager	Patrick Kanouse
Development Editor	Andrew Cupp
Project Editor	Interactive Composition Corporation
Copy Editor	Interactive Composition Corporation
Technical Editors	Philip Lowden, Thomas Nosella, Rob Peglar
Book and Cover Designer	Louisa Adair
Composition	Interactive Composition Corporation
Indexer	Tim Wright

CISCO SYSTEMS

Corporate Headquarters
Cisco Systems, Inc.
170 West Tasman Drive
San Jose, CA 95134-1706
USA
www.cisco.com
Tel: 408 526-4000
    800 553-NETS (6387)
Fax: 408 526-4100

European Headquarters
Cisco Systems International BV
Haarlerbergpark
Haarlerbergweg 13-19
1101 CH Amsterdam
The Netherlands
www-europe.cisco.com
Tel: 31 0 20 357 1000
Fax: 31 0 20 357 1100

Americas Headquarters
Cisco Systems, Inc.
170 West Tasman Drive
San Jose, CA 95134-1706
USA
www.cisco.com
Tel: 408 526-7660
Fax: 408 527-0883

Asia Pacific Headquarters
Cisco Systems, Inc.
Capital Tower
168 Robinson Road
#22-01 to #29-01
Singapore 068912
www.cisco.com
Tel: +65 6317 7777
Fax: +65 6317 7799

Cisco Systems has more than 200 offices in the following countries and regions. Addresses, phone numbers, and fax numbers are listed on the
Cisco.com Web site at www.cisco.com/go/offices.

Argentina • Australia • Austria • Belgium • Brazil • Bulgaria • Canada • Chile • China PRC • Colombia • Costa Rica • Croatia • Czech Republic
Denmark • Dubai, UAE • Finland • France • Germany • Greece • Hong Kong SAR • Hungary • India • Indonesia • Ireland • Israel • Italy
Japan • Korea • Luxembourg • Malaysia • Mexico • The Netherlands • New Zealand • Norway • Peru • Philippines • Poland • Portugal
Puerto Rico • Romania • Russia • Saudi Arabia • Scotland • Singapore • Slovakia • Slovenia • South Africa • Spain • Sweden
Switzerland • Taiwan • Thailand • Turkey • Ukraine • United Kingdom • United States • Venezuela • Vietnam • Zimbabwe

About the Author

James Long is a storage networking systems engineer who works for Cisco Systems, Inc., in the Field Sales Organization. James previously held the position of Global Storage Networking Solutions Architect within the Cisco IT Infrastructure Architecture team. During his tenure in the Cisco IT organization, James authored design guides, technology evaluations, and strategic planning documents. Before joining Cisco in 1999, James contracted with AT&T/TCI, Nextel International, and GTE following five years of employment in the open systems VAR community. James has more than 16 years of IT experience spanning server administration, database administration, software development, multiprotocol network design and administration, remote access solutions design and administration, IP telephony and IP contact center design, content distribution design, storage network design, and advanced technology evaluation. James holds numerous technical certifications from Cisco, Microsoft, Novell, SNIA, and CompTIA.

About the Technical Reviewers

Philip Lowden currently works as a storage manager at Cisco Systems, Inc. Prior to this role, he worked for four years at Cisco and six years at Electronic Data Systems as a senior UNIX systems administrator performing production systems architecture and support duties on a variety of host and storage platforms. He was also an officer in the U.S. Air Force for six years. He holds a Masters of Science degree in computer engineering from North Carolina State University, a Bachelor of Science degree in computer science from the University of Nebraska, and a Bachelor of Art degree in English from Saint Meinrad College. He is an SNIA-certified FC-SAN Specialist. Philip is married and has two children.

Thomas Nosella, CCIE No. 1395, is director of engineering within the Cisco Systems Data Center Switching Business Unit, an organization responsible for LAN, server fabric, and storage switching products and solutions. Thomas and his team of technical marketing engineers are responsible for the creation, validation, and promotion of intelligent and scalable designs and solutions for the Ciscos enterprise and service provider customer base. Thomas was one of the initial members of Andiamo Systems, Inc., and helped bring the Cisco MDS 9000 family of SAN switching products to market. Prior to working on storage, Thomas managed enterprise design teams focused on large-scale Ethernet design, server farm design, and content delivery networking. Thomas received his Bachelor of Engineering and Management from McMaster University in Ontario. Thomas received his CCIE certification in 1995.

Rob Peglar is vice president of Technology, Marketing for Xiotech Corporation. A 28-year industry veteran and published author, he has global responsibility for the shaping and delivery of strategic marketing, emerging technologies, and defining Xiotech's product and solution portfolio, including business and technology requirements, marketing direction, planning, execution, technology futures, strategic direction, and industry/customer liaison. Rob serves on the Board of Directors for the Blade Systems Alliance and is the co-author and track chair of the SNIA Virtualization Tutorial. He has extensive experience in the architecture, design, implementation, and operation of large heterogeneous SANs, distributed clustered virtual storage architectures, data management, disaster avoidance, and compliance, and is a sought-after speaker and panelist at leading storage and networking-related seminars and conferences worldwide. He holds the B.S. degree in computer science from Washington University, St. Louis, Missouri and performed graduate work at Washington University's Sever Institute of Engineering. His research background includes I/O performance analysis, queuing theory, parallel systems architecture and OS design, storage networking protocols, and virtual systems optimization.

Dedication

This book is posthumously dedicated to Don Jones. Don was a good man, a good friend, and a good mentor.

Acknowledgments

The quality of this book is directly attributable to the many people that assisted during the writing process. In particular, I would like to thank Mike Blair for his contribution to the SBCCS/ESCON/FICON section, Tom Burgee for his contribution to the optical section, Joel Christner for his contribution to the file-level protocols section, and Alan Conley for his contribution to the management protocols chapter. Additionally, I would like to thank Tuqiang Cao, Mike Frase, and Mark Bakke for their support. A special thank you goes to Tom Nosella, Phil Lowden, and Robert Peglar for serving as technical reviewers. Finally, I am very grateful to Henry White for hiring me at Cisco. Without Henry's confidence in my potential, this book would not have been possible.

This Book Is Safari Enabled

The Safari® Enabled icon on the cover of your favorite technology book means the book is available through Safari Bookshelf. When you buy this book, you get free access to the online edition for 45 days.

Safari Bookshelf is an electronic reference library that lets you easily search thousands of technical books, find code samples, download chapters, and access technical information whenever and wherever you need it.

To gain 45-day Safari Enabled access to this book:

- Go to http://www.ciscopress.com/safarienabled
- Complete the brief registration form
- Enter the coupon code YNQU-PVJQ-4NCS-65PJ-4EA9

If you have difficulty registering on Safari Bookshelf or accessing the online edition, please e-mail customer-service@safaribooksonline.com.

Contents at a Glance

Table of Contents

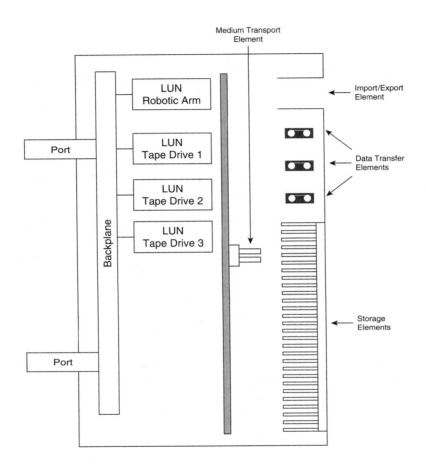

Foreword

It is a great pleasure to write the foreword for this book. Storage networking technologies have been used for computer data storage in almost every major corporation worldwide since the late 90s. Banks, hospitals, credit card companies, airlines, and universities are just a few examples of the organizations that use these technologies. Storage networking gave birth to the concept of the Storage Area Network (SAN), a concept based fundamentally on separating storage and processing resources, with the ability to provision and manage storage as a separate service to the processing resources.

A SAN consists of not only the storage subsystems, but also of the interconnection infrastructure, the data protection subsystems, migration and virtualization technologies, and more. A SAN can have very different characteristics; for example, it can be all contained in a single rack or it might span an entire continent in order to create the most dependable disaster-tolerant configuration. In all cases, a SAN is meant to be more flexible than direct attached storage in accommodating the growth and the changes in an organization.

Several products, based on diverse technologies, are available today as building blocks to design Storage Area Networks. These technologies are quite different and each has its own distinctive properties, advantages, and disadvantages. It is important for an information technology professional to be able to evaluate them and pick the most appropriate for the various customer or organization needs. This is not an easy task, because each technology has a different history, sees the problems from its own point of view, and uses a unique terminology. The associated complex standards documentation, designed for products developers, usually produces more confusion than illumination for the casual reader.

In this book, James takes on the challenge of comparing today's most deployed storage networking architectures. To perform his analysis, he uses a powerful tool, the OSI reference model. By comparing each architecture with the OSI model, James conducts the reader through the nuances of each technology, layer by layer. An appropriate set of parameters is introduced for each layer, and used across the presented technologies to analyze and compare them. In this way, readers familiar with networking have a way to understand the world of storage controllers, while people familiar with controllers will find a different perspective on what they already know.

The first part of the book introduces the world of storage and storage networking. The basics of storage technology, including block storage protocols and file access protocols, are presented, followed by a historical evolution of how they evolved to their current status. The seven OSI layers are also introduced, giving to the reader the tools for the subsequent analysis.

The second part of the book is a deep comparative analysis of today's technologies for networked storage, including iSCSI and Fibre Channel. Each protocol suite is analyzed at the physical and data-link layers; at the network layer; at the transport layer; and finally at the session, presentation, and application layers.

The third and final part of the book relates to advanced functionalities of these technologies, such as quality of service, load-balancing functions, security, and management. In particular, security is an element of continuously increasing importance for storage networking. Because more and more digital data are vital to businesses, keeping these data secure from unauthorized access is crucial. At the same time, this growing mass of data needs to be properly managed, but managing a heterogeneous set of devices is not an easy task. Several underlying protocols for storage management have been defined or are being defined.

Storage networking is a critical concept for today's businesses, and this book provides a unique and helpful way to better understand it. Storage networking is also continuously evolving, and as such this book may be seen as an introduction to the information technology infrastructures of the future.

Claudio DeSanti
Technical Leader Data Center BU, Cisco Systems
Vice-Chairman of the ANSI INCITS T11 Technical Committee

Introduction

The modern business environment is characterized by pervasive use of computer and communication technologies. Corporations increasingly depend on such technologies to remain competitive in the global economy. Customer relationship management, enterprise resource planning, and electronic mail are just a few of the many applications that generate new data every day. All that data must be stored, managed, and accessed effectively if a business is to survive. This is one of the primary business challenges in the information age, and storage networking is a crucial component of the solution.

Objectives

This book has four objectives: document details, explain concepts, dispel misconceptions, and compare protocols. The details of the major protocol suites are documented for reference. To that end, this book aims primarily to disclose rather than assess. In that respect, we give extra effort to objectivity. Additionally, I attempt to explain how each of the major protocol suites operates, and to identify common understandings. Discussions of how the protocols work are included, but you are encouraged to reference the original standards and specifications for a complete understanding of each protocol. This recommendation also ensures you have the latest information. Since many of the standards and specifications referenced in this book are draft versions, they are subject to change. Thus, it is reasonable to expect some of the content in this book will become inaccurate as in-progress specifications are finalized. Finally, comparisons are drawn between the major protocol suites to help you understand the implications of your network design choices. To achieve these objectives, a large amount of reference data must be included. However, this book is written so that you can read it from cover to cover. We have tried to integrate reference data so it is easily and quickly accessible. For this reason, I use tables and bulleted lists extensively.

In support of the stated objectives, we have made every effort to improve clarity. Colloquialisms are avoided throughout the book. Moreover, special attention is paid to the use of the words *may, might, must*, and *should*. The word *may* implies permissibility. The word *might* implies possibility. The word *must* imposes a requirement. The word *should* implies a desirable behavior but does not impose a requirement.

Intended Audiences

This book has two primary audiences. The first audience includes storage administrators who need to learn more about networking. We have included much networking history, and have explained many networking concepts to help acclimate storage administrators to the world of networking. The second audience includes network administrators who need to learn more about storage. This book examines networking technologies in the context of SCSI so that network administrators can fully understand the network requirements imposed by open systems storage applications. Many storage concepts, terms, and technologies exist that network administrators need to know and understand. Although this book provides some storage knowledge for network administrators, other resources should be consulted for a full understanding of storage. One such resource is *Storage Networking Fundamentals: An Introduction to Storage Devices, Subsystems, Applications, Management, and File Systems* (by Marc Farley, ISBN: 1-58705-162-1, Cisco Press).

Organization

This book discusses and compares the networking protocols that underlie modern open systems, block-oriented storage networks. To facilitate a methodical analysis, the book is divided into three parts. The first part introduces readers to the field of storage networking and the Open Systems Interconnection (OSI) reference model. The second part examines in detail each of the major protocol suites layer-by-layer beginning with the lowest layer of the OSI reference model. The third part introduces readers to several advanced networking topics. As the book progresses, each chapter builds upon the previous chapters. Thus, you will benefit most by reading this book from front to back. However, all chapters can be leveraged in any order for reference material. Some of the content in this book is based upon emerging standards and in-progress specifications. Thus, you are encouraged to consult the latest version of in-progress specifications for recent updates and changes.

Storage Networking Landscape

Upon completing this chapter, you will be able to:

- Recount some of the key historical events and current business drivers in the storage market

- Recognize the key characteristics and major benefits of each type of storage network

- Distinguish between file-level and block-level protocols

- Explain the principal differences between mainframe and open systems storage networking

- Describe the basic differences between Synchronous Optical Network (SONET)/Synchronous Digital Hierarchy (SDH), coarse wavelength division multiplexing (CWDM)/dense wavelength division multiplexing (DWDM), and resilient packet ring (RPR)/802.17

- Recognize each storage virtualization model

- Describe how the technologies discussed in this chapter relate to one another

- Locate additional information on the major topics of this chapter

CHAPTER 1

Overview of Storage Networking

This chapter provides an overview of the storage networking landscape. Although this chapter discusses many of the technologies and devices that compose storage networks, many others are omitted for the sake of brevity. The discussion of each topic enlightens rather than educates, because you should have some experience with storage and networks. The goal of this chapter is to provide a context for the discussions that follow in subsequent chapters.

Pervasive use of computer and communication technologies characterizes the modern business environment. Corporations increasingly depend on such technologies to remain competitive in the global economy. Customer relationship management (CRM), enterprise resource planning (ERP), and electronic mail are just a few of the many applications that generate new data every day. If a business is to survive, it must effectively store, manage, and access all data. This is one of the primary business challenges in the information age, and storage networking is a crucial component of the solution.

Brief History of Storage

Early computer systems used various storage media such as punch cards, magnetic tapes, magnetic drums, and floppy magnetic disks for primary storage of data and programs. When IBM invented the hard disk drive in the early 1950s, a new era in storage began. The key benefits introduced include the following:

- Random access capability
- Fast access time
- High throughput
- High capacity
- High reliability
- Media reusability
- Media portability

Some of these features were supported by other storage media, but the hard disk was the first medium to support all of these features. Consequently, the hard disk helped make many advances possible in computing. As evolutionary advances in hard disk technology came to market, they enabled further advances in computing.

Intelligent Interface Models

One of the most important developments in storage technology was the advent of the intelligent interface model. Early storage devices bundled the physical interface, electrical interface, and storage protocol together. Each new storage technology introduced a new physical interface, electrical interface, and storage protocol. The intelligent interface model abstracts device-specific details from the storage protocol and decouples the storage protocol from the physical and electrical interfaces. This allows multiple storage technologies such as magnetic disk, optical disk, and magnetic tape to use a common storage protocol. It also allows the storage protocol to operate over different physical and electrical interfaces.

Serial Transmission Techniques

Another key development in storage was the adoption of serial transmission techniques. Storage interfaces traditionally employ parallel electrical transmission techniques. Parallel electrical transmission has two significant limitations: bandwidth and distance. A common characteristic of electrical signals transmitted in parallel is electromagnetic interference among the wires in a sheath (called crosstalk). Crosstalk increases as the transmission rate increases. The ever-increasing capacities of modern disk drives necessitate ever-increasing transmission rates in their interfaces. Crosstalk makes it difficult to meet this challenge with parallel electrical transmission techniques.

One countermeasure for crosstalk is to shorten the link distance, but distance constraints limit the usefulness of the interface. Cost control is also challenging. The economics of very long-distance cable infrastructure prohibit adoption of parallel transmission techniques. The serial nature of the global voice communications infrastructure provides evidence of this. Even for relatively short distances, such as data center requirements, parallel cabling costs can be adverse. Moreover, parallel cabling presents a logistical challenge. It can be difficult to fit through tight spaces or to bend around corners.

As a result, the storage industry has embraced several serial transmission techniques in recent years. Serial electrical transmission techniques reduce the number of required conductors to one or two per direction. This does not eliminate crosstalk but significantly reduces it. Some of the adopted serial transmission techniques employ optical signaling, which completely eliminates crosstalk. Serial cabling is also less expensive and much easier to install and maintain. These benefits notwithstanding, some standards bodies have chosen to continue work on parallel electrical transmission techniques. The debate about the future of parallel technologies is still active, though serial technologies now clearly have the momentum.

Modern Storage Networks

The adoption of the intelligent interface model and serial transmission techniques made it possible to leverage standard networking technologies for storage connectivity. The loop (also known as ring) topology was common in the early years of open systems storage networking but has since been broadly supplanted by switch-based solutions. Solutions based on Fibre Channel (FC) and Ethernet are most common today.

Drivers for Change

Having the ability to network storage resources does not necessarily make it a good idea. Deploying technology for the sake of technology is not a sound business practice. So why have so many large- and medium-sized enterprises embraced storage networking? There are many reasons, but the primary drivers are the need for efficient management of storage resources and the need for competitive advantages that innovative storage solutions enable.

The volume of data generated each day by the typical modern corporation is greater than ever before. The growth of the Internet and e-commerce have increased the value of data, prompting businesses to store raw data longer, manipulate raw data in new ways, and store more versions of manipulated data. Recently enacted U.S. legislation mandated changes in the retention policies and procedures for financial records of public corporations listed on U.S. exchanges. U.S. companies that have operations in other countries also might be subject to various international regulations in those countries regarding data security and data privacy. Additional U.S. legislation mandated improved patient record-keeping for medical institutions. Recent world events have increased awareness of the need for all corporations, government agencies, and research and educational institutions to replicate data to remote sites for disaster protection. Many of the older enterprise-level applications that were written for optimal functionality at the expense of data life-cycle management cannot be rewritten cost effectively. These and other factors have resulted in storage capacities and growth rates that challenge the efficacy of direct attached storage (DAS) management.

Many corporations report that the cost of storage management is now greater than the cost of storage acquisition. Networking storage resources enables a new management paradigm. New protocols, products, and frameworks for the management of storage promise to reduce the cost of managing large-scale environments. The most prominent industry activity in this area is the Storage Management Initiative Specification (SMI-S) published by the Storage Networking Industry Association (SNIA). Vendor adoption of SMI-S is broad, and consumer interest is high.

Competition is fierce in global markets. The era of U.S. corporate downsizing epitomized the effect of that competition. Any competitive edge is welcome in such a business climate.

Storage networks provide the potential to realize numerous competitive advantages such as the following:

- **Increased throughput**—This allows input/output (I/O) sensitive applications to perform better.

- **Improved flexibility**—Adds, moves, and changes are a fact of life in the operation of any computing or communication infrastructure. Storage networks allow storage administrators to make adds, moves, and changes more easily and with less downtime than otherwise possible in the DAS model.

- **Higher scalability**—Storage networks allow greater numbers of servers and storage subsystems to be interconnected. This allows larger server clusters and web server farms by enabling horizontal expansion, and potentially reduces storage costs by enabling more servers to access shared storage hardware.

- **Data mobility**—Storage networks increase the mobility of stored data for various purposes, such as migration to new hardware and replication to a secondary data center.

- **LAN-free backups**—By deploying a storage area network (SAN), businesses can move network-based backup operations from the local-area network (LAN) to the SAN. This allows nightly operations such as batch processing, log transfers, and device discovery to run normally without competing against backup operations for LAN bandwidth. LAN-free backup was one of the original drivers for enterprises to adopt SAN technology.

- **Server-free backups**—This is made possible by building intelligence into SAN switches and other SAN infrastructure devices to provide Small Computer System Interface (SCSI) EXTENDED COPY (XCOPY) functionality.

- **Advanced volume management**—As virtualization technology migrates into SAN switches, it will enable robust heterogeneous volume management. Host and storage subsystem-based solutions exist today, but each has its limitations. Network-based virtualization promises to eliminate some of those limitations.

Another driver for change is the evolution of relevant standards. An understanding of the standards bodies that represent all aspects of storage functionality enables better understanding of historical storage designs and limitations, and of future directions. In addition to the aforementioned SNIA, other standards bodies are important to storage networking. The American National Standards Institute (ANSI) oversees the activities of the InterNational Committee for Information Technology Standards (INCITS). Two subcommittees of the INCITS are responsible for standards that are central to understanding storage networks. The INCITS T10 subcommittee owns SCSI standards, and the INCITS T11 subcommittee owns Fibre Channel standards. The Internet Engineering Task Force (IETF) has recently emerged as another driving force in storage. The IETF created the IP storage working Group (IPS-WG), which owns all IP-based storage standards. Standards bodies are discussed in more detail in Chapter 2, "OSI Reference Model Versus Other Network Models."

NOTE   The ANSI X3 committee was known officially as the Accredited Standards Committee X3 from 1961 to 1996. The committee was renamed the INCITS in 1996.

What Is a Storage Network?

You can define a storage network in various ways. One strict definition is any network designed specifically to transport only block-level storage protocols and their data. Fibre Channel SANs (FC-SANs) typify this strict definition. Though Fibre Channel can transport non-storage protocols, the vast majority of Fibre Channel SANs deployed today are designed specifically to transport SCSI traffic. Figure 1-1 illustrates a simple Fibre Channel SAN.

Figure 1-1   *Simple Fibre Channel SAN*

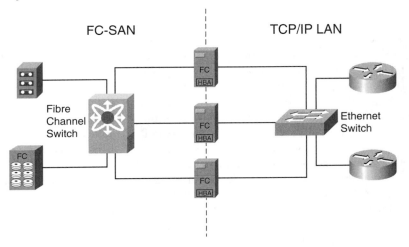

Common use of the phrase "storage area network" and the acronym "SAN" historically has referred to the Fibre Channel SAN model. However, these terms are somewhat ambiguous in light of recent developments such as the ratification of the Internet SCSI (iSCSI) protocol. The iSCSI protocol enables the use of the Transmission Control Protocol (TCP) on the Internet Protocol (IP) on Ethernet in place of Fibre Channel to transport SCSI traffic. An IP network dedicated to the transport of iSCSI traffic is commonly referred to as an IP-SAN. Note that any IP network can transport SCSI traffic; however, a multipurpose IP network that carries SCSI traffic is not called an IP-SAN. Likewise, the acronym FC-SAN is becoming common for the Fibre Channel SAN model. The unqualified term "SAN" is increasingly used to generically refer to both IP-SANs and FC-SANs. Figure 1-2 illustrates a simple IP-SAN.

Figure 1-2 *Simple IP-SAN*

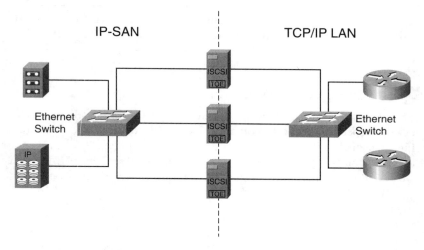

The common definition of a file server is an off-the-shelf operating system (like UNIX or Windows) running on a multipurpose hardware platform (like a PC) configured to share files. By contrast, a network attached storage (NAS) filer typically runs a highly optimized (sometimes specialized) operating system on an optimized hardware platform specifically configured to share files. Another distinction is that UNIX and Windows file servers have native file-level protocols, whereas NAS filers do not. NAS filers are multiprotocol by design and typically support all mainstream file-level protocols. You can create a storage network by connecting NAS clients to NAS filers via a dedicated network. This model uses TCP/IP and Ethernet to transport file-level protocols such as the network file system (NFS) protocol, the common Internet file system (CIFS) protocol, the File Transfer Protocol (FTP) and the HyperText Transfer Protocol (HTTP). There is no common name for this model, but the phrases "filer network" and "file-sharing network" seem appropriate. The phrase "storage area network" is generally not used to describe this model. Figure 1-3 illustrates a simple filer network.

NOTE
There have long been discussions of so-called Internet attached storage (IAS) devices characterized by the use of HTTP to retrieve files from and store files to the storage devices, which are directly attached to an IP network. No standards or other specifications have been produced to define how the operation of these devices would differ from the operation of a normal web server. Because most NAS filers support the use of HTTP for file-level access, IAS can be considered another name for NAS.

Figure 1-3   *Filer Network*

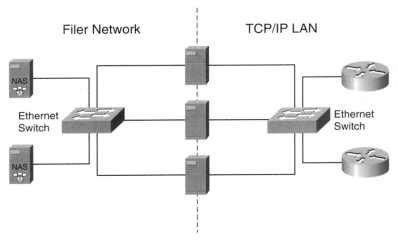

One loose definition for a storage network is any network that transports any file-level or block-level storage protocol and associated data. Although valid, this definition is of little practical use because it essentially includes all the preceding definitions and every traditional computer network on the planet. For example, virtually every Windows-based network transports CIFS, which is the file-level storage protocol native to Microsoft operating systems. Likewise, virtually every UNIX-based network transports NFS, which is the file-level storage protocol native to UNIX operating systems. Even the Internet is included in this definition because the Internet transports FTP, HTTP, and various other protocols designed to transfer files. These points notwithstanding, it might be useful to have a name for traditional data networks that also transport block-level storage protocols. This is because special design considerations for timeslot and wavelength allocations, topology modifications, and quality of service (QoS) mechanisms might be required in addition to hardware and software upgrades for IP and optical networking devices and network management tools, to successfully integrate block-level storage protocols with traditional data and real-time data such as voice over IP (VoIP) and video conferencing. Such changes might be significant enough to warrant a distinction between traditional data networks and these new enhanced networks. A seemingly appropriate, albeit generic, name is *storage-enabled network*; however, the industry hasn't adopted this or any other name yet.

Block Storage Protocol Review: ATA, SCSI, and SBCCS

A storage protocol defines the parameters of communication between storage devices and storage controllers. Storage protocols fall into one of two categories: file-oriented or block-oriented. File-oriented protocols (also known as file-level protocols) read and write variable-length files. Files are segmented into blocks before being stored on disk or tape.

Block-oriented protocols (also known as block-level protocols) read and write individual fixed-length blocks of data. For example, when a client computer uses a file-level storage protocol to write a file to a disk contained in a server, the server first receives the file via the file-level protocol and then invokes the block-level protocol to segment the file into blocks and write the blocks to disk. File-level protocols are discussed in more detail in a subsequent section of this chapter. The three principal block-level storage protocols in use today are advanced technology attachment (ATA), small computer system interface (SCSI), and single-byte command code set (SBCCS).

ATA

ATA is an open-systems standard originally started by the Common Access Method (CAM) committee and later standardized by the ANSI X3 committee in 1994. Several subsequent ATA standards have been published by ANSI. The Small Form Factor (SFF) Committee has published several enhancements, which have been included in subsequent ANSI standards. Each ANSI ATA standard specifies a block-level protocol, a parallel electrical interface, and a parallel physical interface. ATA operates as a bus topology and allows up to two devices per bus. Many computers contain two or more ATA buses. The first ANSI ATA standard is sometimes referred to as ATA-1 or Integrated Drive Electronics (IDE). Many updates to ATA-1 have focused on electrical and physical interface enhancements. The ANSI ATA standards include ATA-1, ATA-2 (also known as enhanced IDE [EIDE]), ATA-3, ATA/ATAPI-4, ATA/ATAPI-5, and ATA/ATAPI-6. The current work in progress is ATA/ATAPI-7. Early ATA standards only supported hard disk commands, but the ATA Packet Interface (ATAPI) introduced SCSI-like commands that allow CD-ROM and tape drives to operate on an ATA electrical interface. Sometimes we refer to these standards collectively as parallel ATA (PATA).

The serial ATA (SATA) Working Group, an industry consortium, published the SATA 1.0 specification in 2001. ANSI is incorporating SATA 1.0 into ATA/ATAPI-7. The SATA Working Group continues other efforts by including minor enhancements to SATA 1.0 that might not be included in ATA/ATAPI-7, the development of SATA II, and, most notably, a collaborative effort with the ANSI T10 subcommittee to "align" SATA II with the Serial Attached SCSI (SAS) specification. The future of serial ATA standards is unclear in light of so many efforts, but it is clear that serial ATA technologies will proliferate.

ATA devices have integrated controller functionality. Computers that contain ATA devices communicate with the devices via an unintelligent electrical interface (sometimes mistakenly called a controller) that essentially converts electrical signals between the system bus and the ATA bus. The ATA/ATAPI command set is implemented in software. This means that the host central processing unit (CPU) shoulders the processing burden associated with storage I/O. The hard disks in most desktop and laptop computers implement ATA. ATA does not support as many device types or as many advanced communication features as SCSI.

The ATA protocol typically is *not* used in storage networks, but ATA disks often are used in storage subsystems that connect to storage networks. These storage devices act as storage protocol converters by speaking SCSI on their SAN interfaces and ATA on their internal ATA bus interfaces. The primary benefit of using ATA disks in storage subsystems is cost savings. ATA disk drives historically have cost less than SCSI disk drives for several reasons. SCSI disk drives typically have a higher mean time between failures (MTBF) rating, which means that they are more reliable. Also, SCSI disk drives historically have provided higher performance and higher capacity. ATA disk drives have gained significant ground in these areas, but still tend to lag behind SCSI disk drives. Of course, these features drive the cost of SCSI disk drives higher. Because the value of data varies from one application to the next, it makes good business sense to store less valuable data on less costly storage devices. Thus, ATA disks increasingly are deployed in SAN environments to provide primary storage to comparatively low-value applications. ATA disks also are being used as first-tier media in new backup/restore solutions, whereby tapes are used as second-tier media for long-term archival or off-site storage. The enhanced backup solutions Initiative (EBSI) is an industry effort to develop advanced backup techniques that leverage the relatively low cost of ATA disks. Figure 1-4 illustrates an ATA-based storage subsystem connected to an FC-SAN.

Figure 1-4   *ATA-Based Storage Connected to FC-SAN*

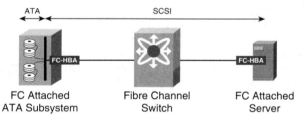

SCSI

SCSI is an open-systems standard originally started by Shugart Associates as the Shugart Associates Systems Interface (SASI) in 1981 and later standardized by the ANSI X3 committee in 1986. Each early SCSI standard specified a block-level protocol, a parallel electrical interface, and a parallel physical interface. These standards are known as SCSI-1 and SCSI-2. Each operates as a bus topology capable of connecting 8 and 16 devices, respectively.

The SCSI-3 family of standards separated the physical interface, electrical interface, and protocol into separate specifications. The protocol commands are separated into two categories: primary and device-specific. Primary commands are common to all types of devices, whereas device-specific commands enable operations unique to each type of device. The SCSI-3 protocol supports a wide variety of device types and transmission technologies. The supported transmission technologies include updated versions of the

SCSI-2 parallel electrical and physical interfaces in addition to many serial interfaces. Even though most of the mapping specifications for transport of SCSI-3 over a given transmission technology are included in the SCSI-3 family of standards, some are not. An example is the iSCSI protocol, which is specified by the IETF.

Most server and workstation computers that employ the DAS model contain either SCSI devices attached via an internal SCSI bus, or they access SCSI devices contained in specialized external enclosures. In the case of external DAS, SCSI bus and Fibre Channel point-to-point connections are common. Computers that access SCSI devices typically implement the SCSI protocol in specialized hardware generically referred to as a storage controller. When the SCSI protocol is transported over a traditional parallel SCSI bus, a storage controller is called a SCSI adapter or SCSI controller. If a SCSI adapter has an onboard CPU and memory, it can control the system bus temporarily, and is called a SCSI host bus adapter (HBA). When the SCSI protocol is transported over a Fibre Channel connection, the storage controller always has a CPU and memory, and is called a Fibre Channel HBA. When a SCSI HBA or Fibre Channel HBA is used, most storage I/O processing is offloaded from the host CPU. When the SCSI protocol is transported over TCP/IP, the storage controller may be implemented via software drivers using a standard network interface card (NIC) or a specialized NIC called a TCP offload engine (TOE), which has a CPU and memory. As its name implies, a TOE offloads TCP processing from the host CPU. Some TOEs also implement iSCSI logic to offload storage I/O processing from the host CPU.

NOTE   A Fibre Channel point-to-point connection is very similar to a Fibre Channel arbitrated loop with only two attached nodes.

All SCSI devices are intelligent, but SCSI operates as a master/slave model. One SCSI device (the initiator) initiates communication with another SCSI device (the target) by issuing a command, to which a response is expected. Thus, the SCSI protocol is half-duplex by design and is considered a command/response protocol. The initiating device is usually a SCSI controller, so SCSI controllers typically are called initiators. SCSI storage devices typically are called targets. That said, a SCSI controller in a modern storage array acts as a target externally and as an initiator internally. Also note that array-based replication software requires a storage controller in the initiating storage array to act as initiator both externally and internally. So it is important to consider the context when discussing SCSI controllers.

The SCSI parallel bus topology is a shared medium implementation, so only one initiator/target session can use the bus at any one time. Separate sessions must alternate accessing the bus. This limitation is removed by newer serial transmission facilities that employ switching techniques. Moreover, the full-duplex nature of switched transmission facilities enables each initiator to participate in multiple simultaneous sessions with one or more targets. Each session employs half-duplex communication, but sessions are multiplexed by the transmission facilities. So, an initiator can issue a command to one target while simultaneously receiving a response from another target. The majority of open-systems storage networks being deployed are Fibre Channel and TCP/IP networks used to transport SCSI traffic. Those environments are the primary focus of this book. Figure 1-5 illustrates a SCSI-based storage subsystem connected to an FC-SAN.

Figure 1-5   *SCSI-Based Storage Connected to FC-SAN*

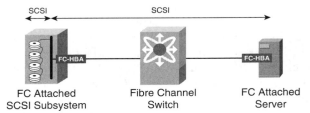

SCSI parallel bus interfaces have one important characteristic, their ability to operate asynchronously or synchronously. Asynchronous mode requires an acknowledgment for each outstanding command before another command can be sent. Synchronous mode allows multiple commands to be issued before receiving an acknowledgment for the first command issued. The maximum number of outstanding commands is negotiated between the initiator and the target. Synchronous mode allows much higher throughput. Despite the similarity of this mechanism to the windowing mechanism of TCP, this mechanism is implemented by the SCSI electrical interface (not the SCSI protocol).

Another important point is the contrasting meaning of the word *synchronous* in the context of the SCSI parallel bus versus its meaning in the context of long-distance storage replication. In the latter context, synchronous refers not to the mode of communication, but to the states of the primary and secondary disk images. The states are guaranteed to be synchronized when the replication software is operating in synchronous mode. When a host (acting as SCSI initiator) sends a write command to the primary storage device, the primary storage device (acting as SCSI target) caches the data. The primary storage device (acting as SCSI initiator) then forwards the data to the secondary storage device at another site. The secondary storage device (acting as SCSI target) writes the data to disk and then sends acknowledgment to the primary storage device, indicating that the command completed successfully. Only after receiving acknowledgment does the primary storage device (acting as SCSI target) write the data to disk and send acknowledgment of successful completion to the initiating host. Because packets can be lost or damaged in transit over long distances, the best way to ensure that both disk images are synchronized is to expect an acknowledgment for each request before sending another request. Using this method, the two disk images can never be more than one request out of sync at any point in time.

TIP	The terms *synchronous* and *asynchronous* should always be interpreted in context. The meanings of these terms often reverse from one context to another.

SBCCS

SBCCS is a generic term describing the mechanism by which IBM mainframe computers perform I/O using single-byte commands. IBM mainframes conduct I/O via a *channel* architecture. A channel architecture comprises many hardware and software components including channel adapters, adapter cables, interface assemblies, device drivers, I/O programming interfaces, I/O units, channel protocols, and so on. IBM channels come in two flavors: byte multiplexer and block multiplexer. Channels used for storage employ block multiplexer communication. I/O units used for storage are called disk control units (CU). Mainframes communicate with CUs via the channel protocol, and CUs translate channel protocol commands into storage I/O commands that the storage device (for example, disk or tape drive) can understand. This contrasts with ATA and SCSI operations, wherein the host initiates the storage I/O commands understood by the storage devices. Figure 1-6 illustrates this contrast.

Figure 1-6 *Mainframe Storage Channel Communication*

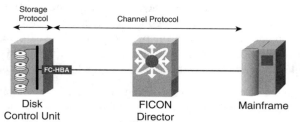

Two block channel protocols follow:

- Direct-coupled interlock (DCI)
- Data streaming (DS)

DCI requires a response for each outstanding command before another command can be sent. This is conceptually analogous to asynchronous mode on a SCSI parallel bus interface. DS can issue multiple commands while waiting for responses. This is conceptually analogous to synchronous mode on a SCSI parallel bus interface. A block channel protocol consists of command, control, and status frames. Commands are known as channel command words (CCW), and each CCW is a single byte. Supported CCWs vary depending on which CU hardware model is used. Some configurations allow an AIX host to appear as a CU to the mainframe. Control frames are exchanged between the channel adapter and the CU during the execution of each command. Upon completion of data transfer, the CU sends ending status to the channel adapter in the mainframe. Command and status frames are acknowledged. Applications must inform the operating system of the I/O request details via operation request blocks (ORB). ORBs contain the memory address where the CCWs to be executed have been stored. The operating system then initiates each I/O operation by invoking the channel subsystem (CSS). The CSS determines which channel adapter to use for communication to the designated CU and then transmits CCWs to the designated CU.

SBCCS is a published protocol that may be implemented without paying royalties to IBM. However, IBM might not support SBCCS if implemented without the control unit port (CUP) feature, and CUP is not available for royalty-free implementation. Furthermore, only IBM and IBM-compatible mainframes, peripherals, and channel extension devices implement SBCCS. So, the open nature of SBCCS is cloudy, and the term pseudo-proprietary seems appropriate. There are two versions of SBCCS; one for enterprise systems connection (ESCON) and one for Fibre Channel connection (FICON).

Mainframes have always played a significant role in the computing industry. In response to advances made in open computing systems and to customer demands, mainframes have evolved by incorporating new hardware, software, and networking technologies. Because this book does not cover mainframes in detail, the following section provides a brief overview of mainframe storage networking for the sake of completeness.

Mainframe Storage Networking: ESCON and FICON

The Bus-and-Tag parallel channel architecture was once the primary storage interface used by IBM mainframes. As mainframes evolved, the ESCON architecture broadly replaced Bus-and-Tag. ESCON is now being replaced by the FICON architecture to avail mainframes of the cost/performance benefits enabled by mainstream adoption of Fibre Channel.

ESCON

ESCON is a proprietary IBM technology introduced in 1990 to overcome the limitations of the Bus-and-Tag parallel channel architecture. ESCON converters were made available to preserve Bus-and-Tag investments by bridging between the two architectures. Today, very little Bus-and-Tag remains in the market. Whereas Bus-and-Tag employs copper cabling and parallel transmission, the ESCON architecture employs optical cabling and serial transmission. The ESCON architecture is roughly equivalent to Layers 1 and 2 of the Open Systems Interconnection (OSI) reference model published by the International Organization for Standardization. We discuss the OSI reference model in detail in Chapter 2, "OSI Reference Model Versus Other Network Models."

In addition to transporting channel protocol (SBCCS) frames, ESCON defines a new frame type at the link level for controlling and maintaining the transmission facilities. ESCON operates as half-duplex communication in a point-to-point topology and supports the optional use of switches (called ESCON directors) to create a mesh of point-to-point connections. ESCON is connection-oriented, meaning that the host channel adapter and CU must exchange link-level frames to reserve resources for a logical connection before exchanging channel protocol frames. The ESCON director circuit-switches all physical connections resulting in a 1:1 ratio of active logical connections to active physical connections. Consequently, each channel adapter supports only one active logical connection at a time. An ESCON director is limited to 256 physical ports (254 usable). No more than two ESCON directors may separate a host channel adapter from a CU. (Daisy-chaining switches in a linear manner is called cascading.)

ESCON originally provided for multi-mode and single-mode host channel adapters. However, the majority of installations use multi-mode channel adapters. The maximum supported distance per link is three kilometers (km) using multi-mode fiber (MMF) or 20 km using single-mode fiber (SMF). By using two ESCON directors and SMF, the distance from host channel adapter to CU theoretically could be extended up to 60 km. However, 43 km was the maximum distance ever officially supported between a host and a CU. Support for SMF interfaces in hosts and CUs was terminated years ago, so SMF is used only between directors today. SMF between directors is called extended distance facility (XDF). It yields a maximum distance of 26 km from host to CU. ESCON remote channel extenders also can be used (in place of directors) to extend the channel distance. In practice, the lack of SMF cable plants during the heyday of ESCON limited most installations to 9 km or less.

ESCON transmissions are encoded via 8b/10b signaling. The ESCON signaling rate is 200 megabits per second (Mbps), which provides a maximum of 20 megabytes per second (MBps) link-level throughput at distances up to 8 km. This equates to 17 MBps of data throughput. Throughput decreases as distance increases beyond 8 km (a condition known as droop). This droop effect results from lack of buffer capabilities and the chatty nature of SBCCS. FICON reduces droop by introducing buffers and reducing SBCCS chatter. ESCON is losing market share to FICON and likely will be deprecated by IBM in the not-too-distant future.

FICON

FICON was introduced in 1998 to overcome the limitations of the ESCON architecture. FICON is the term given to the pseudo-proprietary IBM SBCCS operating on a standard Fibre Channel infrastructure. The version of SBCCS used in FICON is less chatty than the version used in ESCON. The ANSI FC-SB specification series maps the newer version of SBCCS to Fibre Channel. All aspects of FICON infrastructure are based on ANSI FC standards. FICON operates in two modes: bridged (also known as FCV mode) and native (also known as FC mode). Some FICON hardware supports SCSI (instead of SBCCS) on Fibre Channel. This is sometimes called FICON Fibre Channel Protocol (FCP) mode, but there is nothing about it that warrants use of the term FICON. FICON FCP mode is just mainstream open-systems storage networking applied to mainframes.

In bridged mode, hosts use FICON channel adapters to connect to ESCON directors. A FICON bridge adapter is installed in an ESCON director to facilitate communication. A FICON bridge adapter time-division multiplexes up to eight ESCON signals onto a single FICON signal. Investments in late-model ESCON directors and CUs are preserved allowing a phased migration path to FICON over time. Early ESCON directors do not support the FICON bridge adapter. The ESCON SBCCS is used for storage I/O operations in bridged mode.

In native mode, FICON uses a modified version of the SBCCS and replaces the ESCON transmission facilities with the Fibre Channel transmission facilities. FICON native mode resembles ESCON in that it:

- Employs serial transmission on optical cabling
- Is roughly equivalent to Layers 1 and 2 of the OSI reference model
- Is connection-oriented (See Chapter 5, "OSI Physical and Data Link Layers," for a detailed discussion of connection-oriented communication)
- Transports channel protocol and link-level frames
- Supports the point-to-point topology
- Supports the optional use of switches called FICON directors to create a mesh of point-to-point connections (FICON directors are actually just Fibre Channel directors that support transport of SBCCS and management via CUP.)

Unlike ESCON, FICON native mode operates in full-duplex mode. Unlike ESCON directors, Fibre Channel switches employ packet switching to create connections between hosts and CUs. FICON native mode takes advantage of the packet-switching nature of Fibre Channel to allow up to 32 simultaneously active logical connections per physical channel adapter. Like ESCON, FICON is limited to 256 ports per director, but virtual fabrics can extend this scale limitation. FICON native mode retains the ESCON limit of two directors cascaded between a host channel adapter and a CU, though some mainframes support only a single intermediate director.

Fibre Channel transmissions are encoded via 8b/10b signaling. Operating at 1.0625 gigabits per second (Gbps), the maximum supported distance per Fibre Channel link is 500 meters using 50 micron MMF or 10 km using SMF, and the maximum link level throughput is 106.25 MBps. Operating at 2.125 Gbps, the maximum supported distance per Fibre Channel link is 300 meters using 50 micron MMF or 10 km using SMF, and the maximum link-level throughput is 212.5 MBps. By optionally using IBM's mode-conditioning patch (MCP) cable, the maximum distance using 50 micron MMF is extended to 550 meters operating at 1.0625 Gbps. The MCP cable transparently mates the transmit SMF strand to a MMF strand. Both ends of the link must use an MCP cable. This provides a migration path from multi-mode adapters to single-mode adapters prior to cable plant conversion from MMF to SMF. The MCP cable is not currently supported operating at 2.125 Gbps. By using a SMF cable plant end-to-end and two FICON directors, the maximum distance from host channel adapter to CU can be extended up to 30 km. Link-level buffering in FICON equipment (not found in ESCON equipment) enables maximum throughput over long distances. However, throughput decreases as distance increases unless additional link-level buffering is implemented. Increasing the end-to-end device level buffering is also required as distance increases. IBM FICON hosts and CUs currently support sufficient buffering to enable operation at distances up to 100 km (assuming that intermediate link-level buffering is also sufficient). The use of wavelength division multiplexing (WDM) equipment or FICON optical repeaters is required to extend the end-to-end channel to 100 km because no more than two Fibre Channel directors may be cascaded.

The Fibre Channel Protocol for SCSI (FCP) is a mapping for SCSI to be transported on Fibre Channel. In FICON FCP mode, Linux-based mainframes use SCSI in place of SBCCS for storage I/O operations. As mentioned previously, the term FICON really has no meaning in the context of FCP mode. All transmission parameters of FICON FCP mode are comparable to FICON native mode because both use Fibre Channel infrastructure. FICON FCP mode is not supported on OS/390 mainframes.

File Server Protocol Review: CIFS, NFS, and DAFS

When a client accesses a file on a file server or NAS filer, a file-level protocol is used. The most popular Windows and UNIX file-level protocols are CIFS and NFS, respectively. Even though the names of these protocols include *file system,* these are network protocols used to access file systems. These protocols define messaging semantics and syntax that enable file system interaction (such as open, read, and write operations) across a network. Of course, these protocols provide file-system functionality to applications such as open, read, and write operations. Two more popular file-level protocols are FTP and HTTP. However, these protocols are limited in functionality when compared to CIFS and NFS. FTP and HTTP do not support file locking, client notification of state change, or other advanced features supported by CIFS and NFS. FTP and HTTP can be used only to transfer files (simple read and write operations). As such, FTP and HTTP are not considered enabling technologies for modern storage networks. A new file-level protocol known as direct access file system (DAFS) recently appeared in the market. It promises to improve application performance while lowering host CPU utilization. DAFS adoption has been slowed by the requirement to modify application code. To date, DAFS adoption has been led by database application vendors.

CIFS

In Microsoft Windows environments, clients historically requested files from servers via the Server Message Block (SMB) protocol. In 1984, IBM published the basis for the SMB protocol. Based on IBM's work, Microsoft and Intel subsequently published the OpenNET File Sharing Protocol. As the protocol evolved, Intel withdrew from the effort, and the protocol was renamed the SMB File Sharing Protocol; however, SMB provides more than just file-sharing services.

SMB relies upon the services of the Network Basic Input Output System (NetBIOS) rather than Windows Sockets (Winsock) services. NetBIOS on IP networks was standardized by the IETF via request for comment (RFC) 1001 and RFC 1002 in 1987. Those RFCs enabled the use of SMB over IP networks and greatly expanded the market for SMB as IP networks began to rapidly proliferate in the 1990s. SMB remained proprietary until 1992, when the X/Open committee (now known as the Open Group) standardized SMB via the common application environment (CAE) specification (document 209) enabling interoperability with UNIX computers. Even though SMB is supported on various UNIX and Linux operating systems via the open-source software package known as Samba, it is used predominantly by Windows clients to gain access to data on UNIX and Linux servers. Even with the X/Open standardization effort, SMB can be considered proprietary because Microsoft has continued developing the protocol independent of the Open Group's efforts. SMB eventually evolved enough for Microsoft to rename it again. SMB's new name is the CIFS file sharing protocol (commonly called CIFS).

Microsoft originally published the CIFS specification in 1996. With the release of Windows 2000, CIFS replaced SMB in Microsoft operating systems. CIFS typically operates on NetBIOS, but CIFS also can operate directly on TCP. CIFS is proprietary to the extent that Microsoft retains all rights to the CIFS specification. CIFS is open to the extent that Microsoft has published the specification, and permits other for-profit companies to implement CIFS without paying royalties to Microsoft. This royalty-free licensing agreement allows NAS vendors to implement CIFS economically in their own products. CIFS integration enables NAS devices to serve Windows clients without requiring new client software. Unfortunately, Microsoft has not extended its royalty-free CIFS license to the open-source community. To the contrary, open-source implementations are strictly prohibited. This somewhat negates the status of CIFS as an open protocol.

Note that *open* should not be confused with *standard*. Heterogeneous NAS implementations of CIFS, combined with Microsoft's claims that CIFS is a standard protocol, have led to confusion about the true status of the CIFS specification. Microsoft submitted CIFS to the IETF in 1997 and again in 1998, but the CIFS specification was never published as an RFC (not even as *informational*). The SNIA formed a CIFS documentation working group in 2001 to ensure interoperability among heterogeneous vendor implementations. However, the working group's charter does not include standardization efforts. The working group published a CIFS technical reference, which documents existing CIFS implementations. The SNIA CIFS technical reference serves an equivalent function to an IETF informational RFC and is *not* a standard. Even though CIFS is not a de jure standard, it clearly is a de facto standard by virtue of its ubiquity in the marketplace.

A CIFS server makes a local file system, or some portion of a local file system, available to clients by *sharing* it. A client accesses a remote file system by *mapping* a drive letter to the *share* or by *browsing* to the share. When browsing with the Windows Explorer application, a uniform naming convention (UNC) address specifies the location of the share. The UNC address includes the name of the server and the name of the share. CIFS supports file and folder change notification, file and record locking, read-ahead and write-behind caching, and many other functions.

NOTE   The phrase "Universal Naming Convention" is interchangeable with "Uniform Naming Convention" according to Microsoft's website.

NFS

Sun Microsystems created NFS in 1984 to allow UNIX operating systems to share files. Sun immediately made NFS available to the computer industry at large via a royalty-free license. In 1986, Sun introduced PC-NFS to extend NFS functionality to PC operating systems. The IETF first published the NFS v2 specification in 1989 as an informational RFC (1094). NFS v3 was published via an informational RFC (1813) in 1995. Both NFS v2 and NFS v3 were widely regarded as standards even though NFS was not published via a standards track RFC until 2000, when NFS v4 was introduced in RFC 3010. RFC 3530 is the latest specification of NFS v4, which appears to be gaining momentum in the marketplace. NFS v4 improves upon earlier NFS versions in several different areas including security, caching, locking, and message communication efficiency. Even though NFS is available for PC operating systems, it always has been and continues to be most widely used by UNIX and Linux operating systems.

An NFS server makes a local file system, or some portion of a local file system, available to clients by *exporting* it. A client accesses a remote file system by *mounting* it into the local file system at a client-specified *mount point*. All versions of NFS employ the remote-procedure call (RPC) protocol and a data abstraction mechanism known as external data representation (XDR). Both the RPC interface and the XDR originally were developed by Sun and later published as standards-track RFCs.

DAFS

DAFS partially derives from NFS v4. The DAFS protocol was created by a computer industry consortium known as the DAFS Collaborative and first published in 2001. The DAFS protocol was submitted to the IETF in 2001 but was never published as an RFC.

The DAFS protocol is *not* meant to be used in wide-area networks. DAFS is designed to optimize shared file access in low-latency environments such as computer clusters. To accomplish this goal, the DAFS protocol employs remote direct memory access (RDMA). RDMA allows an application running on one host to access memory directly in another host with minimal consumption of operating system resources in either host. The DAFS protocol can be implemented in user mode or kernel mode, but kernel mode negates some of the benefits of RDMA.

RDMA is made possible by a class of high-speed, low-latency, high-reliability interconnect technologies. These technologies are referred to as direct access transports (DAT), and the most popular are the virtual interface (VI) architecture, the Sockets direct protocol (SDP), iSCSI extensions for RDMA (iSER), the Datamover architecture for iSCSI (DA), and the InfiniBand (IB) architecture. RDMA requires modification of applications that were written to use traditional network file system protocols such as CIFS and NFS. For this reason, the DAFS Collaborative published a new application programming interface (API) in 2001. The DAFS API simplifies application modifications by hiding the complexities of the DAFS protocol. The SNIA formed the DAFS Implementers' Forum in 2001 to facilitate the development of interoperable products based on the DAFS protocol.

Another computer industry consortium known as the Direct Access Transport (DAT) Collaborative developed two APIs in 2002. One API is used by kernel mode processes, and the other is used by user mode processes. These APIs provide a consistent interface to DAT services regardless of the underlying DAT. The DAFS protocol can use either of these APIs to avoid grappling with DAT-specific APIs.

Backup Protocols: NDMP and EXTENDED COPY

Of the many data backup mechanisms, two are of particular interest: the Network Data Management Protocol (NDMP) and the SCSI-3 EXTENDED COPY command. These are of interest because each is designed specifically for data backup in network environments, and both are standardized.

NDMP

NDMP is a standard protocol for network-based backup of file servers. There is some confusion about this, as some people believe NDMP is intended strictly for NAS devices. This is true only to the extent that NAS devices are, in fact, highly specialized file servers. But there is nothing about NDMP that limits its use to NAS devices. Network Appliance is the leading vendor in the NAS market. Because Network Appliance was one of two companies responsible for the creation of NDMP, its proprietary NAS filer operating system has supported NDMP since before it became a standard. This has fueled the misconception that NDMP is designed specifically for NAS devices.

The purpose of NDMP is to provide a common interface for backup applications. This allows backup software vendors to concentrate on their core competencies instead of wasting development resources on the never-ending task of agent software maintenance. File server and NAS filer operating systems that implement NDMP can be backed up using third-party software. The third-party backup software vendor does need to explicitly support the operating systems with custom agent software. This makes NDMP an important aspect of heterogeneous data backup.

NDMP separates control traffic from data traffic, which allows centralized control. A central console initiates and controls backup and restore operations by signaling to servers and filers. The source host then dumps data to a locally attached tape drive or to another NDMP-enabled host with an attached tape drive. Control traffic flows between the console and the source/destination hosts. Data traffic flows within a host from disk drive to tape drive or between the source host and destination host to which the tape drive is attached. For large-scale environments, centralized backup and restore operations are easier and more cost-effective to plan, implement, and operate than distributed backup solutions. Figure 1-7 shows the NDMP control and data traffic flows.

Figure 1-7   *NDMP Communication Model*

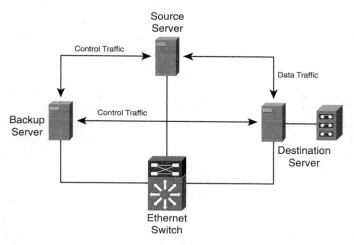

SCSI-3 EXTENDED COPY

EXTENDED COPY was originally developed by the SNIA as Third Party Copy (TPC or 3PC) and later standardized by the ANSI T10 subcommittee in revision 2 of the SCSI-3 primary commands (SPC-2) specification. EXTENDED COPY is meant to further the LAN-free backup model by removing servers from the data path. As with traditional LAN-free backup solutions, control traffic between the media server and the host to be backed up traverses the LAN, and data traffic between the media server and storage devices traverses the SAN. The difference is that EXTENDED COPY allows a SAN switch or other SAN attached device to manage the movement of data from source storage device to destination storage device, which removes the media server from the data path. A device that implements EXTENDED COPY is called a data mover. The most efficient placement of data mover functionality is in a SAN switch or storage array controller. Figure 1-8 shows a typical data flow in a SCSI-3 EXTENDED COPY enabled FC-SAN.

Figure 1-8   *SCSI-3 EXTENDED COPY Data Flow*

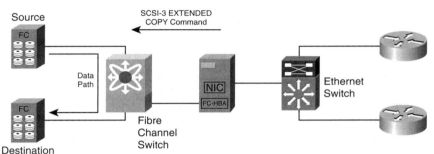

Optical Technologies: SONET/SDH, DWDM/CWDM, and RPR/802.17

Any transmission technology that supports fiber optic cabling can be considered an optical technology. However, the leading communications equipment vendors have long used the phrase *optical technologies* to refer specifically to a subset of transmission technologies that operate at Layer 1 of the OSI reference model (see Chapter 2, "OSI Reference Model Versus Other Network Models") and support very long distances. SONET, SDH, DWDM, and CWDM fall into this category. Operating at OSI Layer 1 is an important characteristic because it permits a broad range of network protocols that operate at OSI Layer 2 or higher to be transported on optical technologies. Resilient packet ring (RPR) technologies combine optical transmission with LAN transport. The only standardized RPR technology is IEEE 802.17, which operates at OSI Layer 2 but is closely bound to OSI Layer 1 optical operations.

SONET/SDH

SONET is the transmission standard for long-haul and metropolitan carrier networks in North America. There are approximately 135,000 metropolitan area SONET rings deployed in North America today. SDH is the equivalent standard used throughout the rest of the world. Both are time division multiplexing (TDM) schemes designed to operate on fiber optic cables, and both provide highly reliable transport services over very long distances. Most storage replication solutions traverse SONET or SDH circuits, though the underlying SONET/SDH infrastructure may be hidden by a network protocol such as Point-to-Point Protocol (PPP) or Asynchronous Transfer Mode (ATM). SONET and SDH are often collectively called SONET/SDH because they are nearly identical. This overview discusses only SONET on the basis that SDH is not significantly different in the context of storage networking.

WDM with frequency division multiplexing (FDM). Two factors distinguish WDM from FDM. First, FDM generally describes older multiplexing systems that process electrical signals. WDM refers to newer multiplexing systems that process optical signals. Second, each frequency multiplexed in an FDM system represents a single transmission source. By contrast, one of the primary WDM applications is the multiplexing of SONET signals, each of which may carry multiple transmissions from multiple sources via TDM. So, WDM combines TDM and FDM techniques to achieve higher bandwidth utilization.

DWDM refers to closely spaced wavelengths; the closer the spacing, the higher the number of channels (bandwidth) per fiber. The International Telecommunication Union (ITU) G.694.1 standard establishes nominal wavelength spacing for DWDM systems. Spacing options are specified via a frequency grid ranging from 12.5 gigahertz (GHz), which equates to approximately 0.1 nm, to 100 GHz, which is approximately 0.8 nm. Many DWDM systems historically have supported only 100 GHz spacing (or a multiple of 100 GHz) because of technical challenges associated with closer spacing. Newer DWDM systems support spacing closer than 100 GHz. Current products typically support transmission rates of 2.5-10 Gbps, and the 40-Gbps market is expected to emerge in 2006.

You can use two methods to transmit through a DWDM system. One of the methods is transparent. This means that the DWDM system will accept any client signal without special protocol mappings or frame encapsulation techniques. Using this method, a client device is connected to a *transparent* interface in the DWDM equipment. The DWDM devices accept the client's optical signal and *shift* the wavelength into the WDM window. The shifted optical signal is then multiplexed with other shifted signals onto a DWDM trunk. Some DWDM-transparent interfaces can accept a broad range of optical signals, whereas others can accept only a narrow range. Some DWDM-transparent interfaces are *protocol aware,* meaning that the interface understands the client protocol and can monitor the client signal. When using the transparent method, the entire end-to-end DWDM infrastructure is invisible to the client. All link-level operations are conducted end-to-end through the DWDM infrastructure.

Using the second method, a client device is connected to a *native* interface in the DWDM equipment. For example, a Fibre Channel switch port is connected to a Fibre Channel port on a line card in a DWDM chassis. The DWDM device terminates the incoming client signal by supporting the client's protocol and actively participating as an end node on the client's network. For example, a Fibre Channel port in a DWDM device would exchange low-level Fibre Channel signals with a Fibre Channel switch and would appear as a bridge port (B_Port) to the Fibre Channel switch. This non-transparent DWDM transport service has the benefit of localizing some or all link-level operations on each side of the DWDM infrastructure. Non-transparent DWDM service also permits aggregation at the point of ingress into the DWDM network. For example, eight 1-Gbps Ethernet (GE) ports could be aggregated onto a single 10-Gbps lambda. The DWDM device must generate a new optical signal for each client signal that it terminates. The newly generated optical signals are in the WDM window and are multiplexed onto a DWDM trunk. Non-transparent DWDM service also supports monitoring of the client protocol signals.

DWDM systems often employ IOAs. IOAs operate on the analog signal (that is, the optical waveform) carried within the fiber. IOAs generally operate on signals in the 1530–1570 nm range, which overlaps the WDM window. As the name suggests, amplification occurs within the fiber. A typical IOA is a box containing a length of special fiber that has been doped during manufacture with a rare earth element. The most common type of IOA is the erbium-doped fiber amplifier (EDFA). The normal fiber is spliced into the special fiber on each side of the EDFA. Contained within the EDFA is an optical carrier generator that operates at 980 nm or 1480 nm. This carrier is injected into the erbium-doped fiber, which excites the erbium. The erbium transfers its energy to optical signals in the 1530–1570 nm range as they pass through the fiber, thus amplifying signals in the center of the WDM window. IOAs can enable analog signals to travel longer distances than unamplified signals, but noise is amplified along with the signal. The noise accumulates and eventually reaches an SNR at which the signal is no longer recognizable. This limits the total distance per span that can be traversed using IOAs. Fortunately, advancements in optical fibers, lasers and filters (also known as graters) have made IOAs feasible for much longer distances than previously possible. Unfortunately, much of the world's metropolitan and long-haul fiber infrastructure was installed before these advancements were commercially viable. So, real-world DWDM spans often are shorter than the theoretical distances supported by EDFA technology. DWDM distances typically are grouped into three categories: inter-office (0–300 km), long-haul (300–600 km), and extended long-haul (600–2000 km). Figure 1-9 shows a metropolitan area DWDM ring.

The operating principles of CWDM are *essentially* the same as DWDM, but the two are quite different from an implementation perspective. CWDM spaces wavelengths farther apart than DWDM. This characteristic leads to many factors (discussed in the following paragraphs) that lower CWDM costs by an order of magnitude. CWDM requires no special skill sets for deployment, operation, or support. Although some CWDM devices support non-transparent service, transparent CWDM devices are more common.

Transparent CWDM involves the use of specialized gigabit interface converters (GBIC) or small form-factor pluggable GBICs (SFP). These are called *colored* GBICs and SFPs because each lambda represents a different color in the spectrum. The native GBIC or SFP in the client device is replaced with a colored GBIC or SFP. The electrical interface in the client passes signals to the colored GBIC/SFP in the usual manner. The colored GBIC/SFP converts the electrical signal to an optical wavelength in the WDM window instead of the optical wavelength natively associated with the client protocol (typically 850 nm or 1310 nm). The client device is connected to a transparent interface in the CWDM device, and the optical signal is multiplexed without being shifted. The colored GBIC/SFP negates the need to perform wavelength shifting in the CWDM device. The network administrator must plan the optical wavelength grid manually before procuring the colored GBICs/SFPs, and the colored GBICs/SFPs must be installed according to the wavelength plan to avoid conflicts in the CWDM device.

Figure 1-9 *Metropolitan Area DWDM Ring*

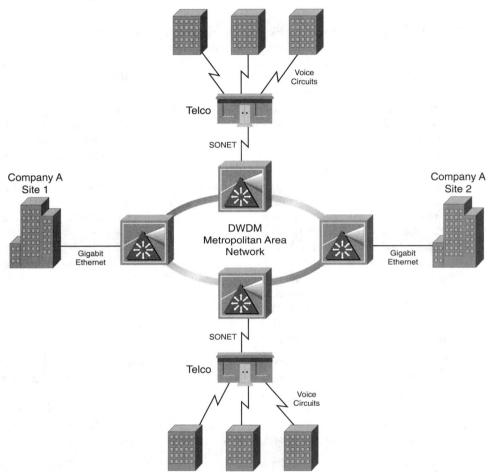

To the extent that client devices are unaware of the CWDM system, and all link-level operations are conducted end-to-end, transparent CWDM service is essentially the same as transparent DWDM service. Transparent CWDM mux/demux equipment is typically passive (not powered). Passive devices cannot generate or repeat optical signals. Additionally, IOAs operate in a small wavelength range that overlaps only three CWDM signals. Some CWDM signals are unaffected by IOAs, so each CWDM span must terminate at a distance determined by the unamplified signals. Therefore, no benefit is realized by amplifying any of the CWDM signals. This means that all optical signal loss introduced by CWDM mux/demux equipment, splices, connectors, and the fiber must be subtracted from the launch power of the colored GBIC/SFP installed in the client. Thus, the client GBIC/SFP determines the theoretical maximum distance that can be traversed. Colored GBICs/SFPs typically are limited to 80 km in a point-to-point configuration, but may reach up to 120 km under ideal conditions. Signal monitoring typically is not implemented in CWDM devices.

TIP   IOAs may be used with CWDM if only three signals (1530 nm, 1550 nm, and 1570 nm) are multiplexed onto the fiber.

Most CWDM devices operate in the 1470-1610 nm range. The ITU G.694.2 standard specifies the wavelength grid for CWDM systems. Spacing is given in nanometers, not gigahertz. The nominal spacing is 20 nm. The sparse wavelength spacing in CWDM systems enables lower product-development costs. Providing such a wide spacing grid enables relaxation of laser tolerances, which lowers laser fabrication costs. Temperature changes in a laser can change the wavelength of a signal passing through the laser. So, lasers must be cooled in DWDM systems. The grid spacing in CWDM systems allows uncooled lasers to be used because a wavelength can change moderately without being confused with a neighbor wavelength. Uncooled lasers are less costly to fabricate. Last, optical filters can be less discerning and still be effective with the wide spacing of the CWDM grid. This lowers the cost of CWDM mux/demux equipment.

RPR/802.17

Cisco Systems originally developed dynamic packet transport (DPT) in 1999. The spatial reuse protocol (SRP) is the basis of DPT. Cisco submitted SRP to the IETF, and it was published as an informational RFC in 2000. SRP was submitted to the IEEE for consideration as the basis of the 802.17 specification. The IEEE decided to combine components of SRP with components of a competing proposal to create 802.17. Final IEEE ratification occurred in 2004. The IETF has formed a working group to produce an RFC for IP over 802.17. Technologies such as DPT and 802.17 are commonly known as RPRs.

Ethernet and SONET interworking is possible in several ways. The IEEE 802.17 standard attempts to take interworking one step further by merging key characteristics of Ethernet and SONET. Traditional service provider technologies (that is, the DS hierarchy and SONET/SDH) are TDM-based and do not provide bandwidth efficiency for data networking. Traditional LAN transport technologies are well suited to data networking, but lack some of the resiliency features required for metropolitan area transport. Traditional LAN transport technologies also tend to be suboptimal for multiservice traffic. The 802.17 standard attempts to resolve these issues by combining aspects of each technology to provide a highly resilient, data friendly, multi-service transport mechanism that mimics LAN behavior across metropolitan areas. Previous attempts to make SONET more LAN-friendly have been less successful than anticipated. For example, ATM and packet over SONET (POS) both bring data-friendly transport mechanisms to SONET by employing row-oriented synchronous payload envelopes (SPE) that take full advantage of concatenated SONET

new disaster recovery solutions. There are several ways to virtualize physical storage resources, and three general categories of implementations:

- Host-based
- Storage subsystem-based
- Network-based

Each has its pros and cons, though network-based implementations seem to have more pros than cons for large-scale storage environments. Enterprise-class virtualization products have appeared in the market recently after years of delays. However, one could argue that enterprise-class virtualization has been a reality for more than a decade if the definition includes redundant array of inexpensive disks (RAID) technology, virtual arrays that incorporate sophisticated virtualization functionality beyond RAID, or host-based volume management techniques. One can think of the new generation of enterprise-class virtualization as the culmination and integration of previously separate technologies such as hierarchical storage management (HSM), volume management, disk striping, storage protocol conversion, and so on. As the new generation of virtualization products matures, the ability to seamlessly and transparently integrate Fibre Channel and iSCSI networks, SCSI and ATA storage subsystems, disk media, tape media, and so on, will be realized. Effectiveness is another story. That might rely heavily on policy-based storage management applications. Automated allocation and recovery of switch ports, logical unit numbers (LUN), tape media, and the like will become increasingly important as advanced virtualization techniques become possible.

Host Implementations

Host-based virtualization products have been available for a long time. RAID controllers for internal DAS and just-a-bunch-of-disks (JBOD) external chassis are good examples of hardware-based virtualization. RAID can be implemented without a special controller, but the software that performs the striping calculations often places a noticeable burden on the host CPU. Linux now natively supports advanced virtualization functionality such as striping and extending via its logical volume manager (LVM) utility. Nearly every modern operating system on the market natively supports mirroring, which is a very simplistic form of virtualization. Mirroring involves block duplication on two physical disks (or two sets of physical disks) that appear as one logical disk to applications. The software virtualization market offers many add-on products from non-operating system vendors.

Host-based implementations really shine in homogeneous operating system environments or companies with a small number of hosts. In large, heterogeneous environments, the number of hosts and variety of operating systems increase the complexity and decrease the efficiency of this model. The host-oriented nature of these solutions often requires different software vendors to be used for different operating systems. Although this prevents storage from being virtualized in a consistent manner across the enterprise, storage can be virtualized in a consistent manner across storage vendor boundaries for each operating system.

Large-scale storage consolidation often is seen in enterprise environments, which results in a one-to-many relationship between each storage subsystem and the hosts. Host-based virtualization fails to exploit the centralized storage management opportunity and imposes a distributed approach to storage management activities such as capacity tracking, LUN allocation and configuration, LUN recovery, and usage trending. On a positive note, host-based implementations make it relatively easy to failover or migrate from one storage subsystem to another, although some storage vendors restrict this capability through the imposition of proprietary host-based failover software.

Storage Subsystem Implementations

The current generation of storage subsystems implement virtualization techniques that can be described as RAID on steroids. One or more controllers in the subsystem manage the physical devices within the subsystem and perform the striping, mirroring, and parity calculation functions in RAID configurations. These controllers have processing power and memory capacity on par with the servers that use the subsystem. In some cases, the controller actually is a high-end personal computer (PC) running specialized operating system software optimized to perform storage-related functions. The subsystem controls the presentation (masking and mapping) of LUNs.

One of the benefits of this model is independence from host operating systems, which allows storage to be virtualized in a consistent manner across all host operating systems. However, this benefit might not extend across storage vendor boundaries. The proprietary nature of most of these solutions prevents storage from being virtualized in a consistent manner across the enterprise.

Another benefit is improved centralization of various management tasks as compared to host-based implementations. This is because there are typically far fewer subsystems than there are hosts. Subsystem-based implementations also enable advanced mirroring and data backup techniques that can be completely transparent to the attached hosts and can be completed without any effect on host CPU or memory resources. One drawback of these solutions is the acquisition cost as compared to host-based implementations with JBOD. Perhaps the most significant drawback is the proprietary nature of these solutions, which can be very costly to enterprises over the life of the subsystem. Much of the functionality of subsystem-based implementations is confined within each subsystem even in homogeneous environments. For example, it is typically not possible to stripe a RAID volume across physical devices in separate subsystems from a single vendor. However, recent advances in distributed cluster storage architecture and advanced virtualization techniques give new promise to such possibilities.

Network Implementations

The widespread adoption of switched FC-SANs has enabled a new virtualization model. Implementing virtualization in the network offers some advantages over subsystem and host implementations. Relative independence from proprietary subsystem-based solutions and host operating system requirements enables the storage administrator to virtualize storage consistently across the enterprise. A higher level of management centralization is realized because there are fewer switches than storage subsystems or hosts. Logical disks can span multiple physical disks in separate subsystems. Other benefits derive from the transparency of storage as viewed from the host, which drives heterogeneity in the storage subsystem market and precipitates improved interoperability. However, some storage vendors are reluctant to adapt their proprietary host-based failover mechanisms to these new network implementations, which might impede enterprise adoption.

Summary

This chapter presents a high-level view of storage networking technologies and select related technologies. We provide insight to the history of storage to elucidate the current business drivers in storage networking. Several types of storage networking technologies are discussed, including open systems file-level, block-level, and backup protocols, and mainframe block-level protocols. We also provide a cursory introduction to the mainstream optical technologies to familiarize you with the long-distance storage connectivity options. We introduce storage virtualization, and briefly compare the various models. Figure 1-11 depicts some of the technologies discussed in this chapter as they relate to each other.

Figure 1-11 *High Level View of Storage Networking*

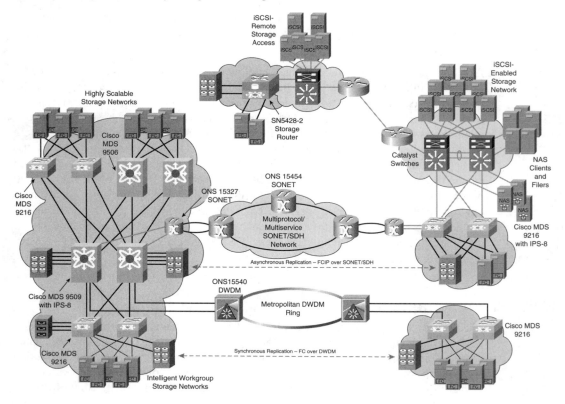

You can find more information on the topics discussed in this chapter and other related topics in standards documents such as IETF RFCs, ANSI T10 and T11 specifications, ITU G series recommendations, and IEEE 802 series specifications. Appendix A lists the specifications most relevant to the topics covered in this book. The websites of industry consortiums and product vendors also contain a wealth of valuable information. Also, the Cisco Systems website contains myriad business and technical documents covering storage technologies, networking technologies, and Cisco's products in a variety of formats including white papers, design guides, and case studies. Last, the Cisco Press storage networking series of books provides comprehensive, in-depth coverage of storage networking topics for readers of all backgrounds.

The subsequent chapters of this book explore select block-oriented, open-systems technologies. The book uses a comparative approach to draw parallels between the technologies. This allows each reader to leverage personal experience with any of the technologies to more readily understand the other technologies. The OSI reference model is used to facilitate this comparative approach.

Review Questions

1 What company invented the modern hard disk drive?

2 Who published the SMI-S?

3 List two competitive advantages enabled by storage networks.

4 What is an IP-SAN?

5 What block-level storage protocol is commonly used in desktop and laptop PCs?

6 What is the latest version of the SCSI protocol?

7 What is the term for an adapter that processes TCP packets on behalf of the host CPU?

8 List the two types of IBM channel protocols.

9 An IBM ESCON director employs what type of switching mechanism?

10 A Fibre Channel switch employs what type of switching mechanism?

11 What company *originally* invented CIFS?

12 What standards body made NFS an industry standard?

13 What type of multiplexing is used by SONET/SDH?

14 What is the WDM window?

15 List one reason the sparse wavelength spacing of CWDM enables lower product costs.

16 In what class of networks is IEEE 802.17?

17 List the two categories of block-oriented virtualization techniques.

Upon completing this chapter, you will be able to:

- Describe the layers of the Open Systems Interconnection (OSI) reference model

- Explain the relationships between the OSI Layers

- Distinguish between a network model and a network implementation

- List the OSI Layers at which the Small Computer System Interface (SCSI) bus, Ethernet, IP, and Fibre Channel (FC) operate

- Define common networking terms used to describe data units

CHAPTER 2

OSI Reference Model Versus Other Network Models

Before delving into the details of the mainstream SCSI networking technologies, we should establish a common frame of reference. This allows accurate comparisons as we examine the details of each technology. The goal of the OSI reference model is to provide such a frame of reference.

OSI Reference Model

The OSI reference model is defined in the 7498 series of documents published by the International Organization for Standardization (ISO). The primary document was originally published in 1984 and then revised and republished in 1994 as ISO/IEC 7498-1:1994. The ISO is responsible for thousands of standards, not all of which relate to information processing and communication. For this reason, the ISO is one of most important international standards bodies in the world. The OSI reference model is widely regarded as the preferred network model by which all networking technologies can be meaningfully compared and contrasted.

NOTE   Notice the acronym ISO does not align with the full name of the organization. The ISO wanted a common acronym to be used by all nations despite language differences. International Organization for Standardization translates differently from one language to the next, so the acronym also would vary from one language to the next. To avoid that problem, they decided that the acronym ISO be used universally despite the language. ISO derives from the Greek word *isos*, meaning *equal*. As a result of choosing this acronym, the organization's name is often documented as International Standardization Organization, which is not accurate.

Network Models, Specifications, and Implementations

A network model typically defines layers and functionality within each layer. A network specification typically defines how to perform the functions defined within each layer of a network model. A network implementation manifests one or more network specifications in hardware or software. The OSI reference model is *not* a network specification. The OSI reference model does not specify protocols, commands, signaling techniques, or other such technical details. Those details are considered implementation-specific and are left to the standards body that defines each specification. The OSI reference model provides common definitions of terms, identifies required network functions, establishes relationships between processes, and provides a framework for the development of open standards that specify how to implement the functions or a subset of the functions defined within the model. Note that the ISO provides separate protocol specifications *based* on the OSI reference model. Those protocol specifications are *not* part of the OSI reference model.

Seven-Layer Model

The OSI reference model comprises seven layers. Each layer may be further divided into sublayers to help implement the model. The common functionality that must be supported for a network to provide end-to-end communication between application processes is broken down into these seven layers. Within each layer, the services that should be implemented to achieve a given level of functionality are defined. Each layer provides services to the layer above and subscribes to the services of the layer below. Each layer accepts data from its upper-layer neighbor and encapsulates it in a header and optional trailer. The result is called a protocol data unit (PDU). The PDU is then passed to the lower-layer neighbor. A PDU received from an upper layer is called a service data unit (SDU) by the receiving layer. The SDU is treated as data and is encapsulated into a PDU. This cycle continues downward through the layers until the physical medium is reached. The logical interface between the layers is called a service access point (SAP). Multiple SAPs can be defined between each pair of layers. Each SAP is unique and is used by a single upper-layer protocol as its interface to the lower-layer process. This enables multiplexing and demultiplexing of upper-layer protocols into lower-layer processes. If a networking technology operates at a single layer, it depends upon all lower layers to provide its services to the layer above. In this way, the layers build upon each other to create a fully functional network model. An implementation of the model is often called a protocol *stack* because of this vertical layering. Figure 2-1 shows the seven OSI layers in relation to each other.

The functions defined within each layer follow:

- **Layer 1**—The physical layer
- **Layer 2**—The data-link layer
- **Layer 3**—The network layer
- **Layer 4**—The transport layer
- **Layer 5**—The session layer
- **Layer 6**—The presentation layer
- **Layer 7**—The application layer

Figure 2-1   *Seven Layers of the OSI Reference Model*

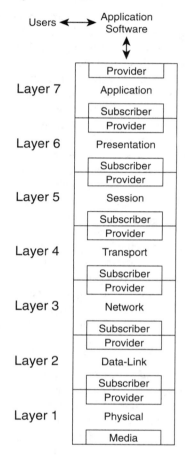

Layer 1—Physical Layer

The physical layer (also known as the PHY layer) is responsible for media-related functions. Data units at this layer are commonly called frames. Details such as physical medium characteristics, physical connector characteristics, electrical and optical signal levels, rules for signal transitions, methods for maintaining direct current (DC) balance, acceptable signal-to-noise ratios, methods for filtering noise, receiver sensitivity, maximum physical link distances, medium error detection and notification procedures, signal timing and synchronization, data encoding techniques, and transmission rates are specified within this layer. Repeaters operate at this layer.

Layer 2—Data-Link Layer

The data-link layer is responsible for transport of data across a physical link. Variable-length data units at this layer are commonly called frames. Fixed-length data units at this layer are commonly called cells. This layer multiplexes network layer protocols into the physical layer process. Details such as medium-access algorithms, duplex settings (half or full), link-level node addressing (also known as physical node addressing), frame types, frame formats, frame sequences, maximum and minimum frame sizes, link-level flow-control mechanisms, handshakes and negotiation methods between Layer 2 entities for support of optional functions, frame and protocol error detection and recovery and notification procedures, protocol timeout values, physical topology, and network layer protocol multiplexing procedures are specified within this layer. A maximum link distance that is shorter than the underlying physical layer technology can support may be imposed by the data-link layer protocol. Multiple similar or dissimilar physical links may be interconnected by Layer 2 devices known as bridges to create an extended Layer 2 network. So, the methods for loop suppression, route discovery and selection, quality of service provisioning, protocol conversion, frame filtering, and frame forwarding are also specified within this layer as appropriate for each technology. Bridging functionality typically is not implemented in end nodes. Data-link layer protocols can operate in connectionless mode or connection-oriented mode. Data-link layer connections facilitate delivery guarantees within a network. So, the procedures for establishment, maintenance, and teardown of connections between pairs of bridges are specified within this layer. If virtual Layer 2 networks are implemented on a shared physical Layer 2 network, this layer is responsible for boundary determination and traffic isolation.

NOTE

In common terminology, *bridge* is somewhat antiquated. It typically refers to a relatively unintelligent device with two ports. The more mainstream term *switch* refers to a bridging device with very high port density, a crossbar for internal port interconnection, advanced intelligence, and other characteristics not found in the bridges of old.

Layer 3—Network Layer

The network layer is responsible for interconnection of physical and virtual Layer 2 networks, network path determination, and forwarding of data between interconnected Layer 2 networks. Data units at this layer are commonly called packets. This layer performs fragmentation of Layer 3 packets received on a network segment that supports a larger packet size than the outbound network segment. Fragments may be reassembled by this layer at a downstream Layer 3 device (rare) or at the destination host before the data is passed to the transport layer (common). This layer also multiplexes transport layer protocols into the data-link layer process.

Details such as network-level node addressing (also known as logical node addressing), network addressing to identify each Layer 2 network, methods for summarization of network addresses, methods for network address discovery, algorithms for path determination, packet types, packet formats, packet sequences, maximum and minimum packet sizes, network-level flow-control mechanisms, network-level quality of service mechanisms, handshakes and negotiation methods between Layer 3 entities for support of optional functions, packet and protocol error detection and recovery and notification procedures, logical topology, and network protocol timeout values are specified within this layer.

Routers operate at this layer. Network layer protocols can operate in connectionless mode or connection-oriented mode. Network layer connections determine the end-to-end path and facilitate delivery guarantees within an internetwork. So the procedures for establishment, maintenance, and teardown of connections between pairs of routers that implement connection-oriented network layer protocols are specified within this layer.

TIP   The phrase *packet switching* is often used to generically describe Layer 3 *and* Layer 2 devices. This sometimes causes confusion because Layer 2 data units are called frames or cells, not packets.

Layer 4—Transport Layer

The transport layer is responsible for end-to-end communication between network nodes. Data units at this layer are commonly called packets. This layer performs segmentation of data received from the session layer into smaller chunks called segments. Segments may or may not be reassembled by this layer at the destination host before the data is passed to the session layer. Likewise, segments that are received out of order may or may not be reordered by this layer at the destination host before the data is passed to the session layer. This layer also multiplexes session layer data streams into the network layer process. Transport layer protocols can operate in connectionless mode or connection-oriented mode. Transport layer connections facilitate end-to-end delivery guarantees. So the procedures for establishment, maintenance, and teardown of connections between pairs of end nodes are specified within this layer. Details such as packet types, packet formats, packet sequences, packet- and protocol-error detection and recovery procedures, node-level flow control mechanisms, node-level queuing mechanisms, connection establishment and maintenance and teardown procedures, maximum segment sizes, segment sequencing and re-ordering procedures, transport protocol timeout values, methods for packet loss detection, and procedures for packet retransmission are specified within this layer.

Layer 5—Session Layer

The session layer is responsible for end-to-end communication between applications. Data units at this layer are commonly called protocol data units (PDU). Session-layer protocols can operate in connectionless mode or connection-oriented mode. Session-layer connections facilitate the orderly exchange of data between applications. Various details are specified within this layer such as the identification of well-known server applications, procedures for dynamic identification of client applications, procedures for session establishment and teardown, mechanisms for resynchronization of a session to a known state, mechanisms for arbitration between presentation-layer protocols to support prioritized access to session layer services, and procedures for suspension and resumption of presentation layer dialogues.

Layer 6—Presentation Layer

The presentation layer is responsible for data representation. Details such as character sets, graphic encoding algorithms, encryption algorithms, and compression algorithms are specified within this layer. This layer identifies the supported data syntaxes and negotiates which to use during each session.

Layer 7—Application Layer

The application layer is responsible for providing the services of the network to application software. An instance of an application running in one host relies on the application layer to identify other hosts running an instance of the application and to verify the target instance is available. This layer also determines an application's quality of service requirements, negotiates security parameters for authentication and authorization and data integrity, negotiates error recovery parameters, negotiates the mode of dialogue between applications, identifies the abstract data syntax to be used, and synchronizes the activities of cooperating applications.

Implementation Considerations

It is possible for end-to-end communication to occur between two nodes that implement only a subset of these layers. The network functionality provided would be less than that achievable by implementing all layers, but might be sufficient for certain applications. Each layer implemented in one network node must also be implemented in a peer node for communication to function properly between that pair of nodes. This is because each layer communicates with its peer layer implemented in another network node. The OSI layer peer relationships are illustrated in Figure 2-2.

Figure 2-2 *Network Node Communication*

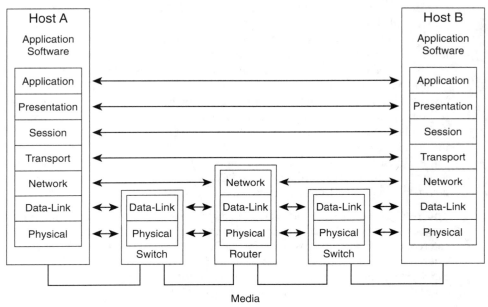

Strict adherence to the OSI reference model is not required of any networking technology. The model is provided only as a reference. Many networking technologies implement only a subset of these layers and provide limited network functionality, thus relying on the complement of other networking technologies to provide full functionality. This compartmentalization of functionality enables a modular approach to the development of networking technologies and facilitates interoperability between disparate technologies. An example of the benefits of this approach is the ability for a connection-oriented physical layer technology to be used by a connectionless data-link layer technology. Some storage networking technologies implement only a subset of functions within one or more of the layers. Those implementation details are discussed in the following sections.

SCSI Bus Interface and the ANSI T10 SCSI-3 Architecture Model

In 1995, the ANSI T10 subcommittee published a three-layer architecture model for the transport of SCSI-3 traffic called the SCSI-3 architecture model (SAM). Two of the three layers are network-oriented, whereas the other is SCSI-oriented. The SAM generically groups all networking technologies into a layer called SCSI Interconnects. Likewise, all protocol mappings that enable SCSI-3 to be transported via SCSI Interconnects are grouped into a single layer called SCSI Transport Protocols. Consequently, the two SAM network layers do not map neatly to the OSI layers. Depending on the actual Interconnect used, the mapping to OSI layers can include one or more layers from the physical layer through the transport layer. Likewise, depending on the actual SCSI Transport Protocol used, the mapping to OSI layers can include one or more layers from the session layer through the application layer. As mentioned in Chapter 1, "Overview of Storage Networking," SCSI-3 is a command/response protocol used to control devices. This can be contrasted with communication protocols, which provide network functionality. Thus, the SCSI-3 command sets compose the third layer of the SAM, which resides above the other two layers. The SCSI-3 command sets are clients to the SCSI Transport Protocols. The SCSI Interconnect and SCSI transport layers are collectively referred to as the SCSI service delivery subsystem. The SCSI-3 command sets are collectively referred to as the SCSI application layer (SAL).

The SCSI parallel bus interfaces are defined by the ANSI T10 subcommittee via the SCSI parallel interface (SPI) series of specifications. The SPI specifications are classified as Interconnects in the SAM. When using an SPI, SCSI commands are transmitted via the Interconnect without the use of a separate SCSI Transport Protocol. The interface between the SCSI command sets and the SPI is implemented as a procedure call similar to the interface between the SCSI command sets and SCSI Transport Protocols.

Each variation of the SPI is a multidrop interface that uses multiple electrical signals carried on physically separate wires to control communication. Such control is normally accomplished via the header of a serialized frame or packet protocol. Some of the other SPI functions include signal generation, data encoding, physical node addressing, medium arbitration, frame generation, and frame error checking. Frame formats are defined for signals on the data wires, one of which contains a data field followed by an optional pad field followed by a cyclic redundancy check (CRC) field. So, the SPI essentially provides OSI physical layer functionality plus a subset of OSI data-link layer functionality. All devices connect directly to a single shared physical medium to create the multidrop bus, and interconnection of buses is not supported. So, there is no need for OSI data-link layer bridging functionality. The concept of OSI data-link layer connection-oriented communication is not applicable to non-bridged environments. Moreover, upper-layer protocol multiplexing is not required because only the SCSI command sets use the SPI. So, many of the services defined within the OSI data-link layer are not required by the SPI. Figure 2-3 compares the SAM to the OSI reference model, lists some specifications, and shows how the SPI specifications map to the OSI layers.

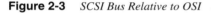

Figure 2-3   *SCSI Bus Relative to OSI*

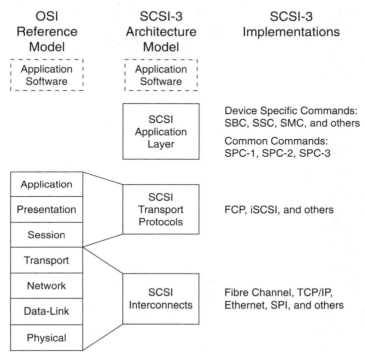

Ethernet and the IEEE 802 Reference Model

The IEEE 802 reference model defines three layers: logical link control (LLC), medium access control (MAC), and physical (PHY). Bridging functions are considered a sublayer within the MAC layer. The LLC and MAC layers map to the OSI data-link layer. The PHY layer maps to the OSI physical layer.

The IEEE 802.3 specification derives from Ethernet II. Today, nearly all Ethernet LANs are 802.3 compliant. A separate amendment, known as 802.3ae, specifies 10-Gbps operation. The frame format of Ethernet II has been merged into 802.3 by allowing the third field of the 802.3 header to be interpreted as either *length* or *type*, depending on the numeric value of the field. The 802.3ae specification uses the same frame format. When the third field is interpreted as *length*, the 802.3 header is followed by the 802.2 header in the PDU. (One notable exception to this rule is the 802.3 raw frame format used by Novell NetWare in the past.) Combined, 802.3 and 802.2 provide full OSI physical layer functionality plus all OSI data-link layer functionality except for bridging-related services. The 802.1D, 802.1G, 802.1H, and 802.1Q specifications provide OSI data-link layer bridging functionality. Alternately, when the third field of the 802.3 header is interpreted as *type*, the 802.2 header is omitted from the PDU. The 802.3 service then provides full OSI physical layer functionality plus limited OSI data-link layer functionality. The *type* field enables identification of the intended upper layer protocol at the destination host (also known as the destination EtherType). This is important because it enables demultiplexing of OSI network layer protocols, which is a subset of the functionality provided by the 802.2 header. Figure 2-4 compares the IEEE 802 reference model to the OSI reference model and lists the relevant Ethernet specifications.

Figure 2-4   *IEEE 802 Relative to OSI*

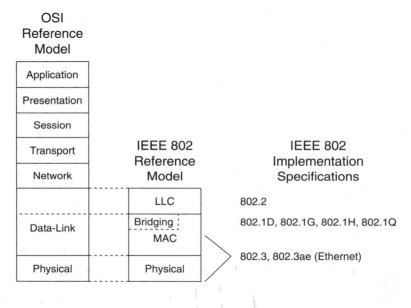

NOTE   IEEE specification names are case sensitive. For example, 802.1q is not the same as 802.1Q. Lower-case letters indicate an amendment to an existing standard, whereas upper-case letters indicate a full standard that might or might not incorporate various amendments.

TCP/IP Suite and the ARPANET Model

The TCP/IP suite originally grew out of the activities of the U.S. military. The TCP/IP suite was the implementation of the four-layer networking model developed by the U.S. military and known as the ARPANET model, which predates the OSI reference model. The principal routed protocols of the TCP/IP suite include Internet Control Message Protocol (ICMP), Address Resolution Protocol (ARP), IP, TCP, and User Datagram Protocol (UDP).

ICMP, ARP, and IP are specified in IETF RFCs 792, 826, and 791 respectively, and all three operate at the OSI network layer. TCP and UDP are specified in IETF RFCs 793 and 768 respectively, and both operate at the OSI transport layer. Of course, there are many routing protocols in the TCP/IP suite such as Enhanced Interior Gateway Routing Protocol (EIGRP), Open Shortest Path First (OSPF), and Border Gateway Protocol (BGP). All IP routing protocols operate at the OSI network layer.

The principal block storage protocols of the TCP/IP suite are routed protocols that operate on TCP. These include Internet SCSI (iSCSI), Fibre Channel over TCP/IP (FCIP), and Internet Fibre Channel Protocol (iFCP) defined in IETF RFCs 3720, 3821, and 4172 respectively. The iSCSI protocol enables delivery of SCSI-3 traffic by providing functionality equivalent to the OSI session, presentation, and application layers. Though iSCSI spans the top three OSI layers, many of the upper-layer protocols in the TCP/IP suite map closely to just one or two of the upper OSI layers. Examples include FCIP and iFCP, each of which map to the OSI session layer. The Common Internet File System (CIFS) and Network File System (NFS) file-level protocols discussed in Chapter 1 also run on TCP. CIFS maps to the OSI application and presentation layers and makes use of NetBIOS at the OSI session layer. NFS spans the top three OSI layers. Figure 2-5 compares the ARPANET model to the OSI reference model and lists the principal protocols of the TCP/IP suite.

Figure 2-5   *ARPANET Relative to OSI*

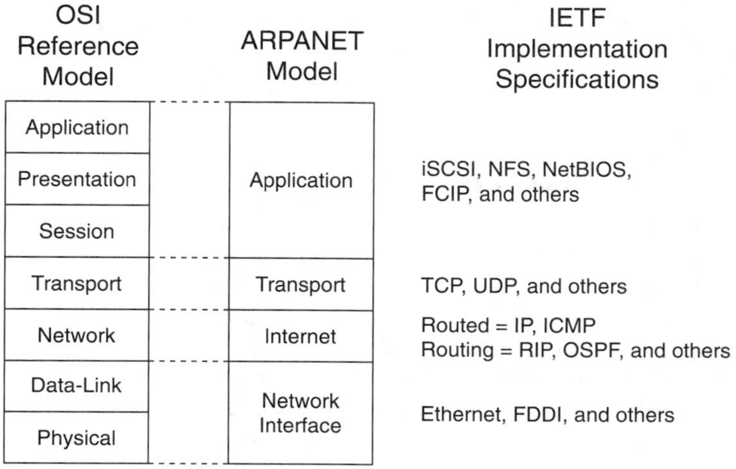

OSI Reference Model	ARPANET Model	IETF Implementation Specifications
Application	Application	iSCSI, NFS, NetBIOS, FCIP, and others
Presentation		
Session		
Transport	Transport	TCP, UDP, and others
Network	Internet	Routed = IP, ICMP Routing = RIP, OSPF, and others
Data-Link	Network Interface	Ethernet, FDDI, and others
Physical		

Fibre Channel Architecture and ANSI T11 Model

The ANSI T11 subcommittee loosely defined a five-layer network model in 1994 as the basis of the Fibre Channel architecture. The layers of the Fibre Channel model are referred to as *levels* in ANSI documentation, but they are called layers within this book. The five layers of the Fibre Channel model are FC-0, FC-1, FC-2, FC-3, and FC-4. Whereas the Fibre Channel model has not changed, the Fibre Channel architecture has undergone numerous changes. The Fibre Channel architecture is currently defined by a large series of specifications published primarily by the ANSI T11 subcommittee.

Fibre Channel Model and the OSI Reference Model

The Fibre Channel model does not map neatly to the OSI reference model. In fact, the Fibre Channel model itself is scantly defined. A quick glance at the Fibre Channel model indicates that the Fibre Channel architecture operates at the OSI physical, data-link, and application layers. However, to fully understand the Fibre Channel model, it is necessary to infer details from the Fibre Channel specifications. This approach is unorthodox, and it undermines the purpose of a network model. These points notwithstanding, we attempt herein to clearly define the Fibre Channel model so that readers can better understand how it relates to the OSI reference model.

Similar to the OSI reference model, the Fibre Channel model layers build upon each other starting with FC-0 as the foundation. One notable exception is the FC-3 layer. The Hunt Group functionality defined within FC-3 builds upon the node-addressing functionality within FC-2. However, the Link Services defined within FC-3 are required for FC-2 operation. So, FC-3 logically resides above *and* below FC-2 in the OSI provider/subscriber paradigm. Despite this, ANSI documentation invariably depicts FC-3 above FC-2 in the vertical stack representing the five layers of the Fibre Channel model. This book depicts FC-3 and FC-2 as peers whenever the Fibre Channel model is diagramed.

Fibre Channel Specifications

ANSI T11 publishes two types of FC specifications: protocol standards and technical reports. Each protocol standard describes a subset of the overall FC functionality. For example, the FC-SW-4 specification describes interswitch behavior. The latest version of each protocol standard is recommended for new product implementations; however, the latest version of a protocol standard does not render obsolete previous versions of the same standard or related standards. This precludes immediate technical obsolescence of products that are based on previous versions of the standard. Unfortunately, this gives rise to interoperability issues. In addition, the protocol standards provide many options to accommodate a wide variety of deployment scenarios. This flexibility also can cause interoperability issues. So, technical reports are published to promote interoperability by restricting the options that might be used in a given environment. For example, the FC-DA specification provides a set of behavioral restrictions for end nodes in arbitrated loop environments and a separate set of behavioral restrictions for end nodes in switched fabric environments. The latest draft version of each in-progress FC specification is available on the ANSI T11 website while the work is in progress. When a specification is completed, the draft versions are archived, and the final version must be purchased for a nominal fee.

The Fibre Channel specifications do not map neatly to the Fibre Channel model. The details of how to implement the functionality defined within each layer of the Fibre Channel model are spread across multiple specification documents. That said, a close look at the Fibre Channel specifications reveals that considerable end-to-end functionality is supported. So, an accurate description is that the Fibre Channel *architecture* operates at the OSI physical, data-link, transport, session, presentation, and application layers. Extrapolating this information to better understand the Fibre Channel *model* indicates the following:

- FC-4 maps roughly to the OSI application and presentation layers.
- FC-3 and FC-2 map roughly to the OSI session, transport, and data-link layers.
- FC-1 and FC-0 map roughly to the OSI physical layer.
- None of the Fibre Channel layers neatly maps to the OSI network layer, but some of the specifications (specifically, the FC-BB series) enable OSI network layer functionality via external protocols.

Originally, the FC-PH series of documents specified much of Fibre Channel's functionality and spanned multiple OSI layers. Later specifications separated portions of the OSI physical layer functionality into a separate series of documents. The OSI physical layer functionality of Fibre Channel is now principally specified in the FC-PI and 10GFC series. The OSI data-link layer functionality is now principally specified in the FC-FS, FC-DA, FC-SW, FC-AL, and FC-MI series. There is no OSI network layer functionality inherent to Fibre Channel, but the FC-BB series provides various methods to leverage external networking technologies, some of which operate at the OSI network layer.

From the Fibre Channel perspective, external networks used to interconnect disparate Fibre Channel storage area networks (FC-SAN) are transparent extensions of the OSI data-link layer service. A subset of the OSI transport layer functionality is provided via the N_port login (PLOGI) and N_port logout (LOGO) mechanisms as specified in the FC-FS, FC-DA, and FC-LS series. A subset of the OSI session layer functionality is provided via the process login (PRLI) and process logout (PRLO) mechanisms as specified in the FC-FS, FC-DA, and FC-LS series. Protocol mappings enable Fibre Channel to transport many types of traffic, including OSI network layer protocols (for example, IP), application level protocols (for example, SCSI-3), and data associated with application-level services (for example, Fibre Channel Name Service). These mappings provide a subset of the OSI presentation layer and application layer functionality. Most of the mappings are defined by the ANSI T11 subcommittee, but some are defined by other organizations. For example, the Single-Byte Command Code Set (SBCCS) mappings are defined in the ANSI T11 subcommittee's FC-SB series, but the SCSI-3 mappings are defined in the ANSI T10 subcommittee's FCP series. Figure 2-6 compares the Fibre Channel model to the OSI reference model and lists the Fibre Channel specifications most relevant to storage networking.

Figure 2-6   *Fibre Channel Relative to OSI*

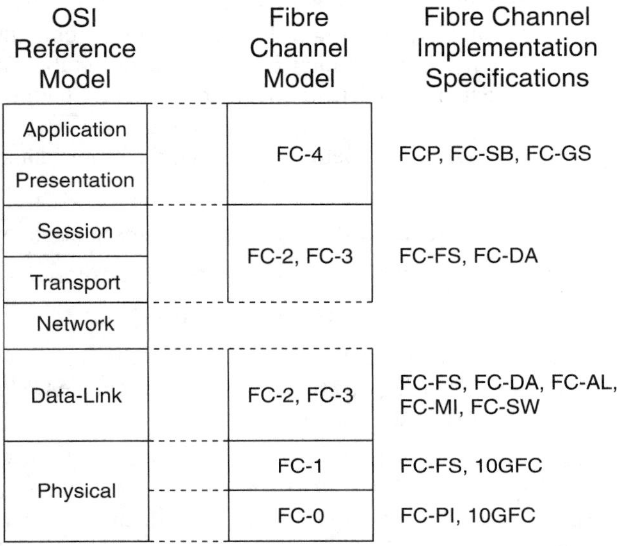

OSI Reference Model	Fibre Channel Model	Fibre Channel Implementation Specifications
Application	FC-4	FCP, FC-SB, FC-GS
Presentation		
Session	FC-2, FC-3	FC-FS, FC-DA
Transport		
Network		
Data-Link	FC-2, FC-3	FC-FS, FC-DA, FC-AL, FC-MI, FC-SW
Physical	FC-1	FC-FS, 10GFC
	FC-0	FC-PI, 10GFC

Summary

The OSI reference model facilitates modular development of communication products, thereby reducing time to market for new products and facilitating faster evolution of existing products. Standards organizations often leverage the OSI reference model in their efforts to specify implementation requirements for new technologies. The ISO does not guarantee interoperability for OSI-compliant implementations, but leveraging the OSI reference model does make interoperability easier and more economical to achieve. This is increasingly important in the modern world of networking.

The protocols discussed in this chapter do not all map to the OSI reference model in a neat and clear manner. However, the functionality provided by each protocol is within the scope of the OSI reference model. The most important things to understand are the concepts presented in the OSI reference model. That understanding will serve you throughout your career as new networking technologies are created. The OSI reference model provides network engineers with the proverbial yardstick required for understanding all the various networking technologies in a relative context. The OSI reference model also brings clarity to the complex interrelation of functionality inherent to every modern networking technology. The OSI reference model is used throughout this book to maintain that clarity.

Review Questions

1 How many layers are specified in the OSI reference model?

2 The data-link layer communicates with which OSI layer in a peer node?

3 What is the OSI term for the interface between vertically stacked OSI layers?

4 How many OSI layers operate end-to-end? List them.

5 Which OSI layer is responsible for bit-level data encoding?

6 Which is the only OSI layer not inherent to the Fibre Channel architecture?

7 Create a mnemonic device for the names and order of the OSI layers.

Upon completing this chapter, you will be able to:

- Discuss the history of the Small Computer System Interface (SCSI) Parallel Interface (SPI), Ethernet, TCP/IP, and Fibre Channel (FC)
- Explain the difference between baud, raw bit, and data bit rates
- Quantify the actual throughput available to SCSI via the SPI, Internet SCSI (iSCSI), and Fibre Channel Protocol (FCP)
- Recognize the various physical topologies
- State which logical topologies are supported by the SPI, Ethernet, IP, and FC
- Define the basic techniques for service and device discovery
- Describe the discovery mechanisms used in SPI, Ethernet, TCP/IP, and FC environments

CHAPTER 3

Overview of Network Operating Principles

This chapter characterizes Ethernet, the TCP/IP suite, and Fibre Channel. These network technologies enable open systems block-oriented storage networking. We also examine the SCSI parallel interface (SPI) for historical perspective. Each section begins with a general characterization of the technology, to give readers a historical perspective on the development of each technology. Each section then examines throughput capabilities, supported topologies, and techniques for discovery of the operating environment. To help readers fully understand the discussion of each technology, this chapter begins with some useful background information.

Conceptual Underpinnings

This section provides the foundational knowledge required to understand throughput, topologies, and discovery techniques.

Throughput

When discussing the throughput of any frame-oriented protocol that operates at OSI Layers 1 and 2, it is important to understand the difference between baud rate, raw bit rate, data bit rate, and upper layer protocol (ULP) throughput rate. The carrier signal is the natural (unmodified) electrical or optical signal. The baud rate is the rate at which the carrier signal is artificially modulated (transformed from one state to another state). Multiple carrier signal transitions can occur between each pair of consecutive artificial state transitions. Baud rate is inherently expressed per second. Bits received from OSI Layer 2 must be encoded into the signal at OSI Layer 1. The number of bits that can be encoded per second is the raw bit rate. The encoding scheme might be able to represent more than one bit per baud, but most schemes represent only one bit per baud. So, the baud rate and the raw bit rate are usually equal. However, the bits encoded often include control bits that were not received from OSI Layer 2. Control bits typically are inserted by the encoding scheme and are used to provide clocking, maintain direct current (DC) balance, facilitate bit error detection, and allow the receiver to achieve byte or word alignment. The number of raw bits per second minus the number of control bits per second yields the data bit rate. This is the number of bits generated at OSI Layer 2 that can be transmitted per second. The data bit rate includes OSI Layer 2 framing bits and payload bits. The ULP throughput rate is the number of payload bits that can be transmitted per second. So, the number of data bits per second minus the number of framing bits per second yields the ULP throughput rate.

Topologies

There are too many design implications associated with each physical topology for this chapter to cover the subject exhaustively. So, this section merely introduces the physical topologies by providing a brief discussion of each. The general points discussed in this section are equally applicable to all networking technologies including the SPI, Ethernet, IP, and Fibre Channel. Note that for any given topology, there might be many names. Each community of network technologists seems to prefer a different name for each topology.

Context should be considered when discussing topology. Discussions of very small-scale networks often include the end nodes in the topological context (see the star and linear paragraphs). When discussing medium- and large-scale networks, communication between network devices is the primary topological concern. So, end nodes usually are excluded from that topological context. This section discusses topologies in both contexts.

Another important point regarding topology is perspective. Link-state protocols based on the Dijkstra algorithm create a logical tree topology in which each network device sees itself as the root of the tree. By contrast, Ethernet's Spanning Tree algorithm creates a tree topology in which every switch recognizes the same switch as the root of the tree. Perspective partially determines the behavior of a network device in a given topology. Additionally, the physical topology (cabling) and logical topology (communication model) often are not the same. This can cause confusion when discussing certain physical topologies in the context of certain protocols.

There are six types of physical topologies:

- Star (sometimes called hub-and-spoke)
- Linear (commonly called bus or cascade)
- Circular (commonly called ring or loop)
- Tree
- Partial Mesh
- Full Mesh

Any of these six physical topologies can be combined to create a hybrid topology. Figures 3-1 through 3-6 illustrate an example of each physical topology. Figure 3-7 illustrates the star topology versus the collapsed ring/loop topology.

Figure 3-1   *Star/Hub-and-Spoke Topology*

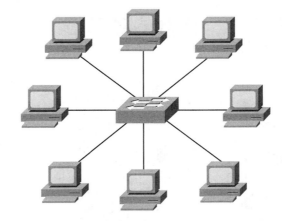

Figure 3-2   *Linear/Bus/Cascade Topology*

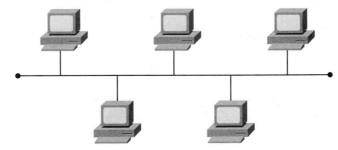

Figure 3-3   *Circular/Ring/Loop Topology*

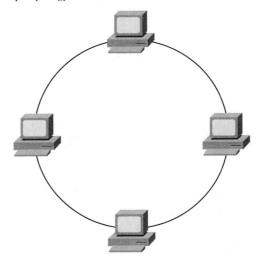

Figure 3-4 *Tree Topology*

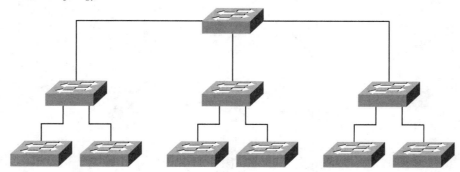

Figure 3-5 *Partial Mesh Topology*

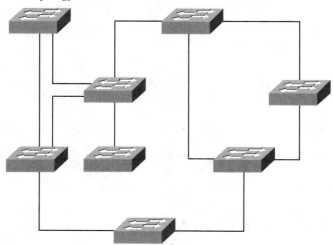

Figure 3-6 *Full Mesh Topology*

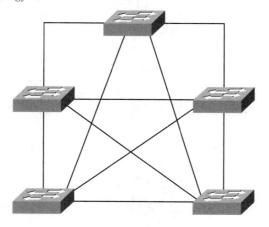

Figure 3-7 *Star Versus Collapsed Ring/Loop*

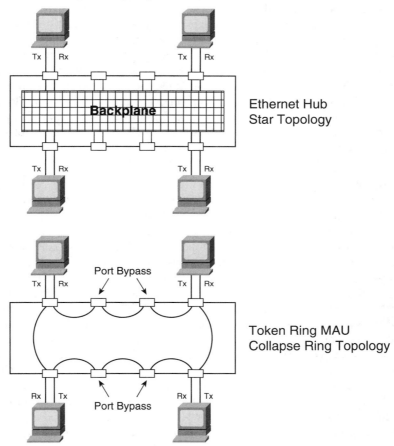

In the star topology, all devices are connected through a single, central network element such as a switch or hub. Without consideration for the end nodes, the star topology is just a single network device. Upon considering the end nodes, the star shape becomes apparent. On the surface, the collapsed ring topology in Figure 3-7 also appears to have a star shape, but it is a circular topology. A collapsed ring/collapsed loop topology is merely a circular topology cabled into a centralized device.

The star topology differs from the collapsed ring/loop topology in the way signals are propagated. The hub at the center of a star topology propagates an incoming signal to every outbound port simultaneously. Such a hub also boosts the transmit signal. For this reason, such hubs are most accurately described as multiport repeaters. By contrast, the multi-access unit (MAU) at the center of the collapsed ring in Figure 3-7 passively connects the transmit wire of one port to the receive wire of the next port. The signal must propagate sequentially from node to node in a circular manner. So, the unqualified terms hub and concentrator are ambiguous. Ethernet hubs are multiport repeaters and support the star topology. Token ring MAUs, FDDI concentrators, and Fibre Channel arbitrated loop (FCAL) hubs are all examples of collapsed ring/loop devices. By collapsing the ring/loop topology, the geometric shape becomes the same as the star topology (even though signal propagation is unchanged). The geometric shape of the star topology (and collapsed ring/loop topology) simplifies cable plant installation and troubleshooting as compared to the geometric shape of a conventional (distributed) ring/loop topology (shown in Figure 3-3). Cable plant simplification is the primary benefit of a collapsed ring/loop topology versus a conventional (distributed) ring/loop topology. However, the star topology provides other benefits not achievable with the collapsed ring/loop topology (because of signal propagation differences). Figure 3-7 illustrates the geometrical similarities and topological differences of the star and collapsed ring/loop topologies.

Network devices connected in a linear manner form a cascade topology. A cascade topology is geometrically the same as a bus topology. However, the term cascade *usually* applies to a topology that connects network devices (such as hubs or switches), whereas the term bus *usually* applies to a topology that connects end nodes. The name indicates the topological context. Note that the bus topology enables direct communication between each pair of attached devices. This direct communication model is an important feature of the bus topology. A cascade topology may require additional protocols for inter-switch or inter-router communication. The connection between each pair of network devices (switch or router) is sometimes treated as a point-to-point (PTP) topology. A PTP topology is a linear topology with only two attached devices (similar to a very small bus topology). Protocols that support multiple topologies often have special procedures or control signals for PTP connections. In other words, the PTP communication model is not always the same as the bus communication model. In fact, many protocols have evolved specifically for PTP connections (for example, high-level data-link control [HDLC] and Point-to-Point Protocol [PPP]). PTP protocols behave quite differently than protocols designed for the bus topology. Some protocols developed for the bus topology also support the PTP topology. However, protocols designed specifically for PTP connections typically do not operate properly in a bus topology.

Devices connected in a circular manner form a ring/loop topology. From a geometrical viewpoint, a ring/loop is essentially a cascade/bus with its two ends connected. However, most protocols behave quite differently in a ring/loop topology than in a cascade/bus topology. In fact, many protocols that support the ring/loop topology are specifically designed for that topology and have special procedures and control signals. Link initialization, arbitration, and frame forwarding are just some of the procedures that require special handling in a ring/loop topology.

Protocols not specifically designed for the ring/loop topology often have special procedures or protocols for using a ring/loop topology. For example, Ethernet's Spanning Tree Protocol (STP) is a special protocol that allows Ethernet to use a circular topology in a non-circular manner (a process commonly known as loop suppression). By contrast, Fibre Channel's loop initialization primitive (LIP) sequences allow Fibre Channel devices to use a circular topology (FCAL) in a circular manner. Conventional logic suggests that a ring/loop topology must contain at least three devices. However, a ring/loop can be formed with only two devices. When only two devices are connected in a ring/loop topology, the geometry is the same as a PTP topology, but communication occurs in accordance with the rules of the particular ring/loop technology. For example, if an FCAL has many devices attached, and all but two are removed, communication between the remaining two devices still must follow the rules of FCAL communication.

Devices connected in a perpetually branching manner form a tree topology. Alternately, a tree topology can have a root with multiple branches that do not subsequently branch. This appears as multiple, separate cascades terminating into a common root. The tree topology generally is considered the most scalable topology. Partial and full mesh topologies can be highly complex. Many people believe that simpler is better in the context of network design, and this belief has been vindicated time and time again throughout the history of the networking industry.

Occam's razor underlies the most scalable, reliable network designs. For this reason, the tree topology, which is hierarchical in nature, has proven to be one of the most effective topologies for large-scale environments. However, complex partial-mesh topologies can also scale quite large if the address allocation scheme is well considered, and the routing protocols are configured with sufficient compartmentalization. The Internet offers ample proof of that.

Service and Device Discovery

Service and device discovery mechanisms in the context of network devices can be quite different from such mechanisms in the context of end nodes. This chapter focuses on the end node context. This section introduces discovery mechanisms and provides a brief discussion of common techniques.

Service discovery mechanisms enable a device to discover the services supported by other devices in its operating environment. Device discovery mechanisms enable a newly added device to discover pre-existing devices in its new operating environment. Pre-existing devices also use device discovery mechanisms to discover newly added devices. Each device typically caches information about other devices (such as name or address) for a limited period of time. As the need arises, device discovery mechanisms are used periodically to re-cache information that has been aged out. Service and device discovery mechanisms often return the names of other devices. In such cases, a name resolution mechanism is required to resolve device names to addresses. When multilayer network technologies are employed, an address resolution mechanism is required to resolve addresses at one OSI layer to addresses at another OSI layer.

The two general approaches to service and device discovery include many variations for each of them. We offer the following examples only to provide insight. They should not be considered comprehensive descriptions.

The first approach is service oriented. A service instance is located, followed by device name resolution, and finally by optional address resolution. For example, a query for a service instance might be sent via some service-locating protocol to a well-known unicast or multicast address, an anycast address, or a broadcast address. A device replying to such queries typically returns a list of device names known to support the service sought by the querying device. The querying device then resolves one of the names to an address and optionally resolves that address to another address. The querying device can then initiate service requests.

The second approach is device-oriented. Devices are discovered first and then queried for a list of supported services. One technique involves the use of a device discovery protocol to query a network by transmitting to a well-known multicast address or even the broadcast address. Devices responding to such a protocol often provide their name or address in the payload of the reply. Another technique is to directly query each unicast address in the address space. A timeout value must be established to avoid a hang condition (waiting forever) when a query is sent to an address at which no active device resides. Address probing typically works well only for technologies that support a small address space. Another technique is to send a query to a central registration authority to discover all registered devices. This is more practical for technologies that support a large address space. In such a case, devices are expected to register upon booting by sending a registration request to a well-known unicast or multicast address or sometimes to the broadcast address. Following a query, name or address resolution might be required depending on the content of the reply sent by the central registration authority. After devices have been discovered and names and addresses have been resolved, some or all of the devices are directly probed for a list of supported services. The querying device may then initiate service requests.

SCSI Parallel Interface

The SPI is most commonly called the SCSI bus. Chapter 1, "Overview of Storage Networking," purposely refers to the SPI as the SCSI bus for the sake of common terminology. Chapter 2, "OSI Reference Model Versus Other Network Models," introduces the more accurate term SPI, which is used in this and in all subsequent chapters. The SPI does not enable modern storage networking per se, but it did shoulder the burden of SCSI transport for many years before the mainstream adoption of open systems storage networks. As such, this trusty technology established many of the criteria by which we judge modern open systems storage networks. We can summarize those criteria as:

- High bandwidth
- Low latency
- No jitter
- Inherent in-order delivery of frames *and* I/O transactions
- Low probability of dropped frames

These criteria are easy to meet when designing a new network technology for small-scale deployments with only one application to transport. However, the modern business climate demands efficiency in all areas, which inevitably leads to infrastructure consolidation. Meeting all of the SPI's legacy requirements in a converged network environment can be quite challenging and complex. So we include a brief discussion of the SPI herein to ensure that readers understand the legacy requirements.

The Right Tool for the Job

The simplicity of the SPI relative to other network technologies is the primary reason that so many people fail to recognize the SPI as a network technology. Indeed, the SPI *is* a network technology, albeit localized and of very small scale and limited capability. The SPI was designed to perform a limited set of functions in a specific environment. Traditionally, a SCSI storage device (target) was used by a single host (initiator) and was deployed inside the chassis of the host or in a separate chassis located very near the host. The host might have used multiple SCSI storage devices, but the total device count generally remained low. The short distance requirements, combined with the low number of attached devices, allowed a simple interconnect to meet the needs of the SCSI protocol. Because SCSI was the only application using the interconnect, no other requirements needed to be considered. Though the SPI might be simple in the context of other network technologies, the latter versions are impressive engineering works in their own right.

SPI Throughput

As is true of most network technologies, the throughput of the SPI has improved significantly since its inception. Four factors determine the maximum supported data transfer rate of each SPI specification. These are data bus width, data transfer mode, signal transition mode, and transceiver type. There are two data bus widths known as narrow (eight bits wide) and wide (16 bits wide). There are three data transfer modes known as asynchronous, synchronous, and paced. There are two signal transition modes known as single transition (ST) and double transition (DT). There are four transceiver types known as single-ended (SE), multimode single-ended (MSE), low voltage differential (LVD), and high voltage differential (HVD). All these variables create a dizzying array of potential combinations. SCSI devices attached to an SPI via any transceiver type always default to the lowest throughput combination for the other three variables: narrow, asynchronous, and ST. Initiators must negotiate with targets to use a higher throughput combination for data transfers. Table 3-1 summarizes the maximum data transfer rate of each SPI specification and the combination used to achieve that rate. Because the SPI is a parallel technology, data transfer rates customarily are expressed in megabytes rather than megabits. Though the SPI-5 specification is complete, very few products have been produced based on that standard. Serial attached SCSI (SAS) was well under way by the time SPI-5 was finished, so most vendors opted to focus their efforts on SAS going forward.

NOTE A 32-bit data bus was introduced in SPI-2, but it was made obsolete in SPI-3. For this reason, discussion of the 32-bit data bus is omitted.

Table 3-1 *SPI Maximum Data Transfer Rates*

Specification	Common Name	Transfer Rate	Negotiated Combination
SPI-2	Ultra2	80 MBps	Wide, Sync, ST, LVD, or HVD
SPI-3	Ultra3 or Ultra160	160 MBps	Wide, Sync, DT, LVD
SPI-4	Ultra320	320 MBps	Wide, Paced, DT, LVD
SPI-5	Ultra640	640 MBps	Wide, Paced, DT, LVD

The SPI consists of multiple wires that are used for simultaneous parallel transmission of signals. Some of these signals are used for control and operation of the SPI, and others are used for data transfer. The set of wires used for data transfer is collectively called the data bus. References to the data bus can be confusing because the data bus is not a separate bus, but is merely a subset of wires within the SPI. The data bus also can be used to transfer certain control information. Use of the data bus is regulated via a state machine. An SPI is always in one of the following eight states (called bus phases):

- BUS FREE
- ARBITRATION
- SELECTION
- RESELECTION
- COMMAND
- DATA
- STATUS
- MESSAGE

The COMMAND, DATA, STATUS, and MESSAGE phases use the data bus, whereas the other four phases do not. The COMMAND, STATUS, and MESSAGE phases always operate in narrow, asynchronous, ST mode. The DATA phase may operate in several modes subject to initiator/target negotiation. The transfer rates in Table 3-1 apply only to data transfer across the data bus during the DATA phase. Data can be transferred across the data bus *only* during the DATA phase. Control information can be transferred across the data bus *only* during the COMMAND, STATUS, and MESSAGE phases. Each DATA phase is preceded and followed by other phases. This is the reason some references to the SPI's throughput describe the maximum transfer rate as a burst rate rather than a sustained rate. However, the intervening phases are the logical equivalent of frame headers and inter-frame spacing in serialized network technologies. During the BUS FREE, ARBITRATION, SELECTION, and RESELECTION phases, the data bus is not used. Those phases transfer information using the control wires of the SPI.

A closer analysis of the SPI's data transfer rate is possible. However, given the SPI's declining importance in modern storage networking solutions, further analysis is not germane to this book. Detailed analysis of data transfer rates is provided for Ethernet and Fibre Channel in subsequent sections.

SPI Topologies

As previously stated, the SPI operates as a multidrop bus. Each attached device is connected directly to a shared medium, and signals propagate the entire length of the medium without being regenerated by attached devices. The device at each end of the bus must have a terminator installed to prevent signal reflection. All intermediate devices must have their terminator removed or disabled to allow end-to-end signal propagation. Each device uses the data bus for both transmission and reception of data. Moreover, there are no dedicated transmit wires or dedicated receive wires in the data bus. There are only *data* wires. Each device implements a dual function driver per data bus wire. Each driver is capable of both transmission and reception. This contrasts with other technologies in which separate transmit and receive wires require separate transmit and receive drivers in the attached devices. In such technologies, the transmit driver of each device is connected to the receive driver of the next device via a single wire. The signal on that wire is perceived as transmit by one device and as receive by the other device. A second wire connects the reciprocal receive driver to the reciprocal transmit driver. Figure 3-8 illustrates the difference.

Figure 3-8   *SPI Common Drivers Versus Dedicated Drivers*

Common Tx/Rx Drivers

Data Bus Wires
1 2 3 4 5 6 7 8

Terminator

Terminator

Dedicated Tx/Rx Drivers

Rx   Tx

Tx   Rx

NIC   NIC

The data bus implementation of the SPI makes the SPI inherently half-duplex. Though it is possible to build dual function drivers capable of simultaneous transmission and reception, the SPI does not implement such drivers. The half-duplex nature of the SPI reflects the half-duplex nature of the SCSI protocol. The SPI was designed specifically for the SCSI protocol, and the multidrop bus is the SPI's only supported topology.

SPI Service and Device Discovery

The SPI uses a device-oriented approach. When an SPI is initialized or reset, the initiator discovers attached devices by sending a TEST UNIT READY command to each address in sequential order. Because the SPI address space is very small, this works well and avoids the complexity of a central registration facility. Name resolution is not required because device names are not implemented by the SPI. Address resolution is not required because the SPI supports only OSI Layer 2 addressing. The initiator then sends, in sequential order, an INQUIRY command to each device that responded to the TEST UNIT READY command. Each device response includes the device type (direct access, sequential access, enclosure services, and so on), the medium type (removable or non-removable), the version number (SPC, SPC-2, or SPC-3), the supported address space (8 or 16) and indicators for support of protocol options (for example, synchronous data transfers and hierarchical Logical Unit Numbers [LUNs]). A response may include optional information such as manufacturer name, hardware model number, or other information. After probing each target device, the initiator issues a REPORT LUNS command to each target device to discover the existence of LUNs. SCSI I/O operations can occur after all LUNs have been discovered, but the initiator may choose to issue additional discovery or configuration commands before beginning I/O operations.

NOTE   The SPI supports multiple initiators, but such a configuration is very rare in the real world. Thus, a single initiator is assumed in all SPI discussions in this book unless otherwise stated.

Ethernet

Many people misunderstand the current capabilities of Ethernet because of lingering preconceptions formed during the early days of Ethernet. In its pre-switching era, Ethernet had some severe limitations. However, most of Ethernet's major drawbacks have been eliminated by the widespread adoption of switching and other technological advances. This section explains how Ethernet has evolved to become the most broadly applicable LAN technology in history, and how Ethernet provides the foundation for new services (like storage networking) that might not be considered LAN-friendly.

Low Overhead Paradigm

To fully appreciate Ethernet, you need to understand that Ethernet began as a low overhead, high efficiency alternative to competing communication technologies. Simplicity was at the heart of the original Ethernet specification developed by Robert Metcalfe and David Boggs in 1973. Ethernet really began to penetrate the LAN market after the IEEE became involved and produced the 802.3 specification. ARCNET and Token Ring were Ethernet's primary competitors when 802.3 debuted. For the remainder of this book, the term Ethernet shall refer to the IEEE 802.3 specification unless otherwise noted.

Ethernet was not designed to outperform supplementary LAN technologies in every way, but rather to provide an alternative that was inexpensive and easy to deploy and support. At 10 Mbps, Ethernet was much faster than ARCNET (2.5 Mbps at that time) and Token Ring (4 Mbps at that time). This was perceived to be advantageous, though the 10 Mbps transmission rate was rarely achieved in real world deployments. Fortunately for Ethernet, very few people realized that at the time. Ethernet had another advantage over ARCNET. Unlike ARCNET, which employed the use of switch blocks to physically configure the address of each node, Ethernet addresses were "burned" into NICs at the factory. This made adds, moves, and changes relatively painless in Ethernet networks compared to ARCNET. A third advantage was Ethernet's prodigious address space. ARCNET's limited address space created challenges for companies as their LANs grew. ARCNET address conflicts often would occur long before a LAN was near the maximum number of nodes unless administrators carefully tracked address assignments. Ethernet was (and still is) carefree in this regard, because every Ethernet address was globally unique.

Ethernet also had several advantages over Token Ring. Unlike Token Ring, Ethernet equipment could be purchased from several vendors. IBM was the only vendor of Token Ring equipment in the early days of LANs. Cabling was another advantage for Ethernet. Most Ethernet networks were based on standard coaxial cabling (commonly called Thinnet and Thicknet) at that time. This made Ethernet cable plants less expensive than Token Ring cable plants, which were based on proprietary IBM Type I cabling. The bus topology also simplified Ethernet cabling compared to Token Ring cabling, which required each ring to be physically looped. A Token Ring MAU enabled the creation of a collapsed ring topology. As mentioned previously, a collapsed ring simplifies the cable plant installation and lowers the cabling costs by centralizing all cable runs. The same could be accomplished with Ethernet by using hubs (sometimes called concentrators) and twisted pair cabling to create a star topology (a configuration called 10BASE-T). The cost of a Token Ring MAU was typically higher than the cost of an Ethernet hub. So, the total cost of a Token Ring solution (with or without MAUs) was typically higher than a comparable Ethernet solution. In the early days of LANs, most companies considered cost more important than other factors.

The Ethernet bus and star topologies required the medium to be shared, and a drawback of shared media is that it supports only half-duplex communication. So, one Ethernet node would transmit while all other nodes received. This limited aggregate throughput and created the need to arbitrate for media access. The arbitration method employed by Ethernet is based on the principle of fairness, which seeks to ensure that all nodes have equal access to the medium. The method of arbitration is called carrier sense multiple access with collision detection (CSMA/CD). ARCNET and Token Ring both employed half-duplex communication at that time, because they too were shared media implementations. ARCNET and Token Ring both employed arbitration based on token passing schemes in which some nodes could have higher priority than others. The CSMA/CD mechanism has very low overhead compared to token passing schemes. The tradeoffs for this low overhead are indeterminate throughput because of unpredictable collision rates and (as mentioned previously) the inability to achieve the maximum theoretical throughput.

As time passed, ARCNET and Token Ring lost market share to Ethernet. That shift in market demand was motivated primarily by the desire to avoid unnecessary complexity, to achieve higher throughput, and (in the case of Token Ring) to reduce costs. As Ethernet displaced ARCNET and Token Ring, it expanded into new deployment scenarios. As more companies became dependent upon Ethernet, its weaknesses became more apparent. The unreliability of Ethernet's coax cabling became intolerable, so Thinnet and Thicknet gave way to 10BASE-T. The indeterminate throughput of CSMA/CD also came into sharper focus. This and other factors created demand for deterministic throughput and line-rate performance. Naturally, the cost savings of Ethernet became less important to consumers as their demand for increased functionality rose in importance. So, 10BASE-T switches were introduced, and Ethernet's 10 Mbps line rate was increased to 100 Mbps (officially called 100BASE-T but commonly called Fast Ethernet and abbreviated as FE). FE hubs were less expensive than 10BASE-T switches and somewhat masked the drawbacks of CSMA/CD. 10BASE-T switches and FE hubs temporarily satiated 10BASE-T users' demand for improved performance.

FE hubs made it possible for Fiber Distributed Data Interface (FDDI) users to begin migrating to Ethernet. Compared to FDDI, FE was inexpensive for two reasons. First, the rapidly expanding Ethernet market kept prices in check as enhancements were introduced. Second, FE used copper cabling that was (at the time) significantly less expensive than FDDI's fiber optic cabling. FE hubs proliferated quickly as 10BASE-T users upgraded and FDDI users migrated. Newly converted FDDI users renewed the demand for deterministic throughput and line rate performance. They were accustomed to high performance because FDDI used a token passing scheme to ensure deterministic throughput. Around the same time, businesses of all sizes in all industries began to see LANs as mandatory rather than optional. Centralized file servers and e-mail servers were proliferating and changing the way businesses operated. So, FE hubs eventually gave way to switches capable of supporting both 10 Mbps and 100 Mbps nodes (commonly called 10/100 auto-sensing switches).

TIP   Auto-sensing is a common term that refers to the ability of Ethernet peers to exchange link level capabilities via a process officially named auto-negotiation. Note that Fibre Channel also supports auto-sensing.

10BASE-T switches had been adopted by some companies, but uncertainty about switching technology and the comparatively high cost of 10BASE-T switches prevented their widespread adoption. Ethernet switches cost more than their hub counterparts because they enable full-duplex communication. Full-duplex communication enables each node to transmit and receive simultaneously, which eliminates the need to arbitrate, which eliminates Ethernet collisions, which enables deterministic throughput and full line-rate performance. Another benefit of switching is the decoupling of transmission rate from aggregate throughput. In switched technologies, the aggregate throughput per port is twice the transmission rate. The aggregate throughput per switch is limited only by the internal switch design (the crossbar implementation, queuing mechanisms, forwarding decision capabilities, and so on) and the number of ports. So, as people began to fully appreciate the benefits of switching, the adoption rate for 10/100 auto-sensing switches began to rise. As switching became the norm, Ethernet left many of its limitations behind. Today, the vast majority of Ethernet deployments are switch-based.

Ethernet's basic media access control (MAC) frame format contains little more than the bare essentials. Ethernet assumes that most protocol functions are handled by upper layer protocols. This too reflects Ethernet's low overhead, high efficiency philosophy. As switching became the norm, some protocol enhancements became necessary and took the form of MAC frame format changes, new frame types, and new control signals.

One of the more notable enhancements is support for link-level flow control. Many people are unaware that Ethernet supports link-level flow control. Again reflecting its low overhead philosophy, Ethernet supports a simple back-pressure flow-control mechanism rather than a credit-based mechanism. Some perceive this as a drawback because back-pressure mechanisms can result in frame loss during periods of congestion. This is true of some back-pressure mechanisms, but does not apply to Ethernet's current mechanism if it is implemented properly. Some people remember the early days of Ethernet when *some* Ethernet switch vendors used a different back-pressure mechanism (but not Cisco). Many switches initially were deployed as high-speed interconnects between hub segments. If a switch began to experience transmit congestion on a port, it would create back pressure on the port to which the source node was connected. The switch did so by intentionally generating a collision on the source node's segment. That action resulted in dropped frames and lowered the effective throughput of all nodes on the source segment. The modern Ethernet back-pressure mechanism is implemented only on full-duplex links, and uses explicit signaling to control the transmission of frames intelligently on a per-link basis. It is still possible to drop Ethernet frames during periods of congestion, but it is far less likely in modern Ethernet implementations. We can further reduce the likelihood of dropped frames through proper design of the MAC sublayer components. In fact, the IEEE 802.3-2002 specification explicitly advises system designers to account for processing and link-propagation delays when implementing flow control. In other words, system designers can and should proactively invoke the flow-control mechanism rather than waiting for all receive buffers to fill before transmitting a flow control frame. A receive buffer high-water mark can be established to trigger flow-control invocation. Because there is no mechanism for determining the round-trip time (RTT) of a link, system designers should take a conservative approach to determining the high-water mark. The unknown RTT represents the possibility of dropped frames. When frames are dropped, Ethernet maintains its low-overhead philosophy by assuming that an upper layer protocol will handle detection and retransmission of the dropped frames.

Ethernet Throughput

As mentioned previously, Ethernet initially operated at only 10 Mbps. Over time, faster transmission rates came to market beginning with 100 Mbps (also called Fast Ethernet [FE]) followed by 1000 Mbps (GE). Each time the transmission rate increased, the auto-sensing capabilities of NICs and switch ports adapted. Today, 10/100/1000 auto-sensing NICs and switches are common. Ethernet achieved a transmission rate of 10 Gbps (called 10Gig-E and abbreviated as 10GE) in early 2003. Currently, 10GE interfaces do not interoperate with 10/100/1000 interfaces because 10GE does not support auto-negotiation. 10GE supports only full-duplex mode and does not implement CSMA/CD.

As previously mentioned, a detailed analysis of Ethernet data transfer rates is germane to modern storage networking. This is because the iSCSI, Fibre Channel over TCP/IP (FCIP), and Internet Fibre Channel Protocol (iFCP) protocols (collectively referred to as IP storage (IPS) protocols) are being deployed on FE and GE today, and the vast majority of IPS deployments will likely run on GE and 10GE as IPS protocols proliferate. So, it is useful to understand the throughput of GE and 10GE when calculating throughput for IPS protocols. The names GE and 10GE refer to their respective data bit rates, not to their respective raw bit rates. This contrasts with some other technologies, whose common names refer to their raw bit rates. The fiber optic variants of GE operate at 1.25 GBaud and encode 1 bit per baud to provide a raw bit rate of 1.25 Gbps. The control bits reduce the data bit rate to 1 Gbps. To derive ULP throughput, we must make some assumptions regarding framing options. Using a standard frame size (no jumbo frames), the maximum payload (1500 bytes), the 802.3 basic MAC frame format, no 802.2 header, and minimum inter-frame spacing (96 bit times), a total of 38 bytes of framing overhead is incurred. The ULP throughput rate is 975.293 Mbps.

The copper variant of GE is somewhat more complex. It simultaneously uses all four pairs of wires in a Category 5 (Cat5) cable. Signals are transmitted on all four pairs in a striped manner. Signals are also received on all four pairs in a striped manner. Implementing dual function drivers makes full-duplex communication possible. Each signal operates at 125 MBaud. Two bits are encoded per baud to provide a raw bit rate of 1 Gbps. There are no dedicated control bits, so the data bit rate is also 1 Gbps. This yields the same ULP throughput rate as the fiber optic variants.

The numerous variants of 10GE each fall into one of three categories:

- 10GBASE-X
- 10GBASE-R
- 10GBASE-W

10GBASE-X is a WDM-based technology that simultaneously uses four lambdas, operates at 3.125 GBaud per lambda, and encodes 1 bit per baud to provide a raw bit rate of 12.5 Gbps. The control bits reduce the data bit rate to 10 Gbps. Using the same framing assumptions used for GE, this yields an ULP throughput rate of 9.75293 Gbps.

10BASE-R operates at 10.3125 GBaud and encodes 1 bit per baud to provide a raw bit rate of 10.3125 Gbps. The control bits reduce the data bit rate to 10 Gbps. Using the same framing assumptions used for GE, this yields the same ULP throughput rate as 10GBASE-X.

10GBASE-W is an exception. 10GBASE-W provides a mapping of 10GE onto SONET STS-192c and SDH VC-4-64c for service provider applications. Only SONET STS-192c is discussed herein on the basis that SDH VC-4-64c is not significantly different in the context of ULP throughput. The STS-192c baud rate of 9.95328 GBaud is lower than the 10GBASE-R PHY baud rate. As mentioned previously, SONET is an OSI Layer 1 technology. However, SONET incorporates robust framing to enable transport of many disparate OSI Layer 2 technologies. The 10GBASE-R PHY merely encodes data received from the MAC, whereas SONET introduces additional framing overhead not present in 10GBASE-R. So, the ULP throughput rate of an STS-192c interface represents the raw bit rate in 10GBASE-W. The WAN interface sublayer (WIS) of the 10GBASE-W PHY is responsible for STS-192c framing. The WIS presents a raw bit rate of 9.5846 Gbps to the physical coding sublayer (PCS) of the 10GBASE-W PHY. 10GBASE-W control bits reduce the data bit rate to 9.2942 Gbps. Using the same framing assumptions used for GE, this yields an ULP throughput rate of 9.06456 Gbps.

Table 3-2 summarizes the baud, bit, and ULP throughput rates of the GE and 10GE variants.

Table 3-2   *Ethernet Baud, Bit, and ULP Throughput Rates*

Ethernet Variant	Baud Rate	Raw Bit Rate	Data Bit Rate	ULP Throughput
GE Fiber Optic	1.25 GBaud	1.25 Gbps	1 Gbps	975.293 Mbps
GE Copper	125 MBaud x 4	1 Gbps	1 Gbps	975.293 Mbps
10GBASE-X	3.125 GBaud x 4	12.5 Gbps	10 Gbps	9.75293 Gbps
10GBASE-R	10.3125 GBaud	10.3125 Gbps	10 Gbps	9.75293 Gbps
10GBASE-W	9.95328 GBaud	9.5846 Gbps	9.2942 Gbps	9.06456 Gbps

NOTE   The IEEE 802.3-2002 specification includes a 1 Mbps variant called 1Base5 that was derived from an obsolete network technology called StarLAN. Discussion of 1Base5 is omitted herein. StarLAN evolved to support 10 Mbps operation and was called StarLAN10. The IEEE's 10BaseT specification was partially derived from StarLAN10.

To transport IPS protocols, additional framing overhead must be incurred. Taking iSCSI as an example, three additional headers are required: IP, TCP, and iSCSI. The TCP/IP section of this chapter discusses IPS protocol overhead.

Ethernet Topologies

Today, Ethernet supports all physical topologies. The original Ethernet I and Ethernet II specifications supported only the bus topology. When the IEEE began development of the first 802.3 specification, they decided to include support for the star topology. However, the communication model remained bus-oriented. Although the 802.3-2002 specification still includes the Thinnet and Thicknet bus topologies (officially called 10BASE2 and 10BASE5 respectively), they are obsolete in the real world. No other bus topologies are specified in 802.3-2002. The star topology is considered superior to the bus topology for various reasons. The primary reasons are easier cable plant installation, improved fault isolation, and (when using a switch) the ability to support full-duplex communication. The star topology can be extended by cascading Ethernet hubs (resulting in a hybrid topology). There are two classes of FE hub. Class I FE hubs cannot be cascaded because of CSMA/CD timing restrictions. Class II FE hubs can be cascaded, but no more than two are allowed per collision domain. Cascading is the only means of connecting Ethernet hubs. FE hubs were largely deprecated in favor of 10/100 switches. GE also supports half-duplex operation, but consumers have not embraced GE hubs. Instead, 10/100/1000 switches have become the preferred upgrade path. While it is technically possible to operate IPS protocols on half-duplex Ethernet segments, it is not feasible because collisions can (and do) occur. So, the remaining chapters of this book focus on switch-based Ethernet deployments.

Unlike Ethernet hubs, which merely repeat signals between ports, Ethernet switches bridge signals between ports. For this reason, Ethernet switches are sometimes called multiport bridges. In Ethernet switches, each port is a collision domain unto itself. Also, collisions can occur only on ports operating in half-duplex mode. Because most Ethernet devices (NICs and switches alike) support full-duplex mode and auto-negotiation, most switch ports operate in full-duplex mode today. Without the restrictions imposed by CSMA/CD, all topologies become possible. There is no restriction on the manner in which Ethernet switches may be interconnected. Likewise, there is no restriction on the number of Ethernet switches that may be interconnected. Ethernet is a broadcast capable technology; therefore loops must be suppressed to avoid broadcast storms. As mentioned previously, this is accomplished via STP. The physical inter-switch topology will always be reduced to a logical cascade or tree topology if STP is enabled. Most switch-based Ethernet deployments have STP enabled by default. The remainder of this book assumes that STP is enabled unless stated otherwise.

A pair of modern Ethernet nodes can be directly connected using a twisted pair or fiber optic cable (crossover cable). The result is a PTP topology in which auto-negotiation occurs directly between the nodes. The PTP topology is obviously not useful for mainstream storage networking, but is useful for various niche situations. For example, dedicated heartbeat connections between clustered devices are commonly implemented via Ethernet. If the cluster contains only two devices, a crossover cable is the simplest and most reliable solution.

Ethernet Service and Device Discovery

There is no service discovery mechanism in Ethernet. No service location protocol is defined by the 802.2-1998, 802.3-2002, or 802.3ae-2002 specifications. Likewise, no procedure is defined for a node to probe other nodes to discover supported services. Reflecting its low-overhead philosophy, Ethernet assumes that ULPs will handle service discovery. Ethernet assumes the same for device discovery. ULPs typically determine the existence of other nodes via their own mechanisms. The ULP address is then resolved to an Ethernet address. Each ULP has its own method for resolving the Ethernet address of another node. The TCP/IP suite uses the Address Resolution Protocol (ARP) specified in RFC 826.

NOTE   A conceptually related protocol is the Reverse Address Resolution Protocol (RARP) specified in RFC 903. RARP provides a means for a device to resolve its own ULP address using its Ethernet address. RARP is operationally similar to ARP but is functionally different. RARP has no bearing on modern storage networks but is still referenced in some product documentation and is still used in some niche environments. RARP is mentioned here only for the sake of completeness, so you will not be confused if you encounter RARP in documentation or in operation. RARP was replaced by BOOTP and DHCP.

Each ULP has a reserved protocol identifier called an Ethertype. Originally, the Ethertype was not included in the 802.3 header, but it is now used in the 802.3 header to identify the intended ULP within the destination node. The Ethertype field enables multiplexing of ULPs on Ethernet. Ethertypes could be used as well known ports (WKPs) for the purpose of ULP discovery, but each ULP would need to define its own probe/reply mechanism to exploit the Ethertype field. This is not the intended purpose of the Ethertype field. Ethertypes are assigned and administered by the IEEE to ensure global uniqueness.

TCP/IP Suite

Many years ago, corporate LANs were characterized by multiple protocols. Each network operating system (NOS) implemented its own protocol at OSI Layer 3. That made life very difficult for systems administrators, network administrators, and users alike. Over time, each NOS vendor began to support multiple protocols. That enabled system and network administrators to converge on one protocol. For better or worse, IP eventually emerged as the predominant OSI Layer 3 protocol for LANs, MANs, and WANs. For many companies, the choice was not based on technical superiority, but rather on the need for Internet connectivity. If any other protocol ever had a chance against IP, the Internet boom sealed its fate. Today, IP is by far the most ubiquitous OSI Layer 3 protocol on earth.

Value of Ubiquitous Connectivity

The primary goal of the ARPANET creators was to transform computer science (and ultimately human society) through communication technology. That said, the creators of the ARPANET probably did not envision the proliferation of IP on today's scale. If they had, they surely would have done some things differently. All things considered, they did far better than could be reasonably expected given the challenges they faced. In the days of the ARPANET (launched in 1969), computer science was characterized primarily by batch processing on isolated machines. The creators of the ARPANET believed that the true power of computers was not in their ability to compute, but in their ability to create communities by providing a new means of communication. So, their challenge was to create the world's first computer network.

The underlying physical infrastructure was to be created by a separate team from the protocol designers. It would be called the interface message processor (IMP). Not knowing the details of the IMP made it very difficult to design the communication protocols. Moreover, each host operating system was unique in those days, so creating communication protocols that could be implemented by a broad range of hosts was very challenging. In the end, it was determined that multiple levels of abstraction would facilitate development of a suitable protocol suite. Thus, the layered network model was born.

The meetings of the ARPANET protocol designers were open forum-style discussions that enabled new, creative ideas to be posited and discussed. The designers were mostly college students who did not have great confidence in their authority to make decisions about the protocols under development. No meeting minutes were taken for the first few meetings. Eventually, notes from each meeting were taken down as *request for comments* (RFCs). The notes were labeled as such because the meeting attendees thought another team of "real" protocol designers would take over eventually, and they did not want to offend the official designers. That seems a bit comical now, but it had a huge effect on the fate of the ARPANET protocols and, eventually, the protocols of the modern Internet. By adopting a system in which uncommitted ideas are documented and then openly reviewed by a broad audience before being formalized into standards, the creators of the ARPANET virtually guaranteed the long-term success of the Internet Protocol suite. The RFC process lends itself to global participation and enables the development of living protocols (protocols that can be adapted as requirements change).

The emphasis on human community, abstraction through layered protocols, and open dialogue about future developments were critical to ensuring the future of TCP/IP. The critical mass of TCP/IP deployments was achieved many years ago. That mass ensures ongoing support by all major application, NOS, and network vendors. Today, development of new protocols and protocol enhancements is undertaken on a voluntary basis by interested parties comprising vendors and users alike. Maintenance of the global address pool, root domain list, protocol documentation, port registry, and other operational constructs is overseen by nonprofit organizations. While no protocol suite is perfect, TCP/IP seems to get closer every day as the result of unprecedented development efforts aimed at meeting the ever-increasing range of demands placed upon TCP/IP. TCP/IP's application support is unrivaled by any other protocol suite, and virtually every operating system supports TCP/IP. Additionally, IP supports virtually every OSI Layer 2 protocol. That powerful combination of attributes forms the basis of TCP/IP's truly ubiquitous connectivity. Ubiquitous connectivity is hugely advantageous for the users of TCP/IP. Ubiquitous connectivity fosters new relationships among computing resources and human communities. In an interesting quote about the thought process that led to the creation of the ARPANET protocols and eventually the modern TCP/IP suite, Stephen Crocker states, "We looked for existing abstractions to use. It would have been convenient if we could have made the network simply look like a tape drive to each host, but we knew that wouldn't do." The recent ratification of the iSCSI protocol, which adapts tape drives and other storage devices to TCP/IP, is testimony of how far TCP/IP has come.

TCP/IP Throughput

IP runs on lower-layer protocols; therefore the achievable throughput depends on the underlying technology. At the low end, IP can run on analog phone lines via PPP and a modem at speeds from 300 bps to 56 Kbps. At the high end, IP can run on SONET OC-192c or 10GE at approximately 10 Gbps. Many factors can affect throughput in IP networks. The maximum transmission unit (MTU) of the underlying technology determines the TCP maximum segment size (MSS) for the source node. The larger the MSS, the more efficiently TCP can use the underlying technology.

Fragmentation of IP packets at intermediate routers also can affect throughput. Fragmentation occurs when a router forwards an IP packet onto an interface with a smaller MTU than the source interface. Once a packet is fragmented, it must remain fragmented across the remainder of the path to the destination node. That decreases the utilization efficiency of the path from the point of fragmentation to the destination node. IP fragmentation also increases the processing burden on the intermediate router that performs the fragmentation, and on the destination node that reassembles the fragments. This can lead to degradation of performance by increasing CPU and memory consumption. Path MTU (PMTU) discovery offers a means of avoiding IP fragmentation by using ICMP immediately before TCP session establishment. (See Chapter 6, "OSI Network Layer," for more information about ICMP and PMTU discovery in IP networks.)

TCP optimization is another critical factor. There are many parameters to consider when optimizing TCP performance. RFC 1323 describes many such parameters. Windowing is central to all TCP operations. The TCP slow start algorithm describes a process by which end nodes begin communicating slowly in an effort to avoid overwhelming intermediate network links. This is necessary because end nodes generally do not know how much bandwidth is available in the network or how many other end nodes are vying for that bandwidth. Thus, a conservative approach to data transmission is warranted. As communication continues, the rate of transmission is slowly increased until a packet drop occurs. The dropped packet is assumed to be the result of an overwhelmed intermediate network link. The slow start algorithm reduces the total number of dropped packets that must be retransmitted, which increases the efficiency of the network as a whole. However, the price paid is that the throughput of every new TCP session is lower than it could be while the end nodes are in the slow start phase. TCP is discussed in more detail in Chapter 7, "OSI Transport Layer," and Chapter 9, "Flow Control and Quality of Service."

As mentioned previously, TCP/IP and IPS protocol overhead reduces the throughput rate available to SCSI. Consider iSCSI; assuming no encryption, three headers must be added before Ethernet encapsulation. Assuming that no optional IP header fields are present, the standard IP header adds 20 bytes. Assuming that no optional TCP header fields are present, the standard TCP header adds another 20 bytes. Assuming that no optional iSCSI header fields are present, the iSCSI basic header segment (BHS) adds another 48 bytes. Table 3-3 summarizes the throughput rates available to SCSI via iSCSI based on the Ethernet ULP throughput rates given in Table 3-2.

Table 3-3   *SCSI Throughput via iSCSI on Ethernet*

Ethernet Variant	Ethernet ULP Throughput	iSCSI ULP Throughput
GE Fiber Optic	975.293 Mbps	918.075 Mbps
GE Copper	975.293 Mbps	918.075 Mbps
10GBASE-X	9.75293 Gbps	9.18075 Gbps
10GBASE-R	9.75293 Gbps	9.18075 Gbps
10GBASE-W	9.06456 Gbps	8.53277 Gbps

The ULP throughput calculation for iSCSI is different than FCIP and iFCP. Both FCIP and iFCP use the common FC frame encapsulation (FC-FE) format defined in RFC 3643. The FC-FE header consists of 7 words, which equates to 28 bytes. This header is encapsulated in the TCP header. Using the same assumptions as in Table 3-3, the ULP throughput can be calculated by adding 20 bytes for the IP header and 20 bytes for the TCP header and 28 bytes for the FC-FE header. Table 3-4 summarizes the throughput rates available to FC via FCIP and iFCP on an Ethernet network.

Table 3-4   *FC Throughput via FCIP and iFCP on Ethernet*

Ethernet Variant	Ethernet ULP Throughput	FCIP/iFCP ULP Throughput
GE Fiber Optic	975.293 Mbps	931.079 Mbps
GE Copper	975.293 Mbps	931.079 Mbps
10GBASE-X	9.75293 Gbps	9.31079 Gbps
10GBASE-R	9.75293 Gbps	9.31079 Gbps
10GBASE-W	9.06456 Gbps	8.65364 Gbps

Note that the ULP in Table 3-4 is FC, not SCSI. To determine the throughput available to SCSI, the FC framing overhead must also be included. If the IP Security (IPsec) protocol suite is used with any of the IPS protocols, an additional header must be added. This further decreases the throughput available to the ULP. Figure 3-9 illustrates the protocol stacks for iSCSI, FCIP and iFCP. Note that neither FCIP nor iFCP adds additional header bits. Certain bits in the FC-FE header are available for ULP-specific usage.

Figure 3-9   *IPS Protocol Stacks*

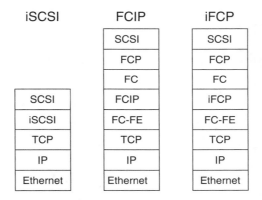

TCP/IP Topologies

IP supports all physical topologies but is subject to the limitations of the underlying protocol. OSI Layer 2 technologies often reduce complex physical topologies into simpler logical topologies. IP sees only the logical topology created by the underlying technology. For example, the logical tree topology created by Ethernet's STP appears to be the physical topology as seen by IP. IP routing protocols can organize the OSI Layer 2 end-to-end logical topology (that is, the concatenation of all interconnected OSI Layer 2 logical topologies) into a wide variety of OSI Layer 3 logical topologies.

Large-scale IP networks invariably incorporate multiple OSI Layer 2 technologies, each with its own limitations. The resulting logical topology at OSI Layer 3 is usually a partial mesh or a hybrid of simpler topologies. Figure 3-10 illustrates a hybrid topology in which multiple sites, each containing a tree topology, are connected via a ring topology.

IP routing is a very complex topic that exceeds the scope of this book. Chapter 10, "Routing and Switching Protocols," introduces some basic routing concepts, but does not cover the topic in depth. One point is worth mentioning: Some IP routing protocols divide a large topology into multiple smaller topologies called areas or autonomous regions. The boundary between the logical topologies is usually called a border. The logical topology on each side of a border is derived independently by the instance of the routing protocol running within each area or autonomous region.

Figure 3-10 *Large-Scale Hybrid Topology*

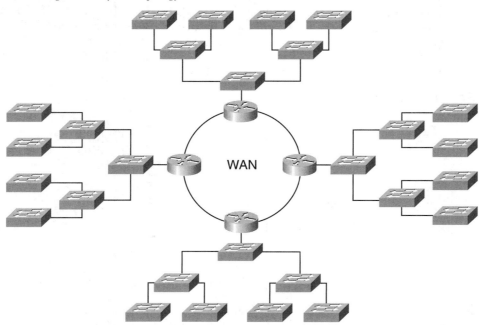

TCP/IP Service and Device Discovery

Service and device discovery in TCP/IP environments is accomplished in different ways depending on the context.

Discovery Contexts

In the context of humans, a user often learns the location of a desired service via non-computerized means. For example, a user who needs access to a corporate e-mail server is told the name of the e-mail server by the e-mail administrator. The World Wide Web (more commonly referred to as the Web) provides another example. Users often learn the name of websites via word of mouth, e-mail, or TV advertisements. For example, a TV commercial that advertises for Cisco Systems would supply the company's URL, http://www.cisco.com/. When the user decides to visit the URL, the service (HTTP) and the host providing the service (www.cisco.com) are already known to the user. So, service and device discovery mechanisms are not required. Name and address resolution are the only required mechanisms. The user simply opens the appropriate application and supplies the name of the destination host. The application transparently resolves the host name to an IP address via the Domain Name System (DNS).

Another broadly deployed IP-based name resolution mechanism is the NetBIOS Name Service (NBNS). NBNS enables Microsoft Windows clients to resolve NetBIOS names to IP addresses. The Windows Internet Name Service (WINS) is Microsoft's implementation of NBNS. DNS and NBNS are both standards specified by IETF RFCs, whereas WINS is proprietary to Microsoft. Once the host name has been resolved to an IP address, the TCP/IP stack may invoke ARP to resolve the Ethernet address associated with the destination IP address. An attempt to resolve the destination host's Ethernet address occurs only if the IP address of the destination host is within the same IP subnet as the source host. Otherwise, the Ethernet address of the default gateway is resolved. Sometimes a user does not know of instances of the required service and needs assistance locating such instances. The Service Location Protocol (SLP) can be used in those scenarios. SLP is discussed in the context of storage in following paragraphs.

In the context of storage, service and device discovery mechanisms are required. Depending on the mechanisms used, the approach may be service-oriented or device-oriented. This section uses iSCSI as a representative IPS protocol. An iSCSI target node represents a service (SCSI target). An iSCSI target node is, among other things, a process that acts upon SCSI commands and returns data and status to iSCSI initiators. There are three ways to inform an iSCSI initiator of iSCSI target nodes:

- Manual configuration (no discovery)
- Semi-manual configuration (partial discovery)
- Automated configuration (full discovery)

Manual Configuration

Manual configuration works well in small-scale environments where the incremental cost and complexity of dynamic discovery is difficult to justify. Manual configuration can also be used in medium-scale environments that are mostly static, but this is not recommended because the initial configuration can be onerous. The administrator must supply each initiator with a list containing the IP address, port number, and iSCSI target name associated with each iSCSI target node that the initiator will access. TCP port number 3260 is registered for use by iSCSI target devices, but iSCSI target devices may listen on other port numbers. The target name can be specified in extended unique identifier (EUI) format, iSCSI qualified name (IQN) format or network address authority (NAA) format (see Chapter 8, "OSI Session, Presentation, and Application Layers"). After an initiator establishes an iSCSI session with a target node, it can issue a SCSI REPORT LUNS command to discover the LUNs defined on that target node.

Semi-Manual Configuration

Semi-manual configuration works well for small- to medium-scale environments. It involves the use of the iSCSI SendTargets command. The SendTargets command employs a device-oriented approach. To understand the operation of the SendTargets command, some background information is needed. There are two types of iSCSI session: discovery and normal. All iSCSI sessions proceed in two phases: login and full feature. The login phase always occurs first. For discovery sessions, the purpose of login is to identify the initiator node to the target entity, so that security filters can be applied to responses. Thus, the initiator node name must be included in the login request. Because target node names are not yet known to the initiator, the initiator is not required to specify a target node name in the login request. So, the initiator does not log in to any particular target node. Instead, the initiator logs into the unidentified iSCSI entity listening at the specified IP address and TCP port. This special login procedure is unique to discovery sessions. Normal iSCSI sessions require the initiator to specify the target node name in the login request. Upon completion of login, a discovery session changes to the full-feature phase. iSCSI commands can be issued only during the full-feature phase. During a discovery session, only the SendTargets command may be issued; no other operations are supported. The sole purpose of a discovery session is to discover the names of and paths to target nodes. Upon receiving a SendTargets command, the target entity issues a SendTargets response containing the iSCSI node names of targets accessible via the IP address and TCP port at which the SendTargets command was received. The response may also contain additional IP addresses and TCP ports at which the specified target nodes can be reached. After discovery of target nodes, a SCSI REPORT Luns command must be issued to each target node to discover LUNs (via a normal iSCSI session).

To establish a discovery session, the initiator must have some knowledge of the target entities. Thus, the initiators must be manually configured with each target entity's IP address and TCP port number. The SendTargets command also may be used during normal iSCSI sessions for additional path discovery to known target nodes.

The SendTargets command contains a parameter that must be set to one of three possible values: ALL, the name of an iSCSI target node, or null. The parameter value ALL can be used only during an iSCSI discovery session. The administrator must configure each initiator with at least one IP address and port number for each target device. Upon boot or reset, the initiator establishes a TCP session and an iSCSI discovery session to each configured target device. The initiator then issues a SendTargets command with a value of ALL to each target device. Each target device returns a list containing all iSCSI target names (representing iSCSI target nodes) to which the initiator has been granted access. The IP address(es), port number(s) and target portal group tag(s) (TPGT) at which each target node can be reached are also returned. (The TPGT is discussed in Chapter 8, "OSI Session, Presentation, and Application Layers.")

After initial discovery of target nodes, normal iSCSI sessions can be established. The discovery session may be maintained or closed. Subsequent discover sessions may be established. If an initiator issues the SendTargets command during a normal iSCSI session, it must specify the name of a target node or use a parameter value of null. When the parameter value is set to the name of an iSCSI target node, the target device returns the IP address(es), port number(s), and TPGT(s) at which the specified target node can be reached. This is useful for discovering new paths to the specified target node or rediscovering paths after an unexpected session disconnect. This parameter value is allowed during discovery and normal iSCSI sessions. The third parameter value of null is similar to the previous example, except that it can be used only during normal iSCSI sessions. The target device returns a list containing all IP address(es), port number(s), and TPGT(s) at which the target node of the current session can be reached. This is useful for discovering path changes during a normal iSCSI session.

The iSCSI RFCs specify no method for automating the discovery of target devices. However, it is technically possible for initiators to probe with echo-request ICMP packets to discover the existence of other IP devices. Given the range of possible IP addresses, it is not practical to probe every IP address. So, initiators would need to limit the scope of their ICMP probes (perhaps to their local IP subnet). Initiators could then attempt to establish a TCP session to port 3260 at each IP address that replied to the echo-request probe. Upon connection establishment, an iSCSI discovery session could be established followed by an iSCSI SendTargets command. Target devices that are not listening on the reserved port number would not be discovered by this method. Likewise, target devices on unprobed IP subnets would not be discovered. This probe method is not recommended because it is not defined in any iSCSI-related RFC, because it has the potential to generate considerable overhead traffic, and because it suffers from functional limitations.

Automated Configuration

Automated configuration is possible via SLP, which is defined in RFC 2165 and updated in RFC 2608. SLP employs a service-oriented approach that works well for medium- to large-scale environments. SLP defines three entities known as the user agent (UA), service agent (SA), and directory agent (DA). The UA is a process that runs on a client device. It issues service-request messages via multicast or broadcast on behalf of client applications. (Other SLP message types are defined but are not discussed herein.) The SA is a process that runs on a server device and replies to service-request messages via unicast *if* the server device is running a service that matches the request. The SLP service type templates that describe iSCSI services are defined in RFC 4018. UAs may also send service request messages via unicast if the server location (name or address) is known. An SA must reply to all unicast service requests, even if the requested service is not supported. A UA may include its iSCSI initiator name in the service request message. This allows SAs to filter requests and reply only to authorized initiators. Such a filter is generically called an access control list (ACL).

For scalability, the use of one or more SLP DAs can be enlisted. The DA is a process that runs on a server device and provides a central registration facility for SAs. If a DA is present, each SA registers its services with the DA, and the DA replies to UAs on behalf of SAs. SA service information is cached in the DA store.

There are four ways that SAs and UAs can discover DAs: multicast/broadcast request, multicast/broadcast advertisement, manual configuration, and Dynamic Host Configuration Protocol (DHCP).

The first way involves issuing a service-request message via multicast or broadcast seeking the DA service. The DA replies via unicast. The reply consists of a DAAdvert message containing the name or address of the DA and the port number of the DA service if a non-standard port is in use.

The second way involves listening for unsolicited DAAdvert messages, which are transmitted periodically via multicast or broadcast by each DA.

The third way is to manually configure the addresses of DAs on each device containing a UA or SA. This approach defeats the spirit of SLP and is not recommended. The fourth way is to use DHCP to advertise the addresses of DAs. DHCP code 78 is defined as the SLP Directory Agent option.

When a DA responds to a UA service request message seeking services other than the DA service, the reply contains the location (host name/IP address and TCP port number if a non-standard port is in use) of all hosts that have registered the requested service. In the case of iSCSI, the reply also contains the iSCSI node name of the target(s) accessible at each IP address. Normal name and address resolution then occurs as needed.

SLP supports a scope feature that increases scalability. SLP scopes enable efficient use of DAs in multi-DA environments by confining UA discovery within administratively defined boundaries. The SLP scope feature offers some security benefits, but it is considered primarily a provisioning tool. Every SA and DA must belong to one or more scopes, but scope membership is optional for UAs. A UA that belongs to a scope can discover services only within that scope. UAs can belong to more than one scope at a time, and scope membership is additive. UAs that do not belong to a scope can discover services in all scopes. Scope membership can be manually configured on each UA and SA, or DHCP can be used. DHCP code 79 is defined as the SLP Service Scope option.

Automated configuration is also possible via the Internet Storage Name Service (iSNS), which is defined in RFC 4171. iSNS employs a service-oriented approach that is well suited to large-scale environments. Like SLP, iSNS provides registration and discovery services. Unlike SLP, these services are provided via a name server modeled from the Fibre Channel Name Server (FCNS). Multiple name servers may be present, but only one may be active. The others act as backup name servers in case the primary name server fails. All discovery requests are processed by the primary iSNS name server; target devices do not receive or reply to discovery requests. This contrasts with the SLP model, in which direct communication between initiators and target devices can occur during discovery. Because of this, the iSNS client is equivalent to both the SLP SA and UA. The iSNS server is equivalent to the SLP DA, and the iSNS database is equivalent to the SLP DA store. Also like SLP, iSNS provides login and discovery control. The iSNS Login Control feature is equivalent to the initiator name filter implemented by SLP targets, but iSNS Login Control is more robust. The iSNS dscovery domain (DD) is equivalent to the SLP scope, but iSNS DDs are more robust. Unlike SLP, iSNS supports centralized configuration, state change notification (SCN), and device mapping.

iSNS clients locate iSNS servers via the same four methods that SLP UAs and SAs use to locate SLP DAs. The first method is a client-initiated multicast/broadcast request. Rather than define a new procedure for this, iSNS clients use the SLP multicast/broadcast procedure. This method requires each iSNS client to implement an SLP UA and each iSNS server to implement an SLP SA. If an SLP DA is present, the iSNS server's SA registers with the DA, and the DA responds to iSNS clients' UA requests. Otherwise, the iSNS server's SA responds directly to iSNS clients' UA requests. The service request message contains a request for the iSNS service.

The second method is a server initiated multicast/broadcast advertisement. The iSNS server advertisement is called the Name Service Heartbeat. In addition to client discovery, the heartbeat facilitates iSNS primary server health monitoring by iSNS backup servers.

The third method is manual configuration. Though this method is not explicitly permitted in the iSNS RFC, support for manual configuration is common in vendor implementations of practically every protocol. As with SLP, this approach is not recommended because it undermines the spirit of iSNS. The fourth method is DHCP. DHCP code 83 is defined as the iSNS option.

All clients (initiators and targets) can register their name, addresses, and services with the name server on the iSNS server upon boot or reset, but registration is not required. Any registered client (including target nodes) can query the name server to discover other registered clients. When a registered iSCSI initiator queries the iSNS, the reply contains the IP address(es), TCP port(s), and iSCSI node name of each target node accessible by the initiator. Unregistered clients are denied access to the name server. In addition, clients can optionally register for state change notification. An SCN message updates registered clients whenever a change occurs in the iSNS database (such as a new client registration). SCN messages are limited by DD membership, so messages are sent only to the affected clients. This is known as regular SCN registration. Management stations can also register for SCN. Management registration allows all SCN messages to be sent to the management node regardless of DD boundaries. Target devices may also register for entity status inquiry (ESI) messages. ESI messages allow the iSNS server to monitor the reachability of target devices. An SCN message is generated when a target device is determined to be unreachable.

DD membership works much like SLP scope membership. Clients can belong to one or more DDs simultaneously, and DD membership is additive. A default DD may be defined into which all clients not explicitly assigned to at least one named DD are placed. Clients in the default DD may be permitted access to all clients in all DDs or may be denied access to all DDs other than the default DD. The choice is implementation specific. Clients belonging to one or more named DDs are allowed to discover only those clients who are in at least one common DD. This limits the probe activity that typically follows target node discovery. As mentioned previously, a SCSI REPORT LUNs command must be issued to each target node to discover LUNs (via a normal iSCSI session). After discovery of target nodes, LUN discovery is usually initiated to every discovered target node. By limiting discovery to only those target nodes that the initiator will use, unnecessary probe activity is curtailed. Management nodes are allowed to query the entire iSNS database without consideration for DD membership. Management nodes also can update the iSNS database with DD and Login Control configuration information that is downloadable by clients, thus centralizing configuration management. The notion of a DD set (DDS) is supported by iSNS to improve manageability. Many DDs can be defined, but only those DDs that belong to the currently active DDS are considered active.

Microsoft has endorsed iSNS as its preferred iSCSI service location mechanism. Additionally, iSNS is required for iFCP operation. However, SLP was recently augmented by the IETF to better accommodate the requirements of FCIP and iSCSI. Thus, it is reasonable to expect that both iSNS and SLP will proliferate in IPS environments.

An iSNS database can store information about iSCSI and Fibre Channel devices. This enables mapping of iSCSI devices to Fibre Channel devices, and vice versa. The common iSNS database also facilitates transparent management across both environments (assuming that the management application supports this). Note that there are other ways to accomplish this. For example, the Cisco MDS9000 cross-registers iSNS devices in the FCNS and vice versa. This enables the Cisco Fabric Manager to manage iSCSI devices via the FCNS.

Fibre Channel

FC is currently the network technology of choice for storage networks. FC is designed to offer high throughput, low latency, high reliability, and moderate scalability. Consequently, FC can be used for a broad range of ULPs. However, market adoption of FC for general purpose IP connectivity is not likely, given Ethernet's immense installed base, lower cost, and comparative simplicity. Also, FC provides the combined functionality of Ethernet and TCP/IP. So, running TCP/IP on FC represents a duplication of network services that unnecessarily increases cost and complexity. That said, IP over FC (IPFC) is used to solve certain niche requirements.

NOTE   Some people think FC has higher throughput than Ethernet and, on that basis, would be a good fit for IP networks. However, Ethernet supports link aggregation in increments of one Gbps. So, a host that needs more than one Gbps can achieve higher throughput simply by aggregating multiple GE NICs. This is sometimes called NIC teaming, and it is very common.

Merger of Channels and Packet Switching

The limitations of multidrop bus technologies such as SPI and the intelligent peripheral interface (IPI) motivated ANSI to begin development of a new storage interconnect in 1988. Though storage was the primary application under consideration, other applications such as supercomputing and high-speed LANs were also considered. ANSI drew from its experience with earlier standards including SPI, IPI, and high-performance parallel interface (HIPPI) while developing FC. IBM's ESCON architecture also influenced the design of FC. ANSI desired FC to support the ULP associated with each of those technologies and others. When ANSI approved the first FC standard in 1994, it supported SCSI, IPI, HIPPI, SBCCS, 802.2, and asynchronous transfer mode (ATM) via separate mapping specifications (FC-4). FC has continued to evolve and now supports additional ULPs.

We can define the concept of a channel in many ways. Historically, a storage channel has been characterized by a physical end-to-end connection (among other things). That is the case with all multidrop bus technologies, and with IBM's ESCON architecture. Preserving the channel characteristics of traditional storage interconnects while simultaneously expanding the new interconnect to support greater distances, higher node counts, and improved utilization of link resources was a major challenge for ANSI. ANSI determined that packet switching could be the answer if properly designed. To that end, ANSI produced a packet-switched interconnect capable of providing various delivery modes including circuit-switched connection emulation (conceptually similar to ATM Circuit Emulation Service [CES]). ANSI made it feasible to transport storage traffic via all defined delivery modes by instituting credit-based link-level flow control and a full suite of timing restrictions. Today, none of the major FC switch vendors support circuit-switched mode, and storage traffic is forwarded through FC-SANs on a hop-by-hop basis. This model facilitates improvements in link-utilization efficiency and enables hosts to multiplex simultaneous sessions.

FC Throughput

FCP is the FC-4 mapping of SCSI-3 onto FC. Understanding FCP throughput in the same terms as iSCSI throughput is useful because FCP and iSCSI can be considered direct competitors. (Note that most vendors position these technologies as complementary today, but both of these technologies solve the same business problems.) Fibre Channel throughput is commonly expressed in bytes per second rather than bits per second. This is similar to SPI throughput terminology, which FC aspires to replace. In the initial FC specification, rates of 12.5 MBps, 25 MBps, 50 MBps, and 100 MBps were introduced on several different copper and fiber media. Additional rates were subsequently introduced, including 200 MBps and 400 MBps. These colloquial byte rates, when converted to bits per second, approximate the *data* bit rate (like Ethernet). 100 MBps FC is also known as one Gbps FC, 200 MBps as 2 Gbps, and 400 MBps as 4 Gbps. These colloquial bit rates approximate the *raw* bit rate (unlike Ethernet). This book uses bit per second terminology for FC to maintain consistency with other serial networking technologies. Today, 1 Gbps and 2 Gbps are the most common rates, and fiber-optic cabling is the most common medium. That said, 4 Gbps is being rapidly and broadly adopted. Additionally, ANSI recently defined a new rate of 10 Gbps (10GFC), which is likely to be used solely for inter-switch links (ISLs) for the next few years. Storage array vendors might adopt 10GFC eventually. ANSI is expected to begin defining a new rate of 8 Gbps in 2006. The remainder of this book focuses on FC rates equal to and greater than 1 Gbps on fiber-optic cabling.

The FC-PH specification defines baud rate as *the encoded bit rate per second*, which means the baud rate and raw bit rate are equal. The FC-PI specification redefines baud rate more accurately and states explicitly that FC encodes 1 bit per baud. Indeed, all FC-1 variants up to and including 4 Gbps use the same encoding scheme (8B/10B) as GE fiber optic variants. 1-Gbps FC operates at 1.0625 GBaud, provides a raw bit rate of 1.0625 Gbps, and provides a data bit rate of 850 Mbps. 2-Gbps FC operates at 2.125 GBaud, provides a raw bit rate of 2.125 Gbps, and provides a data bit rate of 1.7 Gbps. 4-Gbps FC operates at 4.25 GBaud, provides a raw bit rate of 4.25 Gbps, and provides a data bit rate of 3.4 Gbps. To derive ULP throughput, the FC-2 header and inter-frame spacing overhead must be subtracted. Note that FCP does not define its own header. Instead, fields within the FC-2 header are used by

FCP. The basic FC-2 header adds 36 bytes of overhead. Inter-frame spacing adds another 24 bytes. Assuming the maximum payload (2112 bytes) and no optional FC-2 headers, the ULP throughput rate is 826.519 Mbps, 1.65304 Gbps, and 3.30608 Gbps for 1 Gbps, 2 Gbps, and 4 Gbps respectively. These ULP throughput rates are available directly to SCSI.

The 10GFC specification builds upon the 10GE specification. 10GFC supports five physical variants. Two variants are parallel implementations based on 10GBASE-X. One variant is a parallel implementation *similar to* 10GBASE-X that employs four pairs of fiber strands. Two variants are serial implementations based on 10GBASE-R. All parallel implementations operate at a single baud rate. Likewise, all serial variants operate at a single baud rate. 10GFC increases the 10GE baud rates by 2 percent. Parallel 10GFC variants operate at 3.1875 GBaud per signal, provide an aggregate raw bit rate of 12.75 Gbps, and provide an aggregate data bit rate of 10.2 Gbps. Serial 10GFC variants operate at 10.51875 GBaud, provide a raw bit rate of 10.51875 Gbps, and provide a data bit rate of 10.2 Gbps. Note that serial 10GFC variants are more efficient than parallel 10GFC variants. This is because of different encoding schemes. Assuming the maximum payload (2112 bytes) and no optional FC-2 headers, the ULP throughput rate is 9.91823 Gbps for all 10GFC variants. This ULP throughput rate is available directly to SCSI. Table 3-5 summarizes the baud, bit, and ULP throughput rates of the FC and 10GFC variants.

Table 3-5   *FC Baud, Bit, and ULP Throughput Rates*

FC Variant	Baud Rate	Raw Bit Rate	Data Bit Rate	FCP ULP Throughput
1 Gbps	1.0625 GBaud	1.0625 Gbps	850 Mbps	826.519 Mbps
2 Gbps	2.125 GBaud	2.125 Gbps	1.7 Gbps	1.65304 Mbps
4 Gbps	4.25 GBaud	4.25 Gbps	3.4 Gbps	3.30608 Gbps
10GFC Parallel	3.1875 GBaud x 4	12.75 Gbps	10.2 Gbps	9.91823 Gbps
10GFC Serial	10.51875 GBaud	10.51875 Gbps	10.2 Gbps	9.91823 Gbps

Figure 3-11 illustrates the protocol stack for FCP.

Figure 3-11 *FCP Stack*

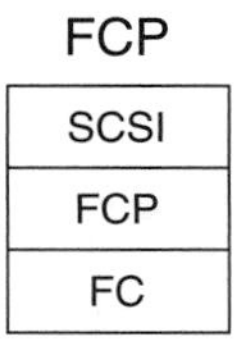

FCP

SCSI
FCP
FC

FC Topologies

FC supports all physical topologies, but protocol operations differ depending on the topology. Protocol behavior is tailored to PTP, loop, and switch-based topologies. Like Ethernet, Fibre Channel supports both shared media and switched topologies. A shared media FC implementation is called a Fibre Channel Arbitrated Loop (FCAL), and a switch-based FC implementation is called a fabric.

FC PTP connections are used for DAS deployments. Companies with SPI-based systems that need higher throughput can upgrade to newer SPI equipment or migrate away from SPI. The FC PTP topology allows companies to migrate away from SPI without migrating away from the DAS model. This strategy allows companies to become comfortable with FC technology in a controlled manner and offers investment protection of FC HBAs if and when companies later decide to adopt FC-SANs. The FC PTP topology is considered a niche.

Most FC switches support FCAL via special ports called fabric loop (FL) ports. Most FC HBAs also support loop protocol operations. An HBA that supports loop protocol operations is called a node loop port (NL_Port). Without support for loop protocol operations, a port cannot join an FCAL. Each time a device joins an FCAL, an attached device resets or any link-level error occurs on the loop, the loop is reinitialized, and all communication is temporarily halted. This can cause problems for certain applications such as tape backup, but these problems can be mitigated through proper network design. Unlike collisions in shared media Ethernet deployments, loop initialization generally occurs infrequently. That said, overall FCAL performance can be adversely affected by recurring initializations to such an extent that a fabric topology becomes a requirement. The FCAL addressing scheme is different than fabric addressing and limits FCAL deployments to 127 nodes (126 if not fabric attached). However, the shared medium of an FCAL imposes a practical limit of approximately 18 nodes. FCAL was popular in the early days of FC but has lost ground to FC switches in recent years. FCAL is still used inside most JBOD chassis, and in some NAS filers, blade centers, and even enterprise-class storage subsystems, but FCAL is now essentially a niche technology for embedded applications.

Like Ethernet, FC switches can be interconnected in any manner. Unlike Ethernet, there is a limit to the number of FC switches that can be interconnected. Address space constraints limit FC-SANs to a maximum of 239 switches. Cisco's virtual SAN (VSAN) technology increases the number of switches that can be physically interconnected by reusing the entire FC address space within each VSAN. FC switches employ a routing protocol called fabric shortest path first (FSPF) based on a link-state algorithm. FSPF reduces all physical topologies to a logical tree topology. Most FC-SANs are deployed in one of two designs commonly known as the core-only and core-edge designs. The core-only is a star topology, and the core-edge is a two-tier tree topology. The FC community seems to prefer its own terminology, but there is nothing novel about these two topologies other than their names. Host-to-storage FC connections are usually redundant. However, single host-to-storage FC connections are common in cluster and grid environments because host-based failover mechanisms are inherent to such environments. In both the core-only and core-edge designs, the redundant paths are usually not interconnected. The edge switches in the core-edge design may be connected to both core switches, but doing so creates one physical network and compromises resilience against network-wide disruptions (for example, FSPF convergence). As FC-SANs proliferate, their size and complexity are likely to increase. Advanced physical topologies eventually might become mandatory, but first, confidence in FSPF and traffic engineering mechanisms must increase. Figures 3-12 and 3-13 illustrate the typical FC-SAN topologies. The remaining chapters of this book assume a switch-based topology for all FC discussions.

Figure 3-12 *Dual Path Core-Only Topology*

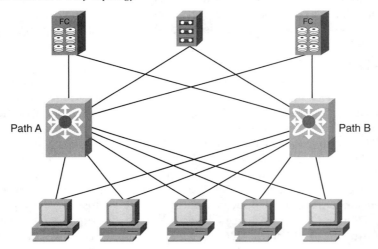

Figure 3-13 *Dual Path Core-Edge Topology*

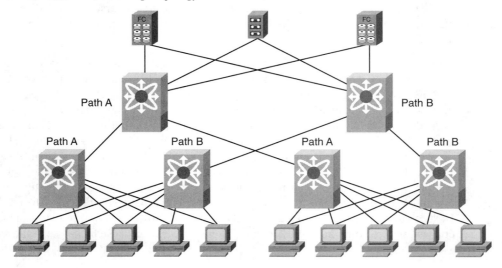

FC Service and Device Discovery

FC employs both service- and device-oriented approaches that are well suited to medium- and large-scale environments. FC provides registration and discovery services via a name server model. The FCNS may be queried for services or devices, but the primary key of the FCNS database is node address. So, a common discovery technique is to query based on node address (device oriented). That said, the device-oriented approach is comparatively inefficient for *initial* discovery of other nodes. So, the FCP specification series suggests querying the FCNS based on service type (service oriented). All nodes (initiators and targets) can register themselves in the FCNS, but registration is optional. This means that FCNS discovery reveals only registered nodes, not all nodes that are physically present. However, practically all FC HBAs are hard coded to register automatically with the FCNS after link initialization. So, unregistered nodes are extremely rare, and FCNS discovery usually provides complete visibility. Unlike the iSNS RFC, the FC specifications do not explicitly state that unregistered nodes cannot query the FCNS.

When a node joins a fabric, an address is assigned to it. The new node does not know which addresses have been assigned to other nodes. So, when using the device-oriented approach, the new node submits a **get next** query to the FCNS asking for all information associated with an arbitrarily chosen node address. The FCNS responds with all information about the next numerically higher node address that has been assigned to a registered node. The address of that node is specified in the next **get next** query submitted by the new node. This process is repeated until the numerically highest address is reached, at which point the FCNS *wraps* to the numerically lowest address that has been assigned to a registered node. The query process then continues normally until the originally specified address is reached. At this point, the new node is aware of every registered node and has all information available about each registered node. LUN discovery can then be initiated to each registered node via the SCSI REPORT LUNS command. The FCNS stores information about which FC-4 ULPs are supported by each node and the capabilities associated with each ULP, assuming that information is supplied by each node during registration. This information allows a new node to limit LUN discovery to just those nodes that support FCP target services. However, a node may query all discovered nodes that support FCP.

Alternately, the new node can submit a **get port identifiers** query. In such a query, a node address is not specified. Instead, an FC-4 protocol is specified along with features of the FC-4 protocol. The name server searches the FCNS database for all registered devices that support the FC-4 protocol and features specified in the query. The response contains a list of node addresses that match the search criteria. This service-oriented approach enables a new node to discover all relevant nodes with a single query.

The FC name service is a subset of the directory service. Implementation of the FC directory service is optional, but all modern FC-SANs implement the directory service. The directory service can be implemented on a host or storage subsystem, but it is most commonly implemented on FC switches. FC globally reserves certain addresses for access to fabric-based services such as the directory service. These reserved addresses are called well known addresses (WKAs). Each FC switch uses the WKA of 0xFFFFFC to represent its internal logical node that provides the directory service. This address is hard coded into FC HBA firmware. Hosts and storage subsystems send FCNS registration and discovery requests to this WKA. Each FC switch processes FCNS requests for the nodes that are physically attached. Each FC switch updates its local database with registration information about locally attached devices, distributes updates to other FCNSs via inter-switch registered state change notifications (SW_RSCNs), listens for SW_RSCNs from other FCNSs, and caches information about non-local devices. FC nodes can optionally register to generate and receive normal RSCNs. This is done via the state change registration (SCR) procedure. The SCR procedure is optional, but practically all FC nodes register because notification of changes is critical to proper operation of storage devices. Registration also enables FC nodes to trigger RSCNs whenever their internal state changes (for example, a change occurs to one of the FC-4 operational parameters). This is done via the RSCN Request procedure.

FC zones are similar to iSNS DDs and SLP scopes. Nodes can belong to one or more zones simultaneously, and zone membership is additive. Zones are considered to be soft or hard. Membership in a soft zone may be determined by node name, node port name, or node port address. Membership in a hard zone is determined by the FC switch port to which a node is connected. A default zone exists into which all nodes not explicitly assigned to at least one named zone are placed. Nodes in the default zone cannot communicate with nodes in other zones. However, communication among nodes within the default zone is optional. The choice is implementation specific. Nodes belonging to one or more named zones are allowed to discover only those nodes that are in at least one common zone. Management nodes are allowed to query the entire FCNS database without consideration for zone membership. The notion of a zone set is supported to improve manageability. Many zones can be defined, but only those zones that belong to the currently active zone set are considered active. Management nodes are able to configure zone sets, zones, and zone membership via the FC zone server (FCZS). RSCNs are limited by zone boundaries. In other words, only the nodes in the affected zone(s) are notified of a change.

Summary

This chapter provides a high-level overview of the lower layer network protocols that compose the SCSI architecture model (SAM) Interconnect technologies. Some historical insight is provided to help readers understand why each technology works the way it does. Key operational characteristics are presented to give readers a "feel" for each technology. Continuing this approach, Chapter 4, "Overview of Modern SCSI Networking Protocols," provides a high-level overview of the upper-layer network protocols that compose the SAM Transport technologies.

Review Questions

1 List the functions provided by bit-level encoding schemes.

2 What must be subtracted from the data bit rate to determine the ULP throughput rate?

3 List the six physical topologies.

4 How can a protocol that is not designed to operate in a circular physical topology overcome this limitation?

5 Describe one situation in which service and device discovery is not required.

6 What additional steps might be required after service/device discovery?

7 How many ULPs was the SPI designed to support? List them.

8 During which SPI bus phases is the data bus used?

9 Why does the SPI device discovery mechanism not scale?

10 What SCSI command enables the discovery of LUNs?

11 Ethernet originally competed against what network technologies?

12 What assumption enables Ethernet to remain a low-overhead protocol?

13 What logical topology is supported by Ethernet?

14 List three characteristics that contributed to the early success of TCP/IP.

15 What is the ULP throughput rate of iSCSI on GE?

16 What iSCSI command enables the discovery of target nodes?

17 What two protocols are available for automated discovery of iSCSI target devices and nodes?

18 Did FC evolve into a multi-protocol transport, or was it designed as such from the beginning?

19 What is the ULP throughput rate of FCP on one Gbps FC?

20 FC protocol operations are defined for what topologies?

21 FC device discovery can be bounded by what mechanism?

Upon completing this chapter, you will be able to:

- Explain the purpose of each Upper Layer Protocol (ULP) commonly used in modern storage networks

- Describe the general procedures used by each ULP discussed in this chapter

CHAPTER 4

Overview of Modern SCSI Networking Protocols

The goal of this chapter is to quickly acclimate readers to the standard upper-layer storage protocols currently being deployed. To that end, we provide a conceptual description and brief procedural overview for each ULP. The procedural overviews are greatly simplified and should not be considered technically complete. Procedural details are provided in subsequent chapters.

iSCSI

This section provides a brief introduction to the Internet Small Computer System Interface (iSCSI) protocol.

iSCSI Functional Overview

As indicated in Chapter 2, "The OSI Reference Model Versus Other Network Models," iSCSI is a Small Computer System Interface (SCSI) Transport Protocol. The Internet Engineering Task Force (IETF) began working on iSCSI in 2000 and subsequently published the first iSCSI standard in 2004. iSCSI facilitates block-level initiator-target communication over TCP/IP networks. In doing so, iSCSI completes the storage over IP model, which supported only file-level protocols (such as Network File System [NFS], Common Internet File System [CIFS], and File Transfer Protocol [FTP]) in the past. To preserve backward compatibility with existing IP network infrastructure components and to accelerate adoption, iSCSI is designed to work with the existing TCP/IP architecture. iSCSI requires no special modifications to TCP or IP. All underlying network technologies supported by IP can be incorporated as part of an iSCSI network, but most early deployments are expected to be based solely on Ethernet. Other lower-layer technologies eventually will be leveraged as iSCSI deployments expand in scope. iSCSI is also designed to work with the existing SCSI architecture, so no special modifications to SCSI are required for iSCSI adoption. This ensures compatibility with a broad portfolio of host operating systems and applications.

iSCSI seamlessly fits into the traditional IP network model in which common network services are provided in utility style. Each of the IP network service protocols performs a single function very efficiently and is available for use by every "application" protocol.

iSCSI is an application protocol that relies on IP network service protocols for name resolution (Domain Name System [DNS]), security (IPsec), flow control (TCP windowing), service location (Service Location Protocol [SLP], and Internet Storage Name Service [iSNS]), and so forth. This simplifies iSCSI implementation for product vendors by eliminating the need to develop a solution to each network service requirement.

When the IETF first began developing the iSCSI protocol, concerns about the security of IP networks prompted the IETF to require IPsec support in every iSCSI product. This requirement was later deemed too burdensome considering the chip-level technology available at that time. So, the IETF made IPsec support optional in the final iSCSI standard (Request For Comments [RFC] 3720). IPsec is implemented at the OSI network layer and complements the authentication mechanisms implemented in iSCSI. If IPsec is used in an iSCSI deployment, it may be integrated into the iSCSI devices or provided via external devices (such as IP routers). The iSCSI standard stipulates which specific IPsec features must be supported if IPsec is integrated into the iSCSI devices. If IPsec is provided via external devices, the feature requirements are not specified. This allows shared external IPsec devices to be configured as needed to accommodate a wide variety of pass-through protocols. Most iSCSI deployments currently do not use IPsec.

One of the primary design goals of iSCSI is to match the performance (subject to underlying bandwidth) and functionality of existing SCSI Transport Protocols. As Chapter 3, "An Overview of Network Operating Principles," discusses, the difference in underlying bandwidth of iSCSI over Gigabit Ethernet (GE) versus Fibre Channel Protocol (FCP) over 2-Gbps Fibre Channel (FC) is not as significant as many people believe. Another oft misunderstood fact is that very few 2-Gbps Fibre Channel Storage Area Networks (FC-SANs) are fully utilized. These factors allow companies to build block-level storage networks using a rich selection of mature IP/Ethernet infrastructure products at comparatively low prices without sacrificing performance. Unfortunately, many storage and switch vendors have propagated the myth that iSCSI can be used in only low-performance environments. Compounding this myth is the cost advantage of iSCSI, which enables cost-effective attachment of low-end servers to block-level storage networks. A low-end server often costs about the same as a pair of fully functional FC Host Bus Adapters (HBAs) required to provide redundant FC-SAN connectivity. Even with the recent introduction of limited-functionality HBAs, FC attachment of low-end servers is difficult to cost-justify in many cases. So, iSCSI is currently being adopted primarily for low-end servers that are not SAN-attached. As large companies seek to extend the benefits of centralized storage to low-end servers, they are considering iSCSI. Likewise, small businesses, which have historically avoided FC-SANs altogether due to cost and complexity, are beginning to deploy iSCSI networks.

That does not imply that iSCSI is simpler to deploy than FC, but many small businesses are willing to accept the complexity of iSCSI in light of the cost savings. It is believed that iSCSI (along with the other IP Storage [IPS] protocols) eventually can breathe new life into the Storage Service Provider (SSP) market. In the SSP market, iSCSI enables initiators secure access to centralized storage located at an SSP Internet Data Center (IDC) by removing the distance limitations of FC. Despite the current adoption trend in low-end environments, iSCSI is a very robust technology capable of supporting relatively high-performance applications. As existing iSCSI products mature and additional iSCSI products come to market, iSCSI adoption is likely to expand into high-performance environments.

Even though some storage array vendors already offer iSCSI-enabled products, most storage products do not currently support iSCSI. By contrast, iSCSI TCP Offload Engines (TOEs) and iSCSI drivers for host operating systems are widely available today. This has given rise to iSCSI gateway devices that convert iSCSI requests originating from hosts (initiators) to FCP requests that FC attached storage devices (targets) can understand. The current generation of iSCSI gateways is characterized by low port density devices designed to aggregate multiple iSCSI hosts. Thus, the iSCSI TOE market has suffered from low demand. As more storage array vendors introduce native iSCSI support in their products, use of iSCSI gateway devices will become less necessary. In the long term, it is likely that companies will deploy pure FC-SANs and pure iSCSI-based IP-SANs (see Figures 1-1 and 1-2, respectively) without iSCSI gateways, and that use of iSCSI TOEs will likely become commonplace. That said, iSCSI gateways that add value other than mere protocol conversion might remain a permanent component in the SANs of the future. Network-based storage virtualization is a good example of the types of features that could extend the useful life of iSCSI gateways. Figure 4-1 illustrates a hybrid SAN built with an iSCSI gateway integrated into an FC switch. This deployment approach is common today.

Figure 4-1 *Hybrid SAN Built with an iSCSI Gateway*

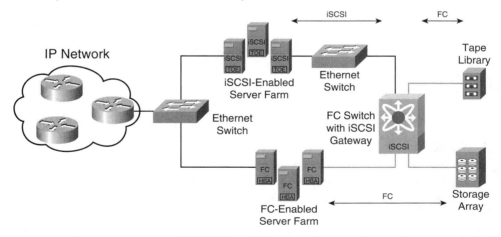

Another way to accomplish iSCSI-to-FCP protocol conversion is to incorporate iSCSI into the portfolio of protocols already supported by Network Attached Storage (NAS) filers. Because NAS filers natively operate on TCP/IP networks, iSCSI is a natural fit. Some NAS vendors already have introduced iSCSI support into their products, and it is expected that most (if not all) other NAS vendors eventually will follow suit. Another emerging trend in

NAS filer evolution is the ability to use FC on the backend. A NAS filer is essentially an optimized file server; therefore the problems associated with the DAS model apply equally to NAS filers and traditional servers. As NAS filers proliferate, the distributed storage that is captive to individual NAS filers becomes costly and difficult to manage. Support for FC on the backend allows NAS filers to leverage the FC-SAN infrastructure that many companies already have. For those companies that do not currently have an FC-SAN, iSCSI could be deployed as an alternative behind the NAS filers (subject to adoption of iSCSI by the storage array vendors). Either way, using a block-level protocol behind NAS filers enables very large-scale consolidation of NAS storage into block-level arrays. In the long term, it is conceivable that all NAS protocols and iSCSI could be supported natively by storage arrays, thus eliminating the need for an external NAS filer. Figure 4-2 illustrates the model in which an iSCSI-enabled NAS filer is attached to an FC-SAN on the backend.

Figure 4-2 *iSCSI-Enabled NAS Filer Attached to an FC-SAN*

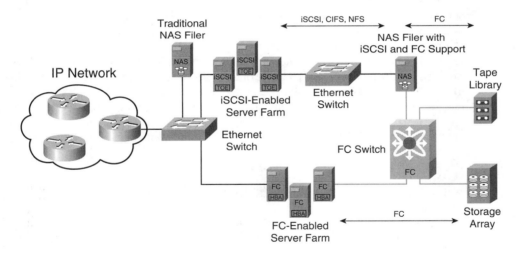

iSCSI Procedural Overview

When a host attached to an Ethernet switch first comes online, it negotiates operating parameters with the switch. This is followed by IP initialization during which the host receives its IP address (if the network is configured for dynamic address assignment via Dynamic Host Configuration Protocol [DHCP]). Next, the host discovers iSCSI devices and targets via one of the methods discussed in Chapter 3, "An Overview of Network Operating Principles." The host then optionally establishes an IPsec connection followed by a TCP connection to each discovered iSCSI device. The discovery method determines what happens next.

If discovery is accomplished via manual or automated configuration, the host optionally authenticates each target within each iSCSI device and then opens a normal iSCSI session with each successfully authenticated target. SCSI Logical Unit Number (LUN) discovery is the final step. The semi-manual discovery method requires an additional intermediate step. All iSCSI sessions are classified as either discovery or normal. A discovery session is used exclusively for iSCSI target discovery. All other iSCSI tasks are accomplished using normal sessions. Semi-manual configuration requires the host to establish a discovery session with each iSCSI device. Target discovery is accomplished via the iSCSI **SendTargets** command. The host then optionally authenticates each target within each iSCSI device. Next, the host opens a normal iSCSI session with each successfully authenticated target and performs SCSI LUN discovery. It is common for the discovery session to remain open with each iSCSI device while normal sessions are open with each iSCSI target.

Each SCSI command is assigned an iSCSI Command Sequence Number (CmdSN). The iSCSI CmdSN has no influence on packet tracking within the SCSI Interconnect. All packets comprising SCSI commands, data, and status are tracked in flight via the TCP sequence-numbering mechanism. TCP sequence numbers are directional and represent an increasing byte count starting at the initial sequence number (ISN) specified during TCP connection establishment. The TCP sequence number is not reset with each new iSCSI CmdSN. There is no explicit mapping of iSCSI CmdSNs to TCP sequence numbers. iSCSI complements the TCP sequence-numbering scheme with PDU sequence numbers. All PDUs comprising SCSI commands, data, and status are tracked in flight via the iSCSI CmdSN, Data Sequence Number (DataSN), and Status Sequence Number (StatSN), respectively. This contrasts with the FCP model.

FCP

This section provides a brief introduction to FCP.

FCP Functional Overview

As indicated in Chapter 2, "The OSI Reference Model Versus Other Network Models," FCP is a SCSI Transport Protocol. FCP was produced by ANSI T10 to facilitate block-level initiator-target communication over FC networks. FCP development began in 1991, and the first standard was published in 1996. In the FC network model, FCP is an FC-4 protocol. FCP uses the existing frame formats and services defined by the FC specifications, so no special modifications to FC are required by FCP. In theory, this allows FCP to share an FC network with other ULPs, but the vast majority of FC networks are deployed exclusively for FCP. FCP works with the existing SCSI architecture, so no special modifications to SCSI are required for FCP adoption. This ensures compatibility with a broad portfolio of host operating systems and applications.

Like the IP network model, the FC network model provides a robust set of network services to "application" protocols (that is, FC-4 protocols). FCP leverages the network services defined by the FC specifications. This simplifies FCP implementation for product vendors by reducing development overhead. Note that even OSI Session Layer login procedures are defined by the FC specifications (not the FCP specifications). This contrasts with the IP network model, in which each "application" protocol specifies its own OSI session layer login procedures. That said, FC-4 protocols are not required to use the services defined by the FC specifications.

There is a general perception that FC networks are inherently secure because they are physically separate (cabled independently) from the Internet and corporate intranets. This tenet is erroneous, but the FC user community is not likely to realize their error until FC security breaches become commonplace. For example, the vast majority of hosts that are attached to an FC-SAN are also attached to an IP network. If a host is compromised via the IP network, the host becomes a springboard for the intruder to access the FC-SAN. Moreover, FC-SANs are commonly extended across IP networks for disaster recovery applications. Such SAN extensions expose FC-SANs to a wide variety of attacks commonly perpetrated on IP networks. Authentication and encryption mechanisms are defined in the FC specifications, so FCP does not define its own security mechanisms. Unlike iSCSI, no security mechanisms are mandatory for FCP deployment. This fact and the misperception about the nature of FC network security have resulted in the vast majority of FC-SANs being deployed without any authentication or encryption.

Because FCP can be transported only by FC, the adoption rate of FCP is bound to the adoption rate of FC. The adoption rate of FC was relatively low in the late 1990s, in part because of the comparatively high cost of FC infrastructure components, which relegated FCP to high-end servers hosting mission-critical applications. Around 2000, FC adoption reached critical mass in the high-end server market. Simultaneously, performance improvements were being realized as companies began to view switched FC networks as the best practice instead of Fibre Channel Arbitrated Loop (FC-AL). In the years following, the adoption rate of switched FC increased dramatically. Consequently, FC prices began to drop and still are dropping as the FC market expands and competition increases. Furthermore, in response to competition from iSCSI, some FC HBA vendors have recently introduced "light" versions of their HBAs that provide less functionality at a lower cost than traditional FC HBAs. FCP is now being used by mid-range and high-end servers hosting a wide variety of business applications.

In the traditional FC-SAN design, each host and storage device is dual-attached to the network. (As previously noted, there are some exceptions to this guideline.) This is primarily motivated by a desire to achieve 99.999 percent availability. Conventional wisdom suggests that the network should be built with redundant switches that are not interconnected to achieve 99.999 percent availability. In other words, the network is actually two separate networks (commonly called path A and path B), and each end node (host or storage) is connected to both networks. Some companies take the same approach with their traditional IP/Ethernet networks, but most do not for reasons of cost. Because the traditional FC-SAN design doubles the cost of network implementation, many companies are actively seeking alternatives. Some companies are looking to iSCSI as the answer, and others are considering single path FC-SANs. Figures 3-12 and 3-13 illustrate typical dual path FC-SAN designs.

FC switches are market-classified as director class or fabric class. A director-class FC switch has no single point of failure in its architecture and provides 99.999 percent availability. Director-class FC switches also tend to have very high port density. By contrast, a fabric-class FC switch is similar to a traditional Ethernet switch in that it does not provide 99.999 percent availability. Fabric-class FC switches also tend to have limited port density. Some FC switch vendors employ completely different architectures in their director-class products versus their fabric-class products. This can result in functional disparity. In large-scale deployments, port density requirements often dictate the use of director-class FC switches. However, smaller environments can supplant the use of dual fabric-class FC switches with the use of a single director-class FC switch. This approach appeals to some companies because it fully protects the switch investment as the company grows, and it allows the company to take advantage of director-class functionality that might be missing from the fabric-class switches. However, availability can suffer if the director-class FC switch is physically damaged, or if a software bug in the switch's operating system causes an unplanned outage. Only dual path FC-SANs can protect against these risks.

A key difference between the FC and IP network models is support for routing protocols in the end nodes. Nearly all hosts attached to an IP network implement an IP routing protocol or static IP routing capability. If more than one router is attached to an Ethernet network, each host can decide which router to use when forwarding packets to non-local subnets. However, the forwarding decision is made at the network layer, not at the data-link layer. FC attached hosts do not implement a network layer protocol. Thus, an FC attached host merely forwards frames to the attached FC switch. This is equivalent to Ethernet frame processing in an IP attached host. Note that FC switches can perform load balancing, just as Ethernet switches and IP routers can. Chapter 10, "Routing and Switching Protocols," provides more detail about frame/packet forwarding mechanisms within networks. Chapter 11, "Load Balancing," provides more detail about load-balancing mechanisms within networks and hosts.

FCP Procedural Overview

When a host attached to an FC switch first comes online, it logs into the switch to exchange operating parameters and receive its FC address. Next, the host establishes an FC connection to the Fibre Channel Name Server (FCNS) and discovers FCP targets as discussed in Chapter 3, "An Overview of Network Operating Principles." The host then establishes an FC connection to each discovered FC device that contains a target. An FCP session is then established with each target. LUN discovery follows.

Each SCSI command is mapped to an FCP I/O operation. Each FCP I/O operation is identified by its Fully Qualified Exchange Identifier (FQXID), which is composed of the initiator's FC address, the target's FC address, an FC Exchange Identifier assigned by the initiator, and an FC Exchange Identifier assigned by the target. An FC Exchange Identifier is integral to frame tracking within the SCSI Interconnect. All frames comprising SCSI commands, data, and status are tracked in flight via the FC Sequence ID (SEQ_ID) and

Sequence Count (SEQ_CNT) mechanisms. Each SEQ_ID value identifies a single sequence of related frames within the context of an Exchange Identifier. Each SEQ_CNT value identifies a single frame within the context of a SEQ_ID. SEQ_ID values do not have to increase contiguously from one Exchange to the next. This contrasts with the iSCSI model.

FCIP

This section provides a brief introduction to Fibre Channel Over TCP/IP (FCIP).

FCIP Functional Overview

As indicated in Chapter 2, "The OSI Reference Model Versus Other Network Models," FCIP maps to the OSI session layer. The IETF began working on FCIP in 2000 and published the first standard in 2004 (RFC 3821). FCIP provides FC backbone functionality as defined in the ANSI T11 FC-BB series of specifications. Like iSCSI, FCIP seamlessly fits into the traditional IP network service model. This simplifies FCIP implementation for product vendors by reducing development overhead. IPsec support is mandatory for every FCIP product, and the FCIP standard stipulates which specific IPsec features must be supported. That said, use of IPsec is optional, and most FCIP deployments currently do not use IPsec.

FCIP enables interconnection of two switched FC-SANs using TCP/IP. This enables "distance applications" such as data replication from a primary site to a disaster recovery site. A point-to-point tunnel is created through an IP network, and FC traffic is transparently encapsulated or de-encapsulated at the tunnel endpoints. For multi-site connectivity, a separate tunnel must be created between each pair of FC-SANs. For this reason, each FCIP entity is architecturally capable of supporting multiple tunnels simultaneously. Each FCIP entity acts like a host on the IP network and does not require support for IP routing protocols. FCIP tunnels are long-lived. Once a tunnel is established, the two FC-SANs merge to form a single logical FC-SAN. All FC switches on each side of the tunnel see the remote FC switches as if they were local. All FC devices at both ends of the tunnel share a single address space. The FCIP tunnel is completely transparent to all FC devices. So, all aspects of the FC network architecture operate as if the tunnel were not present, and FC timers must be enforced end-to-end across the tunnel. FCIP's transparency enables all FC-4 protocols to be transported between the connected FC-SANs. FC-ALs can be attached to the FC switches within each FC-SAN, but low-level FC-AL signals (called primitives) cannot traverse an FCIP tunnel. This is not a problem because FCIP entities are either integrated into an FC switch or embodied in an external bridge device that connects to an FC switch, so low-level FC-AL signals never reach the FCIP entities. Figure 4-3 illustrates an FCIP tunnel connecting two physical FC-SANs.

Figure 4-3   *FCIP Tunnel Connecting Two Physical FC-SANs*

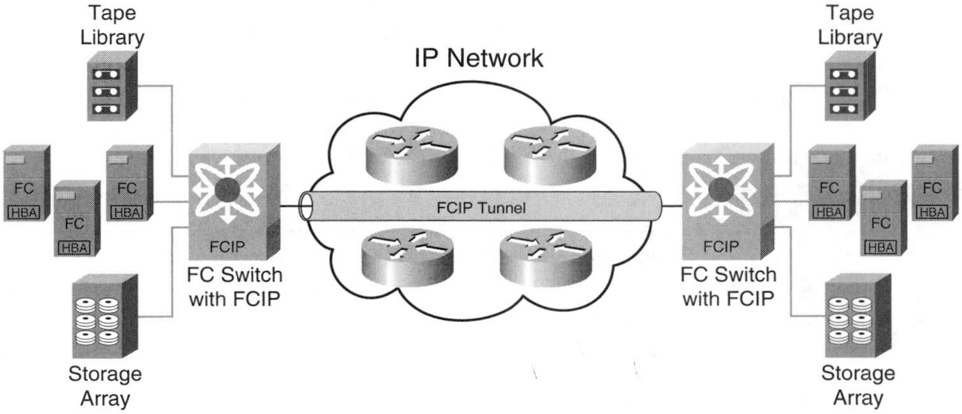

The two switches at the FCIP tunnel endpoints establish a standard FC inter-switch link (ISL) through the tunnel. Essentially, the FCIP tunnel appears to the switches as a cable. Each FCIP tunnel is created using one or more TCP connections. Multiple tunnels can be established between a pair of FC-SANs to increase fault tolerance and performance. Each tunnel carries a single FC ISL. Load balancing across multiple tunnels is accomplished via FC mechanisms just as would be done across multiple FC ISLs in the absence of FCIP. As mentioned in Chapter 3, "An Overview of Network Operating Principles," encapsulation is accomplished per the Fibre Channel Frame Encapsulation (FC-FE) specification (RFC 3643). Eight bytes of the encapsulation header are used by each encapsulating protocol (such as FCIP) to implement protocol-specific functionality. The remainder of the encapsulation header is used for purposes common to all encapsulating protocols, such as identifying the encapsulating protocol and enforcing FC timers end-to-end.

Connectivity failures within the transit IP network can disrupt FC operations. Obviously, a circuit failure that results in FCIP tunnel failure will segment the FC-SAN and prevent communication between the FC-SAN segments. Unfortunately, the effect of the disruption is not limited to cross-tunnel traffic. Local connectivity is temporarily disrupted in each FC-SAN segment while the FC routing protocol reconverges and Registered State Change Notifications (RSCNs) are processed by end nodes. Additionally, one of the FC-SAN segments must select a new principle switch (see Chapter 5, "The OSI Physical and Data-Link Layers," for details). The local effect of routing protocol reconvergence and principal switch selection can be eliminated via proprietary isolation techniques, but there currently is no mechanism within the FCIP standard to isolate FC-SANs from IP connectivity failures. This is generally considered to be the only significant drawback of FCIP.

FCIP Procedural Overview

Following data-link layer initialization, IP initialization occurs. The FCIP tunnel parameters can be configured manually or discovered via SLPv2. Once the tunnel parameters are known, an IPsec connection is optionally established followed by TCP connection establishment. The FCIP endpoint that initiated the TCP connection (the tunnel initiator) then transmits an FCIP Special Frame (FSF). The FSF contains the FC identifier and FCIP endpoint identifier of the tunnel initiator, the FC identifier of the intended destination, and a 64-bit randomly selected number that uniquely identifies the FSF. The receiver verifies that the contents of the FSF match its local configuration. If the FSF contents are acceptable, the unmodified FSF is echoed back to the tunnel initiator. After the tunnel initiator receives and verifies the FSF, the FCIP tunnel may carry FC traffic.

NOTE   The term *identifier* is used generically in this section. As discussed in Chapter 5, "The OSI Physical and Data-Link Layers," the terms *identifier* and *name* each have specific meaning throughout the subsequent chapters of this book.

A time stamp is inserted into the header of each FCIP packet transmitted. The receiver checks the time stamp in each packet. If the time stamp indicates that the packet has been in flight longer than allowed by the FC timers, the packet is dropped. TCP is not responsible for retransmitting the dropped packet because the packet is dropped after TCP processing completes. FCP and FC error detection and recovery mechanisms are responsible for retransmitting the lost FC frame or notifying SCSI.

iFCP

This section provides a brief introduction to Internet Fibre Channel Protocol (iFCP).

iFCP Functional Overview

As indicated in Chapter 2, "The OSI Reference Model Versus Other Network Models," iFCP maps to the OSI session layer. The IETF began working on iFCP in 2000 and published the first standard in 2005 (RFC 4172). iFCP originally sought to supplant FC switching and routing mechanisms with Ethernet switching and IP routing mechanisms by replacing the FC fabric with an IP network. However, end nodes would be FC-attached to iFCP gateway devices. Only the iFCP gateway devices would communicate with each other via TCP/IP. The login procedures of FC would still be used by end nodes, but the IP network would provide the FC network services (in particular, the FCNS and FC Zone Server [FCZS]). Rather than augment the existing IP network services (such as SLP), a new service (iSNS) was created to provide the functionality of the FCNS and FCZS. As iSCSI development progressed in parallel to iFCP, modifications were made to iSNS to meet the needs of iSCSI. However, iSCSI can be deployed without iSNS. By contrast, iFCP requires iSNS. Figure 4-4 illustrates the original design concept of iFCP that was submitted to the IETF.

Figure 4-4 *Original iFCP Design Concept*

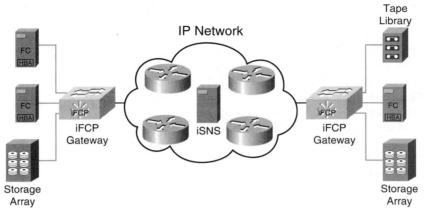

The motivation behind this approach is to reduce the total solution cost by leveraging cost-effective IP-based technology and widely available IP skill sets, extend the reach of FC attached devices beyond the FC limits, and enable the integration of FC and IP management operations. Unfortunately, the cost savings are undermined by the requirement for end nodes to be attached via FC. If the end nodes were attached via IP/Ethernet, the cost would be lower, but the solution would closely resemble iSCSI. Because iSCSI was designed to provide an IP/Ethernet alternative to FC-SANs, iSCSI provides a much more elegant and cost-effective solution than iFCP. Another challenge for iFCP is that only one vendor produces iFCP gateways today, and its iFCP products do not currently provide sufficient FC port densities to accommodate the connectivity requirements of most modern FC-SANs. So, iFCP gateways are usually deployed in conjunction with FC switches. Combined, these factors relegate iFCP usage to FC-SAN interconnectivity. Thus, iFCP competes against FCIP despite the original iFCP design goals. Figure 4-5 illustrates the current deployment practice.

Figure 4-5 *Current iFCP Deployment Practice*

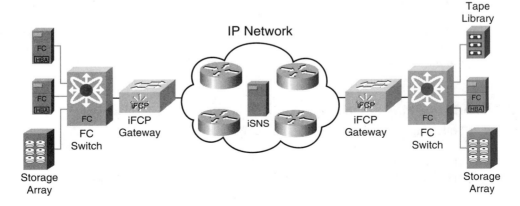

The remainder of this section focuses on FC-SAN interconnectivity. iFCP gateways can operate in address transparency mode so that all FC devices share a single address space across all connected FC-SANs. This mode allows IP network failures to disrupt the attached FC-SANs just as FCIP does. For this reason, iFCP is rarely deployed in address transparency mode, and iFCP gateway support for address transparency mode is optional. iFCP gateways can also operate in address-translation mode. Devices in each FC-SAN communicate with devices in other FC-SANs using FC addresses allocated from the local FC-SAN address space. In this mode, the effect of IP network failures is mitigated. Each FC-SAN operates autonomously, as does the IP network. Network services are provided to FC attached devices via the FC switches. The state of FC network services in each FC-SAN must be replicated to the iSNS for propagation to other FC-SANs. Support for address translation mode is mandatory. Translation mode is customary in almost every deployment, so the remainder of this section focuses on translation mode.

iFCP operation is transparent to end nodes, and encapsulation is accomplished per the FC-FE specification (RFC 3643). However, connectivity across the IP network is handled differently than FCIP. Instead of creating a single tunnel to carry all FC traffic, each iFCP gateway creates a unique iFCP session to the appropriate destination iFCP gateway for each initiator-target pair that needs to communicate. This model might work well in the originally intended iFCP deployment scenario, but it can impede performance in the current iFCP deployment scenario by limiting the size of the TCP window available to each iFCP session. Two factors complicate this potential problem. First, iFCP sessions are created dynamically in response to PLOGI requests and are gracefully terminated only in response to LOGO requests. Second, PLOGI sessions are typically long-lived.

Like FCIP, IPsec support is mandatory for every iFCP product, and the iFCP standard stipulates which specific IPsec features must be supported. That said, use of IPsec is optional, and most iFCP deployments currently do not use IPsec. iFCP supports attachment of FC-ALs to FC switches within each FC-SAN, but low-level FC-AL signals (primitives) cannot traverse an iFCP session. This is not a problem because each iFCP gateway is usually connected to an FC switch, so FC-AL primitives never enter the iFCP gateways. iFCP gateways act like hosts on the IP network and do not require support for IP routing protocols. Multiple iFCP gateways may be deployed in each FC-SAN to increase fault tolerance and performance. Load balancing iFCP sessions across multiple iFCP gateways is implementation-specific. iFCP supports all FC-4 protocols when operating in transparent mode. However, it is possible for address translation mode to prevent certain FC-4 protocols from operating properly. Currently, iFCP is deployed only in FCP environments.

iFCP Procedural Overview

Following data-link layer initialization, IP initialization occurs. Next, iFCP gateways discover each other via iSNS. Likewise, configuration parameters for the iFCP fabric are discovered via iSNS. Once the iFCP fabric parameters are known, an IPsec connection is optionally established between each pair of iFCP gateways. As FC devices register in the

FCNS of each FC-SAN, the attached iFCP gateway propagates the registration information to the iSNS. The iSNS then propagates the information to each of the other iFCP gateways. Upon receipt, each iFCP gateway updates the FCNS of its attached FC-SAN with the remote node information and creates an entry in its address translation table for the remote node. At this point, the iFCP fabric is ready for initiator-target communication. TCP connections can be handled in two ways. An iFCP gateway can proactively establish and maintain multiple TCP connections to other gateways. These are called unbound TCP connections. When a PLOGI request is received, the iFCP gateway creates an iFCP session and binds it to one of the unbound TCP connections. Alternately, an iFCP gateway can wait until it receives a PLOGI request and then establish a TCP connection immediately followed by iFCP session establishment. While a TCP connection is bound to an iFCP session, it cannot be used by other iFCP sessions. iFCP enforces FC frame lifetimes in the same manner as FCIP. Likewise, detection and recovery of FC frames that are lost due to timeout are handled by FCP and FC. Due to limited vendor support and a low adoption rate, further examination of iFCP is currently outside the scope of this book.

Summary

This chapter provides a high-level overview of the upper-layer network protocols that comprise the SAM Transport Protocols. The protocols reviewed are all standards and, with the exception of iFCP, are commonly deployed in modern storage networks. The use of iSCSI and FCP for initiator-target communication is discussed, as is the use of FCIP and iFCP for long-distance FC-SAN connectivity across IP networks. The overviews in this chapter complement the information provided in Chapter 3, "An Overview of Network Operating Principles," in an effort to prime readers for the technical details provided in Part II, "The OSI Layers." Part II begins by examining the details of operation at OSI Layers 1 and 2.

Review Questions

1   How does iSCSI complement the traditional storage over IP model?

2   Is iSCSI capable of supporting high-performance applications?

3   How does the FC network service model resemble the IP network service model?

4   What is the guiding principle in traditional FC network designs?

5   What does FCIP create between FC-SANs to facilitate communication?

6   Which FC-4 protocols does FCIP support?

7   Is iFCP currently being deployed for its originally intended purpose?

8   Which address mode is most commonly used in modern iFCP deployments?

OSI Layers

Upon completing this chapter, you will be able to:

- Describe the physical layer characteristics of the SCSI parallel interface (SPI), Ethernet, and Fibre Channel (FC)

- Relate the addressing schemes used by the SPI, Ethernet, and FC to the SCSI architecture model (SAM) addressing scheme

- Differentiate the SPI, Ethernet, and FC mechanisms for name and address assignment and resolution

- Explain how the SPI, Ethernet, and FC govern media access

- Delineate the physical, logical, and virtual network boundaries observed by the SPI, Ethernet, and FC

- List the frame formats of the SPI and deconstruct the frame formats of Ethernet and FC

- Enumerate and describe the delivery mechanisms supported by the SPI, Ethernet, and FC

- Characterize the link aggregation capabilities of the SPI, Ethernet, and FC

- Chronicle the stages of link initialization for the SPI, Ethernet, and FC

CHAPTER 5

OSI Physical and Data-Link Layers

This chapter provides an in-depth review of the operational details of the SPI, Ethernet, and Fibre Channel at OSI Layers 1 and 2.

Conceptual Underpinnings

Networking professionals understand some of the topics discussed in this chapter, but not others. Before we discuss each network technology, we need to discuss some of the less understood conceptual topics, to clarify terminology and elucidate key points. This section provides foundational knowledge required to understand addressing schemes, address formats, delivery mechanisms, and link aggregation.

Addressing Schemes

The SPI, Ethernet, IP, and Fibre Channel all use different addressing schemes. To provide a consistent frame of reference, we discuss the addressing scheme defined by the SAM in this section. As we discuss addressing schemes of the SPI, Ethernet, IP, and Fibre Channel subsequently, we will compare each one to the SAM addressing scheme. The SAM defines four types of objects known as application client, logical unit, port, and device. Of these, three are addressable: logical unit, port, and device.

The SCSI protocol implemented in an initiator is called a SCSI application client. A SCSI application client can initiate only SCSI commands. No more than one SCSI application client may be implemented per SCSI Transport Protocol within a SCSI initiator device. Thus, no client ambiguity exists within an initiator device. This eliminates the need for SCSI application client addresses.

The SCSI protocol implemented in a target is called a SCSI logical unit. A SCSI logical unit can execute only SCSI commands. A SCSI target device may (and usually does) contain more than one logical unit. So, logical units require addressing to facilitate proper forwarding of incoming SCSI commands. A SCSI logical unit is a processing entity that represents any hardware component capable of providing SCSI services to SCSI application clients. Examples include a storage medium, an application-specific integrated circuit (ASIC) that supports SCSI enclosure services (SES) to provide environmental monitoring services, a robotic arm that supports SCSI media changer (SMC) services, and so forth. A SCSI logical unit is composed of a task manager and a device server. The task manager is responsible for queuing and managing the commands received from one or more SCSI application clients, whereas the device server is responsible for executing SCSI commands.

SCSI ports facilitate communication between SCSI application clients and SCSI logical units. A SCSI port consists of the hardware and software required to implement a SCSI Transport Protocol and associated SCSI Interconnect. One notable exception is the SPI, which does not implement a SCSI Transport Protocol.

A SCSI initiator device is composed of at least one SCSI port and at least one SCSI application client. A SCSI target device consists of at least one SCSI port, one task router per SCSI port, and at least one SCSI logical unit. Each task router directs incoming SCSI commands to the task manager of the appropriate logical unit. An FC HBA or iSCSI TOE is considered a SCSI device. This is somewhat confusing because the term *device* is commonly used to generically refer to a host, storage subsystem, switch, or router. To avoid confusion, we use the terms *enclosure* and *network entity* in the context of SCSI to describe any host, storage subsystem, switch, or router that contains one or more SCSI devices. A SCSI device often contains only a single SCSI port, but may contain more than one. For example, most JBOD chassis in use today contain dual-port disk drives that implement a single SCSI logical unit. Each disk drive is a single SCSI device with multiple ports. Likewise, many intelligent storage arrays contain multiple SCSI ports and implement a single SCSI device accessible via all ports. However, most multi-port FC HBAs in use today implement a SCSI application client per port (that is, multiple single-port SCSI devices). Many of the early iSCSI implementations are software-based to take advantage of commodity Ethernet hardware. In such an implementation, a multi-homed host (the network entity) typically contains a single SCSI device that consists of a single SCSI software driver (the application client) bound to a single iSCSI software driver (the SCSI Transport Protocol) that uses multiple IP addresses (the initiator ports making up the SCSI Interconnect) that are assigned to multiple Ethernet NICs.

The SAM defines two types of addresses known as name and identifier. A name positively identifies an object, and an identifier facilitates communication with an object. Names are generally optional, and identifiers are generally mandatory. Names are implemented by SCSI Interconnects and SCSI Transport Protocols, and identifiers are implemented only by SCSI Interconnects. The SAM addressing rules are not simple, so a brief description of the rules associated with each SAM object follows:

- Device names are optional in the SAM. However, any particular SCSI Transport Protocol may require each SCSI device to have a name. A device name never changes and may be used to positively identify a SCSI device. A device name is useful for determining whether a device is accessible via multiple ports. A device may be assigned only one name within the scope of each SCSI Transport Protocol. Each device name is globally unique within the scope of each SCSI Transport Protocol. Each SCSI Transport Protocol defines its own device name format and length.

- Device identifiers are not defined in the SAM. Because each SCSI device name is associated with one or more SCSI port names, each of which is associated with a SCSI port identifier, SCSI device identifiers are not required to facilitate communication.

- Port names are optional in the SAM. However, any particular SCSI Transport Protocol may require each SCSI port to have a name. A port name never changes and may be used to positively identify a port in the context of dynamic port identifiers. A port may be assigned only one name within the scope of each SCSI Transport Protocol. Each port name is globally unique within the scope of each SCSI Transport Protocol. Each SCSI Transport Protocol defines its own port name format and length.

- Port identifiers are mandatory. Port identifiers are used by SCSI Interconnect technologies as source and destination addresses when forwarding frames or packets. Each SCSI Interconnect defines its own port identifier format and length.

- Logical unit names are optional in the SAM. However, any particular SCSI Transport Protocol may require each SCSI logical unit to have a name. A logical unit name never changes and may be used to positively identify a logical unit in the context of dynamic logical unit identifiers. A logical unit name is also useful for determining whether a logical unit has multiple identifiers. That is the case in multi-port storage arrays that provide access to each logical unit via multiple ports simultaneously. A logical unit may be assigned only one name within the scope of each SCSI Transport Protocol. Each logical unit name is globally unique within the scope of each SCSI Transport Protocol. Each SCSI Transport Protocol defines its own logical unit name format and length.

- Logical unit identifiers are mandatory. A logical unit identifier is commonly called a logical unit number (LUN). If a target device provides access to multiple logical units, a unique LUN is assigned to each logical unit on each port. However, a logical unit may be assigned a different LUN on each port through which the logical unit is accessed. In other words, LUNs are unique only within the scope of a single target port. To accommodate the wide range of LUN scale and complexity from a simple SPI bus to a SAN containing enterprise-class storage subsystems, the SAM defines two types of LUNs known as flat and hierarchical. Each SCSI Transport Protocol defines its own flat LUN format and length. By contrast, the SAM defines the hierarchical LUN format and length. All SCSI Transport Protocols that support hierarchical LUNs must use the SAM-defined format and length. Up to four levels of hierarchy may be implemented, and each level may use any one of four defined formats. Each level is 2 bytes long. The total length of a hierarchical LUN is 8 bytes regardless of how many levels are used. Unused levels are filled with null characters (binary zeros). Support for hierarchical LUNs is optional.

NOTE   In common conversation, the term LUN is often used synonymously with the terms disk and volume. For example, one might hear the phrases *present the LUN to the host, mount the volume,* and *partition the disk* all used to describe actions performed against the same unit of storage.

SCSI logical unit numbering is quite intricate. Because LUNs do not facilitate identification of nodes or ports, or forwarding of frames or packets, further details of the SAM hierarchical LUN scheme are outside the scope of this book. For more information, readers are encouraged to consult the ANSI T10 SAM-3 specification and Annex C of the original ANSI T10 FCP specification. A simplified depiction of the SAM addressing scheme is shown in Figure 5-1. Only two levels of LUN hierarchy are depicted.

Figure 5-1 *SAM Addressing Scheme*

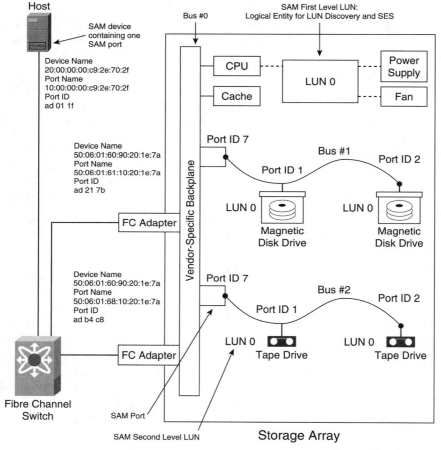

A separate addressing scheme is used to identify physical elements (storage shelves, media load/unload slots, robotic arms, and drives) within a media changer. Each element is assigned an address. In this scenario, the element address scheme is the conceptual equivalent of the logical block addressing (LBA) scheme used by magnetic disks. Just as SCSI initiators can copy data from one block to another within a disk, SCSI initiators can move media cartridges from one element to another within a media changer. Because media cartridges can be stored in any location and subsequently loaded into any drive, a barcode label (or equivalent) is attached to each media cartridge to enable identification as cartridges circulate inside the media changer. This label is called the volume tag. Application software (for example, a tape backup program) typically maintains a media catalog to map volume tags to content identifiers (for example, backup set names). An initiator can send a **read element status** command to the logical unit that represents the robotic arm (called the media transport element) to discover the volume tag at each element address. The initiator can then use element addresses to move media cartridges via the **move medium** command. After the robotic arm loads the specified media cartridge into the specified drive, normal I/O can occur in which the application (for example, a tape backup program) reads from or writes to the medium using the drive's LUN to access the medium, and the medium's LBA scheme to navigate the medium. Element and barcode addressing are not part of the SAM LUN scheme. The element and barcode addressing schemes are both required and are both complementary to the LUN scheme. Further details of physical element addressing, barcode addressing, and media changers are outside the scope of this book. For more information, readers are encouraged to consult the ANSI T10 SMC-2 specification. A simplified depiction of media changer element addressing is shown in Figure 5-2 using tape media.

Figure 5-2   *Media Changer Element Addressing*

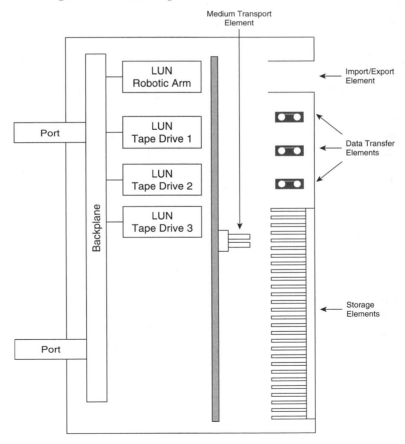

Address Formats

Several address formats are in use today. All address formats used by modern storage networks are specified by standards organizations. In the context of addressing schemes, a standards body that defines an address format is called a network address authority (NAA) even though the standards body might be engaged in many activities outside the scope of addressing. Some network protocols use specified bit positions in the address field of the frame or packet header to identify the NAA and format. This enables the use of multiple address formats via a single address field. The most commonly used address formats include the following:

- MAC-48 specified by the IEEE
- EUI-64 specified by the IEEE
- IPv4 specified by the IETF
- IQN specified by the IETF
- WWN specified by the ANSI T11 subcommittee
- FC Address Identifier specified by the ANSI T11 subcommittee

The IEEE formats are used for a broad range of purposes, so a brief description of each IEEE format is provided in this section. For a full description of each IEEE format, readers are encouraged to consult the IEEE 802-2001 specification and the IEEE 64-bit Global Identifier Format Tutorial. Descriptions of the various implementations of the IEEE formats appear throughout this chapter and Chapter 8, "OSI Session, Presentation, and Application Layers." Description of IPv4 addressing is deferred to Chapter 6, "OSI Network Layer." Note that IPv6 addresses can be used by IPS protocols, but IPv4 addresses are most commonly implemented today. Thus, IPv6 addressing is currently outside the scope of this book. Description of iSCSI qualified names (IQNs) is deferred to Chapter 8, "OSI Session, Presentation, and Application Layers." Descriptions of world wide names (WWNs) and FC address identifiers follow in the FC section of this chapter.

The IEEE 48-bit media access control (MAC-48) format is a 48-bit address format that guarantees universally unique addresses in most scenarios. The MAC-48 format supports locally assigned addresses which are not universally unique, but such usage is uncommon. The MAC-48 format originally was defined to identify physical elements such as LAN interfaces, but its use was expanded later to identify LAN protocols and other non-physical entities. When used to identify non-physical entities, the format is called the 48-bit extended unique identifier (EUI-48). MAC-48 and EUI-48 addresses are expressed in dash-separated hexadecimal notation such as 00-02-8A-9F-52-95. Figure 5-3 illustrates the IEEE MAC-48 address format.

Figure 5-3 *IEEE MAC-48 Address Format*

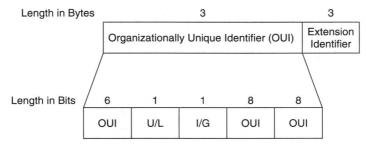

A brief description of each field follows:

- The IEEE registration authority committee (RAC) assigns a three-byte organizationally unique identifier (OUI) to each organization that wants to produce network elements or protocols. No two organizations are assigned the same OUI. All LAN interfaces produced by an organization must use that organization's assigned OUI as the first half of the MAC-48 address. Thus, the OUI field identifies the manufacturer of each LAN interface.

- Embedded within the first byte of the OUI is a bit called the universal/local (U/L) bit. The U/L bit indicates whether the Extension Identifier is universally administered by the organization that produced the LAN interface or locally administered by the company that deployed the LAN interface.

- Embedded within the first byte of the OUI is a bit called the individual/group (I/G) bit. The I/G bit indicates whether the MAC-48 address is an individual address used for unicast frames or a group address used for multicast frames.

- The Extension Identifier field, which is three bytes long, identifies each LAN interface. Each organization manages the Extension Identifier values associated with its OUI. During the interface manufacturing process, the U/L bit is set to 0 to indicate that the Extension Identifier field contains a universally unique value assigned by the manufacturer. The U/L bit can be set to 1 by a network administrator via the NIC driver parameters. This allows a network administrator to assign an Extension Identifier value according to a particular addressing scheme. In this scenario, each LAN interface address may be a duplicate of one or more other LAN interface addresses. This duplication is not a problem if no duplicate addresses exist on a single LAN. That said, local administration of Extension Identifiers is rare. So, the remainder of this book treats all MAC-48 Extension Identifiers as universally unique addresses.

The growing number of devices that require a MAC-48 address prompted the IEEE to define a new address format called EUI-64. The EUI-64 format is a 64-bit universally unique address format used for physical network elements and for non-physical entities. Like the MAC-48 format, the EUI-64 format supports locally assigned addresses which are not universally unique, but such usage is uncommon. MAC-48 addresses are still supported but are no longer promoted by the IEEE. Instead, vendors are encouraged to use the EUI-64 format for all new devices and protocols. A mapping is defined by the IEEE for use of MAC-48 and EUI-48 addresses within EUI-64 addresses. EUI-64 addresses are expressed in hyphen-separated hexadecimal notation such as 00-02-8A-FF-FF-9F-52-95. Figure 5-4 illustrates the IEEE EUI-64 address format.

Figure 5-4   *IEEE EUI-64 Address Format*

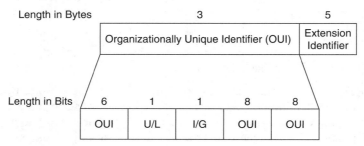

A brief description of each field follows:

- OUI—identical in format and usage to the OUI field in the MAC-48 address format.
- U/L bit—identical in usage to the U/L bit in the MAC-48 address format.
- I/G bit—identical in usage to the I/G bit in the MAC-48 address format.
- Extension Identifier—identical in purpose to the Extension Identifier field in the MAC-48 address format. However, the length is increased from 3 bytes to 5 bytes. The first two bytes can be used to map MAC-48 and EUI-48 Extension Identifier values into the remaining three bytes. Alternately, the first 2 bytes can be concatenated with the last 3 bytes to yield a 5-byte Extension Identifier for new devices and protocols. Local administration of Extension Identifiers is rare. So, the remainder of this book treats all EUI-64 Extension Identifiers as universally unique addresses.

Note the U/L and I/G bits are rarely used in modern storage networks. In fact, some FC address formats omit these bits. However, omission of these bits from FC addresses has no effect on FC-SANs.

Delivery Mechanisms

Delivery mechanisms such as acknowledgement, frame/packet reordering, and error notification vary from one network technology to the next. Network technologies are generally classified as connection-oriented or connectionless depending on the suite of delivery mechanisms employed. However, these terms are not well defined. Confusion can result from assumed meanings when these terms are applied to disparate network technologies because their meanings vary significantly depending on the context.

In circuit-switched environments, such as the public switched telephone network (PSTN), the term *connection-oriented* implies a physical end-to-end path over which every frame or packet flows. A connection is established hop-by-hop by using a signaling protocol (such as Signaling System v7 [SS7]) to communicate with each switch in the physical end-to-end path. Once the connection is established, no information about the source node or destination node needs to be included in the frames or packets. By contrast, packet-switched environments use the term connection-oriented to describe logical connections made between end nodes. For example, in IP networks, TCP is used to form a logical connection between end nodes. Packets associated with a single logical connection may traverse different physical paths. Each router in the path must inspect each IP packet as it enters the router and make a forwarding decision based on the destination information contained in the packet header. This means that packets can be delivered out of order, so reordering protocols are sometimes implemented by end nodes to process packets arriving out of order before they are passed to ULPs. A logical connection such as this is typically characterized by a unique identifier (carried in the header of each packet), reserved resources in the end nodes (used to buffer frames or packets associated with each connection), and negotiated connection management procedures such as frame/packet acknowledgement and buffer management.

In circuit-switched environments, the term connectionless generally has no meaning. By contrast, the term connectionless is used in packet-switched environments to describe the absence of an end-to-end logical connection. For example, UDP is combined with IP to provide connectionless communication. Most packet-switching technologies support both connectionless and connection-oriented communication.

This book occasionally uses the terms connection-oriented and connectionless, but readers should consider the context each time these terms are used. Readers should not equate the collection of delivery mechanisms that define connection-oriented communication in a given network technology with any other network technology. This book attempts to avoid the use of the terms connection-oriented and connectionless, opting instead to refer to specific delivery mechanisms as appropriate. The remainder of this section discusses the details of each type of delivery mechanism so that readers can clearly understand the subsequent descriptions of network technologies. The delivery mechanisms discussed in this section include the following:

- Detection of missing frames or packets (drops)
- Detection of duplicate frames or packets
- Detection of corrupt frames or packets
- Acknowledgement
- Guaranteed delivery (retransmission)
- Flow control (buffering)
- Guaranteed bandwidth
- Guaranteed latency

- Fragmentation, reassembly, and PMTU discovery
- In-order delivery and frame/packet reordering

The SAM does not explicitly require all of these delivery guarantees, but the SAM does *assume* error-free delivery of SCSI requests or responses. How the SCSI Transport Protocol or SCSI Interconnect accomplish error-free delivery is self-determined by each protocol suite. Client notification of delivery failure is explicitly required by the SAM. That implies a requirement for detection of failures within the SCSI Transport Protocol layer, the SCSI Interconnect layer, or both. A brief discussion of each delivery mechanism follows.

Dropped Frames or Packets

Several factors can cause drops. Some examples include the following:

- Buffer overrun
- No route to the destination
- Frame/packet corruption
- Intra-switch forwarding timeout
- Fragmentation required but not permitted
- Administrative routing policy
- Administrative security policy
- Quality of Service (QoS) policy
- Transient protocol error
- Bug in switch or router software

For these reasons, no network protocol can guarantee that frames or packets will never be dropped. However, a network protocol may guarantee to detect drops. Upon detection, the protocol may optionally request retransmission of the dropped frame or packet. Because this requires additional buffering in the transmitting device, it is uncommon in network devices. However, this is commonly implemented in end nodes. Another option is for the protocol that detects the dropped frame or packet to notify the ULP. In this case, the ULP may request retransmission of the frame or packet, or simply notify the next ULP of the drop. If the series of upward notifications continues until the application is notified, the application must request retransmission of the lost data. A third option is for the protocol that detects the dropped frame or packet to take no action. In this case, one of the ULPs or the application must detect the drop via a timeout mechanism.

Duplicate Frames or Packets

Duplicates can result from several causes. This might seem hard to imagine. After all, how is a duplicate frame or packet created? Transient congestion provides a good example. Assume that host A sends a series of packets to host B using a protocol that guarantees delivery. Assume also that there are multiple paths between host A and host B. When load balancing is employed within the network, and one path is congested while the other is not, some packets will arrive at host B while others are delayed in transit. Host B might have a timer to detect dropped packets, and that timer might expire before all delayed packets are received. If so, host B may request retransmission of some packets from host A. When host A retransmits the requested packets, duplicate packets eventually arrive at host B. Various actions may be taken when a duplicate frame or packet arrives at a destination. The duplicate can be transparently discarded, discarded with notification to the ULP, or delivered to the ULP.

Corrupt Frames or Packets

Corrupt frames or packets can result from several causes. Damaged cables, faulty transceivers, and electromagnetic interference (EMI) are just some of the potential causes of frame/packet corruption. Even when operating properly, optical transceivers will introduce errors. OSI physical layer specifications state the minimum interval between transceiver errors. This is known as the bit error ratio (BER). For example, 1000BASE-SX specifies a BER of $1:10^{12}$. Most network protocols include a checksum or CRC in the header or trailer of each frame or packet to allow detection of frame/packet corruption. When a corrupt frame or packet is detected, the protocol that detects the error can deliver the corrupt frame or packet to the ULP (useful for certain types of voice and video traffic), transparently drop the corrupt frame or packet, drop the corrupt frame or packet with notification to the ULP, or drop the frame or packet with notification to the transmitter. In the last case, the transmitter may abort the transmission with notification to the ULP, or retransmit the dropped frame or packet. A retransmit retry limit is usually enforced, and the ULP is usually notified if the limit is reached.

Acknowledgement

Acknowledgement provides notification of delivery success or failure. You can implement acknowledgement as positive or negative, and as explicit or implicit. Positive acknowledgement involves signaling from receiver to transmitter when frames or packets are successfully received. The received frames or packets are identified in the acknowledgement frame or packet (usually called an ACK). This is also a form of explicit acknowledgement. Negative acknowledgement is a bit more complicated. When a frame or packet is received before all frames or packets with lower identities are received, a negative acknowledgement frame or packet (called an NACK) may be sent to the transmitter for the frames or packets with lower identities, which are assumed missing. A receiver timeout value is usually implemented to allow delivery of missing frames or packets prior to NACK transmission. NACKs may be sent under other circumstances, such as when a frame or packet is received but determined to be corrupt. With explicit acknowledgement, each frame or packet that is successfully received is identified in an ACK, or each frame or packet that is dropped is identified in a NACK. Implicit acknowledgement can be implemented in several ways.

For example, a single ACK may imply the receipt of all frames or packets up to the frame or packet identified in the ACK. A retransmission timeout value is an example of implicit NACK.

The SAM does not require explicit acknowledgement of delivery. The SCSI protocol expects a response for each command, so frame/packet delivery failure eventually will generate an implicit negative acknowledgement via SCSI timeout. The SAM assumes that delivery failures are detected within the service delivery subsystem, but places no requirements upon the service delivery subsystem to take action upon detection of a delivery failure.

Guaranteed Delivery

Guaranteed delivery requires retransmission of every frame or packet that is dropped. Some form of frame/packet acknowledgement is required for guaranteed delivery, even if it is implicit. Frames or packets must be held in the transmitter's memory until evidence of successful delivery is received. Protocols that support retransmission typically impose a limit on the number of retransmission attempts. If the limit is reached before successful transmission, the ULP is usually notified.

Flow Control and QoS

Flow control attempts to minimize drops due to buffer overruns. Buffer management can be proactive or reactive. Proactive buffer management involves an exchange of buffering capabilities before transmission of data frames or packets. The downside to this approach is that the amount of available buffer memory determines the maximum distance that can be traversed while maintaining line rate throughput. The upside to this approach is that it prevents frames or packets from being dropped due to buffer overrun. Reactive buffer management permits immediate transmission of frames or packets. The receiver must then signal the transmitter in real time when buffer resources are exhausted. This eliminates the relationship between distance and available buffer memory, but it allows some in-flight frames or packets to be dropped because of buffer overrun. Flow control can be implemented between two directly connected devices to manage the buffers available for frame reception. This is known as device-to-device, buffer-to-buffer, or link-level flow control. Flow control can also be implemented between two devices that communicate across an internetwork to manage the buffers available for frame/packet processing. This is known as end-to-end flow control.

Another key point to understand is the relationship between flow control and QoS. Flow control limits the flow of traffic between a pair of devices, whereas QoS determines how traffic will be processed by intermediate network devices or destination nodes based on the relative priority of each frame or packet. Flow control and QoS are discussed further in Chapter 9, "Flow Control and Quality of Service."

The networking industry uses the phrases *quality of service* and *class of service* inconsistently. Whereas quality of service generally refers to queuing policies based on traffic prioritization, some networking technologies use class of service to convey this meaning. Ethernet falls into this category, as some Ethernet documentation refers to Class of Service instead of Quality of Service. Other networking technologies use class of service to convey the set of delivery mechanisms employed. FC falls into this category.

Guaranteed Bandwidth

Circuit-switching technologies like that used by the PSTN inherently dedicate end-to-end link bandwidth to the connected end nodes. The drawback of this model is inefficient use of available bandwidth within the network. Packet-switching technologies seek to optimize use of bandwidth by sharing links within the network. The drawback of this model is that some end nodes might be starved of bandwidth or might be allotted insufficient bandwidth to sustain acceptable application performance. Thus, many packet-switching technologies support bandwidth reservation schemes that allow end-to-end partial or full-link bandwidth to be dedicated to individual traffic flows or specific node pairs.

Guaranteed Latency

All circuit-switching technologies inherently provide consistent latency for the duration of a connection. Some circuit-switching technologies support transparent failover at OSI Layer 1 in the event of a circuit failure. The new connection might have higher or lower latency than the original connection, but the latency will be consistent for the duration of the new connection. Packet-switching technologies do not inherently provide consistent latency. Circuit emulation service, if supported, can guarantee consistent latency through packet-switched networks. Without circuit-emulation services, consistent latency can be achieved in packet-switching networks via proper network design and the use of QoS mechanisms.

Fragmentation, Reassembly, and PMTU Discovery

Fragmentation is discussed in Chapter 3, "Overview of Network Operating Principles," in the context of IP networks, but fragmentation also can occur in other networks. When the MTU of an intermediate network link or the network link connecting the destination node is smaller than the MTU of the network link connecting the source node, the frame or packet must be fragmented. If the frame or packet cannot be fragmented, it must be dropped. Once a frame or packet is fragmented, it typically remains fragmented until it reaches the destination node. When fragmentation occurs, header information is updated to indicate the data offset of each fragment so that reassembly can take place within the destination node. The network device that fragments the frame or packet and the destination node that reassembles the fragments both incur additional processing overhead. Furthermore, protocol overhead increases as a percentage of the data payload, which contributes to suboptimal use of network bandwidth. For these reasons, it is desirable to have a common MTU across all network links from end to end. When this is not possible, it is desirable to dynamically discover the smallest MTU along the path between each pair of communicating end nodes. Each network technology that supports fragmentation typically specifies its own PMTU discovery mechanism.

Fragmentation should not be confused with segmentation. Fragmentation occurs in a network after a frame or packet has been transmitted by a node. Segmentation occurs within a node before transmission. Segmentation is the process of breaking down a chunk of application data into smaller chunks that are equal to or less than the local MTU. If PMTU is supported, the PMTU value is used instead of the local MTU. The goal of segmentation is to avoid unnecessary fragmentation in the network without imposing any additional processing burden on applications. Segmentation reduces application overhead by enabling applications to transmit large amounts of data without regard for PMTU constraints. The tradeoff is more overhead imposed on the OSI layer that performs segmentation on behalf of the application. Remember this when calculating protocol throughput, because the segmenting layer might introduce additional protocol overhead.

In-order Delivery

If there is only one path between each pair of nodes, in-order delivery is inherently guaranteed by the network. When multiple paths exist between node pairs, network routing algorithms can suppress all but one link and optionally use the suppressed link(s) as backup in the event of primary link failure. Alternately, network routing algorithms can use all links in a load-balanced fashion. In this scenario, frames can arrive out of order unless measures are taken to ensure in-order delivery. In-order delivery can be defined as the receipt of frames at the destination node in the same order as they were transmitted by the source node. Alternately, in-order delivery can be defined as delivery of data to a specific protocol layer within the destination node in the same order as they were transmitted by the same protocol layer within the source node. In both of these definitions, in-order delivery applies to a single source and a single destination. The order of frames or packets arriving at a destination from one source relative to frames or packets arriving at the same destination from another source is not addressed by the SAM and is generally considered benign with regard to data integrity.

In the first definition of in-order delivery, the network must employ special algorithms or special configurations for normal algorithms to ensure that load-balanced links do not result in frames arriving at the destination out of order. There are four levels of granularity for load balancing in serial networking technologies; frame level, flow level, node level, and network level.

Frame-level load balancing spreads individual frames across the available links and makes no effort to ensure in-order delivery of frames. Flow-level load balancing spreads individual flows across the available links. All frames within a flow follow the same link, thus ensuring in-order delivery of frames within each flow. However, in-order delivery of flows is not guaranteed. It is possible for frames in one flow to arrive ahead of frames in another flow without respect to the order in which the flows were transmitted. Some protocols map each I/O operation to an uniquely identifiable flow. In doing so, these protocols enable I/O operation load balancing. If the order of I/O operations must be preserved, node-level load balancing must be used.

Node-level load balancing spreads node-to-node connections across the available links, thus ensuring that all frames within all flows within each connection traverse the same link. Multiple simultaneous connections may exist between a source and destination. Node-level load balancing forwards all such connections over the same link. In this manner, node-level load balancing ensures in-order delivery of all frames exchanged between each pair of nodes. Node-level load balancing can be configured for groups of nodes at the network level by effecting a single routing policy for an entire subnet. This is typically (but not always) the manner in which IP routing protocols are configured. For example, a network administrator who wants to disable load balancing usually does so for a routing protocol (affecting all subnets reachable by that protocol) or for a specific subnet (affecting all nodes on that single subnet). In doing so, the network administrator forces all traffic destined for the affected subnet(s) to follow a single link. This has the same affect on frame delivery as implementing a node-level load-balancing algorithm, but without the benefits of load balancing.

Conversely, network-level load balancing can negate the intended affects of node-level algorithms that might be configured on a subset of intermediate links in the end-to-end path. To illustrate this, you need only to consider the default behavior of most IP routing protocols, which permit equal-cost path load balancing. Assume that node A transmits two frames. Assume also that no intervening frames destined for the same subnet are received by node A's default gateway. If the default gateway has two equal-cost paths to the destination subnet, it will transmit the first frame via the first path and the second frame via the second path. That action could result in out-of-order frame delivery. Now assume that the destination subnet is a large Ethernet network with port channels between each pair of switches. If a node-level load-balancing algorithm is configured on the port channels, the frames received at each switch will be delivered across each port channel with order fidelity, but could still arrive at the destination node out of order. Thus, network administrators must consider the behavior of all load-balancing algorithms in the end-to-end path. That raises an important point; network-level load balancing is not accomplished with a special algorithm, but rather with the algorithm embedded in the routing protocol. Also remember that all load-balancing algorithms are employed hop-by-hop.

In the second definition of in-order delivery, the network makes no attempt to ensure in-order delivery in the presence of load-balanced links. Frames or packets may arrive out of order at the destination node. Thus, one of the network protocols operating within the destination node must support frame/packet reordering to ensure data integrity.

The SAM does not *explicitly* require in-order delivery of frames or packets composing a SCSI request/response. However, because the integrity of a SCSI request/response depends upon in-order delivery of its constituent frames, the SAM *implicitly* requires the SCSI service delivery subsystem (including the protocols implemented within the end nodes) to provide in-order delivery of frames. The nature of some historical SCSI Interconnects, such as the SPI, inherently provides in-order delivery of all frames. With frame-switched networks, such as FC and Ethernet, frames can be delivered out of order. Therefore, when designing and implementing modern storage networks, take care to ensure in-order frame delivery. Note that in-order delivery may be guaranteed without a guarantee of delivery. In this scenario, some data might be lost in transit, but all data arriving at the destination node will be delivered to the application in order. If the network does not provide notification of non-delivery, delivery failures must be detected by an ULP or the application.

Similarly, the SAM does not require initiators or targets to support reordering of SCSI requests or responses or the service delivery subsystem to provide in-order delivery of SCSI requests or responses. The SAM considers such details to be implementation-specific. Some applications are insensitive to the order in which SCSI requests or responses are processed. Conversely, some applications fail or generate errors when SCSI requests or responses are not processed in the desired order. If an application requires in-order processing of SCSI requests or responses, the initiator can control SCSI command execution via task attributes and queue algorithm modifiers (see ANSI T10 SPC-3). In doing so, the order of SCSI responses is also controlled. Or, the application might expect the SCSI delivery subsystem to provide in-order delivery of SCSI requests or responses. Such applications might exist in any storage network, so storage network administrators typically side with caution and assume the presence of such applications. Thus, modern storage networks are typically designed and implemented to provide in-order delivery of SCSI requests and responses. Some SCSI Transport protocols support SCSI request/response reordering to facilitate the use of parallel transmission techniques within end nodes. This loosens the restrictions on storage network design and implementation practices.

Reordering should not be confused with reassembly. Reordering merely implies the order of frame/packet receipt at the destination node does not determine the order of delivery to the application. If a frame or packet is received out of order, it is held until the missing frame or packet is received. At that time, the frames/packets are delivered to the ULP in the proper order. Reassembly requires frames/packets to be held in a buffer until all frames/packets that compose an upper layer protocol data unit (PDU) have been received. The PDU is then reassembled, and the entire PDU is delivered to the ULP. Moreover, reassembly does not inherently imply reordering. A protocol that supports reassembly may discard all received frames/packets of a given PDU upon receipt of an out-of-order frame/packet belonging to the same PDU. In this case, the ULP must retransmit the entire PDU. In the context of fragmentation, lower-layer protocols within the end nodes typically support reassembly. In the context of segmentation, higher layer protocols within the end nodes typically support reassembly.

Link Aggregation

Terminology varies in the storage networking industry related to link aggregation. Some FC switch vendors refer to their proprietary link aggregation feature as *trunking*. However, trunking is well defined in Ethernet environments as the tagging of frames transmitted on an inter-switch link (ISL) to indicate the virtual LAN (VLAN) membership of each frame. With the advent of virtual SAN (VSAN) technology for FC networks, common sense dictates consistent use of the term trunking in both Ethernet and FC environments.

NOTE   One FC switch vendor uses the term *trunking* to describe a proprietary load-balancing feature implemented via the FC routing protocol. This exacerbates the confusion surrounding the term *trunking*.

By contrast, link aggregation is the bundling of two or more physical links so that the links appear to ULPs as one logical link. Link aggregation is accomplished within the OSI data-link layer, and the resulting logical link is properly called a port channel. Cisco Systems invented Ethernet port channels, which were standardized in March 2000 by the IEEE via the 802.3ad specification. Standardization enabled interoperability in heterogeneous Ethernet networks. Aggregation of FC links is not yet standardized. Thus, link aggregation must be deployed with caution in heterogeneous FC networks.

Transceivers

Transceivers can be integrated or pluggable. An integrated transceiver is built into the network interface on a line card, HBA, TOE, or NIC such that it cannot be replaced if it fails. This means the entire interface must be replaced if the transceiver fails. For switch line cards, this implication can be very problematic because an entire line card must be replaced to return a single port to service when a transceiver fails. Also, the type of connector used to mate a cable to an interface is determined by the transceiver. So, the types of cable that can be used by an interface with an integrated transceiver are limited. An example of an integrated transceiver is the traditional 10/100 Ethernet NIC, which has an RJ-45 connector built into it providing cable access to the integrated electrical transceiver.

By contrast, a pluggable transceiver incorporates all required transmit/receive componentry onto a removable device. The removable device can be plugged into an interface receptacle without powering down the device containing the interface (hot-pluggable). This allows the replacement of a failed transceiver without removal of the network interface. For switch line cards, this enables increased uptime by eliminating scheduled outages to replace failed transceivers. Also, hot-pluggable transceivers can be easily replaced to accommodate cable plant upgrades. In exchange for this increased flexibility, the price of the transceiver is increased. This results from an increase in research and development (R&D) costs and componentry. Pluggable transceivers are not always defined by networking standards bodies. Industry consortiums sometimes form to define common criteria for the production of interoperable, pluggable transceivers. The resulting specification is called a multi-source agreement (MSA). The most common types of pluggable transceivers are

- Gigabit interface converter (GBIC)
- Small form-factor pluggable (SFP)

A GBIC or SFP can operate at any transmission rate. The rate is specified in the MSA. Some MSAs specify multi-rate transceivers. Typically, GBICs and SFPs are not used for rates below 1 Gbps. Any pluggable transceiver that has a name beginning with the letter X operates at 10 Gbps. The currently available 10-Gbps pluggable transceivers include the following:

- 10 Gigabit small form-factor pluggable (XFP)
- XENPAK
- XPAK
- X2

XENPAK is the oldest 10 gigabit MSA. The X2 and XPAK MSAs build upon the XENPAK MSA. Both X2 and XPAK use the XENPAK electrical specification. XFP incorporates a completely unique design.

SCSI Parallel Interface

This section explores the details of SPI operation. Though the SPI is waning in popularity, there is still a significant amount of SPI-connected storage in production environments today.

SPI Media, Connectors, Transceivers, and Operating Ranges

The SPI supports only copper media, but various copper media and connectors can be used depending on the SPI version. Media and connectors are specified as shielded or unshielded. Shielded components are used for external connections between enclosures, and unshielded components are used for connections inside an enclosure. Table 5-1 summarizes the supported configurations for each SPI version.

Table 5-1   *SPI Media and Connectors*

Version	Media	Connectors
SPI-2	Unshielded flat ribbon cable	50-pin unshielded
	Unshielded flat twisted-pair ribbon cable	68-pin unshielded
	Unshielded round twisted-pair cable	80-pin unshielded
	Shielded round twisted-pair cable	50-pin shielded
	Printed Circuit Board (PCB) backplane	68-pin shielded
SPI-3	Unshielded planar cable	50-pin unshielded
	Unshielded round twisted-pair cable	68-pin unshielded
	Shielded round twisted-pair cable	80-pin unshielded
	PCB backplane	50-pin shielded
		68-pin shielded
SPI-4	Unshielded planar bulk cable	50-pin unshielded
	Unshielded round twisted-pair bulk cable	68-pin unshielded
	Shielded round twisted-pair bulk cable	80-pin unshielded
	PCB backplane	50-pin shielded
		68-pin shielded
SPI-5	Unshielded planar bulk cable	50-pin unshielded
	Unshielded round twisted-pair bulk cable	68-pin unshielded
	Shielded round twisted-pair bulk cable	80-pin unshielded
	PCB backplane	50-pin shielded
		68-pin shielded

As discussed in Chapter 3, "Overview of Network Operating Principles," the SPI uses four transceiver types known as single-ended (SE), multimode single-ended (MSE), low voltage differential (LVD), and high voltage differential (HVD). The SPI operating range is determined by the transceiver type, the medium, the number of attached devices, and the data rate. Table 5-2 summarizes the operating range (expressed in meters) supported by each SPI version.

Table 5-2   *SPI Operating Ranges*

Version	Operating Range (m)
SPI-2	1.5–25
SPI-3	1.5–25
SPI-4	1.5–25
SPI-5	2–25

SPI Encoding and Signaling

As explained in Chapter 3, "Overview of Network Operating Principles," many networking technologies encode data bits received from OSI Layer 2 into a different bit set before transmission at OSI Layer 1. However, the SPI does not. Instead, the SPI implements a complex system of electrical signaling at OSI Layer 1 to provide similar functionality. The SPI implements multiple electrical signaling schemes depending on the transceiver type, data transfer mode, and data rate. Additionally, the SPI electrical signaling schemes provide much of the OSI Layer 2 functionality that is normally provided via control frames and header fields. Several different electrical signals are raised and lowered in concert to maintain clock synchronization, negotiate bus phases, establish peer sessions, control the flow of data, recover from bus errors, and so on. This approach reflects the parallel nature of the SPI. Because this approach is quite different from the methods employed by serial networking technologies, in-depth discussion of the SPI signaling rules is not germane to the understanding of modern storage networks. Readers who are interested in these details are encouraged to consult the latest version of the ANSI T10 SPI specification.

SPI Addressing Scheme

The SPI does not implement any equivalent to SAM device or port names. However, the SPI does implement an equivalent to SAM port identifiers. These are known simply as SCSI Identifiers (SCSI IDs). SPI devices use SCSI IDs when transmitting frames to indicate the intended destination device. On an 8-bit wide data bus, up to eight SCSI IDs are supported ranging from 0 to 7. On a 16-bit wide data bus, up to 16 SCSI IDs are supported ranging from 0 to 15.

SPI Name Assignment and Resolution

The SPI does not implement SAM names, so name assignment and resolution mechanisms are not required.

SPI Address Assignment and Resolution

The SCSI ID of each device must be manually configured. An SPI device typically has a jumper block, toggle-switch block, or other physical selector that is used to configure the SCSI ID. Some storage controllers support software-based SCSI ID configuration via a setup program embedded in the controller's BIOS. A protocol called SCSI configured automatically (SCAM) was defined in SPI-2 for automatic SCSI ID assignment on SPI buses. SCAM promised to bring plug-and-play functionality to the SPI. However, SPI-3 made SCAM obsolete, thus preserving the static nature of SCSI IDs. The SPI implements only OSI Layer 2 addresses, so address resolution is not required.

SPI Media Access

Because all SPI attached devices use a common set of pins for transmission and reception, only one device can transmit at any point in time. Media access is facilitated through an arbitration process. Each device is assigned an arbitration priority based on its SCSI ID. The highest priority is 1, which is always assigned to SCSI ID 7. Typically, only one initiator is attached to an SPI bus, and it is assigned SCSI ID 7 by convention. This convention ensures the initiator is able to take control of the bus at any time. For historical reasons, the remaining priority assignments are not as straightforward as one might expect. Table 5-3 lists the SPI priorities and associated SCSI IDs.

Table 5-3   *SPI Priorities and SCSI IDs*

Priority	1	2	3	4	5	6	7	8	9	10	11	12	13	14	15	16
SCSI ID	7	6	5	4	3	2	1	0	15	14	13	12	11	10	9	8

NOTE   It is possible for multiple initiators to be connected to a single SPI bus. Such a configuration is used for clustering solutions, in which multiple hosts need simultaneous access to a common set of LUNs. However, most SPI bus deployments are single initiator configurations.

There are two methods of arbitration; normal arbitration, and quick arbitration and selection (QAS). Normal arbitration must be supported by every device, but QAS support is optional. QAS can be negotiated between pairs of devices, thus allowing each device to use normal arbitration to communicate with some devices and QAS arbitration to communicate with other devices. This enables simultaneous support of QAS-enabled devices and non-QAS devices on a single SPI bus.

Using normal arbitration, priority determines which device gains access to the bus if more than one device simultaneously requests access. Each device that loses an arbitration attempt simply retries at the next arbitration interval. Each device continues retrying until no higher priority devices simultaneously arbitrate, at which point the lower priority device can transmit. This can result in starvation of low-priority devices. So, an optional fairness algorithm is supported to prevent starvation. When fairness is used, each device maintains a record of arbitration attempts. Higher priority devices are allowed to access the bus first, but are restrained from arbitrating again until lower priority devices that lost previous arbitration attempts are allowed to access the bus.

The intricacies of this arbitration model can be illustrated with an analogy. Suppose that a director of a corporation goes to the company's cafeteria for lunch and arrives at the cashier line at precisely the same time as a vice president. The director must allow the vice president to go ahead based on rank. Now suppose that the corporation's president arrives. The president must get in line behind the director despite the president's superior rank. Also, the director may not turn around to schmooze with the president (despite the director's innate desire to schmooze upwardly). Thus, the director cannot offer to let the president go ahead. However, the director can step out of line (for example, to swap a chocolate whole milk for a plain low-fat milk). If the director is out of line long enough for the cashier to service one or more patrons, the director must re-enter the line behind all other employees.

QAS is essentially normal arbitration with a streamlined method for detecting when the bus is available for a new arbitration attempt. Normal arbitration requires the SPI bus to transition into the BUS FREE phase before a new arbitration attempt can occur. QAS allows a QAS-enabled device to take control of the bus from another QAS-enabled device without changing to BUS FREE. To prevent starvation of non-QAS-enabled devices, the initiator can arbitrate via QAS and, upon winning, force a BUS FREE transition to occur. Normal arbitration must then be used by all devices for the ensuing arbitration cycle. In this respect, the convention of assigning the highest priority to the initiator allows the initiator to police the bus. The fairness algorithm is mandatory for all QAS-enabled devices when using QAS, but it is optional for QAS-enabled devices during normal arbitration.

SPI Network Boundaries

All SPI bus implementations are physically bounded. It is not possible to create an internetwork of SPI buses because no OSI Layer 2 bridging capability is defined. Therefore, the SPI does not support logical boundaries. Likewise, the concept of a virtual SPI bus is not defined in any specification. Note that it is possible to expand a single SPI bus via SCSI expanders that provide OSI Layer 1 repeater functionality. In fact, some SCSI enclosures employ an expander between each pair of drives to facilitate hot-pluggable operation. However, SPI expanders do not affect the operation of an SPI bus at OSI Layer 2. Therefore, an SPI bus is always a single physical segment bounded by its terminators.

SPI Frame Formats

The SPI implements various frame formats, each of which is used during a specific bus phase. Three frame formats are defined for the DATA phase: data, data group, and information unit. The frame format used depends on the data transfer mode. During asynchronous transfer, only the data format may be used. During synchronous transfers, the data, data group, and information unit formats may be used. During paced transfer, only the information unit format may be used.

During asynchronous transfer, only data is transmitted. There is no header or trailer. There is no formal frame format aside from stipulated bit and byte positions for data. A separate electrical signal is used to indicate odd parity for the data bits. By contrast, a data group frame has a data field, an optional pad field and a parallel CRC (pCRC) trailer field. Likewise, an information unit frame has a data field, an optional pad field, and an information unit CRC (iuCRC) trailer field. The difference between a data group and an information unit has less to do with frame format than with protocol behavior during data transfer.

SPI Delivery Mechanisms

The SPI represents a very simple network. So, delivery mechanisms are inherently simplified. The SPI implements the following delivery mechanisms:

- It is not possible for frames to be dropped on an SPI bus by any device other than the receiver. This is because there are no intermediate processing devices. Electrical signals pass unmodified through each device attached to an SPI bus between the source and destination devices. If the receiver drops a frame for any reason, the sender must be notified.

- When a device drives a signal on an SPI bus, the destination device reads the signal in real time. Thus, it is not possible for duplicate frames to arrive at a destination.

- Corrupt data frames are detected via the parity signal or the CRC field. Corrupt frames are immediately dropped by the receiver, and the sender is notified.

- The SPI supports acknowledgement as an inherent property of the SPI flow control mechanism.

- Devices attached to an SPI bus are not required to retransmit dropped frames. Upon notification of frame drop, a sender may choose to retransmit the dropped frames or abort the delivery request. If the retransmission limit is reached or the delivery request is aborted, the ULP (SCSI) is notified.

- The SPI supports flow control in different ways depending on the data transfer mode (asynchronous, synchronous, or paced). Flow control is negotiated between each initiator/target pair. In all cases, the flow-control mechanism is proactive.

- The SPI does not provide guaranteed bandwidth. While a device is transmitting, the full bandwidth of the bus is available. However, the full bandwidth of the bus must be shared between all connected devices. So, each device has access to the bus less frequently as the number of connected devices increases. Thus, the effective bandwidth available to each device decreases as the number of connected devices increases. The fairness algorithm also plays a role. Without fairness, high-priority devices are allowed access to the bus more frequently than low-priority devices.

- The SPI inherently guarantees consistent latency.

- Fragmentation cannot occur on the SPI bus because all devices are always connected via a single network segment.

- The SPI intrinsically supports in-order delivery. Because all devices are connected to a single physical medium, and because no device on an SPI bus buffers frames for other devices, it is impossible for frames to be delivered out of order.

SPI Link Aggregation

The SPI-2 specification supported link aggregation as a means of doubling the data bus width from 16 bits to 32 bits. Link aggregation can be tricky even with serial links, so it is impressive that the ANSI T10 subcommittee defined a means to aggregate parallel links. The limited distance and single-segment nature of the SPI simplified some aspects of the SPI link aggregation scheme, which made ANSI's job a bit easier. The SPI 32-bit data bus signals were spread across two parallel links to load-balance at the byte level. The parallel nature of the SPI made byte-level load balancing possible. The SPI 32-bit data bus was made obsolete by SPI-3. No subsequent SPI specification defines a new link-aggregation technique.

SPI Link Initialization

The SPI bus is itself a cable. Therefore, initialization of an SPI bus is actually initialization of the devices attached to the bus. Therefore, SPI bus initialization cannot begin until one or more devices power on. The bus phase is BUS FREE after devices power on until an initiator begins target discovery. As described in Chapter 3, "Overview of Network Operating Principles," target discovery is accomplished via the TEST UNIT READY and INQUIRY commands. Upon completing its internal power-on self test (POST), a target device is capable of responding to the TEST UNIT READY and INQUIRY commands. Upon completing its internal POST, a initiator device is capable of issuing the TEST UNIT READY and INQUIRY commands. To initiate these commands, the initiator must arbitrate for access to the bus. During initial arbitration, only the initiator attempts bus access. Upon winning arbitration, target discovery ensues as described in Chapter 3, "Overview of Network Operating Principles." After target discovery completes, normal bus communication ensues.

Ethernet

This section explores the details of Ethernet operation. Because Ethernet has long been sufficiently stable to operate as a plug-and-play technology, it is assumed by many to be a simple technology. In fact, the inner workings of Ethernet are quite intricate. Ethernet is a very mature technology. It is considered the switching technology of choice for almost every network environment. However, IPS protocols are relatively immature, so Ethernet is trailing FC market share in block-level storage environments. As IPS protocols mature, additional IPS products will come to market, and Ethernet will gain market share in block-level storage environments. Thus, it is important to understand Ethernet's inner workings.

Ethernet Media, Connectors, Transceivers, and Operating Ranges

Ethernet supports a very broad range of media, connectors, and transceivers. Today, most deployments are based on copper media for end node connectivity, but ISLs are often deployed on fiber media. Copper media and transceivers are less expensive than their fiber counterparts, but they do not support the same distances as their fiber counterparts. As transmission rates increase, the single-segment distance that can be traversed decreases. This phenomenon is prompting a slow industry-wide movement away from copper media. As new 10GE products come to market, the cable-plant upgrades from copper to optical that began when GE products came to market are expected to continue.

Table 5-4 summarizes the media, connectors, transceivers, and operating ranges that are specified in IEEE 802.3-2002. The nomenclature used to represent each defined GE implementation is [data rate expressed in Mbps concatenated with the word "BASE"]-[PHY designator]. The term 1000BASE-X refers collectively to 1000BASE-SX, 1000BASE-LX and 1000BASE-CX.

Table 5-4   *802.3-2002 Media, Connectors, Transceivers, and Operating Ranges*

GE Variant	Medium	Modal Bandwidth	Connectors	Transceiver	Operating Range (m)
1000BASE-LX	9 μm SMF	N/A	Duplex SC	1310nm laser	2–5000
1000BASE-LX	50 μm MMF	500 MHz*km	Duplex SC	1310nm laser	2–550
1000BASE-LX	50 μm MMF	400 MHz*km	Duplex SC	1310nm laser	2–550
1000BASE-LX	62.5 μm MMF	500 MHz*km	Duplex SC	1310nm laser	2–550
1000BASE-SX	50 μm MMF	500 MHz*km	Duplex SC	850nm laser	2–550
1000BASE-SX	50 μm MMF	400 MHz*km	Duplex SC	850nm laser	2–500
1000BASE-SX	62.5 μm MMF	200 MHz*km	Duplex SC	850nm laser	2–275
1000BASE-SX	62.5 μm MMF	160 MHz*km	Duplex SC	850nm laser	2–220
1000BASE-T	100 ohm Category 5 UTP	N/A	RJ-45	Electrical	0–100
1000BASE-CX	150 ohm twinax	N/A	DB-9, HSSDC	Electrical	0–25

The MT-RJ and LC fiber optic connectors are not listed in Table 5-4 because they are not specified in IEEE 802.3-2002. However, both are quite popular, and both are supported by most GE switch vendors. Many transceiver vendors offer 1000BASE-LX-compliant GBICs that exceed the optical requirements specified in 802.3-2002. These transceivers are called 1000BASE-LH GBICs. They typically support a maximum distance of 10km. Another non-standard transceiver, 1000BASE-ZX, has gained significant popularity. 1000BASE-ZX uses a 1550nm laser instead of the standard 1310nm laser. The 1000BASE-ZX operating range varies by vendor because it is not standardized, but the upper limit is typically 70–100km.

Table 5-5 summarizes the media, connectors, transceivers, and operating ranges that are specified in IEEE 802.3ae-2002 and 802.3ak-2004. The nomenclature used to represent each defined 10GE implementation is [data rate expressed in bps concatenated with the word "BASE"]-[transceiver designator concatenated with encoding designator].

Table 5-5 *802.3ae-2002 and 802.3ak-2004 Media, Connectors, Transceivers, and Operating Ranges*

10GE Variant	Medium	Modal Bandwidth	Connectors	Transceiver	Operating Range (m)
10GBASE-EW	9 μm SMF	N/A	Unspecified	1550nm laser	2–40k *
10GBASE-EW	9 μm SMF	N/A	Unspecified	1550nm laser	2–30k
10GBASE-ER	9 μm SMF	N/A	Unspecified	1550nm laser	2–40k *
10GBASE-ER	9 μm SMF	N/A	Unspecified	1550nm laser	2–30k
10GBASE-LW	9 μm SMF	N/A	Unspecified	1310nm laser	2–10k
10GBASE-LR	9 μm SMF	N/A	Unspecified	1310nm laser	2–10k
10GBASE-LX4	9 μm SMF	N/A	Unspecified	1269-1356nm CWDM lasers	2–10k
10GBASE-LX4	50 μm MMF	500 MHz*km	Unspecified	1269–1356nm CWDM lasers	2–300
10GBASE-LX4	50 μm MMF	400 MHz*km	Unspecified	1269–1356nm CWDM lasers	2–240
10GBASE-LX4	62.5 μm MMF	500 MHz*km	Unspecified	1269–1356nm CWDM lasers	2–300
10GBASE-SW	50 μm MMF	2000 MHz*km	Unspecified	850nm laser	2–300
10GBASE-SW	50 μm MMF	500 MHz*km	Unspecified	850nm laser	2–82
10GBASE-SW	50 μm MMF	400 MHz*km	Unspecified	850nm laser	2–66
10GBASE-SW	62.5 μm MMF	200 MHz*km	Unspecified	850nm laser	2–33
10GBASE-SW	62.5 μm MMF	160 MHz*km	Unspecified	850nm laser	2–26
10GBASE-SR	50 μm MMF	2000 MHz*km	Unspecified	850nm laser	2–300
10GBASE-SR	50 μm MMF	500 MHz*km	Unspecified	850nm laser	2–82
10GBASE-SR	50 μm MMF	400 MHz*km	Unspecified	850nm laser	2–66
10GBASE-SR	62.5 μm MMF	200 MHz*km	Unspecified	850nm laser	2–33
10GBASE-SR	62.5 μm MMF	160 MHz*km	Unspecified	850nm laser	2–26
10GBASE-CX4	100 ohm twinax	N/A	IEC 61076-3-113	Electrical	0–15

Though IEEE 802.3ae-2002 does not specify which connectors may be used, the duplex SC style is supported by many 10GE switch vendors because the XENPAK, X2, and XPAK MSAs specify duplex SC. The XFP MSA supports several different connectors, including duplex SC. Note that 10GBASE-EW and 10GBASE-ER links that are longer than 30km are considered *engineered links* and must provide better attenuation characteristics than normal SMF links.

Ethernet Encoding and Signaling

As stated in Chapter 3, "Overview of Network Operating Principles," bit-level encoding schemes are used to provide clocking, maintain DC balance, facilitate bit error detection, and allow the receiver to achieve byte or word alignment with the transmitter. Bit-level encoding schemes often define special control characters and frames which cannot be used to represent upper-layer data. Serial networking technologies typically use these special control frames along with designated fields in the headers of data frames to signal between devices. The information signaled between devices includes supported communication parameters, start of frame, end of frame, type of frame, priority of frame (for QoS), flow-control status, destination address, source address, ULP (for protocol multiplexing), error information, and so on. Ethernet uses several encoding schemes. This section discusses GE and 10GE encoding. FE encoding, while potentially relevant to modern storage networks, is considered outside the scope of this book. Table 5-6 lists the encoding scheme used by each GE and 10GE implementation and the associated BER objective.

Table 5-6   *GE and 10GE Encoding Schemes, and BER Objectives*

Ethernet Variant	Encoding Scheme	BER Objective
1000BASE-LX	8B/10B	10^{12}
1000BASE-SX	8B/10B	10^{12}
1000BASE-T	8B1Q4	10^{10}
1000BASE-CX	8B/10B	10^{12}
10GBASE-EW	64B/66B with WIS	10^{12}
10GBASE-ER	64B/66B	10^{12}
10GBASE-LW	64B/66B with WIS	10^{12}
10GBASE-LR	64B/66B	10^{12}
10GBASE-LX4	8B/10B	10^{12}
10GBASE-SW	64B/66B with WIS	10^{12}
10GBASE-SR	64B/66B	10^{12}
10GBASE-CX4	8B/10B	10^{12}

The 8B/10B encoding scheme generates 10-bit characters from 8-bit characters. Each 10-bit character is categorized as data or control. Control characters are used to indicate the start of control frames. Control frames can be fixed or variable length. Control frames can contain control and data characters. The set of characters in each control frame must be in a specific order to convey a specific meaning. Thus, control frames are called ordered sets.

Fiber-based implementations of GE use the 8B/10B encoding scheme. GE uses only five of the control characters defined by the 8B/10B encoding scheme. These control characters are denoted as K23.7, K27.7, K28.5, K29.7, and K30.7. GE uses variable-length ordered sets consisting of one, two, or four characters. GE defines eight ordered sets. Two ordered sets are used for auto-negotiation of link parameters between adjacent devices. These are called Configuration ordered sets and are denoted as /C1/ and /C2/. Each is four characters in length consisting of one specified control character followed by one specified data character followed by two variable data characters. The last two data characters represent device configuration parameters. Two ordered sets are used as fillers when no data frames are being transmitted. These are called Idle ordered sets. They are denoted as /I1/ and /I2/, and each is two characters in length. Idles are transmitted in the absence of data traffic to maintain clock synchronization. The remaining four ordered sets are each one character in length and are used to delimit data frames, maintain inter-frame spacing, and propagate error information. These include the start_of_packet delimiter (SPD) denoted as /S/, end_of_packet delimiter (EPD) denoted as /T/, carrier_extend denoted as /R/, and error_propagation denoted as /V/.

Copper-based implementations of GE use the 8B1Q4 encoding scheme. The 8B1Q4 encoding scheme is more complex than the 8B/10B encoding scheme. Eight data bits are converted to a set of four symbols, which are transmitted simultaneously using a quinary electrical signal. The individual symbols are not categorized as data or control, but each four-symbol set is. There are 31 four-symbol sets designated as control sets. These are used to delimit data frames, maintain inter-frame spacing, and propagate error information. Like 8B/10B implementations of GE, 8B1Q4 implementations support auto-negotiation of link parameters between adjacent devices. This is accomplished via the fast link pulse (FLP). The FLP is *not* a four-symbol set, but it is defined at OSI Layer 1, and it does have ordered bit positions. The FLP consists of 33 bit positions containing alternating clock and data bits: 17 clock bits and 16 data bits. The FLP data bits convey device capabilities.

Some 10GE implementations use 8B/10B encoding but do so differently than GE. The following definitions and rules apply to CWDM and parallel implementations. 10GE uses seven control characters denoted as K27.7, K28.0, K28.3, K28.4, K28.5, K29.7, and K30.7. With the exception of K30.7, these are used to identify ordered sets. The K30.7 control character is used for error control and may be transmitted independently. 10GE implementations based on 8B/10B use 10 fixed-length ordered sets consisting of four characters. Three ordered sets are defined to maintain clock synchronization, maintain inter-frame spacing, and align parallel lanes. These are collectively classified as Idle and include Sync Column denoted as ‖K‖, Skip Column denoted as ‖R‖, and Align Column denoted as ‖A‖. Five ordered sets are defined to delimit data frames. These are collectively classified as Encapsulation and include Start Column denoted as ‖S‖, Terminate Column in Lane 0 denoted as $\|T_0\|$, Terminate Column in Lane 1 denoted as $\|T_1\|$, Terminate Column in Lane 2 denoted as $\|T_2\|$, and Terminate Column in Lane 3 denoted as $\|T_3\|$. Two ordered sets are defined to communicate link-status information. These include Local Fault denoted as ‖LF‖ and Remote Fault denoted as ‖RF‖.

Serial implementations of 10GE use the 64B/66B encoding scheme. The 64B/66B encoding scheme generates a 64-bit block from two 32-bit words received from the 10-Gigabit Media Independent Interface (XGMII). Two bits are prepended to each 64-bit block to indicate whether the block is a data block or a control block. Data blocks contain only data characters. Control blocks can contain control and data characters. There are 15 formats for control blocks. The first byte of each control block indicates the format of the block and is called the block type field. The remaining seven bytes of each control block are filled with a combination of 8-bit data characters, 7-bit control characters, 4-bit control characters, and single-bit null character fields.

There are two 7-bit control characters: Idle and Error. These are used to maintain interframe spacing, maintain clock synchronization, adapt clock rates, and propagate error information. There is one four-bit control character: the Sequence ordered set character denoted as /Q/. 10GE ordered sets are embedded in control blocks. Each ordered set is fixed length and consists of a single 4-bit control character followed or preceded by three 8-bit data characters. The Sequence ordered set is used to adapt clock rates. One other ordered set is defined, but it is not used. The null character fields are interpreted as Start or Terminate control characters, which delimit data frames. The value of the block type field implies that a frame delimiter is present and conveys the position of the null character fields. This eliminates the need for explicit coding of information in the actual Start and Terminate control characters. In fact, these control characters are completely omitted from some frame-delimiting control blocks.

Further details of each encoding scheme are outside the scope of this book. The 8B/10B encoding scheme is well documented in clause 36 of the IEEE 802.3-2002 specification and clause 48 of the IEEE 802.3ae-2002 specification. The 8B1Q4 encoding scheme is well documented in clause 40 of the IEEE 802.3-2002 specification. The 64B/66B encoding scheme is well documented in clause 49 of the IEEE 802.3ae-2002 specification.

Ethernet Addressing Scheme

Ethernet does not implement any equivalent to SAM device or port names. However, Ethernet does implement an equivalent to SAM port identifiers. Ethernet devices use MAC-48 addresses to forward frames. Use of the MAC-48 address format in all Ethernet implementations simplifies communication between Ethernet devices operating at different speeds and preserves the legacy Ethernet frame formats. In the context of Ethernet, a MAC-48 address is often called a MAC address. In this book, the terms MAC-48 address and MAC address are used interchangeably.

Ethernet Name Assignment and Resolution

Ethernet does not implement SAM names, so name assignment and resolution mechanisms are not required.

Ethernet Address Assignment and Resolution

Each Ethernet interface has a single MAC address "burned in" during the interface manufacturing process. If a NIC has more than one port, each port is assigned its own MAC address during the interface manufacturing process. This eliminates the need for network administrators to manage the Ethernet address space. A NIC's MAC address is used as the source address in all frames (unicast, multicast, and broadcast) transmitted from that NIC and as the destination address in all unicast frames sent to that NIC. Ethernet multicast addressing is currently outside the scope of this book. Broadcast traffic is sent to the reserved MAC address FF-FF-FF-FF-FF-FF. All Ethernet devices that receive a frame sent to the broadcast address process the frame to determine the ULP. If the ULP carried within the frame is active within the receiving node, the payload of frame is passed to the specified ULP for further processing. Otherwise, the frame is discarded.

Because the MAC-48 addressing scheme provides global uniqueness, VLANs can be merged without risk of address conflicts. Note that some host operating system vendors subscribe to the philosophy that a multihomed host (that is, a host with multiple network interfaces) should be uniquely identified across all its Ethernet interfaces. By using and advertising a single MAC address (taken from one of the installed Ethernet interfaces) on all installed Ethernet interfaces, the host assumes a single Ethernet identity as viewed by all other attached network devices. This requires network administrators to take extra steps to ensure that network communication occurs as desired between the attached networks.

In IP networks, Ethernet address resolution can occur in two ways: dynamically or statically. As discussed in Chapter 3, "Overview of Network Operating Principles," ARP facilitates dynamic resolution of an Ethernet address when the IP address of the destination node is known. To dynamically discover the Ethernet address of another node, the IP stack in the source node invokes ARP to broadcast a frame containing its own IP address, its own Ethernet MAC address, the IP address of the destination node, and an empty field for the Ethernet MAC address of the destination node. All nodes attached to the Ethernet network receive and process this frame by updating their ARP tables with a new entry that maps the IP address of the source node to the Ethernet MAC address of the source node. In addition, the destination node replies to the originator of the ARP request. The unicast reply contains all the information from the original request frame, and the missing Ethernet MAC address. Upon receipt, the originator of the ARP request updates its ARP table with a new entry that maps the IP address of the destination node to the Ethernet MAC address of the destination node. Alternately, system administrators can create static mappings in the ARP table on each host. Static mappings typically are used only in special situations to accomplish a particular goal.

Ethernet Media Access

As stated in Chapter 3, "Overview of Network Operating Principles," Ethernet uses CSMA/CD to arbitrate access to shared media. In switched implementations, arbitration is not required because full-duplex communication is employed on "private" media accessed by only one pair of devices. It is possible for a node to negotiate half-duplex mode when connected to a switch, but this suboptimal condition typically is corrected by the network administrator as soon as it is discovered. Collision-free line-rate performance is achievable if a switched Ethernet network is designed as such. This book does not discuss CSMA/CD in depth because modern storage networks built on Ethernet are switched.

Ethernet Network Boundaries

An Ethernet network can be physically or logically bounded. Physical boundaries are delimited by media terminations (for example, unused switch ports) and end node interfaces (for example, NICs). No control information or user data can be transmitted between Ethernet networks across physical boundaries. Logical boundaries are delimited by OSI Layer 3 entities (for example, logical router interfaces within a multilayer switch). No OSI Layer 2 control information is transmitted between Ethernet networks across logical boundaries. User data is transmitted between Ethernet networks across logical boundaries by removing the Ethernet header and trailer, processing the packet at OSI Layer 3, and then generating a new Ethernet header and trailer. In the process, the source and destination Ethernet addresses are changed. Figure 5-5 illustrates the physical boundaries of an Ethernet network.

Figure 5-5   *Ethernet Network Boundaries*

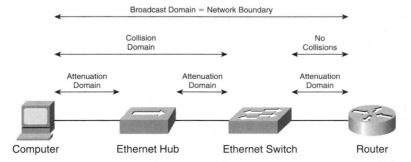

An Ethernet network also can have virtual boundaries. The IEEE 802.1Q-2003 specification defines a method for implementing multiple VLANs within a single physical LAN. In the simplest scenario, each switch port is statically assigned to a single VLAN by the network administrator. As frames enter a switch from an end node, the switch prepends a tag to indicate the VLAN membership of the ingress port (known as the Port VLAN Identifier (PVID)). The tag remains intact until the frame reaches the egress switch port that connects the destination end node. The switch removes the tag and transmits the frame to the destination end node. Ethernet switches use PVIDs to ensure that no frames are forwarded between VLANs. Thus, VLAN boundaries mimic physical LAN boundaries. User data can be forwarded between VLANs only via OSI Layer 3 entities.

Note that the PVID can be assigned dynamically via the Generic Attribute Registration Protocol (GARP) VLAN Registration Protocol (GVRP). When GVRP is used, the PVID is typically determined by the MAC address of the end node attached to the switch port, but other classifiers are permitted. GVRP allows end nodes to be mobile while ensuring that each end node is always assigned to the same VLAN regardless of where the end node attaches to the network. Note also that a switch port can belong to multiple VLANs if the switch supports VLAN trunking as specified in IEEE 802.1Q-2003. This is most commonly used on ISLs, but some NICs support VLAN trunking. An end node using an 802.1Q-enabled NIC may use a single MAC address in all VLANs or a unique MAC address in each VLAN. In the interest of MAC address conservation, some 802.1Q-enabled NICs use a single MAC address in all VLANs. This method allows NIC vendors to allocate only one MAC address to each 802.1Q-enabled NIC. For these end nodes, GVRP cannot be configured to use the MAC address as the PVID classifier. Also, switch vendors must take special measures to forward frames correctly in the presence of this type of end node. These are the same measures required in environments where a host operating system advertises a single MAC address on all NICs installed in a multihomed host. An end node using an 802.1Q-enabled NIC may not forward frames between VLANs except via an OSI Layer 3 process.

Ethernet Frame Formats

The basic Ethernet frame format has changed little since the early days of Ethernet. Today, there are two variations of the basic frame format. These differ from each other only slightly. However, two other frame formats are defined, which build upon the basic format by including one or two additional subheaders. Figure 5-6 illustrates the IEEE 802.3-2002 frame format, which is one of the two variations of the basic frame format.

Figure 5-6   *IEEE 802.3-2002 Frame Format*

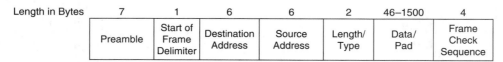

Length in Bytes	7	1	6	6	2	46–1500	4
	Preamble	Start of Frame Delimiter	Destination Address	Source Address	Length/ Type	Data/ Pad	Frame Check Sequence

The Preamble and Start of Frame Delimiter are not considered part of the actual frame. These fields are discussed in this section for the sake of completeness. A brief description of each field follows:

- Preamble—7 bytes long and contains seven repetitions of the sequence "10101010". This field is used by the receiver to achieve steady-state synchronization.

- Start of Frame Delimiter (SFD)—1 byte long and contains the sequence "10101011", which indicates the start of a frame.

- Destination Address (DA)—6 bytes long and indicates the node(s) that should accept and process the frame. The DA field may contain an individual, multicast or broadcast address.

- Source Address (SA)—6 bytes long and indicates the transmitting node. The SA field may only contain an individual address.

- Length/Type—2 bytes long and has two possible interpretations. If the numeric value is equal to or less than 1500, this field is interpreted as the length of the Data/Pad field expressed in bytes. If the numeric value is greater than or equal to 1536, this field is interpreted as the Ethertype. For jumbo frames, which are not yet standardized, this field must specify the Ethertype to be compliant with the existing rules of interpretation.

- Data/Pad—variable in length and contains either ULP data or pad bytes. If no ULP data is transmitted, or if insufficient ULP data is transmitted to meet the minimum frame size requirement, this field is padded. The format of pad bytes is not specified. Minimum frame size requirements stem from CSMA/CD, but these requirements still apply to full-duplex communication for backward compatibility.

- Frame Check Sequence (FCS)—4 bytes long and contains a CRC value. This value is computed on the DA, SA, Length/Type and Data/Pad fields.

The other variation of the basic frame format is the Ethernet II frame format. Most Ethernet networks continue to use the Ethernet II frame format. The only differences between the Ethernet II format and the 802.3-2002 format are the SFD field and the Length/Type field. In the Ethernet II format, the recurring preamble bit pattern continues for eight bytes and is immediately followed by the DA field. The Ethernet II format does not support the length interpretation of the Length/Type field, so the field is called Type. Figure 5-7 illustrates the Ethernet II frame format.

Figure 5-7   *Ethernet II Frame Format*

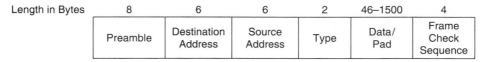

When the IEEE first standardized Ethernet, the Length/Type field could only be interpreted as length. A mechanism was needed to facilitate ULP multiplexing to maintain backward compatibility with Ethernet II. So, an optional subheader was defined. The current version is specified in IEEE 802.2-1998. This subheader embodies the data component of the Logical Link Control (LLC) sublayer. This subheader is required only when the 802.3-2002 frame format is used and the Length/Type field specifies the length of the data field. When present, this subheader occupies the first three or four bytes of the Data/Pad field and therefore reduces the maximum amount of ULP data that the frame can transport. Figure 5-8 illustrates the IEEE 802.2-1998 subheader format.

Figure 5-8   *IEEE 802.2-1998 Subheader Format*

Length in Bytes	1	1	1 or 2
	Destination Service Access Point	Source Service Access Point	Control

A brief description of each field follows:

- Destination Service Access Point (DSAP)—1 byte long. It indicates the ULP(s) that should accept and process the frame's ULP data.

- Source Service Access Point (SSAP)—1 byte long. It indicates the ULP that transmitted the ULP data.

- Control (CTL)—1 or 2 bytes long. It facilitates exchange of control information between ULP entities in peer nodes.

Like Ethertypes, service access points (SAPs) are administered by the IEEE to ensure global uniqueness. Because the Type field in the Ethernet II header is 16 bits, the 8-bit DSAP field in the LLC subheader cannot accommodate as many ULPs. So, another optional subheader was defined by the IETF via RFC 1042 and was later incorporated into the IEEE 802 Overview and Architecture specification. Referred to as the Sub-Network Access Protocol (SNAP), this subheader is required only when the 802.3-2002 frame format is used, the Length/Type field specifies the length of the data field, the 802.2-1998 subheader is present, and the ULP is not an IEEE registered SAP. When present, this subheader follows a 3-byte LLC subheader and occupies an additional 5 bytes of the Data/Pad field. Thus, the maximum amount of ULP data that the frame can transport is further reduced. The DSAP and SSAP fields of the LLC subheader each must contain the value 0xAA or 0xAB, and the CTL field must contain the value 0x03 to indicate that the SNAP subheader follows. The two fields of the SNAP subheader are sometimes collectively called the Protocol Identifier (PID) field. Figure 5-9 illustrates the IEEE 802-2001 subheader format.

Figure 5-9   *IEEE 802-2001 Subheader Format*

A brief description of each field follows:

- OUI—3 bytes long. It contains the IEEE-assigned identifier of the organization that created the ULP.

- Ethertype—2 bytes long. It contains the IEEE-assigned ULP identifier.

In shared media environments, frames of different formats can traverse a shared link. However, each Ethernet interface is normally configured to use only one frame format. All devices using a given frame format can communicate, but they are isolated from all devices using other frame formats. When a device receives a frame of a different format, the frame is not understood and is dropped. One notable exception is a protocol analyzer that can support promiscuous mode. Promiscuous mode enables a device to transmit and receive all frame formats simultaneously. In switched environments, a similar phenomenon of isolation occurs. Each switch port must be configured to use only one frame format. Each end node must use the same frame format as the switch port to which it is attached. When a switch forwards multicast and broadcast traffic, only those switch ports using the same frame format as the source node can transmit the frame without translation. All other switch ports must translate the frame format or drop the frame. Translation of every frame can impose unacceptable performance penalties on a switch, and translation is not always possible. For example, some Ethernet II frames cannot be translated to LLC format in the absence of the SNAP subheader. So, Ethernet switches do not translate frame formats. (VLAN trunking ports are a special case.) Thus, Ethernet switches drop frames when the frame format of the egress port does not match the frame format of the source node. This prevents ARP and other protocols from working properly and results in groups of devices becoming isolated. For this reason, most Ethernet networks employ a single frame format on all switch ports and attached devices.

As previously stated, VLANs require each frame sent between switches to be tagged to indicate the VLAN ID of the transmitting node. This prevents frames from being improperly delivered across VLAN boundaries. There are two frame formats for Ethernet trunking: the IEEE's 802.1Q-2003 format and Cisco Systems' proprietary ISL format. Today, most Ethernet networks use the 802.1Q-2003 frame format, which was first standardized in 1998. So, Cisco Systems' proprietary frame format is not discussed herein. Figure 5-10 illustrates the IEEE 802.1Q-2003 frame format.

Figure 5-10 *IEEE 802.1Q-2003 Frame Format*

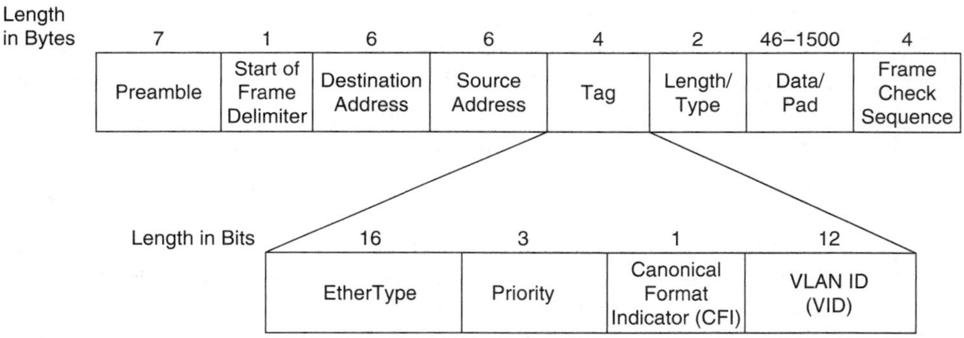

A brief description of each Tag sub-field follows:

- EtherType—2 bytes long and must contain the value 0x8100 to indicate that the following two bytes contain priority and VLAN information. This allows Ethernet switches to recognize tagged frames so special processing can be applied.

- Priority—3 bits long. It is used to implement QoS.

- Canonical Format Indicator (CFI) bit—facilitates use of a common tag header for multiple, dissimilar network types (for example, Ethernet and Token Ring).

- VLAN ID (VID)—12 bits long. It contains a binary number between 2 and 4094, inclusive. VIDs 0, 1, and 4095 are reserved.

The brief field descriptions provided in this section do not encompass all the functionality provided by each of the fields. For more information, readers are encouraged to consult the IEEE 802.3-2002, 802.2-1998, 802-2001, and 802.1Q-2003 specifications.

Ethernet Delivery Mechanisms

Ethernet is often mistakenly considered to be a connectionless technology. In fact, Ethernet provides three types of service via the LLC sublayer. These include the following:

- Unacknowledged, connectionless service (Type 1)
- Acknowledged, connection-oriented service (Type 2)
- Acknowledged, connectionless service (Type 3)

Most Ethernet switches provide only unacknowledged, connectionless service (Type 1), which contributes to the public's misunderstanding of Ethernet's full capabilities. Because the other two service types are rarely used, the delivery mechanisms employed by the LLC sublayer to provide those types of service are outside the scope of this book. Ethernet networks that provide Type 1 service implement the following delivery mechanisms:

- Ethernet devices do not detect frames dropped in transit. When an Ethernet device drops a frame, it does not report the drop to ULPs or peer nodes. ULPs are expected to detect the drop via their own mechanisms.

- Ethernet devices do not detect duplicate frames. If a duplicate frame is received, Ethernet delivers the frame to the ULP in the normal manner. ULPs are expected to detect the duplicate via their own mechanisms.

- Ethernet devices can detect corrupt frames via the FCS field. Upon detection of a corrupt frame, the frame is dropped. Regardless of whether an intermediate switch or the destination node drops the frame, no notification is sent to any node or ULP. Some Ethernet switches employ cut-through switching techniques and are unable to detect corrupt frames. Thus, corrupt frames, are forwarded to the destination node and subsequently dropped. However, most Ethernet switches employ a store-and-forward architecture capable of detecting and dropping corrupt frames.

- Ethernet devices do not provide acknowledgement of successful frame delivery.

- Ethernet devices do not support retransmission.

- Ethernet devices support link-level flow control in a reactive manner. Ethernet devices do not support end-to-end flow control. See Chapter 9, "Flow Control and Quality of Service," for more information about flow control.

- Bandwidth is not guaranteed. Monitoring and trending of bandwidth utilization on shared links is required to ensure optimal network operation. Oversubscription on shared links must be carefully calculated to avoid bandwidth starvation during peak periods.

- Consistent latency is not guaranteed.

- The IEEE 802.3-2002 specification does not define methods for fragmentation or reassembly because the necessary header fields do not exist. An MTU mismatch results in frame drop. Thus, each physical Ethernet network must have a common MTU on all links. That means PMTU discovery is not required within an Ethernet network. MTU mismatches between physically separate Ethernet networks are handled by an ULP in the device that connects the Ethernet networks (for example, IP in a router). Likewise, an ULP is expected to provide end-to-end PMTU discovery.

- In-order delivery is not guaranteed. Ethernet devices do not support frame reordering. ULPs are expected to detect out-of-order frames and provide frame reordering.

Ethernet Link Aggregation

Clause 43 of IEEE 802.3-2002 defines a method for aggregation of multiple Ethernet links into a single logical link called a Link Aggregation Group. Link Aggregation Groups are commonly called Ethernet port channels or EtherChannels. Despite the fact that the term EtherChannel is copyrighted by Cisco Systems, the term is sometimes used generically to describe Ethernet port channels implemented on other vendors' equipment. Automation of link aggregation is supported via the IEEE's Link Aggregation Control Protocol (LACP). With LACP, links that can be aggregated will be aggregated without the need for administrative intervention. The LACP frame format contains 31 fields totaling 128 bytes. Because of the complexity of this protocol, granular description of its operation is currently outside the scope of this book. Before standardization of LACP in 2000, Cisco Systems introduced automated link aggregation via the Port Aggregation Protocol (PAgP). The details of PAgP have not been published by Cisco Systems. Thus, further disclosure of PAgP within this book is not possible. Both link aggregation protocols are in use today. The protocols are quite similar in operation, but they are not interoperable.

Automated link aggregation lowers (but does not eliminate) administrative overhead. Network administrators must be wary of several operational requirements. The following restrictions apply to Ethernet port channels:

- All links in a port channel must use the same aggregation protocol (LACP or PAgP).
- All links in a port channel must connect a single pair of devices (that is, only point-to-point configurations are permitted).
- All links in a port channel must operate in full-duplex mode.
- All links in a port channel must operate at the same transmission rate.
- If any link in a port channel is configured as non-trunking, all links in that port channel must be configured as non-trunking. Likewise, if any link in a port channel is configured as trunking, all links in that port channel must be configured as trunking.
- All links in a non-trunking port channel must belong to the same VLAN.
- All links in a trunking port channel must trunk the same set of VLANs.

- All links in a non-trunking port channel must use the same frame format.
- All links in a trunking port channel must use the same trunking frame format.

Some of these restrictions are not specified in 802.3-2002, but they are required for proper operation. Similarly, there is no de jure limit on the maximum number of links that may be grouped into a single port channel or the maximum number of port channels that may be configured on a single switch. However, product design considerations may impose practical limits that vary from vendor to vendor. The 802.3-2002 specification seeks to minimize the probability of duplicate and out-of-order frame delivery across an Ethernet port channel. However, it is possible for these outcomes to occur during reconfiguration or recovery from a link failure.

Ethernet Link Initialization

Ethernet link initialization procedures are the same for node-to-node, node-to-switch, and switch-to-switch connections. However, different procedures are observed for different types of media. FE and GE links may be configured manually or configured dynamically via auto-negotiation. 10GE does not currently support auto-negotiation. Most NICs, router interfaces, and switch ports default to auto-negotiation mode. Ethernet auto-negotiation is implemented in a peer-to-peer fashion.

Clause 37 of IEEE 802.3-2002 defines auto-negotiation for 1000BASE-X. As previously stated, auto-negotiation is accomplished via ordered sets in 1000BASE-X implementations. Therefore, 1000BASE-X implementations do not support auto-negotiation of the transmission rate because bit-level synchronization must occur before ordered sets can be recognized. So, if a 1000BASE-X device is connected to a 100BASE-FX (fiber-based FE) device, the link will not come up. When two 1000BASE-X devices are connected, operating parameters other than transmission rate are negotiated via the Configuration ordered sets /C1/ and /C2/ (collectively denoted as /C/). All capabilities are advertised to the peer device by default, but it is possible to mask some capabilities. If more than one set of operating parameters is common to a pair of connected devices, a predefined priority policy determines which parameter set will be used. The highest common capabilities are always selected. As previously stated, each /C/ ordered set carries two bytes of operating parameter information representing the transmitter's 16-bit configuration register (Config_Reg). Immediately following link power-on, alternating /C1/ and /C2/ ordered sets containing zeroes in place of the Config_Reg are transmitted by each device. This allows the other device to achieve bit-level synchronization.

Upon achieving bit-level synchronization, the receiving device begins searching the incoming bit stream for the Comma bit pattern (contained within the /K28.5/ control character) and begins transmitting alternating /C1/ and /C2/ ordered sets containing the Config_Reg. Upon recognition of the Comma bit pattern in three consecutive /C/ ordered sets without error, the receiving device achieves word alignment and begins searching the incoming bit stream for the Config_Reg. Upon recognition of three consecutive, matching Config_Regs without error, the receiving device sets the Acknowledge bit to one in its

Config_Reg, continues transmitting until the Link_Timer expires (10ms by default) and begins resolving a common parameter set. If a matching configuration is resolved, normal communication ensues upon expiration of the Link_Timer. If successful negotiation cannot be accomplished for any reason, the network administrator must intervene. Figure 5-11 illustrates the 1000BASE-X Configuration ordered sets.

Figure 5-11 *1000BASE-X Configuration Ordered Sets*

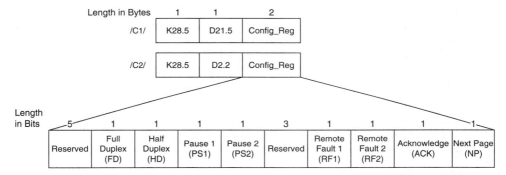

A brief description of each field follows:

- **Full duplex (FD) bit**—used to indicate whether full duplex mode is supported.

- **Half duplex (HD) bit**—used to indicate whether half duplex mode is supported.

- **Pause 1 (PS1) and Pause 2 (PS2) bits**—used together to indicate the supported flow-control modes (asymmetric, symmetric, or none).

- **Remote Fault 1 (RF1) and Remote Fault 2 (RF2) bits**—used together to indicate to the remote device whether a fault has been detected by the local device and, if so, the type of fault (offline, link error, or auto-negotiation error).

- **Acknowledge (ACK) bit**—used to indicate successful recognition of at least three consecutive matching Config_Regs.

- **Next Page (NP) bit**—indicates that one or more /C/ ordered sets follow, and each contains parameter information in one of two alternative formats: message page or unformatted page. A message page must always precede an unformatted page to indicate how to interpret the unformatted page(s). An unformatted page can be used for several purposes.

The preceding description of the 1000BASE-X link initialization procedure is simplified for the sake of clarity. For more detail about /C/ ordered set usage, Next Page formats, field interpretations, and auto-negotiation states, readers are encouraged to consult clause 37 and all associated annexes of IEEE 802.3-2002.

Clause 28 of IEEE 802.3-2002 defines auto-negotiation for all Ethernet implementations that use twisted-pair cabling. As previously stated, auto-negotiation is accomplished via the FLP in twisted-pair based GE implementations. The FLP mechanism is also used for auto-negotiation in 100-Mbps twisted-pair based Ethernet implementations (100BASE-TX, 100BASE-T2, and 100BASE-T4). A special mechanism is defined for 10BASE-T implementations because 10BASE-T does not support the FLP. Because 10BASE-T is irrelevant to modern storage networks, only the FLP mechanism is discussed in this section. The 16 data bits in the FLP are collectively called the link code word (LCW). The LCW represents the transmitter's 16-bit advertisement register (Register 4), which is equivalent to the 1000BASE-X Config_Reg. Like 1000BASE-X, all capabilities are advertised to the peer device by default, but it is possible to mask some capabilities. If more than one set of operating parameters is common to a pair of connected devices, a predefined priority policy determines which parameter set will be used. The highest common capabilities are always selected. Unlike 1000BASE-X, the FLP is independent of the bit-level encoding scheme used during normal communication. That independence enables twisted-pair based Ethernet implementations to auto-negotiate the transmission rate. Of course, it also means that all operating parameters must be negotiated prior to bit-level synchronization. So, the FLP is well defined to allow receivers to achieve temporary bit-level synchronization on a per-FLP basis. The FLP is transmitted immediately following link power-on and is repeated at a specific time interval.

In contrast to the 1000BASE-X procedure, wherein /C/ ordered sets are initially transmitted without conveying the Config_Reg, twisted-pair based implementations convey Register 4 via the LCW in every FLP transmitted. Upon recognition of three consecutive matching LCWs without error, the receiving device sets the Acknowledge bit to one in its LCW, transmits another six to eight FLPs, and begins resolving a common parameter set. If a matching configuration is resolved, transmission of the Idle symbol begins after the final FLP is transmitted. Transmission of Idles continues until bit-level synchronization is achieved followed by symbol alignment. Normal communication then ensues. If successful negotiation cannot be accomplished for any reason, the network administrator must intervene. Figure 5-12 illustrates the Ethernet FLP LCW.

Figure 5-12 *Ethernet FLP Link Code Word*

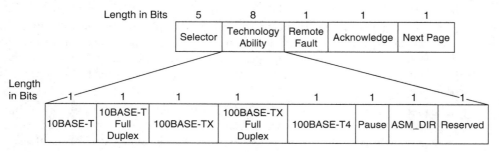

A brief description of each field follows:

- **Selector**—5 bits long. It indicates the technology implemented by the local device. Valid choices include 802.3, 802.5, and 802.9.

- **Technology Ability**—8 bits long. It indicates the abilities of the local device. Abilities that can be advertised include transmission rate (10-Mbps or 100-Mbps), duplex mode (half or full), and flow-control mode (asymmetric, symmetric, or none). To negotiate 1000-Mbps operation, the Next Page field must be used.

- **Remote Fault bit**—used to indicate to the remote device that a fault has been detected by the local device. When a fault is detected, the Remote Fault bit is set to 1, and auto-negotiation is re-initiated. The Next Page field may be optionally used to indicate the nature of the fault.

- **Acknowledge bit**—used to indicate successful recognition of at least three consecutive matching FLPs.

- **Next Page bit**—indicates that one or more FLPs follow, containing LCW information in one of two alternative formats: message page or unformatted page. A message page must always precede an unformatted page to indicate how to interpret the unformatted page(s). An unformatted page can be used for several purposes, including negotiation of 1000-Mbps operation.

The preceding description of the twisted-pair based Ethernet link initialization procedure is simplified for the sake of clarity. For more detail about FLP usage, Next Page formats, field interpretations, and auto-negotiation states, readers are encouraged to consult clause 28 and all associated annexes of IEEE 802.3-2002.

The IEEE 802.3-2002 specification recommends that manual configuration be achieved not by disabling auto-negotiation, but by masking selected capabilities when advertising to the peer device. This choice is vendor dependent. The remainder of this paragraph describes the procedures followed when auto-negotiation is disabled. When manually configuring an interface, the network administrator typically is allowed to specify the transmission rate and duplex mode of each twisted-pair interface. For fiber interfaces, the transmission rate is fixed and cannot be altered, but the duplex mode can be specified. Some products allow additional granularity in manual configuration mode. In the absence of additional granularity, network administrators must consult the product documentation to determine the default values of operating parameters that cannot be explicitly configured.

As previously stated, the order of events following power-on depends on the media type. For 1000BASE-X, bit level synchronization is achieved followed by word alignment. Normal communication is then attempted. If compatible operating parameters are configured, successful communication ensues. Otherwise, the link might come up, but frequent errors occur. For twisted-pair interfaces, bit-level synchronization is attempted. If successful, symbol alignment occurs. Otherwise, the link does not come online. Once symbol alignment is achieved, normal communication is attempted. If compatible operating parameters are configured, successful communication ensues. Otherwise, the link might come up, but frequent errors occur. If a manually configured link cannot come up or experiences frequent errors because of operating parameter mismatch, the network administrator must intervene.

Fibre Channel

Compared to Ethernet, FC is a complex technology. FC attempts to provide functionality equivalent to that provided by Ethernet plus elements of IP, UDP, and TCP. So, it is difficult to compare FC to just Ethernet. FC promises to continue maturing at a rapid pace and is currently considered the switching technology of choice for block-level storage protocols. As block-level SANs proliferate, FC is expected to maintain its market share dominance in the short term. The long term is difficult to predict in the face of rapidly maturing IPS protocols, but FC already enjoys a sufficiently large installed base to justify a detailed examination of FC's inner workings. This section explores the details of FC operation at OSI Layers 1 and 2.

FC Media, Connectors, Transceivers, and Operating Ranges

FC supports a very broad range of media, connectors, and transceivers. Today, most FC deployments are based on fiber media for end node and ISL connectivity. Most 1-Gbps FC products employ the SC style connector, and most 2-Gbps FC products employ the LC style. Copper media is used primarily for intra-enclosure connectivity. For this reason, copper media is not discussed herein. Table 5-7 summarizes the media, connectors, transceivers, and operating ranges that are specified in ANSI T11 FC-PH, FC-PH-2, FC-PI, FC-PI-2, and 10GFC. Data rates under 100 MBps are excluded from Table 5-7 because they are considered historical. The nomenclature used to represent each defined FC implementation is [data rate expressed in MBps]-[medium]-[transceiver]-[distance capability]. The distance capability designator represents a superset of the defined operating range for each implementation.

Table 5-7   *Fibre Channel Media, Connectors, Transceivers, and Operating Ranges*

FC Variant	Medium	Modal Bandwidth	Connectors	Transceiver	Operating Range (m)
100-SM-LL-V	9 μm SMF	N/A	Duplex SC, Duplex SG, Duplex LC	1550nm laser	2–50k
100-SM-LL-L	9 μm SMF	N/A	Duplex SC	1300nm laser	2–10k
100-SM-LC-L	9 μm SMF	N/A	Duplex SC, Duplex SG, Duplex LC, Duplex MT-RJ	1300nm laser (Cost Reduced)	2–10k
100-SM-LL-I	9 μm SMF	N/A	Duplex SC	1300nm laser	2–2k
100-M5-SN-I	50 μm MMF	500 MHz*km	Duplex SC, Duplex SG, Duplex LC, Duplex MT-RJ	850nm laser	0.5–500
100-M5-SN-I	50 μm MMF	400 MHz*km	Duplex SC, Duplex SG, Duplex LC, Duplex MT-RJ	850nm laser	0.5–450

Table 5-7 *Fibre Channel Media, Connectors, Transceivers, and Operating Ranges (Continued)*

FC Variant	Medium	Modal Bandwidth	Connectors	Transceiver	Operating Range (m)
100-M5-SL-I	50 μm MMF	500 MHz*km	Duplex SC	780nm laser	2–500
100-M6-SN-I	62.5 μm MMF	200 MHz*km	Duplex SC, Duplex SG, Duplex LC, Duplex MT-RJ	850nm laser	0.5–300
100-M6-SN-I	62.5 μm MMF	160 MHz*km	Duplex SC, Duplex SG, Duplex LC, Duplex MT-RJ	850nm laser	2–300
100-M6-SL-I	62.5 μm MMF	160 MHz*km	Duplex SC	780nm laser	2–175
200-SM-LL-V	9 μm SMF	N/A	Duplex SC, Duplex SG, Duplex LC	1550nm laser	2–50k
200-SM-LC-L	9 μm SMF	N/A	Duplex SC, Duplex SG, Duplex LC, Duplex MT-RJ	1300nm laser (Cost Reduced)	2–10k
200-SM-LL-I	9 μm SMF	N/A	Duplex SC	1300nm laser	2–2k
200-M5-SN-I	50 μm MMF	500 MHz*km	Duplex SC, Duplex SG, Duplex LC, Duplex MT-RJ	850nm laser	0.5–300
200-M5-SN-I	50 μm MMF	400 MHz*km	Duplex SC, Duplex SG, Duplex LC, Duplex MT-RJ	850nm laser	0.5–260
200-M6-SN-I	62.5 μm MMF	200 MHz*km	Duplex SC, Duplex SG, Duplex LC, Duplex MT-RJ	850nm laser	0.5–150
200-M6-SN-I	62.5 μm MMF	160 MHz*km	Duplex SC, Duplex SG, Duplex LC, Duplex MT-RJ	850nm laser	0.5–120
400-SM-LL-V	9 μm SMF	N/A	Duplex SC, Duplex SG, Duplex LC	1550nm laser	2–50k

continues

Table 5-7 *Fibre Channel Media, Connectors, Transceivers, and Operating Ranges (Continued)*

FC Variant	Medium	Modal Bandwidth	Connectors	Transceiver	Operating Range (m)
400-SM-LC-L	9 μm SMF	N/A	Duplex SC, Duplex SG, Duplex LC, Duplex MT-RJ	1300nm laser (Cost Reduced)	2–10k
400-SM-LL-I	9 μm SMF	N/A	Duplex SC	1300nm laser	2–2k
400-M5-SN-I	50 μm MMF	500 MHz*km	Duplex SC, Duplex SG, Duplex LC, Duplex MT-RJ	850nm laser	2–175
400-M5-SN-I	50 μm MMF	400 MHz*km	Duplex SC, Duplex SG, Duplex LC, Duplex MT-RJ	850nm laser	0.5–130
400-M6-SN-I	62.5 μm MMF	200 MHz*km	Duplex SC, Duplex SG, Duplex LC, Duplex MT-RJ	850nm laser	0.5–70
400-M6-SN-I	62.5 μm MMF	160 MHz*km	Duplex SC, Duplex SG, Duplex LC, Duplex MT-RJ	850nm laser	0.5–55
1200-SM-LL-L	9 μm SMF	N/A	Duplex SC, Duplex SG, Duplex LC, Duplex MT-RJ	1310nm laser	2–10k
1200-SM-LC4-L	9 μm SMF	N/A	Duplex SC, Duplex SG, Duplex LC, Duplex MT-RJ	1269–1356nm CWDM lasers	2–10k
1200-M5E-SN4-I	50 μm Enhanced MMF	1500 MHz*km	Duplex SC, Duplex SG, Duplex LC, Duplex MT-RJ	772–857nm CWDM lasers	0.5–550
1200-M5E-SN4P-I	50 μm Enhanced MMF	2000 MHz*km	MPO	850nm Parallel lasers	0.5–300
1200-M5E-SN-I	50 μm Enhanced MMF	2000 MHz*km	Duplex SC, Duplex SG, Duplex LC, Duplex MT-RJ	850nm laser	0.5–300

Table 5-7   *Fibre Channel Media, Connectors, Transceivers, and Operating Ranges (Continued)*

FC Variant	Medium	Modal Bandwidth	Connectors	Transceiver	Operating Range (m)
1200-M5-LC4-L	50 μm MMF	500 MHz*km	Duplex SC, Duplex SG, Duplex LC, Duplex MT-RJ	1269–1356nm CWDM lasers	0.5–290
1200-M5-LC4-L	50 μm MMF	400 MHz*km	Duplex SC, Duplex SG, Duplex LC, Duplex MT-RJ	1269–1356nm CWDM lasers	0.5–230
1200-M5-SN4-I	50 μm MMF	500 MHz*km	Duplex SC, Duplex SG, Duplex LC, Duplex MT-RJ	772-857nm CWDM lasers	0.5–290
1200-M5-SN4P-I	50 μm MMF	500 MHz*km	MPO	850nm Parallel lasers	0.5–150
1200-M5-SN-I	50 μm MMF	500 MHz*km	Duplex SC, Duplex SG, Duplex LC, Duplex MT-RJ	850nm laser	0.5–82
1200-M5-SN-I	50 μm MMF	400 MHz*km	Duplex SC, Duplex SG, Duplex LC, Duplex MT-RJ	850nm laser	0.5–66
1200-M6-LC4-L	62.5 μm MMF	500 MHz*km	Duplex SC, Duplex SG, Duplex LC, Duplex MT-RJ	1269–1356nm CWDM lasers	0.5–290
1200-M6-SN4-I	62.5 μm MMF	200 MHz*km	Duplex SC, Duplex SG, Duplex LC, Duplex MT-RJ	772–857nm CWDM lasers	0.5–118
1200-M6-SN4P-I	62.5 μm MMF	200 MHz*km	MPO	850nm Parallel lasers	0.5–75
1200-M6-SN-I	62.5 μm MMF	200 MHz*km	Duplex SC, Duplex SG, Duplex LC, Duplex MT-RJ	850nm laser	0.5–33
1200-M6-SN-I	62.5 μm MMF	160 MHz*km	Duplex SC, Duplex SG, Duplex LC, Duplex MT-RJ	850nm laser	0.5–26

FC Encoding and Signaling

The following definitions and rules apply only to switched FC implementations. FC-AL is not discussed herein. All FC implementations use one of two encoding schemes. Table 5-8 lists the encoding scheme used by each FC and 10GFC implementation and the associated BER objective.

Table 5-8 *FC and 10GFC Encoding Schemes and BER Objectives*

FC Variant	Encoding Scheme	BER Objective
100-SM-LL-V	8B/10B	10^{12}
100-SM-LL-L	8B/10B	10^{12}
100-SM-LC-L	8B/10B	10^{12}
100-SM-LL-I	8B/10B	10^{12}
100-M5-SN-I	8B/10B	10^{12}
100-M5-SL-I	8B/10B	10^{12}
100-M6-SN-I	8B/10B	10^{12}
100-M6-SL-I	8B/10B	10^{12}
200-SM-LL-V	8B/10B	10^{12}
200-SM-LC-L	8B/10B	10^{12}
200-SM-LL-I	8B/10B	10^{12}
200-M5-SN-I	8B/10B	10^{12}
200-M6-SN-I	8B/10B	10^{12}
400-SM-LL-V	8B/10B	10^{12}
400-SM-LC-L	8B/10B	10^{12}
400-SM-LL-I	8B/10B	10^{12}
400-M5-SN-I	8B/10B	10^{12}
400-M6-SN-I	8B/10B	10^{12}
1200-SM-LL-L	64B/66B	10^{12}
1200-SM-LC4-L	8B/10B	10^{12}
1200-M5E-SN4-I	8B/10B	10^{12}
1200-M5E-SN4P-I	8B/10B	10^{12}
1200-M5E-SN-I	64B/66B	10^{12}
1200-M5-LC4-L	8B/10B	10^{12}
1200-M5-SN4-I	8B/10B	10^{12}
1200-M5-SN4P-I	8B/10B	10^{12}
1200-M5-SN-I	64B/66B	10^{12}

Table 5-8   *FC and 10GFC Encoding Schemes and BER Objectives (Continued)*

FC Variant	Encoding Scheme	BER Objective
1200-M6-LC4-L	8B/10B	10^{12}
1200-M6-SN4-I	8B/10B	10^{12}
1200-M6-SN4P-I	8B/10B	10^{12}
1200-M6-SN-I	64B/66B	10^{12}

FC implementations operating at 100-MBps, 200-MBps, and 400-MBps use the 8B/10B encoding scheme. Only one of the control characters defined by the 8B/10B encoding scheme is used: K28.5. FC uses fixed-length ordered sets consisting of four characters. Each ordered set begins with K28.5. FC defines 31 ordered sets. FC uses ordered sets as frame delimiters, Primitive Signals, and Primitive Sequences. Multiple frame delimiters are defined so that additional information can be communicated. The start-of-frame (SOF) delimiters indicate the class of service being requested and the position of the frame within the sequence (first or subsequent). The end-of-frame (EOF) delimiters indicate the position of the frame within the sequence (intermediate or last) and whether the frame is valid or invalid or corrupt. Primitive Signals include idle, receiver_ready (R_RDY), virtual_circuit_ready (VC_RDY), buffer-to-buffer_state_change (BB_SC), and clock synchronization (SYN). Idles are transmitted in the absence of data traffic to maintain clock synchronization and in the presence of data traffic to maintain inter-frame spacing. An R_RDY is transmitted after processing a received frame to increment the receive buffer counter (the number of Buffer-to-Buffer_Credits [BB_Credits]) used for link-level flow control. A VC_RDY is transmitted only by a switch port after forwarding a received frame to increment the transmitting node's buffer counter used for link-level flow control within a virtual circuit. BB_SC permits BB_Credit recovery. SYN enables time synchronization of the internal clocks of attached nodes (similar to Network Time Protocol [NTP]). Primitive Signals are transmitted for as long as the transmitting device deems appropriate. By contrast, Primitive Sequences are transmitted continuously until the receiving device responds. Primitive Sequences are used to convey the state of a port, recover from certain types of errors, establish bit-level synchronization, and achieve word alignment. Primitive Sequences include offline state (OLS), not operational state (NOS), link reset (LR), and link reset response (LRR).

The encoding scheme of CWDM and parallel implementations of 10GFC is a combination of definitions and rules taken from the CWDM and parallel implementations of 10GE and the lower-speed FC implementations. 10GFC uses the same seven control characters as 10GE. The rules for their use in 10GFC are the same as in 10GE. However, 10GFC ordered set definitions closely match those of lower-speed FC implementations. There are only six differences in the ordered set definitions. The 10GE Sync_Column, Skip_Column, Align_Column, Local_Fault, and Remote_Fault ordered sets are used in 10GFC. The NOS ordered set used in lower-speed FC implementations is not used in

10GFC (replaced by Remote_Fault). In total, 10GFC uses 35 fixed-length ordered sets. Each consists of four characters, but the composition of each 10GFC ordered set is different than the equivalent ordered set in lower-speed FC implementations.

Serial implementations of 10GFC use the 64B/66B encoding scheme. The definitions and rules are unchanged from the 10GE implementation.

Further details of each encoding scheme are outside the scope of this book. The 8B/10B encoding scheme is well documented in clause 5 of the ANSI T11 FC-FS-2 specification, and in clauses 9 and 12 of the ANSI T11 10GFC specification. The 64B/66B encoding scheme is well documented in clause 49 of the IEEE 802.3ae-2002 specification and in clause 13 of the ANSI T11 10GFC specification.

FC Addressing Scheme

FC employs an addressing scheme that directly maps to the SAM addressing scheme. FC uses WWNs to positively identify each HBA and port, which represent the equivalent of SAM device and port names, respectively. An FC WWN is a 64-bit value expressed in colon-separated hexadecimal notation such as 21:00:00:e0:8b:08:a5:44. There are many formats for FC WWNs, most of which provide universal uniqueness. Figure 5-13 illustrates the basic ANSI T11 WWN address format.

Figure 5-13 *Basic ANSI T11 WWN Address Format*

A brief description of each field follows:

- **NAA**—4 bits long. It indicates the type of address contained within the Name field and the format of the Name field.
- **Name**—60 bits long. It contains the actual name of the node.

The Name field can contain a locally assigned address in any format, a mapped external address in the format defined by the NAA responsible for that address type, or a mapped external address in a modified format defined by the ANSI T11 subcommittee. External addresses are mapped into the Name field according to the rules defined in the FC-PH and FC-FS series of specifications. Six mappings are defined: IEEE MAC-48, IEEE extended, IEEE registered, IEEE registered extended, IEEE EUI-64, and IETF IPv4. The FC-DA specification series mandates the use of the IEEE MAC-48, IEEE extended, IEEE registered, or IEEE EUI-64 format to ensure universal uniqueness and interoperability. All six formats are described herein for the sake of completeness. Figure 5-14 illustrates the format of the Name field for containment of a locally assigned address.

Figure 5-14 *ANSI T11 Name Field Format for Locally Assigned Addresses*

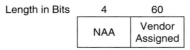

Length in Bits	4	60
	NAA	Vendor Assigned

A brief description of each field follows:

- **NAA**—4 bits long. It is set to 0011.
- **Vendor Assigned**—60 bits long. It can contain any series of bits in any format as defined by the vendor. Therefore, universal uniqueness cannot be guaranteed.

Figure 5-15 illustrates the format of the Name field for containment of an IEEE MAC-48 address.

Figure 5-15 *ANSI T11 Name Field Format for IEEE MAC-48 Addresses*

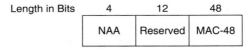

Length in Bits	4	12	48
	NAA	Reserved	MAC-48

A brief description of each field follows:

- **NAA**—4 bits long. It is set to 0001.
- **Reserved**—12 bits long. It may not be used. These bits are set to 0.
- **MAC-48**—48 bits long. It contains an IEEE MAC-48 address generated in accordance with the rules set forth by the IEEE. The U/L and I/G bits have no significance and are set to 0.

Figure 5-16 illustrates the format of the Name field for containment of an IEEE extended address.

Figure 5-16 *ANSI T11 Name Field Format for IEEE Extended Addresses*

Length in Bits	4	12	48
	NAA	Vendor Assigned	MAC-48

A brief description of each field follows:

- **NAA**—4 bits long. It is set to 0010.
- **Vendor Assigned**—12 bits long. It can contain any series of bits in any format as defined by the vendor.
- **MAC-48**—48 bits long. It contains an IEEE MAC-48 address generated in accordance with the rules set forth by the IEEE. The U/L and I/G bits have no significance and are set to 0.

Figure 5-17 illustrates the format of the Name field for containment of an IEEE Registered address.

Figure 5-17 *ANSI T11 Name Field Format for IEEE Registered Addresses*

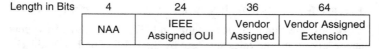

Length in Bits	4	24	36
	NAA	IEEE Assigned OUI	Vendor Assigned

A brief description of each field follows:

- **NAA**—4 bits long. It is set to 0101.
- **OUI**—24 bits long. It contains the vendor's IEEE assigned identifier. The U/L and I/G bits have no significance and are set to 0.
- **Vendor Assigned**—36 bits long. It can contain any series of bits in any format as defined by the vendor.

The IEEE registered extended format is atypical because it is the only WWN format that is not 64 bits long. An extra 64-bit field is appended, yielding a total WWN length of 128 bits. The extra length creates some interoperability issues. Figure 5-18 illustrates the format of the Name field for containment of an IEEE registered extended address.

Figure 5-18 *ANSI T11 Name Field Format for IEEE Registered Extended Addresses*

Length in Bits	4	24	36	64
	NAA	IEEE Assigned OUI	Vendor Assigned	Vendor Assigned Extension

A brief description of each field follows:

- **NAA**—4 bits long. It is set to 0110.
- **OUI**—24 bits long. It contains the vendor's IEEE assigned identifier. The U/L and I/G bits have no significance and are set to 0.
- **Vendor Assigned**—36 bits long. It can contain any series of bits in any format as defined by the vendor.
- **Vendor Assigned Extension**—64 bits long. It can contain any series of bits in any format as defined by the vendor.

Figure 5-19 illustrates the format of the Name field for containment of an IEEE EUI-64 address.

Figure 5-19 *ANSI T11 Name Field Format for IEEE EUI-64 Addresses*

Length in Bits	2	22	40
	NAA	Modified IEEE Assigned OUI	Vendor Assigned

A brief description of each field follows:

- **NAA**—2 bits long. It is set to 11. Because the EUI-64 format is the same length as the FC WWN format, the NAA bits must be taken from the EUI-64 address. To make this easier to accomplish, all NAA values beginning with 11 are designated as EUI-64 indicators. This has the effect of shortening the NAA field to 2 bits. Therefore, only 2 bits need to be taken from the EUI-64 address.

- **OUI**—22 bits long. It contains a modified version of the vendor's IEEE assigned identifier. The U/L and I/G bits are omitted from the first byte of the OUI, and the remaining 6 bits of the first byte are right-shifted two bit positions to make room for the 2 NAA bits.

- **Vendor Assigned**—40 bits long. It can contain any series of bits in any format as defined by the vendor.

Figure 5-20 illustrates the format of the Name field for containment of an IETF IPv4 address.

Figure 5-20 *ANSI T11 Name Field Format for IETF IPv4 Addresses*

A brief description of each field follows:

- **NAA**—4 bits long. It is set to 0100.
- **Reserved**—28 bits long.
- **IPv4 Address**—32 bits long. It contains the IP address assigned to the node. The party responsible for assigning the IP address (for example, the product manufacturer or the network administrator) is unspecified. Also unspecified is the manner in which the IP address should be assigned. For example, the product manufacturer could assign an IP address from an Internet Assigned Numbers Authority (IANA) registered address block, or the network administrator could assign an IP address from the RFC 1918 address space. Therefore, this WWN format does not guarantee universal uniqueness.

The FC equivalent of the SAM port identifier is the FC port identifier (Port_ID). The FC Port_ID is embedded in the FC Address Identifier. The FC Address Identifier consists of a hierarchical 24-bit value, and the lower 8 bits make up the Port_ID. The entire FC Address Identifier is sometimes referred to as the FCID (depending on the context). In this book, the phrase FC Address Identifier and the term FCID are used interchangeably *except* in the context of address assignment. The format of the 24-bit FCID remains unchanged from its original specification. This simplifies communication between FC devices operating at different speeds and preserves the legacy FC frame format. FCIDs are expressed in space-separated hexadecimal notation such as '0x64 03 E8'. Some devices omit the spaces when displaying FCIDs. Figure 5-21 illustrates the ANSI T11 Address Identifier format.

Figure 5-21 *ANSI T11 Address Identifier Format*

A brief description of each field follows:

- **Domain ID** is the first level of hierarchy. This field is 8 bits long. It identifies one or more FC switches.

- **Area ID** is the second level of hierarchy. This field is 8 bits long. It identifies one or more end nodes.

- **Port ID** is the third level of hierarchy. This field is 8 bits long. It identifies a single end node. This field is sometimes called the FCID, which is why the term FCID can be confusing if the context is not clear.

The SAM defines the concept of domain as the entire system of SCSI devices that interact with one another via a service delivery subsystem. FC implements this concept of domain via the first level of hierarchy in the FCID (Domain_ID). In a single-switch fabric, the Domain_ID represents the single switch. In a multi-switch fabric, the Domain_ID should represent all interconnected switches according to the SAM definition of domain. However, FC forwards frames between switches using the Domain_ID. So, each switch must be assigned a unique Domain_ID. To comply with the SAM definition of domain, the ANSI T11 FC-SW-3 specification explicitly allows multiple interconnected switches to share a single Domain_ID. However, the Domain_ID is not implemented in this manner by any FC switch currently on the market.

The Area_ID can identify a group of ports attached to a single switch. The Area_ID may not span FC switches. The FC-SW-3 specification does not mandate how fabric ports should be grouped into an Area_ID. One common technique is to assign all ports in a single slot of a switch chassis to the same Area_ID. Other techniques can be implemented.

The Port_ID provides a unique identity to each HBA port within each Area_ID. Alternately, the Area_ID field can be concatenated with the Port_ID field to create a 16-bit Port_ID. In this case, no port groupings exist.

The FC standards allow multiple FC Address Identifiers to be associated with a single HBA. This is known as N_Port_ID virtualization (NPIV). NPIV enables multiple virtual initiators to share a single HBA by assigning each virtual initiator its own FC Address Identifier. The normal FLOGI procedure is used to acquire the first FC Address Identifier. Additional FC Address Identifiers are acquired using the discover F_port service parameters (FDISC) ELS. When using NPIV, all virtual initiators must share the receive buffers on the HBA. NPIV enhances server virtualization techniques by enabling FC-SAN security policies (such as zoning) and QoS policies to be enforced independently for each virtual server. Note that some HBA vendors call their NPIV implementation "virtual HBA technology."

FC Name Assignment and Resolution

FC WWNs are "burned in" during the interface manufacturing process. Each HBA is assigned a node WWN (NWWN). Each port within an HBA is assigned a port WWN (PWWN). Some HBAs allow these values to be overridden by the network administrator. Locally administered WWNs are not guaranteed to be globally unique, so the factory-assigned WWNs are used in the vast majority of deployments.

FC name resolution occurs immediately following link initialization. As discussed in Chapter 3, "Overview of Network Operating Principles," each initiator and target registers with the FCNS. Following registration, each initiator queries the FCNS to discover accessible targets. Depending on the number and type of queries issued, the FCNS replies can contain the NWWN, PWWN, or FCID of some or all of the targets accessible by the initiator. Initiators may subsequently query the FCNS as needed. For example, when a new target comes online, an RSCN is sent to registered nodes. Upon receiving an RSCN, each initiator queries the FCNS for the details of the change. In doing so, the initiator discovers the NWWN, PWWN, or FCID of the new target.

Two alternate methods are defined to enable nodes to directly query other nodes to resolve or update name-to-address mappings. This is accomplished using extended link service (ELS) commands. An ELS may comprise one or more frames per direction transmitted as a single sequence within a new Exchange. Most ELSs are defined in the FC-LS specification. The first ELS is called discover address (ADISC). ADISC may be used only after completion of the PLOGI process. Because the FCID of the destination node is required to initiate PLOGI, ADISC cannot be used to resolve name-to-address mappings. ADISC can be used to update a peer regarding a local FCID change during an active PLOGI session. Such a change is treated as informational and has no effect on the current active PLOGI session.

The second ELS is called Fibre Channel Address Resolution Protocol (FARP). FARP may be used before using PLOGI. Thus, FARP can be used to resolve a NWWN or PWWN to an FCID. This enables an initiator that queries only for NWWN or PWWN following FCNS registration to issue a PLOGI to a target without querying the FCNS again. In theory, this can be useful in fabrics containing large numbers of targets that use dynamic-fluid FCIDs. However, the actual benefits are negligible. FARP can also be useful as a secondary mechanism to the FCNS in case the FCNS becomes unavailable. For example, some FC switches support a feature called *hot code load* that allows network administrators to upgrade the switch operating system without disrupting the flow of data frames. However, this feature halts all fabric services (including the FCNS) for an extended period of time. Thus, initiators that are dependent upon the FCNS cannot resolve FCIDs during the switch upgrade. In reality, this is not a concern because most initiators query the FCNS for NWWN, PWWN, and FCID following FCNS registration. To use FARP, the requestor must already know the NWWN or PWWN of the destination node so that the destination node can recognize itself as the intended responder upon receipt of a FARP request. Even though this is practical for some ULPs, FCP generally relies on the FCNS.

FC Address Assignment and Resolution

By default, a Domain_ID is dynamically assigned to each switch when a fabric comes online via the Domain_ID Distribution process. Each switch then assigns an FCID to each of its attached nodes via the Area_ID and Port_ID fields of the FC Address Identifier. A single switch, known as the principal switch (PS), controls the Domain_ID Distribution process. The PS is dynamically selected via the principal switch selection (PSS) process. The PSS process occurs automatically upon completion of the extended link initialization process. The PSS process involves the following events, which occur in the order listed:

1 Upon entering the non-disruptive fabric reconfiguration state machine, each switch clears its internal Domain_ID list. The Domain_ID list is a cached record of all Domain_IDs that have been assigned and the switch NWWN associated with each. Clearing the Domain_ID list has no effect during the initial configuration of a fabric because each switch's Domain_ID list is already empty.

2 Each switch transmits a build fabric (BF) switch fabric internal link service (SW_ILS) frame on each ISL. A SW_ILS is an ELS that may be transmitted only between fabric elements (such as FC switches). Most SW_ILSs are defined in the FC-SW specification series. If a BF SW_ILS frame is received on an ISL before transmission of a BF SW_ILS frame on that ISL, the recipient switch does not transmit a BF SW_ILS frame on that ISL.

3 Each switch waits for the fabric stability time-out value (F_S_TOV) to expire before originating exchange fabric parameters (EFP) SW_ILS frames. This allows the BF SW_ILS frames to flood throughout the entire fabric before any subsequent action.

4 Each switch transmits an EFP SW_ILS frame on each ISL. If an EFP SW_ILS frame is received on an ISL before transmission of an EFP SW_ILS frame on that ISL, the recipient switch transmits a switch accept (SW_ACC) SW_ILS frame on that ISL instead of transmitting an EFP SW_ILS frame. Each EFP and associated SW_ACC SW_ILS frame contains a PS_Priority field, a PS_Name field and a Domain_ID_List field. The PS_Priority and PS_Name fields of an EFP SW_ILS frame initially contain the priority and NWWN of the transmitting switch. The priority and NWWN are concatenated to select the PS. The lowest concatenated value wins. Upon receipt of an EFP or SW_ACC SW_ILS frame containing a priority-NWWN value lower than the recipient switch's value, the F_S_TOV timer is reset, the new priority-NWWN value is cached, and the recipient switch transmits an updated EFP SW_ILS frame containing the cached priority-NWWN value on all ISLs except the ISL on which the lower value was received. This flooding continues until all switches agree on the PS. Each switch determines there is PS agreement upon expiration of F_S_TOV. The Domain_ID_List field remains empty during the PSS process but is used during the subsequent Domain_ID Distribution process.

Upon successful completion of the PSS process, the Domain_ID Distribution process ensues. Domain_IDs can be manually assigned by the network administrator, but the Domain_ID Distribution process still executes so the PS (also known as the domain address manager) can compile a list of all assigned Domain_IDs, ensure there are no overlapping Domain_IDs, and distribute the complete Domain_ID_List to all other switches in the fabric. The Domain_ID Distribution process involves the following events, which occur in the order listed:

1 The PS assigns itself a Domain_ID.

2 The PS transmits a Domain_ID Assigned (DIA) SW_ILS frame on all ISLs. The DIA SW_ILS frame indicates that the transmitting switch has been assigned a Domain_ID. A received DIA SW_ILS frame is never forwarded by the recipient switch.

3 Each recipient switch replies to the DIA SW_ILS frame with an SW_ACC SW_ILS frame.

4 Each switch that replied to the DIA SW_ILS frame transmits a Request Domain_ID (RDI) SW_ILS frame to the PS. The RDI SW_ILS frame may optionally contain one or more preferred Domain_IDs. During reconfiguration of a previously operational fabric, each switch may list its previous Domain_ID as its preferred Domain_ID. Alternatively, a preferred or static Domain_ID can be manually assigned to each switch by the network administrator. If the transmitting switch does not have a preferred or static Domain_ID, it indicates this in the RDI SW_ILS frame by listing its preferred Domain_ID as 0x00.

5 The PS assigns a Domain_ID to each switch that transmitted an RDI SW_ILS frame. If available, each switch's requested Domain_ID is assigned. If a requested Domain_ID is not available, the PS may assign a different Domain_ID or reject the request. Each assigned Domain_ID is communicated to the associated switch via an SW_ACC SW_ILS frame.

6 Upon receiving its Domain_ID, each switch transmits a DIA SW_ILS frame on all ISLs except the ISL that connects to the PS (called the upstream principal ISL).

7 Each recipient switch replies to the DIA SW_ILS frame with an SW_ACC SW_ILS frame.

8 Each switch that replied to the DIA SW_ILS frame transmits an RDI SW_ILS frame on its upstream principal ISL.

9 Each intermediate switch forwards the RDI SW_ILS frame on its upstream principal ISL.

10 The PS assigns a Domain_ID to each switch that transmitted an RDI SW_ILS frame and replies with an SW_ACC SW_ILS frame.

11 Each intermediate switch forwards the SW_ACC SW_ILS frame(s) on its downstream principal ISL(s) to the requesting switch(es).

12 The Domain_ID assignment process repeats in this manner until all switches have been assigned a Domain_ID. Thus, Domain_ID assignment propagates outward from the PS.

13 Each time the PS assigns a Domain_ID, it transmits an EFP SW_ILS frame containing the updated Domain_ID_List on all ISLs.

14 Each switch directly connected to the PS replies to the EFP SW_ILS frame with an SW_ACC SW_ILS frame and forwards the EFP SW_ILS frame on all ISLs except the Upstream Principal ISL. Thus, the EFP SW_ILS frame propagates outward from the PS until all switches have received it.

The preceding descriptions of the PSS and Domain_ID Distribution processes are simplified to exclude error conditions and other contingent scenarios. For more information about these processes, readers are encouraged to consult the ANSI T11 FC-SW-3 specification. The eight-bit Domain_ID field mathematically accommodates 256 Domain_IDs, but some Domain_IDs are reserved. Only 239 Domain_IDs are available for use as FC switch identifiers. Table 5-9 lists all FC Domain_ID values and the status and usage of each.

Table 5-9 *FC Domain_IDs, Status, and Usage*

Domain_ID	Status	Usage
0x00	Reserved	FC-AL Environments
0x01-EF	Available	Switch Domain_IDs
0xF0-FE	Reserved	None
0xFF	Reserved	WKAs, Multicast, Broadcast, Domain Controllers

As the preceding table indicates, some Domain_IDs are reserved for use in WKAs. Some WKAs facilitate access to fabric services. Table 5-10 lists the currently defined FC WKAs and the fabric service associated with each.

Table 5-10 *FC WKAs and Associated Fabric Services*

Well Known Address	Fabric Service
0x'FF FF F5'	Multicast Server
0x'FF FF F6'	Clock Synchronization Server
0x'FF FF F7'	Security Key Distribution Server
0x'FF FF F8'	Alias Server
0x'FF FF F9'	Quality of Service Facilitator – Class 4
0x'FF FF FA'	Management Server
0x'FF FF FB'	Time Server

Table 5-10   *FC WKAs and Associated Fabric Services (Continued)*

Well Known Address	Fabric Service
0x'FF FF FC'	Directory Server
0x'FF FF FD'	Fabric Controller
0x'FF FF FE'	Fabric Login Server

In the context of address assignment mechanisms, the term FCID refers only to the Area_ID and Port_ID fields of the FC Address Identifier. These two values can be assigned dynamically by the FC switch or statically by either the FC switch or the network administrator. Dynamic FCID assignment can be fluid or persistent. With dynamic-fluid assignment, FCID assignments may be completely randomized each time an HBA port boots or resets. With dynamic-persistent assignment, the first assignment of an FCID to an HBA port may be completely randomized, but each subsequent boot or reset of that HBA port will result in reassignment of the same FCID. With static assignment, the first assignment of an FCID to an HBA port is predetermined by the software design of the FC switch or by the network administrator, and persistence is inherent in both cases.

FC Address Identifiers are not required to be universally unique. In fact, the entire FC address space is available for use within each physical fabric. Likewise, the entire FC address space is available for use within each VSAN. This increases the scalability of each physical fabric that contains multiple VSANs. However, reusing the entire FC address space can prevent physical fabrics or VSANs from being non-disruptively merged due to potential address conflicts. Reusing the entire FC address space also prevents communication between physical fabrics via SAN routers and between VSANs via inter-VSAN routing (IVR) unless network address translation (NAT) is employed. NAT improves scalability by allowing reuse of the entire FC address space while simultaneously facilitating communication across physical fabric boundaries and across VSAN boundaries. However, because NAT negates universal FC Address Identifier uniqueness, potential address conflicts can still exist, and physical fabric/VSAN mergers can still be disruptive. NAT also increases configuration complexity, processing overhead and management overhead. So, NAT represents a tradeoff between communication flexibility and configuration simplicity. Address reservation schemes facilitate communication between physical fabrics or VSANs without using NAT by ensuring that there is no overlap between the addresses assigned within each physical fabric or VSAN. A unique portion of the FC address space is used within each physical fabric or VSAN. This has the effect of limiting the scalability of all interconnected physical fabrics or VSANs to a single instance of the FC address space. However, address reservation schemes eliminate potential address conflicts, so physical fabrics or VSANs can be merged non-disruptively.

Note that some host operating systems use the FC Address Identifier of target ports to positively identify target ports, which is the stated purpose of PWWNs. Such operating systems require the use of dynamic-persistent or static FCIDs in combination with dynamic-persistent or static Domain_IDs. Note also that the processing of preferred

Domain_IDs during the PSS process guarantees Domain_ID persistence in most cases without administrative intervention. In other words, the PSS process employs a dynamic-persistent Domain_ID assignment mechanism by default. However, merging two physical fabrics (or two VSANs) into one can result in Domain_ID conflicts. Thus, static Domain_ID assignment is required to achieve the highest availability of targets in the presence of host operating systems that use FC Address Identifiers to positively identify target ports. As long as static Domain_IDs are used, and the network administrator takes care to assign unique Domain_IDs across physical fabrics (or VSANs) via an address reservation scheme, dynamic-persistent FCID assignment can be used in place of static FCIDs without risk of address conflicts during physical fabric (or VSAN) mergers.

An HBA's FC Address Identifier is used as the destination address in all unicast frames sent to that HBA and as the source address in all frames (unicast, multicast or broadcast) transmitted from that HBA. Two exceptions to the source address rule are defined: one related to FCID assignment (see the FC Link Initialization section) and another related to Class 6 multicast frames. FC multicast addressing is currently outside the scope of this book. Broadcast traffic is sent to the reserved FC Address Identifier 0x'FF FF FF'. Broadcast traffic delivery is subject to operational parameters such as zoning policy and class of service. All FC devices that receive a frame sent to the broadcast address accept the frame and process it accordingly.

NOTE   In FC, multicast addresses are also called Alias addresses. This should not be confused with PWWN aliases that are optionally used during zoning operations. Another potential point of confusion is Hunt Group addressing, which involves the use of Alias addresses in a particular manner. Hunt Groups are currently outside the scope of this book.

FC implements only OSI Layer 2 addresses, so address resolution is not required to transport SCSI. Note that address resolution is required to transport IP. RFC 2625, IP, and ARP over Fibre Channel (IPFC), defines ARP operation in FC environments. ARP over FC can complement FARP, or FARP can be used independently. ARP over FC facilitates dynamic resolution of an IP address to a PWWN. The PWWN is then resolved to an FC Address Identifier using FARP. Alternately, FARP can be used to directly resolve an IP address to an FC Address Identifier. FARP operation is very similar to ARP operation, but FARP can also solicit a PLOGI from the destination node instead of a FARP reply. Regardless of how ARP and FARP are used, the IP address of the destination node must be known to the requestor before transmitting the resolution request. This is consistent with the ARP over Ethernet model described in the preceding Ethernet section of this chapter. As with ARP, system administrators can create static mappings in the FARP table on each host. Typically, we use static mappings only in special situations to accomplish a particular goal.

FC Media Access

As stated in Chapter 3, "Overview of Network Operating Principles," FC-AL is a shared media implementation, so it requires some form of media access control. However, we use FC-AL primarily for embedded applications (such as connectivity inside a tape library) today, so the FC-AL arbitration mechanism is currently outside the scope of this book. In switched FC implementations, arbitration is not required because full-duplex communication is employed. Likewise, the FC PTP topology used for DAS configurations supports full-duplex communication and does not require arbitration.

FC Network Boundaries

Traditional FC-SANs are physically bounded by media terminations (for example, unused switch ports) and end node interfaces (for example, HBAs). No control information or user data can be transmitted between FC-SANs across physical boundaries. Figure 5-22 illustrates the physical boundaries of a traditional FC-SAN.

Figure 5-22 *Traditional FC-SAN Boundaries*

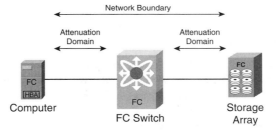

FC-SANs also have logical boundaries, but the definition of a logical boundary in Ethernet networks does not apply to FC-SANs. Like the Ethernet architecture, the FC architecture does not define any native functionality at OSI Layer 3. However, Ethernet is used in conjunction with autonomous OSI Layer 3 protocols as a matter of course, so logical boundaries can be easily identified at each OSI Layer 3 entity. By contrast, normal FC communication does not employ autonomous OSI Layer 3 protocols. So, some OSI Layer 2 control information must be transmitted between FC-SANs across logical boundaries to facilitate native communication of user data between FC-SANs. Currently, there is no standard method of facilitating native communication between FC-SANs. Leading FC switch vendors have created several proprietary methods. The ANSI T11 subcommittee is considering all methods, and a standard method is expected in 2006 or 2007. Because of the proprietary and transitory nature of the current methods, further exploration of this topic is currently outside the scope of this book. Note that network technologies autonomous from FC can be employed to facilitate communication between FC-SANs. Non-native FC transports are defined in the FC-BB specification series. Chapter 8, "OSI Session, Presentation and Application Layers," discusses one such transport (Fibre Channel over TCP/IP [FCIP]) in detail.

FC-SANs also can have virtual boundaries. There is currently only one method of creating virtual FC-SAN boundaries. Invented in 2002 by Cisco Systems, VSANs are now widely deployed in the FC-SAN market. In 2004, ANSI began researching alternative solutions for virtualization of FC-SAN boundaries. In 2005, ANSI selected Cisco's VSAN technology as the basis for the only standards-based solution (called Virtual Fabrics). The new standards (FC-SW-4, FC-FS-2, and FC-LS) are expected to be finalized in 2006. VSANs are similar to VLANs in the way traffic isolation is provided. Typically, each switch port is statically assigned to a single VSAN by the network administrator. Alternately, each switch port can be dynamically assigned to a VSAN via Cisco's dynamic port VSAN membership (DPVM) technology. DPVM is similar in function to Ethernet's GVRP. Like Ethernet, an FC switch port can belong to multiple VSANs. However, this is used exclusively on ISLs; HBAs do not currently support VSAN trunking. As frames enter a switch from an end node, the switch prepends a tag to indicate the VSAN membership of the ingress port. The tag remains intact until the frame reaches the egress switch port that connects the destination end node. The switch removes the tag and transmits the frame to the destination end node. FC switches made by Cisco Systems use VSAN tags to ensure that no frames are forwarded between VSANs. Thus, VSAN boundaries mimic physical FC-SAN boundaries. User data can be forwarded between VSANs only via IVR. IVR is one of the native FC logical boundaries alluded to in the preceding paragraph. IVR can be used with all of the non-native FC transports defined in the FC-BB specification series.

VSANs provide additional functionality not provided by VLANs. The FC specifications outline a model in which all network services (for example, the zone server) may run on one or more FC switches. This contrasts the TCP/IP model, in which network services other than routing protocols typically run on one or more hosts attached to the network (for example, a DHCP server). The FC service model enables switch vendors to instantiate independent network services within each VSAN during the VSAN creation process. This is the case with FC switches made by Cisco Systems. A multi-VSAN FC switch has an instance of each network service operating independently within each VSAN. This enables network administrators to achieve higher availability, security, and flexibility by providing *complete* isolation between VSANs. When facilitating communication between VSANs, IVR selectively exports control information bidirectionally between services in the affected VSANs without fusing the services. This is similar in concept to route redistribution between dissimilar IP routing protocols. The result is preservation of the service isolation model.

FC Frame Formats

FC uses one general frame format for many purposes. The general frame format has not changed since the inception of FC. The specific format of an FC frame is determined by the function of the frame. FC frames are word-oriented, and an FC word is 4 bytes. Figure 5-23 illustrates the general FC frame format.

Figure 5-23 *General FC Frame Format*

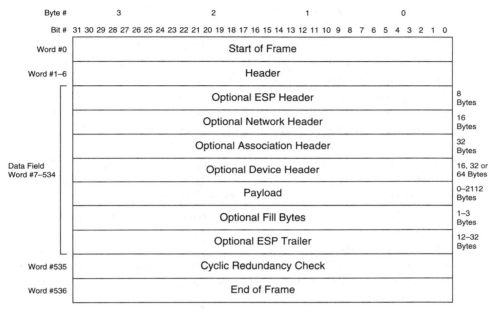

A brief description of each field follows:

- **Start of Frame (SOF) ordered set**—4 bytes long. It delimits the beginning of a frame, indicates the Class of Service, and indicates whether the frame is the first frame of a new sequence or a subsequent frame in an active sequence.

- **Header**—first field of a frame. It is 24 bytes long and contains multiple subfields (see the following subsection).

- **Data**—variable in length. It contains optional headers and ULP data.

- **Optional Encapsulating Security Payload (ESP) header**—8 bytes long. It contains the security parameter index (SPI) and the ESP sequence number. ESP, defined in RFC 2406, provides confidentiality, authentication, and anti-replay protection. ESP usage in FC environments is defined by ANSI in the FC-SP specification. Security is discussed in Chapter 12, "Storage Network Security."

- **Optional Network header**—16 bytes long. It is used by devices that connect FC-SANs to non-native FC networks.

- **Optional Association header**—32 bytes long. It is used to identify a process or group of processes within an initiator or target node. Thus, the Association Header represents an alternative to the Routing Control and Type sub-fields within the Header field. FCP does not use the Association Header.

- **Optional Device header**—16, 32, or 64 bytes long. It is used by some ULPs. The format of the Device Header is variable and is specified by each ULP that makes use of the header. FCP does not use this header.

- **Payload**—variable in length. It contains ULP data. The presence of optional headers in the Data field reduces the maximum size of the payload.

- **Optional Fill Bytes**—variable in length. It ensures that the variable-length payload field ends on a word boundary. The Fill Data Bytes sub-field in the F_CTL field in the Header indicates how many fill bytes are present. This field is not used if the frame contains an ESP header. ESP processing ensures that the payload field is padded if needed. The ESP payload pad field ranges from 0 to 255 bytes.

- **Optional ESP trailer**—variable in length. It contains the Integrity Check Value (ICV) calculated on the FC Header field (excluding the D_ID, S_ID, and CS_CTL/ Priority fields), the ESP Header field and Data field.

- **CRC**—4 bytes long. It contains a CRC value calculated on the FC Header field and Data field.

- **End of Frame (EOF) ordered set**—4 bytes long. It delimits the end of a frame, indicates whether the frame is the last frame of an active sequence, indicates the termination status of an Exchange that is being closed, and sets the running disparity to negative.

As mentioned in Chapter 3, "Overview of Network Operating Principles," the header in the general FC frame format provides functionality at multiple OSI layers. This contrasts the layered header model used in TCP/IP/Ethernet networks wherein a distinct header is present for each protocol operating at OSI Layers 2-4. Figure 5-24 illustrates the FC Header format.

Figure 5-24 *FC Header Format*

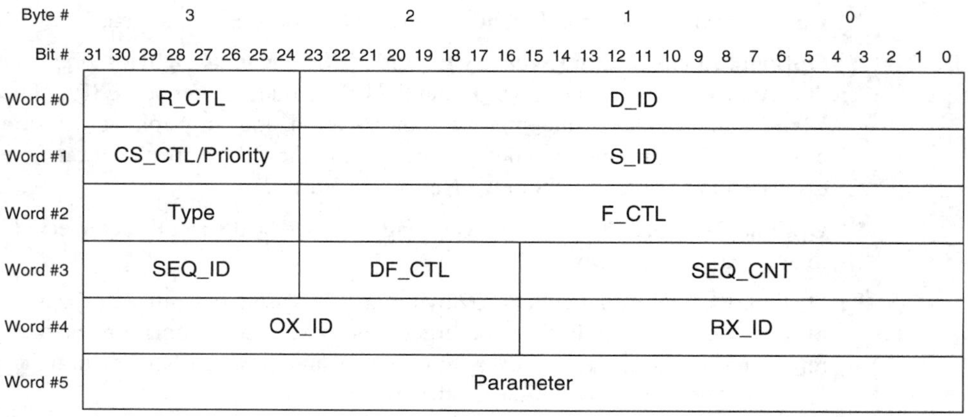

A brief description of each field follows:

- **Routing Control (R_CTL)**—1 byte long. It contains two sub-fields: Routing and Information. The Routing sub-field is 4 bits and indicates the whether the frame is a data frame or link-control frame. This aids the receiving node in routing the frame to the appropriate internal process. Two types of data frames can be indicated: frame type zero (FT_0) and frame type one (FT_1). Two types of link-control frames can be indicated: Acknowledge (ACK) and Link_Response. The value of the Routing sub-field determines how the Information sub-field and Type field are interpreted. The Information sub-field is 4 bits. It indicates the category of data contained within a data frame or the specific type of control operation contained within a link-control frame.

- **Destination ID (D_ID)**—3 bytes long. It contains the FC Address Identifier of the destination node.

- **Class Specific Control (CS_CTL)/Priority**—1 byte long. It can be interpreted as either CS_CTL or Priority. The interpretation of this field is determined by the CS_CTL/Priority Enable bit in the Frame Control field. When used as CS_CTL, this field contains control information such as the connection request policy, virtual circuit identifier, frame preference, and differentiated services codepoint (DSCP) value that is relevant to the CoS indicated by the SOF. When used as Priority in Class 1, 2, 3, or 6 environments, this field indicates the priority of the frame relative to other frames. A minor difference exists between the CS_CTL interpretation and the Priority interpretation regarding QoS. The DSCP values used in the CS_CTL interpretation are defined in the IETF DiffServ RFCs (2597, 3246 and 3260), whereas the priority values used in the Priority interpretation are defined in the ANSI T11 FC-FS specification series. The Priority field also facilitates preemption of a Class 1 or Class 6 connection in favor of a new Class 1 or 6 connection, or Class 2 or 3 frames. Class 4 frames use the Priority field to indicate the virtual circuit identifier.

- **Source ID (S_ID)**—3 bytes long. It contains the FC Address Identifier of the source node.

- **Type**—1 byte long. It contains operation-specific control information when the Routing sub-field of the R_CTL field indicates a control frame. The Type field indicates the ULP when the Routing sub-field of the R_CTL field indicates a data frame.

- **Frame Control (F_CTL)**—3 bytes long. It contains extensive control information. Most notable are the exchange context, sequence context, first_sequence, last_sequence, end_sequence, CS_CTL/priority enable, sequence initiative, retransmitted sequence, continue sequence condition, abort sequence condition, relative offset present, exchange reassembly, and fill data bytes sub-fields. The sequence context bit indicates whether the initiator or target is the source of a sequence. The sequence initiative bit determines which device (initiator or target) may initiate a new sequence. Either the initiator or target possesses the sequence initiative at each point in time. In FC vernacular, *streamed sequences* are simultaneously outstanding sequences transmitted during a single possession of the sequence initiative, and *consecutive non-streamed sequences* are successive sequences transmitted during a single possession of the sequence initiative. If a device transmits only one sequence during a single possession of the sequence initiative, that sequence is simply called a sequence.

- **Sequence ID (SEQ_ID)**—1 byte long. It is used to group frames belonging to a series. The SEQ_ID is set by the initiator for sequences transmitted by the initiator. Likewise, the SEQ_ID is set by the target for sequences transmitted by the target. The initiator and target each maintain a SEQ_ID counter that is incremented independently. SEQ_ID values can be incremented sequentially or randomly. SEQ_ID values are meaningful only within the context of a S_ID/D_ID pair and may be reused by a source device during simultaneous communication with other destination devices. However, each series of frames transmitted by a source device to a given destination device must have a unique SEQ_ID relative to other frame series that are simultaneously outstanding with that destination device. This requirement applies even when each frame series is associated with a unique OX_ID.

- **Data Field Control (DF_CTL)**—1 byte long. It indicates the presence or absence of each optional header. In the case of the Device Header, this field also indicates the size of the optional header.

- **Sequence Count (SEQ_CNT)**—2 bytes long. It is used to indicate the sequential order of frames within a SEQ_ID. SEQ_CNT values are meaningful only within the context of a SEQ_ID or consecutive series of SEQ_IDs between a S_ID/D_ID pair. Because SEQ_ID values are unidirectional between each S_ID/D_ID pair, the SEQ_CNT field must be used with the sequence context bit in the F_CTL field to uniquely identify each frame within an Exchange. The SEQ_CNT field is incremented by one for each frame transmitted within a sequence. The SEQ_CNT field is reset after each consecutive non-streamed sequence and after transferring the sequence initiative. The SEQ_CNT field is not reset after each sequence in a set of streamed sequences.

- **Originator Exchange ID (OX_ID)**—2 bytes long. It is used to group related sequences (that is, sequences associated with a single ULP operation). The OX_ID is assigned by the initiator. Each OX_ID may be unique for the source node across all destination nodes or may be unique only between the source node and a given destination node. FCP maps each I/O operation to an OX_ID.

- **Responder Exchange ID (RX_ID)**—2 bytes long. It is similar to the OX_ID field but is assigned by the target.

- **Parameter**—4 bytes long. When the Routing sub-field of the R_CTL field indicates a control frame, the Parameter field contains operation-specific control information. When the Routing sub-field of the R_CTL field indicates a data frame, the interpretation of this field is determined by the Relative Offset Present bit in the F_CTL field. When the Relative Offset Present bit is set to 1, this field indicates the position of the first byte of data carried in this frame relative to the first byte of all the data transferred by the associated SCSI command. This facilitates payload segmentation and reassembly. When the Relative Offset Present bit is set to 0, this field may contain ULP parameters that are passed to the ULP indicated in the Type field.

The S_ID, D_ID, OX_ID, and RX_ID fields are collectively referred to as the fully qualified exchange identifier (FQXID). The S_ID, D_ID, OX_ID, RX_ID, and SEQ_ID fields are collectively referred to as the sequence qualifier. The fields of the sequence qualifier can be used together in several ways. The preceding descriptions of these fields are highly simplified and apply only to FCP. FC implements many control frames to facilitate link, fabric, and session management. Many of the control frames carry additional information within the Data field. Comprehensive exploration of all the control frames and their payloads is outside the scope of this book, but certain control frames are explored in subsequent chapters. For more information about the general FC frame format, readers are encouraged to consult the ANSI T11 FC-FS-2 specification. For more information about control frame formats, readers are encouraged to consult the ANSI T11 FC-FS-2, FC-SW-3, FC-GS-3, FC-LS, and FC-SP specifications.

FC Delivery Mechanisms

Like Ethernet, FC supports several delivery mechanisms. Each set of delivery mechanisms is called a class of service (CoS). Currently, there are six CoS definitions:

- **Class 1**—Acknowledged, connection-oriented, full bandwidth service
- **Class 2**—Acknowledged, connectionless service
- **Class 3**—Unacknowledged, connectionless service
- **Class 4**—Acknowledged, connection-oriented, partial bandwidth service
- **Class 6**—Acknowledged, connection-oriented, full bandwidth, multicast service
- **Class F**—Acknowledged, connectionless service

NOTE   Class 5 was abandoned before completion. Class 5 was never included in any ANSI standard.

Classes 1, 2, 3, 4, and 6 are referred to collectively as Class N services; the N stands for node. The F in Class F stands for fabric because Class F traffic can never leave the fabric. In other words, Class F traffic can never be accepted from or transmitted to a node and may be exchanged only between fabric infrastructure devices such as switches and bridges. FC devices are not required to support all six classes. Classes 1, 4, and 6 are not currently supported on any modern FC switches. Classes 2 and 3 are supported on all modern FC switches. Class 3 is currently the default service on all modern FC switches, and most FC-SANs operate in Class 3 mode. Class F support is mandatory on all FC switches.

Class 1 provides a dedicated circuit between two end nodes (conceptually similar to ATM CES). Class 1 guarantees full bandwidth end-to-end. Class 2 provides reliable delivery without requiring a circuit to be established. All delivered frames are acknowledged, and all delivery failures are detected and indicated to the source node. Class 3 provides unreliable delivery that is roughly equivalent to Ethernet Type 1 service. Class 4 provides a virtual circuit between two end nodes. Class 4 is similar to Class 1 but guarantees only fractional bandwidth end-to-end. Class 6 essentially provides multiple Class 1 circuits between a single initiator and multiple targets. Only the initiator transmits data frames, and targets transmit acknowledgements. Class F is essentially the same as Class 2 but is reserved for fabric-control traffic.

Class 3 is currently the focus of this book. The following paragraphs describe Class 3 in terms applicable to all ULPs. For details of how Class 3 delivery mechanisms are used by FCP, see Chapter 8, "OSI Session, Presentation, and Application Layers." Class 3 implements the following delivery mechanisms:

- Destination nodes can detect frames dropped in transit. This is accomplished via the SEQ_CNT field and the error detect time-out value (E_D_TOV). When a drop is detected, all subsequently received frames within that sequence (and possibly within that exchange) are discarded, and the ULP within the destination node is notified of the error. The source node is not notified. Source node notification is the responsibility of the ULP. For this reason, ULPs that do not implement their own delivery failure notification or delivery acknowledgement schemes should not be deployed in Class 3 networks. (FCP supports delivery failure detection via timeouts and Exchange status monitoring.) The frames of a sequence are buffered to be delivered to the ULP as a group. So, it is not possible for the ULP to receive only part of a sequence. The decision to retransmit just the affected sequence or the entire Exchange is made by the ULP within the initiator before originating the Exchange. The decision is conveyed to the target via the Abort Sequence Condition sub-field in the F_CTL field in the FC Header. It is called the Exchange Error Policy.

- Destination nodes can detect duplicate frames. However, the current specifications do not explicitly state how duplicate frames should be handled. Duplicates can result only from actions taken by a sequence initiator or from frame forwarding errors within the network. A timer, the resource allocation time-out value (R_A_TOV), is used to avoid transmission of duplicate frames after a node is unexpectedly reset. However, a node that has a software bug, virus, or other errant condition could transmit duplicate frames. It is also possible for frame-forwarding errors caused by software bugs or other errant conditions within an FC switch to result in frame duplication. Recipient behavior in these scenarios is currently subject to vendor interpretation of the specifications.

- FC devices can detect corrupt frames via the CRC field. Upon detection of a corrupt frame, the frame is dropped. If the frame is dropped by the destination node, the ULP is notified within the destination node, but the source node is not notified. If the frame is dropped by a switch, no notification is sent to the source or destination node. Some FC switches employ cut-through switching techniques and are unable to detect corrupt frames. Thus, corrupt frames are forwarded to the destination node and subsequently dropped. All FC switches produced by Cisco Systems employ a store-and-forward architecture capable of detecting and dropping corrupt frames.

- Acknowledgement of successful frame delivery is not supported. (Note that some other Classes of Service support acknowledgement.)

- Retransmission is not supported. (Note that some other Classes of Service support retransmission.) ULPs are expected to retransmit any data lost in transit. FCP supports retransmission. Likewise, SCSI supports retransmission by reissuing failed commands.

- Link-level flow control is supported in a proactive manner. End-to-end flow control is not supported. (Note that some other Classes of Service support end-to-end flow control.) See Chapter 9, "Flow Control and Quality of Service," for more information about flow control.

- Bandwidth is not guaranteed. Monitoring and trending of bandwidth utilization on shared links is required to ensure optimal network operation. Oversubscription on shared links must be carefully calculated to avoid bandwidth starvation during peak periods. (Note that some other Classes of Service support bandwidth guarantees.)

- Consistent latency is not guaranteed.

- The specifications do not define methods for fragmentation or reassembly because the necessary header fields do not exist. An MTU mismatch results in frame drop. To avoid MTU mismatches, end nodes discover the MTU of intermediate network links via fabric login (FLOGI) during link initialization. A single MTU value is provided to end nodes during FLOGI, so all network links must use a common MTU size. End nodes also exchange MTU information during PLOGI (see Chapter 7, "OSI Transport Layer"). Based on this information, transmitters do not send frames that exceed the MTU of any intermediate network link or the destination node.

- Guaranteed in-order delivery of frames within a sequence is not required. Likewise, guaranteed in-order delivery of sequences within an exchange is not required. However, end nodes can request in-order delivery of frames during FLOGI. FC switches are not required to honor such requests. If honored, the entire network must support in-order delivery of frames within each sequence *and* in-order delivery of sequences within each exchange. This requires FC switch architectures, port channel load-balancing algorithms, and FSPF load-balancing algorithms to be specially developed to ensure in-order delivery of frames across load-balanced port channels and equal-cost FSPF paths, even during port-channel membership changes and network topology changes. All FC switches produced by Cisco Systems architecturally guarantee in-order delivery within a single switch. For multi-switch networks, all FC switches produced by Cisco Systems employ port-channel load-balancing algorithms and FSPF load-balancing algorithms that inherently ensure in-order delivery in a stable topology. For unstable networks, Cisco Systems provides an optional feature (disabled by default) called In-Order Delivery that ensures in-order frame delivery during topology changes. This is accomplished by intentionally delaying in-flight frames during topology changes. The feature must be enabled to honor (in a manner fully compliant with the FC-FS series of specifications) in-order delivery requests made by end nodes during FLOGI. Many modern HBA drivers do not request in-order delivery during FLOGI, so out-of-order frame delivery is possible in many Class 3 networks. End nodes can detect out-of-order frames via the Sequence Qualifier fields in combination with the SEQ_CNT field. The E_D_TOV timer begins immediately upon detection of an out-of-order frame. A frame error occurs if the missing frame is not received before E_D_TOV expiration. The events that follow a frame error are determined by the error-handling capabilities of each node, which are discovered during PLOGI between each pair of nodes (see Chapter 7, "OSI Transport Layer"). Subject to these capabilities, an Exchange Error Policy is specified by the source node on a per-exchange basis. This policy determines whether the exchange recipient ignores frame errors (called the process policy), discards only the affected sequence upon detection of a frame error (called the single sequence discard policy) or discards the entire affected exchange upon detection of a frame error (called the multiple sequence discard policy). Receipt of an out-of-order frame is not considered a frame error if the missing frame is received before E_D_TOV expiration. Unfortunately, the specifications do not explicitly require or prohibit frame reordering within the destination node in this scenario. So, recipient behavior is determined by the HBA vendor's interpretation of the specifications. Currently, no HBA produced by any of the three leading HBA vendors (Emulex, QLogic, and JNI/AMCC) reorders frames in this scenario. Instead, this scenario is treated the same as the frame error scenario.

NOTE   Note that the ability of a destination node to reorder frames is present in every CoS because the Sequence Qualifier fields and SEQ_CNT field are contained in the general header format used by every CoS. However, the requirement for a recipient to reorder frames is established per CoS. This contrasts the IP model wherein each transport layer protocol uses a different header format. Thus, in the IP model, the choice of transport layer protocol determines the recipient's ability and requirement to reorder packets.

FC Link Aggregation

Currently, no standard exists for aggregation of multiple FC links into a port channel. Consequently, some FC switch vendors have developed proprietary methods. Link aggregation between FC switches produced by different vendors is possible, but functionality is limited by the dissimilar nature of the load-balancing algorithms. No FC switch vendors currently *allow* port channels between heterogeneous switches. Cisco Systems supports FC port channels in addition to automation of link aggregation. Automation of link aggregation is accomplished via Cisco's FC Port Channel Protocol (PCP). PCP is functionally similar to LACP and PAgP. PCP employs two sub-protocols: the bringup protocol and the autocreation protocol. The bringup protocol validates the configuration of the ports at each end of an ISL (for compatibility) and synchronizes Exchange status across each ISL to ensure symmetric data flow. The autocreation protocol aggregates compatible ISLs into a port channel. The full details of PCP have not been published, so further disclosure of PCP within this book is not possible. As with Ethernet, network administrators must be wary of several operational requirements. The following restrictions apply to FC port channels connecting two switches produced by Cisco Systems:

- All links in a port channel must connect a single pair of devices. In other words, only point-to-point configurations are permitted.
- All links in a port channel must operate at the same transmission rate.
- If any link in a port channel is configured as non-trunking, all links in that port channel must be configured as non-trunking. Likewise, if any link in a port channel is configured as trunking, all links in that port channel must be configured as trunking.
- All links in a non-trunking port channel must belong to the same VSAN.
- All links in a trunking port channel must trunk the same set of VSANs.

The first two restrictions also apply to other FC switch vendors. The three VSAN-related restrictions only apply to Cisco Systems because VSANs are currently supported only by Cisco Systems. Several additional restrictions that do not apply to Cisco Systems do apply to other FC switch vendors. For example, one FC switch vendor mandates that only contiguous ports can be aggregated, and distance limitations apply because of the possibility of out-of-order frame delivery. Similar to Ethernet, the maximum number of links that may be grouped into a single port channel and the maximum number of port channels that may be configured on a single switch are determined by product design. Cisco Systems supports 16 links per FC port channel and 128 FC port channels per switch. These numbers currently exceed the limits of all other FC switch vendors.

FC Link Initialization

When a FC device is powered on, it begins the basic FC link initialization procedure. Unlike Ethernet, the media type is irrelevant to basic FC link initialization procedures. Like Ethernet, FC links may be manually configured or dynamically configured via auto-negotiation. 10GFC does not currently support auto-negotiation. Most HBAs and switch ports default to auto-negotiation mode. FC auto-negotiation is implemented in a peer-to-peer fashion. Following basic FC link initialization, one of several extended FC link initialization procedures occurs. The sequence of events that transpires is determined by the device types that are connected. The sequence of events differs for node-to-node, node-to-switch, switch-to-switch, and switch-to-bridge connections. Node-to-node connections are used for DAS configurations and are not discussed in this book.

The following basic FC link initialization procedure applies to all FC device types. Three state machines govern the basic FC link-initialization procedure: speed negotiation state machine (SNSM), loop port state machine (LPSM), and FC_Port state machine (FPSM). The SNSM executes first, followed by the LPSM, followed by the FPSM. This book does not discuss the LPSM. When a port (port A) is powered on, it starts its receiver transmitter time-out value (R_T_TOV) timer and begins transmitting OLS at its maximum supported transmission rate. If no receive signal is detected before R_T_TOV expiration, port A begins transmitting NOS at its maximum supported transmission rate and continues until another port is connected and powered on. When another port (port B) is connected and powered on, auto-negotiation of the transmission rate begins. The duplex mode is not auto-negotiated because switch-attached FC devices always operate in full-duplex mode. Port B begins transmitting OLS at its maximum supported transmission rate. Port A continues transmitting NOS at its maximum supported transmission rate. This continues for a specified period of time, then each port drops its transmission rate to the next lower supported rate and continues transmitting for the same period of time. This cycle repeats until a transmission rate match is found or all supported transmission rates (up to a maximum of four) have been attempted by each port.

During each transmission rate cycle, each port attempts to achieve bit-level synchronization and word alignment at each of its supported reception rates. Reception rates are cycled at least five times as fast as transmission rates so that five or more reception rates can be attempted during each transmission cycle. Each port selects its transmission rate based on the highest reception rate at which word alignment is achieved and continues transmission of OLS/NOS at the newly selected transmission rate. When both ports achieve word alignment at the new reception rate, auto-negotiation is complete. When a port is manually configured to operate at a single transmission rate, auto-negotiation remains enabled, but only the configured transmission rate is attempted. Thus, the peer port can achieve bit-level synchronization and word alignment at only one rate. If the configured transmission rate is not supported by the peer device, the network administrator must intervene. After auto-negotiation successfully completes, both ports begin listening for a Primitive Sequence. Upon recognition of three consecutive OLS ordered sets without error, port A begins transmitting LR. Upon recognition of three consecutive LR ordered sets without error, port B begins transmitting LRR to acknowledge recognition of the LR ordered sets. Upon recognition of three consecutive LRR ordered sets without error, port A begins transmitting Idle ordered sets. Upon recognition of the first Idle ordered set, port B begins transmitting Idle ordered sets. At this point, both ports are able to begin normal communication.

To understand the extended FC link initialization procedures, first we must understand FC port types. The ANSI T11 specifications define many port types. Each port type displays a specific behavior during initialization and normal operation. An end node HBA port is called a node port (N_Port). A switch port is called a fabric port (F_Port) when it is connected to an N_Port. A switch port is called an expansion port (E_Port) or a trunking E_Port (TE_Port) when it is connected to another switch port or to a bridge port (B_Port). A device that provides backbone connectivity as defined in the FC-BB specification series is called a bridge. Each bridge device contains at least one B_Port. A B_Port can only be connected to an E_Port or a TE_Port. A TE_Port is a VSAN-aware E_Port capable of conveying VSAN membership information on a frame-by-frame basis. TE_Ports were once proprietary to Cisco Systems but are now included in ANSI's new Virtual Fabric (VF) standard. Switch ports are often called generic ports or G_Ports because they can assume the behavior of more than one port type. If a node is connected, the switch port behaves as an F_Port; if a bridge is connected, the switch port behaves as an E_Port; if another switch is connected, the switch port behaves as an E_Port or TE_Port. To determine the appropriate port type, a switch port may adapt its behavior based on the observed behavior of the connected device during extended link initialization.

All FC switches produced by Cisco Systems behave in this manner. If the connected device does not display any specific behavior (that is, only Idle ordered sets are received), a Cisco Systems FC switch cannot determine which port type is appropriate. So, a wait timer is implemented to bound the wait period. Upon expiration of the wait timer, a Cisco Systems FC switch assumes the role of E_Port. Alternately, a switch port may sequentially assume the behavior of multiple port types during extended link initialization until it discovers the appropriate port type based on the reaction of the connected device. However, this approach can prevent some HBAs from initializing properly. Additional port types are defined for FC-AL environments, but those port types are not discussed in this book.

NOTE   Cisco Systems supports a feature called switch port analyzer (SPAN) on its Ethernet and FC switches. On FC switches, SPAN makes use of SPAN destination (SD) and SPAN trunk (ST) ports. These port types are currently proprietary to Cisco Systems. The SD port type and the SPAN feature are discussed in Chapter 14, "Storage Protocol Decoding and Analysis."

When an N_Port is attached to a switch port, the extended link initialization procedure known as FLOGI is employed. FLOGI is mandatory for all N_Ports regardless of CoS, and communication with other N_Ports is not permitted until FLOGI completes. FLOGI is accomplished with a single-frame request followed by a single-frame response. In switched FC environments, FLOGI accomplishes the following tasks:

- Determines the presence or absence of a switch
- Provides the operating characteristics of the requesting N_Port to the switch

- Provides the operating characteristics of the entire network to the requesting N_Port
- Assigns an FCID to the requesting N_Port
- Initializes the BB_Credit mechanism for link-level flow control

The ANSI T11 specifications do not explicitly state a required minimum or maximum number of Idles that must be transmitted before transmission of the FLOGI request. So, the amount of delay varies widely (between 200 microseconds and 1500 milliseconds) from one HBA model to the next. When the N_Port is ready to begin the FLOGI procedure, it transmits a FLOGI ELS frame with the S_ID field set to 0. Upon recognition of the FLOGI request, the switch port assumes the role of F_Port and responds with a FLOGI Link Services Accept (LS_ACC) ELS frame. The FLOGI LS_ACC ELS frame specifies the N_Port's newly assigned FCID via the D_ID field. Upon recognition of the FLOGI LS_ACC ELS frame, the FLOGI procedure is complete, and the N_Port is ready to communicate with other N_Ports. The FLOGI ELS and associated LS_ACC ELS use the same frame format, which is a standard FC frame containing link parameters in the data field. Figure 5-25 illustrates the data field format of an FLOGI/LS_ACC ELS frame.

Figure 5-25 *Data Field Format of an FC FLOGI/LS_ACC ELS Frame*

Byte #	3	2	1	0
Bit #	31 30 29 28 27 26 25 24	23 22 21 20 19 18 17 16	15 14 13 12 11 10 9 8	7 6 5 4 3 2 1 0
Word #0	LS Command Code			
Word #1–4	Common Service Parameters			
Word #5–6	N_Port Name			
Word #7–8	Node Name or Fabric Name			
Word #9–12	Class 1/6 Service Parameters			
Word #13–16	Class 2 Service Parameters			
Word #17–20	Class 3 Service Parameters			
Word #21–24	Class 4 Service Parameters			
Word #25–28	Vendor Version Level			
Word #29–30	Services Availability			
Word #31	Login Extension Data Length			
Word #32–61	Login Extension Data			
Word #62–63	Clock Synchronization QoS			

A brief description of each field follows:

- **LS Command Code**—4 bytes long. It contains the 1-byte FLOGI command code (0x04) followed by 3 bytes of zeros when transmitted by an N_Port. This field contains the 1-byte LS_ACC command code (0x02) followed by 3 bytes of zeros when transmitted by an F_Port.

- **Common Service Parameters**—16 bytes long. It contains parameters that affect network operation regardless of the CoS. Key parameters include the number of BB_Credits, the BB_Credit management policy, the BB_SC interval, the MTU, the R_T_TOV, the E_D_TOV, the R_A_TOV, the length of the FLOGI payload, and the transmitter's port type (N_Port or F_Port). Some parameters can be manually configured by the network administrator. If manually configured, only the values configured by the administrator will be advertised to the peer device.

- **N_Port Name**—8 bytes long. It contains the PWWN of the N_Port. This field is not used by the responding F_Port.

- **Node Name/Fabric Name**—8 bytes long. It contains the NWWN associated with the N_Port (FLOGI) or the switch (LS_ACC).

- **Class 1/6, 2, 3, and 4 Service Parameters**—Each is 16 bytes long. They contain class-specific parameters that affect network operation. Key parameters relevant to Class 3 include indication of support for Class 3, in-order delivery, priority/preemption, CS_CTL preference, DiffServ, and clock synchronization. Some parameters can be manually configured by the network administrator. If manually configured, only the values configured by the administrator will be advertised to the peer device.

- **Vendor Version Level**—16 bytes long. It contains vendor-specific information.

- **Services Availability**—8 bytes long. It is used only in LS_ACC frames. It indicates the availability of fabric services at the defined WKAs.

- **Login Extension Data Length**—4 bytes long. It indicates the length of the Login Extension Data field expressed in 4-byte words.

- **Login Extension Data**—120 bytes long. It contains the vendor identity and other vendor-specific information.

- **Clock Synchronization QoS**—8 bytes long. It contains operational parameters relevant to the fabric's ability to deliver clock synchronization data. It is used only if the Clock Synchronization service is supported by the switch.

If the operating characteristics of an N_Port change after the N_Port completes FLOGI, the N_Port can update the switch via the FDISC ELS command. The FDISC ELS and associated LS_ACC ELS use the exact same frame format as FLOGI. The meaning of each field is also identical. The LS Command Code field contains the FDISC command code (0x51). The FDISC ELS enables N_Ports to update the switch without affecting any sequences or exchanges that are currently open. For the new operating characteristics to take affect, the N_Port must log out of the fabric and perform FLOGI again. An N_Port may also use FDISC to request assignment of additional FC Address Identifiers.

When a switch port is attached to another switch port, the switch port mode initialization state machine (SPMISM) governs the extended link initialization procedure. The SPMISM cannot be invoked until the LPSM and FPSM determine that there is no FC-AL or N_Port attached. Because the delay between basic link initialization and FLOGI request transmission is unspecified, each switch vendor must decide how its switches will determine whether an FC-AL or N_Port is attached to a newly initialized link. All FC switches produced by Cisco Systems wait 700 ms after link initialization for a FLOGI request. If no FLOGI request is received within that time, the LPSM and FPSM relinquish control to the SPMISM.

All FC switches behave the same once the SPMISM takes control. An exchange link parameters (ELP) SW_ILS frame is transmitted by one of the connected switch ports (the requestor). Upon recognition of the ELP SW_ILS frame, the receiving switch port (the responder) transmits an SW_ACC SW_ILS frame. Upon recognition of the SW_ACC SW_ILS frame, the requestor transmits an ACK frame. The ELP SW_ILS and SW_ACC SW_ILS both use the same frame format, which is a standard FC frame containing link parameters in the data field. The data field of an ELP/SW_ACC SW_ILS frame is illustrated in Figure 5-26.

Figure 5-26 *Data Field Format of an FC ELP/SW_ACC SW_ILS Frame*

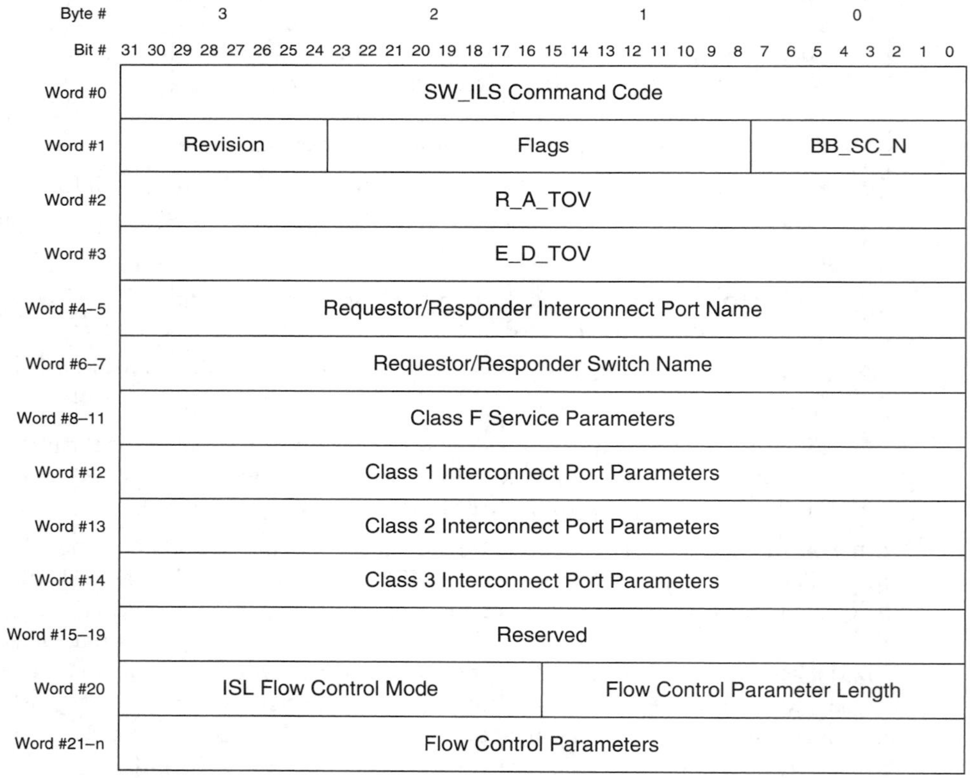

Byte #	3	2	1	0
Bit #	31 30 29 28 27 26 25 24	23 22 21 20 19 18 17 16	15 14 13 12 11 10 9 8	7 6 5 4 3 2 1 0
Word #0	SW_ILS Command Code			
Word #1	Revision	Flags		BB_SC_N
Word #2	R_A_TOV			
Word #3	E_D_TOV			
Word #4–5	Requestor/Responder Interconnect Port Name			
Word #6–7	Requestor/Responder Switch Name			
Word #8–11	Class F Service Parameters			
Word #12	Class 1 Interconnect Port Parameters			
Word #13	Class 2 Interconnect Port Parameters			
Word #14	Class 3 Interconnect Port Parameters			
Word #15–19	Reserved			
Word #20	ISL Flow Control Mode		Flow Control Parameter Length	
Word #21–n	Flow Control Parameters			

NOTE   Each SW_ILS command that expects an SW_ACC response defines the format of the SW_ACC payload. Thus, there are many SW_ACC SW_ILS frame formats.

A brief description of each field follows:

- **SW_ILS Command Code**—4 bytes long. This field contains the ELP command code (0x10000000) when transmitted by a requestor. This field contains the SW_ACC command code (0x02000000) when transmitted by a responder.

- **Revision**—1 byte long. It indicates the ELP/SW_ACC protocol revision.

- **Flags**—2 bytes long. It contains bit-oriented sub-fields that provide additional information about the transmitting port. Currently, only one flag is defined: the Bridge Port flag. If this flag is set to 1, the transmitting port is a B_Port. Otherwise, the transmitting port is an E_Port.

- **BB_SC_N**—1 byte long. It indicates the BB_SC interval. The value of this field is meaningful only if the ISL Flow Control Mode field indicates that the R_RDY mechanism is to be used.

- **R_A_TOV**—4 bytes long. It indicates the transmitter's required value for resource allocation timeout. All devices within a physical SAN or VSAN must agree upon a common R_A_TOV. Some FC switches allow the network administrator to configure this value manually.

- **E_D_TOV**—4 bytes long. It indicates the transmitter's required value for error-detection timeout. All devices within a physical SAN or VSAN must agree upon a common E_D_TOV. Some FC switches allow the network administrator to configure this value manually.

- **Requestor/Responder Interconnect Port Name**—8 bytes long. It indicates the PWWN of the transmitting switch port.

- **Requestor/Responder Switch Name**—8 bytes long. It indicates the NWWN of the transmitting switch.

- **Class F Service Parameters**—6 bytes long. It contains various E_Port operating parameters. Key parameters include the class-specific MTU (ULP buffer size), the maximum number of concurrent Class F sequences, the maximum number of concurrent sequences within each exchange, and the number of End-to-End_Credits (EE_Credits) supported. Some FC switches allow the network administrator to configure one or more of these values manually.

- **Class 1, 2, and 3 Interconnect Port Parameters**—Each is 4 bytes long. They contain class-specific parameters that affect network operation. Key parameters relevant to Class 3 include indication of support for Class 3 and in-order delivery. Also included is the class-specific MTU (ULP buffer size). Some FC switches allow the network administrator to configure one or more of these values manually.

- **Reserved**—20 bytes long.

- **ISL Flow Control Mode**—2 bytes long. It indicates whether the R_RDY mechanism or a vendor-specific mechanism is supported. On some FC switches, the flow-control mechanism is determined by the switch operating mode (native or interoperable).

- **Flow Control Parameter Length**—2 bytes long. It indicates the length of the Flow Control Parameters field expressed in bytes.

- **Flow Control Parameters**—variable in length as determined by the value of the ISL Flow Control Mode field. If the R_RDY mechanism is used, this field has a fixed length of 20 bytes and contains two sub-fields: BB_Credit (4 bytes) and compatibility parameters (16 bytes). The BB_Credit sub-field indicates the total number of BB_Credits available to all Classes of Service. The compatibility parameters sub-field contains four parameters required for backward compatibility.

Following ELP, the ISL is reset to activate the new operating parameters. The ELP requestor begins transmitting LR ordered sets. Upon recognition of three consecutive LR ordered sets without error, the ELP responder begins transmitting LRR to acknowledge recognition of the LR ordered sets. Upon recognition of three consecutive LRR ordered sets without error, the ELP requestor begins transmitting Idle ordered sets. Upon recognition of the first Idle ordered set, the ELP responder begins transmitting Idle ordered sets. At this point, the switches are ready to exchange information about the routing protocols that they support via the exchange switch capabilities (ESC) procedure. The ESC procedure is optional, but all modern FC switches perform ESC. The ELP requestor transmits an ESC SW_ILS frame with the S_ID and D_ID fields each set to 0xFFFFFD. The ESC payload contains a list of routing protocols supported by the transmitter. Upon recognition of the ESC SW_ILS frame, the receiver selects a single routing protocol and transmits an SW_ACC SW_ILS frame indicating its selection in the payload. The S_ID and D_ID fields of the SW_ACC SW_ILS frame are each set to 0xFFFFFD. The ESC SW_ILS frame format is a standard FC frame containing a protocol list in the data field. The data field of an ESC SW_ILS frame is illustrated in Figure 5-27.

Figure 5-27 *Data Field Format of an FC ESC SW_ILS Frame*

Byte #	3	2	1	0
Bit #	31 30 29 28 27 26 25 24	23 22 21 20 19 18 17 16	15 14 13 12 11 10 9 8	7 6 5 4 3 2 1 0
Word #0	SW_ILS Command Code	Reserved	Payload Length	
Word #1–2	Vendor ID String			
Word #3–5	Protocol Descriptor #n			

A brief description of each field follows:

- **SW_ILS Command Code**—1 byte long. It contains the first byte of the ESC command code (0x30). The first byte of the ESC command code is unique to the ESC command, so the remaining 3 bytes are truncated.

- **Reserved**—1 byte long.

- **Payload Length**—2 bytes long. It indicates the total length of all payload fields expressed in bytes.

- **Vendor ID String**—8 bytes long. It contains the unique vendor identification string assigned by ANSI T10 to the manufacturer of the transmitting switch.

- **Protocol Descriptor #n**—multiple Protocol Descriptor fields may be present in the ESC SW_ILS frame. Each Protocol Descriptor field is 12 bytes long and indicates a protocol supported by the transmitter. Three sub-fields are included: vendor ID string (8 bytes), reserved (2 bytes), and protocol ID (2 bytes). The vendor ID string sub-field indicates whether the protocol is standard or proprietary. This sub-field contains all zeros if the protocol is a standard. Otherwise, this sub-field contains the unique vendor identification string assigned by ANSI T10 to the vendor that created the protocol. The reserved sub-field is reserved for future use. The protocol ID sub-field identifies the protocol. Values from 0x0000-0x7FFF indicate standard protocols. Values from 0x8000-0xFFFF indicate proprietary protocols. Currently, only two standard protocols are defined: FSPF (0x0002) and FSPF-Backbone (0x0001).

The corresponding SW_ACC SW_ILS frame format is a standard FC frame containing a single protocol descriptor in the data field. The data field of an SW_ACC SW_ILS frame corresponding to an ESC SW_ILS command is illustrated in Figure 5-28.

Figure 5-28 *Data Field Format of an FC SW_ACC SW_ILS Frame for ESC*

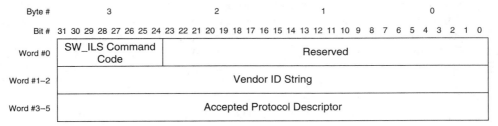

A brief description of each field follows:

- **SW_ILS Command Code**—1 byte long. It contains the first byte of the SW_ACC command code (0x02). The first byte of the SW_ACC command code is unique to the SW_ACC command, so the remaining 3 bytes are truncated.

- **Reserved**—3 bytes long.

- **Vendor ID String**—8 bytes long. It contains the unique vendor identification string assigned by ANSI T10 to the manufacturer of the transmitting switch.
- **Accepted Protocol Descriptor**—12 bytes long. It indicates the routing protocol selected by the transmitter. This field is copied from the ESC SW_ILS frame.

Following ESC, the switch ports optionally authenticate each other (see Chapter 12, "Storage Network Security"). The port-level authentication procedure is relatively new. Thus, few modern FC switches support port-level authentication. That said, all FC switches produced by Cisco Systems support port-level authentication. Upon successful authentication (if supported), the ISL becomes active. Next, the PSS process ensues, followed by domain address assignment. After all Domain_IDs have been assigned, the zone exchange and merge procedure begins. Next, the FSPF routing protocol converges. Finally, RSCNs are generated. To summarize:

- ELP is exchanged between E_Ports
- The new ISL is reset to enable the operating parameters
- ESC is exchanged between E_Ports
- Optional E_Port authentication occurs
- PSS occurs
- Domain_IDs are re-assigned if a Domain_ID conflict exists
- Zone merge occurs
- The FSPF protocol converges
- An SW_RSCN is broadcast to announce the new ISL
- Name server updates are distributed
- RSCNs are generated to announce the new name server records

When a switch port is attached to a bridge port, the switch-to-switch extended link initialization procedure is followed, but ELP is exchanged between the switch port and the bridge port. An equivalent SW_ILS, called exchange B_access parameters (EBP), is exchanged between the bridge ports across the WAN. For details about the EBP SW_ILS, see Chapter 8, "OSI Session, Presentation, and Application Layers." Bridge ports are transparent to all inter-switch operations after ELP. Following ELP, the link is reset. ESC is then performed between the switch ports. Likewise, port-level authentication is optionally performed between the switch ports. The resulting ISL is called a virtual ISL (VISL). Figure 5-29 illustrates this topology.

Any SW_ILS command may be rejected by the responding port via the switch internal link service reject (SW_RJT). A common SW_RJT format is used for all SW_ILS. Figure 5-30 illustrates the data field format of an SW_RJT frame.

Figure 5-29 *FC VISL Across Bridge Devices*

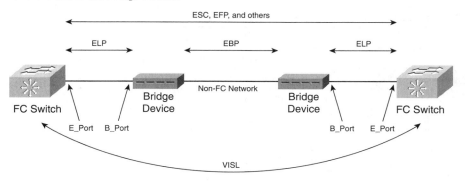

Figure 5-30 *Data Field Format of an FC SW_RJT Frame*

Byte #	3	2	1	0

Bit # 31 30 29 28 27 26 25 24 23 22 21 20 19 18 17 16 15 14 13 12 11 10 9 8 7 6 5 4 3 2 1 0

Word #0	SW_ILS Command Code			
Word #1	Reserved	Reason Code	Reason Code Explanation	Vendor Specific

A brief description of each field follows:

- **SW_ILS Command Code**—4 bytes long. This field contains the SW_RJT command code (0x01000000).
- **Reserved**—1 byte long.
- **Reason Code**—1 byte long. It indicates why the SW_ILS command was rejected. A common set of reason codes is used for all SW_ILS commands. Table 5-11 summarizes the reason codes defined by the FC-SW-4 specification. All reason codes excluded from Table 5-11 are reserved.
- **Reason Code Explanation**—1 byte long. It provides additional diagnostic information that complements the Reason Code field. A common set of reason code explanations is used for all SW_ILS commands. Table 5-12 summarizes the reason code explanations defined by the FC-SW-4 specification. All reason code explanations excluded from Table 5-12 are reserved.
- **Vendor Specific**—1 byte long. When the Reason Code field is set to 0xFF, this field provides a vendor-specific reason code. When the Reason Code field is set to any value other than 0xFF, this field is ignored.

Table 5-11   *SW_RJT Reason Codes*

Reason Code	Description
0x01	Invalid SW_ILS Command Code
0x02	Invalid Revision Level
0x03	Logical Error
0x04	Invalid Payload Size
0x05	Logical Busy
0x07	Protocol Error
0x09	Unable To Perform Command Request
0x0B	Command Not Supported
0x0C	Invalid Attachment
0xFF	Vendor Specific Error

Table 5-12   *SW_RJT Reason Code Explanations*

Reason Code Explanation	Description
0x00	No Additional Explanation
0x01	Class F Service Parameter Error
0x03	Class "n" Service Parameter Error
0x04	Unknown Flow Control Code
0x05	Invalid Flow Control Parameters
0x0D	Invalid Port_Name
0x0E	Invalid Switch_Name
0x0F	R_A_TOV Or E_D_TOV Mismatch
0x10	Invalid Domain_ID_List
0x19	Command Already In Progress
0x29	Insufficient Resources Available
0x2A	Domain_ID Not Available
0x2B	Invalid Domain_ID
0x2C	Request Not Supported
0x2D	Link Parameters Not Yet Established
0x2E	Requested Domain_IDs Not Available
0x2F	E_Port Is Isolated

Table 5-12   *SW_RJT Reason Code Explanations (Continued)*

Reason Code Explanation	Description
0x31	Authorization Failed
0x32	Authentication Failed
0x33	Incompatible Security Attribute
0x34	Checks In Progress
0x35	Policy Summary Not Equal
0x36	FC-SP Zoning Summary Not Equal
0x41	Invalid Data Length
0x42	Unsupported Command
0x44	Not Authorized
0x45	Invalid Request
0x46	Fabric Changing
0x47	Update Not Staged
0x48	Invalid Zone Set Format
0x49	Invalid Data
0x4A	Unable To Merge
0x4B	Zone Set Size Not Supported
0x50	Unable To Verify Connection
0x58	Requested Application Not Supported

The preceding descriptions of the FC link initialization procedures are simplified for the sake of clarity. For more detail about Primitive Sequence usage, speed negotiation states, the FPSM, port types, the SPMISM, frame formats, or B_Port operation, readers are encouraged to consult the ANSI T11 FC-FS, FC-LS, and FC-SW specification series.

Summary

This chapter provides in-depth analysis of the physical layer and data-link layer technologies employed by the SPI, Ethernet, and FC. Many of the details provided are ancillaries to design and troubleshooting efforts rather than daily network operation. That said, a thorough understanding of the details provided can enable network administrators to optimize their daily operations.

Though the SPI is waning in popularity, it is still important to understand that the capabilities and limitations of the SPI influenced the evolution of SCSI performance requirements that must now be met by modern storage networks built on Ethernet or FC. For this reason, the SPI is included in this chapter. Insight to the functional capabilities of Ethernet and FC relative to each other is provided to enable readers to properly employ the use of each technology based on application requirements. Readers should remember that Ethernet is deployed in conjunction with TCP/IP to provide a complete solution. So, the limitations of Ethernet presented in this chapter should not be construed as barriers to deployment. Likewise, many of the capabilities of FC are not examined in this chapter. The subsequent chapters of Part II, "OSI Layers," build upon this chapter to provide a complete picture of each solution.

Review Questions

1   What two components compose a SCSI logical unit?

2   Which SAM addressing construct facilitates communication with an object?

3   What is a standards body that defines an address format commonly called?

4   Which organization assigns organizationally unique identifiers (OUIs)?

5   If fragmentation occurs, where does it occur?

6   Is it possible for a network protocol to guarantee that frames or packets will never be dropped?

7   Why do most packet-switching technologies support bandwidth reservation schemes?

8   Does the SAM explicitly require in-order delivery of frames or packets composing a SCSI request or response?

9   Which term describes tagging of frames transmitted on an ISL to indicate the VLAN or VSAN membership of each frame?

10   The X2 and XPAK MSAs derive their electrical specifications from which MSA?

11   What is the maximum operating range of the SPI?

12   Does the SPI support in-order delivery?

13   Which fiber-optic connectors are supported by GE?

14   What is the maximum operating range of 10GBASE-EW using a normal SMF link?

15   What is the BER of 1000BASE-T?

16   What are the /C1/ and /C2/ ordered sets used for in 1000BASE-SX?

17   An Ethernet MAC address is equivalent to which SAM addressing construct?

18   What is the purpose of GVRP?

19   Which Ethernet frame format is most common today?

20 How many types of service does Ethernet support?

21 Can flow-based load balancing be implemented across an Ethernet port channel?

22 Do copper-based and fiber-based Ethernet implementations follow the same link initialization procedures?

23 What is the most common fiber-optic connector used by 2-Gbps FC devices?

24 What is the maximum operating range of 2-Gbps FC on 62.5 micron MMF?

25 How many 8B/10B control characters does 4-Gbps FC use?

26 What information does the NAA field of an FC WWN provide?

27 What do FC attached SCSI initiators do following receipt of an RSCN frame?

28 Does the header of a FC frame provide functionality at OSI Layers other the data-link layer?

29 Which FC CoS is used by default in most FC-SANs?

30 Does FC currently support automation of link aggregation?

31 What determines the sequence of events during extended FC link initialization?

Upon completing this chapter, you will be able to:

- Draw parallels between common data-link layer terms and network layer terms
- Describe the mapping of IP onto Ethernet and Point-to-Point Protocol (PPP)
- Relate the IPv4 addressing scheme to the SCSI architecture model (SAM) addressing scheme
- Differentiate between the IP naming scheme and the SAM naming scheme
- Explain how IP address assignment works
- Delineate the logical and virtual network boundaries observed by IP
- Deconstruct the packet formats of ICMP and IP
- Enumerate and describe the delivery mechanisms supported by IP
- Describe the relationship of Internet Control Message Protocol (ICMP) to IP
- List the initialization steps required for IP communication

CHAPTER 6

OSI Network Layer

This chapter provides an in-depth review of the operational details of the Internet Protocol (IP).

Internet Protocol

IP is the most ubiquitous network layer protocol in the world. IP's robust support of data-link layer technologies, ability to service multiple transport layer protocols, and functional extensibility have contributed largely to its success. Leveraging IP to transport Small Computer System Interface (SCSI) was inevitable once SCSI was adapted to serial networking technologies.

IPv4 Overview

IP is an open protocol that facilitates network layer communication across internetworks in a packet-switched manner. One or more of the underlying data-link layer networks may operate in a circuit-switched manner, but IP operation at the network layer remains packet-switched. IP provides just the functionality required to deliver packets from a source device to a destination device. Even path determination is left to other network layer protocols called *routing* protocols (see Chapter 10, "Routing and Switching Protocols"). Thus, IP is a *routed* protocol. Likewise, IP relies on other network layer protocols for data confidentiality (see the IPsec section of Chapter 12, "Storage Network Security") and control messaging (see the ICMP section of this chapter).

IPv4 is currently the most widely deployed version of IP. A newer version has been developed (IPv6), but it is not yet widely deployed. IP version numbers are somewhat misleading. The IP header contains a field that identifies the protocol version number. Valid values are 0 through 15. Version numbers 0 and 1 were once assigned to the first and second revisions of a protocol that combined transport layer and network layer functionality. With the third revision, the combined protocol was separated into TCP and IP. That revision of IP was assigned the next available version number (2). Two more revisions of IP were produced and assigned version numbers 3 and 4. When the next revision of IP was pro-duced, it was decided that the version numbers should be reassigned. Version 4 was reassigned to the latest revision of IP, which was the fourth revision of IP as an independent protocol. That revision is now commonly called IPv4. Version number 0 was reserved for intuitive reasons. Version numbers 1 through 3 were left unassigned. Note the first three independent revisions of IP were unstable and never adopted. Because the original two revisions of IP were actually a combined protocol, those revisions were not considered during version-number reassignment. Thus, IPv4 is really the first version of IP ever deployed as a standard protocol.

IPv4 originally was adopted via RFC 760. IPv4 has since been revised, but the protocol version number has not been incremented. Instead, the RFC numbering system is used to identify the current revision of IPv4. RFC 791 is the current revision of IPv4. Subsequent to IPv4 adoption, a completely different network layer protocol was developed by IETF and assigned protocol version number 5. When development of the next generation of IP was undertaken, the new protocol was assigned version number 6 (IPv6). Thus, IPv6 is really the second version of IP ever deployed as a standard protocol. IPv6 was revised multiple times before adoption and one time since adoption, but the protocol version number has not been incremented. Like IPv4, the current revision of IPv6 is tracked via RFC numbers. Originally adopted via RFC 1883, the current revision of IPv6 is RFC 2460.

Development of IPv6 was motivated primarily by the need to expand the address space of IPv4. To extend the life of IPv4 during development of IPv6, new techniques were developed to improve the efficiency of address consumption. Chief among these techniques are private addressing, Network Address Translation (NAT), and variable-length subnet masking (VLSM). These techniques have been so successful that they have significantly slowed adoption of IPv6. Because IPv6 is not yet used in storage networks, the remainder of this book focuses on IPv4 when discussing IP.

When discussing IP, it is customary to use the term *interface* rather than *port*. The purpose is to distinguish between the network layer functionality (the interface) and the data-link layer functionality (the port) in an IP-enabled device. For example, an Ethernet switch can contain a logical IP interface that is used for management access via any Ethernet port. We use customary IP terminology in this chapter when discussing switches or routers because SAM terminology does not apply to networking devices. Networking devices do not implement SCSI; they merely forward encapsulated SCSI packets. However, we use SAM terminology in this chapter when discussing end nodes, to maintain consistency with previous chapters. In the SAM context, an IP interface is a logical SAM port associated with a physical SAM port (such as Ethernet). We discuss this topic in detail in the addressing scheme section of this chapter.

The line between end nodes and networking devices is becoming fuzzy as hybrid devices enter the storage market. Hybrid devices implement SCSI but are installed in networking devices. For example, Cisco Systems produces a variety of storage virtualization modules that are deployed in the MDS9000 family of switches. These virtualization modules should be viewed as end nodes, whereas the MDS9000 switches should be viewed as networking devices. Further discussion of hybrid devices is outside the scope of this book, but readers should be aware of the distinction made herein to avoid confusion when planning the deployment of hybrid devices.

Another difference in terminology between data-link layer technologies and network layer technologies arises in the context of flow control and QoS. The term *buffer* is typically used when discussing data-link layer technologies, whereas the term *queue* is typically used when discussing network layer technologies. A buffer and a queue are essentially the same thing. That said, network layer technologies implement queue management policies that are far more sophisticated than data-link layer buffer management policies. For additional architectural information about the TCP/IP suite, readers are encouraged to consult IETF RFC 1180.

Data-Link Support

One of the most beneficial features of IP is its ability to operate on a very broad range of data-link layer technologies. The IETF is very diligent in adapting IP to new data-link layer technologies as they emerge. Of the many data link layer technologies supported, the most commonly deployed are Ethernet, PPP, high-level data-link control (HDLC), frame relay, asynchronous transfer mode (ATM), and multiprotocol label switching (MPLS). Most Internet Small Computer System Interface (iSCSI) deployments currently employ Ethernet end-to-end. Because Fibre Channel over TCP/IP (FCIP) is a point-to-point technology, most current deployments employ PPP over time-division multiplexing (TDM) circuits for WAN connectivity. Though Internet Fibre Channel Protocol (iFCP) supports mesh topologies, most deployments are currently configured as point-to-point connections that employ PPP over TDM circuits for WAN connectivity. Thus, we discuss only Ethernet and PPP in this section.

Ethernet

As discussed in Chapter 3, "Overview of Network Operating Principles," an Ethertype value is assigned to each protocol carried by Ethernet. Before the IEEE became the official authority for Ethertype assignments, Xerox Corporation fulfilled the role. Xerox assigned Ethertype 0x0800 to IP. When the IEEE took control, they listed many of the Ethertype values as assigned to Xerox. To this day, the IEEE listing of Ethertype assignments still shows 0x0800 assigned to Xerox. However, RFC 894 documents Ethertype 0x0800 as assigned to IP, and the public at large accepts RFC 894 as the final word on this issue. IANA maintains an unofficial listing of Ethertype assignments that properly shows 0x0800 assigned to IP. As discussed in Chapter 5, "OSI Physical and Data-Link Layers," Address Resolution Protocol (ARP) is used to resolve IP addresses to Ethernet addresses. Xerox assigned Ethertype 0x0806 to ARP, but this is not documented via RFC 894, and the IEEE Ethertype listing shows Xerox as the assignee for this value. The unofficial IANA listing of Ethertype assignments properly shows 0x0806 assigned to ARP.

The Ethernet padding mechanism discussed in Chapter 5, "OSI Physical and Data-Link Layers," is sometimes used for IP packets. The minimum size of an Ethernet frame is 64 bytes, but the 802.3-2002 header and trailer are only 18 bytes. The IP header (without options) is only 20 bytes, and there is no minimum length requirement for the payload of an IP packet. Some upper-layer protocols (ULPs) can generate IP packets with payloads less than 26 bytes. Examples include TCP during connection establishment and many ICMP messages. When this occurs, the minimum Ethernet frame length requirement is not met. So, Ethernet inserts padding when the IP packet is framed for transmission. The Ethernet padding is not part of the IP packet, so it does not affect any fields in the IP header.

PPP

In the early 1970s, IBM invented the Synchronous Data Link Control (SDLC) protocol to facilitate mainframe-to-peripheral communication. SDLC proved to be very effective, but it could not be used by open systems. So, IBM submitted SDLC to the ISO. In 1979, the ISO developed the HDLC protocol, which used SDLC's frame format, but differed from SDLC in operation. Like all protocols, HDLC has limitations. One of HDLC's limitations is lack of support for multiple ULPs. To address this and other shortcomings, the IETF developed PPP in 1989 based on HDLC. The original PPP frame format was derived from HDLC but was modified to support multiple ULPs. Each ULP is identified using an IANA-assigned 16-bit protocol number. The protocol number for IPv4 is 0x0021. PPP also enhances HDLC operationally in several ways. The most recent version of PPP is RFC 1661.

PPP is used on serial, point-to-point circuits that inherently provide in-order delivery. Modern storage networks that employ PPP typically do so on DS-1, DS-3, and Synchronous Optical Network (SONET) circuits. PPP consists of three components: a frame format definition, the Link Control Protocol (LCP), and a suite of Network Control Protocols (NCPs). The standard frame format can be used by all ULPs, or deviations from the standard frame format can be negotiated during connection establishment via LCP. LCP is also used to open and close connections, negotiate the MTU (can be symmetric or asymmetric), authenticate peer nodes, test link integrity, and detect configuration errors. Each ULP has its own NCP. An NCP is responsible for negotiating and configuring ULP operating parameters. The NCP for IP is called the IP Control Protocol (IPCP). IPCP was first defined in RFC 1134, which is the original PPP RFC. IPCP was later separated into its own RFC. The most recent version of IPCP is defined in RFC 1332. The PPP protocol number for IPCP is 0x8021. IPCP currently negotiates only four configuration parameters: header compression, IP address assignment, name server assignment, and mobility. Header compression on PPP links is designed for low-speed circuits used for dialup connectivity. Header compression is rarely used on high-speed circuits such as DS-1 and above. IP address assignment, name-server assignment, and mobility are designed for end nodes that require remote access to a network. None of these options apply to FCIP or iFCP deployments.

The original PPP frame format is shown in Figure 6-1.

Figure 6-1 *Original PPP Frame Format*

Length in Bytes	1	1	1	2	0–x	2 or 4	1
	Flag	Address	Control	Protocol	Information/Pad	Frame Check Sequence	Flag

The original PPP frame format has since been modified as shown in Figure 6-2.

Figure 6-2   *Current PPP Frame Format*

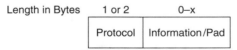

The new frame format allows PPP to be encapsulated easily within a wide variety of other data-link layer frames. This enables multi-protocol support in data-link layer technologies that do not natively support multiple ULPs. The new frame format also allows the leading byte of the protocol number to be omitted if the value is 0x00, which improves protocol efficiency. This improvement applies to IP. When PPP is used on DS-1, DS-3, and SONET circuits, HDLC framing is used to encapsulate the PPP frames. This is called PPP in HDLC-like Framing and is documented in RFC 1662. Some additional requirements apply to PPP when operating on SONET circuits, as documented in RFC 2615 and RFC 3255. Figure 6-3 illustrates PPP in HDLC-like Framing.

Figure 6-3   *PPP in HDLC-Like Framing*

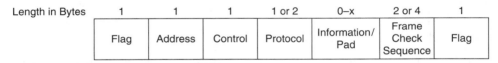

A brief description of each field follows:

- **Flag**—Each is 1 byte long. They are used to delimit frame boundaries.

- **Address**—1 byte long. It contains all ones, which is designated as the broadcast address. All PPP nodes must recognize and respond to the broadcast address.

- **Control**—1 byte long. It identifies the type of frame. For PPP in HDLC-like Framing, this field must contain the Unnumbered Information (UI) code 0x03.

- **Protocol**—Can be 1 or 2 bytes long. It contains the IANA-assigned identifier of the ULP.

- **Information/Pad**—Variable in length. It contains the ULP (for example, IP). This field also may contain pad bytes.

- **FCS**—Can be 2 or 4 bytes long. It contains a cyclic redundancy check (CRC) calculated on the address, control, protocol, and information/pad fields.

Addressing Scheme

IP does not implement an equivalent to SAM device or port names. However, IP does implement a naming mechanism that provides similar functionality to SAM port names under certain circumstances. The primary objective of the Domain Name System (DNS) is to allow a human-friendly name to be optionally assigned to each IP address. Doing so allows humans to use the DNS name of a port or interface instead of the IP address assigned to the port or interface. For example, DNS names usually are specified in web browsers rather than IP addresses. Even though this is a major benefit, it is not the function that SAM port names provide.

Another benefit is that DNS names facilitate persistent identification of ports in the context of dynamically assigned IP addresses. This is accomplished by statically assigning a name to each port within the host operating system, then dynamically registering each port name in DNS along with the IP address dynamically assigned to the port during the boot process. Each time a new IP address is assigned, the port name is re-registered. This permits a single DNS name to persistently identify a port, which is the function that SAM port names provide. However, DNS names are assigned to IP addresses rather than to ports, and IP addresses are routinely reassigned among many ports. Additionally, DNS name assignments are not guaranteed to be permanent. For example, it is possible to change the DNS name of an IP address that is assigned to a port and to reassign the old DNS name to a different IP address that is assigned to a different port. After doing so, the old DNS name no longer identifies the original port. Thus, the SAM port-name objective is not met. The primary purpose of a SAM port name is to positively and persistently identify a single port; therefore each name must be permanently assigned to a single port. It is also possible for a port to be assigned multiple IP addresses. Because each IP address is assigned its own DNS name, multiple DNS names can identify a single port. All these factors illustrate why DNS names are not analogous to SAM port names.

Likewise, DNS names are not analogous to SAM device names. Each host is assigned a host name in its operating system. The host name represents the host chassis and everything contained within it. Host names can be extended to DNS by using the host name as the DNS name of an IP address assigned to the host. That DNS name then represents the host chassis and everything contained within it. As such, that DNS name represents a superset of a SAM device name. Even when a DNS name represents just an IP address (not a host name) on a single-port interface with only one IP address, the DNS name is not analogous to a SAM device name. Because the primary purpose of a SAM device name is to positively and persistently identify a single interface (network interface card [NIC] or host bus adapter [HBA]), each name must be permanently assigned to a single interface. As outlined in the previous paragraph, DNS names do not comply with this requirement.

IP implements the equivalent of SAM port identifiers via IP addresses, which are used to forward packets. In the context of IP storage (IPS) protocols, a node's IP address and data-link layer address both provide SAM port identifier functionality. An IP address facilitates end-to-end forwarding of packets, and a data-link layer address facilitates forwarding of frames between IP interfaces and ports across a single link (in the case of PPP) or multiple links (in the case of Ethernet).

The IPv4 address format is very flexible and well documented in many books, white papers, product manuals, and RFCs. So this section provides only a brief review of the IPv4 address format for readers who do not have a strong networking background. To understand the current IPv4 address format, first it is useful to understand the IPv4 address format used in early implementations. Figure 6-4 illustrates the IPv4 address format used in early implementations as defined in RFC 791.

Figure 6-4   *Early IPv4 Address Format*

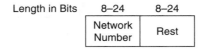

A brief description of each field follows:

- **The Network Number field** could be 1, 2, or 3 bytes long. It contained the address bits that routers used to forward packets. Three classes of networks were defined: A, B, and C. A class A network, identified by a single-byte network address, contained 16,777,216 addresses. A class B network was identified by a 2-byte network address. It contained 65,536 addresses. A class C network was identified by a 3-byte network address. It contained 256 addresses. The total length of an IPv4 address was always 4 bytes regardless of the class of network. In the first byte, a range of values was reserved for each class of network. This was known as a self-describing address format because the value of the network address described the class of the network. Self-describing addresses enabled IP routers to determine the correct number of bits (8, 16, or 24) to inspect when making forwarding decisions. This procedure was known as classful routing.

- **The Rest field** contained the address bits of individual interfaces and ports on each network. The length of the Rest field was determined by the class of the network. A class A network used a 3-byte Rest field. A class B network used a 2-byte Rest field. A class C network used a 1-byte Rest field. In all network classes, the value 0 was reserved in the Rest field as the identifier of the network itself. Likewise, the value equal to all ones in the Rest field was reserved as the broadcast address of the network.

This addressing scheme was called "classful" because the interpretation of addresses was determined by the network class. Network numbers were assigned by IANA to companies, government agencies, and other organizations as requested. As the assignment of network numbers continued, the Internet grew, and the limitations of classful addressing and routing were discovered. The primary concerns were the difficulty of scaling flat networks, the rate of address consumption, and degraded router performance. Organizations that had been assigned class A or B network numbers were struggling to scale their flat networks because of the effect of broadcast traffic. The finite supply of network numbers began to dwindle at an unforeseen pace, which raised concerns about future growth potential. Routing between organizations (a process called inter-domain routing) became problematic because route lookups and protocol convergence required more time to complete as routing tables grew. To resolve these issues, several changes were made to the addressing scheme, address allocation procedures, and routing processes.

One of the changes introduced was a method of segregating large networks into smaller networks called subnetworks or subnets. Subnetting limited the effect of broadcast traffic by creating multiple broadcast domains within each classful network. Before subnetting, each classful network represented a single IP broadcast domain. Class A and B networks experienced severe host and network performance degradation as the number of host attachments increased because

- Broadcast traffic was commonly used in the early days of IP.
- Each additional host attachment introduced additional broadcast traffic.
- Each host was (and still is) required to process each broadcast packet, which consumed processor time.
- Hosts had far less processing power in those days.
- Most networks were based on shared bandwidth data-link layer technologies.
- Each broadcast packet consumed bandwidth.

Another challenge resulted from data-link layer limitations. The most popular LAN technologies severely limited the number of hosts that could be attached to each segment. To accommodate the number of IP addresses available in class A and B networks, multiple LAN segments had to be bridged together. Disparate LAN technologies were often used, which created bridging challenges. Subnetting mitigated the need for bridging by enabling routers to connect the disparate LAN technologies.

Subnetting is accomplished via a masking technique. The subnet mask indicates the number of bits in the IPv4 address that make up the subnet address within each classful network. Subnet masking provides IP routers with a new way to determine the correct number of bits to inspect when making forwarding decisions. Initially, the subnet mask used within each classful network was fixed-length as described in RFC 950. In other words, a classful network could be subdivided into two subnets of equal size, or four subnets of equal size, or eight subnets of equal size, and so on. Figure 6-5 illustrates the subnetted classful IPv4 address format. Note that the total length of the address remained 4 bytes.

Figure 6-5   *Subnetted Classful IPv4 Address Format*

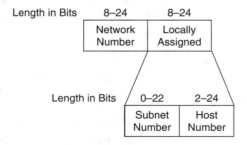

Fixed-length subnetting improved matters, but eventually proved to be less efficient than desired. So, the subnet masking technique was enhanced via RFC 1009 to allow variable-length masks. The new technique is called variable length subnet masking (VLSM). It permits extreme granularity in the allocation of subnets within a network. VLSM resolves the issues associated with scaling flat networks, but only partially resolves the issue of address consumption. So, RFC 1174 and RFC 1466 changed the way network numbers are assigned. Additionally, a method for translating addresses was defined in RFC 1631 (later updated by RFC 3022), and specific network numbers were reserved for "private" use via RFC 1918.

To complement these changes, the concept of address masking was extended to the network portion of the IPv4 address format via RFC 1338. This technique was originally called supernetting, but was later renamed classless inter-domain routing (CIDR) in RFC 1519. CIDR resolves the issues associated with degraded router performance by aggregating multiple contiguous network routes into a summary route. CIDR-enabled routers provide the same functionality as classful routers, but CIDR-enabled routers contain far fewer routes in their routing tables. Eventually, CIDR replaced classful addressing and routing. Today, IP addresses are called "classless" because the historically reserved network number ranges in the first byte no longer have meaning. When an organization is assigned a network number, it is also assigned a network prefix. A network prefix is conceptually similar to a subnet mask, but it indicates the number of bits that make up the network number as opposed to the number of bits that make up the network and subnet numbers. Prefix granularity is achieved by supporting 1-bit increments. CIDR complements VLSM; an organization may subnet its network if needed. Figure 6-6 illustrates the classless IPv4 address format. Note that the total length of the address is still 4 bytes.

Figure 6-6   *Classless IPv4 Address Format*

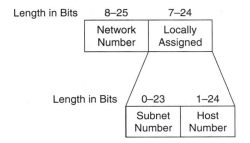

A brief description of each field follows:

- **The Network Number field**—variable in length. It contains the portion of the address that is assigned to individual organizations by the Internet authorities. No network number shorter than 8 bits is assigned to any organization, but CIDR-enabled routers can (and regularly do) make forwarding decisions using summary routes that are shorter than 8 bits. The longest network number assignment is typically 24 bits, but 25-bit network numbers can be assigned at the discretion of the Internet service provider (ISP) through which the assignee organization is connected.

- **The Subnet Number sub-field**—variable in length. It contains the portion of the Locally Assigned field that identifies each subnet within a network. Routers concatenate this sub-field with the Network Number field and use the concatenated bits to make forwarding decisions within a network. The length of this sub-field is indicated by extending the assigned network prefix. Subnetting is optional but strongly encouraged. The values of this field are administered by the assignee organization.

- **The Host Number sub-field**—variable in length. It contains the portion of the Locally Assigned field that identifies each interface and port within a subnet (or within a network if subnetting is not implemented). The values of this field are administered by the assignee organization.

IPv4 addresses are expressed in dotted decimal notation such as 172.45.9.36. A network prefix also can be expressed in dotted decimal notation, but it is called a network mask or netmask when expressed in this notation. The valid decimal values of a netmask are limited to a specific set of numbers that includes 0, 128, 192, 224, 240, 248, 252, 254, and 255. This results from the convention of masking network numbers in a bit-contiguous manner. In other words, the bits that make up a network number are always the leftmost contiguous bits of an IPv4 address. For example, the network number 172.45.8 is expressed as 172.45.8.0 netmask 255.255.248.0. All bit positions in the netmask that are set to 1 represent network number bit positions in the IPv4 address. Thus, 172.45.9.0 netmask 255.255.255.0 indicates the network number 172.45.9. Alternatively, 172.45.9.36 netmask 255.255.248.0 indicates IP address 172.45.9.36 within the 172.45.8 network. In the CIDR context, network prefixes are expressed as /*nn* where *nn* equals the number of leftmost contiguous bits in the IPv4 address that compose the network number. For example, 172.45.8.0/21 is the network prefix notation equivalent to 172.45.8.0 netmask 255.255.248.0. If subnetting is used within a network, the netmask and network prefix must be increased by the assignee organization to include the subnet bits within the Locally Assigned field of the IPv4 address. An extended netmask is called a subnet mask. Likewise, an extended network prefix is called a subnet prefix. To clarify the concepts introduced in this paragraph, Table 6-1 presents an example of dotted decimal notation with equivalent dotted binary notation.

Table 6-1   *IPv4 Address Expressed in Dotted Binary Notation*

Construct	Dotted Decimal Notation	Dotted Binary Notation
IPv4 Address	172.45.9.36	10101100.00101101.00001001.00100100
Netmask	255.255.248.0	11111111.11111111.11111000.00000000
Network Number	172.45.8.0	10101100.00101101.00001000.00000000

The preceding discussion of the IPv4 addressing scheme is highly simplified for the sake of brevity. Comprehensive exploration of the IPv4 addressing scheme is outside the scope of this book. For more information, readers are encouraged to consult IETF RFCs 791, 950, 1009, 1174, 1338, 1466, 1517, 1519, 1520, 1918, and 3022.

Name Assignment and Resolution

Because IP does not implement SAM device or port names, IP does not need SAM name assignment and resolution mechanisms. Each of the IPS protocols is responsible for implementing its own SAM device and port names (if required). Likewise, each of the IPS protocols is responsible for implementing its own SAM name assignment and resolution mechanisms (if required). Alternately, an external protocol may be leveraged for SAM name assignment and resolution. Chapter 8, "OSI Session, Presentation, and Application Layers," discusses the IPS protocols in detail.

As previously mentioned, DNS does not relate to SAM names. However, DNS is an integral component of every IP network, so network administrators undertaking IPS protocol deployment should have a basic understanding of DNS semantics and mechanics. Even though it is possible for system administrators to create static name-to-address mappings in the HOST table on each host, this is typically done only in special situations to accomplish a particular goal. Most name resolution is accomplished dynamically via DNS. DNS employs a hierarchical name space. Except for the lowest level, each level in the hierarchy corresponds to an administrative domain or sub-domain. The lowest level corresponds to individual nodes within a domain or sub-domain. The hierarchy appears as an inverted tree when diagrammed. The root is represented by the "." symbol. The "." symbol also follows the name of each level to signify the boundary between levels. For example, the DNS name "www.cisco.com." indicates the host port named "www" exists in the ".cisco" domain, which exists in the ".com" domain, which exists in the root domain. Note that the "." symbol does not precede "www", which indicates that "www" is a leaf (that is, an end node) in the DNS tree. In practice, the root symbol is omitted because all top-level domains (TLDs) inherently exist under the root, and TLD names are easily recognizable. The most common TLD names are .com, .net, .org, .edu, .gov, and .mil, but others are defined. TLDs are tightly restricted by IANA. The "." symbol is also omitted when referring to the name of an individual level in the hierarchy. For example, "www" exists in the "cisco" domain. Such name references are called unqualified names. A fully qualified domain name (FQDN) includes the full path from leaf to root such as "www.cisco.com".

DNS was designed to be extensible. DNS is used primarily to resolve names to IP addresses, but DNS can be used for other purposes. Each datum associated with a name is tagged to indicate the type of datum. New tags can be defined to extend the functionality of DNS. Indeed, many new tags have been defined since the inception of DNS. The DNS database is too large for the entire Internet to be served by a single DNS server. So, the DNS database is designed to be distributed. Each organization is responsible for and has authority over its own domain and sub-domains. This enables the overhead of creating and deleting DNS records to be distributed among all DNS participants. Each organization's DNS servers are authoritative for that organization's domain. As needed, each DNS server retrieves and temporarily caches foreign records from the authoritative DNS servers of foreign domains. This minimizes server memory requirements and network bandwidth requirements. When a DNS client queries the DNS, the query is usually sent to the topologically nearest DNS server. If a client queries a name that does not exist in the local domain (that is, the domain over which the local server has authority), then the local server queries the authoritative server of the domain directly above the local domain in the DNS hierarchy (called the parent domain). The reply contains the IP address of the authoritative server of the domain in which the queried name exists. The local DNS server then queries the authoritative server of the domain in which the queried name exists. Upon receiving a reply, the local server caches the record. The local server then sends a non-authoritative reply to the DNS client. For more information about DNS, readers are encouraged to consult IETF RFC 1034 and RFC 1035.

Address Assignment and Resolution

On the Internet, public network numbers are assigned to each organization by the ISP through which the organization connects. Ranges of network numbers (called CIDR blocks) are assigned to each ISP by their local Internet registry (LIR). LIRs receive CIDR block assignments from their national Internet registry (NIR). NIRs receive CIDR block assignments from their regional Internet registry (RIR). RIRs receive CIDR block assignments from IANA.

Private network numbers are also available to every organization. RFC 1918 addresses are known as non-routable addresses because no Internet routers are allowed to route to or from private network numbers. For a device using an RFC 1918 address in one network to communicate with a device using an RFC 1918 address in a different network, the private addresses must be translated into public addresses before forwarding packets on the Internet. Likewise, the public addresses must be translated back into private addresses before delivering packets to the end nodes. RFC 1918 reserves the following network numbers for use within each organization:

- 10.0.0.0/8 (10.0.0.0 - 10.255.255.255)
- 172.16.0.0/12 (172.16.0.0 - 172.31.255.255)
- 192.168.0.0/16 (192.168.0.0 - 192.168.255.255)

Within each network, the network number may be subnetted as desired. Subnetting is accomplished by manually configuring the appropriate subnet prefix on each router interface. Within each subnet, individual IP addresses can be statically or dynamically assigned. It is customary to manually configure each router interface with a statically assigned IP address. Although the same can be done for host ports, the preferred method is to automate the process using dynamically assigned addresses. Each host port requires at least three configuration parameters: an IP address, a subnet prefix, and a default gateway. The IP address of the default gateway is used to forward packets to destination addresses that are not connected to the local subnet. These three required parameters (and possibly many other optional parameters) usually are assigned to end nodes via DHCP.

Based on the Bootstrap Protocol (BOOTP), DHCP was originally defined in 1993 via RFC 1531. The most recent DHCP RFC is 2131, which is complemented by RFC 2132 (DHCP options). DHCP is a client-server protocol that employs a distributed database of configuration information. End nodes can access the DHCP database during and after the boot process. When booting, clients discover DHCP servers by transmitting a DHCPDISCOVER message to the local IP broadcast address of 255.255.255.255. DHCP clients do not have an IP address during the boot process, so they use 0.0.0.0 as their IP address until an IP address is assigned. Upon receiving a discovery message, a DHCP server replies with a DHCPOFFER message containing configuration parameters. The client then transmits a DHCPREQUEST message back to the server to accept the offered parameters. The server then replies with a DHCPACK message confirming that the requested parameters have been assigned to the client. The preceding description of DHCP is highly simplified. For more information about DHCP, readers are encouraged to consult IETF RFC 2131 and RFC 2132.

OSI Layer 4 protocols, such as TCP, do not facilitate forwarding of packets, so they do not implement network addresses. DNS names are resolved directly to IP addresses, which are in turn resolved to Ethernet or other data-link layer addresses. Thus, there is no need for an IP address resolution mechanism at OSI Layer 4.

Network Boundaries

An IP network can be logically or virtually bounded. Logical boundaries are delimited by interfaces in networking devices (such as routers, multilayer switches, and firewalls) and by ports in hosts. OSI Layer 3 control information can be transmitted between IP networks. When a router generates control information, it uses one of its own IP addresses as the source address in the header of the IP packets. When OSI Layer 3 control information is forwarded from one IP network to another, the IP packets are forwarded like user data packets. When user data packets are forwarded from one IP network to another, the source and destination IP addresses in the IP header are not modified, but a new data-link layer header and trailer are generated. If a network is subnetted, each subnet operates as an independent network. Figure 6-7 illustrates the logical boundaries of IP networks.

Figure 6-7 *Logical IP Network Boundaries*

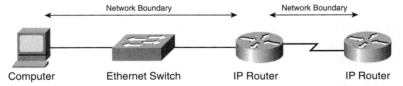

If multiple networks or subnets are configured on a single router interface, network/subnet independence is maintained by protocol behavior. This configuration represents a merit system and is discouraged. Independent operation of multiple networks or subnets on a single router interface can be enforced by creating sub-interfaces on the router interface. Each network or subnet is mapped onto a sub-interface, and each sub-interface is mapped onto a virtual network at the data-link layer (such as an Ethernet VLAN). The virtual network boundaries at the data-link layer then become the virtual network boundaries of the IP networks or subnets. Figure 6-8 illustrates the virtual boundaries of IP networks or subnets using Ethernet VLANs. The "router on a stick" configuration used during the early days of VLANs is shown because it visually depicts the network/subnet separation. However, this configuration is rarely used today. The best current practice (BCP) is a technique called "Layer 3 switching" that collapses the router functionality into the Ethernet switch.

Figure 6-8 *Virtual IP Network Boundaries*

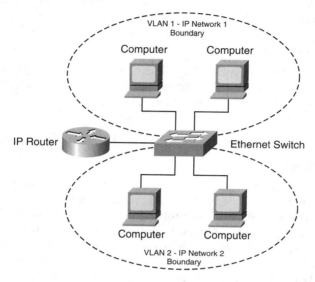

IP packets sent to the local broadcast address of 255.255.255.255 do not cross IP network boundaries. However, routers can be manually configured to convert local broadcast packets to unicast packets and forward the unicast packets. This is typically accomplished on a per-protocol basis. The ULP identifier and destination IP address must be configured on each router interface (or sub-interface) expected to receive and forward local broadcast packets. This configuration promotes service scalability in large environments by enabling organizations to centralize services that must otherwise be accessed via local broadcast packets. For example, an organization may choose to forward all DHCP broadcasts from every subnet to a centralized DHCP server.

In addition to the local broadcast address, IP packets can also be sent to a subnet broadcast address. This is called a directed broadcast because IP routers forward such packets to the destination subnet. No special configuration is required on any of the routers. Upon receiving a directed broadcast, the router connected to the destination subnet converts the packet to a local broadcast and then transmits the packet on the destination subnet. An example of a directed broadcast address is 172.45.9.255 for the subnet 172.45.9.0/24. Local broadcast packets can be forwarded to a directed broadcast address instead of a unicast address. This further promotes service scalability in large environments. For example, an organization that forwards all DHCP broadcasts from every subnet to a centralized DHCP server might overload the server. By using a directed broadcast, multiple DHCP servers can be connected to the destination subnet, and any available server can reply. DHCP and many other services are designed to support this configuration.

Packet Formats

IP uses a header but does not use a trailer. The IP header format defined in RFC 791 is still in use today, but some fields have been redefined. IP packets are word-oriented, and an IP word is 4 bytes. Figure 6-9 illustrates the current IP packet format.

Figure 6-9 *Current IP Packet Format*

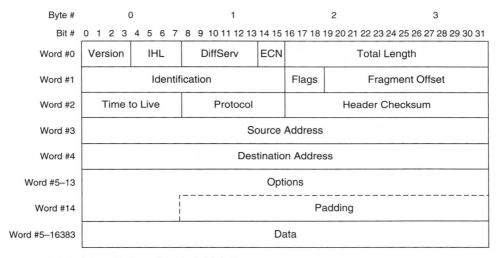

A brief description of each field follows:

- **The Version field**—4 bits long. It indicates the IP version number as previously discussed in this chapter. By parsing this field first, the format of the header can be determined.

- **The Internet Header Length (IHL) field**—4 bits long. It indicates the total length of the IP header expressed in 4-byte words. Valid values are 5 through 15. Thus, the minimum length of an IP header is 20 bytes, and the maximum length is 60 bytes. This field is necessary because the IP header length is variable due to the Options field.

- **The Differentiated Services (DiffServ) field**—6 bits long. It indicates the level of service that the packet should receive from each router. Each of the possible values of this field can be mapped to a QoS policy. Each mapping is called a differentiated services codepoint (DSCP). See Chapter 9, "Flow Control and Quality of Service," for more information about QoS in IP networks.

- **The Explicit Congestion Notification (ECN) field**—2 bits long. It reactively indicates to source nodes that congestion is being experienced. See Chapter 9, "Flow Control and Quality of Service," for more information about flow control in IP networks.

- **The Total Length field**—indicates the overall length of the packet (header plus data) expressed in bytes. An indication of the total packet length is required because the length of the Data field can vary. Because this field is 16 bits long, the maximum length of an IP packet is 65,536 bytes.

- **The Identification field**—16 bits long. It contains a value assigned to each packet by the source node. The value is unique within the context of each source address, destination address, and protocol combination. The value is used to associate fragments of a packet to aid reassembly at the destination node.

- **The Flags field**—3 bits long. It contains a reserved bit, the don't fragment (DF) bit and the more fragments (MF) bit. The DF bit indicates whether a packet may be fragmented by intermediate devices such as routers and firewalls. A value of 0 permits fragmentation, and a value of 1 requires that the packet be forwarded without fragmentation. The MF bit indicates whether a packet contains the final fragment. A value of 0 indicates either that the original packet is unfragmented, or the original packet is fragmented, and this packet contains the last fragment. A value of 1 indicates that the original packet is fragmented, and this packet does not contain the last fragment.

- **The Fragment Offset field**—indicates the offset of the data field in each fragment from the beginning of the data field in the original packet. This field is only 13 bits long, so the offset is expressed in 8-byte units to accommodate the maximum IP packet length. Thus, packets are fragmented on 8-byte boundaries. The minimum fragment length is 8 bytes except for the last fragment, which has no minimum length requirement.

- **The Time To Live (TTL) field**—8 bits long. The original intent of the TTL field was to measure the lifespan of each packet in 1-second increments. However, implementation of the TTL field as a clock proved to be impractical. So, the TTL field is now used to count the number of routers the packet may pass through (called hops) before the packet must be discarded. The value of this field is set by the source node, and each router decrements the value by 1 before forwarding the packet. By limiting the maximum number of hops, infinite forwarding of packets is avoided in the presence of routing loops.

- **The Protocol field**—8 bits long. It contains the number of the network layer protocol or ULP to which the data should be delivered. IANA assigns the IP protocol numbers. Some common network layer protocols are ICMP (protocol 1), Enhanced Interior Gateway Routing Protocol (EIGRP) (protocol 88), and Open Shortest Path First (OSPF) (protocol 89). The most common ULPs are TCP (protocol 6) and UDP (protocol 17).

- **The Header Checksum field**—16 bits long. It contains a checksum that is calculated on all header fields. The value of the checksum field is 0 for the purpose of calculating the checksum. The checksum must be recalculated by each router because the TTL field is modified by each router. Likewise, NAT devices must recalculate the checksum because the source or destination address fields are modified.

- **The Source Address field**—32 bits long. It contains the IP address of the source node.

- **The Destination Address field**—32 bits long. It contains the IP address of the destination node.

- **The Options field**—if present, contains one or more options. Options enable negotiation of security parameters, recording of timestamps generated by each router along a given path, specification of routes by source nodes, and so forth. Options vary in length, and the minimum length is 1 byte. The length of this field is variable, with no minimum length and a maximum length of 40 bytes.

- **The Padding field**—used to pad the header to the nearest 4-byte boundary. The length of this field is variable, with no minimum length and a maximum length of 3 bytes. This field is required only if the Options field is used, and the Options field does not end on a 4-byte boundary. If padding is used, the value of this field is set to 0.

- **The Data field**—if present, may contain another network layer protocol (such as ICMP or OSPF) or an ULP (such as TCP or UDP). The length of this field is variable, with no minimum length and a maximum length of 65,516 bytes.

The preceding field descriptions are simplified for the sake of clarity. For more information about the IPv4 packet format, readers are encouraged to consult IETF RFCs 791, 815, 1122, 1191, 1812, 2474, 2644, 3168, and 3260.

Delivery Mechanisms

IP supports only one set of delivery mechanisms that provide unacknowledged, connectionless service. Transport layer protocols compliment IP to provide other delivery services. IP implements the following delivery mechanisms:

- Because IP was not designed to provide reliable delivery, ICMP was created to provide a means of notifying source nodes of delivery failure. Under certain circumstances, IP must notify source nodes via ICMP when a packet is dropped. Examples include the PMTU discovery process, a TTL expiration, and a packet reassembly timeout. However, IP is not required to send notification to source nodes under all drop conditions. Examples include a queue overrun and an IP Header Checksum error. Additionally, IP does not detect packet drops resulting from external causes. Examples include an Ethernet CRC error and a malformed PPP frame resulting from SONET path failover. The IP process within a source node must notify the appropriate Network Layer protocol or ULP upon receipt of an ICMP error message that indicates a drop has occurred. In the absence of source node notification, detection of dropped packets is the responsibility of the network layer protocol or ULP that generated the packets. Additionally, the subsequent recovery behavior is determined by the network layer protocol or ULP that generated the packets.

- The fields in the IP header can facilitate detection of duplicate packets, but IP makes no effort to detect duplicates for two reasons. First, IP is not responsible for detection of duplicate packets. Second, the Identification field is not used by source nodes in a manner that guarantees that each duplicate is assigned the same identification number as the original packet. So, if a duplicate packet is received, IP delivers the packet to the appropriate network layer protocol or ULP in the normal manner. Detection of duplicates is the responsibility of the network layer protocol or ULP that generated the packets.

- IP devices can detect corrupt IP headers via the Header Checksum field, but IP devices cannot detect corruption in the Data field. Upon detection of a corrupt header, the packet is dropped.

- IP does not provide acknowledgement of successful packet delivery. Each network layer protocol and ULP is expected to define its own acknowledgement mechanism.

- IP does not support retransmission. Each network layer protocol and ULP is expected to define its own retransmission mechanism.

- IP supports four reactive mechanisms for network-level flow control. These include ICMP source-quench, tail-drop, active queue management (AQM), and ECN. ICMP source-quench packets can be generated by routers or destination hosts. When generated by destination hosts, ICMP source-quench packets constitute end-to-end network-level flow control. Tail-drop and AQM both involve dropping packets to trigger a TCP window reduction. ECN enables routers to explicitly notify end nodes via the ECN field in the IP header that congestion was experienced by the packet while in transit. See Chapter 9, "Flow Control and Quality of Service," for more information about flow control.

- Bandwidth is not guaranteed by default, but QoS mechanisms are defined that enable bandwidth guarantees to be implemented. See Chapter 9, "Flow Control and Quality of Service," for more information about QoS. Monitoring and trending of bandwidth utilization on shared links is required to ensure optimal network operation. Oversubscription on shared links must be carefully calculated to avoid bandwidth starvation during peak periods.

- Consistent latency is not guaranteed by default, but QoS mechanisms are defined that enable jitter to be minimized. See Chapter 9, "Flow Control and Quality of Service," for more information about QoS.

- As discussed in Chapter 5, "OSI Physical and Data-Link Layers," it is possible for an IP packet to traverse multiple data-link segments that support different MTU sizes. To handle this, all IP routers must support fragmentation of packets, and all hosts must support reassembly of fragmented packets. To avoid fragmentation, a method for discovering the PMTU is defined in RFC 1191. Routers are required to support RFC 1191. Hosts are encouraged but not required to support RFC 1191. When communication needs to be established to a destination node, the source node generates the first packet based on the local MTU and sets the DF bit to one in the IP header. If the packet needs to be fragmented by a router, the packet is dropped. The router then notifies the source node by sending an ICMP Destination-Unreachable packet. The MTU of the data-link segment that caused the drop is conveyed in the ICMP packet. The IP process within the source node then notifies the appropriate network layer protocol or ULP of the drop and conveys the constricting MTU information. The originating network layer protocol or ULP then segments the payload properly and retransmits. This process repeats until the destination node replies. Reassembly of fragmented packets within the destination node is implementation-specific and may use any of the fields in the IP header. The fields most likely to be used include Total Length, Identification, Fragment Offset, Protocol, Source Address, and Destination Address.

- In-order delivery is not guaranteed. IP does not support packet reordering. Each network layer protocol and ULP is expected to define its own out-of-order packet detection and reordering mechanism.

ICMP

As previously stated, ICMP compliments IP. ICMP is an integral part of IP, yet ICMP uses the services of IP for packet delivery. Figure 6-10 illustrates the architectural relationship of ICMP to IP.

Figure 6-10 *Architectural Relationship of ICMP to IP*

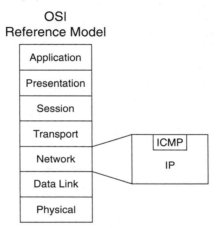

ICMP can be used for many purposes including error notification, congestion notification, route redirection, route verification, address discovery, and so on. Many ICMP message types are defined to accomplish these functions. A common packet format is defined for all ICMP message types. Figure 6-11 illustrates the ICMP packet format.

Figure 6-11 *ICMP Packet Format*

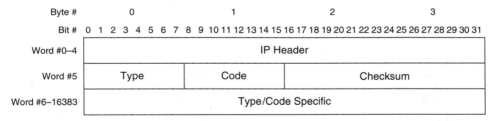

A brief description of each field follows:

- **The Type field** — 1 byte long. It indicates the type of ICMP message.
- **The Code field** — 1 byte long. It indicates the specific ICMP message within each type.
- **The Checksum field** — 2 bytes long. It contains a checksum that is calculated on all ICMP fields including the Type/Code Specific field. The value of the checksum field is zero for the purpose of calculating the checksum. If the total length of the ICMP packet is odd, one byte of padding is added to the Type/Code Specific field for the purpose of calculating the checksum. If padding is used, the value of the pad byte is set to zero.

- **The Type/Code Specific field** is variable in length. It contains additional fields that are defined specifically for each ICMP message.

Currently, 22 types of ICMP message are defined for IPv4. Of these, 15 are in widespread use today. Table 6-2 lists the currently defined ICMP message types for IPv4 and the codes associated with each message type.

Table 6-2 *IPv4 ICMP Message Types and Associated Codes*

Type	Type Description	Code	Code Description
0	Echo Reply	0	Default Code; No Specific Meaning
1–2	Unassigned	-	-
3	Destination Unreachable	0	Network Unreachable
		1	Host Unreachable
		2	Protocol Unreachable
		3	Port Unreachable
		4	Fragmentation Needed But DF Bit Set To One
		5	Source Route Failed
		6	Destination Network Unknown
		7	Destination Host Unknown
		8	Source Host Isolated
		9	Communication With Destination Network Administratively Prohibited
		10	Communication With Destination Host Administratively Prohibited
		11	Network Unreachable For Type of Service (ToS)
		12	Host Unreachable For ToS
4	Source Quench	0	Default Code; No Specific Meaning
5	Redirect	0	Network Redirect
		1	Host Redirect
		2	Network Redirect For ToS
		3	Host Redirect For ToS
6	Alternate Host Address; Not Used	-	-
7	Unassigned	-	-

Table 6-2   *IPv4 ICMP Message Types and Associated Codes (Continued)*

Type	Type Description	Code	Code Description
8	Echo Request	0	Default Code; No Specific Meaning
9	Router/Mobile Agent Advertisement	0	Normal Router
		16	Mobility Agent
10	Router/Mobile Agent Solicitation	0	Default Code; No Specific Meaning
11	Time Exceeded	0	TTL Exceeded In Transit
		1	Fragment Reassembly Time Exceeded
12	Parameter Problem	0	Pointer Field Indicates Erroneous IP Header Field
		1	Required Option Missing
13	Timestamp Request	0	Default Code; No Specific Meaning
14	Timestamp Reply	0	Default Code; No Specific Meaning
15	Information Request	0	Default Code; No Specific Meaning
16	Information Reply	0	Default Code; No Specific Meaning
17	Subnet Mask Request	0	Default Code; No Specific Meaning
18	Subnet Mask Reply	0	Default Code; No Specific Meaning
19–29	Unassigned	-	-
30	Traceroute; Not Used	-	-
31	Datagram Conversion Error; Not Used	-	-
32–36	Unassigned	-	-
37	Domain Name Request; Not Used	-	-
38	Domain Name Reply; Not Used	-	-
39	SKIP; Not Used	-	-
40	Security Failures; Not Used	-	-
41–255	Unassigned	-	-

Comprehensive exploration of all ICMP messages and their payloads is outside the scope of this book. For more information about ICMP, readers are encouraged to consult IETF RFCs 792, 950, 1122, 1256, 1812, and 3344.

Interface and Port Initialization

After a router (or other networking device) interface has been assigned an IP address and administratively enabled, it is ready to communicate with other IP devices. No special initialization procedures must be followed before communication. Likewise, no parameters must be exchanged between IP peers. This reflects the connectionless nature of IP. That said, certain routing protocols and ULPs implement initialization procedures, but the transmission of IP packets to facilitate those procedures does not require any initialization beyond address assignment. Aside from potentially different IP address assignment procedures, host ports can be viewed the same as router interfaces. That is, host ports can communicate with other IP devices immediately following IP address assignment.

Fibre Channel

As previously stated, Fibre Channel (FC) does not inherently provide any OSI Layer 3 functionality. However, the FC-BB specification series enables the use of other network technologies to connect geographically dispersed Fibre Channel storage area networks (FC-SANs). This is commonly called FC-SAN extension. Such extensions are often deployed for disaster recovery applications, and often leverage IP networks.

Summary

The Internet has a long history, which has culminated in a very robust protocol suite. With the advent of IPS protocols, storage network administrators now can leverage that robust protocol suite. An in-depth analysis of IP and ICMP is provided in this chapter to enable storage network administrators to understand the network layer functionality that underlies all IPS protocols. FC does not inherently provide any network layer functionality, so this chapter does not discuss FC. Chapter 7, "OSI Transport Layer," builds upon this chapter by exploring the transport layer functionality of TCP and UDP. Chapter 7 also explores the transport layer functionality of FC.

Review Questions

1 Is IP a routed protocol or a routing protocol?

2 What IP term is equivalent to buffer?

3 What is the Ethertype of IP?

4 Does Ethernet padding affect an IP packet?

5 What are the three components of PPP?

6 Which of the IPCP negotiated options affect FCIP and iFCP?

7   Are DNS names analogous to SAM port names?

8   What is the IP equivalent of a SAM port identifier?

9   What is the granularity of a CIDR prefix?

10   What is the network address of 56.93.17.23/21?

11   What is a non-authoritative DNS reply?

12   Why is NAT required for communication over the Internet between devices using RFC 1918 addresses?

13   How does a host locate available DHCP servers?

14   What enforces virtual IP network boundaries?

15   Why is the Version field the first field in the IP header?

16   What is the maximum length of the Data field in an IP packet?

17   Does IP support notification of drops?

18   How many flow-control mechanisms does IP support?

19   Does IP guarantee in-order delivery?

20   In which layer of the OSI Reference Model does ICMP reside?

21   What is the functional difference between the Type and Code fields in the ICMP header?

Upon completing this chapter, you will be able to:

- Explain the major differences between User Datagram Protocol (UDP) and Transmission Control Protocol (TCP)

- Describe the packet formats used by UDP and TCP

- Characterize each of the TCP options

- Recount the end-to-end delivery mechanisms provided by UDP and TCP

- Chronicle the steps of TCP connection initialization

- Compare and contrast Fibre Channel (FC) functionality to UDP and TCP functionality

- Discuss the frame format used by FC for connection establishment

- Annotate the end-to-end delivery mechanisms provided by FC

- Chronicle the FC connection initialization procedure

CHAPTER 7

OSI Transport Layer

This chapter provides an in-depth review of the operational details of UDP, TCP, and the FC N_Port Login (PLOGI) Extended Link Service (ELS) command.

TCP/IP Suite

As Chapter 6, "OSI Network Layer," stated, IP does not provide reliable delivery. IP delivers packets on a best-effort basis and provides notification of non-delivery in some situations. This is because not all applications require reliable delivery. Indeed, the nature of some applications suits them to unreliable delivery mechanisms. For example, a network management station (NMS) that must poll thousands of devices using the Simple Network Management Protocol (SNMP) could be heavily burdened by the overhead associated with reliable delivery. Additionally, the affect of dropped SNMP packets is negligible as long as the proportion of drops is low. So, SNMP uses unreliable delivery to promote NMS scalability. However, most applications require reliable delivery. So, the TCP/IP suite places the burden of reliable delivery on the transport layer and provides a choice of transport layer protocols. For unreliable delivery, UDP is used. For reliable delivery, TCP is used. This provides flexibility for applications to choose the transport layer protocol that best meets their delivery requirements. For additional architectural information about the TCP/IP suite, readers are encouraged to consult IETF RFC 1180.

UDP

When packet loss has little or no negative impact on an application, UDP can be used. Broadcast traffic is usually transmitted using UDP encapsulation (for example, DHCPDIS-COVER packets defined in IETF RFC 2131). Some unicast traffic also uses UDP encapsulation. Examples of UDP-based unicast traffic include SNMP commands and DNS queries.

UDP Operational Overview

UDP is connectionless. RFC 768 defines UDP, and RFC 1122 defines procedural requirements for UDP. RFC 768 defines the packet format, the packet-level error detection mechanism, and the minimum/maximum packet sizes. UDP leaves all other communication parameters to the upper-layer protocols (ULPs). Thus, UDP adds very little overhead to IP. The only services that UDP provides to ULPs are data-integrity validation (via checksum) and ULP multiplexing.

ULP multiplexing is accomplished by assigning a 16-bit identifier (called a port number) to each session layer protocol. Port numbers are conceptually similar to EtherTypes and PPP protocol numbers at the data-link layer, and IP protocol numbers at the network layer. Both UDP and TCP use port numbers to multiplex ULPs. When a port number is assigned to a session layer protocol, it is assigned for use by UDP and TCP. This is done for several reasons. One reason is that some session layer protocols use both UDP and TCP. For example, DNS uses UDP in most situations, but DNS can use TCP to pass through firewalls that block UDP traffic. Another reason is to simplify network management. For example, a session layer protocol that uses UDP today might be modified in the future to use TCP. If that session layer protocol's UDP port number is not reserved for use with TCP, a different session layer protocol could be assigned that TCP port number. This would require assignment of a new port number for the first session layer protocol to use TCP. This complicates firewall configuration, content switching, protocol decoding, and other network management tasks related to that session layer protocol. IANA manages the range of valid port numbers. The range of valid port numbers is 0 to 65,535. It is divided into the following three categories:

- Well known ports (WKPs) range from 0 to 1023 inclusive.
- Registered Ports range from 1024 to 49,151 inclusive.
- Dynamic Ports range from 49,152 to 65,535 inclusive.

TIP   The meaning of the term *port* varies depending on the context. Readers should not confuse the meaning of port in the context of UDP and TCP with the meaning of port in other contexts (such as switching hardware or the SAM addressing scheme).

IANA assigns WKPs. WKPs derive their name from their reserved status. Once IANA assigns a port number in the WKP range to a session layer protocol, that port number is reserved for use by only that session layer protocol. Assigned WKPs are used on servers to implement popular services for clients. By reserving port numbers for popular services, clients always know which port number to contact when requesting a service. For example, a server-based implementation of DNS "listens" for incoming client queries on UDP port 53. All unassigned WKPs are reserved by IANA and may not be used. IANA does not assign port numbers outside the WKP range. However, IANA maintains a public register of the server-based port numbers used by session layer protocols that have not been assigned a WKP. These are called Registered Ports. The third category is Dynamic Ports. It is used by clients when communicating with servers. Each session layer protocol within a client dynamically selects a port number in the Dynamic Port range upon initiating communication with a server. This facilitates server-to-client communication for the duration of the session. When the session ends, the Dynamic Port number is released and becomes available for reuse within the client.

UDP does not provide data segmentation, reassembly, or reordering for ULPs. So, ULPs that use UDP might suffer performance degradation due to IP fragmentation of large UDP packets. To avoid fragmentation, ULPs that use UDP are required to assess the maximum data segment size that can be transmitted. To facilitate this, UDP transparently provides Session Layer protocols access to the IP service interface. The session layer protocol in the source host queries UDP, which in turn queries IP to determine the local MTU. The session layer protocol then generates packets equal to or less than the local MTU, minus the overhead bytes of the IP and UDP headers. Alternately, path maximum transmission unit (PMTU) discovery can be used. The session layer protocol in the destination host must reorder and reassemble received segments using its own mechanism.

UDP Packet Formats

UDP offers a very limited set of services to ULPs, so the UDP packet format does not need to contain many fields. UDP uses a header but does not use a trailer. UDP packets are word-oriented, and an UDP word is 4 bytes. Figure 7-1 illustrates the UDP packet format.

Figure 7-1 *UDP Packet Format*

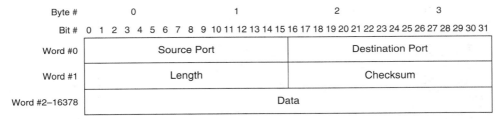

A brief description of each field follows:

- **Source Port** — 16 bits long. It indicates the port number of the session layer protocol within the transmitting host. The receiving host copies this value to the Destination Port field in reply packets.

- **Destination Port** — 16 bits long. It indicates the port number of the session layer protocol within the receiving host. This enables the receiving host to properly route incoming packets to the appropriate session layer protocol. The receiving host copies this value to the Source Port field in reply packets.

- **Length** — 16 bits long. It indicates the overall length of the packet (header plus data) expressed in bytes. Because this field is 16 bits long, the theoretical maximum length of a UDP packet is 65,536 bytes. The actual maximum length of a UDP packet is 65,516 bytes (the maximum size of the Data field in an IP packet).

- **Checksum** — 16 bits long. It contains a checksum that is calculated on the entire UDP packet prepended with a pseudo-header consisting of specific fields from the not-yet-generated IP header. The transport layer must inform the network layer where to send each packet, so certain information in the IP header is known to UDP (and TCP) before generation of the IP header. This enables UDP (and TCP) to generate the IP pseudo-header before calculating the checksum. Figure 7-2 illustrates the IP pseudo-header format. The IP pseudo-header is not transmitted as part of each packet. The IP pseudo-header does not include any IP header fields that are modified by IP routers during normal packet forwarding (such as the TTL field); therefore the UDP checksum does not need to be recalculated by each router. However, NAT devices must recalculate the checksum because they modify the source or destination IP address fields, which are included in the

IP pseudo-header. By including the destination IP address field in the IP pseudo-header, UDP (and TCP) provide protection against accidental delivery of packets to the wrong destination. If the UDP Data field does not end on a 16-bit boundary, it is padded with zeros for the purpose of calculating the checksum. The pad bits are not transmitted as part of each packet. The value of the checksum field is zero for the purpose of calculating the checksum. Many Ethernet NICs now calculate the checksum in hardware, which offloads the processing burden from the host's CPU. Note that use of the Checksum field is optional (unlike TCP). The transmitting host may choose to not calculate a checksum. In this case, the transmitted value of the Checksum field is 0.

- **Data** (if present) — variable in length. It contains an ULP (such as SNMP). The length of this field is variable with no minimum length and a maximum length of 65,508 bytes (65,536 bytes minus 20 bytes of IP header and 8 bytes of UDP header).

Figure 7-2   *IP Pseudo-Header Format*

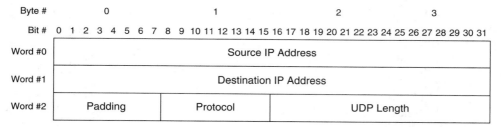

For more information about the UDP packet format, readers are encouraged to consult IETF RFCs 768 and 1122. A new variation of UDP (called UDP-Lite) is documented in RFC 3828. UDP-Lite is optimized for streaming media such as voice and video. As such, UDP-Lite is not applicable to modern storage networks. UDP-Lite is mentioned herein only to prevent confusion.

UDP Delivery Mechanisms

UDP supports only one set of delivery mechanisms that provide unacknowledged, connectionless service. Thus, UDP does not augment the delivery service provided by IP. UDP implements the following delivery mechanisms:

- UDP does not detect packets dropped in transit. When the UDP process within a destination host drops a packet because of checksum failure, UDP does not report the drop to the ULP or source host. When the UDP process within a destination host drops a packet because the destination port number is not active, IP may report the drop to the source host by transmitting an ICMP Type 3 Code 3 message. However, notification is not required. In the absence of notification, ULPs are expected to detect drops via their own mechanisms. Likewise, recovery behavior is determined by the ULP that generated the packets.

- UDP does not detect duplicate packets. If a duplicate packet is received, UDP delivers the packet to the appropriate ULP. ULPs are expected to detect duplicates via their own mechanisms.

- UDP can detect corrupt packets via the Checksum field. Upon detection of a corrupt packet, the packet is dropped.
- UDP does not provide acknowledgement of successful packet delivery. Each ULP is expected to define its own acknowledgement mechanism (if required).
- UDP does not provide retransmission. Each ULP is expected to define its own retransmission mechanism (if required).
- UDP does not provide end-to-end flow control.
- Guaranteeing reserved bandwidth is not a transport layer function. UDP relies on QoS policies implemented by IP for bandwidth guarantees.
- Guaranteeing fixed or minimal latency is not a transport layer function. UDP relies on QoS policies implemented by IP for latency guarantees.
- Fragmentation and reassembly is not a transport layer function. UDP relies on IP for fragmentation and reassembly. To avoid fragmentation, UDP supports PMTU discovery as defined in RFC 1191 by providing ULPs access to the IP service interface. When UDP is notified of a drop via an ICMP Type 3 Code 4 message, the constricting MTU information is passed to the appropriate ULP. The ULP is responsible for resegmenting and retransmitting the data.
- UDP does not guarantee in-order delivery. UDP does not provide packet reordering. Each ULP is expected to define its own out-of-order packet detection and reordering mechanism (if required).

For more information about UDP delivery mechanisms, readers are encouraged to consult IETF RFCs 768, 1122, and 1180.

UDP Connection Initialization

No UDP parameters are exchanged between hosts before communication. This reflects the connectionless nature of UDP.

TCP

When packet loss affects an application negatively, TCP is used. Most unicast traffic uses TCP encapsulation.

TCP Operational Overview

TCP is connection-oriented. Each TCP connection comprises a full-duplex virtual-circuit between a pair of end nodes. Like UDP, TCP provides data integrity validation (via checksum) and ULP multiplexing services (via port numbers). Unlike UDP, TCP provides data segmentation and reordering services, and several end-to-end delivery guarantees to ULPs. RFC 793 defines TCP, whereas RFC 1122 defines procedural requirements for TCP. RFC 793 defines the packet format, minimum and maximum packet sizes, error detection and recovery mechanisms (including a method of packet-loss detection and a procedure for packet retransmission), a flow-control mechanism, connection establishment/maintenance/ teardown procedures, a packet reordering mechanism, and timeout values.

TCP packetizes and transmits data as TCP sees fit. In other words, data received from a ULP may or may not be sent immediately, and separate transmission requests may or may not be aggregated by TCP. For example, a message-based ULP (such as iSCSI) can pass multiple discrete "chunks" of data to TCP. These data chunks are called Protocol Data Units (PDUs). TCP may aggregate multiple PDUs into a single packet for transmission (subject to PMTU constraints).

Likewise, when an ULP passes to TCP a PDU that exceeds the PMTU, TCP may segment and transmit the PDU when and how TCP sees fit. This is known as byte streaming. To TCP, each ULP is the source of a stream of bytes. At the receiving host, TCP does not reassemble segments per se. Because TCP does not segment ULP data as discrete PDUs, TCP cannot reassemble segments into discrete PDUs. So, TCP in a receiving host merely ensures the proper order of received segments before passing data to a ULP. The ULP in the receiving host is responsible for detecting the boundaries between PDUs. Note that TCP in a receiving host may delay passing data to a ULP even when all segments are properly ordered. Sometimes this is done to improve buffer management efficiency. However, a mechanism (the Push bit) is defined to enable ULPs in the transmitting host to instruct TCP in both the transmitting and receiving hosts to immediately forward data (see Chapter 9, "Flow Control and Quality of Service"). In other words, the first PDU received from the ULP may be held by TCP while TCP waits for additional PDUs from the ULP. TCP does not recognize and process data received from a ULP as discrete PDUs.

TCP supports an optional keep-alive mechanism to maintain an open connection during periods of inactivity. The keep-alive mechanism is not included in RFC 793, so RFC 1122 addresses the need for a keep-alive mechanism. RFC 1122 requires the inactivity timer to be configurable. So, most modern TCP implementations support an inactivity timer ranging from a few seconds to many hours. Network administrators determine the optimum value for the inactivity timer based on specific deployment requirements. The TCP keep-alive mechanism works by transmitting an invalid packet, which elicits an acknowledgement packet from the peer host. The transmitting host indicates via the Sequence Number field that it is ready to transmit a byte of data that has already been acknowledged by the peer host. The keep-alive packet contains no data. Upon processing the keep-alive packet, the peer host detects the error in the Sequence Number field and retransmits the most recent acknowledgement packet. This two-packet exchange implicitly notifies each host that the connection is still valid. If the connection is no longer valid, the receiving host returns a reset packet to the transmitting host.

Multiple simultaneous TCP connections can be open between each pair of hosts. In fact, this is required when multiple ULPs are communicating because ULPs may not share a TCP connection. The combination of a TCP port number and an IP address is called a socket. Each TCP connection is uniquely identified by the pair of communicating sockets. This enables each host to use a single socket to communicate simultaneously with multiple remote sockets without confusing the connections. In the context of traditional IP networks, this is common in server implementations. In the context of storage networks, this is common in storage implementations. For example, an iSCSI target (storage array) may use a single socket to conduct multiple simultaneous sessions with several iSCSI initiators (hosts). The storage array's iSCSI socket is reused over time as new sessions are established.

Clients may also reuse sockets. For example, a single-homed host may select TCP port 55,160 to open a TCP connection for file transfer via FTP. Upon completing the file transfer, the client may terminate the TCP connection and reuse TCP port 55,160 for a new TCP connection. Reuse of Dynamic Ports is necessary because the range of Dynamic Ports is finite and would otherwise eventually exhaust. A potential problem arises from reusing sockets. If a client uses a given socket to connect to a given server socket more than once, the first incarnation of the connection cannot be distinguished from the second incarnation. Reincarnated TCP connections can also result from certain types of software crashes. TCP implements multiple mechanisms that work together to resolve the issue of reincarnated TCP connections. Note that each TCP host can open multiple simultaneous connections with a single peer host by selecting a unique Dynamic Port number for each connection.

TCP Packet Formats

TCP offers a rich set of services to ULPs, so the TCP packet format is quite complex compared to UDP. TCP uses a header but does not use a trailer. The TCP header format defined in RFC 793 is still in use today, but some fields have been redefined. TCP packets are word-oriented, and a TCP word is 4 bytes. Figure 7-3 illustrates the TCP packet format.

Figure 7-3   *TCP Packet Format*

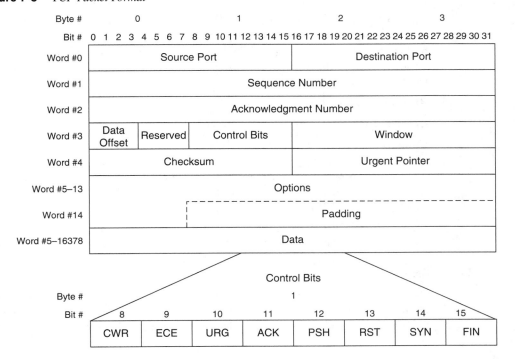

A brief description of each field follows:

- **Source Port**—16 bits long. It indicates the port number of the session layer protocol within the transmitting host. The receiving host copies this value to the Destination Port field in reply packets.

- **Destination Port**—16 bits long. It indicates the port number of the session layer protocol within the receiving host. This enables the receiving host to properly route incoming packets to the appropriate session layer protocol. The receiving host copies this value to the Source Port field in reply packets.

- **Sequence Number**—32 bits long. It contains the sequence number of the first byte in the Data field. TCP consecutively assigns a sequence number to each data byte that is transmitted. Sequence numbers are unique only within the context of a single connection. Over the life of a connection, this field represents an increasing counter of all data bytes transmitted. The Sequence Number field facilitates detection of dropped and duplicate packets, and reordering of packets. The purpose and use of the TCP Sequence Number field should not be confused with the FC Sequence_Identifier (SEQ_ID) field.

- **Acknowledgement Number**—32 bits long. It contains the sequence number of the next byte of data that the receiving host expects. This field acknowledges that all data bytes up to (but not including) the Acknowledgement Number have been received. This technique is known as cumulative acknowledgement. This field facilitates flow control and retransmission. This field is meaningful only when the ACK bit is set to 1.

- **Data Offset** (also known as the TCP Header Length field)—4 bits long. It indicates the total length of the TCP header expressed in 4-byte words. This field is necessary because the TCP header length is variable due to the Options field. Valid values are 5 through 15. Thus, the minimum length of a TCP header is 20 bytes, and the maximum length is 60 bytes.

- **Reserved**—4 bits long.

- **Control Bits**—8 bits long and contains eight sub-fields.

- **Congestion Window Reduced (CWR) bit**—when set to 1, it informs the receiving host that the transmitting host has reduced the size of its congestion window. This bit facilitates flow control in networks that support explicit congestion notification (ECN). See Chapter 9, "Flow Control and Quality of Service," for more information about flow control in IP networks.

- **ECN Echo (ECE) bit**—when set to 1, it informs the transmitting host that the receiving host received notification of congestion from an intermediate router. This bit works in conjunction with the CWR bit. See Chapter 9, "Flow Control and Quality of Service," for more information about flow control in IP networks.

- **Urgent (URG) bit**—when set to 1, it indicates the presence of urgent data in the Data field. Urgent data may fill part or all of the Data field. The definition of "urgent" is left to ULPs. In other words, the ULP in the source host determines whether to mark data urgent. The ULP in the destination host determines what action to take upon receipt of urgent data. This bit works in conjunction with the Urgent Pointer field.

- **Acknowledgement (ACK) bit**—when set to 1, it indicates that the Acknowledgement Number field is meaningful.

- **Push (PSH) bit**—when set to 1, it instructs TCP to act immediately. In the source host, this bit forces TCP to immediately transmit data received from all ULPs. In the destination host, this bit forces TCP to immediately process packets and forward the data to the appropriate ULP. When an ULP requests termination of an open connection, the push function is implied. Likewise, when a packet is received with the FIN bit set to 1, the push function is implied.

- **Reset (RST) bit**—when set to 1, it indicates a request to reset the connection. This bit is used to recover from communication errors such as invalid connection requests, invalid protocol parameters, and so on. A connection reset results in abrupt termination of the connection without preservation of state or in-flight data.

- **Synchronize (SYN) bit**—when set to 1, it indicates a new connection request. Connection establishment is discussed in the following Parameter Exchange section.

- **Final (FIN) bit**—when set to 1, it indicates a connection termination request.

- **Window**—16 bits long. It indicates the current size (expressed in bytes) of the transmitting host's receive buffer. The size of the receive buffer fluctuates as packets are received and processed, so the value of the Window field also fluctuates. For this reason, the TCP flow-control mechanism is called a "sliding window." This field works in conjunction with the Acknowledgement Number field.

- **Checksum**—16 bits long. It is used in an identical manner to the UDP Checksum field. Unlike UDP, TCP requires use of the Checksum field. The TCP header does not have a Length field, so the TCP length must be calculated for inclusion in the IP pseudo-header.

- **Urgent Pointer**—16 bits long. It contains a number that represents an offset from the current Sequence Number. The offset marks the last byte of urgent data in the Data field. This field is meaningful only when the URG bit is set to 1.

- **Options**—if present, it is variable in length with no minimum length and a maximum length of 40 bytes. This field can contain one or more options. Individual options vary in length, and the minimum length is 1 byte. Options enable discovery of the remote host's maximum segment size (MSS), negotiation of selective acknowledgement (SACK), and so forth. The following section discusses TCP options in detail.

- **Padding**—variable in length with no minimum length and a maximum length of 3 bytes. This field is used to pad the header to the nearest 4-byte boundary. This field is required only if the Options field is used, and the Options field does not end on a 4-byte boundary. If padding is used, the value of this field is set to 0.

- **Data**—if present, it is variable in length with no minimum length and a maximum length of 65,496 bytes (65,536 bytes minus 20 bytes of IP header and 20 bytes of TCP header). This field contains ULP data (such as FCIP).

The preceding descriptions of the TCP header fields are simplified for the sake of clarity. For more information about the TCP packet format, readers are encouraged to consult IETF RFCs 793, 1122, 1323, and 3168.

TCP Options

TCP options can be comprised of a single byte or multiple bytes. All multi-byte options use a common format. Figure 7-4 illustrates the format of TCP multi-byte options.

Figure 7-4 *TCP Multi-Byte Option Format*

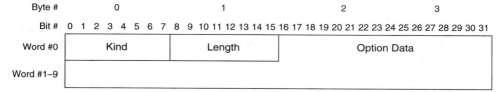

A brief description of each field follows:

- **Kind**—8 bits long. It indicates the kind of option.
- **Length**—8 bits long. It indicates the total length of the option (including the Kind and Length fields) expressed in bytes.
- **Option Data**—if present, it is variable in length and contains option-specific data. The format of this sub-field is determined by the kind of option.

Table 7-1 lists the currently defined TCP options that are in widespread use.

Table 7-1 *TCP Options*

Kind	Length In Bytes	Description
0	1	End of Option List (Pad)
1	1	No-Operation (No-Op)
2	4	Maximum Segment Size (MSS)
3	3	Window Scale (WSopt)
4	2	SACK-Permitted
5	Variable From 10–34	SACK
8	10	Timestamps (TSopt)
19	18	MD5 Signature

Of the options listed in Table 7-1, only the MSS, WSopt, SACK-Permitted, SACK, and TSopt are relevant to modern storage networks. So, only these options are discussed in detail in this section.

Maximum Segment Size

The maximum segment size (MSS) option is closely related to PMTU discovery. Recall that TCP *segments* ULP data before packetizing it. MSS refers to the maximum amount of ULP data that TCP can packetize and depacketize. While this could be limited by some aspect of the TCP software implementation, it is usually limited by the theoretical maximum size of the Data field in a TCP packet (65,496 bytes). Each host can advertise its MSS to the peer host during connection establishment to avoid unnecessary segmentation. Note that the MSS option may be sent only during connection establishment, so the advertised MSS value cannot be changed during the life of an open connection. If the theoretical MSS is advertised, the peer host can send TCP packets that each contain up to 65,496 bytes of ULP data. This would result in severe fragmentation of packets at the network layer due to the ubiquity of Ethernet. So, the best current practice (BCP) is to advertise an MSS equal to the local MTU minus 40 bytes (20 bytes for the IP header and 20 bytes for the TCP header). This practice avoids unnecessary fragmentation while simultaneously avoiding unnecessary segmentation. If a host implements PMTU discovery, TCP uses the lesser of the discovered PMTU and the peer's advertised MSS when segmenting ULP data for transmission. Figure 7-5 illustrates the MSS option format.

Figure 7-5   *TCP Maximum Segment Size Option Format*

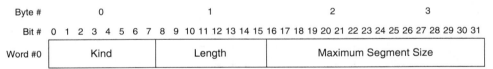

A brief description of each field follows:

- **Kind**—set to 2.
- **Length**—set to 4.
- **Maximum Segment Size**—16 bits long. It indicates the largest segment size that the sender of this option is willing to accept. The value is expressed in bytes.

Window Scale

One drawback of all proactive flow control mechanisms is that they limit throughput based on the amount of available receive buffers. As previously stated, a host may not transmit when the receiving host is out of buffers. To understand the effect of this requirement on throughput, it helps to consider a host that has enough buffer memory to receive only one packet. The transmitting host must wait for an indication that each transmitted packet has been processed before transmitting an additional packet. This requires one round-trip per transmitted packet. While the transmitting host is waiting for an indication that the receive buffer is available, it cannot transmit additional packets, and the available bandwidth is unused. So, the amount of buffer memory required to sustain maximum throughput can be calculated as:

Bandwidth * Round-trip time (RTT)

where bandwidth is expressed in bytes per second, and RTT is expressed in seconds. This is known as the bandwidth-delay product. Although this simple equation does not account for the protocol overhead of lower-layer protocols, it does provide a reasonably accurate estimate of the TCP memory requirement to maximize throughput.

As TCP/IP matured and became widely deployed, the maximum window size that could be advertised via the Window field proved to be inadequate in some environments. So-called long fat networks (LFNs), which combine very long distance with high bandwidth, became common as the Internet and corporate intranets grew. LFNs often exceed the original design parameters of TCP, so a method of increasing the maximum window size is needed. The Window Scale option (WSopt) was developed to resolve this issue. WSopt works by shifting the bit positions in the Window field to omit the least significant bit(s). To derive the peer host's correct window size, each host applies a multiplier to the window size advertisement in each packet received from the peer host. Figure 7-6 illustrates the WSopt format.

Figure 7-6   *TCP Window Scale Option Format*

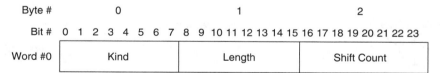

A brief description of each field follows:

- **Kind**—set to 3.
- **Length**—set to 3.
- **Shift Count**—8 bits long. It indicates how many bit positions the Window field is shifted. This is called the scale factor.

Both hosts must send WSopt for window scaling to be enabled on a connection. Sending this option indicates that the sender can both send and receive scaled Window fields. Note that WSopt may be sent only during connection establishment, so window scaling cannot be enabled during the life of an open connection.

Selective Acknowledgement

TCP's cumulative acknowledgement mechanism has limitations that affect performance negatively. As a result, an optional selective acknowledgement mechanism was developed. The principal drawback of TCP's cumulative acknowledgement mechanism is that only contiguous data bytes can be acknowledged. If multiple packets containing non-contiguous data bytes are received, the non-contiguous data is buffered until the lowest gap is filled by subsequently received packets. However, the receiving host can acknowledge only the highest sequence number of the received contiguous bytes. So, the transmitting host must wait for the retransmit timer to expire before retransmitting the unacknowledged bytes. At that time, the transmitting host retransmits all unacknowledged bytes for which the retransmit timer has expired. This often results in unnecessary retransmission of some bytes that were successfully received at the destination. Also, when multiple packets are dropped, this procedure can require multiple roundtrips to fill all the gaps in the receiving host's buffer. To resolve these deficiencies, TCP's optional SACK mechanism enables a receiving host to acknowledge receipt of non-contiguous data bytes. This enables the transmitting host to retransmit multiple packets at once, with each containing non-contiguous data needed to fill the gaps in the receiving host's buffer. By precluding the wait for the retransmit timer to expire, retransmitting only the missing data, and eliminating multiple roundtrips from the recovery procedure, throughput is maximized.

SACK is implemented via two TCP options. The first option is called SACK-Permitted and may be sent only during connection establishment. The SACK-Permitted option informs the peer host that SACK is supported by the transmitting host. To enable SACK, both hosts must include this option in the initial packets transmitted during connection establishment. Figure 7-7 illustrates the format of the SACK-Permitted option.

Figure 7-7 *TCP SACK-Permitted Option Format*

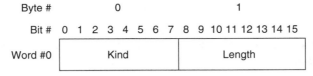

A brief description of each field follows:

- **Kind**—set to 4.
- **Length**—set to 2.

After the connection is established, the second option may be used. The second option is called the SACK option. It contains information about the data that has been received. Figure 7-8 illustrates the format of the SACK option.

Figure 7-8   *TCP SACK Option Format*

Byte #	0	1	2	3

Bit #	0 1 2 3 4 5 6 7	8 9 10 11 12 13 14 15	16 17 18 19 20 21 22 23 24 25 26 27 28 29 30 31
Word #0	Kind	Length	Left Edge of Block 1
Word #1	Left Edge of Block 1		Right Edge of Block 1
Word #2	Right Edge of Block 1		Left Edge of Block 2
Word #3	Left Edge of Block 2		Right Edge of Block 2
Word #4	Right Edge of Block 2		Left Edge of Block 3
Word #5	Left Edge of Block 3		Right Edge of Block 3
Word #6	Right Edge of Block 3		Left Edge of Block 4
Word #7	Left Edge of Block 4		Right Edge of Block 4
Word #8	Right Edge of Block 4		

A brief description of each field follows:

- **Kind**—set to 5.
- **Length**—set to 10, 18, 26, or 34, depending on how many blocks are conveyed. The requesting host decides how many blocks to convey in each packet.
- **Left Edge of Block "X"**—32 bits long. It contains the sequence number of the first byte of data in this block.
- **Right Edge of Block "X"**—32 bits long. It contains the sequence number of the first byte of missing data that follows this block.

TCP's SACK mechanism complements TCP's cumulative ACK mechanism. When the lowest gap in the receive buffer has been filled, the receiving host updates the Acknowledgement Number field in the next packet transmitted. Note that TCP's SACK mechanism provides an explicit ACK for received data bytes currently in the receive buffer, and an explicit NACK for data bytes currently missing from the receive buffer. This contrasts TCP's cumulative ACK mechanism, which provides an implicit ACK for all received data bytes while providing an implicit NACK for all missing data bytes except the byte referenced in the Acknowledgement Number field. Note also the difference in granularity between the retransmission procedures of TCP and FC. Whereas TCP supports retransmission of individual packets, the finest granularity of retransmission in FC is a sequence.

Timestamps

The Timestamps option (TSopt) provides two functions. TSopt augments TCP's traditional duplicate packet detection mechanism and improves TCP's RTT estimation in LFN environments. TSopt may be sent during connection establishment to inform the peer host that timestamps are supported. If TSopt is received during connection establishment, timestamps may be sent in subsequent packets on that connection. Both hosts must support TSopt for timestamps to be used on a connection.

As previously stated, a TCP connection may be reincarnated. Reliable detection of duplicate packets can be challenging in the presence of reincarnated TCP connections. TSopt provides a way to detect duplicates from previous incarnations of a TCP connection. This topic is discussed fully in the following section on duplicate detection.

TCP implements a retransmission timer so that unacknowledged data can be retransmitted within a useful timeframe. When the timer expires, a retransmission time-out (RTO) occurs, and the unacknowledged data is retransmitted. The length of the retransmission timer is derived from the mean RTT. If the RTT is estimated too high, retransmissions are delayed. If the RTT is estimated too low, unnecessary retransmissions occur. The traditional method of gauging the RTT is to time one packet per window of transmitted data. This method works well for small windows (that is, for short distance and low bandwidth), but severely inaccurate RTT estimates can result from this method in LFN environments. To accurately measure the RTT, TSopt may be sent in every packet. This enables TCP to make real-time adjustments to the retransmission timer based on changing conditions within the network (such as fluctuating levels of congestion, route changes, and so on). Figure 7-9 illustrates the TSopt format.

Figure 7-9 *TCP Timestamps Option Format*

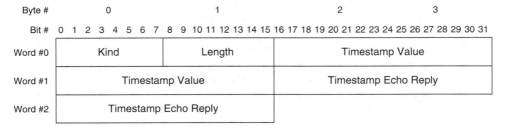

A brief description of each field follows:

- **Kind**—set to 8.
- **Length**—set to 10.
- **Timestamp Value (TSval)**—32 bits long. It records the time at which the packet is transmitted. This value is expressed in a unit of time determined by the transmitting host. The unit of time is usually seconds or milliseconds.
- **Timestamp Echo Reply (TSecr)**—32 bits long. It is used to return the TSval field to the peer host. Each host copies the most recently received TSval field into the TSecr

field when transmitting a packet. Copying the peer host's TSval field eliminates the need for clock synchronization between the hosts.

The preceding descriptions of the TCP options are simplified for the sake of clarity. For more information about the TCP option formats, readers are encouraged to consult IETF RFCs 793, 1122, 1323, 2018, 2385, and 2883.

TCP Delivery Mechanisms

TCP supports only one set of delivery mechanisms that provide acknowledged, connection-oriented service. Thus, TCP augments the delivery service provided by IP. TCP implements the following delivery mechanisms:

- TCP can detect packets dropped in transit via the Sequence Number field. A packet dropped in transit is not acknowledged to the transmitting host. Likewise, a packet dropped by the receiving host because of checksum failure or other error is not acknowledged to the transmitting host. Unacknowledged packets are eventually retransmitted. TCP is connection-oriented, so packets cannot be dropped because of an inactive destination port number except for the first packet of a new connection (the connection request packet). In this case, TCP must drop the packet, must reply to the source host with the RST bit set to 1, and also may transmit an ICMP Type 3 Code 3 message to the source host.

- TCP can detect duplicate packets via the Sequence Number field. If a duplicate packet is received, TCP drops the packet. Recall that TCP is permitted to aggregate data any way TCP chooses. So, a retransmitted packet may contain the data of the dropped packet and additional untransmitted data. When such a duplicate packet is received, TCP discards the duplicate data and forwards the additional data to the appropriate ULP. Since the Sequence Number field is finite, it is likely that each sequence number will be used during a long-lived or high bandwidth connection. When this happens, the Sequence Number field cycles back to 0. This phenomenon is known as *wrapping*. It occurs in many computing environments that involve finite counters. The time required to wrap the Sequence Number field is denoted as Twrap and varies depending on the bandwidth available to the TCP connection. When the Sequence Number field wraps, TCP's traditional method of duplicate packet detection breaks, because valid packets can be mistakenly identified as duplicate packets. Problems can also occur with the packet reordering process. So, RFC 793 defines a maximum segment lifetime (MSL) to ensure that old packets are dropped in the network and not delivered to hosts. The MSL mechanism adequately protected TCP connections against lingering duplicates in the early days of TCP/IP networks. However, many modern LANs provide sufficient bandwidth to wrap the Sequence Number field in just a few seconds. Reducing the value of the MSL would solve this problem, but would create other problems. For example, if the MSL is lower than the one-way delay between a pair of communicating hosts, all TCP packets are dropped. Because LFN environments combine high one-way delay with high bandwidth, the MSL cannot be lowered sufficiently to prevent Twrap from expiring before the MSL. Furthermore, the MSL is enforced via the TTL field in the IP header, and TCP's default TTL value is 60. For reasons of efficiency and performance, most IP networks (including the Internet) are designed to provide any-to-any connectivity with fewer than 60 router hops. So, the MSL never expires in most IP networks. To overcome these deficiencies, RFC 1323 defines a new method of protecting TCP connections against wrapping. The method is called protection against wrapped sequence numbers (PAWS). PAWS uses TSopt to logically extend the Sequence Number field with additional high-order bits so that the Sequence Number field can wrap many times within a single cycle of the TSopt field.

- TCP can detect corrupt packets via the Checksum field. Upon detection of a corrupt packet, the packet is dropped.

- TCP acknowledges receipt of each byte of ULP data. Acknowledgement does not indicate that the data has been processed; that must be inferred by combining the values of the Acknowledgement Number and Window fields. When data is being transmitted in both directions on a connection, acknowledgment is accomplished without additional overhead by setting the ACK bit to one and updating the Acknowledgement Number field in each packet transmitted. When data is being transmitted in only one direction on a connection, packets containing no data must be transmitted in the reverse direction for the purpose of acknowledgment.

- TCP guarantees delivery by providing a retransmission service for undelivered data. TCP uses the Sequence Number and Acknowledgment Number fields to determine which data bytes need to be retransmitted. When a host transmits a packet containing data, TCP retains a copy of the data in a retransmission queue and starts the retransmission timer. If the data is not acknowledged before the retransmission timer expires, a retransmission time-out (RTO) occurs, and the data is retransmitted. When the data is acknowledged, TCP deletes the data from the retransmission queue.

- TCP provides proactive end-to-end flow control via the Window field. TCP implements a separate window for each connection. Each time a host acknowledges receipt of data on a connection, it also advertises its current window size (that is, its receive buffer size) for that connection. A transmitting host may not transmit more data than the receiving host is able to buffer. After a host has transmitted enough data to fill the receiving host's receive buffer, the transmitting host cannot transmit additional data until it receives a TCP packet indicating that additional buffer space has been allocated or in-flight packets have been received *and* processed. Thus, the interpretation of the Acknowledgement Number and Window fields is somewhat intricate. A transmitting host may transmit packets when the receiving host's window size is zero as long as the packets do not contain data. In this scenario, the receiving host must accept and process the packets. See Chapter 9, "Flow Control and Quality of Service," for more information about flow control. Note that in the IP model, the choice of transport layer protocol determines whether end-to-end flow control is used. This contrasts the FC model in which the class of service (CoS) determines whether end-to-end flow control is used.

- Guaranteeing reserved bandwidth is not a transport layer function. TCP relies on QoS policies implemented by IP for bandwidth guarantees.

- Guaranteeing fixed or minimal latency is not a transport layer function. TCP relies on QoS policies implemented by IP for latency guarantees. The PSH bit can be used to lower the processing latency within the source and destination hosts, but the PSH bit has no affect on network behavior.

- Fragmentation and reassembly is not a transport layer function. TCP relies on IP for fragmentation and reassembly. To avoid fragmentation, TCP supports PMTU discovery as defined in RFC 1191. When TCP is notified of a drop via an ICMP Type 3 Code 4 message, TCP resegments and retransmits the data.

- TCP guarantees in-order delivery by reordering packets that are received out of order. The receiving host uses the Sequence Number field to determine the correct order of packets. Each byte of ULP data is passed to the appropriate ULP in consecutive sequence. If one or more packets are received out of order, the ULP data contained in those packets is buffered by TCP until the missing data arrives.

Comprehensive exploration of all the TCP delivery mechanisms is outside the scope of this book. For more information about TCP delivery mechanisms, readers are encouraged to consult IETF RFCs 793, 896, 1122, 1180, 1191, 1323, 2018, 2309, 2525, 2581, 2873, 2883, 2914, 2923, 2988, 3042, 3168, 3390, 3517, and 3782.

TCP Connection Initialization

TCP connections are governed by a state machine. As each new connection is initialized, TCP proceeds through several states. A TCP client begins in the CLOSED state and then proceeds to the SYN-SENT state followed by the ESTABLISHED state. A TCP server begins in the LISTEN state and then proceeds to the SYN-RECEIVED state followed by the ESTABLISHED state. ULP data may be exchanged only while a connection is in the ESTABLISHED state. When the ULP has no more data to transmit, TCP terminates the connection. TCP proceeds through several additional states as each connection is terminated. The state of each connection is maintained in a small area in memory called a transmission control block (TCB). A separate TCB is created for each TCP connection.

RFC 793 defines procedures for establishment, maintenance and teardown of connections between pairs of hosts. Following IP initialization, TCP may initiate a new connection. TCP's connection initialization procedure is often called a three-way handshake because it requires transmission of three packets between the communicating hosts. The initiating host selects an initial sequence number (ISN) for the new connection and then transmits the first packet with the SYN bit set to 1 and the ACK bit set to 0. This packet is called the SYN segment. If the initiating host supports any TCP options, the options are included in the SYN segment. Upon receipt of the SYN segment, the responding host selects an ISN for the new connection and then transmits a reply with both the SYN and ACK bits set to one. This packet is called the SYN/ACK segment. If the responding host supports any TCP options, the options are included in the SYN/ACK segment. The Acknowledgement

Number field contains the initiating host's ISN incremented by one. Upon receipt of the SYN/ACK segment, the initiating host considers the connection established. The initiating host then transmits a reply with the SYN bit set to 0 and the ACK bit set to 1. This is called an ACK segment. (Note that ACK segments occur throughout the life of a connection, whereas the SYN segment and the SYN/ACK segment only occur during connection establishment.) The Acknowledgement Number field contains the responding host's ISN incremented by one. Despite the absence of data, the Sequence Number field contains the initiating host's ISN incremented by one. The ISN must be incremented by one because the sole purpose of the ISN is to synchronize the data byte counter in the responding host's TCB with the data byte counter in the initiating host's TCB. So, the ISN may be used only in the first packet transmitted in each direction. Upon receipt of the ACK segment, the responding host considers the connection established. At this point, both hosts may transmit ULP data. The first byte of ULP data sent by each host is identified by incrementing the ISN by one. Figure 7-10 illustrates TCP's three-way handshake.

Figure 7-10 *TCP Three-Way Handshake*

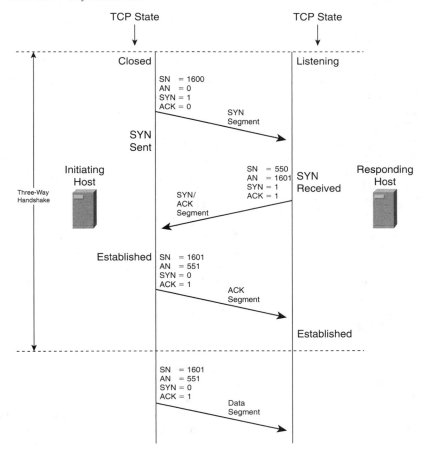

Fibre Channel

As previously stated, the FC network model includes some transport layer functionality. End-to-end connections are established via the PLOGI ELS command. Communication parameters may be updated during an active connection via the discover N_Port parameters (PDISC) ELS command. Segmentation and reassembly services are also supported. The following discussion considers only CoS 3 connections.

FC Operational Overview

PLOGI is mandatory for all N_Ports, and data transfer between N_Ports is not permitted until PLOGI completes. PLOGI may be performed explicitly or implicitly. Only explicit PLOGI is described in this book for the sake of clarity. PLOGI establishes an end-to-end connection between the participating N_Ports. PLOGI is accomplished with a single-frame request followed by a single-frame response. In switched FC environments, PLOGI accomplishes the following tasks:

- Provides the port worldwide name (PWWN) and node worldwide name (NWWN) of each N_Port to the peer N_Port

- Provides the operating characteristics of each N_Port to the peer N_Port

Like a TCP host, an FC node may open and maintain multiple PLOGI connections simultaneously. Unlike a TCP host, only a single PLOGI connection may be open between a pair of nodes at any point in time. This requires all ULPs to share the connection. However, ULPs may not share an Exchange. Similar to TCP connections, PLOGI connections are long-lived. However, keep-alives are not necessary because of the registered state change notification (RSCN) process discussed in Chapter 3, "Overview of Network Operating Principles." Another difference between TCP and FC is the manner in which ULP data is segmented. In the FC model, ULPs specify which PDU is to be transmitted in each sequence. If a PDU exceeds the maximum payload of an FC frame, the PDU is segmented, and each segment is mapped to an FC frame. FC segments a discrete chunk of ULP data into each sequence, so FC can reassemble the segments (frames of a sequence) into a discrete chunk for a ULP (such as FCP). So, receiving nodes reassemble related segments into a PDU before passing received data to a ULP. The segments of each PDU are tracked via the SEQ_CNT field in the FC header. In addition to the SEQ_CNT field, the Sequence Qualifier fields are required to track all data transmitted on a connection. Together, these fields provide equivalent data tracking functionality to the IP Source Address, IP Destination Address, TCP Source Port, TCP Destination Port, and TCP Sequence Number fields.

Two methods are available for segmentation and reassembly of ULP data: SEQ_CNT and relative offset. For each method, two modes are defined. The SEQ_CNT method may use a per-sequence counter (called normal mode) or a per-Exchange counter (called continuously increasing mode). The relative offset method may consider the value of the SEQ_CNT field in the FC header (called continuously increasing mode) or not (called random mode). If the SEQ_CNT method is used, frames received within a single sequence or a consecutive series of sequences are concatenated using the SEQ_CNT field in the FC header. If the relative offset method is used, frames received within a single sequence are concatenated using the Parameter field in the FC header. The method is specified per sequence by the sequence initiator via the Relative Offset Present bit of the F_CTL field in the FC header.

Note that the value of the Relative Offset Present bit must be the same in each frame within each sequence within an Exchange. When the Relative Offset Present bit is set to 1, relative offset is used. When the Relative Offset Present bit is set to 0, SEQ_CNT is used. FCP always uses the relative offset method. To use a particular method, both N_Ports must support that method. The supported methods are negotiated during PLOGI. The SEQ_CNT method must be supported by all N_Ports. The relative offset method is optional. The SEQ_CNT bit in the Common Service Parameters field in the PLOGI ELS indicates support for SEQ_CNT continuously increasing mode. The Continuously Increasing Relative Offset bit, the Random Relative Offset bit, and the Relative Offset By Info Category bit in the Common Service Parameters field in the PLOGI ELS indicate support for each mode of the relative offset method, and for applicability per information category.

Like TCP, FC supports multiple ULPs. So, FC requires a mechanism equivalent to TCP port numbers. This is provided via the Type field in the FC header, which identifies the ULP contained within each frame. Unlike TCP, FC uses the same Type code on the host (initiator) and storage (target) to identify the ULP. Because no more than one PLOGI connection can be open between a pair of nodes at any point in time, there is no need for unique connection identifiers between each pair of nodes. This contrasts with the TCP model, in which multiple TCP connections may be open simultaneously between a pair of nodes. Thus, there is no direct analog for the concept of TCP sockets in the FC model. The S_ID and D_ID fields in the FC header are sufficient to uniquely identify each PLOGI connection. If multiple ULPs are communicating between a pair of nodes, they must share the connection. This, too, contrasts the TCP model in which ULPs are not permitted to share TCP connections.

Multiple information categories are defined in FC. The most commonly used are Solicited Data, Unsolicited Data, Solicited Control, and Unsolicited Control. (Chapter 8, "OSI Session, Presentation, and Application Layers," discusses Solicited Data and Unsolicited Data.) FC permits the transfer of multiple information categories within a single sequence. The ability to mix information categories within a single sequence is negotiated during PLOGI. This is accomplished via the Categories Per Sequence sub-field of the Class 3 Service Parameters field of the PLOGI ELS.

The ability to support multiple simultaneous sequences and Exchanges can improve throughput significantly. However, each sequence within each Exchange consumes resources in the end nodes. Because every end node has limited resources, every end node has an upper limit to the number of simultaneous sequences and Exchanges it can support. During PLOGI, each node informs the peer node of its own limitations. The maximum number of concurrent sequences that are supported across all classes of service is indicated via the Total Concurrent Sequences sub-field of the Common Service Parameters field of the PLOGI ELS. The maximum number of concurrent sequences that are supported within Class 3 is indicated via the Concurrent Sequences sub-field of the Class 3 Service Parameters field of the PLOGI ELS. The maximum number of concurrent sequences that are supported within each Exchange is indicated via the Open Sequences Per Exchange sub-field of the Class 3 Service Parameters field of the PLOGI ELS.

FC Frame Formats

The PLOGI ELS and associated LS_ACC ELS use the exact same frame format as fabric login (FLOGI), which is discussed in Chapter 5, "OSI Physical and Data Link Layers," and diagrammed in Figure 5-25. Figure 5-25 is duplicated in this section as Figure 7-11 for the sake of convenience. Some fields have common meaning and applicability for FLOGI and PLOGI. Other fields have unique meaning and applicability for PLOGI. This section highlights the meaning of each field for PLOGI.

Figure 7-11 *Data Field Format of an FC PLOGI/LS_ACC ELS Frame*

Byte #	3 / 2 / 1 / 0
Bit #	31 30 29 28 27 26 25 24 23 22 21 20 19 18 17 16 15 14 13 12 11 10 9 8 7 6 5 4 3 2 1 0
Word #0	LS Command Code
Word #1–4	Common Service Parameters
Word #5–6	N_Port Name
Word #7–8	Node Name or Fabric Name
Word #9–12	Class 1/6 Service Parameters
Word #13–16	Class 2 Service Parameters
Word #17–20	Class 3 Service Parameters
Word #21–24	Class 4 Service Parameters
Word #25–28	Vendor Version Level
Word #29–30	Services Availability
Word #31	Login Extension Data Length
Word #32–61	Login Extension Data
Word #62–63	Clock Synchronization QoS

A brief description of each field follows:

- **LS command code**—4 bytes long. It contains the 1-byte PLOGI command code (0x03) followed by 3 bytes of zeros when transmitted by an initiating N_Port. This field contains the 1-byte LS_ACC command code (0x02) followed by 3 bytes of zeros when transmitted by a responding N_Port.

- **Common service parameters**—16 bytes long. It contains parameters that affect network operation regardless of the CoS. Key parameters include the MTU, the offset mechanism for segmentation and reassembly, the maximum number of concurrent sequences across all classes of service, the SEQ_CNT policy, and the length of the PLOGI payload (116 or 256 bytes). Some parameters can be configured by the network administrator manually. If manually configured, only the values configured by the administrator will be advertised to the peer device.

- **N_Port name**—8 bytes long. It contains the PWWN of the N_Port.

- **Node name/fabric name**—8 bytes long. It contains the NWWN associated with the N_Port.

- **Class 1/6, 2, 3, and 4 service parameters**—each 16 bytes long. They contain class-specific parameters that affect network operation. Key parameters relevant to Class 3 include indication of support for Class 3, CS_CTL preference, DiffServ, clock synchronization, the types of Exchange Error Policy supported, the maximum number of concurrent sequences within each class of service, the maximum number of concurrent sequences within each exchange, the class-specific MTU, and the ability to mix information categories within a single sequence. Some parameters can be configured by the network administrator manually. If manually configured, only the values configured by the administrator will be advertised to the peer device.

- **Vendor version level**—16 bytes long. It contains vendor-specific information.

- **Services availability**—8 bytes long. It is used only during FLOGI.

- **Login extension data length**—4 bytes long. It indicates the length of the Login Extension Data field. This field is valid only if the Common Service Parameters field indicates that the PLOGI payload is 256 bytes long. If present, this field must be set to 120.

- **Login extension data**—120 bytes long. It contains the vendor identity and other vendor-specific information. This field is valid only if the Common Service Parameters field indicates that the PLOGI payload is 256 bytes long.

- **Clock synchronization QoS**—8 bytes long. It contains operational parameters relevant to the fabric's ability to deliver clock synchronization data. It is used only if the Clock Synchronization service is supported by the switch. This field is valid only if the Common Service Parameters field indicates that the PLOGI payload is 256 bytes long.

The PDISC ELS and associated LS_ACC ELS use the exact same frame format as PLOGI. The meaning of each field is also identical. The LS Command Code field contains the PDISC command code (0x50). The PDISC ELS enables N_Ports to exchange operating characteristics during an active connection without affecting any sequences or exchanges that are currently open. This is useful when operating characteristics change for any reason. For the new operating characteristics to take affect, the connection must be terminated and re-established. Thus, PDISC is merely a notification mechanism.

FC Delivery Mechanisms

As previously stated, the FC model provides multiple sets of delivery mechanisms via multiple Classes of Service. All Classes of Service are implemented primarily at the data-link layer. This contrasts with the TCP/IP model, in which the choice of transport layer protocol determines which set of delivery mechanisms are supported. The majority of modern FC-SANs are configured to use Class 3. Class 3 delivery mechanisms are discussed in Chapter 5, "OSI Physical and Data-Link Layers," so this section discusses only the additional delivery mechanisms provided by PLOGI.

When a missing frame is detected, the behavior of the receiving node is determined by the Exchange Error Policy in effect for the Exchange in which the error is detected. The Exchange originator specifies the Exchange Error Policy on a per-Exchange basis via the Abort Sequence Condition bits of the F_CTL field of the FC header of the first frame of each new Exchange. The Exchange originator may specify any one of the Exchange Error Policies that are supported by the target node. Initiators discover which Exchange Error Policies are supported by each target node via the Error Policy Supported bits of the Class 3 Service Parameters field of the PLOGI ELS. See Chapter 5, "OSI Physical and Data-Link Layers," for a description of each Exchange Error Policy. Target nodes may support all three policies (Process, Discard Sequence, Discard Exchange) or only the two Discard policies. Regardless of the Exchange Error Policy in effect, detection of a missing frame is always reported to the ULP.

As discussed in Chapter 5, "OSI Physical and Data-Link Layers," the CS_CTL/Priority field of the FC header can be interpreted as CS_CTL or Priority. The CS_CTL interpretation enables the use of DiffServ QoS and frame preference. The Priority/Preemption interpretation enables the use of priority QoS and Class 1 or 6 connection preemption. Each node discovers the fabric's ability to support DiffServ QoS/frame preference and Priority QoS/connection preemption during FLOGI via the DiffServ QoS bit, Preference bit, and Priority/Preemption bit, respectively. All three of these bits are contained in the Class 3 Service Parameters field of the FLOGI ELS. Likewise, during

FLOGI, each node informs the fabric of its own support for each of these features. For each feature supported by both the fabric and the node, the node is permitted to negotiate use of the feature with each peer node during PLOGI. This is accomplished via the same three bits of the Class 3 Service Parameters field of the PLOGI ELS.

Each node discovers the PMTU during FLOGI. However, a node might not be able to generate and accept frames as large as the PMTU. So, each node informs each peer node of its own MTU via the Receive Data Field Size bits of the Class 3 Service Parameters field of the PLOGI ELS. The lower of the PMTU and node MTU is used for all subsequent communication between each pair of nodes. Because PLOGI is required before any end-to-end communication occurs, fragmentation is precluded.

Comprehensive exploration of all aspects of the delivery mechanisms facilitated by PLOGI is outside the scope of this book. For more information about the end-to-end delivery mechanisms employed by FC, readers are encouraged to consult the ANSI T11 FC-FS and FC-LS specification series.

FC Connection Initialization

Class 3 service does not provide guaranteed delivery, so end-to-end buffering and acknowledgements are not required. This simplifies the connection establishment procedure. Following FLOGI, each N_Port performs PLOGI with the FC switch. This is required to facilitate Fibre Channel name server (FCNS) registration and subsequent FCNS queries as discussed in Chapter 3, "Overview of Network Operating Principles." Following PLOGI with the switch, each target N_Port waits for PLOGI requests from initiator N_Ports. Following PLOGI with the switch, each initiator N_Port performs PLOGI with each target N_Port discovered via the FCNS. For this reason, proper FCNS zoning must be implemented to avoid accidental target access, which could result in a breach of data security policy or data corruption (see Chapter 12, "Storage Network Security").

An initiator N_Port begins the PLOGI procedure by transmitting a PLOGI ELS frame to the FC address identifier (FCID) of a target N_Port. The FCID assigned to each target N_Port is discovered via the FCNS. Upon recognition of the PLOGI request, the target N_Port responds to the initiator N_Port by transmitting a PLOGI LS_ACC ELS. Upon recognition of the PLOGI LS_ACC, the PLOGI procedure is complete, and the N_Ports may exchange ULP data.

Note that FC does not implement a connection control block in the same manner as TCP. As previously mentioned, TCP creates a TCB per connection to maintain state for each connection. In FC, state is maintained per exchange rather than per connection. After PLOGI completes, the initiator creates an exchange status block (ESB), assigns an OX_ID to the first Exchange, and associates the OX_ID with the ESB. The ESB tracks the state of sequences within the Exchange. The initiator then creates a sequence status block (SSB), assigns a SEQ_ID to the first sequence, associates the SEQ_ID with the

SSB, and associates the SSB with the ESB. The SSB tracks the state of frames within the sequence. The first frame of the first sequence of the first Exchange may then be transmitted by the initiator. Upon receipt of the first frame, the target N_Port creates an ESB and an SSB. The target N_Port then assigns an RX_ID to the Exchange and associates the RX_ID with the ESB. The value of the RX_ID is often the same as the value of the OX_ID. The target N_Port then associates the SEQ_ID received in the frame with the SSB and associates the SSB with the ESB. The target N_Port may then process the frame and pass the ULP data to the appropriate FC-4 protocol. This entire procedure is repeated for each new Exchange.

Summary

A major difference between the TCP/IP model and the FC model is the manner in which end-to-end delivery mechanisms are implemented. With TCP/IP, the transport layer protocol determines which end-to-end delivery mechanisms are provided. By contrast, FC does not implement distinct transport layer protocols. Instead, the Class of Service determines which end-to-end delivery mechanisms are provided. One feature common to both the TCP/IP and FC models is the ability to negotiate which end-to-end delivery mechanisms will be used between each pair of communicating nodes. For TCP, this is accomplished via the three-way handshake procedure. For UDP, no such negotiation occurs. For FC, this is accomplished via the PLOGI procedure. Whereas the TCP/IP suite offers multiple transport layer protocols, most data is transmitted using TCP and UDP. TCP is connection-oriented and guarantees delivery, while UDP is connectionless and does not guarantee delivery. The nature of the source application determines whether TCP or UDP is appropriate. Similarly, FC offers multiple Classes of Service. However, the vast majority of modern FC-SANs are configured to use only Class 3 service regardless of the nature of the source application. Class 3 service blends the features of TCP and UDP. Like TCP, Class 3 service is connection-oriented. Like UDP, Class 3 service does not guarantee delivery.

Review Questions

1   Is reliable delivery required by all applications?

2   Does UDP provide segmentation/reassembly services?

3   What is the purpose of the Destination Port field in the UDP packet header?

4   Does UDP provide notification of dropped packets?

5   Is the segmentation process controlled by TCP or the ULP?

6   Why is the TCP flow-control mechanism called a sliding window?

7   What is the formula for calculating the bandwidth-delay product?

8 Does TCP guarantee in-order delivery?

9 What is the purpose of the TCP ISN?

10 Is the segmentation process controlled by FC-2 or the ULP?

11 Which two fields in the PLOGI ELS facilitate negotiation of end-to-end delivery mechanisms in modern FC-SANs?

12 How is the missing frame error recovery behavior of an FC node determined?

13 After completing PLOGI with the switch, what does each initiator N_Port do?

Upon completing this chapter, you will be able to:

- Relate the addressing schemes of Internet Small Computer System Interface (iSCSI), Fibre Channel Protocol (FCP), and Fibre Channel over TCP/IP (FCIP) to the SCSI architecture model (SAM) addressing scheme

- Discuss the iSCSI name and address assignment and resolution procedures

- Differentiate the FCIP functional models

- List the session establishment procedures of iSCSI, FCP, and FCIP

- Explicate the data transfer optimizations of iSCSI, FCP, and FCIP

- Decode the packet and frame formats of iSCSI, FCP, and FCIP

- Explain the delivery mechanisms supported by iSCSI, FCP, and FCIP

OSI Session, Presentation, and Application Layers

This chapter explores the operational details of iSCSI, FCP, and FCIP in depth. Currently, this chapter does not examine iFCP because iFCP has limited industry support. The primary focus of this chapter is OSI session layer functionality, but we also explore certain aspects of OSI presentation and application layer functionality.

iSCSI Operational Details

This section provides an in-depth exploration of the operational details of iSCSI. This section complements and builds upon the iSCSI overview provided in Chapter 4, "Overview of Modern SCSI Networking Protocols." You are also encouraged to consult IETF RFC 3347 for an overview of the requirements that shaped the development of iSCSI.

iSCSI Addressing Scheme

iSCSI implements SCSI device names, port names, and port identifiers. Both device and port names are required by iSCSI. The SCSI device name is equivalent to the iSCSI node name. Three types of iSCSI node names are currently defined: iSCSI qualified name (IQN), extended unique identifier (EUI), and network address authority (NAA). Each iSCSI node name begins with a three-letter designator that identifies the type. RFC 3720 requires all iSCSI node names to be globally unique, but some node name types support locally administered names that are not globally unique. As with FC node names, global uniqueness can be guaranteed only by using globally administered names. To preserve global uniqueness, take care when moving iSCSI entities from one operating system image to another.

Currently, the IQN type is most prevalent. The IQN type provides globally unique iSCSI node names. The IQN format has four components: a type designator followed by a dot, a date code followed by a dot, the reverse domain name of the naming authority, and an optional device specific string that, if present, is prefixed by a colon. The type designator is "iqn". The date code indicates the year and month that the naming authority registered its domain name in the DNS. The reverse domain name identifies the naming authority. Sub-domains within the naming authority's primary domain are permitted; they enable delegation of naming tasks to departments, subsidiaries, and other subordinate organizations within the naming authority. The optional device specific string provides a unique iSCSI node name for each SCSI device. If the optional device specific string is not used, only one SCSI device can exist within the naming authority's namespace (as identified by the reverse domain name itself). Therefore, the optional device specific string is a practical requirement for real-world deployments. iSCSI node names of type IQN are variable in length up to a maximum of 223 characters. Examples include

iqn.1987-05.com.cisco:host1
iqn.1987-05.com.cisco.apac.singapore:ccm-host1
iqn.1987-05.com.cisco.erp:dr-host8-vpar1

The EUI type provides globally unique iSCSI node names assuming that the Extension Identifier sub-field within the EUI-64 string is not locally administered (see Chapter 5, "OSI Physical and Data-Link Layers"). The EUI format has two components: a type designator followed by a dot and a device specific string. The type designator is "eui". The device specific string is a valid IEEE EUI-64 string. Because the length of an EUI-64 string is eight bytes, and EUI-64 strings are expressed in hexadecimal, the length of an iSCSI node name of type EUI is fixed at 20 characters. For example

eui.02004567A425678D

The NAA type is based on the ANSI T11 NAA scheme. As explained in Chapter 5, the ANSI T11 NAA scheme supports many formats. Some formats provide global uniqueness; others do not. In iSCSI, the NAA format has two components: a type designator followed by a dot and a device specific string. The type designator is "naa". The device specific string is a valid ANSI T11 NAA string. Because the length of ANSI T11 NAA strings can be either 8 or 16 bytes, iSCSI node names of type NAA are variable in length. ANSI T11 NAA strings are expressed in hexadecimal, so the length of an iSCSI node name of type NAA is either 20 or 36 characters. Examples include

naa.52004567BA64678D
naa.62004567BA64678D0123456789ABCDEF

iSCSI allows the use of aliases for iSCSI node names. The purpose of an alias is to provide an easily recognizable, meaningful tag that can be displayed in tools, utilities, and other user interfaces. Although IQNs are text-based and somewhat intuitive, the device-specific portion might need to be very long and even cryptic to adequately ensure a scalable nomenclature in large iSCSI environments. Likewise, EUI and NAA formatted node names can be very difficult for humans to interpret. Aliases solve this problem by associating a human-friendly tag with each iSCSI node name. Aliases are used only by humans. Aliases might not be used for authentication or authorization. Aliases are variable in length up to a maximum of 255 characters.

SCSI port names and identifiers are handled somewhat differently in iSCSI as compared to other SAM Transport Protocols. iSCSI uses a single string as both the port name and port identifier. The string is globally unique, and so the string positively identifies each port within the context of iSCSI. This complies with the defined SAM functionality for port names. However, the string does not contain any resolvable address to facilitate packet forwarding. Thus, iSCSI requires a mapping of its port identifiers to other port types that can facilitate packet forwarding. For this purpose, iSCSI employs the concept of a network portal. Within an iSCSI device, an Ethernet (or other) interface configured with an IP address is called a network portal. Network portals facilitate packet forwarding, while iSCSI port identifiers serve as session endpoint identifiers. Within an initiator device, each network portal is identified by its IP address. Within a target device, each network portal is identified by its IP address and listening TCP port (its socket). Network portals that share compatible operating characteristics may form a portal group. Within a target device, each portal group is assigned a target portal group tag (TPGT).

SCSI ports are implemented differently for iSCSI initiators versus iSCSI targets. Upon resolution of a target iSCSI node name to one or more sockets, an iSCSI initiator logs into the target. After login completes, a SCSI port is dynamically created within the initiator. In response, the iSCSI port name and identifier are created by concatenating the initiator's iSCSI node name, the letter "i" (indicating this port is contained within an initiator device) and the initiator session identifier (ISID). The ISID is 6 bytes long and is expressed in hexadecimal. These three fields are comma-separated. For example

iqn.1987-05.com.cisco:host1,i,0x00023d000002

The order of these events might seem counter-intuitive, but recall that iSCSI port identifiers do not facilitate packet forwarding; network portals do. So, iSCSI port identifiers do not need to exist before the iSCSI login. Essentially, iSCSI login signals the need for a SCSI port, which is subsequently created and then used by the SCSI Application Layer (SAL).

Recall from Chapter 5 that SAM port names must never change. One might think that iSCSI breaks this rule, because initiator port names seem to change regularly. iSCSI creates and destroys port names regularly, but never changes port names. iSCSI generates each new port name in response to the creation of a new SCSI port. Upon termination of an iSCSI session, the associated initiator port is destroyed. Because the iSCSI port name does not change during the lifetime of its associated SCSI port, iSCSI complies with the SAM persistence requirement for port names.

In a target device, SCSI ports are also created dynamically in response to login requests. The target port name and identifier are created by concatenating the target's iSCSI node name, the letter "t" (indicating this port is contained within a target device) and the TPGT. The target node infers the appropriate TPGT from the IP address at which the login request is received. The TPGT is 2 bytes long and is expressed in hexadecimal. These three fields are comma-separated. For example

iqn.1987-05.com.cisco:array1,t,0x4097

All network portals within a target portal group share the same iSCSI port identifier and represent the same SCSI port. Because iSCSI target port names and identifiers are based on TPGTs, and because a network portal may operate independently (not part of a portal group), a TPGT must be assigned to each network portal that is not part of a portal group. Thus, a network portal that operates independently forms a portal group of one.

Some background information helps us fully understand ISID and TPGT usage. According to the SAM, the relationship between a SCSI initiator port and a SCSI target port is known as the initiator-target nexus (I_T nexus). The I_T nexus concept underpins all session-oriented constructs in all modern storage networking technologies. At any point in time, only one I_T nexus can exist between a pair of SCSI ports. According to the SAM, an I_T nexus is identified by the conjunction of the initiator port identifier and the target port identifier. The SAM I_T nexus is equivalent to the iSCSI session. Thus, only one iSCSI session can exist between an iSCSI initiator port identifier and an iSCSI target port identifier at any point in time.

iSCSI initiators adhere to this rule by incorporating the ISID into the iSCSI port identifier. Each new session is assigned a new ISID, which becomes part of the iSCSI port identifier of the newly created SCSI port, which becomes part of the I_T nexus. Each ISID is unique within the context of an initiator-target-TPGT triplet. If an initiator has an active session with a given target device and establishes another session with the same target device via a different target portal group, the initiator may reuse any active ISID. In this case, the new I_T nexus is formed between a unique pair of iSCSI port identifiers because the target port identifier includes the TPGT. Likewise, any active ISID may be reused for a new session with a new target device. Multiple iSCSI sessions may exist simultaneously between an initiator device and a target device as long as each session terminates on a different iSCSI port identifier (representing a different SCSI port) on at least one end of the session. Initiators accomplish this by connecting to a different target portal group or assigning a new ISID. Note that RFC 3720 encourages the reuse of ISIDs in an effort to promote initiator SCSI port persistence for the benefit of applications, and to facilitate target recognition of initiator SCSI ports in multipath environments.

NOTE   RFC 3720 officially defines the I_T nexus identifier as the concatenation of the iSCSI initiator port identifier and the iSCSI target port identifier (initiator node name + "i" + ISID + target node name + "t" + TPGT). This complies with the SAM definition of I_T nexus identifier. However, RFC 3720 also defines a session identifier (SSID) that can be used to reference an iSCSI session. The SSID is defined as the concatenation of the ISID and the TPGT. Because the SSID is ambiguous, it has meaning only in the context of a given initiator-target pair.

iSCSI may be implemented as multiple hardware and software components within a single network entity. As such, coordination of ISID generation in an RFC-compliant manner across all involved components can be challenging. For this reason, RFC 3720 requires a single component to be responsible for the coordination of all ISID generation activity. To facilitate this rule, the ISID format is flexible. It supports a namespace hierarchy that enables coordinated delegation of ISID generation authority to various independent components within the initiator entity. Figure 8-1 illustrates the general ISID format.

Figure 8-1   *General iSCSI ISID Format*

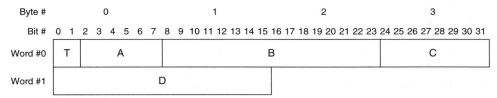

A brief description of each field follows:

- T—This is 2 bits long and indicates the format of the ISID. Though not explicitly stated in RFC 3720, T presumably stands for type.

- A—This is 6 bits long and may be concatenated with the B field. Otherwise, the A field is reserved.

- B—This is 16 bits long and may be concatenated with the A field or the C field. Otherwise, the B field is reserved.

- C—This is 8 bits long and may be concatenated with the B field or the D field. Otherwise, the C field is reserved.

- D—This is 16 bits long and may be concatenated with the C field or used as an independent field. Otherwise, the D field is reserved.

Table 8-1 summarizes the possible values of T and the associated field descriptions.

Table 8-1   *ISID Format Descriptions*

T Value	ISID Format	Field Descriptions
00b	OUI	A & B form a 22-bit field that contains the OUI of the vendor of the component that generates the ISID. The I/G and U/L bits are omitted. C & D form a 24-bit qualifier field that contains a value generated by the component.
01b	EN	A is reserved. B & C form a 24-bit field that contains the IANA enterprise number (EN) of the vendor of the component that generates the ISID. D is a 16-bit qualifier field that contains a value generated by the component.
10b	Random	A is reserved. B & C form a 24-bit field that contains a value that is randomly generated by the component responsible for ISID coordination. A unique value is assigned to each subordinate component that generates ISIDs. D is a 16-bit qualifier field that contains a value generated by subordinate components.
11b	Reserved	All fields are reserved. This T value is currently not used.

The target also assigns a session identifier to each new session. This is known as the target session identifying handle (TSIH). During login for a new session, the initiator uses a

TSIH value of zero. The target generates the TSIH value during login and sends the new value to the initiator in the final login response. In all subsequent packets, the assigned TSIH is used by the initiator to enable the target to associate received packets with the correct session. The TSIH is two bytes long, but the format of the TSIH is not defined in RFC 3720. Each target determines its own TSIH format. For more information about iSCSI device names, port names, port identifiers, and session identifiers, readers are encouraged to consult IETF RFCs 3720, 3721, 3722, and 3980, and ANSI T10 SAM-3.

iSCSI Name Assignment and Resolution

iSCSI is designed to operate with a single node name per operating system image. iSCSI node names can be preset in iSCSI hardware at time of manufacture, dynamically created by iSCSI software at time of installation, or manually assigned by the storage network administrator during initial configuration. If the node name is preset in iSCSI hardware at time of manufacture, RFC 3720 mandates the storage network administrator must be provided a way to change the node name. As previously discussed, iSCSI port names are dynamically assigned by the iSCSI hardware or software upon creation of a SCSI port.

iSCSI name resolution is tied to iSCSI name discovery. Because three methods of target discovery exist (see Chapter 3, "Overview of Network Operating Principles"), three methods of name resolution exist: manual, semi-manual, and automated. A manually configured iSCSI initiator node is given the iSCSI node names of all targets to which access is permitted. The socket(s) associated with each target node also must be manually configured. In this environment, name resolution occurs within the initiator node and does not involve any network service.

A semi-manually configured iSCSI initiator node is given the socket(s) to which the **SendTargets** command should be sent. The SendTargets response contains the TPGT for the network portal at which the request was received. The SendTargets response also contains the iSCSI node name of each target accessible via that portal group. This constitutes reverse name resolution (that is, address-to-name resolution). The SendTargets response also may contain additional socket and TPGT information for each target node name. This constitutes normal name resolution (that is, name-to-address resolution).

When using SLP with a DA, each target entity registers its target nodes in the DA store. Each target node is registered independently as a service URL containing the iSCSI node name, IP address, TCP port, and TPGT. If a target node is accessible via multiple network portals, a service URL is registered for each network portal. Upon booting, an initiator queries the DA to discover accessible targets. The DA response contains the service URL(s) to which access has been administratively granted (based on scope membership). When using SLP without a DA, each SA entity responds to queries it receives. The SA response contains all the service URLs implemented within that target entity to which the initiator has been administratively granted access (based on scope membership). With or without a DA, name resolution is inherent to the discovery process because the service URL contains the iSCSI node name and all relevant network portal information. SLP does not support

RSCN functionality, so initiators must periodically send update requests to the DA or to each SA to discover any new targets that come online after initial discovery.

The iSNS model is very similar to the SLP model. When using iSNS, clients (target and initiator entities) must register with the iSNS server before they can query the iSNS server. Each target entity registers its target node names, network portal information (including IP addresses and TCP port numbers), and TPGT information. Initiator entities query the iSNS server and receive a response containing the iSCSI node name of each target node to which access has been administratively granted (based on Discovery Domain membership). The response also contains the relevant network portal and TPGT information. Thus, name resolution is inherent to the discovery process. iSNS also has the advantage of RSCN support. Clients do not need to periodically query for current status of other devices. Instead, clients may register to receive SCN messages. For more information about iSCSI name resolution, readers are encouraged to consult IETF RFCs 2608, 3720, 3721, 4018, and 4171.

iSCSI Address Assignment and Resolution

As previously discussed, iSCSI port identifiers are dynamically assigned by the iSCSI hardware or software upon creation of a SCSI port. However, iSCSI port identifiers are not addresses per se. To facilitate forwarding of iSCSI packets, IP addresses are required. IP address assignment is handled in the customary manner (manually or via DHCP). No special addressing requirements are mandated by iSCSI, and no special addressing procedures are implemented by network entities that host iSCSI processes. After an IP address is assigned to at least one network portal within an iSCSI device, iSCSI can begin communication. Likewise, address resolution is accomplished via the customary mechanisms. For example, IP addresses are resolved to Ethernet address via ARP. IP address assignment and resolution are transparent to iSCSI.

iSCSI Session Types, Phases, and Stages

As discussed in Chapter 3, iSCSI implements two types of session: discovery and normal. Both session types operate on TCP. Each discovery session uses a single TCP connection. Each normal session can use multiple TCP connections for load balancing and improved fault tolerance. A discovery session is used to discover iSCSI target node names and network portal information via the SendTargets command. A normal session is used for all other purposes. Discovery sessions are optional, and normal sessions are mandatory. We discussed discovery sessions in Chapter 3, so this section focuses on normal sessions.

The login phase always occurs first and is composed of two stages: security parameter negotiation and operational parameter negotiation. Each stage is optional, but at least one of the two stages must occur. If the security parameter negotiation stage occurs, it must occur first. Authentication is optional. If authentication is implemented, it occurs during the security parameter negotiation stage. Therefore, the security parameter negotiation stage must occur if authentication is implemented. Currently, authentication is the only security parameter negotiated during this stage.

Although the operational parameter negotiation stage is optional according to RFC 3720, it is a practical requirement for real-world deployments. Each initiator and target device must support the same operational parameters to communicate successfully. It is possible for the default settings of every iSCSI device to match, but it is not probable. So, negotiable parameters must be configured manually or autonegotiated. Manually setting all negotiable parameters on every iSCSI device can be operationally burdensome. Thus, the operational parameter negotiation stage is implemented by all iSCSI devices currently on the market. Support for unsolicited writes, the maximum burst length and various other parameters are negotiated during this stage.

Following the login phase, the iSCSI session transitions to the full feature phase. During the full feature phase of a normal session, initiators can issue iSCSI commands as well as send SCSI commands and data. Additionally, certain iSCSI operational parameters can be re-negotiated during the full feature phase. When all SCSI operations are complete, a normal iSCSI session can be gracefully terminated via the iSCSI Logout command. If a normal session is terminated unexpectedly, procedures are defined to clean up the session before reinstating the session. Session cleanup prevents processing of commands and responses that might have been delayed in transit, thus avoiding data corruption. Procedures are also defined to re-establish a session that has been terminated unexpectedly, so SCSI processing can continue from the point of abnormal termination. After all normal sessions have been terminated gracefully, the discovery session (if extant) can be terminated gracefully via the iSCSI Logout command. For more information about iSCSI session types, phases, and stages, readers are encouraged to consult IETF RFC 3720. Figure 8-2 illustrates the flow of iSCSI sessions, phases, and stages.

Figure 8-2 *iSCSI Session Flow*

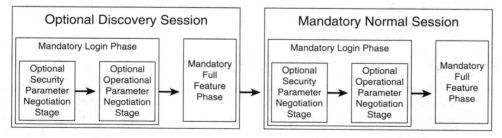

iSCSI Data Transfer Optimizations

iSCSI handles data transfer very flexibly. To understand the data transfer options provided by iSCSI, some background information about SCSI I/O operations is required. SCSI defines the direction of data transfer from the perspective of the initiator. Data transfer from initiator to target (write command) is considered outbound, and data transfer from target to initiator (read command) is considered inbound. The basic procedure for a SCSI read operation involves three steps. First, the initiator sends a SCSI read command to the target.

Next, the target sends the requested data to the initiator. Finally, the target sends a SCSI status indicator to the initiator. The read command specifies the starting block address and the number of contiguous blocks to transfer. If the data being retrieved by the application client is fragmented on the storage medium (that is, stored in non-contiguous blocks), then multiple read commands must be issued (one per set of contiguous blocks). For each set of contiguous blocks, the initiator may issue more than one read command if the total data in the set of contiguous blocks exceeds the initiator's available receive buffer resources. This eliminates the need for a flow-control mechanism for read commands. A target always knows it can send the entire requested data set because an initiator never requests more data than it is prepared to receive. When multiple commands are issued to satisfy a single application client request, the commands may be linked together as a single SCSI task. Such commands are called SCSI linked commands.

The basic procedure for a SCSI write operation involves four steps. First, the initiator sends a SCSI write command to the target. Next, the target sends an indication that it is ready to receive the data. Next, the initiator sends the data. Finally, the target sends a SCSI status indicator to the initiator. The write command specifies the starting block address and the number of contiguous blocks that will be transferred by this command. If the data being stored by the application client exceeds the largest contiguous set of available blocks on the medium, multiple write commands must be issued (one per set of contiguous blocks). The commands may be linked as a single SCSI task. A key difference between read and write operations is the initiator's knowledge of available receive buffer space. When writing, the initiator does not know how much buffer space is currently available in the target to receive the data. So, the target must inform the initiator when the target is ready to receive data (that is, when receive buffers are available). The target must also indicate how much data to transfer. In other words, a flow-control mechanism is required for write operations. The SAM delegates responsibility for this flow-control mechanism to each SCSI Transport Protocol.

In iSCSI parlance, the data transfer steps are called phases (not to be confused with phases of an iSCSI session). iSCSI enables optimization of data transfer through *phase-collapse*. Targets may include SCSI status as part of the final data PDU for read commands. This does not eliminate any round-trips across the network, but it does reduce the total number of PDUs required to complete the read operation. Likewise, initiators may include data with write command PDUs. This can be done in two ways. Data may be included as part of the write command PDU. This is known as *immediate data*. Alternately, data may be sent in one or more data PDUs immediately following a write command PDU without waiting for the target to indicate its readiness to receive data. This is known as *unsolicited data*. In both cases, one round-trip is eliminated across the network, which reduces the total time to completion for the write operation. In the case of immediate data, one data PDU is also eliminated. The initiator must negotiate support for immediate data and unsolicited data during login. Each feature is negotiated separately. If the target supports phase-collapse for write commands, the target informs the initiator (during login) how much data may be sent using each feature. Both features may be supported simultaneously. Collectively, immediate data and unsolicited data are called *first burst data*. First burst data may be sent only once per write command (the first sequence of PDUs). For more information about iSCSI phase-collapse, readers are encouraged to consult IETF RFC 3720.

NOTE   In the generic sense, immediate data is actually a subset of unsolicited data. Unsolicited data generically refers to any data sent to the target without first receiving an indication from the target that the target is ready for the data transfer. By that generic definition, immediate data qualifies as unsolicited data. However, the term *unsolicited data* has specific meaning in the context of iSCSI. Note that data sent in response to an indication of receiver readiness is called *solicited data*.

iSCSI PDU Formats

iSCSI uses one general PDU format for many purposes. The specific format of an iSCSI PDU is determined by the type of PDU. RFC 3720 defines numerous PDU types to facilitate communication between initiators and targets. Of these, the primary PDU types include login request, login response, SCSI command, SCSI response, data-out, data-in, ready to transfer (R2T), selective negative acknowledgment (SNACK) request, task management function (TMF) request, TMF response, and reject. All iSCSI PDUs begin with a basic header segment (BHS). The BHS may be followed by one or more additional header segments (AHS), a header-digest, a data segment, or a data-digest. The data-digest may be present only if the data segment is present. iSCSI PDUs are word-oriented, and an iSCSI word is 4 bytes. All iSCSI PDU segments and digests that do not end on a word boundary must be padded to the nearest word boundary. RFC 3720 encourages, but does not require, the value of 0 for all padding bits. Figure 8-3 illustrates the general iSCSI PDU format.

Figure 8-3   *General iSCSI PDU Format*

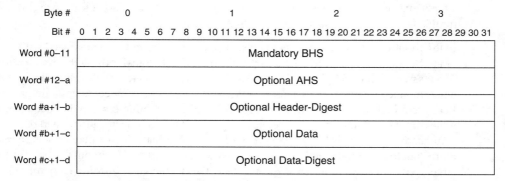

A brief description of each field follows:

- **BHS**—This is 48 bytes long. It is the only mandatory field. The BHS field indicates the type of PDU and contains most of the control information used by iSCSI.

- **Optional AHS**—Each is variable in length. The purpose of the AHS field is to provide protocol extensibility. Currently, only two AHS types are defined: extended command descriptor block (CDB) and expected bidirectional read data length.

- **Optional Header-Digest**—Each is variable in length as determined by the kind of digest used. This field provides additional header integrity beyond that of the IP and TCP checksums. During login, each initiator-target pair negotiates whether a header digest will be used and, if so, what kind. Separating the header digest from the data digest improves the operational efficiency of iSCSI gateways that modify header fields.
- **Optional Data**—This is variable in length. It contains PDU-specific data.
- **Optional Data-Digest**—This is variable in length as determined by the kind of digest used. This field provides additional data integrity beyond that of the IP and TCP checksums. During login, each initiator-target pair negotiates whether a data digest will be used and, if so, what kind.

The remainder of this section focuses on the BHS because the two defined AHSs are less commonly used. Details of the BHS are provided for each of the primary iSCSI PDU types. Figure 8-4 illustrates the general format of the iSCSI BHS. All fields marked with "." are reserved.

Figure 8-4   *iSCSI BHS Format*

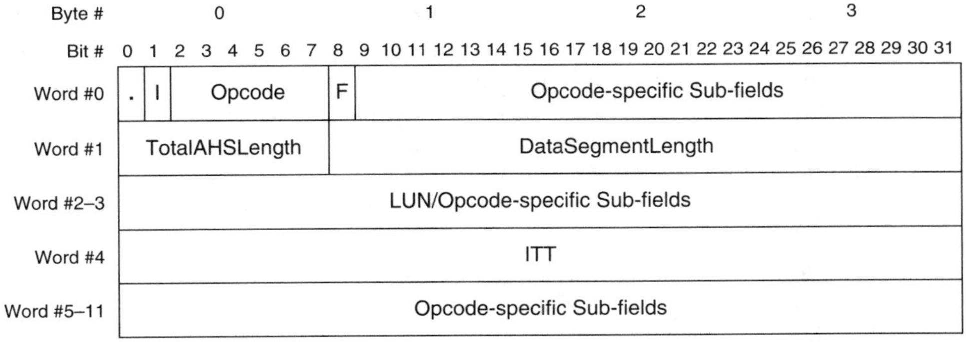

A brief description of each field follows:

- **Reserved**—This is 1 bit.
- **I**—This is 1 bit. I stands for immediate delivery. When an initiator sends an iSCSI command or SCSI command that should be processed immediately, the I bit is set to 1. When this bit is set to 1, the command is called an immediate command. This should not be confused with immediate data (phase-collapse). When this bit is set to 0, the command is called a non-immediate command.
- **Opcode**—This is 6 bits long. The Opcode field contains an operation code that indicates the type of PDU. Opcodes are defined as initiator opcodes (transmitted only by initiators) and target opcodes (transmitted only by targets). RFC 3720 defines 18 opcodes (see Table 8-2).
- **F**—This is 1 bit. F stands for final PDU. When this bit is set to 1, the PDU is the final (or only) PDU in a sequence of PDUs. When this bit is set to 0, the PDU is followed by one or more PDUs in the same sequence. The F bit is redefined by some PDU types.

- **Opcode-specific Sub-fields**—These are 23 bits long. The format and use of all Opcode-specific sub-fields are determined by the value in the Opcode field.

- **TotalAHSLength**—This is 8 bits long. It indicates the total length of all AHS fields. This field is needed because the AHS fields are variable in number and length. The value is expressed in 4-byte words and includes padding bytes (if any exist). If no AHS fields are present, this field is set to 0.

- **DataSegmentLength**—This is 24 bits long. It indicates the total length of the Data segment. This field is needed because the Data segment is variable in length. The value is expressed in bytes and does not include padding bytes (if any exist). If no Data segment is present, this field is set to 0.

- **LUN field and the Opcode-specific Sub-fields**—These are 64 bits (8 bytes) long. They contain the destination LUN if the Opcode field contains a value that is relevant to a specific LUN (such as a SCSI command). When used as a LUN field, the format complies with the SAM LUN format. When used as Opcode-specific sub-fields, the format and use of the sub-fields are opcode-specific.

- **Initiator Task Tag (ITT)**—This is 32 bits long. It contains a tag assigned by the initiator. An ITT is assigned to each iSCSI task. Likewise, an ITT is assigned to each SCSI task. A SCSI task can represent a single SCSI command or multiple linked commands. Each SCSI command can have many SCSI activities associated with it. A SCSI task encompasses all activities associated with a SCSI command or multiple linked commands. Likewise, an ITT that represents a SCSI task also encompasses all associated activities of the SCSI command(s). An ITT value is unique only within the context of the current session. The iSCSI ITT is similar in function to the FC fully qualified exchange identifier (FQXID).

- **Opcode-specific Sub-fields**—These are 224 bits (28 bytes) long. The format and use of the sub-fields are opcode-specific.

Table 8-2 summarizes the iSCSI opcodes that are currently defined in RFC 3720. All opcodes excluded from Table 8-2 are reserved.

Table 8-2 *iSCSI Operation Codes*

Category	Value	Description
Initiator	0x00	NOP-out
Initiator	0x01	SCSI command
Initiator	0x02	SCSI task management request
Initiator	0x03	Login request
Initiator	0x04	Text request
Initiator	0x05	SCSI data-out
Initiator	0x06	Logout request
Initiator	0x10	SNACK request
Initiator	0x1C-0x1E	Vendor-specific codes

Table 8-2   *iSCSI Operation Codes (Continued)*

Category	Value	Description
Target	0x20	NOP-in
Target	0x21	SCSI response
Target	0x22	SCSI task management response
Target	0x23	Login response
Target	0x24	Text response
Target	0x25	SCSI data-in
Target	0x26	Logout response
Target	0x31	Ready to transfer (R2T)
Target	0x32	Asynchronous message
Target	0x3C-0x3E	Vendor-specific codes
Target	0x3F	Reject

The first login request of a new session is called the leading login request. The first TCP connection of a new session is called the leading connection. Figure 8-5 illustrates the iSCSI BHS of a Login Request PDU. Login parameters are encapsulated in the Data segment (not shown) as text key-value pairs. All fields marked with "." are reserved.

Figure 8-5   *iSCSI Login Request BHS Format*

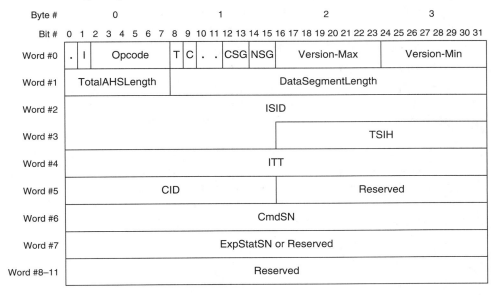

A brief description of each field follows. The description of each field is abbreviated unless a field is used in a PDU-specific manner:

- **Reserved**—This is 1 bit.
- **I**—This is always set to 1.
- **Opcode**—This is 6 bits long. It is set to 0x03.
- **T**—This is the F bit redefined as the T bit. T stands for transit. This bit is set to 1 when the initiator is ready to change to the next login stage.
- **C**—This is 1 bit. It indicates whether the set of text keys in this PDU is complete. C stands for continue. When the set of text keys is too large for a single PDU, the C bit is set to 1, and another PDU follows containing more text keys. When all text keys have been transmitted, the C bit is set to 0. When the C bit is set to 1, the T bit must be set to 0.
- **Reserved**—This is 2 bits long.
- **CSG**—This is 2 bits long. It indicates the current stage of the login procedure. The value 0 indicates the security parameter negotiation stage. The value 1 indicates the operational parameter negotiation stage. The value 2 is reserved. The value 3 indicates the full feature phase. These values also used are by the NSG field.
- **NSG**—This is 2 bits long. It indicates the next stage of the login procedure.
- **Version-Max**—This is 8 bits long. It indicates the highest supported version of the iSCSI protocol. Only one version of the iSCSI protocol is currently defined. The current version is 0x00.
- **Version-Min**—This is 8 bits long. It indicates the lowest supported version of the iSCSI protocol.
- **TotalAHSLength**—This is 8 bits long.
- **DataSegmentLength**—This is 24 bits long.
- **ISID**—This is 48 bits (6 bytes) long. For a new session, this value is unique within the context of the initiator-target-TPGT triplet. For a new connection within an existing session, this field indicates the session to which the new connection should be added.
- **TSIH**—This is 16 bits long. For a new session, the initiator uses the value 0. Upon successful completion of the login procedure, the target provides the TSIH value to the initiator in the final Login Response PDU. For a new connection within an existing session, the value previously assigned to the session by the target must be provided by the initiator in the first and all subsequent Login Request PDUs.
- **ITT**—This is 32 bits long.

- **Connection Identifier (CID)**—This is 16 bits long. The initiator assigns a CID to each TCP connection. The CID is unique only within the context of the session to which the connection belongs. Each TCP connection may be used by only a single session.

- **Reserved**—This is 16 bits long.

- **Command Sequence Number (CmdSN)**—This is 32 bits long. The initiator assigns a unique sequence number to each non-immediate SCSI command issued within a session. This field enables in-order delivery of all non-immediate commands within a session even when multiple TCP connections are used. For a leading login request, the value of this field is arbitrarily selected by the initiator. The same value is used until login successfully completes. The same value is then used for the first non-immediatenon-immediate SCSI Command PDU. The CmdSN counter is then incremented by one for each subsequent new non-immediate command, regardless of which TCP connection is used. If the login request is for a new connection within an existing session, the value of this field must reflect the current CmdSN of that session. The first non-immediate SCSI Command PDU sent on the new TCP connection also must use the current CmdSN value, which can continue to increment while login processing occurs on the new connection. Both initiator and target track this counter. The iSCSI CmdSN is similar in function to the FCP command reference number (CRN).

- **ExpStatSN or Reserved**—This is 32 bits long. It may contain the iSCSI Expected Status Sequence Number. Except during login, the initiator uses the ExpStatSN field to acknowledge receipt of SCSI Response PDUs. The target assigns a status sequence number (StatSN) to each SCSI Response PDU. While the CmdSN is session-wide, the StatSN is unique only within the context of a TCP connection. For a leading login request, this field is reserved. If the login request is for a new connection within an existing session, this field is reserved. If the login request is for recovery of a lost connection, this field contains the last value of ExpStatSN from the failed connection. If multiple Login Request PDUs are sent during recovery, this field is incremented by one for each Login Response PDU received. Thus, during login, this field is either not used or is used to acknowledge receipt of Login Response PDUs.

- **Reserved**—This is 128 bits (16 bytes) long.

Each Login Request PDU or sequence of Login Request PDUs precipitates a Login Response PDU or sequence of Login Response PDUs. Figure 8-6 illustrates the iSCSI BHS of a Login Response PDU. Login parameters are encapsulated in the Data segment (not shown) as text key-value pairs. All fields marked with "." are reserved.

Figure 8-6 *iSCSI Login Response BHS Format*

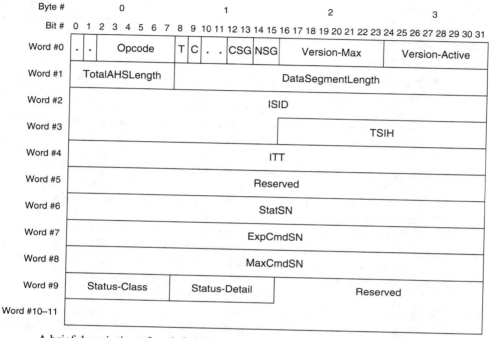

A brief description of each field follows. The description of each field is abbreviated unless a field is used in a PDU-specific manner:

- **Reserved**—This is 1 bit.
- **Reserved**—This is the 1 bit redefined as Reserved.
- **Opcode**—This is 6 bits long. It is set to 0x23.
- **T bit**—This is the F bit redefined as the T bit. This bit is set to 1 when the target is ready to change to the next login stage. The target may set this bit to 1 only if the most recently received Login Request PDU had a T bit value of 1.
- **C**—This is 1 bit.
- **Reserved**—This is 2 bits long.
- **CSG**—This is 2 bits long.
- **NSG**—This is 2 bits long.
- **Version-Max**—This is 8 bits long.
- **Version-Active**—This is 8 bits long. It indicates the highest iSCSI protocol version that both the target and the initiator have in common. If no version is common to both target and initiator, the target rejects the login request, and this field reverts to Version-Min.

- **TotalAHSLength**—This is 8 bits long.
- **DataSegmentLength**—This is 24 bits long.
- **ISID**—This is 48 bits (6 bytes) long.
- **TSIH**—This is 16 bits long.
- **ITT**—This is 32 bits long.
- **Reserved**—This is 32 bits long.
- **Status Sequence Number (StatSN)**—This is 32 bits long. iSCSI assigns a sequence number to each new Login Response PDU and each new SCSI Response PDU sent within a session. This field enables recovery of lost status and Login Response PDUs. When multiple TCP connections are used, the value of StatSN is maintained independently for each TCP connection. Mandatory support for connection allegiance makes this possible. For the first login response sent on each TCP connection, the value of this field is arbitrarily selected by the target. Each time a new Login Response PDU or a new SCSI Response PDU is transmitted, the StatSN of the associated TCP connection is incremented by one. A retransmitted SCSI Response PDU carries the same StatSN as the original PDU. This field is valid only when the Status-Class field is set to 0.
- **Expected Command Sequence Number (ExpCmdSN)**—This is 32 bits long. This field enables the target to acknowledge receipt of commands. Both initiator and target track this counter. The target calculates this value by adding 1 to the highest CmdSN received in a valid PDU. The initiator does not calculate this value. Instead, the initiator uses the value received most recently from the target. This field is valid only when the Status-Class field is set to 0.
- **Maximum Command Sequence Number (MaxCmdSN)**—This is 32 bits long. Whereas lower layers of the OSI model implement flow control at the granularity of a byte or a frame or packet, this field enables flow control at the granularity of a SCSI command. The maximum number of SCSI commands that the target can queue is determined by the resources (such as memory) within the target. This field allows the target to inform the initiator of available resources at a given point in time. Both initiator and target track this counter. The target increments its MaxCmdSN counter by 1 each time it transmits a SCSI Response PDU. The initiator does not calculate this value. Instead, the initiator uses the value received most recently from the target. The maximum number of commands the target can accept from the initiator at a given point in time is calculated as the current value of the target's MaxCmdSN counter minus the current value of the target's CmdSN counter. When the target's CmdSN counter equals its MaxCmdSN counter, the target cannot accept new commands within this session. This field is valid only when the Status-Class field is set to 0.
- **Status-Class**—This is 8 bits long. It indicates the status of the most recently received Login Request PDU. A value of 0 indicates that the request was understood and processed properly. A value of 1 indicates that the initiator is being redirected. Redirection usually indicates the target IP address has changed; a text key-value pair must be included in the Data segment to indicate the new IP address. A value of 2

indicates that the target has detected an initiator error. The login procedure should be aborted, and a new login phase should be initiated if the initiator still requires access to the target. A value of 3 indicates that the target has experienced an internal error. The initiator may retry the request without aborting the login procedure. All other values are currently undefined but not explicitly reserved.

- **Status-Detail**—This is 8 bits long. It provides more detail within each category of Status-Class. This field is meant to be used by sophisticated iSCSI initiator implementations and may be ignored by simple iSCSI initiator implementations.

- **Reserved**—This is 80 bits long.

Following login, the initiator may send SCSI commands to the target. Figure 8-7 illustrates the iSCSI BHS of a SCSI Command PDU. All fields marked with "." are reserved.

Figure 8-7   *iSCSI SCSI Command BHS Format*

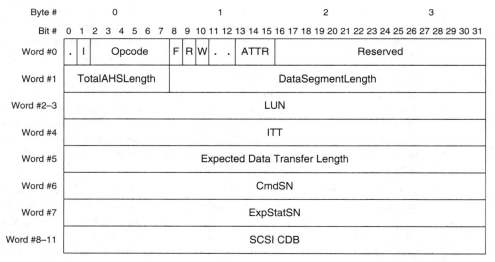

A brief description of each field follows. The description of each field is abbreviated unless a field is used in a PDU-specific manner:

- **Reserved**—This is 1 bit.
- **I**—This is 1 bit.
- **Opcode**—This is 6 bits long. It is set to 0x01.
- **F**—This is 1 bit.
- **R**—This is 1 bit. It indicates a read command when set to 1. For bidirectional commands, both the R and W bits are set to 1.
- **W**—This is 1 bit. It indicates a write command when set to 1. For bidirectional commands, both the R and W bits are set to 1.
- **Reserved**—This is 2 bits long.

- **ATTR**—This is 3 bits long. It indicates the SCSI Task Attribute. A value of 0 indicates an untagged task. A value of 1 indicates a simple task. A value of 2 indicates an ordered task. A value of 3 indicates a Head Of Queue task. A value of 4 indicates an Auto Contingent Allegiance (ACA) task. All other values are reserved. For more information about SCSI Task Attributes, see the ANSI T10 SAM-3 specification.

- **Reserved**—This is 16 bits long.

- **TotalAHSLength**—This is 8 bits long.

- **DataSegmentLength**—This is 24 bits long.

- **LUN**—This is 64 bits (8 bytes) long.

- **ITT**—This is 32 bits long.

- **Expected Data Transfer Length**—This is 32 bits long. It indicates the total amount of data expected to be transferred unidirectionally by this command. This field is expressed in bytes. When the data transfer is bidirectional, this field represents the write data, and the Expected Bidirectional Read Data Length AHS must follow the BHS. This field is set to 0 for certain commands that do not transfer data. This field represents an estimate. After all data is transferred, the target informs the initiator of how much data was actually transferred.

- **CmdSN**—This is 32 bits long. It contains the current value of the CmdSN counter. The CmdSN counter is incremented by 1 immediately following transmission of a new non-immediate command. Thus, the counter represents the number of the next non-immediate command to be sent. The only exception is when an immediate command is transmitted. For an immediate command, the CmdSN field contains the current value of the CmdSN counter, but the counter is not incremented after transmission of the immediate command. Thus, the next non-immediate command to be transmitted carries the same CmdSN as the preceding immediate command. The CmdSN counter is incremented by 1 immediately following transmission of the first non-immediate command to follow an immediate command. A retransmitted SCSI Command PDU carries the same CmdSN as the original PDU. Note that a retransmitted SCSI Command PDU also carries the same ITT as the original PDU.

- **ExpStatSN**—This is 32 bits long.

- **SCSI CDB**—This is 128 bits (16 bytes) long. Multiple SCSI CDB formats are defined by ANSI. SCSI CDBs are variable in length up to a maximum of 260 bytes, but the most common CDB formats are 16 bytes long or less. Thus, the most common CDB formats can fit into this field. When a CDB shorter than 16 bytes is sent, this field is padded with zeros. When a CDB longer than 16 bytes is sent, the BHS must be followed by an Extended CDB AHS containing the remainder of the CDB. All CDBs longer than 16 bytes must end on a 4-byte word boundary, so the Extended CDB AHS does not require padding.

The final result of each SCSI command is a SCSI status indicator delivered in a SCSI Response PDU. The SCSI Response PDU also conveys iSCSI status for protocol operations. Figure 8-8 illustrates the iSCSI BHS of a SCSI Response PDU. All fields marked with "." are reserved.

Figure 8-8 *iSCSI SCSI Response BHS Format*

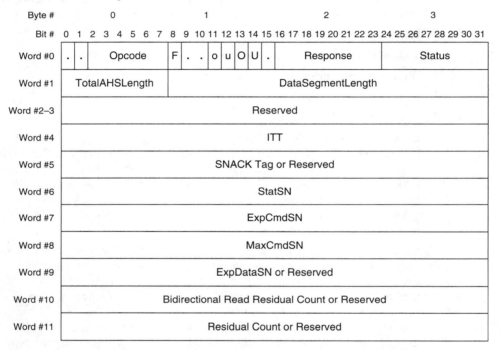

A brief description of each field follows. The description of each field is abbreviated unless a field is used in a PDU-specific manner:

- **Reserved**—This is 1 bit.
- **Reserved**—This is the 1 bit redefined as Reserved.
- **Opcode**—This is 6 bits long and is set to 0x21.
- **F bit**—This is always set to 1.
- **Reserved**—This is 2 bits long.
- **o**—This is 1 bit. The o stands for overflow. When a bidirectional command generates more read data than expected by the initiator, this bit is set to 1. This condition is known as a Bidirectional Read Residual Overflow. This bit is not used for unidirectional commands. This bit is valid only if the Response field is set to 0x00.
- **u**—This is 1 bit. The u stands for underflow. When a bidirectional command generates less read data than expected by the initiator, this bit is set to 1. This condition is known as a Bidirectional Read Residual Underflow. This bit is not used for unidirectional commands. This bit is valid only if the Response field is set to 0x00.

- **O**—This is 1 bit. The O stands for overflow. When a bidirectional command generates more write data than expected by the initiator, this bit is set to 1. This condition is known as a Bidirectional Write Residual Overflow. When a unidirectional read command generates more data than expected by the initiator, this bit is set to 1. When a unidirectional write command generates more data than expected by the initiator, this bit is set to 1. In both unidirectional cases, this condition is known as a Residual Overflow. This bit is valid only if the Response field is set to 0x00.

- **U**—This is 1 bit. The U stands for underflow. When a bidirectional command generates less write data than expected by the initiator, this bit is set to 1. This condition is known as a Bidirectional Write Residual Underflow. When a unidirectional read command generates less data than expected by the initiator, this bit is set to 1. When a unidirectional write command generates less data than expected by the initiator, this bit is set to 1. In both unidirectional cases, this condition is known as a Residual Underflow. This bit is valid only if the Response field is set to 0x00.

- **Reserved**—This is 1 bit.

- **Response**—This is 8 bits long and contains a code that indicates the presence or absence of iSCSI protocol errors. The iSCSI response code is to the SCSI service delivery subsystem what the SCSI status code is to SAL. An iSCSI response code of 0x00 is known as Command Completed at Target. It indicates the target has completed processing the command from the iSCSI perspective. This iSCSI response code is roughly equivalent to a SCSI service response of LINKED COMMAND COMPLETE or TASK COMPLETE. This iSCSI response code is also roughly equivalent to an FCP_RSP_LEN_VALID bit set to zero. An iSCSI response code of 0x00 conveys iSCSI success but does not imply SCSI success. An iSCSI response code of 0x01 is known as Target Failure. It indicates failure to process the command. This iSCSI response code is roughly equivalent to a SCSI service response of SERVICE DELIVERY OR TARGET FAILURE. This iSCSI response code is also roughly equivalent to an FCP_RSP_LEN_VALID bit set to 1. iSCSI response codes 0x80-0xff are vendor-specific. All other iSCSI response codes are reserved.

Note	The SCSI service response is passed to the SAL from the SCSI service delivery subsystem within the initiator. The SCSI service response indicates success or failure for delivery operations. Whereas the iSCSI response code provides status between peer layers in the OSI Reference Model, the SCSI service response provides inter-layer status between provider and subscriber.

- **Status**—This is 8 bits long. This field contains a status code that provides more detail about the final status of the SCSI command and the state of the logical unit that executed the command. This field is valid only if the Response field is set to 0x00. Even if the Response field is set to 0x00, the target might not have processed the command successfully. If the status code indicates failure to process the command successfully, error information (called SCSI sense data) is included in the Data segment. All iSCSI devices must support SCSI autosense. iSCSI does not define status codes. Instead, iSCSI uses the status codes defined by the SAM. Currently, 10 SCSI status codes are defined in the SAM-3 specification (see Table 8-3). All other values are reserved:

- **TotalAHSLength**—This is 8 bits long.

- **DataSegmentLength**—This is 24 bits long.

- **Reserved**—This is 64 bits (8 bytes) long.

- **ITT**—This is 32 bits long.

- **SNACK Tag or Reserved**—This is 32 bits long. Each SNACK Request PDU is assigned a tag by the initiator. If the initiator sends one or more SNACK Request PDUs for read data after the SCSI Response PDU has been received, the SCSI Response PDU must be discarded. After retransmitting the missing data, the target retransmits the SCSI Response PDU containing the SNACK Tag of the most recently received SNACK Request PDU. The SAM mandates that no more than one status indicator be sent for each SCSI command. However, a single status indicator may be sent more than once. So, a retransmitted SCSI Response PDU always carries the same StatSN as the original PDU. This represents multiple instances of a single status indicator. The initiator must be able to distinguish between multiple instances of the status indicator to process the most recent instance. This field enables the initiator to detect and discard older SCSI Response PDUs. Only the SCSI Response PDU containing the most recent SNACK Tag is considered valid. If the target does not receive any SNACK Request PDUs before sending status, this field is reserved.

- **StatSN**—This is 32 bits long.

- **ExpCmdSN**—This is 32 bits long.

- **MaxCmdSN**—This is 32 bits long. If a SCSI Response PDU is dropped, the target and initiator can temporarily lose synchronization of their MaxCmdSN counters. During this time, the initiator does not know that the target can accept another command. Depending on the current level of I/O activity, this can result in slight performance degradation. Upon receipt of the retransmitted SCSI Response PDU, the MaxCmdSN counters resynchronize, and performance returns to normal.

- **ExpDataSN or Reserved**—This is 32 bits long. This field contains the expected data sequence number. It enables the initiator to verify that all Data-In/Data-Out PDUs were received without error. The target assigns a data sequence number (DataSN) to each Data-In PDU sent during a read command. Likewise, the initiator assigns a DataSN to each Data-Out PDU sent during a write command. For read commands, the ExpDataSN is always calculated as the current DataSN plus one. Therefore, a value of DataSN plus one is always reported in the SCSI Response PDU regardless of whether the read command completes successfully. For write commands, the initiator resets the value of DataSN to 0 upon transmission of the first PDU in each new sequence of PDUs, and the target resets the value of ExpDataSN to 0 after successful reception of each sequence of PDUs. Therefore, a value of 0 is reported in the SCSI Response PDU if the write command completes successfully. If the write command completes unsuccessfully, the value reported in the SCSI Response PDU may vary depending on choices made by the target. In the case of bidirectional commands, the target uses this field to report the number of Data-In and R2T PDUs transmitted. This field is reserved if a command does not complete or if no Data-In PDUs were sent during a read command.

- **Bidirectional Read Residual Count or Reserved**—This is 32 bits long. When the o bit or the u bit is set to 1, this field indicates the residual read byte count for a bidirectional command. When neither the o bit nor the u bit is set to 1, this field is reserved. This field is not used for unidirectional commands. This field is valid only if the Response field is set to 0x00.

- **Residual Count or Reserved**—This is 32 bits long. When either the O bit or the U bit is set to 1, this field indicates the residual read byte count for a read command, the residual write byte count for a write command, or the residual write byte count for a bidirectional command. When neither the O bit nor the U bit is set to 1, this field is reserved. This field is valid only if the Response field is set to 0x00.

Table 8-3 summarizes the SCSI status codes that are currently defined in the SAM-3 specification. All SCSI status codes excluded from Table 8-3 are reserved.

Table 8-3   *SCSI Status Codes*

Status Code	Status Name	Associated SCSI Service Response
0x00	GOOD	TASK COMPLETE
0x02	CHECK CONDITION	TASK COMPLETE
0x04	CONDITION MET	TASK COMPLETE
0x08	BUSY	TASK COMPLETE
0x10	INTERMEDIATE	LINKED COMMAND COMPLETE
0x14	INTERMEDIATE-CONDITION MET	LINKED COMMAND COMPLETE
0x18	RESERVATION CONFLICT	TASK COMPLETE
0x28	TASK SET FULL	TASK COMPLETE
0x30	ACA ACTIVE	TASK COMPLETE
0x40	TASK ABORTED	TASK COMPLETE

Outbound data is delivered in Data-Out PDUs. Figure 8-9 illustrates the iSCSI BHS of a Data-Out PDU. All fields marked with "." are reserved. Each Data-Out PDU must include a Data segment.

Figure 8-9   *iSCSI Data-Out BHS Format*

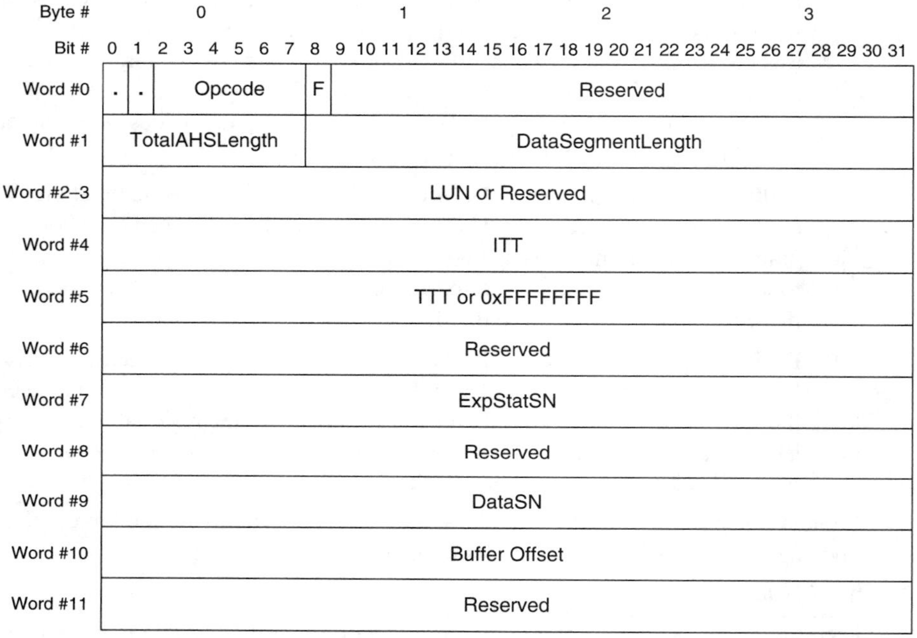

A brief description of each field follows. The description of each field is abbreviated unless a field is used in a PDU-specific manner:

- **Reserved**—This is 1 bit.
- **Reserved**—This is the 1 bit redefined as Reserved.
- **Opcode**—This is 6 bits long. It is set to 0x05.
- **F**—This is 1 bit.
- **Reserved**—This is 23 bits long.
- **TotalAHSLength**—This is 8 bits long.
- **DataSegmentLength**—This is 24 bits long.
- **LUN or Reserved**—This is 64 bits (8 bytes) long. Each R2T PDU provides a LUN. All Data-Out PDUs sent in response to an R2T PDU must carry in this field the LUN provided by the R2T PDU. Upon receipt, the target uses this field and the TTT or 0xFFFFFFFF field to associate the Data-Out PDU with a previously transmitted R2T PDU. For Data-Out PDUs containing first burst data, this field is reserved.
- **ITT**—This is 32 bits long.
- **Target Transfer Tag (TTT) or 0xFFFFFFFF**—This is 32 bits long. Each R2T PDU provides a TTT. All Data-Out PDUs sent in response to an R2T PDU must carry in this field the TTT provided by the R2T PDU. Upon receipt, the target uses this field and the LUN or Reserved field to associate the Data-Out PDU with a previously transmitted R2T

PDU. For Data-Out PDUs containing first burst data, this field contains the value 0xFFFFFFFF.

- **Reserved**—This is 32 bits long.
- **ExpStatSN**—This is 32 bits long.
- **Reserved**—This is 32 bits long.
- **Data Sequence Number (DataSN)**—This is 32 bits long. This field uniquely identifies each Data-Out PDU within each sequence of PDUs. The DataSN is similar in function to the FC SEQ_ID. Each SCSI write command is satisfied with one or more sequences of PDUs. Each PDU sequence is identified by the ITT (for unsolicited data) or the TTT (for solicited data). This field is incremented by one for each Data-Out PDU transmitted within a sequence. A retransmitted Data-Out PDU carries the same DataSN as the original PDU. The counter is reset for each new sequence within the context a single command.
- **Buffer Offset**—This is 32 bits long. This field indicates the position of the first byte of data delivered by this PDU relative to the first byte of all the data transferred by the associated SCSI command. This field enables the target to reassemble the data properly.
- **Reserved**—This is 32 bits long.

Inbound data is delivered in Data-In PDUs. Figure 8-10 illustrates the iSCSI BHS of a Data-In PDU. All fields marked with "." are reserved. Each Data-In PDU must include a Data segment.

Figure 8-10 *iSCSI Data-In BHS Format*

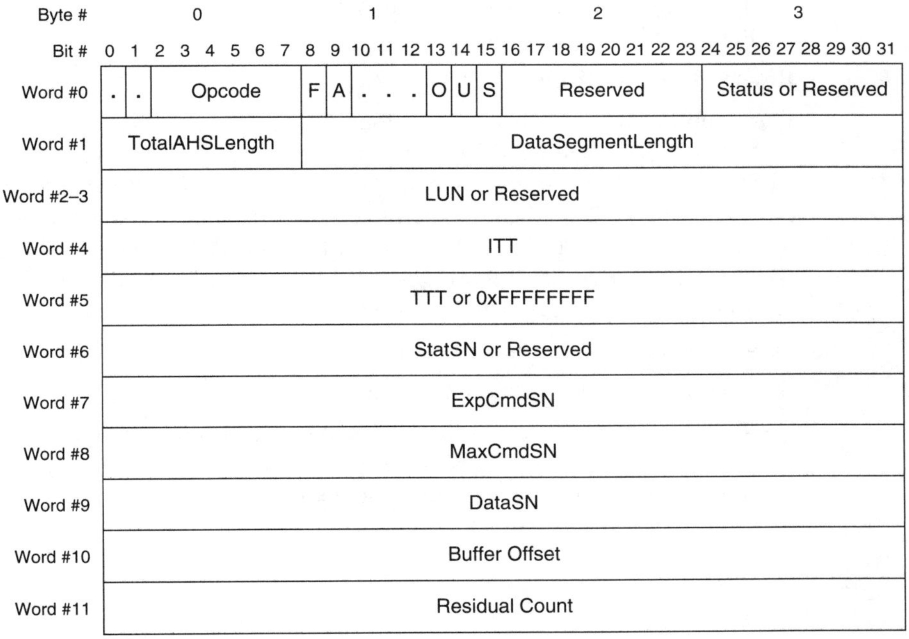

A brief description of each field follows. The description of each field is abbreviated unless a field is used in a PDU-specific manner:

- **Reserved**—This is 1 bit.

- **Reserved**—This is the 1 bit redefined as Reserved.

- **Opcode**—This is 6 bits long. It is set to 0x25.

- **F bit**—This may be set to 1 before sending the final Data-In PDU. Doing so indicates a change of direction during a bidirectional command. When used to change the direction of transfer, this bit is similar in function to the FC Sequence Initiative bit in the F_CTL field in the FC Header.

- **A**—This is 1 bit. The A stands for Acknowledge. The target sets this bit to 1 to request positive, cumulative acknowledgment of all Data-In PDUs transmitted before the current Data-In PDU. This bit may be used only if the session supports an ErrorRecoveryLevel greater than 0 (see the iSCSI Login Parameters section of this chapter).

- **Reserved**—This is 3 bits long.

- **O and U bits**—These are used in the same manner as previously described. These bits are present to support phase-collapse for read commands. For bidirectional commands, the target must send status in a separate SCSI Response PDU. iSCSI (like FCP) does not support status phase-collapse for write commands. These bits are valid only when the S bit is set to 1.

- **S**—This is 1 bit. The S stands for status. When this bit is set to 1, status is included in the PDU.

- **Reserved**—This is 8 bits long.

- **Status or Reserved**—This is 8 bits long. When the S field is set to 1, this field contains the SCSI status code for the command. Phase-collapse is supported only when the iSCSI response code is 0x00. Thus, a Response field is not required because the response code is implied. Furthermore, phase-collapse is supported only when the SCSI status is 0x00, 0x04, 0x10, or 0x14 (GOOD, CONDITION MET, INTERMEDIATE, or INTERMEDIATE-CONDITION MET, respectively). When the S field is set to zero, this field is reserved.

- **TotalAHSLength**—This is 8 bits long.

- **DataSegmentLength**—This is 24 bits long.

- **LUN or Reserved**—This is 64 bits (8 bytes) long and contains the LUN if the A field is set to 1. The initiator copies the value of this field into a similar field in the acknowledgment PDU. If the A field is set to 0, this field is reserved.

- **ITT**—This is 32 bits long.

- **TTT or 0xFFFFFFFF**—This is 32 bits long. It contains a TTT if the A field is set to 1. The initiator copies the value of this field into a similar field in the acknowledgment PDU. If the A field is set to 0, this field is set to 0xFFFFFFFF.

- **StatSN or Reserved**—This is 32 bits long. It contains the StatSN if the S field is set to 1. Otherwise, this field is reserved.

- **ExpCmdSN**—This is 32 bits long.

- **MaxCmdSN**—This is 32 bits long.

- **DataSN**—This is 32 bits long. It uniquely identifies each Data-In PDU within a sequence of PDUs. The DataSN is similar in function to the FC SEQ_ID. Each SCSI read command is satisfied with a single sequence of PDUs. Each PDU sequence is identified by the CmdSN. This field is incremented by 1 for each Data-In PDU transmitted within a SCSI task. A retransmitted Data-In PDU carries the same DataSN as the original PDU. The DataSN counter does not reset within a single read command or after each linked read command within a single SCSI task. Likewise, for bidirectional commands in which the target periodically sets the F field to 1 to allow the transfer of write data, the DataSN counter does not reset after each sequence. This field is also incremented by one for each R2T PDU transmitted during bidirectional command processing. In other words, the target maintains a single counter for both DataSN and R2T Sequence Number (R2TSN) during bidirectional command processing.

- **Buffer Offset**—This is 32 bits long.

- **Residual Count**—This is 32 bits long. It is used in the same manner as previously described. This field is present to support phase-collapse for read commands. This field is valid only when the S field is set to 1.

The target signals its readiness to receive write data via the R2T PDU. The target also uses the R2T PDU to request retransmission of missing Data-Out PDUs. In both cases, the PDU format is the same, but an R2T PDU sent to request retransmission is called a Recovery R2T PDU. Figure 8-11 illustrates the iSCSI BHS of a R2T PDU. All fields marked with "." are reserved.

Figure 8-11 *iSCSI R2T BHS Format*

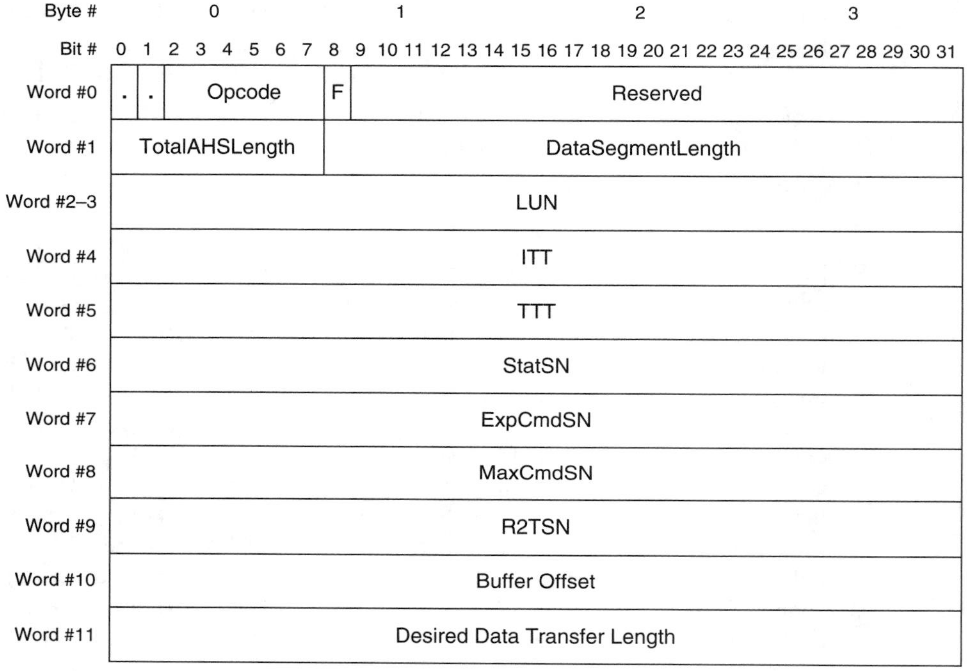

A brief description of each field follows. The description of each field is abbreviated unless a field is used in a PDU-specific manner:

- **Reserved**—This is 1 bit.
- **Reserved**—This is the 1 bit redefined as Reserved.
- **Opcode**—This is 6 bits long. It is set to 0x31.
- **F bit**—This is always set to 1.
- **Reserved**—This is 23 bits long.
- **TotalAHSLength**—This is 8 bits long. It is always set to 0.
- **DataSegmentLength**—This is 24 bits long. It is always set to 0.
- **LUN**—This is 64 bits (8 bytes) in length.
- **ITT**—This is 32 bits in length.
- **TTT**—This is 32 bits long. It contains a tag that aids the target in associating Data-Out PDUs with this R2T PDU. All values are valid except 0xFFFFFFFF, which is reserved for use by initiators during first burst.
- **StatSN**—This is 32 bits long. It contains the StatSN that will be assigned to this command upon completion. This is the same as the ExpStatSN from the initiator's perspective.

- **ExpCmdSN**—This is 32 bits long.
- **MaxCmdSN**—This is 32 bits long.
- **R2TSN**—This is 32 bits long. It uniquely identifies each R2T PDU within the context of a single SCSI task. Each task is identified by the ITT. This field is incremented by 1 for each new R2T PDU transmitted within a SCSI task. A retransmitted R2T PDU carries the same R2TSN as the original PDU. This field is also incremented by 1 for each Data-In PDU transmitted during bidirectional command processing.
- **Buffer Offset**—This is 32 bits long. It indicates the position of the first byte of data requested by this PDU relative to the first byte of all the data transferred by the SCSI command.
- **Desired Data Transfer Length**—This is 32 bits long. This field indicates how much data should be transferred in response to this R2T PDU. This field is expressed in bytes. The value of this field cannot be 0 and cannot exceed the negotiated value of MaxBurstLength (see the iSCSI Login Parameters section of this chapter).

iSCSI supports PDU retransmission and PDU delivery acknowledgment on demand via the SNACK Request PDU. Each SNACK Request PDU specifies a contiguous set of missing single-type PDUs. Each set is called a run. Figure 8-12 illustrates the iSCSI BHS of a SNACK Request PDU. All fields marked with "." are reserved.

Figure 8-12 *iSCSI SNACK Request BHS Format*

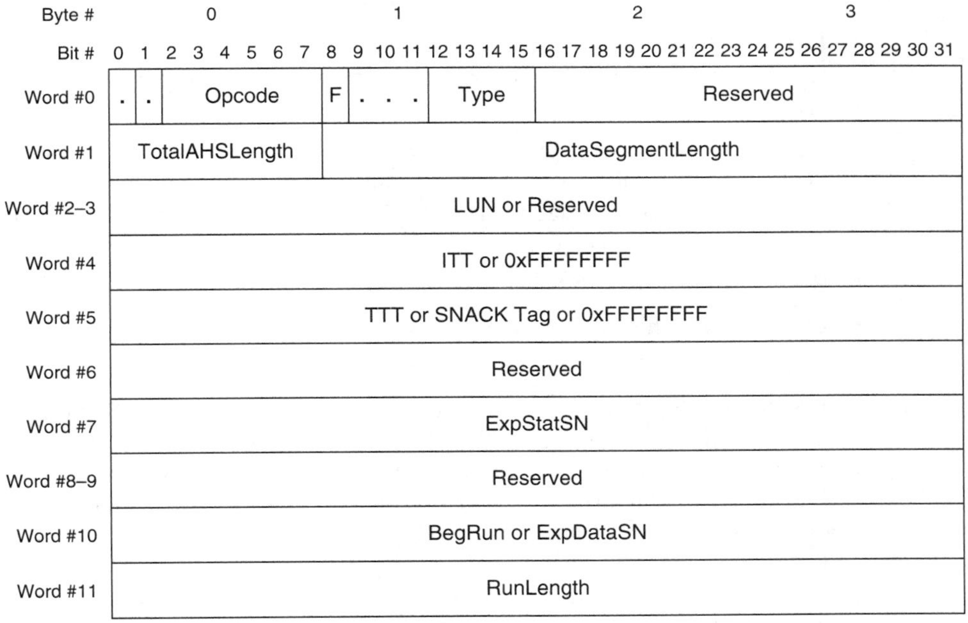

A brief description of each field follows. The description of each field is abbreviated unless a field is used in a PDU-specific manner:

- **Reserved**—This is 1 bit.

- **Reserved**—This is the 1 bit redefined as Reserved.

- **Opcode**—This is 6 bits long. It is set to 0x10.

- **F bit**—This is always set to 1.

- **Reserved**—This is 3 bits long.

- **Type**—This is 4 bits long. The SNACK Request PDU serves multiple functions. So, RFC 3720 defines multiple SNACK Request PDU types. This field indicates the PDU function. The PDU format is the same for all SNACK Request PDUs regardless of type, but some fields contain type-specific information. All PDU types must be supported if an ErrorRecoveryLevel greater than 0 is negotiated during login (see the iSCSI Login Parameters section of this chapter). Currently, only four PDU types are defined (see Table 8-4). All other types are reserved.

- **Reserved**—This is 16 bits long.

- **TotalAHSLength**—This is 8 bits long.

- **DataSegmentLength**—This is 24 bits long.

- **LUN or Reserved**—This is 64 bits (8 bytes) long. It contains a LUN if the PDU type is DataACK. The value in this field is copied from the LUN field of the Data-In PDU that requested the DataACK PDU. Otherwise, this field is reserved.

- **ITT or 0xFFFFFFFF**—This is 32 bits long. It is set to 0xFFFFFFFF if the PDU type is Status or DataACK. Otherwise, this field contains the ITT of the associated task.

- **TTT or SNACK Tag or 0xFFFFFFFF**—This is 32 bits long. It contains a TTT if the PDU type is DataACK. The value in this field is copied from the TTT field of the Data-In PDU that requested the DataACK PDU. This field contains a SNACK Tag if the PDU type is R-Data. Otherwise, this field is set to 0xFFFFFFFF.

- **Reserved**—This is 32 bits long.

- **ExpStatSN**—This is 32 bits long.

- **Reserved**—This is 64 bits (8 bytes) long.

- **BegRun or ExpDataSN**—This is 32 bits long. For Data/R2T and Status PDUs, this field contains the identifier (DataSN, R2TSN or StatSN) of the first PDU to be retransmitted. This value indicates the beginning of the run. Note that the SNACK Request does not request retransmission of data based on relative offset. Instead, one or more specific PDUs are requested. This contrasts the FCP model. For DataACK PDUs, this field contains the initiator's ExpDataSN. All Data-in PDUs up to but not including the ExpDataSN are acknowledged by this field. For R-Data PDUs, this field must be set to 0. In this case, all unacknowledged Data-In PDUs are retransmitted. If no Data-In PDUs have been acknowledged, the entire read sequence is retransmitted beginning at DataSN 0. If some Data-In PDUs have been acknowledged, the first retransmitted Data-In PDU is assigned the first unacknowledged DataSN.

- **RunLength**—This is 32 bits long. For Data/R2T and Status PDUs, this field specifies the number of PDUs to retransmit. This field may be set to 0 to indicate that all PDUs with a sequence number equal to or greater than BegRun must be retransmitted. For DataACK and R-Data PDUs, this field must be set to 0.

Table 8-4 summarizes the SNACK Request PDU types that are currently defined in RFC 3720. All PDU types excluded from Table 8-4 are reserved.

Table 8-4   *iSCSI SNACK Request PDU Types*

Type	Name	Function
0	Data/R2T	Initiators use this PDU type to request retransmission of one or more Data-In or R2T PDUs. By contrast, targets use the Recovery R2T PDU to request retransmission of one or more Data-Out PDUs.
1	Status	Initiators use this PDU type to request retransmission of one or more Login Response PDUs or a SCSI Response PDU. By contrast, targets do not request retransmission of SCSI Command PDUs.
2	DataACK	Initiators use this PDU type to provide explicit, positive, cumulative acknowledgment for Data-In PDUs. This frees buffer space within the target device and enables efficient recovery of dropped PDUs during long read operations. By contrast, targets do not provide acknowledgment for Data-Out PDUs. This is not necessary because the SAM requires initiators to keep all write data in memory until a SCSI status of GOOD, CONDITION MET, or INTERMEDIATE-CONDITION MET is received.
3	R-Data	Initiators use this PDU type to request retransmission of one or more Data-In PDUs that need to be resegmented. The need for resegmentation occurs when the initiator's MaxRecvDataSegmentLength changes during read command processing. By contrast, targets use the Recovery R2T PDU to request retransmission of one or more Data-Out PDUs if the target's MaxRecvDataSegmentLength changes during write command processing. Even when resegmentation is not required, initiators use this PDU type. If a SCSI Response PDU is received before all associated Data-In PDUs are received, this PDU type must be used to request retransmission of the missing Data-In PDUs. In such a case, the associated SCSI Response PDU must be retransmitted after the Data-In PDUs are retransmitted. The SNACK Tag must be copied into the duplicate SCSI Response PDU to enable the initiator to discern between the duplicate SCSI Response PDUs.

iSCSI initiators manage SCSI and iSCSI tasks via the TMF Request PDU. Figure 8-13 illustrates the iSCSI BHS of a TMF Request PDU. All fields marked with "." are reserved.

Figure 8-13 *iSCSI TMF Request BHS Format*

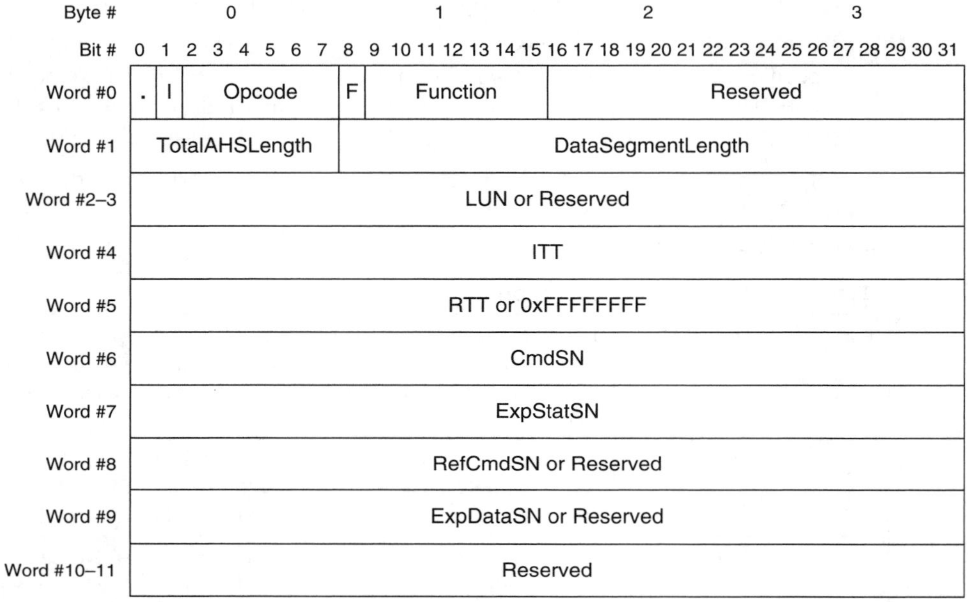

A brief description of each field follows. The description of each field is abbreviated unless a field is used in a PDU-specific manner:

- **Reserved**—This is 1 bit.
- **I**—This is 1 bit.
- **Opcode**—This is 6 bits long. It is set to 0x02.
- **F bit**—This is always set to 1.
- **Function**—This is 7 bits long. It contains the TMF Request code of the function to be performed. iSCSI currently supports six of the TMFs defined in the SAM-2 specification and one TMF defined in RFC 3720 (see Table 8-5). All other TMF Request codes are reserved.
- **Reserved**—This is 16 bits long.
- **TotalAHSLength**—This is 8 bits long. It is always set to 0.
- **DataSegmentLength**—This is 24 bits long. It is always set to 0.
- **LUN or Reserved**—This is 64 bits (8 bytes) long. It contains a LUN if the TMF is ABORT TASK, ABORT TASK SET, CLEAR ACA, CLEAR TASK SET, or LOGICAL UNIT RESET. Otherwise, this field is reserved.
- **ITT**—This is 32 bits long. It contains the ITT assigned to this TMF command. This field does not contain the ITT of the task upon which the TMF command acts.

- **Referenced Task Tag (RTT) or 0xFFFFFFFF**—This is 32 bits long. If the TMF is ABORT TASK or TASK REASSIGN, this field contains the ITT of the task upon which the TMF command acts. Otherwise, this field is set to 0xFFFFFFFF.

- **CmdSN**—This is 32 bits long. It contains the CmdSN of the TMF command. TMF commands are numbered the same way SCSI read and write commands are numbered. This field does not contain the CmdSN of the task upon which the TMF command acts.

- **ExpStatSN**—This is 32 bits long.

- **RefCmdSN or Reserved**—This is 32 bits long. If the TMF is ABORT TASK, this field contains the CmdSN of the task upon which the TMF command acts. The case of linked commands is not explicitly described in RFC 3720. Presumably, this field should contain the highest CmdSN associated with the RTT. This field is reserved for all other TMF commands.

- **ExpDataSN or Reserved**—This is 32 bits long. It is used only if the TMF is TASK REASSIGN. Otherwise, this field is reserved. For read and bidirectional commands, this field contains the highest acknowledged DataSN plus one for Data-In PDUs. This is known as the data acknowledgment reference number (DARN). If no Data-In PDUs were acknowledged before connection failure, this field contains the value 0. The initiator must discard all unacknowledged Data-In PDUs for the affected task(s) after a connection failure. The target must retransmit all unacknowledged Data-In PDUs for the affected task(s) after connection allegiance is reassigned. For write commands and write data in bidirectional commands, this field is not used. The target simply requests retransmission of Data-Out PDUs as needed via the Recovery R2T PDU.

- **Reserved**—This is 64 bits long.

Table 8-5 summarizes the TMF Request codes that are currently supported by iSCSI. All TMF Request codes excluded from Table 8-5 are reserved.

Table 8-5   *iSCSI TMF Request Codes*

TMF Code	TMF Name	Description
1	ABORT TASK	This function instructs the Task Manager of the specified LUN to abort the task identified in the RTT field. This TMF command cannot be used to terminate TMF commands.
2	ABORT TASK SET	This function instructs the Task Manager of the specified LUN to abort all tasks issued within the associated session. This function does not affect tasks instantiated by other initiators.
3	CLEAR ACA	This function instructs the Task Manager of the specified LUN to clear the ACA condition. This has the same affect as ABORT TASK for all tasks with the ACA attribute. Tasks that do not have the ACA attribute are not affected.

continues

Table 8-5   *iSCSI TMF Request Codes (Continued)*

TMF Code	TMF Name	Description
4	CLEAR TASK SET	This function instructs the Task Manager of the specified LUN to abort all tasks identified by the task set type (TST) field in the SCSI Control Mode Page. This function can abort all tasks from a single initiator or all tasks from all initiators.
5	LOGICAL UNIT RESET	This function instructs the Task Manager of the specified LUN to abort all tasks, clear all ACA conditions, release all reservations, reset the logical unit's operating mode to its default state and set a Unit Attention condition. In the case of hierarchical LUNs, these actions also must be taken for each dependent logical unit.
6	TARGET WARM RESET	This function instructs the Task Manager of LUN 0 to perform a LOGICAL UNIT RESET for every LUN accessible via the target port through which the command is received. This function is subject to SCSI access controls and also may be subject to iSCSI access controls.
7	TARGET COLD RESET	This function instructs the Task Manager of LUN 0 to perform a LOGICAL UNIT RESET for every LUN accessible via the target port through which the command is received. This function is *not* subject to SCSI access controls but may be subject to iSCSI access controls. This function also instructs the Task Manager of LUN 0 to terminate all TCP connections for the target port through which the command is received.
8	TASK REASSIGN	This function instructs the Task Manager of the specified LUN to reassign connection allegiance for the task identified in the RTT field. Connection allegiance is reassigned to the TCP connection on which the TASK REASSIGN command is received. This function is supported only if the session supports an ErrorRecoveryLevel of two. This function must always be transmitted as an immediate command.

Each TMF Request PDU precipitates one TMF Response PDU. Figure 8-14 illustrates the iSCSI BHS of a TMF Response PDU. All fields marked with "." are reserved.

A brief description of each field follows. The description of each field is abbreviated unless a field is used in a PDU-specific manner:

- **Reserved**—This is 1 bit.
- **Reserved**—This is the 1 bit redefined as Reserved.

- **Opcode**—This is 6 bits long. It is set to 0x22.
- **F bit**—This is always set to 1.
- **Reserved**—This is 7 bits long.
- **Response**—This is 8 bits long. This field indicates the completion status for the TMF command identified in the ITT field. RFC 3720 currently defines eight TMF Response codes (see Table 8-6). All other values are reserved.
- **Reserved**—This is 8 bits long.
- **TotalAHSLength**—This is 8 bits long. It is always set to 0.
- **DataSegmentLength**—This is 24 bits long. It is always set to 0.
- **Reserved**—This is 64 bits (8 bytes) long.
- **ITT**—This is 32 bits long.
- **Reserved**—This is 32 bits long.
- **StatSN**—This is 32 bits long.
- **ExpCmdSN**—This is 32 bits long.
- **MaxCmdSN**—This is 32 bits long.
- **Reserved**—This is 96 bits (12 bytes) long.

Figure 8-14 *iSCSI TMF Response BHS Format*

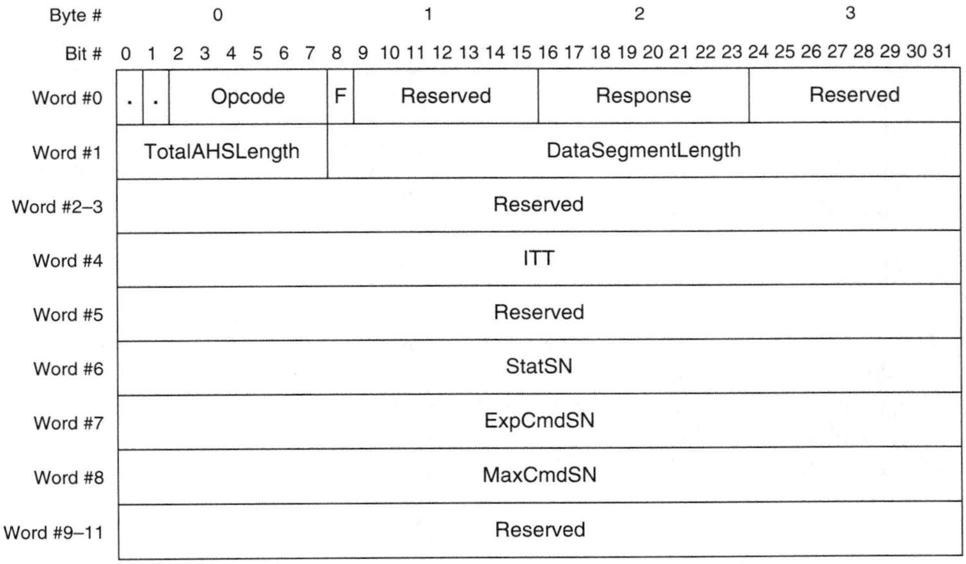

Table 8-6 summarizes the TMF Response codes that are currently supported by iSCSI. All TMF Response codes excluded from Table 8-6 are reserved.

Table 8-6 *iSCSI TMF Response Codes*

TMF Code	TMF Name	Description
0	Function Complete	The TMF command completed successfully.
1	Task Does Not Exist	The task identified in the RTT field of the TMF request PDU does not exist. This response is valid only if the CmdSN in the RefCmdSN field in the TMF request PDU is outside the valid CmdSN window. If the CmdSN in the RefCmdSN field in the TMF request PDU is within the valid CmdSN window, a function complete response must be sent.
2	LUN Does Not Exist	The LUN identified in the LUN or Reserved field of the TMF request PDU does not exist.
3	Task Still Allegiant	Logout of the old connection has not completed. A task may not be reassigned until logout of the old connection successfully completes with reason code "remove the connection for recovery".
4	Task Allegiance Reassignment Not Supported	The session does not support ErrorRecoveryLevel 2.
5	TMF Not Supported	The target does not support the requested TMF command. Some TMF commands are optional for targets.
6	Function Authorization Failed	The initiator is not authorized to execute the requested TMF command.
255	Function Rejected	The initiator attempted an illegal TMF request (such as ABORT TASK for a different TMF task).

The Reject PDU signals an error condition and rejects the PDU that caused the error. The Data segment (not shown in Figure 8-15) must contain the header of the PDU that caused the error. If a Reject PDU causes a task to terminate, a SCSI Response PDU with status CHECK CONDITION must be sent. Figure 8-15 illustrates the iSCSI BHS of a Reject PDU. All fields marked with "." are reserved.

Figure 8-15 *iSCSI Reject BHS Format*

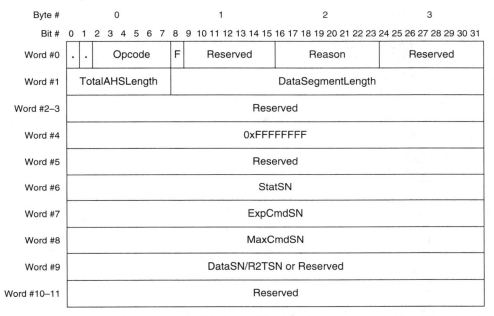

A brief description of each field follows. The description of each field is abbreviated unless a field is used in a PDU-specific manner:

- **Reserved**—This is 1 bit.
- **Reserved**—This is the 1 bit redefined as Reserved.
- **Opcode**—This is 6 bits long. It is set to 0x3F.
- **F bit**—This is always set to 1.
- **Reserved**—This is 7 bits long.
- **Reason**—This is 8 bits long. This field indicates the reason the erroneous PDU is being rejected. RFC 3720 currently defines 11 Reject Reason codes (see Table 8-7). All other values are reserved.
- **Reserved**—This is 8 bits long.
- **TotalAHSLength**—This is 8 bits long. It is always set to 0.
- **DataSegmentLength**—This is 24 bits long.
- **Reserved**—This is 64 bits (8 bytes) long.
- **ITT**—This is 32 bits long. It is set to 0xFFFFFFFF.
- **Reserved**—This is 32 bits long.
- **StatSN**—This is 32 bits long.
- **ExpCmdSN**—This is 32 bits long.

- **MaxCmdSN**—This is 32 bits long.

- **DataSN/R2TSN or Reserved**—This is 32 bits long. This field is valid only when rejecting a Data/R2T SNACK Request PDU. The Reject Reason code must be 0x04 (Protocol Error). This field indicates the DataSN or R2TSN of the next Data-In or R2T PDU to be transmitted by the target. Otherwise, this field is reserved.

- **Reserved**—This is 64 bits (8 bytes) long.

Table 8-7 summarizes the Reject Reason codes that are currently supported by iSCSI. All Reject Reason codes excluded from Table 8-7 are reserved.

Table 8-7   *iSCSI Reject Reason Codes*

Reason Code	Reason Name
0x02	Data-Digest Error
0x03	SNACK Reject
0x04	Protocol Error
0x05	Command Not Supported
0x06	Immediate Command Rejected—Too Many Immediate Commands
0x07	Task In Progress
0x08	Invalid DataACK
0x09	Invalid PDU Field
0x0a	Long Operation Reject—Cannot Generate TTT—Out Of Resources
0x0b	Negotiation Reset
0x0c	Waiting For Logout

The preceding discussion of iSCSI PDU formats is simplified for the sake of clarity. Comprehensive exploration of all the iSCSI PDUs and their variations is outside the scope of this book. For more information, readers are encouraged to consult IETF RFC 3720 and the ANSI T10 SAM-2, SAM-3, SPC-2, and SPC-3 specifications.

iSCSI Login Parameters

During the Login Phase, security and operating parameters are exchanged as text key-value pairs. As previously stated, text keys are encapsulated in the Data segment of the Login Request and Login Response PDUs. Some operating parameters may be re-negotiated after the Login Phase completes (during the Full Feature Phase) via the Text Request and Text Response PDUs. However, most operating parameters remain unchanged for the duration of a session. Security parameters may not be re-negotiated during an active session. Some text keys have a session-wide scope, and others have a connection-specific scope. Some text keys may be exchanged only during negotiation of the leading connection for a new session. Some text keys require a response (negotiation), and others do not (declaration). Currently, RFC 3720 defines 22 operational text keys. RFC 3720 also defines a protocol extension mechanism that enables the use of public and private text keys that are not defined in RFC 3720. This section describes the standard operational text keys and the extension mechanism. The format of all text key-value pairs is:

      <key name>=<list of values>

The SessionType key declares the type of iSCSI session. Only initiators send this key. This key must be sent only during the Login Phase on the leading connection. The valid values are Normal and Discovery. The default value is Normal. The scope is session-wide.

The HeaderDigest and DataDigest keys negotiate the use of the Header-Digest segment and the Data-Digest segment, respectively. Initiators and targets send these keys. These keys may be sent only during the Login Phase. Values that must be supported include CRC32C and None. Other public and private algorithms may be supported. The default value is None for both keys. The chosen digest must be used in every PDU sent during the Full Feature Phase. The scope is connection-specific.

As discussed in Chapter 3, the SendTargets key is used by initiators to discover targets during a Discovery session. This key may also be sent by initiators during a Normal session to discover changed or additional paths to a known target. Sending this key during a Normal session is fruitful only if the target configuration changes after the Login Phase. This is because, during a Discovery session, a target network entity must return all target names, sockets, and TPGTs for all targets that the requesting initiator is permitted to access. Additionally, path changes occurring during the Login Phase of a Normal session are handled via redirection. This key may be sent only during the Full Feature Phase. The scope is session-wide.

The TargetName key declares the iSCSI device name of one or more target devices within the responding network entity. This key may be sent by targets only in response to a SendTargets command. This key may be sent by initiators only during the Login Phase of a Normal session, and the key must be included in the leading Login Request PDU for each connection. The scope is session-wide.

The TargetAddress key declares the network addresses, TCP ports, and TPGTs of the target device to the initiator device. An address may be given in the form of DNS host name, IPv4 address, or IPv6 address. The TCP port may be omitted if the default port of 3260 is used. Only targets send this key. This key is usually sent in response to a SendTargets command, but it may be sent in a Login Response PDU to redirect an initiator. Therefore, this key may be sent during any phase. The scope is session-wide.

The InitiatorName key declares the iSCSI device name of the initiator device within the initiating network entity. This key identifies the initiator device to the target device so that access controls can be implemented. Only initiators send this key. This key may be sent only during the Login Phase, and the key must be included in the leading Login Request PDU for each connection. The scope is session-wide.

The InitiatorAlias key declares the optional human-friendly name of the initiator device to the target for display in relevant user interfaces. Only initiators send this key. This key is usually sent in a Login Request PDU for a Normal session, but it may be sent during the Full Feature Phase as well. The scope is session-wide.

The TargetAlias key declares the optional human-friendly name of the target device to the initiator for display in relevant user interfaces. Only targets send this key. This key usually is sent in a Login Response PDU for a Normal session, but it may be sent during the Full Feature Phase as well. The scope is session-wide.

The TargetPortalGroupTag key declares the TPGT of the target port to the initiator port. Only targets send this key. This key must be sent in the first Login Response PDU of a Normal session unless the first Login Response PDU redirects the initiator to another TargetAddress. The range of valid values is 0 to 65,535. The scope is session-wide.

The ImmediateData and InitialR2T keys negotiate support for immediate data and unsolicited data, respectively. Immediate data may not be sent unless both devices support immediate data. Unsolicited data may not be sent unless both devices support unsolicited data. Initiators and targets send these keys. These keys may be sent only during Normal sessions and must be sent during the Login Phase on the leading connection. The default settings support immediate data but not unsolicited data. The scope is session-wide for both keys.

The MaxOutstandingR2T key negotiates the maximum number of R2T PDUs that may be outstanding simultaneously for a single task. This key does not include the implicit R2T PDU associated with unsolicited data. Each R2T PDU is considered outstanding until the last Data-Out PDU is transferred (initiator's perspective) or received (target's perspective). A sequence timeout can also terminate the lifespan of an R2T PDU. Initiators and targets send this key. This key may be sent only during Normal sessions and must be sent during the Login Phase on the leading connection. The range of valid values is 1 to 65,535. The default value is one. The scope is session-wide.

The MaxRecvDataSegmentLength key declares the maximum amount of data that a receiver (initiator or target) can receive in a single iSCSI PDU. Initiators and targets send this key. This key may be sent during any phase of any session type and is usually sent during the Login Phase on the leading connection. This key is expressed in bytes. The range of valid values is 512 to 16,777,215. The default value is 8,192. The scope is connection-specific.

The MaxBurstLength key negotiates the maximum amount of data that a receiver (initiator or target) can receive in a single iSCSI sequence. This value may exceed the value of MaxRecvDataSegmentLength, which means that more than one PDU may be sent in response to an R2T Request PDU. This contrasts the FC model. For write commands, this key applies only to solicited data. Initiators and targets send this key. This key may be sent only during Normal sessions and must be sent during the Login Phase on the leading connection. This key is expressed in bytes. The range of valid values is 512 to 16,777,215. The default value is 262,144. The scope is session-wide.

The FirstBurstLength key negotiates the maximum amount of data that a target can receive in a single iSCSI sequence of unsolicited data (including immediate data). Thus, the value of this key minus the amount of immediate data received with the SCSI command PDU yields the amount of unsolicited data that the target can receive in the same sequence. If neither immediate data nor unsolicited data is supported within the session, this key is invalid. The value of this key cannot exceed the target's MaxBurstLength. Initiators and targets send this key. This key may be sent only during Normal sessions and must be sent during the Login Phase on the leading connection. This key is expressed in bytes. The range of valid values is 512 to 16,777,215. The default value is 65,536. The scope is session-wide.

The MaxConnections key negotiates the maximum number of TCP connections supported by a session. Initiators and targets send this key. Discovery sessions are restricted to one TCP connection, so this key may be sent only during Normal sessions and must be sent during the Login Phase on the leading connection. The range of valid values is 1 to 65,535. The default is value is 1. The scope is session-wide.

The DefaultTime2Wait key negotiates the amount of time that must pass before attempting to logout a failed connection. Task reassignment may not occur until after the failed connection is logged out. Initiators and targets send this key. This key may be sent only during Normal sessions and must be sent during the Login Phase on the leading connection. This key is expressed in seconds. The range of valid values is 0 to 3600. The default value is 2. A value of 0 indicates that logout may be attempted immediately upon detection of a failed connection. The scope is session-wide.

The DefaultTime2Retain key negotiates the amount of time that task state information must be retained for active tasks after DefaultTime2Wait expires. When a connection fails, this key determines how much time is available to complete task reassignment. If the failed connection is the last (or only) connection in a session, this key also represents the session timeout value. Initiators and targets send this key. This key may be sent only during Normal sessions and must be sent during the Login Phase on the leading connection. This key is expressed in seconds. The range of valid values is 0 to 3600. The default value is 20. A value of 0 indicates that task state information is discarded immediately upon detection of a failed connection. The scope is session-wide.

The DataPDUInOrder key negotiates in-order transmission of data PDUs within a sequence. Because TCP guarantees in-order delivery, the only way for PDUs of a given sequence to arrive out of order is to be transmitted out of order. Initiators and targets send this key. This key may be sent only during Normal sessions and must be sent during the Login Phase on the leading connection. The default value requires in-order transmission. The scope is session-wide.

The DataSequenceInOrder key negotiates in-order transmission of data PDU sequences within a command. For sessions that support in-order transmission of sequences and retransmission of missing data PDUs (ErrorRecoveryLevel greater than zero), the MaxOustandingR2T key must be set to 1. This is because requests for retransmission may be sent only for the lowest outstanding R2TSN, and all PDUs already received for a higher outstanding R2TSN must be discarded until retransmission succeeds. This is inefficient. It undermines the goal of multiple outstanding R2T PDUs. Sessions that do not support retransmission must terminate the appropriate task upon detection of a missing data PDU, and all data PDUs must be retransmitted via a new task. Thus, no additional inefficiency is introduced by supporting multiple outstanding R2T PDUs when the ErrorRecoveryLevel key is set to 0. Initiators and targets send the DataSequenceInOrder key. This key may be sent only during Normal sessions and must be sent during the Login Phase on the leading connection. The default value requires in-order transmission. The scope is session-wide.

The ErrorRecoveryLevel key negotiates the combination of recovery mechanisms supported by the session. Initiators and targets send this key. This key may be sent only during the Login Phase on the leading connection. The range of valid values is 0 to 2. The default value is 0. The scope is session-wide.

The OFMarker and IFMarker keys negotiate support for PDU boundary detection via the fixed interval markers (FIM) scheme. Initiators and targets send these keys. These keys may be sent during any session type and must be sent during the Login Phase. The default setting is disabled for both keys. The scope is connection-specific.

The OFMarkInt and IFMarkInt keys negotiate the interval for the FIM scheme. These keys are valid only if the FIM scheme is used. Initiators and targets send these keys. These keys may be sent during any session type and must be sent during the Login Phase. These keys are expressed in 4-byte words. The range of valid values is 1 to 65,535. The default value is 2048 for both keys. The scope is connection-specific.

A mechanism is defined to enable implementers to extend the iSCSI protocol via additional key-value pairs. These are known as private and public extension keys. Support for private and public extension keys is optional. Private extension keys are proprietary. All private extension keys begin with "X-" to convey their proprietary status. Public extension keys must be registered with the IANA and must also be described in an informational RFC published by the IETF. All public extension keys begin with "X#" to convey their registered status. Private extension keys may be used only in Normal sessions but are not limited by phase. Public extension keys may be used in either type of session and are not limited by phase. Initiators and targets may send private and public extension keys. The scope of each extension key is determined by the rules of that key. The format of private extension keys is flexible but generally takes the form:

X-ReversedVendorDomainName.KeyName

The format of public extension keys is mandated as:

X#IANA-Registered-String

For more information about iSCSI text key-value pairs, readers are encouraged to consult IETF RFC 3720.

iSCSI Delivery Mechanisms

The checksum used by TCP does not detect all errors. Therefore, iSCSI must use its own CRC-based digests (as does FC) to ensure the utmost data integrity. This has two implications:

- When a PDU is dropped due to digest error, the iSCSI protocol must be able to detect the beginning of the PDU that follows the dropped PDU. Because iSCSI PDUs are variable in length, iSCSI recipients depend on the BHS to determine the total length of a PDU. The BHS of the dropped PDU cannot always be trusted (for example, if dropped due to CRC failure), so an alternate method of determining the total length of the dropped PDU is required. Additionally, when a TCP packet containing an iSCSI header is dropped and retransmitted, the received TCP packets of the affected iSCSI PDU and the iSCSI PDUs that follow cannot be optimally buffered. An alternate method of determining the total length of the affected PDU resolves this issue.

- To avoid SCSI task abortion and re-issuance in the presence of digest errors, the iSCSI protocol must support PDU retransmission. An iSCSI device may retransmit dropped PDUs (optimal) or abort each task affected by a digest error (suboptimal).

Additionally, problems can occur in a routed IP network that cause a TCP connection or an iSCSI session to fail. Currently, this does not occur frequently in iSCSI environments because most iSCSI deployments are single-subnet environments. However, iSCSI is designed in a such a way that it supports operation in routed IP networks. Specifically, iSCSI supports connection and session recovery to prevent IP network problems from affecting the SAL. This enables iSCSI users to realize the full potential of TCP/IP. RFC 3720 defines several delivery mechanisms to meet all these requirements.

Error Recovery Classes

RFC 3720 permits each iSCSI implementation to select its own recovery capabilities. Recovery capabilities are grouped into classes to simplify implementation and promote interoperability. Four classes of recoverability are defined:

- Recovery within a command (lowest class)
- Recovery within a connection
- Recovery of a connection
- Recovery of a session (highest class)

RFC 3720 mandates the minimum recovery class that may be used for each type of error. RFC 3720 does not provide a comprehensive list of errors, but does provide representative examples. An iSCSI implementation may use a higher recovery class than the minimum required for a given error. Both initiator and target are allowed to escalate the recovery class. The number of tasks that are potentially affected increases with each higher class. So, use of the lowest possible class is encouraged. The two lowest classes may be used in only the Full Feature Phase of a session. Table 8-8 lists some example scenarios for each recovery class.

Table 8-8   *iSCSI Error Recovery Classes*

Class Name	Scope of Affect	Example Error Scenarios
Recovery Within A Command	Low	Lost Data-In PDU, Lost Data-Out PDU, Lost R2T PDU
Recovery Within A Connection	Medium-Low	Request Acknowledgement Timeout, Response Acknowledgement Timeout, Response Timeout
Recovery Of A Connection	Medium-High	Connection Failure (see Chapter 7, "OSI Transport Layer"), Explicit Notification From Target Via Asynchronous Message PDU
Recovery Of A Session	High	Failure Of All Connections Coupled With Inability To Recover One Or More Connections

Error Recovery Hierarchy

RFC 3720 defines three error recovery levels that map to the four error recovery classes. The three recovery levels are referred to as the Error Recovery Hierarchy. During the Login Phase, the recovery level is negotiated via the ErrorRecoveryLevel key. Each recovery level is a superset of the capabilities of the lower level. Thus, support for a higher level indicates a more sophisticated iSCSI implementation. Table 8-9 summarizes the mapping of levels to classes.

Table 8-9   *iSCSI Error Recovery Hierarchy*

ErrorRecoveryLevel	Implementation Complexity	Error Recovery Classes
0	Low	Recovery Of A Session
1	Medium	Recovery Within A Command, Recovery Within A Connection
2	High	Recovery Of A Connection

At first glance, the mapping of levels to classes may seem counter-intuitive. The mapping is easier to understand after examining the implementation complexity of each recovery class. The goal of iSCSI recovery is to avoid affecting the SAL. However, an iSCSI implementation may choose not to recover from errors. In this case, recovery is left to the SCSI application client. Such is the case with ErrorRecoveryLevel 0, which simply terminates the failed session and creates a new session. The SCSI application client is responsible for reissuing all affected tasks. Therefore, ErrorRecoveryLevel 0 is the simplest to implement. Recovery within a command and recovery within a connection both require iSCSI to retransmit one or more PDUs. Therefore, ErrorRecoveryLevel 1 is more complex to implement. Recovery of a connection requires iSCSI to maintain state for one or more tasks so that task reassignment may occur. Recovery of a connection also requires iSCSI to retransmit one or more PDUs on the new connection. Therefore, ErrorRecoveryLevel 2 is the most complex to implement. Only ErrorRecoveryLevel 0 must be supported. Support for ErrorRecoveryLevel 1 and higher is encouraged but not required.

PDU Boundary Detection

To determine the total length of a PDU without relying solely on the iSCSI BHS, RFC 3720 permits the use of *message synchronization schemes*. Even though RFC 3720 encourages the use of such schemes, no such scheme is mandated. That said, a practical requirement for such schemes arises from the simultaneous implementation of header digests and ErrorRecoveryLevel 1 or higher. As a reference for implementers, RFC 3720 provides the details of a scheme called fixed interval markers (FIM). The FIM scheme works by inserting an 8-byte marker into the TCP stream at fixed intervals. Both the initiator and target may insert the markers. Each marker contains two copies of a 4-byte pointer that indicates the starting byte number of the next iSCSI PDU. Support for the FIM scheme is negotiated during the Login Phase.

PDU Retransmission

iSCSI guarantees in-order data delivery to the SAL. When PDUs arrive out of order due to retransmission, the iSCSI protocol does not reorder PDUs per se. Upon receipt of all TCP packets composing an iSCSI PDU, iSCSI places the ULP data in an application buffer. The position of the data within the application buffer is determined by the Buffer Offset field in the BHS of the Data-In/Data-Out PDU. When an iSCSI digest error, or a dropped or delayed TCP packet causes a processing delay for a given iSCSI PDU, the Buffer Offset field in the BHS of other iSCSI data PDUs that are received error-free enables continued processing without delay regardless of PDU transmission order. Thus, iSCSI PDUs do not need to be reordered before processing. Of course, the use of a message synchronization scheme is required under certain circumstances for PDU processing to continue in the presence of one or more dropped or delayed PDUs. Otherwise, the BHS of subsequent PDUs cannot be read. Assuming this requirement is met, PDUs can be processed in any order.

Retransmission occurs as the result of a digest error, protocol error, or timeout. Despite differences in detection techniques, PDU retransmission is handled in a similar manner for data digest errors, protocol errors and timeouts. However, header digest errors require special handling. When a header digest error occurs, and the connection does not support a PDU boundary detection scheme, the connection must be terminated. If the session supports ErrorRecoveryLevel 2, the connection is recovered, tasks are reassigned, and PDU retransmission occurs on the new connection. If the session does not support ErrorRecoveryLevel 2, the connection is not recovered. In this case, the SCSI application client must re-issue the terminated tasks on another connection within the same session. If no other connections exist with the same session, the session is terminated, and the SCSI application client must re-issue the terminated tasks in a new session. When a header digest error occurs, and the connection supports a PDU boundary detection scheme, the PDU is discarded. If the session supports ErrorRecoveryLevel 1 or higher, retransmission of the dropped PDU is handled as described in the following paragraphs. Note that detection of a dropped PDU because of header digest error requires successful receipt of a subsequent PDU associated with the same task. If the session supports only ErrorRecoveryLevel 0, the session is terminated, and the SCSI application client must re-issue the terminated tasks in a new session. The remainder of this section focuses primarily on PDU retransmission in the presence of data digest errors.

Targets explicitly notify initiators when a PDU is dropped because of data digest failure. The Reject PDU facilitates such notification. Receipt of a Reject PDU for a SCSI Command PDU containing immediate data triggers retransmission if ErrorRecoveryLevel is 1 or higher. When an initiator retransmits a SCSI Command PDU, certain fields (such as the ITT, CmdSN, and operational attributes) in the BHS must be identical to the original PDU's BHS. This is known as a retry. A retry must be sent on the same connection as the original PDU unless the connection is no longer active. Receipt of a Reject PDU for a SCSI Command PDU that does not contain immediate data usually indicates a non-digest error that prevents retrying the command. Receipt of a Reject PDU for a Data-Out PDU does not trigger retransmission. Initiators retransmit Data-Out PDUs only in response to Recovery R2T PDUs. Thus, targets are responsible for requesting retransmission of missing Data-Out PDUs if ErrorRecoveryLevel is 1 or higher. Efficient recovery of dropped data during write operations is accomplished via the Buffer Offset and Desired Data Transfer Length fields in the Recovery R2T PDU. In the absence of a Recovery R2T PDU (in other words, when no Data-Out PDUs are dropped), all Data-Out PDUs are implicitly acknowledged by a SCSI status of GOOD in the SCSI Response PDU. When a connection fails and tasks are reassigned, the initiator retransmits a SCSI Command PDU or Data-Out PDUs as appropriate for each task in response to Recovery R2T PDUs sent by the target on the new connection. When a session fails, an iSCSI initiator does not retransmit any PDUs. At any point in time, an initiator may send a No Operation Out (NOP-Out) PDU to probe the sequence numbers of a target and to convey the initiator's sequence numbers to the same target. Initiators also use the NOP-Out PDU to respond to No Operation IN (NOP-In) PDUs received from a target. A NOP-Out PDU may also be used for diagnostic purposes or to adjust timeout values. A NOP-Out PDU does not directly trigger retransmission.

Initiators do not explicitly notify targets when a Data-In PDU or SCSI Response PDU is dropped due to data digest failure. Because R2T PDUs do not contain data, detection of a missing R2T PDU via an out-of-order R2TSN means a header digest error occurred on the original R2T PDU. When a Data-In PDU or SCSI Response PDU containing data is dropped, the initiator requests retransmission via a Data/R2T SNACK Request PDU if

ErrorRecoveryLevel is 1 or higher. Efficient recovery of dropped data during read operations is accomplished via the BegRun and RunLength fields in the SNACK Request PDU. The target infers that all Data-In PDUs associated with a given command were received based on the ExpStatSN field in the BHS of a subsequent SCSI Command PDU or Data-Out PDU. Until such acknowledgment is inferred, the target must be able to retransmit all data associated with a command.

This requirement can consume a lot of the target's resources during long read operations. To free resources during long read operations, targets may periodically request explicit acknowledgment of Data-In PDU receipt via a DataACK SNACK Request PDU. When a connection fails and tasks are reassigned, the target retransmits Data-In PDUs or a SCSI Response PDU as appropriate for each task. Initiators are not required to explicitly request retransmission following connection recovery. All unacknowledged Data-In PDUs and SCSI Response PDUs must be automatically retransmitted after connection recovery. The target uses the ExpDataSN of the most recent DataACK SNACK Request PDU to determine which Data-IN PDUs must be retransmitted for each task. Optionally, the target may use the ExpDataSN field in the TMF Request PDU received from the initiator after task reassignment to determine which Data-In PDUs must be retransmitted for each task. If the target cannot reliably maintain state for a reassigned task, all Data-In PDUs associated with that task must be retransmitted. If the SCSI Response PDU for a given task was transmitted before task reassignment, the PDU must be retransmitted after task reassignment. Otherwise, the SCSI Response PDU is transmitted at the conclusion of the command or task as usual. When a session fails, an iSCSI target does not retransmit any PDUs. At any point in time, a target may send a NOP-In PDU to probe the sequence numbers of an initiator and to convey the target's sequence numbers to the same initiator. Targets also use the NOP-In PDU to respond to NOP-Out PDUs received from an initiator. A NOP-In PDU may also be used for diagnostic purposes or to adjust timeout values. A NOP-In PDU does not directly trigger retransmission.

iSCSI In-Order Command Delivery

According to the SAM, status received for a command finalizes the command under all circumstances. So, initiators requiring in-order delivery of commands can simply restrict the number of outstanding commands to one and wait for status for each outstanding command before issuing the next command. Alternately, the SCSI Transport Protocol can guarantee in-order command delivery. This enables the initiator to maintain multiple simultaneous outstanding commands.

iSCSI guarantees in-order delivery of non-immediate commands to the SAL within a target. Each non-immediate command is assigned a unique CmdSN. The CmdSN counter must be incremented sequentially for each new non-immediate command without skipping numbers. In a single-connection session, the in-order guarantee is inherent due to the properties of TCP. In a multi-connection session, commands are issued sequentially across all connections. In this scenario, TCP cannot guarantee in-order delivery of non-immediate commands because TCP operates independently on each connection. Additionally, the configuration of a routed IP network can result in one connection using a "shorter" route to the destination node than other connections. Thus, iSCSI must augment TCP by ensuring that non-immediate commands are processed in order (according to the CmdSN) across multiple connections. So, RFC 3720 requires each target to process non-immediate commands in the same order as transmitted by the initiator. Note that a CmdSN is assigned to each TMF Request PDU. The rules of in-order delivery also apply to non-immediate TMF requests.

Immediate commands are handled differently than non-immediate commands. An immediate command is not assigned a unique CmdSN and is not subject to in-order delivery guarantees. The initiator increments its CmdSN counter after transmitting a new non-immediate command. Thus, the value of the initiator's CmdSN counter (the current CmdSN) represents the CmdSN of the next non-immediate command to be issued. The current CmdSN is also assigned to each immediate command issued, but the CmdSN counter is not incremented following issuance of immediate commands. Moreover, the target may deliver immediate commands to the SAL immediately upon receipt regardless of the CmdSN in the BHS. The next non-immediate command is assigned the same CmdSN. For that PDU, the CmdSN in the BHS is used by the target to enforce in-order delivery. Thus, immediate commands are not acknowledged via the ExpCmdSN field in the BHS. Immediate TMF requests are processed like non-immediate TMF requests. Therefore, marking a TMF request for immediate delivery does not expedite processing.

NOTE   The order of command delivery does not necessarily translate to the order of command execution. The order of command execution can be changed via TMF request as specified in the SCSI standards.

---

iSCSI Connection and Session Recovery

When ErrorRecoveryLevel equals 2, iSCSI supports stateful recovery at the connection level. Targets may choose whether to maintain state during connection recovery. When state is maintained, active commands are reassigned, and data transfer resumes on the new connection from the point at which data receipt is acknowledged. When state is not maintained, active commands are reassigned, and all associated data must be transferred on the new connection. Connections may be reinstated or recovered. Reinstatement means that the same CID is reused. Recovery means that a new CID is assigned. RFC 3720 does not clearly define these terms, but the definitions provided herein appear to be accurate. When MaxConnections equals one, and ErrorRecoveryLevel equals two, the session must temporarily override the MaxConnections parameter during connection recovery. Two connections must be simultaneously supported during recovery. Additionally, the failed connection must be cleaned up before recovery to avoid receipt of stale PDUs following recovery.

In a multi-connection session, each command is allegiant to a single connection. In other words, all PDUs associated with a given command must traverse a single connection. This is known as connection allegiance. Connection allegiance is command-oriented, not task-oriented. This can be confusing because connection recovery involves *task* reassignment. When a connection fails, an active command is identified by its ITT (not CmdSN) for reassignment purposes. This is because SCSI defines management functions at the task level, not at the command level. However, multiple commands can be issued with a single ITT (linked commands), and each linked command can be issued on a different connection within a single session. No more than one linked command can be outstanding at any point in time for a given task, so the ITT uniquely identifies each linked command during connection recovery. The PDUs associated with each linked command must traverse the connection on which the command was issued. This means a task may be spread across multiple connections over time, but each command is allegiant to a single connection at any point in time.

When a session is recovered, iSCSI establishes a new session on behalf of the SCSI application client. iSCSI also terminates all active tasks within the target and generates a SCSI response for the SCSI application client. iSCSI does not maintain any state for outstanding tasks. All tasks must be reissued by the SCSI application client.

The preceding discussion of iSCSI delivery mechanisms is simplified for the sake of clarity. For more information about iSCSI delivery mechanisms, readers are encouraged to consult IETF RFCs 3720 and 3783.

FCP Operational Details

This section provides an in-depth exploration of the operational details of FCP. This section complements and builds upon the FCP overview provided in Chapter 4. You are also encouraged to consult the ANSI T11 FC-DA specification series to fully understand which combinations of FC and FCP features are permitted in real-world deployments.

FCP Addressing Scheme

FCP leverages the FC addressing scheme described in Chapter 5. No additional names or addresses are defined by the ANSI T10 FCP-3 specification.

FCP Name Assignment and Resolution

Name assignment for FCP devices and ports occurs as described in Chapter 5. For name resolution, FCP leverages the FCNS as described in Chapters 3 and 5. The FCP-3 specification suggests using a service-oriented approach during initial discovery of fabric attached devices. However, discovery behavior is not mandated by the FCP-3 specification. So, FCP devices may query the FCNS in a wide variety of ways. FCP devices may also leverage the ELS commands described in Chapter 5.

FCP Address Assignment and Resolution

Address assignment for FCP ports occurs as described in Chapter 5. No additional procedures or special requirements are defined by the FCP-3 specification.

FCP Session Establishment

Unlike iSCSI, FCP does not implement multiple session types, phases and stages. Instead of establishing a discovery session with the target device, FCP initiators establish a session with the FCNS to perform discovery operations. Likewise, targets establish a session with the FCNS. This session is long-lived and remains active until the initiator or target goes offline. Initiators establish the same type of FCP session with target devices to perform I/O operations.

An FCP session is established with a simple two-way handshake. FCP processes establish communication via the process login (PRLI) ELS command defined in the FC-LS specification. Only initiators may send a PRLI Request. A single PRLI Request followed by a single LS_ACC ELS can establish a session between two FCP devices. Alternately, a single PRLI Request and a single LS_ACC ELS may be exchanged for the purpose of discovering the FCP operating parameters (called *service parameters* in FCP parlance) supported by a pair of FCP devices. In this case, another PRLI Request and another LS_ACC ELS are required to establish a session. Like iSCSI, some FCP service parameters are negotiated, and others are simply declared. Negotiated FCP parameters are called requirements, and all others are called capabilities. After a session is established, the relationship between the communicating FCP processes is called an image pair. An FCP image pair must exist before SCSI data transfer is permitted between FC devices. As with PLOGI, PRLI may be performed explicitly or implicitly. Only explicit PRLI is described in this book for the sake of clarity.

Whereas iSCSI natively supports the exchange of all required operating parameters to establish a new session, FCP relies on SCSI for the exchange of certain service parameters. This is accomplished via the **scsi mode sense** and **mode select** commands. The **mode sense** command is used to discover the service parameters supported by a target device or logical units within a target device. The **mode select** command is used to inform a target device or logical units within a target device which service parameters to use. Because SCSI commands cannot be issued until after PRLI completes, the use of **scsi mode** commands to establish FCP service parameters requires modification of FCP session behavior after session establishment. The FCP-3 specification does not define how this modification should be accomplished. So, one of the logical unit device servers (usually LUN 0) must communicate **scsi mode** parameters to the FCP port(s) via proprietary means. This is handled within each SCSI device (no network communication). For more information about FCP's use of the **scsi mode** commands, see the FCP Login Parameters section of this chapter. For more information about FCP session establishment, readers are encouraged to consult the ANSI T10 FCP-3 and SPC-3 specifications, and the ANSI T11 FC-FS-2 and FC-LS specifications.

FCP Data Transfer Optimizations

FCP does not support equivalent functionality to iSCSI phase-collapse for the final data-in information unit (IU) and SCSI status. However, FCP supports equivalent functionality to iSCSI phase-collapse for first burst data. Support for unsolicited first burst data is negotiated via PRLI, but PRLI does not support negotiation of the first burst buffer size. Therefore, the first burst buffer size must be negotiated using the SCSI MODE commands with the Disconnect-Reconnect mode page or via proprietary means. FCP does not support immediate data. For more information about FCP first burst optimization, readers are encouraged to consult the ANSI T10 FCP-3 and SPC-3 specifications.

When DWDM or SONET is used to extend an FC-SAN, end-to-end latency can be sufficiently significant to affect performance. As a result, FC switch vendors and SAN extension vendors are responding with proprietary features that reduce round-trip delay in such environments. For example, FC switches produced by Cisco Systems can reduce round-trip delay for write data transfers via a feature called FC write acceleration (FCWA). FCWA provides local spoofing of the target signal (an FCP_XFER_RDY IU) that indicates readiness to receive write data. The switch at the remote site performs the necessary buffering to avoid dropped frames. Unlike the standardized FCP first burst optimization, FCWA operates on every data IU transmitted by an initiator. Another key difference in the behavior of these two optimizations is that FCWA does not eliminate the need for flow-control signaling, whereas unsolicited first burst data is sent without receiving a transfer request from the target.

FCP IU Formats

In FCP parlance, a protocol data unit is called an information unit. The FCP-3 specification defines five types of IU: FCP_CMND, FCP_DATA, FCP_XFER_RDY, FCP_RSP, and FCP_CONF. This section describes all five IUs in detail.

This section also describes the details of the link services most commonly used by FCP. As discussed in Chapter 5, the FC specifications define many link services that may be used by end nodes to interact with the FC-SAN and to manage communication with other end nodes. Three types of link service are defined: basic, extended, and FC-4. Each basic link service (BLS) command is composed of a single frame that is transmitted as part of an existing Exchange. Despite this, BLS commands are ignored with regard to the ability to mix information categories within a single sequence as negotiated during PLOGI. The response to a BLS command is also a single frame transmitted as part of an existing Exchange. BLSs are defined in the FC-FS specification series. The BLS most commonly used by FCP is abort sequence (ABTS). As stated in Chapter 5, an ELS may be composed of one or more frames per direction transmitted as a single sequence per direction within a new Exchange. Most ELSs are defined in the FC-LS specification. The ELSs most commonly used by FCP include PRLI and read exchange concise (REC). An FC-4 link service may be composed of one or more frames and must be transmitted as a new Exchange. The framework for all FC-4 link services is defined in the FC-LS specification, but the specific functionality of each FC-4 link service is defined in an FC-4 protocol specification. The FCP-3 specification defines only one FC-4 link service called sequence retransmission request (SRR). This section describes the ABTS, PRLI, REC, and SRR link services in detail.

FCP IUs are encapsulated within the Data field of the FC frame. An FCP IU that exceeds the maximum size of the Data field is sent as a multi-frame Sequence. Each FCP IU is transmitted as a single Sequence. Additionally, each Sequence composes a single FCP IU. This one-to-one mapping contrasts the iSCSI model. Fields within the FC Header indicate the type of FCP IU contained in the Data field. Table 8-10 summarizes the values of the relevant FC Header fields.

Table 8-10 *FC Header Field Values for FCP IUs*

FCP IU	R_CTL Routing	R_CTL Information Category	Type	F_CTL Relative Offset Present	DF_CTL
FCP_CMND	0000b	0110b	0x08	0b	0x00 or 0x40
FCP_DATA	0000b	0001b	0x08	1b	0x00 or 0x40
FCP_XFER_RDY	0000b	0101b	0x08	0b	0x00 or 0x40
FCP_RSP	0000b	0111b	0x08	0b	0x00 or 0x40
FCP_CONF	0000b	0011b	0x08	0b	0x00 or 0x40

Only one of the members of an FCP image pair may transmit FCP IUs at any point in time. The sequence initiative (SI) bit in the F_CTL field in the FC Header controls which FCP device may transmit. To transmit, an FCP device must hold the sequence initiative. If an FCP device has more than one FCP IU to transmit, it may choose to hold the sequence initiative after transmitting the last frame of a Sequence. Doing so allows the FCP device to transmit another FCP IU. This is known as Sequence streaming. When the FCP device has no more FCP IUs to transmit, it transfers the sequence initiative to the other FCP device. During bidirectional commands, the sequence initiative may be transferred many times at intervals determined by the participating FCP devices.

When an FC frame encapsulates an FCP_CMND IU, the Parameter field in the FC Header can contain a task identifier to assist command retry. If command retry is not supported, the Parameter field is set to 0. Command retry is discussed in the FCP Delivery Mechanisms section of this chapter. Unlike iSCSI, FCP uses a single command IU (FCP_CMND) for SCSI commands and TMF requests. Figure 8-16 illustrates the format of the FCP_CMND IU. Note that FCP IUs are word-oriented like FC frames, but the FCP specification series illustrates FCP IU formats using a byte-oriented format. This book also illustrates FCP IU formats using a byte-oriented format to maintain consistency with the FCP specification series.

Figure 8-16 *FCP_CMND IU Format*

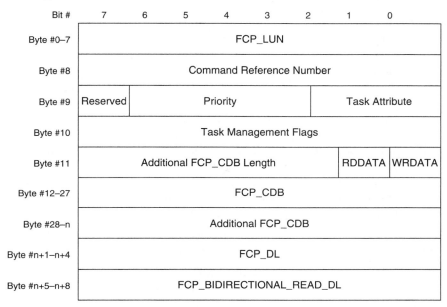

A brief description of each field follows:

- **FCP_LUN**—This is 64 bits (8 bytes) long. It contains the destination LUN. The format of this field complies with the SAM LUN format.

- **Command Reference Number (CRN)**—This is 8 bits long. If in-order command delivery is enabled, the initiator assigns a unique reference number to each SCSI command issued within a session. Note that the FCP_CMND IU does not have a field to identify the SCSI task. Instead, each SCSI task is identified by the fully qualified exchange identifier (FQXID). The FQXID is composed of the S_ID, D_ID, OX_ID, and RX_ID fields in the FC Header. Thus, each FC Exchange represents a SCSI task. This requires SCSI linked commands to be transmitted in a single Exchange. A retransmitted FCP_CMND IU carries the same CRN as the original IU. However, a retransmitted FCP_CMND IU uses a new FQXID, so the initiator's internal mapping of the SCSI task tag to an FQXID must be updated. The FCP CRN is similar in function to the iSCSI CmdSN. The FC FQXID is similar in function to the iSCSI ITT.

- **Reserved**—This is 1 bit.

- **Priority**—This is 4 bits long. It determines the order of execution for tasks in a task manager's queue. This field is valid only for SIMPLE tasks.

- **Task Attribute**—This is 3 bits long. A value of 0 indicates a SIMPLE task. A value of 1 indicates a HEAD OF QUEUE task. A value of 2 indicates an ORDERED task. A value of 4 indicates an ACA task. All other values are reserved. For more information about SCSI Task Attributes, see the ANSI T10 SAM-3 specification.

- **Task Management Flags**—This is 8 bits long. This field is used to request a TMF. If any bit in this field is set to 1, a TMF is requested. When a TMF is requested, the FCP_CMND IU does not encapsulate a SCSI command. Thus, the Task Attribute, Additional FCP_CDB Length, RDDATA, WRDATA, FCP_CDB, Additional FCP_CDB, FCP_DL, and FCP_Bidirectional_Read_DL fields are not used. No more than one bit in the Task Management Flags field may be set to 1 in a given FCP_CMND IU. Bit 1 represents the Abort Task Set TMF. Bit 2 represents the Clear Task Set TMF. Bit 4 represents the Logical Unit Reset TMF. Bit 6 represents the Clear ACA TMF. All other bits are reserved. Note that the Abort Task TMF is not supported via this field. Instead, the ABTS BLS is used. Despite its name, the ABTS BLS can be used to abort a single sequence or an entire Exchange. When the FCP_CMND IU encapsulates a SCSI command, the Task Management Flags field must be set to 0.

- **Additional FCP_CDB Length**—This is 6 bits long. This field indicates the length of the Additional FCP_CDB field expressed in 4-byte words. When the CDB length is 16 bytes or less, this field is set to 0. When a TMF is requested, this field is set to 0.

- **RDDATA**—This is 1 bit. It indicates a read command when set to 1. For bidirectional commands, both the RDDATA and WRDATA bits are set to 1.

- **WRDATA**—This is 1 bit. It indicates a write command when set to 1. For bidirectional commands, both the RDDATA and WRDATA bits are set to 1.

- **FCP_CDB**—This is 128 bits (16 bytes) long. It contains a SCSI CDB if the Task Management Flags field is set to 0. When a CDB shorter than 16 bytes is sent, this field is padded. The value of padding is not defined by the FCP-3 specification. Presumably, zeros should be used for padding. When a CDB longer than 16 bytes is sent, this field contains the first 16 bytes of the CDB.

- **Additional FCP_CDB**—This is variable in length. When a CDB longer than 16 bytes is sent, this field contains all bytes of the CDB except the first 16 bytes. All CDBs longer than 16 bytes must end on a 4-byte word boundary, so this field does not require padding. When the CDB length is 16 bytes or less, this field is omitted from the FCP_CMND IU. Likewise, when a TMF is requested, this field is omitted from the FCP_CMND IU.

- **FCP_DL**—This is 32 bits long. It indicates the total amount of data expected to be transferred unidirectionally by this command. This field is expressed in bytes. When the data transfer is bidirectional, this field represents the write data, and the FCP_Bidirectional_Read_DL field must be present in the FCP_CMND IU. This field is set to 0 for certain commands that do not transfer data. This field represents an estimate. After all data is transferred, the target informs the initiator of how much data was transferred.

- **FCP_BIDIRECTIONAL_READ_DL**—This is 32 bits long. It indicates the total amount of read data expected to be transferred by a bidirectional command. When the SCSI command is unidirectional, this field is omitted from the FCP_CMND IU. This field represents an estimate. After all data is transferred, the target informs the initiator how much data was transferred.

Unlike iSCSI, FCP uses a single IU (FCP_DATA) for both data-out and data-in operations. The only difference in IU format for data-out versus data-in operations is the manner in which the SI bit in the FC Header is handled. For data-out operations, the sequence initiative is transferred from initiator to target after transmission of each FCP_DATA IU. This enables the target to transmit an FCP_XFER_RDY IU to continue the operation or an FCP_RSP IU to complete the operation. For data-in operations, the sequence initiative is held by the target after transmission of each FCP_DATA IU. This enables the target to transmit another FCP_DATA IU to continue the operation or an FCP_RSP IU to complete the operation. For all FCP_DATA IUs, the Parameter field in the FC Header contains a relative offset value. The FCP_DATA IU does not have a defined format within the Data field of the FC frame. The receiver uses only the FC Header to identify an FCP_DATA IU, and ULP data is directly encapsulated in the Data field of the FC frame. An FCP_DATA IU may not be sent with a payload of 0 bytes.

NOTE   The FC-FS-2 specification mandates the Information Category sub-field of the R_CTL field in the FC Header must be set to *solicited data* even when the initiator sends unsolicited first burst data.

When an FC frame encapsulates an FCP_XFER_RDY IU, the Parameter field in the FC Header is set to 0. In contrast to the iSCSI model, FCP implements a one-to-one relationship between FCP_XFER_RDY IUs and FCP_DATA IUs. The FC-FS-2 specification categorizes the FCP_XFER_RDY IU as a Data Descriptor. The FC-FS-2 specification also defines the general format that all Data Descriptors must use. Figure 8-17 illustrates the general format of Data Descriptors. Figure 8-18 illustrates the format of the FCP_XFER_RDY IU.

Figure 8-17 *Data Descriptor Format*

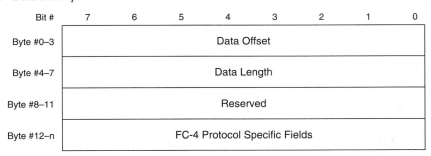

Figure 8-18 *FCP_XFER_RDY IU Format*

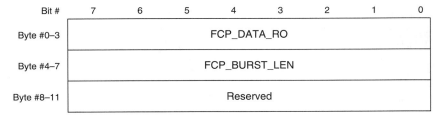

A brief description of each field follows:

- **FCP_DATA_RO**—This is 32 bits long. This field indicates the position of the first byte of data requested by this IU relative to the first byte of all the data transferred by the SCSI command.

- **FCP_BURST_LEN**—This is 32 bits long. This field indicates how much data should be transferred in response to this FCP_XFER_RDY IU. This field is expressed in bytes. The value of this field cannot be 0 and cannot exceed the negotiated value of maximum burst size (see the FCP Login Parameters section of this chapter).

- **Reserved**—This is 32 bits long.

The final result of each SCSI command is a SCSI status indicator delivered in an FCP_RSP IU. The FCP_RSP IU also conveys FCP status for protocol operations. When an FC frame encapsulates an FCP_RSP IU, the Parameter field in the FC Header is set to 0. Unlike iSCSI, FCP uses a single response IU (FCP_RSP) for SCSI commands and TMF requests. Figure 8-19 illustrates the format of the FCP_RSP IU.

Figure 8-19 *FCP_RSP IU Format*

Bit #	7	6	5	4	3	2	1	0
Byte #0–7	Reserved							
Byte #8–9	Retry Delay Timer							
Byte #10	FCP_BIDI_RSP	FCP_BIDI_READ_RESID_UNDER	FCP_BIDI_READ_RESID_OVER	FCP_CONF_REQ	FCP_RESID_UNDER	FCP_RESID_OVER	FCP_SNS_LEN_VALID	FCP_RSP_LEN_VALID
Byte #11	SCSI Status Code							
Byte #12–15	FCP_RESID							
Byte #16–19	FCP_SNS_LEN							
Byte #20–23	FCP_RSP_LEN							
Byte #24–x	FCP_RSP_INFO							
Byte #x+1–y	FCP_SNS_INFO							
Byte #y+1–y+4	FCP_BIDIRECTIONAL_READ_RESID							

A brief description of each field follows:

- **Reserved**—This is 64 bits (8 bytes) long.

- **Retry Delay Timer**—This is 16 bits long. This field contains one of the retry delay timer codes defined in the SAM-4 specification. These codes provide additional information to the initiator regarding why a command failed and how long to wait before retrying the command.

- **FCP_BIDI_RSP**—This is one bit. This field indicates whether the FCP_RSP IU provides status for a bidirectional command. When this bit is set to 1, the FCP_BIDI_READ_RESID_UNDER, FCP_BIDI_READ_RESID_OVER, and FCP_BIDIRECTIONAL_READ_RESID fields are valid. When this bit is set to 0, the FCP_BIDI_READ_RESID_UNDER, FCP_BIDI_READ_RESID_OVER, and FCP_BIDIRECTIONAL_READ_RESID fields are ignored.

- **FCP_BIDI_READ_RESID_UNDER**—This is one bit. When this bit is set to 1, the FCP_BIDIRECTIONAL_READ_RESID field is valid. When this bit is set to 1, the FCP_BIDI_READ_RESID_OVER bit must be set to 0. When this bit is set to 0, the command transferred at least as many read bytes as expected.

- **FCP_BIDI_READ_RESID_OVER**—This is 1 bit. When this bit is set to 1, the FCP_BIDIRECTIONAL_READ_RESID field is valid. When this bit is set to 1, the FCP_BIDI_READ_RESID_UNDER bit must be set to 0. When this bit is set to 0, the command did not transfer more read bytes than expected.

- **FCP_CONF_REQ**—This is 1 bit. When this bit is set to 1, the target is requesting an FCP_CONF IU from the initiator. When this bit is set to 0, the initiator does not send an FCP_CONF IU to the target.

- **FCP_RESID_UNDER**—This is 1 bit. When this bit is set to 1, the FCP_RESID field is valid. When this bit is set to 1, the FCP_RESID_OVER bit must be set to 0. When this bit is set to 0, the command transferred at least as many bytes as expected. For bidirectional commands, this bit represents the write direction.

- **FCP_RESID_OVER**—This is 1 bit. When this bit is set to 1, the FCP_RESID field is valid. When this bit is set to 1, the FCP_RESID_UNDER bit must be set to 0. When this bit is set to 0, the command did not transfer more bytes than expected. For bidirectional commands, this bit represents the write direction.

- **FCP_SNS_LEN_VALID**—This is 1 bit. When this bit is set to 1, the FCP_SNS_LEN and FCP_SNS_INFO fields are valid. When this bit is set to 0, the FCP_SNS_LEN and FCP_SNS_INFO fields are ignored.

- **FCP_RSP_LEN_VALID**—This is 1 bit. For TMF requests, this bit must be set to 1 because TMF completion status is provided via the FCP_RSP_INFO field. So, FCP delivery status cannot be explicitly communicated via this field when also communicating TMF completion status. For SCSI commands, this bit may be set to 1 or 0. The remainder of this paragraph focuses on transport of SCSI commands. This bit indicates the presence or absence of FCP errors. In other words, this bit is to the

SCSI service delivery subsystem what the SCSI status code is to SAL. When this bit is set to 1, the FCP_RSP_LEN and FCP_RSP_INFO fields are valid, and the SCSI Status Code field is ignored. This is roughly equivalent to a SCSI service response of SERVICE DELIVERY OR TARGET FAILURE. This is also roughly equivalent to an iSCSI response code of 0x01 (target failure). Setting this bit to 0 indicates that the target has completed processing the command from the FCP perspective. When this bit is set to 0, the FCP_RSP_LEN and FCP_RSP_INFO fields are ignored, and the SCSI Status Code field is valid. This is roughly equivalent to a SCSI service response of LINKED COMMAND COMPLETE or TASK COMPLETE. This is also roughly equivalent to an iSCSI response code of 0x00 (command completed at target). Setting this bit to 0 conveys FCP success but does not imply SCSI success.

- **SCSI Status Code**—This is 8 bits long. This field contains a status code that provides more detail about the final status of the SCSI command and the state of the logical unit that executed the command. This field is valid only if the FCP_RSP_LEN_VALID bit is set to 0. Even if the FCP_RSP_LEN_VALID bit is set to 0, the target might not have successfully processed the command. If the status code indicates failure to successfully process the command, SCSI sense data is included in the FCP_SNS_INFO field. All FCP devices must support SCSI autosense. Like iSCSI, FCP uses the status codes defined by the SAM (see Table 8-3).

- **FCP_RESID**—This is 32 bits long. When the FCP_RESID_UNDER bit is set to 1, this field indicates the number of bytes that were expected but not transferred. When the FCP_RESID_OVER bit is set to 1, this field indicates the number of bytes that were not transferred because they were not expected. Unexpected bytes cannot be transferred because the receiver does not have sufficient receive buffer space (as determined by the FCP_DL field in the FCP_CMND IU). When both the FCP_RESID_UNDER bit and the FCP_RESID_OVER bit are set to 0, this field is ignored.

- **FCP_SNS_LEN**—This is 32 bits long. When the FCP_SNS_LEN_VALID bit is set to 1, this field indicates the length of the FCP_SNS_INFO field expressed in bytes. When the FCP_SNS_LEN_VALID bit is set to 0, this field is ignored.

- **FCP_RSP_LEN**—This is 32 bits long. When the FCP_RSP_LEN_VALID bit is set to 1, this field indicates the length of the FCP_RSP_INFO field expressed in bytes. When the FCP_RSP_LEN_VALID bit is set to 0, this field is ignored. Valid values include 4 and 8. All other values are invalid.

- **FCP_RSP_INFO**—This is variable in length. It currently may be either 4 or 8 bytes long. Figure 8-20 illustrates the 8-byte format of this field. When the FCP_RSP_LEN_VALID bit is set to 1, this field can contain an FCP response code that provides TMF completion status or SCSI service delivery subsystem diagnostic information about an FCP error (the FCP equivalent to SCSI autosense data). Table 8-11 summarizes the FCP response codes defined by the FCP-3 specification. All response codes excluded from Table 8-11 are reserved. When the FCP_RSP_LEN_VALID bit is set to 0, this field is omitted from the FCP_RSP IU.

- **FCP_SNS_INFO**—This is variable in length. When the FCP_SNS_LEN_VALID bit is set to 1, this field contains SCSI autosense data. When the FCP_SNS_ LEN_VALID bit is set to 0, this field is omitted from the FCP_RSP IU.

- **FCP_BIDIRECTIONAL_READ_RESID**—This is 32 bits long. When the FCP_BIDI_READ_RESID_UNDER bit is set to 1, this field indicates the number of read bytes that were expected but not transferred. When the FCP_BIDI_READ_ RESID_OVER bit is set to 1, this field indicates the number of read bytes that were not transferred because they were not expected. Unexpected read bytes cannot be transferred because the initiator does not have sufficient receive buffer space (as determined by the FCP_BIDIRECTIONAL_READ_DL field in the FCP_CMND IU). When both the FCP_BIDI_READ_RESID_UNDER bit and the FCP_BIDI_READ_RESID_OVER bit are set to 0, this field is ignored.

Figure 8-20 *FCP_RSP_INFO Field Format*

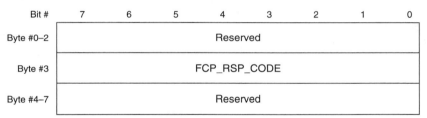

Table 8-11 *FCP Response Codes*

Response Code	Description
0x00	TMF Complete
0x01	FCP_DATA Length Different Than FCP_BURST_LEN
0x02	FCP_CMND Fields Invalid
0x03	FCP_DATA Parameter Mismatch With FCP_DATA_RO
0x04	TMF Rejected
0x05	TMF Failed
0x09	TMF Incorrect LUN

The FCP_CONF IU is sent by an initiator only when requested via the FCP_CONF_REQ bit in the FCP_RSP IU. The FCP_CONF IU confirms the initiator received the referenced FCP_RSP IU. The target associates an FCP_CONF IU with the appropriate FCP_RSP IU via the FQXID. For all FCP_CONF IUs, the Parameter field in the FC Header is set to 0. The FCP_CONF IU does not have a defined format within the Data field of the FC frame. Additionally, the FCP_CONF IU has no payload. The target uses only the FC Header to determine a given FC frame is actually an FCP_CONF IU. The FCP_CONF IU is not supported for TMF requests. Similarly, the FCP_CONF IU is not supported for intermediate commands in a chain of SCSI-linked commands. For SCSI-linked commands, the FCP_CONF IU may be requested for only the last command of the task.

The PRLI ELS is the explicit mechanism by which a session is established between two FCP devices. Support for PRLI is optional. PRLI is the primary, but not the only, mechanism by which service parameters are exchanged. Only initiators can send a PRLI. Possible responses to PRLI include LS_ACC and Link Service Reject (LS_RJT). PRLI and its associated responses are each encapsulated in the Data field of an FC frame. The fields in the FC Header indicate the payload is a PRLI, LS_ACC, or LS_RJT. Table 8-12 summarizes the values of the relevant FC Header fields. A single format is defined in the FC-LS specification for both PRLI and its associated LS_ACC. Figure 8-21 illustrates the format of PRLI and its associated LS_ACC.

Table 8-12 *FC Header Field Values for PRLI and LS_ACC ELS*

ELS	R_CTL Routing	R_CTL Information Category	Type	F_CTL Relative Offset Present	DF_CTL
PRLI	0010b	0010b	0x01	0b	0x00 or 0x40
LS_ACC	0010b	0011b	0x01	0b	0x00 or 0x40
LS_RJT	0010b	0011b	0x01	0b	0x00 or 0x40

Figure 8-21 *PRLI and Associated LS_ACC ELS Format*

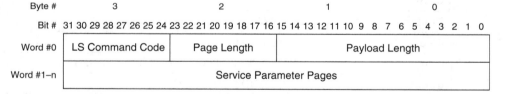

A brief description of each field follows:

- **LS Command Code**—This is 8 bits long. For a PRLI Request, this field is set to 0x20. For an LS_ACC, this field is set to 0x02.

- **Page Length**—This is 8 bits long. This field indicates the length of each Service Parameter Page expressed in bytes. This field is set to 0x10, so each Service Parameter Page is 16 bytes (4 words) long.

- **Payload Length**—This is 16 bits long. This field indicates the total length of the PRLI Request or LS_ACC expressed in bytes. Valid values range from 20 to 65,532.

- **Service Parameter Pages**—This is variable in length. This field may contain one or more Service Parameter Pages, but no more than one Service Parameter Page may be sent per image pair. The FC-LS specification defines the general format of the PRLI Service Parameter Page and the LS_ACC Service Parameter Page.

Like iSCSI, FCP negotiates some service parameters, while others are merely declared. The FCP-3 specification defines the specific format of the PRLI Service Parameter Page. Figure 8-22 illustrates the FCP-specific format of the PRLI Service Parameter Page.

Figure 8-22 *PRLI Service Parameter Page Format for FCP*

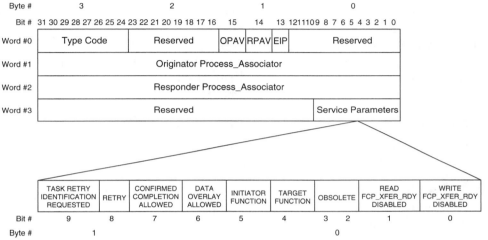

A brief description of each field follows:

- **Type Code**—This is 8 bits long. This field is set to 0x08 and identifies the FC-4 protocol as FCP.

- **Reserved**—This is 8 bits long.

- **ORIGINATOR PROCESS_ASSOCIATOR VALID (OPAV)**—This is 1 bit. This bit is always set to 0, indicating that the ORIGINATOR PROCESS_ ASSOCIATOR field is not used.

- **RESPONDER PROCESS_ASSOCIATOR VALID (RPAV)**—This is 1 bit. This bit is always set to 0, indicating that the RESPONDER PROCESS_ASSOCIATOR field is not used.

- **ESTABLISH IMAGE PAIR (EIP)**—This is 1 bit. When this bit is set to 1, the initiator requests both the exchange of service parameters and the establishment of an image pair. When this bit is set to 0, the initiator requests only the exchange of service parameters.

- **Reserved**—This is 13 bits long.

- **ORIGINATOR PROCESS_ASSOCIATOR**—This is 32 bits long. It is not used.

- **RESPONDER PROCESS_ASSOCIATOR**—This is 32 bits long. It is not used.

- **Reserved**—This is 22 bits long.

- **Service Parameters**—This is 10 bits long. It contains nine sub-fields.

- **TASK RETRY IDENTIFICATION REQUESTED**—This is 1 bit. When this bit is set to 1, the initiator requests support for task retry identification. If the target agrees, the Parameter field in the FC Header of each FCP_CMND IU contains a task retry identifier. When this bit is set to 0, the initiator does not support task retry identification, and the Parameter field in the FC Header of each FCP_CMND IU is set to 0.

- **RETRY**—This is 1 bit. When this bit is set to 1, the initiator requests support for retransmission of sequences that experience errors. If the target agrees, the SRR link service is used. When this bit is set to 0, the initiator does not support retransmission of sequences, and the SRR link service is not used.

- **CONFIRMED COMPLETION ALLOWED**—This is 1 bit. When this bit is set to 1, the initiator declares support for the FCP_CONF IU, and the target may request confirmation via the FCP_CONF_REQ bit. When this bit is set to 0, the initiator does not support the FCP_CONF IU, and the target may not request confirmation via the FCP_CONF_REQ bit.

- **DATA OVERLAY ALLOWED**—This is 1 bit. When this bit is set to 1, the initiator declares support for data overlay. Data overlay is the transfer of data to or from a single buffer offset multiple times per SCSI command. When this bit is set to 0, the initiator does not support data overlay, and the target must transfer data to or from a sequentially increasing buffer offset.

- **INITIATOR FUNCTION**—This is 1 bit. When this bit is set to 1, initiator functionality is supported. When this bit is set to 0, initiator functionality is not supported. Because the PRLI Request ELS can be sent only by initiators, this bit is always set to 1.

- **TARGET FUNCTION**—This is 1 bit. When this bit is set to 1, target functionality is supported. When this bit is set to 0, target functionality is not supported. Some devices, such as storage array ports used for replication, support both initiator and target functionality simultaneously. Those devices set this bit to 1. Most hosts support only initiator functionality. They set this bit to 0.

- **OBSOLETE**—This is 2 bits long. It is not used.

- **READ FCP_XFER_RDY DISABLED**—This is 1 bit. This bit is always set to 1.

- **WRITE FCP_XFER_RDY DISABLED**—This is 1 bit. Despite its misleading name, this bit is applicable only to first burst data. When this bit is set to 1, the initiator requests support for unsolicited data. If the target agrees, the initiator may send one unsolicited FCP_DATA IU per SCSI write command. When this bit is set to 0, the initiator does not support unsolicited data.

In the absence of errors, the target responds to PRLI with LS_ACC. The FCP-3 specification defines the specific format of the LS_ACC Service Parameter Page. Figure 8-23 illustrates the FCP-specific format of the LS_ACC Service Parameter Page.

Figure 8-23 *LS_ACC Service Parameter Page Format for FCP*

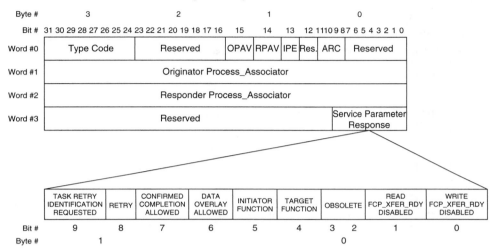

A brief description of each field follows:

- **Type Code**—This is 8 bits long. This field is set to 0x08. It identifies the FC-4 protocol as FCP.

- **Reserved**—This is 8 bits long.

- **ORIGINATOR PROCESS_ASSOCIATOR VALID (OPAV)**—This is 1 bit. This bit is always set to 0, indicating that the ORIGINATOR PROCESS_ASSOCIATOR field is not used.

- **RESPONDER PROCESS_ASSOCIATOR VALID (RPAV)**—This is 1 bit. This bit is always set to 0, indicating that the RESPONDER PROCESS_ASSOCIATOR field is not used.

- **IMAGE PAIR ESTABLISHED (IPE)**—This is 1 bit. This bit is valid only if the EIP bit is set to 1 in the PRLI Request. When this bit is set to 1, the target confirms the establishment of an image pair. When this bit is set to 0, the target is only exchanging service parameters.

- **Reserved**—This is 1 bit.

- **Accept Response Code (ARC)**—This is 4 bits long. This field contains a code that confirms that the image pair is established, or provides diagnostic information when the image pair is not established. Table 8-13 summarizes the PRLI Accept Response Codes defined in the FC-LS specification. All response codes excluded from Table 8-13 are reserved.

Table 8-13 *PRLI Accept Response Codes*

Response Code	Description
0001b	The PRLI Request was executed without error.
0010b	The target has no resources available. The PRLI Request may be retried.
0011b	The target is still initializing. The PRLI Request may be retried.
0100b	This code does not apply to FCP.
0101b	The target has been preconfigured such that it cannot establish the requested image pair. The PRLI Request may not be retried.
0110b	The PRLI Request was executed, but some service parameters were not set as requested.
0111b	The target cannot process a multi-page PRLI Request. The PRLI Request may be retried as multiple single-page PRLI Requests.
1000b	One or more service parameters are invalid.

- **Reserved**—This is 8 bits long.
- **ORIGINATOR PROCESS_ASSOCIATOR**—This is 32 bits long. It is not used.
- **RESPONDER PROCESS_ASSOCIATOR**—This is 32 bits long. It is not used.
- **Reserved**—This is 22 bits long.
- **Service Parameter Response**—This is 10 bits long. It contains nine sub-fields.
- **TASK RETRY IDENTIFICATION REQUESTED**—This is 1 bit. When this bit is set to 1, the target confirms support for task retry identification. When this bit is set to 0, the target does not support task retry identification.
- **RETRY**—This is 1 bit. When this bit is set to 1, the target confirms support for retransmission of dropped frames. When this bit is set to 0, the target does not support retransmission of dropped frames.
- **CONFIRMED COMPLETION ALLOWED**—This is 1 bit. When this bit is set to 1, the target declares support for the FCP_CONF IU. When this bit is set to 0, the target does not support the FCP_CONF IU.
- **DATA OVERLAY ALLOWED**—This is 1 bit. This bit is always set to 0 in the LS_ACC. This bit is used only by initiators to declare support for data overlay. If the initiator declares support for data overlay, the target may choose whether to transfer data using random offsets or sequential offsets.
- **INITIATOR FUNCTION**—This is 1 bit. Some devices set this bit to 1, but most set this bit to 0.

- **TARGET FUNCTION**—This is 1 bit. This bit is usually set to 1. If this bit is set to 0, an image pair cannot be established. This bit must be set to 1 if the IPE bit is set to 1.
- **OBSOLETE**—This is 2 bits long. It is not used.
- **READ FCP_XFER_RDY DISABLED**—This is 1 bit. This bit is always set to 1.
- **WRITE FCP_XFER_RDY DISABLED**—This is 1 bit. When this bit is set to 1, the target confirms support for unsolicited data. When this bit is set to 0, the target does not support unsolicited data.

If the PRLI is not valid, the target responds with LS_RJT. A single LS_RJT format is defined in the FC-LS specification for all ELS commands. Figure 8-24 illustrates the format of LS_RJT.

Figure 8-24 *LS_RJT ELS Format*

Byte #	3	2	1	0

| | Bit # 31 30 29 28 27 26 25 24 | 23 22 21 20 19 18 17 16 | 15 14 13 12 11 10 9 8 | 7 6 5 4 3 2 1 0 |

| Word #0 | LS Command Code | Unused | | |
| Word #1 | Reserved | Reason Code | Reason Explanation | Vendor Specific |

A brief description of each field follows:

- **LS Command Code**—This is 8 bits long. It is set to 0x01.
- **Unused**—This is 24 bits long. It is set to 0.
- **Reserved**—This is 8 bits long.
- **Reason Code**—This is 8 bits long. It indicates why the ELS command was rejected. A common set of reason codes is used for all ELS commands. Table 8-14 summarizes the reason codes defined by the FC-LS specification. All reason codes excluded from Table 8-14 are reserved.

Table 8-14 *LS_RJT Reason Codes*

Reason Code	Description
0x01	Invalid LS Command Code
0x03	Logical Error
0x05	Logical Busy
0x07	Protocol Error
0x09	Unable To Perform Command Request

continues

Table 8-14 *LS_RJT Reason Codes (Continued)*

Reason Code	Description
0x0B	Command Not Supported
0x0E	Command Already In Progress
0xFF	Vendor Specific Error

- **Reason Explanation**—This is 8 bits long. It provides additional diagnostic information that complements the Reason Code field. It uses a unique set of reason explanations for each ELS command. Table 8-15 summarizes the reason explanations defined by the FC-LS specification that are relevant to PRLI. All reason explanations excluded from Table 8-15 are either irrelevant to PRLI or reserved.

- **Vendor Specific**—This is 8 bits long. When the Reason Code field is set to 0xFF, this field provides a vendor-specific reason code. When the Reason Code field is set to any value other than 0xFF, this field is ignored.

Table 8-15 *LS_RJT Reason Explanations for PRLI*

Reason Explanation	Description
0x00	No Additional Explanation
0x1E	PLOGI Required
0x2C	Request Not Supported

The REC ELS enables an initiator to ascertain the state of a given Exchange in a target. Support for REC is optional. When an initiator detects an error (for example, a timeout), the initiator may use REC to determine what, if any, recovery steps are appropriate. Possible responses to REC include LS_ACC and LS_RJT. REC and its associated responses each are encapsulated in the Data field of an FC frame. The fields in the FC Header indicate the payload is a REC, LS_ACC, or LS_RJT. Table 8-16 summarizes the values of the relevant FC Header fields. If command retry is supported, the Parameter field in the FC Header contains the Task Retry Identifier of the Exchange referenced in the REC. If command retry is not supported, the Parameter field in the FC Header is set to 0. The formats of REC and its associated responses are defined in the FC-LS specification. Figure 8-25 illustrates the format of REC.

Table 8-16 *FC Header Field Values for REC and LS_ACC ELS*

ELS	R_CTL Routing	R_CTL Information Category	Type	F_CTL Relative Offset Present	DF_CTL
REC	0010b	0010b	0x01	0b	0x00 or 0x40
LS_ACC	0010b	0011b	0x01	0b	0x00 or 0x40
LS_RJT	0010b	0011b	0x01	0b	0x00 or 0x40

Figure 8-25 *REC ELS Format*

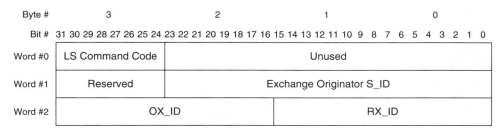

A brief description of each field follows:

- **LS Command Code**—This is 8 bits long. It is set to 0x13.
- **Unused**—This is 24 bits long. It is set to 0.
- **Reserved**—This is 8 bits long.
- **Exchange Originator S_ID**—This is 24 bits long. This field contains the FCID of the FC device that originated the Exchange about which state information is sought. Inclusion of this field in the payload enables an FC device to query state information for an Exchange originated by a different FC device. Without this field, the REC recipient would have to rely on the S_ID field in the FC Header, thus disabling third-party queries.
- **OX_ID**—This is 16 bits long. This field contains the OX_ID of the Exchange about which state information is sought. The REC recipient uses this field in combination with the RX_ID field to identify the proper Exchange.
- **RX_ID**—This is 16 bits long. This field contains the RX_ID of the Exchange about which state information is sought. The REC recipient uses this field in combination with the OX_ID field to identify the proper Exchange. If the value of this field is 0xFFFF (unassigned), the REC recipient uses the Exchange Originator S_ID field in combination with the OX_ID field to identify the proper Exchange. If the value of this field is anything other than 0xFFFF, and the REC recipient has state information for more than one active Exchange with the specified OX_ID-RX_ID combination, the REC recipient uses the Exchange Originator S_ID field in combination with the OX_ID and RX_ID fields to identify the proper Exchange.

In the absence of errors, the target responds to REC with LS_ACC. Figure 8-26 illustrates the format of LS_ACC sent in response to REC.

Figure 8-26 *LS_ACC ELS Format for REC ELS*

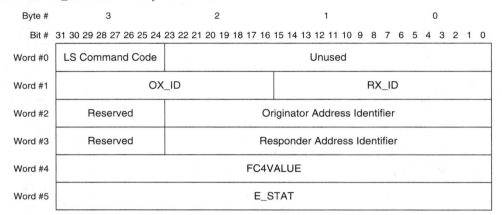

A brief description of each field follows:

- **LS Command Code**—This is 8 bits long. It is set to 0x02.

- **Unused**—This is 24 bits long. It is set to zero.

- **OX_ID**—This is 16 bits long. This field contains the OX_ID of the Exchange about which state information is sought.

- **RX_ID**—This is 16 bits long. This field contains the RX_ID of the Exchange about which state information is sought. If the RX_ID specified in the REC request is 0xFFFF, the REC recipient may set this field to the value previously assigned. This situation occurs when a target receives a new command (thus creating state information for the Exchange), but the initial reply is dropped, so the initiator does not know the assigned value of RX_ID.

- **Reserved**—This is 8 bits long.

- **Originator Address Identifier**—This is 24 bits long. This field contains the FCID of the FC device that originated the Exchange about which state information is sought.

- **Reserved**—This is 8 bits long.

- **Responder Address Identifier**—This is 24 bits long. This field contains the FCID of the FC device that responded to the Exchange about which state information is sought. The value of this field might be different than the value of the D_ID field in the FC Header of the REC request if the REC recipient contains more than one FC port.

- **FC4VALUE**—This is 32 bits long. The meaning of this field is defined by each FC-4 protocol specification. The FCP-3 specification defines this field as the total byte count received or sent by the Exchange about which state information is sought. This field can report the byte count for only one direction of transfer. However, the FCP-3 specification does not explicitly prohibit reporting the total byte count for both directions when the REC request references a bidirectional Exchange.

- **E_STAT**—This is 32 bits long. Each FC device maintains state information about each of its active Exchanges in a chunk of memory called the exchange status block (ESB). The ESB is defined in the FC-FS-2 specification. One of the fields in the ESB is called E_STAT. The E_STAT field in the ESB is 4 bytes long. It contains a broad array of information about the Exchange. The E_STAT field of the ESB is encapsulated in the E_STAT field within the LS_ACC ELS.

If the REC is not valid, or if the target does not support REC, the target responds with LS_RJT. Figure 8-24 illustrates the format of LS_RJT. Table 8-14 summarizes the LS_RJT reason codes. Table 8-17 summarizes the reason explanations defined by the FC-LS specification that are relevant to REC. All reason explanations excluded from Table 8-17 are either irrelevant to REC or reserved.

Table 8-17   *LS_RJT Reason Explanations for REC*

Reason Explanation	Description
0x00	No Additional Explanation
0x15	Invalid Originator S_ID
0x17	Invalid OX_ID-RX_ID Combination
0x1E	PLOGI Required

The ABTS BLS enables an initiator or target to abort a sequence or an entire Exchange. As with all BLS commands, support for ABTS is mandatory. ABTS may be transmitted even if the number of active sequences equals the maximum number of concurrent sequences negotiated during PLOGI. Likewise, ABTS may be transmitted by an FCP device even if it does not hold the sequence initiative. This exception to the sequence initiative rule must be allowed because the sequence initiative is transferred with the last frame of each sequence, but the receiving device neither acknowledges receipt of frames nor notifies the sender of dropped frames (see Chapter 5). Thus, the transmitting device typically detects errors via timeout after transferring the sequence initiative. As a result, ABTS can be sent only by the device that sent the sequence being aborted. Each ABTS is transmitted within the Exchange upon which the ABTS acts. Moreover, the SEQ_ID in the FC Header of the ABTS must match the SEQ_ID of the most recent sequence transmitted by the device that sends the ABTS. In other words, a device may abort only its most recently transmitted sequence or Exchange. The sequence initiative is always transferred with ABTS so the receiving device can respond. The responding device may hold the sequence initiative after responding, or transfer the sequence initiative with the response. Possible responses to an ABTS include the basic accept (BA_ACC) BLS and the basic reject (BA_RJT) BLS. The action taken upon receipt of an ABTS is governed by the Exchange Error Policy in affect for the Exchange impacted by the ABTS. ABTS and its associated responses are each encapsulated in the Data field of an FC frame. The fields in the FC Header indicate that the payload is a BLS command or a BLS response. Table 8-18 summarizes the values of the relevant FC Header fields. Bit 0 in the Parameter field in the FC Header conveys whether the ABTS acts upon a single sequence (set to 1) or an entire Exchange (set to 0). The ABTS does not have a defined format within the Data field of the FC frame. Additionally, the ABTS has no payload. The ABTS recipient uses only the FC Header to determine that a given FC frame is actually an ABTS. The formats of the BA_ACC and BA_RJT are defined in the FC-FS-2 specification. A unique BA_ACC format is defined for each BLS command. Figure 8-27 illustrates the format of the BA_ACC associated with ABTS.

Table 8-18 *FC Header Field Values for ABTS and Responses*

BLS	R_CTL Routing	R_CTL Information Category	Type	F_CTL Relative Offset Present	DF_CTL
ABTS	1000b	0001b	0x00	0b	0x00 or 0x40
BA_ACC	1000b	0100b	0x00	0b	0x00 or 0x40
BA_RJT	1000b	0101b	0x00	0b	0x00 or 0x40

Figure 8-27 *BA_ACC Format for ABTS BLS*

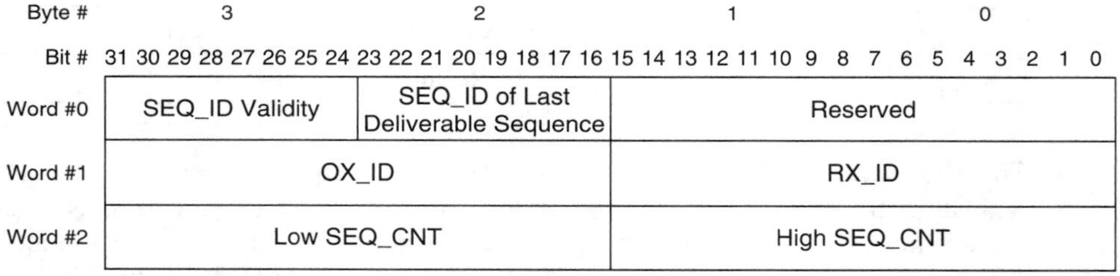

A brief description of each field follows:

- **SEQ_ID Validity**—This is 8 bits long. When this field is set to 0x80, the SEQ_ID Of Last Deliverable Sequence field contains a valid SEQ_ID. When this field is set to 0x00, the SEQ_ID Of Last Deliverable Sequence field is ignored.

- **SEQ_ID of Last Deliverable Sequence**—This is 8 bits long. When the SEQ_ID Validity field is set to 0x80, this field contains the SEQ_ID of the last sequence successfully delivered to the SAL. When the SEQ_ID Validity field is set to 0x00, the transmitter does not provide any information about the last deliverable sequence, and the entire Exchange must be aborted.

- **Reserved**—This is 16 bits long.

- **OX_ID**—This is 16 bits long. This field contains the OX_ID of the Exchange upon which the ABTS acts.

- **RX_ID**—This is 16 bits long. This field contains the RX_ID of the Exchange upon which the ABTS acts.

- **Low SEQ_CNT**—This is 16 bits long. When aborting a sequence, this field contains the SEQ_CNT of the last frame of the last sequence successfully delivered to the SAL. When aborting an Exchange, this field is set to 0x0000.

- **High SEQ_CNT**—This is 16 bits long. When aborting a sequence, this field contains the SEQ_CNT of the ABTS frame. When aborting an Exchange, this field is set to 0xFFFF. The range of SEQ_CNT values covered by the Low SEQ_CNT field and the High SEQ_CNT field is combined with the FQXID to generate the Recovery Qualifier. The Recovery Qualifier is valid for a period equal to R_A_TOV. For the transmitter of the ABTS, the R_A_TOV timer begins upon receipt of the BA_ACC. SEQ_CNT values within the Recovery Qualifier range may not be reused while the Recovery Qualifier is valid. Upon expiration of the R_A_TOV timer, the transmitter of the ABTS transmits a Reinstate Recovery Qualifier (RRQ) ELS. The RRQ ELS retires the Recovery Qualifier and enables the reuse of counter values covered by the Recovery Qualifier.

A common BA_RJT format is defined for all BLS commands. Figure 8-28 illustrates the format of the BA_RJT.

Figure 8-28 *BA_RJT Format*

Byte #	3	2	1	0
Bit #	31 30 29 28 27 26 25 24	23 22 21 20 19 18 17 16	15 14 13 12 11 10 9 8	7 6 5 4 3 2 1 0
Word #0	Reserved	Reason Code	Reason Explanation	Vendor Specific

A brief description of each field follows:

- **Reserved**—This is 8 bits long.
- **Reason Code**—This is 8 bits long. It indicates why the ABTS was rejected. Table 8-19 summarizes the reason codes defined by the FC-FS-2 specification. All reason codes excluded from Table 8-19 are reserved.

Table 8-19 *BA_RJT Reason Codes*

Reason Code	Description
0x01	Invalid Command Code
0x03	Logical Error
0x05	Logical Busy
0x07	Protocol Error
0x09	Unable To Perform Command Request
0xFF	Vendor Specific Error

- **Reason Explanation**—This is 8 bits long. It provides additional diagnostic information that complements the Reason Code field. Table 8-20 summarizes the reason explanations defined by the FC-FS-2 specification. All reason explanations excluded from Table 8-20 are reserved.

Table 8-20 *BA_RJT Reason Explanations*

Reason Explanation	Description
0x00	No Additional Explanation
0x03	Invalid OX_ID-RX_ID Combination
0x05	Sequence Aborted, No Sequence Information Provided

- **Vendor Specific**—This is 8 bits long. When the Reason Code field is set to 0xFF, this field provides a vendor-specific reason code. When the Reason Code field is set to any value other than 0xFF, this field is ignored.

The SRR link service enables an initiator to request retransmission of data during a read command, request that the target request retransmission of data during a write command, or request retransmission of the FCP_RSP IU during a read or write command. Only initiators may send an SRR. Support for SRR is optional. If SRR is supported by both initiator and target, REC and task retry identification also must be supported by both devices. The Parameter field in the FC Header contains the Task Retry Identifier of the Exchange referenced by the SRR payload. SRR may not be used during bidirectional commands. This limitation does not apply to iSCSI, which supports retransmission during bidirectional commands. The sequence initiative of the Exchange referenced by the SRR is always transferred to the target upon receipt of an SRR. This allows the target to transmit the requested IU. The sequence initiative of the SRR Exchange is also transferred to the target. Possible responses to SRR include the SRR Accept and the FCP Reject (FCP_RJT). The SRR and its associated responses are each encapsulated in the Data field of an FC frame. The fields in the FC Header indicate that the payload is an FC-4 link service request or an FC-4 link service response. Table 8-21 summarizes the values of the relevant FC Header fields. The formats of SRR and its associated responses are defined in the FCP-3 specification. Figure 8-29 illustrates the format of SRR.

Table 8-21 *FC Header Field Values for SRR and Responses*

FC-4 LS	R_CTL Routing	R_CTL Information Category	Type	F_CTL Relative Offset Present	DF_CTL
SRR	0011b	0010b	0x08	0b	0x00 or 0x40
SRR Accept	0011b	0011b	0x08	0b	0x00 or 0x40
FCP_RJT	0011b	0011b	0x08	0b	0x00 or 0x40

Figure 8-29 *SRR Link Service Format*

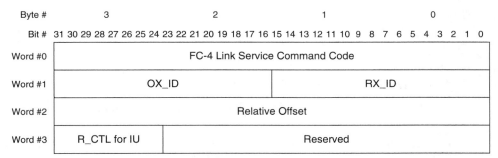

A brief description of each field follows:

- **FC-4 Link Service Command Code**—This is 32 bits long. It is set to 0x14000000.

- **OX_ID**—This is 16 bits long. This field contains the OX_ID of the Exchange for which retransmission is requested.

- **RX_ID**—This is 16 bits long. This field contains the RX_ID of the Exchange for which retransmission is requested.

- **Relative Offset**—This is 32 bits long. When an initiator requests retransmission of an FCP_RSP IU, this field is ignored. When an initiator requests retransmission of data or requests that the target request retransmission of data, this field contains the offset of the lowest numbered byte that needs to be retransmitted. The two low-order bits in this field are always set to 0, so the requested data always begins on a 4-byte word boundary. Note that the SRR link service does not request retransmission of one or more specific IUs. Instead, data is requested based on the relative offset provided in this field. This contrasts with the iSCSI model. In theory, the relative offset approach constitutes a more efficient recovery mechanism because it enables the requestor to specify only those data bytes that need to be retransmitted. However, the SRR link service lacks the ability to specify the upper boundary of data to be retransmitted. Thus, all data bytes with a relative offset equal to or greater than the value specified in this field must be retransmitted. This limitation mitigates the data retransmission efficiencies that FCP could realize compared to iSCSI.

- **R_CTL for IU**—This is 8 bits long. This field specifies the type of IU being requested. This field contains one of the values defined in the FC-FS-2 specification for the R_CTL field in the FC Header. Valid values are 0x01 (solicited data), 0x05 (data descriptor) and 0x07 (command status).

- **Reserved**—This is 24 bits long.

In the absence of errors, the target responds to SRR with SRR Accept. Figure 8-30 illustrates the format of SRR Accept.

Figure 8-30 *SRR Accept Format*

A brief description of the field follows:

- **FC-4 Link Service Command Code**—This is 32 bits long. It is set to 0x02000000.

Upon receipt of an FCP_RJT, the initiator must abort the entire Exchange referenced by the SRR. Figure 8-31 illustrates the format of FCP_RJT.

Figure 8-31 *FCP_RJT Format*

A brief description of each field follows:

- **FC-4 Link Service Command Code**—This is 32 bits long. It is set to 0x01000000.

- **Reserved**—This is 8 bits long.

- **Reason Code**—This is 8 bits long. It indicates why the SRR link service was rejected. Table 8-22 summarizes the reason codes defined by the FCP-3 specification. All reason codes excluded from Table 8-22 are reserved.

- **Reason Explanation**—This is 8 bits long. It provides additional diagnostic information that complements the Reason Code field. Table 8-23 summarizes the reason explanations defined by the FCP-3 specification. All reason explanations excluded from Table 8-23 are reserved.

- **Vendor Specific**—This is 8 bits long. When the Reason Code field is set to 0xFF, this field provides a vendor specific reason code. When the Reason Code field is set to any value other than 0xFF, this field is ignored.

The preceding discussion of FCP IU and FC link service formats is simplified for the sake of clarity. Comprehensive exploration of FCP IU and FC link service usage is outside the scope of this book. For more information, readers are encouraged to consult the ANSI T10 SAM-3, SAM-4, and FCP-3 specifications, and the ANSI T11 FC-FS-2 and FC-LS specifications.

Table 8-22   *FCP_RJT Reason Codes*

Reason Code	Description
0x01	Invalid FCP FC-4 Link Service Command Code
0x03	Logical Error
0x05	Logical Busy
0x07	Protocol Error
0x09	Unable To Perform Command Request
0x0B	Command Not Supported
0xFF	Vendor Specific Error

Table 8-23   *FCP_RJT Reason Explanations*

Reason Explanation	Description
0x00	No Additional Explanation
0x03	Invalid OX_ID-RX_ID Combination
0x2A	Unable To Supply Requested Data

FCP Additional Login Parameters

While most FCP service parameters are negotiated or declared via the PRLI mechanism described in the preceding section, some FCP service parameters are negotiated via the SCSI MODE SENSE and MODE SELECT commands. Detailed exploration of the SCSI MODE commands is outside the scope of this book, but readers should at least be aware of the service parameters that FCP negotiates via the SCSI MODE commands. So, this section provides a brief description of the service parameters relevant to FCP that are negotiated via the SCSI MODE commands. Three SCSI mode pages are relevant to FCP service parameter negotiation. They are the Disconnect-Reconnect mode page, the Protocol Specific Logical Unit mode page, and the Protocol Specific Port mode page.

The Disconnect-Reconnect mode page is used to optimize performance between an initiator port and a target port. Three parameters are relevant to fabric-attached FCP devices: Maximum Burst Size, First Burst Size, and Data Overlay. The Maximum Burst Size is the maximum number of bytes that may be transferred in a single FCP_DATA IU. Because FCP mandates a one-to-one relationship between IUs and sequences, this parameter also determines the maximum number of bytes that may be transferred in a single sequence. However, this parameter might not equate to the maximum number of bytes transferred during a single possession of the sequence initiative, because sequence streaming is allowed. The First Burst Size is the maximum number of bytes that may be transferred in a single unsolicited FCP_DATA IU. This parameter is ignored if the WRITE

FCP_XFER_RDY DISABLED bit in the PRLI Request or associated LS_ACC ELS is set to 0. Data overlay is negotiated via the enable modify data pointers (EMDP) bit. The EMDP bit overrides the value of the DATA OVERLAY ALLOWED bit in the PRLI Request.

The Protocol Specific Logical Unit mode page as implemented by FCP is called the FC Logical Unit Control mode page. The FC Logical Unit Control mode page is used to configure certain logical unit service parameters. In particular, FCP implements the enable precise delivery checking (EPDC) bit. The EPDC bit enables or disables in-order command delivery (called precise delivery in FCP parlance). Unlike iSCSI, FCP does not mandate precise delivery. Instead, FCP allows precise delivery to be negotiated with each logical unit.

The Protocol Specific Port mode page as implemented by FCP is called the FC Port Control mode page. The FC Port Control mode page is used to configure certain target port service parameters. For fabric-attached devices, FCP implements the sequence initiative resource recovery time-out value ($RR\_TOV_{SEQ\_INIT}$). This timer determines the minimum amount of time a target port must wait for a response after transferring the sequence initiative. If this timer expires before a response is received, the target port may begin error recovery procedures. For more information about FCP's use of the SCSI MODE commands, readers are encouraged to consult the ANSI T10 SPC-3 and FCP-3 specifications.

FCP Delivery Mechanisms

FCP leverages the delivery mechanisms implemented by FC. Additionally, the FCP-3 specification defines several mechanisms for detecting and recovering from errors. Like iSCSI, FCP supports error recovery at the task (Exchange) level and the IU (sequence) level. In other words, an FCP device may choose to abort each task affected by an error (suboptimal) or retransmit just the dropped IUs (optimal). The choice is subject to the Exchange Error Policy in effect for the Exchange affected by the error. Like iSCSI, FCP does not support frame level error recovery. However, iSCSI benefits from frame level retransmission as implemented by TCP, whereas FCP does not because FC does not support frame level retransmission (see Chapter 5).

Error Detection

Like iSCSI, FCP mandates that both initiators and targets are responsible for detecting errors. Errors are detected via timeouts, FC primitives, FC Header fields, FCP IU fields, the ABTS BLS, and the REC ELS. Initiators and targets must be able to detect the link errors, protocol errors, and timeouts defined in the FC specifications. Additionally, initiators and targets must be able to detect protocol errors and timeouts using FCP IU fields. Last, initiators and targets must be able to accept and process the ABTS BLS as a means of error detection. The only error detection mechanism that is optional is the REC ELS.

Exchange Level Error Recovery

The initiator is responsible for performing error recovery, but the target may optionally invoke recovery action under certain conditions. At the Exchange level, the error recovery procedure is called Recovery Abort. Recovery Abort is defined in the FC-FS-2 specification. The FCP-3 specification defines rules for using Recovery Abort. Recovery Abort is used to abort an Exchange and to recover the associated resources within the initiator and target devices. All initiators must be able to invoke Recovery Abort. All targets must be able to execute Recovery Abort in response to initiator invocation. Recovery Abort may be invoked in response to an error or by a TMF request. When Recovery Abort is invoked, the SCSI application client must reissue the aborted SCSI task.

If the target detects a frame error, the target discards all frames associated with the Exchange. The target takes no further action and waits for the initiator to detect the error via timeout. Upon detecting an error (via timeout or otherwise), the initiator optionally sends a REC to the target. If the REC confirms that an error has occurred, or if the initiator chose not to send a REC, the initiator sends an ABTS to the target. Bit 0 in the Parameter field in the FC Header is set to 0 indicating that the scope of the ABTS is the entire Exchange. The target takes the necessary internal actions to ensure the affected logical unit is notified. The target then responds with a BA_ACC. The Last_Sequence bit in the F_CTL field in the FC Header of the BA_ACC must be set to 1 (to terminate the Exchange). Upon receiving the BA_ACC, the initiator begins the R_A_TOV timer and notifies the SCSI application client. The SCSI application client may then reissue the command. Upon expiration of the R_A_TOV timer, the initiator sends an RRQ to the target. The RRQ enables reuse of the counter values covered by the Recovery Qualifier. When the initiator receives an LS_ACC in response to the RRQ, the Recovery Abort procedure is complete.

If the initiator does not receive an LS_ACC in response to the REC within two times the R_A_TOV, the REC exchange is aborted via Recovery Abort. The REC may be retried in a new exchange, or the initiator may choose to send an ABTS without retrying REC. If the initiator does not receive a BA_ACC within two times the R_A_TOV, the initiator may send another ABTS. If the second BA_ACC is not received within two times the R_A_TOV, the initiator must explicitly logout the target. The initiator must then perform PLOGI and PRLI to continue SCSI operations with the target, and all previously active SCSI tasks must be reissued by the SCSI application client.

Sequence Level Error Recovery

Initiators and targets are not required to support sequence level error recovery. Sequence level error recovery involves the abortion of a single sequence and the retransmission of the missing data. Upon detecting an error (via timeout or otherwise), the initiator optionally sends a REC to the target. If the REC confirms an error has occurred, or if the initiator chose not to send a REC, the initiator sends an ABTS to the target. Bit 0 in the Parameter field in the FC Header is set to 1, indicating that the scope of the ABTS is a single sequence. The target discards all frames associated with the sequence identified by the ABTS. The target then responds with a BA_ACC. The Last_Sequence bit in the F_CTL field in the FC Header must be set to 0. Upon receiving the BA_ACC, the initiator sends an SRR. Upon receiving the SRR, the target responds with an SRR Accept. The target then retransmits the requested data. In the case of a write command, the SRR requests an FCP_XFER_RDY IU that requests the missing data. The SEQ_CNT field in the FC Header of the first frame of retransmitted data is set to 0 even if continuously increasing SEQ_CNT is in affect for the connection. Note the retransmitted data can be (and often is) transferred from a relative offset that was already used in the Exchange being recovered. This is allowed even if the DATA OVERLAY ALLOWED bit is set to 0 during PRLI.

If the initiator does not receive an LS_ACC in response to the REC within two times the R_A_TOV, the REC exchange is aborted via Recovery Abort. The REC may be retried in a new exchange, or the initiator may choose to send an ABTS without retrying REC. If the initiator does not receive a BA_ACC within two times the R_A_TOV, the initiator may send another ABTS. If the second BA_ACC is not received within two times the R_A_TOV, the initiator must explicitly logout the target. The initiator must then perform PLOGI and PRLI to continue SCSI operations with the target, and all previously active SCSI tasks must be reissued by the SCSI application client. If a BA_ACC is received, but the initiator does not receive an SRR Accept within two times the R_A_TOV, both the SRR Exchange and the Exchange being recovered must be aborted via Recovery Abort.

FCP IU Boundary Detection

Because each FCP IU maps to a single sequence, IU boundaries can be easily detected via the SEQ_ID field in the FC Header. The SEQ_ID field is present in the FC Header of every FC frame, so IU boundaries can be detected even when one or more frames are dropped. So, FCP does not require a message synchronization scheme. This contrasts with the iSCSI model.

FCP In-Order Command Delivery

Like iSCSI, FCP supports in-order command delivery (precise delivery). Unlike iSCSI, precise delivery is optional for FCP devices. Another key difference is the scope of enforcement. Whereas iSCSI enforces in-order command delivery for all commands between each initiator-target pair, FCP enforces precise delivery on a per-LUN basis. The initiator sends an FC Logical Unit Control mode page to each LUN that is discovered by the **report luns** command. For each LUN that responds with the EPDC bit set to 1, commands are delivered in-order. In practice, the enforcement difference is purely academic because most modern storage arrays support precise delivery on all LUNs for performance reasons. However, the per-LUN nature of precise delivery has a real effect on the way FCP implements command numbering. A separate CRN counter is maintained for each LUN that supports precise delivery. In other words, a CRN counter is implemented per I_T_L nexus.

NOTE	The order of command delivery does not necessarily translate to the order of command execution. The order of command execution can be changed via TMF request as specified in the SCSI standards.

The CRN field is set to 0 in every FCP_CMND IU that conveys a TMF request regardless of whether the LUN supports precise delivery. Likewise, the CRN field is set to 0 in every FCP_CMND IU that conveys a SCSI command to LUNs that do not support precise delivery. By contrast, the CRN field contains a value between 1 and 255 in each FCP_CMND IU that conveys a SCSI command to LUNs that support precise delivery. The CRN counter for a given LUN is incremented by 1 for each command issued to that LUN. However, certain SCSI commands (such as **inquiry** and **test unit ready**) do not require precise delivery and may be assigned a value of 0 for the CRN field even when issued to LUNs that support precise delivery. When the CRN counter reaches 255, the value wraps back to one for the next command. The limited number range of the CRN counter exposes FCP devices to possible ambiguity among commands in environments that support sequence level error recovery. State information about each Exchange and sequence must be maintained for specific periods of time to support retransmission. Eventually, the initiator will issue a new command using an OX_ID that was previously used within the session. If the target is still maintaining state for the old command associated with the reused OX_ID, the target could confuse the two commands. To mitigate this risk, task retry identification must be implemented. The Task Retry Identifier effectively extends the CRN counter by providing an additional identifier for each command. The Task Retry Identifier must be consistent in all IUs and link services related to a single command (FCP_CMND, REC, SRR).

NOTE	In high I/O environments, the limited CRN counter might seem to pose a risk to performance. However, each LUN uses a separate CRN counter, which effectively mitigates any risk to performance by increasing the total CRN address space. In the unlikely event that an initiator needs to issue more than 255 ordered commands to a single LUN before the first command completes, the CRN counter limit would prevent issuance of the 256th command. However, when so many commands are simultaneously outstanding, it indicates that the LUN cannot execute commands as quickly as the application requires. Thus, the LUN is the performance bottleneck, not the CRN counter.

FCP Connection and Session Recovery

FCP does not support stateful connection or session recovery. If a connection fails, FCP notifies the SAL of the I_T nexus loss, and all state related to the connection and session is cleared. The initiator must perform PLOGI and PRLI to continue SCSI operations with the target, and all previously active SCSI tasks must be reissued by the SCSI application client. If a session fails, FCP notifies the SAL of the I_T nexus loss, and all state related to the session is cleared. The initiator must perform PRLI to continue SCSI operations with the target, and all previously active SCSI tasks must be reissued by the SCSI application client.

The preceding discussion of FCP delivery mechanisms is simplified for the sake of clarity. For more information about FCP delivery mechanisms, readers are encouraged to consult Chapter 5 and the ANSI T10 FCP-3 specification.

FCIP Operational Details

This section provides an in-depth exploration of the operational details of FCIP. This section complements and builds upon the FCIP overview provided in Chapter 4.

Architecture and Functional Models

TCP/IP is one of four technologies that enable geographically dispersed FC-SANs to be connected via non-FC network links (called SAN extension). The other three are SONET, asynchronous transfer mode (ATM), and transparent generic framing procedure (GFP-T). These four technologies are collectively called FC backbone networks. FC backbone networks serve as transparent virtual links between FC-SANs. The architecture and functional models for FC backbone networks are defined in the FC-BB specification series published by ANSI T11. The FC-BB-3 specification defines a model interface between FC and IP networks, and procedures for connection authentication and management, addressing, time synchronization, frame forwarding, error detection, and error recovery. The FC-BB-3 specification also mandates the protocol by which FCIP devices may be dynamically discovered. If dynamic discovery is supported, SLPv2 must be used. The FC-BB-3 specification requires all FC backbone networks to support Class F frames. Class 2, 3, and 4 frames may be optionally supported. Class 1 and 6 frames are not supported. FC primitive signals and primitive sequences are transmitted across only GFP-T links. The other three FC backbone networks do not forward FC primitives across non-FC links.

Additional specifications published by IETF define the details of FCIP functionality within the architecture defined in the FC-BB series. Generic procedures for encapsulating/ de-encapsulating FC frames in TCP packets, mapping FC frame delimiters into 8-bit codes, and measuring unidirectional transit time between FC-BB devices are defined in RFC 3643. FCIP is defined in RFC 3821, which builds upon RFC 3643 by defining protocol-specific procedures for FC frame encapsulation and de-encapsulation, connection establishment and management, flow control, and tunnel security. Detailed procedures for optional dynamic discovery of FCIP devices using SLPv2 are defined in RFC 3822.

NOTE	The FC-BB specification series explicitly discusses FCIP. By contrast, iFCP is not explicitly discussed.

The FC backbone architecture provides WAN connectivity for FC-SANs as shown in Figure 8-32. The details of the inner workings of each FC-BB device are determined by the functional model of the FC-BB device. The functional model is determined by the type of non-FC network to which the FC-BB device connects. The FC-BB-3 specification defines two functional models for FC-BB devices that connect to IP networks: virtual E_Port (VE_Port) and B_Access. The VE_Port model is implemented by FC switches with integrated FCIP functionality. Currently, Cisco Systems is the only FC-SAN vendor that supports the VE_Port model. The B_Access model is implemented by FCIP devices that are external to FC switches. Devices that implement the B_Access functional model are called FCIP bridges. This can be confusing because bridges operate at OSI Layers 1 and 2, yet FCIP operates at OSI Layer 5. To clarify, FCIP bridges operate at OSI Layers 1 and 2 regarding FC-SAN facing functions, but they operate at OSI Layers 1 through 5 regarding WAN facing functions. The interface within an FCIP bridge to which an FC switch connects is called a B_Port (see Chapter 5). B_Ports support limited FC-SAN functionality.

Figure 8-32 *FC Backbone Architecture*

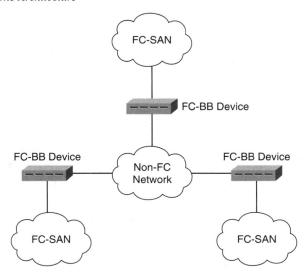

VE_Port Functional Model

An FCIP device that supports the VE_Port functional model has three conceptual components: the FC Interface, the IP Interface, and the FC-BB_IP Interface. The FC Interface implements FC-0 through FC-2 and interacts with the FC-SAN. The IP Interface implements TCP and IP and interacts with the IP network. The FC-BB_IP Interface resides between the other two interfaces and maps FC-2 functions to TCP functions. The FC-BB_IP Interface is composed of a switching element, an FC Entity, an FCIP Entity, a control and service module (CSM), and a platform management module (PMM). Figure 8-33 illustrates the relationships between the components of the VE_Port functional model.

Figure 8-33 *VE_Port Functional Model-Component Relationships*

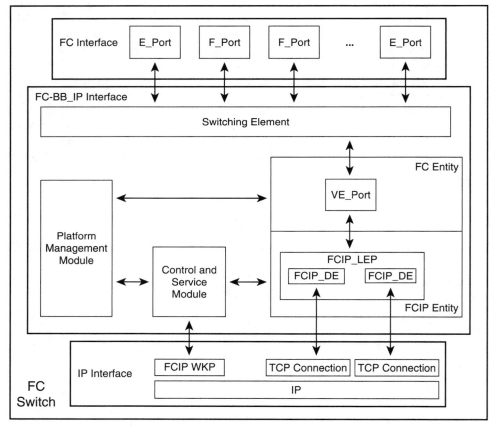

F_Ports, E_Ports, and VE_Ports communicate through the Switching Element. Each FC Entity may contain one or more VE_Ports. Likewise, each FCIP Entity may contain one or more FCIP link end points (FCIP_LEPs). Each VE_Port is paired with exactly one FCIP_LEP. The four primary functions of a VE_Port are:

- Receive FC frames from the Switching Element, generate a timestamp for each FC frame, and forward FC frames with timestamps to an FCIP_DE.

- Receive FC frames and timestamps from an FCIP_DE, validate each FC frame's timestamp, and forward valid FC frames to the Switching Element.

- Transmit Class F frames to the peer VE_Port.
- Respond to Class F frames received from the peer VE_Port.

Each FC Entity is paired with exactly one FCIP Entity. Each FC-BB_IP Interface may contain one or more FC/FCIP Entity pairs. Each FCIP link terminates into an FCIP_LEP. Each FCIP_LEP may contain one or more FCIP data engines (FCIP_DEs). Each FCIP link may contain one or more TCP connections. Each TCP connection is paired with exactly one FCIP_DE. The six primary functions of an FCIP_DE are:

- Receive FC frames and timestamps from a VE_Port via the FC Frame Receiver Portal (a conceptual port).
- Encapsulate FC frames and timestamps in TCP packets.
- Transmit TCP packets via the Encapsulated Frame Transmitter Portal (a conceptual port).
- Receive TCP packets via the Encapsulated Frame Receiver Portal (a conceptual port).
- De-encapsulate FC frames and timestamps from TCP packets.
- Transmit FC frames and timestamps to a VE_Port via the FC Frame Transmitter Portal (a conceptual port).

NOTE   The terms *FCIP tunnel* and *FCIP link* are synonymous.

Figure 8-34 illustrates the FCIP_DE conceptual model.

Figure 8-34 *FCIP_DE Conceptual Model*

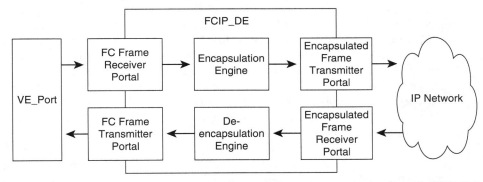

The CSM is responsible for establishing the first TCP connection in each FCIP link (FCIP link initialization). To facilitate this, the CSM listens on the FCIP WKP for incoming TCP connection requests. IANA has reserved TCP port number 3225 as the FCIP WKP. The SAN administrator may optionally configure the CSM to listen on a different TCP port. The CSM is also responsible for establishing additional TCP connections within existing FCIP

Links. When a new FCIP link is requested, the CSM creates an FC/FCIP Entity pair. The FCIP Entity encapsulates FC frames without inspecting the FC frames. So, the FCIP Entity cannot determine the appropriate IP QoS setting based on the FC Header fields. Thus, the FC Entity determines the appropriate IP QoS policies for FC frames that are passed to the FCIP Entity. The FC Entity accesses IP QoS services via the CSM. The CSM is also responsible for TCP connection teardown, FCIP link dissolution, and FC/FCIP Entity pair deletion.

Whereas the FC Entity is responsible for generating a timestamp for each FC frame passed to the FCIP Entity, the PMM is responsible for ensuring that the timestamp is useful at the remote end of the FCIP link. This is accomplished by synchronizing the clocks of the FC switches at each end of an FCIP link. Two time services may be used for this purpose: FC Time Service or Simple Network Time Protocol (SNTP). SNTP is most commonly used. The total unidirectional transit time, including processing time for FCIP encapsulation and de-encapsulation, is defined as the FCIP transit time (FTT). Upon receipt of an FC frame and timestamp from an FCIP Entity, the FC Entity subtracts the value of the timestamp from the current value of FC switch's internal clock to derive the FTT. If the FTT exceeds half of the E_D_TOV, the frame is discarded. Otherwise, the frame is forwarded to the destination FC end node.

The PMM is also responsible for discovery of remote FCIP devices. An FC switch may be manually configured with the IP address, TCP port, and FCIP Entity Name of a remote FCIP device. Alternately, SLPv2 may be used for dynamic discovery of FCIP devices. The PMM interfaces with the SLPv2 service and makes discovered information available to the CSM. The PMM is also responsible for certain security functions (see Chapter 12, "Storage Network Security") and general housekeeping functions such as optional event and error logging.

After an FCIP link is established, the VE_Ports at each end of the link can communicate. VE_Port pairs communicate via a virtual ISL (VISL). Each FCIP link maps to a single VISL. The FCIP link logically resides under the VISL and serves the equivalent function of a physical cable between the FC switches. VE_Ports communicate over a VISL in the same manner that E_Ports communicate over a physical ISL. For example, VE_Ports use Class F frames (ELP, ESC, and others) to initialize and maintain a VISL. Likewise, FC frames are routed across a VISL in the same manner as a physical ISL. When an FC-SAN is connected to multiple remote FC-SANs, the FSFP protocol decides which VISL to use to reach a remote FC-SAN. After FC frames are encapsulated in TCP packets, IP routing protocols are responsible for forwarding the IP packets through the IP network. At the destination FC-SAN, the FSFP protocol makes the final forwarding decisions after FC frame de-encapsulation. Figure 8-35 illustrates the communication that occurs at each layer between FC switches that employ the VE_Port functional model. Note that the layers in Figure 8-35 do not correlate to the OSI layers. Note also that Figure 8-35 indicates which Classes of Service are permitted by the standards. In practice, only Classes 3 and F are used.

Figure 8-35 *VE_Port Functional Model—Layered Communication*

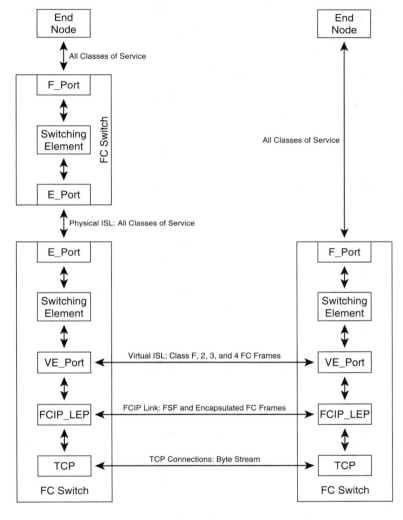

B_Access Functional Model

The B_Access functional model is very similar to the E_Port functional model. In most respects, the two models are identical. The primary differences are the replacement of the VE_Port with the B_Access port within the FC Entity and the use of a B_Port within the FC Interface to connect to an external FC switch. Figure 8-36 illustrates the relationships between the components of the B_Access functional model.

Figure 8-36 *B_Access Functional Model—Component Relationships*

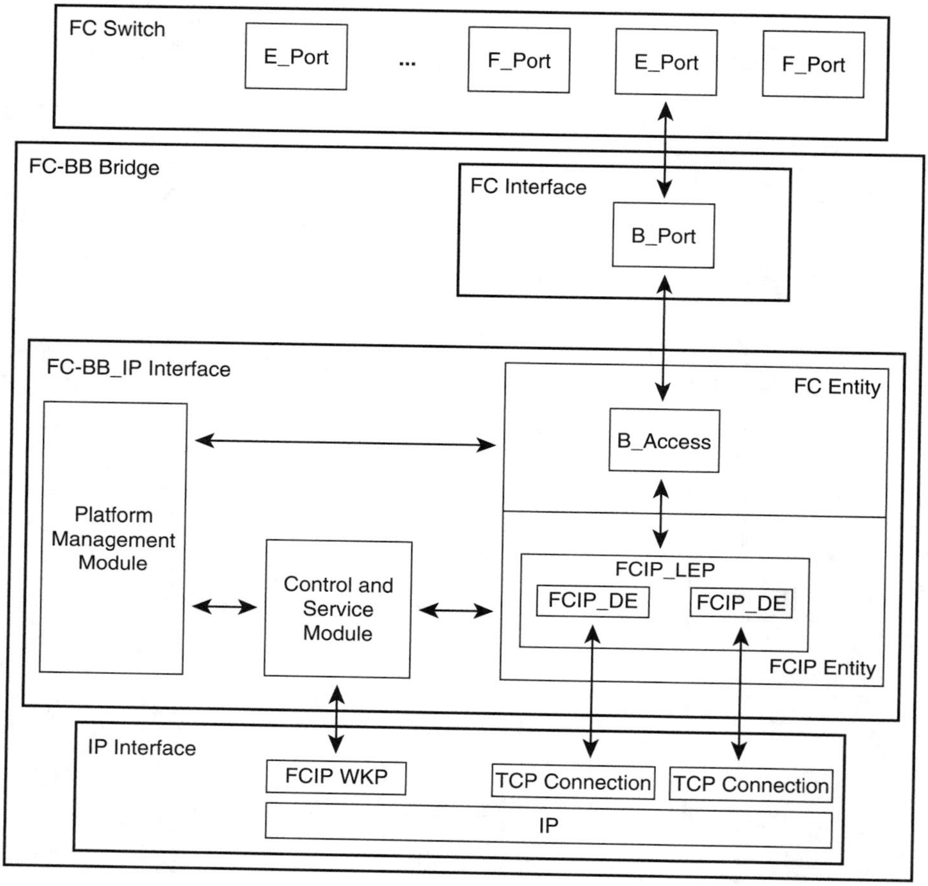

Communication between B_Access peers is similar to communication between VE_Port peers. The primary difference is the use of the Exchange B_Access Parameters (EBP) SW_ILS. As discussed in Chapter 5, the ELP SW_ILS is exchanged between the E_Port in the FC switch and the B_Port in the FC-BB bridge device. The parameters conveyed via ELP must then be conveyed across the WAN between FC-BB devices. The EBP SW_ILS performs this function. All other SW_ILS frames that are normally exchanged between FC switches over a physical ISL are exchanged between FC switches over the VISL provided by the FC-BB devices (see Figure 5-29 in Chapter 5). Figure 8-37 illustrates the communication that occurs at each layer between FC switches and FC_BB bridge devices that employ the B_Access functional model. Note that the layers in Figure 8-37 do not correlate to the OSI layers. Note also that Figure 8-37 indicates which Classes of Service are permitted by the standards. In practice, only Classes 3 and F are used.

Figure 8-37 *B_Access Functional Model—Layered Communication*

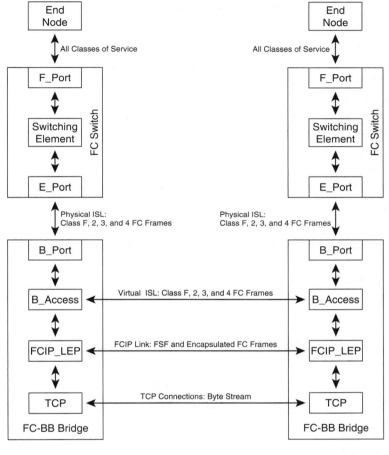

For more information about the FC backbone architecture and functional models, readers are encouraged to consult the ANSI T11 FC-BB-3 specification, and the IETF RFCs 3821 and 3822.

FCIP Addressing Scheme

FCIP does not provide host access to storage as does iSCSI and FCP. Therefore, the FCIP addressing scheme does not map to the SAM addressing scheme. That said, FCIP does use globally unique WWNs to distinguish each instance of an FCIP component from other instances and to facilitate reliable authentication. Such WWNs comply with the ANSI T11 WWN format. FCIP assigns WWNs as follows:

- Each VE_Port is assigned a WWN. This is called the VE_Port_Name.

- Each B_Access is assigned a WWN. This is called the B_Access_Name.
- Each FC/FCIP Entity pair is assigned a WWN. This is called the FC/FCIP Entity identifier.

FCIP also uses WWNs that are assigned by FC. FC assigns WWNs as follows:

- Each FC switch is assigned a WWN regardless of the presence of FCIP devices. This is called the Switch_Name.
- Each FC-SAN is identified by the Switch_Name of the Principal Switch regardless of the presence of FCIP devices. This is called the Fabric_Name.
- Each F_Port is assigned a WWN regardless of the presence of FCIP devices. This is called the F_Port_Name.
- Each E_Port is assigned a WWN regardless of the presence of FCIP devices. This is called the E_Port_Name.
- Each B_Port is assigned a WWN. This is called the B_Port_Name.

An FCIP_LEP that requests establishment of an FCIP Link is called an FCIP Link Originator. An FCIP_LEP that responds to such a request is called an FCIP Link Acceptor. In the VE_Port functional model, each FCIP Link Originator/Acceptor is identified by the following:

- Switch_Name
- FC/FCIP Entity identifier
- VE_Port_Name

In the VE_Port functional model, each FCIP Link is identified by the following:

- Switch_Name of the FCIP Link Originator
- FC/FCIP Entity identifier of the FCIP Link Originator
- VE_Port_Name of the FCIP Link Originator
- Switch_Name of the FCIP Link Acceptor

In the B_Access functional model, each FCIP Link Originator/Acceptor is identified by the following:

- Fabric_Name
- FC/FCIP Entity identifier
- B_Access_Name

In the B_Access functional model, each FCIP Link is identified by the following:

- Fabric_Name of the FCIP Link Originator
- FC/FCIP Entity identifier of the FCIP Link Originator

- B_Access_Name of the FCIP Link Originator
- Fabric_Name of the FCIP Link Acceptor

FCIP is very flexible regarding IP addressing. IP addresses may be assigned using one or more of the following methods:

- A single IP address may be shared by all FCIP Entities within an FC switch or FC-BB bridge device
- Each FCIP Entity within an FC switch or FC-BB bridge device may be assigned an IP address
- Each FCIP_LEP within each FCIP Entity may be assigned an IP address
- Each FCIP_DE within each FCIP_LEP may be assigned an IP address

Furthermore, FCIP devices at each end of an FCIP link are not required to implement IP addressing via the same method. For more information about FCIP addressing, readers are encouraged to consult the ANSI T11 FC-BB-3 specification.

FCIP Packet and Frame Formats

RFC 3643 defines the generic packet format to be used by all protocols that transport FC across IP networks. Figure 8-38 illustrates the generic FC Frame Encapsulation (FC-FE) format. Note that the entire FC frame, including frame delimiters, is encapsulated.

Figure 8-38 *FC Frame Encapsulation Format*

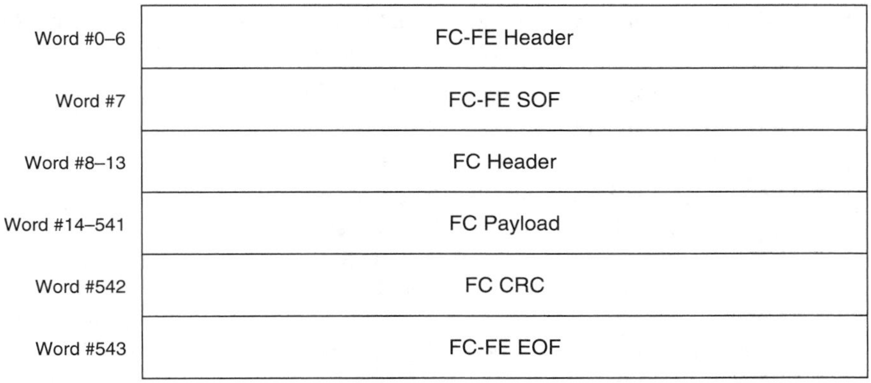

Word #0–6	FC-FE Header
Word #7	FC-FE SOF
Word #8–13	FC Header
Word #14–541	FC Payload
Word #542	FC CRC
Word #543	FC-FE EOF

The encapsulation header is word-oriented, and an FC-FE word is four bytes. The FC-FE header contains many ones complement fields to augment the TCP checksum. Figure 8-39 illustrates the FC-FE header format.

Figure 8-39 *FC-FE Header Format*

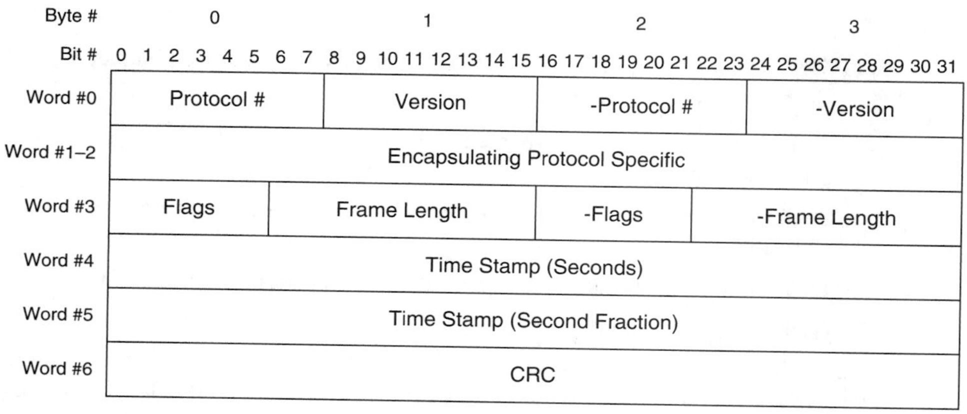

A brief description of each field follows:

- **Protocol #**—This is 8 bits long. This field contains the IANA assigned protocol number of the encapsulating protocol. FCIP is protocol 1.

- **Version**—This is 8 bits long. This field indicates which version of FC-FE is being used. In essence, this field indicates the format of the packet. Currently, only version 1 is valid.

- **-Protocol #**—This is 8 bits long. This field contains the ones complement of the Protocol # field. This field is used to validate the value of the Protocol # field.

- **-Version**—This is 8 bits long. This field contains the ones complement of the Version field. This field is used to validate the value of the Version field.

- **Encapsulating Protocol Specific**—This is 64 bits (8 bytes) long. This field is used by the encapsulating protocol (such as FCIP) in a manner defined by the encapsulating protocol.

- **Flags**—This is 6 bits long. This field currently contains a single flag called the CRC Valid (CRCV) flag. Bits 0 through 4 are reserved and must be set to 0. The CRCV flag occupies bit 5. When the CRCV bit is set to 1, the CRC field is valid. When the CRCV bit is set to 0, the CRC field is ignored. FCIP always sets the CRCV bit to 0. This is because FCIP encapsulates the FC CRC field for end-to-end data integrity verification, and FCIP does not modify FC frames during encapsulation/de-encapsulation. Thus, the FC-FE CRC field is redundant.

- **Frame Length**—This is 10 bits long. This field indicates the total length of the FC-FE packet (FC-FE header through FC-FE EOF) expressed in 4-byte words.

- **-Flags**—This is 6 bits long. This field contains the ones complement of the Flags field. This field is used to validate the value of the Flags field.

- **-Frame Length**—This is 10 bits long. This field contains the ones complement of the Frame Length field. This field is used to validate the value of the Frame Length field.

- **Time Stamp (Seconds)**—This is 4 bytes long. This field may be set to 0 or contain the number of seconds that have passed since 0 hour on January 1, 1900. As discussed in the VE_Port functional model section of this chapter, the value of this field is generated by the FC Entity. The format of this field complies with SNTPv4.

- **Time Stamp (Second Fraction)**—This is 4 bytes long. This field may be set to 0 or contain a number of 200-picosecond intervals to granulate the value of the Time Stamp (Seconds) field. As discussed in the VE_Port functional model section of this chapter, the value of this field is generated by the FC Entity. The format of this field complies with SNTPv4.

- **CRC**—This is 4 bytes long. This field is valid only if the CRCV flag is set to 1. This field is ignored in FCIP implementations and must be set to 0.

RFC 3821 defines the format of the Encapsulating Protocol Specific field (Words 1 and 2) as implemented by FCIP. Figure 8-40 illustrates the FCIP format of the Encapsulating Protocol Specific field.

Figure 8-40 *FCIP Format of Encapsulating Protocol Specific Field*

Byte #	0	1	2	3
Bit #	0 1 2 3 4 5 6 7	8 9 10 11 12 13 14 15	16 17 18 19 20 21 22 23	24 25 26 27 28 29 30 31
Word #1	Protocol #	Version	-Protocol #	-Version
Word #2	pFlags	Reserved	-pFlags	-Reserved

A brief description of each field follows:

- **Word 1**—This contains an identical copy of Word 0 in the FC-FE header.

- **Protocol Specific Flags (pFlags)**—This is 8 bits long. This field currently contains two flags called the Changed (Ch) flag and the special frame (SF) flag. The Ch flag occupies bit 0. Bits 1 through 6 are reserved and must be set to 0. The SF flag occupies bit 7. When the SF flag is set to 1, the FCIP packet contains an FCIP special frame (FSF) instead of an FC frame. When the SF flag is set to 0, the FCIP packet contains an FC frame. The Ch flag may be set to 1 only when the SF flag is set to 1. When the Ch flag is set to 1, the FSF has been changed by the FCIP Link Acceptor. When the Ch flag is set to 0, the FSF has not been changed by the FCIP Link Acceptor.

- **Reserved**—This is 8 bits long. It must be set to 0.

- **-pFlags**—This is 8 bits long. This field contains the ones complement of the pFlags field. This field is used to validate the value of the pFlags field.

- **-Reserved**—This is 8 bits long. It must be set to all ones.

The FC frame delimiters must be encapsulated because they serve several purposes rather than merely delimiting the start and end of each FC frame (see Chapter 5). However, FC frame delimiters are 8B/10B encoded words (40 bits long). Some of the 10-bit characters that compose FC SOF and EOF words have no 8-bit equivalent. Therefore, FC SOF and

EOF words cannot be decoded into 32-bit words for transmission across an IP network. The solution to this problem is to represent each SOF and EOF word with an 8-bit code that can be encapsulated for transmission across an IP network. These codes are called Ordered Set Codes (OS-Codes). They are defined in the FC-BB-3 specification. The OS-Codes relevant to FC-FE are also listed in RFC 3643. Table 8-24 summarizes the OS-Codes that are relevant to FC-FE.

Table 8-24   *OS-Codes Relevant to FC-FE*

OS-Code	Frame Delimiter	Class of Service
0x28	SOFf	F
0x2D	SOFi2	2
0x35	SOFn2	2
0x2E	SOFi3	3
0x36	SOFn3	3
0x29	SOFi4	4
0x31	SOFn4	4
0x39	SOFc4	4
0x41	EOFn	F, 2, 3, 4
0x42	EOFt	F, 2, 3, 4
0x49	EOFni	F, 2, 3, 4
0x50	EOFa	F, 2, 3, 4
0x44	EOFrt	4
0x46	EOFdt	4
0x4E	EOFdti	4
0x4F	EOFrti	4

The format of the FC-FE SOF field is illustrated in figure 8-41. The FC-FE EOF field uses the same format (substituting EOF values for SOF values) and follows the same rules for sub-field interpretation.

Figure 8-41   *FC-FE SOF Field Format*

A brief description of each field follows:

- **First SOF**—This is 8 bits long. This field contains the OS-Code that maps to the FC SOF ordered set associated with the encapsulated FC frame.
- **Second SOF**—This is identical to the first SOF field.
- **First -SOF**—This is 8 bits long. This field contains the ones complement of the first SOF field.
- **Second -SOF**—This is identical to the first -SOF field.

When a TCP connection is established, the first packet transmitted by the FCIP Link Originator must be an FSF. The FCIP Link Acceptor may not transmit any packets until it receives the FSF. Upon receipt of the FSF, the FCIP Link Acceptor must transmit the FSF back to the FCIP Link Originator before transmitting any other packets. The FCIP Link Originator may not send additional packets until the echoed FSF is received. The FSF serves the following five purposes:

- Conveys the originator's Switch_Name or Fabric_Name and FC/FCIP Entity Identifier to the acceptor
- Discovers the Switch_Name or Fabric_Name associated with a known destination socket (if SLPv2 discovery is not used)
- Conveys the intended destination Switch_Name or Fabric_Name to the acceptor (if SLPv2 discovery is used)
- Declares the originator's operational parameters to the acceptor
- Facilitates authentication of TCP connection requests

NOTE   Despite the FC-BB mandate that discovery be accomplished using SLPv2, RFC 3821 permits limited discovery using the FSF. However, RFC 3821 encourages the use of SLPv2 because SLPv2 supports discovery of more configuration parameters, is more extensible, and is more secure.

Figure 8-42 illustrates the FSF format.

Figure 8-42 *FCIP Special Frame Format*

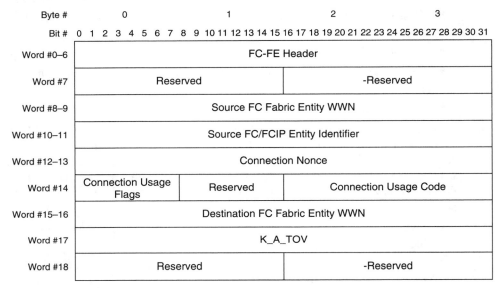

A brief description of each field follows:

- **FC-FE header**—This occupies the first 7 words.

- **Reserved**—This is 16 bits long. It must be set to 0.

- **-Reserved**—This is 16 bits long. It must be set to all ones.

- **Source FC Fabric Entity WWN**—This is 64 bits (8 bytes) long. This field contains the Switch_Name or Fabric_Name of the device that originated the FSF.

- **Source FC/FCIP Entity Identifier**—This is 64 bits (8 bytes) long. This field contains the FC/FCIP Entity Identifier of the FC/FCIP Entity pair that originated the FSF.

- **Connection Nonce**—This is 64 bits (8 bytes) long. This field contains a 64-bit random number that uniquely identifies the TCP connection request. This field is used to authenticate additional TCP connection requests within an existing FCIP link (see Chapter 12).

- **Connection Usage Flags**—This is 8 bits long. This field indicates the Classes of Service that the FCIP link is intended to transport. In practice, only Classes 3 and F are transported. FCIP does not restrict the link usage to comply with the information conveyed by this field. This field is only used to facilitate collaborative control of IP QoS settings by the FC Entity and FCIP Entity.

- **Reserved**—This is 8 bits long and must be set to 0.

- **Connection Usage Code**—This is 16 bits long. This field is meant to contain FC-defined information related to IP QoS settings. RFC 3821 refers to the FC-BB-2 specification for detailed information about the use of this field. However, the FC-BB-2 and FC-BB-3 specifications both state that this field is reserved.

- **Destination FC Fabric Entity WWN**—This is 64 bits (8 bytes) long. This field contains the Switch_Name or Fabric_Name of the intended destination device. If the value of this field matches the receiving device's Switch_Name or Fabric_Name, the unchanged FSF is echoed back to the FCIP Link Originator with the Ch flag set to 0. If this field contains a WWN that does not match the receiving device's Switch_Name or Fabric_Name, the receiving device may correct the value of this field and echo the FSF back to the FCIP Link Originator with the Ch flag set to 1, or simply close the TCP connection without replying. Upon receipt of the changed FSF, the FCIP Link Originator must close the TCP connection. Having discovered the correct destination FC Fabric Entity WWN, the FCIP Link Originator may re-attempt to establish an FCIP link. If the FCIP Link Originator knows the socket of another FCIP device but does not know the FC Fabric Entity WWN of the device, the FCIP Link Originator may establish a TCP connection with that device and then send an FSF with this field set to 0. Upon receipt of the FSF, the receiving device may correct the value of this field and echo the FSF back to the FCIP Link Originator with the Ch flag set to 1, or simply close the TCP connection without replying. Upon receipt of the changed FSF, the FCIP Link Originator must close the TCP connection. Having discovered the destination FC Fabric Entity WWN, the FCIP Link Originator may re-attempt to establish an FCIP link.

- **Keep Alive Time-Out Value (K_A_TOV)**—This is 32 bits (4 bytes) long. This field indicates the maximum interval at which a Link Keep Alive (LKA) ELS should be sent in the absence of other traffic on an FCIP link. The default value for K_A_TOV is half of the E_D_TOV.

- **Reserved**—This is 16 bits long. It must be set to 0.

- **-Reserved**—This is 16 bits long. It must be set to all ones.

The FC-BB-3 specification defines the LKA ELS. Remember that a SW_ILS is an ELS that may be transmitted only between fabric elements. The LKA is exchanged only between VE_Port peers and B_Access peers. So, one might think that the LKA is a SW_ILS. However, the valid responses to an LKA are LS_ACC and LS_RJT (not SW_ACC and SW_RJT). Another key difference is that, unlike most SW_ILSs that must be transmitted in Class F Exchanges, the LKA may be transmitted using any Class of Service supported by the FCIP link. Thus, the FC-BB-3 specification refers to the LKA as an ELS instead of as an SW_ILS. The LKA serves two purposes: the LKA keeps an FCIP link active when no other traffic is traversing the link, and the LKA verifies link connectivity when no FCIP traffic is received for an abnormal period of time. In the case of multi-connection links, the LKA may be sent on each TCP connection. The number of unacknowledged LKAs that signify loss of connectivity is configurable, and the default value is 2. When a TCP connection failure is detected via LKA, the FC Entity may attempt to re-establish the connection (via the FCIP Entity) or redirect the affected flows to one of the surviving TCP connections within the FCIP link (assuming that another TCP connection is available). When an FCIP link failure is detected via LKA, the FC Entity must attempt to re-establish the FCIP link (via the FCIP entity). Support for the LKA is optional. If supported, at least one LKA should be sent per K_A_TOV during periods of inactivity, but LKAs may be sent more frequently. The LKA may be sent during periods of bidirectional activity, but the LKA serves no useful purpose during such periods. For implementations that support TCP keep-alives, the LKA might be unnecessary. However, the LKA is sent from one FC Entity to another. So, the LKA verifies connectivity across more of the end-to-end path than TCP keep-alives. For this reason, SAN administrators who wish to eliminate redundant keep-alive traffic should consider disabling the TCP keep-alive. Because the default K_A_TOV is lower than the typical TCP keep-alive interval, disabling the TCP keep-alive should have no negative side affects. If the TCP keep-alive is used, and the FCIP Entity detects a failed TCP connection, the FCIP Entity must notify the FC Entity and provide diagnostic information about the failure. The FC Entity decides whether to re-establish the TCP connection (via the FCIP Entity). An LKA may be rejected via the LS_RJT ELS, but receipt of an LS_RJT serves the purpose of keeping the link active and verifies connectivity to the peer FC Entity regardless of the Reject Reason Code. The FC-BB-3 specification does not define any Reject Reason Codes or Reason Explanations that are unique to the LKA. Receipt of an LS_ACC ELS signifies a successful response to an LKA. Both the LKA and its associated LS_ACC use the same frame format. Figure 8-43 illustrates the data field format of an LKA/LS_ACC ELS frame.

Figure 8-43 *Data Field Format of an FC LKA/LS_ACC ELS Frame*

Byte #	3	2	1	0
Bit #	31 30 29 28 27 26 25 24	23 22 21 20 19 18 17 16	15 14 13 12 11 10 9 8	7 6 5 4 3 2 1 0
Word #0	LS Command Code	Unused	Unused	Unused

A brief description of each field follows:

- **LS Command Code**—This is 8 bits long. This field contains the LKA command code (0x80) or the LS_ACC command code (0x02).

- **Unused**—These are each 8 bits long. They must be set to 0.

The FC-BB-3 specification defines the EBP SW_ILS. When using the B_Access functional model, the EBP complements the ELP. One B_Access portal transmits an EBP to another B_Access portal to exchange operating parameters similar to those exchanged via the ELP. The valid responses to an EBP are SW_ACC and SW_RJT. The SW_ACC contains the responder's operating parameters. No other frames may be transmitted before successful exchange of the EBP. The normal switch-to-switch extended link initialization procedure occurs after the EBP exchange (see Chapter 5). Both the EBP and its associated SW_ACC use the same frame format. Figure 8-44 illustrates the data field format of an EBP/ SW_ACC SW_ILS frame.

Figure 8-44 *Data Field Format of an FC EBP/SW_ACC SW_ILS Frame*

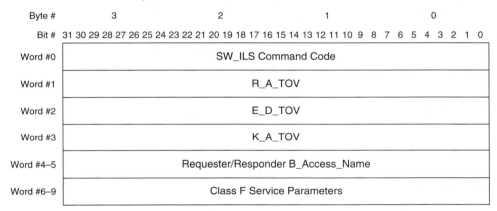

A brief description of each field follows:

- **SW_ILS Command Code**—This is 4 bytes long. This field contains the EBP command code (0x28010000) when transmitted by a requestor. This field contains the SW_ACC command code (0x02000000) when transmitted by a responder.

- **R_A_TOV**—This is 4 bytes long. This field contains the sender's required R_A_TOV expressed in milliseconds.

- **E_D_TOV**—This is 4 bytes long. This field contains the sender's required E_D_TOV expressed in milliseconds.

- **K_A_TOV**—This is 4 bytes long. This field contains the sender's required K_A_TOV expressed in milliseconds.

- **Requester/Responder B_Access_Name**—This is 8 bytes long. In an EBP frame, this field contains the requester's B_Access_Name. In an SW_ACC frame, this field contains the responder's B_Access_Name.

- **Class F Service Parameters**—This is 16 bytes long. The format and use of this field are identical to its format and use in an ELP frame (see Chapter 5). This field contains various B_Access operating parameters. Key parameters include the class-specific MTU (ULP buffer size), the maximum number of concurrent Class F sequences, the maximum number of concurrent sequences within each exchange, and the number of end-to-end Credits (EE_Credits) supported. Some FC switches allow the network administrator to manually configure one or more of these values.

If a parameter mismatch occurs, the EBP command is rejected with an SW_RJT (see Chapter 5). The reason codes defined in the FC-SW-4 specification are used for EBP. However, the FC-BB-3 specification redefines the reason code explanations that are used for EBP. Table 8-25 summarizes the EBP reject reason code explanations. All reason code explanations excluded from Table 8-25 are reserved.

Table 8-25 *EBP Reject Reason Code Explanations*

Reason Code Explanation	Description
0x00	No Additional Explanation
0x01	Class F Service Parameter Error
0x02	Invalid B_Access_Name
0x03	K_A_TOV Mismatch
0x04	E_D_TOV Mismatch
0x05	R_A_TOV Mismatch

For more information about the FCIP packet formats and FC-BB frame formats, readers are encouraged to consult the IETF RFCs 3643 and 3821, and the ANSI T11 FC-BB-2, FC-BB-3, FC-LS, FC-SW-3, and FC-SW-4 specifications.

FCIP Session Establishment

FCIP link initialization cannot begin until the underlying technology at OSI Layers 1 and 2 (usually Ethernet) completes its initialization procedure. Next, an IP address must be assigned to each port that will support FCIP traffic. Most often, this is accomplished manually using static IP addresses. If IP security is implemented, IPsec initialization occurs next. The PMM then optionally initiates FCIP device discovery via SLPv2 and passes the discovered information to the CSM. Alternately, the CSM may retrieve peer FCIP device information from the local config file. The FCIP Link Originator may then establish the first TCP connection with each of its peer FCIP devices. After the TCP three-way handshake completes, the FCIP Link Originator transmits an FSF and then waits for the echoed FSF to arrive. At this point, the FCIP link is fully active.

The FC switch-to-switch extended link initialization procedure described in Chapter 5 then begins (excluding the transmission of FC primitives). To summarize that procedure:

1 ELP is exchanged between VE_Ports or EBP is exchanged between B_Access portals.

2 The VISL is reset to enable the operating parameters.

3 ESC is exchanged between VE_Ports or E_Ports.

4 Optional VE_Port or E_Port authentication occurs.

5 PSS occurs.

6 Domain_IDs are re-assigned if a Domain_ID conflict exists.

7 Zone merge occurs.

   8 The FSPF protocol converges.

   9 An SW_RSCN is broadcast to announce the new VISL.

   10 Name Server updates are distributed.

   11 RSCNs are generated to announce the new Name Server records.

At this point, the two FC-SANs are merged into one FC-SAN. N_Ports can query their local Name Server to discover the new target devices in the remote segment of the merged FC-SAN. Additionally, Class 2, 3, and 4 frames can be exchanged between N_Ports across the new VISL.

FCIP Delivery Mechanisms

In FCIP environments, FC frame delivery failures can occur in any of three arenas: the IP network, the FC network, and the FC-BB_IP device. The delivery mechanisms of TCP, IP, and underlying technologies (such as Ethernet and SONET) are responsible for FCIP packet delivery in the IP network. For example, the TCP Sequence Number can be used to detect the loss of a TCP packet. Likewise, FC delivery mechanisms are responsible for FC frame delivery in the FC network. For example, the destination N_Port can detect a corrupt FC frame using the FC CRC. The handoff between these networks occurs within the FC-BB_IP device as previously described. During the handoff, certain problems can occur that result in dropped FC frames and/or TCP connection loss. These potential problems can be categorized as follows:

- Time synchronization issues
- FC frame corruption not detected by the TCP checksum
- Flow-control issues
- PDU boundary detection issues

If the FC Entities at each end of an FCIP link lose time synchronization, the timestamps delivered to the receiving FC Entity might result in dropped FC frames. Each incoming encapsulated FC frame must have an FTT equal to or less than half the E_D_TOV. Frames that do not meet this requirement must be discarded by the receiving FC Entity. When this happens, the destination N_Port is responsible for detecting the dropped frame and taking the appropriate action based on the Exchange Error Policy in effect for the impacted Exchange. For this reason, SAN administrators should ensure the time server infrastructure is redundant, and the relevant FC time-out values are set correctly to accommodate the FTT (taking jitter into account).

NOTE   Class F frames may be transmitted with a timestamp value of 0.

As previously discussed, the TCP checksum does not detect all bit errors. Therefore, the receiving FCIP Entity is required to validate each FC frame before forwarding it to the FC Entity. The receiving FCIP Entity must verify:

- The SOF and EOF values are appropriate
- The FC header is valid
- The FC frame length is valid

Additionally, the FCIP Entity must verify that each packet received contains the proper content (for example, an FSF in the first packet received on each TCP connection). Invalid FC frames may be dropped by the FCIP Entity or forwarded to the FC Entity with an EOF that indicates that the frame is invalid. Forwarded invalid FC frames are dropped by the destination N_Port. FC is responsible for re-transmission in accordance with the Exchange Error Policy in affect for the affected Exchange.

The FC-BB-3 specification requires FC-BB_IP devices to coordinate the TCP/IP flow-control mechanisms with the FC flow-control mechanisms. Specifically, the FC Entity must cooperate with the FCIP Entity to manage flow control in both the IP network and the FC-SAN as if the two networks were one. In principle, this is accomplished by managing the number of BB_Credits advertised locally based on the size of the peer FCIP device's advertised TCP window. However, no specific methods are mandated or provided by the ANSI or IETF standards. So, the implementation choice is vendor-specific. If this requirement is not implemented properly, dropped FC frames or TCP packets can result.

NOTE   The challenges of mapping flow-control information between the FC and IP networks apply equally to iFCP implementations.

FCIP packets enter the TCP byte stream without the use of a message synchronization scheme. If an FCIP_DE loses message synchronization, it may take any one of the following actions:

- Search the incoming TCP byte stream for a valid FCIP header and discard all bytes received until a valid FCIP header is found.
- Close the TCP connection and notify the FC Entity.
- Attempt to recover message synchronization for an implementation-specific period of time and then, if message synchronization is not recovered, close the TCP connection and notify the FC Entity.

If message synchronization cannot be recovered, and the TCP connection is closed, the FC Entity is responsible for re-establishing the TCP connection (via the FCIP Entity). Regardless of whether message synchronization is recovered, the affected N_Ports are responsible for detecting and re-transmitting all dropped FC frames in accordance with the Exchange Error Policy in effect for the affected Exchanges.

When the FCIP Entity detects an error, the FC Entity is notified via proprietary means. The FC Entity may notify the PMM via proprietary means for the purpose of error logging. The FC Entity must convert each error notification into a registered link incident report (RLIR). The RLIR is then forwarded to the domain controller of the switch. For certain errors, the FC Entity also forwards the RLIR to the management server of the switch. For more information about the FCIP delivery mechanisms and error reporting procedures, readers are encouraged to consult the IETF RFC 3821,and the ANSI T11 FC-BB-2, FC-BB-3, and FC-LS specifications.

FCIP Data Transfer Optimizations

Today, FCIP is used primarily for replicating data across long distances for the purpose of backup or disaster recovery. WAN circuits are often very expensive and represent a recurring cost. So, SAN administrators are always looking for ways to use their WAN circuits more efficiently. To that end, every major FCIP vendor supports one or more data transfer optimization features. The most common is data compression. Data compression works by replacing large, recognizable bit patterns with smaller bit patterns at the transmitting node. The receiving node then looks for the known smaller bit patterns in the incoming bit stream and replaces those patterns with the associated larger bit pattern. Data compression involves computational overhead, so hardware-based implementations are preferred because they offer dedicated computing power for compression operations. Cisco Systems supports hardware-based compression on some FCIP products and software-based compression on other FCIP products.

Another common optimization is the use of Ethernet jumbo frames. Using jumbo frames has the affect of reducing protocol overhead on the wire and reducing processing overhead on the end nodes. Note that the default Ethernet MTU of 1500 bytes is smaller than the largest FC frame size of 2148 bytes (including SOF and EOF). After adding the FC-FE header, TCP header and IP header, the largest encapsulated FC frame size is 2234 bytes. Thus, each FC frame must occupy more than one Ethernet frame. A common practice in FCIP environments is to increase the Ethernet MTU on the FCIP ports to 2300 bytes, which is large enough to accommodate a full-size FC frame and all associated FC-FE/TCP/IP encapsulation overhead (even if TCP options are used). Of course, this technique is fruitful only if jumbo frames are supported end-to-end, otherwise excessive fragmentation will occur (see Chapter 5). Cisco Systems supports jumbo frames on all FCIP products.

NOTE   MTU discovery during FLOGI does not account for FCIP links. FCIP links are completely transparent to N_ports. Also, the MTU of each FC-SAN that will be merged via FCIP must be the same.

As mentioned in the FCP section of this chapter, some of the newer optimizations being offered seek to accelerate SCSI operations. The most common technique is to spoof the FCP_XFER_RDY signal to eliminate excessive round trips across the WAN during SCSI write operations. Most, but not all, SAN extension vendors support some kind of FCP_XFER_RDY spoofing technique. Cisco Systems supports two FCP_XFER_RDY spoofing techniques on all FCIP products. One, for disk I/O, is called FCIP write acceleration (FCWA). The other, for tape I/O, is called FCIP tape acceleration (FCTA).

Summary

This chapter concludes a multi-chapter examination of the operational details of the primary storage networking technologies being deployed today: iSCSI, FCP, and FCIP. The discussions provided in this chapter focus on OSI session layer functionality to give readers a firm understanding of how each technology meets the requirements of the SAM Transport Protocol model without delving too deeply into the application-oriented functionality of SCSI. The information provided in this chapter should prepare readers to design and deploy storage networks with greater understanding of the implications of their design choices.

Review Questions

1 Name the three types of iSCSI names.

2 Why does RFC 3720 encourage the reuse of ISIDs?

3 What key feature does iSNS support that SLP does not support?

4 In the context of iSCSI, what is the difference between immediate data and unsolicited data?

5 What is the function of the iSCSI R2T PDU?

6 Can security parameters be re-negotiated during an active iSCSI session?

7 Why must iSCSI use its own CRC-based digests?

8 Does iSCSI support stateful recovery of active tasks in the presence of TCP connection failures?

9 Does FCP natively support the exchange of all required operating parameters to establish a new session?

10 Does FCP support immediate data?

11 How many bytes long is the FCP_DATA IU header?

12 What is the name of the FC-4 link service defined by the FCP-3 specification?

13 FCP mandates a one-to-one relationship between which two data constructs?

14 When an FCP target that supports only Exchange level error recovery detects a frame error, what action does the target take?

15 What determines the functional model of an FC-BB device?

16 How many FC Entities may be paired with an FCIP Entity?

17 Does the FCIP addressing scheme map to the SAM addressing scheme?

18 Why must the FC frame delimiters be encapsulated for transport across FC backbone networks?

19 Which field in the FSF may be set to zero for the purpose of discovery?

20 What procedure begins after an FCIP link becomes fully active?

21 Why must jumbo frames be supported end-to-end if they are implemented?

PART III

Advanced Network Functionality

Upon completing this chapter, you will be able to:

- List all of the flow control and QoS mechanisms related to modern storage networks
- Describe the general characteristics of each of the flow control and QoS mechanisms related to modern storage networks

CHAPTER **9**

Flow Control and Quality of Service

The chapters in Part I, "The Storage Networking Landscape," and Part II, "The OSI Layers," introduce the flow control and QoS mechanisms used in modern storage networks. Building upon those chapters, this chapter provides a comprehensive inventory of the flow control and QoS mechanisms used by Ethernet, IP, TCP, Internet SCSI (iSCSI), Fibre Channel (FC), Fibre Channel Protocol (FCP), and Fibre Channel over TCP/IP (FCIP). Readers are encouraged to review the flow control and QoS discussion at the beginning of Chapter 5, "The OSI Physical and Data Link Layers," before reading this chapter. Additionally, readers are encouraged to review the frame/packet format descriptions and delivery mechanism discussions in the chapters in Part II, "The OSI Layers," before reading this chapter. Finally, readers are encouraged to review the data transfer optimization discussions in Chapter 8, "The OSI Session, Presentation, and Application Layers," before reading this chapter.

Conceptual Underpinnings of Flow Control and Quality of Service

To fully understand the purpose and operation of flow-control and QoS mechanisms, first readers need to understand several related concepts. These include the following:

- The principle of operation for half-duplex upper layer protocols (ULPs) over full-duplex network protocols
- The difference between half-duplex timing mechanisms and flow-control mechanisms
- The difference between flow control and Quality of Service (QoS)
- The difference between the two types of QoS algorithms
- The relationship of delivery acknowledgement to flow control
- The relationship of processing delay to flow control
- The relationship of network latency to flow control
- The relationship of retransmission to flow control
- The factors that contribute to end-to-end latency

As previously mentioned, SCSI is a half-duplex command/response protocol. For any given I/O operation, either the initiator or the target may transmit at a given point in time. The SCSI communication model does not permit simultaneous transmission by both initiator and target within the context of a single I/O operation. However, SCSI supports full-duplex communication across multiple I/O operations. For example, an initiator may have multiple I/O operations outstanding simultaneously with a given target and may be transmitting in some of those I/O operations while receiving in others. This has the affect of increasing the aggregate throughput between each initiator/target pair. For this to occur, the end-to-end network path between each initiator/target pair must support full-duplex communication at all layers of the OSI model.

Readers should be careful not to confuse half-duplex signaling mechanisms with flow-control mechanisms. Communicating FCP devices use the Sequence Initiative bit in the FC Header to signal which device may transmit at any given point in time. Similarly, iSCSI devices use the F bit in the iSCSI Basic Header Segment (BHS) to signal which device may transmit during bidirectional commands. (iSCSI does not explicitly signal which device may transmit during unidirectional commands.) These mechanisms do not restrict the flow of data. They merely control the timing of data transmissions relative to one another.

Flow control and QoS are closely related mechanisms that complement each other to improve the efficiency of networks and the performance of applications. Flow control is concerned with pacing the rate at which frames or packets are transmitted. The ultimate goal of all flow-control mechanisms is to avoid receive buffer overruns, which improves the reliability of the delivery subsystem. By contrast, QoS is concerned with the treatment of frames or packets after they are received by a network device or end node. When congestion occurs on an egress port in a network device, frames or packets that need to be transmitted on that port must be queued until bandwidth is available. While those frames or packets are waiting in queue, other frames or packets may enter the network device and be queued on the same egress port. QoS policies enable the use of multiple queues per port and determine the order in which the queues are serviced when bandwidth becomes available. Without QoS policies, frames or packets within a queue must be transmitted according to a simple algorithm such as First In First Out (FIFO) or Last In First Out (LIFO). QoS mechanisms enable network administrators to define advanced policies for the transmission order of frames or packets. QoS policies affect both the latency and the throughput experienced by a frame or packet. The QoS concept also applies to frames or packets queued within an end node. Within an end node, QoS policies determine the order in which queued frames or packets are processed when CPU cycles and other processing resources become available.

All QoS algorithms fall into one of two categories: queue management and queue scheduling. Queue management algorithms are responsible for managing the number of frames or packets in a queue. Generally speaking, a frame or packet is not subject to being dropped after being admitted to a queue. Thus, queue management algorithms primarily deal with queue admission policies. By contrast, queue scheduling algorithms are responsible for selecting the next frame or packet to be transmitted from a queue. Thus, queue scheduling algorithms primarily deal with bandwidth allocation.

End-to-end flow control is closely related to delivery acknowledgement. To understand this, consider the following scenario. Device A advertises 10 available buffers to device B. Device B then transmits 10 packets to device A, but all 10 packets are transparently dropped in the network. Device B cannot transmit any more packets until device A advertises that it has free buffers. However, device A does not know it needs to send another buffer advertisement to device B. The result is a deadlock condition preventing device B from transmitting additional frames or packets to device A. If the network notifies device B of the drops, device B can increment its transmit buffers for device A. However, notification of the drops constitutes negative acknowledgement. Device A could send a data packet to device B containing in the header an indication that 10 buffers are available in device A. Although this does not constitute an acknowledgement that the 10 packets transmitted by device B were received and processed by device A, it does provide an indication that device B may transmit additional packets to device A. If device B assumes that the first 10 packets were delivered to device A, the result is an unreliable delivery subsystem (similar to UDP/IP and FC Class 3). If device B does not assume anything, the deadlock condition persists. Other contingencies exist, and in all cases, either a deadlock condition or an unreliable delivery subsystem is the result. Because the goal of flow control is to avoid packet drops due to buffer overrun, little motivation exists for implementing end-to-end flow control on unreliable delivery subsystems. So, end-to-end flow control is usually implemented only on reliable delivery subsystems. Additionally, end-to-end flow-control signaling is often integrated with the delivery acknowledgement mechanism.

End-to-end flow control is also closely tied to frame/packet processing within the receiving node. When a node receives a frame or packet, the frame or packet consumes a receive buffer until the node processes the frame or packet or copies it to another buffer for subsequent processing. The receiving node cannot acknowledge receipt of the frame or packet until the frame or packet has been processed or copied to a different buffer because acknowledgement increases the transmitting node's transmit window (TCP) or EE_Credit counter (FC). In other words, frame/packet acknowledgement implies that the frame or packet being acknowledged has been processed. Thus, processing delays within the receiving node negatively affect throughput in the same manner as network latency. For the effect on throughput to be negated, receive buffer resources must increase within the receiving node as processing delay increases. Another potential impact is the unnecessary retransmission of frames or packets if the transmitter's retransmission timer expires before acknowledgement occurs.

Both reactive and proactive flow-control mechanisms are sensitive to network latency. An increase in network latency potentially yields an increase in dropped frames when using reactive flow control. This is because congestion must occur before the receiver signals the transmitter to stop transmitting. While the pause signal is in flight, any frames or packets already in flight, and any additional frames or packets transmitted before reception of the pause signal, are at risk of overrunning the receiver's buffers. As network latency increases, the number of frames or packets at risk also increases. Proactive flow control precludes this scenario, but latency is still an issue. An increase in network latency yields an increase in buffer requirements or a decrease in throughput. Because all devices have finite memory resources, degraded throughput is inevitable if network latency continues to increase over time. Few devices support dynamic reallocation of memory to or from the receive buffer pool based on real-time fluctuations in network latency (called jitter), so the maximum expected RTT, including jitter, must be used to calculate the buffer requirements to sustain optimal throughput. More buffers increase equipment cost. So, more network latency and more jitter results in higher equipment cost if optimal throughput is to be sustained.

Support for retransmission also increases equipment cost. Aside from the research and development (R&D) cost associated with the more advanced software, devices that support retransmission must buffer transmitted frames or packets until they are acknowledged by the receiving device. This is advantageous because it avoids reliance on ULPs to detect and retransmit dropped frames or packets. However, the transmit buffer either consumes memory resources that would otherwise be available to the receive buffer (thus affecting flow control and degrading throughput) or increases the total memory requirement of a device. The latter is often the design choice made by device vendors, which increases equipment cost.

The factors that contribute to end-to-end latency include transmission delay, serialization delay, propagation delay, and processing delay. Transmission delay is the amount of time that a frame or packet must wait in a queue before being serialized onto a wire. QoS policies affect transmission delay. Serialization delay is the amount of time required to transmit a signal onto a wire. Frames or packets must be transmitted one bit at a time when using serial communication technologies. Thus, bandwidth determines serialization delay. Propagation delay is the time required for a bit to propagate from the transmitting port to the receiving port. The speed of light through an optical fiber is 5 microseconds per kilometer. Processing delay includes, but is not limited to, the time required to:

- Classify a frame or a packet according to QoS policies
- Copy a frame or a packet into the correct queue
- Match the configured policies for security and routing against a frame or a packet and take the necessary actions
- Encrypt or decrypt a frame or a packet
- Compress or decompress a frame or a packet
- Perform accounting functions such as updating port statistics
- Verify that a frame or a packet has a valid CRC/checksum
- Make a forwarding decision
- Forward a frame or a packet from the ingress port to the egress port

The order of processing steps depends on the architecture of the network device and its configuration. Processing delay varies depending on the architecture of the network device and which steps are taken.

Ethernet Flow Control and QoS

This section summarizes the flow-control and QoS mechanisms supported by Ethernet.

Ethernet Flow Control

As discussed in Chapter 5, "The OSI Physical and Data Link Layers," Ethernet supports reactive flow control via the Pause Operation Code (Pause Opcode). All 10-Gbps Ethernet implementations inherently support flow control and do not need to negotiate its use. 1000BASE-X negotiates flow control using the Pause bits in the Configuration ordered sets. Twisted-pair-based Ethernet implementations use the Technology Ability field to negotiate flow control. Except for 10-Gbps Ethernet implementations, three options may be negotiated: symmetric, asymmetric, or none. Symmetric indicates that the device is capable of both transmitting and receiving the Pause Opcode. Asymmetric indicates that the device is capable of either receiving or transmitting the Pause Opcode. None indicates that the Pause Opcode is not supported. All 10-Gbps Ethernet implementations support symmetric operation. A Pause Opcode may be sent before a queue overrun occurs, but many Ethernet switches do not behave in this manner.

Ethernet switches often employ "tail-drop" to manage flows. Tail-drop is not a mechanism per se, but rather a behavior. Tail-drop is the name given to the process of dropping packets that need to be queued in a queue that is already full. In other words, when a receive queue fills, additional frames received while the queue is full must be dropped from the "tail" of the queue. ULPs are expected to detect the dropped frames, reduce the rate of transmission, and retransmit the dropped frames. Tail-drop and the Pause Opcode often are used in concert. For example, when a receive queue fills, a Pause Opcode may be sent to stem the flow of new frames. If additional frames are received after the Pause Opcode is sent and while the receive queue is still full, those frames are dropped. For more information about Ethernet flow control, readers are encouraged to consult the IEEE 802.3-2002 specification.

Ethernet QoS

Ethernet supports QoS via the Priority field in the header tag defined by the IEEE 802.1Q-2003 specification. Whereas the 802.1Q-2003 specification defines the header tag format, the IEEE 802.1D-2004 specification defines the procedures for setting the priority bits. Because the Priority field is 3 bits long, eight priority levels are supported. Currently, only seven traffic classes are considered necessary to provide adequate QoS. The seven traffic classes defined in the 802.1D-2004 specification include the following:

- Network control information
- Voice applications
- Video applications
- Controlled load applications

- Excellent effort applications
- Best effort applications
- Background applications

The 802.1D-2004 specification defines a recommended set of default mappings between the seven traffic classes and the eight Ethernet priority values. In Ethernet switches that support seven or more queues per port, each traffic class can be mapped into its own queue. However, many Ethernet switches support fewer than seven queues per port. So, the 802.1D-2004 specification also defines recommendations for traffic class groupings when traffic classes must share queues. These mappings and groupings are not mandated, but they promote interoperability between Ethernet devices so that end-to-end QoS can be implemented successfully in a plug-and-play manner (even in multi-vendor environments).

Currently, no functionality is defined in the Ethernet specifications for the Pause Opcode to interact with the Priority field. So, the Pause Opcode affects all traffic classes simultaneously. In other words, an Ethernet switch that supports the Pause Opcode and multiple receive queues on a given port must send a Pause Opcode via that port (affecting all traffic classes) if any one of the queues fills. Otherwise, tail-drop occurs for the queue that filled. However, tail-drop can interact with the Priority field. Many Ethernet switches produced by Cisco Systems support *advanced tail-drop*, in which queuing thresholds can be set for each Ethernet priority level. Tail-drop then affects each traffic class independently. When a particular traffic class exceeds its queue threshold, frames matching that traffic class are dropped while the queue remains above the threshold defined for that traffic class. Other traffic classes are unaffected unless they also exceed their respective thresholds. The Pause Opcode needs to be sent only if all queues filled simultaneously. Alternately, the Pause Opcode may be sent only when one or more of the high-priority queues fill, thus avoiding tail-drop for high-priority traffic while permitting tail-drop to occur for lower-priority traffic. In this manner, the Pause Opcode can interact with the Priority field, but this functionality is proprietary and is not supported by all Ethernet switches. For more information about Ethernet QoS, readers are encouraged to consult the IEEE 802.1Q-2003 and 802.1D-2004 specifications.

IP Flow Control and QoS

This section summarizes the flow-control and QoS mechanisms supported by IP.

IP Flow Control

IP employs several flow-control mechanisms. Some are explicit, and others are implicit. All are reactive. The supported mechanisms include the following:

- Tail-drop
- Internet Control Message Protocol (ICMP) Source-Quench

- Active Queue Management (AQM)
- Explicit Congestion Notification (ECN)

Tail-drop is the historical mechanism for routers to control the rate of flows between end nodes. It often is implemented with a FIFO algorithm. When packets are dropped from the tail of a full queue, the end nodes detect the dropped frames via TCP mechanisms. TCP then reduces its window size, which precipitates a reduction in the rate of transmission. Thus, tail-drop constitutes implicit, reactive flow control.

ICMP Source-Quench messages can be used to explicitly convey a request to reduce the rate of transmission at the source. ICMP Source-Quench messages may be sent by any IP device in the end-to-end path. Conceptually, the ICMP Source-Quench mechanism operates in a manner similar to the Ethernet Pause Opcode. A router may choose to send an ICMP Source-Quench packet to a source node *in response to* a queue overrun. Alternately, a router may send an ICMP Source-Quench packet to a source node *before* a queue overruns, but this is not common. Despite the fact that ICMP Source-Quench packets can be sent before a queue overrun occurs, ICMP Source-Quench is considered a reactive mechanism because some indication of congestion or potential congestion must trigger the transmission of an ICMP Source-Quench message. Thus, additional packets can be transmitted by the source nodes while the ICMP Source-Quench packets are in transit, and tail-drop can occur even after "proactive" ICMP Source-Quench packets are sent. Upon receipt of an ICMP Source-Quench packet, the IP process within the source node must notify the appropriate Network Layer protocol or ULP. The notified Network Layer protocol or ULP is then responsible for slowing its rate of transmission. ICMP Source-Quench is a rudimentary mechanism, so few modern routers depend on ICMP Source-Quench messages as the primary means of avoiding tail-drop.

RFC 2309 defines the concept of AQM. Rather than merely dropping packets from the tail of a full queue, AQM employs algorithms that attempt to proactively avoid queue overruns by selectively dropping packets prior to queue overrun. The first such algorithm is called Random Early Detection (RED). More advanced versions of RED have since been developed. The most well known are Weighted RED (WRED) and DiffServ Compliant WRED. All RED-based algorithms attempt to predict when congestion will occur and abate based on rising and falling queue level averages. As a queue level rises, so does the probability of packets being dropped by the AQM algorithm. The packets to be dropped are selected at random when using RED. WRED and DiffServ Compliant WRED consider the traffic class when deciding which packets to drop, which results in administrative control of the probability of packet drop. All RED-based algorithms constitute implicit flow control because the dropped packets must be detected via TCP mechanisms. Additionally, all RED-based algorithms constitute reactive flow control because some indication of potential congestion must trigger the packet drop. The proactive nature of packet drop as implemented by AQM algorithms should not be confused with proactive flow-control mechanisms that exchange buffer resource information before data transfer occurs, to completely avoid frame/packet drops. Note that in the most generic sense, sending an ICMP Source-Quench message before queue overrun ocurs based on threshold settings could be considered a form of AQM. However, the most widely accepted definition of AQM does not include ICMP Source-Quench.

ECN is another method of implementing AQM. ECN enables routers to convey congestion information to end nodes explicitly by marking packets with a congestion indicator rather than by dropping packets. When congestion is experienced by a packet in transit, the congested router sets the two ECN bits to 11. The destination node then notifies the source node (see the TCP Flow Control section of this chapter). When the source node receives notification, the rate of transmission is slowed. However, ECN works only if the Transport Layer protocol supports ECN. TCP supports ECN, but many TCP implementations do not yet implement ECN. For more information about IP flow control, readers are encouraged to consult IETF RFCs 791, 792, 896, 1122, 1180, 1812, 2309, 2914, and 3168.

IP QoS

IP QoS is a robust topic that defies precise summarization. That said, we can categorize all IP QoS models into one of two very general categories: stateful and stateless. Currently, the dominant stateful model is the Integrated Services Architecture (IntServ), and the dominant stateless model is the Differentiated Services Architecture (DiffServ).

The IntServ model is characterized by application-based signaling that conveys a request for flow admission to the network. The signaling is typically accomplished via the Resource Reservation Protocol (RSVP). The network either accepts the request and admits the new flow or rejects the request. If the flow is admitted, the network guarantees the requested service level end-to-end for the duration of the flow. This requires state to be maintained for each flow at each router in the end-to-end path. If the flow is rejected, the application may transmit data, but the network does not provide any service guarantees. This is known as best-effort service. It is currently the default service offered by the Internet. With best-effort service, the level of service rendered varies as the cumulative load on the network varies.

The DiffServ model does not require any signaling from the application prior to data transmission. Instead, the application "marks" each packet via the Differentiated Services Codepoint (DSCP) field to indicate the desired service level. The first router to receive each packet (typically the end node's default gateway) conditions the flow to comply with the traffic profile associated with the requested DSCP value. Such routers are called conditioners. Each router (also called a hop) in the end-to-end path then forwards each packet according to Per Hop Behavior (PHB) rules associated with each DSCP value. The conditioners decouple the applications from the mechanism that controls the cumulative load placed on the network, so the cumulative load can exceed the network's cumulative capacity. When this happens, packets may be dropped in accordance with PHB rules, and the affected end nodes must detect such drops (usually via TCP but sometimes via ICMP Source-Quench). In other words, the DiffServ model devolves into best-effort service for some flows when the network capacity is exceeded along a given path.

Both of these QoS models have strengths and weaknesses. At first glance, the two models would seem to be incompatible. However, the two models can interwork, and various RFCs have been published detailing how such interworking may be accomplished. For more information about IP QoS, readers are encouraged to consult IETF RFCs 791, 1122, 1633, 1812, 2205, 2430, 2474, 2475, 2815, 2873, 2963, 2990, 2998, 3086, 3140, 3260, 3644, and 4094.

TCP Flow Control and QoS

This section summarizes the flow-control and QoS mechanisms supported by TCP.

TCP Flow Control

TCP flow control is a robust topic that defies precise summarization. TCP implements many flow-control algorithms, and many augmentations have been made to those algorithms over the years. That said, the primary TCP flow-control algorithms include slow start, congestion avoidance, fast retransmit, and fast recovery. These algorithms control the behavior of TCP following initial connection establishment in an effort to avoid congestion and packet loss, and during periods of congestion and packet loss in an effort to reduce further congestion and packet loss.

As previously discussed, the TCP sliding window is the ever-changing receive buffer size that is advertised to a peer TCP node. The most recently advertised value is called the receiver window (RWND). The RWND is complemented by the Congestion Window (CWND), which is a state variable within each TCP node that controls the amount of data that may be transmitted. When congestion is detected in the network, TCP reacts by reducing its rate of transmission. Specifically, the transmitting node reduces its CWND. At any point in time, a TCP node may transmit data up to the Sequence Number that is equal to the lesser of the peer's RWND plus the highest acknowledged Sequence Number or the CWND plus the highest acknowledged Sequence Number. If no congestion is experienced, the RWND value is used. If congestion is experienced, the CWND value is used. Congestion can be detected implicitly via TCP's acknowledgement mechanisms or timeout mechanisms (as applies to dropped packets) or explicitly via ICMP Source-Quench messages or the ECE bit in the TCP header.

When ECN is implemented, TCP nodes convey their support for ECN by setting the two ECN bits in the IP header to 10 or 01. A router may then change these bits to 11 when congestion occurs. Upon receipt, the destination node recognizes that congestion was experienced. The destination node then notifies the source node by setting to 1 the ECE bit in the TCP header of the next transmitted packet. Upon receipt, the source node reduces its CWND and sets the CWR bit to 1 in the TCP header of the next transmitted packet. Thus, the destination TCP node is explicitly notified that the rate of transmission has been reduced. For more information about TCP flow control, readers are encouraged to consult

IETF RFCs 792, 793, 896, 1122, 1180, 1323, 1812, 2309, 2525, 2581, 2914, 3042, 3155, 3168, 3390, 3448, 3782, and 4015.

TCP QoS

TCP interacts with the QoS mechanisms implemented by IP. Additionally, TCP provides two explicit QoS mechanisms of its own: the Urgent and Push flags in the TCP header. The Urgent flag indicates whether the Urgent Pointer field is valid. When valid, the Urgent Pointer field indicates the location of the last byte of urgent data in the packet's Data field. The Urgent Pointer field is expressed as an offset from the Sequence Number in the TCP header. No indication is provided for the location of the first byte of urgent data. Likewise, no guidance is provided regarding what constitutes urgent data. An ULP or application decides when to mark data as urgent. The receiving TCP node is not required to take any particular action upon receipt of urgent data, but the general expectation is that some effort will be made to process the urgent data sooner than otherwise would occur if the data were not marked urgent.

As previously discussed, TCP decides when to transmit data received from a ULP. However, a ULP occasionally needs to be sure that data submitted to the source node's TCP byte stream has actually be sent to the destination. This can be accomplished via the push function. A ULP informs TCP that all data previously submitted needs to be "pushed" to the destination ULP by requesting (via the TCP service provider interface) the push function. This causes TCP in the source node to immediately transmit all data in the byte stream and to set the Push flag to one in the final packet. Upon receiving a packet with the Push flag set to 1, TCP in the destination node immediately forwards all data in the byte stream to the required ULPs (subject to the rules for in-order delivery based on the Sequence Number field). For more information about TCP QoS, readers are encouraged to consult IETF RFCs 793 and 1122.

iSCSI Flow Control and QoS

This section summarizes the flow-control and QoS mechanisms supported by iSCSI.

iSCSI Flow Control

The primary flow-control mechanism employed by iSCSI is the Ready To Transfer (R2T) Protocol Data Unit (PDU). iSCSI targets use the R2T PDU to control the flow of SCSI data during write commands. The Desired Data Transfer Length field in the R2T PDU header controls how much data may be transferred per Data-Out PDU sequence. The R2T PDU is complemented by several other mechanisms. The MaxOutstandingR2T text key controls how many R2T PDUs may be outstanding simultaneously. The use of implicit R2T PDUs (unsolicited data) is negotiated via the InitialR2T and ImmediateData text keys. When unsolicited data is supported, the FirstBurstLength text key controls how much data may be transferred in or with the SCSI Command PDU, thus performing an equivalent function to the Desired Data Transfer Length field. The MaxRecvDataSegmentLength text key controls how much data may be transferred in a single Data-Out or Data-In PDU. The MaxBurstLength text key controls how much data may be transferred in a single PDU sequence (solicited or unsolicited). Thus, the FirstBurstLength value must be equal to or less than the MaxBurstLength value. The MaxConnections text key controls how many TCP connections may be aggregated into a single iSCSI session, thus controlling the aggregate TCP window size available to a session. The MaxCmdSN field in the Login Response BHS and SCSI Response BHS controls how many SCSI commands may be outstanding simultaneously. For more information about iSCSI flow control, readers are encouraged to consult IETF RFC 3720.

iSCSI QoS

iSCSI depends primarily on lower-layer protocols to provide QoS. However, iSCSI provides support for expedited command processing via the I bit in the BHS of the Login Request PDU, the SCSI Command PDU, and the TMF Request PDU. For more information about iSCSI QoS, readers are encouraged to consult IETF RFC 3720.

FC Flow Control and QoS

This section summarizes the flow-control and QoS mechanisms supported by FC.

FC Flow Control

The primary flow-control mechanism used in modern FC-SANs (Class 3 fabrics) is the Buffer-to-Buffer_Credit (BB_Credit) mechanism. The BB_Credit mechanism provides link-level flow control. The FLOGI procedure informs the peer port of the number of BB_Credits each N_Port and F_Port has available for frame reception. Likewise, the Exchange Link Parameters (ELP) procedure informs the peer port of the number of BB_Credits each E_Port has available for frame reception. Each time a port transmits a frame, the port decrements the BB_Credit counter associated with the peer port. If the BB_Credit counter reaches zero, no more frames may be transmitted until a Receiver_Ready (R_RDY) primitive signal is received. Each time an R_RDY is received, the receiving port increments the BB_Credit counter associated with the peer port. Each time a port processes a received frame, the port transmits an R_RDY to the peer port. The explicit, proactive nature of the BB_Credit mechanism ensures that no frames are ever dropped in FC-SANs because of link-level buffer overrun. However, line-rate throughput can be very difficult to achieve over long distances because of the high BB_Credit count requirement. Some of the line cards available for FC switches produced by Cisco Systems support thousands of BB_Credits on each port, thus enabling long-distance SAN interconnectivity over optical networks without compromising throughput. When FC-SANs are connected over long-distance optical networks, R_RDY signals are sometimes lost. When this occurs, throughput drops slowly over a long period. This phenomenon can be conceptualized as *temporal droop*. This phenomenon also can occur on native FC inter-switch links (ISLs), but the probability of occurrence is much lower with local connectivity. The FC-FS-2 specification defines a procedure called BB_Credit Recovery for detecting and recovering from temporal droop. For more information about FC flow control, readers are encouraged to consult the ANSI T11 FC-FS-2 and FC-BB-3 specifications.

FC switches produced by Cisco Systems also support a proprietary flow control feature called FC Congestion Control (FCC). Conceptually, FCC mimics the behavior of ICMP Source-Quench. When a port becomes congested, FCC signals the switch to which the source node is connected. The source switch then artificially slows the rate at which BB_Credits are transmitted to the source N_Port. Cisco Systems might submit FCC to ANSI for inclusion in a future FC standard.

FC QoS

FC supports several QoS mechanisms via fields in the FC header. The DSCP sub-field in the CS_CTL/Priority field can be used to implement differentiated services similar to the IP DiffServ model. However, the FC-FS-2 specification currently reserves all values other than zero, which is assigned to best-effort service. The Preference subfield in the CS_CTL/Priority field can be used to implement a simple two-level priority system. The FC-FS-2 specification requires all Class 3 devices to support the Preference subfield. No requirement exists for every frame within a sequence or Exchange to have the same preference value. So, it is theoretically possible for frames to be delivered out of order based on inconsistent values in the Preference fields of frames within a sequence or Exchange. However, this scenario is not likely to occur because all FC Host Bus Adapter (HBA) vendors recognize the danger in such behavior. The Priority subfield in the CS_CTL/Priority field can be used to implement a multi-level priority system. Again, no requirement exists for every frame within a sequence or Exchange to have the same priority value, so out-of-order frame delivery is theoretically possible (though improbable). The Preemption subfield in the CS_CTL/Priority field can be used to preempt a Class 1 or Class 6 connec-tion to allow Class 3 frames to be forwarded. No modern FC switches support Class 1 or Class 6 traffic, so the Preemption field is never used. For more information about FC QoS, readers are encouraged to consult the ANSI T11 FC-FS-2 specification.

FCP Flow Control and QoS

This section summarizes the flow-control and QoS mechanisms supported by FCP.

FCP Flow Control

The primary flow-control mechanism employed by FCP is the FCP_XFER_RDY IU. FCP targets use the FCP_XFER_RDY IU to control the flow of SCSI data during write commands. The FCP_BURST_LEN field in the FCP_XFER_RDY IU header controls how much data may be transferred per FCP_DATA IU. The FCP_XFER_RDY IU is complemented by a variety of other mechanisms. The Class 3 Service Parameters field in the PLOGI ELS header determines how many FCP_XFER_RDY IUs may be outstanding simultaneously. This is negotiated indirectly via the maximum number of concurrent sequences within each Exchange. The use of implicit FCP_XFER_RDY IUs (unsolicited data) is negotiated via the WRITE FCP_XFER_RDY DISABLED field in the PRLI Service Parameter Page.

When unsolicited data is supported, the First Burst Size parameter in the SCSI Disconnect-Reconnect mode page controls how much data may be transferred in the unsolicited FCP_DATA IU, thus performing an equivalent function to the FCP_BURST_LEN field. The Maximum Burst Size parameter in the SCSI Disconnect-Reconnect mode page controls how much data may be transferred in a single FCP_DATA IU (solicited or unsolicited). Thus, the First Burst Size value must be equal to or less than the Maximum Burst Size value. FCP does not support negotiation of the maximum number of SCSI commands that may be outstanding simultaneously because the architectural limit imposed by the size of the CRN field in the FCP_CMND IU header is 255 (versus 4,294,967,296 for iSCSI). For more information about FCP flow control, readers are encouraged to consult the ANSI T10 FCP-3 and ANSI T11 FC-LS specifications.

FCP QoS

FCP depends primarily on lower-layer protocols to provide QoS. However, FCP provides support for expedited command processing via the Priority field in the FCP_CMND IU header. For more information about FCP QoS, readers are encouraged to consult the ANSI T10 FCP-3 specification.

FCIP Flow Control and QoS

This section summarizes the flow-control and QoS mechanisms supported by FCIP.

FCIP Flow Control

FCIP does not provide any flow-control mechanisms of its own. The only FCIP flow-control functionality of note is the mapping function between FC and TCP/IP flow-control mechanisms. FCIP vendors have implemented various proprietary features to augment FCIP performance. Most notable are the FCP_XFER_RDY IU spoofing techniques. In some cases, even the FCP_RSP IU is spoofed. For more information about FCIP flow control, readers are encouraged to consult IETF RFC 3821 and the ANSI T11 FC-BB-3 specification.

FCIP QoS

FCIP does not provide any QoS mechanisms of its own. However, RFC 3821 requires the FC Entity to specify the IP QoS characteristics of each new TCP connection to the FCIP Entity at the time that the TCP connection is requested. In doing so, no requirement exists for the FC Entity to map FC QoS mechanisms to IP QoS mechanisms. This may be optionally accomplished by mapping the value of the Preference subfield or the Priority subfield in the CS_CTL/Priority field of the FC header to an IntServ/RSVP request or a DiffServ DSCP value. FCIP links are not established dynamically in response to received FC frames, so the FC Entity needs to anticipate the required service levels prior to FC frame reception. One method to accommodate all possible FC QoS values is to establish one TCP connection for each of the seven traffic classes identified by the IEEE 802.1D-2004 specification. The TCP connections can be aggregated into one or more FCIP links, or each TCP connection can be associated with an individual FCIP link. The subsequent mapping of FC QoS values onto the seven TCP connections could then be undertaken in a proprietary manner. Many other techniques exist, and all are proprietary. For more information about FCIP QoS, readers are encouraged to consult IETF RFC 3821 and the ANSI T11 FC-BB-3 specification.

Summary

The chapter reviews the flow-control and QoS mechanisms supported by Ethernet, IP, TCP, iSCSI, FC, FCP, and FCIP. As such, this chapter provides insight to network performance optimization. Application performance optimization requires attention to the flow-control and QoS mechanisms at each OSI Layer within each protocol stack.

Review Questions

1 What is the primary function of all flow-control mechanisms?

2 What are the two categories of QoS algorithms?

3 What is the name of the queue management algorithm historically associated with tail-drop?

4 Which specification defines traffic classes, class groupings, and class-priority mappings for Ethernet?

5 What is the name of the first algorithm used for AQM in IP networks?

6 What are the names of the two dominant QoS models used in IP networks today?

7 What is the name of the TCP state variable that controls the amount of data that may be transmitted?

8 What is the primary flow-control mechanism employed by iSCSI?

9 What are the names of the two QoS subfields currently available for use in FC-SANs?

10 What is the primary flow-control mechanism employed by FCP?

11 Are FCIP devices required to map FC QoS mechanisms to IP QoS mechanisms?

Upon completing this chapter, you will be able to:

- Explain the meaning of key networking terms based on the context
- Describe the effect of routing loops
- Differentiate between the types of routing protocols
- List the routing and switching protocols used by Ethernet, IP, and Fibre Channel (FC)
- Recite some of the key characteristics of each routing and switching protocol

CHAPTER 10

Routing and Switching Protocols

This chapter provides a brief introduction to the concepts and protocols related to routing and switching within Ethernet, IP, and FC networks. Many books have been written on the topic of routing and switching protocols, so this chapter does not delve into the details of the topic. This chapter seeks only to provide an overview of routing and switching protocols for readers who do not have a networking background. Multicast protocols are not covered.

Conceptual Underpinnings of Routing and Switching Protocols

To fully understand the operation of routing and switching protocols, you need to first understand several related concepts. These include:

- The traditional definitions of the terms *routing* and *switching*
- The new definition of the term *routing* as used by FC switch vendors
- The potential effect of loops within a topology
- The types of broadcast traffic that can be generated
- The difference between distance vector protocols and link-state protocols
- The difference between Interior Gateway Protocols (IGPs) and Exterior Gateway Protocols (EGPs)

In traditional IP and Ethernet terminology, the term routing describes the process of forwarding Layer 3 packets, whereas the terms bridging and switching describe the process of forwarding Layer 2 frames. This chapter uses the term switching instead of bridging when discussing Layer 2 forwarding. In both cases, the forwarding process involves two basic steps: path determination and frame/packet forwarding. Path determination (sometimes called path selection) involves some type of table lookup to determine the correct egress port or the next hop address. Frame/packet forwarding is the process of actually moving a received frame or packet from the ingress port to a queue associated with the appropriate egress port. Buffer management and scheduling algorithms then ensure the frame or packet is serialized onto the wire. The basic difference between routing and switching is that routing uses Layer 3 addresses for path determination, whereas switching uses Layer 2 addresses.

FC is a switching technology, and FC addresses are Layer 2 constructs. Therefore, FC switches do not "route" frames according to the traditional definition of routing. That said, the ANSI T11 FC-SW series of specifications refers to switching functionality, based on the Fabric Shortest Path First (FSPF) protocol, as "routing." FSPF must use FC addresses for path determination, therefore FSPF is actually a switching protocol according to the traditional definition. Moreover, many FC switch vendors have recently begun to offer FC routing products. Although the architectures of such offerings are quite different, they all accomplish the same goal, which is to connect separate FC-SANs without merging them. Since all FC routing solutions must use FC addresses for path determination, all FC routing solutions are actually FC switching solutions according to the traditional definition. However, FSPF employs a link-state algorithm, which is traditionally associated with Layer 3 routing protocols. Additionally, all FC routing solutions provide functionality that is similar to inter-VLAN IP routing. So, these new definitions of the term routing in the context of FC-SANs are not so egregious.

When a source node injects a frame or packet into a network, the frame or packet consumes network resources until it is delivered to the destination node. This is normal and does not present a problem as long as network resources are available. Of course, the underlying assumption is that each frame or packet will exit the network at some point in time. When this assumption fails to hold true, network resources become fully consumed as new frames or packets enter the network. Eventually, no new frames or packets can enter the network. This scenario can result from routing loops that cause frames or packets to be forwarded perpetually. For this reason, many routed protocols (such as IP) include a Time To Live (TTL) field (or equivalent) in the header. In the case of IP, the source node sets the TTL value, and each router decrements the TTL by one as part of the routing process. When the value in the TTL field reaches 0, the IP packet is discarded. This mechanism enables complex topologies in which loops might exist. However, even with the TTL mechanism, loops can cause problems. As the number of end nodes connected to an IP network grows, so does the network itself. The TTL mechanism limits network growth to the number of hops allowed by the TTL field. If the TTL limit is increased to enable network growth, the lifetime of looping packets is also increased. So, the TTL mechanism cannot solve the problem of loops in very large IP networks. Therefore, routing protocols that support complex topologies must implement other loop-suppression mechanisms to enable scalability. Even in small networks, the absence of a TTL mechanism requires the routing or switching protocol to suppress loops.

NOTE   The TTL field in the IP header does not limit the *time* each packet can live. The lifetime of an IP packet is measured in hops rather than time.

Protocols that support hierarchical addressing can also support three types of broadcast traffic:

- Local
- Directed
- All-networks

A local broadcast is sent to all nodes on the local network. A local broadcast contains the local network address in the high-order portion of the destination address and the all-nodes designator in the low-order portion of the destination address. A local broadcast is not forwarded by routers.

A directed broadcast is sent to all nodes on a specific, remote network. A directed broadcast contains the remote network address in the high-order portion of the destination address and the all-nodes designator in the low-order portion of the destination address. A directed broadcast is forwarded by routers in the same manner as a unicast packet until the broadcast packet reaches the destination network.

An all-networks broadcast is sent to all nodes on all networks. An all-networks broadcast contains the all-networks designator in the high-order portion of the destination address and the all-nodes designator in the low-order portion of the destination address. An all-networks broadcast is forwarded by routers. Because Ethernet addressing is flat, Ethernet supports only local broadcasts. IP addressing is hierarchical, but IP does not permit all-networks broadcasts. Instead, an all-networks broadcast (sent to IP address 255.255.255.255) is treated as a local broadcast. FC addressing is hierarchical, but the high-order portion of an FC address identifies a domain (an FC switch) rather than a network. So, the all-networks broadcast format equates to an all-domains broadcast format. FC supports only the all-domains broadcast format (no local or directed broadcasts). An all-domains broadcast is sent to D_ID 0xFF FF FF and is subject to zoning constraints (see Chapter 12, "Storage Network Security").

NOTE   Some people consider *broadcast* and *multicast* to be variations of the same theme. In that context, a broadcast is a simplified version of a multicast.

Each routing protocol is generally considered to be either a distance vector protocol (such as Routing Information Protocol [RIP]) or a link-state protocol (such as Open Shortest Path First [OSPF]). With a distance vector protocol, each router advertises its routing table to its neighbor routers. Initially, the only entries in a router's routing table are the networks to which the router is directly connected. Upon receipt of a distance vector advertisement, each receiving router updates its own routing table and then propagates its routing table to its neighbor routers. Thus, each router determines the best path to a remote network based on information received from neighbor routers. This is sometimes called *routing by rumor* because each router must make forwarding decisions based on unverified information.

By contrast, a router using a link-state protocol sends information about only its own interfaces. Such an advertisement is called a Link State Advertisement (LSA). Upon receipt of an LSA, each receiving router copies the information into a link-state database and then forwards the unmodified LSA to its neighbor routers. This process is called *flooding*. Thus, each router makes forwarding decisions based on information that is known to be accurate because the information is received from the actual source router.

In short, distance vector protocols advertise the entire routing table to adjacent routers only, whereas link-state protocols advertise only directly connected networks to all other routers. Distance vector protocols have the benefit of comparatively low processing overhead on routers, but advertisements can be comparatively large. Link-state protocols have the benefit of comparatively small advertisements, but processing overhead on routers can be comparatively high. Some routing protocols incorporate aspects of both distance vector and link state protocols. Such protocols are called hybrid routing protocols. Other variations also exist.

Routing protocols also are categorized as interior or exterior. An interior protocol is called an Interior Gateway Protocol (IGP), and an exterior protocol is called an Exterior Gateway Protocol (EGP). IGPs facilitate communication within a single administrative domain, and EGPs facilitate communication between administrative domains. An administrative domain can take the form of a corporation, an Internet Service Provider (ISP), a division within a government, and so on. Each administrative domain is called an Autonomous System (AS). Routing between Autonomous Systems is called inter-AS routing. To facilitate inter-AS routing on the Internet, IANA assigns a globally unique AS number to each AS.

Ethernet Switching Protocols

The protocol originally employed to make forwarding decisions in Ethernet networks was the Spanning Tree Protocol (STP). Early versions of STP were not sensitive to service interruptions. For example, a physical topology change often resulted in temporary cessation of frame forwarding that could last up to one minute. That historical behavior contributes to the public's lingering misunderstanding of modern Ethernet networks. Many enhancements have been made to STP over the years. In particular, physical topology changes are now detected and resolved much more quickly. In properly designed Ethernet networks, frame-forwarding disruptions of less than 1 second can be achieved during physical topology changes. Furthermore, STP was officially replaced by the Rapid Spanning Tree Protocol (RSTP) in 2004. RSTP improves certain operating characteristics of STP while maintaining backward compatibility with STP. So, switches running STP can be connected to switches running RSTP, thus facilitating phased migration. However, the full benefits of RSTP are not available in mixed networks. The configuration restrictions are identical for both protocols.

RSTP is a variation of the distance vector model. Each switch learns the location of MAC addresses by inspecting the Source Address field in the header of Ethernet frames received on each switch port. Thus, RSTP operation is completely transparent to end nodes. The learned addresses are entered into a forwarding table that associates each address with an egress port (the port on which the address was learned). No information is stored regarding the distance to each address. So, RSTP is a vector based protocol. No information is exchanged between switches regarding the reachability of MAC addresses. However, switches do exchange information about the physical topology so that loop suppression may occur. In multi-VLAN environments, the Multiple Spanning Tree Protocol (MSTP) may be used. MSTP is a variation of RSTP that enables an independent spanning tree to be established within each VLAN on a common physical network.

Because none of the Ethernet header formats include a TTL field (or equivalent), Ethernet frames can be forwarded indefinitely in topologies that have one or more loops. For example, when a broadcast frame (such as an ARP request) is received by a switch, the switch forwards the frame via all active ports except for the ingress port. If a loop exists in the physical topology, the forwarded broadcast frame eventually returns to the same switch and is forwarded again. Meanwhile, new broadcast frames are generated by the attached nodes. Those frames are forwarded in the same manner as the first broadcast frame. This cycle continues until all available bandwidth on all active ports is fully consumed by re-circulating broadcast frames. This phenomenon is called a broadcast storm. RSTP suppresses all loops in the physical topology to prevent broadcast storms and other congestion-related failures. The resulting logical topology is a tree that spans to facilitate connectivity between all attached nodes. Connectivity is always symmetric, which means that frames exchanged between a given pair of end nodes always traverse the same path in both directions. For more information about Ethernet switching protocols, readers are encouraged to consult the IEEE 802.1Q-2003 and 802.1D-2004 specifications.

IP Routing Protocols

IP supports a broad variety of IGPs. In the distance vector category, IP supports the Routing Information Protocol (RIP) and the Interior Gateway Routing Protocol (IGRP). In the hybrid category, IP supports the Enhanced Interior Gateway Routing Protocol (EIGRP). In the link-state category, IP supports the Open Shortest Path First (OSPF) protocol and the Integrated Intermediate System to Intermediate System (Integrated IS-IS) protocol. IP also supports two EGPs: the Exterior Gateway Protocol (EGP) and the Border Gateway Protocol (BGP).

RIP is the original distance vector protocol. RIP and its successor, RIP version 2 (RIPv2), enjoyed widespread use for many years. Today, RIP and RIPv2 are mostly historical. RIP employs classful routing based on classful IP addresses. RIP distributes routing updates via broadcast. RIPv2 enhances RIP by supporting classless routing based on variable-length subnet masking (VLSM) methodologies. Other enhancements include the use of multicast for routing update distribution and support for route update authentication. Both RIP and RIPv2 use hop count as the routing metric and support load balancing across equal-cost paths. RIP and RIPv2 are both IETF standards. For more information about classful/classless routing and VLSM, see Chapter 6, "The OSI Network Layer."

IGRP is a Cisco Systems proprietary protocol. IGRP was developed to overcome the limitations of RIP. The most notable improvement is IGRP's use of a composite metric that considers the delay, bandwidth, reliability, and load characteristics of each link. Additionally, IGRP expands the maximum network diameter to 255 hops versus the 15-hop maximum supported by RIP and RIPv2. IGRP also supports load balancing across unequal-cost paths. IGRP is mostly historical today.

EIGRP is another Cisco Systems proprietary protocol. EIGRP significantly enhances IGRP. Although EIGRP is often called a hybrid protocol, it advertises routing-table entries to adjacent routers just like distance vector protocols. However, EIGRP supports several features that differ from typical distance vector protocols. Among these are partial table updates (as opposed to full table updates), change triggered updates (as opposed to periodic updates), scope sensitive updates sent only to affected neighbor routers (as opposed to blind updates sent to all neighbor routers), a "diffusing computation" system that spreads the route calculation burden across multiple routers, and support for bandwidth throttling to control protocol overhead on low-bandwidth WAN links. EIGRP is a classless protocol that supports route summaries for address aggregation, load balancing across unequal-cost paths, and route update authentication. Though waning in popularity, EIGRP is still in use today.

OSPF is another IETF standard protocol. OSPF was originally developed to overcome the limitations of RIP. OSPF is a classless protocol that employs Dijkstra's Shortest Path First (SPF) algorithm, supports equal-cost load balancing, supports route summaries for address aggregation, and supports authentication. To promote scalability, OSPF supports the notion of *areas*. An OSPF area is a collection of OSPF routers that exchange LSAs. In other words, LSA flooding does not traverse area boundaries. This reduces the number of LSAs that each router must process and reduces the size of each router's link-state database. One area is designated as the backbone area through which all inter-area communication flows. Each area has one or more Area Border Routers (ABRs) that connect the area to the backbone area. Thus, OSPF implements a two-level hierarchical topology. All inter-area routes are calculated using a distance-vector algorithm. Despite this fact, OSPF is not widely considered to be a hybrid protocol. OSPF is very robust and is in widespread use today.

IS-IS was originally developed by Digital Equipment Corporation (DEC). IS-IS was later adopted by the ISO as the routing protocol for its Connectionless Network Protocol (CLNP). At one time, many people believed that CLNP eventually would replace IP. So, an enhanced version of IS-IS was developed to support CLNP and IP simultaneously.

The enhanced version is called Integrated IS-IS. In the end, the IETF adopted OSPF as its official IGP. OSPF and Integrated IS-IS have many common features. Like OSPF, Integrated IS-IS is a classless protocol that employs Dijkstra's SPF algorithm, supports equal-cost load balancing, supports route summaries for address aggregation, supports authentication, and supports a two-level hierarchical topology. Some key differences also exist. For example, Integrated IS-IS uses the Dijkstra algorithm to compute inter-area routes.

EGP was the first exterior protocol. Due to EGP's many limitations, many people consider EGP to be a *reachability* protocol rather than a full routing protocol. EGP is mostly historical today. From EGP evolved BGP. BGP has since evolved from its first implementation into BGP version 4 (BGP-4). BGP-4 is widely used today. Many companies run BGP-4 on their Autonomous System Border Routers (ASBRs) for connectivity to the Internet. Likewise, many ISPs run BGP-4 on their ASBRs to communicate with other ISPs. Whereas BGP-4 is widely considered to be a hybrid protocol, BGP-4 advertises routing table entries to other BGP-4 routers just like distance vector protocols. However, a BGP-4 route is the list of AS numbers (called the AS_Path) that must be traversed to reach a given destination. Thus, BGP-4 is called a path vector protocol. Also, BGP-4 runs over TCP. Each BGP-4 router establishes a TCP connection to another BGP-4 router (called a BGP-4 peer) based on routing policies that are administratively configured. Using TCP relaxes the requirement for BGP-4 peers to be topologically adjacent. Connectivity between BGP-4 peers often spans an entire AS that runs its own IGP internally. A TCP packet originated by a BGP-4 router is routed to the BGP-4 peer just like any other unicast packet. BGP-4 is considered a policy-based routing protocol because the protocol behavior can be fully controlled via administrative policies. BGP-4 is a classless protocol that supports equal-cost load balancing and authentication.

NOTE   BGP-4's use of TCP can be confusing. How can a routing protocol operate at OSI Layer 3 and use TCP to communicate? The answer is simple. For a router to operate, it must gather information from peer routers. Various mechanisms exist for gathering such information. Once the information is gathered, the subsequent functions of path determination and packet forwarding are executed at OSI Layer 3. In the case of BGP-4, the peer communication function leverages TCP, but AS_Path creation and packet forwarding are executed at OSI Layer 3.

The sheer volume of information associated with IP routing protocols can be very intimidating to someone who is new to IP networking. For more information on IP routing protocols, readers can consult the numerous IETF RFCs in which the protocols are defined and enhanced. Alternately, readers can consult one of the many books written about this subject. A very comprehensive analysis of all IP routing protocols is available in the two-volume set by Jeff Doyle entitled *Routing TCP/IP, volumes I and II*.

FC Switching Protocols

FSPF is the protocol used for routing within an FC-SAN. FSPF is a link-state protocol, but each vendor may choose which link-state algorithm to use. Dijkstra's algorithm is the most widely known link-state algorithm, but the ANSI T11 FC-SW-4 specification does not require the use of Dijkstra's algorithm. Well-defined interactions between switches ensure interoperability even if multiple link-state algorithms are used within a single FC-SAN. Additionally, the FC-SW-4 specification neither requires nor precludes the ability to load-balance, so FC switch vendors may choose whether and how to implement such functionality. In most other respects, FSPF is similar to other link-state protocols.

Routing between FC-SANs is currently accomplished via proprietary techniques. ANSI recently began work on standardization of inter-fabric routing, but no such standards currently exist. Each FC switch vendor currently takes a different approach to solving this problem. All these approaches fall into one of two categories: integrated or appliance-based. The integrated approach is conceptually similar to *Layer 3 switching,* wherein the ASICs that provide Layer 2 switching functionality also provide inter-fabric routing functionality as configured by administrative policy. The appliance-based approach requires the use of an external device that physically connects to each of the FC-SANs between which frames need to be routed. This approach is conceptually similar to the original techniques used for inter-VLAN IP routing (often called the router-on-a-stick model).

Summary

This chapter introduces readers to the routing and switching protocols used by Ethernet, IP, and FC. The traditional and new definitions of the terms *switching* and *routing* are discussed. The issues related to topological loops are discussed. The three types of broadcast traffic are discussed: local, directed, and all-networks. Multicast is not discussed. The categories of routing protocols are discussed: distance vector versus link state, and interior versus exterior. RSTP and MSTP are discussed in the context of Ethernet. RIP, IGRP, EIGRP, OSPF, Integrated IS-IS, EGP, and BGP-4 are discussed in the context of IP. FSPF is discussed in the context of FC.

Review Questions

1 What are the two basic steps that every switching and routing protocol performs?

2 What is the primary purpose of a TTL mechanism?

3 Does IP permit all-networks broadcasts?

4 Is RSTP backward-compatible with STP?

5 Does EIGRP support load balancing across unequal-cost paths?

6 How many levels in the topological hierarchy does OSPF support?

7 How do BGP-4 peers communicate?

8 Which link-state algorithm does FSPF use?

Upon completing this chapter, you will be able to:

- Explain the purpose of load balancing

- List the load-balancing techniques and mechanisms supported by Ethernet, IP, Fibre Channel (FC), Internet Small Computer System Interface (iSCSI), Fibre Channel Protocol (FCP), and Fibre Channel over TCP/IP (FCIP)

- Describe some of the key characteristics of each load-balancing technique and mechanism supported by Ethernet, IP, FC, iSCSI, FCP, and FCIP

- Differentiate between the methods of load balancing with Dynamic Multi-Pathing (DMP) software

CHAPTER 11

Load Balancing

This chapter provides a brief introduction to the principles of load balancing. We briefly discuss the load-balancing functionality supported by Ethernet, IP, FC, iSCSI, FCP, and FCIP, and the techniques employed by end nodes.

Conceptual Underpinnings of Load Balancing

The primary goal of load balancing is to improve throughput. Load balancing requires multiple routes or links, which often are implemented to improve redundancy. Multiple levels of load balancing may be implemented simultaneously. Indeed, this is often the case. Routing protocols often load-balance across multiple links, some of which are logical links composed of multiple physical links. Likewise, session-oriented protocols often load-balance across multiple sessions, while each session is composed of multiple Transport Layer connections. To avoid undesirable behavior in such environments, network and storage administrators must understand the operation of each protocol that performs load balancing and the interaction between those protocols.

The phrase *load sharing* is often used interchangeably with the phrase *load balancing*, but some people distinguish between these phrases. Load sharing can mean that multiple paths are used with each path bearing an arbitrary load. By contrast, load balancing can imply that some effort is made to balance the traffic load evenly across each available path. This distinction is important to note when reading white papers, design guides, and the like. So, readers are encouraged to consider the context when either of these terms is used. Both terms are used interchangeably within this book.

Load Balancing with Networking Technologies

This section provides an overview of the load-balancing functionality supported by Ethernet, IP, and FC.

Ethernet Load Balancing

As discussed in Chapter 5, "The OSI Physical and Data Link Layers," Ethernet supports the aggregation of multiple physical links into a single logical link. However, the load-balancing algorithm is not specified by IEEE 802.3-2002. It may be chosen by each Ethernet switch vendor. The chosen load-balancing algorithm must be able to transmit all frames associated with a conversation on a single link. A conversation is defined as a series of frames exchanged between a single pair of end nodes that the transmitting end node requires to be delivered in order. This rule ensures interoperability between switches that use different load-balancing algorithms. Because there is no way to discern a conversation from unordered frames using just the Ethernet header fields, many Ethernet switch vendors historically have employed algorithms that load-balance all traffic based on source or destination addresses. This ensures that all traffic exchanged between a given pair of end nodes traverses a single link within an Ethernet port channel. Newer techniques use fields in the protocol headers at OSI Layers 3 and 4 to identify flows. After a flow is identified, the flow identifier is used to implement flow-based load balancing within an Ethernet port channel. Flow-based algorithms improve the utilization of each link within a port channel by distributing the load more evenly across all available links.

A complementary technique exists based on the implementation of multiple VLANs on a single physical infrastructure. The Multiple Spanning Tree Protocol (MSTP) calculates an independent spanning tree in each VLAN. This enables network administrators to modify link costs independently within each VLAN. When done properly, each inter-switch link (ISL) within a shared infrastructure is utilized. For example, some VLANs might prefer ISL A to reach switch X, while other VLANs prefer ISL B to reach switch X. If ISL A fails, all VLANs use ISL B to reach switch X. Likewise, if ISL B fails, all VLANs use ISL A to reach switch X. ISLs A and B are both operational, and the total traffic load is spread across both ISLs. When this technique is not employed, all VLANs use the same ISL to reach switch X, while the other ISL remains operational but unused until the primary ISL fails.

IP Load Balancing

Each IP routing protocol defines its own rules for load balancing. Most IP routing protocols support load balancing across equal cost paths, while some support load balancing across equal and unequal cost paths. While unequal-cost load balancing is more efficient in its use of available bandwidth, most people consider unequal-cost load balancing to be more trouble than it is worth. The comparatively complex nature of unequal-cost load balancing makes configuration and troubleshooting more difficult. In practice, equal-cost load balancing is almost always preferred.

The router architecture and supported forwarding techniques also affect how traffic is load-balanced. For example, Cisco Systems routers can load balance traffic on a simple round-robin basis or on a per-destination basis. The operating mode of the router and its interfaces determines which load-balancing behavior is exhibited. When process switching is configured, each packet is forwarded based on a route table lookup. The result is round-robin load balancing when multiple equal-cost paths are available. Alternately, route table lookup information can be cached on interface cards so that only one route table lookup is required per destination IP address. Each subsequent IP packet sent to a given destination IP address is forwarded on the same path as the first packet forwarded to that IP address. The result is per-destination load balancing when multiple equal-cost paths are available. Note that the source IP address is not relevant to the forwarding decision.

Each IP routing protocol determines the cost of a path using its own metric. Thus, the "best" path from host A to host B might be different for one routing protocol versus another. Likewise, one routing protocol might determine two or more equal cost paths exists between host A and host B, while another routing protocol might determine only one best cost path exists. So, the ability to load-balance is somewhat dependent upon the choice of routing protocol. When equal-cost paths exist, administrators can configure the number of paths across which traffic is distributed for each routing protocol.

A complementary technology, called the Virtual Router Redundancy Protocol (VRRP), is defined in IETF RFC 3768. VRRP evolved from Cisco Systems' proprietary technology called Hot Standby Router Protocol (HSRP). VRRP enables a "virtual" IP address to be used as the IP address to which end nodes transmit traffic (the default gateway address). Each virtual IP address is associated with a "floating" Media Access Control (MAC) address.

VRRP implements a distributed priority mechanism that enables multiple routers to potentially take ownership of the virtual IP address and floating MAC address. The router with the highest priority owns the virtual IP address and floating MAC address. That router processes all traffic sent to the floating MAC address. If that router fails, the router with the next highest priority takes ownership of the virtual IP address and floating MAC address. VRRP can augment routing protocol load-balancing functionality by distributing end nodes across multiple routers. For example, assume that an IP subnet containing 100 hosts has two routers attached via interface A. Two VRRP addresses are configured for interface A in each router. The first router has the highest priority for the first VRRP address and the lowest priority for the second VRRP address. The second router has the highest priority for the second VRRP address and the lowest priority for the first VRRP address. The first 50 hosts are configured to use the first VRRP address as their default gateway. The other 50 hosts are configured to use the second VRRP address as their default gateway. This configuration enables half the traffic load to be forwarded by each router. If either router fails, the other router assumes ownership of the failed router's VRRP address, so none of the hosts are affected by the router failure.

The Gateway Load Balancing Protocol (GLBP) augments VRRP. GLBP is currently proprietary to Cisco Systems. Load balancing via VRRP requires two or more default gateway addresses to be configured for a single subnet. That requirement increases administrative overhead associated with Dynamic Host Configuration Protocol (DHCP) configuration and static end node addressing. Additionally, at least one IP address per router is consumed by VRRP. GLBP addresses these deficiencies by dissociating the virtual IP address from the floating MAC address. GLBP enables all routers on a subnet to simultaneously own a single virtual IP address. Each router has a floating MAC address associated with the virtual IP address. One router responds to all ARP requests associated with the virtual IP address. Each ARP reply contains a different floating MAC address. The result is that all end nodes use a single default gateway address, but the end nodes are evenly distributed across all available GLBP capable routers. When a router fails, one of the other routers takes ownership of the floating MAC address associated with the failed router.

FC Load Balancing

As discussed in Chapter 5, "The OSI Physical and Data Link Layers," FC supports the aggregation of multiple physical links into a single logical link (an FC port channel). Because all FC link aggregation schemes are currently proprietary, the load-balancing algorithms are also proprietary. In FC, the load-balancing algorithm is of crucial importance because it affects in-order frame delivery. Not all FC switch vendors support link aggregation. Each of the FC switch vendors that support link aggregation currently implements one or more load-balancing algorithms. Cisco Systems offers two algorithms. The default algorithm uses the source Fibre Channel Address Identifier (FCID), destination FCID, and Originator Exchange ID (OX_ID) to achieve load balancing at the granularity of an I/O operation. This algorithm ensures that all frames within a sequence and all sequences within an exchange are delivered in order across any distance. This algorithm also improves link utilization within each port channel. However, this algorithm does not guarantee that exchanges will be delivered in order. The second algorithm uses only the source FCID and destination FCID to ensure that all exchanges are delivered in order.

As previously stated, load balancing via Fabric Shortest Path First (FSPF) is currently accomplished in a proprietary manner. So, each FC switch vendor implements FSPF load balancing differently. FC switches produced by Cisco Systems support equal-cost load balancing across 16 paths simultaneously. Each path can be a single ISL or multiple ISLs aggregated into a logical ISL. When multiple equal-cost paths are available, FC switches produced by Cisco Systems can be configured to perform load balancing based on the source FCID and destination FCID or the source FCID, destination FCID, and OX_ID.

Similar to Ethernet, FC supports independent configuration of FSPF link costs in each Virtual Storage Area Network (VSAN). This enables FC-SAN administrators to optimize ISL bandwidth utilization. The same design principles that apply to Ethernet also apply to FC when using this technique.

Load Balancing with Session-Oriented Technologies

This section provides an overview of the load-balancing functionality supported by iSCSI, FCP, and FCIP.

iSCSI Load Balancing

iSCSI supports load balancing at the Transport Layer and at the Session Layer. Transport Layer load balancing is accomplished via multiple TCP connections within a single session. A discovery iSCSI session may use only one TCP connection. However, a normal iSCSI session may use more than one TCP connection. Each TCP connection may be established via a different network portal. When more than one TCP connection is associated with a session, iSCSI load-balances SCSI commands across the TCP connections. The maximum number of TCP connections supported within a single session is negotiated during the operational parameter negotiation stage of the login phase. After a normal session reaches the full feature phase on the first TCP connection, additional TCP connections may be added to the session. The login phase must be completed on each new TCP connection before the new TCP connection may be added to an existing session. When adding a new TCP connection to an existing session, the initiator sends the Target Session Identifying Handle (TSIH) of the existing session to the target. This enables the target to associate the new connection with the correct session. The iSCSI Command Sequence Number (CmdSN) is used to ensure in-order delivery of SCSI commands that are transmitted on different TCP connections.

When multiple sessions are established between an initiator/target pair, Dynamic Multi-Pathing (DMP) software must be used to load-balance SCSI traffic across the sessions. DMP software treats each iSCSI session as a path. DMP software is available from every major storage array vendor and some independent software vendors (ISV). Limited DMP functionality is now built into certain operating systems. DMP software is implemented as a transparent, logical layer above iSCSI and below the operating system's SCSI initiator. DMP software can load-balance SCSI traffic based on several algorithms. The choice of algorithms varies from one DMP product to the next. However, iSCSI connection allegiance restricts the granularity of DMP load balancing to a single SCSI command. This restriction exists because each TCP connection can belong to only one iSCSI session. So, the iSCSI Protocol Data Units (PDU) associated with a single SCSI command cannot be distributed across multiple iSCSI sessions. Upon receiving a SCSI PDU from the SCSI initiator, the DMP software makes a load-balancing decision and then passes the SCSI PDU to iSCSI with an indication of which session to use. iSCSI then makes a load-balancing decision based on the CmdSN (if multiple TCP connections exist within the selected session).

NOTE   By placing the network portals of a multihomed target device in different Internet Storage Name Service (iSNS) Discovery Domains (DDs), iSNS can be used to facilitate load balancing. For example, a network entity containing two SCSI target nodes (nodes A and B) and two NICs (NICs A and B) may present both nodes to initiators via both NICs. Selective DD assignment can force initiator A to access target node A via NIC A while forcing initiator B to access node B via NIC B.

FCP Load Balancing

Unlike the iSCSI model, FCP cannot leverage multiple Transport Layer connections between an initiator/target pair. This is because FC does not support multiple, simultaneous PLOGI connections between a pair of FC N_Ports. However, load balancing at the Session Layer is supported by FCP. Like the iSCSI model, DMP software is required to load-balance across multiple FCP sessions. DMP software treats each FCP session as a path. The DMP software is implemented as a transparent, logical layer above FCP and below the operating system's SCSI initiator. Like iSCSI, all FCP Information Units (IUs) associated with a single SCSI command must traverse the same FCP session. So, the granularity of DMP load balancing in the FCP model is a single SCSI command (like the iSCSI model).

FCIP Load Balancing

FCIP supports load balancing across multiple TCP connections within a single FCIP link, and across multiple FCIP links. When multiple TCP connections exist within a single FCIP link, load balancing across the TCP connections is accomplished using the source FCID and destination FCID. The ANSI T11 FC-BB-3 specification prohibits the use of any frame-based, sequence-based or Exchange-based algorithms. This restriction ensures that all frames, sequences, and Exchanges are delivered in-order between each pair of communicating FC Entities. When multiple FCIP links exist between a pair of FC-SANs, the FSPF protocol makes the load-balancing decisions. The ANSI T11 FC-SW-4 specification does not restrict the choice of FSPF load-balancing algorithms; therefore the load-balancing behavior is determined by the choice of FC switching equipment. Note that Cisco Systems supports FCIP link aggregation. When multiple FCIP links are aggregated into a single logical FCIP link (called an FCIP port channel), the FSPF protocol sees only one virtual inter-switch link (VISL). In this case, load balancing across the FCIP links within the FCIP port channel is accomplished using the same proprietary algorithms discussed in the FC port channel paragraph of this chapter.

End Node Load-Balancing Techniques

End nodes can load-balance SCSI commands across multiple iSCSI or FCP sessions using DMP software. Two basic approaches exist: LUN-to-path mapping and SCSI command distribution. When a host uses the LUN-to-path mapping approach, all I/O operations initiated to a given LUN are mapped to a single session (the active session). Recall from Chapter 8, "The OSI Session, Presentation and Application Layers," that an iSCSI or FCP session is identified by the concatenation of the initiator port identifier and the target port identifier. So, the active session is inherently associated with only one of the available paths (the active path) between the host and storage array. A different path is designated within the DMP configuration as the backup path in case the active path fails. Upon failure of the active path, the DMP software establishes a new session via the backup path and resumes I/O to the LUN via the new session. Load balancing is accomplished by distributing the active sessions across the available paths. For example, all I/O for LUN 13 traverses path A, and path B is the backup path for LUN 13. Simultaneously, all I/O for LUN 17 traverses path B, and path A is the backup path for LUN 17. Obviously, the LUN-to-path mapping approach enables load balancing only when multiple LUNs are being accessed simultaneously. When a host uses the SCSI command distribution approach, all I/O operations initiated to all LUNs are distributed across all available paths. The DMP software establishes a session via each available path and then determines which LUNs are accessible via each session. For any given SCSI command, the session is selected by the configured DMP algorithm. Some algorithms simply perform round-robin distribution. Other algorithms attempt to distribute commands based on real-time utilization statistics for each session. Many other algorithms exist. Note that optimal use of all available paths requires LUN access via each path, which is controlled by the storage array configuration. The SCSI command distribution approach enables load balancing even if the host is accessing only one LUN.

Summary

This chapter briefly introduces readers to the principles of load balancing. The goals of load balancing are discussed, and some common terminology. Ethernet port channeling and MSTP configuration options are reviewed. Routing protocols, VRRP and GLBP are examined in the context of IP. FC port channeling, FSPF and per-VSAN FSPF configuration options are covered. iSCSI connection-level and session-level techniques are explored. FCP session-level load balancing is compared to iSCSI. FCIP connection-level and tunnel-level options are discussed. Finally, end node configurations using DMP software are discussed.

Review Questions

1 What is the primary goal of load balancing?

2 Which protocol enables network administrators to modify link costs independently within each VLAN?

3 In IP networks, is load balancing across equal-cost paths more or less common than load balancing across unequal-cost paths?

4 Is the FSPF load-balancing algorithm defined in the FC specifications?

5 Does iSCSI require any third-party software to perform load balancing at the Transport Layer?

6 Does FCP support Transport Layer load balancing?

7 Does FCIP support Exchange-based load balancing across TCP connections within an FCIP link?

8 Name the two techniques commonly used by end nodes to load-balance across DMP paths.

Upon completing this chapter, you will be able to:

- Define some of the most common security terms

- Explain the benefits of Role Based Access Control (RBAC) and Authentication, Authorization, and Accounting (AAA)

- Describe the features of the most common AAA protocols and management protocols

- Enumerate the security services supported by Ethernet, IP, TCP, Internet Small Computer System Interface (iSCSI), Fibre Channel (FC), Fibre Channel Protocol (FCP), and Fibre Channel over TCP/IP (FCIP)

CHAPTER **12**

Storage Network Security

This chapter highlights some of the most prevalent security protocols related to modern storage networks. Many books have been written solely on the topic of information security, so this chapter does not delve into the details of the topic.

Conceptual Underpinnings of Storage Network Security

Security can mean many things to many people. In the world of data communications, security is concerned primarily with the protection of in-flight data (as opposed to data-at-rest) and device access. Many services are required to provide a complete security solution. The major services related to in-flight data include the following:

- **Data origin authentication** is the service that verifies that each message actually originated from the source claimed in the header.

- **Data integrity** is the service that detects modifications made to data while in flight. Data integrity can be implemented as connectionless or connection-oriented.

- **Anti-replay protection** is the service that detects the arrival of duplicate packets within a given window of packets or a bounded timeframe.

- **Data confidentiality** is the service that prevents exposure of application data to unauthorized parties while the data is in flight.

- **Traffic flow confidentiality** is the service that prevents exposure of communication parameters (such as original source and destination addresses) to unauthorized parties.

In many computing environments, multiple administrators are granted access to production systems for the purpose of management. Additionally, management responsibilities are sometimes divided among different teams or departments in large organizations. To facilitate shared management responsibilities in a scalable manner with minimal complexity, the concept of Role Based Access Control (RBAC) was introduced in 1992. RBAC simplifies multi-access security administration in large-scale environments. Consequently, RBAC has emerged as the preferred solution for multi-access security control. The RBAC model was standardized by ANSI INCITS in 2004 via the 359-2004 standard. The 359-2004 standard defines the RBAC reference model and provides the RBAC functional specification. The RBAC reference model is composed of five basic elements: users, roles, permissions, operations, and objects. The RBAC functional specification defines the requisite features of an RBAC implementation. In 2005, ANSI INCITS formed the Cyber Security (CS1) subcommittee to continue work on RBAC and other security initiatives. Although the reference model and functional specification defined in the 359-2004 standard are broadly applicable to many environments, various organizations outside of ANSI are working on RBAC standards for specific environments that have specialized requirements. Today, most information technology vendors support RBAC in their products.

RBAC is complemented by a set of technologies called authentication, authorization, and accounting (AAA). AAA implemented as a client/server model in which all security information is centrally stored and managed on an AAA server. The devices under management act as clients to the AAA server by relaying user credentials and access requests to the AAA server. The AAA server replies authoritatively to the managed devices. The user is granted or denied access based on the AAA server's reply. The traditional alternate is to create, store, and manage user identification and password information on each managed device (a distributed model). The AAA model requires significantly less administration than the distributed model. AAA is also inherently more secure because the central database can be protected by physical security measures that are not practical to implement in most distributed environments. Consequently, AAA is currently deployed in most large organizations. Many AAA products are available as software-only solutions that run on every major operating system. As its name suggests, AAA provides three services. The authentication service verifies the identification of each or device. The authorization service dynamically grants access to network and compute resources based on a preconfigured access list associated with the user's credentials. This enables granular control of who can do what rather than granting each authenticated user full access to all resources. Authorization is handled transparently, so the user experience is not tedious. The accounting service logs actions taken by users and devices. Some AAA servers also support the syslog protocol and integrate syslog messages into the accounting log for consolidated logging. The accounting service can log various data including the user's ID, the source IP address, protocol numbers, TCP and UDP port numbers, time and date of access, the commands executed and services accessed, the result of each attempt (permitted or denied), and the location of access. The accounting service enables many applications such as customer billing, suspicious activity tracing, utilization trending, and root cause analysis.

AAA Protocols

Communication between an AAA client and an AAA server occurs using one of several protocols. The most prevalent AAA protocols are the Remote Authentication Dial In User Service (RADIUS) and the Terminal Access Controller Access Control System Plus (TACACS+). A third protocol, Kerberos, is used for authentication in server environments. A fourth protocol, Secure Remote Password (SRP), is leveraged by many application protocols as a substitute for native authentication procedures.

RADIUS is defined in IETF RFC 2865, and RADIUS source code is freely distributed. As its name implies, RADIUS was originally implemented to authenticate remote users trying to access a LAN via analog modem connections. Remote users dial into a Network Access Server (NAS), which relays the user's credentials to a RADIUS server. Thus, the NAS (not the user) is the RADIUS client. RADIUS is still used for remote user authentication, but

RADIUS is now commonly used for other authentication requirements, too. For example, network administrators are often authenticated via RADIUS when accessing routers and switches for management purposes. To prevent unauthorized access to the RADIUS database, RADIUS client requests are authenticated by the RADIUS server before the user's credentials are processed. RADIUS also encrypts user passwords prior to transmission. However, other information (such as user ID, source IP address, and so on) is not encrypted. RADIUS implements authentication and authorization together. When a RADIUS server replies to a client authentication request, authorization information is included in the reply. A RADIUS server can reply to a client request or relay the request to another RADIUS server or other type of authentication server (such as Microsoft Active Directory). Communication between client and server is accomplished via variable-length keys in the form of Attribute-Length-Value. This enables new attributes to be defined to extend RADIUS functionality without affecting existing implementations. Note that RADIUS uses UDP (not TCP). Whereas the decision to use UDP is justified by a variety of reasons, this sometimes causes a network or security administrator to choose a different AAA protocol.

TACACS began as a protocol for authenticating remote users trying to access the ARPANET via analog modem connections. TACACS is defined in IETF RFC 1492. TACACS was later augmented by Cisco Systems. The proprietary augmentation is called Extended TACACS (XTACACS). Cisco subsequently developed the TACACS+ protocol based on TACACS and XTACACS. However, TACACS+ is a significantly different protocol and is incompatible with TACACS and XTACACS. Cisco Systems has deprecated TACACS and XTACACS in favor of TACACS+. Similar to RADIUS, the TACACS+ client (NAS, router, switch, and others) relays the user's credentials to a TACACS+ server. Unlike RADIUS, TACACS+ encrypts the entire payload of each packet (but not the TACACS+ header). Thus, TACACS+ is considered more secure than RADIUS. TACACS+ supports authentication, authorization, and accounting functions separately. So, any combination of services can be enabled via TACACS+. TACACS+ provides a more granular authorization service than RADIUS, but the penalty for this granularity is increased communication overhead between the TACACS+ client and server. Another key difference between TACACS+ and RADIUS is that TACACS+ uses TCP, which makes TACACS+ more attractive than RADIUS to some network and security administrators.

Kerberos was originally developed by the Massachusetts Institute of Technology (MIT) in the mid 1980s. The most recent version is Kerberos V5 as defined in IETF RFC 4120. Kerberos V5 is complemented by the Generic Security Services API (GSS-API) defined in IETF RFC 4121. Kerberos provides an encrypted authentication service using shared secret keys. Kerberos can also support authentication via public key cryptography, but this is not covered by RFC 4120. Kerberos does not provide an authorization service, but Kerberos does support pass-through to other authorization services. Kerberos does not provide an accounting service.

Another popular authentication protocol is the SRP protocol as defined in IETF RFC 2945. SRP provides a cryptographic authentication mechanism that can be integrated with a broad variety of existing Internet application protocols. For example, IETF RFC 2944 defines an SRP authentication option for Telnet. SRP implements a secure key exchange that enables additional protection such as data integrity and data confidentiality.

Management Protocols

The Simple Network Management Protocol (SNMP) is currently the most widely used management protocol. Early versions of SNMP restrict management access via *community strings*. A community string is specified by a management host (commonly called a management station) when connecting to a managed device. The managed device grants the management station access to configuration and state information based on the permissions associated with the specified community string. Community strings may be configured to grant read-only or read-write access on the managed device. Early versions of SNMP transmit community strings as clear text strings (said to be "in the clear"). SNMP version 3 (SNMPv3) replaces the community string model with a user-based security model (USM). SNMPv3 provides user authentication and data confidentiality. IETF RFC 3414 defines the USM for SNMPv3.

The Telnet protocol is very old. It is a staple among IP-based application protocols. Telnet was originally defined through a series of IETF RFCs in the 1970s. The most current Telnet specification is RFC 854. Telnet enables access to the command line interface (CLI) of remote devices. Unfortunately, Telnet operates in the clear and is considered insecure. Multiple security extensions have been defined for Telnet via a large number of RFCs. Telnet now supports strong authentication and encryption options. A suite of Unix commands (collectively called the R-commands) provides similar functionality to Telnet, but the suite of R-commands operates in the clear and is considered insecure. The suite includes Remote Login (RLOGIN), Remote Shell (RSH), Remote Command (RCMD) and Remote Copy (RCP) among other commands. Another protocol called Secure Shell (SSH) was developed by the open source community in the late 1990s to overcome the security limitations of Telnet and the suite of R-commands. The most commonly used free implementation of SSH is the OpenSSH distribution. SSH natively supports strong authentication and encryption. Among its many features, SSH supports *port forwarding,* which allows protocols like Telnet and the R-command suite to operate over an encrypted SSH session. The encrypted SSH session is transparent to Telnet and other forwarded protocols.

The File Transfer Protocol (FTP) is commonly used to transfer configuration files and system images to and from infrastructure devices such as switches, routers, and storage arrays. FTP supports authentication of users, but authentication is accomplished by sending user credentials in the clear. Once a user is authenticated, the user may access the FTP server. In other words, successful authentication implies authorization. No mechanism is defined for the user to authenticate the server. Additionally, data is transferred in the clear. To address these security deficiencies, IETF RFC 2228 defines several security extensions to FTP. The extensions provide secure bi-directional authentication, authorization, data integrity, and data confidentiality. Any or all of these extensions may be used by an FTP implementation. Secure implementations of FTP should not be confused with the SSH File Transfer Protocol (SFTP). SFTP is in the development stage and is currently defined in an IETF draft RFC. However, SFTP is already in widespread use. Despite its misleading name, SFTP is not FTP operating over SSH. SFTP is a relatively new protocol that supports many advanced features not supported by FTP. SFTP provides a secure file transfer service and implements some features typically associated with a file system. SFTP does not support authentication. Instead, SFTP relies on the underlying secure transport to authenticate users. SFTP is most commonly used with SSH, but any secure transport can be leveraged. Another option for moving configuration files and system images is the RCP command/protocol. As previously stated, RCP operates in the clear and is considered insecure. The Secure Copy (SCP) command/protocol is based on RCP, but SCP leverages the security services of SSH. SCP is not currently standardized.

NOTE   FTP deployed with security extensions is generically called secure FTP. However, secure FTP is not abbreviated as SFTP. SSH File Transfer Protocol is officially abbreviated as SFTP. Note that the Simple File Transfer Protocol is also officially abbreviated as SFTP. Readers are encouraged to consider the context when the acronym SFTP is encountered.

Ethernet Security

The IEEE 802.1X-2001 specification provides a port-based architecture and protocol for the authentication and authorization of Ethernet devices. The authorization function is not granular and merely determines whether access to the LAN is authorized following successful authentication. A device to be authenticated (such as a host) is called a supplicant. A device that enforces authentication (such as an Ethernet switch) is called an authenticator. The authenticator relays supplicant credentials to an authentication server, which permits or denies access to the LAN. The authentication server function may be implemented within the authenticator device. Alternately, the authentication server may be centralized and accessed by the authenticator via RADIUS, TACACS+, or other such protocol. A port in an Ethernet switch may act as authenticator or supplicant. For example, when a new Ethernet switch is attached to a LAN, the port in the existing Ethernet switch acts as authenticator, and the port in the new Ethernet switch acts as supplicant.

VLANs can be used as security mechanisms. By enforcing traffic isolation policies along VLAN boundaries, Ethernet switches protect the devices in each VLAN from the devices in other VLANs. VLAN boundaries can also isolate management access in Ethernet switches that support VLAN-aware RBAC.

IP Security

Security for IP-based communication is provided via many mechanisms. Central to these is the IP Security (IPsec) suite of protocols and algorithms. The IPsec suite is defined in many IETF RFCs. Each IPsec RFC falls into one of the following seven categories:

- Architecture
- Encapsulating Security Payload
- Authentication Header
- Encryption Algorithms
- Authentication Algorithms
- Key Management Protocols
- Domain of Interpretation

The primary IPsec RFCs include the following:

- **2401** — Security Architecture for the Internet Protocol
- **2406** — IP Encapsulating Security Payload (ESP)
- **2402** — IP Authentication Header (AH)
- **2409** — Internet Key Exchange (IKE)
- **2408** — Internet Security Association and Key Management Protocol (ISAKMP)
- **2407** — IP Security Domain of Interpretation (DOI) for ISAKMP

The IPsec suite provides the following services:

- Access control
- Data origin authentication
- Connectionless data integrity
- Anti-replay protection
- Data confidentiality
- Limited traffic flow confidentiality

IPsec is implemented at the OSI Network Layer between two peer devices, so all IP-based ULPs can be protected. IPsec supports two modes of operation: transport and tunnel. In transport mode, a security association (SA) is established between two end nodes. In tunnel mode, an SA is established between two gateway devices or between an end node and a gateway device. A security association is a unidirectional tunnel identified by a Security Parameter Index (SPI), the protocol used (ESP) and the destination IP address. Two SAs must be established (one in each direction) for successful communication to occur.

IP routers and switches also support Access Control Lists (ACL). An ACL permits or denies protocol actions based on a highly granular permissions list applied to the ingress or egress traffic of a specified interface or group of interfaces. An ACL can be applied to inter-VLAN traffic or intra-VLAN traffic. Inter-VLAN traffic is filtered by applying an ACL to a router interface. This is sometimes called a Router ACL (RACL). Intra-VLAN traffic is filtered by applying an ACL to all non-ISL switch ports in a given VLAN. An intra-VLAN ACL is sometimes called a VLAN ACL (VACL).

TCP Security

TCP does not natively provide secure communication aside from limited protection against mis-delivery via the Checksum field in the TCP header. TCP-based applications can rely on IPsec for security services. Alternately, TCP-based applications can rely on an OSI Transport Layer protocol (other than TCP) for security services. The Transport Layer Security (TLS) protocol is one such option. TLS is currently defined in IETF RFC 2246. TLS operates above TCP (but within the Transport Layer) and provides peer authentication, connection-oriented data integrity, and data confidentiality. TLS operation is transparent to all ULPs. TLS is comprised of two sub-protocols: the TLS Record Protocol and the TLS

Handshake Protocol. TLS is sometimes referred to as the Secure Sockets Layer (SSL). However, SSL is a separate protocol that was originally developed by Netscape for secure web browsing. HTTP is still the primary consumer of SSL services. TLS v1.0 evolved from SSL v3.0. TLS and SSL are not compatible, but TLS implementations can negotiate the use of SSL when communicating with SSL implementations that do not support TLS.

iSCSI Security

As previously discussed, iSCSI natively supports bi-directional authentication. iSCSI authentication occurs as part of the initial session establishment procedure. iSCSI authentication is optional and may transpire using clear text messages or cryptographically protected messages. For cryptographically protected authentication, IETF RFC 3720 permits the use of SRP, Kerberos V5, the Simple Public-Key GSS-API Mechanism (SPKM) as defined in RFC 2025, and the Challenge Handshake Authentication Protocol (CHAP) as defined in RFC 1994. Vendor-specific protocols are also permitted for cryptographically protected authentication. For all other security services, iSCSI relies upon IPsec.

Additional iSCSI security can be achieved by masking the existence of iSCSI devices during the discovery process. Both Internet Storage Name Service (iSNS) Discovery Domains and Service Location Protocol (SLP) Scopes can be leveraged for this purpose. Both of these mechanisms provide limited access control by confining device discovery within administratively defined boundaries. However, this form of security is based on a merit system; no enforcement mechanisms are available to prevent direct discovery via probing. Readers are encouraged to consult IETF RFC 3723 for background information related to iSCSI security.

Fibre Channel Security

Most FC security mechanisms are defined in the Fibre Channel Security Protocols (FC-SP) specification. The FC-SP model is largely based on the IPsec model. The FC-SP specification defines the following security services:

- Device authentication
- Device authorization
- Connectionless data integrity
- Data confidentiality
- Cryptographic key management
- Security policy definition and distribution

Multiple authentication protocols are supported, including Diffie-Hellmann CHAP (DH-CHAP), the Fibre Channel Authentication Protocol (FCAP), and the Fibre Channel Password Authentication Protocol (FCPAP). DH-CHAP uses shared secrets. FCAP leverages the public key infrastructure (PKI). FCPAP is based on SRP. The authorization service enables the following policies:

- Binding restrictions to control which devices (N_Ports, B_Ports, and so on) may join a fabric, and to which switch(es) a given device may connect

- Binding restrictions to control which switches may join a fabric and which switch pairs may form an ISL

- Management access restrictions to control which IP hosts may manage a fabric and which IP protocols may be used by management hosts

The authentication and binding procedures are based on Worldwide Names (WWN). The optional ESP_Header defined in the Fibre Channel Framing and Signaling (FC-FS) specification series provides the data integrity and confidentiality services. Key management is facilitated by an FC-specific variant of IKE.

Perhaps the most known FC security mechanism is the FC zoning service. The FC zoning service is defined in the Fibre Channel Generic Services (FC-GS) specification series. FC zoning restricts which device pairs may communicate. FC zoning traditionally operates in two modes: soft zoning and hard zoning. Soft zoning is a merit system in which certain WWNs are masked during the discovery process. The Fibre Channel Name Server (FCNS) provides each host a list of targets that the host is permitted to access. The list is derived from WWN-based policies defined in the Fibre Channel Zone Server (FCZS). However, no enforcement mechanism is implemented to prevent hosts from accessing all targets. By contrast, hard zoning enforces communication policies that have traditionally been based on switch ports (not WWNs). The line between soft and hard zoning is beginning to blur because newer FC switches support hard zoning based on WWNs.

Virtual Fabrics (VF) can also be used as security mechanisms. By enforcing traffic isolation policies along VF boundaries, FC switches protect the devices in each VF from the devices in other VFs. VF boundaries can also isolate management access in FC switches that support VF-aware RBAC.

Modern storage arrays commonly support another security mechanism called Logical Unit Number (LUN) masking. LUN masking hides certain LUNs from initiators when the storage array responds to the SCSI REPORT LUNS command. Note that LUN masking was developed to ensure data integrity, and the security benefits are inherent side affects. FC switches produced by Cisco Systems support enforcement of LUN masking policies via the FC zoning mechanism (called LUN zoning).

FCP Security

FCP does not natively support any security services. FCP relies on the security services provided by the FC architecture.

FCIP Security

FCIP does not natively support any IP-based security mechanisms. FCIP relies upon IPsec for all IP-based security services. Additional FCIP security can be achieved by masking the existence of FCIP devices during the discovery process. Because FCIP does not support discovery via iSNS, only SLP Scopes can be leveraged for this purpose. However, this form of security is based on a merit system; no enforcement mechanisms are available to prevent direct discovery via probing.

Following FCIP link establishment, the FC virtual inter-switch link (VISL) may be secured by FC-SP procedures. For example, after an FCIP link is established, the peer FC switches may be authenticated via FC-SP procedures during E_Port (VISL) initialization. If authentication fails, no SCSI data can transit the FCIP link even though an active TCP connection exists. One limitation of this approach is the inability to authenticate additional TCP connections that are added to an existing FCIP link. From the perspective of the FC fabric, the additional TCP connections are transparent. Therefore, FC-SP procedures cannot be used to validate additional TCP connections. For this reason, the ANSI T11 FC-BB specification series defines the Authenticate Special Frame (ASF) Switch Internal Link Service (SW_ILS). The ASF is used to authenticate additional TCP connections before they are added to an existing FCIP link. When a new TCP connection is requested for an existing FCIP link, the receiving FCIP Entity passes certain information about the connection request to the FC Entity. The FC Entity uses that information to send an ASF to the claimed requestor. The claimed requestor validates the ASF with a Switch Accept (SW_ACC) SW_ILS if the TCP connection request is valid. Until the ASF transmitter receives an SW_ACC, SCSI data may not traverse the new TCP connection. Readers are encouraged to consult IETF RFC 3723 for background information related to FCIP security.

Summary

This chapter highlights the primary security protocols used by modern storage networks. An introduction to in-flight data protection services, RBAC, and AAA is followed by a brief discussion of the most commonly used AAA and management protocols. An overview of Ethernet, IP, and TCP security is provided by reviewing the IEEE 802.1X-2001 specification, the IPsec suite, and SSL/TLS, respectively. iSCSI authentication and discovery are discussed and followed by a discussion of FC security as defined in the FC-SP specification. To conclude this chapter, a summary of FCIP security mechanisms is provided.

Review Questions

1 List the five primary protection services for in-flight data.

2 Which management protocol supports "port forwarding"?

3 What type of security model does Ethernet implement?

4 Which standard defines the IPsec architecture?

5 Is SSL compatible with TLS?

6 Is iSCSI authentication mandatory?

7 Which security architecture was leveraged as the basis for the FC-SP architecture?

8 Which standard defines the ASF SW_ILS?

Upon completing this chapter, you will be able to:

- List the requisite components of a management system
- Explain the role of standards in management
- Describe the two primary IP-based management frameworks and supporting protocols
- Characterize the Fibre Channel (FC) Management Service and supporting services
- Name the two primary in-band Small Computer System Interface (SCSI) management techniques

CHAPTER 13

Storage Management Protocols

Management is a diverse and complex topic. Additionally, the storage industry is currently undergoing widespread evolution with regard to management technologies and techniques. For example, disparate management tools, each designed for a specific purpose, are converging into holistic tools that provide enterprise-wide management. Therefore, this chapter seeks only to provide readers with an overview of the management concepts and protocols relevant to modern storage networks. This chapter covers both legacy and modern protocols.

Conceptual Underpinnings of Storage Management Protocols

To understand management protocols, readers must first understand certain principles of management. Typically, several components work together to compose a management system. At the heart of the management system is a centralized management host called a management station. In some cases, the management station is actually a group of clustered hosts. The management station typically communicates with a software component, called an agent, on each device to be managed. The agent accesses hardware-based instrumentation to make management data (such as events, states, and values) available to the management station. A data model is required to ensure that management data is structured using a well defined format. A well defined protocol facilitates communication between the management station and agents. The types of actions that the management station may perform on the managed devices are determined by the capabilities of the agents, management station, communication protocol, and administrative policies. The administrative policies cover such things as authentication, authorization, data privacy, provisioning, reclamation, alerting, and event response.

NOTE   Some management stations communicate with agent-less devices. An agent-less device exposes management information via one or more mechanisms embedded in the system BIOS or integrated into the operating system.

Standards play an important role in the cost of management systems. In the absence of standards, each product vendor must develop a proprietary management agent. Each new product results in a new proprietary agent. That increases product development costs. Additionally, management station vendors must adopt multiple proprietary interfaces to manage heterogeneous devices with proprietary agents. That increases the number of lines of software code in the management station product. The increased code size often increases the occurrence of bugs, slows product performance, increases product development costs, slows product adaptation to accommodate new managed devices, and complicates code maintenance when changes are made to one or more existing agents. Standards address these challenges so that product development efforts can be focused on high-level management functionality instead of basic communication challenges. As a result, prices fall and innovation occurs more rapidly. Much of the innovation currently taking place in storage and network management seeks to automate provisioning and reclamation tasks.

Several categories of storage-related management applications exist. One such category is called Storage Resource Management (SRM) that provides the ability to discover, inventory, and monitor disk and tape resources. Some SRM products support visualization of the relationship between each host and its allocated storage resources. Many SRM vendors are actively augmenting their products to include policy-based, automated provisioning and reclamation. SRM applications are sold separately from the storage resources being managed. SAN management is another category. SAN management applications are often called fabric managers. SAN management provides the ability to discover, inventory, monitor, visualize, provision, and reclaim storage network resources. Most FC switch vendors bundle a SAN management application with each FC switch at no additional charge. However, advanced functionality is often licensed or sold as a separate SAN management application. Note that the line between SRM and SAN management is blurring as convergence takes place in the storage management market.

Data management is another category. Data management is sometimes called Hierarchical Storage Management (HSM). HSM should not be confused with Information Lifecycle Management (ILM). HSM provides policy-based, automated migration of data from one type of storage resource to another. HSM policies are usually based on frequency or recency of data access. The goal of HSM is to leverage less-expensive storage technologies to store data that is used infrequently. HSM products have existed for decades. They originated in mainframe environments. The concept of ILM recently evolved from HSM. ILM performs essentially the same function as HSM, but ILM migration policies are based on the business value of data rather than solely on frequency and recency of use. The word *information* implies knowledge of the business value of the *data*. In other words, all data must be classified by the ILM application. The phrase *tiered storage* is often used in conjunction with ILM. ILM applications migrate data between tiers of storage. Each storage tier provides a unique level of performance and reliability. Thus, each storage tier has a unique cost basis. The concept of tiered storage originally derives from the HSM context. However, storage tiers were typically defined as different types of storage media (disk, tape, and optical) in the HSM context. In the ILM context, storage tiers are typically defined as different levels of functionality or business value. For example, high-performance SCSI disk might be used as tier one, while low-performance ATA disk is used as tier two. The underlying premise of all ILM applications is that businesses are willing and able to classify their data accurately so that ILM policies can be executed against the data. In practice, that premise is not entirely sound, and the adoption rate for ILM applications is likely to reflect the challenge of data classification until a practical and efficient data classification methodology is developed.

TCP/IP Management

Management of IP-based devices is accomplished via the Internet Standard Management Framework (ISMF). The ISMF and supporting specifications are summarized in IETF RFC 3410. Many people erroneously refer to the Simple Network Management Protocol (SNMP) when they really mean to refer to the ISMF. While SNMP is a key component of the framework, several other components are required for the framework to be of any use. The five major components of the framework are as follows:

- A modeling language, called the Structure of Management Information (SMI), for describing management data
- A virtual store, called the Management Information Base (MIB), for organizing and storing management data
- A protocol (SNMP) for communication between management stations and managed devices
- A security model to provide authentication, authorization, and data protection services (such as data confidentiality)
- Management applications to manipulate the information retrieved from managed devices

SMI is based on the ISO's Abstract Syntax Notation One (ASN.1). The most recent version of the SMI is called SMIv2. It is defined in RFC 2578. SMIv2 defines data types, an object model, and syntax rules for MIB module creation. The framework views each management datum as an object. Management objects are stored in the MIB. The most recent version of the MIB is called MIB-II. It is defined in RFC 1213. Many proprietary extensions have been made to the MIB without compromising the standard object definitions. This is possible because the MIB is modular. The internal structure of the MIB is an inverted tree in which each branch represents a group of related management objects (called a module). MIB modules are sometimes called MIBs. Vendors can define their own MIB modules and graft those modules onto the standard MIB. An agent in a managed device uses the MIB to organize management data retrieved from hardware instrumentation. Management stations access the MIB in managed devices via SNMP requests sent to agents. SNMP version 2 (SNMPv2) is the most recent and capable version of the communication protocol. SNMPv2 is defined in RFC 3416.

Chapter 12, "Storage Network Security," states that SNMPv2 uses a community-based security model, whereas SNMPv3 uses a user-based security model. More accurately stated, SNMPv2 combined with a community-based security model is called SNMPv2c, and SNMPv2 combined with a user-based security model is called SNMPv3. The fact that the same communication protocol (SNMPv2) is used by SNMPv2c and SNMPv3 is commonly misunderstood. SNMPv2 typically operates over UDP, but TCP is also supported. However, the RFC that defines a mapping for SNMP over TCP is still in the experimental state. Another common misconception is the notion that SNMP is a management application. In actuality, SNMP is an enabling technology (a protocol) for management applications. Most SNMP operations occur at the direction of a management application layered on top of SNMP.

Management stations can read MIB object values by issuing the GetRequest Protocol Data Unit (PDU) or one of its variants. Management stations can modify MIB object values by issuing the SetRequest PDU. The SetRequest PDU can be used to configure device operations, clear counters, and so on. Note that SNMP supports limited device configuration functionality. Each GetRequest PDU, variant of the GetRequest PDU, and SetRequest PDU elicits a Response PDU. Managed devices can also initiate communication. When an event transpires or a threshold is reached, a managed device can reactively send notification to the management station via the Trap PDU. A Trap PDU does not elicit a Response PDU (unacknowledged). Alternately, reactive notification can be sent via the InformRequest PDU. Each InformRequest PDU elicits a Response PDU (acknowledged).

Worthy of mention is a class of MIB modules used for Remote Network Monitoring (RMON). In the past, network administrators had to deploy physical devices to remotely monitor the performance of a network. To manage those specialized devices, a MIB module (the RMON MIB) was developed. Over time, the functionality of remote network monitoring devices was integrated into the actual network devices, thus eliminating the need for physically separate monitoring devices. The RMON MIB was also integrated into the self-monitoring network devices. As new classes of network devices came to market, self-monitoring functionality adapted. New MIB modules were defined to manage the new devices, and the RMON MIB module was also augmented. Today, several variants of the RMON MIB are defined and in widespread use.

Another management framework, called Web-Based Enterprise Management (WBEM), was developed by the Distributed Management Task Force (DMTF). WBEM seeks to unify the management of all types of information systems including storage arrays, servers, routers, switches, protocol gateways, firewalls, transaction load balancers, and even applications. WBEM aspires to go beyond the limits of SNMP. One example is WBEM's support for robust provisioning and configuration. WBEM uses the Common Information Model (CIM) as its object model. Like the MIB object model, CIM supports vendor extensions without compromising interoperability. However, CIM goes beyond the MIB object model by supporting the notion of relationships between objects. CIM also supports methods (operations) that can be invoked remotely. CIM enables a wide variety of disparate management applications to share management data in a common format. WBEM is modular so that any modeling language and communication protocol can be used. The Extensible Markup Language (XML) is the most commonly used modeling language to implement CIM, which is defined in the xmlCIM Encoding specification. HTTP is the most commonly used communication protocol, which is defined in the CIM Operations Over HTTP specification. The CIM-XML specification brings together the xmlCIM Encoding specification and the CIM Operations Over HTTP specification. WBEM supports discovery via SLP, which is generally preferred over the direct probing behavior of SNMP-based management stations. In the WBEM framework, an agent is called a CIM provider or a CIM server, and a management station is called a CIM client.

Web Services is a technology suite produced by the Organization for the Advancement of Structured Information Standards (OASIS). The Web Services architecture is built upon the Simple Object Access Protocol (SOAP), the Universal Description, Discovery and Integration (UDDI) protocol, the Web Service Definition Language (WSDL), and XML. The DMTF began work in 2005 to map the Web Services for Management (WS-Management) specification and the Web Services Distributed Management (WSDM) specification onto WBEM. Upon completion, WS-Management and WSDM will be able to manage resources modeled with CIM.

The first CIM-based storage management technology demonstration occurred in October 1999 at an industry trade show called Storage Networking World. Various working groups within the Storage Networking Industry Association (SNIA) continued work on CIM-based management projects. Simultaneously, a group of 16 SNIA member companies developed a WBEM-based storage management specification called Bluefin. The goal of Bluefin was to unify the storage networking industry on a single management interface. The group of 16 submitted Bluefin to SNIA in mid-2002. SNIA subsequently created the Storage Management Initiative (SMI) to streamline the management projects of the various SNIA working groups and to incorporate those efforts with Bluefin to produce a single storage management standard that could be broadly adopted.

The resultant standard is called the Storage Management Initiative Specification (SMI-S), which leverages WBEM to provide a high degree of interoperability between heterogeneous devices. Storage and networking vendors have developed object models for storage devices and storage networking devices, and work continues to extend those models. Additionally, object models for storage services (such as backup/restore, snapshots, clones, and volume management) are being developed. SNIA continues to champion SMI-S today in the hopes of fostering widespread adoption of the new standard. Indeed, most storage and storage networking vendors have already adopted SMI-S to some extent. ANSI has also adopted SMI-S v1.0.2 via the INCITS 388-2004 specification. SNIA also conducts conformance testing to ensure vendor compliance.

Another common function supported on storage and storage networking devices is *call home*. Call home is similar to SNMP traps in that they both reactively notify support personnel when certain events transpire. Unlike SNMP traps, call home is usually invoked only in response to hardware or software failures. That said, some devices allow administrators to decide which events generate a call home. Many devices support call home over modem lines, which explains the name of the feature. Call home functionality is not standardized, so the communication protocols and message formats are usually proprietary (unlike SNMP traps). That said, some devices support call home via the Simple Mail Transfer Protocol (SMTP), which operates over TCP/IP in a standardized manner as defined in IETF RFC 2821.

Similar to SNMP traps and call home, the Syslog protocol can be used to log details about device operation. The Syslog protocol was originally developed by University of California at Berkeley for use on UNIX systems. The popularity of the Syslog protocol precipitated its adoption on many other operating systems and even on networking devices. Though Syslog was never standardized, IETF RFC 3164 documents the behavior of many Syslog implementations in the hopes of improving interoperability. Like SNMP traps, Syslog messages are not acknowledged. Another useful management tool is the accounting function of the AAA model discussed in Chapter 12, "Storage Network Security." Accounting data can be logged centrally on an AAA server or locally on the managed device. Today, most devices support some level of accounting.

IP operates over every major OSI Layer 2 protocol including FC. The ANSI T11 Fibre Channel Link Encapsulation (FC-LE) specification defines a mapping for IP and ARP onto FC. However, the FC-LE specification fails to adequately define all necessary aspects of IP operation over FC. So, the IETF filled in the gaps by producing RFC 2625. Together, the two specifications provide sufficient guidance for IP over FC (IPFC) to be implemented reliably.

IPFC originally was envisioned as a server-oriented transport for use in clustered server environments, localized grid computing environments, tiered application environments, High Performance Computing (HPC) environments, and so on. However, IPFC can also be used for management purposes. Any given device (server or otherwise) that is attached to a FC fabric is inevitably also attached to an IP network. If a device loses its primary IP connection (perhaps because of a hardware failure), IPFC can be used to access the device over the FC fabric. This "back door" approach ensures that management stations can access devices continuously even in the presence of isolated communication failures. However, very few administrators are willing to compromise the reliability of SCSI operations by introducing a second ULP into their FC-SANs. Moreover, modern server platforms are commonly configured with dual Ethernet NICs for improved redundancy on the LAN. Consequently, IPFC is rarely used for management access. In fact, IPFC is rarely used for any purpose. Low latency Ethernet switches and InfiniBand switches are generally preferred for high performance server-to-server communication. Thus, IPFC is currently relegated to niche applications.

FC Management

The ANSI T11 Fibre Channel Generic Services (FC-GS) specification series defines several services that augment the functionality of FC-SANs. Among these is an in-band management service. The FC Management Service is actually composed of many supporting services. The FC Management Service currently includes:

- A Fabric Configuration Server
- A Performance Server
- A Fabric Zone Server
- A Security Policy Server
- An Unzoned Name Server
- A Host Bus Adapter (HBA) Management Server

The FC Management Service is distributed. It typically runs on the FC switches that compose a fabric. Each switch in a fabric maintains an identical copy of the management information for the entire fabric. This enables a single point of access for management of an FC-SAN. In other words, a management application (such as a fabric manager) can connect to a single switch to access all management information for all switches in the fabric.

The Fabric Configuration Server supports discovery of the fabric topology and operating characteristics. When a fabric manager connects to a FC switch, connectivity information for all devices in the fabric is visualized using data extracted from the Fabric Configuration Server. The Performance Server collects and aggregates performance statistics for the entire fabric. Management applications can query any FC switch to access performance statistics for the entire fabric. The Performance Server also supports threshold monitoring. As discussed in Chapter 12, "Storage Network Security," the Fabric Zone Server restricts communication between devices attached to an FC-SAN. Though FC zones are security-focused, the Fabric Zone Server is integral to the management service. This is because the Fabric Zone Server is the mechanism by which FC zones are configured and managed. The Security Policy Server facilitates the definition and management of security policies related to the Fibre Channel Security Protocols (FC-SP) specification. The Unzoned Name Server provides full access to the FC Name Server (FCNS) database for management applications. Initiators and targets are subject to zone policies that restrict access to the information in the FCNS database. However, management applications require unrestricted access to the FCNS database. The HBA Management Server enables HBAs to register certain data (called HBA management information) with the FC fabric. This enables management applications to query the FC fabric for HBA management information instead of querying the end nodes directly. The mechanisms for HBA management information registration and retrieval are defined by the Fabric Device Management Interface (FDMI).

A standard Application Programming Interface (API) for HBAs complements the FC Management Service. The so-called HBA API is defined in the ANSI T11 SM-HBA specification. It supports direct management of HBAs. Vendor-supplied agents implement proprietary APIs. A standard API enables management application vendors to write software without the overhead of HBA-specific API calls. Thus, the HBA API enables management applications to discover, monitor, and manage heterogeneous HBAs consistently across disparate operating systems and server platforms. Note that the same information can be gathered from the FC fabric via the Performance Server, the HBA Management Server, and the FCNS.

The FC-GS specification series also defines a notification service called the Event Service. Fabric attached devices can register with the Event Server to receive notification of events. Currently, a limited number of events are supported. Like the FC Management Service, the Event Service is distributed.

The FC-LS specification defines various Extended Link Service (ELS) commands that can be issued by a fabric device to ascertain state information about devices, connections, Exchanges, and sequences. Examples include Read Exchange Status Block (RES), Read Sequence Status Block (RSS), Read Connection Status (RCS), Read Link Error Status Block (RLS), and Read Port Status Block (RPS). These commands are issued directly from one device to another.

SCSI Management

SCSI enclosures provide electrical power, thermal cooling, and other support for the operation of SCSI target devices. Two in-band techniques for management of SCSI enclosures warrant mention. The first is the SCSI Accessed Fault-Tolerant Enclosures (SAF-TE) specification. The most recent SAF-TE specification was produced by the nStor Corporation and the Intel Corporation in 1997. SAF-TE provides a method of monitoring fault-tolerant SCSI enclosures using the following six SCSI commands:

- INQUIRY
- READ BUFFER
- REQUEST SENSE
- SEND DIAGNOSTIC
- TEST UNIT READY
- WRITE BUFFER

All six of these commands are defined in the ANSI T10 SCSI Primary Commands (SPC) specification series. SAF-TE is a proprietary specification that is published in an open manner. SAF-TE is not a de jure standard. That said, the goal of SAF-TE is to provide a nonproprietary method for heterogeneous SCSI controllers to monitor heterogeneous storage enclosures. SAF-TE is implemented as a SCSI processor inside the enclosure. The SAF-TE SCSI processor supports target functionality. The SCSI controller (initiator) periodically polls the SAF-TE target using the aforementioned commands to detect changes in enclosure status such as temperature and voltage levels. The SAF-TE target can also assert indicators (for example, lights and audible alarms) to indicate the status of enclosure components such as fans, power supplies, and hot-swap bays.

The second in-band technique is called SCSI Enclosure Services (SES). SES is defined in the ANSI T10 SES specification series. SES provides a method of monitoring and managing the components of a SCSI enclosure. SES is conceptually similar to SAF-TE, and SES has the same goal as SAF-TE. However, SES is a standard, and ANSI development of SES is ongoing. Like SAF-TE, SES is implemented as a SCSI target. SES operation is similar to SAF-TE, but SCSI controllers (initiators) use only two commands to access SES:

- SEND DIAGNOSTIC
- RECEIVE DIAGNOSTIC RESULTS

Both of these commands are defined in the ANSI T10 SPC specification series.

Summary

This chapter provides an introduction to management concepts by discussing the components of a management system and the role of standards in the realm of management. Certain categories of management applications are then described. The two predominant IP-based management frameworks, ISMF and WBEM, are reviewed and followed by a brief description of SMI-S, call home, Syslog, Accounting, and IPFC. The FC Management Service and its constituent parts are explained. Concluding the FC section is a description of the HBA API, the FC Event Service and management related ELS commands. Finally, two SCSI in-band management techniques, SAF-TE and SES, are examined.

Review Questions

1 List two aspects of management that are currently undergoing rapid innovation.

2 List the five major components of the ISMF.

3 WBEM usually operates over which communication protocol?

4 List the constituent parts of the FC Management Service.

5 List two in-band techniques for management of SCSI enclosures.

Upon completing this chapter, you will be able to:

- Explain the need for protocol decoders
- Describe the methods available to capture traffic
- List the types of protocol decoders
- Explain the need for traffic analyzers
- List the types of traffic analyzers

CHAPTER 14

Protocol Decoding and Traffic Analysis

This chapter provides an overview of the concepts and tools related to protocol decoding and analysis. The material in this chapter is more relevant to troubleshooting activities than to day-to-day operations. Though troubleshooting occurs less frequently than daily maintenance and configuration changes, every storage network administrator should be familiar with the tools available for troubleshooting.

The Purpose of Protocol Decoding

Most storage networking products include some integrated tools for troubleshooting. For example, Cisco Systems supports the **show** and **debug** commands via the Command Line Interface (CLI) on all switches in the MDS9000 family. The **show** command displays detailed state information about switch hardware, software, tables in memory, and so on. The **debug** command displays detailed, real-time information about fabric operations such as N_Port login/logout, Fabric Shortest Path First (FSPF) updates, zoneset activation, authentication requests, and so on. These commands are invaluable when a problem arises. However, these commands cannot display the actual header fields of the frames that are passing through the switch. In some situations, the root cause of a problem is an end node. To troubleshoot such situations effectively, the administrator must use the troubleshooting tools supplied by the vendor of the suspect device. Those tools are often incapable of displaying all the requisite information to resolve the problem. For example, a server might be properly configured but unable to login to a storage array because of a software bug in the Host Bus Adapter (HBA) driver. Many other examples exist in which the best (and sometimes only) way to identify the root cause of a problem is to analyze the protocols by capturing frames as they transit the network. This is known as traffic capture and protocol decode.

Methods of Traffic Capture

Historically, administrators had to disconnect a suspect device from one of its adjacent devices to connect a protocol decoder. The protocol decoder would be inserted between the suspect device and its adjacent device (usually a switch or hub). That was required to facilitate traffic capture. This method is known as in-line traffic capture. The disadvantages of this approach include the following:

- The suspect device must be taken offline temporarily to connect the protocol decoder and again to subsequently disconnect the protocol decoder.

- The act of inserting another device into the data stream can introduce additional problems or mask the original problem.

- A one-to-one relationship exists between the suspect device and the protocol decoder, so only one device can be decoded at any point in time unless multiple protocol decoders are available. Note that protocol decoders tend to be very expensive.

- An administrator must be physically present to connect and configure the protocol decoder.

The advantages of in-line traffic capture include the following:

- All types of frames can be captured including low-level primitives that are normally terminated by the physically adjacent device.

- OSI Layer 1 issues related to faulty cabling and connectors can be detected.

To mitigate the drawbacks of in-line traffic capture, Cisco Systems developed an alternate approach (out-of-line). The Switch Port Analyzer (SPAN) feature was introduced on the Catalyst family of Ethernet switches in the mid-1990s. The MDS9000 family of switches also supports SPAN. SPAN is also known as port mirroring and port monitoring. SPAN transparently copies frames from one or more ports to a specified port called a SPAN Destination (SD) port. In most cases, the SD port can be any port in the switch. A protocol decoder is attached to the SD port. The disadvantages of this approach include the following:

- Low-level primitives that are normally terminated by the device physically adjacent to the suspect device cannot be captured.

- OSI Layer 1 issues related to faulty cabling and connectors cannot be detected.

The advantages of out-of-line traffic capture include the following:

- The protocol decoder can be connected to the switch in a non-disruptive manner.

- No new devices are introduced into the original data stream, so no additional problems are created.

- Multiple SPAN sessions can be configured and activated simultaneously. Thus, the one-to-one relationship between the suspect device and the protocol decoder is removed. This reduces the total number of protocol decoders required to troubleshoot large networks.

- SPAN traffic can be forwarded between switches via the Remote SPAN (RSPAN) feature. RSPAN *further* reduces the total number of protocol decoders required to troubleshoot large networks.

- After the protocol decoder is connected to the switch, an administrator can configure and activate SPAN/RSPAN sessions remotely.

Another approach is to use a signal splitter such as a "tap" or "Y-cable," but this approach has its own set of drawbacks that precludes widespread adoption. So, signal splitters are used to meet niche requirements, and the in-line and out-of-line approaches are used to meet mainstream requirements.

Types of Protocol Decoders

Several types of products are available to facilitate traffic capture and protocol decoding. The traditional implementation is a special-purpose hardware-based product that can capture and decode frames. Such devices are often portable PCs with high-speed expansion slots for add-in cards. Special add-in cards are used in place of conventional network cards to ensure that traffic can be captured at high throughput rates with no frame drops. Special capture/decode software is pre-loaded by the vendor, and administrators do not install any additional software. This type of device can be inserted in-line, connected to a signal splitter, or connected to an SD port on a switch produced by Cisco Systems.

A similar but less expensive solution is a software-based traffic capture and decode product. Several such products are available; some must be purchased, and some are free. The best-known free product is Ethereal. Ethereal is a GUI-based open source package, which has very robust capabilities. Software-based products can be installed on any PC and use any conventional network card, but the performance characteristics of the PC hardware and network card determine the reliability of the traffic capture process. In some cases, frames are dropped during capture because the PC hardware or conventional network card are incapable of receiving frames at high speeds. For this reason, administrators are advised to install a dedicated network card for traffic capture rather than using a single network card for all purposes. This type of solution can be inserted in-line, connected to a signal splitter, or connected to an SD port on a switch produced by Cisco Systems. Because of the potential for dropped frames, administrators are advised not to use this type of solution in-line.

Another option is to separate the traffic capture function from the protocol decode function. That is the case with the Cisco Systems FC Port Analyzer Adapter (PAA). The PAA is supported with the MDS9000 family of switches. The PAA is a small special-purpose device with one FC interface and one Ethernet interface. The FC interface is attached to an MDS9000 switch port configured as an SD port. The Ethernet interface is typically connected via straight-through cable to a dedicated Ethernet NIC in a PC that has a software-based protocol decode package installed. Alternately, the Ethernet interface can be connected to an Ethernet switch via cross-over cable, but the PC with a software-based protocol decode package must be connected in the same Ethernet broadcast domain. Currently, only Ethereal is supported. The PAA captures FC frames, encapsulates them in Ethernet frames, and then forwards the Ethernet frames to the PC. The Ethernet frames are de-encapsulated by Ethereal, and then the FC frames are decoded by Ethereal.

A fourth option is to integrate a software-based traffic capture and decode product into the control plane of a switch. That is the case with the MDS9000 family. The text-based implementation of Ethereal (called Tethereal) is built into the operating system of the MDS9000 family (called SANOS). This feature is called the Cisco Fabric Analyzer. It can be used to capture and decode control traffic such as FLOGI requests and RSCNs. Captured frames can be decoded in real time, saved to a file for future decoding, or encapsulated in TCP/IP and forwarded in real time to a PC that has Ethereal installed.

A fifth option is to integrate a hardware-based capture and decode product into a switch. That is the case with the Cisco Systems Network Analysis Module (NAM). The NAM is available for the Catalyst family of switches. The NAM can capture and decode frames from multiple ports simultaneously. The NAM provides access to the decoded frames via an integrated web server.

Protocol Decoder Screenshots

This section contains screenshots of frames decoded by Ethereal. The frames were captured using SPAN and a PAA attached to an MDS9000 series switch. Figure 14-1 shows an Internet Small Computer System Interface (iSCSI) Login Request Protocol Data Unit (PDU). Figure 14-2 shows the associated iSCSI Login Response PDU. Figure 14-3 shows an iSCSI SCSI Command PDU. Figure 14-4 shows the associated iSCSI SCSI Response PDU. Figure 14-5 shows a Fibre Channel (FC) N_Port Login (PLOGI) Extended Link Service (ELS). Figure 14-6 shows the associated FC PLOGI Link Services Accept (LS_ACC) ELS. Figure 14-7 shows an FC Process Login (PRLI) ELS. Figure 14-8 shows the associated FC PRLI LS_ACC ELS. Figure 14-9 shows an FCP_CMND Information Unit (IU). Figure 14-10 shows the associated FCP_DATA IU. Figure 14-11 shows the associated FCP_RSP IU.

Figure 14-1 *iSCSI Login Request PDU*

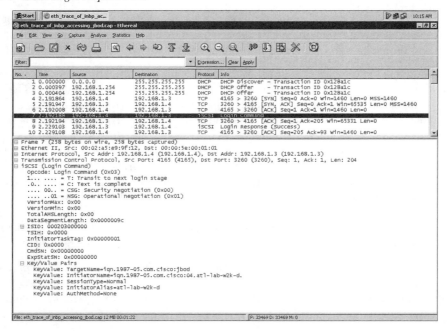

Figure 14-2 *iSCSI Login Response PDU*

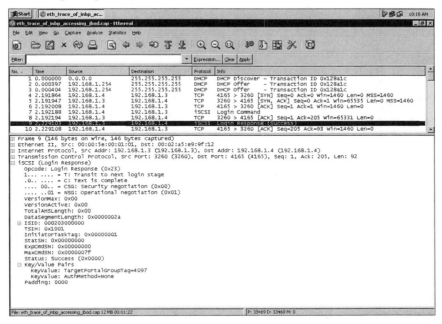

Figure 14-3 *iSCSI SCSI Command PDU*

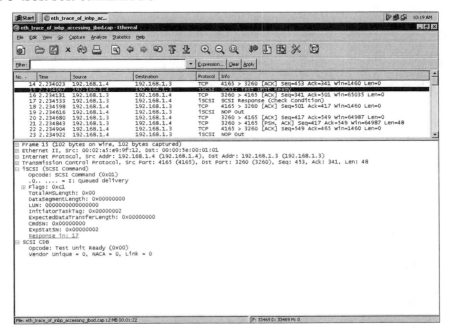

Figure 14-4 *iSCSI SCSI Response PDU*

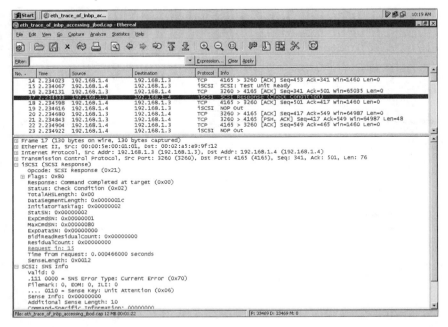

Figure 14-5 *FC PLOGI ELS*

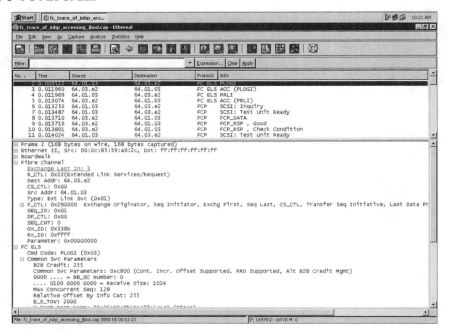

Figure 14-6 *FC PLOGI LS_ACC ELS*

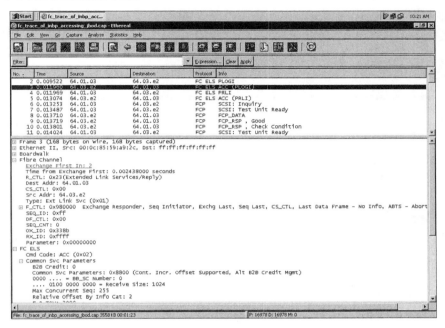

Figure 14-7 *FC PRLI ELS*

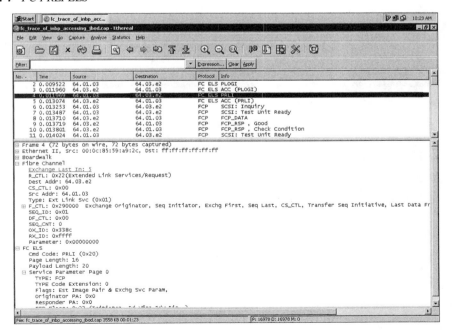

Figure 14-8 *FC PRLI LS_ACC ELS*

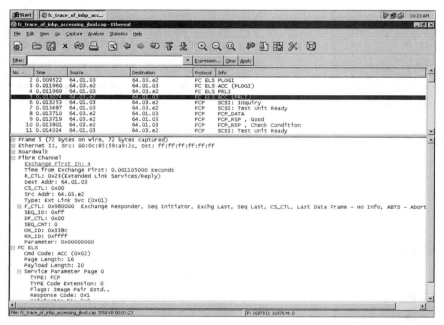

Figure 14-9 *FCP_CMND IU*

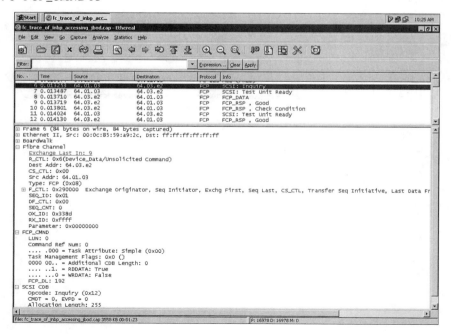

Figure 14-10 *FCP_DATA IU*

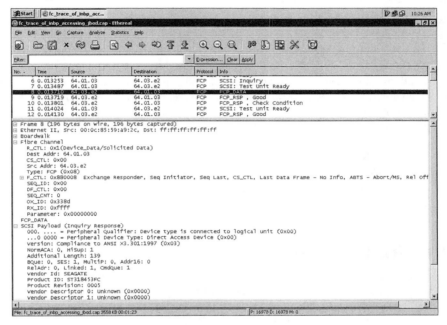

Figure 14-11 *FCP_RSP IU*

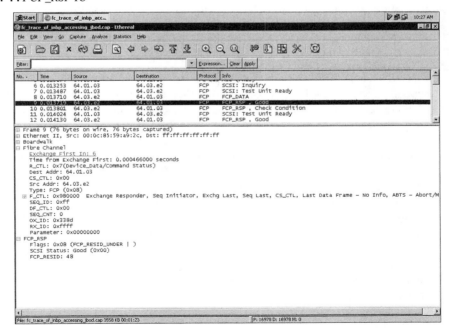

Purpose of Traffic Analysis

Traffic analysis can be accomplished using the Remote Network Monitor (RMON) family of Management Information Base (MIB) modules. However, MIB-based monitoring provides a limited view of network activity. To augment MIB-based monitoring, frames can be captured and analyzed. By analyzing captured frames, traffic patterns can be discerned at all layers of the OSI Reference Model, and application data can be inspected to reveal each application's behavioral patterns. In this respect, traffic analysis is closely related to protocol decoding. Whereas a protocol decoder breaks down frames field-by-field at all layers of the OSI Reference Model for troubleshooting purposes, a traffic analyzer inspects frame headers and payloads to identify trends and generate detailed performance statistics. Additionally, traffic analyzers often have built-in reporting capabilities to display compiled data in useful formats. Both protocol decoding and traffic analysis begin by capturing traffic. For this reason, many of the products that support protocol decoding also support traffic analysis.

Types of Traffic Analyzers

Like protocol decoders, traffic analyzers are available in various forms. Some are hardware-based devices designed expressly for capturing and analyzing traffic. Such devices are often built using standard PC hardware and network cards that meet stringent performance criteria. Other solutions are software based. While software-based solutions are not suitable for high throughput networks, this type of solution provides improved flexibility by enabling administrators to install the traffic analyzer on an existing PC or laptop. In both cases, the traffic analyzer is connected to a switch using a signal splitter or the SPAN/RSPAN features on switches produced by Cisco Systems. Traffic analyzers are generally not connected in-line.

Cisco Systems offers three additional options for traffic analysis. The MDS9000 family supports in-line analysis of FC and SCSI traffic via the Storage Services Module (SSM). The SSM can analyze only the traffic that passes through the SSM, so the hosts or storage arrays to be analyzed must be connected to the SSM. The SSM has traffic analysis capabilities built into the Application Specific Integrated Circuits (ASICs) that process and forward FC frames. This type of in-line solution supports the highest performance of any traffic analysis solution. Another option for the MDS9000 family is to use the SPAN/RSPAN features. By spanning traffic to a PAA, all traffic passing through the FC fabric can be analyzed. The PC to which the PAA is attached must have the Cisco Traffic Analyzer installed. The Cisco Traffic Analyzer is a software-based tool. The third option is to copy traffic to a NAM installed in a Catalyst switch using the SPAN/RSPAN features. Conceptually, the NAM is similar to the hardware-based traffic analyzers described in the previous paragraph. However, the NAM supports much higher performance because it is directly connected to the crossbar in the switch. The NAM also supports basic traffic analysis using a suite of RMON-based MIBs.

Summary

This chapter introduces the concepts of traffic capture and protocol decoding and explains why they are needed. Various methods for capturing traffic are discussed and followed by descriptions of the various types of protocol decoders. Screenshots of decoded frames are included to help readers understand the value of protocol decoding. The concept of traffic analysis is then presented and followed by descriptions of the various types of traffic analyzers.

Review Questions

1 Why are protocol decoders necessary?

2 List the three methods of traffic capture.

3 Name the most popular free GUI-based protocol decoder.

4 What is the purpose of traffic analysis?

5 What is the highest performance solution available for traffic analysis?

Appendixes

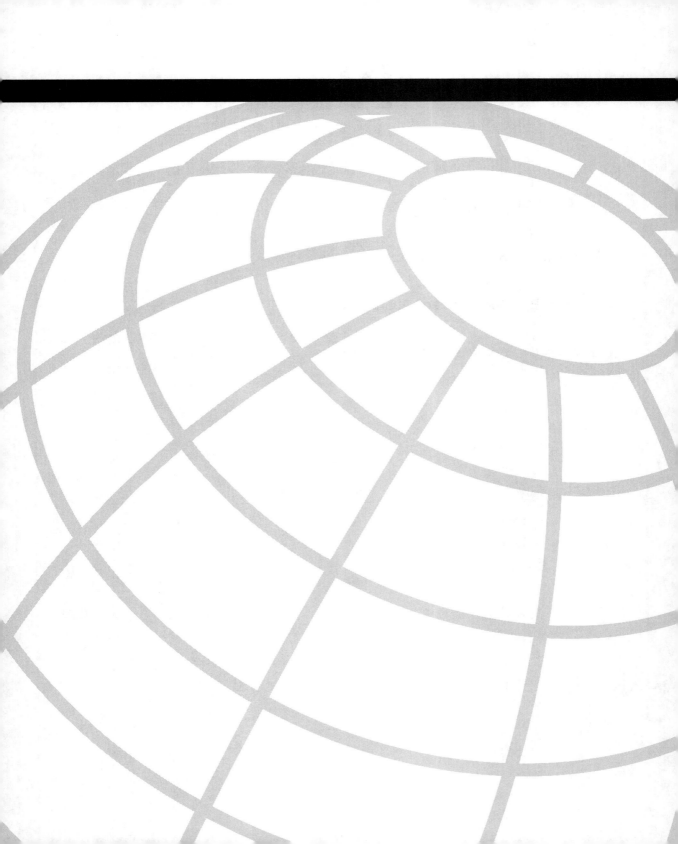

Standards and Specifications

This appendix provides a convenient, all-inclusive list of the standards and specifications referenced throughout the book. In most cases, the documents listed can be acquired directly from the publishing organization. Many of the documents listed can be downloaded free of charge, but some documents must be purchased. In the latter case, draft versions are often available free of charge.

American National Standards Institute (ANSI) InterNational Committee for Information Technology Standards (INCITS) T10

SCSI Architecture Model - 3 (SAM-3)

402-2005

2/14/2005

Serial Attached SCSI (SAS)

376-2003

10/30/2003

Serial Attached SCSI - 1.1 (SAS-1.1)

Project 1601-D

Draft Revision 10

9/21/2005

Serial Attached SCSI - 2 (SAS-2)

Project 1760-D

Draft Revision 1

11/13/2005

SCSI / ATA Translation (SAT)

Project 1711-D

Draft Revision 7

11/18/2005

SCSI Primary Commands - 3 (SPC-3)

408-2005

10/25/2005

SCSI Enclosure Services (SES)

305-1998

1/1/1998

SCSI Enclosure Services (SES) - Amendment 1

305-1998/AM1-2000

12/13/2000

SCSI Enclosure Services - 2 (SES-2)

Project 1559-D

Draft Revision 13

11/12/2005

SCSI Parallel Interface - 2 (SPI-2)

302-1998

4/14/1998

SCSI Parallel Interface - 3 (SPI-3)

336-2000

11/1/2000

SCSI Parallel Interface - 4 (SPI-4)

362-2002

12/1/2002

SCSI Parallel Interface - 5 (SPI-5)

367-2003

7/10/2003

SCSI Fibre Channel Protocol - 2 (FCP-2)

350-2003

10/8/2003

SCSI Fibre Channel Protocol - 3 (FCP-3)

Project 1560-D

Draft Revision 4

9/13/2005

SCSI RDMA Protocol (SRP)

365-2002

12/1/2002

SCSI RDMA Protocol - 2 (SRP-2)

Project 1524-D

Draft Revision 00a

7/7/2003

ANSI INCITS T11

Single-Byte Command Code Sets - 2 Mapping Protocol (FC-SB-2)

372-2003

7/25/2003

Single-Byte Command Code Sets - 3 Mapping Protocol (FC-SB-3)

Project 1357-D

Draft Revision 6.9

08/10/2005

Fibre Channel - 10 Gigabit (10GFC)

364-2003

11/6/2003

Fibre Channel - Arbitrated Loop (FC-AL-2)

332-1999

4/1/1999

Fibre Channel – Backbone – 2 (FC-BB-2)

372-2003

7/25/2003

Fibre Channel - Backbone - 3 (FC-BB-3)

Project 1639-D

Draft Revision 6.9

8/10/2005

Fibre Channel - Device Attach (FC-DA)

TR-36-2004

2/1/2005

Fibre Channel - Device Attach – 2 (FC-DA-2)

Draft Revision 1.0

11/18/2004

Fibre Channel - Framing and Signaling (FC-FS)

373-2003

10/27/2003

Fibre Channel - Framing and Signaling - 2 (FC-FS-2)

Project 1619-D

Draft Revision 0.9

8/9/2005

Fibre Channel - Generic Services - 4 (FC-GS-4)

387-2004

8/3/2004

Fibre Channel - Generic Services - 5 (FC-GS-5)

Project 1677-D

Draft Revision 8.2

10/4/2005

Storage Management HBA API (SM-HBA)

386-2004

8/3/2004

Fibre Channel - Link Services (FC-LS)

Project 1620-D

Draft Revision 1.2

6/7/2005

Fibre Channel - Methodologies for Interconnects - 2 (FC-MI-2)

TR-39-2005

1/1/2005

Fibre Channel - Physical Interfaces – 2 (FC-PI-2)

Project 1506-D

Draft Revision 9.0

7/5/2005

Fibre Channel - Physical Interfaces – 3 (FC-PI-3)

Project 1235-DT

Draft Revision 1.0

11/29/2004

Fibre Channel—Security Protocols (FC-SP)

Project 1570-D

Draft Revision 1.73

10/3/2005

Fibre Channel - Switch Fabric - 3 (FC-SW-3)

384-2004

5/25/2004

Fibre Channel - Switch Fabric - 4 (FC-SW-4)

Project 1674-D

Draft Revision 7.6

11/22/2005

Fibre Channel Switch API (FC-SWAPI)

399-2004

11/29/2004

Distributed Management Task Force (DMTF)

Representation of Common Information Model (CIM) in Extensible Markup Language (XML)

DSP0201

Version 2.2

12/9/2004

Common Information Model (CIM) Operations over HyperText Transfer Protocol (HTTP)

DSP0200

Version 1.2

12/9/2004

Common Information Model (CIM) Schema

Version 2.10.1

10/3/2005

Common Information Model (CIM) Infrastructure Specification

DSP0004

Version 2.3

10/4/2005

Web-Based Enterprise Management (WBEM) Discovery Using Service Location Protocol (SLP)

DSP0205

Version 1.0

1/27/2004

Institute of Electrical and Electronics Engineers (IEEE)

Standard for Local and Metropolitan Area Networks: Overview and Architecture

802-2001

3/8/2002

Media Access Control (MAC) Bridges

802.1D-2004

2/9/2004

Virtual Bridged Local Area Networks

802.1Q-2003

5/7/2003

Port-Based Network Access Control

802.1X-2001

6/14/2001

Logical Link Control

802.2-1998

5/7/1998

Carrier Sense Multiple Access with Collision Detection (CSMA/CD) Access Method and Physical Layer Specifications

802.3-2002

3/8/2002

Media Access Control (MAC) Parameters, Physical Layers and Management Parameters for 10Gbps Operation

802.3ae-2002

8/30/2002

Physical Layer and Management Parameters for 10Gbps Operation, Type 10GBASE-CX4

802.3ak-2004

3/1/2004

Resilient Packet Ring (RPR) Access Method and Physical Layer Specifications

802.17-2004

9/24/2004

OUI and Company_ID Tutorials

http://standards.ieee.org/regauth/oui/tutorials/

Internet Engineering Task Force (IETF)

User Datagram Protocol

RFC 768

Internet Protocol

RFC 791

Internet Control Message Protocol

RFC 792

Transmission Control Protocol

RFC 793

IP Datagram Reassembly Algorithms

RFC 815

An Ethernet Address Resolution Protocol

RFC 826

Telnet Protocol Specification

RFC 854

A Standard for the Transmission of IP Datagrams over Ethernet Networks

RFC 894

Congestion Control in IP/TCP Internetworks

RFC 896

Internet Standard Subnetting Procedure

RFC 950

Protocol Standard for a NetBIOS Service on a TCP/UDP Transport: Concepts and methods

RFC 1001

Protocol Standard for a NetBIOS Service on a TCP/UDP Transport: Detailed Specifications

RFC 1002

Domain Names - Concepts and Facilities

RFC 1034

Domain Names - Implementation and Specification

RFC 1035

Requirements for Internet Hosts -- Communication Layers

RFC 1122

IAB Recommended Policy on Distributing Internet Identifier Assignment and IAB Recommended Policy Change to Internet "Connected" Status

RFC 1174

A TCP/IP Tutorial

RFC 1180

Path MTU Discovery

RFC 1191

Management Information Base for Network Management of TCP/IP-based internets: MIB-II

RFC 1213

TCP Extensions for High Performance

RFC 1323

An Access Control Protocol, Sometimes Called TACACS

RFC 1492

Applicability Statement for the Implementation of Classless Inter-Domain Routing (CIDR)

RFC 1517

Classless Inter-Domain Routing (CIDR): an Address Assignment and Aggregation Strategy

RFC 1519

Exchanging Routing Information Across Provider Boundaries in the CIDR Environment

RFC 1520

Integrated Services in the Internet Architecture: an Overview

RFC 1633

Requirements for IP Version 4 Routers

RFC 1812

Address Allocation for Private Internets
RFC 1918

PPP Challenge Handshake Authentication Protocol (CHAP)
RFC 1994

TCP Selective Acknowledgment Options
RFC 2018

The Simple Public-Key GSS-API Mechanism (SPKM)
RFC 2025

Internet Registry IP Allocation Guidelines
RFC 2050

Dynamic Host Configuration Protocol
RFC 2131

DHCP Options and BOOTP Vendor Extensions
RFC 2132

Resource ReSerVation Protocol (RSVP) -- Version 1 Functional Specification
RFC 2205

FTP Security Extensions
RFC 2228

The TLS Protocol Version 1.0
RFC 2246

Recommendations on Queue Management and Congestion Avoidance in the Internet
RFC 2309

Protection of BGP Sessions via the TCP MD5 Signature Option
RFC 2385

Security Architecture for the Internet Protocol
RFC 2401

IP Authentication Header
RFC 2402

IP Encapsulating Security Payload (ESP)
RFC 2406

The Internet IP Security Domain of Interpretation for ISAKMP
RFC 2407

Internet Security Association and Key Management Protocol (ISAKMP)
RFC 2408

The Internet Key Exchange (IKE)
RFC 2409

A Provider Architecture for Differentiated Services and Traffic Engineering (PASTE)
RFC 2430

Definition of the Differentiated Services Field (DS Field) in the IPv4 and IPv6 Headers
RFC 2474

An Architecture for Differentiated Services

RFC 2475

Known TCP Implementation Problems

RFC 2525

Structure of Management Information Version 2 (SMIv2)

RFC 2578

TCP Congestion Control

RFC 2581

Assured Forwarding PHB Group

RFC 2597

Service Location Protocol, Version 2

RFC 2608

Service Templates and Service: Schemes

RFC 2609

DHCP Options for Service Location Protocol

RFC 2610

PPP over SONET/SDH

RFC 2615

IP and ARP over Fibre Channel

RFC 2625

Integrated Service Mappings on IEEE 802 Networks

RFC 2815

Simple Mail Transfer Protocol

RFC 2821

Remote Authentication Dial In User Service (RADIUS)

RFC 2865

TCP Processing of the IPv4 Precedence Field

RFC 2873

An Extension to the Selective Acknowledgement (SACK) Option for TCP

RFC 2883

Congestion Control Principles

RFC 2914

TCP Problems with Path MTU Discovery

RFC 2923

Telnet Authentication: SRP

RFC 2944

The SRP Authentication and Key Exchange System

RFC 2945

A Rate Adaptive Shaper for Differentiated Services

RFC 2963

Computing TCP's Retransmission Timer

RFC 2988

Next Steps for the IP QoS Architecture

RFC 2990

A Framework for Integrated Services Operation over Diffserv Networks

RFC 2998

Traditional IP Network Address Translator (Traditional NAT)

RFC 3022

Enhancing TCP's Loss Recovery Using Limited Transmit

RFC 3042

Definition of Differentiated Services Per Domain Behaviors and Rules for their Specification

RFC 3086

Per Hop Behavior Identification Codes

RFC 3140

End-to-end Performance Implications of Links with Errors

RFC 3155

The BSD syslog Protocol

RFC 3164

The Addition of Explicit Congestion Notification (ECN) to IP

RFC 3168

Vendor Extensions for Service Location Protocol, Version 2

RFC 3224

An Expedited Forwarding PHB (Per-Hop Behavior)

RFC 3246

New Terminology and Clarifications for Diffserv

RFC 3260

Small Computer System Interface protocol over the Internet (iSCSI) Requirements and Design Considerations

RFC 3347

Internet Protocol Small Computer System Interface (iSCSI) Cyclic Redundancy Check (CRC)/Checksum Considerations

RFC 3385

Increasing TCP's Initial Window

RFC 3390

Introduction and Applicability Statements for Internet Standard Management Framework

RFC 3410

User-based Security Model (USM) for version 3 of the Simple Network Management Protocol (SNMPv3)

RFC 3414

Version 2 of the Protocol Operations for the Simple Network Management Protocol (SNMP)

RFC 3416

TCP Friendly Rate Control (TFRC): Protocol Specification

RFC 3448

A Conservative Selective Acknowledgment (SACK)-based Loss Recovery Algorithm for TCP

RFC 3517

Fibre Channel (FC) Frame Encapsulation

RFC 3643

Policy Quality of Service (QoS) Information Model

RFC 3644

Internet Small Computer System Interface (iSCSI)

RFC 3720

Internet Small Computer System Interface (iSCSI) Naming and Discovery

RFC 3721

String Profile for Internet Small Computer System Interface (iSCSI) Names

RFC 3722

Securing Block Storage Protocols over IP

RFC 3723

Virtual Router Redundancy Protocol (VRRP)

RFC 3768

The NewReno Modification to TCP's Fast Recovery Algorithm

RFC 3782

Small Computer System Interface (SCSI) Command Ordering Considerations with iSCSI

RFC 3783

Fibre Channel Over TCP/IP (FCIP)

RFC 3821

Finding Fibre Channel over TCP/IP (FCIP) Entities Using Service Location Protocol version 2 (SLPv2)

RFC 3822

T11 Network Address Authority (NAA) Naming Format for iSCSI Node Names

RFC 3980

The Eifel Response Algorithm for TCP

RFC 4015

Finding Internet Small Computer System Interface (iSCSI) Targets and Name Servers by Using Service Location Protocol version 2 (SLPv2)

RFC 4018

Analysis of Existing Quality-of-Service Signaling Protocols

RFC 4094

The Kerberos Network Authentication Service (V5)

RFC 4120

The Kerberos Version 5 Generic Security Service Application Program Interface (GSS-API) Mechanism: Version 2

RFC 4121

Internet Storage Name Service (iSNS)

RFC 4171

iFCP - A Protocol for Internet Fibre Channel Storage Networking

RFC 4172

Bootstrapping Clients using the Internet Small Computer System Interface (iSCSI) Protocol

RFC 4173

The IPv4 Dynamic Host Configuration Protocol (DHCP) Option for the Internet Storage Name Service

RFC 4174

Storage Networking Industry Association (SNIA)

Common Internet File System (CIFS) Technical Reference

Revision 1.0

3/1/2002

Storage Management Initiative Specification (SMI-S)

Version 1.0.2

2/23/2004

Direct Access File System (DAFS) Collaborative

Direct Access File System (DAFS) Application Programming Interface (API)

Version 1.0

11/17/2001

Direct Access File System (DAFS) Protocol

Version 1.0

9/1/2001

International Organization for Standardization (ISO)/ International Electrotechnical Commission (IEC)

Information technology - Open Systems Interconnection – Basic Reference Model: The Basic Model

International Standard 7498-1

Second Edition

11/15/1994

International Telecommunication Union-Telecommunication Standardization Sector (ITU-T)

Spectral grids for WDM applications: DWDM frequency grid

Recommendation G.694.1

6/2002

Spectral grids for WDM applications: CWDM wavelength grid

Recommendation G.694.2

6/2002

Vendor Documents

IBM Enterprise Systems Connection (ESCON) Implementation Guide

SG24-4662-00

7/1996

IBM FICON Native Implementation and Reference Guide

SG24-6266-01

10/2002

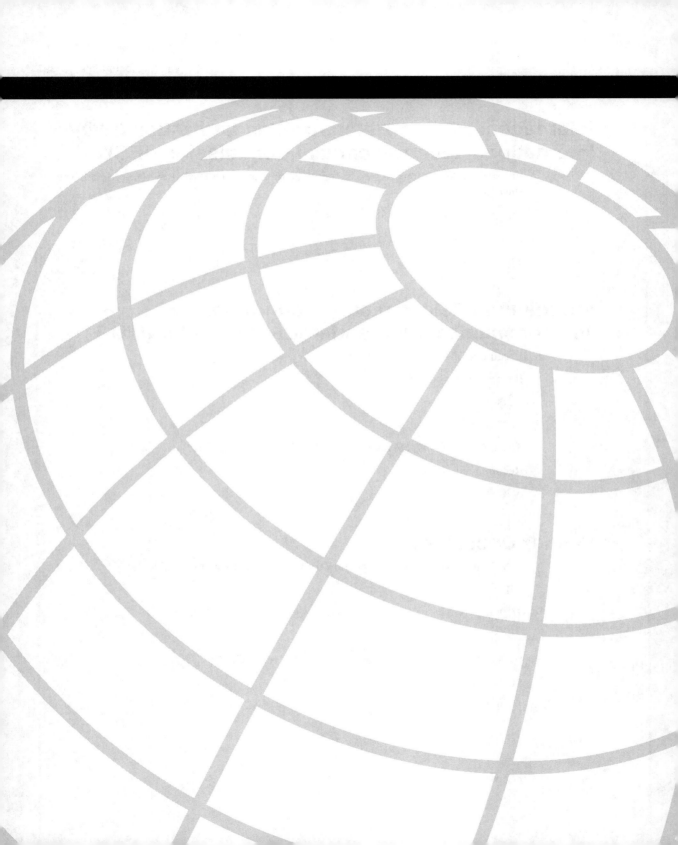

APPENDIX B

Acronyms and Abbreviations

10GE   10-Gbps Ethernet

10GFC   10-Gbps Fibre Channel

10GigE   10-Gbps Ethernet

3PC   Third Party Copy

AAA   Authentication, Authorization and Accounting

ABR   Area Border Router

ABTS   Abort Sequence

ACA   Auto Contingent Allegiance

ACK   Acknowledge

ACL   Access Control List

ADISC   Discover Address

AH   Authentication Header

AHS   Additional Header Segment

ANSI   American National Standards Institute

API   Application Programming Interface

AQM   Active Queue Management

ARC   Accept Response Code

ARP   Address Resolution Protocol

AS   Autonomous System

ASBR   Autonomous System Border Router

ASF   Authenticate Special Frame

ASIC   Application Specific Integrated Circuit

ASN.1   Abstract Syntax Notation One

ATA   Advanced Technology Attachment

ATAPI   Advanced Technology Attachment Packet Interface

ATM   Asynchronous Transfer Mode

B_Port   Bridge Port

BA_ACC   Basic Accept

BA_RJT   Basic Reject

BB_SC   Buffer-to-Buffer_State_Change

BBC   Buffer-to-Buffer_Credit

BCP   Best Current Practice

BER   Bit Error Ratio

BER   Bit Error Rate

BF   Build Fabric

BGP   Border Gateway Protocol

BGP-4   Border Gateway Protocol version 4

BHS   Basic Header Segment

BLS   Basic Link Service

BOOTP   Bootstrap Protocol

CAE   Common Application Environment

CAM   Common Access Method

CCW   Channel Command Word

CDB   Command Descriptor Block

CES   Circuit Emulation Service

CFI   Canonical Format Indicator

Ch   Changed

CHAP   Challenge Handshake Authentication Protocol

CID   Connection Identifier

CIDR   Classless Inter-Domain Routing

CIFS   Common Internet File System

CIM   Common Information Model

CLI   Command Line Interface

CLNP   Connectionless Network Protocol

CmdSN   Command Sequence Number

COS   Class of Service

CPU   Central Processing Unit

CRC   Cyclic Redundancy Check

CRCV   Cyclic Redundancy Check Valid

CRN   Command Reference Number

CS_CTL   Class Specific Control

CS1   Cyber Security

CSM   Control and Service Module

CSMA/CD   Carrier Sense Multiple Access with Collision Detection

CSS   Channel Sub-System

CTL   Control

CU   Control Unit

CUP   Control Unit Port

CWDM   Coarse Wavelength Division Multiplexing

CWND   Congestion Window

CWR   Congestion Window Reduced

D_ID   Destination ID

DA   Datamover Architecture for iSCSI

DA   Directory Agent

DA   Destination Address

DAFS   Direct Access File System

DARN   Data Acknowledgement Reference Number

DAS   Direct Attached Storage

DAT   Direct Access Transport

DataSN   Data Sequence Number

DC   Direct Current

DCI   Direct-Coupled Interlock

DD   Discovery Domain

DDS   Discovery Domain Set

DEC   Digital Equipment Corporation

DF   Don't Fragment

DF_CTL   Data Field Control

DH-CHAP   Diffie-Hellmann Challenge Handshake Authentication Protocol

DHCP   Dynamic Host Configuration Protocol

DIA   Domain_ID Assigned

DiffServ   Differentiated Services

DMP   Dynamic Multi-Pathing

DMTF   Distributed Management Task Force

DNS   Domain Name System

DOI   Domain of Interpretation

DPT   Dynamic Packet Transport

DS   Data Streaming

DS   Digital Signal Services

DS-0   Digital Signal 0

DSAP   Destination Service Access Point

DSCP   Differentiated Services Codepoint

DT   Double Transition

DWDM   Dense Wavelength Division Multiplexing

E_D_TOV   Error Detect Time-Out Value

E_Port   Expansion Port

EBP   Exchange B_Access Parameters

EBSI   Enhanced Backup Solutions Initiative

ECE   ECN Echo

ECN   Explicit Congestion Notification

EDFA   Erbium-doped fiber amplifier

EEC   End-to-End_Credit

EFP   Exchange Fabric Parameters

EGP   Exterior Gateway Protocol

EIDE   Enhanced Integrated Drive Electronics

EIGRP   Enhanced Interior Gateway Routing Protocol

EIP   Establish Image Pair

ELP   Exchange Link Parameters

ELS   Extended Link Service

EMDP   Enable Modify Data Pointers

EMI   Electro-Magnetic Interference

EN   Enterprise Number

EOF   End-of-Frame

EOR   Electro-Optical Repeater

EPD   End_of_Packet Delimiter

EPDC   Enable Precise Delivery Checking

ESB   Exchange Status Block

ESC   Exchange Switch Capabilities

ESCON   Enterprise Systems Connection

ESI   Entity Status Inquiry

ESP   Encapsulating Security Payload

EUI   Extended Unique Identifier

ExpCmdSN   Expected Command Sequence Number

F_CTL   Frame Control

F_Port   Fabric Port

F_S_TOV   Fabric Stability Time-Out Value

FARP   FC Address Resolution Protocol

FCAL   Fibre Channel Arbitrated Loop

FCAP   Fibre Channel Authentication Protocol

FCC   FC Congestion Control

FC-FE   Fibre Channel Frame Encapsulation

FCIP   Fibre Channel over TCP/IP

FCIP_DE   Fibre Channel over TCP/IP Data Engine

FCIP_LEP   Fibre Channel over TCP/IP Link End Point

FCNS   Fibre Channel Name Server

FCP   Fibre Channel Protocol for SCSI

FCP_CMND   Fibre Channel Protocol Command

FCP_CONF   Fibre Channel Protocol Confirmation

FCP_DATA   Fibre Channel Protocol Data

FCP_RJT   Fibre Channel Protocol Reject

FCP_RSP   Fibre Channel Protocol Response

FCP_XFER_RDY   Fibre Channel Protocol Transfer Ready

FCPAP   Fibre Channel Password Authentication Protocol

FCS   Frame Check Sequence

FCTA   Fibre Channel Tape Acceleration

FCWA   Fibre Channel Write Acceleration

FCZS   Fibre Channel Zone Server

FD   Full Duplex

FDDI   Fiber Distributed Data Interface

FDISC   Discover F_Port Service Parameters

FDM   Frequency Division Multiplexing

FDMI   Fabric Device Management Interface

FE   Fast Ethernet

FICON   Fibre Channel Connection

FIFO   First in First Out

FIM   Fixed Interval Marker

FIN Final

FL Fabric Loop

FL_Port Fabric Loop Port

FLOGI Fabric Login

FLP Fast Link Pulse

FPSM FC_Port State Machine

FQDN Fully Qualified Domain Name

FQXID Fully Qualified Exchange Identifier

FSF FCIP Special Frame

FSPF Fabric Shortest Path First

FT_0 Frame Type Zero

FT_1 Frame Type One

FTP File Transfer Protocol

FTT FCIP Transit Time

GARP Generic Attribute Registration Protocol

GBIC Gigabit Interface Converter

Gbps Gigabits per second

GE Gigabit Ethernet

GFP-T Transparent Generic Framing Procedure

GHz Gigahertz

GigE Gigabit Ethernet

GLBP Gateway Load Balancing Protocol

GSS-API Generic Security Services Application Programming Interface

GVRP GARP VLAN Registration Protocol

HBA Host Bus Adapter

HCA Host Channel Adapter

HD Half Duplex

HDLC High-Level Data Link Control

HIPPI   High-Performance Parallel Interface

HPC   High Performance Computing

HSM   Hierarchical Storage Management

HSRP   Hot Standby Router Protocol

HTTP   HyperText Transfer Protocol

HVD   High Voltage Differential

I/G   Individual/Group

I/O   Input/Output

I_T Nexus   Initiator-Target Nexus

I_T_L Nexus   Initiator-Target-Logical Unit Nexus

IANA   Internet Assigned Numbers Authority

IAS   Internet Attached Storage

IB   InfiniBand

ICMP   Internet Control Message Protocol

ICV   Integrity Check Value

IDC   Internet Data Center

IDE   Integrated Drive Electronics

IETF   Internet Engineering Task Force

iFCP   Internet Fibre Channel Protocol

IGP   Interior Gateway Protocol

IGRP   Interior Gateway Routing Protocol

IHL   Internet Header Length

IKE   Internet Key Exchange

ILM   Information Lifecycle Management

IMP   Interface Message Processor

INCITS   InterNational Committee for Information Technology Standards

IntServ   Integrated Services

IO   Input/Output

IOA   In-fiber Optical Amplifier

IOPS   I/O Operations Per Second

IP   Internet Protocol

IPCP   Internet Protocol Control Protocol

IPFC   Internet Protocol over Fibre Channel

IPI   Intelligent Peripheral Interface

IPS   Internet Protocol Storage

IPsec   Internet Protocol Security

IPS-WG   Internet Protocol Storage Working Group

IPv4   Internet Protocol version 4

IPv6   Internet Protocol version 6

IQN   iSCSI Qualified Name

ISAKMP   Internet Security Association and Key Management Protocol

iSCSI   Internet Small Computer System Interface

iSER   iSCSI Extensions for RDMA

ISID   Initiator Session Identifier

IS-IS   Intermediate System to Intermediate System

ISL   Inter-Switch Link

ISMF   Internet Standard Management Framework

ISN   Initial Sequence Number

iSNS   Internet Storage Name Service

ISO   International Organization for Standardization

ISP   Internet Service Provider

ISV   Independent Software Vendor

ITT   Initiator Task Tag

ITU   International Telecommunication Union

iuCRC   information unit Cyclic Redundancy Check

IVR   Inter-VSAN Routing

JBOD   Just a Bunch of Disks

K_A_TOV   Keep Alive Time-Out Value

Kbps   Kilobits per second

KBps   Kilobytes per second

LACP   Link Aggregation Control Protocol

LAN   Local Area Network

LBA   Logical Block Addressing

LCP   Link Control Protocol

LCW   Link Code Word

LFN   Long Fat Network

LIFO   Last in First Out

LIP   Loop Initialization Primitive

LIR   Local Internet Registry

LKA   Link Keep Alive

LLC   Logical Link Control

LOGO   Logout

LPSM   Loop Port State Machine

LR   Link Reset

LRR   Link Reset Response

LS_ACC   Link Services Accept

LS_RJT   Link Service Reject

LSA   Link State Advertisement

LUN   Logical Unit Number

LVD   Low Voltage Differential

LVM   Logical Volume Manager

MAC   Media Access Control

MAN   Metropolitan Area Network

MAU   Multi-Access Unit

MaxCmdSN   Maximum Command Sequence Number

Mbps   Megabits per second

MBps   Megabytes per second

MCP   Mode-Conditioning Patch

MF   More Fragments

MIB   Management Information Base

MIT   Massachusetts Institute of Technology

MMF   Multi-Mode Fiber

MPLS   Multiprotocol Label Switching

MSA   Multi-Source Agreement

MSE   Multimode Single-Ended

MSL   Maximum Segment Lifetime

MSS   Maximum Segment Size

MSTP   Multiple Spanning Tree Protocol

MTBF   Mean Time Between Failures

MTTF   Mean Time to Failure

MTU   Maximum Transmission Unit

N_Port   Node Port

NAA   Network Address Authority

NACK   Negative Acknowledgement

NAM   Network Analysis Module

NAS   Network Attached Storage

NAS   Network Access Server

NAT   Network Address Translation

NBNS   NetBIOS Name Service

NCP   Network Control Protocol

NDMP   Network Data Management Protocol

NetBIOS   Network Basic Input Output System

NFS   Network File System

NIC   Network Interface Card

NIR   National Internet Registry

NL   Node Loop

NL_Port   Node Loop Port

NMS   Network Management Station

No-OP   No-Operation

NOP-In   No Operation In

NOP-Out   No Operation Out

NOS   Network Operating System

NOS   Not Operational State

NPIV N_Port_ID Virtualization

NTP   Network Time Protocol

NWWN   Node Worldwide Name

OC   Optical Carrier

OLS   Offline State

OPAV   Originator Process_Associator Valid

Opcode   Operation Code

ORB   Operation Request Block

OS-Code   Ordered Set Code

OSI   Open Systems Interconnect

OSPF   Open Shortest Path First

OUI   Organizationally Unique Identifier

OX_ID   Originator Exchange ID

P2P   Point-to-Point

PAA   Port Analyzer Adapter

PAgP   Port Aggregation Protocol

PATA   Parallel Advanced Technology Attachment

PAWS   Protection Against Wrapped Sequence numbers

PC   Personal Computer

PCB   Printed Circuit Board

PCM   Pulse Code Modulation

pCRC   parallel Cyclic Redundancy Check

PCS   Physical Coding Sublayer

PDISC   Discover N_Port Parameters

PDU   Protocol Data Unit

PHB   Per Hop Behavior

PID   Protocol Identifier

PKI   Public Key Infrastructure

PLOGI   N_Port Login

PMM   Platform Management Module

PMTU   Path Maximum Transmission Unit

POS   PPP over SONET

POST   Power on Self Test

PPP   Point-to-Point Protocol

PRLI   Process Login

PRLO   Process Logout

PS   Principal Switch

PS1   Pause 1

PS2   Pause 2

PSH   Push

PSS   Principal Switch Selection

PSTN   Public Switched Telephone Network

PTP   Point-To-Point

PVID   Port VLAN Identifier

PWWN   Port Worldwide Name

QAS   Quick Arbitration and Selection

QoS   Quality of Service

R&D   Research and Development

R_A_TOV   Resource Allocation Time-Out Value

R_CTL   Routing Control

R_RDY   Receiver_Ready

R_T_TOV   Receiver Transmitter Time-Out Value

R2T   Ready to Transfer

R2TSN   Ready to Transfer Sequence Number

RAC   Registration Authority Committee

RACL   Router Access Control List

RADIUS   Remote Authentication Dial In User Service

RAID   Redundant Array of Inexpensive Disks

RARP   Reverse Address Resolution Protocol

RBAC   Role Based Access Control

RCMD   Remote Command

RCP   Remote Copy

RCS   Read Connection Status

RDI   Request Domain_ID

RDMA   Remote Direct Memory Access

REC   Read Exchange Concise

RED   Random Early Detection

RES   Read Exchange Status Block

RF1   Remote Fault 1

RF2   Remote Fault 2

RFC   Request For Comment

RIP   Routing Information Protocol

RIPv2   Routing Information Protocol version 2

RIR   Regional Internet Registry

RLIR   Registered Link Incident Report

RLOGIN   Remote Login

RLS   Read Link Error Status Block

RMON   Remote Network Monitor

RPAV   Responder Process_Associator Valid

RPC   Remote Procedure Call

RPR   Resilient Packet Ring

RPS   Read Port Status Block

$RR\_TOV_{SEQ\_INIT}$ Sequence Initiative Resource Recovery Time-Out Value

RRQ   Reinstate Recovery Qualifier

RSCN   Registered State Change Notification

RSH   Remote Shell

RSPAN   Remote Switch Port Analyzer

RSS   Read Sequence Status Block

RST   Reset

RSTP   Rapid Spanning Tree Protocol

RSVP   Resource Reservation Protocol

RTO   Retransmission Time-Out

RTT   Round-Trip Time

RTT   Referenced Task Tag

RWND   Receiver Window

RX_ID   Responder Exchange ID

S_ID   Source ID

SA   Service Agent

SA   Source Address

SA   Security Association

SACK   Selective Acknowledgement

SAF-TE   SCSI Accessed Fault-Tolerant Enclosures

SAL   SCSI Application Layer

SAM   SCSI-3 Architecture Model

SAN   Storage Area Network

SANOS   Storage Area Network Operating System

SAP   Service Access Point

SAS   Serial Attached SCSI

SASI   Shugart Associates Systems Interface

SATA   Serial Advanced Technology Attachment

SBCCS   Single-Byte Command Code Set

SCAM   SCSI Configured Automatically

SCN   State Change Notification

SCP   Secure Copy

SCR   State Change Registration

SCSI   Small Computer System Interface

SD   SPAN Destination

SDH   Synchronous Digital Hierarchy

SDLC   Synchronous Data Link Control

SDP   Sockets Direct Protocol

SDU   Service Data Unit

SE   Single-Ended

SEQ_CNT   Sequence Count

SEQ_ID   Sequence Identifier

SES   SCSI Enclosure Services

SF   Special Frame

SFD   Start of Frame Delimiter

SFF   Small Form Factor

SFP   Small Form-factor Pluggable

SFTP   SSH File Transfer Protocol

SI   Sequence Initiative

SLA   Service Level Agreement

SLP   Service Location Protocol

SMB   Server Message Block

SMC   SCSI Media Changer

SMF   Single-Mode Fiber

SMI   Structure of Management Information

SMI   Storage Management Initiative

SMI-S   Storage Management Initiative Specification

SMTP   Simple Mail Transfer Protocol

SNACK   Selective Negative Acknowledgment

SNAP   Sub-Network Access Protocol

SNIA   Storage Networking Industry Association

SNMP   Simple Network Management Protocol

SNMPv2   Simple Network Management Protocol version 2

SNMPv3   Simple Network Management Protocol version 3

SNR   Signal-to-Noise Ratio

SNSM   Speed Negotiation State Machine

SNTP   Simple Network Time Protocol

SOA   Semiconductor Optical Amplifier

SOF   Start-of-Frame

SONET   Synchronous Optical Network

SPAN   Switch Port Analyzer

SPC   SCSI-3 Primary Commands

SPD   Start_of_Packet Delimiter

SPE   Synchronous Payload Envelope

SPF   Shortest Path First

SPI   SCSI Parallel Interface

SPI   Security Parameter Index

SPKM   Simple Public-Key GSS-API Mechanism

SPMISM   Switch Port Mode Initialization State Machine

SRM   Storage Resource Management

SRP   Spatial Reuse Protocol

SRP   Secure Remote Password

SRR   Sequence Retransmission Request

SSAP   Source Service Access Point

SSB   Sequence Status Block

SSH   Secure Shell

SSID   Session Identifier

SSL   Secure Sockets Layer

SSM   Storage Services Module

SSP   Storage Service Provider

ST   Single Transition

ST   SPAN Trunk

StatSN   Status Sequence Number

STP   Spanning Tree Protocol

STS-1   Synchronous Transport Signal level 1

SW_ACC   Switch Internal Link Service Accept

SW_ILS   Switch Internal Link Service

SW_RJT   Switch Internal Link Service Reject

SW-RSCN   Switch Registered State Change Notification

SYN   Synchronize

TACACS+   Terminal Access Controller Access Control System Plus

TCB   Transmission Control Block

TCP   Transmission Control Protocol

TDM   Time Division Multiplexing

TE_Port   Trunking Expansion Port

TLD   Top Level Domain

TLS   Transport Layer Security

TMF   Task Management Function

TOE   TCP Offload Engine

TOS   Type of Service

TPC   Third Party Copy

TPGT   Target Portal Group Tag

TSecr   Timestamp Echo Reply

TSIH   Target Session Identifying Handle

TSopt   Timestamps Option

TST   Task Set Type

TSval   Timestamp Value

TTL   Time to Live

TTT   Target Transfer Tag

U/L   Universal/Local

UA   User Agent

UDP   User Datagram Protocol

UI   Unnumbered Information

ULP   Upper Layer Protocol

UNC   Uniform Naming Convention

UNC   Universal Naming Convention

URG   Urgent

URL   Universal Resource Locator

USM   User-based Security Model

VACL   VLAN Access Control List

VC_RDY   Virtual_Circuit_Ready

VE_Port   Virtual Expansion Port

VF   Virtual Fabric

VI   Virtual Interface

VID   VLAN ID

VISL   Virtual Inter-Switch Link

VLAN   Virtual Local Area Network

VLSM   Variable Length Subnet Mask

VoIP   Voice over Internet Protocol

VRRP   Virtual Router Redundancy Protocol

VSAN   Virtual Storage Area Network

WBEM   Web-Based Enterprise Management

WDM   Wavelength Division Multiplexing

WINS   Windows Internet Name Service

Winsock   Windows Sockets

WIS   WAN Interface Sublayer

WKA   Well Known Address

WKP   Well Known Port

WRED   Weighted Random Early Detection

WSopt   Window Scale Option

WWN   Worldwide Name

WWNN   Worldwide Node Name

WWPN   Worldwide Port Name

XCOPY   EXTENDED COPY

XDF   Extended Distance Facility

XDR   External Data Representation

XFP   10-Gigabit Small Form-factor Pluggable

XGMII   10-Gigabit Media Independent Interface

XML   Extensible Markup Language

XTACACS   Extended Terminal Access Controller Access Control System

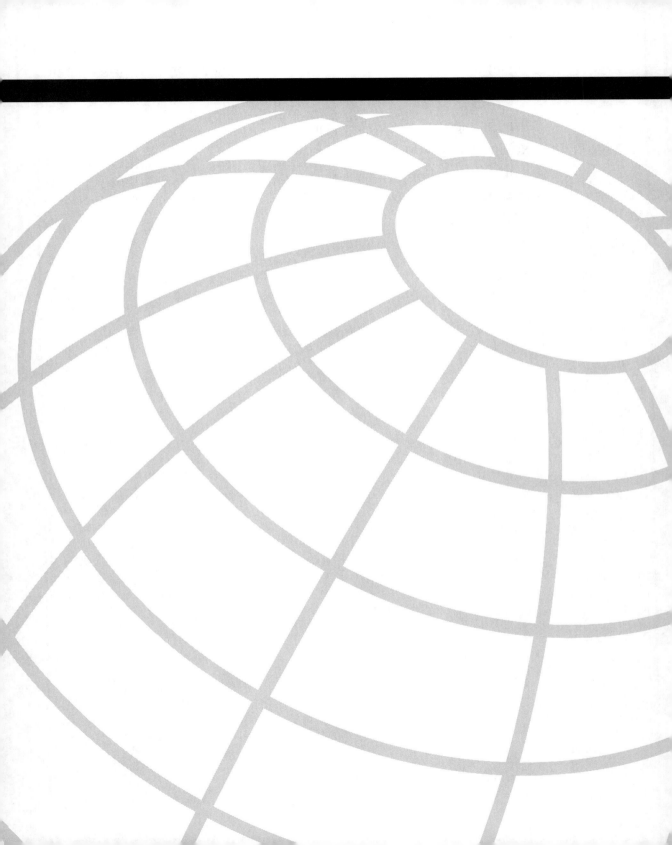

Answers to Review Questions

Chapter 1

1 What company invented the modern hard disk drive?

Answer: IBM.

2 Who published the SMI-S?

Answer: The SNIA.

3 List two competitive advantages enabled by storage networks.

Answer: Any two of the following are correct: increased throughput, improved flexibility, higher scalability, LAN-free backups, server-free backups, advanced volume management.

4 What is an IP-SAN?

Answer: An IP network designed specifically to transport only iSCSI traffic.

5 What block-level storage protocol is commonly used in desktop and laptop PCs?

Answer: ATA.

6 What is the latest version of the SCSI protocol?

Answer: SCSI-3.

7 What is the term for an adapter that processes TCP packets on behalf of the host CPU?

Answer: TCP Offload Engine (TOE).

8 List the two types of IBM channel protocols.

Answer: Byte multiplexer and block multiplexer.

9 An IBM ESCON director employs what type of switching mechanism?

Answer: Circuit switching.

10 A Fibre Channel switch employs what type of switching mechanism?

Answer: Packet switching.

11 What company *originally* invented CIFS?

Answer: While Microsoft gave CIFS its name, the original protocol was invented by IBM.

12 What standards body made NFS an industry standard?

Answer: The IETF.

13 What type of multiplexing is used by SONET/SDH?

Answer: Time Division Multiplexing (TDM).

14 What is the WDM window?

Answer: A wavelength range typically between 1500–1600 nm.

15 List one reason the sparse wavelength spacing of CWDM enables lower product costs.

Answer: Any one of the following is correct: laser tolerances can be relaxed, uncooled lasers can be used, optical filters can be less discerning.

16 In what class of networks is IEEE 802.17?

Answer: Resilient Packet Ring (RPR) networks.

17 List the two categories of block-oriented virtualization techniques.

Answer: Striping and extending.

Chapter 2

1 How many layers are specified in the OSI reference model?

Answer: Seven. Many popular networking technologies divide the seven OSI Layers into sublayers, but these optional subdivisions are not specified within the OSI reference model.

2 The data-link layer communicates with which OSI layer in a peer node?

Answer: The Data Link Layer.

3 What is the OSI term for the interface between vertically stacked OSI layers?

Answer: The Service Access Point (SAP).

4 How many OSI layers operate end-to-end? List them.

Answer: Four: Transport, Session, Presentation and Application.

5 Which OSI layer is responsible for bit-level data encoding?

Answer: The Physical Layer.

6 Which is the only OSI layer not inherent to the Fibre Channel architecture?

Answer: The Network Layer.

7 Create a mnemonic device for the names and order of the OSI layers.

Answer: Any answer that helps the reader remember the names and the order of the OSI Layers is correct. A popular mnemonic device is "All People Seem To Need Data Processing".

Chapter 3

1 List the functions provided by bit-level encoding schemes.

Answer: Clocking, DC balance, bit error detection and byte/word alignment.

2 What must be subtracted from the data bit rate to determine the ULP throughput rate?

Answer: Inter-frame spacing and framing overhead.

3 List the six physical topologies.

Answer: Star, linear, circular, tree, partial mesh and full mesh.

4 How can a protocol that is not designed to operate in a circular physical topology overcome this limitation?

Answer: By implementing special procedures or protocols that create a non-circular logical topology.

5 Describe one situation in which service and device discovery is not required.

Answer: Either of the following is correct: when a human learns of the service/device name or address via some non-computerized method or when a device has been manually configured.

6 What additional steps might be required after service/device discovery?

Answer: Name and/or address resolution depending on the contents of the discovery reply.

7 How many ULPs was the SPI designed to support? List them.

Answer: One; SCSI.

8 During which SPI bus phases is the data bus used?

Answer: COMMAND, DATA, STATUS and MESSAGE.

9 Why does the SPI device discovery mechanism not scale?

Answer: Each address in the address space must be probed.

10 What SCSI command enables the discovery of LUNs?

Answer: REPORT LUNS.

11 Ethernet originally competed against what network technologies?

Answer: Primarily ARCNET and Token Ring.

12 What assumption enables Ethernet to remain a low-overhead protocol?

Answer: That ULPs will provide the required functionality that is missing from Ethernet.

13 What logical topology is supported by Ethernet?

Answer: Tree.

14 List three characteristics that contributed to the early success of TCP/IP.

Answer: Emphasis on human community, abstraction through layered protocols and open dialogue about future developments.

15 What is the ULP throughput rate of iSCSI on GE?

Answer: 918.075 Mbps.

16 What iSCSI command enables the discovery of target nodes?

Answer: SendTargets.

17 What two protocols are available for automated discovery of iSCSI target devices and nodes?

Answer: SLP and iSNS.

18 Did FC evolve into a multi-protocol transport, or was it designed as such from the beginning?

Answer: FC was designed to be multi-protocol from the beginning.

19 What is the ULP throughput rate of FCP on one Gbps FC?

Answer: 826.519 Mbps.

20 FC protocol operations are defined for what topologies?

Answer: PTP, loop and switch based (fabric).

21 FC device discovery can be bounded by what mechanism?

Answer: Zoning.

Chapter 4

1 How does iSCSI complement the traditional storage over IP model?

Answer: By introducing support for block-level operations.

2 Is iSCSI capable of supporting high-performance applications?

Answer: Yes.

3 How does the FC network service model resemble the IP network service model?

Answer: Both models provide a robust set of services that are available to all "application" protocols.

4   What is the guiding principle in traditional FC network designs?

Answer: Implement dual independent paths to achieve 99.999% availability.

5   What does FCIP create between FC-SANs to facilitate communication?

Answer: A point-to-point tunnel

6   Which FC-4 protocols does FCIP support?

Answer: All FC-4 protocols.

7   Is iFCP currently being deployed for its originally intended purpose?

Answer: No.

8   Which address mode is most commonly used in modern iFCP deployments?

Answer: Translation mode.

Chapter 5

1   What two components compose a SCSI logical unit?
Answer: A task manager and a device server.

2   Which SAM addressing construct facilitates communication with an object?
Answer: The SAM Port Identifier.

3   What is a standards body that defines an address format commonly called?
Answer: A Network Address Authority (NAA).

4   Which organization assigns organizationally unique identifiers (OUIs)?
Answer: The IEEE Registration Authority Committee (RAC).

5   If fragmentation occurs, where does it occur?
Answer: In a network.

6   Is it possible for a network protocol to guarantee that frames or packets will never be dropped?
Answer: No.

7   Why do most packet-switching technologies support bandwidth reservation schemes?
Answer: Because it is possible for some end nodes to be starved of bandwidth or be allotted insufficient bandwidth to sustain acceptable application performance.

8   Does the SAM explicitly require in-order delivery of frames or packets comprising a SCSI request or response?
Answer: No.

9   Which term describes tagging of frames transmitted on an ISL to indicate the VLAN or VSAN membership of each frame?

Answer: Trunking.

10 The X2 and XPAK MSAs derive their electrical specifications from which MSA?

Answer: XENPAK.

11 What is the maximum operating range of the SPI?

Answer: 25m.

12 Does the SPI support in-order delivery?

Answer: Yes, intrinsically.

13 Which fiber-optic connectors are supported by GE?

Answer: Duplex SC, MT-RJ and LC.

14 What is the maximum operating range of 10GBASE-EW using a normal SMF link?

Answer: 30km.

15 What is the BER of 1000BASE-T?

Answer: $10^{10.}$

16 What are the /C1/ and /C2/ ordered sets used for in 1000BASE-SX?

Answer: Auto-negotiation of link operating parameters.

17 An Ethernet MAC address is equivalent to which SAM addressing construct?

Answer: The SAM Port Identifier.

18 What is the purpose of GVRP?

Answer: Dynamic PVID assignment.

19 Which Ethernet frame format is most common today?

Answer: Ethernet II.

20 How many types of service does Ethernet support?

Answer: Three.

21 Can flow-based load balancing be implemented across an Ethernet port channel?

Answer: Yes.

22 Do copper-based and fiber-based Ethernet implementations follow the same link initialization procedures?

Answer: No.

23 What is the most common fiber-optic connector used by 2-Gbps FC devices?

Answer: LC.

24 What is the maximum operating range of 2-Gbps FC on 62.5 micron MMF?

Answer: 150m.

25 How many 8B/10B control characters does 4-Gbps FC use?

Answer: One.

26 What information does the NAA field of an FC WWN provide?

Answer: The type of address contained within the Name field and the format of the Name field.

27 What do FC attached SCSI initiators do following receipt of an RSCN frame?

Answer: Query the FCNS.

28 Does the header of a FC frame provide functionality at OSI Layers other the data-link layer?

Answer: Yes.

29 Which FC CoS is used by default in most FC-SANs?

Answer: CoS 3.

30 Does FC currently support automation of link aggregation?

Answer: No, but some proprietary methods have recently appeared in the market.

31 What determines the sequence of events during extended FC link initialization?

Answer: The type of devices connected by the link.

Chapter 6

1 Is IP a routed protocol or a routing protocol?
Answer: Routed.

2 What IP term is equivalent to buffer?
Answer: Queue.

3 What is the Ethertype of IP?
Answer: 0x0800.

4 Does Ethernet padding affect an IP packet?
Answer: No.

5 What are the three components of PPP?

Answer: A frame format definition, the Link Control Protocol (LCP) and a suite of Network Control Protocols (NCPs).

6 Which of the IPCP negotiated options affect FCIP and iFCP?

Answer: None.

7 Are DNS names analogous to SAM port names?

Answer: No.

8 What is the IP equivalent of a SAM port identifier?

Answer: IP address.

9 What is the granularity of a CIDR prefix?

Answer: One bit.

10 What is the network address of 56.93.17.23/21?

Answer: 56.93.16.0.

11 What is a non-authoritative DNS reply?

Answer: A reply that is sent to a DNS client by a DNS server that does not have authority over the domain referenced in the reply.

12 Why is NAT required for communication over the Internet between devices using RFC 1918 addresses?

Answer: Because RFC 1918 addresses are not Internet routable.

13 How does a host locate available DHCP servers?

Answer: By broadcasting a DHCPDISCOVER packet.

14 What enforces virtual IP network boundaries?

Answer: Data Link Layer virtual network mechanisms.

15 Why is the Version field the first field in the IP header?

Answer: It enables the receiving device to determine the format of the IP header.

16 What is the maximum length of the Data field in an IP packet?

Answer: 65,516 bytes.

17 Does IP support notification of drops?

Answer: Yes.

18 How many flow-control mechanisms does IP support?

Answer: Four.

19 Does IP guarantee in-order delivery?

Answer: No.

20 In which layer of the OSI Reference Model does ICMP reside?

Answer: The Network Layer.

21 What is the functional difference between the Type and Code fields in the ICMP header?

Answer: The Type field indicates the category of message, while the Code field identifies the specific message.

Chapter 7

1 Is reliable delivery required by all applications?
Answer: No.

2 Does UDP provide segmentation/reassembly services?

Answer: No.

3 What is the purpose of the Destination Port field in the UDP packet header?

Answer: It enables the receiving host to properly route incoming packets to the appropriate Session Layer protocol.

4 Does UDP provide notification of dropped packets?

Answer: Notification is optional and is supported only in certain situations.

5 Is the segmentation process controlled by TCP or the ULP?

Answer: TCP performs segmentation and controls the process.

6 Why is the TCP flow-control mechanism called a sliding window?

Answer: Because the advertised receive buffer size is allowed to fluctuate dynamically.

7 What is the formula for calculating the bandwidth-delay product?

Answer: Bandwidth * Round-Trip Time (RTT)

8 Does TCP guarantee in-order delivery?

Answer: Yes.

9 What is the purpose of the TCP ISN?

Answer: To synchronize the data byte counter in the responding host's TCB with the data byte counter in the initiating host's TCB.

10 Is the segmentation process controlled by FC-2 or the ULP?

Answer: FC-2 performs segmentation, but the ULP controls the process.

11 Which two fields in the PLOGI ELS facilitate negotiation of end-to-end delivery mechanisms in modern FC-SANs?

Answer: The Common Service Parameters field and the Class 3 Service Parameters field.

12 How is the missing frame error recovery behavior of an FC node determined?

Answer: The Exchange Error Policy is specified by the Exchange originator on a per-Exchange basis via the Abort Sequence Condition bits of the F_CTL field of the FC header of the first frame of each new Exchange.

13 After completing PLOGI with the switch, what does each initiator N_Port do?

Answer: Each initiator N_Port queries the FCNS and then performs PLOGI with each target N_Port discovered via the FCNS.

Chapter 8

1 Name the three types of iSCSI names.

Answer: IQN, EUI and NAA.

2 Why does RFC 3720 encourage the reuse of ISIDs?

Answer: To promote initiator SCSI port persistence for the benefit of applications and to facilitate target recognition of initiator SCSI ports in multi-path environments.

3 What key feature does iSNS support that SLP does not support?

Answer: RSCN.

4 In the context of iSCSI, what is the difference between immediate data and unsolicited data?

Answer: Immediate data is sent in the SCSI Command PDU, whereas unsolicited data accompanies the SCSI Command PDU in a separate Data-Out PDU.

5 What is the function of the iSCSI R2T PDU?

Answer: The iSCSI target signals its readiness to receive write data via the R2T PDU.

6 Can security parameters be re-negotiated during an active iSCSI session?

Answer: No.

7 Why must iSCSI use its own CRC-based digests?

Answer: Because the TCP checksum cannot detect all bit errors.

8 Does iSCSI support stateful recovery of active tasks in the presence of TCP connection failures?

Answer: Yes.

9 Does FCP natively support the exchange of all required operating parameters to establish a new session?

Answer: No. FCP relies on SCSI Mode commands for the exchange of certain operating parameters.

10 Does FCP support immediate data?

Answer: No.

11 How many bytes long is the FCP_DATA IU header?

Answer: Zero. The receiver uses only the FC Header to identify an FCP_DATA IU, and ULP data is directly encapsulated in the Data field of the FC frame.

12 What is the name of the FC-4 link service defined by the FCP-3 specification?

Answer: Sequence Retransmission Request (SRR).

13 FCP mandates a one-to-one relationship between which two data constructs?

Answer: IUs and sequences.

14 When an FCP target that supports only Exchange level error recovery detects a frame error, what action does the target take?

Answer: The FCP target discards all frames associated with the Exchange. The target takes no further action and waits for the initiator to detect the error via timeout.

15 What determines the functional model of an FC-BB device?

Answer: The type of non-FC network to which the FC-BB device connects.

16 How many FC Entities may be paired with an FCIP Entity?

Answer: One.

17 Does the FCIP addressing scheme map to the SAM addressing scheme?

Answer: No.

18 Why must the FC frame delimiters be encapsulated for transport across FC backbone networks?

Answer: Because they serve several purposes rather than merely delimiting the start and end of each FC frame.

19 Which field in the FSF may be set to zero for the purpose of discovery?

Answer: The Destination FC Fabric Entity WWN field.

20 What procedure begins after an FCIP link becomes fully active?

Answer: The FC switch-to-switch extended link initialization procedure.

21 Why must jumbo frames be supported end-to-end if they are implemented?

Answer: To avoid excessive fragmentation.

Chapter 9

1 What is the primary function of all flow-control mechanisms?

Answer: Reduce the probability of or completely avoid receive buffer overruns.

2 What are the two categories of QoS algorithms?

Answer: Queue management and queue scheduling.

3 What is the name of the queue management algorithm historically associated with tail-drop?

Answer: FIFO.

4 Which specification defines traffic classes, class groupings, and class-priority mappings for Ethernet?

Answer: The IEEE 802.1D-2004 specification.

5 What is the name of the first algorithm used for AQM in IP networks?

Answer: Random Early Detection (RED).

6 What are the names of the two dominant QoS models used in IP networks today?

Answer: The Integrated Services Architecture (IntServ) and the Differentiated Services Architecture (DiffServ).

7 What is the name of the TCP state variable that controls the amount of data that may be transmitted?

Answer: The Congestion Window (CWND).

8 What is the primary flow-control mechanism employed by iSCSI?

Answer: The R2T PDU.

9 What are the names of the two QoS subfields currently available for use in FC-SANs?

Answer: Preference and Priority.

10 What is the primary flow-control mechanism employed by FCP?

Answer: The FCP_XFER_RDY IU.

11 Are FCIP devices required to map FC QoS mechanisms to IP QoS mechanisms?

Answer: No.

Chapter 10

1 What are the two basic steps that every switching and routing protocol performs?

Answer: Path determination and frame/packet forwarding.

2 What is the primary purpose of a TTL mechanism?

Answer: To limit the congestion caused by routing loops.

3 Does IP permit all-networks broadcasts?

Answer: No.

4 Is RSTP backward-compatible with STP?

Answer: Yes.

5 Does EIGRP support load balancing across unequal-cost paths?

Answer: Yes.

6 How many levels in the topological hierarchy does OSPF support?

Answer: Two.

7 How do BGP-4 peers communicate?

Answer: Via TCP.

8 Which link-state algorithm does FSPF use?

Answer: The choice of algorithm is vendor dependent.

Chapter 11

1 What is the primary goal of load balancing?

Answer: To improve throughput.

2 Which protocol enables network administrators to modify link costs independently within each VLAN?

Answer: MSTP.

3 In IP networks, is load balancing across equal-cost paths more or less common than load balancing across unequal-cost paths?

Answer: More common.

4 Is the FSPF load-balancing algorithm defined in the FC specifications?

Answer: No.

5 Does iSCSI require any third-party software to perform load balancing at the Transport Layer?

Answer: No.

6 Does FCP support Transport Layer load balancing?

Answer: No.

7 Does FCIP support Exchange-based load balancing across TCP connections within an FCIP link?

Answer: No.

8 Name the two techniques commonly used by end nodes to load-balance across DMP paths.

Answer: LUN-to-path mapping and SCSI command distribution.

Chapter 12

1 List the five primary protection services for in-flight data.

Answer: Data origin authentication, Data integrity, Anti-replay, Data confidentiality and Traffic flow confidentiality.

2 Which management protocol supports "port forwarding"?

Answer: SSH.

3 What type of security model does Ethernet implement?

Answer: Port based.

4 Which standard defines the IPsec architecture?

Answer: IETF RFC 2401.

5 Is SSL compatible with TLS?

Answer: No.

6 Is iSCSI authentication mandatory?

Answer: No.

7 Which security architecture was leveraged as the basis for the FC-SP architecture?

Answer: IPsec.

8 Which standard defines the ASF SW_ILS?

Answer: The ANSI T11 FC-BB specification series.

Chapter 13

1 List two aspects of management that are currently undergoing rapid innovation.

Answer: Automated provisioning and reclamation.

2 List the five major components of the ISMF.

Answer: The SMI, the MIB, the SNMP, a security model and management applications.

3 WBEM usually operates over which communication protocol?

Answer: HTTP.

4 List the constituent parts of the FC Management Service.

Answer: A Fabric Configuration Server, a Performance Server, a Fabric Zone Server, a Security Policy Server, an Unzoned Name Server and an HBA Management Server.

5 List two in-band techniques for management of SCSI enclosures.

Answer: SAF-TE and SES.

Chapter 14

1 Why are protocol decoders necessary?

Answer: Because the tools integrated into server, storage and network devices are sometimes insufficient to resolve communication problems.

2 List the three methods of traffic capture.

Answer: In-line, out-of-line and signal splitter.

3 Name the most popular free GUI-based protocol decoder.

Answer: Ethereal.

4 What is the purpose of traffic analysis?

Answer: To identify trends and generate detailed performance statistics.

5 What is the highest performance solution available for traffic analysis?

Answer: An in-line ASIC-based product.

GLOSSARY

A

advanced technology attachment (ATA). The block-level protocol historically used in laptops, desktops, and low-end server platforms. *See also* direct attached storage (DAS).

anti-replay protection. A security service that detects the arrival of duplicate packets within a given window of packets or a bounded timeframe.

anycast. An IP routing feature that supports regionalized duplication of IP addresses; facilitates efficient location of globally distributed services.

application specific integrated circuit (ASIC). An integrated circuit that performs a specific function.

asynchronous replication. A method of replicating data across long distances in which the states of the source and target disk images may be significantly out of sync at any point in time.

ATA Packet Interface (ATAPI). An enhancement to the ATA protocol that enables support for device types other than magnetic disk.

autonomous system (AS). An administrative domain in which a common policy set is used for the configuration of routing protocols.

auto-sensing. The ability to detect the transmission rate of an attached Ethernet port; a subset of the auto-negotiation features supported by Ethernet.

B

back-pressure. Any mechanism that slows transmission by creating congestion along the backward path.

basic link service. Special Fibre Channel procedures and frame payloads that provide basic low-level networking functions.

bit error ratio (BER). The ratio of erroneous bits to valid bits in a data stream. Minimum BER requirements are stated in Layer 1 technology specifications to indicate the minimum acceptable transmit fidelity.

block-level protocol.   A protocol used to store and retrieve data via storage device constructs.

block multiplexer.   One of two classes of mainframe channel protocols.

bridge.   A device that operates at the OSI data-link layer to connect two physical network segments. A bridge can connect segments that use the same communication protocol (transparent bridge) or dissimilar communication protocols (translational bridge). A bridge can forward or filter frames.

byte multiplexer.   One of two classes of mainframe channel protocols.

C

carrier sense multiple access with collision detection (CSMA/CD).   The medium access control algorithm used by Ethernet technologies.

channel protocol.   A generic term for any protocol used by a mainframe to control devices via its channel interface.

checksum.   A mathematical calculation capable of detecting bit-level errors; used to verify the integrity of a frame or packet. Some checksum algorithms can detect multi-bit errors; others can detect only single-bit errors.

class of service (CoS).   (1) A synonym for QoS. (2) A field in the 802.1Q header used to mark Ethernet frames for QoS handling. (3) The mode of delivery in Fibre Channel networks.

classful network.   An IP network address that complies with the addressing definitions in RFC 791.

classless interdomain routing (CIDR).   A set of procedures for forwarding IP packets on the Internet using network addresses that do not comply with the addressing definitions in RFC 791.

coarse wavelength division multiplexing (CWDM).   A simplified implementation of dense wavelength division multiplexing (DWDM).

command descriptor block (CDB).   *See* SCSI Command Descriptor Block (CDB).

command/response protocol.   A protocol used to control devices. The devices can operate as peers, or as masters or slaves.

Common Internet File System (CIFS).   A file-level protocol native to Windows used to access storage across a network.

communication protocol.   Any protocol that provides some or all of the functionality defined in one or more of the OSI layers.

connection allegiance.   An iSCSI term referring to the mandatory requirement that all PDUs associated with a single SCSI command must traverse a single TCP connection.

crosstalk.   Signal interference on a conductor caused by another signal on a nearby conductor.

cut-through switching.   A method of switching in which the forwarding of each frame begins while the frame is still being received. As soon as sufficient header information is received to make a forwarding decision, the switch makes a forwarding decision and begins transmitting the received bits on the appropriate egress port. This method was popular during the early days of Ethernet switching but is no longer used except in high performance computing (HPC) environments.

cyclic redundancy check (CRC).   A mathematical calculation capable of detecting multi-bit errors; used to verify the integrity of a frame or packet.

D

data confidentiality.   A security service that prevents exposure of application data to unauthorized parties while the data is in flight.

data integrity.   A security service that detects modifications made to data while in flight. Data integrity can be implemented as connectionless or connection-oriented.

data origin authentication.   A security service that verifies that each message actually originated from the source claimed in the header.

data streaming (DS) protocol.   The synchronous block multiplexer protocol used by mainframes to access storage.

dense wavelength division multiplexing (DWDM).   A physical layer wide area transport technology that combines frequency division multiplexing techniques with time division multiplexing techniques.

differentiated services architecture (DiffServ).   A stateless QoS model used in IP networks as defined in IETF RFC 2475.

direct access file system (DAFS).   A file-level protocol for accessing storage across a Direct Access Transport (DAT).

Direct Access Transport (DAT).   A class of interconnect technologies based on Remote direct memory access (RDMA).

direct attached storage (DAS).   Disk or tape storage that is directly attached to a single host. It is typically attached via SPI, SAS, PATA, or SATA.

direct-coupled interlock (DCI) protocol.   The asynchronous block multiplexer protocol used by mainframes to access storage.

disk control unit.   A device class within a mainframe storage channel architecture used to control physical storage devices.

disk drive.   A generic term referring to a floppy drive or a hard drive.

distance vector protocol.   A category of routing protocols characterized by the exchange of routing table entries between topologically adjacent routers.

droop.   The resulting lag in throughput that results from link buffer exhaustion. Droop occurs when the round-trip time of a link is greater than the time required to transmit sufficient data to fill the receiver's link-level buffers.

dynamic multi-pathing (DMP).   A generic term describing the ability of end nodes to load balance across multiple iSCSI or FCP sessions.

Dynamic Packet Transport (DPT).   An RPR implementation developed by Cisco Systems and used, in part, as the basis for IEEE 802.17.

E

electromagnetic interference (EMI).   The degradation of a signal caused by exposure to environmental electricity or magnetism.

electro-optical repeater (EOR).   A type of semiconductor optical amplifier (SOA).

enhanced IDE (EIDE).   The common term for ATA-2.

enterprise systems connection (ESCON).   A proprietary channel architecture used by IBM mainframes to access storage.

erbium-doped fiber amplifier (EDFA).   A type of in-fiber optical amplifier that amplifies wavelengths in the WDM window.

Ethernet II.   A network specification published by Digital Equipment Corporation, Intel, and Xerox. Ethernet II evolved from Ethernet, which was originally created by Bob Metcalfe while working at Xerox PARC. Ethernet II is sometimes called DIX, DIX Ethernet, or Ethernet DIX. DIX stands for Digital, Intel, and Xerox.

EtherType.   The system used by Ethernet and Ethernet II to assigned a unique numeric identifier to each OSI network layer protocol. EtherType is equivalent in function to the destination SAP (DSAP) used by IEEE 802.3.

exchange.   The highest level FC transmission construct. An exchange is composed of sequences. Each sequence is composed of one or more frames. Each SCSI task maps to a single FC Exchange.

exchange error policy.   The Fibre Channel policy that determines how the exchange recipient will handle frame and sequence errors. The exchange originator specifies the error policy in the first frame of each new exchange.

exchange status block (ESB).   A small area in memory used to maintain the state of each FC exchange.

EXTENDED COPY.   *See* SCSI-3 EXTENDED COPY.

extended fabric.   An FC-SAN that spans a long distance by leveraging one of the technologies defined in the ANSI T11 FC-BB specification series.

extended link service (ELS).   Special Fibre Channel procedures and frame payloads that provide advanced low-level networking functions.

extent.   A set of contiguous storage blocks. Multiple extents can be concatenated and presented to an application as a single logical volume. The individual extents of a concatenated logical volume do not need to be contiguous and can reside on a single physical disk or on physically separate disks. Data blocks are written to a single extent until it fills. Data blocks are then written to the next extent in the logical volume until it fills. When the last extent is filled, the logical volume is full.

Exterior Gateway Protocol (EGP).   Any of the routing protocols commonly used between Autonomous Systems.

External Data Representation (XDR).   A presentation layer protocol used by NFS.

F

fabric. The term used in Fibre Channel environments to describe a switched network.

fabric manager. A SAN management application that provides the ability to discover, inventory, monitor, visualize, provision, and reclaim storage network resources.

failover. The process by which a service is moved from a failed component to a backup component.

fast link pulse (FLP). A well-defined series of electrical pulses representing 17 clock signals and 16 bits of configuration information that is used for auto-negotiation of Ethernet link parameters in copper-based implementations.

FC-SAN. Acronym for Fibre Channel (FC) storage area network (SAN). A SAN built on FC for the purpose of transporting SCSI or SBCCS traffic.

Fibre Channel Connection (FICON). A proprietary channel architecture based on an open-systems networking technology and used by IBM mainframes to access storage.

file-level protocol. A protocol used to store and retrieve data via file system constructs.

File Transfer Protocol (FTP). A file-level protocol used for rudimentary access to storage across an IP network.

floppy disk. A round, thin platter of celluloid-like material covered with a magnetic substance. Data blocks on a floppy disk are accessed randomly, but capacity, throughput, and reliability are very low relative to hard disks. Floppy disks are classified as removable media.

floppy disk drive. *See* floppy drive.

floppy drive. A device used to read from and write to floppy disks.

fragmentation. The process by which an intermediate network device fragments an in-transit frame into multiple frames for the purpose of MTU matching. Fragmentation occurs when the MTU of an intermediate network link is smaller than the MTU of the transmitter's directly connected link.

frequency-division multiplexing (FDM).   A technique for multiplexing signals onto a shared medium in which a fixed percentage of the bandwidth of the medium is simultaneously allotted to each source full time.

full-duplex.   A method of communication in which a device can transmit and receive data simultaneously. *See also* half-duplex.

G–H

gigabit interface converter (GBIC).   A small hardware device used to adapt an interface to a medium. GBICs allow a port in a router or switch, and a NIC in a host, to be connected to several media via several connectors.

half-duplex.   A method of communication in which a device can transmit and receive data but not simultaneously. *See also* full-duplex.

hardcoded.   Encoded into a device by the manufacturer. For example, a device that contains compiled software code (such as BIOS or firmware) might behave a certain way regardless of configuration parameters applied by the device administrator. Such behavior is said to be hardcoded into the device because the behavior cannot be changed.

hard disk.   A storage medium and drive mechanism enclosed as a single unit. The medium itself is made of aluminum alloy platters covered with a magnetic substance and anchored at the center to a spindle. Data blocks on a hard disk are accessed randomly. Hard disks provide high capacity, throughput, and reliability relative to floppy disks. Hard disks are classified as permanent media.

hard disk drive.   *See* hard disk.

hard drive.   *See* hard disk.

hierarchical storage management (HSM).   A method of automating data migration between storage mediums that are organized in a hierarchical manner. Primary storage represents the top tier and typically takes the form of relatively expensive, high-performance disk media. Tape media typically constitutes the lowest tier. Many tiers can be defined, and policies are set to initiate migration of data up or down through the hierarchy.

host bus adapter (HBA).   A hardware interface to an open-systems storage network. An HBA is installed in the PCI bus, Sbus, or other expansion bus of a host.

host channel adapter (HCA). A hardware interface to a mainframe storage network. An HCA is installed in a mainframe.

hot-pluggable. The ability to insert into an electrical device, or remove from it, another electrical device without powering off either device.

HyperText Transfer Protocol (HTTP). A file-level protocol originally used to access text files across a network. HTTP is now often used for read-only access to files of all types and also can be used for writing to files.

I

in-fiber optical amplifier (IOA). An optical fiber that has been doped with a rare earth element. Certain wavelengths excite the rare earth element, which in turn amplifies other wavelengths.

initiator-target nexus (I_T Nexus). A SCSI term referring to the relationship between an Initiator port and a Target port.

in-order delivery. (1) The receipt of frames at the destination node in the same order that they were transmitted by the source node. (2) The delivery of data to a specific protocol layer within the destination node in the same order that it was transmitted by the same protocol layer within the source node.

input/output (I/O). A generic term referring to the acts of reading blocks from and writing blocks to a storage device, providing information to and drawing information from a computer, or transmitting frames onto and receiving frames from a network.

input/output operations per second (IOPS). A common metric for gauging the storage throughput requirements of an application.

Integrated Drive Electronics (IDE). The common term for ATA-1.

integrated services architecture (IntServ). A stateful QoS model used in IP networks as defined in IETF RFC 1633.

Interior Gateway Protocol (IGP). Any of the routing protocols commonly used within an Autonomous System.

Internet Assigned Numbers Authority (IANA). The global authority that assigns numbers such as parameters, ports, and protocols for use on the global Internet.

Internet attached storage (IAS). *See* network attached storage (NAS).

Inter-switch link (ISL).   A network link that connects two switches.

interworking.   The process of mixing disparate network technologies together in a manner that facilitates interaction.

IP-SAN.   Acronym for Internet Protocol (IP) storage area network (SAN). A SAN built on IP for the purpose of transporting SCSI-3 traffic.

J–K

jitter.   Variance in the amount of delay experienced by a frame or packet during transit.

just-a-bunch-of-disks (JBOD).   A chassis containing disks. JBOD chassis do not support the advanced functionality typically supported by storage subsystems.

keepalives.   Frames or packets sent between two communicating devices during periods of inactivity to prevent connection timeouts from occurring.

L

lambda.   A Greek letter. The symbol for lambda is used to represent wavelength. The term lambda is often used to refer to a signal operating at a specific wavelength.

LAN-free backup.   A technique for backing up data that confines the data path to a SAN.

line rate.   The theoretical maximum rate at which OSI Layer 2 frames can be forwarded onto a link. Line rate varies from one networking technology to another. For example, the line rate of IEEE 802.3 10BaseT is different than the line rate of IEEE 802.5 16-Mbps Token Ring.

link aggregation.   The bundling of two or more physical links in a manner that causes the links appear to ULPs as one logical link.

link-state Protocol.   A category of routing protocols characterized by the exchange of link-state information propagated via a flooding mechanism.

logical block addressing (LBA).   An addressing scheme used to locate real blocks on a storage medium such as disk or tape. LBA constitutes the lowest level of addressing used in storage and does not represent a virtualized address scheme.

logical unit number (LUN).   The identification of a logical partition in SCSI environments.

M

magnetic drum. One of the earliest mediums for storing computer commands and data. A magnetic drum is a cylindrical metal surface covered with a magnetic substance.

magnetic tape. A long, thin strip of celluloid-like material covered with a magnetic substance. Data blocks on a magnetic tape are accessed sequentially, so tape is normally used as secondary storage (for data backup and archival) versus primary storage.

management station. A centralized host or cluster of hosts at the heart of a management system.

maximum transmission unit (MTU). The maximum payload size supported by a given interface on a given segment of an OSI Layer 2 network. MTU does not include header or trailer bytes. MTU is used to indicate the maximum data payload to ULPs.

mean time between failures (MTBF). A metric for the reliability of a repairable device expressed as the mean average time between failures of that device. MTBF is calculated across large numbers of devices within a class.

mean time to failure (MTTF). A metric for the reliability of non-repairable devices expressed as the mean average time between the first use of devices within a class and the first failure of devices within the same class. MTTF is calculated across large numbers of devices within a class.

mirror set. A set of partitions on physically separate disks to which data blocks are written. Each block is written to all partitions.

mode-conditioning patch (MCP) cable. A special cable used by IBM mainframes to convert the transmit signal of a single mode optical interface to multi-mode.

multidrop interface. A bus interface supporting multiple device connections. Examples include the SCSI Parallel Interface (SPI), IEEE 802.3 10Base2, and IEEE 802.3 10Base5.

multi-source agreement (MSA). A voluntary agreement among multiple interested parties on the specifications of a transceiver. An MSA represents a consortium-based transceiver standard. MSAs allow switch, router, NIC, and HBA manufacturers to purchase transceivers from multiple sources without interoperability concerns. MSAs also allow transceiver manufacturers to sell to multiple consumers without engineering a unique interface for each switch, router, NIC, and HBA.

N

network address authority (NAA).   Any standards body that defines an address format.

network architecture.   The totality of specifications and recommendations required to implement a network.

network attached storage (NAS).   A class of storage devices characterized by file-level access, multiprotocol support, and specialized operating system software often implemented on specialized hardware.

Network basic input output system (NetBIOS).   A session layer protocol historically used by IBM and Microsoft upper-layer protocols.

Network Data Management Protocol (NDMP).   A standard protocol used by backup software to control backup operations in a network environment.

Network File System (NFS).   A file-level protocol native to UNIX that is used to access storage across a network.

network implementation.   The manifestation of one or more network specifications in hardware or software.

network interface card (NIC).   A hardware interface to a network. A NIC is installed in the PCI bus, Sbus, or other expansion bus of a host.

network model.   A reference tool that typically defines network functionality and divides that functionality into layers.

network specification.   A document that typically defines how to perform the functions defined within a layer of a network model.

O–P

ones complement.   A mathematical system used to represent negative numbers in computer systems.

ordered set.   A special construct used to implement low-level networking functions. An ordered set is usually 2 or 4 bytes long. Each byte has a specific meaning, and the bytes must be transmitted in a specific order.

organizationally unique identifier (OUI).   The IEEE-RAC assigned 24-bit value that is used as the first three bytes of an EUI-48 or EUI-64 address. The OUI identifies the organization that administers the remaining bits of the EUI-48 or EUI-64 address.

parallel ATA (PATA).   A series of specifications for ATA operation on parallel bus interfaces.

parallel SCSI.   A series of specifications for SCSI operation on parallel bus interfaces.

path maximum transmission unit (PMTU).   The smallest MTU along a given OSI Layer 3 end-to-end path.

phase-collapse.   An iSCSI term referring to the ability to piggyback data with a SCSI command. Alternately, SCSI status may be piggybacked with data.

pluggable transceiver.   A hot-pluggable transceiver.

primitive sequence.   A Fibre Channel Ordered Set that is continuously transmitted under certain circumstances until the receiving device responds.

primitive signal.   A Fibre Channel Ordered Set that is transmitted under certain circumstances for as long as the transmitting device deems appropriate.

protection switching.   A technique employed by wide area optical technologies to transparently switch from a failed circuit to a standby circuit.

protocol data unit (PDU).   An OSI layer data entity composed of a header, upper neighbor layer SDU, and optional trailer.

protocol decoder.   A product that dissects frame header fields to reveal exactly what is happening on the wire.

protocol stack.   Vertically stacked communication protocols representing an implementation of a layered network model.

punch card.   One of the earliest media for entering commands and data into a computer. A punch card is a slip of cardstock with holes punched at specific positions (row and column) to represent data.

Q–R

quality of service (QoS).   The level of delivery service guaranteed by a network with regard to bandwidth, latency, and frequency of access to media. QoS is usually applied via a system of traffic classification, frame/packet marking, and input/output queuing in switches or routers.

redundant array of inexpensive disks (RAID).   A technology for mirroring or striping data across a set of disks. Striping can be done with or without the generation of parity data.

remote direct memory access (RDMA).   A method by which an application on a host can directly access a memory address on another host. RDMA is often used in clustering environments to improve the performance of cooperating applications.

remote-procedure call (RPC).   An application layer protocol used by NFS for invocation of procedures implemented on remote hosts.

repeater.   A device that terminates an OSI physical layer transmission, interprets the digitally encoded signal, regenerates the signal, and retransmits the signal on a different link than whence it was received.

resilient packet ring (RPR).   A class of data-link layer metropolitan area transport technologies that combine characteristics of TDM-based optical rings with LAN technologies.

router.   A device that operates at the OSI network layer to connect two data-link layer networks. A router can forward or filter packets. Routers typically employ advanced intelligence for processing packets.

routing.   The combined act of making forwarding decisions based on OSI Layer 3 information and forwarding packets.

S

SAM identifier.   An identifier assigned to a SCSI port or SCSI logical unit. SAM identifiers are used to facilitate communication.

SAM logical unit identifier.   An identifier that is unique within the context of the SCSI port through which the logical unit is accessed. The identifier assigned to a logical unit can change. A SAM logical unit identifier is commonly called a SCSI logical unit number (LUN).

SAM name.   An identifier assigned to a SCSI device or SCSI port that is globally unique within the context of the SCSI Transport Protocol implemented by the SCSI device. SCSI names are used to positively identify a SCSI device or SCSI port. SCSI names never change.

SAM port identifier.   An identifier that is unique within the context of the SCSI service delivery subsystem to which the port is connected. The identifier assigned to a SCSI port can change.

SAN manager.   *See* fabric manager.

SCSI application client.   The SCSI protocol implemented in an initiator.

SCSI application protocol.   A generic term encompassing both the SCSI application client and the SCSI logical unit.

SCSI asynchronous mode.   A mode of communication in which each request must be acknowledged before another request can be issued.

SCSI command descriptor block (CDB).   The data structure by which a SCSI command is conveyed from an initiator to a target.

SCSI device.   A NIC, HBA, or other endpoint that contains one or more ports and supports the SCSI protocol.

SCSI domain.   A complete I/O system composed of SCSI devices that contain SCSI ports that communicate via a SCSI service delivery subsystem.

SCSI enclosure.   A chassis that contains one or more SCSI devices.

SCSI identifier (SCSI ID).   The SPI term for SAM port identifier.

SCSI initiator.   The device that initiates a transfer of data between two SCSI devices.

SCSI interconnect.   A networking technology that can be used to facilitate communication between SCSI ports. A SCSI interconnect developed specifically for the SCSI protocol may transport the SCSI protocol natively. A general-purpose SCSI interconnect requires a SCSI Transport Protocol.

SCSI logical unit (LU).   The processing entity within a SCSI target device that presents a storage medium to SCSI application clients and executes SCSI commands on that medium.

SCSI logical unit number (LUN).   The address assigned to a logical unit. From the perspective of a host, a LUN is often called a volume.

SCSI parallel interface (SPI).   A physical and electrical interface specification supporting parallel transmission in a bus topology.

SCSI port.   A port in a SCSI device.

SCSI service delivery subsystem.   A generic term that refers to a SCSI interconnect technology or the combination of a SCSI interconnect technology and a SCSI Transport Protocol.

SCSI synchronous mode.   A mode of communication in which one or more requests can be issued without first receiving acknowledgement for previously issued requests.

SCSI target.   The device that responds to a request for transfer of data between two SCSI devices.

SCSI transport protocol.   A protocol mapping that enables the SCSI protocol to be transported on a general-purpose SCSI Interconnect.

SCSI-3 EXTENDED COPY.   A SCSI-3 command that enables a third-party device (neither the initiator nor the target) to control the movement of data as requested by a SCSI initiator.

segmentation.   The process by which an end node segments a large chunk of ULP data into multiple smaller chunks that can be framed for transmission without exceeding the MTU of the egress port in the NIC, HBA, or other network interface.

semiconductor optical amplifier (SOA).   A device that converts an optical signal to an electrical signal, amplifies it, and then converts it back to optical.

sequence qualifier.   A sequence identifier that is guaranteed to be unique during the R_A_TOV and is composed of the S_ID, D_ID, OX_ID, RX_ID, and SEQ_ID fields of the header of a Fibre Channel frame. The sequence qualifier is used for error recovery.

sequence status block (SSB).   A small area in memory used to maintain the state of each FC Sequence.

Serial ATA (SATA).   A new series of specifications for ATA operation on serial bus interfaces.

serial attached SCSI (SAS).   A new series of specifications for SCSI operation on serial bus interfaces.

Server Message Block (SMB).   The predecessor to CIFS.

server-free backup.   A technique for backing up data that removes the requesting server from the data path and confines the data path to a SAN.

service access point (SAP).   The interface between vertically stacked OSI layers.

service data unit (SDU).   The PDU of an OSI layer from the viewpoint of the lower neighbor layer.

signal-to-noise ratio (SNR).   An expression of the strength of data-bearing signals relative to the strength of non-data-bearing signals present on a conductor.

silent discard.   To drop a frame or packet without any notification to the source node or the ULP. The dropped frame or packet may be counted in an error log.

single-byte command code set (SBCCS).   The block-multiplexer protocol historically used in mainframes. *See also* Enterprise Systems Connection (ESCON) and Fibre Channel Connection (FICON).

Small Computer System Interface (SCSI).   The block-level protocol historically used in open systems such as workstations and high-end server platforms. *See also* direct attached storage (DAS).

small form-factor pluggable (SFP).   A relatively new type of gigabit interface converter (GBIC) in smaller physical form that allows higher port density on switch and router line cards.

spatial reuse protocol (SRP).   A protocol developed by Cisco Systems that optimizes bandwidth in ring topologies.

SPI.   *See* SCSI parallel interface.

starvation.   A condition in which some nodes are denied sufficient access to a medium to sustain normal communication sessions.

storage area network (SAN).   A generic term referring to any network dedicated to the transport of block-level storage protocols.

storage channel.   A communication architecture used by mainframes to access storage.

storage resource management (SRM).   A storage management application that provides the ability to discover, inventory, and monitor disk and tape resources. Automated storage provisioning and reclamation functions are also supported by some SRM applications. Some SRM applications also support limited SAN management functionality.

storage subsystem.   A chassis or set of modular enclosures that contain disks. Storage subsystems typically contain one or more disk controllers and support advanced functionality such as caching, RAID (mirroring and striping), and LUN management. This term is interchangeable with storage array.

store-and-forward switching.   A method of switching in which the forwarding of each frame begins after the entire frame has been received. As soon as sufficient header information is received to make a forwarding decision, the switch makes a forwarding decision but does not begin transmitting until the rest of the frame is received. This method is currently the de facto standard for Ethernet switching in non-HPC environments.

stripe set.   A set of partitions on physically separate disks to which data and optional parity blocks are written. One block is written to one partition, then another block is written to another partition, and so on until one block is written to each partition. The cycle then repeats until all blocks are written. The set of partitions is presented to applications as a single logical partition.

switch.   A multiport bridge that employs a mechanism for internal port interconnection. A switch has the ability to simultaneously forward frames at line rate across multiple ports. A switch typically employs advanced intelligence for processing frames.

switch internal link service (SW_ILS).   Special Fibre Channel procedures and frame payloads that provide advanced low-level networking functions and operate internal to a fabric (that is, between switches).

switching.   The combined act of making forwarding decisions based on OSI Layer 2 information and forwarding frames.

synchronous digital hierarchy (SDH).   A physical layer wide area transport technology based on time division multiplexing. SDH is an international standard.

Synchronous Optical Network (SONET).   A physical layer wide area transport technology based on time division multiplexing. SONET is a North American standard.

synchronous replication.   A method of replicating data across long distances in which the states of the source and destination disk images are never more than one write request out of sync at any point in time. Both the source and destination disk devices must successfully complete the write request before SCSI status is returned to the initiator.

T

TCP offload engine (TOE).   An intelligent hardware interface to a network. A TOE is capable of processing TCP and IP packets on behalf of the host CPU. A TOE is installed in the PCI bus, Sbus, or other expansion bus of a host.

TCP port number.   A 16-bit identifier assigned by IANA to each well-known session layer protocol that operates over TCP. Each port number that IANA assigns may be used by TCP or UDP. Unassigned port numbers may be used by vendors to identify their own proprietary session layer protocols. A range of port numbers is reserved for use by clients to initiate TCP connections to servers.

TCP sliding window.   The mechanism by which a host dynamically updates its peer host regarding the current size of its receive buffer.

TCP socket.   A connection end-point identifier derived by concatenating the IP address of a host with the port number of a session layer protocol within the host.

third party copy (3PC).   The predecessor to the SCSI-3 EXTENDED COPY command.

time division multiplexing (TDM).   A technique for multiplexing signals onto a shared medium in which the full bandwidth of the medium is allotted to each source sequentially for a fixed and limited period of time.

top level domain (TLD).   A domain within the Domain Name System (DNS) that resides immediately under the root domain.

traffic analyzer.   A product that inspects frame headers and payloads to generate network performance reports.

traffic capture.   The process of capturing frames in transit for further analysis.

traffic flow confidentiality.   A security service that prevents exposure of communication parameters (such as original source and destination addresses) to unauthorized parties.

transmission control block (TCB).   A small area in memory used to maintain the state of each TCP connection.

transmission rate.   The rate at which bits are serialized onto a link.

trunk.   A link between two switches.

trunking.   The process of tagging frames before transmission on an ISL to indicate the VLAN or VSAN membership of each frame.

type of service (ToS). A field in the IP Header that was previously used to specify Quality of Service (QoS) requirements on a per-packet basis. This field was redefined in RFC 2474 as the Differentiated Services (DiffServ) field.

U–V–W

UDP port number. *See* TCP port number.

uniform naming convention (UNC). The resource identification mechanism used by CIFS.

uniform resource locator (URL). The resource identification mechanism used by HTTP, FTP, and other sockets-based applications.

virtual LAN (VLAN). A logical Ethernet LAN implemented within a larger physical Ethernet LAN.

virtual SAN (VSAN). A logical Fibre Channel SAN implemented within a larger physical Fibre Channel SAN.

virtualization. The abstraction of physical resources into logical resources.

volume. A unit of storage. A volume can be a block-level entity such as a LUN, or a file-level entity such as an NFS mount point. A volume can also be a tape cartridge or other removable media.

volume serial number (VSN). *See* volume tag.

volume tag. An identifier used to track physical units of removable storage.

WDM window. Wavelengths generally in the range of 1500–1600 nanometers.

well known address (WKA). A reserved address that is used for access to a network service.

well known logical unit. A logical unit that supports specified functions, which facilitate initiator control of a target device.

Windows sockets (Winsock). An adaptation of UNIX sockets to Windows. Winsock provides session, presentation, and application layer functionality to applications running on Windows operating systems.

INDEX

Numerics

1Base5, 71
8B/10B encoding scheme, 135
8B1Q4 encoding scheme, 136
10/100 auto-sensing switches, 68
10GE, throughput, 70
10GFC, throughput, 86
64B/66B encoding scheme, 137
1000BASE-X Configuration ordered sets,
   fields, 147

A

AAA, 386
Abort Sequence (Abort Sequence) BLS, 295
ABTS BLS, 313–314
Accept format (SRR), fields, 317
ACK segments, 235
acknowledgements, SAM delivery mechanisms,
   119–120
ACLs (access control lists), 390
address masking, 201
address resolution, FC, 162–166
addressing
   DNS, 197
   Ethernet, 137–138
   EUI-64 format, 115–116
   FC, 158–160
      ANSI T11 WWN address fields, 156
   FCAL, 87
   FCIP, 331–333
   FCP, 293
   IPv4, 198
      dotted decimal notation, 202
      fields, 199
      subnetting, 199
   iSCSI, 245
      I_T nexus, 248
      IP address assignment, 251
      ISIDs, 247–249
      port names, 246
   MAC-48 format, 114–115
   NAAs, 114

SAM
   element addressing scheme, 112
   identifiers, 110
   LUNs, 111
   names, 110
   SPI, 128
ADISC (Discover Address), 161
adoption rate of FCP, 98
advanced tail-drop, 356
advanced volume management, 8
agents, 395
aliases, 246
ALL parameter (SendTargets
   command), 80
all-networks broadcasts, 369
ANSI (American National Standards
   Institute), 8
ANSI T11 subcommittee
   Ethernet address formats, 156–159
   Fibre Channel specifications, 50–51
ANSI X3 committee, 9
anti-replay protection, 385
APIs, HBA API, 401
application layer, 44
AQM, as IP flow control mechanism, 357
arbitration processes, SPI, 129–130
areas, 372
ARPANET model, 48
   comparing with OSI reference model, 49
AS (autonomous system), 370
ASBRs (autonomous system boundary
   routers), 373
ASF (ANSI T11 FC-BB) specification, 393
ASN.1 (Abstract Syntax Notation One), 397
assigning WKPs, 218
asymmetric flow control, 355
ATA (advanced technology attachment)
   protocol, 12–13
authentication
   FC-SP model, DH-CHAP, 391
   ISCSI, 391
   Kerberos, 387
   RADIUS, 386
   SRP protocol, 387
   supplicants, 389
   TACACS+, 387

ciscopress.com

CISCO SYSTEMS

Cisco Press

3 STEPS TO LEARNING

STEP 1

STEP 2

STEP 3

First-Step

Fundamentals

**Networking
Technology Guides**

STEP 1 **First-Step**—Benefit from easy-to-grasp explanations.
No experience required!

STEP 2 **Fundamentals**—Understand the purpose, application,
and management of technology.

STEP 3 **Networking Technology Guides**—Gain the knowledge
to master the challenge of the network.

NETWORK BUSINESS SERIES

The Network Business series helps professionals tackle the
business issues surrounding the network. Whether you are a
seasoned IT professional or a business manager with minimal
technical expertise, this series will help you understand the
business case for technologies.

Justify Your Network Investment.

Look for Cisco Press titles at your favorite bookseller today.

Visit **www.ciscopress.com/series** for details on each of these book series.

Learning is serious business. **Invest wisely.**

Cisco Press

FUNDAMENTALS SERIES
ESSENTIAL EXPLANATIONS AND SOLUTIONS

When you need an authoritative introduction to a key networking topic, **reach for a Cisco Press Fundamentals book**. Learn about network topologies, deployment concepts, protocols, and management techniques and **master essential networking concepts and solutions**.

1-57870-168-6

Look for Fundamentals titles at your favorite bookseller

802.11 Wireless LAN Fundamentals
ISBN: 1-58705-077-3

**Cisco CallManager Fundamentals:
A Cisco AVVID Solution**
ISBN: 1-58705-008-0

Cisco LAN Switching Fundamentals
ISBN: 1-58705-089-7

Cisco Unity Fundamentals
ISBN: 1-58705-098-6

Data Center Fundamentals
ISBN: 1-58705-023-4

IP Addressing Fundamentals
ISBN: 1-58705-067-6

IP Routing Fundamentals
ISBN: 1-57870-071-X

Network Security Fundamentals
ISBN: 1-58705-167-2

Storage Networking Fundamentals
ISBN: 1-58705-162-1

Voice over IP Fundamentals
ISBN: 1-57870-168-6

Coming in Fall 2005
**Cisco CallManager Fundamentals:
A Cisco AVVID Solution**, Second Edition
ISBN: 1-58705-192-3

Visit **www.ciscopress.com/series** for details about the Fundamentals series and a complete list of titles.

Cisco Press

Learning is serious business.

Invest wisely.

John F. Kennedy

Significant Figures in World History

John F. Kennedy

A Reference Guide to His Life and Works

Ian James Bickerton

ROWMAN & LITTLEFIELD
Lanham • Boulder • New York • London

Published by Rowman & Littlefield
An imprint of The Rowman & Littlefield Publishing Group, Inc.
4501 Forbes Boulevard, Suite 200, Lanham, Maryland 20706
www.rowman.com

6 Tinworth Street, London, SE11 5AL, United Kingdom

British Library Cataloguing in Publication Information Available

Library of Congress Cataloging-in-Publication Data

Names: Bickerton, Ian J., author.
Title: John F. Kennedy : a reference guide to his life and works / Ian James
   Bickerton.
Description: Lanham : Rowman & Littlefield, [2019] I Series: Significant
   figures in world history I Includes bibliographical references and index.
Identifiers: LCCN 2019016322 (print) I LCCN 2019018194 (ebook) I ISBN
   9781538120569 (Electronic) I ISBN 9781538120552 (cloth : alk. paper)
Subjects: LCSH: Kennedy, John F. (John Fitzgerald), 1917–1963—Encyclopedias. I
   United States—Politics and government—1961–1963—Encyclopedias.
Classification: LCC E841 (ebook) I LCC E841 .B53 2019 (print) I DDC
   973.922092 [B] —dc23
LC record available at https://lccn.loc.gov/2019016322

Contents

Preface

John Fitzgerald Kennedy's election as president in November 1960 and his assassination three years later in November 1963 were truly transformative events in the history of the United States. Not simply because Kennedy was a young and charismatic president, but because, as the first president to be born in the 20th century, his presidency marked the end of an era; it symbolized the end of the legacy of the 19th century. Many Americans saw in the dynamic, self-confident John "Jack" Kennedy the embodiment and standard bearer heralding the onset of "the American Century" that *Life* magazine owner Henry Luce had predicted. But it was not to be.

That unrealized outcome posed a tantalizing question that fascinates Americans and millions across the world to this day: just what would the United States be today if Kennedy had served two terms—as he, and others, had every right to anticipate? The poignancy of this central question is heightened by the assassination less than five years later of Jack's brother, Robert F. Kennedy. Once again, many Americans assumed that had Robert been elected president in 1968, he would have picked up Jack's torch and completed the unfinished business begun by his brother. Robert's death compounded the tragedy and loss of Jack.

The study of any president presents its own challenges to understanding the man and the office. That astute student of the constitution, former president Harry S. Truman, once observed: "The presidency is the most peculiar office in the world. There's never been one like

it." The president is both more and less than a king, and also more and less than a prime minister. He is alone at the top. And one of the main challenges in assessing a president's performance is the question of determining the factors that contribute to a president's decision. Quite simply, the solitary authority of the person in the Oval Office makes complete knowledge of the answer to this question impossible. John F. Kennedy himself readily acknowledged this reality: "The essence of ultimate decision remains impenetrable to the observer—often, indeed, to the decider himself."

I once asked Truman, long after he had left office: what had led him to recognize the state of Israel on 14 May 1948 on a de facto basis so quickly after the new state's declaration of independence, coming as it did just minutes after the announcement made by David Ben-Gurion? Truman's answer epitomized both the man and the power of his office: "Somebody had to do something," he said, "so I did it." And, of course, he could. Kennedy reflected on this question of decision making more than once. Less than four months before his murder, he wrote of the presidency: "No one in the country is more assailed by divergent advice and clamorous counsel. . . . There will always be the dark and tangled stretches in the decision-making process." Many other presidents have made similar observations about their decision making, but Truman, at least, did not appear to agonize as Kennedy did over his decisions. Once he had made a decision, he told me, he slept well, and he had few regrets.

Nevertheless, what we can say is that many of the characteristics of the office of president we witness in the early decades of the 21st century are very much the result of initiatives introduced during the short time of the Kennedy years. Kennedy expanded the authority of the executive—especially in relation to foreign relations—leading to the virtually unrestrained control exercised by recent incumbents in the White House. He increased the power of presidential advisors at the expense of traditional departmental heads. He made extensive use of modern media to reach out directly to the people, bypassing potential objections from congressional opponents.

Today's presidents are still addressing all the great issues of the 1960s that Kennedy faced—the struggle of equal rights for African Americans and for women, the challenges of ethnic diversity, the limitation and control of nuclear weapons, and the Cold War and its legacy. But above all—and this is perhaps what is lacking in today's America—John F. Kennedy used his extraordinary oratorical ability and the power of his office to reformulate and extoll the traditional values of the nation, giving pride, inspiration, and optimism to both Americans and to the world with an eloquence and conviction not heard for many years before or, for that matter, since, with, perhaps, the exception of Barack Obama. Those brief three years offered Americans a new beginning.

History is more than a collection of facts, names, and dates, and it is not written in a vacuum. Although John F. Kennedy and his administration, when preoccupied with foreign affairs, focused primarily on the Cold War, Cuba, and Vietnam, since the totally unexpected terrifying suicidal aircraft attacks on New York and Washington on 11 September 2001, successive U.S. administrations have shifted attention toward, and launched major military offensives upon, the nations of the Middle East—the region from which these devastating events originated. And since we are the heirs of the past, in the A–Z section of this volume, I have devoted some time to exploring Kennedy's tenuous relationships and policies with Middle Eastern countries to present a

historical context to assist in identifying the antecedents leading to 11 September 2001.

Preparing this reference guide has revived many memories of my time in the United States as a graduate student in the mid-1960s. I remember the 1964 election of Lyndon B. Johnson, the subsequent protests against the war in Vietnam, the assassinations of Martin Luther King and Bobby Kennedy, and the protests and race riots of summer 1968, with National Guardsmen and tanks on the streets in major American cities. I had worked as a volunteer for Robert Kennedy in the California primary, and his death, as well as that of King, and the increasing divisions and hatreds within the country led me to flee the United States to return to an academic position in Australia.

In this volume, I have attempted to capture the essence of this remarkable president. I have begun with a thorough chronology, followed by an introductory chapter. Individual alphabetized entries follow, covering people and events that constituted the political landscape in the Kennedy era. In this section, the subject of each entry is considered only in so far as it relates directly to John F. Kennedy. It is hoped that this volume is useful as a starting point for those wishing to increase their awareness of, and conduct research into, the 35th American president. The book also contains useful appendices, beginning with selected primary documents; followed by membership of the 87th and 88th Congresses, the U.S. Supreme Court, executive departments, regulatory commissions and independent agencies, and governors; and concludes with a selected bibliography.

In order to make this book as useful a reference tool as possible and to help locate information, extensive cross-references have been provided in the dictionary section.

Within individual entries, terms that have their own entries are in boldface type the first time they appear.

Related terms that have their own entries but are not used in the entry at hand are included as *See also* cross-references.

See cross-references direct the reader to the entries that deal with topics that do not have their own entries.

I would like to thank my good friend and colleague Joseph Siracusa of RMIT University, Melbourne, for his encouragement throughout my work on this project. Without his unstinting support, knowledge, and wisdom, I would never have completed the task. Numerous colleagues also added their suggestions as to what to include and exclude. Any errors are, of course, my own. I should also like to thank April Snider and Jessica McCleary for their close attention to the text and their support throughout the preparation of the work. I would also like to thank my partner, Jenny Learmont, who, with unfailing good grace, has allowed me to interrupt her own busy schedule.

Acronyms and Abbreviations

ABM	antiballistic missile
ACDA	Arms Control and Disarmament Agency
AFL-CIO	American Federation of Labor/Congress of Industrial Organizations
AID	Agency for International Development
AIM	American Indian Movement
AWOC	Agricultural Workers Organizing Committee
CACSW	Citizens Advisory Council on the Status of Women
CBS	Columbia Broadcasting System
CEA	Council of Economic Advisers
CIA	Central Intelligence Agency
COINTELPRO	Counterintelligence program
COMSAT	Communications Satellite Corporation
CORE	Congress of Racial Equality
EEC	European Economic Community
EEOC	Equal Employment Opportunity Commission
ERA	Equal Rights Amendment
ExComm	Executive Committee of the National Security Council
FAO	Food and Agriculture Organization
FBI	Federal Bureau of Investigation
FSM	Free Speech Movement
FTC	Federal Trade Commission
GCD	general and complete disarmament
GOP	Grand Old Party (Republican)
HHFA	Housing and Home Finance Agency
IAEA	International Atomic Energy Agency
ICBM	intercontinental ballistic missile
JFK	John Fitzgerald Kennedy
KGB	Soviet secret service
LBJ	Lyndon Baines Johnson
MAD	Mutual Assured Destruction
MFDP	Mississippi Freedom Democratic Party
MIRV	multiple independently targeted reentry vehicles
MIT	Massachusetts Institute of Technology
MLF	Multilateral Defense Force

MRBM	medium-range ballistic missile
NAACP	National Association for the Advancement of Colored People
NATO	North Atlantic Treaty Organization
NBC	National Broadcasting Corporation
NFWA	National Farm Workers Association
NLF	National Liberation Front (of South Vietnam)
NSC	National Security Council
OAS	Organization of American States
OEO	Office of Economic Opportunity
PCEEO	President's Committee on Equal Employment Opportunities
PCSW	Presidential Commission on the Status of Women
SALT I	Strategic Arms Limitation Treaty I
SAM	surface-to-air missile
SAS	Student Afro-American Society
SCLC	Southern Christian Leadership Conference
SDS	Students for a Democratic Society
SEATO	Southeast Asia Treaty Organization
SLBM	submarine-launched ballistic missile
SNCC	Student Nonviolent Coordinating Committee
SRBM	short-range ballistic missile
SWP	Socialist Workers Party
UAW	United Automobile Workers
UFWOC	United Farm Workers Organizing Committee
UN	United Nations
UNESCO	United Nations Educational, Scientific and Cultural Organization
VISTA	Volunteers in Service to America
WHO	World Health Organization

Chronology

JOHN F. KENNEDY'S CHILDHOOD AND EDUCATION

1917 29 May: John F. Kennedy (JFK) is born in Brookline, Massachusetts, the second of what would eventually be a family of nine children. His father, Joseph P. Kennedy Sr., was a banker, financier, and diplomat; his mother, Rose Fitzgerald, was a member of a prominent Boston family.

1917–1926 Kennedy lives at 83 Beals Street in Brookline and attends the Dexter school there.

1925 20 November: Robert F. Kennedy, JFK's brother, is born.

1926 The Kennedy family moves to New York City, residing at 252nd Street and Independence Avenue, Riverdale-on-Hudson. John "Jack" Kennedy attended fourth, fifth, and sixth grades at the Riverdale Country Day School.

1929 The family moves to Bronxville, New York, and Joseph P. Kennedy Sr. buys what becomes the main house in the Kennedy compound at Hyannis Port, Massachusetts.

1930 Kennedy spends one year at a Catholic preparatory school, Canterbury, in New Milford, Massachusetts.

1931 At the age of 14, he enrolls at Choate, a private school in Wallingford, Connecticut.

1932 Edward M. Kennedy, JFK's brother, is born.

1935 Kennedy graduates from Choate, 64th in a class of 112. He goes to England that summer to study at the London School of Economics but returns prematurely to the United States because of an attack of jaundice. JFK enters Princeton University but drops out in December after a recurrence of jaundice.

1936 JFK enrolls at Harvard University; he is more excited by sport than academic subjects. He joins the undergraduate newspaper, the *Crimson*, but is not very interested in politics.

1937 June–August: Kennedy tours Europe with a close friend from Choate. He visits France, Spain, and Italy, where he has an audience with the pope. Upon his return to Harvard, he becomes more interested in his studies, particularly international relations. **December:** Joseph P. Kennedy Sr. is appointed as the ambassador to the United Kingdom by President Franklin D. Roosevelt.

1938 29 May: JFK receives a $1 million trust fund established by his father upon reaching the age of 21.

1939 JFK spends the second semester of his junior year at Harvard in Europe, traveling in Poland, Russia, Turkey, Germany, and France. He also works briefly in his father's embassy office in London.

1940 21 June: Kennedy graduates from Harvard cum laude with a BS degree. In order to obtain honors in his major field, political science, he writes an undergraduate thesis titled "Appeasement in Europe." **July:** His honors thesis is published as *Why England Slept*, a critical analysis of Britain's apathy and lack of military preparedness before World War II. The book receives praise from reviewers and becomes a best seller. **Fall:** JFK enrolls at Stanford University for graduate study in business and quits after six months.

1941 February: JFK travels throughout South America.

WORLD WAR II

1941 September: Prior to the Japanese attack on Pearl Harbor, Kennedy enlists in the United States Navy.

1943 March: JFK is given command of PT-109 based at Tulagi in the Solomon Islands with the rank of lieutenant. **2 August:** His torpedo boat is rammed by a Japanese destroyer in the South Pacific. For heroism in rescuing an injured man and leading his crew to safety, he was awarded the Purple Heart and Navy and Marine Corps Medal. **December:** Because of malaria and a recurring back injury, he returns to the United States.

1944 12 August: JFK's brother, Joseph P. Kennedy Jr., the oldest son in the family, is killed while piloting an airplane over England.

1945 April: JFK receives an honorable discharge from the U.S. Navy. **June:** As a special correspondent for the *New York Journal-American*, he covers the San Francisco conference founding the United Nations (UN). He ends his journalistic career after reporting on the British elections from London that same summer.

CONGRESS

1946 June: Kennedy enters upon his political career by winning the Democratic nomination for congressman from Massachusetts' Eleventh District. **5 November:** He is elected to Congress.

1947 January: At 29, JFK takes a seat in the House of Representatives and then serves three terms. **4 June:** He is one of 79 congressmen to vote against the Taft-Hartley bill. (Kennedy generally favored President Truman's domestic policies in the areas of social welfare; on taxation and business regulation, he was progressive. On the economy and efficiency in government, he was conservative, and on civil liberties, he was ambivalent.)

1949 25 January: In a speech in Congress, JFK attacks President Harry S. Truman's foreign policy for having let China "fall" to the communists. **February:** He attacks the administration for inadequate military and defense spending.

1952 April: Kennedy announces he will seek the senate seat held by Henry Cabot Lodge Jr. His brothers and family assist him in his campaign. **4 November:** He defeats Lodge to become the U.S. senator from Massachusetts. Dwight D. Eisenhower is elected president.

1953 31 July: JFK's brother Robert resigns as a lawyer-investigator for Joseph McCarthy's Senate subcommittee. (The liberal record of both Kennedys was later hurt by this connection with the controversial McCarthy.) **12 September:** Kennedy marries Jacqueline Bouvier.

1954 21 October: JFK enters a Manhattan hospital for a back operation.

1955 February: Kennedy undergoes a second back operation. While convalescing, he writes *Profiles in Courage*, a book of brief biographies of courageous American politicians. The book is published in 1956 and wins the Pulitzer Prize for Biography in 1957.

1956 August: Kennedy nominates Adlai Stevenson II for president at the Democratic National Convention. JFK loses to Estes

Kefauver in his bid for the vice presidential nomination.

1957 27 November: JFK becomes a father for the first time with the birth of a daughter, Caroline Bouvier Kennedy.

1958 4 November: Kennedy is reelected to a second term as senator by nearly one million votes.

PRESIDENCY

1960 2 January: JFK holds a press conference where he states, "I am announcing today my candidacy for the presidency of the United States." **9 January:** Vice President Richard M. Nixon announces his candidacy for the Republican presidential nomination. **1 February:** Civil rights demonstrators begin a sit-in movement to integrate public accommodations in Greensboro, North Carolina. **8 March:** JFK wins the New Hampshire Democratic primary with a record 42,969 votes. **5 April:** JFK wins the Wisconsin Democratic presidential primary by a four-to-three margin over Senator Hubert H. Humphrey. **8 April:** The Senate invokes cloture and, by a vote of 71–18, passes a civil rights bill that gives increased authority to the federal courts and Civil Rights Commission to prevent the intimidation of black voters in the South. **26 April:** JFK wins the Pennsylvania Democratic presidential primary by 49,838 votes. **5 May:** An American U-2 spy plane is downed over the Soviet Union. **10 May:** JFK defeats Humphrey in the West Virginia Democratic primary by 77,305 votes. Humphrey withdraws from the presidential race. **20 May:** JFK wins the Oregon primary over Senator Wayne Morse. **13 July:** JFK wins the Democratic presidential nomination on the first ballot at the Los Angeles convention. (The vote is 806 for Kennedy, 409 for his chief rival, Lyndon B. Johnson. Johnson is chosen as vice presidential candidate at the following session.) **25 July:** Richard M. Nixon easily wins the Republican presidential nomination on the first ballot in Chicago. **9 August:** The United Nations Security Council orders Katanga Province to end its secession

from the Congo. **12 September:** JFK delivers a speech in Houston facing the Catholic issue: "Contrary to common newspaper usage, I am not the Catholic candidate for President. I am the Democratic Party's candidate for President." **26 September:** Kennedy and Nixon hold the first of four televised debates between the presidential candidates, which are the first televised presidential debates. **8 November:** Kennedy defeats Nixon in the presidential election by 113,057 votes out of 68,000,000 and receives 303 of the 537 electoral votes. Nixon received 219; Senator Harry F. Byrd (D-Va.), 15. JFK is the youngest man and the first Catholic to be elected president. **14 November:** Kennedy meets with Vice President Nixon at Key Biscayne, Florida. **17 November:** The Central Intelligence Agency (CIA) briefs Kennedy on its involvement in training Cuban exiles in Guatemala to overthrow Fidel Castro. **18 November:** President Dwight D. Eisenhower orders U.S. naval units to patrol Central American waters to prevent potential communist-led invasions of either Guatemala or Nicaragua. **25 November:** John F. Kennedy Jr. is born.

1961 3 January: The United States breaks off diplomatic relations with Cuba. **4 January:** The Organization of American States votes to impose limited economic sanctions against the Dominican Republic. **17 January:** In his farewell address, Eisenhower warns against the influence of a "military-industrial complex." **19 January:** JFK has his last meeting with President Eisenhower where Southeast Asia and Cuba are discussed. **20 January:** Kennedy is inaugurated as the 35th president of the United States; he is the first president to be born in the 20th century. **21 January:** Kennedy names his cabinet appointees: State Department, Dean Rusk; Treasury, C. Douglas Dillon; Defense, Robert S. McNamara; Attorney General, Robert F. Kennedy; Postmaster General, J. Edward Day (replaced by John A. Gronouski, 30 September 1963); Interior, Stewart L. Udall; Agriculture, Orville Freeman; Commerce, Luther Hodges; Labor, Arthur J. Goldberg (replaced by W. Willard Wirtz, 31 August 1962); and Health, Education

and Welfare, Abraham Ribicoff (replaced by Anthony J. Celebrezze, 31 July 1962). He also names his presidential staff appointees: David Bell, budget director; McGeorge Bundy, special assistant for national security affairs; Richard Goodwin, assistant special counsel to the president; Lawrence O'Brien, special assistant for legislative liaison; Kenneth O'Donnell, appointments secretary; Pierre Salinger, press secretary; Arthur Schlesinger Jr., special assistant on Latin American affairs; Theodore Sorensen, special counsel to the president; Walt M. Rostow, deputy special assistant to the president for national security; Jerome B. Wiesmer, science advisor; Walter Heller, head of the Council of Economic Advisors; and Ralph Dungan, special assistant in charge of personnel. JFK's other key appointments include Chester A. Bowles, undersecretary of state; George W. Ball, undersecretary for economic affairs; Robert V. Roosa, undersecretary for monetary affairs; H. H. Fowler, undersecretary of the Treasury; Adolf A. Berle Jr., special adviser on Latin American affairs and chairman of the Latin American Task Force; Edward R. Murrow, head of the United States Information Agency; Newton N. Minow, chairman of the Federal Communications Commission; Averell Harriman, ambassador at large; Adlai Stevenson II, ambassador to the United Nations; George McGovern, director of the Food for Peace Program; Thomas K. Finletter, United States representative to NATO; Glenn T. Seaborg, chairman of the Atomic Energy Commission; and James E. Webb, head of the National Aeronautics and Space Administration. **25 January:** In his first presidential news conference, JFK supports the idea of a neutral Laos. **28 January:** Kennedy approves a South Vietnam counterinsurgency plan that calls for government reform and military restructuring as the basis for expanded U.S. assistance. **30 January:** JFK delivers his first State of the Union message stressing dangers abroad and economic problems at home. **7 February:** Kennedy orders a ban on most trade with Cuba. **16 February:** JFK warns of the risk of war if Belgium takes unilateral action in the Congo. **20 February:** In a special message to Congress, he asks for a five-year, $5.625

billion program of federal aid to education. **1 March:** Kennedy establishes the Peace Corps by executive order and names his brother-in-law, R. Sargent Shriver Jr., as director. **6 March:** JFK issues an executive order establishing the Committee on Equal Employment Opportunity. **13 March:** He proposes that Latin America join the United States in an Alliance for Progress, a 10-year, $20 billion program of economic and social development. **21 March:** Great Britain, the United States, and the Soviet Union resume their three-power nuclear test ban conference in Geneva, Switzerland. **23 March:** In a televised news conference, Kennedy discusses the situation in Laos. **28 March:** JFK announces the initiation of a program to rapidly increase U.S. military strength. **12 April:** Soviet cosmonaut Yuri Gagarin becomes the first man to orbit the Earth. **17 April:** CIA-trained Cuban exiles begin the Bay of Pigs invasion. **20 April:** Cuba reports the defeat and capture of the invasion force. **24 April:** Kennedy accepts full responsibility for the Cuban invasion. **5 May:** JFK signs a bill raising the minimum wage from $1.00 to $1.25 per hour, extending coverage to more than four million Americans. Alan B. Shepard makes the first U.S. manned suborbital flight. **9–15 May:** Vice President Johnson visits Southeast Asia and recommends a "strong program of action" in Vietnam. **14 May:** A Freedom Riders' bus is stoned and burned in Anniston, Alabama. **21 May:** Four hundred U.S. marshals are sent to Alabama after 20 people are hurt in racial violence stemming from the Freedom Rides. **25 May:** Kennedy asks Congress for $1.8 billion to expand the space program and calls for a manned lunar landing by 1970. **31 May–6 June:** JFK meets with British and French leaders in Europe. **3–4 June:** Kennedy and Khrushchev hold an inconclusive summit meeting in Vienna. **9 June:** President Ngo Dinh Diem requests U.S. troops for training the South Vietnamese army. **30 June:** Kennedy signs a bill liberalizing Social Security benefits for 4.4 million people; he also signs a housing bill offering wide-ranging assistance to home buyers. **20 July:** Kennedy signs a bill doubling federal efforts to halt water pollution. **25 July:** JFK calls for $3.25

billion to meet commitments in the wake of the Berlin crisis and asks Congress for the power to increase the size of the armed forces by 217,000. **13 August:** East Germany seals its border with West Berlin to halt the flow of refugees to the West. Work begins on the Berlin Wall. **16 August:** The United States and 19 other American countries adopt the Alliance for Progress charter at Punta del Este, Uruguay. **18–21 August:** Vice President Johnson visits Berlin to reaffirm the U.S. commitment there. U.S. troops are stationed in West Berlin. **30 August:** The House votes 242–170 against consideration of the administration's school aid bill. **September–December:** East Germany hampers U.S. access to East Berlin. **1 September:** The Soviet Union resumes atmospheric nuclear tests. **5 September:** Kennedy announces that the United States will resume underground nuclear tests. Following several mid-air hijackings, Kennedy signs a bill making the crime of airplane hijacking punishable by death or imprisonment. **11 September:** Congress approves a two-year extension of the Civil Rights Commission. **16 September:** The United States backs UN military action in Katanga (the Congo). **20 September:** The Agency for International Development (AID) is created; Nancy Fowler Hamilton is named its head. **25 September:** Kennedy delivers a "Proposal for General and Complete Disarmament in a Peaceful World" in a major foreign policy address to the UN. **26 September:** JFK signs a bill establishing the U.S. Arms Control and Disarmament Agency. **1 October:** South Vietnam requests a bilateral defense treaty with the United States. **4 October:** An international group of protestors urging unilateral disarmament and an end to nuclear testing demonstrates in Moscow. **27 October:** U.S. and Soviet tanks confront each other at the Berlin border; they withdraw the next day. **1 November:** Fifty thousand demonstrators turn out in 60 U.S. cities for the Women Strike for Peace. **3 November:** After a trip to South Vietnam, General Maxwell Taylor reports to Kennedy that prompt U.S. military, economic, and political action can lead to victory without a U.S. takeover of the war. **26 November:** The "Thanksgiving Day Massacre" results in a

major high-level reorganization of the State Department. Chester Bowles is replaced by George Ball as undersecretary of state. **7 December:** The United States begins its transport of UN troops to the Congo to end Katanga's secession. **15 December:** Kennedy renews the U.S. commitment to preserve the independence of South Vietnam and pledges U.S. assistance to its defense effort. **15–17 December:** With his wife, Jacqueline, Kennedy makes a triumphant goodwill tour to Puerto Rico, Venezuela, and Colombia. **20 December:** The *New York Times* reports that 2,000 U.S. uniformed troops and specialists are stationed in Vietnam.

1962 2 January: The United States begins a series of diplomatic "probes" of Moscow regarding Berlin. **6 January:** The United States resumes diplomatic ties with the Dominican Republic after a 14-month suspension. **16 January:** The United States and Common Market agree to mutual tariff reductions. **21 January:** In a 264–150 decision, the House votes down an administration plan to create an urban affairs and housing department. **29 January:** The United States, the Soviet Union, and Great Britain nuclear test ban conference at Geneva adjourns after a three-year period; talks remain deadlocked. **3 February:** Kennedy orders a near complete end to U.S. trade with Cuba. **8 February:** The Defense Department announces the creation of a Military Assistance Command in South Vietnam with General Paul D. Haskins as commander. **14 February:** JFK announces that U.S. troops in South Vietnam are instructed to use weapons for defensive purposes. **20 February:** John Glenn becomes the first American to orbit the Earth. **26 February:** The U.S. Supreme Court holds that no state can require racial segregation of interstate or intrastate transportation. **1 March:** In the biggest antitrust case in U.S. history, a federal district court orders E. I. du Pont de Nemours and Company to divest itself of 63 million shares of General Motors stock. **2 March:** Kennedy announces his decision to resume atmospheric nuclear tests. **14 March:** The 17-nation UN disarmament conference opens in Geneva. **18 March:** In a message to

Khrushchev, Kennedy proposes the joint exploration of outer space. **19 March:** Michael Harrington's *The Other America: Poverty in the United States* is published. **22 March:** The United States begins its involvement in the Vietnam Strategic Hamlet (rural pacification) Program. **26 March:** The U.S. Supreme Court holds that the distribution of seats in state legislatures is subject to the constitutional scrutiny of the federal courts. **29 March:** The Federal Bureau of Investigation arrests Billie Sol Estes on fraud charges. **31 March:** The United Steelworkers Union and U.S. Steel Corporation formally ratify a pact providing for a 10-cent-per-hour fringe benefit increase. The agreement is the most modest contract improvement since 1942. **3 April:** The Defense Department orders the integration of all military reserve units except the National Guard. **10 April:** The U.S. Steel Corporation announces a $6-per-ton steel price increase; other steel companies follow suit. **13 April:** Reacting to administration pressure, the major steel companies rescind their price increases. **25 April:** The United States opens a nuclear test series in the air over the Pacific. **9 May:** The Senate votes, 43–53, to reject cloture on a bill outlawing literacy tests in federal elections. **15 May:** Kennedy orders 5,000 Marines and 50 jet fighters to Thailand in response to communist insurgency in Laos. **24 May:** Scott Carpenter becomes the second American to orbit the Earth. **25 May:** The American Federation of Labor/Congress of Industrial Organizations (AFL-CIO) announces a drive for a 25-hour work week to reduce unemployment. **28 May:** Shares on the New York Stock Exchange lose $20.8 billion in the biggest one-day drop in prices since 1929. **June:** Students for a Democratic Society (SDS) adopts the "Port Huron Statement" in its second annual convention, held at Port Huron, Michigan. **25 June:** The Supreme Court outlaws an official New York State school prayer. **29 June:** JFK and his wife embark on a three-day state visit to Mexico; they are received by President Lopez Mateos and an enthusiastic Mexican people. **10 July:** Telstar relays live pictures from the United States to Europe. **17 July:** The Senate votes, 52–48, to table a compromise Medicare plan.

23 July: Fourteen nations sign the Geneva Accords guaranteeing the neutrality of Laos. **25 July:** Kennedy approves a Puerto Rican plebiscite on the political status of the island. **26 July:** JFK signs a bill providing for public welfare laws emphasizing family rehabilitation and training instead of dependency. **July–August:** Martin Luther King Jr. leads a series of unsuccessful demonstrations in Albany, Georgia, for the integration of public facilities. **14 August:** The Senate, in a 63–27 vote, invokes cloture for the first time since 1927; the move ends a liberal filibuster against the president's communications satellite bill. **27 August:** Congress approves a constitutional amendment barring poll tax requirements for voting in federal elections. **14 September:** Kennedy signs a $900 million public works bill. **24 September:** The House of Representatives grants Kennedy's request for special limited power to call up to 150,000 reservists for one year and to extend active duty tours without declaring a state of emergency. **1 October:** Three thousand troops quell Mississippi rioting and arrest 200 people as James Meredith enrolls at the University of Mississippi. Arthur J. Goldberg is appointed associate justice of the Supreme Court. **2 October:** The United States bars its ports to all ships carrying cargoes to Cuba. Kennedy signs a bill authorizing a $100 million UN loan. **11 October:** Kennedy signs the Trade Expansion Act, which reduces tariffs and gives the president greater discretionary power in making trade agreements. **14 October:** U.S. intelligence receives the first photographic evidence of Soviet offensive missiles in Cuba. **22 October:** Kennedy announces a "quarantine" of Cuba to force the removal of Soviet missiles. **28 October:** Soviet premier Nikita Khrushchev agrees to dismantle the Soviet missiles in Cuba and withdraw Russian weapons under UN supervision. **2–10 November:** The United States supplies emergency military aid to India in its border war with communist China. **6 November:** The Democrats increase their Senate majority by four but lose six House seats in the midterm election. JFK's brother Edward M. Kennedy wins the Massachusetts Senate seat. Richard M. Nixon loses the California gubernatorial race. **20 November:** The United

States lifts its naval blockade of Cuba. Kennedy signs an executive order banning racial discrimination in housing built or purchased with federal funds. **24 November:** The Pentagon awards General Dynamics the F-111 (TFX) fighter/bomber contract. **21 December:** Kennedy and Prime Minister Harold Macmillan sign the Nassau pact, granting Great Britain Polaris missiles and pledging the commitment of U.S. and British atomic weapons to a multilateral NATO nuclear force. **31 December:** The United States cancels the joint U.S.–Great Britain Skybolt missile project.

1963   January: UN troops reunify the Congo. **14 January:** Kennedy delivers State of the Union address calling for tax reform and tax cuts. **24 January:** JFK proposes a $13.6 billion tax cut over a three-year period. **26 January:** The Senate Permanent Investigations Subcommittee begins a probe of the TFX contract award. **1 February:** Secretary of State Rusk announces authorization of resumption of underground nuclear tests in Nevada. **21 February:** Kennedy proposes a hospital insurance plan to be financed through Social Security. **24 February:** A Senate panel reports that annual U.S. aid to South Vietnam is $400 million and that 12,000 Americans are stationed there "on dangerous assignment." **28 February:** Kennedy sends a civil rights message to Congress that stresses the need to ensure blacks have the right to vote. **15 March:** Kennedy signs the $435 million Manpower and Development Act. **19 March:** In a San José, Costa Rica, meeting, Kennedy and six Latin American presidents pledge resistance to Soviet aggression in the Western Hemisphere. **28 March:** A federal jury convicts Billie Sol Estes of mail fraud and conspiracy. **1 April:** A federal grand jury indicts the U.S. Steel Corporation and six other manufacturers for price fixing. **2 April:** Led by Martin Luther King Jr., the Southern Christian Leadership Conference begins an integration campaign in Birmingham, Alabama. **9 April:** Wheeling Steel Corporation announces a $6-per-ton price increase. Other major steel companies follow suit. **10 April:** The U.S. atomic submarine *Thresher* is lost with 129 crewmen aboard. **22 April:** Twenty-two

units of the 7th Fleet are sent to the Gulf of Siam as a "precautionary" measure during fighting in Laos. **2–7 May:** Major civil rights demonstrations take place in Birmingham, Alabama. Police assaults and arrests lead to black riots. **9 May:** Birmingham leaders announce an agreement calling for the phased integration of business facilities and the establishment of a permanent biracial committee. **11 May:** Kennedy and Prime Minister Lester Pearson announce a joint defense agreement. Canada agrees to accept nuclear warheads for missiles located in its territory. **12 May:** Kennedy dispatches federal troops to bases near Birmingham, Alabama, when riots break out there. **20 May:** The Supreme Court rules that state and local governments cannot interfere with peaceful sit-in demonstrations for racial integration in public places of business. **27 May:** The Supreme Court prohibits an "indefinite delay" in the desegregation of public schools. **31 May:** Police in Jackson, Mississippi, arrest 600 black children involved in an integration demonstration. **10 June:** Kennedy signs a bill requiring employers subject to the Fair Standards Act to pay equal wages for equal work, regardless of the sex of the worker. He also delivers a major policy address at American University calling for a reexamination of Cold War attitudes and announces new test ban negotiations with Moscow. **11 June:** The first African Americans enroll at the University of Alabama over the protest of Governor George C. Wallace. **12 June:** Medgar W. Evers, field secretary for the Mississippi chapter of the National Association for the Advancement of Colored People (NAACP), is murdered following mass demonstrations in Jackson, Mississippi. **17 June:** The Supreme Court prohibits the use of the Lord's Prayer and Bible reading in public schools. **19 June:** Kennedy asks Congress to enact extensive civil rights legislation to give all citizens equal opportunity in employment, public accommodations, voting, and education. **26 June:** On a visit to West Berlin, Kennedy delivers his "Ich bin ein Berliner" address, which promises continued support of that city. **8 July:** The United States bans virtually all financial transactions with Cuba in a move toward economic isolation of

that country. **12 July:** Modified martial law is imposed in Cambridge, Maryland, after racial strife in that city. **15 July:** The United States, Great Britain, and the Soviet Union open disarmament talks in Moscow. **18 July:** The United States and Mexico agree on a settlement of the disputed El Chamizal border area between El Paso, Texas, and Ciudad Juárez, Chihuahua. **18–19 July:** The United States suspends relations with, and aid to, Peru following a military coup. **25 July:** The United States, the Soviet Union, and Great Britain initial a test ban treaty in Moscow that prohibits nuclear testing in the atmosphere, space, and under water. **2 August:** The United States cuts off all economic assistance to Haiti to show its disapproval of the dictatorial government of François Duvalier. **7 August:** A son, Patrick Bouvier Kennedy, is born to the president and Mrs. Kennedy. **9 August:** Patrick Bouvier Kennedy dies. **21 August:** The South Vietnam government attacks Buddhist Pagodas. **28 August:** More than 200,000 participate in the March on Washington and hear Martin Luther King Jr. deliver his "I Have a Dream" speech. **30 August:** The Washington-Moscow hotline is made operational. **10 September:** Kennedy federalizes the Alabama National Guard to prevent its use against the desegregation of public schools. **15 September:** A bomb blast in a Birmingham, Alabama, church kills four African American girls. **20 September:** Kennedy addresses the United Nations General Assembly and proposes cooperation with the Soviet Union, including outer space exploration. **24 September:** The Senate, 80–19, ratifies the Limited Nuclear Test Ban Treaty. **24–28**

September: Kennedy visits 11 western states to encourage stronger conservation measures. **25 September:** Following a successful military coup against President Juan Bosch, the United States suspends diplomatic relations and economic aid to the Dominican Republic. **10 October:** Kennedy signs a bill controlling possibly hazardous drugs such as thalidomide. **11 October:** The final report of the President's Commission on the Status of Women is presented. **24 October:** Kennedy signs the Maternal and Child Health and Mental Retardation Bill. **1 November:** South Vietnamese generals stage a successful coup. President Diem and Ngo Dinh Nhu are assassinated. **21 November:** Kennedy requests economic advisors prepare "War on Poverty" programs for 1964. **22 November:** Kennedy is assassinated in Dallas, Texas, by Lee Harvey Oswald; he is the youngest president to die in office. Lyndon B. Johnson is sworn in as the 36th president of the United States. **23 November:** Jack Ruby kills Oswald in Dallas. The incident is seen live on television. **25 November:** Kennedy is given a state funeral in Washington and burial with full military honors in the Arlington National Cemetery; the ceremony is attended by many foreign dignitaries, including heads of state, and watched on television by millions of Americans. **29 November:** The Warren Commission is set up to investigate the assassination of Kennedy.

1964 September: The Warren Commission concludes that the shots that killed Kennedy and wounded Governor John Connally were fired by Oswald acting alone.

Introduction

John Fitzgerald Kennedy began his administration with a clarion cry to Americans to ask not what their country could do for them but what they could do for their country. A thousand days later it ended with a stunned and bereft nation asking how it had come to this; that their young, charismatic, and energetic leader had been slain by an assassin—one of their own. Reflecting on Kennedy's brief time in office on Sunday, 24 November 1963, Daniel P. Moynihan observed on American television: "I don't think there is any point in being Irish if you don't know that the world is going to break your heart eventually. I guess we thought we had a little more time. So did he."

It is perhaps ironic that John F. Kennedy appears to have been more loved and esteemed outside the United States than within the nation. In 1990, a consortium from the Danish business community commissioned a number of huge commemorative tapestries be made tracing the history of Denmark from its beginning as a Viking nation to the present, to be hung in the Great Hall of Christiansborg Palace in Copenhagen to celebrate the Queen's 50th birthday. There are 17 tapestries altogether, designed by the artist Bjørn Nørgaard, and are collectively known as Bjørn Nørgaard's History of Denmark; they were hung in the year 2000. In a large panel depicting the major events and individuals of the 20th century, there are only two Americans presented—together with other world leaders including Mao Zedong, Vladimir Lenin, Winston Churchill, Charles de Gaulle, and Mahatma Gandhi, to name a few. The two Americans are Woodrow Wilson and John F. Kennedy—not Franklin D. Roosevelt with his "New Deal" to fight the Great Depression of the 1930s; not Dwight D. Eisenhower who led the victorious Allied armies that liberated Europe from Hitler; not even Harry S. Truman whose decision to drop the atomic bombs on Japan must surely rank among the most momentous and earthshattering actions of any American president before or since—but, instead, we see John F. Kennedy. Wilson we can understand—the president who arrived to a hero's welcome in Paris at the end of World War I; the man who brought us the Fourteen Points and the League of Nations. But Kennedy's presence in this truly amazing tapestry demonstrates the impact and power of charisma and hope over the prosaic realities of U.S. politics. Surrounding himself with the best and the brightest, Kennedy projected the aura of a modern King Arthur and declared himself a Berliner. He promised Europeans a Grand Strategy that would set the United States and Europe upon a new path to peace and prosperity—but it was a promise cruelly cut short by his untimely death.

Assessing or summarizing the life, character, and achievements of John F. Kennedy is a daunting task, partly because his life, and his term as president, was cut so short, partly because he was an enigmatic, complex person, but mainly, perhaps, because most of the early commentators who engaged in this enterprise were so partisan as to render their views of little real value. Some, Kennedy's enemies, saw a rich, entitled young man—under the abiding influence of a domineering, womanizing father and an emotionally distant, strictly Catholic

mother—who remained a reckless playboy throughout his life. Others—Kennedy's advisers, close friends, and colleagues—created the image of a president presiding over a modern-day Camelot, in which everything was bright and rosy.

In January 1962, however, one astute observer, theologian Thomas Merton, a friend of the president's sister-in-law, Ethel Kennedy, and regarded by many as the leading spiritual writer of his generation, wrote presciently of his president and fellow Catholic, John Kennedy:

> I have little confidence in Kennedy, I think he cannot measure up to the magnitude of his task, and lacks creative imagination and the deeper kind of sensitivity that is needed. Too much the *Time* and *Life* mentality, than which I can imagine nothing further, in realty, from, say Lincoln. What is needed is really not shrewdness or craft, but what the politicians don't have; depth, humanity and a certain totality of self-forgetfulness and compassion, not just for individuals but for man as a whole: a deeper kind of dedication. Maybe Kennedy will break through into that someday by miracle. But such people are before long marked out for assassination.

That prophecy may well be the story of the life and times of John F. Kennedy. George Ball, who served under Kennedy first as undersecretary of state for economic affairs and then as undersecretary of state, later recalled that the sense of ever-present doom proved especially poignant for John Kennedy. It was especially strong during Kennedy's early weeks in the White House, Ball noted, as the president felt critically menaced both by enemies abroad and adversaries at home. Kennedy lacked his predecessor's high reputation for military command, while his limited electoral victory in 1960 cast doubt on the breadth of his mandate.

John F. Kennedy displayed all the strengths and weaknesses said of him, and more that were unsaid. He was both reckless and courageous; he exuded vitality while suffering chronic ill health and experiencing intense physical pain. He could be charming and brutal, witty and boring. Although he maintained an outward appearance of aplomb and invulnerability, he never forgot that the American people were comparing him with Eisenhower, a looming father figure whose established reputation not only for overwhelming military but also for political victories had given him political self-assurance. Kennedy's political assets were far less impressive. In Congress, his reputation had been more for absenteeism than serious achievement. He had never belonged to the inner circle of senators; nor was he confident of an always capricious public support. His major political assets were his good looks and the glamour of a golden boy with a glamorous, beautiful young wife.

Much about John F. Kennedy's character, judgment, and accomplishments was hidden from the American public. The Kennedys made their own rules. The father, a prodigious philanderer, set an example for his sons. It was obvious that Jack's infidelity made his wife, Jacqueline Bouvier Kennedy, angry and unhappy, historian Robert Dallek reports, "but she chose to live with it." Apparently, she never confronted him with what she knew. The American public knew little of the president's disrespect and lack of consideration of the numerous women he slept with, belying the public picture of family harmony the White House projected. Had evidence of Kennedy's serial marital infidelities while president been made public and deemed unacceptable conduct, the course of American history, especially that of American women, may well have been dramatically altered. The public was unaware that his Pulitzer Prize–winning book *Profiles in Courage* was largely ghostwritten by his speechwriter Ted Sorensen, and that Kennedy's father, Joseph, had asked *New York Times* columnist Arthur Krock, his political adviser and a long-time member of the Pulitzer Prize board, to persuade others to vote for it. This was not the first time Krock had assisted a Kennedy publication at the request of Kennedy Sr. Krock, former Washington bureau chief of the *Times*, had redrafted Kennedy's Harvard college thesis, originally titled "Appeasement at Munich," into what became *Why England Slept.* Wiretapping of Martin Luther King Jr.

and the abuse of the Internal Revenue Service to discredit his political opponents were also kept secret from the public.

Jack Kennedy grew up in a dysfunctional family environment. His father, Joe Kennedy, was an overbearing, coarse, and unethical bully. He constantly humiliated Jack's mother, Rose, who simply endured their marriage. Rose was remote and distant. She was essentially an absent mother in terms of affection and warmth toward her nine children, and she regarded their upbringing as an exercise in management, devoid of any real warmth. The children were left in the charge of an endless succession of governesses. This emotionally deprived home environment doubtless contributed to Jack's later womanizing, which has been described as pathological in its intensity.

Almost everyone associated with Kennedy noted that he was a man driven by a desire for power and a determination to win. He had learned from his father that it was essential to be tough and act boldly. Yet in reality Kennedy suffered from ill health that required frequent injections of cortisone and other painkilling medications and often needed a supporting back-brace for his ongoing osteoporosis caused in part by the back injury he sustained in World War II. A sickly, scrawny boy in a large family that worshipped physical beauty and athletic prowess, Jack Kennedy nevertheless grew up spoiled and overprivileged. Though he lived through the Great Depression, he seemed unaware of it until his years at Harvard. Perhaps this cloistered existence is what dulled him to the needs and discontents of African Americans in his presidency—though this did not happen with his younger brother, Bobby. At an early age, Jack became accustomed to his father pulling strings for him. The deaths of his brother and sister accentuated this. His older brother, Joe, died over England (British radar upset the delicate wiring on his explosive-laden plane: the American bases in the South of England had turned their radar off but had not asked their allies to do the same). And he lost his favorite sister, Kathleen, a fellow rebel who defied her Catholic parents in marrying the Protestant heir to the Duke of Devonshire, in a plane crash in the Rhône Valley with her husband.

At the end of World War II, Kennedy was committed to the idea of preventing another war, and as a journalist for the Hearst press, he attended the San Francisco conference in April–May 1945 that created the United Nations. In his announcement of his candidacy for Congress on 22 April 1946, he declared his determination to work for peace. However, by 1954, in his second year in the Senate, he had succumbed to the rhetoric and practice of the Cold War. He urged an increase of the defense budget to guarantee "a clear margin of victory over our enemies." In 1960, he campaigned for the presidency on the promise to eliminate what he described as "a missile gap" despite an overwhelming superiority held by the United States.

Liberals, in particular, were cool toward Kennedy's candidacy. "Most liberals," Dallek writes, "subscribed to the view of Kennedy as an ambitious but superficial playboy with little more to commend him than his good looks and charm. On none of the issues most important to them—McCarthyism, Civil Rights and labor unions—had Jack been an outspoken advocate." Liberal hearts were with Hubert Humphrey and Adlai Stevenson. Jack Kennedy had grown up in a racially segregated United States, and he had shown little interest in redressing the discrimination toward, and the injustices experienced by, African Americans that were, by and large, taken for granted. In the 1950s, African Americans made up less than 5 percent of the population of Massachusetts and experienced de facto segregation. They were relegated to attending separate schools, eating in separate restaurants, shopping in separate department stores, and attending separate movie theaters—as they were in most states. Boston's public schools were not desegregated until 1965. There were only three or four African Americans in the U.S. House of Representatives during Kennedy's congressional years, and none in the Senate—nor any while he was president. Washington, D.C., itself, with a 35 percent (reaching 50 percent in 1957) African American population had begun the process of desegregation in the

early 1950s. Prior to running for president, John Kennedy seemed indifferent to the issue of race in the United States.

Kennedy was as pragmatic as he was ambitious. Whether his marriage to Jacqueline Bouvier in 1953 was a genuine love match is a matter of conjecture, but there is no doubt that it was a political master-stroke. Together with his father's wealth, and Jackie's beauty and prestigious Southern family, Kennedy knew that the 1960 election presented the best chance for a successful run at the presidency; otherwise, he reasoned, he would languish in the Senate for another eight years while his more senior, experienced colleagues occupied the White House.

John F. Kennedy was elected in the November 1960 presidential election with the narrowest of popular vote margins on record; Kennedy's margin was 118,000 votes out of 68.8 million cast—a plurality of less than 0.05 percent of the total vote. The electoral column was a different story, however, with a Kennedy margin of 303 to 219. The 1960 election was notable in that, for the first time, citizens in Hawaii and Alaska were able to vote in a presidential election; both had become states in 1959. Kennedy was one of the youngest presidents ever elected and the first candidate to rely heavily on television. As well as being the first president to be born in the 20th century, he was also the first Irish Catholic president. Kennedy faced considerable opposition because of concern over his Catholicism, but appearing before an influential gathering of Protestant ministers in Houston in September 1960, in a short address that Ted Sorensen thought was the most important of the campaign, he succeeded in neutralizing the religion question. He stated: "Contrary to common newspaper usage, I am not the Catholic candidate for president. I am the Democratic Party's candidate for president, who happens also to be a Catholic. I do not speak for my church on public matters, and the church does not speak for me."

The 1960 election was also a milestone in terms of the impact of television on electoral politics. In retrospect, the outcome of the election seems to have turned on the first televised debate between Senator Kennedy and Vice President Richard M. Nixon. Nixon, who had been vice president under President Eisenhower for eight years, and who had a number of notable achievements on his record, was a formidable, intelligent candidate with broad experience and a sophisticated understanding of foreign affairs. Kennedy's movie star good looks and smooth performance overshadowed the haggard, pale appearance of Nixon, who had recently been hospitalized, and who looked far less appealing to the television audience, having declined to use makeup. Those who heard the debate on the radio and did not see it were equally divided in their adjudication of the outcome between the two candidates. For those who saw the debate on television, Kennedy came out ahead by a substantial margin. In his nomination acceptance speech in Los Angeles in July 1960, Kennedy made it clear that his goal was to "get the country moving again." Americans, he said, stood "on the edge of a New Frontier—of the 1960s—a frontier of unknown opportunities and perils—a frontier of unfilled hopes and threats." In the elections of 1960, the Democrats retained control of Congress with a slightly reduced margin. However, Republicans and Southern Democrats in Congress (the conservative coalition) still outnumbered moderate and liberal Democrats, so Kennedy's task in gaining passage of his legislative program was not going to be easy.

The young, vibrant, eloquent 43-year-old Kennedy generated excitement and hope that he was committed to solving problems in new ways. In his inaugural speech of 20 January 1961, he declared, "We observe today not a victory of party but a celebration of freedom—symbolizing an end as well as a beginning, signifying renewal as well as change." In contrast to what many Americans saw as the aging and uninspiring administration that preceded him, Kennedy exemplified youth, energy, and innovation. Despite his cynicism, detachment, and cold-bloodedness, he projected an idealism that inspired many people to follow his example and go into politics. He gave politics the appearance of a noble endeavor. People were captivated by Kennedy's style, quick wit, and sense of humor—and by his good looks

and beautiful, talented wife. "I am the man who accompanied Jacqueline Kennedy to Paris," he once joked. People saw a cultured man who invited Robert Frost to read a specially written poem at his inauguration, and who asked Pablo Casals to play music at the White House. Thousands of young lawyers and others flocked to Washington to be part of the New Frontier; they joined the Peace Corps or the Agency for International Development.

Americans looked forward to economic progress, peace, and stability under the new president as a younger generation took the reins of government. Not surprisingly, Kennedy's immediate appointees were excited at the prospect of the next four years. Many were, or became, friends; Douglas Dillon, Arthur M. Schlesinger Jr., John Kenneth Galbraith, Robert McNamara, Joseph Alsop, and Phil and Kay Graham all socialized at dinner parties in Georgetown. However, Kennedy's presidency can be more accurately seen as a series of crises, some more serious than was apparent at the time. Although his years in Congress and the Senate had been undistinguished, during his presidential campaign Kennedy had stressed the need for a vigorous foreign policy to halt Soviet expansionism. He was very much a Cold War warrior. Despite his advocacy of diplomacy to resolve international issues, Kennedy was quick to threaten and use military force and increased defense expenditure by 13 percent. Knowing that there was no self-described "missile gap" and that the United States had a vastly superior nuclear capacity to the Soviet Union, he nevertheless expanded America's nuclear arsenal.

John F. Kennedy brought his own style of management to the presidency, but he did not alter the architecture of U.S. power he inherited. He embraced and strengthened it. He, like those who followed him, believed that the United States was the world's "indispensable nation." Following World War II, America's policy elites believed in a world in which there could be no way except the American Way. The architecture of the world order that Washington built after World War II was a global system that rested upon a delicate duality:

an idealistic community of sovereign nations equal under the rule of international law joined tensely, even tenuously, to an American imperium grounded in the realpolitik of its military and economic power. The United States helped form an international community that would promote peace and shared prosperity through such permanent institutions as the United Nations (1945), the International Monetary Fund (1945), and the General Agreement on Tariffs and Trade (1947), the predecessor to the World Trade Organization. To govern such a world order through the rule of law, Washington also helped establish the International Court of Justice at The Hague and would later promote both human rights and women's rights. In addition, Washington also strengthened its own military, diplomatic, economic (and clandestine) organizations to advance U.S. global dominion. An unmatched military circled the globe, using overseas bases and backed by the most formidable nuclear arsenal on the planet, as well as massive air and naval forces, and an unparalleled array of client armies. Complementing this military strength was an active worldwide diplomatic corps, working to promote close bilateral ties with allies like the United Kingdom, Australia, and others, as well as multilateral alliances like the North Atlantic Treaty Organization (NATO), the Southeast Asia Treaty Organization (SEATO), and the Organization of American States (OAS).

Kennedy's predecessor, Dwight D. Eisenhower, tended to delegate and share power with Congress and a broad-ranging government committee structure that reflected his military chain of command approach to policy making. Kennedy took office with a new vision for the presidency. He sought to concentrate as much power as possible, especially in foreign affairs, into his own hands. He was determined to use mass media (namely, television) to take his policies directly to the American people, employing his skills of persuasion, backroom maneuvering, and public prestige to implement his agenda. Days before he was sworn in as president, he outlined his approach to the National Press Club. Eisenhower had a "detached, limited concept of the presidency," he said. The 1960s, he asserted,

required a president to "place himself in the very thick of the fight . . . prepared to exercise the fullest powers of his office . . . to ensure enactment of that legislation—even when conflict is the result." Kennedy disbanded many of Eisenhower's committees and relied instead upon more informal groups made up of young, like-minded zealots who believed liberal democratic capitalism was engaged in a life-and-death struggle with communism and did not question the proposition that the American system was destined to prevail everywhere. Although the number of full-time White House staff remained roughly that of the Eisenhower administration (around 270–275), because of Kennedy's reliance upon special groups, the number of "special" advisers leapt from around 30 under Eisenhower to more than 100 with the new president. Kennedy filled the upper ranks of his administration with allies, such as his brother Robert, George Ball, Walt W. Rostow, and a small National Security Council staff under the direction of McGeorge Bundy, who were keen to wield American military muscle to deter "evil-doers" and expand America's empire. They continued along the path of sundry mistakes and moral compromises that marred U.S. policy from the 1940s through the 1960s and into the 1980s and beyond.

Kennedy may not have created the "Imperial Presidency"—a term coined by Arthur M. Schlesinger Jr. in his important best-selling book of that title published in 1973, in which he described the expansion of presidential power beyond that envisioned by the Founders, resulting in the exclusion of the Congress, the press, the public, and the Constitution in foreign policy decisions—but he certainly contributed to its consolidation and expansion. The imperial presidency was created in response to foreign policy issues, and, once established, it then extended into domestic issues. Kennedy took advantage of the trend begun in 1947, increasing presidential power over the federal budget with slight modifications by Congress thereby giving the president important controls over the economy and social priorities. In the decade after the Korean War, most liberal and conservative members of Congress agreed on presidential control of foreign policy.

One issue that dogged the imperial presidency was the key question of secrecy. As Schlesinger argues, secrecy appeals to leaders of nations that value openness and accountability because it enables them to withhold information from, and also to lie to, the public. Kennedy used this tool in the case of the Bay of Pigs operation and in his Vietnam policy. Perhaps the United States would have avoided those disasters had the public known of Central Intelligence Agency (CIA) activities during that period. On the other hand, Schlesinger defends Kennedy's handling of the 1962 Cuban missile crisis, arguing that it supports the view that independent and unilateral—even secret—presidential action in extreme circumstances is, at times, required.

Americans welcomed Kennedy's peace initiatives, the creation of the Peace Corps and the Alliance for Progress, and the accelerated and enlarged space program Kennedy announced. They were pleased with the way he handled the Cuban missile crisis and his approach to arms control and the agreement to limit nuclear testing. And they liked the Trade Expansion Act. In domestic policy, Kennedy was less a leader than his public image suggested. He was slow to embrace support for the civil rights of black Americans and the emerging women's movement. Nor did he do much in the way of initiating a national universal health care program.

John F. Kennedy was an eloquent and inspiring orator. He was fortunate to have a speech writer in Ted Sorensen, who was not only a highly gifted writer but also crafted Kennedy's speeches to match and highlight the cadences and the timbre of his voice using the alliteration and repetition that became the hallmark of Kennedy's addresses. Kennedy was also capable of mastering a long and complicated brief in an astonishingly short time. He was at his best when proclaiming a grandiose, ambitious program or advocating an idealistic, aspirational policy, although the execution rarely matched the promise. Who can forget his defiant and moving "Ich bin ein Berliner" declaration when visiting the Berlin

Wall in 1963 or his American University, Washington, DC, commencement address titled "A Strategy of Peace," delivered on Monday, 10 June 1963, in which he stated: "I realize that the pursuit of peace is not as dramatic as the pursuit of war. . . . But we have no more urgent task."

Within three months, the new president faced his first challenge in foreign policy. Kennedy had inherited a secret plan hatched by the CIA during the Eisenhower administration to overthrow the regime of Fidel Castro in Cuba. The plan involved sponsoring an invasion of Cuba by anti-Castro refugees. Since he had called for stronger anti-Castro actions during the election campaign, Kennedy quickly endorsed the plan himself. Although the chairman of the Senate Foreign Relations Committee, J. William Fulbright, urged him not to go ahead, he was assured by his own military advisers and the CIA that the chance of success was good. In the early hours of 17 April 1961, an "army" of roughly 2,000 Cuban refugees trained and equipped by the CIA landed at the Bahia de Cochinos (Bay of Pigs) on Cuba's southern coast. The plan was ill conceived and poorly executed. Castro's forces quickly overwhelmed the army of refugees. The accompanying popular uprising, which U.S. intelligence had confidently predicted, failed to materialize. The administration's cover story collapsed immediately, and it was clear that despite the president's denial of U.S. involvement, Washington was indeed behind the putative invasion. The situation deteriorated even further when the Soviet Union threatened all-out war if the United States should invade Cuba. Kennedy replied that America intended no military invasion. Castro, the target of the invasion and subsequent CIA assassination attempts, was politically strengthened through the ensuing crackdown on those suspected of disloyalty at home. Kennedy's misadventure cost American prestige dearly. Moreover, the president took the failure personally, harboring a sensitivity to the issue for the remainder of his presidency; the disaster subsequently became an important factor in how he viewed his options in the foreign policy crises for the rest of his time in office. Kennedy learned from the experience to keep tight control from the Oval Office.

Shortly after the Bay of Pigs invasion, Kennedy announced an Alliance for Progress (Alianza para el Progresso) for Latin America—essentially a continuation and expansion of the Latin American aid program launched in the closing months of the Eisenhower administration. The president envisaged a 10-year plan of economic development and social progress and reform that many characterized as a sort of Marshall Plan for Latin America. Despite the fanfare, the Alliance for Progress got off to a disappointingly slow start. Although the United States had disbursed more than $1.5 billion for such items as residential housing, hospitals, and schools, two years after its inauguration at Punta del Este the Alliance for Progress had made a relatively small contribution to the self-sustaining economic growth on which the eventual success of the program depended. In addition, entrenched resistance to reforms in landholding and taxation hindered the promotion of political democracy in the Western Hemisphere.

Kennedy had more success with the establishment of the Peace Corps, which enlisted idealistic young Americans to volunteer to work in humanitarian programs in Africa and Asia. He challenged Americans to contribute to national and international public service, calling in his inaugural address for Americans to form a "grand and global alliance" to fight tyranny, poverty, and disease. On 1 March 1961, Kennedy temporarily established the Peace Corps through Executive Order 10924 under the auspices of the Department of State and appointed his brother-in-law, R. Sargent Shriver Jr., to act as the Corps' first director at a token salary of $1 per year. In September 1961, shortly after Congress formally endorsed the Peace Corps by making it a permanent program, the first volunteers left to teach English in Ghana, the first black African nation to achieve independence (in 1957) and whose government had since become an outspoken advocate of anticolonialism. Contingents of volunteers soon followed to Tanzania and India. By the turn of the century, the Peace Corps had sent more than 170,000 American volunteers to more than 135 nations.

Seven weeks after the Bay of Pigs disaster, Kennedy's confidence was shaken when he met with Soviet premier Nikita Khrushchev in Vienna for a two-day conference to discuss East-West relations in Germany and Laos. Although the meeting was superficially businesslike, the situation was tense. Khrushchev stated that, unless the four occupying powers could agree on a peace treaty or treaties with Germany within six months, the Kremlin would conclude a separate treaty with Walter Ulbricht's East German regime and terminate the West's rights to traverse East German territory to access West Berlin. Such Soviet action would have totally undermined the viability of West Berlin as a Western outpost and a symbol of Western resolve. Despite being subjected to a boastful, bullying tirade from the Soviet leader, Kennedy refused to be intimidated. During a post-summit report to the nation in July, Kennedy reaffirmed the Western commitment to West Berlin, declaring that NATO countries would not allow the communists to drive them out of the city, an enclave of two million people living in freedom. To increase the flexible options available to the Western alliance, 45,000 U.S. troops were moved to Europe, and France and West Germany increased NATO forces. The Soviets canceled their time limit but, in the early hours of 13 August, began sealing the border between East and West Berlin with barbed wire and other fortifications. Over the coming months, a wall was built. Khrushchev's move had the desired effect of ending West Berlin's role as an escape route for those seeking to escape from communist East Germany; however, it did not constitute a direct threat to U.S. interests, and the U.S. response was a relatively mild protest. Khrushchev followed up by initiating a new series of nuclear tests in the atmosphere, ending an informal moratorium begun in 1958.

The year 1962 brought yet another, more serious challenge to Kennedy. By the end of 1961, the Cold War was heating up. The United States and the Soviet Union in October 1962 came face-to-face—or, as U.S. secretary of state Dean Rusk aptly put it, "eyeball to eyeball"—in what has often been described as the moment when the world was in most peril

of nuclear disaster. And on this occasion, Kennedy's decisive action promoted him to the leadership position that had eluded him during the previous year.

In May 1962, Khrushchev and Castro had conspired to ship Soviet nuclear missiles to Cuba, ostensibly intended to protect Cuba from a much-rumored U.S. invasion. In addition, they agreed that more than 40,000 Soviet troops would be sent to Cuba along with nuclear-capable bombers, battlefield nuclear weapons, and nuclear missiles capable of reaching most of the continental United States. The Soviets hoped in this way to neutralize the nuclear superiority of the United States, which in turn would strengthen their negotiating position on issues such as Berlin. During September, when informed of a buildup of defensive conventional weapons on the island, including advanced air defense systems and Soviet "technicians," Kennedy issued a statement that if any offensive weapons were found "the gravest consequences would arise." In mid-October, when American U-2 planes discovered missile installations capable of launching offensive missiles, Kennedy secretly summoned his top advisers—later known as ExComm (Executive Committee of the National Security Council)—to the White House to devise a response. By 21 October, Kennedy had settled on an interim response: a naval "quarantine" (in reality, a blockade) accompanied by an ultimatum that military action would follow if the missiles and their sites were not removed.

On the evening of 22 October 1962, reading the carefully crafted speech prepared for him by Sorensen, with one or two stumbles, Kennedy, in a somber and unemotional voice, announced the discovery of the existence in Cuba of Soviet missile sites under construction together with some offensive missiles in a televised address to an unprepared and stunned nation. There was no flamboyance, no amusing or witty ripostes; this was not a spoiled, carefree, and rich playboy speaking. This was a deadly serious, mature president, very conscious of his responsibilities. Denouncing the cloak of secrecy and deception under which the missiles had been spirited

into Cuba, Kennedy voiced a grave warning to the Kremlin: The United States would "regard any nuclear missile launched from Cuba against any nation in the Western Hemisphere as an attack by the Soviet Union on the United States requiring a full retaliatory response upon the Soviet Union." On 24 October, the world waited anxiously for the Soviet response to the quarantine/blockade. The world watched on television as some Soviet ships en route to Cuba voluntarily turned back or stopped dead in the water. Others, known to be carrying inoffensive cargoes, were allowed to proceed. Khrushchev did not challenge the blockade; Kennedy's strategy had worked. By 28 October, Khrushchev agreed to withdraw the "offensive weapons" in return for an American guarantee against a future invasion of Cuba. President Kennedy also secretly agreed to remove obsolete American Jupiter missiles in Turkey.

The Cuban missile crisis had unexpected flow-on effects. It provided renewed momentum for arms control efforts, as both Moscow and Washington recognized that they might not be so fortunate next time. After discovering the difficulty of communication in times of crisis, the White House and the Kremlin negotiated the so-called Hotline Agreement, signed in July 1963, which provided for special crisis-communication satellites between the superpowers. More significantly, the United States and the Soviet Union, together with Great Britain, concluded the Limited Nuclear Test Ban Treaty, which prohibited nuclear testing in the atmosphere, in outer space, and under water. This treaty has correctly been cited as the first real success in limiting the arms race.

With regard to Europe, Kennedy sought to strengthen the Western alliance. He formulated a Grand Design for Europe, which would enable a flexible Western defense in a time of crisis using allied conventional forces strong enough to permit a "pause" in any future fighting that would be sufficient to enable the combatants to negotiate a cease-fire or give the aggressor time to reflect on the next step rather than relying on all-out nuclear action. These anticipated conventional forces—including 300,000 U.S. military personnel

already committed to the European theater—demanded more from Europe. The trouble was that the Western European leaders were intent on building their own cooperative economic institutions leading toward a Common Market; they did not share the U.S. paranoia and sense of insecurity and, consequently, resisted Kennedy's vision.

In addition to the crises over Cuba and Berlin, Kennedy had to deal with developments in Asia that posed even greater challenges for the United States over the long term. During the 1950s, Laos had been unable to form a stable government, and the civil war being fought in that country had the potential to escalate into a major conflict between Washington and Moscow. The United States had assumed the task of training and supplying the Royal Laotian Army, while the Soviet Union aided the government's opponents who were mostly communists. Kennedy and Khrushchev in their Vienna summit agreed upon the formation of a neutral and independent Laos, with the result that a 14-nation conference met at Geneva in May 1961. While negotiations were under way, another communist offensive in the region threatened to spill over into Thailand, a SEATO ally of the United States. Almost 2,000 marines from the Seventh Fleet landed in Thailand, followed by token forces from Great Britain, Australia, and New Zealand, ending the crisis, and on 21 July 1962, the 14 nations of the conference agreed to respect the independence, sovereignty, neutrality, and territorial integrity of the kingdom of Laos.

However, shortly after assuming office Kennedy received an appeal for increased military spending from President Ngo Dinh Diem of the Republic of Vietnam (South Vietnam). For the previous several years, Diem's government had been engaged in a guerrilla war with insurgents (the Viet Cong), who had established control of many rural areas. Whether this conflict was a war of aggression by the North against the South, or a genuine civil war with Ho Chi Minh of the Democratic Government of North Vietnam coming to the aid of his communist brethren, there could be little doubt that guerrilla warfare was erupting all

over Vietnam. The president sent General Maxwell D. Taylor—and a few months later Vice President Johnson—on a fact-finding mission to Vietnam and elsewhere in Asia. Both men agreed that the communist threat had to be stopped, so Kennedy promised to increase American assistance. Kennedy felt he had to draw a line against what he saw as Soviet-inspired communist aggression in the region. Persuaded that Vietnam represented "the cornerstone of the Free World in Southeast Asia, the keystone of the arch, the finger in the dike," Kennedy steadily expanded the American presence there. It never occurred to him, or his advisers, that the conflict was a genuine war of national liberation, and that the communists had the support of the people of Vietnam. They had forgotten that around 40 years previously, Ho Chi Minh had initially turned to the United States for support but had been rebuffed. The number of U.S. "advisers" in Vietnam rose from 650 when Eisenhower left office to 16,500 before the end of 1963. By May 1964, more than 200 Americans had been killed, about half of them in battle.

As the war against the Viet Cong dragged on with no end in sight, the Kennedy administration gradually came to the realization that President Diem's unpopularity among his own noncommunist population was part of the problem. The State Department tacitly agreed to the overthrow of the government and the assassination of Diem by a group of army officers on 1 November 1963, and Kennedy promptly recognized the new government, hoping for a more united and renewed effort against the Viet Cong. By the end of the month, Kennedy had also been assassinated, so the question of whether he was looking for alternatives to escalating America's military involvement in Vietnam remains unanswered. What can be said is that Kennedy set in motion actions in what would become, up to that time, America's longest war.

Turning to domestic affairs, we can say Kennedy had mixed success in achieving his goals. He took office at a time when the economy was in trouble. The United States was experiencing its fourth major recession since World War II with seven years of diminished economic growth and nine years of falling farm income. Business bankruptcies had reached their highest level since the 1930s, farm incomes had been squeezed 24 percent since 1951, and 5.5 million people were looking for work. His saw his priorities as protecting the unemployed, increasing the minimum wage, lowering taxes, and stimulating the economy, particularly in the business and housing sectors. Hence, the "New Frontier." Despite some congressional opposition, in 1961 the administration managed to expand Social Security benefits. The minimum wage was increased in stages to reach $1.25 per hour, benefiting more than 27 million workers. The Area Redevelopment Act authorized loans, grants, and technical assistance to depressed industrial and rural areas. As a result of these pump-priming initiatives, by the end of the president's first year in office the recession had faded. In 1962, Kennedy's legislative program met with mixed results. On the positive side of the ledger, the president requested and received intact the Trade Expansion Act, giving him authority to negotiate for the reduction and removal of tariffs, as well as creating a new program of "adjustments assistance" aid to industries and workers especially hard hit by competitive imports. Congress also enacted an accelerated Public Works Act and the Manpower Retraining Bill. The Communications Satellite Act, which authorized the creation of a privately owned and financed corporation, was also enacted in 1962. Some of the administration's legislative program relating to social welfare, agricultural, and civil rights proposals did not succeed in gaining passage through Congress. However, the Higher Education Facilities Act, which authorized a five-year federal program for the growth and continuation or improvement of public and private higher education facilities, the Drug Industry Act, which established additional safeguards in the processing and prescription of drugs, and aid for research into mental illness and retardation were passed.

Kennedy was determined to keep inflation low and firmly believed that it was essential that business and labor work together to keep their total increases in profits and wages in line with productivity. He felt betrayed and was

furious when the U.S. Steel Corporation, the nation's preeminent steel producer, suddenly announced large price increases for its products on 10 April 1961, only five days after the company had signed a new two-year, "noninflationary" contract with the United Steelworkers of America. The administration had spent almost a year persuading both sides to exercise restraint. The president, who recalled his father's words "that all businessmen were sons-of-bitches, but I never believed it till now," used all the power of his office to force a rollback. After 72 hours, U.S. Steel backed down and rescinded the increase. The president had proved his point, but business criticism of the administration reached an intensity not seen since the New Deal days of Franklin Roosevelt.

Kennedy was cautious, but persistent, in his approach to civil rights and achieving equal rights for African Americans. Facing strong opposition from opponents of civil rights legislation in Congress, Kennedy made use of executive powers to improve the situation of African Americans, particularly those facing difficulties in the Deep South. He desegregated interstate transportation systems with their related terminals and appointed several African Americans to high office, most notably Thurgood Marshall to the U.S. Circuit Court, Carl Rowan as ambassador to Finland, and Robert Weaver to the Housing and Home Financing Agency. He appointed Vice President Johnson chair of the President's Committee on Equal Employment to combat racial discrimination in the employment policies of firms holding government contracts. Also Robert Kennedy brought more than 50 suits against restrictive voting registration laws in four states on behalf of African Americans seeking to cast their ballots. Finally, Kennedy's executive order of 20 November 1962 sought to eliminate racial (as well as religious) discrimination in housing financed with federal aid.

Kennedy's biggest tests in the area of civil rights related to the desegregation of schools and universities in the South in 1962 and 1963. In January 1961, James H. Meredith, a black Mississippian and veteran of eight years in the U.S. Air Force, had applied for admission to the University of Mississippi, where no black had ever been enrolled. His application was rejected. In May, Meredith filed suit in the U.S. District Court of Appeals for southern Mississippi, contending that his admission had been denied squarely on racial grounds. Sixteen months later, in fall 1962, the federal courts ordered Meredith's admission. The governor of Mississippi, Ross Barnett, a states' rightser and white supremacist, chose to defy the order and bar Meredith's enrolment. Knowing that there would come a time when, to quote candidate Kennedy, "[t]he next President of the United States cannot stand above the battle engaging in vague little sermons on brotherhood," the White House tried persuasion with Barnett, federalized the Mississippi National Guard, and ordered an escort of federal marshals to accompany Meredith to the campus. On 1 October 1962, Meredith was allowed to enroll during an ugly riot that took thousands of Guardsmen and soldiers 15 hours to quell. Hundreds were injured and two were killed. Meredith graduated from the University of Mississippi the next year.

By spring 1963, the civil rights movement, together with broadly based support for black equality, had gained considerable momentum. Both the North and the South witnessed civil rights demonstrations on a massive scale. Led by Dr. Martin Luther King Jr., black Americans had reached the point where "We're through with tokenism and gradualism. . . . We can't wait any longer." Slowly, inexorably, racial barriers came down in the hotels, universities, and recreational facilities of southern cities. In Birmingham, Alabama, King and his followers were met by the stereotypical southern police chief—in this instance, Director of Public Safety "Bull" Connor, complete with cattle prods, police dogs, and fire hoses. The Kennedy administration was brought into the foreground of the struggle for racial equality. When the governor of the state of Alabama, George C. Wallace, threatened to bar the entry of black students to the University of Alabama, he met the same fate as Governor Barnett of Mississippi, as Kennedy once again federalized the state National Guard. Moving a step further, the administration called on Congress to enact comprehensive legislation to protect

and guarantee blacks their basic rights—measures supported by a huge "March on Washington" in June 1963, with 250,000 people in attendance. Unlike Eisenhower, Kennedy gave the marchers his moral support and left no one in doubt about his administration's position. Even so, the president could not force Congress to enact his legislative program, nor could he prevent the senseless murder of the leader of the Mississippi branch of the NAACP, Medgar Evers, or the killing of four children in a bomb attack on a Birmingham church in September 1963.

John F. Kennedy adopted the same cautious approach to the question of gender equality as he did to that of racial equality. While not an opponent of equal pay for women, he was far from a champion of women's rights. Once again, he used his executive powers to appoint women to significant positions in government, and he established the President's Commission on the Status of Women. But he was, basically, not very interested in advancing the cause of women.

On 22 November 1963, President Kennedy was shot and killed by an assassin, later identified as Lee Harvey Oswald, while riding through downtown Dallas in a motorcade. Oswald, who had once defected to the Soviet Union and had been active in the pro-Castro Fair Play for Cuba Committee, was quickly identified and subsequently arrested by Dallas police. Within 30 minutes of the shooting, 75 million Americans had heard the news; by late afternoon, 90 million Americans, or 99.8 percent of the adult population, had heard of the president's death. "It had been the greatest simultaneous experience in the history of their or any other people," wrote William Manchester. Events moved rapidly. While still in police custody, Oswald was himself shot and killed by an obscure Dallas nightclub owner, Jack Ruby; the entire drama was captured on national television. Theories of conspiracies filled the air. The official Warren Report—the study of the presidential commission headed by U.S. Supreme Court chief justice Earl Warren in 1964—concluded that Oswald alone killed the president and that there was no conspiracy. The commission also found that Ruby acted alone in killing Oswald. Subsequent studies of the event tend, overall, to support those conclusions.

Kennedy's death was mourned around the world as well as in the United States. Following his assassination, columnist and friend Richard Rovere wrote of him in the *New Yorker* (30 November 1963): "It can be said of him that he did not fear the weather, and did not trim his sails, but instead challenged the wind itself to improve its direction and to cause it to blow more softly and more kindly over the world and its people." However, as many commentators have noted, Kennedy's time in the White House was too short to allow any meaningful evaluation of his presidency—or even of the man himself. The issue at the heart of any assessment is "what might have been," rather than what was actually achieved. And, of course, to that question we have no answer.

Entries A–Z

ABERNATHY, RALPH DAVID (1926–1990). Ralph David Abernathy was born on 11 March 1926, in Linden, Alabama, the 10th of 12 children, and raised on his parents' 500-acre farm in Morengo County. He was ordained a Baptist minister in 1948, and he earned a BS from Alabama State University in Montgomery in 1950 and an MA in sociology from Atlanta University the next year.

Abernathy was appointed pastor of the First Baptist Church in Montgomery, Alabama, in 1951. When **Martin Luther King Jr.** became pastor at the city's Dexter Avenue Baptist Church in 1954, the two young ministers soon became close friends. In December 1955, King was chosen by the local black community to lead the historic Montgomery bus boycott. Throughout the protest, King later wrote, Abernathy was his "closest associate and most trusted friend," aiding King in organization and strategy. In January 1957, shortly after the boycott's end, Abernathy's home and church were bombed.

Abernathy helped found the Southern Christian Leadership Conference (SCLC) in 1957. He was elected secretary-treasurer at the same time that King was elected the organization's president. Abernathy became King's top aide in the SCLC. He moved to Atlanta, site of the SCLC's headquarters in 1961, and became pastor of the West Hunter Street Baptist Church there.

During the 1961 **Freedom Rides**, Abernathy, then still in Montgomery, opened his church to the interstate riders; he was arrested on 25 May, when he accompanied other ministers in a protest at Montgomery's segregated bus terminal. In December 1961, Abernathy joined King in aiding a desegregation campaign in Albany, Georgia. The two were arrested for leading a march there in December, found guilty of the charges stemming from that arrest in February 1962, and began serving their 45-day jail sentences together in July. However, they were soon released from jail when someone anonymously paid their fines.

In January 1963, Abernathy went to Birmingham to plan demonstrations and to build support for the protest among local black leaders. The massive campaign began on 3 April. On 12 April, Good Friday, King, Abernathy, and others headed a march to city hall in defiance of a court injunction prohibiting further demonstrations. They were arrested once again, and King and Abernathy remained in jail until 20 April. Abernathy then helped in negotiations with the city's white leadership and, on 10 May, reached an agreement ending the dramatic Birmingham campaign. When a bomb exploded at a black church in Birmingham on 15 September 1963, killing four young black girls, Abernathy was one of seven black leaders who met with President John F. Kennedy four days later to discuss the Birmingham situation.

Abernathy was with King when he was assassinated in Memphis, Tennessee, on 4 April 1968; he was immediately named King's successor as president of the SCLC. Under Abernathy's leadership, the SCLC remained committed to King's principles of nonviolence

and interracial cooperation and went forward with the planned Poor People's Campaign in spring and summer 1968.

He resigned from the SCLC in 1977 and served as a pastor of a Baptist church in Atlanta. His autobiography, *And the Walls Came Tumbling Down*, was published in 1989. Abernathy died of a heart attack, five weeks after his 64th birthday, on 30 April 1990.

AFFIRMATIVE ACTION. On 6 March 1961, President John F. Kennedy signed Executive Order 10925, which required government contractors to "take affirmative action to ensure that applicants are employed and that employees are treated during employment without regard to their race, creed, color, or national origin." It established the President's Committee on Equal Employment Opportunity. Kennedy appointed Vice President **Lyndon B. Johnson** to chair the committee, and U.S. secretary of labor **Arthur J. Goldberg** was placed in charge of the committee's operations. This was perhaps the first use of the term *affirmative action* in its present sense, and it was intended to give equal opportunities in the workforce to all U.S. citizens rather than to give special treatment to **African Americans** or any others who faced discrimination.

The term *affirmative action* itself did not come into popular use until a few years later, when it was used to describe a national program designed to advance equality for African Americans. In late 1962 or early 1963, **James Farmer**, founder of the **Congress of Racial Equality**, met with Vice President Johnson, and suggested a program he labeled "Compensatory Preferential Treatment" as a means of advancing equality for African Americans. **Whitney Young** claimed to have discussed the same idea with John F. Kennedy. In 1965, as president, Johnson renamed Farmer's proposal as "affirmative action" in a speech at Howard University and offered it as a national program. Johnson stated: "You do not take a person who, for years, has been hobbled by chains and liberate him, bring him up to the starting line in a race and then say, 'you are free to compete with all the others,' and still justly believe that you have been completely fair."

The term was applied to a national program that made positive efforts, through preferential selection, to place African Americans, women, and minorities in educational institutions and occupations from which they had been historically excluded. Such efforts were opposed by conservatives and became highly controversial because they operated counter to the idea that entry to educational and workplace opportunities should be based on merit. *See also* DEMOCRATIC PARTY.

AFRICA. Africa took up a considerable amount of time in the John F. Kennedy administration and aroused much controversy. Kennedy sought to find common ground between the ideal of supporting newly independent Third-World nations and the reality of American self-interest at the same time as he tried to limit the spread of an expanding **Cold War** into Africa. The continent was undergoing dramatic changes as decolonization swept the region, with most of the former colonies gaining independence during the 1960s. Some colonizers—Portugal in particular, and Belgium to a lesser extent—were reluctant to relinquish sovereignty, resulting in bitter wars for independence followed by internal civil wars lasting a decade or more.

During his congressional and senatorial years, Kennedy was a strong advocate of U.S. support for independence and self-determination of the newly emerging African nations. He opposed continued French rule in Indochina and Algeria, for example. His anticolonial stance gained him the acquaintance and sympathy of future African leaders such as Kwame Nkrumah in Ghana and Guinean leader Ahmed Sékou Touré. During the 1960 presidential campaign, Kennedy repeatedly faulted the Eisenhower administration for neglecting "the needs and aspirations of the African people" and stressed that the United States should be on the side of anticolonialism and self-determination. And, upon assuming the presidency, he named young, energetic appointees, dubbed "the best and the brightest," to several African embassies. Kennedy turned to **G. Mennen "Soapy" Williams**, former longtime governor of Michigan, to

represent him and manage his team, seeking moderate changes in African affairs. In 1962, he approved American aid to assist economic growth, prosperity, and political maturity.

However, Kennedy gradually moved away from his position of generally supporting the new nations. The turning point took place in the Republic of the Congo. The Congo had become independent from Belgium in June 1960 and was immediately torn apart by what Kennedy described as "civil strife, political unrest and public disorder." In July 1960, Moïse Tshombe, leader of Katanga Province, declared its independence from the Congo, and in the ensuing civil war, the Congo's first prime minister, Patrice Lumumba, having failed in a request to the Eisenhower administration for support, called upon the **Soviet Union** for assistance to quash the rebellion. The Soviets responded by sending weapons and technicians. Western officials, including members of the U.S. Central Intelligence Agency (CIA), had been concerned about the inroads of communism within the Congo government and were now alarmed at the prospect of the Soviets gaining a foothold in Africa. Belgium supported the secession of Katanga, seeking to retain rights to mine minerals in the copper- and diamond-rich breakaway state.

Three days prior to Kennedy's inauguration on 20 January 1961, despite the presence of a **United Nations** (UN) peacekeeping force, Lumumba, who had been captured after fleeing the capital, Léopoldville, was executed in Elisabethville, Katanga. Kennedy had originally hoped to forge a centrist coalition among the warring groups to create a stable government, but when that failed he supported the more conservative, anticommunist elements. On 2 October 1962, Kennedy signed a UN bond issue bill to guarantee American assistance in financing UN peacekeeping operations seeking to bring order to the Congo. Supported by UN troops, Léopoldville defeated the secessionist movements in Katanga and South Kasai by early 1963. However, the UN peacekeeping operation faced ongoing difficulties until it left in 1964. Following the continuing extreme instability

and civil unrest, the CIA and Belgium backed the anticommunist Joseph-Désiré Mobutu in a coup that overthrew the government in November 1965. The United States willingly overlooked Mobutu's many faults, and he would rule the country for three decades, earning a reputation for corruption, nepotism, embezzlement, and human rights violations. In Angola, Kennedy followed a different policy. He hoped to see an orderly transition toward Angolan independence without a colonial war and possible Soviet intervention. Over the course of time, he found that he had to choose between Portugal and Angolan independence; he chose North Atlantic Treaty Organization member Portugal.

While Kennedy was praised for accepting the world's diversity, as well as for improving the United States' standing in Africa, he had to adjust his ideals to the turbulent and often bloody reality that frequently accompanied the independence movements and to deep disagreements within his own administration between conservative Europeanists and pro-African, pro-UN liberals.

AFRICAN AMERICANS. The descriptive names widely used to describe black people of African descent residing in the United States have changed over time. During the years of the Kennedy administration, *Negro* or *colored people* were the most commonly used names. The earliest **civil rights** organizations still functioning at that time were the **National Association for the Advancement of Colored People** (NAACP), founded in 1909, and the United Negro College Fund (1944). But by the middle of the 1960s, influenced by the black power/black pride movements, those terms gave way to *black* and *Afro-American*. Then in the late 1980s, black spokesmen such as Jesse Jackson insisted that *African American* was more in keeping with the U.S. tradition of joining the term *American* with the name of their ancestors' geographical origin and permitted people to look at their ethnic origins with pride while still retaining an American national identity. By the second decade of the 21st century, the term *black* had become more prominent.

John F. Kennedy successfully courted the votes of African Americans in his presidential campaign. In doing so, he relied upon advisers who included some African American strategists led by the longtime former editor of the *Chicago Defender*, Louis E. Martin, whom the *Washington Post* once called "the godfather of black politics." Martin had years of experience in advising **Democratic Party** candidates in national politics stretching back to Franklin Delano Roosevelt. While top Kennedy surrogates downplayed his civil rights record in the South, Martin's team targeted specific messages to black voters. It was a "strategy of association." Martin had helped found the National Newspaper Publishers Association in 1940 and, assisted by black Washington attorneys Frank Reeves and Marjorie Lawson, customized Kennedy's image for their friends at leading black newspapers across the country. Martin (with others) had a hand in persuading candidate Kennedy to place a timely call to Coretta Scott King when her husband Martin was in jail. In the end, Kennedy gained around 73 percent of the African American vote. Kennedy acknowledged the importance of, and indicated his commitment to move forward in achieving equality for, African Americans at his inauguration, inviting Marian Anderson to sing "The Star-Spangled Banner" on that occasion.

Remarkably, given his slowness in following up on his promises to end discrimination against African Americans, John F. Kennedy was almost immediately elevated to sainthood by African Americans following his assassination. Within a week of the president's burial, George Barbour wrote of Kennedy in the *Pittsburgh Courier*: "He never wavered and in appointments, speeches, application of presidential power, secured direct benefits for the Negro unparalleled in modern history, and this strengthened the character of a great country."

Kennedy's appointments of African Americans to positions in his administration included the following:

Andrew T. Hatcher, associate White House press secretary, was the first black man to hold the number two communications spot in the White House, behind his longtime political compatriot **Pierre Salinger**. Simeon Booker, in a profile in *Ebony* magazine in October 1963, claimed that Hatcher pinch-hit for Salinger "200 days . . . as the official White House spokesman at press briefings, on the mikes and on the job," including during the Mississippi Meredith case. "The appointment was enough to jar 'the old pros' who had long become accustomed to Negroes serving only as porters, messengers, maids, clerks and valets at the White House."

Dr. **Robert C. Weaver** became the administrator of the Housing and Home Finance Agency. The *Chicago Defender* noted Weaver's was "the highest appointive federal office ever held by an American Negro." Kennedy tried to elevate Weaver to a full cabinet member but was rebuffed by Southern Democrats around the same time he pushed to open up federal housing for blacks. (**Lyndon Baines Johnson**, the legislator's legislator, eventually made it happen, naming Weaver his first housing and urban development secretary in 1966.)

Other appointees included George L. P. Weaver, assistant secretary of labor for internal affairs; Carl Rowan, deputy assistant secretary of state for public affairs (later Johnson's director of the U.S. Information Agency, after Edward R. Murrow, and a nationally syndicated columnist); Dr. Grace Hewell, program coordination officer for the Department of Health, **Education** and Welfare; Christopher C. Scott, deputy assistant postmaster general for transportation; Dr. Mabel Murphy Smythe, member of the U.S. Advisory Commission on Educational Exchange, Department of State; John P. Duncan, commissioner of the District of Columbia; and Clifford Alexander Jr., National Security Council (later secretary of the army under President Carter). Lieutenant Commander Samuel Gravely of the USS *Falgout* was the first black U.S. Navy commander to lead a combat ship.

Additionally, Kennedy selected A. Leon Higginbotham Jr. to be a member of the five-man Federal Trade Commission, which, in September 1962, made him the first African American ever to be appointed to a federal regulatory agency—and at only age 35,

Higginbotham was a distinguished Philadelphia attorney who had graduated from Yale Law School and served as the city's NAACP chapter president and former assistant district attorney. He and his wife Evelyn Brooks Higginbotham later taught at Harvard.

Kennedy appointed ambassadors Carl Rowan (to Finland), Clifton Wharton (to Norway), and Mercer Cook (to Niger); Kennedy's U.S. attorneys included Cecil Poole (Northern California) and Merle McCurdy (Northern Ohio). For the President's Committee on Equal Employment Opportunity, Kennedy selected Alice Dunnigan, John Hope, Azie Taylor (later U.S. treasurer under President Carter), Hobart Taylor, John Wheeler, and Howard Woods.

Kennedy's federal judge appointees included James Benton Parsons, Northern District of Illinois, the first black federal district judge to serve inside the continental United States; Wade McCree, Eastern District of Michigan; Marjorie Lawson, Juvenile Court of the District of Columbia; and "Mr. Civil Rights" himself (as Louis Martin referred to him), **Thurgood Marshall**, the Second Circuit, U.S. Court of Appeals. A. Leon Higginbotham would have made number five when Kennedy nominated him for a district court judgeship in October 1963, but after the assassination, he was held over until Johnson submitted his name again in January 1964.

During the 1960s, there were many African Americans prominent in the fields of art (Aaron Douglas), filmmaking (Gordon Parks, **Dick Gregory**), music (Louis Armstrong), literature (**James Baldwin**), politics (Shirley Chisholm, Robert C. Weaver), and sports (Muhammad Ali).

Leading African Americans promoting civil rights included Dr. **Martin Luther King Jr.**, Hubert "Rap" Brown, **Medgar W. Evers**, and **Roy Wilkins**. The civil rights movement spawned such widely different African American–led organizations as the Student Nonviolent Coordinating Committee, the **Congress of Racial Equality**, and the Black Panthers.

Despite the dramatic events surrounding desegregation of schools that had occurred during the Eisenhower administration, Kennedy was slow to recognize the significance of the change taking place in race relations in the United States and the need for leadership by the chief executive. Until the equally dramatic events of 1963, to Kennedy the discrimination faced by, and the treatment of, African Americans was not a high priority. It was left to his successor Lyndon B. Johnson (and later Kennedy's brother Robert) to champion civil rights and oversee the passage of significant legislation directed at improving the lives of African Americans.

AIKEN, GEORGE DAVID (1892–1984). George David Aiken was born on 20 August 1892, in Dummerston, Vermont, and was raised on a farm near Brattleboro, Vermont. After graduating from high school, he entered the nursery business and became one of the nation's leading experts in the commercial cultivation of wildflowers. In 1930, he embarked on a highly successful political career in Vermont and, following election to the Vermont House of Representatives, underwent a meteoric rise, winning the governorship in 1937. He was elected to the U.S. Senate in 1940 and, over the next 34 years, had little difficulty winning reelection. In 1954, Aiken sponsored the Water Facilities Act, which provided federal aid to rural communities seeking to develop an adequate water supply. Aiken considered this bill to be critical for the development of rural America and believed it was one of the most important bills he ever sponsored.

During the Kennedy years, Aiken was the ranking Republican on the Senate Agriculture and Forestry Committee. He also served on the Senate Foreign Relations Committee and on the Joint Atomic Energy Committee. Aiken was generally associated with the moderate wing of the **Republican Party**. He voted for the Kennedy administration's 1961 minimum-wage bill and its school aid proposal. He broke ranks with the conservative majority on the Agriculture Committee to support an amendment requiring U.S. farmers to pay Mexican "bracero" farm workers the same wages as U.S. workers. In July 1962, however, he initially voted against the administration's Medicare bill, later reversing that decision in 1965

to vote in favor of a similar health care bill, which became law in July of that year.

When Aiken retired from the Senate in 1974, he was 82 and the chamber's oldest member. He died in Montpelier, Vermont, on 19 November 1984.

ALBERT, CARL BERT (1908–2000). The son of a poor cotton farmer and coal miner, Carl Bert Albert was born on 10 May 1908, in McAlester, Oklahoma. He graduated Phi Beta Kappa from the University of Oklahoma in 1931 and received a Rhodes Scholarship to study at Oxford University, where he earned a BA in jurisprudence and a BCL. After practicing law and serving in the army, in 1946 Albert won a seat in the U.S. House of Representatives from Oklahoma's impoverished third district. In Congress, Albert consistently backed liberal measures but also voted for legislation favored by oil companies, which formed a major interest group in his state. He uniformly supported the lower chamber's Democratic leadership. Because of his relatively short height, he was affectionately known as the "Little Giant from Little Dixie."

From his earliest days as a representative, he carefully observed the operations of the House to familiarize himself with its procedures and with the voting patterns of its members. Speaker **Sam Rayburn** (D-Tex.) and House majority leader **John W. McCormack** (D-Mass.) appointed him to serve as majority whip in 1955. As whip, Albert was a conciliator and compromiser who preferred winning votes by persuasion rather than by threats. Known as a quiet, scholarly, and modest man, Albert worked behind the scenes and shunned publicity. When President John F. Kennedy took office in 1961, Albert assumed the additional function of advising the White House on the congressional reception of the administration's programs. He soon proved his acute sensitivity to House opinion. Shortly after the death of Rayburn in October 1961, Albert, assuming that McCormack would be elected to the speakership, began to seek backing for McCormack's former post as majority leader. As a House insider with extensive contacts among his colleagues, Albert

was chosen by the Democratic caucus later in the month. As majority leader, Albert's functions included devising Democratic floor strategy and speaking on behalf of administration programs. In January 1963, he helped secure the permanent expansion of the Rules Committee. It had originally been enlarged in 1961 to create a liberal majority, thereby preventing the panel from blocking administration bills. In seeking support for the president's programs, Albert retained his low-key, conciliatory approach. A hard worker, he continued performing some of the functions of the whip and tried to maintain contact with all Democratic representatives. After Kennedy's assassination, Albert was a strong supporter of Johnson administration policies, including the **Vietnam War**. In 1971, he succeeded McCormack as speaker.

Albert retired from Congress in 1976. In 1977, he returned to McAlester, where he maintained an office until 1998. He died aged 91 at the McAlester Regional Health Center on 4 February 2000.

ALLEN, JAMES EDWARD, JR. (1911–1971). A Presbyterian minister's son, James E. Allen Jr. was born on 25 April 1911, in Elkins, West Virginia. He received his BA from Elkins College in 1932 and worked for six years in the West Virginia State Department of **Education**. Allen then went to Harvard to study educational administration, gaining a PhD in 1945. Eight years after joining the staff of the Commissioner of the New York State Department of Education in 1947, he became commissioner. His task was the administration and planning of the state's local school systems and universities. He established a liberal record.

In January 1961, Allen claimed to have refused President John F. Kennedy's offer of appointment as U.S. commissioner of education. In June 1962, Allen ordered all school boards in the state to obey a U.S. **Supreme Court** decision banning a public-school prayer approved by the New York State Board of Regents despite widespread community opposition. He was also active in the desegregation of schools in New York's school districts. He devised a plan to improve educational

opportunities in New York City districts with large black or Puerto Rican populations.

Allen remained New York's state commissioner of education until 1969, overseeing the revitalization of the state university system. He was later briefly appointed U.S. commissioner of education by President **Richard M. Nixon** in February 1969 but was fired in June 1970 because his vigorous support of school desegregation antagonized the president's southern and conservative supporters.

Allen and his wife died in a private-plane crash at Peace Springs, Arizona, on 16 October 1971.

ALLIANCE FOR PROGRESS. In March 1961, President John F. Kennedy proposed a 10-year plan for Latin America with the aim of countering the perceived emerging communist threat from Cuba to U.S. interests and dominance in the region. The program, termed the *Alliance for Progress*, was launched at an inter-American conference at Punta del Este, Uruguay, in August 1961. The ambitious plan envisioned the U.S. supplying or guaranteeing $20 billion over 10 years in return for which Latin American countries were to pledge a capital investment of $80 billion to be spent in land and tax reforms, housing projects and health improvements, and the establishment of democratic governments. The plans of the participating Latin American countries were to be supervised by an inter-American board of experts. It was hoped these investments and reforms would result in an annual increase of 2.5 percent in per capita income.

The alliance failed to live up to Kennedy's expectations. American businesses did not invest as expected, and the State Department was not enthusiastic. Most of the U.S. aid money was spent at home; a 1967 study revealed that 90 percent of all aid commodity expenditures had gone to U.S. corporations. Latin American nationalists saw the scheme as another tool used by the United States to maintain hegemony in the hemisphere; elites resisted the proposed reforms and kept the U.S. money themselves while the gap between the rich and poor increased. The alliance proved to be a short-lived public relations success, achieving only a few real, limited, economic improvements. Adult illiteracy was reduced, and the number of people attending universities doubled or even tripled. Many health clinics were built across Latin America, but progress in improving health care faltered because of population growth.

On assuming the presidency, **Lyndon B. Johnson** removed key Kennedy appointees Edwin A. Martin and Teodoro Moscoso, and he combined State Department and Agency for International Development (AID) activities under **Thomas C. Mann**, former ambassador to Mexico, a trusted fellow Texan and staunch supporter of U.S. business interests. Under Mann, the alliance turned its resources to military purposes and internal security forces. The Organization of American States disbanded the permanent committee created to implement the alliance in 1973. *See also* CUBAN MISSILE CRISIS.

ALLOTT, GORDON LLEWELLYN (1907–1989). Gordon Allott was born on 2 January 1907, in Pueblo, Colorado, and graduated from the University of Colorado Law School. He served in World War II and, in 1950, was elected as lieutenant governor of Colorado. Four years later, he upset a popular Democrat in the contest for the U.S. Senate and easily won reelection in 1960.

Allott devoted his energies to opposing most of the Kennedy administration's legislation. He cast the only vote against the president's nomination of **Robert F. Kennedy** as attorney general, declaring that the younger Kennedy lacked "the legal experience to qualify him" for the post. In June 1961, Allott opposed the president's pledge to place an American on the moon as a "useless contest with the Russians." The only senator to vote against the National Aeronautics and Space Administration's request of $1.8 billion for fiscal year 1962, Allott warned of the probable costs of the moon mission, which he estimated at between $20 billion and $30 billion.

An unashamed and vocal hawk, Allott wanted government to concentrate its space efforts on orbital missions, including weapon-carrying space vehicles. He cosponsored a

resolution introduced by Senator Thomas Dodd (D-Conn.) in August 1961 requesting the president to resume the testing of nuclear weapons. He did, however, vote with the administration in favor of the **Limited Nuclear Test Ban Treaty** in September 1963.

Allott was also the leading Senate opponent of the administration's wilderness preservation legislation. During the Senate's 1961 debate, he won the support of the U.S. Chamber of Commerce, the Farm Bureau Federation, and mining and cattle industry interests to limit the area requested for preservation by the administration. Although the administration measure passed the Senate, it failed to reach the House floor, due in large part to the opposition of Representative **Wayne Aspinall** (D-Colo.), chairman of the House Interior and Insular Affairs Committee. Senate colleagues again continued to frustrate Allott's efforts to weaken the administration's request, which passed the Senate in April 1963. Aspinall's continued resistance to the bill, however, forced the White House to compromise, and the final Wilderness Act of 1964 incorporated many of the amendments Allott had fought for in the Senate. He died on 17 January 1989 in Englewood, Colorado.

ALSOP, JOSEPH WRIGHT, JR. (1910–1989). Joseph Wright Alsop Jr. was born on 11 October 1910, the son of socially prominent parents who were politically active in Republican politics. His mother was a distant relative of President Teddy Roosevelt, and both parents served in the Connecticut state legislature. Alsop grew up in Avon, Connecticut; he attended the Groton School and graduated from Harvard University in 1932. He became one of a select group of journalists and syndicated newspaper columnists who were close friends of John F. Kennedy. By the late 1950s, he and his brother **Stewart Alsop** were well-established members of the affluent, well-educated, and connected civilians living in Washington known as the **Georgetown Set**.

Through family connections, Joseph Alsop joined the staff of the *New York Herald Tribune* where he quickly gained a reputation as a brilliant journalist. In 1937, he became coauthor of his first newspaper column. During World War II, Alsop joined Claire Chennault's American Volunteer Group in China as staff historian/correspondent, and he helped publicize the efforts of the Flying Tigers—the American volunteer pilots who fought against the Japanese in the run-up to and during World War II. After the war, Alsop teamed with his brother Stewart on another syndicated column for the *Herald Tribune*. In 1958, their partnership ended amicably, and Joseph Alsop continued the column, first for the *Herald Tribune* and then for the increasingly influential *Washington Post*.

Despite his Republican affiliations, Joseph described both himself and his brother as "New Deal liberals." He was a very early supporter of the presidential ambitions of Democratic senator John F. Kennedy and became a close friend and influential adviser to Kennedy after his election to the presidency in November 1960. Alsop urged the nomination of **Lyndon B. Johnson** for vice president, and he recommended that Republican **C. Douglas Dillon** be appointed secretary of the treasury.

No position was more paramount to Alsop than America's supremacy. In the late 1940s, he was among the earliest opinion journalists to call for a massive U.S. military buildup against the **Soviet Union**. At the same time, he consistently urged American policy makers to oppose communist insurgencies throughout the globe. Those lacking his ardor were likened to British leaders in the 1930s who had failed to recognize Hitler's designs on Europe. Alsop greatly admired Kennedy and his administration. "I cannot recall a single broad area of policy on which I really disagreed with President Kennedy," Alsop later wrote. He frequently socialized with the president and was on similarly good terms with Kennedy's successor Lyndon B. Johnson. To both presidents and his readers, Alsop strongly promoted U.S. support of South Vietnam, under siege from communist guerrillas. He applauded Johnson's decision to commit U.S. forces in **Vietnam** and then insisted that America was winning the war. He forcefully attacked the views of critical young war correspondents, most notably David Halberstam, Malcolm

Browne, and Neil Sheehan, regarding them as "commie sympathizers." He also believed by the mid-1960s that communists were infiltrating the **civil rights** movement. His hardline, bordering upon fanatical, hostility to the Soviet Union alienated many of his more liberal friends and led to a decline in the influence of his column. Alsop's steadfast endorsement of U.S. involvement in Vietnam cost him dearly as the conflict became unpopular and split the Washington foreign policy establishment and many readers. "I cannot tell you how isolated and suddenly out of fashion I feel," he wrote in 1966. He quit his column in 1974.

On his retirement, he devoted himself to the study of Greek antiquities. He died of cancer in Washington, DC, on 28 August 1989. His memoir was published posthumously as *I've Seen the Best of It: Memoirs* (1992). *See also* APPEASEMENT.

ALSOP, STEWART JOHONNOT OLIVER (1914–1974). Stewart Johonnot Oliver Alsop was born on 17 May 1914. Like his older brother, **Joseph Alsop**, he grew up in Avon, Connecticut, and was educated at the Groton School and at Yale University, from which he graduated in 1936. After a few years with the publishing firm Doubleday Doran in New York, Stewart served in World War II with the Office of Strategic Services and parachuted into occupied France shortly after D-Day. In 1945, Alsop teamed with his brother Joseph on a thrice-weekly "Matter of Fact" column syndicated through the *New York Herald Tribune*. Both men became renowned for their painstaking research, indefatigable legwork, and regular trips to foreign capitals. They became part of a small cadre of journalists in Washington who, because of their privileged background and social connections, and their hard-line hostility to communism and the **Soviet Union**, had access to and influenced the Kennedy and, later, the Johnson administrations.

In November 1949, the Alsop brothers were denounced before the United Nations General Assembly by Soviet foreign minister Andrey I. Vishinsky because they had advocated the creation of new air bases in India, the **Middle East**, and North Africa.

From 1958 to 1968, Stewart Alsop served as a contributing editor of the *Saturday Evening Post*. In December 1962 in collaboration with John F. Kennedy confidant Charles Bartlett, Alsop published an article (which Kennedy had seen in draft form) in the *Post* asserting that **Adlai Stevenson II**, then U.S. ambassador to the **United Nations**, had strongly "dissented" from the Kennedy administration's decision to impose a naval blockade of Cuba, urging instead a more cautionary role. The article created a furor, implying, as it did, that Stevenson advocated "a Munich"—the greatest of sins in the eyes of a **Cold War** warrior! Despite vigorous denials by Kennedy, Stevenson, and various Kennedy aides that any such dissension had taken place, Alsop and Bartlett maintained their story was accurate.

In 1968, Alsop joined *Newsweek* magazine as a political columnist. He defended the **Vietnam War** through much of the Johnson administration. Alsop's 1968 book *The Center* denounced academics and "liberal intellectual" critics of administration policy. He died of cancer at the age of 60 on 26 May 1974, in Washington, DC.

AMERICAN INDIANS. *See* FIRST AMERICANS.

ANDERSON, CLINTON PRESBA (1895–1975). Born on 23 October 1895, in Centerville, South Dakota, by the 1960s Clinton Presba Anderson had become one of the most influential members of the U.S. Senate. Anderson was raised in rural South Dakota and attended Dakota Wesleyan University and the University of Michigan. Tuberculosis prevented him from serving in World War I. He moved to New Mexico, where the climate helped him recuperate. From 1918 to 1922, he worked as a reporter for the *Albuquerque Journal* and helped uncover evidence relating to the Teapot Dome scandal. In the mid-1920s, he made his fortune as head of his own insurance agency, the Mountain States Casualty Company.

In 1928, he became chairman of the New Mexico Democratic Party; in 1930, he was appointed president of Rotary International; and in 1933, he was chosen state treasurer.

Anderson helped administer New Deal relief and unemployment compensation programs in New Mexico. He was elected to Congress in 1940 and served for three terms. Early in 1945, he headed a congressional probe into food shortages and black-market operations in the distribution of meat. President **Harry S. Truman** was so impressed by Anderson's report that he appointed him secretary of agriculture in spring 1945. Anderson held the post for three years. In 1948, he won election to the Senate, where he served for the next 23 years.

During the 1960s, Anderson's influence was based on his seniority, chairmanship of several important committees, and close ties to the John F. Kennedy and later the **Lyndon B. Johnson** administrations. Anderson was generally regarded as one of the more liberal members of a powerful group of Democratic senators who set the pace of upper-house business. He failed, however, to overcome the resistance of Southern Democrats, as well as some conservative Republicans in his efforts to limit the use of the filibuster in the Senate.

Anderson was closely involved in shaping water resources legislation, a subject of vital interest to arid New Mexico. He also served as floor manager for a number of successful water reclamation project bills, including the Navaho–San Juan water storage project, which irrigated a considerable expanse of New Mexico's land by diverting Colorado River water into the Rio Grande Valley. From 1961 to 1963, Anderson was chairman of the Senate Interior and Insular Affairs Committee. He also joined with Representative Cecil R. King (D-Calif.) to sponsor legislation that mandated increases in Social Security taxes to provide hospital care for old-age assistance beneficiaries. The King-Anderson Medicare bill, which was strongly backed by the administration, was defeated every year between 1961 and 1964 because of the stiff opposition of the American Medical Association and Representative **Wilbur Mills** (D-Ark.), the powerful chairman of the House Ways and Means Committee. In summer 1965, a version of the bill became law, thanks in part to a change of attitude by Representative Mills and a sweeping congressional victory for Medicare advocates in the 1964 elections.

In January 1963, Anderson became chairman of the Senate Aeronautical and Space Sciences Committee, a post he held for the next nine years. Anderson headed this committee during the boom years of the American space program, which he supported enthusiastically. Led by Anderson, the Aeronautics Committee was generous when handling National Aeronautics and Space Administration requests for funds. During the Johnson years, Anderson supported the administration on key domestic legislation. However, because he backed the administration's **Vietnam** policy, supported large-scale military appropriations, and opposed strict gun control legislation, he began to lose his standing with liberal elements of the **Democratic Party**. Anderson, in ill health, retired from the Senate in 1972. He died at the age of 80 on 11 November 1975, in Albuquerque, New Mexico. *See also* JAVITS, JACOB KOPPEL; RIBICOFF, ABRAHAM ALEXANDER.

ANDERSON, GEORGE WHELAN, JR. (1906–1992). George Whelan Anderson was born in New York City on 15 December 1906. He entered the United States Naval Academy in 1923 and graduated with the class of 1927. He served in the Pacific theater during World War II, and he rose through the ranks to become commander of the Sixth Fleet in the Mediterranean in 1959. In June 1961, the secretary of the navy, John Connally, named Anderson successor to Admiral Arleigh A. Burke as chief of naval operations.

As chief commanding officer for the U.S. Navy, Anderson assumed responsibility in October 1962 for setting up the "quarantine" to prevent the **Soviet Union** from continuing to deliver missiles to **Cuba**. On Sunday afternoon, 21 October, President John F. Kennedy met with Anderson, who assured the president that any Russian vessel approaching Cuba could be stopped by crippling but not sinking it. The secretary of defense, **Robert S. McNamara**, who was responsible for the overall planning and supervision of the action, was not so sure and, three days later in a heated meeting with Anderson, stressed that the quarantine had been ordered not to humiliate the Russians but

to prevent further arming of their missile bases in Cuba. McNamara was afraid that a miscalculation by the navy could touch off nuclear war. The secretary pressed Anderson on matters of tactics. Which ship would make the first interception? Were Russian-speaking officers on board? How would Russian submarines be dealt with? What would be done if a Soviet captain refused to answer questions about cargo? Anderson then picked up a copy of the Manual of Naval Regulations and shouted, "It's all in there." McNamara snapped back, "I don't give a damn what John Paul Jones would have done, I want to know what you are going to do, now." Anderson advised McNamara to return to his office and let the navy handle the problem. McNamara obliged, but it had become apparent that the two men could never again have a sound working relationship.

Anderson and McNamara also disagreed over the Defense Department's choice of General Dynamics as the prime contractor for the new TFX jet fighter. Appearing before the Senate Permanent Investigations Subcommittee in April 1963, Anderson testified that the aircraft would be far too heavy for most carriers. McNamara, in turn, challenged Anderson's recommendation that new surface ships utilize nuclear power, charging that nuclear-powered ships were too costly. Anderson later deplored the "lack of trust and confidence between military and civilian echelons." "Any president," said John F. Kennedy in spring 1963, "should have the right to choose carefully his military advisers."

Kennedy then broke with precedent and refused to appoint Anderson to a second term as chief of naval operations. To placate Anderson's many supporters on Capitol Hill, Kennedy named Anderson ambassador to Portugal. He held this post from August 1963 until March 1966. In March 1969, Anderson was appointed to the president's Foreign Intelligence Advisory Board. Anderson also served as director of several corporations, including National Airlines and Value Line Funds. He died on 20 March 1992 of heart failure in McLean, Virginia.

APPEASEMENT. Since the outbreak of World War II, the term *appeasement* has been a derogatory word associated with a nation's unwillingness to resort to military force in the face of demands or actions by a foreign power deemed to endanger national security. This association stems from the unsuccessful attempts by Britain and France (with the moral support of the United States) in Munich in September 1938 to negotiate with German chancellor Adolf Hitler to prevent his planned occupation of Czechoslovakia. Appeasement, according to this line of argument, results from an inability to fight or a fundamental misconception of reality. In the case of Czechoslovakia, interests were literally given away without any concessions being extracted from Germany. The Munich Agreement also became a metaphor for weakness in foreign policy, and the fear of being called an "appeaser" encouraged statesmen to stand up and resist. It also turned firmness into an essential virtue in the conduct of foreign policy. This "lesson" of the Munich conference has, in this sense, permeated the American political world since World War II.

The Munich analogy was increasingly cited by American politicians during the **Cold War**, especially during the **Vietnam War**. For example, **Dwight D. Eisenhower** invoked Munich in 1954, when he sought British support to use American air and naval power in Indochina to save the French from defeat at the hands of the communists. In a letter to Winston Churchill, he used the Munich analogy in an attempt to persuade the British to support American actions: "If I may refer again to history; we failed to halt Hirohito, Mussolini and Hitler by not acting in unity and in time. That marked the beginning of many years of stark tragedy and desperate peril. May it not be that our nations have learned something from that lesson?"

The lessons of Munich had had particular meaning for John F. Kennedy. His father had been Roosevelt's ambassador to Great Britain at the time of the Munich conference, and he had been a 21-year-old university student when the meeting took place. **Joseph P. Kennedy, Sr.** had been a long-term supporter of Great Britain's policy of appeasement and never repented. His son had, however, formed

his own beliefs with the coming of World War II. John F. Kennedy disagreed with appeasement so fervently that his honors thesis at Harvard was titled "Appeasement at Munich." This work was published after his graduation under the title *Why England Slept* (1940) and became a best seller. The book argued that appeasement was a weak policy that the United States should avoid at all costs.

Kennedy invoked the Munich analogy to support his confrontational policies in relation to **Vietnam** and to **Cuba**. "Vietnam," he stated, "represents the cornerstone of the Free World in Southeast Asia, the keystone of the arch, the finger in the dike. Burma, Thailand, India, Japan, the Philippines and, obviously, Laos and Cambodia are among those whose security would be threatened if the red tide of Communism overflowed into Viet-Nam." He argued that a healthy Vietnamese economy was essential to the economy of all of Southeast Asia. For these reasons, added Kennedy, "the fundamental tenets of this nation's foreign policy, in short, depend in considerable measure upon a strong and free Vietnamese nation." Under Kennedy, the number of American troops in South Vietnam increased steadily, reaching some 14,500 before the end of 1963. Technically, these personnel were engaged only in transportation, training, and advice, but these activities invariably exposed them to combat. Few questioned why they were there.

During the **Cuban missile crisis**, Kennedy pointedly used the Munich analogy in his speech of 22 October 1962, when he announced that he would implement a quarantine on communist Cuba in response to the discovery that the **Soviet Union** had been placing offensive weapons there. Explaining his decision, the president reminded the nation that "[t]he 1930s taught us a clear lesson: Aggressive conduct, if allowed to grow unchecked and unchallenged, ultimately leads to war." The transcripts of the Executive Committee of the National Security Council show that the Munich analogy was extensively used in governmental discussions during the crisis. The chairman of the Joint Chiefs of Staff, General Curtis LeMay, wanted a more aggressive policy than the blockade imposed by Kennedy

and argued that "[t]his blockade and political action, I see leading into war. I don't see any other solution. It will lead right into war. This is almost as bad as the appeasement at Munich."

As it was, in the wake of the Cuban missile crisis, Kennedy's ambassador to the **United Nations, Adlai Stevenson II**, was accused of appeasement because at one point in the pre-crisis talks regarding what path the United States should take in the face of the Soviet threat, Stevenson had suggested that the president "should consider offering to withdraw from the Guantanamo naval base as part of a plan to demilitarize, neutralize and guarantee the territorial integrity of Cuba . . . [and offer] to remove the Jupiter [missiles in Turkey] in exchange for the Russian missiles from Cuba." Kennedy vehemently disagreed, of course, and Stevenson was subsequently charged with wanting "a Munich." Journalist **Joseph Alsop**, who attributed the statement to a "non-admiring official," used his comments to discredit Stevenson. As a result, the article made Stevenson's arguments for trading the Turkish bases seem less rational than they really were. This charge of being a "Municheer" was especially damaging to Stevenson's political reputation. The irony, of course, was that the removal of the Jupiter missiles from Turkey did play a secret role in resolving the crisis.

ARAB NATIONALISM. *See* MIDDLE EAST.

AREA REDEVELOPMENT ACT (1961). The Area Redevelopment Act was passed on 1 May 1961. It was one of a series of programs initiated by the Kennedy administration designed to modernize economic and social conditions in an attempt to redress the economic problems faced by communities experiencing substantial hardship. The act was directed primarily toward the Appalachia region and grew out of unsuccessful attempts by Senator Paul Douglas of Illinois in the 1950s to pass federal legislation to assist these depressed states as well as the appeals by the governors of the Appalachian states for assistance.

By the late 1950s, the Appalachian region was experiencing serious economic lag, social deprivation, environmental degradation,

and political isolation. The administration selected 852 localities as redevelopment areas and an additional 106 communities as areas of substantial unemployment for assistance. The Area Redevelopment Act established the Area Redevelopment Administration (ARA), which was housed in the Department of Commerce; the ARA identified the challenges these communities faced as "exodus of industry, displacement of labor by technological change, excessive dependence on declining industries, influx of job-seekers, changing weapons requirements in military procurement, and chronic rural poverty." It was estimated that the unemployment rate in the designated areas was 33 percent higher than that in the rest of the country.

Candidate John F. Kennedy had campaigned hard in West Virginia promising a kind of "New Deal" to address the poverty of the region, and he was rewarded by the voters of that state in the hard-fought presidential election. He immediately set about to act on his promises and authorized work that led to the formation of the ARA. The president and administration officials indicated that the focus of the new organization should be on long-term solutions to these communities' economic problems, not primarily current unemployment levels.

The program, however, was hampered by low-level funding, and the bulk of funds allocated did not go to the development of human resources such as **education** and health but, rather, to brick-and-mortar projects. A disproportionate amount went to West Virginia and to tourism projects. In its first year, $394 million was allocated to invigorate the private sector and, thereby, create new jobs, and an additional $4.5 million annually was set aside, over four years, for vocational training programs. Federal funds of up to 50 percent of the costs, along with grants and loans, were also made available for eligible federal, state, and local capital-improvement projects.

Serious floods in March 1963, especially in Kentucky, led to the creation of the President's Appalachian Regional Commission (PARC) in April to accelerate and invigorate the development programs. Following the assassination of

Kennedy in November 1963, the work of PARC was carried on by the Johnson administration. *See also* YARBOROUGH, RALPH WEBSTER.

ARMS CONTROL. By the time John F. Kennedy entered the White House in January 1961, arms control was essentially an effort by the two **Cold War** superpowers to limit the spread of nuclear weapons beyond those nations already possessing them—namely, themselves and the United Kingdom—in the face of pressures from their respective allies to build their own nuclear arsenals. Kennedy had to balance his belief in the necessity of, and reliance upon, military strength with his view that the control of armaments, especially the development and deployment of nuclear weapons by countries other than the United States, was essential for the success of his foreign policy.

By the early 1960s, it had become increasingly evident that the chaos and destruction emanating from a nuclear conflict would cause devastating international damage, despite disclaimers by the superpowers that nuclear weapons would ever be used. Kennedy voiced these conflicting ideals in his inaugural address. He appealed to the **Soviet Union** to join the United States "to invoke the wonders of science instead of its terrors. Together let us explore the stars, conquer the deserts, eradicate disease, tap the ocean depths, and encourage the arts and commerce." He pointed out that the instruments of war had far outpaced the instruments of peace, and he urged nations to renew their quest for peace "before the dark powers of destruction unleashed by science engulf all humanity in planned or accidental self-destruction." Stimulated by the development and deployment of nuclear weapons and delivery systems with global reach, the desire to control armaments, and thereby reduce the likelihood of widespread warfare, had increased greatly in the decade and a half since the first use of atomic weapons by the United States. Despite disclaimers by the superpowers that nuclear weapons would ever be used, many academics, diplomats, and citizens urged the negotiation of measures that could rein in the expansion of the new

military systems. The trouble was that nuclear weapons were an essential component of U.S. defense/foreign policy, and, in addition, seeking to limit the spread of nuclear arms frequently conflicted with other foreign policy objectives such as support for Israel or ensuring the cooperation of Pakistan. Arms limitation, and nonproliferation, were subordinated to these other priorities.

Appalled that less than 100 people in the U.S. government were at work on disarmament planning under President **Dwight D. Eisenhower**, Kennedy set out to create a specific agency for the work. In September 1961, he created the **Arms Control and Disarmament Agency** (ACDA) to study various arms control mechanisms and gained congressional approval for its establishment. The ACDA conducted, supported, and coordinated "research for arms control and disarmament policy formulation"; prepared for and managed "U.S. participation in international arms control and disarmament negotiations"; and prepared, operated, and directed "U.S. participation in international arms control and disarmament systems." In the 1960s, the agency became the driving force behind many of the early proposals, such as a nuclear Non-Proliferation Treaty, that were opposed by the State and Defense Departments.

Nuclear arms control was first included on the agenda of the United Nations General Assembly under the somewhat clumsy heading **General and Complete Disarmament** at the request of the Soviet Union. Premier **Nikita Khrushchev** addressed the assembly at its annual meeting on 18 September 1959 and proposed a new disarmament program in three stages aimed at eliminating all armed forces and armaments within a four-year period, but little action had resulted. Serious efforts to achieve arms control measures began when presidential adviser **John J. McCloy** and Soviet deputy foreign minister Valerian Zorin issued "agreed principles regarding disarmament" in September 1961. The so-called Zorin-McCloy agreement sought a general strategy to assure that war would not be used as a way of settling international disputes and an outline for future arms control negotiations between Washington and Moscow. Following this agreement, President Kennedy told the General Assembly, on 25 September 1961, that signing a nuclear test ban treaty—which had escaped the Eisenhower administration—should be a priority. "This can be done now," he challenged. "Test ban negotiations need not and should not await general disarmament." Additionally, he urged four more measures: (1) halting the production of fissionable materials for use in weapons and the transfer of such materials to nonnuclear powers; (2) prohibiting the transfer of nuclear weapons to nations that do not have them; (3) keeping nuclear weapons from outer space; and (4) destroying strategic missiles and aircraft that could deliver nuclear bombs. These themes were included in the United States' proposal for general and complete disarmament submitted to the Eighteen-Nation Disarmament Committee in 1962. The stumbling block to a final agreement was the issue of verification and inspection. The United States insisted upon an approach requiring international inspection to ensure compliance at each stage of disarmament, which the Soviets regarded as too intrusive. At that time, the United States possessed around 3,500 nuclear warheads, six times the number stockpiled by the Soviet Union. Almost 3,000 of the U.S. warheads could be delivered by the always airborne Strategic Air Command long-range bombers.

After the **Cuban missile crisis** in October 1962, and although they were unable to negotiate a comprehensive test ban treaty, in July 1963 Kennedy and Soviet and UK negotiators signed a **Limited Nuclear Test Ban Treaty** (LTBT), an agreement that prohibited atmospheric, outer space, and undersea testing. This agreement was subsequently adopted by scores of other nations. While the LTBT ended the atmospheric testing of nuclear weapons, it did not end the **arms race**. It literally drove it underground where U.S. testing continued for the next three decades. The policies followed by Kennedy's successor, **Lyndon B. Johnson**, were basically those of the Kennedy administration.

ARMS CONTROL AND DISARMAMENT AGENCY (ACDA). The idea of an independent statutory agency for the planning, negotiating, and implementation of **arms control** and disarmament agreements was first suggested in the United States by Senator **Hubert H. Humphrey** of Minnesota. The Arms Control and Disarmament Agency was created by Act of Congress on 26 September 1961. The legislation, describing the new body as "an Agency of Peace," was drafted by presidential adviser **John J. McCloy**, and the agency served under the direction of the Department of State as adviser to the president and the National Security Council, as well as the secretary of state. It stipulated that the agency was to strengthen American security by "formulating, advocating, negotiating, implementing and verifying effective arms control, nonproliferation, and disarmament policies, strategies, and agreements" and by directing American "participation in international arms control and disarmament systems." The agency's initial directors—William C. Foster (1961–1969) and Gerard C. Smith (1969–1972)—worked closely as principal advisers to the president and secretary of state on matters related to arms control and disarmament. However, the ACDA faced problems from the outset. It was planned as a bureaucratic counterweight to the Department of Defense, but some legislators and bureaucrats suggested it would be populated by pacifists and individuals who wanted to surrender to the Soviets. Also, given the centrality of nuclear weapons to U.S. defense strategy, the ACDA, in seeking to ensure that arms control was fully integrated into the development and conduct of U.S. national security policy, was tasked with reconciling an inherent contradiction.

ARMS RACE. The arms race was a major component of the **Cold War**, as the United States and the **Soviet Union** vied for more and more sophisticated weaponry. Nuclear weapons were a central feature of this contest, as well as new delivery systems, as each nation invested heavily in what became a game of technological escalation aimed at producing more and better military devices. The United States' successful test of a hydrogen bomb (H-bomb) in 1952 made possible the creation of warheads that were smaller than the World War II atomic bomb (A-bomb) but 2,500 times more powerful than their predecessors. The Soviets developed similar bombs a few years later, and China followed suit in 1967.

These developments were followed in the 1960s with improved delivery systems that included missiles of several types, including short-range, medium-range, and intercontinental (ICBM) ballistic missiles. Initially, these missiles and their nuclear warheads were land based, but in 1960, the United States launched its first submarine that carried 16 Polaris missiles, only to see these new weapons be countered by Soviet submarines equipped with nuclear-tipped missiles. The growth in the number of targeted warheads grew dramatically with the introduction of multiple, independently targeted reentry vehicles (MIRVs), which allowed a single missile to carry 10 or more warheads. In an attempt to defend against these new missile-delivered warheads, both nations experimented with antiballistic missile systems. However, the advent of MIRVed ICBMs employing an array of decoys presented a challenge that was not solved during the Cold War. The two superpowers now possessed weapons that could obliterate cities and cause tens of millions of casualties; indeed, they possessed enough warheads to virtually destroy the world.

Recognition of this fact meant that each nation possessed weapons they dare not use for fear of being destroyed themselves by retaliatory strikes. The concept of **nuclear deterrence** was borne from the fact there could be no winners in a nuclear war; the secretary of defense, **Robert S. McNamara**, labeled the situation that of "mutually assured destruction." Finally determining that they could not find security through engineering, leadership in Moscow and Washington turned slowly to political mechanisms referred to as **arms control** agreements.

THE ARTS AND JOHN F. KENNEDY. The Kennedys made the arts part of their lives in the White House. Jack Kennedy enjoyed literature

and poetry, especially works of the Romantic-era English poet Lord Byron (mad, bad, and dangerous) and the American contemporary poet Robert Frost. Reputedly a speed reader, he read widely but never considered himself an intellectual or an original thinker. His favorite book by all accounts was David Cecil's biography of Lord Melbourne (2 volumes, 1939 and 1954); just why is not clear, other than it is an elegantly written and brilliant evocation of a golden age in British history and a revealing, insightful portrait of its charismatic prime minister. Cecil also portrays, of course, the sexual indulgences and total disregard of the ruling class of the time for the conventional norms of monogamous marriage. **Jacqueline Kennedy** loved poetry as well and was also deeply committed to both music and the visual arts. There is little evidence that Jack was particularly sophisticated about the arts. His musical tastes ran to Broadway show tunes and Irish ballads rather than Mozart or Beethoven. Once, when asked about the president's taste in music, the first lady replied that his favorite piece was "Hail to the Chief."

However, John F. Kennedy did understand the importance of what Theodore Roosevelt had called the "bully pulpit," and he was convinced that it was essential for the president to demonstrate a regard for and recognition of cultural and intellectual excellence. As a result, he readily welcomed the idea of inviting Robert Frost to read a poem at the inauguration and agreed to invite more than 50 other writers, painters, poets, and musicians to the ceremonies. At an April 1962 White House dinner for Nobel Prize winners, Kennedy delighted his distinguished guests by calling them "the most extraordinary collection of talent, of human knowledge, that has ever been gathered together at the White House, with the possible exception of when Thomas Jefferson dined alone."

The Kennedys' support for the arts extended beyond contemporary artists to the next generation of Americans and included, for example, a series of "Concerts for Young People" at the White House sponsored by the first lady to encourage the study and performance of music by America's youth.

In May 1962, the Kennedys invited the French minister of culture, André Malraux, to the White House and hosted a dinner in his honor attended by many of the nation's leading artists, writers, and musicians. In doing so, they hoped to focus national attention on the role of the arts in America and encourage the development of Washington as a cultural center. In his toast, President Kennedy affirmed that "creativity is the hardest work there is." He observed that the White House "was becoming a sort of eating place for artists. But," he added in his usual self-deprecating way, "they never ask us out." Malraux honored the president and first lady by promising Jackie Kennedy at the end of the dinner that he would send to her France's most famous cultural treasure, *La Gioconda* (the *Mona Lisa*). In December 1962, a special loan was made directly to the president and to the American people by the government of the French Republic. Malraux accompanied the painting to the United States where more than 700,000 people saw it at the National Gallery of Art and more than a million others viewed it at the Metropolitan Museum of Art. President Kennedy expressed his appreciation for the loan and stated, "We will continue to press ahead to develop an independent artistic force and power of our own."

In spring 1962, Kennedy created the position of special consultant on the arts. He recognized that the role of the federal government in the arts was historically and constitutionally limited but, nonetheless, wanted to have access to advice in those areas where public policy had an artistic dimension—such as in the design of public buildings. In May 1962, he strongly endorsed a report on federal architecture emphasizing that the design of new buildings should provide "visual testimony to the dignity, enterprise, vigor, and stability of the American government." The report, which introduced *The Guiding Principles for Federal Architecture*, also stated that "where appropriate, fine art should be incorporated in the designs [of federal buildings], with emphasis on the work of living American artists." The General Services Administration Art in Architecture Program was then established to commission American artists to integrate their

creative contributions in meaningful ways with an equally vibrant federal architecture.

In general terms, American art in the 1960s followed the trend, established in the 1950s, to develop a modern and futuristic style reflecting the budding space age. The works of Alexander Calder (mobiles and sculpture) and Helen Frankenthaler (non-representational art) focused on interpretation that sought to inspire viewers to see art in their own way. Calder changed the course of modern art "by developing a new method of sculpting: by bending and twisting wire, he essentially 'drew' three-dimensional figures in space . . . [and was] renowned for the invention of the mobile, whose suspended, abstract elements move and balance in changing harmony." Andy Warhol emerged as a leader in the 20th-century pop art movement with his imagery of common consumer items. In its reaction against abstract expressionism, pop art sought to remove distinctions between "good" and "bad" taste. *See also* JOHN F. KENNEDY CENTER FOR THE PERFORMING ARTS; NATIONAL ENDOWMENTS FOR ARTS AND HUMANITIES.

ASPINALL, WAYNE NORVIEL (1896–1983). Wayne Norviel Aspinall was born on 3 April 1896, in Middleburg, Ohio. His family moved to Colorado in 1904, and after serving in World War I, Aspinall graduated from the University of Denver in 1919 where he also gained a law degree in 1925. He spent several years as a fruit grower and lawyer, and he became a leading figure in the Colorado legislature. He was elected to the U.S. House of Representatives as a Democrat in 1948 where he remained until 1973. During the years 1959 to 1973, he was chairman of the House Interior and Insular Affairs Committee.

Aspinall represented a western Colorado district heavily dependent upon agriculture, timber, and mining. He was immediately assigned to the Public Lands Committee (later renamed Interior and Insular Affairs Committee) and became a leader in sponsoring water reclamation legislation for Colorado and the West. Aspinall favored local control over water and land resources rather than centralized control,

and he was a strong advocate of dams and water reclamation projects. He advocated a "multiple-use" conservation policy to open the government's extensive western wilderness holdings to both commercial and recreational development. This approach was generally backed by the forest products, cattle, and mining industries and brought him into conflict with the increasingly powerful environmental lobby.

As chairman of the Interior and Insular Affairs Committee, Aspinall played a decisive role in first defeating and then substantially reshaping the Kennedy administration's wilderness preservation legislation. For several years, conservationist groups had unsuccessfully pressed for a law that would protect wilderness lands under Forest Service jurisdiction against commercial exploitation. The Senate finally approved a strong conservation bill in September 1961. The proposed legislation gave the president authority to include new lands in the wilderness system unless Congress vetoed the additions within a specified time. Under Aspinall's direction, the House Interior Committee effectively rewrote the bill to allow public lands to be declared wilderness only by an express vote of Congress itself. Backed by conservation groups, President Kennedy and U.S. interior secretary **Stewart Udall** opposed Aspinall's proposed revisions and the bill died in committee. At the time Aspinall commented, "[Conservationist] extremists . . . have created an atmosphere which makes impossible the enactment of any wilderness legislation during this Congress."

The Senate passed another Kennedy-backed wilderness bill on 9 April 1963. Aspinall, in turn, delayed the measure in the Interior Committee. On 20 November, he met with President Kennedy and agreed to report a modified wilderness bill out of committee in return for administration support of an Aspinall-controlled commission to make a general review of public land-management policies. The resulting Wilderness Act, signed by President **Lyndon B. Johnson** on 3 September 1964, protected mining and grazing rights in the new wilderness areas until 1984 and required Congress to act before additional

lands could be placed in the wilderness system beyond an initial 9.1 million acres—a figure reduced from the 55 million acres requested by Kennedy. The final law was considered a defeat for the growing wilderness preservation movement.

Aspinall died in his hometown of Palisade, Colorado, on 9 October 1983. *See also* AL-LOTT, GORDON LLEWELLYN.

ASSASSINATION OF JOHN F. KENNEDY.

John F. Kennedy's assassination at 12:30 p.m. on 22 November 1963 stunned Americans and shocked much of the world. Americans were thrown into profound grief for their fallen leader regardless of party affiliation, economic circumstances, ethnic identity, or geographic location, and many around the globe shared their distress. The nation came to a standstill and watched mesmerized as **television** captured the poignant images of Kennedy's widowed wife and her two young children, John-John, aged three years, and Caroline, aged five, standing grief stricken as the solemn funeral procession of a horse-drawn caisson followed by a riderless (caparisoned) horse with boots reversed in the stirrups passed by on its way to Arlington cemetery in Virginia.

Over the previous two days, hundreds of thousands had passed by Kennedy's casket placed on the catafalque constructed for Abraham Lincoln's coffin in the Capitol building rotunda to pay their final respects to the president. **Jacqueline Kennedy** and daughter **Caroline Kennedy** had knelt to kiss the American flag on the casket, and President **Lyndon B. Johnson** had laid a wreath of red and white carnations.

Although he was the fourth U.S. president to be assassinated, the death of America's 35th president—the youngest ever to be elected—at the hands of an assassin was the most dramatic political event in the United States in the 20th century. What made Kennedy's assassination even more shocking than might otherwise have been the case was its unexpectedness, the manner in which it was carried out, and, of course, the young age of Kennedy at the time of his death. As James Reston wrote in the *New York Times*, for many

in the United States and around the world, "[w]hat was killed in Dallas was not only the President but the promise."

Kennedy was in Texas to raise money for the **Democratic Party** and to kick-start his own campaign for reelection in 1964. The visit was not without its risks. Kennedy was not popular in Dallas, a city that was the stronghold of the John Birch Society, Dixiecrats, and ultraright Republican extremists who had previously greeted former Illinois governor **Adlai Stevenson II** and Texas's own Lyndon B. Johnson with considerable hostility. There was also a split within the Democratic Party between the supporters of conservative governor John Connally and the moderate liberal supporters of Senator **Ralph Yarborough**. But on this clear day, all appeared to be going well. Kennedy, traveling in a motorcade in an open convertible through the center of the city, was responding joyfully to the large, enthusiastic crowd, surrounded by Secret Service and FBI agents detailed to protect him. He was accompanied by his wife, Jacqueline "Jackie," who wore a striking pink outfit, and Governor John Connally and his wife, Nellie. Suddenly, witnesses heard three shots ring out, and the 46-year-old president was shot in the throat and then in the head. Connally was also hit.

At first, it was hoped that the shooting was not fatal. The car carrying Kennedy, Jackie, and Connally and his wife sped off to the nearby Parkland Memorial Hospital where it was hoped the president could be saved. The sight of Jackie retrieving/holding Kennedy's stricken head after he had been hit must surely rank as the most distressing and moving image in modern U.S. political history. However, at 1:00 p.m. CST Kennedy was pronounced dead, and a short time later CBS anchor **Walter Cronkite**, scarcely holding back his tears, announced the news to the nation. Shortly after, Kennedy's body was transferred to Air Force One at the Dallas airport and Vice President Lyndon B. Johnson was sworn in as president by federal judge Sarah T. Hughes in the presence of Jackie.

For decades following the assassination, Americans could relate where they were at the time they saw or heard of John Kennedy's

assassination. More than half of Kennedy's cabinet was on board a Boeing 707 over the Pacific Ocean headed to Japan on a goodwill trip when a news bulletin reported that three shots had been fired at the president's motorcade in Dallas. On board the cabinet plane, the news, at first, was incomplete. When word came that Kennedy had been shot in the head, U.S. agriculture secretary Orville Freeman and his wife, Jane, recalled that the group tried to stay optimistic. Then U.S. secretary of state **Dean Rusk** announced the awful news: "Ladies and gentlemen, it is official. We have had official word—the president has died. God save our nation." The Freemans remembered that "everybody was emotional, most of us shed tears." The delegation returned to Andrews Air Force Base in the middle of the night, several hours after Air Force One had landed with newly sworn-in president Lyndon B. Johnson, Jackie Kennedy, the casket, the Secret Service, and the Kennedy and Johnson entourages.

Meanwhile, in Dallas, a search was under way for Kennedy's assassin. It was ascertained that the shots had been fired from the sixth floor of the Texas Book Depository building adjacent to Dealey Plaza where the motorcade had been targeted. Later that afternoon, the suspected shooter, **Lee Harvey Oswald**, a former marine, was arrested in a nearby picture theater in Dallas after witnesses saw him shoot a Dallas police officer, J. D. Tippit, who had been seeking to interrogate him. The public knew little about Oswald, but authorities were aware that between 1957 and 1959 he had briefly lived in the **Soviet Union** and then, disaffected from communism, had returned to the United States. Oswald was an active and vocal supporter of Cuban leader **Fidel Castro** and had traveled to Mexico in the months prior to November 1963. Two days later, before he could be interrogated at any length by local police or federal law officers, he was shot dead by Dallas nightclub owner **Jack Ruby**, who had entered the police station parking garage while Oswald was being transferred. Oswald is reported to have said little more than he was "just a patsy."

President Johnson immediately set up a commission of inquiry to discover the facts surrounding the assassination and appointed Chief Justice **Earl Warren** to head it. Other members included Senator Richard Russell (D-Ga.), Senator John Sherman Cooper (R-Ky.), Representative Hale Boggs (D-La.), Representative Gerald Ford (R-Mich.), **Allen Dulles** (former director of the Central Intelligence Agency [CIA]), and **John J. McCloy** (former U.S. high commissioner to Germany). After an exhaustive investigation lasting 10 months, the **Warren Commission** concluded in an 888-page report presented to President Johnson on 24 September 1964 that Kennedy had been shot by a lone assassin, Lee Harvey Oswald; that Oswald had fired three shots at Kennedy; that he had acted alone; and that Jack Ruby also acted alone when he killed Oswald before he could stand trial. No radio or television stations had broadcast the assassination live as most media crews were waiting instead at the Dallas Trade Mart in anticipation of the president's arrival. Those members of the media who were with the motorcade were riding at the rear of the procession. The Warren Commission relied heavily on the visual record of Kennedy's last seconds recorded on a silent 8 mm film of the 26.6 seconds before, during, and immediately following the assassination filmed by garment manufacturer and amateur cameraman Abraham Zapruder, in what became known as the Zapruder film.

The findings of the commission were immediately rejected by many critics who believed it left as many questions unanswered as it had addressed, and that the assassination had been the result of a conspiracy. Most Americans could not believe that Oswald was capable of carrying out this act without assistance of some kind. Speculation about a conspiracy continued and grew to the point that, in 1976, a House of Representatives Select Committee on Assassinations (HSCA) was established to investigate Kennedy's assassination (and that of **Martin Luther King Jr.**). The HSCA concluded in a report in March 1979 that Kennedy was probably assassinated as a result of a conspiracy. The House committee agreed with the Warren Commission that three shots had been fired by Oswald but believed additional acoustic analysis of an

open microphone on a nearby police motorcycle suggested that a fourth shot may have been fired. The committee, however, was unable to identify the other gunman or the extent of the conspiracy. It did rule out the Soviet and Cuban governments, organized Cubans opposed to Fidel Castro, the Mafia, the Federal Bureau of Investigation (FBI), the CIA, and the Secret Service, although it could not rule out that individual members of those organizations were involved.

In 1988, the Justice Department's assistant attorney general formally reviewed the recommendations of the HSCA report and concluded "that no persuasive evidence can be identified to support the theory of a conspiracy in . . . the assassination of President Kennedy."

In October 2017, except for a few files that remain classified, all remaining government documents (around 2,800 files or some 5,000 pages) relating to the assassination were released under Section 5 of the President John F. Kennedy Assassination Records Collection Act of 1992. Initial readings of these records indicate that, although they provide additional details about Oswald and Ruby, they throw little new light on the events of that day. If anything, the files appear to reveal a good deal of confusion within the FBI and CIA and suggest the agencies may have tried to cover up their own inadequacies in monitoring Oswald prior to 22 November. Public opinion polls indicate that a majority of Americans continue to believe (60 percent according to a 2013 poll) there was a conspiracy to kill Kennedy. Some conspiracy theories even extend to include members of Kennedy's security detail.

One interesting facet concerning speculation about Kennedy's assassination came to light in November 2013 when the Israeli archives released the transcript of the cabinet meeting of 1 December 1963 in which the then Israeli foreign minister, Golda Meir, who had been in Washington for Kennedy's funeral, reported on her experience. Meir had met Kennedy in Palm Springs, Florida, late in December 1962, and the two appeared to have formed a strong bond.

Meir noted that there was widespread feeling that the world had changed with the assassination of Kennedy, not just for Americans but for the world. There was, she added, the added feeling of personal loss felt by millions. Meir then told the cabinet: "In my opinion, there are some 'dark corners' that I doubt will be ever be cleared. . . . The fact is there is something strange about the Dallas police." She was concerned that Oswald, "who was registered as a Castro man," was allowed to enter the book depository without any inspection of the package he was carrying and that Jack Ruby, known to the police and also recognized by Oswald, was allowed to enter the police station with a weapon. She concluded her remarks about the assassination: "If he [Oswald] was an emissary of Castro—if there's a clandestine group of Castro sympathizers that murdered the president, and it's organized in a way that they silence the murderer. . . . I would say this is as severe as Kennedy's murder. . . . Not only am I not a detective, I don't even like detective stories, but I ask myself—I think that Ruby was someone's emissary."

The handwritten Hebrew script above the typed cable reads as follows: "Israel-Washington: Harman* hereunder is the phrasing of the telegram that was sent directly to Rusk. For your information." [*Avraham Harman was the Israeli ambassador to the United States at the time.] *Courtesy of Israeli National Archives.*

Eternal flame over John F. Kennedy's grave. *Courtesy of Library of Congress.*

Meir's letter of condolence to U.S. secretary of state Dean Rusk immediately on hearing the news was typical of the response of many world leaders to the assassination of Kennedy. Two hundred and twenty representatives from more than 90 countries attended Kennedy's state funeral on Monday, 25 November 1963.

Around one million people lined the route of the funeral procession, from the Capitol back to the White House, then to St. Matthew's Cathedral, and finally to Arlington National Cemetery. Millions more watched as all three major networks televised the proceedings.

B

BADEAU, JOHN STOTHOFF (1903–1995). John Stothoff Badeau was born in Pittsburgh, Pennsylvania, on 24 February 1903. He gained a BS in civil engineering while attending Union Theological College in Schenectady, New York; a BD at Rutgers University; and an MA at Union Theological Seminary, Columbia University, where he also studied Arabic and Muslim philosophy. He was ordained a minister of the Dutch Reformed Church of America in 1928 (later converting to Presbyterianism). The United Mission assigned him to Iraq where he worked as a civil and sanitary engineer for the Mission in Mesopotamia.

In 1936, he was appointed professor of religion and philosophy at the American University of Cairo, and between 1946 and 1953, he was president of the university. During World War II, he had served in the Office of War Information in the **Middle East**. After returning to New York, he joined the Near East Foundation in New York, and in May 1961, he was the foundation's president when John F. Kennedy appointed him ambassador to the United Arab Republic (UAR).

Badeau's was a political appointment rather than one of a foreign service officer. Badeau had not previously met Kennedy and believed he was recommended for the post by Chester Bowles or **Dean Rusk**, whom he had known through the Near East Foundation. A number of factors played a role in Kennedy's choice. First, in picking Badeau, Kennedy bypassed the New York State Democratic organization of Michael H. Prendergast and Carmine G. DeSapio. This was one of the many moves by which Kennedy hoped to break the power of the New York machine. Second, the choice of Badeau illustrated Kennedy's desire to appoint scholars and experts as ambassadors to act as his personal emissaries, rather than rely on career service officers or political figures. Most important, Badeau was well known and liked in **Egypt**. Because U.S.-Egyptian relations had been strained since the Suez crisis of 1956, Kennedy wanted to start the relationship anew and establish a friendly association with President Gamal Abdel Nasser, head of the most powerful state in the Arab world. Badeau eased tensions between Nasser and the White House over their opposing views about Israel by suggesting that the two countries place "the Israel question" in an "ice box" and instead concentrate on issues relating to mutually beneficial future cooperation between the two nations.

The 1963 civil war in Yemen complicated the precarious relations between the United States and the UAR and threatened the already unstable Middle East. Following the overthrow of the monarchy in Yemen and the formation of the republic of Yemen in 1962, civil war broke out. The monarchies, **Jordan** and **Saudi Arabia**, backed royalist forces seeking to regain power, while Egypt and the United States supported the Yemeni republicans. The Kennedy administration believed that a republican Yemen constituted the best chance for maintaining political stability in the area. The decision was also consistent with Kennedy's avowed policy of backing the forces of change in international conflicts, as long as

these forces were anticommunist. Although the U.S. and Egyptian positions appeared identical, the United States strongly objected to the UAR military attacks on Saudi territory, believing it would threaten Saudi political stability and possibly Saudi oil supplies to the United States. These developments hindered Badeau's attempt at a rapprochement with Cairo.

In April 1963, the president sent Ellsworth Bunker as a special envoy to confer with Nasser to bolster ties, an action that somewhat weakened Badeau's influence with the UAR president. But it was a matter of too little too late. Partly because of the increasing American involvement in **Vietnam**, the Kennedy administration had drastically reduced economic aid to the UAR, which had been the cornerstone of the U.S. policy of conciliation. By the time of Kennedy's assassination, Cairo was moving closer to the communist bloc. This trend was underscored by Chou En-lai's visit to Cairo in December 1963.

Badeau resigned as ambassador in May 1964 to become head of the Middle East Institute at Columbia University. He remained there until his retirement in 1971. He continued to lecture occasionally at Georgetown University until his death in 1995 at the age of 92.

BAEZ, JOAN (1941–). Joan Chandos Baez was born on 9 January 1941 on Staten Island, New York, the middle of three daughters of a Mexican-born father and a Scottish-born mother. The family moved to California where her father earned his PhD in mathematics and physics in 1950. She was raised as a Quaker and because, in part, of the racial discrimination she experienced growing up due to her Mexican heritage, she became involved in causes of social equality at an early age.

Joan Baez is a folksinger/songwriter, with a lifelong commitment to political and social activism in the fields of nonviolence, **civil rights**, human rights, and the environment. During the Kennedy years, she epitomized folk music, and her songs, which encompass a wide range of music from counterculture through gospel music, revealed her commitment to social justice and civil rights. For many Americans,

Joan Baez was the sound of the civil rights movement. She has been actively performing for more than 60 years. She popularized the protest songs of Pete Seeger and mentored and interpreted the songs of **Bob Dylan**.

Baez was born with a natural soprano singing voice, and at the age of 13, she attended a concert by Pete Seeger, who was to become a legend in his own lifetime as the towering figure in American folk music. (His song, "Where Have All the Flowers Gone?" remains the benchmark for protest songs.) Baez recalls that she was so moved that she began singing Seeger's songs publicly. When her father accepted a faculty position at MIT in 1958 and the family moved to Massachusetts, she began performing in Boston and nearby Cambridge. At that time, Cambridge was in the center of the relatively new up-and-coming folk-music scene. In 1959, she sang at the Newport Folk Festival, and the following year she released her first album, *Joan Baez*.

Baez was immediately acknowledged as having an exceptional talent and a great affinity for interpreting and promulgating songs of social and political protest. She became prominent for her songs championing civil rights and denouncing the **Vietnam War**. She mentored and interpreted the songs of her friend Bob Dylan, whose songs "The Times They Are a-Changin'," "Hard Rain," and especially "Blowin' in the Wind" became the anthems of the anti–Vietnam War movement during the Kennedy and Johnson years—and beyond. Together, not only for Americans but also worldwide, Baez and Dylan came to personify folk music, and its message of protest. Baez wrote of Dylan, in terms that could equally apply to herself: "Bob Dylan's name would be so associated with the radical movements of the sixties that he, more than all the others who followed . . . would go down forever in the history books as a leader of dissent and social change" (Joan Baez, *And a Voice to Sing With: A Memoir* [New York: Simon & Schuster, 2009], 93). During the 1960s, in particular, her albums topped the charts. She was widely regarded as the foremost folksinger/songwriter of her generation and was widely emulated.

Baez became close friends with Dr. **Martin Luther King Jr.** When she discovered in 1961 that no black Americans were permitted to attend her concerts when she performed in the South, she had written into her contracts that she would sing only in desegregated venues. She was with King when he delivered his "I Have a Dream" speech in Washington in August 1964 and led the 350,000 assembled mass of people in singing "We Shall Overcome," aligning herself completely with the struggle for black civil rights. She went on to sing that song in December 1964 just before several thousand free speech movement supporters at the University of California, Berkeley, occupied Sproul Hall in a demonstration that first brought national attention to the growing student movement. She also sang at the first major national demonstration against the war in **Vietnam**, held in Washington, DC, in April 1965. In 1966, she walked arm in arm with King during a march in Mississippi.

Baez was also a pacifist, and in 1965, she founded the Institute for the Study of Nonviolence in Palo Alto, California. She advocated the use of nonviolent tactics to oppose the Vietnam War and refused to pay federal income tax. She also participated in "Stop the Draft Week" protests in Oakland, California, in October 1967. In 1968, Baez married David Harris, a leader of the Resistance, a draft resistance group, and in 1969, she gave birth to their son, Gabriel. Harris was briefly imprisoned for failing to report for induction into the army. The couple later divorced.

Baez continued to oppose the war and was one of a group of four Americans who visited North Vietnam in 1972, where she met with U.S. prisoners of war. She was in Hanoi during the U.S. Christmas 1972 bombing raids. Baez is as committed as ever to political activism, using her music to combat the evils of racism, violence, and environmental depredation.

BAILEY, JOHN MORAN (1904–1975). Born on 23 November 1904, in Hartford, Connecticut, John Moran Bailey grew up there. He received a BS degree from Catholic University in 1926 and an LLB degree from Harvard Law School in 1929. Following his admission to the

bar, Bailey quickly immersed himself in local Democratic politics. In 1932, he became a member of the Democratic State Committee and, in 1946, won the chairmanship. Allying himself with Representative **Abraham A. Ribicoff** (D-Conn.), Bailey created a powerful Democratic organization, gaining the governor's chair for Ribicoff in 1954 and a U.S. Senate seat for Thomas Dodd in 1958.

In national politics, Bailey proved a steadfast supporter of Senator John F. Kennedy. At the 1956 Democratic National Convention, he worked for Kennedy's nomination as vice president. Under his name, Kennedy strategists released "the Bailey Memorandum," which claimed that the senator, as a Roman Catholic, would add enormous strength among Catholic voters to the party's presidential campaign.

Although Kennedy's race for second place on the 1956 ticket failed, his managers again utilized the memorandum during the senator's drive for the presidential nomination four years later. With Congressman Eugene J. Keough (D-N.Y.), Bailey led efforts in 1960 to round up convention support for Kennedy among New England and New York delegates. All 114 New England votes and 104 of New York's 114 votes were cast for Kennedy, who won on the first ballot. Following Kennedy's nomination, Bailey strongly endorsed the selection of Senator **Lyndon B. Johnson** (D-Tex.) for vice president. Between the convention and general election, Bailey worked primarily as a liaison with other state party leaders, while successfully directing the Connecticut Kennedy-Johnson campaign.

Kennedy named Bailey as chairman of the Democratic National Committee in January 1961 and gave him a major voice in the distribution of party patronage. Beginning in October 1961, the president assigned to Bailey, who was normally regarded as a political technician rather than a spokesman, the task of defending the administration against criticisms made by the Republican National Committee chairman, Representative William E. Miller (R-N.Y.). As national committee chairman, Bailey's main task was to maintain Democratic majorities in Congress. In the 1962 elections, the **Democratic Party** avoided

the usual off-year losses for the party occupying the White House. The Democrats gained four Senate seats while losing only four in the House of Representatives. The number of Democratic governors remained unchanged at 34, although the GOP captured state houses in several large, industrial states. In Connecticut, where Bailey continued as state chairman, the Democrats retained the governorship and elected Ribicoff to the U.S. Senate. On 12 November 1963, President Kennedy and his aides met with Bailey to plan the 1964 presidential campaign. Kennedy designated Stephen Smith, his brother-in-law, and Bailey as codirectors of the effort. Although he remained party chairman after Kennedy's death 10 days later, Bailey played a limited role in the presidential campaign of Lyndon B. Johnson.

Bailey died on 10 April 1975 and is buried in Cedar Hills cemetery in Hartford. *See also* O'BRIEN, LAWRENCE FRANCIS, JR.

BALDWIN, JAMES (1924–1987). James Arthur "Jimmy" Baldwin (2 August 1924–1 December 1987) was an American essayist, novelist, and social critic. Although he lived much of his life in France, his essays, especially *Notes of a Native Son* (1955), explore primarily the experience of racial, sexual, and class discrimination in mid-20th-century America. His major publications include *The Fire Next Time* (1963) and *No Names in the Street* (1972).

Baldwin grew up in Harlem in a large family ruled by a very strict stepfather who was a preacher. During his adolescence, he tried preaching, and although more successful than his father, he gave it up at age 17 and left home, moving to Greenwich Village. He took up writing, but after experiencing racial and sexual discrimination as a gay man, at the age of 24 Baldwin left for France, where in 1953 he finished *Go Tell It on the Mountain*, in which he described the religious experience in Harlem.

Although he lived abroad and devoted most his energies to creative writing, Baldwin continued to take an active interest in the **civil rights** movement in America. During the early 1960s, Baldwin was probably the most widely read and discussed black writer

in America. In *The Crisis of the Negro Intellectual*, Harold Cruse characterized Baldwin as "the chief spokesman for the Negro among the intellectual class" during the early years of the decade. In *The Fire Next Time*, two essays published in 1963, Baldwin argued that black people in America "are very well placed indeed to precipitate chaos and ring down the curtain on the American dream." He went on to predict that "if we do not dare everything, the fulfillment of the prophecy, recreated from the Bible in song by a slave, is upon us: 'God gave Noah the rainbow sign, no more water, the fire next time.'" Read in light of the 1965 Watts riot and later violence in inner cities across the nation, *The Fire Next Time* was a prophetic and insightful study of American race relations.

In May 1963, Baldwin arranged a meeting between President John F. Kennedy and a dozen black leaders and artists. Baldwin returned from Europe in March 1965 to participate in a march from Selma to Montgomery, Alabama, led by **Martin Luther King Jr.** In February 1967, he resigned from the advisory board of *Liberator*, a black nationalist monthly with which he had been associated since 1961, in protest against the magazine's publication of allegedly anti-Semitic articles. His writings also dealt increasingly with the topic of homosexuality. In fact, Baldwin's work as a whole focused more on conflict and the human condition than simply the lives of **African Americans**. His writing also earned Baldwin extensive scrutiny by the Federal Bureau of Investigation, which compiled a file of more than 1,700 pages on the author. In 1983, he became a professor at the University of Massachusetts. He died of cancer four years later in France. *See also* HOWE, IRVING.

BALL, GEORGE WILDMAN (1909–1994). George Wildman Ball was born in Des Moines, Iowa, on 21 December 1909 in Des Moines, Iowa, the third son of Amos and Edna Wildman Ball. His mother was a teacher, and his father was a Scottish immigrant who became a vice president of Standard Oil of Indiana. Following his graduation from Northwestern University Law School in 1933, Ball worked for the

Farm Credit Administration and Treasury Department. In 1935, he returned to Illinois and joined a Chicago law firm, where **Adlai Stevenson II** was one of his colleagues. Ball reentered government service in 1942 in the Office of Lend-Lease Administration and, in 1944, was appointed director of the U.S. Strategic Bombing Survey.

After the war, Ball resumed private law practice and became a specialist on international trade. He worked closely with Jean Monnet on plans for the new European Coal and Steel Community. He later represented this organization and several other Common Market agencies in the United States. In 1952 and 1956, Ball played an important role in Stevenson's presidential campaign, and in 1960, he served as Stevenson's manager at the Los Angeles convention. Despite Ball's support of Stevenson, President John F. Kennedy, impressed with a report on economic and commercial policy that the lawyer had written, designated Ball as undersecretary of state for economic affairs in January 1961.

His dissenting views stemmed rather from his belief that Southeast Asia was peripheral to American interests, diverting attention from the main arena, which he said lay in Europe. This theme—that a united Western Europe was the key to American foreign policy because it would strengthen the Atlantic alliance and provide a cushion between the United States and the **Soviet Union**—was, in fact, the touchstone of Mr. Ball's vision of global politics. Ball became an administration troubleshooter, shuttling between Athens, Ankara, and Nicosia to mediate crises over Cyprus and dashing off to Pakistan, the Congo, the Dominican Republic, and other trouble spots to ease tensions or halt fighting. He was a prodigious toiler and traveler, often working six days a week and 70 hours at a stretch, and he was usually at his best under pressure.

During the early months of the Kennedy administration, Ball was primarily involved in the formation of U.S. trade policy. Concerned with America's continued adverse balance of payments and anticipating increased problems after Great Britain's expected entrance into the Common Market, Ball advocated a complete revision of U.S. trade policy to bring down tariff levels and give the president flexibility to meet new conditions. These proposals were embodied in the **Trade Expansion Act** of 1962, which Ball helped draft. This measure cut tariffs by 50 percent and 100 percent on many foreign goods and gave the president wide discretionary powers to retaliate against foreign import restrictions.

In addition to his activities as economic adviser, Ball was concerned with U.S. policy toward the Congo, where the secession of mineral-rich Katanga Province shortly after Belgium had granted independence in June 1960 threatened the viability of the central government. Despite his close connection with Western Europe and sympathy for the plight of the Belgians, Ball supported the policy of the State Department's "New Africa" group, led by men such as Harlan Cleveland, which advocated the use of force against Katanga if necessary to achieve reunification. Ball lobbied behind the scenes at the **United Nations** (UN) and within the Kennedy administration for the adoption of this policy. Reunification was achieved in January 1963 through the use of UN troops backed by American military support.

In November 1961, Ball replaced Chester Bowles as undersecretary of state, the second-ranking position in the State Department. The change was made because of Kennedy's desire to place trusted aides in the State Department, which he felt had not performed effectively, and because of continual clashes between Bowles and Kennedy advisers, particularly Attorney General **Robert Kennedy**. During the **Cuban missile crisis** of October 1962, Ball served as a member of the Executive Committee of the National Security Council, the committee of high-ranking advisers formed to counsel the president after the discovery of Soviet offensive missiles in **Cuba**. After Kennedy proclaimed a "quarantine" of Cuba on October 22, Ball directed the arrangement of a program to inform the allies of the U.S. decision and to write a legal justification of the action. During the early 1960s, Ball also became increasingly involved with the growing war in **Vietnam**. In 1961, when the

administration was discussing policy options in Vietnam, Ball opposed the recommendation of **Maxwell D. Taylor** and **Walt W. Rostow** to introduce combat forces into that country because he felt it would lead to an ever-increasing involvement. The recommendation was not approved. Ball strongly opposed the regime of South Vietnamese president Ngo Dinh Diem and his brother Ngo Dinh Nhu. In August 1963, he urged that American support of the government be withdrawn to force either a change of policy or a coup. Following the August 1963 attack of Nhu's secret police on Buddhist dissidents, Ball, in conjunction with **Michael Forrestal, W. Averell Harriman**, and Roger Hilsman, drafted the "August 24 Cable" sent to **Henry Cabot Lodge Jr.**, the new U.S. ambassador to Vietnam. The message stated that the United States could not accept Nhu's crackdown. It also informed Lodge that "Diem must be given [a] chance to rid himself of Nhu" but cautioned that if Diem did not take that step, the United States "must face the possibility that Diem himself cannot be preserved." Lodge was also instructed to privately inform South Vietnamese generals contemplating a coup that if Nhu remained, the United States would "give them direct support in any interim period of breakdown [of the] central government mechanism." The coup failed to take place immediately because of the generals' inability to achieve a favorable balance of forces in the Saigon area and because of doubts about the firmness of U.S. commitments to Diem's overthrow. However, a coup, staged by different military leaders, was eventually carried out in November 1963.

During the **Lyndon B. Johnson** administration, Ball objected to the large-scale troop commitments and intensive bombing raids against North Vietnam ordered by the president. Convinced that he could not change American policy, he left office in September 1966 to return to his law firm and to investment banking. A quiet man who remained personally loyal to Johnson and U.S. secretary of state **Dean Rusk**, his determined opposition to the war became widely known only after the publication of the Pentagon Papers in 1971. *See also* JOHNSON, URAL ALEXIS.

BARNETT, ROSS ROBERT (1898–1987). Ross Robert Barnett was born in the hamlet of Standing Pine in Leake County, near Carthage, Mississippi, on 22 January 1898, the youngest of 10 children in a farm family. His father was a veteran of the Confederate army. Ross worked his way through high school and Mississippi College and served in the U.S. Army in World War I. He then earned his living as a high school coach and teacher and taught Sunday school while attending the Mississippi School of Law at Oxford.

He opened a law office in Jackson, the state capital, and built a lucrative civil practice. He served as president of the Mississippi Bar Association in the 1940s and, in 1956, was among the southern attorneys who helped John Kasper, a racist agitator convicted in Tennessee after school-integration violence. After three attempts, Barnett was elected governor of Mississippi in 1959 and took office in January 1960. White supremacy was virtually Mr. Barnett's sole campaign theme. A member of the segregationist Citizens Councils, Barnett preached white supremacy during his campaign with what one observer called a "Bible-pounding evangelistic fervor." Repeatedly he promised he would "rot in jail" before he would "let one Negro ever darken the sacred threshold of our white schools."

During the years of his rule, Barnett strongly supported the segregationist cause in his state and promoted some initiatives aimed at celebrating the Confederacy. In Barnett's first 10 weeks in office, 24 new segregation bills were introduced in the state legislature. Although his administration was marked by achievements in industrializing Mississippi, Governor Barnett was best remembered for his role in the riots of 1 October 1962, the day after **James H. Meredith**, a 29-year-old black U.S. Air Force veteran, sought to enroll at the University of Mississippi campus in Oxford. Barnett defied three federal court orders mandating the admission of Meredith to the University of Mississippi in September 1962. There had been no desegregation in any of the state's public schools until then, and shortly after the final court order for Meredith's admission was handed down on 10 September,

Barnett promised to oppose it, declaring, "We will not surrender to the evil and illegal forces of tyranny." The resulting confrontation was the sharpest clash between a state and the federal government since the Civil War.

Governor Barnett denied Meredith admission to the university after pressuring the legislature to cloak him with legal authority usually exercised by the state's College Board. As early efforts to register Meredith were unsuccessful and public disorders seemed imminent, Governor Barnett and Attorney General **Robert Kennedy** held a number of tense telephone conversations, with Kenney hoping to persuade the governor to comply with the court orders and thus obviate the need to call in federal troops. Kennedy later recalled that among the strategies he and Barnett discussed, one involved the governor physically blocking Meredith and a force of U.S. marshals when they came on the campus that day, but then stepping aside when the marshals drew guns. President Kennedy entered the behind-the-scenes negotiations on 29 September and, in three phone conversations with Barnett, worked out a new arrangement in which Barnett would go to Oxford on 1 October, ostensibly planning to deny Meredith admission again while Meredith himself would enroll in Jackson. This plan, like the former, was also abandoned.

On 29 September, President Kennedy federalized members of the National Guard, and the governor finally yielded. Federal marshals and state police entered the campus late that afternoon, while Meredith was flown in from Memphis and taken to his dormitory room around 6 p.m. At 9 p.m., Barnett issued a statement declaring that the state was "surrounded by armed forces" and "physically overpowered" but calling on Mississippians to "preserve the peace and avoid bloodshed."

When Mr. Meredith and federal marshals arrived at the school, an army of segregationists assembled just off the campus. They poured onto the campus when the Highway Patrol was withdrawn from the entrances. The ensuing riot lasted into the early morning hours, ending only after Kennedy called in both the National Guard and the army. Two men died during the

night of violence, and more than 350 were injured. At 8 a.m. on 1 October, Meredith finally registered at the university.

The United States Court of Appeals for the Fifth Circuit cited Governor Barnett for contempt for his part in the affair, and he was assessed a penalty of $10,000 a day and sentenced to jail. He never served prison time or paid the fine, and the charges finally were dropped in 1965.

Mr. Barnett, who could not succeed himself, left office when his term ran out in 1964 and returned to the practice of law. He sought to make a political comeback in 1967, entering the Democratic gubernatorial contest, but he suffered a humiliating defeat when he finished a weak fourth in the party primary. He died at the age of 89 on 6 November 1987. *See also* CIVIL RIGHTS.

BAY OF PIGS. In April 1961, within three months of assuming office, John F. Kennedy was faced with one of the defining moments of his presidency. It involved **Cuba.** Two years earlier, in 1959, **Fidel Castro** had seized power in Cuba, overthrowing a dictatorial ally of the United States. Castro nationalized foreign (mainly U.S.) assets, forged close ties with the Soviet bloc, and promised to support revolutionary movements throughout Latin America. As a result, in 1960, President **Dwight D. Eisenhower** had broken off diplomatic relations with Cuba.

Kennedy discovered that the Central Intelligence Agency (CIA) had organized and designed a carefully planned counterrevolutionary movement to overthrow the Castro regime in spring 1961. At the time of Kennedy's inauguration, some 2,000 to 3,000 rebel Cuban soldiers were training in the United States and Guatemala for an invasion of the island. The CIA leadership believed that the guerrilla invasion would assuredly ignite a revolution and free the country from communist domination. Most of Kennedy's advisers had serious doubts about the plan and its underlying assumptions. Chester Bowles concluded that it was "a highly risky operation" with little chance of success. He penned a note to U.S. secretary of state **Dean Rusk:** "If you agree that this operation

would be a mistake, I suggest that you personally and privately communicate your views to the President." Rusk indeed shared Bowles's doubts but preferred to wait for the president to seek his advice. General Edward Lansdale, the government's leading expert on **counterinsurgency**, took his misgivings to Paul Nitze, the assistant secretary of defense for international security affairs. Despite sharing Lansdale's misgivings, Nitze supported the project, explaining in his memoirs: "The Soviet Union had inserted itself in our backyard . . . in the form of the Castro regime in Cuba. Like a spreading cancer, it should, if possible, be excised from the Americas." Kennedy himself doubted the wisdom of the invasion but gave grudging consent. He assured the nation that he would never commit American troops to any assault on Cuba.

On 17 April 1961, around 1,300 Cuban assault troops struck the Cienaja de Zapata swamps of Las Villas Province (Bay of Pigs) on the south coast of Cuba. There was no popular uprising. Kennedy's refusal to back the invasion with U.S. air power assured Castro's control of the skies. Cuban regulars quickly demolished the invading forces. The president accepted blame for the fiasco with good grace. So favorable was the public response to such executive candor that Kennedy's popularity soared. "My God," he commented. "It's worse than Eisenhower." The invasion's failure demonstrated both that the Castro regime enjoyed substantial national support and that guerrillas, operating in hostile territory, have little assurance of victory. Upon reflection, Kennedy and his staff agreed that the decision not to use American forces was the correct one.

However, the failure of the Bay of Pigs invasion did not end Washington's determination to remove Castro. Washington's growing obsession with Castro received considerable impetus when the Cuban leader, basking in the prestige of victory, began to convert Cuba into a Soviet model with a single governing party, a command economy, and stronger economic ties to the Soviet bloc. The Soviets, in exchange, rewarded Castro with shipments of tanks and artillery, along with the necessary advisers and technicians. For the Kennedy administration,

Castro's ties to the Kremlin rendered him the agent of international communism in the Western Hemisphere. On 30 November, the president issued a memorandum committing the United States to help the Cuban people overthrow Castro. Thereafter, the administration sent sabotage units of Cuban émigrés into Cuba under a covert action plan called Operation Mongoose, with General Lansdale in command. A planning document of 20 February 1962 set the target dates of the operation. After the necessary internal preparations, guerrilla operations would begin in August and September 1962; during October, an open revolt would establish the new government. Another document, of 14 March 1962, declared that "the U.S. will make maximum use of indigenous resources, internal and external, but recognizes that final success will require decisive U.S. military intervention."

Attorney General **Robert Kennedy**, determined to get Castro after the Bay of Pigs, was Mongoose's driving force. During 1962, the Kennedy administration embarked on a variety of maneuvers to weaken the Castro regime. In January, the foreign ministers of the Organization of American States (OAS) met in Punta del Este, Uruguay, to deal with the issue of Castro's alliance with the Soviet bloc. Secretary Rusk sought diplomatic sanctions against Cuba. Seven Latin American states, including the larger ones, issued a memorandum on 24 January recognizing "the incompatibility between the present regime in Cuba and the inter-American system," but they opposed sanctions. Rusk now limited his objective to the suspension of Cuba from the Council of the OAS. In his plea to the delegates on 25 January, he declared that the United States had no quarrel with the Cuban people, or even with the principles of the Cuban Revolution, but rather "with the use of Cuba as a 'bridgehead in the Americas' for Communist efforts to destroy free governments in this hemisphere." On 31 January, the conference adopted the seven-nation memorandum. On the resolution excluding Cuba, the vote was a bare two-thirds, 14 to 1 (Cuba), with six abstentions. The convention recognized the right of any country to sever trade relations with Cuba.

On 2 February, the United States instituted a complete embargo. During succeeding weeks, the administration undermined Cuban trade negotiations with Israel, **Jordan**, **Iran**, Greece, and Japan. "In short," concluded historian Raymond Garthoff, "by the spring of 1962 the United States had embarked on a concerted campaign of overt and covert political, economic, psychological, and clandestine operations to weaken the Castro regime." Military contingency plans had anticipated a possible air and ground assault against Cuba. In December 1962, the captured invaders were ransomed for U.S. $53 million in food and medicine, supplied by private donations. *See also* COLD WAR; CUBAN MISSILE CRISIS.

BELL, DAVID ELLIOTT (1919–2000). David Elliott Bell was born in Jamestown, North Dakota, on 20 January 1919, and raised in Palo Alto, California, where his father taught at Stanford University. He graduated from Pomona College and then gained an MA in economics at Harvard University. He joined the Bureau of the Budget in 1942, served in the U.S. Marine Corps, and then returned to the bureau in 1945. Between 1947 and 1953, Bell taught at Harvard's Graduate School of Public Administration, but he served the federal government in several administrations specializing in drafting presidential budget messages and speeches on economic affairs. He was White House executive assistant under President **Harry S. Truman** and economic adviser to Pakistan under President **Dwight D. Eisenhower**, becoming a recognized authority on the economic problems of underdeveloped countries. Bell worked for **Adlai Stevenson II** in his 1952 presidential campaign and then returned to Harvard. Although Bell did not work for John F. Kennedy's election, **Clark Clifford** recommended him to Kennedy for the post of budget director. Kennedy announced the appointment on 2 December 1960, citing Bell's experience in working with both the bureau and the White House and his experience in the area of foreign aid.

The post of budget director had become more critical since Franklin Roosevelt's time, as the government's role in the economy expanded. The Bureau of the Budget not only made the final judgment on allocations to federal programs but also made policy by sponsoring legislation, encouraging certain programs, and discouraging others. More than most agencies, it worked closely with Congress.

Kennedy publicly stated that he wanted a balanced budget, but he felt that the economic recession and high unemployment rate inherited from the Eisenhower years constituted a higher priority. The Kennedy administration and Bell faced a deficit of some $2.8 billion left by the Eisenhower administration. Bell, with the assistance of **Ted Sorensen**, **Myer Feldman**, and **Lawrence O'Brien**, helped draft Kennedy's complete legislative program for 1962. One of the most important parts of the program was the request for a large tax cut. Although Bell thought it would leave a large budget deficit and stimulate inflation, he held that a tax cut of around $10 billion would finally end the recession of 1960–1961. Balancing the budget, on the other hand, he believed would bring any recovery to a halt below full employment levels. Because of congressional opposition, the tax reduction was not enacted until February 1964.

Kennedy appointed Bell as administrator of the Agency for International Development (AID) in November 1962. AID was a newly created semiautonomous agency within the State Department, designed to coordinate and rationalize foreign aid programs. AID's guiding principles owed much to the economic development theories of **Walt W. Rostow** and to the Ford Foundation's experience in the underdeveloped world. Whereas Eisenhower's foreign aid policy concentrated on grants intended for military and short-range purposes, the Kennedy administration planned to offer long-term loans and credits to governments and native entrepreneurs. In addition, AID sought to train a cadre of experts in foreign aid. Attempts were made to enlist the skills of individuals in American private enterprise, thereby making foreign aid more representative of a national consensus. As head of AID, Bell had to work under constant public and congressional criticism. Congress cut Kennedy's foreign aid

request for the fiscal year 1963 by $1 billion to a final appropriation of $3.9 billion.

Bell hoped for congressional approval of around $5 billion in foreign aid for fiscal year 1964, but by that time, attacks on the program had grown even more vociferous. Congressional liberals, such as Senator **Wayne Morse** (D-Ore.), turned against "waste" in foreign aid, while conservatives, such as Senator **Barry M. Goldwater** (R-Ariz.), wanted to eliminate all economic foreign aid, saving only the military programs. The final appropriation was only $3 billion despite the protests of Bell and other members of the administration.

Bell resigned as head of AID in June 1966 to become a vice president of the Ford Foundation, a private independent institution dedicated to advancing social justice in the United States and in developing nations. When he left the government in 1966, an editorial in the *Washington Post* called him "the most successful administrator of foreign aid since the Marshall Plan," adding that he "managed to build and retain the confidence of Congress through a combination of precision, patience and staying power." The editorial said he was "flexible in attitude but willing to fight for principle."

He retired from the Ford Foundation in 1980. From 1981 until taking emeritus status in 1988, he was professor of population sciences and international health at Harvard's School of Public Health. He also had been chairman of the population sciences department and director of the Center for Population Studies. Bell died of leukemia on 6 September 2000 in Cambridge, Massachusetts.

BERLE, ADOLF AUGUSTUS, JR. (1895– 1971). Adolf Augustus Berle Jr. was born in Boston, Massachusetts, on 29 January 1895. His father was a highly regarded Congregational minister of German background. Given a home **education** by his parents, he entered Harvard College at the age of 14 where he earned an MA and graduated in law in 1916. He served in U.S. Army intelligence during World War I and attended the Paris Peace Conference. He moved to New York City and began a long teaching career, mainly at

Columbia University. He was a champion of liberal causes and became one of Franklin D. Roosevelt's original "brain trusters," advising Roosevelt in the 1932 campaign and preparing much of the early New Deal legislation. Until 1938, Berle also was involved in New York City government, where he helped Mayor Fiorello H. La Guardia reorganize the city's finances.

Prior to the presidency of John F. Kennedy, Berle had considerable experience with Latin America. In 1938, Roosevelt appointed him assistant secretary of state for Latin American affairs, a position he held until 1944. He then served as ambassador to Brazil, where he supported military insurgents who overthrew the dictatorship of Getulio Vargas in 1945. Berle was both an architect and an instrument of Roosevelt's "Good Neighbor" policy, and he earned a popularity in Latin America unusual for a North American.

During the 1950s, Berle confined himself to his law practice, to his activity with the New York State Liberal Party, and to participation in some of the studies sponsored by the Rockefeller Brothers Fund. Berle moved to support Kennedy during the 1960 presidential elections, and the president-elect asked him to head a six-man task force designed to make recommendations on both immediate Latin American problems and long-range policy. The task force report, reflecting Berle's fear of **Fidel Castro**'s **Cuba**, stated that the communists intended to "convert the Latin American social revolution into a Marxist attack on the United States itself." Believing that the social revolution was inevitable, Berle advised the United States to decrease its support of right-wing dictatorships and openly support democratic-progressive political movements. The recommendations, made in January 1961, found their most significant expression in the new administration's "**Alliance for Progress**," which marked a change from the Latin American policy pursued in the Eisenhower-Dulles years. His idea of the alliance was a more vigorous version of the Good Neighbor policy.

To Berle, Latin America in 1960 resembled Europe in 1947, and the situation called for a new Marshall Plan to defeat the communist

effort to bring the **Cold War** to the Southern Hemisphere. His task force, in fact, advised that a State Department undersecretaryship for the Western Hemisphere be set up, "thus ending stepchild status of this area in U.S. policy." Berle, however, decided to serve as head of an interdepartmental task force on Latin America with authority at least equal to that of an assistant secretary of state. The task force was to be directly responsible to the president and the secretary of state. Berle served in his new post from January through July 1961.

He played no role in planning the **Bay of Pigs** invasion, although his advice was occasionally solicited. He wrote that he "did not dissent," although he disliked the covert nature of the Central Intelligence Agency's plan and the agency's indifference to the politics of the Cuban exiles whom they trained.

When Berle left his post in July 1961, he was on good terms with Kennedy but was disturbed that the State Department was so slow in implementing new policies. He had also warned the United States to take more forceful action against Castro with the cooperation of the other American nations, but he found that the inter-American machinery, particularly the Organization of American States, was ineffective.

Berle remained active until his death on 17 March 1971, in New York City, writing on Latin America and economics, offering his advice to the government, and participating in New York City politics.

BERLIN CRISIS OF 1961. Berlin had been a contentious issue between the United States and the **Soviet Union** since the end of World War II, when the city had been occupied by Soviet forces. Since 1945, the city had been divided between Allied forces in the western sector and Soviet forces in the eastern sector. Germany itself was also divided into two sectors: the Federal Republic of Germany (West Germany) and the German Democratic Republic (East Germany). Berlin was located in the eastern sector. The goal of the United States was the unification of the two sectors; the Soviet Union wished the two sectors to remain separate states. The situation stayed unresolved and a flashpoint of tension between the United States and the Soviet Union when John F. Kennedy assumed the presidency.

In his inaugural address, Kennedy acknowledged his readiness to negotiate with the Soviets over Berlin, and soon thereafter, he announced his intention "to explore promptly all possible areas of cooperation with the Soviet Union." From the outset of his administration, Kennedy saw the question of the future of Berlin as a test of his toughness in dealing with his Soviet counterpart **Nikita Khrushchev**. He was confident that United States nuclear supremacy would enable him to confront Khrushchev on outstanding issues, including Berlin, with some prospect of success.

In March, Kennedy requested Dean Acheson recommend an American policy for Berlin. In his report, Acheson warned against advocating any change in the status of Berlin. Unless the United States took an uncompromising stand on the Berlin question, Acheson asserted, the Soviet Union would dominate Europe and, eventually, Asia and **Africa**. Acheson also recommended a huge increase in the military budget.

Kennedy visited Vienna in June 1961 to meet the Soviet leader to discuss Berlin, and he received a shock. Khrushchev told Kennedy that unless the Western powers accepted the conversion of West Berlin into a free city by 31 December 1961, the Soviet Union would negotiate a treaty with East Germany and assign it control of the access routes into West Berlin. Kennedy replied that the West intended to assert its international right to remain in the city, even at the risk of war.

On his return to Washington, Kennedy announced, on July 25, that he would request Congress to allocate a supplemental defense budget increase of $3.2 billion for an immediate buildup in conventional forces. This expenditure would increase the U.S. Army's manpower from 875,000 to one million. Within weeks, the United States dispatched an additional 40,000 troops to Europe. At the same time, Kennedy requested standing authority to call up Army Reserves and triple the draft calls. Kennedy's auxiliary defense program

President John F. Kennedy and Dean Acheson standing in the doorway of Acheson's home at 2805 P Street NW, Washington, DC, after a meeting. *Courtesy of Library of Congress.*

pushed the tension over Berlin to a new high. He proclaimed "Captive Nations Week" and urged the American people to recommit themselves to the support and just aspirations of all suppressed peoples and affirmed the American goal of German reunification.

At a North Atlantic Treaty Organization meeting on 4 August, France and West Germany supported Kennedy's approach, including the use of military action in defense of West Berlin's freedom and viability. East Germany controlled the access routes to West Berlin. Anticipating a crisis, the East German government, in July, began to restrict movements of East Germans into West Berlin. The resulting anxiety sent a flood of East Germans across the line, including hundreds of professionals. Around 47,000 people fled during the first 12 days of August. On the night of 9 August, the communists sealed the border between East and West Berlin. They stopped cars and pedestrians at the Brandenburg Gate as well as all service on the communist-run elevated rail line. Beginning with a barricade of barbed wire, the East Germans eventually sealed off West Berlin completely by erecting a concrete wall; the "Berlin Wall." Germans watched in despair. Western leaders complained that the barricades broke the four-power agreement on Berlin, but they shrank from the risk of initiating a war.

Determined to demonstrate his strength of purpose, Kennedy sent a U.S. battle group from Mannheim down the autobahn through the East German checkpoints into West Berlin. He sent Vice President **Lyndon B. Johnson** to Bonn, the West German capital, as well as to West Berlin itself, to further reassure the West Germans of U.S. support. Johnson told a Bonn audience that the United States did not intend to retreat. The deadlock continued until October 1961, when Khrushchev announced that he would withdraw his 31 December deadline if the Western powers revealed some willingness to negotiate.

This Berlin crisis died, as did those that preceded it, with the both sides reluctant to fight over Berlin. The Western powers refused to compromise on their principle of self-determination, and the Soviet bloc succeeded

in impeding East German movement into the West German Republic. Berlin remained a symbol of their values for both sides. *See also* CUBAN MISSILE CRISIS; KAYSEN, CARL.

BISSELL, RICHARD MERVIN, JR. (1909–1994). Richard Mervin Bissell Jr. was born in Hartford, Connecticut, to a wealthy and prominent family, on 18 September 1909. His father was president of Hartford Fire Insurance. He was educated at the Groton School (where one of his classmates was **Joseph Alsop**); Yale University, where he gained a PhD in economics in 1939; and the London School of Economics. He taught economics at Yale and the Massachusetts Institute of Technology. During World War II, he worked for several government agencies supervising allied shipping. Bissell was appointed assistant administrator of the Marshall Plan in 1948 and served in that capacity until 1951, including a brief tenure as acting administrator.

On his return to the United States, Bissell moved to Washington, DC, where he became a member of the **Georgetown Set**, a group of influential journalists, politicians, and government officials. In 1954, at the urging of then deputy director of plans (DDP) Frank Wisner—a fellow member of the Georgetown Set—he joined the Central Intelligence Agency (CIA) as special assistant to Director **Allen W. Dulles.** Prior to and during the Kennedy administration as CIA deputy director for plans, he was in charge of covert activities to overthrow or remove Cuban leader **Fidel Castro**.

Although Bissell was one of the few top CIA officials without a long intelligence background, he conceived and supervised the program of U-2 spy-plane flights over the **Soviet Union** and other countries. He also helped develop the SR-71 high-altitude surveillance plane, and he was an early advocate of surveillance satellites. On 1 January 1959, Bissell assumed the office of the CIA's DDP, thereby becoming responsible for covert operations.

In response to a direction by President **Dwight D. Eisenhower** in March 1960, Bissell instructed the CIA to recruit and train a force of Cuban exiles capable of guerrilla action against the Cuban government as part of

a covert attempt to replace the Castro regime with one more acceptable to the United States. According to a Senate Select Committee report released in 1975, in September 1960 Bissell authorized an attempt on the life of Fidel Castro, which involved CIA cooperation with organized crime leaders Sam Giancana and John Roselli. The Mafia bosses were happy to cooperate as they were angry at Castro's closure of their illegal operations in Cuba, and, in turn, the Mafia provided the CIA with plausible deniability in subsequent events. Bissell claimed that Dulles was fully informed of these activities. It was unclear whether President Eisenhower had authorized or was aware of the plans, nor could the Senate Committee report determine whether Kennedy was ever informed of the plans to assassinate Castro. Among other projects Bissell supervised around this time was an unsuccessful effort, started in August 1960, to assassinate Congolese leader Patrice Lumumba.

On 18 November 1960, Bissell and Dulles briefed president-elect John F. Kennedy on the training of the exile force taking place at a CIA camp in Guatemala with plans for landing them in Cuba at a place known as the **Bay of Pigs**. On 29 November, after a more detailed briefing, despite the advice of the Pentagon to abandon the project and the reservations of his advisers Chester Bowles, **Theodore Sorensen**, and Arthur Schlesinger, Kennedy ordered the planning to proceed. After a series of top-level meetings, at which Dulles and Bissell presented and defended the CIA invasion plan, in early April 1961, Kennedy, in a vain attempt to ensure plausible deniability, gave his approval for a plan of action that he had severely curtailed. The CIA plan called for two air strikes against the Cuban air force, one before and one simultaneous with a landing at the Bay of Pigs. Kennedy halved the number of aircraft to be used and refused naval support.

The operation launched on 17 April did not go well, and it was soon apparent that the CIA plan had serious weaknesses. By 19 April, the invasion force was completely defeated. Any chance that Bissell had of being appointed to the CIA directorship vanished. According to the account offered by David Wise and Thomas

B. Ross in *The Invisible Government*, Kennedy had been planning major changes in the CIA before the Cuban invasion. After the Bay of Pigs fiasco, the top CIA leadership was quietly replaced. Dulles's resignation was accepted on 27 September 1961, and Bissell resigned on 17 February 1962. Others were also let go.

Bissell received a secret intelligence medal for his years of service and shortly thereafter became head of the Institute of Defense Analysis, a Pentagon think tank set up to evaluate weapons systems. He remained there until 1964, when he became an executive of the United Aircraft Corporation. In February 1994, Bissell died at his home in Farmington, Connecticut.

BLACK, EUGENE ROBERT, SR. (1898–1992). Eugene Robert Black Sr. was born on 1 May 1898, in Atlanta, Georgia. His father, also born in Atlanta and named Eugene Robert Black I (7 January 1873–19 December 1934), was chairman of the Federal Reserve from 9 May 1933 to his death from a heart attack on 15 August 1934. The son, Eugene Sr., graduated from the University of Georgia in 1917. He served as an ensign in the U.S. Navy during World War I. Following the war, he became an investment banker and, by 1933, was a vice president of Chase National Bank.

Black was appointed undersecretary of the treasury in 1936 but returned to Chase a few months later because of the financial sacrifice that government service involved. During the postwar era, he became increasingly active in Chase Bank's international operations. In 1947, President **Harry S. Truman** appointed Black an executive director of the World Bank at the insistence of **John J. McCloy**, the bank's president. McCloy was anxious to reverse the liberal lending policies of his predecessor and place the bank in the hands of individuals who could be depended on to pursue sound lending policies acceptable to the financial community. In May 1949, when McCloy resigned, Black was named president of the World Bank.

During the 1950s, he guided the institution in making loans for industrial, agricultural, and power development, particularly in Europe and Asia. Black conceived of the bank in terms

of a traditional lending institution rather than as an instrument of foreign aid through which governments of capital-exporting states could assist underdeveloped areas. He remained with the World Bank until January 1963.

In December 1962, President John F. Kennedy, reacting to criticism of the newly created Agency for International Development and fearing that his 1963 foreign aid bill would have difficulty passing Congress, appointed Black to a committee of generally conservative businessmen asked to study the U.S. foreign aid program. Kennedy hoped that the panel would recommend the continuation of the program and generate support for it among businessmen and conservatives in Congress. The committee, however, reacted negatively to the proposals. Black, in particular, disapproved of bilateral foreign aid, fearing that it would clearly introduce international politics into the bank's development program. The final report of the committee, issued in March 1963, maintained that aid was indispensable to national security, but it disappointed Kennedy by suggesting that the total value of aid be reduced.

When Black became the third president of the World Bank it was a relatively unknown organization and had not yet developed a clear vision of its role and potential. Under Black's leadership, the bank began to focus on the issues associated with lending to developing countries. Black was extremely skillful as a negotiator and earned an international reputation as a mediator of wise judgment and absolute integrity.

Black saw international mediation as an essential aspect of the bank's business. In 1962, he helped resolve the long-standing dispute between India and Pakistan over the use of water resources in the Indus Basin. Black was also successful in the settlement of claims arising from the nationalization of the Suez Canal.

Perhaps the most striking feature of his presidency is the extent to which he came to personify the institution. Black was much liked as chief executive officer of the bank. His tenure of office was so long, the stamp of his personality so strong, and his responsibility for

its evolving pattern so clear that the bank became widely known as Black's Bank.

In August 1963, Black was named to a panel formed to study the development of a commercial supersonic airplane. The report, issued in March 1964, backed development but suggested a reorganization of the program under an independent agency directly responsible to the president and urged increasing the government's share in the cost of development. During the **Lyndon B. Johnson** administration, Black continued to serve on panels reviewing U.S. aid policy, particularly in Southeast Asia. Black died on 20 February 1992, aged 93, in Oakwood, Oklahoma. *See also* EISENHOWER, DWIGHT DAVID.

BOHLEN, CHARLES EUSTIS (1904–1974). Charles Eustis Bohlen was born in Clayton, New York, on 30 August 1904, into a wealthy, well-connected family of German background. His mother Celestine Eustis, and later his wife, were both from families of diplomats. He graduated with a degree in history from Harvard College in 1927 and joined the foreign service in 1929. He learned Russian and familiarized himself with Russian literature, art, and music, and he specialized in Soviet affairs. He joined the first U.S. embassy in the **Soviet Union** and served as a Russian translator at the Teheran, Yalta, and Potsdam Conferences. In 1947, he became a key adviser to President **Harry S. Truman**. Despite objections from Senator Joseph McCarthy (R-Wis.), who regarded him as an "appeaser," **Dwight D. Eisenhower** appointed Bohlen ambassador to Moscow in 1953. In 1960, Bohlen was made special assistant for Soviet affairs in the State Department. In Washington, he associated with **George Kennan, Joseph Alsop, Philip Graham** and **Katharine Graham, Clark Clifford**, the Rostow brothers, Paul Nitze, and others—the group that became known as the **Georgetown Set**.

John F. Kennedy was attracted by Bohlen's charm, shrewdness, and breadth of experience, and he asked his advice on a wide range of foreign policy issues, especially those involving Soviet-American relations. Bohlen was highly regarded for his blend of pragmatic expertise and firsthand information that made him one

of the leading Soviet experts in the State Department. He was known for his bluntness and "realist"—hard-line—approach to the Soviet Union. Although Bohlen claimed to know little of Asia, in March 1961 Kennedy sought his advice on the civil war being waged in Laos since 1959 between the American-supported royalist government of General Phoumi Nosavan and the neutralist forces of Prince Souvanna Phouma who were supported by communist rebels (the Pathet Lao) and North Vietnamese forces. Bohlen advised the president to back the neutralists because the corrupt Phoumi regime had little popular support. By early 1961, the ongoing conflict had brought much of Laos under communist control. Bohlen helped Kennedy draft a statement, aimed at the Soviet Union, asking for a cease-fire and, at the same time, warning that the United States would intervene if the military campaign continued.

The president also consulted Bohlen on possible Soviet responses to the planned April 1961 **Bay of Pigs** invasion of **Cuba**. Bohlen assured Kennedy that the Soviet Union would not act militarily but would merely use the invasion as political propaganda—provided the effort either succeeded or failed quickly. The invasion took place on 17 April, and the next day Kennedy received a letter from Soviet premier **Nikita Khrushchev** denouncing the attack. Bohlen helped Kennedy draft a reply, which stated that the Soviet Union should "recognize that free peoples in all parts of the world do not accept the claim of historical inevitability of Communist revolution."

In summer 1961, Kennedy asked Bohlen to accompany **Lyndon B. Johnson** to West Berlin, where the vice president had been sent to boost the morale of the Berliners and assure them of American support in the face of Soviet and East German attempts to cut off access to the city. Upon returning from the 18–21 August trip, Bohlen wrote a report to the president recommending that the United States be prepared to react vigorously, using any measures necessary short of war, to clear signs of harassment or attempts to erode Western rights in the city. He warned that any American hesitancy would depress morale in West Berlin.

In August 1962, at a time when relations between the United States and France were undergoing some strain because of President Charles de Gaulle's desire to pursue an independent French foreign policy, Kennedy appointed Bohlen ambassador to France. Before he could assume his post at the end of October, the **Cuban missile crisis** absorbed the attention of Washington policy makers. According to Kennedy adviser **Theodore Sorensen**, Bohlen participated in early discussions surrounding the crisis. During an Executive Committee meeting on 18 October 1962, **Dean Rusk** read a letter Bohlen had written the previous night during deliberations. In it, Bohlen advocated dealing with Khrushchev through firm diplomatic action, and if the Russian response was unsatisfactory, informing U.S. allies of the country's intentions and then asking Congress for a declaration of war. To everyone's surprise, Bohlen had not canceled his reservation aboard an ocean liner to take him to his Paris post as ambassador immediately rather than wait until after the crisis had been resolved. He was thus absent for most of what was arguably the most important confrontation between the two superpowers during the **Cold War**. As it happened, Bohlen's advice was rejected, and on 23 October, the administration ordered a "quarantine" of Cuba to prevent shipments of additional missiles and demand removal of those already in place.

Bohlen strongly believed that the United States was inextricably involved in the affairs of Europe and that American policy makers had to adjust to its changing responsibilities in Europe. He helped maintain good relations with France by convincing Kennedy to avoid an open conflict with de Gaulle, no matter what the provocation. In December 1967, Bohlen returned to the United States to take the position of deputy undersecretary of state for political affairs and retired from the foreign service in January 1969. Bohlen died of cancer at the age of 69 on 1 January 1974 in Washington, DC.

BOUVIER, JACQUELINE LEE (1929–1994). *See* KENNEDY, JACQUELINE LEE BOUVIER.

BRINKLEY, DAVID (1920–2003). During the Kennedy administration, David Brinkley, together with his coanchor, newscaster Chet Huntley, was a national celebrity, broadcasting the early evening NBC News slot. He established a reputation for his dry wit and economical style of reporting.

Brinkley was born on 10 July 1920, in Wilmington, North Carolina, the son of a railroad worker. After graduating from high school in 1938, he worked as a reporter for the Wilmington (North Carolina) *Star-News*. He attended the University of North Carolina at Chapel Hill, Emory University, and Vanderbilt University until 1940, when he joined the U.S. Army. Discharged in 1942, Brinkley then worked for the United Press news agency as a reporter in the South.

Brinkley joined the National Broadcasting Company in 1943 in Washington, DC. In 1956, he teamed with Chet Huntley during the 1956 political conventions. In October of that year, the team took over the early evening NBC News slot and, after one month, captured a 36 percent share of the national audience. The program, which was later renamed the *Huntley-Brinkley Report*, followed a carefully orchestrated format designed to portray Huntley, reporting from New York, as a conservative, and Brinkley, reporting from Washington, as an antiestablishment maverick, although both men shared the same liberal philosophy.

During the late 1950s and throughout the 1960s, the Huntley-Brinkley team consistently led the competition from ABC and CBS in the Nielsen ratings and earned 10 Emmy and two Peabody awards. When, in September 1963, the three major networks expanded their evening news formats from 15 to 30 minutes, President John F. Kennedy seized the opportunity to speak to the estimated audience of 50 million viewers and agreed to be interviewed by all three networks.

Kennedy was unhappy with the edited version of his first interview, with CBS correspondent **Walter Cronkite**, believing that Cronkite had distorted his opinion of South Vietnamese president Ngo Dinh Diem, leaving the impression that Kennedy had lost confidence in Diem. Consequently, the president insisted that he exercise final approval of the televised version of his Huntley-Brinkley appearance. In the interview, he told the reporters that he had no intention of reducing U.S. aid to **Vietnam**. Kennedy also supported the **domino theory**, stating that the fall of South Vietnam "would give the impression that the wave of the future in Southeast Asia was China and the Communists."

During the late 1960s and early 1970s, Brinkley coanchored NBC News's coverage of such stories as the Watergate affair, the funeral of **Lyndon B. Johnson**, the flights of Apollo 10 and 11, and the 1968 and 1972 national political conventions. When Chet Huntley retired from NBC in August 1970, Brinkley continued to anchor the new *NBC Nightly News* until August 1971, when he was replaced by veteran newsman John Chancellor. Five times a week Brinkley continued to present *David Brinkley's Journal* from Washington, DC. Brinkley died in 2003 at his home in Houston, Texas.

BUNDY, McGEORGE (1919–1996). McGeorge Bundy was born in Boston, Massachusetts on 30 March 1919, the third son in a well-connected and highly distinguished New England family. The family had a long history of political and legal activity. His father, Harvey Bundy, had worked closely with Henry L. Stimson during several tours of high-government service, and Stimson proved a great influence on the younger Bundy. Bundy and his older brother, **William Putnam Bundy**, were raised in a milieu that stressed family position and personal achievement. McGeorge Bundy was one of the young, brash, and bright advisers who gave the Kennedy administration its reputation for intellectual prowess and ideological toughness. He was also one of President **Lyndon B. Johnson**'s "Wise Men," as well as a key figure in the development of U.S. **Vietnam** policy throughout the war.

McGeorge Bundy was a brilliant scholar, graduating first in his class from the Groton School and first from Yale University in 1940. In 1941, he became a junior fellow at Harvard University. He served in the U.S. Army during World War II and participated in the planning of

the invasions of Sicily and France. Following his discharge in 1946, he helped Stimson research and write his autobiography.

In April 1948, Bundy went to Washington to work for the agency responsible for implementing the Marshall Plan. He left his government position in September to join Thomas Dewey's presidential campaign as a foreign policy adviser. Following Dewey's defeat, Bundy became a political analyst for the prestigious Council on Foreign Relations. In 1949, he was appointed a lecturer in government at Harvard, teaching a course in modern foreign policy. He rose rapidly within the department, becoming a full professor in 1954. In 1953, he had been appointed dean of arts and sciences, the second-ranking position at Harvard.

A nominal Republican, Bundy backed **Dwight D. Eisenhower** in 1952 and 1956. However, he withdrew his support of the **Republican Party** after its 1960 nomination of **Richard M. Nixon**. Instead, Bundy helped organize a scientific and professional committee in support of Senator John F. Kennedy. Following his election, Kennedy, impressed with Bundy's intellectual brilliance, organizational ability, and philosophical pragmatism, offered him several positions in the State and Defense Departments and on the U.S. disarmament team. Bundy was not interested in these appointments but accepted one as the president's special assistant for national security affairs.

Bundy's position suited his philosophical background and prior experience. He was, in the words of Joseph Kraft, an "organizer of process," more interested in the process of informed decision making than in advocating particular policies. It was Bundy's job to gather information from the Defense and State Departments and the intelligence agencies and to present this information to the president in a concise fashion. More important, he also controlled access to the president. These functions gave him great power in determining the issues that received priority and the policy options from which Kennedy could choose.

Bundy was also responsible for organizing the meetings of the National Security Council and helped assemble the task forces that Kennedy often used in place of State Department officials to deal with special diplomatic problems. Because of Bundy's background, he generally drew men from the ranks of the academic and business establishments for these assignments and, therefore, indirectly determined the way many issues would be tackled. Bundy's influence became even greater following the April 1961 **Bay of Pigs** invasion. Angered by what he considered the State Department's poor advice during the months prior to the attack, Kennedy began relying more and more upon Bundy for foreign policy information and counsel.

At Kennedy's urging, Bundy reorganized and streamlined his staff, and he gathered at the White House a group of scholars and intellectuals such as **Carl Kaysen** and Ralph Dungan who became important forces in formulating the administration of foreign policy. Bundy also set up a communications system that equaled those of the State and Defense Departments and that permitted him to have the information available to these bureaucracies. By the end of 1961, he had come close to achieving what Arthur M. Schlesinger Jr. described as Kennedy's desire to have a small semi-secret office to run foreign affairs "while maintaining the State Department as a facade." Bundy became, in Kennedy's words, one of his "inner circle," the very small group of advisers whom the president consulted daily and whose counsel he trusted in times of crisis.

The role Bundy played in the Kennedy administration was most evident during the **Cuban missile crisis** of 1962. Late in the afternoon of 15 October, Bundy was informed of the presence of Soviet missiles in **Cuba**. He delayed telling the president about this discovery until the next morning, ostensibly to give the intelligence agencies time to compile all necessary data and to permit Kennedy to rest before dealing with a potential nuclear confrontation. Bundy was then instructed to set up the meetings of the Executive Committee of the National Security Council (ExComm), a special panel to advise the president, and gain bipartisan support for administration action. This group included many men with much experience in foreign affairs, among them Dean

Acheson, Robert Lovett, and **John J. McCloy**. At the meetings, Bundy was anxious to keep the process of decision making open until all policy ramifications had been explored. He acted as something of a devil's advocate. At the ExComm meeting held on 17 October, when majority sentiment seemed to favor an air strike to remove the missiles, Bundy advocated using a diplomatic approach. Two days later, when sentiment favored a blockade, Bundy advocated an armed strike. Because a blockade was technically an act of war, Kennedy instituted a "quarantine" of Cuba on 23 October.

In the early 1960s, Bundy began an involvement in Vietnam affairs that would grow during the remainder of his government service. Following the August 1963 attack on Buddhist dissidents by the regime of Ngo Dinh Diem, the Kennedy administration began a reevaluation of American policy toward the South Vietnamese government. During the two-month debate on the subject, some advisers such as Roger Hilsman advocated U.S. withdrawal of support in hope of precipitating a coup. Others, such as U.S. secretary of defense **Robert S. McNamara**, insisted that the United States continue to support Diem but demand governmental reform. Bundy believed that the United States should not thwart any coup that seemed potentially successful but should have the "option of judging and warning on any plan with poor prospects of success." On 1 November 1963, South Vietnamese generals staged a successful coup. The United States had given no direct aid to the rebels but made no move to stop the change in government.

Following Kennedy's assassination, Bundy remained a special assistant to President Lyndon B. Johnson and played a major role in the decision to send U.S. troops to the Dominican Republic in 1965. He was a major force in the formation of the administration's Vietnam policy and advocated the bombing of North Vietnam in 1965. Unable to accommodate himself to Johnson's personality, Bundy left government in February 1966 to become president of the Ford Foundation. In 1968, he came out in opposition to further troop increases in Vietnam and supported de-escalation. *See*

also FORRESTAL, MICHAEL VINCENT; NEW FRONTIER; ROSTOW, WALT WHITMAN.

BUNDY, WILLIAM PUTNAM (1917–2000). William Bundy was born in Washington, DC, on 24 September 1917. As coordinator of military assistance programs during the Kennedy administration, Bundy often remained in the shadow of his younger brother, **McGeorge Bundy**. Yet, by the end of the decade, William Bundy emerged as one of the prime architects of and spokesmen for the **Lyndon B. Johnson** administration's policy in Southeast Asia.

Bundy attended the Groton School and Yale University, graduating from Yale in 1939, one year ahead of his younger brother. After service in the U.S. Army, Bundy received a law degree from Harvard Law School in 1947 and joined Covington and Burling, a Washington, DC, law firm that traditionally supplied young lawyers for high government positions. In 1950, Bundy joined the Central Intelligence Agency (CIA), where he became a protégé of Director **Allen Dulles**. He was assigned to the office of national estimates and was put in charge of overall evaluation of international intelligence. In 1960, Bundy took a leave of absence from the CIA to become staff director of President **Dwight D. Eisenhower**'s Commission on National Goals, which had been established to formulate broad, long-term objectives and programs for the United States.

President Kennedy appointed Bundy deputy assistant secretary of defense in charge of international security affairs in January 1961. In this post, he was responsible for coordinating military aid programs throughout the world. In fall 1962, when communist China invaded disputed areas on its border with India, Bundy organized the shipment of American arms to India and attempted to get other U.S. allies to supply that country. Shortly after assuming office, Bundy began an involvement in **Vietnam** policy making that would continue and increase during the Johnson administration.

Following the erosion of the South Vietnamese military position and the deterioration of morale in Saigon during 1961, President Ngo Dinh Diem asked the United States to sign a

defense treaty and increase military aid to his country. Bundy was one of the officials chosen to make recommendations on the proposal. In an October 1961 memorandum to U.S. secretary of defense **Robert S. McNamara**, Bundy told his superior, "It is now or never if we are to arrest the gains being made by the Viet Cong." He suggested that "an early hard-hitting operation" would limit communist expansion and give Diem a chance to reform and strengthen his government. In Bundy's opinion, any delay would lessen U.S. chances of success.

Kennedy, reluctant to make a major U.S. commitment, decided not to send ground forces to Vietnam but to concentrate on prompt deployment of support troops and equipment in November 1961. During the Johnson administration, Bundy became one of the president's principal policy advisers on Vietnam. Although he only reluctantly supported the administration's large-scale troop commitments in 1964, Bundy backed increased American intervention during the last half of the decade. In 1969, Bundy resigned his position as assistant secretary of state for Far Eastern and Pacific affairs to become a visiting professor at the Massachusetts Institute of Technology's Center for International Studies. In 1972, he became editor of the quarterly *Foreign Affairs*.

BUSH, PRESCOTT SHELDON (1895–1972). Prescott Sheldon Bush was born in Columbus, Ohio, on 15 May 1895. A Yale graduate and World War I veteran, he entered the banking industry after the war and, in 1930, became a partner in Brown Brothers, Harriman in New York City. Maintaining a residence in Connecticut, he assumed the chairmanship of the state's Republican Finance Committee in 1947 and defeated Representative **Abraham A. Ribicoff** (D-Conn.) for election to the Senate in 1952. He proved to be one of the **Dwight D. Eisenhower** administration's most loyal Senate supporters, voting with the White House on more than 90 percent of all votes recorded in the 1953 session.

One of Prescott Bush's sons, George H. W. Bush, served in the Nixon and Ford administrations and as Reagan's vice president, before he was elected as the 41st president. Prescott Bush's grandson, George W. Bush, secured the presidency in the elections of 2000 and 2004.

As a Republican, Prescott Bush generally opposed legislation put forward by the Kennedy administration, crossing the aisle only on foreign policy issues. In 1961, he failed to defeat the White House's aid-to-**education** bill in the Senate, and he voted against the president's Medicare bill in July 1962. He supported Kennedy, however, on the Treasury Department's proposed purchase of $100 million worth of **United Nations** bonds in April 1962. Bush also approved of the creation of the **Peace Corps** as "a sounder approach than our foreign aid program" and "certainly . . . less expensive."

In September 1962, Kennedy sought to expand the power of the presidency in relation to tariffs and trade. Under existing legislation (the 1951 Trade Agreements Extension Act), the president was required to submit to the U.S. Tariff Commission a list of items upon which he planned to negotiate reciprocal reductions, and the commission would then inform him of the duty level or "peril point" below which a tariff cut, if implemented, might hurt an affected industry. Kennedy wanted to eliminate some of the existing procedural and substantive restrictions on the president and did not want to be accountable to Congress for cuts below these "peril points." The new White House–sponsored bill reflected his views, and the old "peril point" section was removed, allowing the president to negotiate trade agreements and remove tariffs altogether on some items. Bush opposed the idea and tried to maintain the "peril point" provisions. "Why do we have a Tariff Commission," Bush asked, "if we are unwilling to trust its judgment on the safe limits for tariff change?" The White House effectively lobbied to frustrate Bush's efforts, and the Senate narrowly defeated (by two votes) a Bush amendment that would have retained the existing guidelines; in the end, only seven senators joined Bush in voting against the passage of the **Trade Expansion Act** of 1962.

In May 1962, the 67-year-old Bush, citing reasons of health, announced his decision not to run for reelection. Abraham Ribicoff,

secretary of health, education, and welfare under Kennedy, recaptured his seat for the Democrats in the November election. Prescott Bush died in New York City on 8 October 1972.

BYRD, ROBERT CARLYLE (1917–2010). Robert Carlyle Byrd was born on 20 November 1917, in North Wilkesboro, North Carolina, as Cornelius Calvin Sale, the fifth child of a woman who died in the great influenza epidemic within a year of his birth. After her death, Sale was adopted by his aunt, who renamed him Robert Carlyle Byrd and took him to Bluefield, West Virginia.

During World War II, he worked as a shipyard welder and briefly belonged to the Ku Klux Klan. He won election to the West Virginia House of Delegates in 1946 and, after serving in both houses of the state legislature, became a member of the U.S. House of Representatives from Charleston in 1953.

In 1958, Byrd defeated an incumbent Republican for the U.S. Senate with 59.2 percent of the vote and soon emerged as the most powerful Democrat in the state. Byrd supported Senate majority leader **Lyndon B. Johnson** (D-Tex.) for the 1960 Democratic presidential nomination. When Johnson declined to enter the West Virginia primary, Byrd supported Senator **Hubert H. Humphrey** and actively worked against Senator John F. Kennedy, the frontrunner for the party's nomination. Many observers expected Kennedy's Catholicism to hurt his chances in the overwhelmingly Protestant state, but Byrd discounted any religious bias in his support of Johnson and Humphrey. "I wouldn't have supported Kennedy," Byrd remarked in 1972, "if he had been a Missionary Baptist." Despite the state's Protestantism, Kennedy swept the primary with 61 percent of the vote, carrying Byrd's hometown of Sophia. After opposing John Kennedy in the primary, Byrd campaigned for the 1960 Democratic ticket of Kennedy and Johnson. Byrd gave 27 speeches in Texas during the campaign,

urging Texans to vote for that ticket, especially Southern Baptists who were furious with Johnson for being on a ticket with a Catholic.

After Kennedy's victory in November 1960, the two made up and worked together. It is ironic how close Byrd and Kennedy became, given how different they were: Byrd was a rural Appalachian, and Kennedy came from urban New England; Byrd was a fundamentalist, while Kennedy was the first Catholic president; Byrd came from a poor working-class family, while the Kennedys came from wealth and affluence. Byrd remained a segregationist for some years and distrusted Kennedy's links to organized labor.

According to the *Congressional Quarterly*, Byrd supported the Kennedy administration in 1961–1962 on 85 percent of the roll call votes for which the president announced a position. However, Byrd voted against the **Limited Nuclear Test Ban Treaty** in September 1963 and opposed the administration's 1963 **civil rights** bill.

After eight years of night classes, Byrd earned a law degree from American University in Washington, DC, in June 1963. Kennedy spoke at the commencement ceremony and presented Byrd with his law degree. Reelected in 1964 and 1970, Byrd became secretary to the Senate Democratic Conference in 1967, and in 1971, he defeated **Ted Kennedy** to become Democratic whip and then defeated Hubert Humphrey to become Senate majority leader in 1977. Byrd and Ted Kennedy later became allies and friends in the Senate.

Byrd's major contribution while in Congress was to ensure that the Senate would serve both as a strong check on—and a vital ally of—the president. Upon his death on 28 June 2010, the Democratic senator had served 51 years in the Senate and had cast more than 18,600 votes. He was the longest-serving senator and longest-serving member in the history of the U.S. Congress and widely regarded as the custodian of the Senate.

C

CABINET APPOINTMENTS. In making his cabinet appointments, John Kennedy relied on the advice of a number of individuals. Robert Lovett was perhaps the most important, but Dean Acheson—**Harry S. Truman**'s secretary of state—**Clark Clifford, John J. McCloy, R. Sargent Shriver Jr.** and John's brother, **Robert Kennedy**, also played important roles in the selection process. Lovett had been a Republican Wall Street international investment banker who had served as undersecretary of state and secretary of defense in the Truman administration. Lovett and the other former government officials declined to accept any appointment under Kennedy and the president-elect saw their advice as objective and free of special pleading. He also asked advice from his friends in the press, **Joseph Alsop, Philip Graham,** and **Walter Lippmann**. Kennedy told Acheson he wanted a "ministry of talent."

Kennedy tried to balance party affiliation and geographic distribution as well as expertise and experience. He also sought a balance between youth and experience. **C. Douglas Dillon** and **Robert S. McNamara** were ideologically Republicans while Orville Freeman and **Stewart Udall** were liberal Democrats. **Dean Rusk**, chosen as secretary of state, was the oldest at 52 years of age. They did not always get along with each other. **Abraham A. Ribicoff** was regarded by Postmaster General **J. Edward Day** as difficult, and Rusk (from Georgia), who was never really comfortable with the New England set, was overshadowed—and often overruled—by the more dynamic and self-confident McNamara. **Arthur J. Goldberg** and Dillon were personal friends of the Kennedys and socialized with the president. Some were rewarded for their support of the candidate, and he wedded that to his geographical spread. Udall was from the West (Arizona) and **Luther Hodges** from the South (North Carolina).

Kennedy's most controversial appointment was that of his brother Robert to the position of attorney general. John liked the idea but was hesitant because he felt it would not be well received. John's father, Joe, was determined that the post should go to Robert, and in the end, he won out over advice against the appointment.

CAMELOT MYTH. The notion that the Kennedy administration could be thought of as representing in some way a period akin to that of the British mythical legend of King Arthur and Camelot was the creation of **Jacqueline Kennedy**. It has become perhaps the most popular and lasting of the various myths surrounding President John F. Kennedy's legacy. His wife, Jacqueline Bouvier Kennedy—beautiful, multilingual, and intelligent—offered this creative contribution as the public mourned the president's death. She arranged for an exclusive interview with journalist Theodore White, author of *The Making of the President, 1960*, which portrayed Kennedy favorably, and whom she knew was friendly to the Kennedy family. During their discussion, Mrs. Kennedy stressed the image that would provide the basis for the public's adoring memory of

Kennedy and his administration by pointing to the president's fondness of the popular Broadway musical *Camelot*. Kennedy, she claimed, especially enjoyed the music of Alan Jay Lerner, a former classmate of his, and the couple would often listen to the title song. According to Jackie, Kennedy was particularly fond of the song's final phrase: "Don't ever let it be forgot, that once there was a spot, for one brief shining moment that was Camelot." She insisted that the president was an idealist who especially liked heroes such as King Arthur—which White knew not to be true. In her attempt to provide a positive message to an ugly event, she said: "There will be great presidents again, but there will never be another Camelot." Presidential historian Stephen E. Ambrose later observed of Jackie: "She wanted to take control of history, and in many ways she managed to do so."

White's influential essay carrying the Camelot story, which appeared in a special issue of *Life* magazine on 3 December 1963, received an extremely wide circulation and found an estimated readership of more than 30 million. To the grieving public, the uplifting message appeared to be grounded on certain logic. After all, at 43 he was the youngest man ever to be elected president, and his extraordinary press conferences suggested he was perhaps the most intelligent, articulate, and amusing president yet. Moreover, with his young, beautiful wife, who was adored in international circles, and his dynastic family, it was easy to equate Kennedy with the legend of King Arthur. Later, White indicated that he regretted his role in the transmission of the Camelot myth. "I was her instrument in labelling the myth," he admitted. "So the epitaph of the Kennedy administration became Camelot—a magic moment in American history when gallant men danced with beautiful women, when great deeds were done, when artists, writers and poets met at the White House and the barbarians beyond the walls were held back."

Over the years, critics, especially historians, have ridiculed the Camelot myth as a distortion of Kennedy's actions, beliefs, and policies. Ironically, Camelot is not exactly the most uplifting epitaph for John F. Kennedy. While Jackie meant the comparison to be positive, highlighting the hope and potential ushered in with the inauguration, the book that served as the basis for the musical that she was referencing, T. H. White's *The Once and Future King* (published in 1958), tells the story of a weak leader who fails in the face of other people's lust for power or each other. Nonetheless, the Kennedy presidential years are still regarded in the public memory as a brief, bright, and shining moment.

CANADA. John F. Kennedy's first trip abroad as president was to Canada. The timing of the visit indicates the importance Kennedy placed on matters relating to the **Cold War**. It took place on 16–18 May 1961, in the middle of the racially motivated violence against the **Freedom Riders** in Alabama; a time when **civil rights** activists might have expected the full attention of the president. In the late 1950s, most Americans took Canada for granted; Canada had joined with the United States in creating a North American Air Defense Command (NORAD) in 1957, and the economies of the two countries were overwhelmingly linked—if not inseparable. Canadians, on the other hand, were becoming increasingly concerned that their country was becoming too Americanized and too dependent upon the United States. They especially wanted to develop their status as an independent power in the Cold War, not simply be tied to the policies coming out of Washington. John Diefenbaker, a 61-year-old populist who had been elected as prime minister in 1957, did not wish to join the Organization of American States (OAS), nor did he want U.S. nuclear weapons deployed in Canada, both policies espoused by the Kennedy administration. During his visit to Ottawa, Kennedy used a speech before the Parliament urging Canadians to join the OAS as a way of pressuring Diefenbaker to agree. "Nothing is more vital than the unity of the United States and Canada," Kennedy told his audience in his 17 May address to Parliament. The ploy did not work; it was seen as a personal affront by the anti-American Canadian prime minister, and it simply reinforced his dislike of Kennedy

and his opposition to the American idea. The Canadian government, however, did support Kennedy's position in the 1961 crisis in Berlin and, despite some reservations, did not raise strong objections to Kennedy's policy toward **Vietnam**. The animosity in the relationship between Diefenbaker and Kennedy was starkly revealed during the **Cuban missile crisis** of October 1962. Although there was no doubt that the Canadian public supported the actions of the Kennedy administration and that Canada would live up to its responsibilities under the NORAD and North Atlantic Treaty Organization agreements, Diefenbaker was indecisive and reluctant to voice his support. He resented that Kennedy had informed him of his actions rather than consulted with him first as required under the NORAD arrangements. Accordingly, he called instead for a **United Nations**–sponsored mission to **Cuba** to investigate the situation on the island. That did not go down well in Washington.

It was only after Diefenbaker was defeated in general elections in early 1963, to be replaced by a more sympathetic Lester Pearson, that relations with Canada improved during the Kennedy years.

CAPEHART, HOMER EARL (1897–1979). Homer Earl Capehart was born in Algiers, Indiana, on 6 June 1897, and grew up on his father's tenant farm. Following noncombat duty in World War I, Capehart became wealthy as the owner of a profitable jukebox company.

He was elected to the U.S. Senate from Indiana in 1944, and he became one of the more conservative, anticommunist Republican members of Congress, winning reelection in 1950 and 1956. During the 87th Congress, Capehart was one of the strongest opponents of the policies of John F. Kennedy. He voted against Medicare, housing subsidies, and the 1961 school aid bill. According to *Congressional Quarterly*, Capehart opposed Kennedy on 82 percent of the key roll call votes for which the president's position had been announced. In October 1962, Kennedy charged the Indiana Republican with having a "19th-century voting record" on domestic and foreign policy issues.

Capehart achieved national attention during the 1962 congressional elections when he attacked what he described as the Kennedy administration's failure in relation to **Cuba**. He and Senator Kenneth B. Keating (R-N.Y.), called for "a crackdown on Cuba" in response to the presence of Soviet troops on the island nation. Prior to the American discovery of Soviet missile launching facilities in Cuba on 16 October, Kennedy had consistently dismissed the claims of Keating and Capehart as campaign rhetoric. However, although he did not follow Capehart's original suggestion to invade the island, Kennedy felt the actual existence of Soviet weapons on Cuba assured the Indiana senator of reelection. "Would you believe it?" presidential adviser **Theodore Sorensen** reported the president as saying, "Homer Capehart is the Winston Churchill of our time." The president was delighted when the young 34-year-old Democrat Birch E. Bayh, actively endorsed by the state American Federation of Labor/Congress of Industrial Organizations, narrowly defeated Capehart in the 1962 elections. Capehart retired and resided in Indianapolis until his death on 3 September 1979. *See also* DIRKSEN, EVERETT McKINLEY; KHRUSHCHEV, NIKITA SERGEYEVICH.

CASTRO, FIDEL (1926–2016). Fidel Castro Ruz was born in Birán, Oriente Province, **Cuba**, the son of a wealthy Spanish farmer, on 13 August 1926. He governed the Republic of Cuba as prime minister from 1959 to 1976 and then as president from 1976 to 2008.

Castro was educated by Jesuits and received a law degree from the University of Havana in 1950. He adopted Marxism and became a revolutionary activist. In 1953, he was jailed following the failure of a coup—namely, the July uprising against dictator Fulgencio Batista. Freed and then exiled, he lived in Mexico and the United States before returning to launch a guerrilla campaign against Batista from the Sierra Maestra region of Oriente Province.

In February 1959, Castro succeeded in ousting Batista, became premier, and immediately set out to reform Cuban society along Marxist-Leninist lines. In 1960, he became

a hero in Cuba because he nationalized oil companies and sugar producers, as well as cracking down on mobsters, but his seizure of American companies aroused the relentless enmity of the United States. On 3 January 1961, the United States withdrew diplomatic recognition of the Cuban government and closed the embassy in Havana.

Because his policies drove many middle-class Cubans into exile, the American government assumed that Castro was deeply unpopular; it encouraged and financially supported a growing band of Cuban exiles determined to overthrow him. Fearing such a U.S.-backed coup, Castro had purchased Soviet, French, and Belgian weaponry and, by early 1960, had doubled the size of Cuba's armed forces. The Central Intelligence Agency–backed coup failed, and the disaster at the **Bay of Pigs** in 1961 only made Castro more powerful. Following the Bay of Pigs fiasco, the United States began the formulation of new plans aimed at destabilizing the Castro government. These activities were collectively known as the "Cuban Project." It was a coordinated program of political, psychological, and military sabotage, involving intelligence operations as well as assassination attempts on key political leaders, including Castro himself.

In 1962, President Kennedy broadened the partial trade restrictions imposed by President **Dwight D. Eisenhower** to a ban on virtually all trade with Cuba. Castro turned increasingly to the **Soviet Union** for assistance and announced that Cuba was a socialist state and that he was a Marxist-Leninist. His hostility to what he saw as Yankee imperialism was implacable, and he welcomed Soviet missiles that led to the crisis with the Kennedy administration in October 1962.

The resolution of the **Cuban missile crisis**, which did not include discussions with Castro, led to strains in the friendship between Castro and Khrushchev, and although relations between the Soviets and Cuba were repaired, they were never as close in subsequent years.

On 31 July 2006, because of his poor health, Castro delegated his presidential duties to his brother Raúl Castro, and on 24 February 2008, the National Assembly of People's Power unanimously voted Raúl as president.

The U.S. embargo against Cuba continued in varying forms until President Barack Obama formally reestablished relations between Cuba and the United States on 20 July 2015, with the opening of a Cuban embassy in Washington and a U.S. embassy in Havana.

Fidel Castro died on the night of 25 November 2016. Upon his death, Indian prime minister Narendra Modi described him as "one of the most iconic personalities of the 20th century."

The United States continues to exercise complete jurisdiction and control over Guantánamo Bay under a lease arrangement signed in 1903. The current government of Cuba regards the U.S. presence as illegal. *See also* ASSASSINATION OF JOHN F. KENNEDY; BERLE, ADOLF AUGUSTUS, JR.; PRESIDENTIAL ELECTION OF 1960.

CELEBREZZE, ANTHONY JOSEPH (1910–1998). Anthony Joseph Celebrezze was born in Anzi, Italy, on 4 September 1910 and grew up in the slums of Cleveland. While working as a manual laborer for the New York Central Railroad, he attended Ohio Northern Law School. He entered politics in 1950 and won election to the Ohio senate, where he became a close ally of Governor Frank J. Lausche (D-Ohio). Three years later, Celebrezze won the endorsement of the influential *Cleveland Press* and defeated the local Democratic organization's candidate in the 1953 mayoralty primary, winning in the general election in November. Celebrezze remained a popular mayor and easily won reelection a record-breaking five times. In the 1961 election, he received an unprecedented 73.8 percent of the total vote, winning every one of the city's 33 wards. He considered a run for the governorship of Ohio in 1958, but in his only major political defeat, he lost the Democratic gubernatorial primary to former Toledo mayor Michael V. DiSalle.

President John F. Kennedy designated Celebrezze to succeed **Abraham A. Ribicoff** as secretary of the Department of Health, **Education**, and Welfare (HEW) in July 1962. The president wanted an Italian American for a

cabinet-level position, and Celebrezze, who had requested appointment to the federal circuit court, suited Kennedy's purposes. The president had known Celebrezze for many years and respected the Cleveland politician's skills as an urban administrator. According to presidential adviser **Theodore Sorensen**, the president found Celebrezze more amusing than helpful at cabinet meetings, with a tendency for analyzing "every world and national problem in terms of his experiences in Cleveland."

With the aid of Undersecretary Wilbur J. Cohen and **education** commissioner Francis Keppel, Celebrezze reorganized his 112-program department, once called "unmanageable" by Abraham Ribicoff. In January 1963, Celebrezze separated the public assistance and child health and welfare functions from the Social Security Administration and transferred these programs to a new Welfare Administration.

As chief of HEW, Celebrezze worked for the passage of the administration's Medicare and aid-to-education measures in 1962 and 1963. He was a strong advocate of increased federal funds for private and public universities to accommodate the needs of a rapidly increasing college-age population. The administration included broad discretionary authority for HEW in its June 1963 **civil rights** bill to enforce desegregation guidelines by granting HEW the power to deny funds for any federal program to states or institutions that practiced racial segregation. In November 1963, Celebrezze championed federal funding of medical care for the elderly. Congress, however, moved slowly on civil rights legislation and rejected Medicare and the administration's 1962 and 1963 aid-to-education bills.

After the Democrats increased their congressional ranks following the 1964 elections, President **Lyndon B. Johnson** reintroduced these measures with far greater success. Celebrezze continued as HEW secretary until August 1965. On 19 August 1965, Johnson appointed Celebrezze to a seat on the United States Court of Appeals for the Sixth Circuit, where he served until he retired in 1980. He died in Cleveland on 29 October 1998.

CELLER, EMANUEL (1888–1981). Emanuel Celler, the grandson of German Jewish immigrants, was born into a middle-class family in Brooklyn, New York, on 6 May 1888. He graduated from Columbia Law School in 1912 and practiced law in New York until 1922, when he ran for Congress as a Democrat in Brooklyn's 10th congressional district. His victory began a half century career in the House of Representatives, where Celler established himself as a liberal Democrat and a staunch civil libertarian.

He rose to the chairmanship of the House Judiciary Committee in 1949 and chaired that committee for the next 22 years. Celler conducted highly publicized investigations into insurance companies in 1949, the steel industry in 1950, and monopoly practices in baseball in 1951. He coauthored the Celler-Kefauver Anti-Merger Act of 1950, a major piece of antitrust legislation. In the late 1950s, Celler's committee held hearings on government antitrust enforcement procedures and on the anticompetitive practices of regulatory agencies, particularly the Civil Aeronautics Board. Long an advocate of **civil rights** legislation, Celler was the principal architect of the 1957 Civil Rights Act, the first federal civil rights legislation in 82 years, and of the supplementary Civil Rights Act passed in 1960.

Celler cooperated closely with John F. Kennedy and his administration. In April 1962, when Kennedy clashed with the steel industry over a projected price increase, Celler assisted Kennedy by announcing that he would hold hearings on the steel price situation. He also played a key role in the development of civil rights legislation during the Kennedy administration. He had prepared civil rights recommendations for Kennedy during his campaign for the presidency, and with Kennedy's backing, Celler sponsored the Twenty-Fourth Amendment, approved by Congress in August 1962 and ratified in 1964, which abolished the poll tax in federal elections.

In February 1963, Kennedy sent to Congress a modest civil rights bill limited largely to the protection of voting rights. Celler, who had proposed much stronger legislation in

May 1961, urged Kennedy to broaden his bill to include public accommodations and employment. The rising tempo of the civil rights movement—in particular, the April 1963 demonstrations in Birmingham, Alabama—finally brought Kennedy to support legislation of the type Celler advocated. Kennedy and Celler worked closely to secure a strong bill, which Celler then shepherded through the Judiciary Committee in late October. Celler also guided the bill, which became the landmark **Civil Rights Act of 1964**, through the full House in February 1964. He went on to play an important role in the passage of the 1965 Voting Rights Act, the Immigration and Naturalization Act of 1965, and the 1968 Civil Rights Act.

Following his failure to be reelected in 1972, Celler returned to his work as a lawyer in New York City. He died in Brooklyn on 15 January 1981.

CHAPPAQUIDDICK INCIDENT. The term *Chappaquiddick incident* refers to the events surrounding the death, on 18–19 July 1969, of Mary Jo Kopechne, a woman who had worked in the office of Senator **Robert Kennedy** during his 1968 presidential campaign.

In January 1969, **Edward "Ted" Kennedy**, aged 38, became the youngest-ever majority whip in the Senate. Many saw it as a step toward a third family member running for the presidency. Ted and Bobby's tightly knit cohort of campaign workers were still not over the shock and sorrow of Bobby's death the previous June. The annual July regatta at Edgartown, Massachusetts, seemed like a good occasion to get the group back together. After the boat race, Ted and his friends decided to have a party on Chappaquiddick Island, adjacent to Martha's Vineyard.

On the morning of 19 July 1969, Kopechne's body was discovered underwater inside an automobile belonging to Senator Kennedy in a tidal channel on Chappaquiddick Island. The tragedy occurred following a party hosted by Senator Kennedy as a reunion for the group of six women (which included 28-year-old Mary Jo Kopechne), sometimes called "the boiler-room girls," who had served on Robert F. Kennedy's 1968 presidential campaign. Also present were six men—Ted Kennedy, Kennedy's chauffeur, and three close friends and a cousin of Kennedy's. Kennedy's car had veered off a narrow bridge and into a deep tidal channel. Kennedy escaped the car, and Kopechne did not; the senator did not immediately report the incident.

After the discovery of the submerged vehicle by locals the next morning, Kennedy gave a statement to police saying that on the previous night Kopechne was his passenger when he took a wrong turn and accidentally drove his car off a narrow bridge into the water. After pleading guilty to a charge of leaving the scene of an accident after causing injury—a misdemeanor rather than a felony—Kennedy received a suspended sentence. A number of inquiries were held, and the incident became a national scandal and undoubtedly influenced Kennedy's decision not to run for president in 1972 and 1976.

There are two dimensions to the incident that make it worthy of note: the first is the behavior of Senator Ted Kennedy and its impact upon his subsequent career, and the second is the impact of the event on the women who worked for Senator Robert Kennedy.

Many questions remain unanswered. Why did Kennedy turn right onto the rugged dirt path to the small dike bridge, instead of left along the paved road to the ferry? To what extent was alcohol a factor? Why was the car going fast enough to flip off the low bridge? How did Ted get out of the sunken car, and why didn't Mary Jo? Why did it take so long for Ted to report the accident?

In the days immediately following the discovery of Kopechne's body, several senior **Democratic Party** advisers and speechwriters, including **Ted Sorensen**, **Robert S. McNamara**, Richard Goodwin, and Ken O'Donnell, traveled to Martha's Vineyard, and a week later, on Sunday, 26 July, Kennedy made a **television** speech to "the people of Massachusetts" explaining what had happened. Many observers saw it less as an explanation and more as a public relations pitch. The response was overwhelmingly supportive of Kennedy's actions; he was reelected to the Senate in 1970 by an overwhelming majority.

The five surviving women who attended the party at Chappaquiddick suffered greatly, both personally and professionally. Although they had significant responsibility in the national campaign for Bobby Kennedy, they were portrayed as girls of no significance—even described as party girls. Then, for several years on each anniversary, they were pursued by the press, subjected to hate mail, demeaning descriptions of their work, and veiled accusations about their moral rectitude. They were wiretapped by the **Richard M. Nixon** administration and criticized for inconsistencies in their recollections. Nevertheless, they refused offers of payment to tell all. They declined to be interviewed at length for their "story" even as Kennedy polished his career as a "lion of the Senate." They refused to take a public stand against what appeared to be a clear example of male misbehavior toward women.

CHARYK, JOSEPH VINCENT (1920–2016). Joseph Vincent Charyk was born in Canmore, Alberta, **Canada**, on 9 September 1920, into a Ukrainian family. Charyk earned his bachelor's degree in engineering and physics from the University of Alberta and his PhD in aeronautics from the California Institute of Technology. He taught aeronautics at Princeton University from 1946 to 1955. He then joined the missile research facilities of Lockheed Aircraft and Aeronautics Systems and, in 1959, accepted a one-year appointment as chief scientist of the U.S. Air Force. In January 1960, he was appointed undersecretary of the air force. He was widely credited as the founder of the geosynchronous communications satellite industry.

As undersecretary of the U.S. Air Force, Charyk supported the Defense Department's grant of the TFX fighter/bomber contract to General Dynamics despite the lower cost of the Boeing Company's design. Charyk contended that the Boeing design was scientifically inferior to that of General Dynamics.

In 1961, President Kennedy appointed Charyk to become the first director of the National Reconnaissance Office, and, following its incorporation in February 1963, Kennedy named Charyk president and chief operating officer of the Communications Satellite Corporation (Comsat). The corporation was a privately owned, profit-making company established by Congress; it had been formed to create and maintain a global network of commercial communications satellites. In 1964, Comsat became the manager of the International Telecommunications Consortium. This system leased satellite service to any member of the International Telecommunications Union, an association that included virtually all nations except communist China.

As president of Comsat, Charyk was the technological expert responsible for the design of the actual satellite system adopted. This system relied on the placement of satellites in synchronous orbits circling the earth at a rate of speed and altitude that would keep each over a fixed point. The system was begun with the launching of the Early Bird satellite in April 1964. By 1970, Comsat had orbited satellites over every continent except Antarctica. During the late 1960s, Charyk was unable to maintain Comsat's domestic monopoly on the ownership of ground stations and satellites. In 1966, the company was required to share ownership of its transmission stations with communications carriers such as the American Telephone and Telegraph Company. Broadcasting networks and communications corporations were allowed to enter the satellite field in 1972. Charyk was appointed by President Ronald Reagan to the National Telecommunication Security Advisory Council in 1982, and he was made its chairman in 1984. He died on 28 September 2016 at the age of 96.

CHAVEZ, CESAR (1927–1993). Cesar Chavez was born on 31 March 1927 in Yuma, Arizona, into a family of six children, and he grew up in a small adobe home. His family owned a grocery store and a ranch, but their land was lost during the Great Depression and the family then moved to California to become migrant farm workers. Young Cesar left school in the seventh grade to become a full-time farm field-worker in California. After taking part in several unsuccessful strikes of farm workers, he began to consider ways of organizing Mexican Americans in California. In 1952, he joined the San Jose branch of

the Community Service Organization (CSO), which fostered grassroots efforts to meet the problems of poor people. As a CSO worker, and later director, Chavez organized voter registration drives among Mexican Americans and set up services to provide information on such matters as immigration laws and welfare regulations. He left the CSO in 1962, when the organization turned down his proposal to create a union of farm workers. With their meager savings, Chavez and his wife, Helen, immediately established the National Farm Workers Association (NFWA—later to become the United Farm Workers Organizing Committee [UFWOC]).

Under the leadership of Chavez, membership of the NFWA grew rapidly in the fields and migrant worker camps of southern and central California, and in September 1965, the NFWA joined with 800 striking Filipino grape pickers in Delano. The following year Chavez led 60 union members in a 300-mile march from Delano to Sacramento to dramatize union demands for recognition. The march ended with a demonstration of more than 10,000 people in the state capital. Under Chavez, the farm workers' strike had elements of both a labor struggle and a **civil rights** movement with strong religious overtones.

The drama of the strike and Chavez's personal magnetism brought together a broad coalition of national support, ranging from civil rights and church groups to traditional labor leaders. Senator **Robert F. Kennedy** and Walter Reuther, leader of the United Auto Workers (UAW) union, appeared at farm workers' rallies; the UAW also contributed to the UFWOC strike fund. The farm workers' struggle soon became a defining issue in both California and national politics. Democratic governor Edmund G. Brown's sympathy for the growers cost him much liberal support in his state, while the farm workers' enthusiastic endorsement of Senator Kennedy helped increase his national standing. Chavez's actions also earned him the attention of the Federal Bureau of Investigation, which developed a 2,000-page file on his activities. Gradually, publicity and labor unrest began to tell on the California growers. The first employers to acknowledge

union demands were the growers of wine grapes, who marketed their own brands and were highly vulnerable to boycott. Between April and September 1966, the major wine manufacturers of California signed contracts with the UFWOC recognizing the union as the sole bargaining agent of the grape pickers. Chavez died on 23 April 1993, of unspecified natural causes, in San Luis, Arizona.

CHICANO MOVEMENT. The Chicano movement, also known as the Chicano **civil rights** movement, the Mexican American civil rights movement, and El Movimiento, was part of the widespread American civil rights movement of the 1960s. The Chicano movement had three major goals: restoration of land, rights for farm workers, and **education** reforms. The Chicano movement sought to enhance all political, social, economic, and cultural activities of Mexican Americans. In New Mexico, the political dimensions included efforts to restore Spanish-era land grants to their original owners, while in California and elsewhere in the West, it involved the election and appointment of Mexican Americans to government offices. Political activities also involved the desegregation of schools and responsible authorities to review complaints of police brutality.

Prior to the 1960s, however, Latinos lacked influence in the national political arena. In 1960, the strength of the Mexican American vote was unknown. As it happened, John F. Kennedy enjoyed overwhelming support from Mexican American voters in 1960, and their votes helped him narrowly win the presidential election. Kennedy and his wife, Jackie, connected with Mexican Americans because they were warm and charming, and Catholic, the primary religion in the Mexican American community. Jackie also made a point of reaching out by speaking Spanish to the Mexican American community. Kennedy was so popular among Mexican Americans that "Viva Kennedy" clubs were formed in 1960. These clubs encouraged the Mexican American community to become proactive and "get out there and vote."

Kennedy, however, did not entirely live up to his promise to Mexican Americans. He didn't

appoint more Mexican Americans to high political positions and didn't pass legislation to benefit the Mexican American community. It was left to his brother **Robert Kennedy** to meet community expectations. Robert became a great supporter of Mexican farm worker activist **Cesar Chavez**. John F. Kennedy's legacy was important, however, because he highlighted the growing voting power of Mexican Americans in American society. Kennedy's power was so great that Mexican American political coalitions continued because of his influence.

The **assassination of John F. Kennedy** holds special poignancy for Mexican Americans. On 21 November 1963, the night prior to Kennedy's assassination, Kennedy and Jackie—along with Vice President **Lyndon B. Johnson** and his wife Lady Bird—had attended a formal gala dinner in Houston given by the League of United Latin American Citizens, and during the course of the evening, Jackie spoke to the dinner guests in Spanish on behalf of her husband. The dinner had a mariachi band performing, and Kennedy reportedly told Jackie he was enjoying the music.

CIVIL DEFENSE. Civil (or civilian) defense took on new dimensions in the United States following World War II with the advent of nuclear weapons and the onset of the **Cold War** with its implication that it could at any moment turn into a hot war with potentially staggering human and industrial losses. The National Security Act of 1947 included a National Security Resources Board (NSRB), and in 1950, the NSRB prepared a 162-page document outlining a model civil defense structure for the United States. However, Congress never came close to meeting the budget requests of federal civil defense agencies. Civil defense programs included identifying and marking public locations where citizens could shield themselves from the blast and radiation effects of a nuclear bomb. Citizens often took it upon themselves to prepare for such a catastrophe—preparations that usually focused on construction of a family fallout shelter. In November 1957, a commission appointed by President **Dwight D. Eisenhower** (headed by California attorney

Horace R. Gaither) to explore the feasibility of a nationwide program of shelters, reported that shelters were of limited value against an attack by intercontinental ballistic missiles. Nevertheless, following his summit meeting with Premier **Nikita Khrushchev** at Vienna on 3–4 June 1961, and the October 1962 **Cuban missile crisis**, President Kennedy launched an ambitious effort to install fallout shelters throughout the United States. While these shelters would not have provided protection against the blast and heat effects of nuclear weapons, it was believed they would have provided some protection against the radiation effects that followed. Civil defense officials also launched an educational effort, composing songs and TV presentations such as "Duck and Cover," in which Bert the Turtle advocated that children "duck and cover" when they "see the flash." Evacuation plans were also considered but almost immediately rejected as impractical. By the end of the decade, most officials and citizens recognized that the destructiveness of nuclear warheads rendered civil defense programs futile, while the nuclear balance, and subsequent negotiations between the superpowers seeking to control this weaponry, offered the greatest prospect for safety.

CIVIL RIGHTS. Efforts to ensure equality before the law for **African Americans**, known as the civil rights movement, was one of the major domestic matters facing John F. Kennedy when he assumed the presidency in January 1961. Indeed, it had emerged as a major issue during the 1960 presidential campaign. Some of the most dramatic events of the Kennedy presidency centered on the struggle for civil rights.

The background to this situation was long in the making. Despite the passage of the Fourteenth Amendment to the constitution guaranteeing the rights of African Americans to "equal protection of the laws" in 1868, African Americans had lived in a nation segregated along racial lines and had been attacked, lynched, and discriminated against for much of the previous century. In Washington, serious attempts to redress the unequal circumstances of African Americans began in the 1950s.

In 1954, the U.S. **Supreme Court** ruled unanimously in *Brown v. Board of Education* that racial segregation in public schools was unconstitutional because it was "inherently unequal" in quality and, therefore, a violation of the rights of black children. This decision effectively overturned the 1896 Supreme Court's ruling in *Plessy v. Ferguson* that segregated schools were legal so long as they provided "separate but equal" education for black and white children. The court required the desegregation of public education "with all deliberate speed." Faced with the opposition of the majority of southern political leaders who responded with defiance, legal challenges, delays, or token compliance, school desegregation proceeded very slowly.

In 1957, the governor of Arkansas promised to resist the desegregation of Little Rock's Central High School. Faced with this critical situation, President **Dwight D. Eisenhower**, who until that time had remained aloof from the integration movement, felt compelled to federalize the National Guard to escort the excluded nine black students into the school. Even after Little Rock, school integration was painfully slow and mostly token in nature. By the end of the 1950s, less than 10 percent of black children in the South were attending integrated schools.

Meanwhile, segregation in general continued. Following the arrest, in December 1955, of Rosa Parks, the secretary of the Montgomery, Alabama, chapter of the **National Association for the Advancement of Colored People** (NAACP), for refusing to surrender her seat in a city bus to a white person, **Martin Luther King Jr.**, then a 26-year-old Baptist minister, led a black boycott of the bus company. A year later, in December 1956, the Supreme Court ruled segregated seating in Montgomery buses was unconstitutional and drew national attention to the issue.

These and many other acts of white resistance to granting African Americans civil rights, drew attention to the disparity between white and black Americans in voting participation in federal and state elections. In 1957, President Eisenhower introduced, and on 9 September signed, the 1957 Civil Rights Act,

the first such act for 82 years. The goal of the legislation was to ensure African Americans had the right to vote. Up to 1957, because of a variety of discriminatory and other deterrent activities by (mainly southern) segregationists, only 20 percent of African Americans had registered to vote. The act essentially kick-started the civil rights legislative program that was to include the **Civil Rights Act of 1964** and the 1965 Voting Rights Act. The person who steered the passage of the 1957 act through the Senate was **Lyndon B. Johnson**. Democratic senator Strom Thurmond of South Carolina, an ardent segregationist, mounted a one-man filibuster of more than 24 hours—the longest one-person filibuster in history—in an attempt to keep the bill from becoming law.

Civil rights activists, black and white, continued their campaign for equality—sit-ins, stand-ins, and pray-ins against segregated establishments in more than 65 cities in 12 states across the South—and these events formed the backdrop against which the 1960 presidential election campaign was conducted. When Dr. King was arrested for leading civil rights protests in Georgia, candidate John F. Kennedy called Coretta Scott King and offered to help secure Dr. King's safe release. Kennedy was subsequently publicly endorsed by Martin Luther King Sr. The African American vote went solidly for Kennedy across the nation (more than 70 percent), providing the winning edge in several key states.

Kennedy was slow to respond to civil rights issues and did little in his first year of office (1961) to meet the high expectations of black Americans. Conscious of his narrow margin of victory he was more concerned to protect his small working margin in Congress and reluctant to lose southern support for legislation (such as housing, which would help minorities and the poor), than pressing for civil rights legislation. He did not lead the movement for racial equality; rather, he responded to the emerging situation led by grassroots activists. He did utilize his executive authority, however, by appointing an unprecedented number of African Americans to high-level positions in the administration and strengthened the Civil Rights Commission. He spoke out in favor of

school desegregation, praised a number of cities for integrating their schools, and put Vice President Johnson in charge of the President's Committee on Equal Employment Opportunity. He also acquiesced in the use of direct violent confrontation, using federal marshals and the National Guard to counter white supremacist violence. But it was not until 11 June 1963, when faced with the refusal of the governor of Alabama to allow African American students to enroll at the University of Alabama, that he identified himself personally with the cause, announcing in a nationally televised address that civil rights were "a moral issue . . . as old as the Scriptures . . . and as clear as the constitution." He asked the American people, "who among us would be content to have the color of his skin changed and stand in [the Negro's] place? Who among us would then be content with counsels of patience and delay?" The time had come, he declared, for the nation to fulfill its promise of equality for all.

In 1961, Kennedy instructed his attorney general, **Robert Kennedy**, to prosecute violations of voting rights. However, millions of black Americans and the civil rights movement would not wait for this trickle-down approach to take effect. In May 1961, the **Congress of Racial Equality**, led by **James Farmer**, organized integrated "**Freedom Rides**" to defy segregation in interstate transportation (seating on buses and in waiting rooms, restrooms, and restaurants in bus stations). Freedom Riders were arrested and beaten in southern states. In Alabama, a bus was burned and its riders attacked with baseball bats and tire irons. Attorney General Kennedy sent 400 federal marshals to protect the Freedom Riders and urged the Interstate Commerce Commission to order the desegregation of interstate travel (which became effective in September 1961).

Mississippi defied the courts and the administration in late September 1962 by refusing to desegregate its state university. **James H. Meredith**, a black U.S. Air Force veteran, was denied admission to "Ole Miss" with the acquiescence of Governor **Ross Barnett**. Meredith had attempted to register four times without success. Lengthy telephone conversations between the president, the attorney

general, and Barnett failed to produce a solution. President Kennedy eventually federalized the National Guard and sent federal marshals to the campus. After a riot in which two died and dozens were injured, Meredith registered, and segregation ended at the University of Mississippi.

Matters came to a head in 1963. In the spring of that year, Martin Luther King Jr. organized desegregation protests in Birmingham, Alabama, which he called the most segregated city in America. The city administration, led by Director of Public Safety **Theophilus "Bull" Connor**, refused to yield. King mobilized sit-ins and marches by thousands of schoolchildren—which began on Good Friday. Backed by the state's new segregationist governor, **George Wallace**, the Birmingham police used dogs and high-pressure fire hoses to put down the demonstrations. The march in Birmingham was joined by 800 African American schoolchildren who walked out of their classrooms to join the march. Their bravery and determination in the face of the dogs and high-pressure hoses turned on them, captured in photos and newspaper articles across the country, helped accomplish what their parents had failed to do; sway public opinion in support of the civil rights movement. King, along with nearly 1,000 children, was arrested. Kennedy, as a demonstration of federal authority, sent several thousand troops to an Alabama air base. The violence was broadcast on **television** to the nation and the world. The Kennedy administration moved rapidly to respond to the crisis by speeding up the drafting of a comprehensive civil rights bill.

In June 1963, the defiant Governor Wallace, who had vowed at his inauguration to defend "segregation now, segregation tomorrow, and segregation forever," carried out his promise to "stand in the schoolhouse door" to prevent two black students from enrolling at the University of Alabama. After federalizing the Alabama National Guard to protect the students and secure their admission, the president addressed the nation that evening about civil rights. Kennedy defined the crisis as a moral issue, as well as a constitutional and legal matter, and announced that major

civil rights legislation would be submitted to Congress to guarantee equal access to public facilities, to end segregation in education, and to provide federal protection of the right to vote.

In August 1963, more than 200,000 Americans of all races celebrated the centennial of President Abraham Lincoln's Emancipation Proclamation by participating in a "March on Washington." The event was led by key civil rights figures such as A. Phillip Randolph, **Roy Wilkins**, **Bayard Rustin**, and **Whitney Young**, but the most memorable moment came when Martin Luther King Jr. delivered his "I Have a Dream" speech. Kennedy's comprehensive civil rights bill had cleared several hurdles in Congress by fall 1963, including winning the endorsement of House and Senate Republican leaders. It was not passed, however, before 22 November 1963, when President Kennedy was assassinated. The bill was left in the hands of Lyndon B. Johnson (formerly a U.S. senator for Texas), who assumed the presidency. Johnson used his connections with southern white congressional leaders and the outpouring of emotion from the country in response to the death of Kennedy to urge Congress to pass the Civil Rights Bill as a way to honor Kennedy. This bill was passed on 2 July 1964, and it was a crucial step in achieving the civil rights movement's initial goal: full legal equality for minority citizens. It was followed in 1965 by a comprehensive Voting Rights Act. *See also* EVERS, MEDGAR WILEY; MARSHALL, THURGOOD.

CIVIL RIGHTS ACT OF 1964. The landmark legislation known as the Civil Rights Act of 1964 forbade discrimination in the United States based on race, color, religion, sex,

Civil rights leaders talking with reporters after meeting with President John F. Kennedy following the March on Washington, Washington, DC, 1963. *Courtesy of Library of Congress.*

Civil rights leaders meeting with President John F. Kennedy in the Oval Office of the White House after the March on Washington, Washington, DC, 1963. *Courtesy of Library of Congress.*

or national origins. It altered the American political, social, and economic landscape by banning discrimination in public facilities, government, and employment, and by abolishing segregation by race in schools, housing, and hiring. President Kennedy had urged the passage of such a bill in his **civil rights** speech of 11 June 1963, when he asked for legislation that would extend to all individuals "the kind of equality of treatment which we would want for ourselves." Senate majority leader **Mike Mansfield** introduced the bill in Congress, but neither he nor Kennedy was able to achieve its passage. After Kennedy's death, President **Lyndon B. Johnson** addressed Congress and the nation for the first time as president on 27 November 1963. He urged the passage of the Civil Rights Bill as a tribute to Kennedy so that "the ideas and the ideals which [he] so nobly represented

. . . will be translated into effective action." Johnson employed his considerable influence to persuade Congress to act on the bill, and despite an 83-day filibuster in the Senate by conservatives and segregationists, it was overwhelmingly passed and signed into law on 2 July 1964.

Enforcement of the act grew slowly as judicial decisions upheld its intent. Although the initial intent of the bill was to guarantee the rights of African Americans, it was amended prior to passage to protect the civil rights of all individuals and, for the first time, specifically women. The inclusion of women in the 1964 act was due to the influence of a Virginia segregationist, Representative Howard W. Smith, who chaired the House Rules Committee. Although he opposed civil rights protections for African Americans, his support of such measures for women was due to the urging of his

long-time friend, Alice Paul, a leader in the suffrage movement since 1917.

The repercussions that evolved from the passage of the Civil Rights Act altered national politics. Southern states that had long provided the Democrats with majorities in the House and Senate shifted their political allegiance to the Republicans. As a sign of the impending change, the election of 1964 found five states in the Deep South going to the Republican candidate, two of which had not voted Republican since 1876. Spurred by the assassination of Dr. **Martin Luther King Jr.** a week before, Congress passed on 11 April the Civil Rights Act of 1968, which was intended to be a supplement to the 1964 act. Although the 1964 legislation had prohibited discrimination in housing, it lacked federal provisions for enforcement. The 1968 Civil Rights Act, also known as the Fair Housing Act, expanded earlier legislation by banning discrimination in the sale, rental, and financing of housing based on race, religion, national origin, and (later added) sex. It additionally extended protection to civil rights workers.

CLAY, LUCIUS DUBIGNON (1897–1978).

Lucius Dubignon Clay was born in Marietta, Georgia, on 23 April 1897, the son of a U.S. senator and a descendant of the noted American statesman Henry Clay—known as "the great compromiser." In contrast, Lucius, who graduated from West Point in 1918, was known in his military career as "the great uncompromiser." During World War II, he was appointed director of material and coordinated the production and movement of supplies to the battlefront. Following the war, on the recommendation of General **Dwight D. Eisenhower**, Clay was appointed U.S. deputy military governor of the American zone in Germany in 1945 and then military governor and commanding general of U.S. forces in Europe from 1947 to 1949. He became deeply involved in the reconstruction of post–World War II Germany and, as the result of his successful management of the Allied airlift to supply the western sector of the city, became the symbol of U.S. determination to break the Russian blockade of Berlin in 1948. Clay retired from

military service in 1949 and accepted a position as chairman of the board and chief executive officer of the Continental Can Company.

In August 1961, when the Kremlin and East Germany threatened to cut off Western access to East Berlin and make Berlin a "free city," theoretically independent of both Eastern and Western control, President Kennedy asked Clay to act as his personal representative to West Berlin. Not one for diplomatic niceties, Clay insisted upon asserting Western access rights into the Soviet sector. On several occasions, he ordered American diplomats to drive into the Eastern zone. When, on 27 October, East German authorities stopped American officials entering East Berlin, Clay ordered armed convoys to accompany the diplomats to ensure entry. In the ensuing crisis, American and Soviet tanks faced each other across the border for the first time in the postwar era. After a tense standoff, both sides withdrew their armored forces in a step-by-step process.

Relieved but alarmed, Kennedy, like Truman before him, felt the need for the administration in Washington to control U.S. responses—especially military ones—in such situations rather than allow local military commanders unlimited freedom to act. Clay denied he was unhappy with Kennedy's decision, but in May 1962, when the crisis had subsided, he resigned and returned to the United States and resumed his business activities.

Kennedy did call upon Clay later in December 1962 to be part of a committee of businessmen to report on U.S. foreign assistance programs. The president hoped a favorable report would help in garnering support within the business community and conservative members of Congress. While the report, released in March 1963, did acknowledge that foreign aid was indispensable to national security, its tone was such that conservatives in Congress used it to drastically reduce the 1963 foreign aid budget.

Clay supported the **Lyndon B. Johnson** administration's policy on **Vietnam**. In 1970, he retired as chairman of the board of the Continental Can Company. Clay died in Chatham, Massachusetts, on 16 April 1978, aged 81. *See also* BERLIN CRISIS OF 1961.

CLIFFORD, CLARK McADAMS (1906–1998). Born in Fort Scott, Kansas, on 25 December 1906, Clark McAdams Clifford graduated in law from Washington University in St. Louis and specialized in corporation and labor law. Ambitious, urbane, and with courtly manners, he became a highly successful attorney. He was an invaluable adviser to three **Democratic Party** presidents, **Harry S. Truman**, John F. Kennedy, and **Lyndon B. Johnson**.

In 1944, Clifford was commissioned a lieutenant in the U.S. Naval Reserve; a year later he became the assistant to President Harry S. Truman's naval aide, James K. Vardaman. He succeeded Vardaman in that role in 1946. Following the completion of his naval service in June 1946, Truman appointed him as special counsel to the president.

Clifford was essentially a realist in the context of the **Cold War**. He helped draft the Truman Doctrine and the National Security Act of 1947. Clifford also helped plan the political strategy that led to Truman's election in 1948 and that laid the basis for much Fair Deal legislation. He and Truman became close friends. He advised the president on many contentious issues including Truman's recognition of Israel. Returning to private practice in 1950, Clifford became one of the most influential lawyers in Washington, representing some of America's largest corporations in their dealings with the government.

In 1959, Senator John F. Kennedy appointed Clifford his personal attorney, and he acted as an adviser to Kennedy during the senator's campaign for the presidency in 1960. Following the failure of U.S. intelligence agencies that led to the abortive **Bay of Pigs** invasion of **Cuba** in 1961, Kennedy created the Foreign Intelligence Advisory Board to oversee and restructure these agencies and appointed Clifford to the new panel. He became its chairman from April 1963 until January 1968.

Kennedy also used Clifford as his negotiator when, in April 1962, the steel industry increased prices against the president's wishes. Clifford met secretly with U.S. Steel chairman Roger Blough and persuaded the corporation to rescind its price increase.

Clifford also served as a trusted adviser to President Johnson, in both domestic and foreign affairs. In 1967, Johnson sent him on a tour of **Vietnam** and Southeast Asia to assess U.S. prospects in the ongoing and increasingly divisive **Vietnam War**. In January 1968, he succeeded **Robert S. McNamara** as secretary of defense. Clifford's advice was decisive in persuading Johnson to de-escalate the Vietnam War in March 1968.

Before returning to his private law practice, on 20 January 1969 Clifford was presented with the Presidential Medal of Freedom with Distinction by Johnson on the president's last day in office.

In 1980, at the request of the president, Clifford acted as Jimmy Carter's special presidential emissary in an unsuccessful effort to reassure India that the U.S. decision to supply arms for Pakistan was an appropriate response to Soviet military intervention in Afghanistan.

In his later years, Clifford was implicated in an international scandal surrounding the financial dealings of the Bank of Credit and Commerce International, in which he was a major figure. Speaking of his situation, he lamented: "I have a choice of either seeming stupid or venal." Nonetheless, his reputation as a distinguished public servant who played an important part in the formulation of postwar foreign and domestic policy remains intact.

He died in 10 October 1998 in Bethesda, Maryland, of natural causes at the age of 91 and is buried at Arlington National Cemetery. *See also* BELL, DAVID ELLIOTT; GOLDBERG, ARTHUR JOSEPH.

COLD WAR. The Cold War, the economic and political rivalry between the United States and the **Soviet Union** and their respective allies for preeminence among world powers short of outright military conflict, dominated the 1950s and 1960s through the 1980s. In the United States, it created a bipartisan consensus between Republicans and Democrats as to the shape and direction of the nation's foreign policy. That policy was the doctrine of containment, a policy toward the Soviet Union of restricting what was seen as Russian expansionist tendencies. The goal of U.S. Cold War

policy was to maintain—even extend—the economic and military predominance throughout the world the United States believed it possessed at the end of World War II.

This global competition between the United States and the Soviet Union was fueled by ideology, geopolitics, economics, militarization, and patriotic culture. Although falling short of a "hot" war between the two superpowers (granted hostilities frequently involved client states), this conflict lasted from 1946 to 1991. Public officials and citizens—and there were many on both sides—rarely ever considered an issue from the other side's perspective; those ruled by their fervent ideological animosity were known as "Cold Warriors" and played a significant role in constantly feeding international tensions.

In retrospect, the Cold War manifested itself in periods of differing intensity. Following a relative calm in the mid-1950s following the end of the Korean War, it flared sharply during John F. Kennedy's presidency with confrontations over the Western nation's enclaves in Berlin, the construction of the Berlin Wall in August 1961, and the **Bay of Pigs** intervention, and it reached its apogee during the **Cuban missile crisis** in 1962. At the same time, Kennedy and his advisers were entangled in the unfolding series of crises in Laos and **Vietnam**.

Kennedy's inaugural address was a rousing, but nonetheless ominously expansionist, call to action; the United States would pay any price, would bear any burden, oppose any foe, in defense of liberty, he proclaimed. In his first State of the Union address, he proposed the **Peace Corps** and outlined a "Food for Peace" foreign aid program. In March 1961, he announced the **Alliance for Progress**, and among the first questions he faced was whether to go ahead with the **Dwight D. Eisenhower** administration's plans to launch a covert operation against the **Fidel Castro** government of **Cuba**.

Although many Americans anticipated a more aggressive approach toward the Soviet Union from Kennedy, the new young president proved surprisingly cautious in his decision making and was reluctant to commit U.S. troops to war. He was torn between a

considered, pragmatic approach and a desire to act quickly and decisively to solve problems. His reliance upon ambassadors and special personal envoys, rather than formal meetings of the National Security Council (NSC), reflected a quest for innovative solutions. As a result of the debacle of the Bay of Pigs invasion, he sought alternatives to military intervention, at the same time stating that his administration would embark upon "a relentless struggle in very corner of the globe against communism." In the following year, the administration adopted a punitive policy toward Cuba and the Castro regime.

Kennedy's approach to Cuba not only reflected the Cold War mind-set of the president and his administration but also set the tone for his relations with Latin America as a whole. Kennedy and his inner cadre of advisers had a mission to save impoverished Latin American nations from the clutches of communism and left-wing radicals. They saw the need for and welcomed modernization and land and tax reform in corrupt dictatorships of the region, but they feared revolution—thus the hostility toward Castro. Kennedy wanted to embark on U.S. industrial and economic development assistance to Latin American countries as a means of preventing radical and subversive activities. The centerpiece of Kennedy's solution to lessen aggression and subversion in Latin America—especially in countries like Brazil, Colombia, and Venezuela—was to accelerate economic growth and social progress through a policy known as the "**Alliance for Progress**," which he announced on 13 March 1961. An international conference to inaugurate the alliance attended by the American republics was held in Punta del Este in August, but given Cuba's opposition to the program, it had little chance of success.

In June 1961, when faced with an ultimatum from **Nikita Khrushchev** that implied an outbreak of (possibly nuclear) war over Western access to West Berlin, Kennedy rejected State Department proposals that involved any military attempt to reopen access to the city. Similarly, in July through October 1961, against the advice of his senior national security advisers, Kennedy accepted

the notion of a neutral government in Laos rather than embark on U.S. or Southeast Asia Treaty Organization military intervention to install a pro-American government to prevent the success of a communist insurgency. Kennedy did, however, make the critical decision for a substantial increase in the advisory presence in South Vietnam, although he refused to declare the independence of South Vietnam a vital interest of the United States. Kennedy was reluctant to become involved in what was essentially a civil war in Vietnam, but because he embraced the **domino theory**, he authorized an increase in U.S. military forces in that country. By November 1963, the number of U.S. military forces in Vietnam had reached around 16,700 and was to substantially increase in the next decade with devastating consequences for the United States and Vietnam; the Cold War had prevailed over Kennedy.

But perhaps Kennedy's biggest crisis in the Cold War occurred in October 1962 over the discovery on 14 October of the placement of Soviet missiles in Cuba. The discovery of the missiles led to a tense, 13-day political and military standoff between the leaders of the United States and the Soviet Union. Kennedy was presented with two options. The first, supported initially by **Robert S. McNamara**, was to do nothing as, he argued, the missiles did not alter the overall strategic balance between the Soviet Union and the United States. The second, supported by the Joint Chiefs of Staff, was to launch a full-scale air strike followed by an invasion of Cuba. The president chose a third course of action: a naval quarantine of Cuba, largely because the air force could not guarantee the success of even a limited air strike. In a **television** address on 22 October, Kennedy notified Americans about the presence of the missiles, explained his decision to enact a naval blockade around Cuba, and made it clear the United States was prepared to use military force if necessary to neutralize this perceived threat to national security. Following this news, many people feared the world was on the brink of nuclear war. Soviet ships bound for Cuba stopped short of U.S. ships on 24 October, but on Saturday 27 October, a U.S. U-2 spy plane was shot down over Cuba and the pilot killed.

Later that day, Kennedy held two meetings with his advisers; the first with 15 members of the Executive Committee of the NSC (ExComm) and the second with only nine members of the ExComm. After lengthy discussion with this group, Kennedy agreed to inform Khrushchev that, in return for the Soviet removal of the missiles, the United States would not invade Cuba, and to have **Robert Kennedy** privately inform the Russian ambassador that the United States would remove its Jupiter missiles from Turkey—a condition demanded by the Soviet leader.

The Cuban missile crisis was a sobering moment. The following year, a direct "hotline" communication link was installed between Washington and Moscow to help defuse similar situations, and in 1963, the superpowers signed a **Limited Nuclear Test Ban Treaty**— a treaty that was subsequently adopted by scores of other nations. Following the resolution of the Cuban missile crisis, tensions relaxed, and a series of negotiations were undertaken by officials in Moscow and Washington, some reaching mutual understandings and others not. Several of the successful arrangements were arms-control agreements reached with the Soviets by the Kennedy and Johnson administrations.

In 1963–1964, the United States and the Soviets each unilaterally announced military budget cuts. In 1965, however, with the United States involved in Vietnam, the Americans began increasing their expenditures and the program was terminated. A 1964 proposal for a cutback in production of enriched uranium and plutonium for nuclear weapons did not attract much interest in Moscow.

CONGRESS OF RACIAL EQUALITY (CORE). The Congress of Racial Equality is an African American **civil rights** organization formed in Chicago in 1942. The founding group of 50 members—28 of whom were men and 22 women, roughly one-third black and two-thirds white—had evolved out of the Chicago branch of the pacifist organization Fellowship of Reconciliation. Inspired by the nonviolent

resistance teachings of Mahatma Gandhi, the stated purpose of CORE was "to bring about equality for all people regardless of race, creed, sex, age, disability, sexual orientation, religion or ethnic background." Core has played a pivotal role for **African Americans** in the civil rights movement.

Led by **James L. Farmer** and others, CORE launched a series of direct-action protests against racial discrimination. These included tactics involving sit-ins, jail-ins, and **Freedom Rides**. The 1954 decision in *Brown v. Board of Education* revitalized the declining civil rights movement, and CORE began to focus its attention on segregation in the South. The 1961 Freedom Ride was modeled after an earlier Journey of Reconciliation. In 1963, the group planned the March on Washington, and in the following year, they participated with other groups in the Mississippi Freedom Summer project, during which three young CORE members were killed.

CONNOR, THEOPHILUS EUGENE "BULL"

(1897–1973). Theophilus Eugene Connor was born on 11 July 1897, in Selma, Alabama. His mother died when he was a child, and it is reposted that he lived with relatives or traveled extensively across the United States with his father, Hugh, who worked as a railroad dispatcher and telegrapher. The young Connor never finished high school, though he did learn his father's trade. He later received the moniker "Bull" from friends inspired by the cartoon character B.U.L. Conner.

After his marriage in 1920, Connor and his family moved to Birmingham, Alabama, where he became well known as a radio sports personality. He eventually turned to politics, serving on the Alabama state legislature for one term in the mid-1930s. In 1937, he became Birmingham's public safety commissioner, winning multiple reelections to the position throughout the 1940s and then running unsuccessfully for the governorship. He was reelected as Birmingham's public safety commissioner in the late 1950s through the early 1960s.

In the late 1950s and early 1960s, Birmingham was known as one of the American South's most rigidly segregated cities. Connor was a Southern Democrat and a staunch proponent of racist social policies. He attended many Democratic Party national conventions as a delegate and was part of the faction who walked out of the 1948 convention in protest of the **civil rights** platform, thus becoming part of the Dixiecrat movement. Connor became a known foe in the civil rights movement. He refused to provide police protection for the Freedom Riders who arrived in Birmingham on 14 March 1961 (Mother's Day), although he knew that they would be besieged upon their arrival in the city. Despite some local efforts to remove him from office because of his hard-line racist policies by replacing the existing commissioner form of government with a mayor–city council system, Connor continued to hold power.

In spring 1963, **Martin Luther King Jr.** and Fred Shuttlesworth led a series of civil rights demonstrations to end segregation in Birmingham. Connor ordered the arrest and jailing of hundreds of student protesters. He eventually ordered authorities to besiege peaceful protesters, many of whom were quite young, with nightsticks, water hoses, and attack dogs. Shocking images of these events were broadcast throughout the United States and around the world, thus accelerating integration in the city and galvanizing the Kennedy administration into action, thereby helping to set into motion the creation of the **Civil Rights Act of 1964**.

The Kennedy administration responded to the national and worldwide indignation against Connor's policing methods by exerting strong pressure on Birmingham's business community to negotiate with black leaders. On 10 May 1963, Shuttlesworth announced an agreement that provided for gradual desegregation of the city's major public accommodations and the hiring of blacks in jobs previously reserved for whites. President Kennedy, in a conversation with civil rights leaders shortly afterward, said, "I don't think you should be totally harsh on 'Bull' Connor. He has done more for civil rights than almost anybody else."

Toward the end of May, Connor was forced out of office by the state supreme court, though he was soon elected to the public

service commission, winning a second term as well. Connor remained an unyielding foe of integration. He died in Birmingham on 10 March 1973 after suffering a stroke.

COUNTERINSURGENCY. Counterinsurgency is a military tactic designed to defeat insurgents by utilizing means short of full-scale warfare. Its purpose is to win the hearts, minds, and the acquiescence of a population who are engaged in defending themselves against a group or groups who are seeking to destabilize or overthrow their government by the use of force. The basic question is this: How much force should be employed in a situation that is not a battlefield situation? The use of too much firepower creates blood feuds, homeless people, and societal disruption that fuels and perpetuates the insurgency. The populations being protected must accept that counterinsurgency actions benefit them and ensure their security.

Successfully applying the tactical techniques of counterinsurgency, as President Kennedy discovered, especially in the case of **Vietnam**, was "complicated." The Kennedy administration searched through various historical episodes to uncover the secrets to defeating inspired insurgent or guerrilla forces but could find no magic formula. American and South Vietnamese forces relied heavily upon the use of airpower, artillery, Agent Orange, free fire zones, and search and destroy tactics, all of which too often resulted in the destruction of hamlets, small cities, and cropland. Most U.S. commanders viewed counterinsurgency and pacification tactics with disdain and adopted as their strategy the "war of attrition." *See also* VIETNAM WAR.

CRONKITE, WALTER LELAND (1916–2009). Walter Cronkite was born on 4 November 1916 in St. Joseph, Missouri. He lived in Kansas City, Missouri, until the age of 10 when his parents moved to Houston, Texas. He attended the University of Texas at Austin for two years while simultaneously working as the state capital reporter for the Scripps-Howard Bureau in 1935 and 1936. During World War II, Cronkite had a distinguished career as a correspondent

for United Press International. He joined the Columbia Broadcasting System (CBS) in July 1950 as a member of the network's Washington staff and soon became one of its most important correspondents, acting as anchor for the 1952 and 1956 political conventions.

Among the most popular of his CBS programs during the 1950s were *You Are There* and the *Morning Show*. He became the anchor of CBS Television's *Evening News* in April 1962. In September 1963, the broadcast expanded from 15 to 30 minutes.

Cronkite was among the first to broadcast news of the **assassination of John F. Kennedy**. He anchored the CBS News coverage during the first hours after bullets hit the president in Dallas on 22 November 1963. He was reluctant to announce Kennedy's death until it was officially confirmed, and when he did so, it was in a deeply emotional manner. In a 2003 interview referring to his coverage of Kennedy's assassination, Cronkite stated: "when you finally had to say it's official, the President is dead . . . pretty tough words in a situation like that. And they were, um, hard to come by." In a 2006 **television** interview, Cronkite recalled: "I choked up, I really had a little trouble . . . my eyes got a little wet . . . [what Kennedy had represented] was just all lost to us. Fortunately, I grabbed hold before I was actually [crying]." According to historian Douglas Brinkley, Cronkite provided a sense of perspective throughout the unfolding sequence of disturbing events.

He later put together a story about that fateful day for the National Public Radio program *All Things Considered*, which combined his recollections together with several recordings from the day of the assassination few had heard before. "UPI teletypes around the world started ticking out the news," Cronkite recalled. "One of them was on the communications deck of Aircraft 972—the plane which held two-thirds of Kennedy's Cabinet, including Secretary of State **Dean Rusk**— was 900 miles west of Honolulu, en route to Japan, where the radio officer blinked in disbelief at what he read." Cronkite commented that "government was being improvised in the air," as small but necessary decisions, like the

equipment needed to transport the coffin, were being made en route.

During the mid-1960s, Cronkite's ratings dropped as a result of the popularity of NBC's Huntley-Brinkley news program, and he was removed from his customary position as anchor for the 1964 political conventions. By the middle of the 1960s, the majority of Americans regarded television as their main source of news, and the **Vietnam War** was a—if not the—major news story. When the first declared U.S. combat troops went into South Vietnam in 1965, Cronkite supported the **Lyndon B. Johnson** administration's actions; nevertheless, the news broadcaster won considerable praise for his balanced reporting. By 1968, he had changed his mind, and on 27 February, in a special, prime-time report, Cronkite declared that the war was a stalemate and that the United States would most likely have to accept a negotiated settlement. Johnson despaired, "If I've lost Cronkite, I've lost the country."

Renowned for his relaxed manner and a lucid style that was especially evident during "live" events, Cronkite's evening news program was broadcast by over 200 affiliated stations and led the competition with an estimated audience of 26 million by 1973. For years, polls indicated he was regarded as "the most trusted man in America."

He retired from CBS in 1981 but remained active in the television field on many levels. Cronkite died on 17 July 2009, at his home in New York City, at the age of 92. He is believed to have died from cerebrovascular disease.

CUBA. Cuba is a Caribbean island 90 miles southeast of the Florida Keys, and its close proximity to the United States, together with its pro-Moscow communist government, led successive American administrations to fear the island both as a base for subversive activities throughout the Western Hemisphere and as a platform for a Soviet attack on the U.S. mainland. These fears led to the **Bay of Pigs** invasion, the **Cuban missile crisis**, and American efforts to isolate the government and assassinate its leader, **Fidel Castro.**

CUBAN MISSILE CRISIS. Kennedy's biggest test in the **Cold War** occurred in October 1962 over the presence of Soviet missile sites in Cuba. Unknown to most Americans, between 1959 and 1961, the United States had deployed medium-range nuclear armed ballistic missiles, Jupiters, in North Atlantic Treaty Organization member countries Turkey and Italy, as part of its containment policy toward the **Soviet Union.** Despite the disparity between his nuclear capability and that of the United States, Soviet leader **Nikita Khrushchev** planned to counter this threat—and hopefully deter any further attempts by Washington to remove **Fidel Castro** from power—by locating nuclear armed intercontinental ballistic missiles in **Cuba.**

The discovery of the missiles was first made by a U-2 spy plane flying over Cuba in September. At the time of U.S. sighting, no missiles had been commissioned, but the discovery of the partly constructed missile sites led to a tense, 13-day political and military standoff between the leaders of the United States and the Soviet Union.

On 16 October, Kennedy's advisers presented him with four options. The first was to handle the matter through diplomacy, and to do nothing militarily, because, as Robert S. McNamara argued correctly, the Soviet missiles did not alter the overall strategic balance between the Soviet Union and the United States. Despite Kennedy's assertions during the 1960 presidential campaign that the United States was losing the missile race with the Soviet Union, he knew that the United States maintained an overwhelming nuclear superiority over the Soviets. The second option was to try to trade off America's missiles in Turkey for the Soviet missiles in Cuba; the third was to implement a selective blockade of Cuba to prevent the passage of Russian missiles to Cuba. The fourth option, supported by the Joint Chiefs of Staff, was to launch a full-scale air strike followed by an invasion of Cuba. The president chose the third course of action: a naval blockade of Cuba—which he termed a "quarantine" to avoid the implication

that he was initiating a state of war—largely because the air force could not guarantee the success of even a limited air strike.

In a **television** address on 22 October, a somber Kennedy notified a stunned American population about the presence of the missiles, explained his decision to employ the navy to prevent the passage of Soviet ships to Cuba, and made it clear the United States was prepared to use military force if necessary to neutralize this perceived threat to national security. He threatened that the launch of a single missile from Cuba would result in "a full retaliatory response upon the Soviet Union"—by which he meant a massive nuclear attack—by the United States. He had delayed any public announcement to ensure maximum (electoral) impact before the upcoming November midterm congressional elections. Following this news, many people feared the world was on the brink of nuclear war. Soviet ships bound for Cuba stopped short of U.S. ships on 24 October, but on Saturday, 27 October, a U.S. U-2 spy plane was shot down over Cuba and the pilot killed. Later that day, Kennedy held two meetings with his advisers; the first with 15 members of the Executive Committee of the National Security Council (ExComm) and the second with only nine members of the ExComm. After lengthy discussion with this group, Kennedy decided to complement the blockade with diplomacy. That night acting as his brother's emissary, **Robert Kennedy** met secretly with Soviet ambassador Anatoly Dobrynin in Washington. He demanded the immediate withdrawal of the missiles, but he also informed Dobrynin that, in return for the Soviet removal of the missiles, the United States would not invade Cuba, and that the U.S. would remove its Jupiter missiles—a condition demanded by the Soviet leader. Vulnerable to air strikes, the outdated and limited-capability Jupiters, which had been superseded in 1961 by the more mobile submarine-launched Polaris missiles, were removed from Turkey in mid-April 1963.

The situation was much more dangerous than anyone knew at the time. Khrushchev had not, in fact, authorized the shooting down of the U-2, and Robert Kennedy, in threatening

an invasion of Cuba unless the missiles were removed immediately, did not know that the Soviets already had around 100 "tactical" nuclear weapons together with Soviet forces located in Cuba as defense against such an American invasion. Furthermore, the number of Soviet military personnel in Cuba was not the 8,000–10,000 estimated by the Pentagon but, instead, numbered around 40,000 troops. Any clashes between U.S. Marines and Soviet forces could well have quickly escalated out of control with catastrophic results. The Cuban missile crisis was a sobering moment. The following year, a direct "hotline" communication link was installed between Washington and Moscow to help defuse similar situations, and the superpowers signed two treaties to limit aboveground testing and the number of nuclear weapons each side would build.

Kennedy's approach to the Cuban missile crisis not only reflected the Cold War mind-set of the president and his administration but also set the tone for his relations with Latin America as a whole. Kennedy and his New England, Ivy League–educated inner cadre of advisers had a mission to save impoverished Latin American nations from the clutches of communism and left-wing radicals. They saw the need for and welcomed modernization and land and tax reform in corrupt dictatorships of the region, but they feared revolution—thus the hostility

Soviet ambassador to the United States Anatoly F. Dobrynin and Soviet foreign minister Andrei Gromyko talking with President Kennedy, who is seated in a rocking chair, at the White House, Washington, DC. *Courtesy of Library of Congress.*

toward Fidel Castro. Kennedy wanted to embark on U.S. industrial and economic development assistance to Latin American countries as a means of preventing radical and subversive activities. The centerpiece of Kennedy's solution to lessen aggression and subversion in Latin America—especially in countries like Brazil, Colombia, and Venezuela—was to accelerate economic growth and social progress through the "**Alliance for Progress**," which he announced on 13 March 1961. An international conference to inaugurate the alliance attended by the American republics was held in Punta del Este in August, but given Cuba's opposition to the program, it had little chance of success.

D

DALEY, RICHARD J. (1902–1976). Richard J. Daley was born on 15 May 1902 in Chicago, in an Irish working-class neighborhood near the Union Stockyards, not far from the house where he later resided as mayor. Trained as a clerk and bookkeeper at the Christian Brothers De La Salle Institute, Daley later attended De-Paul University, from which he earned a law degree in 1934. Daley was elected to the Illinois House of Representatives in 1936 and, for the next decade, served there and in the state senate. As a state legislator, he earned a reputation for reliability and a sense of discretion. These qualities won him appointment as Cook County comptroller, a position that gave him access to politically sensitive material on patronage and public works contracts.

In 1953, he became chairman of the Cook County Democratic Central Committee and thus head of the **Democratic Party** in Chicago, a position he held for 23 years. Two years later, in April 1955, Daley was elected as the 38th mayor of Chicago and had little difficulty winning reelection. He served as mayor for a total of 21 years, holding both positions until his death in office in December 1976. In 1960, Daley came to prominence as a power broker in national politics. At the Democratic National Convention held in Los Angeles, he controlled an estimated three-quarters of the 69 Illinois delegate votes. He was instrumental in rejecting **Adlai E. Stevenson II**'s late bid for a third presidential nomination and helped secure the first ballot nomination for Senator John F. Kennedy. In the tightly contested November general election, the Cook County Democratic organization worked hard to turn out the urban vote; it swung Illinois into the Democratic column by a mere 10,000 votes. Benjamin Adamowski, the losing Republican candidate for state's attorney, charged that "Daley has stolen the White House." A limited and incomplete recount reduced Kennedy's margin of victory but failed to give **Richard M. Nixon** the 27 Illinois electoral votes.

He was later to become infamous for his conduct and remarks at the 1968 Democratic National Convention held in Chicago. Richard Daley died in Chicago of a massive heart attack on 20 December 1976.

DAY, J. EDWARD (1914–1996). James Edward Day was born on 11 October 1914, in Jacksonville, Illinois. He attended public schools in Springfield, Illinois; received his BA from the University of Chicago in 1935; and then attended Harvard Law School. While at Harvard, he served as the treasurer of the Lincoln's Inn Society from 1936 to 1937 and was the legislative editor of the *Harvard Law Review*. He graduated from Harvard Law in 1938.

Day went to work for the firm of Sidney, Austin, Burgess, and Harper in Chicago. During World War II, he trained as an officer in the Naval Reserve (1940–1942) and was called to active duty as an ensign in 1942. He was discharged as a lieutenant in 1945, returning to work for his law firm.

In 1948, after **Adlai Stevenson II** was elected governor of Illinois, Day worked for Stevenson as legislative assistant and later as

state insurance commissioner. He next signed on with the Prudential Insurance Company in 1953 and moved to Los Angeles to take charge of Prudential's western operations in 1957. In addition to his involvement in **Democratic Party** politics, he became active in community and philanthropic organizations while in Los Angeles.

Working with Stevenson, Day became a close friend of the Illinois governor and was part of his 1952 and 1956 presidential campaign teams. When Stevenson indicated he would not continue as a candidate for the 1960 nomination, Day switched his allegiance to Senator John F. Kennedy, although the two had never previously met. He was a Kennedy delegate to the 1960 convention.

In order to strike a greater geographic balance within his cabinet, president-elect Kennedy named Day postmaster general, a decision that surprised most in Kennedy's circle as Day was virtually unknown in Washington. His own explanation for his appointment was the quip: "I went to Harvard, I served in the Navy and my wife went to Vassar."

His experience with Prudential, and his sharp wit, stood him in good stead, and he soon proved himself a highly capable administrator. Day stabilized and then decreased the postal service deficit through modest rate increases. He also introduced the ZIP code (Zoning Improvement Plan) system of mail delivery, which sped up deliveries and cut costs. It also enabled the introduction of mass marketing by providing a quick and easy way of identifying potential customers by income level.

He did not have the best relationship with the Kennedy administration, however. Kennedy's style was to leave cabinet secretaries to their own devices, and the president had little interest in the inner workings of the postal service. However, for years the postal service had been a rich mine for political lobbying and patronage by members of Congress and the executive branch of government, and Day was determined to lessen appointments made through patronage in favor of appointments made through a merit-based system. This caused friction with members of the White House wishing to make political

appointments, and within the postal service itself. Some cabinet members also—especially **Abe Ribicoff**—quarreled with the postmaster. Day found himself involved in frustrating and time-consuming disputes with subordinates and with the West Wing. Well known for his flamboyant lifestyle, he resigned in 1963 due to personal financial difficulties, and he rejoined the private sector.

In later years, Day was known for his wit and was the author of several books, including a memoir and a work of fiction. He died in Hunt Valley, Maryland, on 29 October 1996.

DEMOCRATIC PARTY. With the election of John F. Kennedy, the Democratic Party regained the White House after eight years of **Republican Party** rule with the presidency of **Dwight D. Eisenhower.** Kennedy's victory over his adversary **Richard M. Nixon** was a very narrow one, and while Eisenhower had offered stability and warned against any extension of the "military-industrial complex," Kennedy promised to take America to a **"New Frontier."** After the somewhat uninspiring administration of Eisenhower, Kennedy's youth and energy promised to revitalize American society. Kennedy and the Democratic Party provided space and opportunity for the forces of reform that had begun to take root the decade before, such as the **civil rights** and feminist movements. Following Kennedy's death, **Lyndon B. Johnson** accelerated the party's reform program, laying the foundations of what he termed a "Great Society." He supported **affirmative action** and attempted to break down many of the traditional social barriers. However, the pace of change was deemed too slow by many younger, more radical Americans with the result that the nation experienced considerable social and political upheaval. One dramatic outcome of all this was the collapse of the Democratic Party in the South as a reaction to the granting of equality to **African Americans.** The situation was not helped by Kennedy's determination to demonstrate America's military strength and power on the world stage. The Democratic Party's assertiveness led to a series of crises that appeared to take the world to the brink of nuclear disaster.

Domestically the escalation of American involvement in **Vietnam** divided the nation and resulted in long-term political and social unrest if not outright violence.

DILLON, CLARENCE DOUGLAS (1909–2003). Clarence Douglas Dillon was born on 21 August 1909, in Geneva, Switzerland, and attended the Groton School and Harvard College before his father bought him a seat on the New York Stock Exchange for $185,000 in 1931. His father was one of the country's most successful Wall Street investment bankers, and in 1938, Douglas became vice president of his father's company, Dillon, Read. The company's president was James Forrestal. Following the example of Forrestal, he joined the navy in 1940 and saw action in the Pacific toward the end of the war. With peace he became chairman of the board of Dillon, Read and rapidly expanded the firm's domestic and foreign holdings.

An active Republican, Dillon worked with John Foster Dulles in the 1948 presidential campaign of Governor Thomas E. Dewey and was active in drafting **Dwight D. Eisenhower** in the 1952 presidential race. In 1953, Eisenhower appointed Dillon ambassador to France, where he served until 1957, when he returned to Washington to become undersecretary of state for economic affairs. He contributed heavily to the 1960 presidential campaign of Vice President **Richard M. Nixon** and was considered a natural appointment to a Nixon cabinet.

C. Douglas Dillon, although a staunch Republican, was the most influential member of President John F. Kennedy's economic policymaking team. Like Kennedy, he came from a wealthy family, and he persuaded the president that his administration's economic priority should be to reduce the U.S. balance of payments deficit. He was a conservative in economic matters and urged the government to limit the availability of so-called easy money.

President Kennedy shared Dillon's outlook on economic matters and hoped the selection of Dillon as secretary of the treasury in January 1961 would reassure the financial community, which was apprehensive about the "easy money" proclivities of the incoming Democratic administration. Throughout the Kennedy administration, Dillon enjoyed easy access to the president and was one of Kennedy's few political associates who socialized with him as well.

The preoccupation of Kennedy and Dillon with the balance of payments question in the first two years of the Kennedy administration blocked the path of more aggressive fiscal and monetary stimulation of the economy or heavier spending on social programs. The chief advocate of the latter approach within the Kennedy administration was Walter W. Heller, chairman of the President's Council of Economic Advisers (CEA). Heller and Dillon represented the two major opposing poles of economic thought in the administration's policy-making councils. Heller advocated the active promotion of economic growth by the federal government employing the Keynesian techniques of fiscal stimulation via spending and tax cuts. Dillon voiced the Treasury Department's traditional opposition to deficit spending and generally resisted unorthodox proposals emanating from the CEA.

For the most part, President Kennedy chose Dillon's cautious strategy over Heller's activist approach. Kennedy's decision in May 1961 not to recommend the substantial public works program urged by Heller and U.S. secretary of labor **Arthur J. Goldberg** was an important early victory for Dillon. For almost two years, Dillon also succeeded in blocking Heller's proposal for a sizable tax cut, although later he joined President Kennedy in favoring a $10 billion fiscal stimulus.

Controlling inflation and encouraging exports were broader elements in the balance of payments strategy. Dillon backed the **Trade Expansion Act** of 1962, which was designed to invigorate U.S. foreign trade by giving the president discretionary tariff-cutting authority. However, despite confident predictions in fall 1962 that the U.S. payments deficit would be eliminated by the end of 1963, the annual deficits continued unabated.

Kennedy also used Dillon for foreign policy assignments. He made Dillon head of the American delegation sent to Punta del Este, Uruguay, to inaugurate the **Alliance**

for **Progress** in August 1961. There Dillon pledged $20 billion in low-interest loans over the next 10 years to improve Latin America's living standards. "We welcome the revolution of rising expectations," Dillon said, "and we intend to transform it into a revolution of rising satisfactions." Dillon also sat on the National Security Council and took part in the tense deliberations during the **Cuban missile crisis** of October 1962. Dillon retired as treasury secretary in March 1965. He received the Presidential Medal of Freedom on 6 July 1989. Dillon died in New York City on 10 January 2003. *See also* ALSOP, JOSEPH WRIGHT, JR.; BELL, DAVID ELLIOTT; GRAHAM, PHILIP LESLIE; MANN, THOMAS CLIFTON.

DIRKSEN, EVERETT McKINLEY (1896–1969). Everett McKinley Dirksen was born in Pekin, Illinois, on 4 January 1896, the son of poor German immigrants. He grew up on his family's farm and then worked while attending the University of Minnesota. During World War I, Dirksen served in the balloon corps. He returned to Pekin following the armistice and became active in local politics before being elected in 1932 to the House of Representatives as a Republican, where he served until 1948. Dirksen ran for and won a seat in the U.S. Senate in 1950. Dirksen's political skill, rumpled appearance, and convincing if sometimes flowery, overblown oratory (which made his critics call him "the Wizard of Ooze") brought him national prominence. Sponsored by the powerful conservative leader Senator Henry Styles Bridges (R-N.H.), Dirksen became Senate minority whip in January 1957, the party's second-ranking position in the upper chamber. Two years later he won election as minority leader defeating a more liberal-moderate candidate. Although he had not initially backed **Dwight D. Eisenhower** as Republican candidate for the presidency, he proved a loyal and effective legislative leader. Dirksen established an unusual degree of party unity among his Republican colleagues, giving up his own choice committee assignments to younger or more liberal members and employing flattery rather than threats to those reluctant to vote with the leadership.

The Republicans' loss of the White House in the elections of 1960 left Dirksen as the single most powerful GOP leader in Washington. The Senate leader played both a partisan and cooperative role with the new Kennedy administration. He frequently condemned the president's domestic policies in characteristically flowery prose and in an easily recognized, husky voice. "It may be called the New Frontier," he remarked in May 1961, "but the Kennedy program is the old New Deal taken out of an old warming oven." At the suggestion of former president Eisenhower, Dirksen and House minority leader Charles A. Halleck (R-Ind.) began a weekly review of Kennedy administration policies, dubbed the "Ev and Charlie Show" by Washington journalists. Dirksen led the Republican minority in defeating the administration's proposals for an Urban Affairs Department, a new farm bill, and school construction authorization. A fervent opponent of governmental regulation of business, Dirksen played an adversary role in the investigation chaired by Senator Estes Kefauver (D-Tenn.) into the pricing policies of the pharmaceutical industry.

Despite his conservative stands on domestic issues, Dirksen consistently displayed a bipartisan attitude toward the Kennedy administration's foreign policy initiatives. In April 1961, he opposed Republican attacks on the White House for its role in the disastrous **Bay of Pigs** invasion, and he strongly endorsed the president's policies in Laos and Berlin. The Illinois Republican continued to support foreign aid requests by the White House and worked for the Treasury Department purchase of $100 million worth of **United Nations** (UN) bonds in April 1962. More partisan Republican leaders, however, did not always approve of Dirksen's cooperative attitude. Senator **Barry M. Goldwater** (R-Ariz.), for example, termed Dirksen's stand on the UN bond issue "a surrender." Dirksen's unqualified endorsement of Kennedy's foreign policy, however, did not go unrewarded. Amid a close contest for reelection in October 1962, Dirksen received a presidential summons to Washington for a congressional briefing on the **Cuban missile crisis**. When senators advised the president

to invade the Caribbean island and destroy missile sites, Dirksen helped end the debate when he inquired of U.S. secretary of defense **Robert S. McNamara** about the casualty rate in such an attack. McNamara's estimates, heavy both in men and material, helped bolster the president's plan merely to blockade the island. Immediately following the meeting, Dirksen and other Republican congressional leaders drafted a statement endorsing Kennedy's action. A few days later, the president told Dirksen that he fully expected him to win reelection, a prediction that the Republican leader subsequently leaked to the press and that hampered the final stage of his Democratic opponent's campaign. Dirksen won reelection with 52.9 percent of the vote.

He greatly assisted the administration's negotiation of the **Limited Nuclear Test Ban Treaty** with the **Soviet Union** in July 1963. Dirksen initially opposed the agreement, but the White House actively sought his assistance when it became apparent that some powerful Southern Democratic senators were seeking to block Senate ratification of the treaty. The Republican leader endorsed the treaty upon receiving the president's "unqualified and unequivocal assurances" that Kennedy would continue to support weapons development. Dirksen's position prevented Republican defections and countered the Southern Democrat's opposition, assuring passage. The Senate ratified the Moscow Treaty in September 1963 by a vote of 80 to 19, with only eight Republican votes against the pact compared to 11 nays by Democratic members.

In June 1963, Dirksen and Senate majority leader **Mike Mansfield** (D-Mont.) introduced an omnibus **civil rights** bill. Their proposal included the right of a government agency to cut off federal funds to any state or institution that refused to comply with desegregation guidelines. However, Dirksen declined to support the president's request for a provision to provide a federal guarantee to blacks of the right to use all public accommodations on constitutional grounds, and excluded it from his bill. Nonetheless during the legislative maneuvering over what became the **Civil Rights Act of 1964**, Dirksen changed his position

on this issue. Seven months after Kennedy's death, with Dirksen's strong support, Congress passed the first comprehensive civil rights measure since Reconstruction. During the **Lyndon B. Johnson** years, Dirksen aided the administration in the enactment of additional civil rights legislation while opposing most of the "Great Society" program. He became one of the strongest supporters of Johnson's **Vietnam** policy and remained minority leader until his death in Washington, DC, on 7 September 1969. *See also* HUMPHREY, HUBERT HORATIO.

DOMINO THEORY. The domino theory is an idea that appears to have been born during administration of **Harry S. Truman**. In 1946, Truman used the notion to gain support for a firm stand against the **Soviet Union**'s occupation of the northern portion of **Iran**. The idea was that if one country in a region fell to the communists then all neighboring countries would also fall to them. The dominoes in danger of falling in 1946 were Turkey, Iraq, and other oil suppliers in the region. In 1947, Truman used the same idea to gain approval for the Truman Doctrine, which promised assistance to Greece and Turkey, by raising the specter of communism spreading into Western Europe.

In April 1954, **Dwight D. Eisenhower** employed the concept in relation to Indochina. The president used the image to generate congressional and public support for a policy of support of the South Vietnamese government, at that time locked in conflict with what was seen as a communist insurgency. Eisenhower argued that if the communists were allowed to achieve power in **Vietnam**, then the growing communist groups in Southeast Asia would gain the momentum and materiel support to seize power in Laos, Cambodia, Burma, Thailand, Malaysia, and Indonesia. There was little evidence to support the idea, but once articulated at the highest level, as it was, it soon became an uncontestable mantra.

President Kennedy continued to use the same theme, adding the fantasy that the Philippines, New Zealand, and Australia were possible dominoes in line. In his inaugural address, the new president endorsed Ngo Dinh Diem

and his government and declared that communism must be stopped in South Vietnam or it would gradually consume the entire world. Kennedy stated, "No other challenge is more deserving of our effort and energy. . . . Our security may be lost piece by piece, country by country." And he went on to pledge America's willingness to "pay any price, bear any burden, meet any hardship, support any friend, oppose any foe to assure the survival and success of liberty."

Subsequently, almost all presidents have employed the fear of falling dominoes to generate support for the administration's interventionist policies around the world. In recent years, the domino theory has been somewhat overtaken by the equally fanciful catch-cry, "Better to fight our enemies 'over there' so we do not have to fight them at home."

DULLES, ALLEN WELSH (1893–1969). Allen Welsh Dulles was born into a family that had a long history of public service to the United States in foreign affairs. Three family members had been appointed secretary of state: his maternal grandfather, John W. Foster, under President Benjamin Harrison; his uncle, Robert Lansing, under Woodrow Wilson; and his older brother, John Foster Dulles, under **Dwight D. Eisenhower**. Another uncle, John Walsh, had been a minister to England, and Dulles's sister, Elinor Lansing Dulles, was later a State Department official as well. Dulles's father was a Presbyterian minister.

Born in Watertown, New York, on 7 April 1893, after attending private schools in upstate New York and Paris and receiving BA and MA degrees from Princeton University, Dulles entered the diplomatic service in 1916. He observed and reported to Washington on World War I from Switzerland (where he briefly knew Vladimir Lenin), and he was a member of the U.S. delegation to the Versailles Peace Conference. He served four years as chief of the State Department Division of Near Eastern Affairs, until 1926 when he resigned to join his brother at the Wall Street law firm of Sullivan and Cromwell, where he remained for the next 15 years. During World War II, Dulles once again found himself in Switzerland, heading the ultrasecret Office of Strategic Services.

He was subsequently a key figure in the establishment of the Central Intelligence Agency (CIA) after the war. Dulles later said that the act that set up the CIA "has given intelligence a more influential position in our government than intelligence enjoys in any other government in the world." The agency was soon given authority and capacity to conduct covert operations abroad. In 1951, Dulles joined the CIA as deputy director for plans, and he was put in charge of those operations. In February 1953, President Eisenhower appointed him director of central intelligence, making him both head of the CIA and coordinator of all U.S. intelligence activity. During the Eisenhower administration, in part as the result of the close working relationship between Dulles and his brother John Foster Dulles, who was secretary of state from 1953 to 1959, the CIA often intervened in the domestic affairs of other countries and, at times, examined the correspondence of U.S. citizens, violating U.S. laws.

On 10 November 1960, president-elect Kennedy announced that he would retain Dulles as director of central intelligence. Eight days later, Dulles and **Richard M. Bissell**, CIA deputy director, briefed Kennedy on the training of a group of Cuban exiles in Guatemala who were believed to be capable of guerrilla action and were recruited to unify opposition to the Cuban ruler, **Fidel Castro**. The project had been ordered by Eisenhower in March 1960, and the initial plan was to land the force in **Cuba**. On 29 November, after a second, more detailed briefing, Kennedy ordered the planning to proceed. The invasion failed, and controversy surrounds almost every aspect of these and subsequent events.

During the early months of the Kennedy administration, Dulles was also involved in efforts to bolster the deteriorating position of U.S.-supported forces in Laos, where the CIA had long been involved. After the **Bay of Pigs** fiasco, Kennedy felt let down by Dulles and the CIA. On 31 July 1961, administration spokesman **Pierre Salinger** confirmed that Dulles would soon retire. On 27 September,

Kennedy accepted his resignation. (Bissell and CIA deputy director General Charles P. Cabell also left the CIA in the following months.) Dulles returned to his former law firm.

President **Lyndon B. Johnson** appointed Dulles to the **Warren Commission** charged with investigating the **assassination of John F. Kennedy**. In June 1964, following the disappearance of three **civil rights** workers in Philadelphia, Mississippi, Dulles went to Mississippi as Johnson's special emissary to evaluate "law observance problems." Dulles died in Washington, DC, on 30 January 1969. *See also* DAY, J. EDWARD; KENNEDY, ROBERT FRANCIS.

DYLAN, BOB (1941–). Bob Dylan was born Robert Allen Zimmerman on 24 May 1941. He grew up in a middle-class family in Hibbing, Minnesota, a declining mining center. In high school, he led a rock and roll band, and during a short stay at the University of Minnesota, he began publicly performing folk music. In winter 1960–1961, Dylan went to New York City, partially to fulfill his desire to meet the then seriously ill folksinger Woody Guthrie. In New York, Dylan joined a growing circle of folk musicians performing in small Greenwich Village clubs.

Well, my telephone rang it would not stop
It's President Kennedy callin' me up
He said, "My friend, Bob, what do we need to make
  the country grow?
I said, "My friend, John,
Brigitte Bardot, Anita Ekberg, Sophia Loren
Country'll grow."

These satirical lines are from the 22-year-old Bob Dylan's "I Shall Be Free," one of the songs on *The Freewheelin' Bob Dylan* album (released in May 1963). The title of the song suggests the artist did not wish to be co-opted by Kennedy. (Oddly enough, Dylan has never sung "I Shall Be Free" in concert.) Musicologist Daniel Karlin in a June 2018 lecture discussing Dylan and his connection with John F. Kennedy notes that rulers have always wanted to ingratiate themselves with popular entertainers—actors, musicians, comedians—and in this song, Dylan catches just the note of fake bonhomie and coercive familiarity in Kennedy's manner. But Karlin points out that in May 1963 no one really believed that Kennedy had the slightest interest in Dylan, or was even aware of his existence. Dylan is singing about how people like himself think of Kennedy—people who generic politicians regard merely as ballot fodder.

Karlin points out that many think of Kennedy and Dylan as, somehow, embodying the same spirit of youthful promise, the same optimism of the early 1960s—as if "Blowin' in the Wind" blew through the White House, or that Kennedy, too, was the sworn enemy of the "Masters of War." However, the two men came from very different worlds, and Dylan's understanding of what "your country" meant differed from Kennedy's. Dylan had arrived in New York on 24 January 1961, four days after the inauguration, and paid his first visit to terminally ill Woody Guthrie. To Dylan, Guthrie was a tribal elder who meant far more to him than Kennedy. From where he was standing in 1961, Dylan might not have felt himself one of the "fellow citizens," or even "fellow Americans," whom Kennedy addressed in his speeches. Kennedy arrived in Washington full-fed with power; Dylan, according to the first line of his early piece "Song to Woody," was virtually penniless: "I'm out here a thousand miles from my home."

Many of Dylan's songs dealt with social themes. Some, like "A Hard Rain's a-Gonna Fall," described a fundamental corruption Dylan saw pervading U.S. society. Others chronicled specific cases of injustice, particularly violence and discrimination against blacks. Dylan was encouraged by the **civil rights** and antiwar movements and that, in the cultural awakening of the early 1960s, a new spirit was beginning to emerge. When the singing group Peter, Paul and Mary recorded his song "Blowin' in the Wind," it became a best-selling record, introducing Dylan's writing to millions of listeners and turning the song itself into something of an anthem for supporters of the civil rights movement.

By May 1963, Dylan was singing about race and the civil rights movement. In July 1963, he performed a new song, "Only a Pawn

in Their Game," about the murder of the **National Association for the Advancement of Colored People** activist **Medgar W. Evers**, at a voter registration drive in Greenwood, Mississippi. Later that month he performed a set at the Newport Folk Festival, which amounted to a declaration of allegiance to the liberal Left: "With God on Our Side," "Talkin' John Birch Paranoid Blues," and "A Hard Rain's a-Gonna Fall"—followed by renditions of "Blowin' in the Wind," and "We Shall Overcome" alongside **Joan Baez**; Theo Bikel; Peter, Paul and Mary; Pete Seeger; and the Freedom Singers.

Summer and autumn 1963 saw the rising tide of Dylan's conscious political engagement. The high-water mark was his performance of "When the Ship Comes In" and "Only a Pawn in Their Game" on 28 August at the March on Washington, on the steps of the Lincoln Memorial. The composition of "The Times They Are a-Changin'" dates from this period; recorded for the album of that name on 24 October, it immediately became the focal point of the concerts Dylan was playing, starting two days later at Carnegie Hall. Less than a month later, on 22 November, Kennedy was assassinated in Dallas.

Dylan had become a major influence on millions of young Americans by 1964, especially after the release of his popular album *The Times They Are a-Changin'*. For his largely white, middle-class audience, Dylan articulated a growing, if inchoate dissatisfaction with the existing society, chronicling the plight and struggles of the poor, the abused, and the victims of discrimination. His songs often had a lyricism and grace that transcended the norm of much popular music. By writing about such a wide range of subjects, Dylan helped expand the range and depth of popular music in general. By late 1964, Dylan was turning away from explicitly political themes and, as a result, was strongly criticized by many political activists.

He won a Grammy Award in 1975 for best artist, following the release of the popular album *Blood on the Tracks*. Overall, he would record 43 albums, with more than 57 million copies sold, on his way to becoming one of America's most influential musicians. According to *Rolling Stone* magazine, Dylan "not only revolutionized popular music by incorporating poetry into his compositions, he also helped create a more inclusive and progressive social consciousness in American culture." *See also* MUSIC AND JOHN F. KENNEDY.

E

ECONOMIC MANAGEMENT. John F. Kennedy inherited a weak economy with high unemployment as he entered the White House in 1961. During his 1960 presidential campaign, Kennedy promised, if elected, "to get America moving again" with economic growth of 4–6 percent annually and unemployment at 4 percent. He asked Americans to be prepared to meet the challenges of a "**New Frontier.**" To accomplish his goals, President Kennedy called upon the federal government to play a major role in the economy as employer, regulator, and welfare provider.

Kennedy's initial move was to send Congress an ambitious and broad-ranging 12-step program for economic growth and recovery: (1) monetary policy and debt management; (2) housing and community development; (3) temporary unemployment insurance extension; (4) expansion of the United States Employment Service; (5) aid to dependent children of the unemployed; (6) distressed area redevelopment program; (7) distribution of surplus food; (8) improvements in the old-age, survivors, and disability insurance program; (9) early payment of veterans life insurance dividends; (10) minimum-wage increase and expanded coverage; (11) accelerating procurement and construction; and (12) government procurement in labor surplus areas. Few of these proposals were immediately enacted, but many were reconstituted by his successor in **Lyndon B. Johnson**'s "Great Society" programs.

In 1962, Kennedy proposed a reduction in taxes. He argued that taxes were too high but tax revenue too low. The solution, he asserted, was to achieve a more prosperous, expanding economy that could bring a budget surplus. And the way to achieve that outcome was to reduce taxes, which would create rising consumer demand that, in turn, would encourage industrial production and increase employment. Meanwhile, a book published in 1962 by **Michael Harrington** titled *The Other America* revealed shocking details of poverty and want in the United States. The book chronicled the plight of "the unskilled workers, the migrant farm workers, the aged, the minorities, and all of the others who live in the economic underworld of American life." Real, desperate poverty represented a disturbing challenge to Americans' sense of their nation—a sentiment that would later support Johnson's "War on Poverty."

Nevertheless, by 1963 the Kennedy administration had succeeded in stabilizing inflation, providing record high corporate profits, and turning around the stock market; unfortunately, unemployment remained high at 6.7 percent. When Kennedy was assassinated in late November, Lyndon B. Johnson inherited a strong, steady economy for the first two years with only a 2 percent inflation rate and annually some $4–6 billion in extra revenue. Eager to spread the benefits of America's successful economy, Johnson dramatically increased federal spending on his "Great Society" program and on the expanded **Vietnam War**, which improved the economy in the near term. However, by the end of the decade failure to raise taxes to pay for these activities led to accelerating

inflation, which eroded the prosperity. *See also* DILLON, CLARENCE DOUGLAS; EQUAL PAY ACT OF 1963; GOLDBERG, ARTHUR JOSEPH; SORENSEN, THEODORE CHAIKIN.

EDUCATION. Education was important to John F. Kennedy. He spoke publicly about it frequently. **Ted Sorensen**, the president's speechwriter, quotes Kennedy as saying: "Our progress as a nation can be no swifter than our progress in education. The human mind is our fundamental resource." Perhaps the strongest statement on the importance he placed on education was made at Vanderbilt University in May 1963: "Liberty without learning is always in peril; and learning without liberty is always in vain. Any educated citizen who seeks to subvert the law, to suppress freedom, or to subject other human beings to acts that are less than human, degrades his heritage, ignores his learning and betrays his obligations."

Education was important to Kennedy because he saw it as means to advance the nation in the **Cold War**, in the space race, and in achieving America's economic and technological superiority. He initiated several legislative measures to improve education in several areas: graduation rates, science, and teacher training. Soviet successes in space—the October 1957 launch of Sputnik 1, the first earth satellite in space, and the launch of Yuri Gagarin into space in April 1961—had focused the attention of U.S. leaders on the need for more and better science teachers and science education in schools and universities. Kennedy responded in a speech on 25 May 1961, before a joint session of Congress, in which he proposed space exploration to put astronauts on the moon, as well as other projects including nuclear rockets and weather satellites. He was, however, unable to gain passage of a massive federal aid to education bill, limited, as he emphasized, to public schools as required by recent **Supreme Court** rulings against federal aid to parochial schools.

On 6 February 1962, he sent another message to Congress setting out the argument that education was the right—and the necessity and the responsibility—of all Americans. He also lamented that far too many students dropped out from high school. "Too many—an estimated one million a year—leave school before completing high school—the bare minimum for a fair start in modern-day life." At Rice University on 12 September 1962, Kennedy repeated his goal to land a man on the moon by the end of the decade, a goal that would be directed to educational institutions: "The growth of our science and education will be enriched by new knowledge of our universe and environment, by new techniques of learning and mapping and observation, by new tools and computers for industry, medicine, the home as well as the school." On 22 October 1963, before the National Academy of Sciences, which was celebrating its 100th anniversary, he emphasized the overall importance of science to the country: "The question in all our minds today is how science can best continue its service to the Nation, to the people, to the world, in the years to come."

According to Sorensen an estimated one-third of all principal Kennedy programs made some form of education a central element. With regard to **civil rights**, he sought to hasten high school desegregation. Kennedy included provisions for teacher training in his "**New Frontier**" programs. Under the policies of the New Frontier, legislation was passed to expand scholarships and student loans with increases in funds for libraries and school lunches. There were also funds directed to teach the deaf, children with disabilities, and children who were gifted. In addition, literacy training was authorized under Manpower Development as well as an allocation of presidential funds to stop dropouts and, in 1963, a Vocational Education Act. This act was enacted to offer new and expanded vocational education programs to bring job training into harmony with the industrial, economic, and social realities being brought about by automation, urbanization, and rapidly increasing population pressures. It made training available to unemployed and employed workers of all ages at all levels for all fields in both rural and urban areas.

EGYPT. Egypt, with a population of around 30 million in the mid-1960s, has been a

presidential republic since 1956. The monarchy was abolished in 1953 following a military coup the previous year, and in 1954, Gamal Abdel Nasser assumed the presidency. The new regime embarked upon a policy of massive nationalization termed "Arab Socialism," and relations with the United States became strained during the **Dwight D. Eisenhower** years, leading Nasser to seek stronger ties with the **Soviet Union** and alliances with other Arab states—especially **Syria**, with whom it formed the short-lived United Arab Republic (1958–1961)—although Egypt continued to be known officially as the "United Arab Republic" until 1971. The Kennedy administration sought to improve relations with Nasser, without great success. *See also* MIDDLE EAST.

EISENHOWER, DWIGHT DAVID (1890–1969). Dwight D. Eisenhower was born on 14 October 1890, the third of seven sons, in Denison, Texas, to a farming family of Swiss descent. He grew up in Abilene, Kansas, where he earned the nickname "Ike" and worked in a variety of jobs to help his brothers through college.

Eisenhower served two terms as president during 1953–1961. Prior to his election, as general of the army, Eisenhower commanded the western Allied forces in the invasion of Europe and defeat of Germany in World War II, and he was the first supreme commander of North Atlantic Treaty Organization (NATO) forces (1950–1952).

In 1915, Eisenhower graduated from West Point. He served in World War I, and during the interwar years under the tutelage of his mentor, General Douglas MacArthur, he successfully navigated his way through the ranks until he was given command of Allied forces on the western front in World War II. Between 1942 and 1944, he oversaw the Allied invasions of North Africa, Sicily, Italy, and Normandy. In November 1945, President **Harry S. Truman** named Eisenhower as U.S. Army chief of staff. In the seven years following the end of World War II, he moved from leadership positions in the army to the worlds of **education** and politics.

Eisenhower resigned as chief of staff in February 1948 to become president of Columbia University. In 1951, he assumed command of forces newly organized under NATO. In 1952, Eisenhower ran for the Republican presidential nomination and, in a closely fought contest, defeated conservative senator Robert A. Taft (R-Ohio). The most popular war hero since Ulysses S. Grant, with a wide grin and a pleasing personality, Eisenhower easily defeated his Democratic opponent, **Adlai E. Stevenson II**, both in 1952 and again in 1956. Eisenhower's eight years in office proved less notable for accomplishment than for the deliberate avoidance of foreign and domestic conflict.

Kennedy was elected to the Senate in the same election that brought Eisenhower to the White House. Kennedy supported the Eisenhower administration's decision in 1953 to end United States–**United Nations** (UN) intervention in the Korean War and its efforts in 1954 to reach agreement with the **Soviet Union** to limit nuclear weapons, as well as Eisenhower's "Atoms for Peace" program. He was also a strong supporter of efforts to create mutual security alliances similar to NATO and the policy of "massive nuclear retaliation" to limit Soviet expansion.

While Eisenhower supported the Republican candidate for president, **Richard M. Nixon**, in the 1960 election campaign, he did not use his considerable prestige and popularity to actively campaign for Nixon. Nor did Kennedy directly attack Eisenhower, his leadership, or even his policies during the campaign. The result was that Kennedy narrowly defeated Nixon.

However, there were significant differences between the foreign policy views of Eisenhower and Kennedy. In his farewell address in January 1961, Eisenhower expressed his concern about the burgeoning growth of the "military-industrial complex" in America, which he believed led to huge expenditure on the manufacture of weapons of war at the expense of nonmilitary infrastructure. He opposed the Kennedy administration's increases in defense spending, and in June 1962, he urged a reduction of the defense budget. In November

1963, he also suggested that the United States withdraw five of its six divisions stationed in Europe.

The biggest split between Eisenhower and Kennedy occurred over the failed April 1961 **Bay of Pigs** invasion of **Cuba**. Kennedy publicly took full responsibility for the operation, but many Democrats attributed the planning of the invasion to Eisenhower. In June 1961, the former president admitted that he had ordered the training and equipping of Cuban refugees in March 1960, but he insisted in September 1961 that "there was absolutely no planning for an invasion" of Cuba during his tenure in office. The Kennedy administration immediately challenged his assertion. Evidence revealed later largely discredited Eisenhower's claims of noninvolvement.

Determined to defend his administration from criticisms by the Kennedy administration of his domestic policies, in May 1962 Eisenhower attacked Kennedy's call for a cabinet-level urban affairs department. Eisenhower saw the move as an effort by Kennedy to augment his personal authority and described the Kennedy administration as a "clique" of "callow youths." Despite these partisan attacks, Eisenhower endorsed Kennedy's trade bill and UN loan proposal in 1962 and the **Limited Nuclear Test Ban Treaty** in 1963.

Although he remained liked and respected in his last years, Eisenhower exercised little control over national events, including those within his own party. He published the first volume of his presidential memoirs, *Mandate for Change*, in March 1963. The second volume appeared in 1965. His health deteriorated steadily after 1964, and he died on 28 March 1969, in Washington, DC. *See also* APPEASEMENT; ARMS CONTROL; JOHN F. KENNEDY CENTER FOR THE PERFORMING ARTS; KHRUSHCHEV, NIKITA SERGEYEVICH.

EQUAL PAY ACT OF 1963. On 10 June 1963, President Kennedy signed the Equal Pay Act into law. The act, part of Kennedy's **New Frontier** program, amended the Fair Labor Standards Act passed in 1938 and aimed at abolishing wage disparity based on gender. It was a first step toward workplace equality.

During the signing, the president stated the act "affirms our determination that when women enter the labor force they will find equality in their pay envelopes."

The act had been drafted by **Esther Peterson**, head of the **Women's Bureau** of the Department of Labor. It prohibited employers who were subject to the Fair Labor Standards Act from paying employees differently, based on gender, for work that required "equal skill, effort, and responsibility." At that time, the average woman worker earned only 60 percent of the average wage for men. Throughout America's history, women had been paid less than men even when employed in identical jobs. Perhaps the most dramatic illustration of this discrimination was "Rosie the Riveter," illustrating the disparity in wages during World War II—women widely heralded, patriotic, but underpaid. Despite the National War Labor Board plea of equal pay for equal work, employers failed to answer the voluntary request; moreover, when the war ended most of the women were forced out of their jobs to make room for returning veterans. In the early 1960s, newspapers listed jobs for men and women separately, with the higher-level and higher-paid jobs almost exclusively under "Help Wanted—Male." Even when the same jobs were placed under both male and female listings, the pay scales were lower for women. The new equal pay law, however, applied only to women working minimum-wage jobs. Exceptions were allowed if related to seniority or merit systems, based on quantity or quality of work or any other variable, as long as it was not based on gender. As Kennedy acknowledged, there was still much work to be done.

ESTES, BILLIE SOL (1925–2013). Billie Sol Estes was born on 10 January 1925, near Clyde, Texas, the son of an impoverished farmer and lay preacher. He grew up in a spartan and fundamentalist household in West Texas. In 1951, Estes moved to Pecos, Texas, where a cotton boom was under way, and, utilizing federal price guarantees, within two years he had become a prosperous cotton farmer with interests in a several other enterprises.

Over the next decade, Estes accumulated considerable wealth by price-cutting and exploiting federal assistance programs in various fraudulent and illegal manipulations. He also built up large debts. While building his fortune, Estes also became involved in **Democratic Party** affairs, contributing to the campaigns of Senator **Ralph Yarborough** and Representative J. T. Rutherford, both of Texas. From December 1960 to January 1962, he donated $12,300 to the national party; traveled to Washington, DC, frequently; and made the acquaintance of many leading government officials. In July 1961, Estes was appointed to the Agriculture Department's National Cotton Advisory Committee. In February 1962, news of the many illegal activities of Estes became public, and on 29 March, he was arrested by the Federal Bureau of Investigation. Soon the entire range of Estes's business affairs was exposed, including his fraudulent dealings with the Agriculture Department. These revelations, combined with Estes's links to the Democratic Party at the national level, produced the first important scandal of the John F. Kennedy administration.

In May 1962, the Agriculture Department fined Estes more than $500,000, and in November, a Texas court convicted him of fraud, theft, and conspiracy. He was sentenced to eight years in prison. In March 1963, a federal jury found Estes guilty of mail fraud and conspiracy, for which he received a 15-year sentence. All charges in both trials stemmed from Estes's activities involving the fraudulent rental of nonexistent fertilizer tanks. In July 1971, Estes was released from prison after having served almost 6.5 years of his federal term. By the spring of 1975, he was employed by the Permian Petroleum Company in Abilene, Texas. In 1997, he was indicted for tax evasion.

In 2003, Estes published a book, *JFK, the Last Standing Man*, claiming that **Lyndon B. Johnson** was involved in the **assassination of John F. Kennedy**. Estes died at his home in DeCordova, Texas, on 14 May 2013 at the age of 88.

EUROPE AND THE UNITED KINGDOM. U.S. relations with Europe were always going to be a priority for Kennedy. John F. Kennedy came to the presidency a mere 15 years after the end of the world's most catastrophic war—a war that he had fought in; a war that had resulted in the deaths of more than 20 million people; a war that had witnessed the use of the atomic bomb, the most destructive weapon of war yet devised; and a war that had left Europe devastated and divided and whose future was subject in large part to the ongoing differing, seemingly incompatible, visions of the United States and the **Soviet Union**. Kennedy saw close ties with an economically strong, united, and prosperous Western Europe as essential for the security of the United States and for stability, if not peace, in other regions of the world. This strategic framework—combined with a binary view of the world locked in a struggle between good and evil, a compulsion to win in any contest, and an unshakable belief in the efficacy of force—led Kennedy to view the Soviet Union as an implacable foe that had to be met with the threat, if not the actual use, of military force. At the same time, Kennedy knew he had to avoid an all-out nuclear war with the Soviet Union, and he did search for alternative peaceful outcomes.

The **Cold War** was at its height. In January 1961, Soviet premier **Nikita Khrushchev** announced that the Soviet Union would support wars of national liberation. Kennedy interpreted this statement as a direct threat to the "free world." In the course of exploratory letters between Khrushchev and Kennedy following the latter's election victory, on 22 February 1961, the president suggested a summit meeting for an informal exchange of views. The two met in Vienna, Austria, in early June. In the meantime, Kennedy experienced the embarrassment of the failed **Bay of Pigs (Cuba)** invasion, which took place in April. Berlin (as well as the future of Laos) dominated the Vienna summit discussion. The issue regarding Berlin was whether the United States would/should accept the Soviet Union signing a separate peace treaty with East Germany, which would mean that the United States would require the permission of the East German government for access to West Berlin. The Soviets feared a resurgent united

Germany, while the United States refused to give up access to West Berlin. The two agreed to postpone any action until December 1961 to consider an interim agreement.

Kennedy responded to Khrushchev's challenge over Berlin with a determination to strengthen Atlantic unity as the foundation of a stronger, more effective, Western alliance. Through what he called his "Grand Design for Europe," the president hoped to integrate U.S. economic, political, and military policies toward Western Europe. The scheme included the **Trade Expansion Act** to reduce tariffs and create an Atlantic-wide free trade area and greater conformity in the West's economic and political institutions to enable them to meet the requirements imposed by a dangerous world.

U.S. relations with Europe faced a number of interrelated challenges. Among the more contentious issues was the nature, location, and control of U.S. military forces, especially nuclear weapons, in Europe and interstate rivalry within Western Europe itself. The key question for both the United States and Europe was this: What was the extent of America's commitment to defend Europe?

From the outset, Europeans favored their own independent nuclear deterrents, an approach the Kennedy administration opposed. In 1958, France's leader, Charles de Gaulle, challenged the wisdom of binding the defenses of the North Atlantic Treaty Organization (NATO) to the nuclear power of the United States. The situation was further complicated by the U.S. refusal to share nuclear materials and information with its European allies. On 5 September 1960, de Gaulle issued an edict forbidding nuclear weapons on French soil unless France shared in their control. Thereupon, the United States shifted its atomic bomb–carrying aircraft from French to British and German bases.

De Gaulle urged Europe's continental powers to take responsibility for their own defense and, under French leadership, come into their own as a third force in world politics. The U.S. government responded by suggesting an arrangement whereby the European nuclear force, closely linked with that of the United States, would encompass a future French deterrent as well. That objective, however, required a more effective political and economic union in Europe, one that included Britain. To that end, the Kennedy administration placed the full force of its influence and prestige behind Britain's bid for membership in the European Common Market. Earlier Britain had refused to join either the Coal and Steel Community or the European Economic Community (EEC). Traditionally, Britain had avoided ties to the continent, but in 1961, British leaders questioned their country's isolation from Europe. In April of that year, Prime Minister Harold Macmillan informed U.S. officials of Britain's desire to enter the EEC and elicited Washington's support. The British quest for EEC membership faced strong opposition among British conservatives and socialists, who feared that the EEC's agricultural policies would eliminate Britain's Commonwealth preferences. Macmillan's effort to accommodate Britain's imperial economic interests, especially those of the Commonwealth, cast doubts on British fitness for membership in the EEC or Washington's capacity to help.

In Ann Arbor, Michigan, on 6 June 1962, U.S. defense secretary **Robert S. McNamara** declared that "limited nuclear capabilities, operating independently, are dangerous, expensive, prone to obsolescence, and lacking in credibility as a deterrent." He asked that NATO partners leave full responsibility for nuclear warfare to the United States.

In Philadelphia, on 4 July 1962 (U.S. Independence Day), Kennedy declared that the United States contemplated the European movement toward union, as embodied especially in the Common Market, with hope and admiration. "We do not," he said, "regard a strong and united Europe as a rival, but a partner." The president refused to define what kind of partnership he had in mind, but Kennedy's design for Europe required, above all, a flexible Western defense. He stressed the need for a "wider choice than humiliation or all-out nuclear action." He advocated strengthening allied conventional forces strongly enough to permit a "pause" in any future fighting sufficient to enable the combatants

to negotiate a cease-fire or give the aggressor time to contemplate the consequences of further military escalation. The United States was already maintaining 300,000 military personnel in the European theater. The European nations, however, which were then enjoying unprecedented economic growth and prosperity, refused to contribute their share to the existing conventional forces in Europe.

The problem was that Kennedy's new emphasis on the need for a flexible response seemed to endanger the credibility of the nuclear deterrent and undermine further Europe's confidence in the American commitment to its defense. The Kremlin fully realized that any Western decision to resist even a minor Soviet assault could quickly degenerate into a nuclear war. Furthermore there was no clarity on the question of nuclear control; some Europeans feared that the United States, in an effort to avoid the extremity of a nuclear exchange, might refuse to act until much of Europe again lay in ruins.

By 1962, the cost of keeping U.S. troops in Europe had already undermined the nation's balance-of-payments structure, while Western Europe's gold and dollar reserves exceeded the combined holdings of the United States and Great Britain. Some Europeans acknowledged that Western Europe had become the special beneficiary of U.S. insecurities. As Italian leader Altiero Spinelli observed in July 1962, "Western Europe, thanks to American protection, has become a paradise of political, military and social irresponsibility."

Late in 1962, the Kennedy administration discovered a possible answer to the dilemma of nuclear control in a mixed-manned multilateral defense force. Great Britain pushed the Americans into this proposal when, in November, the administration responded to improvements in the Polaris submarine missile by canceling the Skybolt project. Britain had joined the United States in developing this air-to-ground missile; launched from bombers, it could reach targets 1,000 miles away. Britain regarded the Skybolt project as an American guarantee of its nuclear future. Britain's defense minister accused the Kennedy administration of attempting to deprive his country

of a national nuclear deterrent. London's bitter reaction compelled Washington to find a substitute quickly.

On 21 December 1962, Kennedy and Macmillan conferred in Nassau. There the president agreed to provide Britain with Polaris missiles. To resolve the question of control, the two leaders accepted the principle of a Multilateral Defense Force (MLF) of nuclear-armed naval vessels, initially submarines but later surface ships, manned by mixed NATO crews. The proposal contained no arrangement for an integrated strategy; nor did it diminish U.S. control of its nuclear weapons.

De Gaulle, in a dramatic press conference on 14 January 1963, challenged every facet of the American Grand Design. In rejecting the British application for Common Market membership, the French leader charged that Britain was not sufficiently European minded to break its ties with the United States and the Commonwealth. He was, he said, simply advancing the emancipation of Europe. British membership in the Common Market would lead to the formation of "a colossal Atlantic Community under American dependence and leadership." France could accomplish little without sacrifice, he informed a French audience in April, "but we do not wish to be protégés or satellites; we are allies among allies, defenders among the defenders." De Gaulle rejected the principle of the MLF with equal determination. "France has taken note of the Anglo-American Nassau agreement," he declared. "As it was conceived, undoubtedly no one will be surprised that we cannot subscribe to it." De Gaulle dismissed completely the question of the integration of nuclear forces. France, he said, would provide its own nuclear deterrent. The French leader admitted that U.S. defense strategy covered all European targets; what he questioned, he noted, was the American willingness to engage in a nuclear exchange over issues that Washington might regard as secondary. In an apparent effort to protect Europe even further from U.S. influence, de Gaulle, one week after his January press conference, announced the signing of a Franco-German treaty whereby the two governments agreed to "consult before any decision on all important

questions of foreign policy . . . with a view to reaching as far as possible parallel positions." American officials, wondering about the treaty's implications, soon discovered that many German leaders were embarrassed by Chancellor Adenauer's decision to sign the document in Paris. Actually, in Adenauer's absence members of the German Foreign Office had prepared a preamble that upheld all the Federal Republic's obligations under previous multilateral treaties.

The West German government sent its top Foreign Office spokesmen to Washington to assure U.S. officials of West Germany's reliability as a member of NATO. The preamble, in effect, repudiated de Gaulle's objectives. Recognizing his failure to enlist Germany in his anti-Anglo-Saxon crusade, de Gaulle proceeded to ignore the new German treaty and conduct French diplomacy without reference to Bonn. Still, de Gaulle had placed the movement for trans-Atlantic partnership in temporary eclipse. In Washington, de Gaulle's news conference evoked expressions of muffled rage. Kennedy answered the French leader in a press conference on 8 February, noting regretfully that France had denied Britain membership in the Common Market. He challenged de Gaulle's assertion that the United States did not deal with Europe as an equal partner. The president reminded the press that the United States had supported every move toward European unity so that Europe could speak with a stronger voice, accept greater burdens and responsibilities, and take advantage of great opportunities. To promote the MLF, Kennedy dispatched Ambassador Livingston T. Merchant to open negotiations with the NATO governments on the question of membership in the new defense force.

Only West Germany indicated a willingness to join and defray its share of the cost. Critics noted that the multinational force satisfied no outstanding strategic requirement and offered Europe no significant responsibility for **nuclear deterrence**. To many international observers, the new defense project was simply an effort to involve West Germany in a system of nuclear defense without upsetting the delicate Cold War balance in Europe. If the MLF placed a

German in control of nuclear power, it endangered the peace of Europe—as the Kremlin made clear. Conversely, if the MLF perpetuated U.S. control of allied nuclear defenses, it served no purpose whatever. Not without justification, **George Ball** termed the MLF an "absurd contrivance." To demonstrate his desire to bridge the Atlantic gap with new forms of allied cooperation, Kennedy, in late June 1963, visited West Germany, Ireland, England, and Italy. The trip quickly assumed the form of a ceremonial spectacle. In West Germany, the president stressed the concept of partnership. At historic Paulskirche in Frankfurt, he designated the United States and West Germany as "partners for peace." In a clear thrust at de Gaulle, he added: "Those who would separate Europe from America or split one ally from another—could only give aid and comfort to the men who make themselves our adversaries and welcome any Western disarray. The United States cannot withdraw from Europe, unless and until Europe should wish us gone. We cannot distinguish its defenses from our own. We cannot diminish our contributions to Western security or abdicate the responsibility of power." At Bonn, the president offered the same assurance: "Your safety is our safety, your liberty is our liberty, and an attack on your soil is an attack on our own." Kennedy effectively challenged de Gaulle's persistent warnings of America's unreliability; he had no measurable effect on French policy. De Gaulle's reading of French economic interests still determined the course of Common Market decisions. When the United States, during autumn 1963, pressed the allies for greater defense contributions, de Gaulle replied that the American concept of a "pause" would not prevent nuclear war as effectively as reliance on instant nuclear retaliation. Nothing in the entire spectrum of Soviet behavior could disprove his contention. *See also* BUNDY, McGEORGE.

EVERS, MEDGAR WILEY (1925–1963). Medgar Wiley Evers was born on 2 July 1925, in Decatur, Mississippi. After graduating from Alcorn A & M College in 1952, Evers took a job with a black-owned insurance company in Mound Bayou, Mississippi, and joined the

National Association for the Advancement of Colored People (NAACP).

At an NAACP meeting late in 1953, Evers volunteered to try to desegregate the University of Mississippi. He applied to the university's law school in January 1954, but his application was rejected. Evers and the NAACP decided not to take his case to court. Evers became the association's first state field secretary in Mississippi in December 1954, and he opened an office in Jackson, the state capital, in January 1955. Over the next nine years, Evers worked to increase NAACP membership and to encourage **African Americans** in Mississippi to register to vote. He traveled throughout the state explaining the **Supreme Court**'s 1954 school desegregation decision to black parents.

Once described as "the heartbeat of any integration activity in the state of Mississippi," Evers kept in touch with the increased tempo of **civil rights** work in the state during the John F. Kennedy years. After 1960, the **Student Nonviolent Coordinating Committee** and the **Congress of Racial Equality** began voter registration drives in Mississippi. The Justice Department filed several voting discrimination suits, and black students from colleges and high schools staged occasional sit-ins and protests. In fall 1960, Evers assisted **James H. Meredith** in his efforts to enter the University of Mississippi at Oxford, still an all-white institution, and supported him until his graduation in 1963.

In August 1962, Evers and his wife signed a petition to the Jackson school board asking for desegregation of the city's schools. When the board took no action, they joined in a federal court suit to integrate the schools—the first such case to be filed by individuals in Mississippi. In May 1963, Evers led a major NAACP antisegregation drive in Jackson, demanding fair employment opportunities for blacks in city jobs, the desegregation of all public facilities and accommodations in Jackson, an end to discriminatory business practices, and the appointment of a biracial committee to achieve these goals. Jackson mayor Allen Thompson rejected all the demands, and on 17 May, Evers called for a consumer boycott, which quickly spread from a few local products and

one department store to all the stores in Jackson's main shopping area. The mayor finally met with an NAACP committee on 28 May, but when black leaders reported afterward that he had agreed to several of their key demands, the mayor denied their statements. Black college students in Jackson began sitting in at local lunch counters that day, and on 30 May, a student march was attacked by the police and 600 participants arrested.

On 1 June, Evers himself was arrested for picketing. Released from jail soon after, Evers led a daily campaign of mass meetings, marches, picketing, and prayer vigils. On the evening of 11 June, with the Jackson protests still in high gear, Evers listened to President Kennedy's nationwide address in which he announced that he was submitting the Civil Rights Bill to Congress. Evers spoke at a mass rally in Jackson and then drove home. Around 12:20 a.m., as he walked from his car to the door of his house, Evers was shot in the back by a sniper. He died within an hour.

Evers had received little publicity for his work while alive, but his death made him a celebrated martyr of the civil rights movement. Funeral services were held in Jackson on 15 June, and some 3,000 blacks marched that day behind a hearse bearing Evers's body. On 19 June, Evers was buried in Arlington National Cemetery. The Jackson demonstrations he had led were suspended on 17 June while another local black leader met with President Kennedy in Washington. After a call from the president and Attorney General **Robert Kennedy**, Mayor Thompson met with a committee of black leaders on 18 June. Later he announced that the city would hire six blacks as policemen and eight blacks as school crossing guards and would promote another eight blacks in the sanitation department. On 23 June, the Federal Bureau of Investigation arrested Byron De La Beckwith, a fertilizer salesman from Greenwood, Mississippi, and a member of the segregationist White Citizens Council. He was indicted by a county grand jury in July in connection with Evers's murder and was tried twice early in 1964. Both trials ended in hung juries. *See also* WILKINS, ROY

OTTOWAY.

F

FARMER, JAMES LEONARD, JR. (1920–1999). James Leonard Farmer Jr. was born on 12 January 1920, in Marshall, Texas. A gifted child, he attended Wiley College, a school for blacks in Marshall where his father was a professor; he graduated in 1938. Three years later he received a BD degree at Howard University, where he became well versed in pacifist thought.

Farmer joined the Fellowship of Reconciliation, a Christian pacifist organization, and became its race relations secretary until 1945. During this time, he helped found the Committee of Radical Equality, later renamed the **Congress of Racial Equality** (CORE), first as a local Chicago group in spring 1942 and then as a national organization in June 1943. CORE was an interracial association that applied Gandhian techniques of nonviolent direct action to racial segregation and discrimination in the United States, pioneering the use of sit-ins and other forms of nonviolent protest.

Farmer became national director of CORE on 1 February 1961, and on 13 March he issued a call for a **Freedom Ride** through the South to challenge segregation at interstate bus terminals. The first 13 riders, including Farmer, left Washington, DC, by bus on 4 May, with New Orleans as their destination. However, that ride ended on 14 May after one bus was burned in Anniston, Alabama, and several riders were severely beaten there and in Birmingham, Alabama. Farmer and 26 other riders attempted a second Freedom Ride later in the month from Montgomery, Alabama, to Jackson, Mississippi, in two heavily guarded buses. They were arrested in Jackson when they tried to use the white waiting room at the bus terminal and, when found guilty of breach of the peace, went to jail rather than pay their fines. Farmer spent 39 days in jail and then continued organizing more rides through the summer. As Farmer later noted, the Freedom Rides "catapulted CORE into fame," making it a major **civil rights** organization and Farmer a black leader of national stature. The rides ended after the Interstate Commerce Commission issued an order on 22 September prohibiting segregation in all interstate bus terminals.

As CORE national director, Farmer continued to travel extensively. In August 1963, Farmer went to Plaquemines, Louisiana, where local **African Americans** aided by CORE workers had begun demonstrations to achieve desegregation in the town. The protests intensified on 19 August when Farmer led a mass march of 500 blacks that was broken up by police. Farmer was arrested along with key local leaders and remained in jail until 29 August. He then led another march of 600 blacks to the county courthouse on 1 September. This protest was also broken up by police using tear gas, fire hoses, and electric cattle prods. State troopers then began a house-to-house search for the demonstration leaders, especially Farmer.

Farmer escaped Plaquemines hidden in a hearse that took him over back roads to New Orleans. Under Farmer, CORE became known as one of the most militant and creative groups in the civil rights movement, and Farmer himself developed a reputation as a tough and

audacious **civil rights** leader of great physical courage.

Farmer was a cochairman of the 1963 March on Washington, but he missed the 28 August march because he was then in the Plaquemines jail. He led sit-ins at the New York World's Fair on its opening day in April 1964 and participated in highly publicized demonstrations in Bogalusa, Louisiana, in April and July 1965.

He resigned from CORE on 1 March 1966, intending to launch a program for improving literacy and job skills among the chronically unemployed. However, he eventually abandoned this project when an expected grant from the Office of Economic Opportunity did not materialize. Farmer later worked as an organizer for several unions and as program director for the **National Association for the Advancement of Colored People**, but he remained in touch with CORE and its activities. Farmer died on 9 July 1999 in Fredericksberg, Virginia. *See also* GREGORY, DICK CLAXTON; KING, MARTIN LUTHER, JR.

FELDMAN, MYER (1914–2007). Myer Feldman was born in Philadelphia, Pennsylvania, on 22 June 1914, of recently arrived parents from Ukraine. His father, a tailor, died in 1918 during the great influenza epidemic, and Myer attended Girard College, a segregated private school for fatherless boys, in Philadelphia. He later went to the University of Pennsylvania on a scholarship where he graduated with a law degree in 1938. He joined the armed forces in 1942 serving in the U.S. Army Air Forces. Following the war, he served as counsel to the U.S. Senate Banking and Currency Committee where he met **Theodore C. Sorensen** and Senator John F. Kennedy.

Myer "Mike" Feldman was an invaluable presidential aide to Kennedy, but he was virtually unknown to the public. The *New York Post* called him "the White House's anonymous man." He played an integral role in planning Kennedy's campaign for the presidency and, upon Kennedy's death, did much the same for **Lyndon B. Johnson** in 1964. When he left the White House in January 1965, Theodore Sorensen wrote him: "You were far more

indispensable than the public knows to John Kennedy's success as a Senator, candidate and President. He knew it, however; and I know he would want me to express his deep gratitude."

Feldman joined Kennedy's staff as a legislative assistant in 1958. During the 1960 presidential campaign, Feldman was director of research for the Democratic ticket. When Kennedy was preparing to counter critics of his Roman Catholicism in a crucial campaign speech in Houston, Feldman found Irish-sounding names of Texans who had died at the Alamo for Kennedy to use in the speech. More importantly, he helped prepare Kennedy for the televised debate with **Richard M. Nixon**.

After winning the election, President Kennedy appointed Feldman to the post of deputy special counsel, and he served directly under Sorensen, who was special counsel to the president. Feldman was among a group who had breakfast with the president before news conferences. He was a behind-the-scenes liaison to Israel, a principal adviser on domestic policy, and the channel for business requests, like tariffs and air routes. "If Mike ever turned dishonest, we could all go to jail," Kennedy said, according to Mr. Sorensen.

Soon after his inauguration, President Kennedy asked Feldman to monitor progress on immigration legislation in Congress. The administration was seeking a complete overhaul of existing immigration policies and specifically targeted the national origins quota system for elimination. Many different plans were proposed, but an acceptable compromise proved extremely difficult until the Immigration and Nationality Act was signed into law by President Johnson on 3 October 1965. Although Feldman had left the White House by that time, the legislation would not have been possible without his work on the issue over the previous four years.

Feldman was responsible for briefing the president on matters pertaining to trade and tariffs. He traveled to Hakone, Japan, in November 1961 to attend the conference of the Joint U.S.-Japan Committee on Trade and Economic Affairs. When Congress passed the **Trade Expansion Act** in 1962, the White

House gained an expanded role in negotiating tariffs with foreign countries. The next period of international trade negotiations (the General Agreement on Tariffs and Trade), held from 1964 to 1967, was named the "Kennedy Round" in honor of the deceased president and his administration's efforts in this field.

Feldman served as the main White House adviser on matters related to Israel and acted as liaison to the American Jewish community. When Feldman suggested to Kennedy that he might not be the right person due to his bias in favor of Israel, Kennedy responded that his "bias" was exactly why he wanted him for the position. In that role, Feldman had access to all diplomatic cables and intelligence reports on the **Middle East**. He helped shape the administration's strategy on Israel and the Middle East.

When the president wanted to have direct policy discussions, he often sent Feldman on a secret diplomatic mission to confer with Israeli leaders David Ben-Gurion and Golda Meir face-to-face about matters including arms sales, Palestinian refugees, and whether Israel was building a nuclear weapon. He was also highly influential as President Kennedy's liaison to the Jewish community. In his own words, this role included "domestic issues of special interest to the community, our attitude toward Israel, **United Nations** actions affecting the Near East, [and] political matters."

After President Kennedy's death, President Johnson retained Feldman and promoted him to counsel in April 1964. During Johnson's presidential campaign, Feldman led the effort to compile information on opponent **Barry M. Goldwater**. Johnson dubbed Feldman his "prime minister" to Israel in recognition of his contributions to important foreign policy decisions. After leaving the White House in February 1965, Feldman returned to private law practice in Washington, DC. He made a considerable fortune buying and selling radio stations and helped finance the condominium boom in Washington in the 1970s. Feldman died in Bethesda, Maryland, on 1 March 2007, aged 92, after a long period suffering from Alzheimer's disease.

FIRST AMERICANS. During the 1960 presidential election campaign, American Indians felt an affinity with the **Democratic Party** candidate John F. Kennedy. Indian country hadn't fared so well during eight years of a Republican Eisenhower administration. In those years, 64 tribes were terminated. Kennedy, however, called for an end to termination, and he pledged to "end practices that have eroded Indian rights and resources, reduced the Indians' land base and repudiated Federal responsibility." The policy of termination severed the special relationships of tribes with the federal government, divided reservations into private ownership, and sought to assimilate Indians into full citizenship. On 28 October 1960, Kennedy wrote to Oliver La Farge, president of the Association on American Indian Affairs, stating that "[m]y administration would see to it that the Government of the United States discharges its moral obligation to our first Americans by inaugurating a comprehensive program for the improvement of their health, **education**, and economic well-being. There would be no change in treaty or contractual relationships without the consent of the tribes concerned. No steps would be taken by the Federal Government to impair the cultural heritage of any group. There would be protection of the Indian land base, credit assistance, and encouragement of tribal planning for economic development." He pledged to reverse termination policies, making a "specific promise of a positive program to improve the life of a neglected and disadvantaged group of our population," adding an assurance that he wanted an America in which "there would be no room for areas of depression, poverty, and disease."

Kennedy's platform appeared to mark a real change in policy toward Indian affairs. His outreach to the National Congress of American Indians, Association on American Indian Affairs, and the Friends Committee on National Legislation sparked hope that Indian tribes would soon see the day when they would gain the human right of self-determination. Just days after Kennedy's narrow election victory, the National Congress of American Indians, which was meeting in Denver, called its annual convention "Self-Determination, Not Termination."

Shortly after taking office in 1961, Kennedy appointed a task force to study the conditions and circumstances of American Indians and to make recommendations. This Task Force on Indian Affairs recommended an end to termination policy after it found that in previous years the Bureau of Indian Affairs had emphasized termination over self-sufficiency. But Kennedy's administration failed to act; indeed, in his first year in office Kennedy supported the construction of the Kinzua Dam on Seneca land in Pennsylvania. Kennedy sent the Seneca a letter expressing his condolences for the lost land, but supporting the dam, construction of which had begun in 1960. "It is not possible to halt the construction of the Kinzua Dam," he wrote. All alternate plans were deemed "clearly inferior to the Kinzua project from the viewpoint of cost, amount of land to be flooded and number of people who would be dislocated." The dam submerged nearly 10,000 acres of Seneca land, forced 600 residents to relocate and led to the destruction and desecration of homes and gravesites. In September 1961, he authorized limited federal funds be made available to build 150 homes on the Pine Ridge Oglala Sioux Indian Reservation.

On 15 August 1962, President Kennedy hosted on the lawns of the White House a gathering of 90 tribal leaders from the National Congress of American Indians being held that year in Chicago. They read to the president a Declaration of Indian Purpose. In his prepared remarks, Kennedy acknowledged the social ills still plaguing Indian country and recognized that their mission "reminds us all of a very strong obligation which any American, whether he was born here or came here from other parts of the world, has to every American Indian." He understood, he said, the importance of the nation's trust and treaty responsibilities by adding that he hoped the Indian national summit would "be a reminder to all Americans of the number of Indians whose housing is inadequate, whose education is inadequate, whose employment is inadequate, whose health is inadequate, whose security and old age is inadequate—a very useful reminder that there is still a good deal of unfinished business."

Kennedy did not complete this unfinished business. The following month, in September 1962, he signed the final termination bill, calling for the Ponca Tribe of Nebraska to be removed from federal oversight by 1966. More than 400 Poncas were removed from tribal rolls, and all their remaining land and holdings were dissolved.

In assessing Kennedy's relationship with American Indians, historian Thomas Clarkin, (in his 2001 book *Federal Indian Policy in the Kennedy and Johnson Administrations*), concluded that although termination was already a clearly troubled policy, "Kennedy never took that last step to end termination. He was a transitional figure. He knew it wasn't working, but he never put a mechanism in place wherein Indians were making decisions for themselves in the federal process. . . . Kennedy was interested in helping people, helping Indians, but he did not acknowledge treaties or sovereignty or the relationship between Indians and the government."

FITZGERALD, ROSE (1890–1995). *See* KENNEDY, ROSE FITZGERALD.

FORRESTAL, MICHAEL VINCENT (1927–1989). Michael Vincent Forrestal was born in New York City on 26 November 1927. He served as a presidential adviser and was a close associate of **W. Averell Harriman** during the Kennedy administration. Forrestal's major concern during his tenure at the White House was America's growing commitment in **Vietnam**.

Forrestal, the son of James V. Forrestal, the first U.S. secretary of defense, had been Harriman's assistant when the ambassador was director of the Marshall Plan from 1948 to 1950. At Harriman's request, in January 1962 Forrestal was appointed a senior staff member of President Kennedy's National Security Council under **McGeorge Bundy**.

At that time, former ambassador and elder statesman Harriman was assistant secretary of state for Far Eastern affairs. In 1962, he secured a neutralist government for Laos, established by agreements signed in Geneva, and helped negotiate the Partial Nuclear Test Ban

Treaty in 1963. Forrestal coordinated policy among Harriman, the president, and other government agencies during their negotiations. In April 1963, Harriman was appointed undersecretary of state for political affairs.

In December 1962, Forrestal was sent on a fact-finding mission to Vietnam with Roger Hilsman, head of intelligence services in the State Department. In a joint report, the two men concluded that the only people who supported President Ngo Dinh Diem and his brother, Ngo Dinh Nhu, were Americans and Vietnamese leaders with close ties to the Diem family.

Although Forrestal and Hilsman were skeptical about the optimistic assessment of the war offered by many high-ranking American officials and questioned the value of the strategic hamlet program initiated by Kennedy earlier that year, their report was essentially optimistic: "Our overall judgment, in sum, is that we are probably winning, but certainly more slowly than we had hoped. At the rate it is now going the war will last longer than we would like, cost more in terms of both lives and money than we anticipated." In expressing this view, they contributed to the escalation of U.S. involvement in Vietnam.

In May 1963, Forrestal accompanied Abram Chayes to Indonesia to negotiate a treaty on the eventual nationalization of American oil interests in that country. By August 1963, because of the increasingly harsh response to protests against the Diem regime, Forrestal was convinced that Diem should be replaced, and he cabled **Henry Cabot Lodge Jr.**, the new ambassador to Vietnam, indicating that the United States would support a coup led by Vietnamese generals. A coup was carried out the following November.

Forrestal did not exercise the same influence during the administration of Kennedy's successor, **Lyndon B. Johnson**, because the president entrusted Vietnam affairs to his own closest senior advisers. He was moved to the State Department in July 1964, where he worked on the Vietnam pacification program. He tried without success to limit the scale of the U.S. air war in Vietnam and wrote a paper outlining the measures needed to achieve a negotiated settlement of the war, but the administration never seriously considered it. In January 1965, he quietly left government to return to his law practice. He died in New York City on 11 January 1989 and is buried at Arlington National Cemetery. *See also* BALL, GEORGE WILDMAN; DILLON, CLARENCE DOUGLAS.

FREEDOM RIDE (1961). "Freedom Ride" was the name given to a program called the Journey of Reconciliation introduced by the **Congress of Racial Equality** (CORE) in May 1961. It was a strategy designed to test the resolve of the Kennedy administration to act in support of the **civil rights** movement whose members had overwhelmingly supported John F. Kennedy in the 1960 presidential election. The plan was for an interracial group of riders to board buses bound for the South, with the whites sitting in the back, the blacks in the front, and at bus stops, the whites would go into blacks only areas, and vice versa. The Freedom Riders expected—indeed planned on—meeting resistance. According to **James Farmer**, the CORE director, "We felt we could count on the racists of the South to create a crisis so that the federal government would be compelled to enforce the law. When we began the ride, I think all of us were prepared for as much violence as could be thrown at us. We were prepared for the possibility of death."

The riders departed Washington, DC, on 4 May 1961 and planned to arrive in New Orleans on 17 May—the seventh anniversary of *Brown v. Board of Education*. Meeting little trouble in the upper South, the riders split into two groups to travel through Alabama. The first group was stoned by a mob of some 200 in Anniston; they escaped, but the bus's tires were slashed. When they halted to change tires, the bus was set on fire. The second group fared no better, for as they entered Birmingham they were also met by a mob, which severely beat the riders. The wounded riders wanted to continue the journey, but the bus company was unwilling to risk more buses or the lives of its white drivers. A group of Nashville students elected to take over the Freedom Ride. Attorney General **Robert F. Kennedy** put pressure on the

bus company and on the local police to maintain order. On 17 May, the Birmingham police placed the Nashville riders in protective custody, drove them to the Tennessee border, and left them by the highway. As soon as they were able, the riders returned to Birmingham, where Robert Kennedy and other officials arranged for them to continue their journey. Departing on 20 May, the riders came under attack at the bus station in Montgomery where, as the police were absent, a mob beat them. Robert Kennedy had had enough; he sent in federal marshals to provide the riders protection. But when pressing on into Mississippi, they were met not with violence but by the local courts. The riders were arrested for trespassing, and many were sentenced to jail time. None of the Freedom Riders made it to New Orleans, but they had forced the Kennedy administration to take a position on civil rights.

FRIEDAN, BETTY (1921–2006). Betty Friedan was born on 4 February 1921 in Peoria, Illinois, into a family of Russian and Hungarian background. She graduated from Smith College in 1942 with a degree in psychology. After a postgraduate year at Berkeley, Friedan worked as a labor journalist. Friedan gained national attention in 1963 with the publication of *The Feminine Mystique*, in which she argued that, in the years after World War II, a "mystique" promoted by advertisers, educators, women's magazines, and psychologists had convinced American women that fulfillment for them lay only in a life of domesticity. The result, she asserted, was that women, living primarily, if not solely, as homemakers, abandoned any efforts at self-realization or personal achievement and submerged their own identities into those of their husbands and children. The outcome was not happiness but what Friedan called "the problem that has no name"—a sense of emptiness and malaise and a lack of personal identity.

The book became an immediate best seller, not only heralding the arrival of but significantly contributing to the contemporary wave of U.S. feminism. Friedan lectured extensively on the position of women over the next several years, and in October 1966, she cofounded the

National Organization for Women (NOW) to press for "true equality" for women. As NOW's first president, Friedan helped build an organization that emphasized **education**, legislation, and court action to win equal rights for women. During 1967 and 1968, NOW members picketed the *New York Times*, charging that its use of "Male" and "Female" headings in classified advertisements discriminated against women. NOW also brought a suit against the Equal Employment Opportunity Commission (EEOC) for permitting such column headings and pressured the EEOC to step up its enforcement of Title VII of the **Civil Rights Act of 1964**, which prohibited sex discrimination in employment. Under Friedan's direction, NOW lobbied for the repeal of antiabortion laws in New York State and for the passage of the Equal Rights Amendment in Washington. She remained an active, if at times controversial, leader in the women's liberation movement until her death. According to leading feminist Germaine Greer, Betty Friedan "changed the course of human history almost single-handedly." Friedan died of congestive heart failure at her home in Washington, DC, on 4 February 2006, her 85th birthday.

FULBRIGHT, JAMES WILLIAM (1905–1995). James William Fulbright was born on 9 April 1905 in Sumner, Missouri, but grew up in Fayetteville, Arkansas, in a socially and economically prominent family. During the Kennedy administration, he was chairman of the Senate Foreign Relations Committee (SFRC), a position he assumed in 1959 and held until he left Congress in 1974—the longest-serving chairman in the committee's history. As chair of the SFRC, he was a strong supporter of Kennedy, although he did not always agree with the president's policies.

Fulbright (known to his friends and colleagues as Bill) graduated from the University of Arkansas in 1925, studied at Oxford on a Rhodes Scholarship, and then returned to the United States in 1928 to take a law degree at George Washington University. After serving as a lawyer in the antitrust division of the Justice Department in 1934 and as an instructor at George Washington Law School in 1935,

he took a faculty position at the University of Arkansas in 1936. In 1939, he was appointed the university's president, which was a difficult post due to state government indifference.

In 1942, Fulbright was elected to Congress. He quickly indicated his interest in shaping the role of the United States in world affairs. As a member of the House Foreign Affairs Committee, he introduced the "Fulbright Resolution" calling for U.S. participation in an international organization to maintain peace, and he supported the establishment of the **United Nations**. Two years later he ran for and was elected to the Senate, and for the next two decades, he was repeatedly returned to the upper house. On most domestic issues, he was conservative, especially those involving **civil rights**.

However, the senator's main preoccupation throughout his career was foreign affairs. In 1946, Fulbright introduced legislation in the Senate establishing an international exchange program that resulted in the creation of a fellowship program that bears his name, the Fulbright Program, sponsored by the Bureau of Educational and Cultural Affairs of the Department of State. Around 294,000 "Fulbrighters"—111,000 from the United States and 183,000 from other countries—have participated in the program since its inception. Currently, the Fulbright Program operates in more than 155 countries.

When Senator John F. Kennedy was appointed to the SFRC in January 1957, he joined Fulbright, who became the committee's chairman in 1959. Although he attended very few of the committee's meetings, Kennedy admired and respected the experienced Fulbright. As a member of the congressional "Southern Democrats," Fulbright supported **Lyndon B. Johnson** at the 1960 **Democratic Party** convention. He was, nevertheless, widely mentioned as a possible choice for secretary of state following Kennedy's election. Kennedy rejected the Arkansas senator because his civil rights record would have made it difficult for him to deal with African nations. Besides, Fulbright made it clear he did not want the job.

During the Kennedy administration, Fulbright used his position as chair of the SFRC to advocate a reappraisal of the basic tenets upon which Soviet-American diplomacy had been conducted. In a series of speeches and articles and in two books, *Prospects for the West* (1963) and *Old Myths and New Realities* (1964), Fulbright urged the United States to abandon the postwar assumption that Russia and the United States were locked in uncompromising ideological combat. He believed the United States should use foreign aid to assist the economic growth vital for the development of free societies to counter the spread of communism.

During the opening months of 1961, when the administration debated whether to carry out a planned invasion of **Cuba** by U.S.-trained Cuban exiles, Fulbright opposed the action. In a 30 March meeting with the president, the senator questioned the exiles' political leadership and popular support and reminded Kennedy that, regardless of the outcome, the United States would be condemned as imperialist. The senator again presented his objections to an attack in a 4 April meeting with the president and his highest military and civilian advisers. His recommendations went unheeded, and the invasion was launched on 17 April. Two days later, **Fidel Castro** crushed it.

Fulbright took a dramatically different stand during the **Cuban missile crisis** the following year. At the 22 October 1962 meeting with congressional leaders in which the president advised them of his decision to blockade the island to force removal of the missiles, Fulbright stood alone in opposing the move. He agreed with Kennedy that decisive action was imperative to show the **Soviet Union** that the United States would not tolerate missiles so close to its territory. However, he argued that the United States should avoid direct military confrontation with Russia, and since a blockade could lead to a clash with Russian ships, he stated that an invasion of Cuba itself was a more prudent step. He maintained that the president's measure would be more likely to provoke a nuclear war than an invasion in which Americans would presumably be fighting only Cubans. Kennedy did not accept this advice; instead, on 24 October, he instituted the naval "quarantine." Fulbright later

acknowledged that Kennedy's decision had been a wise one.

Fulbright was also concerned by the events taking place in Southeast Asia—that is, in Laos and **Vietnam**. In June 1961, he delivered a major address to the Senate outlining his thoughts on the U.S. role in the nationalist struggles of developing nations. He recommended that the United States place more emphasis on long-term economic assistance rather than military aid, as it had been providing Laos and South Vietnam to that point. As long as that emphasis continued, he asserted, America's efforts were doomed to failure. This region became his major preoccupation for the remainder of his Senate career.

Fulbright became an increasingly vocal critic of America's military involvement in Vietnam. Although he helped draft and supported the 1964 Gulf of Tonkin Resolution, which gave President Johnson almost unlimited authority to send American troops to Vietnam, he soon questioned the moral right of the United States to attempt to destroy a small country for what, in his view, were slight political gains. The senator, therefore, used the Senate Foreign Relations Committee as a forum to attack the policies of the Johnson and Nixon administrations in Indochina. By the end of the decade, he had become the preeminent symbol of growing congressional discontent with the **Vietnam War**.

His defeat in the elections of 1974 was attributed to his preoccupation with foreign affairs at the expense of his constituents' interests. Bill Fulbright died in Washington, DC, after a stroke on 9 February 1995 at the age of 89.

G

GALBRAITH, JOHN KENNETH (1908–2006). John Kenneth Galbraith was born on 15 October 1908 in Iona Station, Canada, and raised in rural Ontario. Following his graduation from the University of Toronto in 1931, he studied economics at the University of California, Berkeley, where he earned a PhD in 1934. During the next five years Galbraith taught at Harvard University and then joined the economics department at Princeton University. After a year at Princeton, Galbraith took the first of several government posts as a high-ranking policy maker in the wartime mobilization effort and remained in government service until 1949, when he returned to Harvard and rapidly established himself as the nation's leading Keynesian economist. In 1947 he helped to establish a progressive policy organization Americans for Democratic Action (ADA) in support of the cause of economic and social justice.

Galbraith advocated the transfer of resources from the private sector to the public sector to eliminate poverty, equalize social and economic opportunity, and generate faster economic growth. He worked on Adlai Stevenson's campaign staff in 1952 and 1956. From 1956 to 1960, he was chairman of the Democratic Advisory Council's economic panel. In 1960, Galbraith was an early supporter of Senator John F. Kennedy's presidential nomination and worked to overcome distrust of the candidate within the **Democratic Party**'s liberal wing. Following Kennedy's victory, Galbraith served on the president's foreign economic policy task force and advised the administration on important appointments.

Seeking to appoint capable men from outside the foreign service to high diplomatic posts, Kennedy named Galbraith ambassador to India in March 1961. Kennedy's choice was based on Galbraith's familiarity with India's staggering economic problems, his personal acquaintance with Indian prime minister Jawaharlal Nehru, and his prestige as an economic and social analyst. The president also admired Galbraith for his intelligence, trenchant wit, and independence, and believed that as ambassador he could overcome the State Department's inertia to explore new policies toward India. Galbraith came to India during a period when U.S.–Indian relations had been strained by the American policy of supplying military aid to Pakistan and by U.S. actions in Laos and Berlin. Things did not go well at first. Nehru had personal objections to U.S. policies in Europe and Southern Asia and the State Department refused to abandon its old policies and act on the ambassador's recommendations. In the winter of 1961, Galbraith attempted unsuccessfully to prevent India's military takeover of Goa, but relations between the United States and India improved following the outbreak of a China–India border conflict in October 1962. Throughout the crucial months of October and November, Galbraith helped the aged, ill Nehru plan India's defenses and organized American military aid. The ambassador also directed diplomatic efforts designed to prevent a possible Pakistani attack on India.

Kennedy asked Galbraith to visit South Vietnam in November 1961 and provide an independent assessment of the situation, but the president did not act on Galbraith's advice to focus on a political rather than a military solution to **Vietnam**'s problems. In June 1962 Kennedy also failed to heed Galbraith's objections to the president's proposed massive $11 billion tax cuts. The cuts were enacted in 1964. Somewhat frustrated, Galbraith returned to Harvard in early 1963 and continued to publish works of economic history and analysis that argued for the nationalization of some industries, especially defense contractors, and favored a thorough system of wage and price controls. Galbraith died in Cambridge, Massachusetts, on 29 April 2006 at the age of 97. *See also* HARRIMAN, WILLIAM AVERELL; VIETNAM

GENERAL AND COMPLETE DISARMAMENT (GCD). During the early years of the **Cold War**, both the **Soviet Union** and the United States made several unrealistic and broad-ranging public proposals calling for "general and complete disarmament"—primarily for propaganda reasons. Both sides wanted to influence neutral countries and world opinion in their favor. On 18 September 1959, Soviet premier **Nikita Khrushchev** had offered the UN General Assembly a plan for GCD. President Kennedy responded with his own plan at the **United Nations** (UN) on 25 September 1961. Kennedy's plan included not only signing a nuclear test ban pact, halting the production of fissionable materials used for weapons, and several other prohibitions but also included a rigorous inspection regime. There was little in the plan that had not been suggested by previous administrations, nor did it offer any new ideas that might prompt Moscow to forego its longstanding objections to on-site inspections to verify compliance with any of the proposals. In 1962, revised versions of both proposals were formally sent to the UN Eighteen-Nation Disarmament Committee created in December 1961 where portions of the proposals eventually reappeared as **arms control** measures designed to deal with specific problems, such as the nuclear Non-Proliferation Treaty and the

Outer Space Treaty. At the time they were offered, however, neither government expected much to materialize from their proposals. *See also* ARMS CONTROL AND DISARMAMENT AGENCY (ACDA).

GEORGETOWN SET. In 1945–1948, a group of former Office of Strategic Services veterans from World War II found themselves living in the exclusive Georgetown enclave of Washington, DC, and began meeting at each other's houses to discuss the state of the world and the importance of maintaining the preeminent role of the United States. Because of their location, wealth and prominence, experience and expertise, and close connections with high-ranking officials in whatever administration was in office, within a short time the group expanded and they became known as the Georgetown Set. Among the original members of this group of spies, diplomats, journalists, government officials, and political pundits were Frank Wisner, **Walt W. Rostow**, **Stewart Alsop**, Thomas Braden, **Philip Graham**, and David K. E. Bruce. By the end of the 1950s, the group included Ben Bradlee, **George Kennan**, Dean Acheson, Desmond FitzGerald, **Joseph Alsop**, Tracy Barnes, James Truitt, **Clark Clifford**, Eugene Rostow, **Charles "Chip" Bohlen**, Cord Meyer, James Angleton, **William Averell Harriman**, **John J. McCloy**, Felix Frankfurter, John Sherman Cooper, James Reston, **Allen W. Dulles**, and Paul Nitze. Several wives accompanied their husbands to these gatherings. Members of what was later called the Georgetown Ladies' Social Club included **Katharine Meyer Graham**, Mary Pinchot Meyer, Antoinette Pinchot, Anne Truitt, Sally Reston, Polly Wisner, Joan Braden, Lorraine Cooper, Evangeline Bruce, Avis Bohlen, Janet Barnes, Tish Alsop, Cynthia Helms, Marietta FitzGerald, Phyllis Nitze, and Annie Bissell.

John F. Kennedy also frequented the parties and gatherings of this bright and ambitious group of Washington insiders, many of whom had attended the same schools, Groton, Harvard, and Yale. They acted as informal advisers, sounding boards, and supporters of Kennedy on foreign policy matters. In addition to being close friends of Kennedy, all were

Cold War warriors driven by a hatred and fear of the Soviet Union and communism.

GLENN, JOHN H. (1921–2016). John H. Glenn was born in Cambridge, Ohio, on 18 July 1921. He became fascinated by flight and took his first flight in an airplane with his father when he was eight years old. He became a naval pilot in the U.S. Marine Corps in 1943 and saw action in the Pacific, where he was awarded several medals. He remained on active duty during the Korean War and later became a naval test pilot. In 1957, he set a speed record in the first nonstop, transcontinental supersonic flight. In April 1959, Glenn and six others were selected from 110 military test pilots to become the first American astronauts. On 20 February 1962, Glenn became the first Project Mercury astronaut to orbit the earth, circling the globe three times in just under five hours. The flight made Glenn the first American to orbit the Earth, the third American in space, and the fifth human in space. Glenn's flight allayed fears that America had lagged helplessly behind the Soviets in the space race and made him a national hero. He received a ticker-tape parade in New York. Several days after his flight, Glenn addressed a joint session of Congress in support of the space program's long-range goals, saying "exploration and the pursuit of knowledge have always paid dividends in the long run." He became "so valuable to the nation as an iconic figure," according to NASA administrator Charles Bolden, that Kennedy would not "risk putting him back in space again." He became a friend of the Kennedy family, and on 23 February 1962, President Kennedy gave him the NASA Distinguished Service Medal for his *Friendship 7* flight. Glenn was promoted to the rank of colonel in October 1964 and retired from the Marine Corps on 1 January 1965. Glenn was elected to the U.S. Senate in November 1974, where he served until January 1999. He died 8 December 2016 in Columbus, Ohio, at the age of 95.

Astronaut John Glenn in Washington with John F. Kennedy, 1962. *Courtesy of Library of Congress.*

GOLDBERG, ARTHUR JOSEPH (1908–1990).

Arthur Joseph Goldberg was born on 8 August 1908, on the West Side of Chicago, Illinois, the youngest of eight children to Joseph and Rebecca (Pearlstein) Goldberg, who had migrated from the Russian Empire. After graduating from high school in 1924, he took classes at DePaul University before entering law school at Northwestern University, graduating magna cum laude in 1929 and obtaining a doctorate in juridical science the following year. While at Northwestern, he became editor of the *Illinois Law Review* (now *Northwestern Law Review*).

After working briefly with a Chicago law firm, he opened his own practice specializing in labor law in 1933. He quickly became a prominent labor attorney and, in 1938, represented the Congress of Industrial Organizations (CIO) when newspaper employees went on strike seeking more favorable working conditions. Goldberg enlisted and served in the Office of Strategic Services, the precursor to the Central Intelligence Agency, during World War II and worked with underground European labor groups and organizations. He returned to his law practice after the war and, in 1948, was appointed general counsel for the CIO and United Steelworkers of America (USW). He then moved to Washington, DC, where in 1955 he served as an expert adviser during the merger of the American Federation of Labor (AFL) and CIO.

Goldberg was the principal author of the AFL-CIO ethical practices code and cooperated closely with Senator John F. Kennedy during the 1958–1959 McClellan Committee investigation of corrupt union practices. He achieved national recognition when he guided USW negotiations during the 116-day national steel strike in 1959 and 1960. Goldberg was among the earliest labor backers of Kennedy's presidential primary campaign, and in December 1960, the new president chose him as his secretary of labor over five elected union officials nominated by AFL-CIO president George Meany. According to labor historian Thomas R. Brooks, Kennedy chose Goldberg because he needed a secretary of labor who could administer the reform provisions of the Landrum-Griffin Act, which had recently been enacted over strong trade union opposition. Goldberg, who was "from the unions but not of them," was the "perfect appointee."

Goldberg brought remarkable energy to his job as secretary of labor, taking a "hands-on" approach. He oversaw a remarkable and important increase in government supervision of peacetime labor-management relations.

During 1961, he personally intervened to settle a New York tugboat strike in January, a wildcat strike of flight engineers in February, a California agricultural work stoppage in March, and a musicians' dispute at New York's Metropolitan Opera in August. In May 1961, he helped negotiate a no-strike, no-lockout pledge covering construction work at U.S. missile and space bases. President Kennedy then appointed Goldberg to chair an 11-man Missile Sites Labor Commission to handle subsequent labor disputes at the bases.

One of the first challenges facing Goldberg and President Kennedy in early 1961 was the high level of unemployment throughout the nation, which hovered around 6.7 percent. After visiting several midwestern states at Kennedy's request, Goldberg reported that the country was in a "full fledged recession." This gave added urgency to the adoption by the administration of the heretofore unsuccessful legislative proposals of Senator Paul Douglas (D-Ill.) to aid these "depressed areas" with a comprehensive federal aid package. The administration pledged $380 million to fund a new Area Redevelopment Agency to be administered by the secretary of commerce. Goldberg vigorously backed the proposal and lobbied conservative members of Congress to adopt the plan. The bill setting up the agency passed both houses of Congress in April and was signed by the president on 1 May 1961.

Goldberg provided further assistance by persuading all 50 states to extend unemployment benefits by 13 weeks and to share the additional costs. The minimum wage was increased from $1 to $1.25 per hour over two years, and the minimum-wage coverage was extended to an additional 3.6 million workers, the first such extension since 1938. In June, the administration increased social security

benefits by $800 million. The Senate also passed an employment training bill, but the House delayed passage of the $435 package until March 1962. Goldberg was less successful, however, in improving the working conditions of Californian and Texan American farm workers.

In seeking to set guidelines for wage growth within inflationary limits and national security considerations, Goldberg and the Kennedy administration faced considerable opposition, not the least of which came from the unions Goldberg had championed. The issue came to a head in March–April 1962. In February and March, Goldberg was instrumental in reaching a noninflationary settlement between the steelworkers and management, in which the USW accepted a 2.5 percent increase in wages and the steel industry agreed not to raise the price of steel. However, on 10 April U.S. Steel chairman Roger Blough unexpectedly announced that U.S. Steel was raising the price of its steel by around $6 per ton. Kennedy and Goldberg were outraged by what they considered a betrayal and double cross. Five other steel companies followed suit the next day. Goldberg offered his resignation, which Kennedy refused; together with **Ted Sorensen**, Goldberg prepared a speech condemning the price rise, which Kennedy delivered in a nationally televised press conference.

With former Truman adviser **Clark Clifford**, Goldberg met secretly with U.S. Steel executives during the next two days, threatening harsh legislation unless the steel price increases were withdrawn. By the afternoon of 14 April, Bethlehem Steel announced it would rescind its price increase. A few hours later, U.S. Steel followed suit. The crisis was over.

Goldberg's time in the cabinet was short, however, because the declining health and subsequent resignation of **Supreme Court** justice Felix Frankfurter, who had recently suffered a stroke, caused Kennedy to nominate Goldberg to fill the vacant seat. Goldberg took his seat on the bench on 28 September 1962. Goldberg spent 34 months on the Supreme Court bench. According to legal scholar Henry J. Abraham, the former secretary of labor showed a "zest for innovation in

the law that left an imprint far out of proportion to the brief period he served." His liberal perspective on jurisprudence helped shift the court's focus toward broader constructions of constitutional rights at a time when the **civil rights** movement dominated the American legal system.

Goldberg championed the right to privacy (in *Griswold v. Connecticut*) and authored the court's landmark 5–4 decision in *Escobedo v. Illinois*, holding that confessions cannot be used in court if police question a suspect without letting him consult a lawyer or without warning him that his answers may be used against him. Goldberg also strongly opposed the death penalty, going so far as to write an internal Supreme Court memorandum in 1963 that construed it as cruel and unusual punishment. This dissent inspired attorneys nationwide to challenge the constitutionality of capital punishment.

Goldberg's time on the bench came to an abrupt halt in 1965 when President **Lyndon B. Johnson** asked him to step down in order to become the U.S. ambassador to the **United Nations** (UN) and work toward mitigating the war in **Vietnam**, a decision he later came to regret. His most significant achievement while at the UN was the role he played in drafting Security Council Resolution 242, which was passed in November 1967 after the June 1967 **Middle East** War. The measure, which calls for a just and lasting peace in the Middle East, was the cornerstone of diplomatic efforts to achieve peace in the region for several years. He resigned from the UN in 1968.

He made an unsuccessful run for the governorship of New York in 1970, losing in a landslide to incumbent Nelson Rockefeller. He returned to practicing law in Washington, and served as U.S. ambassador to the Belgrade Conference on Human Rights in 1977 under President Jimmy Carter. He was awarded the Presidential Medal of Freedom in 1978.

Arthur Goldberg died in New York on 19 January 1990 at the age of 81 from coronary artery disease. He was interred at Arlington National Cemetery in Virginia for his service to his country. *See also* DILLON, CLARENCE DOUGLAS; HUMPHREY, HUBERT HORATIO.

GOLDWATER, BARRY MORRIS (1909–1998). Barry Morris Goldwater was born in Phoenix, Arizona, on 2 January 1909, the son of Baron M. "Barry" Goldwater, a businessman and retailer, and Josephine Williams Goldwater. Although raised an Episcopalian, Goldwater was the grandson of a Jewish immigrant from Poland, Michel Goldwasser. Goldwater's father, Baron, settled in Phoenix, where he opened a successful women's clothing store. Indifferent in high school, he attended Staunton Military Academy in Virginia, graduating as the top military cadet in 1928. After his father's death the following year, Goldwater joined the family business. In 1934, he married Margaret "Peggy" Johnson; the couple had two sons and two daughters. By 1937, Goldwater had become president of Goldwater's Inc. Although over 30 and hampered by poor vision, Goldwater was accepted for active duty in the U.S. Army Air Forces during World War II. By the end of the war, he had risen to the rank of colonel and later became a brigadier general in the Air National Guard.

He returned to Phoenix after the war and embarked on a political career as a member of the Phoenix city council; he was one of a successful reform slate of candidates. On the city council, Goldwater gained a lasting reputation for candor, integrity, and humor. In 1952, he ran for the U.S. Senate and, although regarded as an underdog, successfully rode **Dwight D. Eisenhower**'s coattails to an upset victory. Goldwater's political success paralleled the transformation of Arizona from an old western Democratic populist state to one dominated by Sunbelt Republican conservatism.

In the Senate, Goldwater soon revealed himself to be a hard-line anticommunist (he was one of 22 senators who voted against the censure of Joseph McCarthy) and staunch advocate of free enterprise and states' rights. In 1958, he easily won reelection. The defeat of the Nixon-Lodge Republican ticket to John F. Kennedy in the 1960 presidential election opened the door for a serious conservative challenge to the moderate Northern-Eastern Establishment that had dominated the Republican Party since the 1940s. Goldwater, whose political credo, *The Conscience of a Conservative* (1960), had become a best seller thanks largely to his following among grass-roots conservatives, especially those in the southern states. In a bitter and divisive convention in San Francisco in July 1964, he won the Republican presidential nomination. True to his image as a man of uncompromising principle, Goldwater chose conservative New York congressman William E. Miller as his running mate, and his rousing acceptance speech took on his moderate critics directly: "Extremism in the defense of liberty is no vice, and . . . moderation in the pursuit of justice is no virtue."

Goldwater's general election campaign was a disaster. **Lyondon Johnson** campaigned as his predecessor's successor, maintaining a booming economy and securing passage of the **Civil Rights Act of 1964**. Goldwater's outspoken nature, uncompromising southwestern conservatism, and hard-line anti-Soviet stance also made it easy for the incumbent to depict him as an intemperate ideologue who could not be trusted with the huge U.S. nuclear arsenal. On the domestic front, Goldwater's votes against the 1964 Civil Rights Act (on grounds that it violated states' rights) and his public speculations about privatizing the Tennessee Valley Authority also enabled the Democrats to portray him as an extremist. These strategies led to Goldwater's landslide defeat in the fall. He won only 38.5 percent of the popular vote and carried only six states (Georgia, Alabama, Louisiana, Mississippi, South Carolina, and his home state of Arizona) with a combined total of 52 electoral votes to Johnson's 486.

Goldwater returned to the Senate in 1968 and reestablished himself as a leader of Republican conservatives in that body. In 1974, he played a decisive role in the Watergate drama when he informed President **Richard M. Nixon** that he would likely be convicted in a Senate impeachment trial. Having lost Goldwater's support, Nixon realized that his position was hopeless and resigned the presidency. As chair of the Senate Select Intelligence Committee during the 1980s, Goldwater was frequently critical of the Ronald Reagan administration. His views on a wide range of domestic issues became quite idiosyncratic after his final

retirement from the Senate in 1986, but they added to his reputation for candor and integrity and brought him sympathy from a broader ideological audience.

Despite the decisive repudiation of Goldwater in 1964, his "New Right" conservatism led in time to Ronald Reagan's sweeping presidential victories in the 1980s. The electoral, economic, and social base of the Republican party shifted decisively in 1964, and Barry Goldwater ultimately proved to be one of the most influential losing presidential nominees in U.S. history. Goldwater died of natural causes at his home in Paradise Valley, Arizona, on 29 May 1998 at the age of 89.

GRAHAM, KATHARINE "KAY" MEYER (1917–2001). Katharine "Kay" Meyer Graham was born in 1917 into a wealthy family in New York City, to Agnes Elizabeth (née Ernst) and Eugene Meyer. Her father made a fortune during World War I. He had founded the Allied Chemical Company to replace the German aniline dyes that were unobtainable by the American textile industry because of the war. He served as the chairman of the War Finance Corporation, and Kay grew up in luxury in the Meridian Park section of Washington, where the prewar aristocracy had their homes. From 1930 to 1933, Kay's father served as chairman of the Federal Reserve, and in June 1933, he bought the *Washington Post* at a bankruptcy auction, for $825,000. Kay's mother was a bohemian intellectual, art lover, and political activist in the **Republican Party**, who shared friendships with people as diverse as Auguste Rodin, Marie Curie, **Thomas C. Mann**, Albert Einstein, and Eleanor Roosevelt. Although her father was Jewish, her mother was a Lutheran, and Kay was baptized a Lutheran. After attending Madeira in Virginia, the smartest private school for young ladies, Kay went on to Vassar. One of Kay's best friends at school was President Grant's granddaughter. She would have liked to go to the London School of Economics, but her father refused to allow it, and she went to the University of Chicago instead.

In 1940, she married **Philip Graham**, a young man who had made it into the emerging American power elite from the unlikely background of rural South Dakota via Florida. The Grahams moved to Georgetown, where their mansion was the equal of the elegant Georgian-style homes of John F. Kennedy, **W. Averell Harriman, Joseph Alsop**, and other members of the elite. Katharine, attractive and wealthy—if a little shy—and her husband were soon in great demand in Washington.

Although her family were Republicans and her husband, before becoming a major Democratic power behind the scenes, voted for the Republican Eisenhower in 1952, she herself was much more liberal in her political leanings. With the Kennedy inauguration in 1961, the Grahams and their friends became prominent both socially and politically. So when Katharine took responsibility for the family business, just before Kennedy's assassination, she might have been, as she had always thought of herself, a wife inexperienced in the ways of business, but she was also on friendly—and in many cases, tennis and family-supper—terms with most of the inner circle in Washington and a founding member of that well-born, well-heeled circle known as the **Georgetown Set**.

Her gatherings were bipartisan. Her personal friends included the pianist Rudolf Serkin; **Adlai Stevenson II**, whom she did not find as attractive as did many other liberal women; Jean Monnet; and later, Warren Buffett, the immensely successful investor from Omaha who built up a large position in the Washington Post Company's stock and became Graham's most trusted business mentor. She had no shortage of contacts and advice from the Robert McNamaras, the McGeorge Bundys, and members of Congress, and while in New York, she joined the Truman Capote set, graced by such luminaries as Pamela Harriman, Babe Paley (wife of the owner of CBS), and Marella Agnelli, whose husband owned Fiat.

Kay Graham led the *Washington Post* for more than two decades, overseeing its most famous period: the Watergate coverage that eventually led to the resignation of President **Richard M. Nixon**. Her memoir, *Personal History*, won the Pulitzer Prize in 1998. She received numerous awards for her contributions to U.S. journalism, **education**, and public service.

On 17 July 2001, Graham died after a fall in Sun Valley, Idaho, where she was attending an international business conference. Her death marked the passing of an era. For many years, Graham had been regarded as the most powerful woman in Washington. Her passing was reported in every newspaper and every radio and **television** news broadcast in the nation. She is buried in a plot beside that of her husband in Oak Hill Cemetery, across the street from her former home in Georgetown.

GRAHAM, PHILIP LESLIE (1915–1963). Philip Leslie Graham was born into a Lutheran family in Terry, South Dakota. He was raised in Miami, Florida, where his father, Ernest R. "Cap" Graham, worked as a farmer and in real estate. He was elected to the Florida State Senate. His mother, Florence Morris, had been a schoolteacher in the Black Hills of South Dakota. Graham was one of four children.

Graham attended Miami High School and, in 1936, earned a BA degree in economics from the University of Florida. He then studied at Harvard Law School, where he graduated with a law degree magna cum laude in 1939; he was also editor of the *Harvard Law Review*. In 1939–1940, he was law clerk to U.S. **Supreme Court** justice Stanley F. Reed, and the following year he clerked for Justice Felix Frankfurter, who had been one of his professors at Harvard. Graham was a brilliant young man, tall, bespectacled, and scholarly looking; a brilliant legal career was predicted for him.

However, fate, in the form of marriage, took him in a different direction. On 5 June 1940, Graham married Katharine Meyer, the daughter of Eugene Meyer, a multimillionaire and the owner of the *Washington Post*, at that time a struggling and little-known newspaper. During World War II, Graham enlisted in 1942 as a private in the U.S. Army Air Corps, and in 1945, he was sent to the Pacific theater as an intelligence officer in the newly formed Far East Air Force, where he rose to the rank of major.

In 1946, President **Harry S. Truman** appointed Meyer the first president of the World Bank, and Meyer passed the position of publisher of the *Post* to Graham. Meyer left the World Bank after a very short tenure and returned as chairman of the board of the Washington Post Company but kept Graham on as publisher. In 1948, Meyer transferred his company shares to his daughter and her husband. **Katharine Graham** received 30 percent as a gift. Phil received 70 percent of the stock, with his purchase financed by his father-in-law. Meyer remained a close adviser to his son-in-law until his death in 1959, at which time Graham assumed the titles of president and chairman of the board of the Post Company.

While running the *Washington Post* and other parts of the Post Company, Graham played a backstage role in national and local politics. He and his wife helped create the **Georgetown Set**. In 1960, he helped persuade his friend John F. Kennedy to take his even closer friend **Lyndon B. Johnson** on his ticket as the vice presidential candidate, personally talking with both men multiple times during the 1960 Democratic National Convention in Los Angeles, California. During the 1960 campaign, he wrote the drafts for several speeches that Johnson gave. After Kennedy and Johnson were elected in November, he successfully lobbied for the appointment of **C. Douglas Dillon** as secretary of the treasury, and he had multiple discussions with Kennedy about other appointments. Following Kennedy's inauguration, he continued to write occasional drafts of speeches, primarily for Johnson, but also for the president and for **Robert F. Kennedy**. In 1961, Kennedy named Graham to serve as an incorporator for the Communications Satellite Corporation, known as COMSAT, a joint venture between the private sector and government for satellite communications. In October 1961, he was appointed chairman of the group.

In Katharine Graham's memoirs, titled *Personal History*, she notes that her husband was always intense and spontaneous but occasionally lapsed into periods of depression. In 1957, he had a severe manic episode, and at the time, no medicines were available for effective treatment. He retired to the couple's farm in Marshall, Virginia, to recuperate. Thereafter, periods in which he functioned brilliantly alternated with periods in which he was morose and erratic and isolated himself. He often

drank heavily and would become extremely argumentative and blunt. His behavior became more erratic as his undiagnosed bipolar disorder took control. In 1962, Graham met Australian journalist Robin Webb, and they began an affair. The following year his behavior at a newspaper publishing convention was so manic he was flown back to Washington and committed for five days to Chestnut Lodge, a psychiatric hospital in Rockville, Maryland. On leaving the hospital, Graham briefly left his wife for Webb, announced that he planned to divorce his wife and immediately remarry, and indicated that he wanted to purchase sole control of the Post Company. However, in June 1963, in a fit of depression, he broke off his affair and returned home. On 20 June he entered Chestnut Lodge for the second time and was formally diagnosed with manic depression (now called bipolar disorder). He was treated with psychotherapy. On 3 August 1963, after requesting release from the hospital, Graham traveled to the family farm in Virginia and committed suicide with a 28-gauge shotgun.

GREGORY, DICK CLAXTON (1932–2017). Dick Claxton Gregory was born on 12 October 1932 in St. Louis, Missouri, and raised by his impoverished mother. He ran track for his St. Louis high school and attended predominantly white Southern Illinois University on an athletic scholarship. After serving in the army, where he was encouraged to develop his comedic skills, he drifted through several jobs before launching his career as a comedian in 1958 at a black nightclub in Chicago. He remained largely unknown outside of black audiences until 1961, when he appeared at the Chicago Playboy Club as a replacement for a white comedian. He was so successful in his limited number of appearances that the Playboy Club offered him a contract extension from several weeks to three years. By 1962, he had become a national figure, with **television** appearances, comedy albums, and a large network of supporters, blacks and whites alike.

Gregory became a pioneer in stand-up comedy with his "no-holds-barred" sets, in which he drew on current events, especially racial issues, for much of his material to mock bigotry and racism. In his comedy routines, he provided ironic commentary on many social issues. Gregory became involved in **civil rights** in November 1962, when he spoke at a voter registration rally in Jackson, Mississippi. He became friendly with **Medgar W. Evers**, leader of the Mississippi **National Association for the Advancement of Colored People**, and subsequently toured the South, speaking at civil rights rallies and demonstrations. On 7 October 1963, he gave a two-hour public speech in Selma, Alabama, two days before the voter registration drive known as "Freedom Day." When local governments in Mississippi stopped distributing federal food surpluses to poor blacks in areas where the **Student Nonviolent Coordinating Committee** had taken an active role in voter registration campaigns, Gregory chartered a plane to bring in several tons of food.

In the mid-1960s, Gregory gave up nightclub performances to devote himself to college appearances aimed at encouraging student activism. For the remainder of the decade, he became increasingly involved in opposition to the **Vietnam War** and political activism in areas including environmental protection, feminism, and the rights of **Native Americans**. Always an individualist, Gregory did not identify himself with any single civil rights or peace organization. However, his celebrity status enabled him to act alone for the causes he espoused. In November 1967, he began a series of fasts, lasting from 40 to 80 days, to dramatize his stance on the war and other issues including pollution, diet, and health.

Gregory reduced his political activism after 1969, partly for financial reasons. He resumed his nightclub performances in 1970 but left show business again in August 1973. This transition reflected a change in Gregory's lifestyle; he moved with his family from Chicago to a farm outside of Boston and devoted himself to pursuing a "natural" life, including a vegetarian diet, breathing exercises, and running. Gregory published a number of books at various stages of his career, including *From the Back of the Bus* (1964) and *Write Me In* (1972). Gregory died of heart failure in Washington, DC, on 19 August 2017, at the age of 84. *See also* AFRICAN AMERICANS.

H

HARRIMAN, WILLIAM AVERELL (1891–1986). William Averell Harriman was born in New York City on 15 November 1891, the son of railroad baron Edward Henry Harriman and Mary Williamson Averell. He attended the Groton School in Massachusetts before going on to Yale, graduating in 1913. He then inherited one of the largest fortunes in America.

Harriman established himself as an accomplished diplomat during World War II when he acted for President Franklin D. Roosevelt and became the first U.S. minister and then ambassador to the **Soviet Union** from 1941 to 1946. He served as President **Harry S. Truman**'s secretary of commerce and, after helping implement the Marshall Plan in Europe, became Truman's national security adviser during the Korean War. In 1954, Harriman was elected governor of New York, but he was not a success as a politician and served only one term.

Harriman, however, became a widely respected foreign policy elder within the **Democratic Party**, and John F. Kennedy offered the 69-year-old a roving ambassadorship. Still vital, hardworking, and ambitious, Harriman accepted, ready, in his own words, "to start at the bottom and work [my] way up." The president first assigned Harriman to help resolve the lingering political-military crisis in Laos. Harriman was among those in the new administration who urged the neutralization of Laos as a solution to the crisis there. He met with Soviet premier **Nikita Khrushchev** in February 1961 and reported to Washington that the Russian leader had made it plain that he did not want a war over Laos. After Harriman

met with Souvanna Phouma in New Delhi in March, he recommended that the administration support Souvanna's efforts to form a new neutralist government. At the same time, Harriman urged a limited commitment of troops to Thailand to underline American opposition to a communist takeover in Laos. His proposal was offered in opposition to suggestions from the Joint Chiefs of Staff that as many as 60,000 troops be deployed in Laos. Kennedy publicly adopted Harriman's perspective on 23 March 1961, when he called for "a truly neutral government, not a Cold War pawn," in Laos. In November, Kennedy appointed Harriman assistant secretary of state for Far Eastern affairs.

Harriman handled several important diplomatic assignments for the Kennedy administration. When, in October 1962, China invaded the mountainous regions along India's northern frontier, Prime Minister Jawaharlal Nehru asked for Western support. Harriman led an American delegation to the subcontinent to survey Indian military requirements. Along with U.S. ambassador **John Kenneth Galbraith**, Harriman pressed India to resolve its dispute with Pakistan over Kashmir to avoid the possibility that military aid to the subcontinent would pit one American-supplied army against another. Before American pressure could win results, the Chinese declared a unilateral cease-fire, and the incentive for resolving the India-Pakistan dispute evaporated.

Kennedy promoted Harriman to undersecretary of state for political affairs in March 1963 and, two months later, put him in charge

of negotiating the **Limited Nuclear Test Ban Treaty** with the Soviets in Moscow. On 25 July, Harriman initialed the treaty for the United States, and it was ratified by the Senate and signed by President Kennedy on 7 October 1963.

As the American role in **Vietnam** expanded, Harriman maintained a skeptical attitude toward a purely military solution to the civil war there. Along with Roger Hilsman, the new assistant secretary of state for Far Eastern affairs, and **Michael Forrestal**, a White House aide assigned to work on Vietnam, Harriman repeatedly questioned the military's optimistic reports on the progress of the **counterinsurgency** in Southeast Asia. There were some who questioned whether Harriman was acting without consulting with Kennedy. With the **assassination of John F. Kennedy** and the continuing escalation of the **Vietnam War**, Harriman's influence in government declined, until President Johnson called on the former governor to serve as chairman of the American delegation to the Paris peace talks on Vietnam in May 1968. Harriman died on 26 July 1986 in Yorktown Heights, New York, at the age of 94. *See also* LODGE, HENRY CABOT, JR.

HARRINGTON, EDWARD MICHAEL, JR.

(1928–1989). Edward Michael Harrington Jr. was born in St. Louis and was educated by the Jesuits at St. Louis University High School and at Holy Cross College. In 1951, he moved to New York, where he began drifting toward socialism. After spending a year working with the Catholic Worker movement, Harrington joined the Young People's Socialist League and eventually became a leader of the Socialist Party. In the early 1960s, he became convinced that the anticommunist, socialist movement of which he was part could be most effective by working within the **Democratic Party** in an effort to "realign" it in a more progressive direction. Harrington was active in civil liberties, **civil rights**, and peace groups throughout the 1950s and early 1960s. His 1962 book, *The Other America: Poverty in the United States*, was important in directing public attention toward the large number of people living in chronic poverty within the "affluent society."

These people, Harrington claimed, especially the elderly and the rural poor of Appalachia, had become invisible to the larger society. The poor, as he described them, were not just a segment of Americans without money but actually constituted "a separate culture, another nation with its own way of life."

President Kennedy read Harrington's book in fall 1963, shortly before he ordered the Council of Economic Advisers (CEA) to begin planning an antipoverty program. On **Lyndon B. Johnson**'s first full day in office, CEA chair Walter Heller advised the president that, four days earlier, Kennedy had approved the planning of a major antipoverty program. The new president gave the project his highest priority, and on 8 January 1964, in his first State of the Union address, Johnson declared an "unconditional war on poverty in America." Later that month, poverty program planners asked Harrington to Washington. With Paul Jacobs, a former union organizer and West Coast radical, and **Peace Corps** official Frank Mankiewicz, Harrington began two weeks of meetings with high-ranking government officials to prepare proposals for the new program. In their final memo, Mankiewicz, Jacobs, and Harrington argued that the elimination of poverty would require major changes in the allocation of government resources and certain basic structural changes in society. Newly appointed poverty program head **R. Sargent Shriver Jr.** incorporated part of the memo in his report to Johnson, who at the time responded favorably.

After Kennedy's death, Harrington continued to be active the U.S. politics. He became involved in the growing anti–**Vietnam War** movement and, in 1965, published *The Accidental Century* followed by *Toward a Democratic Left* in 1968. He continued to write until his death from cancer in 1989.

HARTKE, RUPERT VANCE (1919–2003).

Vance Hartke was born in Stendal, Indiana, and raised in a small mining town in southwestern Indiana. He served in the Coast Guard during World War II and returned to his studies at the Indiana University Law School, from which he graduated in 1948. Hartke then practiced law in Evansville, Indiana, while earning

a reputation as a skilled organizer for the local **Democratic Party**. He was elected mayor of Evansville in 1955; three years later, after a strenuous campaign, he won election to the U.S. Senate. He was the first Democrat to represent Indiana in the upper house in 20 years.

Hartke proved to be a strong supporter of the Kennedy administration, voting for its school aid, minimum-wage, housing, and Medicare bills. From 1961 to 1963, the liberal Americans for Democratic Action gave him high ratings. Hartke did not play an influential role in the Senate during the Kennedy years, although he did serve on the powerful Commerce and Finance Committees. In 1961, Hartke successfully amended Social Security legislation, raising to $1,800 the limit on earnings of retired individuals exempted from benefit deductions. He was also a member of the Senate District of Columbia Committee, and in 1962 he managed the law that abolished the mandatory death penalty for first-degree murder convictions in Washington. He also supported a key provision of the administration's 1962 tax revision bill requiring automatic withholding of taxes on interest and dividend payments, although the measure was defeated on the floor of the Senate following intensive lobbying against it by savings and loan associations.

In Indiana, the manufacture of steel was an important industry. In an effort to encourage greater purchase of domestic steel products, in April 1963 Hartke introduced legislation requiring manufacturers to label containers made with foreign steel with the metal's country of origin. Congress, however, took no action on the bill. In 1964, Hartke won reelection with 55 percent of the vote, a substantial margin for a liberal running in an essentially conservative state. During the campaign, Hartke received large cash contributions from a Chicago-based mail-order firm. A year later he requested and won appointment to the Senate Post Office Committee, where he worked to forestall planned postal rate increases for third-class mail. Hartke's opponents charged that he was guilty of conflict of interest; this accusation, coupled with his outspoken opposition to American involvement in **Vietnam**, made his

reelection in 1970 problematic. Hartke defeated his opponent by only 4,235 votes; his claim to his seat was not finally settled until 18 months after the election. Hartke died in Falls Church, Virginia, on 27 July 2003, at the age of 84.

HAYDEN, TOM (1939–2016). Tom Hayden was born to parents of Irish heritage on 11 December 1939 in Royal Oak, Michigan. After attending parochial schools, he went to the University of Michigan in 1957 on a tennis scholarship. Majoring in English, he became the editor of the *Michigan Daily*, the student paper. Most of Hayden's political activity took place after the **assassination of John F. Kennedy**, but it was Kennedy's presidential campaign in 1960 that inspired the young journalist, and his first involvement in national events took place during the Kennedy administration.

In May 1960, Hayden attended a **civil rights** conference sponsored by the recently revitalized **Students for a Democratic Society** (SDS), and that fall, he would help organize VOICE, a University of Michigan student group affiliated with SDS that soon became its largest chapter. After graduating from Michigan, Hayden was hired in fall 1961 as one of two paid SDS field secretaries. Working out of Atlanta, he wrote articles and a pamphlet, *Revolution in Mississippi*, about the southern civil rights movement. Hayden himself participated in the **Freedom Ride** and was beaten in McComb, Mississippi, in October 1961, and that December, he was arrested with 10 others in a **Student Nonviolent Coordinating Committee** (SNCC) effort to desegregate Albany, Georgia, transit facilities. Hayden wrote the initial drafts of the manifesto produced by the June 1962 SDS convention at Port Huron, Michigan.

The "Port Huron Statement" became the most widely known formulation of New Left ideology. "We are people of this generation, bred in at least modest comfort, housed now in universities, looking uncomfortably at the world we inherit," the statement declared. At the same convention, Hayden was elected to a one-year term as SDS president. Hayden helped plan and carry out an SDS

experiment in community organizing, the Economic Research and Action Project (ERAP), which began in September 1963, supported by a $5,000 donation from the United Auto Workers. The following summer, Hayden himself joined an ERAP group in Newark, New Jersey. Attempting to apply SNCC tactics in the North, Hayden and other SDS members spent two years in a predominantly black Newark neighborhood trying to develop local organizations and community campaigns on a broad range of issues. The Newark project, the most successful and long-lasting ERAP effort, ended following the July 1967 Newark riots.

During the years 1965 through 1968, Hayden became a leading protester against the **Vietnam War**—even visiting North Vietnam several times—and was also prominent in the civil rights movement. He ended up in jail briefly for his activities as one of the "Chicago Seven" who disrupted the 1968 **Democratic Party** convention in Chicago in 1968, before his conviction was reversed. He held several academic positions and authored/edited 19 books.

Hayden was elected to the California Assembly in 1982 and the state senate in 1992. He retired in 1999. He was the former husband of actress Jane Fonda and the father of their son, actor Troy Garity. Hayden died in Santa Monica, California, on 23 October 2016, at the age of 76 after a lengthy illness, and he is survived by his third wife, Barbara Williams (born 1953), a Canadian-born American actress whom he married in 1993.

HEALTH CARE POLICY. Heath care policy—especially for elderly Americans—was an important issue for John F. Kennedy. The costs associated with his own father's stroke in December 1961 had made him realize that it was virtually impossible for those less wealthy to bear the economic burden of serious illnesses. Health care was also a highly controversial subject, and the president knew that, in order to gain the support of Congress and the public for federally funded medical services for the aged, he had to tread cautiously. As a senator in 1960, Kennedy had sponsored a medical care measure, and following his election, at a

news conference on 20 December, he included medical care for the aged among five fields to which he assigned top legislative priority for the 87th Congress. On 10 January 1961, a Kennedy task force on health and Social Security headed by Wilbur J. Cohen, a University of Michigan professor (and later assistant secretary of health, **education**, and welfare) issued a report recommending that hospitalization and health services for the aged should be financed by Social Security. On 13 February, representative Cecil R. King (D-Calif.) and **Clinton P. Anderson** (D-N.M.) in the Senate introduced such a plan in Congress. In broad terms, the plan—later to become "Medicare" when implemented by the **Lyndon B. Johnson** administration in 1964—expanded the original 1935 Social Security Act's old-age pension program by providing individuals 65 years or older with basic hospital insurance and supplementary medical insurance to assist in paying for doctors' bills and drug costs. Working men and women would contribute to their own old age health insurance program through Social Security, which employers would match, to finance the program. The Kennedy administration proposal was to levy an additional .25 percent in Social Security payroll taxes on both employers and employees, increase the earnings base, and earmark the additional revenue to pay hospital and nursing bills (up to specified limits) of individuals eligible for Social Security old-age pensions. The plan would spread the costs of medical care for the aged among the younger working population and eventually over the lifespan of recipients. Under the bill, it was estimated that 14,250,000 individuals 65 or over (out of a total aged population of 16,750,000) would be eligible for benefits under either the Social Security or related railroad retirement systems. Little progress was made, however, as a majority of the House Ways and Means Committee was hostile to the Social Security approach, and the controversial issue carried forward to 1962.

However, on 5 October 1961 Congress did pass the Community Health Services and Facilities Act of 1961 (H.R. 4998—Public Law 87-395), which expanded and improved

community health services and facilities for the health care of the aged and other individuals, by providing funds for the greater availability of community health services and facilities to assist in meeting the health needs of the chronically ill and aged, as well as increasing and expanding medical research.

In spring 1962, Kennedy launched a concerted effort to have his medical care package passed by Congress. The president had political and personal reasons to act at this time. Kennedy's pollster Lou Harris advised him that he needed domestic accomplishments for his reelection and that Medicare would be an important one. The issue was also essential to the labor movement and the American Federation of Labor/Congress of Industrial Organizations (AFL-CIO), key **Democratic Party** allies, and so would be incredibly helpful for Democrats facing congressional election that year. Kennedy also wanted to be remembered as the president who achieved landmark legislation in the field of health care. And, this time, at the suggestion of **Wilbur Mills**, the powerful chairman of the House Ways and Means Committee who had initially opposed the legislation being attached to the Social Security Act, the president's plan was to attach appropriate provisions to a welfare bill.

On 20 May, Kennedy gave a major address to almost 20,000 older voters in Madison Square Garden, New York City, urging his audience to mobilize support for the health care plan he had presented to Congress. The address was broadcast live on all three **television** networks. On the same day, the AFL-CIO held 33 rallies across the country. However, the bill continued to face strong opposition in Congress and from the American Medical Association (AMA). Kennedy planned to socialize medicine, a spokesman for the AMA claimed, stating: "We doctors fear that the American public is in danger of being blitzed, brainwashed, and band-wagoned," arguing the laws already on the books allowed people to be covered through private programs. Although Congress was, in general, friendly toward Kennedy at this time, the legislation he proposed was soon caught up in labyrinthine discussions

and negotiations for three weeks and failed to pass. On 13 June 1963, Kennedy once again spoke on the importance of providing health insurance for senior citizens in a speech delivered before the National Council of Senior Citizens.

Mental Health

On 24 October 1963, Kennedy signed the Maternal and Child Health and Mental Retardation Planning Amendments to the Social Security Act, a bill sponsored by Wilbur Mills and **Abraham Ribicoff**. The act provided funding to states to improve programs for those with intellectual disabilities. He was especially sensitive to this matter as his younger sister Rosemary had been born with such a condition. At the signing, Kennedy stated: "An estimated 15 to 20 million people in our country live in families where there is a mentally retarded person who must accept support of some kind throughout his entire life. This condition affects more of our children and more of our people than blindness, cerebral palsy, and rheumatic heart disease combined."

A week later on 31 October, he signed the Mental Retardation Facilities and Community Mental Health Centers Construction Act. Kennedy observed that, as a result of this act, "[t]he mentally ill need no longer be alien to our affections or beyond the help of our communities." This act authorized a four-year, $329 million mental health program of grants to states and private and public institutions for construction of centers connected with universities and affiliated hospitals for research into the causes of mental retardation and facilities for treatment of such cases; for construction of community centers for care and treatment of mental patients; and for training of teachers of mentally challenged, mentally ill, and handicapped children. The act funded community mental health centers to provide better care than mental hospitals. Or, at least, that was the plan. Instead, states closed their mental hospitals. Funding was inadequate, and later cut, for the community centers. Only 5 percent of patients treated at the centers were psychotic. This was the beginning of deinstitutionalization.

HODGES, LUTHER (1898–1974). Luther Hodges was born on 9 March 1898, in Pittsylvania County, Virginia, the son of a tenant farmer. He became governor of North Carolina and then secretary of commerce in John F. Kennedy's cabinet.

The family moved to Leaksville, North Carolina, where Hodges worked part time in a textile mill while attending school. He waited on tables and carried out various jobs in a mill in order to pay expenses to attend the University of North Carolina. He also took a job as a book salesman.

Hodges gained in BA degree in 1919 after a brief interruption when he served in the army during World War I at Camp David, Illinois. He joined a textile company and soon became secretary to the general manager of Marshall Field's eight textile mills in the Leaksville area. By 1939, he was general manager of all 29 of his company's mills in the United States and abroad.

Hodges headed the textile division of the Office of Price Administration in 1944 and, immediately after the war, became a special consultant to the secretary of agriculture, **Clinton P. Anderson**. In 1950, he resigned as vice president in charge of textile mills and sales for Marshall Field and Company to take the position of head of the industry division of the Economic Cooperation Administration in West Germany set up by the **Harry S. Truman** administration.

Two years later, at the age of 54, he embarked upon a political career and was elected lieutenant governor of North Carolina. Upon the death of the incumbent, Hodges became governor and was elected by a landslide in his own right for the term 1956–1960. He established a national reputation as governor, altering the tax structure and embarking on an intensive industrialization program for the state. He led the move to establish the Research Triangle in North Carolina, concentrating research facilities into a single geographical area.

Regarded as a leading moderate in terms of race relations in the South, he supported John F. Kennedy in his 1960 presidential campaign. Kennedy appointed him secretary of commerce in 1961. He set out to aggressively promote U.S. exports and played a leading role in the passage of the **Trade Expansion Act** of 1962. He urged the expansion of nonstrategic trade with the bloc: "Sell them anything they can eat, drink or smoke" was his slogan. Domestically, he participated in the creation of the Area Redevelopment Administration, a program designed to assist economic growth in areas of the United States—particularly in Appalachia and the South—experiencing high unemployment.

After Hodges retired as secretary of commerce in January 1965, he was elected chairman of the board of a financial consultant company whose purpose was the investment of U.S. stocks to be sold worldwide. He was also president of International Rotary in 1967–1968. Hodges died on 6 October 1974 in Chapel Hill, North Carolina.

HOOVER, J. EDGAR (1895–1972). J. Edgar Hoover was born on 1 January 1895 in Washington, DC, and raised there, where his father worked for the Coast and Geodetic Survey. In 1913, he graduated from Central High School as class valedictorian. He then studied law at George Washington University (at night) while working in the Library of Congress as an indexer. After receiving his law degree in 1916, Hoover joined the Justice Department as a clerk, distinguishing himself by his enthusiasm, thoroughness, and willingness to work overtime. In 1919, he was named special assistant to Attorney General A. Mitchell Palmer, who was then engaged in rounding up thousands of alleged communists and revolutionaries for possible deportation under the provisions of the Wartime Sedition Act. In 1921, Hoover was appointed assistant director of the Bureau of Investigation (the name was changed to the Federal Bureau of Investigation [FBI] in 1935), and three years later he was named director.

Hoover served as director of the FBI under every president from Calvin Coolidge to **Richard M. Nixon** and was to become one of the most controversial figures in 20th-century America. During the John F. Kennedy years, Hoover clashed frequently with his superior, Attorney General **Robert F. Kennedy**, who

attempted to bring the bureau under his control. Hoover, nonetheless, maintained his autonomy and continued to dominate the FBI as he had for more than a generation.

Hoover assumed the directorship at a time when the bureau had been demoralized by revelations linking it to the scandals of the Harding administration. Over the next half century, Hoover improved morale and recruited an honest and well-disciplined staff. He transformed the bureau from a small, virtually powerless group with few resources and restricted functions into one of the largest, most powerful, best known, and best-resourced bureaucracies in Washington. After World War II, the FBI became increasingly involved in investigating alleged communist subversion within the United States. Information gathered by FBI agents played an important part in the prosecution of Julius and Ethel Rosenberg and Alger Hiss. By the end of the 1950s, in the popular mind, the suppression of communism had become the FBI's preeminent responsibility.

In the Kennedy years, Hoover, as head of a 13,000-man agency, was a formidable political figure. He was virtually immune from criticism on Capitol Hill and maintained close relations with House Speaker John McCormack and Representative John J. Rooney (chairman of the House appropriations subcommittee responsible for approving Justice Department budgets) to ensure his budget requests were approved. Hoover's position within the FBI was so secure that president-elect Kennedy approved his reappointment before even naming his brother Robert attorney general. Relations between Robert F. Kennedy and Hoover were at first cordial. Hoover for many years had been a friend of Kennedy's father, **Joseph P. Kennedy Sr.** However, as Robert attempted to exert his authority over the FBI—an agency that absorbed more than 40 percent of the Justice Department's budget—his differences with Hoover became evident. Hoover, who had been accustomed to speaking directly with presidents, was now forced to communicate through the attorney general's office. He also resented the rule stipulating that FBI press releases be cleared through the Justice Department Information Office.

Hoover resisted Robert F. Kennedy's efforts to suppress crime syndicates, claiming that no single individual or coalition of racketeers dominated organized crime across the nation. Hoover did eventually agree to establish a special division within the bureau to work exclusively on organized crime investigations. Hoover was also unsympathetic to the **civil rights** movement believing that communists were attempting to infiltrate civil rights organizations such as the **National Association for the Advancement of Colored People**. He opposed the attorney general's efforts to have the Justice Department hire more blacks and other minorities. The FBI refused to promote all but a very few **African Americans** and Puerto Ricans to the prestigious rank of "agent." In the 1960s, the FBI did little to protect civil rights workers in the South even when they were in great danger. Only after the slaying of three civil rights workers in Philadelphia, Mississippi, in summer 1964 did the FBI begin to make its presence felt in civil rights cases. One of the most controversial aspects of FBI investigative work concerned its use of wiretapping of telephones and secret electronic listening devices to record private conversations without congressional approval. In October 1963, the FBI began tapping **Martin Luther King Jr.**'s phone lines; the taps remained in effect until April 1965. Robert F. Kennedy authorized these actions. According to Sanford J. Ungar, a student of the bureau, Hoover personally detested Dr. King, whom he considered a dangerous demagogue and associate of known communists. He used information acquired from the phone taps to attempt to discredit King as a civil rights leader.

The final straw for Robert Kennedy came on 22 November 1963, when, at 1:45 p.m., Hoover called Robert at his home in Virginia; according to William Manchester, who relates the story in his *Death of a President*, the FBI director, without any preamble, declared, "I have news for you, the president has been shot." Following the president's death, the FBI conducted its own investigation of the **assassination of John F. Kennedy** and, in December 1963, concluded that a single gunman, **Lee Harvey Oswald**, acting without accomplices,

had murdered the president. The **Warren Commission** subsequently upheld this finding but criticized the bureau for having failed to inform the Secret Service that the FBI file on Oswald suggested that he may have been a potential assassin. Following the assassination, Robert Kennedy's relations with Hoover deteriorated rapidly. Indeed, the two men never spoke again.

In May 1964, **Lyndon B. Johnson** waived mandatory retirement for Hoover. President Nixon did likewise in 1971. In the Nixon years, administration officials argued that the FBI was not sufficiently aggressive in its campaign against antiwar student organizations, and it consequently encouraged the Central Intelligence Agency to infiltrate and disrupt these groups. Hoover's reputation declined in the years immediately before and after his death due to revelations of widespread illegal activities carried out by the bureau. Hoover died on 2 May 1972.

HOTLINE AGREEMENT (1963). On 20 June 1963, the United States and the **Soviet Union** signed a "Memorandum of Understanding between the United States of America and the Union of Soviet Socialist Republics regarding the Establishment of a Direct Communications Link," which became known as the hotline agreement. It was designed to help speed up communications between the two governments and prevent the possibility of accidental nuclear war. The hotline agreement was the first attempt during the **Cold War** to control the use of nuclear weapons. The pact was prompted by the difficulties the leaders of the two countries incurred when seeking to communicate with each other during the **Cuban missile crisis** of October 1962. The hotline not only provided a direct, open communications link between the superpowers but also acknowledged that nuclear weapons and intercontinental delivery systems required better communications and cooperation to prevent an accidental war. Contrary to public belief, the hotline was not a red telephone that sat in the Oval Office of the White House. The initial system called for two terminal points with teletypes, a full-time duplex telegraph circuit, and a full-time duplex radiotelegraph circuit between Moscow and Washington, DC. It proved its worth early during the Arab-Israeli War in 1967 when President **Lyndon B. Johnson** employed it to eliminate any misunderstanding between the superpowers.

HOWE, IRVING (1920–1993). Irving Howe was born the son of immigrant parents from Eastern Europe on 11 June 1920. He was raised in the slums of the East Bronx. He graduated from the City College of New York in 1940. As a young man growing up during the Great Depression, Leon Trotsky was one of his heroes. Howe was committed to left-wing politics and remained a committed democratic socialist throughout his life.

During the 1940s and 1950s, Howe became known as a leading American literary and social critic. A prolific writer on a broad range of subjects, he was a frequent contributor to *Partisan Review* and other "little magazines." He wrote or coauthored 11 books over a 15-year period and edited 11 more. Among his works were *The U.A.W. and Walter Reuther* (1949), *William Faulkner: A Critical Study* (1952), *Politics and the Novel* (1957), and with Lewis Coser, *The American Communist Party: A Critical History* (1957). Howe pursued an academic career as a professor of English at Brandeis University from 1953 to 1961 and at Stanford University from 1961 to 1963 (two unhappy years). In 1963, he was appointed distinguished professor of English at Hunter College of the City University of New York, where he remained until his retirement in 1986. Among his best-known works was *World of Our Fathers: The Journey of the East European Jews to America and the Life They Found and Made* (1976), a best-selling social history of the immigrant Jewish community in New York.

Howe was a vocal opponent of both Soviet totalitarianism and McCarthyism and questioned standard Marxist doctrine. In 1953, Howe and several other like-minded socialists founded *Dissent*, a journal "devoted to radical ideas and the values of socialism and democracy." During the 1950s, *Dissent* defended the civil liberties of American communists at

the same time it criticized the celebration of American capitalism. Nevertheless, he was happy to see John F. Kennedy elected president. In the 1960s, Howe saw *Dissent* as the organ of an informal and loosely knit group of intellectual members of the "democratic Left." It would be, he hoped, a bastion of defense for left-wing political views, while at the same time, it would resist being subjugated by a Moscow-directed communism. He came into conflict with the New Left, seeing in the radicals of that movement (including **Tom Hayden**) a tendency to violence, irrationalism, and intolerance. The gulf between Howe and the New Left was widened further by the explosive issue of the **Vietnam War**. Critical of Washington's conduct of the war in the mid-1960s, Howe favored a bombing halt and a negotiated peace but supported maintenance of a U.S. military presence in South Vietnam in order to prevent a massacre of anti–National Liberation Front elements.

Howe remained active in both political and literary circles; however, his influence waned, and he confessed to feeling out of place with the newer generation of literary critics. One of his friends, Leon Wieseltier, literary editor of the *New Republic*, said of Howe: "He lived in three worlds, literary, political and Jewish, and he watched them change almost beyond recognition. He saw the end of socialism. He saw literature be mauled by second-rate deconstructionists and third-rate sociologists of race, class and gender. And he saw the world of Yiddish disappear." Irving Howe died in New York's Sinai Hospital, on 5 May 1993, of cardiovascular disease.

HUMPHREY, HUBERT HORATIO (1911–1978). Hubert Horatio Humphrey Jr. was born in Wallace, South Dakota, on 27 May 1911, the son of the owner of the town's drugstore. He attended the University of Minnesota and earned a master's degree from Louisiana State University and worked for the Works Progress Administration, the Minnesota war service program, and the War Manpower Commission. At one point, he helped run his father's pharmacy. In 1943, he became a professor of political science at Macalester College. In the

same year, he unsuccessfully ran for mayor of Minneapolis but was elected two years later, in 1945. In 1947, he cofounded Americans for Democratic Action, a liberal anticommunist group. In 1948, he was elected to the U.S. Senate and successfully advocated for the inclusion of a proposal to end racial segregation in the 1948 Democratic National Convention's party platform. He served until becoming the 38th vice president of the United States from 1965 to 1969. He returned to the Senate from 1971 until 1978.

During the Kennedy administration, Humphrey was selected as assistant majority leader, or Senate majority whip. He was perhaps the most liberal senator in the chamber—a champion of the welfare state, a fierce advocate of domestic social reform, and a staunch anticommunist. He placed his crusading zeal behind passage of the administration's program. In the 1950s, he had eased his way into the Senate "establishment," toning down his fervid ideological approach and working closely with the Democratic leader, Senator **Lyndon B. Johnson**. In foreign affairs, he softened his anticommunism with Wilsonian idealism. He became a leading advocate of disarmament and distribution of surplus food to needy nations.

As majority whip, Humphrey's task was to round up votes for the administration's measures, and Humphrey plunged into the job with characteristic exuberance, becoming a more effective advocate for the Kennedy program, in the eyes of many senators, than the majority leader, Senator **Mike Mansfield**, who was as reserved as Humphrey was extroverted. In the aftermath of the **assassination of John F. Kennedy**, Humphrey helped smooth the transition to the Johnson administration. In his last year as majority whip, he was floor manager of the historic **Civil Rights Act of 1964**, the climax of Humphrey's long advocacy of the cause of equal rights.

Chosen by Johnson as his vice presidential running mate in August 1964 and elected in November, Humphrey was an enthusiastic defender of Johnson's domestic and foreign policies throughout the next four years. His unwavering support for Johnson's **Vietnam** policy cost him the support of many antiwar

Democrats in his 1968 presidential campaign. Humphrey lost the election to Republican **Richard M. Nixon** by a narrow margin. After a short interval, he returned to national politics and remained in the Senate from January 1971 until his death. He died of cancer at home in Waverly, Minnesota, on 13 January 1978.

Humphrey summed up his philosophy and his life's work when he stated in one of his last speeches: "It was once said that the moral test of Government is how that Government treats those who are in the dawn of life, the children; those who are in the twilight of life, the elderly; and those who are in the shadows of life, the sick, the needy and the handicapped."

I

INTERNATIONAL RELATIONS: KENNEDY'S APPROACH. In 1941, the *Time-Life* publisher, Henry Luce, in an article that appeared in the 7 February 1941 issue of *Life*, coined his famous phrase, "The American Century." His intent, at that point during World War II, was to prod his fellow citizens into action. He called upon the United States to "accept wholeheartedly our duty and our opportunity as the most powerful and vital nation in the world . . . to exert upon the world the full impact of our influence, for such purposes as we see fit and by such means as we see fit. . . . It is in this spirit that all of us are called, each to his own measure of capacity, and each in the widest horizon of his vision, to create the first great American Century." As president, John F. Kennedy took this plea to heart and did all he could to use his power to ensure the United States would act righteously to overcome evil in the world.

Kennedy came to office a mere 15 years after the most destructive war ever waged. The ties between the United Kingdom, the **Soviet Union**, China and the United States had fractured soon after the war's end, and the United States—supported by its allies and together with its former enemies, Germany, Italy, and Japan—was locked in a worldwide struggle for economic and political predominance against the Soviet Union and China. Although the United States suffered only 2 percent of Allied deaths in defeating the Third Reich compared to 65 percent of deaths sustained by the Soviet Union, Americans believed they had the right to shape the world in America's image. They saw themselves fighting a "Cold War" against implacable dictatorial foes seeking worldwide domination.

The decade and a half following World War II had witnessed enormous changes on the world international scene. Between 1946 and 1960, more than 35 new countries of the so-called Third World declared independence from their former colonial rulers—18 in 1960 alone. United States policy makers were faced with the prospect of dealing with numerous regimes they regarded as anti-Western and left-wing (if not Marxist) oriented, many of whom were militarist in nature. In addition to nationalizing and confiscating foreign, including U.S., enterprises and properties, many of the nascent revolutionary movements welcomed the support of the Soviet Union. The United States under Kennedy and the Soviet Union led by **Nikita Khrushchev** competed to gain the favor of the growing number of nationalist independence movements around the world. Whatever high hopes for lessening tensions with the Soviet Union and forging closer ties with emerging nations he may have brought to the White House, Kennedy quickly discovered the world was not as he thought.

The field of foreign affairs was the primary area in which Kennedy wished to differentiate himself from his predecessor. During the 1960 presidential campaign, he had repeatedly criticized the Eisenhower administration for failing to take stronger action against the Soviet Union's invasion of Hungary in 1956 and for falling behind the Soviets in missile production (the **missile gap**). Kennedy's inaugural address was a rousing call to action; he

proclaimed that the United States would pay any price and would bear any burden in defense of liberty. John F. Kennedy liked to think that his personal charm was a potent factor in shaping U.S. relations with other countries. He was confident that by personal activism expressed through frequent contact and correspondence with foreign leaders he could do better, and he frequently acted as his own secretary of state. The young new president stood in stark contrast to the retiring president and promised a new style and approach in seeking change at home and abroad. He was impatient with the approach of the **Dwight D. Eisenhower** administration and frustrated by what he regarded as the lack of progress in dealing with America's place in the world. Addressing the Democratic National Convention in Los Angeles on 15 July 1960, Kennedy dismissed Eisenhower's foreign policy as "eight years of drugged and fitful sleep." He had some, but limited, exposure to U.S. foreign relations in the Senate.

Many anticipated Kennedy would move away from the established hard-line anticommunist dogmas of the previous administration and adopt policies reflecting a deeper appreciation of the world's growing complexities. In speaking of foreign policy, Kennedy used the terms *revolution, progress, modernization,* and *development* to describe his policies. He stated that he wanted to rely less on security pacts and ideological dogma and apply a more pragmatic approach to tackling international issues stemming from poverty, oppression, and emerging nationalism in a postwar, postcolonial, and rapidly evolving world. For many listening, Kennedy's inaugural address, delivered before the Capitol on a windy 20 January 1961, carried the promise of a fresh approach to the country's external relations. The new president appealed to the Soviets to join Americans in seeking "to invoke the wonders of science instead of its terrors." "Together," he continued, "let us explore the stars, conquer the deserts, eradicate disease, tap the ocean depths, and encourage the arts and commerce." Kennedy urged nations to renew their quest for peace "before the dark powers of destruction unleashed by science

engulf all humanity in planned or accidental self-destruction."

But Kennedy also revealed the ambivalence that would characterize his approach to foreign affairs: "We dare not," he warned, "tempt them with weakness. For only when our arms are sufficient can we be certain beyond doubt that they will never be employed." He declared that under his leadership the United States would "pay any price, bear any burden, meet any hardship, support any friend, oppose any foe to assure the survival and success of liberty." Throughout his campaign for the presidency, Kennedy had pursued a hard-line, uncompromising crusade against the Soviet Union. In Alexandria, Virginia, on 24 August 1960, he dwelled on the extreme dangers facing the country. For a decade, he warned, the tide had been running out for the United States and the communist enemy. At Salt Lake City, on 23 September he was more specific: "The enemy is the communist system itself—implacable, insatiable, unceasing in its drive for world domination. For this is not a struggle for the supremacy of arms alone—it is also a struggle for supremacy between two conflicting ideologies." Kennedy repeated these fears in his first State of the Union message on 30 January 1961. For him, the United States had entered a period of national peril. Ten days in office, he averred, had taught him "the harsh enormities of the trials through which we must pass in the next four years. Each day the crises multiply. Each day their solution grows more difficult. Each day we draw nearer the hour of maximum danger, as weapons spread and hostile forces grow stronger." Neither the Soviet Union nor communist China, he declared, "has yielded its ambitions for world domination." Shortly thereafter, the president informed the American people: "I am convinced that history will record the fact that this bitter struggle reached its climax in the late nineteen fifties and the early nineteen sixties." For Kennedy, and for many of the nation's elite, the Soviet-American competition dominated international life. In a presumed world of global conflict, military power remained the decisive, essential factor. For the United States, therefore, nuclear

supremacy was essential to assure credibility to any national defense strategy.

As president, Kennedy, as do all presidents, surrounded himself with men who shared his own views. He selected as his closet advisers men who believed as he did that the United States would deal effectively with the communist world only through uncompromising toughness. He thought that the Moscow-Beijing axis, if not monolithic, remained united in essentials and was dangerous to the non-communist world. Only an armed United States could carry the burden for peace and stability everywhere. Accordingly, he selected **Dean Rusk** as secretary of state over Chester Bowles, **Adlai Stevenson II**, and **J. William Fulbright**. Although those three intellectuals had been critical of past decisions, especially those relating to Asia, Kennedy knew he could trust Rusk to carry out his wishes. His choice of **Robert S. McNamara**, former president of the Ford Motor Company and an expert on statistical analysis, as the new secretary of defense added to the sense of toughness in the new administration. In external affairs, no less than in football and politics, Kennedy was out to win. Supported by key White House advisers **McGeorge Bundy** and **Walt W. Rostow**, he welcomed every confrontation with the conviction that he could not lose. The style and external brilliance of the administration did not conceal its intensity, its propensity for action, and its supreme confidence in its capacity to command any crisis.

In background, **education**, outlook, and experience, the men Kennedy surrounded himself with represented the nation's anticommunist Establishment. For journalist David Halberstam, they possessed the Establishment's conviction that they "knew what was right and what was wrong for the country, linked to one another, but not to the country." Later, **John Kenneth Galbraith**, Harvard economist and Kennedy's choice as U.S. ambassador to India, said of them:

We knew that their expertise was nothing, and that it was mostly a product of social background and a certain kind of education, and that they were men who had not travelled around the world and knew nothing of this country and the world. All they knew was the difference between a Communist and an anti-Communist. But that made no difference; they had this mystique and it still worked and those of us who doubted it . . . were like Indians firing occasional arrows into the campsite from the outside.

The president was determined to fulfill his campaign pledge on national defense. His message to Congress on 28 March 1961 asked for a $2.3 billion increase in the defense budget, targeted primarily for new strategic missile systems. "Our defense," he declared, "must be designed to reduce the danger of irrational and unpremeditated general war—the danger of an unnecessary escalation of a small war into a larger one, or of miscalculation or misinterpretation of an incident or enemy initiative."

By the early 1960s, however, the uncertainties created by nationalist movements across Asia and **Africa**, together with Europe's remarkable recovery from World War II, demanded not larger military budgets but, rather, a reassessment of the underlying attitudes leading to the perceived insecurities of a bipolar world. The trends were clear, but despite his claim to be offering a new foreign policy, Kennedy offered little more than aspirations and slogans in place of a coherent body of doctrine or even a well-articulated strategic plan to address the new and rapidly changing realities.

Kennedy's basic philosophy on the way the United States should conduct its foreign policy was a result of his observations and experience before and during World War II. He had witnessed the failure of the Munich Agreement in 1939, which many thought would bring peace instead of war, and, like most of his contemporaries, he internalized the lesson that the agreement represented weakness in foreign policy. For future statesmen, Munich was to become the archetype of failure of will in the face of moral confrontation; strength and firmness were henceforth the essential virtues in the conduct of foreign policy. The lessons of Munich had particular relevance for John F. Kennedy. At the time of the Munich conference, his father

had been President Roosevelt's ambassador to Great Britain, and he had been a 21-year-old university student when the meeting took place. **Joseph P. Kennedy Sr.** had been a long-term supporter of Great Britain's policy of **appeasement** and continued to be so throughout the war. His son had, however, formed his own beliefs with the coming of World War II. He disagreed with appeasement so fervently that his honors thesis at Harvard was titled "Appeasement at Munich." This work was published after his graduation under the title *Why England Slept* (1940), and it argued that appeasement was a weak policy that the United States should avoid at all costs. This "lesson" of the Munich conference has, in this sense, permeated the American political world since World War II. The Munich analogy was increasingly cited by American politicians during the **Cold War**, especially during the **Vietnam War**. As early as 1954, when the French were nearing defeat in **Vietnam**, President Dwight D. Eisenhower used it to persuade British prime minister Winston Churchill to support U.S. air and naval power in Indochina: "If I may refer again to history," the president wrote, "we failed to halt Hirohito, Mussolini and Hitler by not acting in unity and in time. That marked the beginning of many years of stark tragedy and desperate peril. May it not be that our nations have learned something from that lesson?" John F. Kennedy certainly thought and acted upon the same assumptions. He saw America's strong support for an independent Vietnam as crucial to the free world, and during the **Cuban missile crisis**, Kennedy pointedly used the Munich analogy in his speech of 22 October 1962, in which he explained his decision to quarantine **Cuba** to the American public. He reminded the nation that "[t]he 1930s taught us a clear lesson: Aggressive conduct, if allowed to grow unchecked and unchallenged, ultimately leads to war." The transcripts of the Executive Committee of the National Security Council show that the Munich analogy was extensively used in governmental discussions during the crisis. The chairman of the Joint Chiefs of Staff, General Curtis LeMay, even informed Kennedy in one meeting that his preference for a blockade rather than a more aggressive military action was "almost as bad as the appeasement at Munich." In the end, the crisis was resolved by a combination of the deployment of force and negotiations that saw both sides make concessions.

Although many Americans anticipated a more aggressive approach toward the Soviet Union from Kennedy, he proved surprisingly cautious in his decision making. His reliance upon ambassadors and special personal envoys, rather than formal meetings of the National Security Council, reflected his search for innovative solutions. As a result of the debacle of the **Bay of Pigs** invasion of Cuba in April 1961, he increasingly sought alternatives to military intervention. In June 1961, when faced with an ultimatum from Nikita Khrushchev that implied an outbreak of (possibly nuclear) war over Western access to West Berlin, Kennedy rejected State Department proposals that involved any military attempt to reopen access to the city. Similarly, in July through October 1961, against the advice of his senior national security advisers, Kennedy accepted the notion of a neutral government in Laos rather than embark on U.S. or Southeast Asia Treaty Organization military intervention to install a pro-American government to prevent the success of a communist insurgency. Kennedy did, however, make the critical decision for a substantial increase in the advisory presence in South Vietnam, although he refused to declare the independence of South Vietnam a vital interest of the United States.

IRAN. The modern state of Iran, located strategically between the **Soviet Union** and the Persian Gulf, emerged as part of the Arab nationalist uprising that took place against the Ottoman Empire in the first decade of the 20th century. A second revolutionary movement directed against foreign influence (this time, British) occurred in the 1920s, and in 1925, Reza Khan, founder of the Pahlavi dynasty, was placed on the throne of Iran. The country was reoccupied by the British and the Soviet Union during World War II. By 1951, the British, utilizing the power of the Anglo-Iranian Oil Company—an Anglo-American consortium—had established a controlling influence over the

affairs of the country. However, nationalist/ communist elements within the parliament succeeded in nationalizing the oil industry in March 1951 and, in April, named Mohammad Mossadegh as premier.

In August 1953, with U.S. Central Intelligence Agency backing, Mossadegh was deposed and imprisoned. With Western support, the shah (since 1941 Mohammad Raza, the son of Reza Khan) quickly established a repressive regime aimed at maintaining his position and protecting foreign oil interests. Iran joined the Baghdad Pact formed in 1955 aimed at containing Soviet expansion. At this point, Iran was the world's second-largest oil-producing country. Efforts begun in the early 1960s by the shah to modernize Iran, encouraged by the United States and overseen by his secret police, created considerable hostility among the population, especially the unemployed and religious leaders, but U.S. observers took little notice until it was too late to halt the opposition to the shah. *See also* MIDDLE EAST.

ISRAEL/PALESTINE. Following the decision by the United Kingdom to relinquish its 30-year mandate over Palestine, in November 1947 the **United Nations** General Assembly (UNGA) voted to partition the 10,000-square-kilometer territory in which, the assembly proposed, two independent states, one Arab and the other Jewish, would be constituted after a transitional period, with Jerusalem to become an international city. Subsequently, on 14 May 1948, the state of Israel was proclaimed, and the few remaining British troops withdrew from Haifa the following day. The United States and the **Soviet Union** extended recognition to the new state almost immediately following the proclamation, and other nations followed. The Arabs of Palestine refused to recognize the new state, and thousands had been displaced during the conflict that had ensued following the November 1947 UNGA resolution. The area allocated by the United Nations to the Arab state was occupied by Jordanian and Egyptian forces, and Israel and its neighbors remained in a state of war. Over the next two decades, Israel aligned itself strongly with the United States and remains a staunch ally to this day. *See also* MIDDLE EAST.

J

JACKSON, HENRY MARTIN (1912–1983). Henry Martin Jackson, known affectionally as "Scoop Jackson," was born in Everett, Washington, on 31 May 1912, the son of Norwegian immigrants. He graduated with a law degree from the University of Washington in 1935 and, three years later, was elected prosecuting attorney of Snohomish County, Washington. His political career began in 1940, when he was elected to the U.S. House of Representatives at the young age of 28. He quickly established himself as a liberal, voting for social welfare measures, against the creation of the House Un-American Activities Committee, and in support of President **Harry S. Truman**'s veto of the Internal Security Act in 1950. He was a strenuous supporter of the labor movement and **civil rights**—many regarded him as one of the last of the "New Dealers." Despite a Republican landslide in 1952, Jackson was elected to the U.S. Senate. As a senator, he continued to support liberal domestic legislation, but his major interest was foreign policy and military matters. He joined the Senate Armed Services Committee and was strident in his insistence that the U.S. maintain military superiority over the **Soviet Union**. Jackson became intimately acquainted with the inner workings of the Defense and State Departments. Some political observers attributed Jackson's support for large defense expenditures to the presence of major defense industries in his state; the Boeing aircraft company was the state's largest employer. At the 1960 Democratic National Convention, Senator John F. Kennedy passed over Jackson as a possible vice presidential running mate, instead he was asked to run the presidential campaign as chairman of the Democratic National Committee. When he realized that **Robert F. Kennedy** was the real director of the Kennedy election effort, he resigned the chairmanship.

Jackson's commitment to military solutions during the Kennedy administration caused some friction between the president and the Washington senator. Jackson opposed Kennedy's efforts to improve relations with the Soviets and to limit the **arms race**. In 1961, he joined conservatives in a nearly successful effort to prevent the creation of the **Arms Control and Disarmament Agency**. In March 1962, Jackson won widespread publicity as the result of a speech at the National Press Club in which he criticized what he considered to be "the undue influence of UN considerations in our national decision making." He argued that American military power, not the **United Nations**, was the foundation of world peace.

The following year Jackson expressed reservations about the **Limited Nuclear Test Ban Treaty** with the Soviet Union. He ultimately backed the agreement but interpreted it as a loose commitment that could be unilaterally abrogated. Jackson also disagreed with the Pentagon's decision in November 1962 to award General Dynamics—rather than Boeing—the contract to build the swing-wing TFX fighter/bomber plane. During an investigation carried out by the Government Operations subcommittee from February to November 1963, most committee members,

including Jackson, were critical of the Pentagon decision.

In the years following the Kennedy administration, Jackson was a firm supporter of the **Vietnam War**, advocated U.S. support for Israel, and supported the rights of Soviet Jews. He twice unsuccessfully ran—in 1972 and 1976—for the Democratic presidential nomination. While still serving in the Senate, Jackson died of a massive heart attack in Everett, Washington, on 1 September 1983, at the age of 71.

JAVITS, JACOB KOPPEL (1904–1986). Jacob Koppel Javits was born on 18 May 1904, the son of a tenement janitor and Tammany Hall ward heeler on New York City's Lower East Side. He held part-time jobs while studying law at New York University. After he was admitted to the bar in 1927, he and his older brother established a law firm specializing in bankruptcy and corporate reorganization. During World War II, too old for active service, he served in the Chemical Warfare Service in Washington, DC. Rejecting what he saw as the corruption of Tammany Hall politics, he became a supporter of the liberal policies of New York City mayor Fiorello La Guardia and joined the **Republican Party** during the 1930s. In 1945, he was the chief of research for a Republican mayoral candidate in New York City. The following year, he received his party's nomination in an Upper West Side congressional district. Running on a liberal platform, he was the first Republican to carry the district since 1920.

Javits and John F. Kennedy came to the U.S. House of Representatives in the same year. Although on opposite sides, they became good friends and worked together on labor bills and legislation dealing with the provision of public health. Javits generally voted against the Republican majority on major bills. He opposed the successful effort to override President **Harry S. Truman**'s veto of the Taft-Hartley Act in 1947, favored anti–poll tax bills in 1947 and 1949, and voted against appropriations for the House Un-American Activities Committee in 1948. Between 1954 and 1956, Javits served as New York State's attorney general, defeating Democrat Franklin

D. Roosevelt Jr. In 1956, he was elected to the Senate, defeating New York City mayor Robert F. Wagner Jr. by almost 500,000 votes.

In the Senate, Javits continued to function as a Republican maverick, supporting progressive social legislation. Javits consistently won a large share of New York City's vote because of his liberal positions and Jewish religious affiliation, while his party label enabled him to carry easily the traditionally Republican regions upstate. In his 1962 reelection, he accomplished the rare Republican feat of carrying New York City. In the Senate, however, Javits's liberalism and his combative style barred him from entering the ranks of the chamber's Republican leadership. Despite differences over some issues, Javits and Kennedy continued their personal friendship. For example, Javits was more liberal than Kennedy on **civil rights**. In his 1960 book *Discrimination, U.S.A.*, Javits wrote that "racial segregation or discrimination is inconsistent with freedom," and during the early 1960s, he uniformly supported civil rights measures. He praised the civil rights bill proposed by Kennedy in June 1963. Javits offered an amendment in 1961 to expand the number of workers covered by minimum-wage legislation. In 1962, he cosponsored, with Senator **Clinton P. Anderson** (D-N.M.), an administration-backed Social Security Medicare bill. The next year Javits was the only Republican on the Banking and Currency Committee who supported a mass-transit aid bill and was one of six Republicans who voted for the measure on the Senate floor. He was also a strong supporter of Israel.

Although Javits was best known as a supporter of liberal legislation, he contended that the Republican Party should support a mixed economy in which business and government would cooperate to further the national welfare. Accordingly, in 1962, Javits, in opposition to his party's views, supported the Kennedy administration's communications satellite, which provided for private ownership of the satellite system and public controls over the corporation.

In the years following Kennedy's assassination, Javits supported Governor Nelson A. Rockefeller's 1964 presidential bid, and

he refused to endorse the candidacy of conservative Republican senator **Barry M. Goldwater** (R-Ariz.). Initially a supporter of the **Vietnam War**, Javits expressed doubts about its conduct in 1967. In the late 1960s and early 1970s, Javits became a leading advocate of consumer protection legislation. In 1974, he was reelected to a fourth term in the Senate, but due to his declining health, he failed to win the Republican primary in 1980. Javits died in West Palm Beach, Florida, on 7 March 1986 at the age of 81.

JOHN F. KENNEDY CENTER FOR THE PERFORMING ARTS. A national cultural center had been suggested during the Franklin Roosevelt administration, when, in 1933, first lady Eleanor Roosevelt discussed ideas for the Emergency Relief and Civil Works Administration to create employment for unemployed actors during the Great Depression. In 1938, Congress passed a resolution calling for construction of a "public building which shall be known as the National Cultural Center," but nothing came of it until the mid-1950s, when, on 4 September 1958, President **Dwight D. Eisenhower** signed into law the National Cultural Center Act, which provided momentum for the project. This was the first time that the federal government helped finance a structure dedicated to the performing arts.

Because of his desire to bring culture to the nation's capital, President John F. Kennedy provided leadership and support for the project. Edward Durell Stone was selected as architect in June 1959. In 1961, a board of trustees was formed with **Jacqueline Kennedy** as honorary chairman of the center and former first lady Mamie Eisenhower as cochairman. Two months after John F. Kennedy's death, new legislation transformed the center into a memorial for the assassinated president, quickly generating $23 million in funding. The total cost of construction was $70 million. President **Lyndon B. Johnson** dug the ceremonial first shovel of earth signaling the start of construction on 2 December 1964. The opening gala event, with **Rose Kennedy** and **Ted Kennedy** present in the presidential

John F. Kennedy. *Courtesy of Library of Congress.*

box, took place on 8 September 1971 with a performance of Leonard Bernstein's *Mass.*

Its location—out of the way on the banks of the Potomac River—and design—a huge low-rise rectangle—were, as is usual in such matters, controversial, but it is a striking building with excellent acoustics, designed with a double roof to keep out the noise of commercial aircraft taking off and landing at nearby Ronald Reagan airport. *See also* SMITH, JEAN KENNEDY.

JOHN F. KENNEDY'S IRISH HERITAGE. John F. Kennedy was the great-grandson of Irish immigrants and the first and only Irish Catholic American elected as president of the United States.

He was the offspring of two families whose roots can be traced to Ireland. The Fitzgerald family was from western Ireland in the rural County Limerick village of Bruff, and some of the Fitzgeralds migrated to America between 1846 and 1855 because of the devastating potato famine. At about the same time, Patrick Kennedy, a cooper, left his ancestral home in

Dunganstown, County Wexford, and sailed for the United States. The Fitzgeralds and Kennedys lived and worked in Boston, seeking to take advantage of the economic opportunity offered in America. On arrival, they experienced harsh, widespread discrimination against Irish Catholic immigrants. The early Kennedys and Fitzgeralds worked as peddlers, coopers, and common laborers; later they became clerks, tavern owners, and retailers. By the end of the century, Patrick "P. J." Kennedy and John "Honey Fitz" Fitzgerald, the president's maternal grandfather, had become successful Boston politicians, with Honey Fitz serving twice as mayor of Boston and as a member of the U.S. Congress.

John Fitzgerald Kennedy appeared to relish his Irish heritage. His father, **Joseph P. Kennedy Sr.**, while U.S. ambassador to the United Kingdom, had made an important contribution to negotiations prior to the outbreak of World War II, allowing Ireland to stay out of the war, and in July 1938, Irish prime minister Eamon de Valera, as chancellor of the National University, rewarded him with an honorary doctorate. John F. Kennedy first visited Ireland in July 1945 when he went as a young journalist writing articles for the Hearst newspaper chain, partly in order to raise his public profile for a run at Congress the following year. He stopped off in Ireland again in August 1947 to visit his sister **Kathleen Kennedy**, who was staying at Lismore Castle, which her late husband, William Cavendish, the Marquess of Hartington, had been due to inherit before he was killed in the war. His visit was to allow him to track down his relatives in Dunganstown, County Wexford. When he found the farmhouse, so the story goes, he held his hand out and introduced himself as "your cousin John from Massachusetts." As president, Kennedy visited Ireland in June 1963. He was welcomed by the president of Ireland, de Valera, as a "distinguished son of our race." Kennedy remarked to the people of New Ross, Ireland: "When my great-grandfather left here to become a cooper in East Boston, he carried nothing with him except two things: a strong religious faith and a strong desire for liberty. I am glad to say that all of his great-grandchildren have valued that

inheritance." And after receiving the Freedom of the City of Galway on 29 June, Kennedy commented: "If the day was clear enough, and if you went down to the bay and you looked west, and your sight was good enough, you would see Boston, Massachusetts, and if you did, you would see down working on the docks there some Dougherty's and Flaherty's and Ryan's and cousins of yours who have gone to Boston and made good."

On display in the John F. Kennedy Presidential Library and Museum is the Fitzgerald family Bible, brought from Ireland by President Kennedy's forebears. The Bible is an 1850 edition of the Douay English translation, containing a handwritten chronicle of the Fitzgerald family from 1857 and including a record of the birth of John Fitzgerald Kennedy on 29 May 1917. In the museum's Oval Office exhibit is a fragment of a pennant flown on the *Raleigh*, a ship commanded by John Barry, a founder of the U.S. Navy and former commander of the USS *Constitution*. Barry, who served during the Revolutionary War as one of the first captains of the Constitutional Navy, was born in County Wexford. President Kennedy displayed the pennant in the White House Oval Office, and during his visit to Wexford on 27 June 1963, he placed a wreath at the John Barry statue.

JOHNSON, LYNDON BAINES (1908–1973). Lyndon Baines Johnson was born on 27 August 1908, on a farm in Stonewall in the hill country of south-central Texas. He attended local public schools and graduated from Southwest Texas State Teachers College in 1930. Between 1927 and 1930, he taught intermittently in local primary and secondary schools, and in 1931, he became secretary to a Texas congressman. In 1934, he married Claudia Alta Taylor, known as Lady Bird, an accomplished woman who was credited with being a steadying influence on the sometimes mercurial Johnson. In 1935, President Franklin D. Roosevelt appointed Johnson Texas state administrator of the National Youth Administration, a New Deal relief agency for young people. Johnson ran for Congress in 1937 on a strong New Deal platform. After

serving in the U.S. Navy in Australia and the South West Pacific during World War II, he was elected to the U.S. Senate in 1948. Befriended by powerful senator Richard Russell (D-Ga.), a member of the Senate "Establishment," Johnson rose quickly through the Senate hierarchy, attaining the post of Senate minority leader in 1953 and that of majority leader two years later. In 1955, he made a rapid recovery from a massive heart attack.

As majority leader, Johnson established a near-legendary reputation for his command of the legislative process and his assessment of the needs, ambitions, and weaknesses of individual senators. Johnson's political stance moved from conservative to moderate during the 1950s, and he helped gain passage for the Civil Rights Acts of 1957 and 1960, despite considerable southern opposition. On 5 July 1960, Johnson made a late announcement of his candidacy for the Democratic presidential nomination but was defeated by John F. Kennedy, who won the Democratic presidential nomination at the Los Angeles convention on 13 July, with 806 delegates to Johnson's 409. Kennedy then surprised his northern liberal and labor backers by selecting Johnson as his running mate, although Johnson had declared repeatedly that he would not accept the second spot on the ticket. It was Kennedy's belief that he needed Johnson to carry the southern and western votes in the general election. Johnson's nomination was generally considered to be a critical factor in the Kennedy-Johnson ticket's narrow margin of victory over Vice President **Richard M. Nixon** and **Henry Cabot Lodge Jr.** in the November election.

There was a good deal of competition and uneasiness bordering on hostility between Kennedy and his vice president. The ambitious Johnson sought to broaden the powers of the vice presidency so as to exert the control over Senate Democrats that he had exercised as majority leader. However, he was unsuccessful. He then attempted to strengthen his powers within the executive branch by drafting an executive order stipulating that the vice president was to have "general supervision" over certain governmental areas, particularly the National Aeronautics and Space

Administration (NASA). The president declined to sign the order. According to columnists Rowland Evans and Robert Novak, from then on Johnson "did absolutely nothing to advance the Kennedy legislative program."

Kennedy did, however, appoint Johnson as chairman of the National Aeronautics and Space Council, which was organized to formulate **space policy** and mediate disputes between military and civilian leaders. He was instrumental in securing the February 1961 appointment of Texas businessman James E. Webb as director of NASA, and he participated in all major decisions involving the space program during the Kennedy administration. Following Commander Alan Shepard's brief but successful space flight in May 1961 (after the orbit of the earth by Soviet cosmonaut Yuri Gagarin earlier in April), Kennedy joked to Johnson: "You know, Lyndon, nobody knows that the vice-president is the chairman of the Space Council. But if that flight had been a flop, I guarantee you that everybody would have known that you were the chairman." Johnson was not amused. Replying to critics angered over the cost of the "race to the moon" program, Johnson warned in October 1963 that abandonment of the effort would be tantamount to a "conspicuous withdrawal and retreat." In association with his Space Council duties, Johnson was also chairman of a committee to study supersonic transport (SST). The question of financing the SST prototype brought him into direct conflict with U.S. secretary of defense **Robert S. McNamara** and others within the administration who believed that private industry should pay for at least one-third of the project. Johnson wanted a large, if not total, federal underwriting of the costs.

To keep Johnson busy and to utilize his formidable negotiating skills, on 6 March 1961, Kennedy designated him chairman of the newly created President's Committee on Equal Opportunity, established to prevent racial discrimination in employment by businesses having contracts with the federal government. In February 1962, Johnson succeeded in having 31 leading defense contractors agree to eliminate job discrimination,

but in late 1962, Attorney General **Robert F. Kennedy** and Secretary of Labor Willard Wirtz urged Johnson to move faster. Later that year, Wirtz, angered at Johnson's reluctance to act, began to systematically reduce the committee's influence by transferring many of its functions to government agencies that had large defense contracts with private business.

Johnson told his biographer Doris Kearns that the vice presidency "is filled with trips around the world, chauffeurs, men saluting, people clapping, chairmanships of councils, but in the end, it is nothing. I detested every minute of it." During his vice presidency, Johnson visited more than 34 countries on trips likened to domestic campaign swings. Their main function was to spread goodwill rather than to initiate policy. The widely publicized 1961 U.S. visit of a camel driver, whom Johnson had met on an earlier trip to Pakistan, vividly illustrated to many observers Johnson's decline in power and prestige since his days as majority leader. The vice president's most important trip was his May 1961 mission to Southeast Asia where, on 12 May, Johnson addressed the South Vietnamese General Assembly and declared that the United States was ready "immediately" to help expand South Vietnam's armed forces and to "meet the needs of your people on education, rural development, new industry and long-range economic development."

Tension increased between Kennedy and Johnson in 1962 and 1963 because of persistent rumors, denied by the president, that Johnson would be "dropped" from the 1964 national Democratic ticket. The indictment of Bobby Baker, former secretary to the majority leader and Johnson protégé, who was charged with having used his job and political influence for his own personal gain in fall 1963, did not help matters.

On 21 November 1963, President Kennedy and his wife flew to Texas with Johnson and his wife on a pre-campaign swing designed to reconcile rival factions of the Texas Democratic Party. The next day, 22 November, Kennedy was assassinated while riding in a Dallas motorcade. At 2:49 p.m. the same day, Lyndon B. Johnson was sworn in aboard Air Force

One as the 36th president of the United States. In a brief address to the nation that evening at Andrews Air Force Base in Washington, DC, Johnson said, "This is a sad time for all people. We have suffered a loss that cannot be weighed. . . . I will do my best, that is all I can do. I ask for your help and God's."

During the early weeks of his administration, Johnson earned unanimous praise for his success in maintaining national stability. He initiated a series of conferences with congressional leaders, cabinet members, and advisers; reaffirmed U.S. commitments in foreign affairs; asked the cabinet and important Kennedy staffers to remain in service; and pledged on 28 November "to work for a new American greatness." The next month Johnson established the **Warren Commission** to investigate the **assassination of John F. Kennedy**. During the following year, Johnson secured congressional passage for several dormant Kennedy legislative proposals, including the tax-cut bill and the **Civil Rights Act of 1964**. Johnson was elected to a full presidential term in 1964, defeating Republican presidential candidate Senator **Barry M. Goldwater** (R-Ariz.) by an electoral vote margin of 486 to 52.

In January 1969, after the election of Richard M. Nixon as president, Johnson retired to his Texas ranch to work on his memoirs and to oversee the construction of the Johnson Library at the University of Texas. During the next four years, Johnson's health declined. He died of a heart attack on 22 January 1973, in Stonewall, Texas. *See also* AFFIRMATIVE ACTION; ALSOP, JOSEPH WRIGHT, JR.; BERLIN CRISIS OF 1961; CIVIL RIGHTS; HUMPHREY, HUBERT HORATIO; WARREN, EARL.

JOHNSON, URAL ALEXIS (1908–1997). U. Alexis Johnson was born on 17 October 1908 in Falun, Kansas. He joined the State Department in 1935, and for most of his career, he served in the Far East and was highly regarded in Washington as an expert in that area throughout the postwar period. President Kennedy appointed him deputy undersecretary of state for political affairs in April 1961, making him the highest-ranking career foreign service officer in the State Department.

Vice President Lyndon B. Johnson standing among a group of Vietnamese soldiers and Americans during a visit to Saigon, South Vietnam, 1962. *Courtesy of Library of Congress.*

In response to a request for increased United States military aid from South Vietnamese president Ngo Dinh Diem in October 1961, Johnson was one of the officials chosen by Kennedy to make recommendations on the proposal. In a document titled the "Concept of Intervention in Vietnam," he advised an increased U.S. troop commitment, which he believed would lead to the defeat of the Vietcong and render **Vietnam** secure under a noncommunist government. General **Maxwell D. Taylor** and presidential adviser **Walt W. Rostow** also made recommendations. Kennedy decided to defer a major commitment of ground forces and, by April 1962, had opted for a policy known as the strategic hamlet program; this plan sought to relocate much of the rural population into fortified villages, which could be used as defense, political, and educational units by the Saigon government. In January 1962, Johnson had become part of a special (counterinsurgency) group created at the suggestion of General Taylor to integrate the government's effort to support **counterinsurgency** measures in Laos, South Vietnam, and Thailand. This group was concerned mainly with keeping the importance of counterinsurgency before the Defense and State Departments and with training personnel for guerrilla warfare. By spring 1963, Johnson had joined the chorus of self-serving administration optimists and announced that the war was being handled successfully and that the

strategic hamlet program "was the most important reason for guarded optimism."

Johnson also served as a member of the Executive Committee of the National Security Council, the special bipartisan committee formed to advise Kennedy on the crisis following the discovery of Soviet missiles in **Cuba** in October 1962. When the president decided to use a blockade to force the missile withdrawal, Johnson, along with Undersecretary of State **George Ball** and Assistant Secretary of State Edwin Martin, was designated to inform American allies, prepare for the meeting of the Organization of American States called to discuss the issue, and write a legal justification for the action.

During the **Lyndon B. Johnson** administration, the undersecretary continued his involvement in Vietnam both in Washington, DC, and as deputy ambassador in Saigon. In July 1966, he succeeded Edwin Reischauer as ambassador to Japan. President **Richard M. Nixon** appointed Johnson chief of the U.S. delegation to the strategic Arms Limitation Talks in 1973. He again served as ambassador to Japan from 1973 to 1977. Johnson died in Raleigh, North Carolina, on 24 March 1997.

JOHNSTON, OLIN DEWITT (1896–1965). Olin Dewitt Johnston was born on 18 November 1896 in Honea Path, South Carolina, and grew up in rural South Carolina. He served with the U.S. Army in World War I and

then graduated from Wofford College in 1921. Johnston received an MA degree in rural economics from the University of South Carolina in 1923 and a law degree from that university the next year. After a career in local politics, Johnston was elected governor of South Carolina in 1934 and again in 1942. Although a vigorous supporter of most New Deal programs, he also earned a reputation as a militant segregationist.

In 1944, Johnston was elected to the U.S. Senate. Four years later, he became chairman of the Post Office and Civil Service Committee. During the Kennedy administration, Johnston voted with the conservative coalition on more than 60 percent of all major issues, according to *Congressional Quarterly*. However, Johnston remained a strong advocate of his state's textile mill workers. In 1962, Johnston cosponsored a constitutional amendment to nullify the **Supreme Court**'s decision banning prayer in public schools. In 1963, Johnston supported ratification of the **Limited Nuclear Test Ban Treaty**. He declared that rejection of the treaty would be "telling the world it must look forward only to an endless dark age of Cold War and ever-threatening nuclear attack." Johnston maintained a militant stance against **civil rights** legislation and joined with other Southern Democrats in 1963 to prevent the Kennedy administration's civil rights bill from reaching the Senate floor. He voted against the **Civil Rights Act of 1964**. True to his working-class origins, later the same year he supported the Social Security and Medicare bills. Johnston died of cancer on 18 April 1965 in Columbia, South Carolina.

JORDAN. The Hashemite Kingdom of Jordan occupies the area east of the river Jordan that made up the former British mandate of Palestine. It is bounded on the north by **Syria**, in the northeast by Iraq, in the south by **Saudi Arabia**, and in the west by Israel. It became independent in 1946, and the amir, Abdullah, assumed the title of king. In 1948, Jordan occupied and, in 1950, formally annexed western Palestine (including East Jerusalem) now known as the West Bank. In July 1951, King Abdullah was assassinated by a Palestinian while visiting the al-Aqsa Mosque in Jerusalem, and after a short interim, Abdullah's grandson, Hussein, was crowned king in 1953. When Kennedy assumed office, Jordan's population, which included almost 500,000 Palestinian refugees in the West Bank, was under two million. Under Hussein, the kingdom remained a close ally of Great Britain, and relations between Jordan and its Arab neighbors were fractious. *See also* MIDDLE EAST.

JORDAN, BENJAMIN EVERETT (1896–1974). Benjamin Everett Jordan was born in Ramseur, North Carolina, on 8 September 1896, the son of a Methodist minister. From humble beginnings, he worked his way up in the textile industry to become a wealthy North Carolina textile manufacturer. He began to participate in Democratic state politics as a fund-raiser in the mid-1930s. From 1949 to 1954, he served as chairman of the Democratic State Executive Committee. Originally associated with the party's liberal wing, he moved into its conservative faction during the early 1950s. In April 1958, Governor **Luther Hodges** appointed Jordan to fill a U.S. Senate vacancy created by the death of W. Kerr Scott. The following November Jordan was elected to complete the final two years of Kerr's term. During the early 1960s, Jordan compiled a conservative voting record on Capitol Hill, although he supported the John F. Kennedy administration's federal school aid bill in 1961 and, the following year, voted for a constitutional amendment banning the use of the poll tax in federal elections. According to *Congressional Quarterly*, Jordan supported the Senate's conservative coalition in 95 percent, 91 percent, and 86 percent of roll-call votes in 1961, 1962, and 1963, respectively.

In 1963, Jordan succeeded Senate majority leader **Mike Mansfield** (D-Mont.) as chairman of the Senate Rules and Administration Committee. During the last days of the Kennedy presidency, the committee began an investigation of the activities of Bobby Baker, secretary to the Senate majority, who had been accused in a civil suit of using his influence to obtain government contracts. The committee completed its investigation in 1965. The majority

report, signed by Jordan, asserted that Baker had been guilty of "gross improprieties." It cleared Baker of some of the charges against him, however, and did not implicate President **Lyndon B. Johnson**, who, as Senate majority leader until his assumption of the vice presidency in 1961, had worked closely with Baker. The committee's three Republicans charged that the majority report was a whitewash. In 1972, Representative Nick Galifianakis (D-N.C.), who had a more liberal voting record than Jordan, defeated the incumbent in the Democratic senatorial primary. On 29 May 1972, Jordan escaped injury during a shooting incident while campaigning at a Raleigh, North Carolina, shopping center. He died in Saxapahaw, North Carolina, on 15 March 1974.

K

KAYSEN, CARL (1920–2010). Carl Kaysen was born on 5 March 1920, in Philadelphia, Pennsylvania. Following his graduation from the University of Pennsylvania in 1940, he worked for the National Bureau of Economic Research before becoming an economist in the Office of Strategic Services in 1942. After World War II, Kaysen received both his MS in 1947 and PhD in 1954 from Harvard University and then joined Harvard's faculty. A specialist in U.S. antitrust policy, he rose to the rank of professor of economics in 1957.

John F. Kennedy appointed Kaysen a White House assistant in November 1961. He was little known to the public, but journalist Joseph Kraft regarded Kaysen as "one of the really influential figures inside the administration." Kraft attributed his effectiveness to the fact that he was not a "celebrity" and, therefore, could maintain good relations with both the White House and the State Department bureaucracy. Kaysen served as deputy special assistant for national security affairs from 1961 until June 1963 working directly under national security adviser **McGeorge Bundy**. A staff memo prepared for Bundy described "the limits of Kaysen's empire, like that of Darius, were undefined and expanding." During the **Berlin crisis** of summer 1961, when the **Soviet Union** threatened to cut off access to the city and make Berlin a "free city" ostensibly independent of Eastern or Western control, Kaysen was one of Kennedy's advisers who rejected Dean Acheson's analysis of the situation. Believing that negotiations would be a sign of weakness, Acheson urged Kennedy to build up U.S. conventional and nuclear forces in preparation for an armed confrontation with the Soviet Union. Instead, Kaysen recommended negotiations supplemented by a military buildup. President Kennedy accepted Kaysen's proposals in July 1961.

As an economist, Kaysen helped reorganize American foreign trade policy to stem the growing U.S. deficit in its international balance of payments in 1961–1962. This development culminated in the **Trade Expansion Act** of 1962, which cut tariffs from 50 to 100 percent on many foreign goods and gave the president wide discretionary powers to retaliate against foreign import restrictions. Kaysen also pressed for a nuclear test ban treaty during the Kennedy administration. Working from the White House, he helped coordinate the efforts of various government agencies and lobbying groups in support of a total test ban agreement. When the Russians rejected this proposal in spring 1962, Kaysen was one of the advisers who recommended that the United States offer the Soviet Union a partial ban outlawing tests in the atmosphere, in the sea, and in outer space. Kaysen accompanied Ambassador **W. Averell Harriman** on the Moscow mission that resulted in the signing of a partial test ban agreement in August 1963. During the ratification hearings on the treaty, he coordinated the administration's effort at the behest of U.S. secretary of defense **Robert S. McNamara**. The treaty was approved by the Senate in September 1963. In 1964, he served as chairman of President **Lyndon B. Johnson**'s Task Force on Foreign Economic Policy.

Kaysen returned to Harvard in 1964. In 1966, he became director of the Institute for Advanced Studies at Princeton University, serving in that role for 10 years before accepting a post at MIT from 1976 until 1987 when he retired. He died on 8 February 2010, aged 89, at his home in Cambridge, Massachusetts.

KENNAN, GEORGE FROST (1904–2005). George Frost Kennan was born in Milwaukee, Wisconsin, on 16 February 1904, and after gaining a BA degree in history at Princeton University in 1925, he entered the newly formed U.S. Foreign Service in 1926. He became fluent in a number of European languages, including Russian, while serving in Eastern and Central European posts, and he was appointed to two tours of duty in Moscow (1933–1935; 1944–1946), becoming recognized as an expert on Soviet-American relations.

Kennan saw himself as a realist rather than an idealist in formulating his foreign policy views. Following World War II, he expressed an idea for a policy to resist what he saw as Soviet expansionism that was to become known as "containment." Encouraged by then secretary of the navy James Forrestal, Kennan published his views in an article titled "The Sources of Soviet Conduct" under the name "X" in the Washington journal *Foreign Affairs* in July 1947, and soon thereafter, he was appointed director of the State Department's policy planning staff and, subsequently, counselor to the department. While director of policy planning, Kennan played an important role in drafting the Marshall Plan for Europe. Because of a public disagreement with John Foster Dulles, president-elect **Dwight D. Eisenhower**'s designated secretary of state, in 1952 Kennan retired from the foreign service and took a position at the Institute for Advanced Studies at Princeton University. Given what he saw as a widespread misunderstanding and (mainly military) misapplication of his concept of containment by subsequent policy makers and commentators, Kennan spent a good deal of his time after leaving government service explaining that he did not regard the **Soviet Union** as presenting a military threat to the United States at the time of his writing the "X" article.

Senator John F. Kennedy was impressed by Kennan's advocacy, in 1957, for the unification of a disarmed and neutralized Germany, and soon after his inauguration, Kennedy offered him the ambassadorship to either Yugoslavia or Poland. Kennan accepted the Belgrade post and was officially designated ambassador on 8 February 1961. Before departing for Belgrade, Kennan took part in discussions with the administration to reassess U.S. policy toward the Soviet Union that led to an invitation to Soviet premier **Nikita Khrushchev** for a face-to-face meeting with the president. That meeting, held in Vienna on 3–4 June 1961, was not a success from Kennedy's point of view as the older, more experienced Soviet leader intimidated the new, young president, and tensions increased between the two countries.

Kennan arrived in Belgrade in early May 1961, at a time when U.S.-Yugoslav relations were deteriorating. In April 1961, President Josip Tito had vehemently denounced the **Bay of Pigs** invasion, and then in September, he adopted a pro-Soviet position in relation to the Soviet resumption of atmospheric nuclear testing. The administration responded by delaying the sale of surplus wheat requested by Yugoslavia under the Food for Peace program until April 1962. Kennan's first months in Belgrade were further complicated by congressional opposition to the delivery of the final components for 130 obsolescent U.S. F-86D jet fighters purchased during the Eisenhower administration. In October 1962, a number of senators objected to the transfer, and although he received an oral assurance from Kennedy that the delivery would go ahead, Kennan reported in his memoirs that the components still had not arrived when he resigned in 1963.

Congressional attempts to manage U.S.-Yugoslav relations continued to frustrate Kennan during 1962. Several legislators, led by Senator William Proxmire (D-Wis.), wanted to prohibit all aid to Yugoslavia and to cancel Yugoslavia's most-favored-nation status, despite the advice of Kennan that such vindictive measures would severely damage Yugoslavia's economy, jeopardize repayment of its debts to

the United States, and force Yugoslavia to seek closer ties to the Soviet Union. When, in late September, Kennedy refused Kennan's pleas to intervene to prevent the congressional revocation of Yugoslavia's most-favored-nation status, the diplomat decided to resign. Kennan's resignation was announced on 17 May 1963. He returned to the United States in July to resume his academic career at Princeton. Kennan continued to comment on U.S. foreign policy until his death at the age of 101, in 2005. *See also* COLD WAR; KHRUSHCHEV, NIKITA SERGEYEVICH.

KENNEDY, CAROLINE BOUVIER (1957–). Caroline Bouvier Kennedy was born on 27 November 1957 in New York City to **Jacqueline Bouvier Kennedy** and John F. Kennedy. Caroline spent her early years living in the White House. She became a writer, editor, and lawyer, and in 2013, she was appointed by President Barack Obama as U.S. ambassador to Japan.

She is the only surviving child of John and Jackie Kennedy.

With two young children, Caroline and her younger brother John Jr., President Kennedy and Jacqueline were thrust into the spotlight as the ideal American family. Caroline was a frequent media darling; people could not get enough of the little girl who walked her father to the Oval Office each morning and rode her pony on the White House lawn.

Caroline was not yet six years old when her father was assassinated by sniper fire on 22 November 1963. Four months previously, on 7 August 1963, her youngest brother, Patrick, was born prematurely; he died two days later from lung failure. During her youth, Caroline grew extremely close to her younger brother. Together, they endured a series of family tragedies, later dubbed "the Kennedy curse." Among them was the assassination of their uncle, U.S. senator **Robert F. Kennedy**, in June 1968, and a year later the death of

Robert and Caroline Kennedy on the beach in Hyannis, 1964. *Courtesy of Library of Congress.*

a former campaign worker during a car accident involving another uncle, U.S. senator **Edward "Ted" Kennedy**. Ted survived, but the incident became a national scandal. Following the death of Robert Kennedy, in October 1968 Caroline's mother married her long-time friend, Greek shipping magnate Aristotle Onassis, who could provide Caroline and John Jr. with security and privacy. Jackie tried hard to shield her children from the public eye. In the ensuing years, they remained close to Ted.

Caroline and her brother became conscientious students. Caroline performed well in a New York private school and went on to attend Radcliffe College (now part of Harvard), where she gained a BA degree in 1979. In addition to her studies, she interned for the *New York Daily News* and worked in the summers as a political intern for her uncle Ted. Caroline then worked at the Metropolitan Museum of Art, where she met her future husband, an interactive-media designer named Edwin Schlossberg. They were married on 19 July 1986. They have three children.

In 1988, she earned a juris doctor from Columbia Law School, graduating in the top 10 percent of her class. She has served on the boards of numerous not-for-profit organizations and was active in the campaigns to elect President Barack Obama in 2008 and 2012. She is also president of the John F. Kennedy Library Foundation, a nonprofit organization dedicated to providing financial support, staffing, and creative resources for the John F. Kennedy Presidential Library and Museum.

On 16 July 1999, Caroline endured another family tragedy when John Jr. died when the airplane he was flying crashed into the Atlantic Ocean off the coast of Martha's Vineyard, Massachusetts. John Jr.'s wife, **Carolyn Bessette Kennedy**, and sister-in-law, Lauren Bessette, were also on board and died.

Caroline Kennedy resigned as the U.S. ambassador to Japan shortly before Donald Trump was sworn in as the 45th president of the United States. She formally left Japan as ambassador on 18 January 2017. In August 2017, she was elected to serve on the board of the Boeing company.

KENNEDY, CAROLYN BESSETTE (1966–1999). Carolyn Bessette was born on 7 January 1966, in White Plains, New York. She was the youngest child of William J. Bessette, a cabinet maker, and Ann Messina, an academic administrator in the New York City public school system. She had two older sisters, twins Lauren and Lisa.

Carolyn moved to a wealthy corner of Connecticut just outside New York City with her mother and sisters at age eight, when her parents divorced. Her mother remarried, to a prominent doctor. After attending Catholic high school, Bessette earned an undergraduate degree in **education** at Boston University. Six feet tall with long, blonde hair, she was regarded as a beauty, and she featured as the cover girl for the "Girls of BU" 1988 calendar.

Upon graduation she worked for the Calvin Klein company in New York. She first met and spoke with John F. Kennedy Jr. when both were running in Central Park, and, so the story goes, she impressed him with her beauty, intelligence, and sincerity. They married in 1996 in a 100-year-old, flower-strewn chapel on a secluded island off the Georgia coast. After her marriage to "John-John," as her husband was often affectionately called, Bessette became the focus of much media attention as a trendsetter.

Bessette and Kennedy, along with her sister Lauren, were killed when their small private plane, piloted by Kennedy, crashed off the coast of Martha's Vineyard on 16 July 1999.

Nearly two years later, Carolyn and Lauren Bessette's parents received a monetary settlement as a result of their wrongful death lawsuit against the Kennedy estate. *See also* KENNEDY, JACQUELINE LEE BOUVIER.

KENNEDY, EDWARD MOORE "TED" (1932–2009). Edward Moore Kennedy was born in Boston on 22 February 1932, the third of the Kennedy brothers and the last of the nine children of **Joseph P. Kennedy Sr.** and **Rose Fitzgerald Kennedy**. As the youngest child (and male), he was spoiled by the family, and his youth consisted of years of privilege and entitlement mixed with tragedy. By the time he was 16, he had experienced the trauma of

the death of two of his siblings—**Joseph Patrick Kennedy Jr.** in World War II and **Kathleen Kennedy** in an airplane crash—and the institutionalization of another, **Rose Marie Kennedy**. In 1951, he entered Harvard, but during his freshman year, he was suspended for cheating on a Spanish exam and subsequently served two years in the U.S. Army before returning to Harvard. He graduated in 1956 at age 24 after a mediocre performance He did little better at the Virginia University Law School, where he gained a hard-earned degree in 1959. In November 1958, he married Joan Bennett. They had three children: Kara (1960–2011), Ted Jr. (1961–), and Patrick (1967–), but by the 1970s, the marriage was in trouble due to Ted's infidelity and Joan's growing alcoholism.

During 1958, Ted had managed his brother John's Senate reelection campaign and, in 1960, also managed Jack's campaign for the presidency in the western states, with mixed results. After Jack's election, in 1962 Ted, who by that time had reached the minimum age of 30 required for Senate election, won the Senate seat for Massachusetts vacated by his older brother, a seat he held for almost 47 years until his death in 2009. Kennedy defeated the equally inexperienced George Cabot Lodge, son of **Henry Cabot Lodge Jr.**, winning with 57 percent of the vote. At the time of his death, Ted Kennedy had become the second most senior member of the Senate and the fourth-longest-serving senator in history.

Like his brothers, Ted Kennedy was a staunch anticommunist, but in the course of his Senate career, he became far more progressive and liberal than they had ever been. He was an eloquent orator and a highly skilled parliamentary negotiator, especially when successfully shepherding legislation through the Senate that required bipartisan support. Kennedy and his staff wrote more than 300 bills that were enacted into law. In the course of his long years in the Senate, he worked with several presidents. He supported the **Vietnam War** at first but then urged withdrawal. Ted championed an interventionist government that emphasized economic and social justice. Among the laws he was instrumental in passing were the Immigration and Nationality Act of 1965, the National Cancer Act of 1971, the COBRA health insurance provision, the Comprehensive Anti-Apartheid Act of 1986, the Americans with Disabilities Act of 1990, the Ryan White AIDS Care Act, the Civil Rights Act of 1991, and the Mental Health Parity Act. He was passionate in advocating a National Health Care Act.

Kennedy's grief at the assassination of his brothers made him very wary of seeking the presidency. In addition, despite his popularity with Massachusetts voters, his career was dogged by scandal—mostly to do with women and his growing dependency upon alcohol. In particular, the controversy surrounding his negligence in contributing to the death by drowning of Mary Jo Kopechne on Chappaquiddick Island, off Martha's Vineyard, Massachusetts, on 18 July 1969 was an ever-present obstacle to whatever presidential aspirations he may have nurtured.

During the 1970s, Kennedy developed a wide-ranging interest in U.S. foreign affairs, including nuclear disarmament, and among the many countries he visited, he stopped over in Hiroshima in January 1978. The same year, he became chairman of the Senate Judiciary Committee with a staff of around 100. He entered the **Democratic Party** primaries in the 1980 presidential campaign but withdrew at the party convention in New York in August when it was clear he would lose the nomination to the incumbent president, Jimmy Carter. He supported the first war against Iraq and invasion of Afghanistan but opposed the invasion of Iraq in 2003.

Kennedy endorsed Barack Obama as the Democratic Party candidate in January 2008, and his endorsement helped Obama secure the nomination and eventually win the election. In May 2008, he suffered a seizure and was diagnosed with brain cancer; 15 months later on 25 August 2009, at the age of 77, he died at his home in Hyannis Port, Massachusetts. His funeral was well attended.

There is no better summary of the life of Ted Kennedy than that offered by the *New York Times* in its obituary: "He was a Rabelaisian figure in the Senate and in life, instantly recognizable by his shock of white hair,

his florid, oversize face, his booming Boston brogue, his powerful but pained stride. He was a celebrity, sometimes a self-parody, a hearty friend, an implacable foe, a man of large faith and large flaws, a melancholy character who persevered, drank deeply and sang loudly. He was a Kennedy." *See also* CHAPPAQUIDDICK INCIDENT; KENNEDY, CAROLINE BOUVIER; KENNEDY, ROBERT FRANCIS; LAWFORD, PATRICIA KENNEDY; NIXON, RICHARD MIL-HOUS; SIRHAN, SIRHAN B.

KENNEDY, ETHEL SKAKEL (1928–). Ethel Skakel was born 11 April 1928, in Chicago, the sixth of seven children of George and Anne Skakel. Her father, a Protestant of Dutch descent, was a very wealthy businessman who made his fortune in the field of chemical engineering; her mother came from a poor Chicago South Side Irish Catholic family.

Ethel shared her mother's devotion to Catholicism. She was an average student but excelled at sports. She attended Manhattan-ville College of the Sacred Heart, where she became friends with a classmate, **Jean Kennedy**, the second-youngest child of **Joseph P. Kennedy Sr.** and **Rose Fitzgerald Kennedy**. Ethel Skakel met **Robert Kennedy** on a ski weekend with Jean. The following year, 1946, Ethel campaigned for John F. Kennedy in his run for Congress. She became Ethel Kennedy when she married Robert in June 1950. After Robert graduated from law school in Charlottesville, Virginia, the young couple moved to Washington, DC.

In 1956, the Kennedys purchased the large 13-bedroom house "Hickory Hill," a six-acre property in McLean, Virginia, from Bobby's brother John and his wife, **Jacqueline Kennedy**. At that time, Ethel was pregnant with their fifth child, Courtney. Ethel and Robert

Bobby and Ethel Kennedy at the White House with Lyndon B. Johnson. *Courtesy of Library of Congress.*

attracted many notable Washingtonians and other international celebrities to parties they hosted at Hickory Hill. At John's request, in 1962 Ethel and Robert embarked upon a 28-day, 14-country goodwill tour as stand-ins for the president and first lady.

Ethel urged Robert to enter the **Democratic Party** primaries for the 1968 presidential election. Devastated by Robert's assassination in Los Angeles on 6 June, she publicly stated that she would never marry again. She was pregnant with her 11th child when he was killed, and she gave birth to their daughter Rory on 12 December 1968.

In the same year, Ethel founded the not-for-profit Robert F. Kennedy Center for Justice and Human Rights, dedicated to advancing human rights through litigation, advocacy, and **education**. She continued to live at the family home, Hickory Hill, until December 2009, when it was sold, and she continued to work actively in Democratic Party politics through the Obama years.

KENNEDY, EUNICE (1921–2009). *See* SHRIVER, EUNICE KENNEDY.

KENNEDY, JACQUELINE LEE BOUVIER (1929–1994). Jacqueline Lee Bouvier was born on 28 July 1929, in Southampton, New York. Her father, John "Black Jack" Vernou Bouvier III, was an affluent Wall Street stockbroker who claimed French aristocratic ancestry. Her mother, Janet Lee Bouvier, was of Irish and English parentage. Jackie spent her early childhood in New York City and Long Island. Following her mother's divorce in 1940 and remarriage in 1942 to Hugh D. Auchincloss II, Jacqueline lived with her new family in McLean, Virginia, and Newport, Rhode Island. She was born and raised a Catholic, and, like her mother, she became an accomplished equestrian.

As the wife of John F. Kennedy, Jacqueline Lee Bouvier (known throughout the world as "Jackie") played an important role as first lady during her husband's presidency. Immediately upon entering the White House, she set about the building's restoration and added significant

works to its collection of art and historical furnishings. She sought to make the White House "the most perfect house in the United States." She also became a strong supporter of the arts nationwide, and an advocate for the historic preservation movement. Jackie also set the standard for style and grace during her husband's presidency, becoming a global fashion icon. She transfixed all who met her with her charm and beauty.

Jackie attended Miss Porter's School for Girls in Connecticut and Vassar College, where she excelled in history, literature, art, and French. In 1949, during her junior year, she studied at the Sorbonne in Paris, and upon returning to the United States, she completed a degree in French literature at George Washington University. She was a talented writer, and while still at George Washington, she won a writing contest sponsored by *Vogue* called the "Prix de Paris," with an essay on "People I Wish I Had Known," beating out 1,279 other contestants. Her subjects were Oscar Wilde, Charles Baudelaire, and Sergei Diaghilev. However, she did not accept the prize of six months working in the *Vogue* Paris office, and instead, in 1952 she went to work as the "Inquiring Camera Girl" for the *Washington Times-Herald*.

During this time, Jackie met the young congressman from Massachusetts, John F. Kennedy, soon to be elected to the U.S. Senate. Encouraged by **Joseph P. Kennedy Sr.** and Jack Bouvier, the two married on 12 September 1953, at St. Mary's Church in Newport. A huge crowd of onlookers waited outside the church for a glimpse of the good-looking young newlyweds. Afterward, 1,200 guests attended the wedding reception at Hammersmith Farm, the nearby Auchincloss estate. Following their wedding, the Kennedys lived in Georgetown, Washington, DC.

In November 1957, the Kennedy's first child, **Caroline Bouvier Kennedy**, was born, and in January 1960, Senator John F. Kennedy announced his candidacy for the presidency of the United States, launching 11 months of cross-country campaigning. A few weeks into the campaign, Jacqueline became

pregnant, and her doctors instructed her to remain at home. There she answered campaign mail, taped TV commercials, gave interviews, and wrote "Campaign Wife," a syndicated column carried across the nation. Shortly after Kennedy's election victory, Jackie's second child, John Fitzgerald Kennedy Jr., was born, and at the age of 31, Jackie became the third-youngest first lady in U.S. history. A third child, Patrick Bouvier Kennedy, lived only 39 hours and died less than four months before President Kennedy's assassination in 1963.

Jackie set out to make the White House a museum that reflected the artistic history of the United States. Her passion for history guided and informed her work as she shared her knowledge and excitement about the past with all Americans, especially with children. Within a month of becoming first lady, she established a White House Fine Arts Committee made up of experts in historic preservation and decorative arts. Items that had been owned by previous presidents and had been part of the White House collection, especially those that had belonged to presidents George Washington, Abraham Lincoln, and James Madison, were located and returned to the White House. She found stored in the White House a desk made from the timbers of the British sailing ship HMS *Resolute*, presented by Queen Victoria in 1878 to President Rutherford B. Hayes, and had it moved into the Oval Office, where it remains today.

Jacqueline Kennedy also redesigned the President's Rose Garden and helped preserve the historical character of Lafayette Square across the street from the White House when it was scheduled for demolition. She was also instrumental in the restoration of Pennsylvania Avenue, the main thoroughfare connecting the White House to Capitol Hill, and supported creation of a national cultural complex, which eventually became the **John F. Kennedy Center for the Performing Arts** in Washington, DC.

Together with her husband, Jackie celebrated American arts and letters and encouraged Americans to take pride in their artistic, as well as their political, heritage. The two transformed the White House into a showcase for cultural and intellectual achievement. Authors, scientists, artists, musicians, and actors mingled with politicians, diplomats, and statesmen. In the East Room, she had a portable stage built for memorable musical and dramatic performances, including a series of concerts for young people.

On 14 February 1962, Jackie conducted a televised tour of the Executive Mansion for CBS Television. A record audience of 56 million viewers tuned in to watch the first lady as she proudly guided them through the newly restored building. The tour was so well received that the Academy of Television Arts and Sciences awarded Jackie an honorary Emmy Award for her achievement.

Jacqueline Kennedy's interest in the cultures of other countries and her fluency in languages made her a popular ambassador around the world. She accompanied her husband on trips to France, Austria, the United Kingdom, Venezuela, Mexico, Costa Rica, and Colombia, and she also traveled as first lady to Italy, Pakistan, and India. After an extraordinarily warm welcome afforded to the French-speaking Jackie during her visit to Paris in May 1961, President Kennedy remarked, "I do not think it altogether inappropriate to introduce myself. . . . I am the man who accompanied Jacqueline Kennedy to Paris, and I have enjoyed it."

On 22 November 1963, John F. Kennedy was assassinated in Dallas, and Jacqueline Kennedy became a widow at age 34. She planned the president's state funeral, which was watched by millions around the world who shared her grief and marveled at her courage and dignity. As the *New York Times* noted in its obituary of her, the images of Jackie Kennedy that remain with most were those of her in Dallas on 22 November 1963: her lunge across the open limousine after the assassin's bullets struck; the Schiaparelli pink suit stained with her husband's blood; her gaunt, stunned face in the blur of the speeding motorcade; and the anguish later at Parkland Memorial Hospital as the doctors gave way to the priest. And at Jack's funeral, the world saw and admired a self-controlled, black-veiled widow who, with her head up, walked beside the coffin and the riderless horse she stipulated

Jacqueline Bouvier Kennedy and John F. Kennedy, in wedding attire, with members of the wedding party, Newport, Rhode Island, 12 September 1953. *Courtesy of Library of Congress.*

take part in the procession; who reminded three-year-old John Jr. to salute at the service; and who looked with solemn dignity upon the proceedings.

Soon after President Kennedy's death, Jackie began the planning to build the John F. Kennedy Presidential Library and Museum, which would commemorate her husband's life. She chose then-unknown Chinese American architect I. M. Pei to design the library and

decided upon a striking location overlooking Boston Harbor. She also worked to create and perpetuate the notion that the Kennedy presidency would be remembered as a modern-day "**Camelot**."

In 1968, Jacqueline Kennedy married Greek shipping magnate Aristotle Onassis on Skorpios, his private island. Following his death in 1975, she embarked on a successful career in publishing.

Hammersmith Farm, Newport, Rhode Island. *Courtesy of Library of Congress.*

On 19 May 1994, Jacqueline Bouvier Kennedy Onassis died of a form of cancer of the lymphatic system at her apartment in New York City. She was 64 years old. She was laid to rest beside President Kennedy in Arlington National Cemetery outside Washington, DC. *See also* ASSASSINATION OF JOHN F. KENNEDY; KENNEDY, CAROLYN BESSETTE; NEW FRONTIER; PRESIDENTIAL ELECTION OF 1960.

KENNEDY, JEAN (1928–). *See* SMITH, JEAN KENNEDY.

KENNEDY, JOHN F., JR. (1960–1998). John Fitzgerald Kennedy Jr. was the second child of John and Jacqueline Kennedy. He was born at Georgetown University Hospital on Thanksgiving Day, 25 November 1960, just two weeks after his father had been elected president. John Jr. had an older sister, Caroline, and a younger brother, Patrick, who died two days after his premature birth in 1963. A daughter, Arabella, had been stillborn four years before his birth. While a child living in the White House, he became known outside the family as "John-John."

Not surprisingly, Jacqueline Kennedy worried about her children's safety, especially after Robert F. Kennedy, their uncle, was assassinated in 1968. She is reported to have remarked at the time: "If they're killing Kennedys, then my children are targets. I want to get out of this country." When John Jr. was eight years old, in October 1968, she married Greek shipping magnate Aristotle Socrates

Onassis, a man 29 years her senior, in part because of his ability to provide the family security. The family moved to an apartment on the Upper East Side in New York.

Kennedy attended private Catholic schools in Manhattan before completing high school at Phillips Academy, Andover, Massachusetts. During his late teenage years, John Jr. worked on projects to alleviate inequality both within the United States and in South Africa and India and accompanied his mother on a visit to Africa. In 1976, Kennedy visited an earthquake disaster zone at Rabinal in Guatemala, helping with heavy building work and distributing food. In 1983 he graduated with a BA in American studies from Brown University. Upon graduation, from 1984 to 1986, he worked for the New York City Office of Business Development, conducting negotiations with developers and city agencies. Kennedy also served on the boards of several family foundations and a number of non-profit organizations. From 1989 he headed Reaching Up, a non-profit group that provided educational and other opportunities for workers who helped people with disabilities.

Kennedy graduated in law from New York University in 1989, and after passing the New York Bar exam on his third attempt in 1990, worked as a prosecutor in the office of the Manhattan District Attorney, Robert M. Morgenthau. "I'm clearly not a major legal genius," he said after the New York tabloids labelled him the "Hunk Who Flunked." However, the law bored him, and after four years he left the district attorney's office.

At 34, he struck out on his own in 1995 and started a glossy, politics-as-lifestyle and fashion monthly magazine, *George*, in a joint venture with Hachette-Filipacchi, a media conglomerate. He seemed to enjoy being provocative, posing semi-nude in *George* and inviting *Hustler* publisher Larry Flynt to be his magazine's guest at the annual White House correspondents' dinner in 1999. Despite publishing some adventurous and controversial articles, the magazine did not do well and eventually folded in 2001.

On 21 September 1996, he married a fashion publicist, Carolyn Bessette, on a barrier island off the coast of Georgia. The couple lived in Manhattan. Kennedy had dreamed of becoming a pilot since childhood, and despite his mother's (and others') disapproval, he began flying lessons and received his pilot's license in Florida in April 1998.

Kennedy died at the age of 38 when the single-engine plane he was flying from New Jersey to Martha's Vineyard, Massachusetts, to attend the wedding of his cousin Rory Kennedy, crashed into the sea in darkness on 16 July 1999. His wife and her sister, Lauren Bessette, were also on the plane. He was survived by his sister, Caroline Kennedy Schlossberg of Manhattan.

As the *New York Times* observed on his death, John F. Kennedy Jr. was touched by both the Kennedy charisma and its curse. Perhaps the most poignant event surrounding the assassination of his father took place on John Jr.'s third birthday, when the bewildered little boy stepped forward and rendered a final salute as his father's flag-draped casket was carried out from St. Matthew's Cathedral. The moment became an iconic image of the decade. Throughout his relatively short, somewhat tumultuous, life, he was rarely out of the public spotlight, hounded by photographers wherever he went. In 1988, *People* magazine called him "the sexiest man alive." Americans cheered when he emerged with his dazzling bride following their secret wedding in 1996. He never sought public office, seeking rather a more private career in publishing. Young, handsome, and charismatic, he was acutely aware that as the son of the slain president he was regarded by many as an obvious potential candidate for the presidency. But, as he commented in a 1993 interview, "It's hard for me to talk about a legacy or a mystique, it's my family. The fact that there have been difficulties and hardships, or obstacles, makes us closer." *See also* KENNEDY, JACQUELINE BOUVIER

KENNEDY, JOSEPH PATRICK, JR. (1915–1944). Joseph Patrick Kennedy Jr., the oldest child of **Joseph P. Kennedy Sr.** and **Rose Fitzgerald Kennedy**, was born on 25 July 1915. He attended the Choate School in

Connecticut and the London School of Economics prior to entering Harvard College, from which he graduated cum laude in 1938. He went on to Harvard Law School but left before his final year to volunteer as a navy flier in World War II. Awarded his wings in May 1942, he flew Caribbean patrols and, in September 1943, was sent to England with the first naval squadron to fly B-24s with the British Naval Command. On 12 August 1944, he was killed when the bomber he was flying exploded over England.

The secret mission on which he lost his life was described by a fellow officer after it was declassified:

> Joe, regarded as an experienced Patrol Plane Commander, and a fellow-officer, an expert in radio control projects, was to take a "drone" Liberator bomber loaded with 21,170 pounds of high explosives into the air and to stay with it until two "mother" planes had achieved complete radio control over the drone. They were then to bail out over England; the "drone," under the control of the mother planes, was to proceed on the mission which was to culminate in a crash-dive on the target, a V-2 rocket launching site in Normandy. The airplane . . . was in flight with routine checking of the radio controls proceeding satisfactorily, when at 6:20 P.M. on August 12, 1944, two explosions blasted the drone resulting in the death of its two pilots.

No final conclusions as to the cause of the explosions have ever been reached. Joe was posthumously awarded the Navy Cross and the Air Medal. In 1946, a destroyer, the USS *Joseph P. Kennedy, Jr.*, destroyer No. 850, was launched at the Fore River shipyards as the navy's final tribute to a gallant officer and his heroic devotion to duty. It is now in a museum in Battleship Cove, Fall River, Massachusetts.

In 1946, the Joseph P. Kennedy Jr. Foundation was established by Ambassador and Mrs. Joseph P. Kennedy Sr. to honor their eldest son. It aims to improve the way society deals with its citizens who have intellectual disabilities (mental retardation) and to help identify and disseminate ways to prevent the causes of intellectual disabilities. *See also* SHRIVER, EUNICE KENNEDY; SMITH, JEAN KENNEDY.

KENNEDY, JOSEPH PATRICK, SR. (1888–1969). Joseph Patrick Kennedy Sr. was born in the Irish enclave of East Boston on 6 September 1888, the first child of Mary Augusta Hickey, the daughter of a successful building contractor, and Patrick Joseph Kennedy, a **Democratic Party** official who held a number of government jobs and had interests in a variety of local businesses, including liquor, banking, and real estate. From childhood, Joe was noted as possessing a magnetic charm. He attended Harvard University, along with a sprinkling of other Catholics. His first job after graduating in 1912 was as a bank examiner for the state. Joe was driven by the need to get rich, the desire to escape the anti-Catholic prejudice of the wealthy classes of New England, and a determination to create a political dynasty through the manipulation of money and mass media. In personality, he was overbearing and coarse, and he was a bully and a physical coward; some said he was dishonest, if not outright crooked. He was also a serial philanderer who sustained a relentless pursuit of women, frequently showgirls and starlets. His son Jack's appetite for sexual conquest replicated that of his father; they both felt a sense of entitlement where women were concerned.

In January 1914, Joe was elected president of a small bank, Columbia Trust Bank, where his father was on the board. In October 1914, he married the well-known and pretty Catholic girl, **Rose Fitzgerald**. Rose was the first-born child of the Boston mayor, John Francis "Honey Fitz" Fitzgerald. They moved into a house on Beals Street in Brookline, a middle-class Protestant neighborhood. Joe began borrowing money to invest in real estate and stocks.

When the United States entered World War I, Joe managed the Fore River Shipyard and, following the war, continued to shrewdly borrow and invest, rapidly increasing his wealth. In

1928, he bought the summer house in Hyannis Port where the family would assemble for decades, and the year after a mansion in Bronxville (just north of New York City) where, he believed, they could escape Brahmin prejudice for good.

He invested in the film industry, and while in charge of Pathe Pictures, he began an extended affair with Gloria Swanson in January 1928. Joe became notorious for his frequently, seemingly compulsive, marital infidelities. Kennedy made a huge fortune from his investments in Hollywood. He sold his interest in Pathe in 1929, making a monster profit. He also profited greatly from the sale of alcohol and residential and commercial real estate in New York and Chicago. Utilizing his Wall Street contacts, Joe continued his stock market activities, buying and selling overvalued stock between 1930 and 1932, more than doubling his net worth. Such was his success and his powers of persuasion that President Franklin D. Roosevelt (FDR) appointed him to chair the newly created Securities and Exchange Commission. With the assistance of a publicity campaign orchestrated by *New York Times* journalist Arthur Krock, he succeeded in restoring confidence in the stock market before resigning in 1935. Indeed, Krock became pivotal in creating the so-called Kennedy myth with his rewriting of Jack's senior thesis *Why England Slept* (1940) for publication.

In return for the public support by a prominent and wealthy Irish Catholic, in January 1938 FDR appointed Joe Kennedy ambassador to the Court of St. James. Given Kennedy's belief that **appeasement** was the only way to keep the peace conflicted with FDR's inclinations toward intervention, it was an odd appointment, bound to end with Kennedy's resignation and banishment from Washington—but not before he had endorsed FDR for a further term in 1940.

The Second World War years were particularly hard for Joe and Rose. Joe intervened to ensure Jack a commission in the navy and an assignment on a patrol torpedo boat. Jack emerged from the war something of a hero after saving the life of a crew member when his

A new informal picture of Joseph P. Kennedy, U.S. ambassador to Great Britain, Washington, DC. *Courtesy of Library of Congress.*

boat was sunk when rammed by a Japanese destroyer. However, **Joseph Patrick Kennedy Jr.**, who had joined the air force as a pilot, lost his life when his B-24 bomber exploded while in flight over England. Joe was shattered, and Rose retreated into solitude and prayer. Further tragedy struck the family when, in May 1948, their daughter **Kathleen Kennedy** was killed when the plane in which she was traveling crashed in France.

Following Joe Jr.'s death, Joe then devoted his energy to ensuring that Jack achieved success in politics. In 1946, he used his political experience and skills—and money—to manage Jack's election to Congress.

In the run-up to the **presidential election of 1960**, Joe once again called upon Arthur Krock of the *Times* to promote Jack's candidacy. Joe did an enormous amount behind the scenes and encouraged the use of **television**, having taught his sons to be as comfortable on camera as he was. Joe was the first to bring Hollywood to Washington, and by January 1961, he had what he wanted: a son

in the White House. On 19 December 1961, Kennedy suffered a stroke at the age of 73. He survived but was left paralyzed on his right side. However, he remained mentally alert. He died at home in Hyannis Port on 18 November 1969. He had outlived three of his four sons and one of his five daughters.

KENNEDY, KATHLEEN (1920–1948). Kathleen "Kick" Kennedy, John F. Kennedy's sister, was born on 20 February 1920, in Brookline, Massachusetts, the second daughter and fourth child of **Joseph P. Kennedy Sr.** and **Rose Fitzgerald Kennedy.** She moved with her family to Bronxville, New York, in 1927 and attended the private Riverdale Country School. After graduating from Riverdale, she went to the Noroton Convent of the Sacred Heart in Greenwich, Connecticut, and spent a year abroad studying at the Holy Child Convent in Neuilly, France.

In 1938, when her father was appointed ambassador to Great Britain, Kathleen sailed with her family to England. There, just days before her 18th birthday, she made her formal entrance as a debutante on 12 May 1938, and her refreshingly open and friendly manner made her an instant hit with British high society. While in England, she worked on various committees for social events, and she met and fell in love with William "Billy" Cavendish, the Marquess of Hartington, the eldest son and heir apparent of the 10th Duke of Devonshire. Kathleen's religion, however, presented a problem for a possible marriage as the Protestant Cavendish family could not contemplate their heirs being raised Catholic and the magnificent Hartford estate being passed into Catholic hands, and the Kennedy family were equally aghast at the prospect of one of theirs marrying out of the faith and their grandchildren belonging to the Church of England. Kathleen returned to the United States with her mother and siblings in fall 1939 after Great Britain declared war. She briefly attended the Finch School in New York and later Florida Commercial College. While in college, Kennedy began volunteering for the Red Cross in New York in summer 1940. She planned benefit luncheons and fashion shows for the Allied Relief Fund to aid British seamen disabled in the war. Kennedy left college in 1941 to begin working for the *Times-Herald* newspaper in Washington, DC, where she reviewed plays and movies in her own bylined column. In June 1943, she returned to London as a volunteer for the Red Cross. Her official position was the program assistant at Hans Crescent, a club in London that offered food, supplies, and accommodations for officers.

On 6 May 1944, despite family opposition, the then 23-year-old Kennedy married Cavendish. Her eldest brother, **Joseph P. Kennedy Jr.**, was the only member of her family in attendance. "Billy," Lord Hartington, a member of the British army, was called up on 20 June, five weeks after their wedding. He was killed in combat on 9 August 1944. Kathleen, now Lady Hartington, remained in England after the death of her husband. After the end of the war, she briefly traveled back to the United States to visit her family but returned to London to live there permanently. Lady Hartington later began a relationship with the 8th Earl Fitzwilliam, once again despite the disapproval of her mother, and died in a plane crash with Fitzwilliam in France on 13 May 1948. She is buried on the Cavendish family burial grounds, in the Church at Edensor outside of Chatsworth, England. Her father attended her funeral. In October 1957, her parents and siblings dedicated a new physical education building in her honor at Manhattanville College in Purchase, New York. John F. Kennedy visited her gravesite in June 1963 when returning from a visit to Ireland.

KENNEDY, PATRICIA (1924–2006). *See* LAWFORD, PATRICIA KENNEDY.

KENNEDY, ROBERT FRANCIS (1925–1968). Robert "Bobby" Kennedy was born in Brookline, Massachusetts, on 20 November 1925. As a youngster, he was largely ignored by his father but favored by his mother. Because of his parents' peripatetic lifestyle, Bobby attended a number of public and private schools before entering Harvard, graduating with a BA degree in political science in 1948. While at Harvard, he helped with his brother John's

1946 congressional campaign. He then gained a law degree from the University of Virginia Law School in 1951. In June 1950, he married **Ethel Skakel** with whom he had 11 children, the last born after his death. He worked for a time in the Justice Department and became a vigorous opponent of communism.

The third of four sons to **Joseph P. Kennedy Sr.** and **Rose Fitzgerald Kennedy**, he remained in the shadow of his two older brothers. Jack's decision to run for the Senate in 1952 proved to be a turning point in his family relationships. Robert proved invaluable in organizing voter turnout for Jack in the run for the Senate and even more so during Jack's run for the presidency in 1960. During the 1960 presidential campaign, Robert defended attacks on Jack because of his religion but made an enemy of **Lyndon B. Johnson** when he tried unsuccessfully to dissuade the Texan senator from accepting his brother's offer to be his running mate. Jack had become so dependent upon his younger brother's advice that he appointed him attorney general, a decision that was widely criticized as nepotism. President Kennedy sought the advice and counsel of his younger brother, who became the president's closest political adviser. He was the president's primary source of administrative information and a general counsel he could trust.

Although initially a hawk in matters relating to international relations, Bobby became more dovish than Jack's other foreign policy advisers. This was evidenced during the **Berlin crisis of 1961** and the **Cuban missile crisis** of 1962. In both instances, the president relied heavily upon Bobby. During the standoff over the presence of Russian missiles in **Cuba**, Jack accepted Bobby's advice to ignore the more belligerent message of Soviet premier **Nikita Khrushchev** as a way to resolve what had become a critical and potentially catastrophic standoff between the two countries.

Robert was also Jack's point-man in the hostile relationship between the president and **J. Edgar Hoover**, the director of the Federal Bureau of Investigation. Hoover hated both the Kennedys, and the feeling was reciprocated. Hoover was particularly unhappy at the Kennedys' intolerance of the ties between organized crime and the organized labor movement, which the Kennedys regarded as a hot bed of corruption. Hoover also disapproved of Jack's extramarital activities.

Robert also led his brother in furthering **civil rights** during the years of the Kennedy administration. Although at times subjected to criticism for his cautious approach as attorney general, many of the initiatives between 1960 and 1963 in furthering and assisting the civil rights movement were the result of the passion and determination of Robert Kennedy.

Following the **assassination of John F. Kennedy**, his successor, President Lyndon B. Johnson, made it clear that Robert would not be his running mate in the 1964 presidential election. Despite the devastation he experienced at his brother's death, in June 1964 Bobby announced he would run for the Senate representing New York, and he was successful. His younger brother **Ted Kennedy** was already a member of the Senate. One of the issues he pursued in the Senate was gun control. He also supported (with some reservations) Johnson's Great Society program; advocated for nuclear nonproliferation, low-cost housing projects in New York City, and California farm workers; and allied himself with civil rights and antipoverty activists, youth, and students. Kennedy will be forever identified with the explosion of citizen activism that characterized the 1960s.

Following the assassination on 4 April 1968 of civil rights leader Dr. **Martin Luther King Jr.**, Bobby made an impassioned plea for reconciliation between blacks and whites in the United States and urged **African Americans** to remain calm, basing his appeal upon his shared experience of the assassination of his brother.

In 1968, opposed to the continuation of American involvement in the **Vietnam War**, Robert announced his decision to run for the presidency, a decision that contributed to that of the incumbent, Johnson, not to do so.

Following his speech at the Ambassador Hotel in Los Angeles in the immediate aftermath of a close victory over his main rival in the **Democratic Party** primary in California, Eugene McCarthy, Robert Kennedy was shot by an assassin, a Palestinian by the name of

John F. Kennedy home, Brookline, Massachusetts. *Courtesy of Library of Congress.*

Sirhan B. Sirhan. He died the following day, 6 June 1968. He was 42 years of age. The Kennedy family had lost another of its sons to an assassin.

Robert's death, like the 1963 assassination of his brother, has been the subject of widespread analysis, with many believing that there was more than one assassin. Following a high requiem Mass in St. Patrick's Cathedral, New York, attended by family members and President Johnson and his wife, in which Ted gave what has become a legendary speech in praise of his brother, Robert's body was transported by a ceremonial funeral train to Washington. Hundreds of thousands of mourners lined the tracks to pay their respects. His body lies next to his brother in the Arlington National Cemetery.

KENNEDY, ROSE FITZGERALD (1890–1995). The mother of John F. Kennedy, Rose Elizabeth Fitzgerald was born in Boston's North End on 22 July 1890, the eldest child of John F. "Honey Fitz" and Mary Josephine Hannon Fitzgerald. The young Rose was first introduced to politics as a child, as her father was a congressman. She graduated from Dorchester High School in June 1906. Although she had been accepted at Wellesley College, her father enrolled her in the Convent of the Sacred Heart, in Boston, at the suggestion of

Archbishop William O'Connell. Late in her life she was to say that not having attended Wellesley was perhaps her greatest regret. However, the religious training she received at the convent became the foundation for her life. On 7 October 1914, Cardinal O'Connell officiated at her marriage to **Joseph P. Kennedy Sr.** in a modest ceremony in a small chapel at the cardinal's residence. The couple's first home was a three-story gray building on Beals Street in Brookline, now a national historic site. At the time of their marriage, Joseph Kennedy was making $10,000 per year as a businessman. When the family left Brookline and moved to Riverdale, New York, about 10 years later, he was a multimillionaire, in part through his dealings as a lone wolf financier and investor. In their first 18 years of marriage, the couple had nine children. **Joseph P. Kennedy Jr.** was born in 1915, John F. Kennedy in 1917, **Rose Marie Kennedy** in 1918, **Kathleen Kennedy** in 1920, **Eunice Kennedy** in 1921, **Patricia Kennedy** in 1924, **Robert F. Kennedy** in 1925, **Jean Kennedy** in 1928, and **Edward Kennedy** in 1932.

Rose Kennedy was considered by many to be a model parent. "Children," she said, "should be stimulated by their parents to see, touch, know, understand, and appreciate." She made the family a self-sustaining unit, with members allowed to go their own way while maintaining interest in the lives of the others. She was obsessive in keeping tabs on her large family. She kept careful records of all her children on index cards, and she had an extensive filing system that she said helped her remember each one's physical condition and other details. As a strict and observant Catholic herself, she raised her children in the faith, but she was reportedly a remote and frequently absent mother.

Rose encouraged her sons' interest in politics. When John ran for the Massachusetts 11th congressional district seat in 1946, the one previously held by Honey Fitz, Rose spurred him on. She loved politics, especially the backroom strategies and behind-the-scenes wheeling and dealing. "She knew all the nuts and bolts," **Pierre Salinger** once

said of her. She hosted many "Kennedy teas" sponsored by the **Democratic Party** during his 1952 campaign to unseat **Henry Cabot Lodge Jr.** In her son's 1960 presidential campaign, she was again a keen participant.

Rose Kennedy rarely talked publicly about her personal life. She took refuge in her religious faith from the errant behavior of her husband and the tragedies she experienced at the deaths of her children. She once remarked to a friend: "Wasn't there a book about Michelangelo called *The Agony and the Ecstasy*? That's what my life has been." During World War II, her eldest son, Joseph Jr., a U.S. Navy pilot, was killed in action on 12 August 1944, when the plane he was flying on a mission exploded in flight. Her second-oldest daughter, Kathleen, wife of the Marquess of Hartington, who was also killed during World War II, died 13 May 1948 in a plane crash in France. Her second son, John, was assassinated in Dallas on 22 November 1963, during his first term as president. Her third son, Robert, who was U.S. attorney general under his brother and later a Democratic senator from New York, was assassinated in Los Angeles on 5 June 1968, while campaigning for president. Her eldest daughter, Rosemary, spent most of her adult life in a home for intellectually disabled people. Her husband suffered a stroke in 1961, and it left him an invalid until his death eight years later.

Rose Fitzgerald Kennedy died in her Hyannis Port, Massachusetts, home on 22 January 1995. She was 104.

KENNEDY, ROSE MARIE "ROSEMARY" (1918–2005). John F. Kennedy's sister, Rose Marie Kennedy, was born on 13 September 1918. She was the third child and eldest daughter of **Joseph P. Kennedy Sr.** and **Rose Fitzgerald Kennedy**. It soon became apparent to her parents that Rosemary was born with some form of developmental disability—although they kept this knowledge hidden from outsiders. She was slower to crawl, slower to walk, and slower to speak than her brothers, and she experienced learning difficulties when she reached school age. However, Rosemary participated in most family activities. She kept a diary as a teenager in which she described people she met, dances and concerts she attended, and a visit to the Franklin D. Roosevelt White House. There were few outward signs of her mental disabilities—she was described as an outwardly easygoing, happy, and very beautiful young woman—and when her father was appointed U.S. ambassador to Britain in 1938, she was presented at court along with her mother and sister **Kathleen Kennedy**. When the family returned to the United States in 1940, however, "Rosemary was not making progress but seemed instead to be going backward," as her younger sister Eunice Kennedy later wrote. "At 22, she was becoming increasingly irritable and difficult."

The following year, Joseph Kennedy was persuaded that a relatively new form of neurosurgery known as a lobotomy would help calm his daughter and prevent her sometimes violent and erratic mood swings. Joseph authorized the operation, without informing his wife. The procedure, which at that time seemed to hold great promise, left Rosemary permanently incapacitated and unable to care for herself. On the recommendation of Boston's Archbishop Richard Cushing, Rosemary was sent to St. Coletta's School for Exceptional Children in Jefferson, Wisconsin, where she would be cared for and live for the rest of her life.

John F. Kennedy, along with other members of the Kennedy family, never publicly acknowledged Rosemary's circumstances. However, as president, John F. Kennedy initiated sweeping legislation designed to improve the quality of life for Americans with disabilities. **Eunice Kennedy Shriver** had a particularly close relationship with her older sister and great empathy for Rosemary and others who faced similar challenges. In 1962, Shriver started a summer day camp in her own backyard for children and adults with intellectual disabilities; the camp evolved into the Special Olympics, now a global competition that involves 1.4 million athletes from 150 countries. Rosemary Kennedy inspired her sister **Jean Kennedy Smith** to start Very Special Arts and her nephew, Anthony Shriver, to start Best Buddies. Hospitals, schools, and other such

facilities around the world have been named in her honor. Rosemary Kennedy died on 7 January 2005, at age 86. *See also* KENNEDY, JOSEPH PATRICK, JR.

KENNEDY, ROSEMARY (1918–2005). *See* KENNEDY, ROSE MARIE "ROSEMARY".

KENNEDY, TED (1932–2009). *See* KENNEDY, EDWARD MOORE "TED".

KHRUSHCHEV, NIKITA SERGEYEVICH (1894–1971). Nikita Sergeyevich Khrushchev was born on 15 April 1894, the son of a coal miner, in the village of Kalinovka, near the present-day border between Russia and Ukraine. He worked as a metal worker and became a political commissar during the Russian Civil War. He worked his way up the Soviet hierarchy, and in 1938, he was appointed governor of Ukraine by Joseph Stalin. During World War II, he was present at the defense of Stalingrad. Soon after the war, he was recalled to Moscow as one of Stalin's close advisers. In the power struggle that followed Stalin's death in early March 1953, Khrushchev emerged as first secretary of the Communist Party of the **Soviet Union** from 1953 to 1964 and premier from 1958 to 1964. He undertook to de-Stalinize the Soviet Union, denouncing Stalin's purges in the so-called (and widely disseminated) secret speech to the Communist Party Congress in February 1956—despite his own previous participation and support for such purges—and he introduced a number of domestic liberal reforms, ushering in a less repressive era. He also built up the Soviet space program. To Communist Party progressives, Khrushchev was a reformer, although it was not until Mikhail Gorbachev assumed leadership that many of the reforms were seriously attempted. Khrushchev was removed from office by his party colleagues in 1964, and he was replaced by Leonid Brezhnev as first secretary and Alexei Kosygin as premier.

Khrushchev was the counterpart to presidents **Dwight D. Eisenhower** and John F. Kennedy during the 1950s and 1960s. Khrushchev was described by his ambassador to Washington, Anatoly Dobrynin, as "committed to the peace process [but he] could not often translate that commitment into concrete agreements. His improvisation, his inclination to bluff, and his bad temper were all overlaid by a strong ideology and this helped turn his discussions with American presidents into heated disputes without helpful results." During the final days of the Kennedy-Nixon presidential campaign, the Soviet premier threw a tantrum at the **United Nations** General Assembly, on 12 October 1960. Responding to accusations that Soviet domination of Eastern Europe was an example of colonialism, Khrushchev took off his shoe and used it to pound on the table, causing a chaotic scene that enshrined the image of Khrushchev as a hot-headed buffoon.

Khrushchev and Kennedy got off to a rocky start, as the Soviet leader tried to dominate the American in their first meeting in Vienna in June 1961, but the dangerous **Cuban missile crisis** in 1962 sharpened both men's interest in peaceful solutions. In early 1963, both Khrushchev and the Kennedy administration moved toward agreement on a partial nuclear test ban and to establish an instant teletype communication system—the "hotline." Although Khrushchev had visited the United States in September 1959 as Eisenhower's guest, their relations had cooled substantially after the U-2 incident in 1960. The Soviet leader had a more positive opinion of Kennedy, however. He wrote in his memoirs: "I had no cause for regret once Kennedy became President. . . . It quickly became clear he understood better than Eisenhower that an improvement in relations was the only rational course. . . . He seemed to have a better grasp of the idea of peaceful coexistence than Eisenhower had. . . . From the beginning, he tried to establish closer contacts with the Soviet Union with an eye to reaching an agreement on disarmament and to avoiding any incident which might set off a military conflict."

During the **Lyndon B. Johnson** administration, Khrushchev continued to move a few steps away from the old Stalinist thinking toward a new policy of peaceful coexistence with the United States and sought to deflate grossly exaggerated threats and end the extreme demonization of capitalist adversaries—subtle

changes that some commentators believe the West failed to recognize at the time.

Following his ouster from office, Khrushchev lived under virtual house arrest outside Moscow, where he began to make tape recordings of his memoirs. He died of a heart attack in a hospital in Moscow on 11 September 1971, at the age of 77.

His memoirs were published and translated into English in two volumes, *Khrushchev Remembers* (1970) and *Khrushchev Remembers: The Last Testament* (1974). Following a series of talks with Khrushchev's son Sergei, a third volume was published in 1990 as *Khrushchev Remembers: The Glasnost Tapes.*

KING, MARTIN LUTHER, JR. (1929–1968). Martin Luther King Jr. was born in Atlanta, Georgia, on 15 January 1929, the son of the pastor of the prestigious Ebenezer Baptist Church. While a student at Morehouse College he was ordained in his father's church in 1947 and received his BA from Morehouse in 1948. He was awarded a divinity degree at Crozer Theological Seminary in Chester, Pennsylvania, in 1951. He then received a PhD in theology at Boston University in June 1955.

In September 1954 King moved to Montgomery, Alabama, to become pastor of the Dexter Avenue Baptist Church and immediately became involved in the **civil rights** movement. In December 1955, the black community in Montgomery began a boycott of the city's segregated buses and formed the Montgomery Improvement Association to continue the protest. King was elected president of the association the same day. Early in 1957, King helped found and was elected president of the Southern Christian Leadership Conference (SCLC), an organization established to coordinate direct action protests in the South and committed to a philosophy of nonviolence. By 1960 King was the most prominent exponent of nonviolent direct action within the civil rights movement. In January 1960, he moved to Atlanta to become co-pastor at his father's church. King welcomed the nonviolent student sit-ins that took place in February and helped form the Student Nonviolent Coordinating Committee (SNCC). In October 1960,

When King was arrested by officials of DeKalb County and was sentenced to four months hard labor in a rural penal camp, his imprisonment caused a nationwide protest. On 26 October presidential candidate John F. Kennedy and his brother Robert Kennedy intervened and helped arrange for King's release. Coming in the last days of the 1960 campaign, the incident has been credited with swinging black voters solidly behind Kennedy, providing him with the margin of victory in at least eleven crucial states.

In May 1961 the **Congress of Racial Equality (CORE)** launched the **Freedom Rides**—protests designed to challenge segregation at southern bus terminals. When a mob attacked the riders as they arrived in Montgomery on 20 May, King rushed to the city and the next day addressed a mass meeting in support of the riders. With James Farmer of CORE and other civil rights leaders, he announced on 23 May that the protests would continue despite threats of more violence. King was named chairman of a Freedom Rides Coordinating Committee, and he rejected Attorney General **Robert Kennedy**'s call for a "cooling-off" period at the end of the month.

During the spring of 1963 King participated in a major desegregation campaign in Birmingham, Alabama. The campaign began on 3 April. Demonstrations began at segregated lunch counters, and a boycott of downtown stores started the same day. A series of daily mass marches was begun on 6 April. Four days later, the city obtained an injunction against further demonstrations that specifically cited King. On 12 April, Good Friday, King led a march toward city hall in defiance of the injunction, was arrested en route, and was placed in solitary confinement. While in prison, King wrote his later famous "Letter from a Birmingham Jail." The letter rebutted charges that the Birmingham campaign was untimely and unwise and detailed the injustices blacks suffered in that city and elsewhere. He threatened a resumption of demonstrations in Birmingham but was reportedly dissuaded from this action by moderate black leaders in the city and by President Kennedy's decision to send an advisory team to Birmingham to

conduct negotiations between black and white leaders. Instead, King decided to focus on Atlanta, and in October he joined other local black leaders in a demand that the pace of desegregation in that city be increased. The rejection of the demands led to a series of demonstrations in Atlanta in December and January in which King joined.

By the end of 1963, King had achieved enormous stature. In January 1964 *Time* magazine selected him as its Man of the Year, and in December 1964 he was awarded the Nobel Peace Prize. To the general public, King was clearly the symbolic leader of the civil rights movement, and within the movement he occupied a unique position. King served as an extraordinary symbol to both blacks and whites and as a unique channel of communication between the races. He articulated the aspirations of Southern blacks for full equality better than any black leader of the day, and he communicated those aspirations to whites more effectively than anyone else. To many whites King seemed a militant, but his willingness to negotiate and compromise also made him appear a "responsible" activist and gave him respectability among white moderates. His philosophy of nonviolence combined a challenge to white society with a promise of its salvation. King repeatedly argued that nonviolence would awaken the conscience of America and make the nation live up to its democratic and religious ideals. King was able to develop and exploit whites' feelings of guilt without alienating them.

It became increasingly difficult for King to continue this role during the latter half of the decade when the civil rights movement began to fragment, when black radicalism and violence increased, and when white opposition to black gains outside the South intensified as the focus of black protest shifted from the small-town South to the urban North. King was an early opponent of the war in **Vietnam**. During the 1960s, he was the target of a six-year Federal Bureau of Investigation campaign that attempted to discredit him. On 4 April 1968, King was assassinated in Memphis, Tennessee, by segregationist and convicted criminal James Earl Ray. *See also* ABERNATHY, RALPH DAVID; BAEZ, JOAN; CIVIL RIGHTS; CONNOR, THEOPHILUS EUGENE "BULL"; KENNEDY, ROBERT FRANCIS; MEREDITH, JAMES H.; MOYNIHAN, DANIEL PATRICK; NATIONAL ASSOCIATION FOR THE ADVANCEMENT OF COLORED PEOPLE (NAACP); RUSTIN, BAYARD; WALLACE, GEORGE CORLEY; WILKINS, ROY

L

LAWFORD, PATRICIA KENNEDY (1924–2006). The sixth child and fourth daughter of **Rose Fitzgerald Kennedy** and **Joseph P. Kennedy Sr.**, Patricia Helen Kennedy was born in Brookline, Massachusetts, on 6 May 1924. She attended the Roehampton Sacred Heart Convent School, a boarding school on the outskirts of London, while her father was ambassador to Great Britain. Kennedy was a good student, especially in mathematics. In 1927, her family moved to Bronxville, New York, where she studied at the Maplehurst Sacred Heart Convent School. She then attended Rosemont College in Rosemont, Pennsylvania, where she directed and acted in various plays and theatrical spectacles. She received a BA from Rosemont in 1945.

Patricia Kennedy was better known to the public as Patricia Lawford, the wife of **Peter Lawford,** whom she married in 1954. However, she was an integral part of the political campaigns of her three brothers, John F. Kennedy, **Robert Kennedy**, and **Ted Kennedy**, and remained part of the Kennedy clan throughout her life. After graduation, Kennedy pursued her theatrical activities. She wanted to become a movie producer, like her father, and a director. She worked as an assistant in NBC's New York production department. She then moved to Los Angeles to work as an assistant for Kate Smith's radio program and, later, for Father Peyton's *Family Theater* and Family Rosary Crusade. On 23 April 1954, Kennedy married Peter Lawford, a debonair, handsome English actor whom she had met through her brother John in 1949. The couple settled into a large

mansion in Malibu. The house became a recreation center for other family members, and the president would spend time lounging at his sister's pool when he was on the West Coast. The Lawfords had four children: Christopher, Sydney, Victoria, and Robin. Patricia and Peter Lawford divorced in 1966.

Although not politically ambitious herself, Patricia Kennedy Lawford understood and lived in the world of politics. She was a tireless supporter of her brothers' political campaigns. For John's congressional race in 1946, she and her sisters and mother held a number of tea parties in which they discussed John's boyhood and his World War II experience. In 1952, the "Kennedy teas" contributed to Kennedy's election to the U.S. Senate in an upset win over the incumbent, **Henry Cabot Lodge Jr.** During the presidential election of 1960, Lawford traveled around the country speaking on her brother's behalf, and she would later play an active role in the Senate and presidential races of her brothers Robert and Ted.

Having been particularly close to Robert, she gathered together memories of him from many people in a book, *The Shining Hour*, which was privately printed for family and friends after his death.

In 1966, Lawford moved with her children to New York City. There she was actively involved in supporting the city's arts scene. She devoted her time to charity auctions and fundraisers for the arts. Lawford founded the National Committee for the Literary Arts, which arranges author lectures and scholarships.

She also worked with the National Center on Addiction and with the John F. Kennedy Presidential Library and Museum on its museum exhibits. Patricia Kennedy Lawford died of pneumonia in Manhattan on 17 September 2006, at the age of 82.

LAWFORD, PETER SYDNEY ERNEST (1923–1984). Peter Sydney Ernest Lawford was born on 7 September 1923, in London, England. His father was a knighted World War I veteran who became an actor after he retired. Lawford was best known as the husband of **Patricia Kennedy** (the sister of President John F. Kennedy) and as a member of the "Rat Pack," a group of Las Vegas and Hollywood entertainers that included Lawford, **Frank Sinatra**, Dean Martin, Sammy Davis Jr., and Joey Bishop, among others.

Lawford's film debut at age eight in the British film *Poor Old Bill* (1931) was followed by a role in *Lord Jeff* (1938). He grew to be a handsome and suave young man, who was being groomed for stardom by MGM in the 1940s. He was the first actor to kiss Elizabeth Taylor on camera and the last to speak to **Marilyn Monroe** before she died. Lawford also organized the famous 1962 birthday party for John F. Kennedy in Madison Square Garden where Monroe sang "Happy Birthday" to the president.

The debonair Lawford enjoyed a reputation as a jet-setting playboy and was a heavy drinker. In 1954, he married Patricia Kennedy. The couple had four children: Christopher, Sydney, Victoria, and Robin. The pair divorced in 1966 as a result of Lawford's growing alcoholism and continuing extramarital affairs. In 1971, he married Mary Rowan, the daughter of comedian Dan Rowan, but the marriage lasted only eight months. In 1975, he married Deborah Gould, and that marriage lasted only two months. In July 1984, just a few months before his death, he married Patricia Seaton after a nine-year courtship.

As part of the famous Hollywood "Rat Pack," Lawford performed with the group in Las Vegas and in films, including *Ocean's Eleven* (1960) and *Sergeants 3* (1962). Lawford became an American citizen on 23 April 1960, and along with other members of the "Rat Pack," helped campaign for Kennedy in the **presidential election of 1960**. Lawford and Sinatra had a falling-out in the early 1960s over brother-in-law **Robert Kennedy**'s objections to Sinatra's alleged Mafia connections. They spoke only once more, when Sinatra called Lawford after his son Frank Sinatra Jr. was kidnapped on 8 December 1963, and the singer needed the help of Lawford's brother-in-law, Robert Kennedy, then attorney general.

In 1972, Lawford had surgery to remove a pancreatic tumor. By that time, he was in ill health as a result of long-time alcoholism. He died on 24 December 1984 of cardiac arrest complicated by kidney and liver failure. Although never considered a very important actor, Lawford's films included *Mrs. Miniver* (1942), *The Picture of Dorian Gray* (1945), *Easter Parade* (1948), *Little Women* (1949), *Royal Wedding* (1950), *It Should Happen to You* (1954), *Ocean's Eleven* (1960), *Pepe* (1960), *Sergeants 3* (1962), *The Longest Day* (1962), *Advise & Consent* (1962), *Harlow* (1965), *The April Fools* (1969), and *Body and Soul* (1981).

LIMITED NUCLEAR TEST BAN TREATY. The Treaty Banning Nuclear Weapons Tests in the Atmosphere, in Outer Space and Underwater, known colloquially as the Limited Nuclear Test Ban Treaty (LNTBT), was signed in Moscow on 5 August 1963 by representatives of the **Soviet Union**, the United States, and the United Kingdom (UK). It had been a long time in the making, and a large majority of the world's states subsequently ratified the treaty. Negotiations had begun toward banning the testing of nuclear weapons during the administrations of **Dwight D. Eisenhower** and Soviet Communist Party chairman **Nikita Khrushchev**. By the mid-to-late 1950s, populations around the world, led by scientists and peace activists, had grown alarmed at the levels of radioactive fallout caused by atmospheric testing. But both sides insisted that continued testing was vital to their national security. A year of tough but desultory negotiations ensued among the United States, the Soviet Union, and the United Kingdom, and in 1958 they agreed to an

informal moratorium of atmospheric testing. However, no agreement could be reached on the question of verification to ensure compliance of the alternative: underground testing.

John F. Kennedy and Nikita Khrushchev did not get off to a good start. Their differences when they met in Vienna in June 1961, and the Berlin crisis over the following four to five months, stalled any initial progress on nuclear arms limitations. On 30 August 1961, the Soviets terminated the testing moratorium that had been in place for three years. Kennedy immediately responded by authorizing **Operation Dominic**, which consisted of 105 nuclear test explosions conducted in 1962–1963—the largest nuclear weapons testing program ever conducted by the United States and the last atmospheric test series conducted. Tests were conducted in the Pacific Ocean and in Nevada; most of them utilized free-fall bombs dropped by B-52 aircraft. Twenty of these "shots" were to test new weaponry, six to test weapons' effects, and others to determine the reliability of the current nuclear inventory. Thor missiles carrying warheads were also employed to experiment with high-altitude nuclear explosions ranging from 30 miles to 248 miles. These tests were called Operation Fishbowl.

In the immediate aftermath of the October 1962 **Cuban missile crisis**, Kennedy sought better relations with the Soviet Union and indicated his willingness to resume negotiations on **arms control** and other tension-reducing measures. Khrushchev also seriously wanted a nuclear test ban treaty and wrote to Kennedy on 27 October 1962 suggesting a resumption of negotiations. Once again negotiations quickly snagged on the question of on-site verification. The U.S. Joint Chiefs insisted upon guaranteed verification and on-site inspection. They were, nonetheless, prepared to accept a limited test ban that permitted underground testing. Some steps in lessening tension were enacted. In January 1963, the North Atlantic Treaty Organization announced the removal of the Jupiter missiles from Turkey. In June, Kennedy and Khrushchev established a direct communications "hotline" between Washington and Moscow; later there would be one connecting London with Moscow. On 30

May 1963, Kennedy, joined by British prime minister Harold Macmillan, suggested a conference in Moscow to resolve the issue, and Kennedy selected veteran diplomat **W. Averell Harriman** to represent the United States at Moscow.

The president laid out his views for doing so in an address to the American University on 10 June 1963, in which he attacked those who denounced any discussion of peace and disarmament as useless until the Soviets adopted a more enlightened attitude toward the world. He explained:

> I also believe we must re-examine our own attitude—as individuals and as a Nation—for our attitude is as essential as theirs. And . . . every thoughtful citizen who despairs of war and wishes to bring peace, should begin by . . . examining his own attitude toward the possibilities of peace, toward the Soviet Union, toward the course of the Cold War. . . . [L]et us not be blind to our differences—but let us also direct attention to our common interests and to the means by which those differences can be resolved. And if we cannot end now our differences, at least we can make the world safe for diversity.

On 2 July, Khrushchev offered a partial treaty, eliminating the problem of inspection by barring tests in the atmosphere, outer space, and underwater but allowing underground tests. On 25 July 1963, Harriman, Lord Hailsham representing Britain, and Andrei Gromyko of the Soviet Union initialed a partial test ban treaty, incorporating these ideas. On 5 August 1963, British foreign secretary Alec Douglas-Home, Soviet foreign minister Gromyko, and U.S. secretary of state Dean Rusk signed the final agreement. In the U.S. Senate, the treaty, formally signed in August, faced strong opposition from the Right, but public opinion mobilized behind the president sufficiently to assure a favorable vote of 81–19, on 24 September, allowing ratification. The United States and the Soviet Union also agreed to support a **United Nations** resolution barring weapons of mass destruction from outer

space, as well as a nonproliferation nuclear weapons treaty that would be developed into treaties under President **Lyndon B. Johnson**.

Some saw the nuclear partial test ban as evidence that Kennedy was committed to a policy of "peaceful coexistence" with the Soviet Union, implying that U.S. security no longer required the pursuit of victory in the **Cold War**. Yet Kennedy remained a committed Cold War warrior. At Fort Worth, on the morning of 22 November 1963, he declared:

> Without the United States, South Vietnam would collapse overnight. Without the United States, the SEATO alliance would collapse overnight. . . . Without the United States there would be no NATO, and gradually Europe would drift into neutralism and indifference. Without the effort of the United

Andrei Gromyko, Soviet minister of foreign affairs, and President John F. Kennedy seated in the Oval Office in the White House during a meeting. *Courtesy of Library of Congress.*

States and the Alliance for Progress, the Communist advance onto the mainland of South America would long ago have taken place.

He assured his listeners: "We are still the keystone in the arch of freedom."

The LNTBT eliminated the dangers of worldwide radioactive fallout but failed in its major goal of ending the nuclear **arms race**. From 1964 to 1968, the United States conducted 140 announced tests, compared with 25 for the Soviet Union. Testing rates exceeded those carried out before the test ban went into effect. Washington had no intention of giving up its nuclear arsenal superiority. *See also* ARMS CONTROL AND DISARMAMENT AGENCY (ACDA); INTERNATIONAL RELATIONS: KENNEDY'S APPROACH.

LINCOLN, EVELYN NORTON (1909–1995). The daughter of John Norton, a member of Congress from Nebraska, Evelyn Norton was born in Polk County, Nebraska, on 25 June 1909. The family moved to Washington, DC, in the 1920s, and she graduated from George Washington University in 1930. While attending law school there, she met her future husband, Harold "Abe" Lincoln (no relation to President Lincoln). The Lincolns lived in New York for several years where her husband taught at New York University; the couple returned to Washington when Abe was offered a government position. Mrs. Lincoln got a job on Capitol Hill working for Congressman B. L. Forrester (D-Ga.).

Seeking to work for a more prominent, promising, and charismatic legislator, in 1952 at the age of 43, she volunteered to work on John F. Kennedy's campaign for the U.S. Senate after reading a few of his press releases. Kennedy, then a 35-year-old bachelor, was seeking a secretary who was an efficient, savvy confidante and whose devotion to him and his ambitions he could totally rely upon. Evelyn Lincoln was Kennedy's personal secretary from January 1953, when he started his first term in the Senate, until his death on 22 November 1963, when she was in the motorcade in Dallas when he was assassinated.

She was perhaps his most trusted confidante, organizing his private as well as his public appointments. She traveled with the Kennedy delegation on his historic trips to Ireland, Britain, and Germany.

According to the *New York Times*, Lincoln's office, next to the president's, became a nerve center at the White House, partly because of the candy dish she kept there along with the humidor full of gift cigars not up to presidential standards, and partly because of the West Wing's layout. She had a direct view of the president in his office. And the president had to walk through her office to get to cabinet meetings. Her office also had a **television** set on which the president and aides watched the nation's first manned space flight and other major events.

Evelyn Lincoln became an early and avid collector of Kennedy memorabilia, saving everything tied to Kennedy, including memos, doodles, photographs, and letters. She even saved some things the Kennedy family said really belonged to them: Kennedy's briefcase, the watch he was wearing when he died, and the possessions he kept in the Oval Office. Robert White, a family friend, who inherited Mrs. Lincoln's collection of Kennedy memorabilia, contended she primarily kept things no one wanted.

Lincoln wrote of her time with Kennedy in her memoir, *My Twelve Years with John F. Kennedy*, published in 1967. She died on 11 May 1995, in Georgetown University Hospital of complications after surgery for cancer.

LIPPMANN, WALTER (1889–1974). Walter Lippmann was born in New York City, on 23 September 1889, to upper-middle-class German Jewish parents, Jacob and Daisy Baum Lippmann. After graduating from New York's Dwight School, he entered Harvard University at the age of 17 and earned his degree in three years, graduating in 1906. Lippmann became a member of the New York Socialist Party alongside Sinclair Lewis. In 1913, Lippmann, Herbert Croly, and Walter Weyl became the founding editors of the *New Republic* magazine. During World War I, in 1918, he was briefly commissioned a captain in the

U.S. Army, and then on being discharged, he became an adviser to President Woodrow Wilson, assisting in the drafting of Wilson's Fourteen Points speech. Lippmann went on to carve a stellar career as a writer, reporter, and political commentator. Over six decades, he wrote a score of books and more than 4,000 columns and is famous for being among the first to introduce the concept of **Cold War**. He has been described as the most influential U.S. journalist of the 20th century.

Because of his calm, impersonal, and almost aloof journalistic style, as well as his access to government decision makers, Walter Lippmann influenced critical taste more than any other journalist of his time. During the 1960 presidential campaign, Lippmann hailed John F. Kennedy as the first candidate since Franklin D. Roosevelt who could stir and unite the American people. "I felt a new generation had to come to power," he wrote. Many observers felt Lippmann's endorsement lent the Kennedy campaign a special air of legitimacy.

However, following Kennedy's election, Lippmann became increasingly critical of the president. Kennedy's cautious economic policies caused him to write in June 1961 that the president was carrying on "in all its essentials the Eisenhower economic philosophy. . . . It's like the Eisenhower Administration 30 years younger." Lippmann also opposed the administration's October 1962 decision to blockade **Cuba** to force the removal of Soviet missiles from that island. He believed that the risk of nuclear confrontation was unnecessary and that the United States should quietly negotiate to exchange the Soviet missiles in Cuba for American missiles in Turkey. In 1963, Lippmann shifted his column from the New York *Herald Tribune* to *Newsweek*. During the next five years, his fear that the United States would become involved in an Asian land war led him to criticize the **Vietnam** policies of both the Kennedy and Johnson administrations. Often regarded as "the dean of American liberal journalists," many of his admirers chose to ignore his dislike of popular democracy and his shift from an early liberalism to an almost despairing conservatism in his later years.

Lippmann retired from *Newsweek* in 1968. He died in New York City on 14 December 1974.

LODGE, HENRY CABOT, JR. (1902–1985). Henry Cabot Lodge Jr. was born in Nahant, Massachusetts, on 5 July 1902 into a distinguished New England family that traced its ancestry back to the Massachusetts Bay Colony. When his father died in 1909, he was raised by his grandfather, Henry Cabot Lodge Sr., the powerful Republican senator who opposed U.S. entry into the League of Nations after World War I. Lodge graduated from Harvard College in 1924, then worked as a reporter and then an editorial writer for the *New York Herald Tribune*. Following four years—1933 to 1937—in the Massachusetts House of Representatives, he was first elected to the U.S. Senate as a Republican in 1936, and following an interval during which he served in the U.S. Army, he remained there for the next 15 years. In 1951, he helped persuade **Dwight D. Eisenhower** to run for the Republican presidential nomination and later managed Eisenhower's primary campaign. Because of his work for Eisenhower, Lodge neglected his own political career and was defeated for reelection in 1952 by John F. Kennedy.

During the Eisenhower years, the former Massachusetts senator served as ambassador to the **United Nations**, representing the United States in important debates on Suez, Lebanon, and Hungary, as well as in clashes with the **Soviet Union** on disarmament and espionage. In 1960, **Richard M. Nixon** chose Lodge as his vice presidential running mate. Nixon assumed that Lodge's East Coast connections would balance his own strength in the West and Midwest and that Lodge's liberalism would offset his more conservative image.

In June 1963, President Kennedy, anxious to gain bipartisan support for American involvement in **Vietnam**, appointed Lodge ambassador to Saigon. While at that post, Lodge served not only as an executor of the administration's plans but also as an important formulator of policy. The ambassador arrived in Saigon on 22 August during the crisis precipitated by the Diem regime's attack on Buddhist dissidents. This attack—carried out

by President Ngo Dinh Diem's brother, Ngo Dinh Nhu—generated fierce criticism not only from foreign governments but also from elements within Vietnam. Several American observers also thought the attack threatened the military effort in that country. After assessing the situation, Lodge concluded that the war could not be won with the unpopular regime in power. In the ensuing months, he worked to convince Washington officials that it should be replaced. He supported the idea of a U.S.-inspired coup. However, the secretaries of defense and state and the chairman of the Joint Chiefs of Staff questioned the efficacy of a coup. The State Department sent Lodge a message ordering him to work for the reform of the Diem regime. Despite Washington's opposition, Lodge remained convinced that the war would not be won with Diem at the helm of South Vietnam, and he tried to persuade U.S. officials that a new, more popular government was necessary. In mid-October 1963, Lodge, with the permission of U.S. officials, increased the pressure on Diem, informing him that U.S. aid for his private guard, which had been used in August to put down the Buddhists, would be suspended until it was transferred to field combat. The U.S. ambassador indirectly informed South Vietnamese generals that the United States would not thwart any proposed coup. As the coup took shape during the last days of October, Lodge worked for forestall any attempt by U.S. officials to oppose it. On 30 October, when several of the president's advisers decided to make one last attempt to deal with Diem and asked Lodge to delay or call off the coup, he informed them that the matter was in Vietnamese hands and he could do nothing to prevent it. A successful coup took place on 1 November 1963.

During the months following the coup, Lodge remained an important force in Vietnamese politics, attempting to aid in the establishment of a stable government and pushing for needed reforms. In May 1964, he resigned his post to return home to try to prevent the nomination of Senator **Barry M. Goldwater** (R-Ariz.) as the Republican presidential candidate. In July 1965, President **Lyndon B. Johnson** sent Lodge back to Vietnam as ambassador,

where he worked to develop the pacification program and to find a formula that would bring the North Vietnamese to the negotiating table. He served at that post until April 1967. Under President Johnson, Lodge was ambassador to West Germany from April 1968 until January 1969. He served as the U.S. chief negotiator at the Paris Peace Talks aimed at ending the **Vietnam War** from January 1969 until June 1970. In June 1970, Lodge was named presidential envoy to the Vatican. Lodge died after a long illness in Beverly, Massachusetts, 27 February 1985. *See also* BALL, GEORGE WILDMAN; HARRIMAN, WILLIAM AVERELL; PRESIDENTIAL ELECTION OF 1960.

LOEB, WILLIAM, III (1905–1981). William Loeb III was born in Washington, DC, on 26 December 1905, and he grew up in fashionable Oyster Bay, New York. His father, also named William, had been a private secretary to President Theodore Roosevelt. William attended the Hotchkiss School and graduated from Williams College, in Williamstown, Massachusetts, in 1927. After two years at Harvard Law School, Loeb took a variety of newspaper jobs before purchasing a string of small New England newspapers in the 1940s and 1950s. He bought a share in New Hampshire's *Manchester Union Leader* in 1946 and gained full control of the newspaper in 1948. The *Union Leader* was the only New Hampshire newspaper with a state-wide circulation, and Loeb used it as a forum for his arch-conservative and often erratic views on U.S. politics. His strength was negative. While he did not give a candidate momentum, he played upon the negatives, which helped erode support. The paper exercised an important influence on the state's politics and, once every four years during the presidential primary, on national politics as well, as the New Hampshire primaries were the candidates' first testing ground.

Using highly personal front-page editorials, Loeb supported Robert Taft (R-Ohio) and Joseph McCarthy (R-Wis.) in the 1950s. Late in the decade, he attacked the national political aspirations of Senator John F. Kennedy and, during the New Hampshire presidential primary in March 1960, supported a ball-point pen manufacturer from Chicago named Paul C. Fisher. It was an indication of hard-core New Hampshire support for Loeb's conservative ideas that the unknown Fisher received almost 13 percent of the Democratic vote in the 8 March primary. On 2 November 1960, six days before the presidential election, Loeb stated in an editorial that Kennedy, "whose father has a half a billion dollars and whose family has $40,000 weddings," was incapable of understanding the problems of the average citizen. On 7 November, the last day of the campaign, Kennedy, standing in front of the *Union Leader* offices in Manchester, declared: "I believe there is probably a more irresponsible newspaper than that one right over there somewhere in the United States, but I've been through 40 states and I haven't found it yet!" The crowd roared again as Kennedy said, "I believe that there is a publisher who has less regard for the truth than William Loeb, but I can't think of his name." Kennedy's strategy had been to attack Loeb 24 hours before the presidential election, so that the publisher— who lived just across the border in Massachusetts—would not have a chance to write an editorial reply before his newspaper's deadline. In the New Hampshire presidential balloting, Kennedy received 135,000 votes, the highest total for any Democrat in history, but he failed to carry the state. After the new president's inauguration, Loeb called him "the No. 1 liar in the United States."

During the Kennedy years, Loeb was involved with antitrust suits between one of his newspapers, the *Haverhill* (Massachusetts) *Journal*, and a group of anti-Loeb New England publishers who had purchased the rival *Gazette*. He borrowed heavily from the Teamsters Union to pay fines he incurred, and, as a result, he gave vigorous editorial support to Teamsters president James R. Hoffa in his running legal battle with Attorney General **Robert F. Kennedy**. Viewing himself as a last bastion of the traditional American way of life—he considered himself a conservative in the tradition of his godfather, Teddy Roosevelt—Loeb proffered a somewhat eccentric ideology. A vigorous anticommunist who saw a Soviet menace on a global scale, he nevertheless

denounced the far-right John Birch Society and called its leader, Robert Welch, a "bloody nut." In 1963, Loeb headed the Coordinating Committee for Fundamental Human Freedoms, a lobby against the **civil rights** bill. He was also a vigorous opponent of increased taxation in New Hampshire.

Loeb gave editorial support to the presidential candidacies of Senator **Barry M. Goldwater** (R-Ariz.) in 1964, **Richard M. Nixon** in 1968, and Los Angeles mayor Sam Yorty in 1972. William Loeb died of cancer in Burlington, Massachusetts, on 13 September 1981, at the age of 75.

M

MANN, THOMAS CLIFTON (1912–1999).
Thomas Clifton Mann was born in the border
town of Laredo, Texas, on 11 November 1912.
His family was deeply religious. He spoke
Spanish almost as fluently as English. After
attending Baylor University and Baylor Law
School, both in Waco, Texas, he joined his father's law firm before joining the State Department in 1942, specializing in Latin American
and economic affairs. He became a foreign
service officer in 1947, attaining ambassadorial rank in El Salvador in 1955. Mann was
named assistant secretary of state for economic affairs in 1957. Along with **C. Douglas
Dillon**, he set a pattern in President **Dwight
D. Eisenhower**'s Latin American policy that
provided a basis for some of the policies of
the John F. Kennedy administration. From
the outset, he believed the main issue for the
United States in this region was not the threat
of a communist invasion but the problem
of U.S. control over "readily accessible essential strategic materials," and he worked
toward that end throughout his career as a
diplomat. He was an advocate of U.S. military
intervention to curb nationalist ambitions in
Latin America. As a beginning, he sought to
influence the prices of Latin American commodities. In 1958, he succeeded in convincing
Latin American coffee-producing countries to
attempt to stabilize quotas and prices. A year
later he brought African nations into the agreement. In 1960, Mann helped negotiate the Act
of Bogota, an inter-American document signed
on 13 September by the hemispheric economic ministers in Bogota outlining measures

for social improvement and economic development within the framework of Operation Pan
America that foreshadowed the **Alliance for
Progress**. According to Arthur Schlesinger Jr.,
Mann was skeptical of the idealism of the **New
Frontier** and the Alliance for Progress but was
a "good bureaucrat and ready enough to go
along with" Kennedy policies. Mann was also
skeptical of the Central Intelligence Agency's
Cuban invasion plan but, like many others, felt
it was impossible to stop preparations that had
proceeded so far.

Kennedy appointed Mann ambassador to
Mexico in March 1961. Mann's first task was
to negotiate a resolution to the longstanding
dispute (known as the Chamizal) between the
United States and Mexico created by a shift
in the course of the Rio Grande separating El
Paso, Texas, and Ciudad Juárez, Chihuahua, in
Mexico. Mann resolved the first problem by negotiating the Chamizal Treaty of 1963, which
ceded part of El Paso to Mexico. Mexico was
also unhappy over the excessive salinity in the
irrigation water that flowed from the Colorado
River into Mexico. This problem was not successfully settled despite talks between Kennedy and Mexican president Fernando Lopez,
a $20 million U.S. agricultural loan, and grants
from the Ford and Rockefeller Foundations.

In December 1963, President **Lyndon B.
Johnson** named Mann as assistant secretary
of state for inter-American affairs. In addition,
Mann was also to head the U.S. Agency for International Development, an organization created by President Kennedy two years earlier.
Mann emphasized private U.S. investment in

Latin America and did not believe the United States should exclusively aid democratic governments or only those that sponsored social and economic reforms. His policy called for nonintervention against dictators if they were friendly to U.S. business interests but intervention against communists regardless of their policies. He believed economic development should precede political and social progress in many countries. Mann left government service in 1966 to lecture and, in 1967, became president of the Automobile Manufacturers Association. He died on 23 January 1999 in Lubbock, Texas. *See also* CUBA.

MANPOWER DEVELOPMENT AND TRAINING ACT (1962).

In May 1961, President John F. Kennedy sent a proposal to Congress aimed at training and retraining workers who were unemployed because of automation and technological change. Several factors prompted Kennedy's proposal. The Great Depression of the 1930s had created unprecedented unemployment, and the new developing postwar technology, driven by the emergence of the atomic age, appeared to threaten workers being replaced by machines. In addition, the **Cold War** required large numbers of skilled technicians. By the end of February 1962, these considerations came together to persuade Congress to pass the Manpower Development and Training Act with considerable Republican support. President Kennedy signed it into law on 15 March. During the 1950s, a number of federal acts had directly or indirectly extended various aid schemes for occupational **education**, but this was the first major U.S. federal job training program.

The initial three-year program authorized training allowances of up to 52 weeks for the unemployed, but it did not exclude participation by employed workers. Some unions, particularly the building trades, had reservations about the legislation, concerned that government training would interfere with apprenticeship programs. On 19 December 1963, **Lyndon B. Johnson** signed an amendment to the original act that provided basic education to prepare a worker for occupational training. The new legislation recognized that payment of allowances was necessary for younger people and lowered the age limit to 17 and 18 years of age because of their high rate of unemployment. Over subsequent years, the intent and focus of this legislation were modified several times, beginning with the Job Corps in 1964 and the Work Incentive Program in 1967.

MANSFIELD, MICHAEL JOSEPH (1903–2001). Michael Joseph Mansfield was born on 16 March 1903, in Brooklyn, New York, the son of Irish Catholic immigrants. Following the death of his mother from pneumonia, three-year-old Michael "Mike" and his two sisters were sent to live with relatives in Great Falls, Montana. From 1918 to 1922, he served successively in the navy, army, and marines. For the next eight years, he worked as a miner and mining engineer in Butte, Montana. Mansfield received BA and MA degrees from Montana State University in 1933 and 1934. He also attended the University of California, Los Angeles, from 1936 to 1937. He remained there to teach Latin American and Far Eastern history. Mansfield lost a Democratic congressional primary in Montana in 1940 but won a seat in the U.S. House of Representatives two years later. Interested in foreign affairs as a result of his academic background, the freshman congressman was assigned to the Foreign Relations Committee. At President Franklin D. Roosevelt's request, he made a tour of inspection in China in 1944. A supporter of President **Harry S. Truman**'s foreign policy, Mansfield served on the U.S. delegation to the 1951–1952 session of the **United Nations** General Assembly. In 1952, Mansfield defeated an incumbent Republican senator and entered the Senate the following year. He was immediately assigned a seat on that body's foreign relations panel. In 1957, Senate majority leader **Lyndon B. Johnson** chose Mansfield as his assistant, or whip. Johnson allegedly chose Mansfield because the latter was a political moderate and an unassertive man, unlikely to challenge the majority leader's authority. In January 1961, Johnson assumed the vice presidency, and the Senate Democratic caucus chose Mansfield to succeed him.

The Montana senator inherited a position that, although unrecognized by either

the Constitution or the Senate rules, gives its occupant great potential power. By tradition, the majority leader has nearly total control over the scheduling of bills and considerable influence over committee appointments and policy through the chairmanship of his party's Steering and Policy Committees and of the full party conference. Johnson had been a forceful and dominant leader, who used all the powers of cajolery and threats at his disposal to shape legislation and control the votes of his Democratic colleagues. He served as floor manager of almost every major bill as the Democrats' chief strategist, parliamentarian, and whip. Mansfield, however, assumed his position as a Democratic administration took office and, therefore, shared with the White House the role of directing the Senate majority. Because of his mild-mannered and scholarly disposition, and his preference to win votes by persuasion, a number of Democratic senators regarded Mansfield as an indecisive and ineffective leader. Mansfield left the arrangement of deals and the use of pressure to his whip, Senator **Hubert H. Humphrey** (D-Minn.). He preferred that committee chairmen acted as floor managers for their own bills. In addition, liberal Democratic senators often criticized Mansfield for working too closely with minority leader **Everett M. Dirksen** (R-Ill.), failing to appreciate that because many Senate Democrats were southern conservatives, he often had to cooperate with Dirksen to win Republican votes for administration measures. The almost universal affection in which he was held enabled Mansfield to exercise considerable influence. Under his guidance, the Senate passed controversial aid-to-education bills in 1961 and mass-transit and area-redevelopment bills in 1963, all of which were blocked in the House of Representatives.

Mansfield did not always agree with the administration on foreign policy, however. In June 1961, he suggested that Berlin be made a free, neutralized city under international guarantees and protection. American diplomats hastened to assure distraught West German officials that the majority leader was speaking only for himself. On 24 November 1963, as President Kennedy's casket lay in state in the Capitol rotunda, Mansfield delivered a eulogy stating: "He gave that we might give of ourselves, that we might give to one another until there would be no room, no room at all, for the bigotry, the hatred, prejudice, and the arrogance which converged in that moment of horror to strike him down."

During the Johnson administration, Mansfield became increasingly critical of the **Vietnam War**, which strained relations with the president. He became more assertive as Democratic leader when the Republicans gained control of the White House in 1969. In March 1976, he announced that he would not seek reelection that year. He was appointed ambassador to Japan in April 1977 by President Jimmy Carter, a role he retained during the Reagan administration until 1988. He died in Washington, DC, on 5 October 2001. *See also* CIVIL RIGHTS; JORDAN, BENJAMIN EVERETT; VIETNAM.

MARSHALL, THURGOOD (1908–1993). Thurgood Marshall was born on 2 July 1908 in Baltimore, Maryland, the second son of Norma and William Marshall. Norma was an elementary schoolteacher, and William worked as a railroad porter. He was descended from slaves on both sides of his family. He attended Frederick Douglass High School in Baltimore, and later graduated valedictorian of the class in 1933 at Howard University Law School in Washington, DC. In 1933, Marshall was named assistant special counsel of the **National Association for the Advancement of Colored People** (NAACP), special counsel in 1938, and director-counsel of the newly created NAACP Legal Defense and Educational Fund in 1940. In the latter two positions, Marshall coordinated the entire NAACP legal program and led the organization to a series of U.S. **Supreme Court** victories in cases challenging racial segregation and discrimination. Marshall argued 32 cases before the Supreme Court as NAACP counsel and won substantive victories in 29. His most notable success was the 1954 school desegregation decision in *Brown v. Board of Education*. In that case, the Supreme Court ruled unanimously that the doctrine of "separate but equal" was unconstitutional and

could not be used to keep schools segregated by race. It was among the first of the court's opinions breaking the barrier of legal racial discrimination. Other significant victories included the 1944 Supreme Court decision invalidating white Democratic primaries and a 1949 decision ending state court enforcement of racially restrictive covenants in housing.

John F. Kennedy nominated Marshall for a judgeship on the Second Circuit Court of Appeals on 23 September 1961, during a Senate recess after southern senators threatened to block his nomination—a so-called recess appointment. Marshall began serving in October. Marshall was later confirmed by the full Senate after the end of his "replacement" term, but Senator James O. Eastland, the Senate Judiciary Committee chairman who opposed Marshall's appointment, delayed hearings on the nomination for nearly eight months and then held six days of hearings stretched out over four months. The committee finally approved his appointment on 7 September 1962, by an 11–4 vote, and the full Senate confirmed the nomination on 11 September by a vote of 54–16.

As a new judge, Marshall had little opportunity to write majority opinions in significant civil or individual rights cases, and most of his written decisions concerned such areas as federal tort claims, admiralty law, or patent and trademark cases. However, his votes on the court and the opinions he did write identified him as a liberal jurist who usually granted the government broad powers in economic matters but barred it from infringing on the constitutional rights of the individual—a pattern he continued as an associate justice of the Supreme Court. Marshall was not actively involved in the **civil rights** movement after his appointment to the court. However, he remained a symbol of the NAACP's achievements through legal action.

President **Lyndon B. Johnson** appointed Marshall U.S. solicitor general in July 1965 and an associate justice of the U.S. Supreme Court in June 1967. Marshall was the first **African American** to hold either post. Marshall served on the court for 24 years, compiling a liberal record that included strong support

for civil rights and constitutional protection of individual rights. Marshall died of heart failure at the National Naval Medical Center in Bethesda, Maryland, on 24 January 1993, at the age of 84.

McCLOY, JOHN JAY (1895–1989). John Jay McCloy was born in Philadelphia, Pennsylvania, on 31 March 1895, the son of John J. McCloy, an auditor for the Penn Mutual Life Insurance Company, and Anna May Snader McCloy. He was a self-made man. His father died when McCloy was six, and his mother turned to nursing to support the family. He went on to become one of that group later called the "Wise Men" who were the architects of American foreign policy in the 30 years following World War II. He worked for four presidents who were Democrats and three who were Republicans from the administration of Franklin D. Roosevelt to that of Ronald Reagan, including the John F. Kennedy administration.

After serving as an artillery officer in the U.S. Army in Europe during World War I, he returned to the United States, graduating from Harvard Law School in 1921; he worked in several New York law firms specializing in international corporate law. In 1940, he accepted the position of consultant to U.S. secretary of war Henry L. Stimson; a year later, he became assistant secretary of war. In that post, he helped obtain congressional approval of the Lend-Lease Act and oversaw the program to intern Japanese Americans in World War II. He also advocated warning the Japanese people before the dropping of the atomic bomb. McCloy resigned his post in 1946 to resume private law practice before becoming head of the World Bank the following year. In 1949, he was appointed military governor and high commissioner for Germany. McCloy left Germany in 1952 and, for the next nine years, served as chairman of the Chase Manhattan Bank. In 1962, he returned to private practice to handle international legal problems for several of the nation's largest oil companies. As a lawyer, he represented scores of corporate clients, including 23 oil companies dealing with the Organization of Petroleum Exporting

Countries. From 1953 to 1965, he was also chairman of the Ford Foundation.

In January 1961, president-elect Kennedy appointed McCloy, a Republican, as his principal disarmament adviser and negotiator. While at that post, McCloy drafted the bill that led to the establishment of the **Arms Control and Disarmament Agency** in September 1961. The agency was designed to coordinate government policy on disarmament and nuclear testing free from the influence of other federal bodies. McCloy negotiated one of the seminal documents of the era: the U.S.-Soviet Joint Statement of Agreed Principles of Arms Control and Disarmament, adopted in September 1961. Painstakingly hammered out by McCloy with the ever-difficult Valerian Zorin (and invariably referred to as the McCloy-Zorin principles), these principles were a road map to the future. They led to the first serious **arms control** agreement, the test ban treaty of 1963. In October 1962, President Kennedy asked McCloy to take part in **United Nations** negotiations on the terms of inspection for the removal of Soviet missiles and the withdrawal of their bombers from **Cuba** during the American blockade of the island. The talks proved unproductive, and the question of inspection was solved only in December, when **Nikita Khrushchev** agreed to permit aerial observation and counting of the weapons as they left.

McCloy served on several presidential commissions during the **Lyndon B. Johnson** administration. In late 1963, Johnson appointed him to the **Warren Commission** probing Kennedy's death. A year later he joined panels dealing with ways of forestalling the spread of nuclear weapons and ensuring world peace. During 1966, McCloy acted as a presidential consultant on the North Atlantic Treaty Organization and was envoy to the multilateral talks held to renegotiate financial arrangements for German compensation of its allies, whose troops helped protect that country.

In 1968, Johnson asked McCloy to become a member of the Senior Advisory Group on **Vietnam**, which recommended de-escalation of the war in March of that year. McCloy made known his opposition to the president's Vietnam policies. In 1974,

a Senate investigation of the petroleum industry revealed that since 1961 McCloy had been in the forefront of attempts to unite U.S. oil companies in their dealings with the producing nations. He had also used his influence to obtain Justice Department approval for the plan in 1971. McCloy's efforts proved fruitless, however, because the U.S. ambassador to **Iran** had agreed to a suggestion by the shah that the oil companies conclude separate price arrangements with the producing states. He died in New York on 11 March 1989 at the age of 93. *See also* ASSASSINATION OF JOHN F. KENNEDY; BLACK, EUGENE ROBERT, SR.; BUNDY, McGEORGE; CUBAN MISSILE CRISIS.

McNAMARA, ROBERT STRANGE (1916–2009). Robert Strange McNamara was born in San Francisco on 9 June 1916, the son of the sales manager of a wholesale shoe business, and was raised in a middle-class section of Oakland. From grammar school to the University of California, Berkeley, to the Harvard Business School, McNamara was an outstanding student. After taking his MBA in 1939, he worked briefly for a San Francisco accounting firm. The next year he returned to Cambridge, Massachusetts, to accept a teaching post in the Harvard Business School.

During World War II, because of his poor vision, McNamara remained at Harvard to instruct U.S. Army Air Corps officers in statistical techniques useful for the management of the war effort. Transferred to the United Kingdom, he used his knowledge of logistics to assist the Air Corps bomber operations and was promoted to lieutenant colonel. By war's end he was in the Far East, where he pioneered ways of assessing the effects of B-29 bombing raids on Japan.

In 1945, McNamara joined a group of young army officers, later dubbed the "whiz kids," who offered their managerial services to the financially troubled Ford Motor Company. He was a great success, becoming general manager and vice president of the automotive division of Ford in the 1950s. In November 1960, McNamara was named company president, the first man outside of the Ford family

to hold that position. McNamara, a registered Republican, had held his new post for only a month when, at the suggestion of New York banker Robert Lovett, upon whom president-elect John F. Kennedy relied for advice on staffing many of his top policy-making positions, Kennedy invited him to join the cabinet as secretary of defense in the new administration. The ambitious, assertive McNamara soon became a favorite of Kennedy, and the two socialized with their friends in Georgetown. One result of the close relationship between Kennedy and McNamara was that the Joint Chiefs of Staff played a far less significant role in policy-making decisions under the new secretary of defense. McNamara was to become one of the most controversial cabinet members of the post–World War II era for his efforts to bring the armed forces under strong civilian control and as a leading architect of American strategy in **Vietnam**. He began to have doubts about the war late in his tenure but did not voice them publicly, much to the anger of many.

Shortly after he assumed office in January 1961, McNamara realized that many operations of the Pentagon were grossly inefficient because the three armed services, the army, navy, and air force, were duplicating efforts that cost the taxpayers billions of dollars. He enlarged his personal staff and moved to centralize decision-making authority. He also created several new divisions controlled by civilians to deal with the common needs of the armed services. He established cost-effectiveness programs that led him to veto construction of nuclear power plants for naval ships. McNamara's budgetary and organizational reforms were highly controversial. Despite McNamara's reluctance to build new weapons systems, the Defense Department budget rose from $45.9 billion in 1960 to $53.6 billion in 1964.

In 1962, following Kennedy's wishes, McNamara supported the development of a new jet fighter with "swing wings" to meet the needs of both the air force and the navy rather than developing the B-70 supersonic bomber, a project favored by U.S. Air Force chief of staff general Curtis LeMay. However, the aircraft, built by General Dynamics, did not perform as expected because of various structural problems, and it ran considerably over budget. Increases in defense spending also resulted from McNamara's adoption of the idea of developing a "second strike" capability, which he believed would reduce the likelihood of accidental nuclear war. To ensure a second-strike capability, McNamara urged the replacement of vulnerable, liquid-fuel intercontinental ballistic missiles (ICBMs) with solid-fuel Polaris and Minutemen ICBMs, which could be widely dispersed and fired quickly from underground or from submarines. In addition, he replaced the Eisenhower administration's doctrine of "massive retaliation" with a policy known as the "flexible response" strategy, in which highly mobile strike forces would be employed in the belief that such actions would thereby lessen the need to resort to nuclear weapons. McNamara won approval for a 300,000-man increase in U.S. fighting strength and authorization for a vast build-up in U.S. capacity to airlift troops. At the same time, he favored an end to the arms race and strongly supported the 1963 **Limited Nuclear Test Ban Treaty**, which he thought might lead to arms limitations talks between the United States and the **Soviet Union**.

McNamara regarded the Kennedy administration's handling of the **Cuban missile crisis** in October 1962 as an example of the successful use of his "flexible response" strategy. Kennedy's decision to follow the advice of his civilian rather than his military advisors when he learned of the presence of Soviet missile launch pads in **Cuba** defused a tense, highly volatile, and dangerous situation. Rather than immediately launch a military strike on the Soviet missile sites, Kennedy imposed a blockade (or a quarantine) of the island to turn back Soviet ships carrying missiles. McNamara carefully supervised the deployment and conduct of the blockade ships to ensure that unnecessary clashes with the Soviets were avoided. After the U.S. Navy intercepted two ships on the high seas, the Russians agreed to withdraw their missiles from Cuba.

McNamara believed the same flexible strategy would work in supressing what was being described as communist guerrilla

activity in Vietnam. Kennedy gave McNamara rather than secretary of state **Dean Rusk** responsibility for handling Vietnam. Throughout the 1950s, U.S. relations with Vietnam had been considered more of a military than a political problem, and the same attitude prevailed in the 1960s. At the end of 1961, an estimated 2,000 American troops were deployed in South Vietnam training Vietnamese military personnel and operating aircraft, transport, and communications facilities. In the spring of 1962, McNamara stated that the United States had no plans for introducing combat forces into South Vietnam, although Americans already there were authorized to fire back if fired upon. However, after visiting Saigon in the fall of 1963 with General **Maxwell D. Taylor**, he advised that the date for the completion of U.S. military involvement had lengthened to the end of 1965 and beyond. At the time of President Kennedy's death, there were some 15,000 American advisers in South Vietnam. McNamara soon realized that the war in Vietnam would not end soon, but he continued to misinform the American people about the lack of progress in the war. Vietnam soon became his overwhelming preoccupation, and in the spring of 1964 Senator **Wayne Morse** (D-Ore.) dubbed the conflict "McNamara's war." McNamara was subsequently involved in the key decisions that led in 1965 to the commitment of U.S. combat troops to South Vietnam and to sustained U.S. bombing of North Vietnam. By 1967, more than half a million American troops were involved in a conflict that was costing the United States $2.5 billion a month.

By the end of the 1960s Soviet nuclear capability was approaching parity with the United States, and the policy of massive retaliation, while a feasible if reckless policy when the U.S. had overwhelming nuclear superiority, was no longer viable. By then, both **Cold War** opponents believed they could absorb a nuclear first strike and still be capable of a retaliatory strike, thereby creating a situation of "assured destruction" (critic Donald Brennen added "mutual" to get the acronym of MAD). Faced with this reality, in September 1967 McNamara formally abandoned the policy of massive

retaliation replacing it with assured destruction, much to the chagrin of U.S. military chiefs.

In November 1967 McNamara announced his resignation as defense secretary, and in April 1968 he became president of the World Bank, a largely U.S.-supported organization devoted to lending money to underdeveloped countries. He later joined the search for "lessons" to be drawn from the **Vietnam War**, publishing a memoir, *In Retrospect* (1995). McNamara died in Washington, D.C., on 6 July 2009, at the age of 93. He is buried at the Arlington National Cemetery in Arlington, Virginia. *See also* ARMS RACE; CUBAN MISSILE CRISIS; FOREIGN POLICY FOR A NEW GENERATION; NUCLEAR DETERRENCE; VIETNAM.

MEDIA AND JOHN F. KENNEDY. Many commentators believe **television** was the most important factor in getting John F. Kennedy elected, and it certainly helped shape his presidency. Kennedy and his wife, **Jacqueline Kennedy**, brought youth, glamour, and excitement to the White House. Kennedy himself used the new medium to inspire young Americans to public service. And then, with the televised coverage of the events following his assassination, Kennedy became not just an icon but an almost mythical figure.

John F. Kennedy was the first television president. The nation had never seen a presidential debate until the little-known senator from Massachusetts faced Republican vice president **Richard M. Nixon** in 1960. He became the first president to allow live coverage of his news conferences. By November 1963, Kennedy had held 64 news conferences, an average of one every 16 days. The first, less than a week after his inauguration, was viewed by an estimated 65 million people. A poll taken in 1961 indicated that 90 percent of those interviewed had watched at least one of Kennedy's first three press conferences. Journalists loved him because he was witty, charming, engaging, and handsome. Americans came to know Kennedy in a more personal way than any of his predecessors. Kennedy was briefly a newspaperman in his youth. He understood the power of the press, and he understood how to put himself and his family in the best light.

"A nation that is afraid to let its people judge the truth and falsehood in an open market is a nation that is afraid of its people," he stated.

Kennedy's first national television exposure took place when he gave the nominating speech for candidate **Adlai Stevenson II** at the 1956 Democratic Convention. He urged the party to unite around "the most eloquent, the most forceful, and our most appealing figure." Impressing the television audience, Kennedy became the most sought-after speaker of the **Democratic Party**, catapulting his presidential run.

Pierre Salinger, press secretary to President Kennedy, noted in an interview for the John F. Kennedy Presidential Library and Museum that

> John F. Kennedy was the first president to effectively use the new medium of television to speak directly to the American people. No other president had conducted live televised press conferences without delay or editing. The fact of the matter is that the time when President Kennedy started televised press conferences there were only three or four newspapers in the entire United States that carried a full transcript of a presidential press conference. Therefore, what people read was a distillation. . . . We thought that they should have the opportunity to see it in full. Although some worried about the risk of mistakes or injudicious statements by the president, and others thought the press showed insufficient respect for the dignity of his office, public response was extremely positive.

The average audience for all the broadcast conferences was 18 million viewers. Though he helped enlarge significantly the role of television as a news medium, President Kennedy himself continued to be a voracious consumer of print journalism. In responding to a question about his reading habits during a December 1962 interview with representatives of the three major television networks, Kennedy gave his overall view of the contributions, as well as the responsibilities, of the press in a free society:

SANDER VANOCUR (NBC): You once said that you were reading more and enjoying it less. Are you still as avid a newspaper reader, magazine—I remember those of us who travelled with you on the campaign, a magazine wasn't safe around you.

THE PRESIDENT: Oh, yes. No, no, I think it is invaluable, even though it may cause you—it is never pleasant to be reading things that are not agreeable news, but I would say that it is an invaluable arm of the presidency, as a check really on what is going on in the administration, and more things come to my attention that cause me concern or give me information. So I would think that Mr. Khrushchev operating a totalitarian system, which has many advantages as far as being able to move in secret, and all the rest—there is a terrific disadvantage not having the abrasive quality of the press applied to you daily, to an administration, even though we never like it, and even though we wish they didn't write it, and even though we disapprove, there isn't any doubt that we could not do the job at all in a free society without a very, very active press. Now, on the other hand, the press has the responsibility not to distort things for political purposes, not to just take some news in order to prove a political point. It seems to me their obligation is to be as tough as they can on the administration but do it in a way which is directed towards getting as close to the truth as they can get and not merely because of some political motivation.

The president was not always so sanguine about the media, especially when it criticized his decisions or actions.

MEREDITH, JAMES H. (1933–). James Howard Meredith was born on 25 June 1933 in Kosciusko, Mississippi, and grew up on a Mississippi farm. He graduated from high school in 1951, and he then spent nine years in the air force. He returned to Mississippi in August 1960 and enrolled that fall at the all-black Jackson State College to complete the college studies he had begun while in the military. Sometime during the semester, Meredith decided to try to enter the all-white University

of Mississippi at Oxford, the state's best public university. His goal was to put pressure on the Kennedy administration to enforce **civil rights** for **African Americans**. In his account of this effort, *Three Years in Mississippi*, published in 1966, Meredith wrote that he believed he had a "divine responsibility," a "mission," to help "break the system of 'White Supremacy'" in Mississippi and direct "civilization toward a destiny of humaneness." Inspired by the inaugural address of President John F. Kennedy, he sent his application for admission to Oxford in January 1961, initiating a 17-month fight to desegregate the University of Mississippi. Supported by the **National Association for the Advancement of Colored People** in his legal struggle with the university to allow his admission, on 1 October 1962, Meredith became the first African American student to enroll at the university. Kennedy ordered the nationalized Mississippi National Guard and federal troops to the campus to overcome the violent opposition to Meredith's admission. Many regard this event as a pivotal moment in the history of civil rights in the United States. In August 1963, despite considerable harassment and isolation by white students, Meredith graduated with a degree in political science. He then went on to receive a master's degree in economics from the University of Ibadan in Nigeria and a law degree from Columbia University in 1968. He later unsuccessfully sought election to political offices. He lives in Jackson, Mississippi.

MIDDLE EAST.

Introduction

In his run for the presidency, John F. Kennedy promised that, if elected, he would embark upon a new "even-handed" approach to the Middle East. As president, he discovered that it was not an easy promise to keep. Kennedy was not entirely unfamiliar with the region and the complexities of the competing interests that were in play there. He sought to achieve a comprehensive peace settlement of the Israel-Arab conflict, believing he could accomplish more than the Eisenhower administration to further U.S. interests and to insulate the region against an increase of Soviet influence. For its

part, the **Soviet Union** was seeking to improve its position in the Muslim world by promoting itself as the champion of Arab revolutionary nationalism.

Kennedy had briefly visited British-mandated Palestine in 1939 and Israel in 1951. Because of his Irish heritage, he empathized with those who had suffered persecution and displacement. Unlike his father, he was not anti-Semitic, and he strongly endorsed President **Harry S. Truman**'s recognition of the state of Israel and U.S. policy of support for the newly founded state. He was also disturbed and stressed at the plight of Palestinian refugees who fled the fighting in 1947–1948, and he strongly advocated their repatriation to their former homes. He recognized that preventing the tensions between Israelis and Palestinians from erupting into outright conflict was a key element to maintaining regional stability. He also recognized that the desire of Arab populations to free themselves from colonial rule and create independent nation-states was another potent force sweeping the region and that the United States should cultivate Arab leaders as friends or they would be lost to communism. There was an added imperative to maintain good relations with Arab leaders—namely, their possession of vast reserves of oil necessary for the recovery and growth of America's European allies. The Middle East's strategic location at the intersection of east and west and north and south added to the region's value as a highly desirable asset in the contest between the United States and the Soviet Union for predominant power and influence. Successful juggling all these elements also depended upon the cooperation of European allies, a task that in itself was fraught with difficulties.

Kennedy made his commitment to even-handedness clear in the organization of his administration. Two of his cabinet members were staunch supporters of Israel and the creation of close ties with the Middle East state—**Abraham Ribicoff** and Abraham Goldberg—and he appointed **Myer Feldman**, one of his key campaign aides, as special counsel to liaise with the U.S. Jewish community. He made these appointments to balance the pro-Arab propensities of senior State Department

and National Security Council members. U.S. secretary of state **Dean Rusk**, assistant secretary of state Phillip Talbot, and National Security Council member Robert Komer all favored closer ties with **Egypt**'s president, Gamal Abdul Nasser. Kennedy's ambassador to Egypt, **John Badeau**, needless to say, also believed that Nasser was the key figure to cultivate peace in the region.

However, events in the volatile and unpredictable Middle East moved quickly in the 32 months Kennedy was president. In short, the Middle East presented Kennedy with monumental challenges, which, in the end, he was no more successful in overcoming than had been his predecessors—or successors, for that matter.

The Middle East experienced a period of political turmoil in the years 1946–1960 as the populations of the region sought to achieve and consolidate national independence. The revolutionary unrest that accompanied the decolonization process was compounded by the conflict between the state of Israel—newly sanctioned by the **United Nations** (UN)—and its Arab neighbors, as well as attempts by the Soviet Union to expand its influence in the region. The overthrow of pro-Western regimes in **Syria** (1949), Egypt (1952), and Iraq (1958), as well as the ongoing challenges to the Jordanian monarchy and the near collapse of the government in Lebanon in 1958, greatly alarmed Washington. President **Dwight D. Eisenhower** sought to strengthen the conservative regimes in **Saudi Arabia**, Lebanon, Iraq, and **Jordan** through arms sales and political support, as well as encouraging regional security arrangements. American policy in the Middle East sought to create and maintain stable, independent, pro-Western regimes; to increase its presence and influence in the region; and to strengthen its partnerships with the United Kingdom and other Western European allies to achieve the above two goals.

The instrument of American policy became the Eisenhower Doctrine, approved by Congress in March 1957. By its terms, the president was authorized to extend economic and military assistance, including troops, to any Middle Eastern nation that requested help against the threat of international communism. No Arab country, with the exceptions of Libya and Lebanon, was eager to embrace the doctrine. Zionism, not communism, was considered the enemy. Moreover, the United States was seen as attempting to weaken Arab unity by insisting that the Arab countries line up on one side or the other in the **Cold War**. Although the United States continued to maintain an important air base at Dhahran (until 1961), and the Saudis were considered to be "allies," the Saudi king did not endorse the Eisenhower Doctrine. Nor did Jordan's King Hussein, even though the United States extended $10 million in financial assistance to Jordan when the king quashed a Nasser-supported communist plot against the monarchy in 1957.

U.S. relations with Egypt were especially fraught during these years, in part because Egypt's pivotal strategic location made it a hotly contested prize in the Cold War struggle between the United States and the Soviet Union, and partly because of its prominence in the Arab resistance to Israel. Efforts to win over Egypt's charismatic and fiercely nationalistic leader Gamal Abdel Nasser to become a friend of America failed. And while the United States made no secret of its friendship and support for Israel, the Eisenhower administration recognized that active intervention in the conflict between the Arab states and Israel would further alienate extremist Arab leaders and provide an opportunity for the Soviet Union to offer them assistance against Israel.

Kennedy and his administration, however, indicated a somewhat greater appreciation of the dynamics and complexities of the Arab world. They began to realize that the achievement of American objectives did not require a specific form of political or economic system. Indeed, many believed that America could aid constructive change in Middle Eastern countries through nonmilitary aid and cultural exchange, to the mutual benefit of the Arabs and the United States. Economic and technical aid was therefore offered to Egypt, especially through Public Law 480, which enabled recipient countries to purchase surplus wheat and other commodities with local currency that remained in the country to generate

development projects. In the early 1960s, for example, the United States supplied around $150 million a year in wheat surpluses, which was more than half the grain consumed in Egypt.

The Kennedy administration had only limited capacity to influence events in the Middle East. Arab leaders were much more inclined to listen to Nasser than to Kennedy, and Israel's main arms supplier was France, not the United States, so Washington could not exert much influence on Israeli leaders. With U.S. attention focused on such volatile hotspots as Berlin and **Cuba**, and increasingly on troubling developments in Southeast Asia and **Vietnam**, the American public was not interested in a greater active commitment in the Middle East. There were already enough problems avoiding conflict with the Soviet Union without adding further risks in that part of the world. Besides, Washington thought Israel could look after itself.

Arab Nationalism

The appeal of Arab nationalism, whether promoted by Nasser or by the ideology of the Arab Renaissance, or *Ba'ath*, Party, became almost irresistible in the 1950s. The Ba'ath Party, formed in Syria in the mid-1950s, combined the idea of Arab unity with that of revolutionary socialism, and its slogan became "Arab freedom, Arab socialism, and Arab unity." Described as being "post-communistic," it rejected Marxist internationalism and allowed for some private ownership in the economic sphere. The party established branches in Lebanon, Jordan, and Iraq. It eventually seized power in Syria and Iraq, although a bitter rivalry marked the relations of the two groups.

In Syria, the Ba'ath Party had assumed increasing power in the mid-1950s and had initiated economic and social changes. Supplied with Soviet arms and equipment but coming under Soviet influence internally as well as externally, and fearful of a communist takeover within Syria, the Ba'ath Party leaders precipitated the 1958 union with Egypt. Ba'ath ideology, however, was inconsistent with the goal of international communism, and it was also

incompatible with the kind of authoritarian, one-man rule personified by Nasser. Moreover, Syria's economy, which had been built up after the war largely by a vigorous middle class, and which, despite Arab socialism, remained more freewheeling than that of Egypt, was sacrificed to Egyptian needs.

The idea of Arab unity, or Pan-Arabism, was also powerful in the years after the Suez War of 1956, and it primarily focused on Nasser. The high point for pan-Arabism was achieved in 1958 when Syria joined Egypt in creating the United Arab Republic (UAR). Yemen, under a hereditary monarch, became a federated member of the UAR. In that same year, the pro-Western monarchy in Iraq was toppled, and one of the first acts of the new military regime was to withdraw from the pro-U.S. Baghdad Pact. The UAR was a complete merger of the two countries rather than a confederation of equals, and Egypt was the dominant partner. In 1961, after Nasser announced drastic nationalization decrees affecting almost 90 percent of industry, manufacturing, and trade, Syria withdrew from the UAR. As the Arabs debated the implications of unity, civilian control was replaced by a Ba'ath military coup in 1963, and yet another in 1966, which brought to the fore General Salah Jadid, the most radical leader until then in the Arab world. Jadid was critical of other Arab leaders whom he accused of passivity, and he openly threatened Israel.

Meanwhile, a civil war had erupted in Lebanon, precipitated in part by the waves rippling out from Egypt. The Christian Lebanese president, Camille Chamoun, concerned about the effect in Lebanon of the coup in Iraq, called in the U.S. Marines on 15 July 1958. There was also instability in Jordan, where King Hussein in 1957 had dismissed his parliament, alleging a communist plot against him inspired by Nasser. On 17 July, Hussein requested the landing of British troops to help stabilize the monarchy.

Despite the prestige that Nasser continued to enjoy with the masses, the internal economic situation in Egypt deteriorated. By the mid-1960s, Egypt was in serious financial straits. Egypt became embroiled in a civil war

in Yemen after 1962 that drained its manpower and money (to the tune of around $1 million per day). A determined but largely frustrated effort to industrialize exhausted Egypt's foreign-currency reserves. Egypt was simply unable to keep up with population growth, unemployment, and inflation.

Egypt

Relations with Gamal Abdel Nasser had gone from bad to worse during the Eisenhower administration. The signing of the short-lived and ill-conceived regional mutual security defense agreement known as the Baghdad Pact in February 1955 masterminded by Washington, which excluded Egypt but included Iraq, led Nasser to seek weapons from the Soviet Union and China. And Eisenhower's comprehensive peace plan for the Arab-Israeli conflict unveiled in August 1955, code-named "Alpha," was rejected by both sides. Then in July 1956, Nasser nationalized the Suez Canal, an action that set in motion events leading to the Suez-Sinai War of October–November 1956, between Egypt on one side and France and Britain on the other, precipitated by a previously agreed upon invasion of Egypt by Israeli forces. Despite the prominent role played by Eisenhower in separating the combatants and ending the hostilities in 1956, U.S. relations with Egypt remained tense. Indeed, the United States adhered to a Western economic boycott of Egypt, refusing to sell surplus wheat and oil. In this way, the United States exhibited its continued friendship for its European allies and its disdain for Nasser. At the same time, this attitude enabled and encouraged the Soviet Union and its satellites to extend their influence.

By the time John Kennedy took office in January 1961, Egypt's Nasser was no longer enthralled by the Soviet Union, and was he prepared to seek a rapprochement with the United States. Nasser was at the height of his popularity as the hero and leader of Arab nationalism. In February 1958, the United Arab Republic, a political union of Syria and Egypt with Nasser as president, was created as a result of a Syrian initiative. Later that year, on 14 July 1958, Iraqi army officers staged a

military coup and overthrew the Hashemite king of Iraq—which had just previously united with Jordan to form a rival Arab Federation. Jordan and Lebanon were alarmed by these developments, and the next day U.S. Marines and British special forces landed in Lebanon and in Jordan, respectively, to protect the two countries from falling to pro-Nasser forces.

John F. Kennedy was especially keen to seek a rapprochement with Egypt, not because of any great attachment to Nasser, but because he hoped a lessening of tension between the Egyptian leader and Washington might be beneficial in countering Soviet growing influence with Egypt's allies in the region, Syria and Iraq. In May 1961, Kennedy wrote the first of several accommodating letters to Nasser, and he appointed John Badeau, a former missionary in Iraq and president of the American University in Cairo as ambassador (and personal representative) to Egypt. In July 1961, on their first meeting, Nasser made clear to U.S. ambassador John Badeau that differences between the two countries over the Israel-Palestine issue should be put to one side—in the ice box—so that they could discuss bilateral matters. One example of this approach was that in September 1962 Kennedy informed the Egyptian leader of the impending American arms sales to Israel in an attempt to lessen Arab hostility to the move. The Kennedy administration indicated that if Nasser turned his attention to internal reforms rather than seeking to further his influence abroad, the United States would provide Egypt with surplus U.S. wheat under Public Law 480 (a foreign assistance program designed to sell off surplus agricultural products). The United States supplied around $150 million a year in wheat surpluses, which was more than one-third of the grain consumed in Egypt.

On 28 September 1961, a group of Syrian army officers unhappy with Nasser's almost total control over Syrian affairs staged a coup and declared Syria's independence from the UAR, although Nasser retained the name until 1971. After a good deal of internal debate—which included a favorable report from Chester Bowles, whom Kennedy appointed as ambassador-at-large to the Third World, and

who visited Egypt in February 1962—on 30 June, Kennedy signed a three-year, $500 million PL40 agreement. This was the high point in U.S.-Egyptian relations during the Kennedy administration.

Egypt's policy in Yemen ended the rapprochement between Kennedy and Nasser. In December 1962, the United States recognized the newly declared Yemen Republic. Nasser then went back on his promise to remove Egyptian troops from Yemen, supporting the revolutionary government against counterrevolutionary royalist forces armed and supported by Saudi Arabia. Throughout 1963, Kennedy unsuccessfully sought the end of fighting in Yemen using a personal emissary. He could not afford to antagonize Crown Prince Faisal of Saudi Arabia and did not want to lose Nasser. In the end, he did both, and the conflict continued.

Iran and Jordan

Perhaps the most immediate critical events to face Kennedy in the Middle East upon assuming office took place in Iran. In May 1961, around 50,000 teachers and students rioted in Tehran seeking better pay, freedom of political activity and expression, and social justice, threatening to topple the government of the pro-Western, dictatorial shah. The Kennedy administration saw Iran as a major area of stability and strategic importance. The main aim of U.S. policy was to keep Iran as a strong and stable ally to minimize Soviet influence and, of course, to protect its oil reserves for the West. The shah played upon Kennedy's fears and perceptions of Soviet intentions while posing as a secular reformer to extract maximum economic and military aid from the United States—which he did with great success. He was aided in this as there were debates within the Kennedy administration as to how far the shah could be pushed to make democratic reforms without pushing him into the arms of the Soviets. There were even some who thought at this early stage that he should not be supported at all.

Following the May 1961 riots, Kennedy immediately set up an Iranian task force headed by State Department officer Armin

Meyer. Meyer reported that sweeping reforms were needed if the regime was to avoid being swept aside by those seeking the democratization and modernization of Iran. Over the next 18 months, the president sent Vice President **Lyndon B. Johnson** and Ambassador Bowles to urge this course upon the shah. In April 1962, Kennedy stressed the urgency of reform upon the shah when, at the president's invitation, the latter visited Washington and Kennedy demonstrated his commitment with a $90 million development aid package.

However, after a brief period of reform— the so-called White Revolution in late 1962— the shah once again cracked down on dissent. When, in June 1963, Ayatollah Ruhollah Khomeini—a radical, anti-shah cleric—was arrested, massive uprisings occurred in five major Iranian cities. Faced with this, the government sent in the army infantry and tanks to crush the riots, which resulted in at least hundreds (some believe thousands) of deaths. Overall, Kennedy's policies were to have only a limited impact on the course of events in Iran. Kennedy had more success when he adopted the same approach with King Hussein of Jordan, providing the young king with $50 million of development aid per year with which to modernize his country.

Israel

The Kennedy years were pivotal in U.S. relations with Israel because, for the first time, Washington agreed to sell major weapons to Israel, setting the two countries on the path toward today's close association. Kennedy's policy toward Israel was in marked contrast to that of his predecessors. Kennedy was not entirely unfamiliar with the circumstances arising from the establishment of Israel in 1948. As a young man, he had visited the region in 1939, and he agreed with Britain's policy of restricting Jews fleeing Nazi Germany from entering Palestine and had kept up with post–World War II developments. Kennedy visited Israel a second time in late 1951 as part of a seven-week Middle East tour with Congressman Franklin Delano Roosevelt Jr., which included Iran, Pakistan, India,

Southeast Asia, Korea, and Japan. He recognized that relations with Israel existed within the context of basic American interests in the area. These included access to the region's oil, uninterrupted communications facilities, the maintenance of general stability, and the protection of strategic interests against the threat of Soviet expansionism. The United States assured Israel that it upheld the principle of the territorial integrity of all countries in the region and would defend Israel against aggression. Although he acknowledged the legitimate aspirations of Arab states for national independence, one of Kennedy's first acts was to send his assistant, **Myer Feldman**, on a secret mission to Tel Aviv to promise Israel U.S. protection by the U.S. Sixth Fleet in the case of an Arab attack. Feldman also offered to sell to Israel Hawk ground-to-air missiles.

During his time in the Oval Office, Kennedy gave Israel frequent assurances of U.S. support. He did not always agree with his secretary of state, Dean Rusk, who had a good knowledge of the Arab-Israeli conflict and knew the intractability of the issues. Rusk believed the best policy was to remain cool and stay out of the kitchen while Kennedy was always looking for new recipes. The closer ties between the United States and Israel flourished in part because Golda Meir and David Ben-Gurion succeeded in forging close personal connections with Kennedy. Kennedy and Meir admired each other. At a dinner in her honor held in Boston on 25 November 1956, the then senator Kennedy observed that "the story of Mrs. Golda Meir is the story of modern Israel," and in a 70-minute informal meeting with Meir in December 1962 at his Palm Beach, Florida, vacation home three months after the sale of Hawk missiles to Israel, Kennedy told the Israeli foreign minister that the United States and Israel had "a special relationship . . . comparable" to that between the United States and Britain "over a wide range of world affairs." Domestic politics—the (so-called) Israel lobby—played little role in this process. Together with the Israeli president, Zalman Shazar, Meir attended Kennedy's funeral in Washington's National Cathedral.

However, Kennedy had little success in using his personal connections to resolve the issue of the future of Palestinian refugees. Intermittent fighting between Israeli troops and Palestinian guerrilla groups had been taking place regularly in the years since Israel's declaration of independence. In fall 1961, concerned that the resentment of hundreds of thousands of Palestinians in refugee camps with little hope of returning to their homes would erupt into violence, Kennedy asked Dr. Joseph Johnson of the Carnegie Endowment to develop a the resettlement plan for Palestinian refugees. Johnson's plan, released in July 1962, which would have allowed for the return of an estimated 100,000 Palestinians under the active supervision of the UN, was rejected by Ben-Gurion Meir who offered to accept only 20,000. Johnson had no luck on his first or on a subsequent trip the next spring in moving the different parties from their respective positions. The Arabs continued to insist on the right of return of all refugees, and the Israelis insisted on recognition by the Arab states and direct negotiation of all outstanding issues, including that of the refugees. The Kennedy administration then determined to link the supply of Hawk missiles and a U.S. security guarantee to an Israeli pledge to cooperate with the Johnson plan.

Israel had been seeking weapons from the United States during previous administrations with only very limited success. Soviet arms sales to Egypt in the mid-to-late 1950s made the matter even more urgent for the Israelis. Israeli prime minister Ben-Gurion met with Kennedy in New York on 30 May 1961 and requested that the United States supply Israel with Hawk surface-to-air missiles to defend his country against air attacks. In reality, the Israeli military regarded the acquisition of these U.S. missiles as more symbolic than a tactical necessity. Kennedy agreed to look into the request but stressed the need for Israel to cooperate in finding a solution to the plight of Palestinian refugees. A year later, Shimon Peres, at the time deputy minister of defense, renewed the request, but the administration took little action. The Israelis initially made their acceptance of the Johnson plan

dependent upon endorsement of the arrangement by Nasser and other Arab states. Nasser did not object to the deal but indicated that other Arab states would find it unacceptable. Nasser was correct; Libya and even pro-American Lebanon strongly objected to the deal, and Jordan's King Hussein made it clear that he, too, should receive Hawk missiles. Israel rejected the plan outright when it was made public at the United Nations General Assembly in New York in September 1962. Nevertheless, agreement for the sale of the Hawk ground-to-air missiles and tanks went ahead at the end of September, and the administration also agreed to ship arms to Saudi Arabia and Jordan. In this way, Kennedy attempted to maintain a balance between Israel and the Arabs, and between the "radical" Arab countries supplied by the Soviet Union and those supplied by the United States.

Golda Meir met with Kennedy in December 1962 in Palm Beach, Florida, to again press for the Hawk missiles. Meir told Kennedy that Israel's need was even greater at that time as Egypt had demonstrated its regional ambitions by intervening in the civil war being fought in Yemen. Nevertheless, Kennedy insisted, and Meir reluctantly agreed that Israel would make efforts to resolve the Palestinian refugee dilemma in exchange for the missiles. Unexpected events in Jordan, Iraq, and Syria in early 1963, however, derailed the Johnson plan. Palestinians rioted against King Hussein, threatening to overthrow the monarch. In February, pro-Nasser militias overthrew the governments of Iraq and Syria and called for a pan-Arab union of Egypt, Iraq, and Syria. If the regime of King Hussein fell, they would occupy all the West Bank. By April, military hostilities between Israel and neighboring Arab states appeared imminent. Kennedy and his advisers were worried that if the United States intervened directly with military forces in support of Israel, the Arab states would turn to the Soviets for support. Ben-Gurion called for a joint Soviet-American security guarantee of Israel as well as the delivery of the promised Hawk missiles. The Kennedy administration rejected the idea of a joint guarantee of Israel, deciding instead to send the Sixth Fleet to the eastern Mediterranean to enable American forces to defend King Hussein if necessary. The crisis in Jordan passed, and while Kennedy reiterated that the United States and Israel had a "special relationship," he refused to issue a formal U.S. guarantee to Israel.

In addition to the hostility displayed by the Arab states to America moving to closer relations with Israel, and the implications this posed for the Cold War, there was one major obstacle to close ties with Israel during the Kennedy years: Israel's determination to build a nuclear weapon. One of Kennedy's major concerns was the administration's suspicion, if not undeniable knowledge, that Israel was secretly building a nuclear bomb. Not only was this activity in opposition to Kennedy's policy of preventing/limiting the spread of nuclear weapons, Israel also refused to allow U.S. inspectors to visit its nuclear reactor site, Dimona, and, as later declassified documents revealed, Israel was deliberately duplicitous in denying it was engaged in the project. Even more ironic is the fact that Israel had advanced its nuclear know-how through a small research reactor provided by the Eisenhower administration in 1958. Fearing that Israel's possession of an atomic bomb would lead to a nuclear **arms race** in the Middle East with the Soviets supplying the Arabs states, Kennedy tried once more to obtain Nasser's cooperation, resurrecting the idea of an arms limitation agreement for the region not unlike that first proposed in the 1950s. In mid-May 1963, the president sent his special coordinator for disarmament, **John J. McCloy**, to Egypt with the idea, but Nasser rejected the notion out of hand. He was determined to obtain his own missiles in response to Israel's acquisition of the Hawks.

Still seeking the elusive U.S. security guarantee, Levi Eshkol, who had succeeded Ben-Gurion as Israeli prime minister in June 1963, voiced some conciliatory proposals, and in October 1963, Kennedy formally confirmed to Eshkol that "the United States would militarily assist Israel in case of attack." Israel denied it was developing a nuclear weapon, and Kennedy did not push too hard to find out what was happening at the location of Israel's nuclear

research base Dimona, a small town in the Negev desert, or to put a stop to the process. Discussions between Kennedy and Ben-Gurion in 1961 through early 1963 were followed by American visits to the Dimona plant with little being learned by the Americans. When Kennedy insisted upon an unrestricted U.S. inspection in May–June 1963, Eshkol reluctantly agreed but ensured that on their visit in late 1963 the inspectors did not discover the full nature of the weapons program work being carried out. The question remained, as the Israelis described it, "a sensitive issue."

Saudi Arabia

Relations between Saudi Arabia and the United States had deteriorated by the time Kennedy took office. Despite repeated American urging, the crown had refused to undertake much-needed social-economic reforms; the country's economy was in crisis, and tension was high between King Saud and his brother, Crown Prince Faisal. In 1961, Prince Faisal refused to renew the lease of the U.S. air base at Dhahran, and Kennedy froze U.S. technical aid to the monarchy. Saudi Arabia's involvement in the civil war being fought in Yemen threatened the future of the monarchy itself.

Saudi Arabia had been engaged in warfare supporting the family of recently crowned imam Mohammed al-Badr who had been overthrown by pro-Nasser military officers seeking to establish a republic in September 1962, and al-Badr escaped to Saudi Arabia. The royalists were supported by the monarchies, Jordan and Saudi Arabia, which supplied military aid, with British encouragement, while the republicans were supported by Nasser who supplied troops and military aircraft from the Soviet Union. Kennedy was concerned that the war would extend beyond Yemen and urged the Saudis to cease their assistance to al-Badr's forces and called for the withdrawal of Nasser's forces from Yemen. Nasser agreed, but Saudi Arabia and Jordan refused. Jordan's King Hussein faced his own problems, desperately fighting Palestinian radicals inspired by Nasser to overthrow his regime.

After some hesitation, in December 1962 the Kennedy administration recognized the new Yemen Arab Republic. In January 1963, Faisal increased his support for the royalist rebels, and Nasser retaliated with air attacks against the royalists inside Saudi Arabia. Kennedy finally decided to station a "token" air defense force in Saudi Arabia in return for suspension of Saudi aid to the royalists, but the proxy conflict between Egypt and Saudi Arabia continued. There seemed no end in sight.

Kennedy's November 1963 assurance to Saudi Arabia, together with that given to Israel in October, more or less ended the even-handed approach adopted by the president. If there was any doubt, in November 1963 the Senate targeted the UAR in passing legislation outlawing PL480 assistance to countries engaged militarily against the United States or its allies.

MILLS, WILBUR DAIGH (1909–1992). Wilbur Daigh Mills was born on 24 May 1909 in Kensett, Arkansas, the son of a country banker. He was educated at Arkansas public schools and Methodist-affiliated Hendrix College before attending Harvard Law School. After gaining his law degree in 1933, he returned to Arkansas and worked in his father's bank because of the Depression. In 1934, he was elected country and probate judge for White County, serving until his election to the House of Representatives in 1938. Mills was to become one of the most powerful men in Congress during the Kennedy and Johnson administrations.

Mills joined the Ways and Means Committee—which handles legislation relating to taxes, Social Security, and foreign trade—in 1943, becoming its chairman in late 1957. By the 1950s he was the House's foremost tax expert. No congressman could match his vast knowledge of the tax laws. Most stood in awe of his mastery of the complex subject matter, applauding his lucid explanations of complicated bills. During the Kennedy administration, Mills held a pivotal position in the enactment of the administration's economic program. In April 1961, Mills introduced the administration's bill to increase Social Security benefits and lower

the retirement age from 65 to 62. He was the floor manager in March 1962 for administration welfare measures that made far-reaching changes in the federal–state public assistance and child welfare programs. The bill, which increased welfare benefits and enlarged the federal government's role, passed the House, 320 to 69. Mills also guided through the House the centerpiece of the administration's 1962 legislative program, the **Trade Expansion Act**. He managed to preserve all the major provisions requested by the president through a nine-month congressional struggle. The House finally passed the bill, 256 to 91, in October 1962. The new law authorized the president to cut tariffs to stimulate the nation's foreign trade. Like all his southern colleagues, however, he voted against all **civil rights** proposals. Mills also blocked the Kennedy administration's Medicare plan to provide medical care for the aged financed through the Social Security system, but he became a key player in the success of the 1965 Medicare bill.

Mills resigned as chairman of the Ways and Means Committee in December 1974 after a highly publicized incident in which he was linked with an Argentine stripper, and then hospitalized for alcoholism and exhaustion. Mills did not run for re-election in 1976. He acknowledged his alcoholism and joined Alcoholics Anonymous and toward the end of his life helped fund research into alcoholism and drug abuse at the University of Arkansas. He died in Searcy, Arkansas, on 2 May 1992.

MISSILE GAP. The **Soviet Union** launched the world's first intercontinental ballistic missile (ICBM) in August 1957, followed by Sputnik, the world's first man-made, earth-orbiting satellite, on 4 October 1957. An inquiry by President **Dwight D. Eisenhower**'s Security Resources Panel, initially chaired by H. Rowan Gaither, secretly reported to the president that the United States appeared to be falling behind the Soviets in the field of technological prowess—especially in the development of ICBMs. The press and the public became alarmed when the report's pessimistic findings of "an increasing threat which may become critical in 1959–1960," were revealed.

During the presidential campaign of 1960, the perceived strategic deficiency of the United States was emphasized by writers and politicians—especially Democrats—and by military leaders who had begun to speak of a "missile gap." John F. Kennedy, first as a senator and then as a presidential candidate, urged spending much more on defense to close the gap. Early in his presidency, Kennedy was told by U.S. secretary of defense **Robert S. McNamara** that there was no missile gap; indeed, on the contrary, the United States possessed many more ICBMs than the Soviet Union. *See also* ARMS RACE.

MITCHELL, CLARENCE M. (1911–1984). Clarence M. Mitchell was born in Baltimore, Maryland, on 8 March 1911. He was raised in a large Episcopalian household, and his brother, Parren Mitchell, was to become the first **African American** to be elected to Congress from Maryland (1971–1987, representing the 7th congressional district). After attending Lincoln College, Pennsylvania, and the University of Minnesota, he became the executive secretary for the National Urban League in St. Paul, Minnesota, in 1937. During World War II, he served on the Fair Employment Practices Committee and the War Manpower Commission. Immediately after the war, he was appointed to head the newly created labor department of the **National Association for the Advancement of Colored People** (NAACP); in 1950, he became the director of the NAACP's Washington, DC, bureau. His major function in that post was to serve as the organization's lobbyist for **civil rights** measures in the legislative and executive branches of the federal government. Mitchell waged a tireless campaign on Capitol Hill, helping to secure passage of civil rights legislation in the 1950s and 1960s, including the Civil Rights Act of 1957, the Civil Rights Act of 1960, the **Civil Rights Act of 1964**, the Voting Rights Act of 1965, and the Fair Housing Act (Title VIII of the Civil Rights Act of 1968). He was so effective, he acquired the nickname, "the 101st U.S. Senator."

The NAACP and other civil rights groups were dissatisfied with John F. Kennedy because of his administration's failure to introduce

significant civil rights legislation. In July 1961, Mitchell denounced the president for ignoring the civil rights pledges of the 1960 Democratic national platform, and he repeated his criticism at the NAACP's annual membership meeting in January 1962. The only difference between the Democratic and Republican Parties in the area of civil rights, he charged at the meeting, was that "the Democrats have more Negroes who can explain why we don't need such rights." In November 1962, Kennedy issued an executive order barring discrimination in federally aided housing. However, the following April, Mitchell charged that the order was not being enforced, and he placed the blame on the president himself, asserting: "The tempo is always taken by the President. . . . I have been in Washington a long time, and I know this is true under any Administration, under any program. If the President wants it to move, it will move." Meanwhile, in 1962 and early 1963, Mitchell, who met frequently with liberal congressmen and senators to map civil rights strategy, appeared before the House **Education** and Labor Committee and other congressional panels in support of measures to combat racial discrimination. Southern civil rights protests in the early 1960s and the violent white reaction to them enlarged the national constituency for antidiscrimination laws, and in June 1963, President Kennedy sent a civil rights bill to Congress. The major sections of the bill provided for the desegregation of public accommodations, the withholding of federal aid from all programs and activities in which racial discrimination was practiced, and federal initiation of public-school desegregation suits. The House Judiciary Committee subcommittee sought to strengthen the bill, but in October, Attorney General **Robert F. Kennedy** urged against it. Mitchell asserted, as he had on earlier occasions, that the difficulty in securing passage of effective civil rights laws was not a lack of support for such measures but the unwillingness of President Kennedy to vigorously press for them. He denounced the attorney general's suggestions and said, "There is no reason for this kind of sell-out. . . . The Administration should be in there fighting for the subcommittee bill."

On the whole, Mitchell was more pleased with President **Lyndon B. Johnson**'s successful efforts on behalf of civil rights legislation in the areas of public accommodations, voting rights, and housing discrimination. Mitchell wrote an editorial column for the *Baltimore Sun* every Sunday until his death in Baltimore on 19 March 1984. More than 2,500 mourners attended his funeral.

MONROE, MARILYN (1926–1962). Marilyn Monroe (born Norma Jeane Mortenson) was born on 1 June 1926 in Los Angeles, California. She spent many (mostly happy) years in foster homes. However, to avoid being sent to an orphanage on 19 June 1942, at the age of 16, she married 21-year-old factory worker James "Jim" Dougherty. Monroe's acting career spanned 16 years and 29 films, and she rose from struggling actress to screen legend. She became one of the most famous actresses, models, and popular singers of the 1950s. She became renowned for playing comic "blonde bombshell" characters, and among her many film credits are *Bus Stop* (1956) and *Some Like It Hot* (1959). She entered into two tumultuous marriages; one with baseball star Joe DiMaggio (January 1954 to October 1955), the other with playwright Arthur Miller (June 1956 to January 1961).

On 19 May 1962, Monroe created a sensation when she sang "Happy Birthday" on stage at President John F. Kennedy's birthday celebration at Madison Square Garden in New York, wearing a revealing, beige, skin-tight dress covered in rhinestones, which made her appear nude. On 5 August 1962, she was found dead in her Brentwood, California, home of an overdose of sleeping pills.

Countless books and articles have been written about Monroe. She has been the subject of films, plays, operas, and songs, and she has influenced artists and entertainers as diverse as Andy Warhol and Madonna. Monroe's enduring popularity stems in part from the contradictions her life entailed. On the one hand, she remains a sex symbol, beauty icon, and famous film star. On the other hand, she also experienced an unstable childhood and a troubled private life, and she struggled

for professional respect. In addition, because of her known association with John F. Kennedy and with **Robert F. Kennedy**, there has been much speculation about the events surrounding her death. She has become part of the broader discussions in the United States about the role of women, the nature of modern feminism, and the impact of mass media, fame, and consumer culture on contemporary society. *See also* LAWFORD, PETER SYDNEY ERNEST.

MORSE, WAYNE LYMAN (1900–1974). Wayne Lyman Morse was born in Madison, Wisconsin, on 20 October 1900. He grew up on a farm with his parents who were supporters of the Progressive Party. He majored in labor economics at the University of Wisconsin, graduating in 1923. From 1924 to 1928, he was an assistant professor of speech at the University of Minnesota, and while there he received a law degree in 1928. The following year Morse took a position as assistant professor of law at the University of Oregon. Two years later, he was appointed dean of the university's law school at the young age of 31. During the 1930s, Morse served as an arbitrator in West Coast labor disputes, and by 1940, he was one of the nation's most prominent labor relations experts. In January 1942, he was appointed a public member of the National War Labor Board.

In 1944, Morse defeated the incumbent U.S. senator in Oregon's Republican primary and went on to defeat his Democratic opponent. In the Senate, he was a contentious and fiercely independent liberal who often refused to modify strongly held views for the sake of legislative compromise. He alienated many senators by what they felt was his self-righteous and scornful attitude toward those who disagreed with him. His propensity for antagonizing his colleagues with his liberal views barred him from playing a major leadership role in the Senate. Morse's admirers, however, saw him as a fearless maverick who placed principle over expediency and who served as a watchdog against injustice.

Morse was an early backer of **Dwight D. Eisenhower** for the 1952 Republican presidential nomination, but he abandoned his support of Eisenhower when the party's national convention adopted what he considered a "reactionary" platform. When Eisenhower selected **Richard M. Nixon** as his running mate in 1952, Morse resigned from the **Republican Party** in October and became an independent. A persistent critic of the Eisenhower administration, early in 1955 he joined the **Democratic Party**, giving it the decisive vote needed to manage the evenly divided Senate. Morse strongly believed in the settlement of international disputes through multilateral cooperation and a system of world law. In 1946, he successfully pressed for American participation in the World Court. A supporter of **civil rights** measures, Morse, as a member of the District of Columbia Committee, was the chief Senate proponent of home rule for the nation's capital, whose population in the 1950s was around 50 percent black. He voted against the 1957 civil rights bill on the grounds that it was too weak.

In December 1959, Morse announced he would enter the race to become the 1960 Democratic candidate for president. He attacked senators John F. Kennedy, **Hubert H. Humphrey** (D-Minn.), and other presidential aspirants in his party as "phony liberals." Morse criticized Kennedy for his failure to sufficiently support the activities and power of the labor movement. He withdrew from the race after he suffered successive primary defeats in the District of Columbia, Maryland, and his home state. Under the Kennedy administration, the White House was occupied for the first time by a president who belonged to the same party as Morse, who was then chairman of the Labor and Public Welfare Committee's **Education** Subcommittee and of the Foreign Relations Committee's American Republics Affairs Subcommittee. He continued to act as an independent critic in many legislative areas and, at the same time, served as a pragmatic conciliator on most matters within the jurisdiction of his subcommittees.

In 1961, Morse successfully guided controversial administration school aid bills through the Senate. Although he personally supported federal aid to private schools,

Kennedy opposed such assistance, and Morse cooperated with the administration in ensuring such loans were excluded from its school aid package. During the early days of the Kennedy administration, however, Morse demonstrated that he was not abandoning his accustomed role as a gadfly. His outspoken opposition in March 1961 to the nomination of Charles M. Meriwether of Alabama as a director of the Export-Import Bank because of the nominee's past connections with a Grand Dragon of the Ku Klux Klan was one such example. Failing to win significant support for his fight against the Meriwether appointment, Morse, at a Foreign Relations Committee hearing, shouted, "Where are the other flaming liberals? . . . In seventeen years I've never backed away from a fight." Many observers believed that Morse's lack of discrimination in choosing causes reduced his effectiveness as a dissenter. In July and August of the following year, Morse led a liberal filibuster against an administration bill creating a private corporation to establish, own, and operate a communications satellite network. He and other liberals argued that the bill represented a gift to private enterprise of millions of the taxpayers' dollars spent on research and development, and they warned that the corporation would be dominated by the American Telephone & Telegraph Company. On 14 August 1962, the Senate, for the first time since 1927, invoked cloture to limit debate, and the bill was passed later in the month.

Morse was particularly vociferous, if rarely successful, on foreign policy matters. In 1963, he unsuccessfully sought to prohibit **Alliance for Progress** aid to any country whose government had come to power through the forcible overthrow of a prior government chosen in a democratic election. He believed that aid to Israel, Taiwan, and Turkey was no longer necessary, but Congress traditionally opposed attacking foreign aid programs on a country-by-country basis. During the mid-1960s, Morse was best known for his vehement opposition to the **Vietnam War**. In August 1964, he and Senator Ernest Gruening (D-Alaska) were the only opponents of the Tonkin Gulf Resolution on Capitol Hill. Morse subsequently attacked the war as unconstitutional and immoral and, in 1966, denounced President **Lyndon B. Johnson** as "drunk with power." In 1968, largely because of his views on the war, Morse—nicknamed the "Tiger of the Senate"—was narrowly defeated by Republican challenger Robert W. Packwood after 24 years in the Senate. Morse attempted to reenter the Senate, but on 22 July 1974, in Portland, Oregon, in the midst of his election campaign, he died of kidney failure. *See also* VIETNAM.

MOYNIHAN, DANIEL PATRICK (1927–2003). Daniel Patrick Moynihan was born in Tulsa, Oklahoma, on 16 March 1927, and grew up in New York City. His father, a former newspaper journalist, deserted the family when Moynihan was 10. What had been a comfortable childhood abruptly became an uncertain life of poverty. Living in "Hell's Kitchen" in New York City, Moynihan was forced to work to pay family expenses. Moynihan graduated from Benjamin Franklin High School in Manhattan in 1943. He worked briefly on the Hudson River docks, attended City College for a year, and then enlisted in the navy in 1944. After the war, he earned a bachelor's degree from Tufts University and an MA from Tuft's Fletcher School of Law and Diplomacy in 1949. He enrolled as a doctoral student at the Fletcher School and carried out graduate study at the London School of Economics as a Fulbright Scholar, earning a PhD in international relations from the Fletcher School in 1961.

During the 1950s, Moynihan served as assistant secretary and later acting secretary to New York governor **W. Averell Harriman**. From 1958 to 1960, he was secretary of the public affairs committee of the New York State **Democratic Party**. During the 1960 presidential campaign, Moynihan wrote a number of position papers on urban affairs for John F. Kennedy. Shortly after he took office Kennedy appointed Moynihan special assistant to the secretary of labor, **Arthur J. Goldberg**. In March 1963, Moynihan was promoted to the post of assistant secretary of labor for policy planning and research. In this job, he undertook an extensive study of employment problems throughout the country. During 1963,

President Kennedy appointed Moynihan, **R. Sargent Shriver Jr.**, James Sundquist, and **Adam Yarmolinsky** to draft the legislation that became the 1964 Economic Opportunity Act.

While active in politics, Moynihan built a reputation in academic circles. As the *New York Times* noted at the time of his death, Moynihan was more a man of ideas than of legislation or partisan conflict; however, it added, he was enough of a politician to win re-election easily. He was erudite and opinionated and recognized new problems before most of his contemporaries. For example, he spent 40 years transforming Pennsylvania Avenue in Washington, DC, from a dingy street into the broad, grand avenue that George Washington and the Founders envisaged. He wrote 18 books, nine of them while a senator.

In 1963, he and Harvard sociologist Nathan Glazer completed an important study, *Beyond the Melting Pot*, which concluded that the various immigrant groups of New York City were not being assimilated but, instead, retained striking individual characteristics from one generation to the next. In March 1965, Moynihan, Paul Barton, and Ellen Broderick released a Labor Department study called *The Negro Family: The Case for National Action*, commonly known as the "Moynihan report." Many **civil rights** leaders, including **Martin Luther King Jr.**, were critical of the report. They considered it to be patronizing and condescending as it suggested that the high rates of juvenile delinquency and illiteracy among black children could be traced to the fact that in nearly 40 percent of black families the father was absent. Moynihan continued his study of black families at Wesleyan University, Middletown, Connecticut, and in June 1966, he was named director of the Harvard-MIT Joint Center for Urban Studies.

In spring 1968, Moynihan served as an adviser to Senator **Robert F. Kennedy** (D-N.Y.) in his quest for the Democratic presidential nomination; after Kennedy was assassinated, Moynihan worked briefly on behalf of the candidacy of Senator Eugene J. McCarthy (D-Minn.). He supported Vice President **Hubert H. Humphrey** in the fall.

Moynihan worked briefly for the **Richard M. Nixon** administration advising on urban affairs. In 1970, he resigned from his post as a presidential assistant and returned to academic life as a sociology professor at Harvard University. In December 1972, he was named ambassador to India. In May 1975, he was appointed U.S. ambassador to the **United Nations**. A year later Moynihan resigned and won the first of four terms as a senator from New York. He died, aged 76, on 26 March 2003 at Washington Hospital Center, Washington, DC, of complications following a ruptured appendix.

MULTILATERAL FORCE (MLF). In 1962, the Kennedy administration canceled "Skybolt," an air-to-ground missile system launched from a bomber, when the improved "Polaris" submarine-launched ballistic missile system proved more effective. In an effort to sooth British sensitivities, President Kennedy proposed a multilateral force (MLF) as an additional instrument of protection for America's allies against a Soviet attack. The administration hoped that North Atlantic Treaty Organization (NATO) allies might regard the MLF as a voice in decision making regarding the use of nuclear weapons, without giving up U.S. veto power over nuclear weapons usage. However, the proposal did not get very far. As Kennedy's national security adviser **McGeorge Bundy** noted, it had little Western European support. France's Charles de Gaulle preferred his own nuclear force, and the Soviets—who were prepared to sign a nuclear test ban—were also opposed to it. To promote the creation of the MLF, Kennedy dispatched Ambassador Livingston T. Merchant to open negotiations with the NATO governments on the question of membership in the new defense force. Only West Germany indicated a willingness to join and defray its share of the cost.

Many of its critics labeled the MLF the "multifarce." They noted that the multinational force satisfied no outstanding strategic requirement and offered Europe no significant responsibility for **nuclear deterrence**. If the MLF placed a German in control of nuclear weapons, it endangered the peace of Europe—as the Kremlin made clear. If, on the

other hand, the MLF perpetuated U.S. control of allied nuclear defenses—as it, in fact, did—it served no purpose whatever as far as the European powers were concerned. Not without justification, **George Ball** termed the MLF an "absurd contrivance." By June 1963, the Kennedy administration's tepid interest in the multilateral defense force had waned, and the matter passed to the **Lyndon B. Johnson** administration. With Congress also opposed to the idea of nuclear sharing, the Johnson administration finally decided to "arrange to let the MLF sink out of sight." The Soviets then joined with the United States and other countries to support the nuclear Non-Proliferation Treaty. *See also* EUROPE AND THE UNITED KINGDOM.

MUSIC AND JOHN F. KENNEDY. Unlike Thomas Jefferson, Jack Kennedy did not play a musical instrument, nor, by most accounts, did he particularly enjoy music. Because of his chronic back pain, he could not join in the latest dance crazes that accompanied the parties held in the White House East Room from time to time. For example, he was disappointed that he could not "twist" to Chubby Checker's "The Twist," one of his favorite tunes. Kennedy did, however, like jazz, and on 19 November 1962, he brought the Paul Winter Sextet to the White House, the first jazz ensemble to play there.

Music was, nevertheless, welcomed into the Kennedy White House. With their leadership, charisma, and style, Jacqueline and John F. Kennedy brought an appreciation for music to a virtual national stage. The Kennedy White House supported a wide range of musical artists and encouraged Americans to seek out a greater involvement with the arts. Gospel singer legend Mahalia Jackson, iconic vocalist Ella Fitzgerald, Dixieland trumpeter Al Hirt, and jazz great Count Basie were among the many leading musicians of the day chosen to participate at the Kennedy inaugural festivities. Leonard Bernstein wrote a "Fanfare for JFK," for the new president, which was premiered at the inaugural gala on 19 January 1961, with the composer conducting.

Classical music, opera, gospel, jazz, and even rock and roll were embraced by the Kennedys, and concerts in the executive mansion were de rigueur events for entertaining dignitaries and heads of state. Influenced by his wife, John hosted many classical concerts, but he was undereducated in this field and took his lead as to when to applaud at these concerts from his social secretary, Letitia Baldrige. Many of the most acclaimed composers of the 20th century were invited to the White House, including Leonard Bernstein and Aaron Copland. Virtuoso cellist Pablo Casals gave a concert performance at the White House on 13 November 1961, perhaps the most celebrated concert given at the White House during the Kennedy years. Among its 200 invited guests were many of the nation's most prominent composers and conductors. Broadway musicals and ballet productions were also performed at the Kennedy White House. Performances included the American Ballet Theatre's production of *Billy the Kid*, with composer Aaron Copland in attendance, and *Brigadoon*, with lyrics by President Kennedy's Harvard classmate Alan Jay Lerner. The popular Alan Jay Lerner and Frederick Loewe musical, *Camelot*, provided what became the unofficial theme of the Kennedy administration.

Kennedy also took care to maintain the traditions of the Marine Corps Band, "The President's Own," ensuring that the orchestra functioned as the president's private band and was on call for White House performances. The Marine Band performed at functions ranging from teas to state dinners and introduced the president and his wife with four ruffles and flourishes, followed by "Hail to the Chief." Kennedy once joked: "I think 'Hail to the Chief' has a nice ring to it!"

Kennedy had a special affinity for Irish music and the bagpipes, "the noble, haunting instruments that especially appealed to the President's Irish heritage." The Air Force Pipers and the Drum and Bugle Corps performed on the South Lawn after the first state dinner of the Kennedy administration on 3 May 1961, for President Habib Bourguiba of Tunisia. And the famous Royal Highland Regiment, the Black

Watch, played at the last state function at the White House, on 13 November 1963. The band presented a special program of piping, marching, and spirited dancing on the South Lawn. Guests for the afternoon were 1,700 children from child-care agencies served by the United Givers Fund, and they managed to devour more than 10,000 cookies. "I don't know when I have seen the President enjoy himself more," wrote **Jacqueline Kennedy** to Major W. M. Wingate-Gray. "The ceremony was one of the most stirring we have ever had at the White House."

The Kennedy years saw a broadening of popular music in the United States. Reflecting the desire for change that characterized American society in the early 1960s, rock, country, soul, and other styles competed for popularity throughout the decade. Songwriters wrote about the ambitions of the counterculture, sexual liberation, and the antiwar and **civil rights** movements. Radio was the primary means of listening to one's favorite artists, but increasingly it was being supplemented if not replaced by **television**'s immensely popular program *American Bandstand*—watched by teens from coast to coast. From this medium,

the young not only heard the latest music but also saw how to dance to it.

When the 1960s began, Elvis Presley returned from the army to join other Caucasian male vocalists at the top of the charts—Bobby Darin, Neil Sedaka, Jerry Lee Lewis, Paul Anka, and Frankie Avalon. Soon, however, the famous black-owned Tamla Motown Record Company popularized rhythm and blues and introduced female performers, such as Gladys Knight and the Pips, the Supremes, and Aretha Franklin, to a wide, appreciative audience. Some **African American** male singers were also highlighted, including Smoky Robinson, James Brown, Jimi Hendrix, and the Temptations.

There was also a revival of folk music, often carrying protest messages, led by **Bob Dylan**, **Joan Baez**, and Peter, Paul and Mary. From California came the Beach Boys (who drew from the Safaris) with music that appealed to teenagers. The British invasion brought the Beatles to American television, along with the Dave Clark Five, with an innovative style of rock music that soon gained wide appeal. The popular white duo the Righteous Brothers employed African American styling to create a new sound.

N

NATIONAL ASSOCIATION FOR THE ADVANCEMENT OF COLORED PEOPLE (NAACP).

The NAACP was an organization initially founded by a group of **African Americans** in 1905, including W. E. B. DuBois, whose aim was to improve the conditions and rights of African Americans. After a shaky start, in February 1909 the group was joined by some non–African Americans, and in the following year it was launched as the National Association for the Advancement of Colored People (NAACP). Its legal team, led by Charles Hamilton Houston and **Thurgood Marshall**, spearheaded a decades-long campaign to reverse the 19th-century "separate but equal doctrine." The NAACP used litigation to press for the full desegregation of the South, which led to the **civil rights** movement of the 1950s and 1960s that initially employed moderate, integrationist goals. The NAACP's efforts culminated in *Brown v. Board of Education* (1954), in which the U.S. **Supreme Court** held state-sponsored segregation of schools was unconstitutional.

Members of the NAACP met with President Kennedy each year he was in office, and the organization was instrumental in convincing President Kennedy to send in the National Guard to protect **James H. Meredith** when he became the first African American to enroll at the University of Mississippi in October 1962. However, many civil rights leaders, such as **Martin Luther King Jr.** of the Southern Christian Leadership Conference (SCLC), believed more direct action was required to achieve their objectives. Though the NAACP was opposed to extra-legal popular actions, many of its members, such as Mississippi field secretary **Medgar W. Evers**, participated in nonviolent demonstrations such as sit-ins to protest the persistence of Jim Crow segregation throughout the South. **Roy Wilkins**, who succeeded Walter White as secretary of the NAACP in 1955, cooperated with A. Philip Randolph and **Bayard Rustin** in organizing the 1963 March on Washington.

With the passage of the civil rights legislation in 1964, the NAACP had finally succeeded in accomplishing its historic goals. With millions of African Americans still living in urban poverty and plagued by crime, job discrimination, and de facto racial segregation, many civil rights activists turned away from the NAACP to more militant, even separatist organizations. These groups—such as the SCLC, the **Student Nonviolent Coordinating Committee**, and the Black Panthers—relied on direct action and mass protests, rather than litigation, to advance their causes. The new philosophies often included themes espoused by the black power movement.

NATIONAL ENDOWMENTS FOR ARTS AND HUMANITIES.

The Kennedy administration provided the inspiration and laid the groundwork for federally funded programs to support the arts and humanities. In 1963, the American Council of Learned Societies, a private, nonprofit federation of 75 scholarly organizations in the humanities and related social sciences founded in 1919, together with the Council of Graduate Schools in America and

the United Chapters of Phi Beta, organized a National Commission on the Humanities tasked with studying "the state of the humanities in America." The commission's report in April 1964 recommended the creation of a National Humanities Foundation. The report generated several proposals, but **Lyndon B. Johnson** gained the approval of Congress for two separate agencies, one for the arts and the other for the humanities. The National Foundation on the Arts and Humanities Act, which established a governing board for each agency, was signed on 29 September 1965. The president of Brown University, Barnaby C. Keeney, who had chaired the 1963 national commission, served as the first chair of the National Endowment for the Humanities (NEH) from 1966 to 1970. Among its many notable activities, the NEH in 1972 established an honorary "Jefferson Lecture in the Humanities." According to the NEH, the lecture is "the highest honor the federal government confers for distinguished intellectual achievement in the humanities," and it has produced some truly outstanding lectures. The NEH has frequently confronted political controversy and attempts to eliminate its funding.

NATIVE AMERICANS. *See* FIRST AMERICANS.

NEW FRONTIER. John F. Kennedy wanted his administration to be identified as one that ushered in a symbolic "New Frontier" in United States history. He first used the phrase in his acceptance speech to the Democratic National Convention at the Los Angeles Memorial Coliseum in June 1960: "We stand today on the edge of a New Frontier—the frontier of the 1960s, the frontier of unknown opportunities and perils, the frontier of unfilled hopes and unfilled threats." "Beyond that frontier," Kennedy continued, "are uncharted areas of science and space, unsolved problems of peace and war, unconquered problems of ignorance and prejudice, unanswered questions of poverty and surplus." He promised an administration that would overcome those problems, including expanding scientific and space research. He concluded his speech with an appeal to the American people: "Ask not what your country can do for you—ask what you can do for your country." The speech received a rapturous reception.

The goal of conquering that new frontier was to become the theme for John F. Kennedy's administration's domestic and foreign programs. It was his commitment to renewal and change after what he regarded as eight years of stagnation under the Republican **Dwight D. Eisenhower.** Using this motif, Kennedy hoped to push through his programs intended to stimulate the domestic economy, provide international aid, boost national defense, and support the space program. At the core of the concept domestically was raising the minimum wage, guaranteeing equal pay for women, rebuilding the inner cities, increasing federal aid for **education**, and developing a Medicare program to assist the elderly. In international relations, it was a weapon to fight the **Cold War.** In terms of legislation enacted, the strategy of appealing to Americans to conquer a new frontier worked. According to biographer Theodore White, under Kennedy more new legislation was approved and passed into law than at any other time since the 1930s. When Congress recessed in the latter part of 1961, 33 out of 53 bills that Kennedy had submitted to Congress had been enacted. A year later, 40 out of 54 bills that the Kennedy administration had proposed had been passed by Congress, and in 1963, the figure was 35 out of 58 "must" bills, enacted.

Domestic New Frontier initiatives included efforts to control monopoly prices (against the wishes of large companies); the installation of the **President's Commission on the Status of Women** to investigate questions regarding women's equality in education, in the workplace, and under the law (established on 14 December 1961); and (initially tentative and cautious) support for the **civil rights** movement. In March 1961, Kennedy asked Congress to endorse an extensive housing program aimed at stimulating the economy, revitalizing cities, and providing affordable housing for middle-income and low-income families. The **Manpower Development and Training Act** of 1962 authorized a three-year

program to retrain workers displaced by new technology. The legislation included employed workers and provided a training allowance for unemployed participants, but it had minimal effect on the economy. Additionally, Kennedy increased the minimum wage and signed the **Equal Pay Act** into law on 10 June 1963, which sought to end sex-based pay discrimination. During the law's first 10 years, 171,000 employees received back pay worth $84 million.

Questions of health, including improving the situation of people with mental illnesses, were also addressed using the rhetoric of the New Frontier. Kennedy proposed a Medical Health Bill for the Aged (later known as Medicare), although Congress refused to pass it. More successfully, Kennedy, who had a mentally challenged sister, submitted the nation's first presidential special message to Congress in 1963 asking for federal support to improve mental health facilities. Congress responded, passing the Mental Retardation Facilities and Community Mental Health Centers Construction Act, with the National Institute of Mental Health assigned responsibility for monitoring community mental health center programs. Mental health facilities subsequently saw a sixfold increase in people using their services.

The New Frontier was useful as a tool to reassure and inspire the American people in fighting the Cold War, and Kennedy launched a number of international initiatives citing the theme of the New Frontier as motivation. The **Peace Corps**, which sent teachers abroad to increase education levels and expand the economies of so-called developing countries, was perhaps the most notable and successful of these programs. The **Alliance for Progress**, which was presented as a program to improve economic, political, and living conditions in Latin America, was another. And in 1961, it was the perfect appeal to a stunned American public with which to enter the space race by asking American scientists to take up the challenge of the newest frontier and put a man on the moon, following the **Soviet Union**'s launch of a cosmonaut into space. The **Limited Nuclear Test Ban Treaty** with the Soviet Union that stopped all nuclear testing in the atmosphere while limiting it to underground

sites was yet another new frontier achievement. Kennedy used national security—the New Frontier—to gain support for the **Trade Expansion Act** of 1962, which authorized him to negotiate reciprocal tariff reductions of up to 50 percent with the European Common Market. Moreover, it provided the basis for U.S. participation in what became known as the "Kennedy Round" of the General Agreement on Tariffs and Trade negotiations dealing with multilateral trade discussions from 1964 to 1967. In sum, the New Frontier was a potent, bracing concept at the time, and it remains an enduring symbol of the administration of John F. Kennedy.

NIXON, RICHARD MILHOUS (1913–1994). Richard M. Nixon was born in Yorba Linda, California, on 9 January 1913, and grew up in Whittier, where he worked in the family grocery store and attended public schools and Whittier College. A competitive student, he won a scholarship to Duke University Law School. He graduated in 1937 and returned to Whittier where he practiced law until 1942, when he went to work for the Office of Price Administration in Washington for seven months and then joined the U.S. Navy.

Soon after the war, Nixon ran as the **Republican Party**'s candidate for a seat in Congress from California's 12th district. He conducted an aggressive, personal campaign in which he capitalized on anticommunist sentiment by questioning the patriotism of his opponent, Representative Jerry Voorhis (D-Calif.). Nixon defeated Voorhis and in Congress became identified with a new postwar brand of Southern California conservatism. As a member of the House Un-American Activities Committee, Nixon gained national recognition in the sensational investigation of Alger Hiss, a former State Department official, which eventually led to Hiss's conviction on perjury charges. Nominated as the Republican candidate in the 1950 U.S. Senate race against Representative Helen Gahagan Douglas (D-Calif.), Nixon won a bitter campaign in which he accused his opponent of being "soft on communism." Nixon's questionable campaign tactics earned him the nickname "Tricky Dick" in liberal circles, but

his vehement anticommunism made him a respected national figure in the **Cold War** climate of the early 1950s. At the 1952 Republican National Convention, Nixon was nominated for vice president to give a conservative balance to a ticket headed by former general **Dwight D. Eisenhower**, the choice of the Republican Eastern Establishment. Elected in 1952 and reelected in 1956, Nixon wielded very little real power, but he received more public exposure than most vice presidents. Nixon's "kitchen debate" with Soviet premier **Nikita Khrushchev** in Moscow in 1959 reinforced the vice president's stature as a spokesman for the West. By 1958, when he began to lay plans for a 1960 presidential race, polls showed that Nixon was already the overwhelming choice of a majority of registered Republicans.

Nixon easily won the nomination as Republican candidate and chose **Henry Cabot Lodge Jr.**, ambassador to the **United Nations** and an easterner, as his running mate. Public opinion polls taken in early August 1960 showed that a slim majority of voters preferred Nixon to Senator John F. Kennedy in the presidential contest. Nixon had the advantage of greater national recognition, claimed to possess executive experience, and had the personal blessing of the still popular incumbent president. Yet Nixon's campaign failed to develop as he had hoped. He could find no issue on which he sharply disagreed with Kennedy. On foreign policy questions, Nixon was unable to outflank Kennedy on the Right since both candidates accepted the basic tenets of U.S. Cold War strategy and employed similar rhetoric. Nixon not only was unable to accuse Kennedy of "softness" toward the communist threat but also found himself on the defensive when Kennedy called for tougher policies against **Fidel Castro's Cuba** and a strengthening of U.S. nuclear defenses. Nixon took a more aggressive stance in defense of Nationalist China's island outpost, but the issue excited little voter interest. According to most political observers, the turning point of the campaign came on 26 September, when the candidates met for the first of four nationally televised debates. At the time, Nixon was still leading in the public opinion polls, but on **television**, he projected a tired appearance, which contrasted sharply with Kennedy's crisp style and good looks. Neither candidate "won" the debate, but the verbal confrontation proved a distinct advantage to Kennedy because it enabled some 70 million viewers to see the Democratic candidate as the mature and forceful equal of the vice president in face-to-face debate.

After the first television debate, the momentum of the Nixon campaign slowed considerably. Increased unemployment in October and the absence of Eisenhower on the campaign trail damaged Nixon's chances. Nixon supporters claimed that poor health kept Eisenhower from active campaigning. When Eisenhower spoke publicly on Nixon's behalf during the last week of the campaign, it was already too late to reverse the trend. In the election, a record turnout gave Kennedy a plurality of 113,507—the smallest of the century—but a comfortable electoral vote margin of 303 to 219. Nixon won more states, but Kennedy took the industrial North and most of the South. Although there was postelection evidence that fraud in Illinois and Texas had given the votes of those key states to Kennedy by narrow margins, Nixon recognized that any investigation would be both time consuming and divisive. He therefore conceded defeat. He later declined Kennedy's offer of a temporary foreign assignment.

In January 1961, he retired to private life and joined the Los Angeles law firm of Adams, Dugue, and Hazeltine. Nixon retained part of his old power base in his home state and, as titular leader of the Republican Party, continued to receive national media coverage. Between June 1961 and 1962, he worked on a book, published in March 1962 as *Six Crises*. The work focused on the major political events of his career and included a defense of his role in the Hiss case and an analysis of his 1960 defeat. *Six Crises* was a financial success and helped keep Nixon's name in the national spotlight. Nixon announced his candidacy for the governorship of California in September 1961. He expected to win in November against a colorless Democratic opponent, Governor Edmund G. Brown, but could not find a controversial issue upon which to peg his campaign.

Nixon lost badly in the November election—by around 300,000 votes—and many commentators asserted that his political career was finished. In his concession speech the following morning, Nixon shocked assembled reporters with an emotional and confused outburst in which he attacked the press for biased reporting throughout his career. Nearing the end of his speech, he said, "I leave you gentlemen now, and you will now write it. You will interpret it. That's your right. But as I leave you I want you to know—just think how much you're going to be missing. You won't have Nixon to kick around anymore, because, gentlemen, this is my last press conference." Many thought that this speech, as much as the electoral defeat, finished Nixon's political career and permanently ruined his relationship with the press.

In June 1963, Nixon moved to New York City and joined the prestigious law firm of Mudge, Stern, Baldwin, and Todd. He continued to speak out on national issues and to visit political leaders abroad. He assumed the role of an "elder statesman" in the Republican Party and attempted to conciliate its liberal and conservative factions. Nixon campaigned loyally for the party's national ticket in 1964 and, following the disastrous Republican defeat that year, became the party's leading fund-raiser. He worked hard for Republican candidates in 1966, captured the party's nomination in 1968, and in a three-way race, won the presidential election in November. Although Nixon was reelected by a landslide in 1972, revelations of criminal misconduct by him and his staff in the cover-up of the Watergate affair forced Nixon to resign the presidency in August 1974. He died of a stroke on 22 April 1994.

NUCLEAR DETERRENCE. The development of nuclear-tipped long-range ballistic missiles with their enormous destructive capacity revived the age-old concept of deterrence—a military strategy in which one power uses the threat of reprisal effectively to preclude an attack from an adversary power—in the years immediately following World War II. As nuclear arsenals expanded in the 1960s, the phrases "deterrence policy" and "deterrence strategy" were used as euphemisms for nuclear policy (short for nuclear weapons policy) and nuclear strategy. **Cold War** strategic theorists gradually linked words such as *credible, effective, stable,* and *mutual* to the concept of a nuclear balance or deterrence. However, it did not prevent military theorists on both sides from speculating about possible methods of expanding and using their nuclear arsenals. A "first strike" could take place when a nation thought it had sufficient nuclear capacity to destroy its foe and thereby achieve victory, while a closely related "preemptive strike" nuclear assault could be launched when a nation anticipated its enemy was preparing a first strike. A "retaliatory strike" or "second strike" capability referred to a nation's ability to absorb a nuclear first strike and still retain sufficient weapons to inflict unacceptable damage on its attacker. In 1954, the **Dwight D. Eisenhower** administration had adopted a policy of "massive retaliation" as a deterrent against a nuclear strike, but by the mid-1960s, the Soviet nuclear capacity was approaching parity with that of the United States—especially in antiballistic missiles—creating a situation of "assured destruction" should a nuclear war between the superpowers occur (critic Donald Brennen added "mutual" to get the acronym MAD). In light of these developments, U.S. secretary of defense **Robert S. McNamara** formally abandoned the policy of massive retaliation; a recognition that deterrence applied equally to both the **Soviet Union** and the United States. Not surprisingly, the idea of MAD did not sit well with American military chiefs preaching "Peace through Strength." The "first principle of deterrence," General Thomas S. Powers wrote in 1965, was "to maintain a credible capability to achieve a military victory under any set of conditions or circumstances." Whether or not victory would be the outcome, by the end of the 1960s the United States and Soviet Union governments believed their military services could absorb a nuclear first strike and still possess sufficient forces for retaliatory strikes; mutual deterrence remained in place, in fact, if not in formal policy. *See also* ARMS RACE.

O

O'BRIEN, LAWRENCE FRANCIS, JR. (1917–1990). Lawrence Francis "Larry" O'Brien Jr. was born on 7 July 1917 in Springfield, Massachusetts. His father was a hotel/restaurant owner who had migrated from County Cork, Ireland, as had his mother, Myra Sweeney. Driven by anti-Irish prejudice, following in his father's footsteps, Larry became a part-time worker in local **Democratic Party** politics. At the young age of 11, he helped in the 1928 presidential campaign of Governor Alfred E. Smith, and he became a passionate Democrat. He worked while attending Northeastern University where he earned a law degree. During World War II, he served in the U.S. Army.

Lawrence F. O'Brien Jr. was a master of modern political organization. He was an assistant to presidents John F. Kennedy and **Lyndon B. Johnson**, as well as an innovative commissioner of the National Basketball Association. After running the congressional campaign of longtime friend Foster Furcolo in 1948, O'Brien became his administrative assistant. However, in 1950 he was approached by Congressman John F. Kennedy to run his 1952 campaign for the Senate seat held by **Henry Cabot Lodge Jr.** That campaign, which relied heavily on the mobilization of volunteers, was successful, despite a Republican landslide with General **Dwight D. Eisenhower** at the head of the GOP's national ticket, and, using the same approach, Kennedy was reelected by a wide margin in 1958.

O'Brien came to national prominence as the organizer of Kennedy's 1960 primary and presidential campaigns. O'Brien introduced into presidential elections the use and organization of large numbers of volunteers to register voters, distribute campaign literature, create files on candidates, and man telephones in strategic primaries—which he detailed in a 64-page document that became known as *O'Brien's Manual*. Theodore H. White wrote in *The Making of the President 1960* that O'Brien's organizational work in the crucial West Virginia primary was "a masterpiece."

White said that the difference between the old and new politics was the difference between inclusion and exclusion. "In a tight old-fashioned machine," he wrote, "the idea is to operate with as few people as possible, keeping decision and action in the hands of as few inside men as possible. In the new style . . . the central idea is to give as many people as possible a sense of participation; participation galvanizes emotions, gives the participant a live stake in the victory of the leader." O'Brien's tactics were to become the gold standard for running campaigns.

Kennedy immediately appointed O'Brien to be his liaison person with Capitol Hill. And, as his special assistant for congressional relations, O'Brien was a crucial bridge between the White House and Congress, helping Kennedy's **New Frontier** programs become law. He helped persuade a Congress dominated by Republicans and Southern Democratic conservatives to back such measures as the establishment of the **Peace Corps**, the **Alliance for Progress**, Medicare, the **Arms Control and Disarmament Agency**, and a two-year extension of the **Civil Rights** Commission. He did so

with persuasion, patience, arm-twisting, and an occasional favor. The task required all his considerable experience and tact.

He began by coordinating the activities of the congressional liaison offices located in more than 40 federal departments and agencies, insisting that they work in concert for the president's legislative priorities instead of for the vested interests of their own agencies and departments. O'Brien initiated a system requiring each liaison office to submit weekly reports of its congressional activity for the previous week and plans for the week ahead. Detailed files were compiled on each member of Congress, covering voting records, prejudices, favorite projects, and political friends.

O'Brien was instrumental in negotiating the passage of the bill increasing the minimum wage from $1.00 to $1.25 over two years by both houses in May 1961, in securing a $389 million area development program (passed by voice vote in the Senate on 20 April and a 223–193 House vote on 26 April), and an omnibus housing bill (passed 28 June by a 53–38 Senate vote and a 229–176 House vote). Among his successes, O'Brien's tight supervision of the executive branch's relations with Congress was decisive in the passage (House, 28 June; Senate, 19 September) of the **Trade Expansion Act** of 1962 by wide margins. In 1963, the administration's only major legislative victory was Senate approval of the **Limited Nuclear Test Ban Treaty** by an 80–14 vote on 24 September. He was with Kennedy when the president fell to a sniper's bullet in Dallas on 22 November 1963. According to O'Brien, before Kennedy was assassinated, significant progress had been made in the drive to enact civil rights legislation, Medicare, and an aid plan for elementary and secondary **education**.

When **Lyndon B. Johnson** succeeded to the presidency, he asked O'Brien to be his postmaster general. In that job, he produced a report that resulted in the establishment of the U.S. Postal Service and the removal of the postmaster generalship from the cabinet. He also reported to Johnson on the political consequences of the rising tide of dismay at the war in **Vietnam**.

In 1968, when Johnson announced he would not seek another term in the White House but instead would concentrate on seeking an end to the war in Southeast Asia, Mr. O'Brien heeded a call from **Robert F. Kennedy** to assist him in his own bid for the presidency. He was with Robert Kennedy when he was shot in a hotel in Los Angeles on 6 June 1968, just after winning the crucial California primary. After the 1968 presidential campaign, he left Washington and moved to New York City as president of McDonnell & Company, an investment banking firm. He later worked in the presidential campaigns of **Hubert H. Humphrey** and George S. McGovern, and he twice served as chairman of the Democratic National Committee (DNC). He was head of the DNC in June 1972 when his office at the Watergate complex in Washington was broken into by burglars who wanted to wiretap his conversations to gain political intelligence. The incident precipitated the scandal that led to Nixon's impeachment and resignation two years later. From 1975 to 1984, O'Brien was commissioner of the National Basketball Association. He died of cancer on 27 September 1990 at New York Hospital–Cornell Medical Center in New York City. *See also* NIXON, RICHARD MILHOUS.

OPERATION DOMINIC I AND II. At the end of August 1961, the **Soviet Union** terminated a three-year moratorium agreement on nuclear weapons testing reached with the **Dwight D. Eisenhower** administration by launching a series of atmospheric tests. John F. Kennedy responded by authorizing "Operation Dominic," which consisted of 105 nuclear test explosions. This was the largest nuclear weapons testing program (1962–1963) ever conducted by the United States and the last atmospheric test series conducted, as a **Limited Nuclear Test Ban Treaty** prohibiting such tests was signed by the two superpowers in the following year. Tests were conducted in the Pacific (labeled Dominic I) and in Nevada (known as Dominic II). Most of the nuclear tests utilized free-fall bombs dropped by B-52 aircraft. Twenty of these "shots" were to test new weaponry, six to test weapons' effects, and others to determine

the reliability of the current nuclear inventory. Thor missiles carrying warheads were also employed to experiment with high-altitude (30–248 miles) nuclear explosions. These tests were called "Operation Fishbowl."

OSWALD, LEE HARVEY (1939–1963). Lee Harvey Oswald was born in New Orleans, Louisiana, on 18 October 1939. His father died before Oswald was born, and in 1944 his mother moved the family from New Orleans to Dallas. Oswald had a troubled upbringing, and at age 17, he quit school to join the U.S. Marines. He never earned a high school diploma, and by that point in his life, he had resided at 22 locations and attended 12 schools. After three unsettled years with the Marines, on 11 September 1959 he received a hardship discharge from active service, claiming his mother needed care. A month later, Oswald traveled to the **Soviet Union** having learned Russian and having saved $1,500 of his Marine Corps salary. While in the Soviet Union, Oswald married, and he and his Russian-born wife, Marina, and child returned to the United States in June 1962, to reside in the Dallas–Fort Worth area. On his return, Oswald could not settle down; he moved from job to job and involved himself in pro-**Fidel Castro** political activities. In October 1963, Oswald began work at the Texas School Book Depository building overlooking Dealey Plaza in Dallas.

According to the **Warren Commission**, which investigated the **assassination of John F. Kennedy**, Lee Harvey Oswald stood at the sixth-floor window of the Book Depository at around 12:30 p.m. on 22 November 1963 and fired three shots that killed President Kennedy and wounded Texas governor John Connally, who was riding with him in the same car. Forty-five minutes after the assassination, Dallas police officer J. D. Tippit, attempting to arrest a man fitting Oswald's description on the street not far from Oswald's rooming house, was shot four times and died instantly.

John F. Kennedy motorcade, Dallas, Texas, 22 November 1963. *Courtesy of Library of Congress.*

Oswald was arrested in a Dallas movie theater at 2:15 p.m. He was armed with a revolver later identified as the one that killed Tippit. At 7:10 p.m., Oswald was charged with the murder of Tippit and, at 1:30 a.m. the next morning, with the murder of the president. Oswald denied that he had committed either crime, stating that he was simply a "patsy." On 24 November 1963, as Oswald was being taken to a car to take him from the city jail to the Dallas County Jail, **Jack Ruby**, a Dallas nightclub proprietor, fatally shot Oswald in the stomach. The incident was televised live around the country.

President **Lyndon B. Johnson** appointed a commission under the chairmanship of Chief Justice **Earl Warren** to investigate the assassination of President Kennedy on 29 November 1963. A year later, it issued a report that declared that Oswald, acting entirely alone, had murdered the president and Tippit and wounded Governor Connally. *See also* HOOVER, J. EDGAR; WALKER, EDWIN ANDERSON.

P

PACIFICATION PROGRAM IN VIETNAM.

Vietnam was not the first time the U.S. Army encountered irregulars; Philippine revolutionaries had provided something of a testing ground for pacification after the Spanish-American War. However, in **Vietnam**, using British successes in Malaya as a model, in 1961 the U.S. Military Assistance and Advisory Group-Vietnam and the South Vietnamese government initiated a pacification program in which they began surrounding villages with barbed wire and other various defenses. The "Strategic Hamlet" program, as it was called, focused on rural areas where armed, trained, and secure villagers in "anti-guerrilla bastions" would be able to isolate the insurgents and deprive the Viet Cong of intelligence, recruits, and supplies. After a year, Saigon authorities were supplying 3,235 such villages and claimed to control 34 percent of the population. However, by 1963, the hamlet system was disbanded because it had proved to be unworkable. The peasants disliked the restraints, and the Viet Cong had only to concentrate their forces to capture an individual village. Thus, while most American officials acknowledged the importance of pacification as a **counterinsurgency** strategy, as was the case more than a half century earlier, they never worked out how to achieve it.

PATROL TORPEDO BOAT 109 (PT-109).

Much of John F. Kennedy's appeal to the American electorate was based on his reputation as a war hero. When asked to explain how he had come to be a hero, the young naval commander, by then an aspiring politician, replied laconically, "It was involuntary. They sank my boat." Lieutenant Kennedy was involved in what is arguably the most famous small-craft engagement in naval history, and it was an unmitigated disaster.

Kennedy was in command of Patrol Torpedo Boat 109 (PT-109) in Blackett Strait, south of Kolombangara in the Solomon Islands, in the early morning of 1 August 1943 when it was struck by a Japanese destroyer and sank. To understand the events that culminated in the sinking of PT-109, it is important to remember that it was dark—deeply, unrelievedly dark. The disorienting effect, even for experienced sailors, of a moonless, starless night on the ocean should not be underestimated. In this profound darkness, PT-109 was one of 15 PT boats sent out to engage, damage, and maybe even turn back the well-known "Tokyo Express," the Japanese navy's more or less regular resupply convoy that enabled resistance to the advance of U.S. forces in the islands farther south. When the patrol actually did come in contact with the Tokyo Express—three Japanese destroyers acting as transports with a fourth serving as escort—the encounter did not go well. Thirty torpedoes were fired, with no more effect than to make the Japanese even more wary than they had been. Boats that had used up their complement of torpedoes were ordered home. The few boats that still had torpedoes remained in the strait, in the doubtful hope of catching the Express on its return voyage. PT-109 was one of the boats left behind.

Kennedy rendezvoused his boat with PT-162 of his own patrol section and PT-169, which had been separated from another section; the three boats then spread out to make a picket line across the strait.

At about 2:30 in the morning, a shape loomed out of the darkness 300 yards off the PT-109's starboard bow. So murky was visibility that it was at first believed to be another PT. When it became apparent that it was one of the Japanese destroyers, Kennedy attempted to turn to starboard to bring his torpedoes to bear, but there was not enough time. The destroyer—later identified as the *Amagiri*, the escort ship of the Express—struck PT-109 just forward of the starboard torpedo tube, ripping away the starboard aft side of the boat. Less than a minute had passed since the first sighting. Over the next several hours, Kennedy, a strong swimmer, showed extraordinary endurance and resourcefulness in saving his crew and himself. He was rewarded with the Navy and Marine Corps Medal, and the injuries he suffered during the incident also qualified him for the Purple Heart. However, the consequences of the event were more far-reaching for John F. Kennedy than simple decorations. The story was picked up by the writer John Hersey, who told it to the readers of the *New Yorker* and *Reader's Digest*, and it followed Kennedy into politics, where it provided a strong foundation for his appeal as a young veteran. For here was a war hero who had not won battles but who had shown courage and dogged will, responsibility for those he led, and the ability to inspire them—and it was hard to compete against these qualities in such a young and otherwise inexperienced political leader.

PEACE CORPS. On 1 March, in one of his first acts as president, John F. Kennedy issued Executive Order 10924 establishing what was to become known as the Peace Corps. The president announced his decision to the nation in a televised broadcast on 2 March, and the program was authorized by Congress on 21 September 1961, with passage of the Peace Corps Act (Public Law 87–293). The act declared the program's purpose as follows:

To promote world peace and friendship through a Peace Corps, which shall make available to interested countries and areas men and women of the United States qualified for service abroad and willing to serve, under conditions of hardship if necessary, to help the peoples of such countries and areas in meeting their needs for trained manpower.

Kennedy appointed his brother-in-law, **R. Sargent Shriver Jr.**, as the first director, and the Peace Corps began recruiting in July 1962; Bob Hope cut radio and **television** announcements hailing the program. Volunteers arrived in five countries during 1961. In just under six years, Shriver developed programs in 55 countries with more than 14,500 volunteers.

The idea of Americans living and working in developing countries around the world, dedicating themselves to the cause of peace and development, had been around for some time. Kennedy had floated the notion as early as December 1951 when the young congressman suggested to a group that "young college graduates would find a full life in bringing technical advice and assistance to the underprivileged and backward Middle East. . . . In that calling, these men would follow the constructive work done by the religious missionaries in these countries over the past 100 years."

Hubert Humphry, the **Democratic Party** senator from Minnesota, had also proposed the creation of such a group as early as 1959. But it did not become popular until Kennedy raised it during his presidential campaign in a speech to university students at the University of Michigan in October 1960. He returned to this theme in his inaugural address when he appealed to the nation: "And so, my fellow Americans: ask not what your country can do for you—ask what you can do for your country."

Kennedy's desire to create the Peace Corps was essentially part of his response to the **Cold War**. He knew that the **Soviet Union** had hundreds of men and women—scientists, physicists, teachers, engineers, doctors, and nurses—who were prepared to spend their lives abroad "in the service of world communism."

He wanted to counter Soviet influence with an equivalent program that prompted individual U.S. citizens to work abroad and involve themselves more actively in the cause of global democracy, development, and freedom along American lines.

The Peace Corps was very popular in the 1960s with recent college graduates whose ideals reflected the generational attitudes of the time—namely, a commitment to peace and international goodwill. However, its popularity waxed and waned. It was more popular with Democratic Party administrations than with Republicans. Following the **Vietnam War** and the Watergate scandal, the Peace Corps no longer commanded such great interest, and government funding for the agency was cut. Due to few recruits and low financial support, President **Richard M. Nixon** placed the Peace Corps under an umbrella agency, ACTION, in July 1971; it remained there until 1979, when President Jimmy Carter declared it autonomous in an executive order.

In 1981, under the Ronald Reagan administration, Congress made the Peace Corps an independent federal agency. At that time, Reagan attempted to diversify the Peace Corps program by expanding it from its traditional concern with **education** and agriculture to more current concerns such as computer literacy and business-related education by initiating several new business-related programs. For the first time, the Peace Corps saw an increase in the number of conservative and Republican volunteers who joined the largely progressive volunteer contingent overseas. The program continued to reflect the evolving and expanding ideology of the United States.

In the 2010s, the Peace Corps has more than 200,000 volunteers serving in more than 139 countries and learning more than 200 languages and dialects. Volunteers serve two-year periods helping to build a self-sustaining, better future within their host country, along with establishing goodwill toward the United States. Life as a Peace Corps volunteer was, and is, not easy, and volunteers face many challenges, ranging from language barriers to poor living conditions. They have been, and

continue to be, subject to personal assaults, rape, and in some cases even murder.

Nevertheless, Kennedy's inspiration led to the formation and continuation of an agency that for the most part has fostered world peace and friendship, and American volunteers abroad continue to help individuals build a better life for themselves, their children, their community, and their country.

PEARSON, ANDREW RUSSELL (1897–1969). Andrew Russell "Drew" Pearson was born in Evanston, Illinois, on 13 December 1897, the son of a Quaker professor. In 1919, he graduated from Swarthmore College and became a foreign correspondent for 10 years before joining the staff of the *Baltimore Sun* in 1929. Pearson first gained renown through an exposé in 1931, "The Washington Merry-Go-Round," written with journalist Robert Allen. In 1932, Allen and Pearson collaborated on a column of the same name, which by 1942 was syndicated in 350 papers. Pearson saw himself as a liberal. He supported **civil rights**, domestic welfare programs, foreign aid, and East–West detente, but his column mainly specialized in exposing the private lives of public figures and in searching out corruption in government. He did so with merciless zeal and occasionally with inadequate regard for accuracy. For more than 30 years, Pearson was the most prominent "muckraking" journalist in the United States.

During the Kennedy administration, Pearson praised President John F. Kennedy for his intelligence but delighted in reviving the Kennedy connection with the late senator Joseph McCarthy (R-Wis.) and detailing the allegedly unscrupulous business dealings of **Joseph P. Kennedy Sr.** Pearson also attributed the government's increased aid to the Diem regime in South Vietnam to Kennedy's Catholicism. In August 1961, Soviet premier **Nikita Khrushchev** consented to an exclusive interview with Pearson. The premier told the columnist that he was "ready at any moment" to negotiate with Western leaders on a realistic settlement of the Berlin question and was willing to guarantee "free city" status for West Berlin with only a token Soviet force stationed

alongside U.S., British, and French troops in the city. Khrushchev added the Western powers should sign a peace treaty with East Germany, to ensure their further access to West Berlin. A Pearson exposé led to the dismissal of deputy Federal Housing Administration commissioner James B. Cash on 20 November 1961 after it became known that Pearson's column the next day would report that Cash had lost $7,000 in a card game at a builders' convention. During the late 1960s, Pearson's column was instrumental in exposing the financial misconduct of Senator Thomas Dodd (D-Conn.); the exposure eventually led to Senate hearings and Dodd's official censure. By 1969, Pearson's column was syndicated by more than 650 newspapers, making it the most widely read column in the United States. Pearson died on 1 September 1969, in Washington, DC. His column was taken over by a long-time associate, Jack Anderson.

PETERSON, ESTHER EGGERTSEN (1906–1997). Esther Eggertsen was born on 9 December 1906 in conservative Provo, Utah, the daughter of Danish immigrants. She grew up in a Mormon family. At age 12, she witnessed her first strike when railway workers pushed for an eight-hour workday in 1918. She graduated from Brigham Young University and moved to New York City; she enrolled at Columbia University's Teachers College where she married Oliver Peterson. In 1932 the two moved to Boston, where she taught at a prep school and volunteered at the Young Women's Christian Association (YWCA).

During the 1930s, Peterson helped end segregation at the YWCA and became involved with the International Ladies Garment Workers Union. In 1938, Peterson became a paid organizer for the American Federation of Teachers and traveled around New England. That year, she also had the first of four children. Although her husband fully supported her in motherhood and career, it wasn't easy balancing work and family, particularly in the 1930s. At one point, she was earning $15 a week, while paying someone $20 a week to look after her child.

She spent a summer in Utah organizing teachers, with help from the newly established National Labor Relations Board. In 1939, she joined the Amalgamated Clothing Workers Union (ACWU) as assistant director for **education** under the wing of ACW leaders Sidney Hillman and Jacob Potofsky. In 1944, the ACWU sent her to Washington, DC, as its legislative representative, where she became the union's first lobbyist. As a labor lobbyist, she participated in the National Committee on Equal Pay, the National Committee on the Status of Women, and the Labor Advisory Council of the **Women's Bureau**.

She was assigned to a new representative from Boston, John F. Kennedy, who—everyone thought at the time—"won't amount to much" anyway. She also initiated her association with labor lawyer **Arthur J. Goldberg**. On Capitol Hill, one of Peterson's main projects involved raising the minimum wage from 40 cents to 75 cents an hour. She also worked on getting workers in other industries covered by the Fair Labor Standards Act, which established minimum wages and work hours.

In 1948, the State Department offered Peterson's husband a position as a diplomat in Sweden. She spent 10 years in Europe and became active in the women's committees of the Swedish Confederation of Trade Unions and the International Confederation of Free Trade Unions.

The family returned to Washington, DC, in 1957, and Peterson joined the Industrial Union Department of the American Federation of Labor/Congress of Industrial Organizations, becoming its first woman lobbyist. By then, Kennedy was a senator, and when he decided to run for president a few years later, Peterson agreed to help work the campaign in Utah.

After Kennedy became president in 1961, Peterson was appointed head of the Women's Bureau in the Department of Labor. She hosted a series of hearings across the country to hear from working women. Peterson proposed and then headed the **President's Commission on the Status of Women** to further study the status of women and develop recommendations to achieve equality. The commission's final report, which became a best seller, addressed

the lack of day care for working parents, equal pay for equal work, and women clustered in low-wage work. The report sparked a national debate over the value of women's work. The commission also laid the groundwork for the National Women's Committee on **Civil Rights** to ensure **African American** women, in particular, were heard in the struggle for civil rights.

Peterson was a driving force behind the passage of the **Equal Pay Act of 1963**. That year, she also was named assistant secretary of labor for labor standards. As the highest-ranking woman in the Kennedy administration, she was responsible for enforcing laws covering minimum wage, work hours, and health and safety protections. For the next 20 years, Peterson was the voice for consumers within the White House and the food industry. Peterson fought for truth in advertising, standardization in packing and pricing, and consumer rights across industries. She died in Washington, DC, on 20 December 1997.

PETROLEUM EXPORTING COUNTRIES' ORGANIZATION (ORGANIZATION OF THE PETROLEUM EXPORTING COUNTRIES [OPEC]). This organization—created at the Baghdad Conference on 10–14 September 1960 by **Iran**, Iraq, Kuwait, **Saudi Arabia**, and Venezuela—was to have a profound impact on American motorists in the 1970s. The founding of OPEC occurred as the early transition of the global economic and political landscape was impacted by the decolonization and the emergence of new independent, underdeveloped nations. OPEC's basic objective was to unify petroleum policies in order to obtain higher and more stable prices for its member states and maintain an efficient and regular supply to consuming nations. Its initial headquarters was established in Geneva, Switzerland, from which it moved to Vienna, Austria, on 1 September 1965. OPEC adopted a "Declaratory Statement of Petroleum Policy in Member Countries" in 1968 that declared the inalienable right of all countries to exercise permanent sovereignty over their natural resources. By the end of the first decade, its membership grew to 10, with the addition of Qatar, Indonesia, Libya, United Arab Emirates,

Algeria, and later to 14, with Nigeria, Ecuador, Angola, and Gabon. *See also* MIDDLE EAST.

PHYSICAL FITNESS. Physical fitness was central to the life of John F. Kennedy. He prided himself on projecting his fitness and relative youth as a strength that compensated for his inexperience in government. The Kennedy family had built a reputation based upon the ideas that vigor (pronounced "vigah" by Jack), vitality, physical beauty, and athletic prowess were paramount. Politically, Kennedy sought to embody the notion that physical strength and fitness indicated preparedness in a **Cold War** in which a nation, if weak, would fail.

Yet Kennedy's medical records reveal the reality that, for most of his life, he lived in poor health. He was almost always sick, often from several conditions at once. John Kennedy grew up a sickly and scrawny boy. Before his third birthday, he came down with a virulent case of scarlet fever—at the time a life-threatening disease. Historian Robert Dallek writes that, from then on, not a year passed without one physical affliction or another. By 1940, Kennedy was in constant moderate to severe back pain from steroids, and in 1954, he underwent surgery for his Addison's disease. Between May 1955 and October 1957, when launching his vice presidential and presidential bids, he was secretly hospitalized nine times. As president, he sometimes took five hot showers a day to ease his pain. He took injections of painkillers and amphetamines to enable him to stay off crutches, which he believed essential to project a picture of robust good health. According to this account, during the first six months of his presidency, Kennedy also had "stomach/colon and prostate problems, high fevers, occasional dehydration, abscesses, sleeplessness and high cholesterol. . . . Medical attention was a fixed part of his routine." All this was kept hidden from public view.

It is not surprising, then, that Kennedy promoted physical fitness. Rather than delegate fitness initiatives as had his predecessor **Dwight D. Eisenhower**, Kennedy attempted to link them directly with the office of the

president. Immediately after his election, he published an article, "The Soft American," in *Sports Illustrated*. The article was an unprecedented announcement of public policy in the mass media by a president-elect. In his article, Kennedy set out four principles that would form the basis of a planned federally funded fitness program. He would create a "White House Committee on Health and Fitness"; fitness would come under the direct oversight of the Department of Health, **Education**, and Welfare; an annual Youth Fitness Congress would be held to be attended by state governors; and fitness—physical fitness—was to become very much the business of the federal government. Among his first acts as president was to convene a fitness conference only a month after the inauguration and to reorganize the President's Council on Youth Fitness established by Eisenhower in 1956. The Kennedy administration was surprisingly successful in raising public awareness of the importance of fitness. Perhaps his most famous intervention in the area of fitness, and an indicator of the extent to which the council became identified with him personally, was his attempt to revive the "50-mile hike," a scheme initiated by Theodore Roosevelt challenging U.S. Marine officers to finish 50 miles in 20 hours. The idea caught the public's imagination, but the President's Council satisfied itself with recommendations to the American people that they engage in a moderate, gradual program of walking for exercise.

Kennedy continued to address the issue of fitness at every opportunity, and the President's Council also began a major publicity campaign through the National Advertising Council. Material was produced for print, radio, **television**, and display advertising. For broadcast alone, 650 television kits and 3,500 radio kits were sent out. The $50,000 budget for the campaign compared favorably with the National Advertising Council's work on war bonds or forest conservation. *See also* SPORT.

PRESIDENTIAL ELECTION OF 1960. This political contest saw **Democratic Party** nominees John F. Kennedy and **Lyndon B. Johnson** opposed to **Republican Party** nominees **Richard M. Nixon** and **Henry Cabot Lodge Jr.** The campaign was fought largely on **Cold War** issues. Kennedy attacked the Republican Eisenhower administration for allowing the United States to appear to fall behind the **Soviet Union** militarily—the so-called **missile gap** critique—and economically, which was a tactic frequently used by both parties during the four-decade contest with the communist regime. The presidential race was one of the closest in history and featured the first **television** debates and, finally, resulted in the first Catholic being elected to the nation's highest office.

PRESIDENT'S COMMISSION ON THE STATUS OF WOMEN. John F. Kennedy's record on women (particularly in his personal life) was mixed, and his cabinet and policy staff were overwhelmingly male. When he was inaugurated, Kennedy himself did not specifically intend to implement a program that would empower women or initiate federal intervention on behalf of women's equality. Nevertheless, his administration did raise the expectations of women in America. The Kennedy administration encouraged the creation of activist networks and legitimated women's demands for action. It provided a structural basis for the organization of the first women's rights groups, and women transitioned from playing a marginal role through token appointments to being able to address women's social and economic position more directly. Although Kennedy neglected appointments of women, he avoided the charge that he was indifferent to the obstacles they faced by the establishment in December 1961 of the President's Commission on the Status of Women and the administration's pursuit of equal pay legislation.

The early 1960s were a turbulent time for women. Spurred by **Betty Friedan's** 1963 book, *The Feminine Mystique*, traditional roles were coming into question. However, the administration's agenda for women was rooted in the post-war era 15 years earlier. World War II had infused discussion of women's roles with new energy.

Throughout the war, in order to win support for the defense effort, the government

Inauguration of President Kennedy on the east portico of the U.S. Capitol, 20 January 1961. *Courtesy of Library of Congress.*

had emphasized national ideals of justice and equality. The contributions of women made many believe that the nation owed them a share in these ideals, some gesture of recognition in the particular form of legislation—an equal rights amendment to the Constitution or, less radical, an equal pay law. But a longing for the social stability that had supposedly characterized the pre-war world dominated the national consciousness and worked against the impulse to recognize women's individual achievements. Americans wanted to re-establish traditional family arrangements at work and at home. Government policy, implemented mid-war, turned from urging women to take war jobs toward ejecting women from those places so that

they—both the jobs and the women—would be available to the homecoming soldiers.

Economic events sabotaged these plans. Post-war inflation led even married women to want to remain in the labor force, despite their having to move to lower-paying, sex-segregated work to do so. Because the clerical and service sectors of the workforce, reserved largely for women workers, expanded more rapidly than the population of young single women, employers gave up their longstanding objection to hiring married women. And married women, for their part, eagerly accepted the places. In 1940, 15 percent of wives worked outside the home; by 1960, 30.5 percent of them would hold jobs.

A key question facing the labor movement and women's rights advocates at that time was whether to support ratification of an Equal Rights Amendment to the U.S. Constitution or, instead, to support protective legislation for women. Protective legislation provided for gender-based workplace restrictions specifically for women to help working women avoid workplace injury and exploitation. However, despite the evidence that indicated protective legislation frequently provided employers with a justification to avoid hiring women altogether or to not pay them the same wages as men, until the 1970s, trade unions/organized labor opposed an Equal Rights Amendment. The Kennedy administration sought to achieve equality for women without alienating its labor supporters. It argued publicly that the United States needed the talents of all its citizens, obviously including women, to win the global challenge against the **Soviet Union**. Esther Peterson proposed an advisory commission to assess the position of American women in society as a way to explore the options available to the administration. Kennedy asked Eleanor Roosevelt to chair the new commission.

On 14 December 1961, Kennedy signed Executive Order 10980 creating the President's Commission on the Status of Women, the first of its kind in the United States. The commission was charged with developing "recommendations for overcoming discriminations in government and private employment on the basis of sex" and was made up of 26 legislative officials and civic leaders. Roosevelt accepted the appointment. It was her last public position; she chaired the commission until her death in November 1962. Peterson was executive vice chairwoman and took over leadership on the death of Roosevelt. Members included Attorney General **Robert F. Kennedy**, a female senator and two congresswomen, Radcliffe College president Mary Bunting, and National Council of Negro Women president Dorothy Height. After meeting for two years, the commission presented its final report to President Kennedy on what would have been Eleanor Roosevelt's 79th birthday, 11 October 1963. The report took a cautious yet careful position. It recognized that women faced serious inequalities, unacceptable in a "free" society while acknowledging the importance of women's traditional gender roles. Reflecting the then-position of labor and Kennedy's ties to the labor movement, the report stated that because women were already entitled to constitutional protection against discrimination by the Fourteenth Amendment, it did not "now" endorse a constitutional amendment. However, some key members of the commission said privately that they would support an equal rights amendment if the **Supreme Court** refused to extend the Fourteenth Amendment to cover women. Kennedy also ordered federal agencies to end sex discrimination in hiring. Then, in June 1963, he signed into law the historic Equal Pay Act, which prohibited "discrimination on account of sex in the payment of wages by employers." *See also* PETERSON, ESTHER; UNITED STATES WOMEN'S BUREAU; WOMEN AND JOHN F. KENNEDY.

PT-109. *See* PATROL TORPEDO BOAT 109 (PT-109).

R

REPUBLICAN PARTY. In the **presidential election of 1960**, the Republican Party, led by **Richard M. Nixon**, vice president to President **Dwight D. Eisenhower**, lost to the Democrats and Senator John F. Kennedy by the astonishing margin of just under 120,000 votes out of a record 68.8 million votes cast, a plurality of less than .05 of the total vote, the smallest percentage difference since 1880. In the 1964 presidential election, the result was much worse. Republican Party conservative senator **Barry M. Goldwater** of Arizona lost in a landslide to President **Lyndon B. Johnson**. The party recovered to narrowly win in the election of 1968. Richard M. Nixon defeated **Democratic Party** candidate **Hubert Humphrey** with 43.4 percent of the popular vote to 42.3 percent.

RIBICOFF, ABRAHAM ALEXANDER (1910–1998). Abraham Ribicoff was born in New Britain, Connecticut, on 9 April 1910, the son of poor Polish Jewish immigrants, Abraham A. Ribicoff, a factory worker, and Rose Sable Ribicoff. After working his way through school, he attended the University of Chicago Law School where he was editor of the *Law Review*; he graduated in 1933. He returned to Hartford and practiced law.

However, Ribicoff was ambitious for a political career, and in 1938 he was elected to the Connecticut state legislature. From 1941 to 1947, he was judge of the Police Court at Hartford. During this period, he became a protégé of powerful Democratic state party chairman **John Moran Bailey**. In 1948, he was elected to Congress and served there until 1952. He

served on the Foreign Affairs Committee and proved to be a loyal supporter of Truman administration foreign and domestic policies. While in Congress, Ribicoff established an enduring friendship with Representative John F. Kennedy (D-Mass.).

In 1954, after an unsuccessful run for the Senate, Ribicoff was elected governor of Connecticut. As governor, he increased state spending on schools and welfare programs and gave greater governing power to local municipalities. He gained national prominence for introducing a much publicized traffic safety campaign to reduce the road accident toll. He was easily reelected for another four years in 1958. By then active on the national political scene, he nominated his good friend and fellow New Englander John F. Kennedy for vice president at the 1956 Democratic National Convention and was one of the first public officials to endorse Kennedy's presidential campaign.

In June 1960, he worked to rally support for Kennedy at the National Governors' Conference. A month later, Ribicoff and **Robert Kennedy** served as floor managers for their candidate at the Democratic National Convention in Los Angeles. Following the 1960 elections, Kennedy offered Ribicoff his choice of cabinet post, including that of attorney general. Ribicoff reportedly turned down the position of attorney general, believing that as a Jew he might create needless controversy within the emerging **civil rights** movement in prosecuting civil rights and school desegregation cases in the South. He chose instead the post of secretary of health, **education**, and welfare

(HEW). Although he did manage to secure a revision of the 1935 Social Security Act that liberalized requirements for aid-to-dependent-children funds from Congress, Ribicoff was unable to gain approval for the administration's Medicare and school aid bills.

During 1961 and 1962, Ribicoff and his talented assistant secretary Wilbur H. Cohen worked for the enactment of the Medicare bill sponsored by Senator **Clinton Anderson** (D-N.M.) and Representative Cecil R. King (D-Calif.), but were unsuccessful because of the powerful opposition of the American Medical Association. He also failed to win enactment of a bill authorizing federal aid to elementary and secondary schools. The issue came down to the question of whether private and parochial schools should receive federal assistance. Groups such as the National Catholic Welfare Conference demanded assistance for parochial schools, while the National Educational Association, representing one million public school-teachers, was bitterly opposed to such aid.

Ribicoff did have some success with the passage of the 1962 Public Welfare Amendments to the Social Security Act, which provided federal assistance (Aid to Dependent Children—ADC) for needy two-parent families rather than one-parent families as had been the case until then. The new amendments, however, did not compel states to broaden their ADC programs, and many continued to exclude two-parent families from assistance. Ribicoff took a more pragmatic approach to the question of whether federal aid should be continued to segregated schools. Although the 1954 **Supreme Court** decision ordered school desegregation to take place with "all deliberate speed," Ribicoff argued that HEW could not legally withhold funds from segregated schools (to speed up that process) without specific congressional authorization. He was aware that if he cut such aid, he would lose the support of southern congressmen and senators for the administration's general school aid bill.

After 18 frustrating months, he resigned, stating that the very size of HEW made it unmanageable. He was elected to the United States Senate in 1962 and served until 3 January 1981. As a senator, Ribicoff was counted on by both the Kennedy and Johnson administrations for support of major social welfare legislation. He consistently won high ratings from the liberal Americans for Democratic Action. Although he initially supported the **Vietnam War**, by 1968 he opposed American involvement, believing that it diverted resources that would be better used in domestic programs.

Ribicoff is perhaps best remembered for the speech he made at the **Democratic Party** presidential convention in 1968 when nominating George McGovern. The Chicago police had been responding to anti–Vietnam War demonstrations with excessive force, and in a vehement denunciation of their actions, Ribicoff declared that "with George McGovern as President of the United States, we wouldn't have to have Gestapo tactics in the streets of Chicago." Although many in the audience applauded, **television** cameras focused in on Chicago mayor **Richard J. Daley** who appeared to be shouting obscenities at Ribicoff. He died in New York City on 22 February 1998. *See also* CELEBREZZE, ANTHONY JOSEPH.

ROSTOW, WALT WHITMAN (1916–2003). Walt Whitman Rostow was born on 7 October 1916, in New York City, the son of Russian Jewish immigrants. He attended Yale University as an undergraduate and graduate student, receiving his PhD in 1940, after having spent two years at Oxford University as a Rhodes Scholar. During World War II, he was an officer in the Office of Strategic Services and helped select bombing targets in Germany. Following the war, he served briefly in the State Department and, from 1947 to 1949, was assistant to the executive secretary of the Economic Commission for Europe. From 1950 to 1960, Rostow taught economics at the Massachusetts Institute of Technology (MIT). While at MIT, he was associated with its Center for International Studies, a group partially funded by the Central Intelligence Agency. Rostow's chief academic interests were the process of economic growth and the direction of U.S. foreign policy. His best-known book, *The Stages of Economic Growth: A Non-communist Manifesto* (1960), presented an economic interpretation of history that challenged Marxist

theories of development. Rostow argued that economic growth was a multistage process stimulated by a widespread desire for the improvement of life as well as the search for profit by the middle class. Rapid growth in a few sectors such as railroads or textiles, he asserted, caused an economic "take-off" toward industrialization and modernization, leading to an "age of high mass consumption."

Rostow did occasional work as a consultant for the **Dwight D. Eisenhower** administration and, in 1958, regularly began to provide Senator John F. Kennedy with ideas and research on foreign affairs. During the 1960 presidential campaign, he was on Kennedy's informal academic advisory council and was credited with writing two widely used Kennedy campaign slogans: "The **New Frontier**" and "Let's Get This Country Moving Again." Kennedy originally intended to appoint Rostow as head of the State Department Policy Planning Council, but secretary of state–designate Dean Rusk preferred to have an old friend, George Mc-Ghee, in the post. Kennedy finally appointed Rostow to be deputy to **McGeorge Bundy**, the special assistant to the president for national security affairs. In this post, Rostow had a major role in advising the president on foreign policy options and planning.

Shortly after Kennedy's inauguration, Rostow was given a report on conditions in **Vietnam**, prepared in the final days of the Eisenhower administration by Brigadier General Edward G. Lansdale. Lansdale was pessimistic and urged a major expansion of U.S. programs in that country. Rostow passed on Lansdale's report to the president, who was greatly impressed by it. The report was the first step in a major administration examination of Vietnam policy. Rostow believed that communist insurgents were "scavengers of the modernization process," preying on dislocations and discontent inherent in the transitional stages of economic growth. He argued that the United States had to speed up the modernization process in these developing countries and, while the process of modernization was under way, prevent guerrilla infiltration by either diplomatic or military means, or else take direct action against its sources. Rostow was thus one

of the earliest administration figures to urge the consideration of bombing North Vietnam or invading and occupying its southern regions. According to David Halberstam in *The Best and the Brightest*, Rostow was "genuinely enthusiastic about a guerrilla confrontation" in South Vietnam. In a memorandum to the president on 12 April 1961, Rostow urged "gearing up the whole Vietnam operation." Shortly after reading this memorandum, Kennedy appointed a task force headed by the deputy secretary of defense, Roswell Gilpatric, to re-evaluate Vietnam policy. The task force recommended a moderate increase in aid but did not clearly call for ground troops to be sent.

Rostow was also involved in deliberations about Laos. An interdepartmental task force on Laos was established in January 1961, and Rostow was the White House voice. During the crisis—which resulted from military setbacks experienced by the U.S.-backed rightist troops in spring 1961—Rostow advocated firm military and political action against the communist forces. When a similar crisis occurred in May 1962, he advised bombing North Vietnam, which he believed to be largely in control of the Laotian communists. Fortunately, in both cases, diplomatic solutions were reached before any major military steps were taken by the United States.

In September 1961, insurgent action in Vietnam increased, and on 1 October, South Vietnamese president Ngo Dinh Diem requested a bilateral treaty with the United States. Rostow proposed, instead, sending a Southeast Asia Treaty Organization force of 25,000 men to guard the Laotian-Vietnamese border, but the idea was rejected by the Joint Chiefs of Staff, who introduced their own plan to send U.S. troops to either Laos or the Central Highlands of Vietnam. On 11 October, Kennedy decided to send Rostow and presidential adviser General **Maxwell D. Taylor** to Vietnam to investigate possible plans for increasing U.S. involvement, including the introduction of combat troops. Rostow was one of the principal authors of the mission's main report, issued on 3 November. The tone of this document was characterized in *The Pentagon Papers* as combining "urgency with optimism."

The report recommended a series of reforms in the Saigon government and military, and an increase in U.S. military involvement from advisory to "limited partnership." In a separate top-secret report, Taylor recommended the introduction of 8,000 combat troops. With the exception of Taylor's call for the introduction of ground troops, most of the mission's recommendations were put into effect.

On 26 November 1961, Kennedy undertook a high-level shuffle of White House and State Department officials. Rostow was appointed a State Department counselor and chairman of the department's Policy Planning Council (PPC). He was no longer directly involved in the White House decision-making process and no longer centrally involved in Vietnam policy. As chair of the PPC, he was in charge of long-range analysis and planning for a broad spectrum of foreign policy areas. Among Rostow's new projects was a program to improve the profile of West Berlin in the face of the construction of the Berlin Wall. He also attended various international planning conferences and, in February 1962, attended a meeting of the North Atlantic Treaty Organization's Permanent Council to seek support for the U.S. policy toward Latin America, particularly for a ban on trade with **Cuba**. At the request of Kennedy and Rusk, Rostow made a week-long trip to India and Pakistan in April 1963 to explore the possibility for a settlement of their dispute over Kashmir and to encourage both sides to seek a negotiated solution. However, in his report to Kennedy, Rostow was deeply pessimistic about the possibility for a peaceful resolution of the dispute in the near future.

In May 1964, President **Lyndon B. Johnson** gave Rostow the additional post of U.S. representative to the Inter-American Committee on the **Alliance for Progress**. In April 1966, he succeeded Bundy as special assistant to the president for national security affairs, and he served in that post for the remainder of the Johnson administration.

Following the election of **Richard M. Nixon** as president in November 1968, Rostow resigned and returned to academic life as a professor of economics and history at the University of Texas, where he taught for the next 30 years. He died on 13 February 2003. *See also* BALL, GEORGE WILDMAN; CUBAN MISSILE CRISIS; JOHNSON, URAL ALEXIS.

RUBY, JACK (1911–1967). Jack Ruby was born Jacob Leon Rubenstein on 25 April 1911, in Chicago, the son of Polish-born Orthodox Jewish parents. He was the fifth of his parents' 10 surviving children, and he had a troubled childhood and adolescence, marked by juvenile delinquency and time spent in foster homes. Ruby quit school at age 16 and worked as a ticket scalper, a hawker of racetrack tip sheets, and an organizer for the Scrap Iron and Junk Handlers Union. Ruby served in World War II in the U.S. Army Air Forces, and in 1947 he moved to Dallas to help his sister open a nightclub; he later shortened his surname to "Ruby." He remained in Dallas, where he owned and managed various clubs for the next 16 years. According to the House of Representatives Select Committee on Assassinations report of 1979, during these years, Ruby developed close ties to many Dallas police officers who frequented his nightclubs, where he provided them with free liquor, prostitutes, and other favors.

On the morning of 24 November 1963, Ruby entered the Dallas Police and Courts Building where **Lee Harvey Oswald**, the alleged assassin of President John F. Kennedy, was being held. (He had, in fact, visited police headquarters the day of Oswald's arrest two days earlier.) At around 11:20 a.m. CST, as Oswald, surrounded by police, reporters, and camera operators, was being escorted to the car that was to take him to the county jail, Ruby pushed his way past police, drew his pistol, and fired one shot into Oswald's abdomen. Oswald died within two hours.

The shooting was witnessed by millions on live **television**. Ruby said he killed Oswald in a temporary fit of depression and rage over the death of the president. He denied that he had ever known Oswald or had been connected in any way with a plot to assassinate the president. Flamboyant San Francisco attorney Melvin Belli, Ruby's defense lawyer (who acted pro bono), requested the trial judge, Joseph

Brantley Brown, to move the proceedings to another location as, Belli argued, Ruby would not get a fair trial in Dallas. Judge Brown refused the request.

In February 1964, jury selection was completed; all but two had seen the shooting on television. Ruby's pleaded not guilty by reason of insanity. Prosecution psychologists and neurologists contended that the evidence, including the electroencephalograms, introduced by the defense, were insufficient to support the plea. On 14 March, the jury found Ruby guilty and directed that he be sentenced to death. Belli called the proceedings a kangaroo court and charged that the Dallas "oligarchy wanted to send Ruby to the public abattoir . . . to cleanse this city of its shame."

After a Dallas state court jury ruled in June 1966 that Ruby was sane and competent to dismiss his lawyers, a new defense team, which included New York attorney William Kuntsler, took the case to the Texas Court of Appeals. In October, that court's three judges—in separate opinions—agreed that Ruby's conviction should be reversed. The holding of Ruby's trial in Dallas had been an error, said the court, and it ordered that he be retried outside Dallas County. However, on 3 January 1967, before he could be tried again, Ruby, who was suffering from cancer, died of a blood clot in the lungs.

Ruby consistently denied that he knew Oswald or that he was connected to a plot to murder President Kennedy. However, given his record of shady and illegal activities in Dallas, it is not surprising that assassination theorists have connected Ruby with various conspiracies to kill Kennedy, despite the lack of detailed, compelling evidence. *See also* ASSASSINATION OF JOHN F. KENNEDY.

RUSK, DAVID DEAN (1909–1994). Dean Rusk was born on 9 February 1909 in Cherokee County, Georgia, the son of a Presbyterian minister. However, his father's poor health resulted in his growing up in a household on the edge of poverty. Rusk worked his way through Davidson College and, following his graduation in 1931, studied at Oxford University on a Rhodes scholarship. Returning to the United States in 1934, he joined the political science department of California's Mills College and in 1938 he became dean of the faculty. During World War II he served in the infantry in the China–Burma–India theater where he came to the attention of General George Marshall. In 1946, he joined the State Department, and, after a short stint as special assistant to Secretary of War Robert P. Patterson, returned to the State Department as director of the Office of Special Political Affairs. During the next five years Rusk served as a close aide to Robert Lovett and Dean Acheson. In 1950, he was appointed assistant secretary of state for Far Eastern affairs. In this position Rusk helped formulate policy during the Korean conflict, supporting military action in Korea but opposing the expansion of the war into Communist China. Rusk left the State Department to become president of the Rockefeller Foundation in 1952.

Following his election in 1960, President John F. Kennedy appointed Rusk his secretary of state at the urging of the New York establishment, with whom Rusk had formed close ties. Kennedy considered foreign affairs to be his personal responsibility and was determined to dominate foreign policy formulation during his administration. He expected to easily control Rusk and the State Department. Rusk attempted to make the department more responsive to new policy trends and to the wishes of the president. Rusk quietly improved relations between the State Department, Congress, and the Central Intelligence Agency and moderated the rivalry between the State and Defense Departments. Although he served the second-longest term of any secretary of state in the twentieth century, he had relatively little impact on foreign policy formulation. Because Kennedy sought to be his own secretary of state, he personally directed day-to-day policymaking on many major issues, such as the East–West conflict over Berlin in the summer of 1961. Kennedy was also reluctant to rely on the traditional department bureaucracy and instead appointed task forces made up of men both from inside and outside of government to deal with particular problems. Rusk's lack of impact can also be attributed to his personality

and his conception of the role of secretary of state. Rusk was by nature a reserved, unassertive man whose chief virtues were patience together with the ability to handle detail and express himself clearly. Rusk believed that the secretary should be the personal adviser of the president. It was the president who defined the nation's overall goals and objectives. His first loyalty was always to his president.

Consequently, Rusk refused to advocate specific policies during most of the important crises of the Kennedy administration. During the March 1961 debates over the proposed invasion of **Cuba** by U.S.-trained Cuban exiles, Rusk, in the words of Arthur Schlesinger Jr., merely listened "inscrutably through the discussions, confining himself to gentle warnings about possible excesses." Rusk again played little part in the policy discussions that followed the discovery of Soviet offensive missiles in Cuba in October 1962. His advice was extremely ambiguous if not inconsistent. At one point he argued against an air strike to destroy the weapons, but later he urged a limited air attack after informing U.S. allies. Then he backed away from that position as well. He followed a similarly inconsistent path with respect to U.S. policy in **Vietnam**. During the Kennedy administration, Rusk attempted to keep the State Department out of Vietnam affairs; by 1963, however, he had become entangled in the conflict, which would occupy his attention for the remainder of the decade. During the **Lyndon B. Johnson** administration, Rusk helped implement the president's Vietnam policy and, despite his own personal misgivings and doubts, he became one of its most eloquent defenders.

Rusk left office in January 1969 and later became a professor of international law at the University of Georgia. He died on 20 December 1994 in Athens, Georgia. *See also* BAY OF PIGS; CUBAN MISSILE CRISIS; MCNAMARA, ROBERT STRANGE; ROSTOW, WALT WHITMAN.

RUSTIN, BAYARD (1912–1987). Bayard Rustin was born on 17 March 1912, in West Chester, Pennsylvania, as an illegitimate child. He was raised by his Quaker grandparents in West Chester and was influenced by the Quakers' pacifist principles. He was a great organizer and used his very considerable organizational skills to great effect in the antiwar and the **civil rights** movements of the 1940s, 1950s, and 1960s.

Rustin rejected segregation at a young age and, in his mid-20s, joined the Young Communist League (YCL), an organization he believed was committed to peace and to equal rights for blacks. He became an organizer for the league in 1938 in New York City and attended the City College of New York at night. Disillusioned by the pro-war response of the YCL during World War II in 1941, Rustin became a socialist and joined the Fellowship of Reconciliation, a pacifist nondenominational religious group that opposed the war and racial injustice.

That same year he met and worked with A. Philip Randolph, president of the Brotherhood of Sleeping Car Porters, in planning a march on Washington to demand fair employment practices in the nation's rapidly growing defense industries. The march itself was canceled when President Franklin D. Roosevelt issued an executive order banning racial discrimination by defense contractors.

During the early 1940s, Rustin also participated in the founding of the **Congress of Racial Equality** (CORE), an offshoot of the Fellowship of Reconciliation. In 1947, he helped organize and participated in CORE's first **Freedom Ride** into the South. At around the same time, he became director of Randolph's Committee against Discrimination in the Armed Forces, which played a major role in securing President **Harry S. Truman**'s 1948 executive order prohibiting discrimination in all branches of the U.S. military.

During World War II, Rustin had served more than two years in jail as a conscientious objector for his refusal to serve in the armed forces. After the war, in 1953, he became executive secretary of the War Resisters League and, in 1958, went to England to assist the Campaign for Nuclear Disarmament in organizing the first of its annual Aldermaston-to-London "ban the bomb" peace marches.

During the 1950s, Rustin also turned his attention to the civil rights movement and

became one of its leading strategists. In 1955, he played a key role in organizing the Montgomery, Alabama, bus boycott led by **Martin Luther King Jr.**, and he subsequently drafted the plan for what became the Southern Christian Leadership Conference. In the late 1950s, he served as an adviser to King.

In 1960, Rustin, acting on behalf of King and Randolph, organized civil rights demonstrations at the Democratic and Republican national conventions. His radical left-wing approach upset some, more conservative, black leaders, for example, Representative Adam Clayton Powell Jr. (D-N.Y.). Randolph, with whom he had established a close working relationship over the previous two decades, was the only leader who maintained his ties with Rustin.

During winter 1962–1963, Randolph asked Rustin to draw up plans for a mass march on Washington, DC. Rustin believed that black demonstrations should concentrate on demands for federal action in the areas of jobs, housing, and **education**. Demonstrations in Birmingham, Alabama, in April and May 1963 that involved masses of black workers who, not satisfied with token integration of public accommodations, insisted upon equal opportunity and full employment, further convinced him of that course of action. His original plans for the march reflected these views. During the two months preceding the demonstration, however, march leaders shifted its emphasis from economic and social reforms to traditional civil rights objectives so as to secure the support of moderate blacks such as **Roy Wilkins**, executive director of the **National Association for the Advancement of Colored People**. Concerned that Rustin's radical background might expose the project to unnecessary attack, Randolph agreed to be the official director of the march, but he appointed Rustin to serve as his deputy, and the latter was the actual organizer of the demonstration.

Rustin was successful in gaining the support of around 100 civil rights, religious, and labor organizations for the march, although the American Federation of Labor/Congress of Industrial Organizations (AFL-CIO), fearing possible disorders, declined to endorse the demonstration. On 28 August, an unprecedented 200,000 to 250,000 individuals participated in a well-ordered and peaceful March on Washington for Jobs and Freedom.

In the mid-1960s, Rustin contended that coalition politics within the framework of the **Democratic Party** was the only feasible means by which blacks could gain economic and social justice. As a minority, he said, blacks acting on their own could not exert sufficient power to influence the federal government to provide decent jobs, housing, and education. Viewing political struggle as essentially a conflict between the interests of workers and of business rather than between races, he urged an alliance of blacks with the established AFL-CIO leadership for the purpose of radically reforming American society. Rustin believed black separatism would merely strengthen the position of a few black businessmen within the **African American** community. In 1964, Rustin became executive director of the newly created A. Philip Randolph Institute. In that post, he attempted to bring black youths into union apprenticeship training programs and to solidify the political links between blacks and unions. He died on 24 August 1987, in New York City. *See also* HARRINGTON, EDWARD MICHAEL, JR.; STONE, ISIDOR FEINSTEIN.

S

SALINGER, PIERRE EMIL GEORGE (1925–2004). Pierre Emil George Salinger was born in San Francisco on 14 June 1925 to a French-born Catholic mother and a New York City–born Jewish father. He was a musical child prodigy and, until the age of 12, was destined to follow a career as a concert pianist. Following World War II when he served in the U.S. Navy, Salinger graduated from the University of San Francisco in 1947. He began his career as a journalist working as night city editor of the *San Francisco Chronicle* and later West Coast and contributing editor for *Collier's* magazine during the 1940s and 1950s. He established a reputation as an investigative reporter and became active in state and national politics.

Salinger served as press officer for **Adlai Stevenson II**'s California campaign in 1952 and supported Robert Graves for California governor in 1954. Salinger first became acquainted with the Kennedys in 1957 when **Robert Kennedy** hired him as an investigator for the Senate Rackets Committee. Senator John F. Kennedy served on this committee and, during his 1960 presidential campaign, made Salinger his press secretary. On 10 November 1960, Salinger, at age 35, became the youngest White House press secretary in history. According to journalist William White, Salinger conveyed "an essentially light-hearted atmosphere" in the White House. He brought his love of music into the White House, and he encouraged President Kennedy's wife, **Jacqueline Kennedy**, in her efforts to bring "high" culture into the White House by inviting leading international classical musicians to perform there. Salinger also innovated the use of "live" **television** and radio broadcasts of presidential press conferences.

Salinger's centralization and control of the dissemination of top-level information—especially following the **Cuban missile crisis** in October 1962—led to charges of "news management" by journalists; a charge vigorously denied by the press secretary. However, in early 1963 the House Government Information Subcommittee conducted hearings on the Kennedy administration's handling of news information during the crisis. Friends of the administration, such as James Reston of the *New York Times*, testified that management of information was not as bad as some critics had suggested, but the managing editor of the Associated Press, Charles S. Rowe, claimed that the public had never been told the full story of the **Cuba** blockade. The administration's denials were not helped by U.S. assistant secretary of defense Arthur Sylvester's statement in December 1962 that the government has "a right, if necessary, to lie to save itself when it's going up into nuclear war." Salinger, in a speech before the National Press Club on 22 March 1963, responded to the charges by denying that the administration had lied to the public, and he turned the tables on the press by proposing a "fundamental study" to determine whether the media itself was managing news.

Despite his high visibility, Pierre Salinger—unlike **Dwight D. Eisenhower**'s press secretary, James Hagerty—had little influence on Kennedy's domestic or foreign policy. He was

with the six members of Kennedy's cabinet traveling by plane to Japan when the president was assassinated. After Kennedy's death, he stayed on as White House press secretary until March 1964, when he resigned to assume the Senate seat in California vacated by Democrat Clair Engle. In the subsequent 1964 senatorial race, Salinger lost decisively to Republican George Murphy. As a campaign manager of the 1968 presidential campaign of Robert Kennedy, Salinger was present at the Ambassador Hotel in Los Angeles when Robert was assassinated. In the late 1970s and into the 1980s, he was a national broadcast journalist for ABC Television News and Sport. Pierre Salinger died of a heart attack in a hospital near his home in France on 16 October 2004, at the age of 79. He is buried at Arlington National Cemetery. *See also* CRONKITE, WALTER LELAND.

SAUDI ARABIA. The development of the rich oil fields in the large, predominantly arid country that occupies much of the Arabian Peninsula in the years immediately following World War II transformed Saudi Arabia from an impoverished desert populated by nomads (bedouins) into a financial giant, containing the world's largest proven oil reserves—estimated to be around 25 percent. United States oil companies, including the Arabian American Oil Company, Texaco, and Standard Oil of New Jersey, were key players in the production of Saudi oil, and, as the British withdrew from the region, U.S. **Middle East** policy began to focus on protecting its interests by building its military strength in the region. In 1953, Saud bin Abdulaziz Al Saud (King Saud) took the throne, but by the early 1960s, intense family rivalries had led to instability and uncertainty in the kingdom. In 1957, the United States extended its lease of the air base at Dhahran it had built after World War II for another five years. The country is an absolute monarchy ruled by the Saud family—a family with around 2,000 important princes—who are members of the highly conservative, puritanical, Wahhabi sect of Islam, and within its borders are two of the holiest cities of Islam, Mecca and Medina.

SHRIVER, EUNICE KENNEDY (1921–2009). Sister of John F. Kennedy, Eunice Kennedy was born in Brookline, Massachusetts, on 10 July 1921, the fifth of **Rose Fitzgerald Kennedy** and **Joseph P. Kennedy Sr.**'s nine children, and their third daughter. She attended the Convent of the Sacred Heart School in Noroton, Connecticut, and Manhattanville College, and she received a BS degree in sociology from Stanford University in 1943. Following graduation, Kennedy began a career devoted to assisting those with mental disabilities and social disadvantage. She first served in the Special War Problems Division of the Department of State and then headed a juvenile delinquency project in the Department of Justice. In 1950, she became a social worker at the Penitentiary for Women in Alderson, West Virginia; the following year she moved to Chicago, Illinois, to work with the House of the Good Shepherd and the Chicago Juvenile Court.

In 1953, Kennedy married **R. Sargent Shriver Jr.**, a graduate of Yale University and Yale Law School and former U.S. Navy officer who had joined her father's firm in Chicago, the Merchandise Mart, in 1948. The Shrivers had five children: Robert III, Maria, Timothy, Mark, and Anthony. In 1957, Eunice Kennedy Shriver took over the direction of the Joseph P. Kennedy Jr. Foundation, established in 1946 as a memorial to her oldest brother, who had been killed in World War II. The foundation's goals were to help prevent mental retardation by identifying its causes and to improve the means by which society deals with citizens who are afflicted.

Under Shriver's leadership, the Joseph P. Kennedy Jr. Foundation helped achieve many significant advances. In June 1962, Shriver began a summer day camp for children and adults with intellectual disabilities at her home in Maryland to explore their capabilities in a variety of sports and physical activities. From that camp came the concept of the Special Olympics, an organization dedicated to empowering people with intellectual disabilities to realize their full potential and develop their skills through year-round training in sports and competition. Shriver continued her work to support people with intellectual disabilities

throughout her life. Today, more than 1.3 million children and adults participate in the Special Olympics, which is active in more than 150 countries. Shriver was recognized throughout the world for her leadership on behalf of individuals with intellectual disabilities, and she received countless honors and awards, including the Presidential Medal of Freedom. Eunice Kennedy Shriver died on 11 August 2009, at the age of 88. *See also* KENNEDY, ROSE MARIE "ROSEMARY".

SHRIVER, R. SARGENT, JR. (1915–2011). Sargent Shriver was born on 9 November 1915 in Westminster, Maryland, to parents who traced their German ancestry back to the founding fathers. He spent his high school years at Canterbury School in New Milford, Connecticut. After graduating from high school, Shriver spent the summer in Germany and returned in fall 1934 to enter Yale University. He received his bachelor's degree in 1938 and then attended Yale Law School, earning an LLB degree in 1941.

Although he was a founding member of the America First Committee—an organization started in 1940 by a group of Yale Law School students—and opposed American involvement in World War II, Shriver volunteered for the U.S. Navy before the attack on Pearl Harbor and spent five years on active duty, mostly in the South Pacific. Following the war, he worked as an assistant editor of *Newsweek* in New York, where he met **Eunice Kennedy**, the third daughter of **Joseph P. Kennedy Sr.** and **Rose Fitzgerald Kennedy**. After a seven-year courtship, Shriver married Eunice on 23 May 1953, at St. Patrick's Cathedral in New York City. Shriver managed the Merchandise Mart, part of Kennedy's business empire, in Chicago, Illinois.

In April 1960, when his brother-in-law, John F. Kennedy, ran for president, Shriver joined Kennedy's presidential campaign staff and worked on the Wisconsin and West Virginia primaries. Although not one of Kennedy's top advisers, he also functioned as a fund-raiser and was active in promoting the candidate in urban areas. It was Shriver who persuaded candidate John F. Kennedy to call

Coretta King in October 1960 to offer his help in obtaining the release of her husband, **Martin Luther King Jr.** Following Kennedy's election, Shriver headed the administration's talent hunt, a systematic attempt to recruit personnel for high government posts. During the new administration, Shriver served as organizer and first director of the **Peace Corps** from 22 March 1961 to 28 February 1966. The establishment of such a volunteer group, first suggested by Senator **Hubert H. Humphrey**, was promised during the last days of Kennedy's campaign. After the inauguration, Shriver immediately began developing plans for the agency. By 1964, more than 100,000 men and women had applied to join the organization, and the program had indeed expanded from 500–1,000 members in 1961 to 10,000 in 1964. Many of the men and women who served in the corps believed that it provided a way of putting their idealism to work by doing something worthwhile for others.

Shriver continued to serve as director of the Peace Corps after Kennedy's assassination and served as special assistant to President **Lyndon B. Johnson**. In February 1964, he was appointed to head President Johnson's War on Poverty. From 1968 to 1970, he served as ambassador to France. Shriver continued to be active in national politics. He was Senator George McGovern's running mate during the 1972 presidential race, and in 1976 he made a brief, unsuccessful attempt to win the Democratic nomination for president. Shriver founded numerous social programs and organizations.

Shriver died on 18 January 2011, in Suburban Hospital in Bethesda, Maryland, at the age of 95. President Barack Obama released a statement, calling Shriver "one of the brightest lights of the greatest generation."

SINATRA, FRANCIS ALBERT "FRANK" (1915–1998). Francis Albert "Frank" Sinatra was born on 12 December 1915, in Hoboken, New Jersey, to an Italian American Catholic family. His father was a firefighter, and his mother was a midwife and active in local **Democratic Party** politics. Sinatra developed an interest in music, particularly big band

jazz, at a young age and began singing professionally as a teenager. By the early 1940s, he had gained an idolatrous nationwide audience of "bobby-soxers" (as teenage girls of that time were called) for his uniquely intimate vocal style. His career went into eclipse late in the decade but revived after he won a 1953 Academy Award for best supporting actor in the film *From Here to Eternity*. For the next 20 years, Sinatra remained at the top of his profession with nightclub acts, **television** shows, recordings, and films. His yearly income was estimated at $4 million. In the early 1960s, Sinatra and several other show-business stars, including singers Dean Martin and Sammy Davis Jr., became known as the "Rat Pack" and frequently performed together. He became one of the best-selling music artists of all time, selling more than 150 million records worldwide.

Sinatra was a long-time Democrat and became an early and active supporter of the presidential candidacy of Senator John F. Kennedy, to whom he had been introduced by a Kennedy in-law, actor and sometime "Rat Pack" member **Peter Lawford**. Sinatra urged liberals in Hollywood to support Kennedy, organized benefits on Kennedy's behalf, and accompanied the senator on several campaign trips. After the election, he escorted **Jacqueline Kennedy** to the Inaugural Gala, where ticket prices ranged from $100 to $10,000. The gala raised $1.4 million to help pay off the Democratic Party's campaign debts. During the next two years, Kennedy became a close friend of Sinatra's and often stayed at the entertainer's house in Palm Springs, California. However, late in the administration, Sinatra's reputed connections with organized crime led to a cooling off between the two men. According to many observers, the friendship was terminated in September 1963 after the Nevada State Gaming Commission charged that Sinatra had violated state law by permitting Mafia leader Sam Giancana to use the gambling facilities of Cal-Neva Lodge, of which Sinatra was the principal stockholder. After the commission ordered Sinatra to sever his financial interests in the state's gambling industry, the entertainer announced that he was

divesting himself of his gambling holdings and would confine his investments to the entertainment industry.

In April 1976, the *New York Times* reported in a series of investigative articles that during the Kennedy administration Attorney General **Robert F. Kennedy** had blocked Justice Department inquiries into the nature and extent of Sinatra's Mafia connections and into his relationship with Judith Campbell Exner, who was an intimate friend of Mafia leaders Sam Giancana and John Roselli. According to the Senate Committee on Intelligence Activities, in the early 1960s both Roselli and Giancana had been involved in Central Intelligence Agency plots to assassinate Cuban prime minister **Fidel Castro**. Early in 1976, Exner publicly acknowledged that she had had a two-year affair with President Kennedy from 1960 until 1962. She said she had been introduced to Kennedy in Las Vegas by Sinatra and that several weeks later Sinatra had introduced her to Giancana and Roselli. Exner speculated that Sinatra had wanted to "set up a [Mafia] Connection" with the White House.

During the **Richard M. Nixon** administration, Sinatra developed a close personal friendship with Vice President Spiro Agnew. In 1972, he changed his political allegiance and contributed $14,000 to Nixon's reelection campaign. In the 1980 presidential election, Sinatra supported Ronald Reagan and donated $4 million to Reagan's campaign. Sinatra arranged Reagan's Inaugural Gala, as he had done for Kennedy 20 years previously. In 1985, Reagan presented Sinatra with the Presidential Medal of Freedom. Frank Sinatra died of a heart attack on 14 May 1998, in Los Angeles, California.

SIRHAN, SIRHAN B. (1944–). Sirhan Bishara Sirhan was born on 19 March 1944 to a Christian Arab family in Jerusalem in what at that time was mandatory Palestine. He experienced the violence that occurred between Arabs and Jews in the struggle that resulted in the establishment of the Jewish state of Israel in May 1948. Sirhan's family fled during the conflict that followed the founding of Israel. In 1957, when Sirhan was 12 years old,

his family arrived in the United States, where Sirhan attended high school in Pasadena, California, and then entered Pasadena City College. He left college in 1966. Sirhan had retained a deep-seated hostility toward Israel and was deeply distressed over Israel's victory in the Six-Day War of June 1967. During spring 1968, Senator **Robert F. Kennedy**, a supporter of Israel, became the focus of his rage. During his campaign in the California presidential primary, Kennedy had promised to send 50 fighter jets to Israel if elected president. By May as Kennedy campaigned, Sirhan considered assassinating him. On 18 May, he wrote in his diary: "My determination to eliminate R.F.K. is becoming more of an unshakeable obsession. . . . R.F.K. must die . . . Robert F. Kennedy must be assassinated before 5 June"—the first anniversary of the 1967 Six-Day War.

On 4 June, Sirhan went to the Ambassador Hotel in Los Angeles, the Kennedy headquarters during the California campaign. Late in the evening, when it became clear that he had won the primary, Kennedy left his suite and made his way to the hotel ballroom to address his cheering campaign workers. After speaking briefly, Kennedy headed for the pressroom, taking a shortcut through the hotel kitchen. Kennedy was shaking hands with the kitchen workers when Sirhan approached him. Shortly after midnight on 5 June, Sirhan opened fire with a .22 caliber pistol. Kennedy, shot in the head and armpit, fell to the floor. Five others were shot and wounded, leading to later speculation that perhaps a second shooter was involved. Sirhan was immediately subdued and apprehended by Kennedy aides and hotel staff. When arrested, Sirhan allegedly stated, "I did it for my country."

Early in the morning of 6 June 1968, 25 hours after the shooting, Kennedy died at the Good Samaritan Hospital in Los Angeles. Sirhan was charged with first-degree murder. At his trial, defense attorneys argued that Sirhan had diminished mental capacity and therefore was not capable of the premeditation required to convict him of first-degree murder. On 17 April, however, the jury found Sirhan guilty of murder. The judge sentenced him to

death in the gas chamber. Robert Kennedy's brother, Senator **Edward Kennedy**, requested that the death penalty be set aside, but Judge Herbert Walker, who had the power to reduce the sentence to life imprisonment, refused to do so. In June 1972, the **Supreme Court** suspended all executions until state legislatures drastically revised their capital punishment statutes. This ruling led to the commutation of Sirhan's sentence to life imprisonment. Several hearings have been held to release Sirhan on parole, but on 10 February 2016, at his 15th parole hearing in a federal courthouse in San Diego—at which the suggestion of a second shooter was again raised—he was once more denied parole.

SKAKEL, ETHEL (1928–). *See* KENNEDY, ETHEL SKAKEL.

SMITH, JEAN KENNEDY (1928–). Jean Ann Kennedy was the eighth of nine children born to **Joseph P. Kennedy Sr.** and **Rose Fitzgerald Kennedy**, on 20 February 1928. After attending Sacred Heart schools in England and the United States, she graduated from Manhattanville College in Westchester County, New York, with a major in English. Interestingly, there she met her two future sisters-in-law: **Ethel Skakel**, who married her older brother **Robert Kennedy** in 1950, and Joan Bennett, who married her younger brother **Ted Kennedy** in 1958. After her brother **Joseph P. Kennedy Jr.** was killed in 1944 in World War II, Jean was chosen in 1945 to christen the USS *Joseph P. Kennedy Jr.*, a newly commissioned navy destroyer. In 1956, Kennedy married Stephen E. Smith, an executive in a transportation company founded by his grandfather, and they took up residence in New York City. The couple kept a lower profile than some other members of the extended Kennedy family. They had two sons, Stephen Jr. and William, and two adopted daughters, Amanda and Kym. Stephen Smith died in 1990.

Jean Kennedy Smith assisted in the congressional campaigns of her brother John F. Kennedy, and in 1960, she traveled around the country during his campaign for the presidency. She and her husband were also present

at the Ambassador Hotel, Los Angeles, in June 1968 when her brother Robert was assassinated. Smith had accompanied President Kennedy on his much-celebrated visit to Ireland in 1963, and three decades later, in 1993, President Clinton nominated her to be U.S. ambassador to Ireland. After confirmation by the Senate, she assumed her duties that June, serving in the position until 1998. The Irish government and the Irish people enthusiastically welcomed her as America's ambassador. She took an active interest in encouraging a peaceful settlement in the long-standing conflict in Northern Ireland, and one of her principal achievements was in persuading the Clinton administration to grant a visa to Gerry Adams, president of Sinn Fein, the political arm of the Irish Republican Army, to visit the United States in 1994. The visit was widely regarded as a key step in the success of the peace process in the years that followed.

Since 1964, Smith has been a member of the board of trustees of the Joseph P. Kennedy Jr. Foundation, which provides grants to promote awareness and advocacy in the field of mental retardation. In 1974, she founded Very Special Arts (VSA), a nonprofit educational affiliate of the **John F. Kennedy Center for the Performing Arts** that provides opportunities in the creative arts for individuals with disabilities. In April 1993, Random House published her book *Chronicles of Courage: Very Special Artists*, written with George Plimpton.

She has also served on the boards of the John F. Kennedy Center for the Performing Arts and the Carnegie Endowment for International Peace. In addition to a number of honorary degrees, Smith has received various awards, including the Jefferson Award for Outstanding Public Service from the American Institutes for Public Service and the Margaret Mead Humanitarian Award from the Council of Cerebral Palsy Auxiliaries. In 2011, she was awarded the Presidential Medal of Freedom, the nation's highest civilian honor, by President Barack Obama, for her work with VSA and people with disabilities. She is the last surviving child of Joe and Rose Kennedy. *See also* KENNEDY, ROSE MARIE "ROSEMARY".

SORENSEN, THEODORE CHAIKIN (1928–2010). Theodore Chaikin Sorensen was born on 8 May 1928—**Harry S. Truman's** 44th birthday, as he was fond of noting—into a politically liberal family in Lincoln, Nebraska. He described himself as a distinct minority: "a Danish-Russian-Jewish-Unitarian." His mother, Annis Chaikin, was a social worker, pacifist, and feminist, and his father, Christian A. Sorensen, was a crusading lawyer and reformer. Sorensen was raised in the progressive tradition of Senator George W. Norris (D-Neb.), a close friend of his father's. Continuing the family's liberal tradition, in 1945 Sorensen registered with the draft as a noncombatant and later campaigned for the integration of universities and municipal facilities in Nebraska while a student at the University of Nebraska Law School. In 1951, Sorensen went to Washington, DC, as an attorney for the Federal Security Agency. A year later, he became a staff researcher for the joint congressional subcommittee studying railroad pensions.

In 1953, he joined the staff of newly elected senator John F. Kennedy, where he helped research and draft legislation. He also prepared the background material for—and cowrote—Kennedy's best-selling, prize-winning book, *Profiles in Courage*, which brought the young senator to national attention. Sorensen was to become Kennedy's closest aide throughout his Senate and presidential career; he was a political strategist and a trusted adviser on everything from election tactics to foreign policy. His relationship with Kennedy was one of total loyalty and dedication, a connection emphasized by his title, special counsel to the president. Although not a close social friend of the senator, he became Kennedy's political alter ego, willingly submitting his personal interests to Kennedy's political ambition. Sorensen later stated that "for those eleven years he was the only human being who mattered to me." According to journalist Patrick Anderson, Sorensen was a liberalizing influence on the senator, particularly in the areas of **civil rights**, international relations, and social welfare. The aide drew Kennedy from the conservative positions he had taken while influenced by his father to more moderate stands on many

issues. At the same time, Kennedy steered the idealistic Sorensen toward a more pragmatic political philosophy. Gradually the two men's philosophies merged until "no one—not even Sorensen—was sure just where his thoughts left and Kennedy's began."

Not personally aggressive in presenting his ideas, Sorensen believed that he could use his facility as a speechwriter to educate Kennedy, present him with policy choices not previously considered, and force him to take a stand on the issues. At the White House, Sorensen's duties became more varied. As the chief White House speechwriter, he helped Kennedy forge a style of public speaking that often captured the nation's imagination and contributed to the flavor of pragmatic optimism that characterized his presidency. **Pierre Salinger** claimed of Sorensen's and Kennedy's relationship: "They hit it off magnificently. Sorensen not only had strong social convictions echoing those of the young senator, but a genius for translating them into eloquent and persuasive language." According to historian Godfrey Hodgson, Sorensen "worked very closely for eight years with Kennedy, travelled with him, shared his political aims and ambitions and acquired a deep and instinctive understanding of Kennedy's sometimes idiosyncratic political philosophy."

Sorensen was credited with writing some of Kennedy's most notable speeches, including the inaugural address. Kennedy's stirring proclamation that "the torch has been passed to a new generation of Americans" and his challenge to Americans to "ask not what your country can do for you, ask what you can do for your country," for example, were both written by Sorensen. Sorensen drew on the Bible, the Gettysburg Address, and the words of Thomas Jefferson and Winston Churchill to help hone and polish that speech. Sorensen was also the author of Kennedy's speech at American University in June 1963. Because of Kennedy's distrust of the federal bureaucracy, Sorensen and his staff were responsible for shaping much of the administration's legislative program, particularly its aid-to-**education** proposals. He was also the spokesman for Kennedy and served as his chief aide in

domestic crises. During summer 1961, when Kennedy contemplated a tax increase to pay for the military buildup in Berlin, Sorensen advised him against the idea as it reflected bad politics and conservative economics. In April 1962, he helped coordinate the administration's drive for a price rollback following steel industry rate increases. After the abortive **Bay of Pigs** invasion of **Cuba** in April 1961, Sorensen's influence increased further. Kennedy had plenty of yes-men. He needed a no-man from time to time. The president trusted Sorensen to play that role in foreign as well as domestic matters, and, in the judgment of U.S. attorney general **Robert F. Kennedy**, he played it well. "If it was difficult," Robert Kennedy said, "Ted Sorensen was brought in." Jack Kennedy believed he had received poor advice from the State and Defense Departments during the months prior to the Bay of Pigs attack, and he began to rely more heavily on trusted aides. Sorensen, therefore, began advising the president on such issues as the American response to the Soviet challenge in Berlin and communist expansion in Laos during 1961 and 1962. In each of these situations, Sorensen urged Kennedy to avoid confrontation and the use of military force and to work for a peaceful solution to the problem.

Sorensen played a leading role in policy formation in the days following the discovery of Soviet missiles in Cuba on 14 October 1962. In the policy meetings of the Executive Committee of the National Security Council (ExComm)—the special group of advisers gathered to counsel the president in the crisis and gain bipartisan support for administration policy—participants were divided: some advocated air strikes against the missile bases, and others urged a blockade of Cuba to force removal of the weapons. Following the tentative decision made on 18 October to recommend the blockade, Sorensen, anxious to gain a stronger consensus, offered to prepare draft papers on both proposals. These statements and his discussions with the ExComm members convinced many of those recommending stronger action that a blockade would be the beginning of the U.S. response, and that if it did not force removal of the weapons an air

strike would follow. Sorensen drafted carefully crafted letters that Kennedy sent directly to the Soviet leader, **Nikita Khrushchev**, setting out the blockade option and warning of the dangers of any escalation. Sorensen also polished the televised speech Kennedy made to the American people on Monday 22 October. The Soviets withdrew the missiles, and further negotiations led to an end to the crisis.

Sorensen was utterly devasted by Kennedy's assassination. He left the White House and spent the next two years writing his book *Kennedy*, a glowing description of the White House years that was published in 1965. In the prologue, Sorensen wrote that the book was "my substitute for the book he [Kennedy] was going to write." Sorensen, initially indecisive about a prospective career, traveled and lectured before joining a leading New York law firm in 1966. In 1970, he made an unsuccessful bid for the Democratic Senate nomination from New York. Ted Sorensen died in New York on 30 October 2010, at the age of 82. *See also* CUBAN MISSILE CRISIS; VIETNAM.

SOVIET UNION. At the conclusion of World War II, the Soviet Union occupied Central Europe and appeared capable of dominating Western Europe unless challenged by the United States. In February 1946, Soviet leader Joseph Stalin gave a speech in Moscow stating that capitalism and communism were incompatible but predicted that communism would eventually defeat the forces of capitalism. A few days later, U.S. diplomat **George Kennan**, in what has become known as his "Long Telegram," confirmed that in his view the Soviet Union would treat the United States as irredeemably hostile. Despite the rejection of Stalin's extreme views by **Nikita Khrushchev** upon the death of the Soviet dictator in 1953 and the adoption in 1956 of a more conciliatory approach of peaceful coexistence, or "managed competition," the "**Cold War**" (the term used to describe the contest between the two superpowers) became intense during the 1960s, heightened by various political disputes coupled with the possession of nuclear weapons. Each side created a mirror image

of the other. Officials in Moscow believed that "the United States was interfering everywhere; that American globalism was a powerful force; that whenever anything happened anywhere, the hand of the United States must have been involved." An identical ideologically driven assessment prevailed in Washington. The situation was made more dangerous by the creation by both superpowers of patron-client relationships. The question arose: Does the dog wag the tail, or does the tail wag the dog? The inability to determine which was which was particularly troubling during periods of confrontation, even in those incidents that arose accidently.

Soviet leadership felt the election of John F. Kennedy as president presented an opportunity to assert its leadership in Europe and in the Third World. However, Moscow found a tougher opponent in Kennedy than anticipated when questions arose in relation to the status of Berlin, the independence of **Cuba**, the **Middle East**, and the future of South Vietnam. Kennedy enthusiastically endorsed the anticommunist absolutes of previous administrations, and both superpowers stood behind their clients, even when it was not necessarily in their own interests. The construction of, testing, and possession of nuclear weapons was also an area of intense concern and dispute. With the testing of the new, deadly hydrogen bombs, Soviet premier Georgy Malenkov in January 1955 publicly warned that a global nuclear war could lead to the end of civilization, essentially rejecting the Stalinist view that communism would inevitably achieve "final victory" over the imperialist capitalist forces. Nikita Khrushchev, when he assumed office as premier early in 1958, took up the same line, which over time morphed into the doctrine of peaceful coexistence. Nonetheless, determined to demonstrate advances in Soviet technology to a global audience, Khrushchev authorized the explosion of a 50-megaton device over an island in northern Russia above the Arctic Circle at an altitude of 4,000 meters on 30 October 1961. The effect was awesome: "The atmospheric disturbance generated by the explosion orbited the earth three times. The flash of light was so bright that it was visible at a

distance of 1,000 kilometers, despite cloudy skies. A gigantic, swirling mushroom cloud rose as high as 64 kilometers." The test led American officials to believe that the Soviets had taken "a qualitative leap which wiped out the American advantage in total number of tests."

Both superpowers entered the 1960s determined to build or maintain nuclear superiority. Nevertheless, concerned about the potential effects of radioactive fallout on the people exposed to radiation resulting from the testing of more destructive nuclear weapons, Moscow and Washington devoted considerable diplomatic time and effort on ways to restrict or reduce these new weapons. There were also concerns about nuclear proliferation. Negotiations to limit nuclear weapons had begun at the **United Nations** as early as 1946, without much progress. In September 1959, Premier Khrushchev submitted a proposal for general disarmament to the United Nations General Assembly that sought to eliminate all armed forces and armaments within a four-year period, but that proposal was not adopted. In his first State of the Union message of 30 January 1961, Kennedy indicated his wish to make **arms control** a central goal of U.S. policy. However, despite the president's promise to resume discussions of steps toward disarmament, whenever agreement seemed in sight, U.S. negotiators insisted upon formal on-site inspections by the International Atomic Energy Commission—established in July 1957—to verify that promises had been kept, a demand that usually thwarted serious efforts. Moscow viewed roving inspectors as spies and the on-site verification process as espionage.

The rapid escalation of, and the tense brinksmanship experienced during, the October 1962 **Cuban missile crisis** compelled leaders in both the United States and the Soviet Union to pursue more aggressively an agreement that could help them avoid the devastating destruction of a nuclear war. Restricting nuclear armaments looked more like a necessity and less like a dream. Following the 1962 crisis, a new direct emergency communication between the White House and the Kremlin, or "hotline," was agreed upon and formalized in June 1963. At Moscow on 15 July, three-power talks (the United States, the Soviet Union, and the United Kingdom) again took up the issue of limiting nuclear tests, which had been stalled for nearly a decade. As both Khrushchev and the Kennedy administration began to move toward agreement on a partial test ban, a major impulse came from nuclear scientists, and the three powers signed an agreement on 5 August 1963, prohibiting nuclear tests in space, in the atmosphere, and underwater. The agreement did not, however, eliminate underground tests. When the partial test ban became effective on 10 October, more than 100 nations agreed to it. Negotiators then turned their attention to preventing the militarization of outer space. From 1960 to 1962, the military leaders of the Soviet Union's space program were lobbying for authorization and funding to build military space stations, presumably capable of launching nuclear missiles against the United States. In Washington, policy makers had to contend with similar enthusiasm emanating from the Pentagon, but they concluded that the economic and political costs did not warrant such a program. President Kennedy briefly considered a diplomatic initiative for a formal ban on military competition in space, but when confronted with Pentagon opposition, he happily turned the matter over to the United Nations. *See also* HOTLINE AGREEMENT; MISSILE GAP; NUCLEAR DETERRENCE.

SPACE POLICY. The parallel efforts by the United States and the **Soviet Union** to employ artificial satellites to explore outer space, to send human beings into space, and to land people on the moon was labeled the "space race." It was sparked by the successful launch of Sputnik by the Soviet Union on 4 October 1957 and lasted until 1975. This competition for civilian and military achievements in space was significant during the **Cold War** as each party sought cultural and technological advantages. In the geopolitical realm, being first in space offered special propaganda advantages, as John F. Kennedy stated in 1961: "In the eyes of the world, first in space means first, period; second in space is second

in everything." Kennedy defined winning the space race as being the first nation to land a person on the moon. After initially being intimidated by Sputnik, the American public became fascinated with rockets and satellites and agreed with President Kennedy that spending U.S. dollars on space projects was important to enhance national prestige as well as other worthwhile objectives. The military aspects of space technology found immediate practical use in spy satellites, which could effectively supply vital information on Soviet activities. The technical development required for space travel applied also to the power plants that lifted intercontinental ballistic missiles.

The Soviets had the early "firsts." Yuri Gagarin was the first man in space when he orbited Earth on 12 April 1961. Stung into action by this remarkable achievement, on 25 May 1961 Kennedy announced to a joint session of Congress that the United States was committed to sending a man to the moon. Initiating the Apollo project recommended to him by the National Aeronautics and Space Administration, created in 1958, the president declared: "I believe that this nation should commit itself to achieving the goal, before this decade is out, of landing a man on the Moon and returning him safely to the Earth. No single space project in this period will be more impressive to mankind, or more important in the long-range exploration of space; and none will be so difficult or expensive to accomplish." On 11–15 August 1962, the Soviets launched the first dual-manned flight, and they sent the first woman into space on 16 June 1963. The first flight involving multiple crew members lifted off Soviet soil on 13 October 1964 carrying three men; it also was the first flight on which the crew did not wear space suits. In a mission that could have ended disastrously, Alexei Leonov took the first space walk in March 1965 but had difficulty returning to the Voskhod 2 capsule, and because of a faulty retrorocket, the capsule landed nearly 1,000 miles from its scheduled destination. America's Alan Shepard followed Gagarin into space 23 days later, but **John Glenn** became the first American to successfully orbit Earth, on 20 February 1962. The following year, on 2 July, the

United States placed the first geosynchronous satellite in space, the success of which meant that its orbit would remain geostationary and satellite transmissions for **television** broadcast were practical. Meanwhile, Kennedy proposed a number of joint ventures, such as a moon landing by Soviet and American astronauts and improved weather-monitoring satellites, but **Nikita Khrushchev** rejected the suggestion, fearing that it was an attempt to gain access to Moscow's superior space technology.

Having chosen the moon as the goal, the Apollo planners sought to design a program that would minimize the risks to the crew, the fiscal burden, and the requirements for technology and astronaut skill. They adopted a plan involving a lunar rendezvous in which the spacecraft, composed of a command/service module and a lunar module, would separate in lunar orbit, and the lunar module would carry two astronauts to the moon's surface

Return of John Glenn's space capsule, 1962. *Courtesy of Library of Congress.*

and back. Kennedy's goal of landing a man on the moon and returning him safely to Earth was achieved with the Apollo 11 mission in July 1969. Neil Armstrong and Buzz Aldrin, the crew of Apollo 11, became the first men to walk on the moon. The lunar program continued into the early 1970s to carry out the initial hands-on scientific exploration of the moon, with a total of six successful landings. *See also* GLENN, JOHN.

SPORT. John F. Kennedy grew up in a household devoted to athletic activity. Tennis, swimming, touch football, water skiing, sailing, and winter sports were family recreational staples. All four Kennedy brothers played football at Harvard. Jack did not progress beyond the junior varsity as illness and injury in his freshman year curtailed his involvement. Health problems often affected young Jack Kennedy's involvement, but he remained determined to be an energetic participant as well as an enthusiastic follower of sports. In later years, all the Kennedy brothers, and in some cases their sisters and wives too, famously enjoyed games of touch football. Kennedy was a baseball fan and, following family tradition, supported the Boston Red Sox. He also loved sailing and was part of the Harvard sailing crew that won the Eastern Collegiate Championship.

As president, Kennedy wished to promote sport and **physical fitness**: "We do not want our children to become a generation of spectators. Rather we want each of them to be a participant in the vigorous life," he asserted. Not surprisingly, in football, he supported the U.S. Navy team and, nominally, the Washington Senators. Interestingly, in 1961 the Washington Redskins were the only team in professional football without an African American player, and, keen to display its commitment to **civil rights**, the Kennedy administration moved to desegregate the Redskins. During the 1950s, around 150 **African Americans** had played in the National Football League—61 in 1960 alone—and by January 1961, the Redskins were the only team not to have played an African American. In late March 1961, the secretary of the interior, **Stewart L. Udall**, threatened federal retribution if the Redskins did not hire an African American player.

Udall's threats caused considerable controversy in the sporting world; indeed in the nation as a whole, sport was seen as leading the move toward integration and equal job opportunities. This was the first time the federal government had sought to desegregate a professional sporting team. The Redskins owner resisted, but Kennedy supported Udall's position; by early 1962, the team included one African America player.

Following tradition, President Kennedy played golf and, despite chronic back pain, remained an accomplished golfer, playing mainly at the Burning Tree Club and Chevy Chase Club in Maryland. He also continued to enjoy touch football, tennis, and softball with family and friends, and he sailed *Victura*, his 26-foot sloop, in Nantucket Sound.

STEVENSON, ADLAI EWING, II (1900–1965). Adlai Ewing Stevenson II was born in Los Angeles, California, on 5 February 1900, the son of Lewis Green Stevenson, a businessman, and Helen Louise Davis. His grandfather, Adlai Ewing Stevenson I, had been President Grover Cleveland's vice president in 1893–1897 and William Jennings Bryan's running mate in 1900.

Stevenson's parents moved to Bloomington, Illinois, when he was six. Stevenson attended Choate and then Princeton, graduating in 1922. He briefly attended Harvard Law School but completed his law degree at Chicago's Northwestern Law School in 1926. He then joined Cutting, Moore & Sidley, an old and respected Chicago firm. He married in 1928, and in 1937 he bought a farm in Libertyville, his home for the rest of his life.

Because of Stevenson's internationalist outlook, his **Democratic Party** allegiance, and his reputation as an eloquent and persuasive public speaker, Colonel Frank Knox, secretary of the navy, appointed Stevenson as his special assistant during World War II. In 1945, at the request of the State Department, Stevenson helped organize public support for the embryonic **United Nations** (UN), and he was appointed deputy chief of the U.S. delegation

to the UN Preparatory Commission. Stevenson played a central part in shaping the UN's structure. He served as senior adviser to the U.S. delegation at the first session of the General Assembly and as alternate delegate to the New York sessions in 1946 and 1947.

In 1948, Stevenson was elected governor of Illinois. He was so successful in cleaning up the state's disreputable political system that he was nominated as the Democratic Party candidate for president in 1952. He lost to national war hero **Dwight D. Eisenhower** by a wide margin. Eisenhower took 55.1 percent of the popular vote and won by 442–89 in the electoral college. Stevenson ran again in 1956 with even less success; Eisenhower took 57.7 percent of the popular vote and won the electoral college by 457 to 73. In 1960, at the Los Angeles Democratic National Convention, he came in fourth when Senator John F. Kennedy was nominated on the first ballot.

However, Stevenson threw himself wholeheartedly behind Kennedy in the campaign against **Richard M. Nixon**. He helped bridge the gap between Kennedy and liberal Democrats, whose support was vital for victory in what was anticipated to be a close race. Many liberals, including Eleanor Roosevelt, thought that Kennedy was devoid of commitment and too willing to compromise on moral issues, but Stevenson's support convinced the influential liberals to support the party's candidate, if only with a show of reluctance. Stevenson thought that, as a reward for his services as well as his past experience, he would be Kennedy's choice for secretary of state, but despite his long experience and knowledge of world affairs, the young president regarded him as indecisive and too senior and independent minded and passed him over for **Dean Rusk**. Equally important in Kennedy's refusal to offer Stevenson the office was the lack of personal rapport between the two men. According to Arthur Schlesinger Jr., Kennedy found Stevenson "prissy" and "indecisive." Instead of making him chief of the State Department, Kennedy offered him the post of U.S. ambassador to the United Nations. The ambassadorship was a post of cabinet rank, but it was not a policy-making office. The White House did

not consult the ambassador during the planning stages of the Cuban **Bay of Pigs** operation in April 1961 and misinformed Stevenson about the invasion's American character. Consequently, Stevenson told the Security Council on 17 April that the United States had committed no aggression against **Cuba**. When it became apparent that the United States had been heavily involved in training and equipping the Cuban exile group, Stevenson was enraged. Kennedy later described his neglecting to inform Stevenson as a "communications failure."

The Bay of Pigs episode had far-reaching repercussions on Stevenson's position. Although his personal integrity at the United Nations was not questioned, his power within the administration's policy-making councils was limited still further. Stevenson, therefore, found himself in the humiliating position of having his speeches censored by men with less foreign affairs experience than himself and being forced to support policies he had had no voice in making.

Kennedy did include Stevenson in policy-making discussions during the **Cuban missile crisis** of 1962. Stevenson's advocacy of early concessions as a means of getting the missiles out of Cuba won him a reputation as a "dove" in a nest of "hawks." The crisis was finally resolved along much the same lines Stevenson had urged, with the United States withdrawing American missiles from Turkey in exchange for the withdrawal of Soviet missiles from Cuba.

With the **assassination of John F. Kennedy** in November 1963, Stevenson hoped for a larger role in shaping foreign policy, but he was to have less influence with President **Lyndon B. Johnson** than with Kennedy. By 1965, he was dubious about Johnson's escalation in **Vietnam**, favoring instead a political settlement. He was even more dubious about Johnson's unilateral dispatch of troops to the Dominican Republic in the face of an alleged but unproven communist uprising. "If we did so badly in the Dominican Republic," he wrote privately, "I now wonder about our policy in Vietnam." Stevenson revitalized the Democratic Party in the 1950s. He not only

redefined the party mission but also brought a new generation of idealists and activists into politics, and many believe Kennedy was the heir and executor of the Stevenson revolution. In failing health, Stevenson suffered a massive fatal heart attack on a London street on 14 July 1965. See also PRESIDENTIAL ELECTION OF 1960.

STEWART, POTTER (1915–1985). Potter Stewart was born in Jackson, Michigan, on 23 January 1915, into a Cincinnati family long prominent in Ohio Republican politics. He graduated from Yale University in 1937 and received a degree from Yale Law School in 1941 before moving from a Wall Street law practice to a leading Cincinnati firm in 1947. There he served two terms as a city councilman and one as vice mayor. In 1954, President **Dwight D. Eisenhower** appointed Stewart to the Sixth Circuit Court of Appeals and named him to the U.S. **Supreme Court** in October 1958.

Stewart was often considered a "swing" justice between the court's liberal and conservative wings, casting the decisive vote particularly in civil liberties cases. He lost his pivotal position when a liberal majority developed on the court in the early 1960s, but Stewart was still evaluated as a moderate justice—conservative on criminal rights questions and more liberal on race discrimination and free expression issues. In June 1961, he was part of a five-man majority that sustained federal laws that required communist action organizations to register with the Justice Department and made active membership in a party advocating violent overthrow of the government illegal. In two February 1961 cases, Stewart's majority opinions upheld the power of the House Un-American Activities Committee to question individuals about their alleged prior membership in the Communist Party. Whether sustaining or invalidating government action, Stewart generally wrote narrowly based opinions limited to the facts of a case. Stewart was the sole dissenter in three cases decided in June 1962 and June 1963 that held the use of a nondenominational prayer, the recitation of the Lord's Prayer, and Bible reading in public schools was unconstitutional. Noncoercive,

nondenominational religious exercises, Stewart argued, did not establish an official religion in violation of the First Amendment, and he suggested that the prohibition of these practices denied individuals the right to free exercise of religion without interference from government. Justice Stewart joined in several decisions expanding the rights of criminal defendants in the John F. Kennedy years. He wrote the majority opinion in a February 1963 case that reversed the convictions of **civil rights** demonstrators in South Carolina for breaching the peace, and he upheld their rights to free speech, assembly, and petition. During the **Lyndon B. Johnson** years, however, he often voted to sustain state convictions of civil rights protesters, and he also dissented in several major criminal rights cases. Even when they disagreed with his views, Supreme Court observers praised Stewart for his clear, concise, and direct opinions. Legal scholars have rated Stewart as a competent and fair-minded, if rather cautious, jurist. Stewart retired in 1981 and died in Hanover, New Hampshire, on 7 December 1985.

STONE, ISIDOR FEINSTEIN (1907–1989). Isidor Feinstein Stone, born on 24 December 1907, in Philadelphia, was raised in Haddonfield, New Jersey. He began working on local newspapers while in high school, and he left the University of Pennsylvania in 1927 during his junior year. He joined the Socialist Party and worked for Norman Thomas's presidential campaign in 1928. From 1933 to 1952, Stone wrote for several New York–based liberal and left-wing publications. He supported Henry Wallace's 1948 Progressive Party presidential candidacy and was strongly opposed U.S. **Cold War** policies. In 1952, he wrote *The Hidden History of the Korean War*, which questioned the prevailing view that North Korean aggression was responsible for initiating that conflict. The following year, 1953, he began publishing *I. F. Stone's Weekly*, an independent newsletter. Among the early targets of the *Weekly* were Senator Joseph R. McCarthy (R-Wis.), the House Un-American Activities Committee, and the practice of blacklisting radicals and alleged radicals. Stone was an

independent radical—he described himself as a democratic socialist—and avoided affiliation with any organized political group. His newsletter did not accept advertising. He did all research, reportorial, and editorial work, and his wife handled the newsletter's business affairs. By 1963, his *Weekly* had a circulation of more than 20,000. Stone was best known for what his admirers believed was his iconoclastic skill in exposing the inconsistencies, mistakes, and hypocrisy of public officials and his ability to detect the early signals of changes in government policies. His journalistic method entailed the diligent sifting and comparing of government publications, which were available to everyone but generally went unread.

Stone did not endorse a presidential candidate in 1960, and he was disturbed by the efforts of the Kennedy administration to combat revolutionary regimes and movements by military means. In April 1961, he warned that American support of the unsuccessful **Bay of Pigs** invasion and of the faltering effort of the Ngo Dinh Diem regime in South Vietnam to suppress the National Liberation Front demonstrated the administration's failure to recognize that communism could be fought successfully only by responding to the aspirations of the people of the world's poor nations. Stone believed that the Kennedy administration recognized the danger of an unlimited nuclear **arms race**, but he found the president's initiatives to reduce U.S.-Soviet tensions wanting. In February 1962, he wrote that Kennedy was "racing so hard for peace that he had to increase the Eisenhower military budget by almost 25 percent." He also questioned the adequacy of the administration's **civil rights** proposals of 1963. In an evaluation of the Kennedy administration written in December 1963, Stone attributed the weaknesses of President Kennedy's programs to a lack of daring. Fearing conservative reaction in Congress, Stone said, the administration failed to press resolutely for antidiscrimination measures and peace initiatives. He concluded that in the last analysis, "Kennedy, when the tinsel was stripped away, was a conventional leader, no more than an enlightened conservative, cautious as an old man for all his youth, with a basic distrust of the people."

In December 1971, he announced that he would cease publication of his newsletter. He became a contributing editor to the *New York Review of Books*, for which he had been writing occasionally since 1964. Stone continued to write about politics until his death on 18 July 1989. *See also* VIETNAM.

STUDENT NONVIOLENT COORDINATING COMMITTEE (SNCC). Known by its initials SNCC (pronounced "snick"), the Student Nonviolent Coordinating Committee played a major role in the **civil rights** movement of the 1960s. Beginning with a modest grant from the Southern Christian Leadership Conference (SCLC—founded in 1957 by **Martin Luther King Jr.** who was its first president) in 1960, Ella Baker, a staff member of the SCLC who also provided a small grant, organized a student conference at Shaw University in Raleigh, North Carolina, that resulted in the formation of the Coordinating Committee. Among the attendees were Stokely Carmichael and Marion Barry, the latter becoming SNCC's first chairman (and who later was elected mayor of Washington, DC). SNCC focused on mobilizing local communities, a policy in which **African American** communities would push for change, forcing the federal government to act once the injustice had become apparent. The most common action of these groups was organizing sit-ins at racially segregated lunch counters throughout the South to protest the pervasiveness of Jim Crow and other forms of racism. SNCC took part in the **Freedom Rides**, the March on Washington for Jobs and Freedom (1963), and the Freedom Summer in Mississippi. After the Freedom Rides, SNCC worked primarily on voter registration and with local protests over segregated public facilities. Registering black voters was extremely difficult and dangerous. In the late 1960s, SNCC's leadership and emphasis began to change under the aegis of the more militant Stokely Carmichael, and it became heavily involved in the black power movement. The organization officially changed its name to the Student National Coordinating Committee in 1969. It passed out of existence in the 1970s following heavy infiltration and suppression by the

Martin Luther King Jr. with leaders at the March on Washington, Washington, DC, 1963. *Courtesy of Library of Congress.*

Federal Bureau of Investigation (FBI), spearheaded as part of COINTELPRO operations during the 1960s and 1970s led by **J. Edgar Hoover.** COINTELPRO (COunter INTELligence PROgram) was a series of covert, and at times illegal, projects conducted by the FBI between 1956 and 1971 aimed at surveilling, infiltrating, discrediting, and disrupting domestic political organizations, including civil rights organizations and personnel such as Martin Luther King Jr. Some of these activities were personally authorized by U.S. attorney general **Robert F. Kennedy.** *See also* HARRINGTON, EDWARD MICHAEL JR.; HOWE, IRVING; NATIONAL ASSOCIATION FOR THE ADVANCEMENT OF COLORED PEOPLE (NAACP).

STUDENTS FOR A DEMOCRATIC SOCIETY

(SDS). In 1961, two radical students at the University of Michigan, Al Haber and **Tom Hayden,** founded Students for a Democratic Society (SDS). They regarded it as a broadened outgrowth of the League for Industrial Democracy, which had sought to educate Americans about socialist ideals in the 1930s. The following year, in June 1962, 59 members, representing 11 SDS chapters, met at Port Huron, Michigan, where they drafted a New Left manifesto—labeled the "Port Huron Statement"—that advocated nonviolence and emphasized the failure of liberal ideals and denounced the military-industrial-academic establishment. Written by Hayden, the 64-page document called for black dignity and equality, condemned war and "anticommunism," and argued that colleges and universities were not doing enough to awaken students from the prevailing atmosphere of apathy. The well-educated, affluent members of SDS were outraged and angry at what they saw as the hypocrisy, corruption, and inequality of the system, which they hoped they could save.

Initially focusing on domestic issues, SDS worked with the Old and New Left for **Lyndon B. Johnson** in the 1964 presidential campaign and was actively involved in the **civil rights** movement. Beginning in 1965 and continuing through the presidency of **Richard M. Nixon**, SDS actively participated in the anti–**Vietnam War** movement, becoming the focal group leading student demonstrations and teach-ins in universities around the country. *See also* HARRINGTON, EDWARD MICHAEL, JR.

SULZBERGER, ARTHUR OCHS (1926–2012). Arthur Ochs Sulzberger was born in New York City on 5 February 1926, a descendant of the Jewish family that purchased the *New York Times* in 1896 and turned it into one of the world's most distinguished newspapers. He served in the U.S. Marines during World War II, graduated from Columbia University in 1951, and began his career as a cub reporter with the *Times* in 1953. He joined the staff of the *Milwaukee Journal* in 1954 but was soon back with the *Times* as a reporter on the foreign news desk, then London correspondent, and finally assistant to his father, Arthur Hays Sulzberger. Arthur Ochs Sulzberger took over the newspaper in 1963 upon the death of his brother-in-law, Orville Dryfoos, who had been *Times* publisher since 1961. The 37-year-old Sulzberger initiated a vast internal organizational shake-up in the paper. By 1966, he had succeeded in improving the circulation of the *Times* to 800,000 for the weekday edition and 1,500,000 for the Sunday edition, and the *Times* had become one of the few morning newspapers published in New York City. Sulzberger continued a tradition of reprinting the complete texts of major political speeches, significant **Supreme Court** decisions, and important congressional reports and resolutions despite the space these items took in the paper at the expense of revenue-producing material. In October 1963, Sulzberger resisted President Kennedy's suggestion that controversial *Times* reporter David Halberstam be transferred from **Vietnam** to another assignment. Sulzberger told the president that Halberstam, whose critical reporting in Vietnam had disturbed the administration, would remain at his post. In

1964, the paper devoted 48 pages to publication of the **Warren Commission** Report on the **assassination of John F. Kennedy**.

During his tenure, Sulzberger also broadened coverage of religion, sports, and women's news. He is perhaps best remembered for his decision, in June 1971, that the *New York Times* publish the Pentagon Papers despite the opposition of the **Richard M. Nixon** administration. In 1997, Sulzberger retired as chairman and chief executive officer. He died of a brain hemorrhage at his home in Southampton, New York, on 29 September 2012, at the age of 86.

SUPREME COURT OF THE UNITED STATES. The Supreme Court is the only court specifically created by the Constitution. Article III of the Constitution states:

> The judicial Power of the United States, shall be vested in one supreme Court, and in such inferior Courts as the Congress may from time to time ordain and establish. The Judges, both of the supreme and inferior Courts, shall hold their Offices during good Behavior [interpreted as being for life] and shall, at stated Times, receive for their Services a Compensation which shall not be diminished during their Continuance in Office.

This body of nine justices—the chief justice and eight associate justices—is the highest judicial body in the United States. The first bill introduced in the U.S. Senate became the Judiciary Act of 1789 that established the court, which was to sit in the nation's capital. The Constitution did not stipulate the exact powers and prerogatives of the Supreme Court nor the organization of the judicial branch as a whole. Thus, it was left to Congress and to the justices of the court through their decisions to develop the federal judiciary and a body of federal law. The court has both original and appellate jurisdiction; the latter, however, makes up most of the court's caseload, since the Founders intended it should have somewhat limited jurisdiction. It was envisaged as acting to check the executive and legislative

branches of government from overreaching their constitutional powers, as well as to adjudicate in disputed legal matters between the federal and state governments. The Supreme Court first assembled on 1 February 1790, in the Merchants Exchange Building in New York City. The president of the United States may nominate anyone to the court, since there are no qualifications of any kind stated in the Constitution, but the appointment requires the "advice and consent" of the Senate. While the Senate Judiciary Committee conducts hearings on candidates to determine their suitability, the entire Senate decides on confirmation. The committee's recommendation is usually necessary to advance a candidate.

Throughout U.S. history, the appointments to, and the decisions of, the court have been contested. Over the past century, the court has increasingly acted in accordance with the wishes of the federal executive. The court under Chief Justice **Earl Warren** (1953–1969), former Republican governor of California nominated by Republican president **Dwight D. Eisenhower**, was responsible for a number of both celebrated and controversial judgments that expanded the application of the Constitution to civil liberties. In perhaps its most famous case, *Brown v. Board of Education*, it declared segregation unconstitutional; in *Griswold v. Connecticut*, it held the Constitution protected a general right to privacy; in *Miranda v. Arizona* it greatly expanded the rights of those accused of crimes; and it held that states could not apportion their senior legislative body in the same manner that the U.S. Senate is apportioned.

In 1962, John F. Kennedy successfully nominated U.S. deputy attorney general (and former Colorado state chair of Kennedy's 1960 presidential campaign) **Byron R. White** (1962–1993) as an associate justice of the court, as well as **Arthur J. Goldberg** (1962–1965), who later resigned to become the U.S. ambassador to the **United Nations**. Kennedy's successor, **Lyndon B. Johnson**, appointed Abe Fortas (1965–1969), first as an associate justice and then failed to obtain his appointment as chief justice after Earl Warren retired. Johnson also appointed **Thurgood Marshall** (1967–1991), the first **African American**, as an associate justice.

SYRIA. The modern state of Syria, one of the oldest inhabited areas of the world, gained its independence from French rule in April 1945. Following a series of military coups, a democratic regime was established in February 1955 with Shukri al-Quwatli as president. On 1 February 1958, President Quwatli and Egyptian president Gamal Abdel Nasser signed an agreement proclaiming the United Arab Republic (UAR). The two countries were united under President Nasser, with one army. However, unhappy with Egyptian domination of their internal affairs, in September 1961 the Syrian army staged a coup and seceded from the UAR, established a new civilian government, and established the Syrian Arab Republic. In March 1963, the Arab Socialist Resurrection Party (the Ba'ath Party) gained predominant control of the government, and Lieutenant General Amin al-Hafiz became premier and de facto president. *See also* MIDDLE EAST.

T

TAYLOR, MAXWELL DAVENPORT (1901–1987). Maxwell Davenport Taylor was born in Keytesville, Missouri, on 26 August 1901. He graduated from the U.S. Military Academy with the fourth-highest average in the class of 1922. Soon after the Japanese attack on Pearl Harbor, Taylor helped organize the 82nd Airborne Division, later commanding its artillery in the Sicilian and Italian campaigns. He was in command of the 101st Airborne by D-Day and parachuted with the division into Normandy. Following World War II, Taylor was superintendent of West Point for three years and then served in command and staff positions in Europe, the Far East, and in Washington, DC, before being named army chief of staff in 1955.

As the army's principal spokesman on defense strategy, Taylor vigorously opposed the **Dwight D. Eisenhower** administration's reliance on massive nuclear retaliation, arguing that there was a continuing need for strong ground forces capable of fighting a conventional war. After he retired from active service in July 1959, Taylor published *The Uncertain Trumpet*, in which he argued his case. Fascinated by the idea of launching anticommunist **counterinsurgency** operations, John F. Kennedy greatly admired Taylor (as did his brother **Robert Kennedy**) and was impressed with his idea of adopting a military "flexible response" approach. During the 1960 presidential campaign, he used Taylor's arguments to support his own attacks on the Eisenhower administration's defense policies.

Following the botched exile invasion of Cuba sponsored by the Central Intelligence Agency (CIA) at the **Bay of Pigs**, Kennedy asked Taylor to lead an investigation of the CIA's role in the fiasco and to evaluate America's capability for conducting unconventional warfare. Not surprisingly, the hawkish Taylor's report concluded that the Defense Department, rather than the CIA, should be responsible for major paramilitary operations. Kennedy was anxious to have a source of independent military advice from a professional detached from the interservice rivalries of the Pentagon, and on 26 June 1961, the president named Taylor to a newly created White House post as military representative of the president. One of the first tasks Kennedy assigned Taylor was to lead a special mission to South Vietnam in the wake of major communist victories in autumn 1961 to assess the military situation and recommend how the United States should respond. The mission, which included the equally hawkish **Walt W. Rostow**, arrived in Saigon on 18 October. After consultations in South Vietnam and Thailand, Taylor and Rostow flew on to Manila on 30 October where Taylor wrote his report for the president. Although it was kept secret at the time, on his return to Washington on 3 November, Taylor recommended—to an uncertain and troubled President Kennedy—sending some 8,000 U.S. combat troops to **Vietnam**. Taylor told Kennedy that U.S. ground troops were necessary to deter the communists from escalating the conflict. U.S.

secretary of defense **Robert S. McNamara** backed Taylor's recommendation.

Resistance from **Dean Rusk** and the State Department, however, was strong. A compromise devised by McNamara emerged on 11 November: the United States would increase military aid, send more military advisers and helicopter pilots, and pressure Ngo Dinh Diem to carry out political reforms—all measures suggested in the Taylor-Rostow report. As a concession to Taylor's request for combat forces, the Pentagon was directed to prepare a plan for sending in troops on a contingency basis. The administration's public position was that Taylor had recommended against the use of American combat troops. Nevertheless, according to David Halberstam in his book *The Best and the Brightest*, the Taylor mission and the decisions made in late 1961 profoundly "changed and escalated the American commitment to Vietnam." Taylor continued to advise the president on Laos, Vietnam, Berlin, and other foreign policy crises during early 1962, until Kennedy appointed him on 20 July to serve as chairman of the Joint Chiefs of Staff (JCS) to replace General Lyman L. Lemnitzer, who was named commander of North Atlantic Treaty Organization forces in Europe. Taylor was approved unanimously by the Senate on 8 August 1962. Taylor returned to South Vietnam on 10–13 September to review the military situation. Meeting newsmen in Manila on 19 September, he declared that "the Vietnamese are on the road to victory." Despite warnings from Charles de Gaulle and **Nikita Khrushchev** not to engage militarily—and blind to the power of revolutionary, nationalist, independence movements—Kennedy went ahead and authorized an increase in U.S. forces in South Vietnam.

Taylor was a major participant in the crucial White House meetings during the **Cuban missile crisis** of October 1962, advocating a strong response to eliminate Soviet missiles from the island. Taylor also played an active role in the deployment of federal troops to protect **James H. Meredith** when he became the first black to register at the University of Mississippi in fall 1963. During his term as chairman of the JCS, Taylor loyally followed administration policies, in contrast to the other joint chiefs, whose assessments were often at odds with President Kennedy's policies. He was the only member of the JCS to join the administration in opposing the development of the RS-70 manned-bomber program. Taylor's support proved essential when the administration sought Senate ratification of the **Limited Nuclear Test Ban Treaty** with the **Soviet Union**.

Reports that the Diem government's repression of Buddhist protestors was hampering the war effort prompted Kennedy to send Taylor and Defense Secretary McNamara on another mission to Vietnam in September 1963. On the surface, their joint report to the president on 2 October continued to express optimism about the military effort and predicted a victory over the communists by 1965. McNamara, however, reportedly had begun to question Taylor's sanguine confidence that the political situation had not affected the war effort. As a result of Diem's inept handling of the Buddhist crisis, the Kennedy administration—with Taylor's concurrence—acquiesced to the military coup that overthrew the Diem regime at the beginning of November. Taylor continued to serve as chairman of the JCS after Kennedy's assassination until June 1964, when President **Lyndon B. Johnson** appointed him ambassador to South Vietnam, a post he filled until July 1965. Taylor spent his last three months at Walter Reed Army Medical Center in Washington, DC, and died at 85 years of age on 19 April 1987. *See also* BALL, GEORGE WILDMAN.

TELEVISION (TV). By the 1960s, television was rapidly becoming perhaps the mainstream form of mass media in the United States. Programming was more sophisticated and sought not only to entertain but also to inform and entertain, appealing to wider audiences. Television provided a new avenue for politicians and political parties to reach the American public. TV broadcasting networks had been established, and they created news and current affairs programs with anchormen like **Walter Cronkite** (CBS) and Chet Huntley and **David Brinkley** (NBC) who became household names. Television began to shape the political landscape in significant ways.

In the world of politics, one of the most noteworthy events was the series of four face-to-face encounters between presidential candidates John F. Kennedy and **Richard M. Nixon** on national television in late September and October 1960. In the first television debates of their kind—actually, newsmen questioned the candidates, and they in turn were allowed to challenge each other's comments—the widespread public view was that the telegenic Kennedy came out ahead; at the very least, he showed he could handle himself. Many commentators argued that the debates tipped the scales in Kennedy's favor in securing his narrow electoral victory. Three years later, news coverage of the **assassination of John F. Kennedy** mesmerized the country, becoming one of the first major tragedies covered by network news.

The activities surrounding the **civil rights** movement, antiwar demonstrations, and the emerging counterculture movement were also broadcast. Protestors and hippies were routinely embraced and condemned. Overseas in the **Vietnam War**, TV cameras were filming what they could of the conflict, rushing it back for the evening news hour, and giving a face and voice to military and civilian activities—what some observers called the "Living Room War." Television journalism and news unquestionably played a significant role in arousing popular feelings about these events and influenced the ultimate political decisions reached.

Entertainment programs also blossomed on TV in the 1960s—some serious, others pure escapism. The most successful prime-time family program was *The Andy Griffith Show*, which ran for most of the decade. Westerns such as *Gunsmoke* and *Wagon Train* were popular from the late 1950s through the 1960s. Popular adult shows included a blend of the supernatural and science fiction in *Bewitched*, *The Addams Family*, *My Favorite Martian*, *I Dream of Jeannie*, *Star Trek*, *The Outer Limits*, and *The Twilight Zone*. *The Beverly Hillbillies* marked the rise of the sitcom, while in the late 1960s, humor was revived with *Rowan and Martin's Laugh-In*. Many performers who first appeared as guest artists on *Laugh-In* later became regular stars in the show, which is now

regarded as one of the great TV classics. Children's shows featuring cartoon characters appeared in 1959 with *Rocky and His Friends*, followed a year later by *The Flintstones*. The success of the cartoon programs led to a trend that featured *Alvin and the Chipmunks*, *The Jetsons*, and *Mr. Magoo*. *See also* MEDIA AND JOHN F. KENNEDY.

TELLER, EDWARD (1908–2003). Edward Teller was born in Budapest, Hungary, on 15 January 1908. After completing his doctorate in physical chemistry at the University of Leipzig in 1930, he studied with Niels Bohr, the distinguished Danish physicist. Teller left Germany when the Nazis came to power and became an American citizen in 1941. During World War II, he worked on the Manhattan Project, which developed the atomic bomb, and from 1949 to 1951 he was an assistant director of the science laboratory at Los Alamos, New Mexico. During the 1950s, Teller taught physics at the University of California. In 1954, he became an associate director of the Atomic Energy Commission (AEC) Lawrence Livermore National Laboratory in Livermore, California.

During the 1950s, Teller became a leading scientific spokesman for the maintenance of U.S. atomic weapons superiority. He believed that American supremacy was the only means of countering what he viewed as an aggressive Soviet arms policy. Described by *Newsweek* as "the principal architect of the H-bomb [hydrogen bomb]," Teller was a leading advocate of that weapon's development. In the 1954 AEC security hearings, he testified against granting J. Robert Oppenheimer a security clearance, claiming that Oppenheimer's opposition to the H-bomb project had delayed its development. Teller also opposed the three-year moratorium on atomic testing that ended in September 1961 when the **Soviet Union** resumed atmospheric explosions, and he favored the renewed U.S. testing, which began later that month. Calling nuclear test ban negotiations "dangerous," he said they "have helped the Soviets" and "have impeded our own testing."

During the August 1963 Senate hearings on the **Limited Nuclear Test Ban Treaty**, Teller

was the most influential scientist to testify against ratification. His principal objection was to the ban's prohibition of atmospheric tests, which were necessary for the further development of antiballistic missiles (ABMs). Teller feared that the Soviets led in ABM production and that the treaty might enable them to increase that lead. Warning that current detection techniques would be ineffective for policing the agreement, Teller also believed that the treaty would inhibit the military's ability to respond in case of war because it stipulated that atomic weapons could be used only three months after repudiation of the agreement. "You will have given away the future safety of our country and increased the dangers of war," he said.

Teller's views were rejected by Joint Chiefs of Staff chairman General **Maxwell D. Taylor** and other military and government officials who testified in support of the treaty. Taylor said that despite Soviet leads in multimegaton bombs and antimissile defenses, the treaty would make it difficult for the Soviet Union to reach the U.S. level of overall nuclear capability. President John F. Kennedy rebutted many of Teller's objections in a news conference in late August and signed the treaty in October.

In addition to his call for atomic superiority, Teller believed that the threat of international communism required an aggressive American stance in other areas. In March 1962, he told a House Science and Astronautics Committee that U.S. security demanded control of the moon. He urged the establishment of a U.S. colony and the development of a nuclear reactor there. Teller was also a founding member of the Citizens Committee for a Free **Cuba**, a group formed in May 1963 that warned the "Castro-Communist infiltration of Latin America" threatened "democratic forces" throughout the hemisphere. Teller died in Stanford, California, on 9 September 2003, at the age of 95.

THEATER IN THE KENNEDY YEARS. John F. Kennedy was not a regular theatergoer. In the 1950s and 1960s, the center of theater in the United States was New York City, although there were many regional theater companies as well. Playwrights like Arthur Miller and Tennessee Williams were by then well known and their plays performed worldwide, and popular stage actors attracted appreciative audiences to Broadway and its offshoots. Perhaps the most famous playwright of the decade was Edward Albee, who wrote *Who's Afraid of Virginia Woolf?* (1962), the highlight of the Broadway stage and later a popular movie. In the 1960s, experimentation in the arts spread into the theater and eventually reached into the movies. The impact of the counterculture movement appeared in such Broadway plays as *Hair*, which included nudity and references to the drug scene. But by 1960, Broadway shows had become prohibitively expensive for experimental offerings, and producers stayed with proven, traditional shows and musicals. The decade's musical offerings were outstanding—these included not only *Hair* but also *Camelot, Hello, Dolly!, Oliver, Man of La Mancha, Funny Girl*, and *A Chorus Line*. Even off-Broadway theater felt the economic pinch, and thus new writers and actors began to appear in off-off-Broadway theater outside of New York City. This expansion of theater activity led by 1966 to more actors being employed outside New York City than in it.

TRADE EXPANSION ACT (1962). The Trade Expansion Act (TEA) of 1962 was a foreign trade policy devised by the Kennedy administration in response to the formation of the European Economic Community (EEC)—or Common Market—formed in 1957. The competitive commercial potential of the Common Market inside and outside of Europe and its protective, unitary external tariff threatened to curtail U.S. exports to European nations. However, the EEC also offered a tremendous market for U.S. products. It promised growth of national economies, political unity for all traders, and a strengthening of the Western alliance. Kennedy's plan to liberalize trade was the centerpiece of his 1962 **New Frontier** legislative agenda, and it was the economic component of a comprehensive diplomatic blueprint for forging an Atlantic partnership with Europe—his so-called Grand Design.

The president hoped that the liberalization of trade would help stem North Atlantic Treaty Organization members' unease concerning the reliability of the United States as an ally as U.S. postwar economic dominance declined, thereby threatening to derail Kennedy's Grand Design before it got off the ground. Kennedy declared that the TEA was "the most important international piece of legislation, I think, affecting economics since the passage of the Marshall plan. . . . It marks a decisive point for the future of our economy, for our relations with our friends and allies, and for the prospects of free institutions and free societies everywhere."

The Trade Expansion Act enacted on 11 October 1962 gave the Kennedy administration unprecedented authority to negotiate tariff reductions—up to 50 percent—on a reciprocal basis with the six countries of the EEC and other nations, for the next five years. The new act gave the president more tariff-cutting authority than had ever been granted by Congress to a president. The 1962 law largely replaced the Trade Agreements Act of 1934 and was designed to facilitate the movement of goods between the United States and the newly formed EEC. Section 232 of the act also provided that under certain circumstances the president was permitted to impose tariffs based on a recommendation from the U.S. secretary of commerce if "an article is being imported into the United States in such quantities or under such circumstances as to threaten or impair the national security." The TEA was widely regarded as the most important legislation passed by the 87th Congress. It was also President Kennedy's largest and most satisfying legislative victory in his first two years in office. The act also enabled the administration to compensate in various ways groups and sectors of the economy that might be disadvantaged by the tariff reductions.

In the following year, the president created the office of the Special Trade Representative (STR), with two deputy representatives, one in Washington, DC, and the other in Geneva, Switzerland, where trade negotiations would be conducted. The STR also was responsible for coordinating interagency interests in the preparation of trade policy. The legislation and the appointment of an STR prepared the way for the United States to participate in the Kennedy Round of the General Agreement on Tariffs and Trade (known as GATT) negotiations, which concluded on 30 June 1967—the day before the act expired.

TRUMAN, HARRY S. (1884–1972). Harry S. Truman was born in Lamar, Missouri, on 8 May 1884. He grew up in Independence, Missouri, and managed a farm near Grandview from 1906 to 1917. He served as an artillery captain during World War I, and upon his return to the United States he started a haberdashery business in Kansas City with his friend Eddy Jacobson. The business failed during the depression of 1922. His political career began soon after, when, backed by the local **Democratic Party** boss Tom Pendergast, he was elected judge of the local Jackson County Court, becoming the presiding judge in 1926. Truman used this basically administrative position to improve the county roads and consolidate his political credentials.

He was elected to the Senate in 1934 running on a platform endorsing President Franklin Roosevelt's New Deal. Because of his reputation for probity, he was selected to chair the "Truman Committee," to investigate abuses in defense spending, and this brought him to national attention. At the Democratic Party convention in 1944 he was chosen to replace Vice President Henry A. Wallace as Roosevelt's running mate. Elected in November, Truman became president upon Roosevelt's death in April 1945.

Truman was truly a transformational president, setting in train the institutional and policy framework that shaped the United States domestically and internationally for the next half century. Perhaps his most important decision was to approve the use of the newly developed atomic bombs on the Japanese cities of Hiroshima and Nagasaki in 1945, and certainly one of his most controversial decisions was to extend almost instantaneous de facto recognition to the newly declared state of Israel in May 1948.

Truman was an internationalist with a strong belief in the need to maintain and build U.S. military and economic power in the world. At home, he advocated labor, social welfare, and **civil rights** reform in a program he called the Fair Deal. Hostile to communism, he supported the Marshall Plan and the North Atlantic Treaty Organization, and in 1950 he committed U.S. forces to assist South Korea. He also commenced U.S. involvement in **Vietnam** by extending military assistance to the French in the Indochina War as part of the strategy to defeat communist expansion.

He was reelected in 1948 despite predictions he would lose to New York governor Thomas E. Dewey. Korea turned out badly, as did Truman's China policy, leading to considerable domestic dissatisfaction. Despite a sweeping "loyalty" program, in his second term the president was attacked by Republicans and by Senator Joseph R. McCarthy for failing to root out communists from the government.

Truman did not run for reelection in 1952. Instead he returned to Independence in 1953 and oversaw the setting up of the Harry S. Truman Presidential Library. From time to time, he issued public statements attacking the **Dwight D. Eisenhower** administration, defending his own record, or supporting Democratic candidates.

Truman was direct and blunt in his manner and speech, in an old-fashioned, midwestern way, although he could also be gracious and courteous. He did not much like John F. Kennedy, or any of the Kennedy family for that matter. He regarded them as part of the New England elite who, he believed, thought they were born to rule. He characterized President Kennedy's father, **Joseph P. Kennedy Sr.**, as a "crook" who "bought his son the nomination for the presidency." He disliked **Robert F. Kennedy** because he had "worked for old Joe McCarthy." Truman said that "the whole Kennedy family" was interested only in "getting the power. They don't care a hoot in hell about using it." Nonetheless, as a Democrat, Truman campaigned vigorously for John Kennedy during the 1960 election campaign. He had nothing but contempt for Kennedy's opponent, Vice President **Richard M. Nixon**. In a speech in Texas, for example, he said that Nixon had "never told the truth in his life." Truman told Nixon backers to "go to hell."

The former president strongly defended the Kennedy administration against **Republican Party** attacks. Kennedy essentially continued many of the policies inaugurated by Truman. Truman supported Kennedy's resumption of atomic tests in September 1961, his fight against the steel price rise in April 1962, the **United Nations** loan bill in October 1962, and Kennedy's confrontation with Premier **Nikita Khrushchev** during the **Cuban missile crisis**. In August 1963, Truman supported the **Limited Nuclear Test Ban Treaty**. However, he opposed Kennedy's proposed $11 billion tax cut in September 1963. Truman died in Kansas City, Missouri, on 26 December 1972, at the age of 88. *See also* PRESIDENTIAL ELECTION OF 1960.

U

UDALL, STEWART LEE (1920–2010). Stewart Lee Udall was born on 31 January 1920, in the small rural town of Saint Johns, Arizona. He was the son of former Arizona Supreme Court justice Levi S. Udall and Louise Lee Udall. The Udalls were a religious family; both his grandfather and his father were prominent members of the Church of Jesus Christ of Latter-day Saints (the Mormon community).

Stewart L. Udall, as secretary of the interior in the Kennedy and Johnson administrations, was one of the most significant figures in the effort to protect America's natural environment. He launched a series of far-reaching conservation reforms. He attended the University of Arizona briefly before leaving as a missionary to the eastern states in 1940. In World War II, he joined the U.S. Air Force as a B-24 Liberator gunner flying over Western Europe. Upon his return from the war, he completed his law degree at the University of Arizona in 1948 and was active in desegregating the University of Arizona cafeteria. He also married Ermalee Webb that year and started his own legal practice. Around two years later, he and his brother, Morris, opened up a firm together in Tucson, Arizona.

Udall did not raise his family as active, church-going Mormons. Nevertheless, he kept close ties with the church and continued to self-identify as a Mormon. He was, he wrote: "Mormon born and bred, and it's inside me. . . . I prize my Mormon heritage and status." Throughout his adult life, he served as an important intermediary for the church on both political and religious matters. Active

in public service and local politics, as a liberal for a few years, in 1954 Stewart ran for Congress and was elected to a district that encompassed almost all of Arizona. Deeply interested in labor reform, he served on the U.S. House of Representatives Committee on Interior and Insular Affairs (1955–1960), and the **Education** and Labor Committee (1955–1956, 1957–1960). During the 85th Congress (1957–1958), Stewart served on a Joint Committee on Navajo-Hopi Indian Administration. Although more liberal than the candidate and initially filled with misgivings, in 1959 Stewart was instrumental in persuading Arizona Democrats to support Senator John F. Kennedy during the 1960 Democratic National Convention. Partly because of his support for Kennedy in the presidential campaign and partly because he was from the western states, President Kennedy appointed Udall to serve as secretary of the interior, a position he held for eight years. Upon his appointment he initiated the first White House conference on conservation since the administration of Theodore Roosevelt. He brought conservation and environmental concerns into the national consciousness and was the guiding force behind landmark legislation that preserved millions of acres of land, expanded the national park system, and protected water and land from pollution. From the Cape Cod seashore in Massachusetts to the untamed wilds of Alaska, Udall left a monumental legacy as a guardian of America's natural beauty. In September 1962, he was the first of Kennedy's cabinet to visit the **Soviet Union** where he met Soviet

premier **Nikita Khrushchev.** Udall also helped spark a cultural renaissance in America by setting in motion initiatives that led to the **John F. Kennedy Center for the Performing Arts** in Washington, Wolf Trap National Park for the Performing Arts, and other centers. He also suggested to Kennedy that he have former U.S. poet laureate Robert Frost read an original poem at the inauguration.

Kennedy's successor, **Lyndon B. Johnson,** kept Udall on as secretary of the interior and gave him personal responsibility over the issuance of oil and gas leases on public lands. Udall restricted these leases and made concern for the environment a key part of Johnson's Great Society. Udall helped secure passage of the Wilderness Act of 1964 (which now protects around 400 million acres of land in 44 states), as well as the Land and Water Conservation Fund Act (1965), the Water Quality Act (1965), the Solid Waste Disposal Act (1965), the Endangered Species Preservation Act (1966), the National Historic Preservation Act (1966), and the Wild and Scenic Rivers Act (1968). In the late 1960s, he succeeded in preventing the building of dams on the Colorado River that would have put vast stretches of the Grand Canyon under water.

Among his other achievements, Udall made Ellis Island in New York Harbor a national monument, protected the Outer Banks of North Carolina, and designated Assateague Island in Maryland and Virginia a national seashore. After he left Washington in 1969, Udall returned to the West and continued to contribute to the nation's affairs as an author, historian, scholar, lecturer, environmental activist, lawyer, naturalist, and citizen of the outdoors. He died at the age of 90 on 20 March 2010 at his home in Santa Fe, New Mexico, the last surviving member of the Kennedy cabinet. President Barack Obama noted: "Stewart Udall left an indelible mark on this nation and inspired countless Americans who will continue his fight for clean air, clean water, and to maintain our many natural treasures."

UNIONS AND JOHN F. KENNEDY. In 1955, the two largest trade union organizations in the United States, the American Federation of Labor (AFL) and Congress of Industrial Organizations (CIO), whose combined membership of 16 million workers represented around one-third of all workers in non-farm industries, merged after a long, disruptive relationship. George Meany, who had served as president of the AFL from 1952 until the merger, subsequently became president of the united AFL-CIO until 1979. The Landrum-Griffin Act, passed in 1959, in which the federal government recognized that unions were a permanent element in the national economy, regulated the way unions conducted their internal affairs. Unions in the private sector were regulated by the National Labor Relations Board, a part of the U.S. Department of Labor, while public sector unions were governed by a combination of federal and state laws. In 1958, New York City public employees were extended collective bargaining rights, effectively shifting political power from Tammany Hall to the public sector unions.

John F. Kennedy recognized the importance of unions and the union movement. He also recognized that one of the biggest challenges facing unions was automation. Numbers in the organized labor movement reached their peak in 1956 and began to decline thereafter, largely as a result of automation in the automobile and mining industries. In 1960, Flint, Michigan, was the center of the auto industry's biggest player, General Motors (GM), and was at its peak population. Flint had one of the highest incomes per household in the country, similar to Detroit, which was number one in per capita income of all U.S. cities. GM employed 80,000 in Flint alone. In January 1961, Kennedy appointed **Arthur J. Goldberg,** who had been special counsel to the AFL-CIO, to be his secretary of labor. Goldberg sought to facilitate collective bargaining and made the federal government available to help settle or prevent strikes. On 17 January 1962, Kennedy issued Executive Order 10988 ("Employee-Management Cooperation in the Federal Sector"), which enabled federal employees to obtain the right to engage in collective bargaining through labor organizations. This executive order was a breakthrough for public sector workers, who were not protected

under the 1935 Wagner Act. However, they were not permitted to strike—federal strikes had been explicitly prohibited in 1947 by the Taft-Hartley Act—or to join the leadership of these groups.

UNITED NATIONS (UN). The international body known as the United Nations was created at the United Nations Conference on International Organization meetings held in San Francisco from April through June 1945. The UN charter drawn up at those meetings came into force in late 1945 in the aftermath of World War II as nations sought ways of maintaining international peace and security through public discussion and resolution of issues short of armed conflict. The UN charter stipulated a General Assembly consisting of all members of the UN, with several subsidiary bodies, and a Security Council of 15 (rotating) members, five of whom (China, France, the United Kingdom, the **Soviet Union**, and the United States) were to be permanent members. The General Assembly was to meet annually in September–December to discuss and make recommendations (usually requiring a two-thirds majority vote) on any matters within its charter, and the Security Council, whose primary role is to maintain peace and security, was to meet whenever members believed peace was threatened. According to its charter, its further aims included the promotion of human rights, fostering social and economic development, protecting the environment, and providing humanitarian aid in cases of famine or natural disaster. The first meetings of the 51 member states who made up the General Assembly, together with the Security Council, took place in London on 10 January 1946. The main headquarters of the UN are located in Manhattan, New York City, and are subject to extraterritoriality. Offices and numerous agencies of the UN are also situated in other major cities around the world.

Things rarely worked out as the original planners hoped they would, largely because the United States and the Soviet Union brought their intense rivalry into UN debates. In 1960, 16 new states from **Africa** were admitted to the UN, bringing the total of states from that continent to 21. By 1964, the total number of states from Africa, Asia, and Latin America reached 77, making it extremely difficult for the United States to generate a two-thirds majority in the General Assembly. The UN's promise became a victim of the emerging **Cold War**, as the United States and Soviet Union used their veto rights in the Security Council to hamstring the work of UN agencies. President John F. Kennedy, in his inaugural address in 1961, recognized the dilemma, calling the UN "our last best hope" for world peace, while at the same time acknowledging that "the instruments of war have far outpaced the instruments of peace." Nevertheless, he declared, "we renew our pledge of support" for the UN in the hope that it would no longer be "merely a forum for invective," and that it would seek "to strengthen its shield of the new and the weak." Kennedy appointed the liberal internationalist **Adlai E. Stevenson II** (1961–1965) as American ambassador to the United Nations as an indication of his support for the work of the UN. In reality, however, Kennedy's actions and policies regarding the UN were ambivalent. For example, in 1962, when Stevenson sought to disentangle Washington's artificial "two China" policy by devising a compromise that would allow communist China to join the UN, the Kennedy administration rejected his proposals. Indeed, Kennedy informed the Taiwan government that he would use the U.S. Security Council veto to prevent their removal from the international body. During the **Cuban missile crisis**, Stevenson, on 25 October 1962, famously confronted the Soviet ambassador to the United Nations, Valerian Zorin, with photographic evidence of the missile sites under construction and declared his intent to "wait until hell freezes over" for a Soviet explanation. At the same time, in some of the most dramatic diplomacy that the United Nations had engaged in, Kennedy and Soviet secretary-general **Nikita Khrushchev** allowed UN acting secretary-general U Thant to become a valuable mediator of peace during the tense hours of the crisis.

At the time of the Kennedy administration, one of the major roles the UN set itself was

to provide economic and technical assistance to new nations seeking to establish their independence from colonization—especially in Africa, which was experiencing rapid decolonization. The Republic of the Congo was one such nation. On 11 July 1960, shortly after the Republic of the Congo declared its independence from Belgium, Katanga, one of the 11 provinces that made up the new country, announced its secession. This action was supported by Belgium but opposed by the Congolese prime minister Patrice Lumumba. Following a Security Council resolution on 14 July 1960, the UN mounted a peacekeeping operation (Opération des Nations Unies au Congo, or ONUC). The operation continued until June 1964. The situation rapidly became something of a test case of the capacity of the UN to carry out its peacekeeping mission. It did not go well, in large part because of U.S. fears of a communist takeover of the newly independent nation. When the Eisenhower administration refused Lumumba's request for military assistance, he sought aid from the Soviet Union which supplied him with a small number of troops. Originally established to provide the Congolese government with the military and technical assistance required following the collapse of many essential services, circumstances caused ONUC to become embroiled in a chaotic internal situation of extreme complexity, in which it had to assume responsibilities that extended beyond normal peacekeeping duties. It included, in addition to a military force that comprised at its peak strength nearly 20,000 officers and men, an important civilian operations component. After more than two years of continued turmoil, in January 1963 UN forces forcibly reunited the mineral-rich province of Katanga with the Congo. However, civilian aid continued in the largest single assistance program undertaken until that time by the UN and its agencies, employing some 2,000 experts at the peak of its operations in 1963–1964. The "peacekeeping activity" almost bankrupted the United Nations, prompting Washington to guarantee its bonds. Even after the end of the Cold War, memories of the Congo operation

haunted UN officials as well as convinced the international organization that peacekeeping should remain consensual and nonthreatening in nature, an attitude it maintained for almost three decades.

Among its many functions, seeking to reduce military conflict and pursuing the elimination of weapons of mass destruction rank as major objectives of the United Nations. In his September 1959 speech to the UN General Assembly, Soviet leader Khrushchev melodramatically put forward a proposal to eliminate all armed forces and armaments within a four-year period. Nothing happened, of course. Two years later, in September 1961, Kennedy more realistically suggested to the same body that a limited nuclear test ban treaty rather than general disarmament should be the UN's priority. He also urged (1) halting the production of fissionable materials for use in weapons and the transfer of such materials to nonnuclear powers, (2) prohibiting the transfer of nuclear weapons to nations that do not have them, (3) keeping nuclear weapons from outer space, and (4) destroying strategic missiles and aircraft that could deliver nuclear bombs. These themes were included in a U.S. proposal for **general and complete disarmament** submitted to the UN-endorsed Eighteen-Nation Disarmament Committee in 1962.

During the 1960s, the UN had greater success in pursuing its humanitarian and development objectives through its specialized agencies—especially as they related to children. These agencies included the United Nations Children's Fund, with its modest humanitarian program; the World Health Organization (WHO), for the health needs of children; the Food and Agriculture Organization and WHO, for the nutritional needs of children; the United Nations Educational, Scientific and Cultural Organization, for the educational needs of children; the UN Bureau of Social Affairs, for the social welfare needs of children; and the International Labour Organization, for the work and livelihood needs of children. The agencies worked on the theory that children's needs should be built into national development plans.

UNITED STATES WOMEN'S BUREAU. The United States Women's Bureau was established by Congress on 5 June 1920, just two months before women achieved the right to vote, and continues its responsibility to carry out Public Law 66-259; 29 U.S.C. 11-16.29 (1920). The role of the bureau was to formulate policies and standards to promote the welfare of wage-earning women, improve their working conditions, increase their efficiency, and advance their opportunities for profitable employment.

However, the bureau had not been highly effective in providing leadership to its members. In 1961, the situation finally changed. During the Kennedy administration, thanks to the president's interest in an activist program and his reliance on the team in the Labor Department, the Women's Bureau assumed the role it had claimed for the previous decades.

Because of his dependence upon the labor movement, John F. Kennedy elevated the visibility of the Women's Bureau and granted the director a genuine role in policy making. While a member of the House, representing a working-class district of Boston, his voting record on bills of interest to labor had been virtually perfect: 100 percent for four of the six years, 90 percent and 88 percent in the remaining two. In the House, Kennedy had been a member of the House Labor Committee and had opposed the Taft-Hartley Act. In the Senate, as chair of the Senate Subcommittee on Labor, Kennedy continued his commitment to rank-and-file workers although he sometimes met with opposition from union leaders over alleged corruption within labor unions.

The Women's Bureau played an instrumental role in the passage of the **Equal Pay Act of 1963**, which amended the Fair Labor Standards Act. It effectively removed the ability to pay employees differently based on sex. John F. Kennedy signed the law on 10 June 1963. During this time, the bureau opposed the Equal Rights Amendment (ERA) introduced by the National Woman's Party in 1923 until Kennedy took office in 1961. The bureau had been committed to maintaining protective labor legislation for women. Instead of supporting an ERA during his presidency, the president created the **President's Commission on the Status of Women**. *See also* PETERSON, ESTHER EGGERTSEN.

V

VIETNAM. Vietnam is located on the eastern Indochinese Peninsula south of China. It covers a total area of just under 128,000 square miles. Its coastline is around 2,140 miles long and varies between 31 miles and 160 miles in width. Vietnam is a mostly hilly, densely forested country with only around 20 percent of level land. The climate is subtropical with high levels of rainfall.

During the 20th century, the French controlled Vietnam until World War II, when the Japanese invaded and took over the country. During the war, an essentially communist nationalist liberation movement known as the Việt Minh emerged under the Vietnamese revolutionary leader Hồ Chí Minh. The Việt Minh occupied Hanoi and proclaimed a provisional government, which asserted national independence on 2 September 1945. However, earlier that year, in July, the Western allies had decided to divide Indochina into half at the 16th parallel and agreed that the region would remain a French possession.

Hồ Chí Minh, hoping to build a modern independent Vietnam, reached out to the United States to assist in convincing the French to withdraw their colonial administration but was rejected by Washington; in 1946, war broke out between the Việt Minh and France that lasted until July 1954, when the French were defeated in the battle of Dien Bien Phu and withdrew their forces from Vietnam. In the subsequent Geneva Conference, French colonial administration was ended, and French Indochina was dissolved and divided into three countries: Vietnam and the kingdoms of Cambodia and Laos. Vietnam was further divided into North and South administrative regions at the Demilitarized Zone, approximately along the 17th parallel north, pending elections scheduled for July 1956. The Geneva Accords did not intend that the partition of Vietnam would be permanent. However, in 1955 the division did become permanent and the internationally recognized State of Vietnam was effectively replaced by the Republic of Vietnam in the South and Hồ Chí Minh's Democratic Republic of Vietnam in the North. By the time John F. Kennedy assumed office in 1961, conflict between the North and the South had escalated to an alarming degree. *See also* VIETNAM WAR.

VIETNAM WAR. In the 1950s, the United States began to intervene in what was largely a civil war between the northern and southern halves of Vietnam, a division that had taken place after World War II. Initially Washington decided that the government of South Vietnam should be provided with military advisers and financial aid. By the time John F. Kennedy became president, the number of American advisers had risen to more than 5,000 and, during his administration, rose to more than 16,000. Military involvement with ground forces was just a matter of time.

The United States involvement in the Vietnam War was a product of the northeastern foreign policy establishment that Kennedy had chosen and relied upon for advice. These academics and graduates of Harvard and Yale believed that the United States had

vital interests in every part of the world, and (not surprisingly) they were supported in this view by senior members of the military and the State Department.

Vietnam—or rather "not losing Vietnam"— became a key element in the U.S. policy of global containment of communism. That program grew out of the "loss" of China and the need to prove the credibility of the United States as a guarantor of the security of the "free world." When first entering politics, John F. Kennedy was opposed to U.S. involvement in the region. In April 1954, he spoke eloquently against it: "To pour money, material, and men into the jungles of Vietnam without at least a remote prospect of victory," he warned, "would be dangerously futile. . . . I am frankly of the belief that no amount of American assistance in Indochina can conquer an enemy which is everywhere and at the same time nowhere." By June 1956, however, he had changed his mind. He had embraced the **domino theory** that had become gospel during the Eisenhower years and declared that Vietnam was "the cornerstone of the free world in Southeast Asia, the keystone in the arch, the finger in the dike." He now believed that all the nations of South and Southeast Asia—Burma, Thailand, India, Japan, the Philippines, Laos, and Cambodia—would be threatened if communism overflowed into Vietnam. By the time Kennedy entered the Oval Office, Viet Cong guerrillas, with Hanoi's encouragement, had gained control of much of the countryside of Vietnam, putting the rhetoric of falling dominoes to the test.

John F. Kennedy found himself trapped by his own rhetoric. He promised a foreign policy of strength and vigor—a "Grand Design" for Europe, an **"Alliance for Progress"** for Latin America, but what did he offer Southeast Asia? Whatever the future held, he, and his "New Frontiersmen," were confident—indeed overconfident—of victory. However, in mid-1961, sobered by the **Bay of Pigs** fiasco and convinced that Congress, the public, and the press would not tolerate another failure, Kennedy confided to John Kenneth Galbraith, "There are just so many concessions that one can make to the Communists in one year and

survive politically." With his credibility thoroughly challenged, it required only his unsettling exchange with **Nikita Khrushchev** in June to send him in search of some promising area of confrontation. "Vietnam," he concluded, "looks like the place." Behind the Kennedy administration's decisions to engage the United States heavily in Vietnamese affairs was not only an inherited sense of responsibility for Vietnam's future but also a fear of anticommunists at home. Kennedy's determination to avoid any retreat in Vietnam reflected his desire to protect his administration from charges of weakness in confronting the communist enemy abroad.

Kennedy quickly became involved. On 28 January 1961, he called a top-level meeting to discuss a report on Vietnam by General Edward C. Lansdale, at that time the leading U.S. expert on **counterinsurgency**. Lansdale advocated a strong economic, political, and military program to help the American groomed and backed, but increasingly repressive, President Ngo Dinh Diem establish his control of the country. Unfortunately, Diem was rapidly losing command of the South Vietnamese countryside as he faced skillful guerrilla warfare and effective Việt Minh recruitment. Unless conditions improved, Lansdale predicted, the Saigon regime faced certain defeat. Lansdale's memorandum gave the president, for the first time, "a sense of the danger and urgency of the problem of Viet-Nam." The National Intelligence Estimate of 28 March corroborated Lansdale's findings, observing that Saigon's situation "seems likely to become increasingly difficult because of rising Communist guerrilla strength and of widening dissatisfaction with Diem's government." During subsequent months, the supposition that Indochinese communism endangered far more than South Vietnam deepened the administration's commitment to Diem's success. In April, **Walt W. Rostow**, deputy special assistant to the president for national security affairs, reinforced Kennedy's conviction that the United States must prevent the communist domination of South Vietnam. Vice President **Lyndon B. Johnson**, on 23 May, following a trip to Southeast Asia, added further confirmation.

As Saigon's authority continued to deteriorate, Kennedy, in October 1961, dispatched General **Maxwell D. Taylor**, his personal military adviser, and Walt Rostow to Vietnam to gather information for a major reassessment of the American position in Southeast Asia. The absence of State Department personnel on the mission revealed the president's growing acceptance of a military solution. Taylor, in his report of 4 November, accused North Vietnam of aggression and attributed Saigon's military failures to favoritism, inefficiency, and corruption. He recommended an initial deployment of 8,000 American troops to defend South Vietnam's northern frontier against infiltration. Taylor offered Washington three stark choices: defeat, reform, or direct U.S. military involvement. Kennedy rejected the first alternative but would not, as yet, embrace the third; reform remained the least expensive and most promising solution.

Kennedy hoped to avoid large-scale American military confrontation in Vietnam. **Robert S. McNamara** reminded him that the United States might become mired in a land war that it could not win. Kennedy shared that pessimism and doubted that the United States would be any more successful than the French in securing the support of the villagers, so essential for success against guerrilla forces. Responding to Taylor's request for troops, Kennedy complained: "They want a force of American troops. . . . They say it's necessary in order to restore confidence and maintain morale. But it will be just like Berlin. The troops will march in; the bands will play; the crowds will cheer; and in four days everyone will have forgotten. Then we will be told we have to send in more troops." But Kennedy could not resist the promises of success and, over time, approved increasingly large shipments of equipment and advisers to South Vietnam. John K. Galbraith wrote to the president warning him of the dangers. The situation in South Vietnam was exceedingly bad, he wrote: "Unless I am mistaken, Diem has alienated his people to a far greater extent than we allow ourselves to know. This is our old mistake. We take the ruler's word and that of our own people who have become committed to him. . . . But I fear that we have one more government which, on present form, no one will support." By January 1962, the United States had given Diem everything he wanted without achieving any measurable influence in Saigon's administration of public policy. Kennedy had assumed, erroneously, that the Saigon government, responding to American encouragement, would institute reforms in order to achieve political and military effectiveness. He soon discovered that by linking American policy to Diem's survival, the administration had provided the Vietnamese leader with incredible leverage over Washington.

Determined to avoid a hard decision that would unleash a torrent of public opposition, Kennedy committed to increments of military and economic aid sufficient only to sustain the administration's objectives but not large enough to require broad national approval. During 1962, the president gradually increased the military aid to South Vietnam from 4,000 military advisers in January to 10,000 by October, while the secretary of defense assured the American people that the government had no policy for introducing combat forces into South Vietnam.

Kennedy wanted a strategy that would bridge the gap between the goal of victory and the reality of limited U.S. involvement. He believed the political-military program of counterinsurgency was such a strategy. Counterinsurgency involved a range of overt and covert activities by special forces, psychological warfare, intelligence collection, and so forth. The idea of counterinsurgency became fashionable, even faddish in the administration. It was argued that "strong, highly mobile forces trained in this type of warfare, some of which must be deployed in forward areas," would be more than a match for any competing force, even in the jungles of Asia. Kennedy placed control of the counterinsurgency forces under a special group of high-ranking State and Defense officials in Washington. In practice, counterinsurgency assumed the form of a "strategic hamlet" program, which was initiated in March 1962 to insulate the peasants of the countryside, with their resources, and thereby deprive the Viet Cong guerrillas of their necessary base of supplies.

The program, however, achieved little; Washington refused to permit the special forces to move against the guerrillas. In the absence of direct U.S. military involvement in the war, the means for victory lay essentially in Saigon's capacity to organize, staff, and direct a successful counterinsurgency campaign across South Vietnam. Ngo Dinh Nhu, Diem's brother and political adviser, quickly emerged as the director of the strategic hamlet program. In April 1962, he adopted the model of counterinsurgency that had succeeded in Malaya. Unfortunately, South Vietnam possessed none of the sociological, political, and ethnic factors that had been crucial to Malaya's apparent triumph over its guerrilla movement. Despite intensive training, the South Vietnamese acquired neither the skills nor the motivation required for effective counterinsurgency operations. When U.S. forces later assumed responsibility for South Vietnam's defense, they reverted to traditional modes of warfare.

Chester Bowles, Kennedy's special adviser on **Africa**, Asia, and Latin America, told Kennedy in June 1963: "As matters now stand, we may find ourselves forced to choose between an escalating war or a humiliating retreat in an area where the strategic conditions are disadvantageous to us." Meanwhile, Washington exuded confidence, with private optimism usually following, rather than preceding, each successive escalation of the American effort. The president summed up the year's successes in his State of the Union message of January 1963: "The spearhead of aggression has been blunted in South Vietnam." With the economic and military increments of early 1963, official optimism became even more pronounced. During March, U.S. secretary of state Dean Rusk declared that "government forces clearly have the initiative in most areas of the country." Nothing seemed to challenge Washington's strong ties to Diem until, in summer 1963, the South Vietnamese leader, with his brother, Ngo Dinh Nhu, instituted a drastic repression of the Buddhists. **Henry Cabot Lodge Jr.**, who became ambassador in August 1963, as well as Kennedy and the White House staff, found Diem's behavior toward the Buddhists embarrassing and unacceptable. Lodge soon discovered a plot among South Vietnam's leading officers to overthrow the Diem regime. Supported by Kennedy and his top advisers, Lodge encouraged Diem's opponents by assuring them that the United States would do nothing to prevent a coup, and Vietnamese officers alone planned and executed the coup on 1 November. Washington officials anticipated the coup but not the assassination of Diem and his brother. Kennedy's own assassination followed three weeks later. At that moment, the United States had 16,000 troops in Vietnam, with a continuing commitment to victory and no plan of escape.

Kennedy's successor Lyndon B. Johnson escalated the war with disastrous results for the Vietnamese and for domestic harmony at home. President **Richard M. Nixon** finally accepted a Paris cease-fire agreement, initialed on 23 January 1973, which became effective on 28 January 1973. The withdrawal of the last U.S. combat units and Hanoi's return of American prisoners of war was completed by 1 April 1973.

American involvement in Vietnam was, by any standard of judgment, the most disastrous episode in the history of U.S. foreign policy. The loss in national treasure and blood was staggering. From 1961 until the collapse of the Thieu regime in late April 1975, U.S. expenditures in Indochina amounted to more than $141 billion or, to put it another way, $7,000 for each of South Vietnam's 20 million people. After finally breaking their silence in 1965, **civil rights** leaders pointedly observed that it cost something near $30,000 to kill a single enemy solider, around three times what was spent to rehabilitate a Job Corps trainee. The loss of life was equally staggering. American casualties alone reached a figure of 350,000, with around 58,000 killed, 40,000 of whom were killed in combat, and 304,000 wounded, with some 74,000 surviving as quadriplegics or multiple amputees. Vietnamese casualties (North and South) reached a figure of more than two million, with more than 241,000 South Vietnamese combat deaths and more than one million combined North Vietnamese and Viet Cong combat deaths. In addition to the known dead, there are 300,000 North

Vietnamese MIAs, in contrast to the 2,000 Americans still missing.

As important as it is to draw attention to the increasing involvement of the United States in Vietnam under Kennedy, the real question that remains unanswered, and the answer to which can never be known, is this: Did John F. Kennedy intend to reduce the level of American involvement and withdraw from the conflict? Kennedy received conflicting advice as to why the administration should do so; the South was doing so well there was no need to remain, or the war was going so badly for the South there was no end in sight. As the situation in Vietnam deteriorated, Senator **Mike Mansfield** urged Kennedy to withdraw the United States from Vietnam's civil conflict, but, according to one account, Kennedy was unwilling to consider such a move before the election of 1964, fearing he would be labeled "weak" on anticommunism during the presidential election campaign. On 2 October 1963, in Washington, DC, U.S. secretary of defense Robert S. McNamara and Joint Chiefs of Staff chairman Maxwell D. Taylor held conversations with Kennedy on their return from Vietnam where they had been sent by the president to assess the situation and the state of the conflict. Both disingenuously stated that "great progress" was being made militarily against the Vietcong and that the government of president Ngo Dinh Diem was stable. Accordingly, they recommended that 1,000

troops could be withdrawn by the end of the year. The president accepted their recommendation. Later that day the White House issued a public statement to this effect, and on 11 October 1963, the National Security Council drew an action memorandum, NSCAM 263, recommending that 1,000 advisers be pulled out. Kennedy saw and approved this course of action, if only, perhaps, to pressure Diem to greater effort and commitment. In any event, less than three weeks later, on 2 November, Diem was overthrown and killed, and three weeks later Kennedy was assassinated. On 26 November, the day after Kennedy's funeral, President Lyndon Johnson approved NSCAM 273, which essentially implemented (instrumented) the agreed withdrawal of 1,000 U.S. military personnel. However, things got worse not better, and within two months the hawkish advisers then argued to the new administration that the United States should fight on. Victory in Vietnam soon proved illusionary. Johnson had been left with a far more dangerous legacy in Southeast Asia than Kennedy had inherited from **Dwight D. Eisenhower**. There is little to suggest that Kennedy would have followed any course other than that taken by Johnson. See also APPEASEMENT; BUNDY, Mc-GEORGE; BUNDY, WILLIAM PUTNAM; FORRESTAL, MICHAEL VINCENT; FULBRIGHT, JAMES WILLIAM; PACIFICATION PROGRAM IN VIETNAM.

WALKER, EDWIN ANDERSON (1909–1993). Edwin Anderson Walker was born in Center Point, Texas, on 10 November 1909. He graduated from the United States Military Academy at West Point in 1931 and began his military career as an artillery officer. He served in Italy in World War II. His experiences as a combat commander during the Korean War led him to believe that a pro-communist conspiracy in Washington, DC, prevented American forces from carrying the war into mainland China.

In September 1957, Walker was a major general and commander of the Arkansas Military District. When asked to maintain order during the integration of Central High School in Little Rock, Arkansas, with regular troops and the federalized National Guard, he offered his resignation. President **Dwight D. Eisenhower** refused to accept it. In 1959, Walker joined the right-wing John Birch Society. The same year, he was sent overseas to command the 13,000-man 24th Infantry Division in Augsburg, West Germany. However, in April 1961 Walker was accused of using his position to indoctrinate troops and their dependents with his right-wing political views. In a speech to 200 members of his division and their families, Walker had declared that 60 percent of the press, along with **Harry S. Truman**, Dean Acheson, and Eleanor Roosevelt, were "Communist influenced." He was relieved of his command by U.S. secretary of defense **Robert S. McNamara** and admonished by the secretary of the army. Reports of this incident created a furor in the United States. The acting judge advocate of the army, Major General Robert H. McCaw, stated that Walker had violated the Hatch Act by "attempting to influence voting in the national election in favor of the ultra-conservative point of view."

Walker resigned from the army in November 1961 "to be free from the power of little men, who, in the name of my country, punish loyal service." On this occasion, his resignation was accepted by President John F. Kennedy. At that time, because of his strong anticommunist views, Walker had become a popular figure on the Right—but his popularity did not last long. Walker's incoherent and paranoid evidence before a special Senate Armed Services Committee headed by Senator John Stennis (D-Miss.) in April 1962 destroyed his reputation as a leader of the Right. Stennis's committee had been investigating charges that the Kennedy administration was "muzzling" military officials to keep them from speaking out against communism. The editor of the conservative journal *National Review*, William F. Buckley, thought Walker's performance was "pitiful," and he relegated him to "history's ashcan."

Walker entered the May 1962 Texas Democratic gubernatorial primary but finished last in a field of six. He was arrested 1 October 1962, in Oxford, Mississippi, for promoting the riots protesting the admission of **James H. Meredith** as the first black student at the University of Mississippi. Charges against Walker were later dropped, but he was unsuccessful in a court

case for libel against the Associated Press and the *New Orleans Times-Picayune,* which had described him as a leader of the riots.

After the **assassination of John F. Kennedy**, the **Warren Commission** revealed that the president's assassin, **Lee Harvey Oswald**, had on 10 April 1963 inexplicably shot at and barely missed General Walker at his home in Dallas. Walker continued his anticommunist activities until the late 1970s. Edwin Walker died of lung cancer at his home in Dallas on 31 October 1993 at the age of 83.

WALLACE, GEORGE CORLEY, JR. (1919–1998). George Corley Wallace Jr. was born in Clio in southeastern Alabama on 25 August 1919, to George Corley Wallace Sr. and his wife, Mozelle (Smith). He was the third of five generations to bear the name "George Wallace." He attended the University of Alabama School of Law, earning a LLB degree in 1942. After serving in the U.S. Army Air Corps during World War II, he was appointed as one of the assistant attorneys general of Alabama late in 1945, and in May 1946, he won his first election as a member to the Alabama House of Representatives and served as a state judge. At that time, he was considered a moderate on racial issues. Wallace was defeated in the Democratic primary of the 1958 Alabama gubernatorial election. He then adopted a hard-line segregationist stance and won election as governor in 1962. Wallace took the oath of office on 14 January 1963, standing on the spot where, nearly 102 years earlier, Jefferson Davis was sworn in as provisional president of the Confederate States of America. In his inaugural speech, Wallace stated: "In the name of the greatest people that have ever trod this earth, I draw the line in the dust and toss the gauntlet before the feet of tyranny, and I say segregation now, segregation tomorrow, segregation forever."

By 1963, Alabama was the only southern state without any desegregated schools. During his campaign for governor, Wallace had promised to "resist any illegal federal court orders" for school desegregation "even to the point of standing at the schoolhouse door in person." He fulfilled that pledge, on

11 June 1963, at the University of Alabama. On 21 May, a federal district court had ordered the enrollment of two black students at the university's main campus in Tuscaloosa, and Wallace immediately announced he would "be present to bar the entrance of any Negro" who attempted to enroll. Hoping to avoid the violence that had accompanied **James H. Meredith**'s entry into the University of Mississippi in September 1962, the Justice Department secured a federal court injunction prohibiting Wallace from interfering with the students' enrollment and sent a team headed by the deputy attorney general, Nicholas Katzenbach, to Tuscaloosa to help arrange for the peaceful entry of the students. President John F. Kennedy placed nearby army troops on alert and issued an executive proclamation ordering Wallace and all others to "cease and desist" from obstructing justice. Despite the court injunction, Wallace stood in the doorway of Foster Auditorium, the university's registration center, on 11 June, blocking the entrance of the two students, Katzenbach, and other Justice Department officials who accompanied them. Katzenbach read the president's proclamation and demanded that Wallace comply with the federal court orders. Standing before a lectern, Wallace responded with his own proclamation, claiming that the federal government was usurping the state's authority to control its own school system. Katzenbach withdrew; the two students were accompanied to their dormitory rooms. President Kennedy federalized the Alabama National Guard and ordered several units onto the campus. At a second confrontation late in the afternoon, the National Guard commander escorted the two students to register, and Wallace was again blocking the doorway. After being asked to step aside, this time Wallace did so. The two students registered, and two days later another black student enrolled at the University Center at Huntsville without incident. Wallace also tried to forestall integration of elementary and secondary schools in fall 1963 in defiance of federal court orders. Only after President Kennedy federalized the National Guard and ordered state troopers not to interfere did black students finally enter the schools.

Wallace subsequently unsuccessfully sought the United States presidency as a Democrat three times, and once as an independent candidate, and was reelected governor of Alabama on two further occasions. He died in Montgomery, Alabama, on 13 September 1998, at the age of 79. *See also* CIVIL RIGHTS.

WARREN, EARL (1891–1974). Earl Warren was born in Los Angeles on 19 March 1891, the son of Scandinavian immigrants. He received a law degree from the University of California, Los Angeles, in 1914. He was appointed deputy city attorney in Oakland, California, in 1919 and later served as district attorney of Alameda County for 13 years. In 1938, he was elected California's state attorney general. Warren was the Republican vice presidential candidate in 1948. He also made an unsuccessful bid for the party's presidential nomination in 1952. In September 1953, assuming him to be a cautious and moderate jurist, President **Dwight D. Eisenhower** named Warren chief justice of the U.S. **Supreme Court**. However, under Warren, the court broke new ground in a variety of fields. The first example of this came on 17 May 1954, when Warren, speaking for a unanimous court, delivered the opinion in *Brown v. Board of Education*, a ruling that held racial segregation in public schools to be unconstitutional.

This decision served as the base from which the Supreme Court went on to outlaw all public discrimination during the 1960s. Under Warren, the Supreme Court also initiated significant changes in the U.S. political system. The court rewrote the laws on the administration of criminal justice and extended its rulings to the states as well as the federal government. It ordered legislative reapportionment on a "one man, one vote" basis, prohibited religious exercises in public schools, significantly broadened the rights of free speech and artistic expression, and restricted the government's power to penalize individual beliefs and associations.

Initially Warren took a middle-of-the-road stance in these matters, but by the late 1950s he had clearly aligned himself with such liberal justices as Hugo Black and William O.

Douglas. During the John F. Kennedy years, when the **civil rights** movement entered a new phase with widespread use of nonviolent protest, Warren delivered the court's first ruling on sit-in demonstrations. In December 1961, he overturned the "breach-of-the-peace" convictions of 16 black protesters on the grounds that there was no evidence to support the original charge. Between June 1962 and May 1963, he joined in voiding the convictions of civil rights demonstrators in several cases that came before the court. Warren also joined the majority in decisions that prohibited the exclusion of blacks from private restaurants situated on state-owned property and held invalid pupil transfer plans designed to thwart school desegregation.

Later Warren court decisions further undermined the force of federal and state antisubversive legislation and expanded the individual's freedom to hold and express dissident political views. In three cases decided in June 1962 and June 1963, Warren joined the majority in holding prayer and Bible reading in public schools to be a violation of the First Amendment's guarantee of freedom of religion. The decisions resulted in a storm of criticism from certain members of Congress and religious leaders, and they generated unsuccessful attempts to adopt a constitutional amendment restoring prayer to public schools.

In November 1963, at the urging of President **Lyndon B. Johnson**, Warren accepted the chairmanship of a commission to investigate the **assassination of John F. Kennedy**. The **Warren Commission**'s report of September 1964 concluded that **Lee Harvey Oswald** had killed President Kennedy and that he had acted alone. Widely acclaimed when it was first published, the report soon became a target of criticism for those who believed that Kennedy's assassination was the result of a conspiracy.

Whatever his actual role, Chief Justice Warren served as a symbol for the entire Supreme Court to both admirers and critics. Attacks on the court for its desegregation, school prayer, and criminal rights rulings often turned into attacks on Warren himself. Despite these criticisms, Warren has been ranked as one of America's greatest chief justices, second

only to John Marshall in the minds of many. His personal dedication to the ideal of equal justice for all Americans and to the protection of individual liberties has been widely praised. All observers agreed that the court he presided over had an enormous impact on American law and life, giving support and impetus to significant social change. According to Leon Friedman, the Warren court helped "establish new goals for the nation, articulate a new moral sense for the people and, in effect, reorganize the political structure of the country itself." During the Lyndon B. Johnson administration, the Supreme Court continued to serve as a focal point of progressive reform and public controversy. It overturned federal laws limiting the rights of members of the Communist Party and handed down decisions on libel law that expanded freedom of the press and a citizen's right to criticize public officials.

Warren himself delivered the court's most controversial criminal rights ruling in the June 1966 *Miranda v. Arizona* case. This decision declared that a suspect in the hands of police authorities must be clearly informed of his or her right to remain silent and right to counsel prior to questioning. The justices sustained federal civil rights laws and prohibited racial discrimination in housing, but they became increasingly divided in rulings concerning civil rights demonstrators. After 16 years on the bench, Warren retired in June 1969. He died in Washington, DC, on 9 July 1974.

WARREN COMMISSION. On 29 November 1963, just a week after assuming office, President **Lyndon B. Johnson** issued Executive Order No. 11130, which established a special investigative commission to "ascertain, evaluate, and report about the facts relating to the assassination of the late President John F. Kennedy." **Earl Warren**, the U.S. chief justice, was appointed chairman of the investigative group, which was quickly labeled the Warren Commission. The other members were Senator Richard B. Russell (D-Ga.), Senator John Sherman Cooper (R-Ky.), Representative Hale Boggs (D-La.), Representative Gerald R. Ford (R-Mich.), former Central Intelligence Agency director **Allen Dulles**, and **John J. McCloy**,

former U.S. high commissioner for Germany. The commission held open hearings to gather evidence and had hoped to complete its work within three months, but the Warren Report was not submitted to Johnson until 24 September 1964. The 888-page report, together with 26 volumes of supporting documents, including the testimony or depositions of more than 550 witnesses and more than 3,100 exhibits, concluded that "[t]he shots which killed President Kennedy and wounded Governor Connally were fired from the sixth-floor window at the south-east corner of the Texas School Book Depository . . . by **Lee Harvey Oswald**." The commission found no evidence to support the rumors that Kennedy had been the victim of an assassination conspiracy. Nor did the commission find any evidence to link Oswald to **Jack Ruby**, the nightclub operator who had gunned down the assassin in the Dallas County Jail on 24 November 1963. The commission was also unable to make any "definitive determination" of the motives for the **assassination of John F. Kennedy** then. Senator Russell had objected to the categorical rejection of the possibility of conspiracy and had originally been unwilling to go beyond the statement that it had indeed been Oswald who fired the shots at President Kennedy and wounded Governor Connally. He had desired to append a dissent to the report but was eventually won over by Chief Justice Warren, who was insistent that the report be unanimous. Although the findings of the commission were immediately rejected by many critics when they were made public on 27 September 1963, the report was generally accepted by the public and the press. However, in the years since the release of the report in 1964, there have been a number of additional investigations, and the release of further documentation, into Kennedy's assassination.

WEAVER, ROBERT C. (1907–1997). Robert C. Weaver was born in Washington, DC, on 29 December 1907 and was raised in a middle-class, largely white, suburb of Washington. His parents encouraged their son in his academic studies, and after attending a segregated high school in Washington, DC, he went on to Harvard University, where he earned BS and MA

degrees. He also completed a PhD in economics in 1934. In December 1955, New York governor **W. Averell Harriman** named Weaver state deputy rent commissioner. In this post, which he held for three years, Weaver earned a reputation for his expertise in city housing problems. In the latter half of 1960, Weaver served as head of the New York City Housing and Redevelopment Board.

In December 1960, President John F. Kennedy announced that he would appoint Weaver administrator of the Housing and Home Finance Agency (HHFA). Weaver thereby became the highest-ranking **African American** in the Kennedy administration. His appointment to the high-level post proved controversial, particularly with southern members of Congress, who opposed Weaver's advocacy of integrated housing. As head of the HHFA, Weaver was responsible for the management of federal housing, home finance, slum clearance, and community development programs. These programs were so important, particularly to the welfare of the nation's cities, that Kennedy urged that they be dealt with at cabinet level. In March 1961, he proposed that Congress authorize creation of a new department of housing and urban affairs, to be headed by Weaver. The Kennedy proposal made no headway in Congress during 1961 because Southern Democrats opposed elevating Weaver to cabinet rank, conservative Republicans viewed the creation of a new cabinet department as a needless expansion of government, and rural congressmen could see no benefit for their constituents. In February 1962, the House rejected the creation of the new department, 264 votes to 150. It remained for the Johnson administration to win approval of a cabinet-rank department.

Weaver was one of the architects of the Kennedy administration's omnibus housing bill, which became law in June 1961. The new law, the most important piece of housing legislation passed since 1949, authorized expenditure of up to $2 billion for construction of low-income public housing, farm dwellings, and housing for the elderly. It increased funds available for the Federal National Mortgage Association for new low-interest home

mortgages and authorized substantial low-interest loans to colleges, universities, and hospitals for the construction of dormitories, dining halls, and student centers. The measure won broad congressional approval because it promised to rejuvenate the depressed home building industry.

Weaver lobbied successfully on behalf of the 1962 Senior Citizens Housing Act and for the Johnson administration's 1964 Housing Act. He was less successful in his efforts to win congressional subsidies for urban mass transit systems. In January 1966, Weaver attained cabinet rank when he was named secretary of the newly created Department of Housing and Urban Development, becoming the first African American to achieve cabinet rank. After serving under Johnson, Weaver held university posts until his retirement in 1978. He died in Manhattan on 17 July 1997, at the age of 89.

WHITE, BYRON RAYMOND (1917–2002). Byron Raymond White was born on 8 June 1917, in Fort Collins, Colorado, into a poor family of German heritage. He grew up in Wellington, a small Colorado town near the Wyoming border, and completed high school there; in 1938, he graduated from the University of Colorado. "Whizzer" White was an outstanding athlete, and he attended Oxford University as a Rhodes Scholar in 1939 before entering Yale Law School in October of that year. After service in the navy in World War II, he completed his legal studies at Yale Law School in November 1946 and served as law clerk to **Supreme Court** chief justice Fred Vinson during the court's 1946–1947 term.

White then entered private practice, joining a prestigious Denver law firm. John F. Kennedy had met White while in the United Kingdom in 1939, and they had remained in touch. White became an early supporter of Kennedy in his bid for the 1960 Democratic presidential nomination. He led the Kennedy forces in Colorado, delivering a majority of the state's 21 votes for Kennedy at the Democratic National Convention, and then headed a nationwide "Citizens for Kennedy-Johnson" organization during the 1960 campaign. Named deputy attorney general in January 1961, White assisted Attorney

General **Robert F. Kennedy** in recruiting highly qualified attorneys for the Justice Department. White proved to be an excellent administrator. He supervised the department's antitrust and **civil rights** suits and was in charge of evaluating candidates for federal judicial appointments. On 20 May 1961, the Freedom Riders—civil rights demonstrators challenging segregated transportation—were assaulted by a mob in Montgomery, Alabama. White personally commanded the more than 500 federal marshals that the attorney general ordered to Montgomery later that day. He also negotiated with Alabama governor John Patterson and the head of the Alabama National Guard during the crisis.

When Associate Justice **Charles Whittaker** retired from the Supreme Court, President Kennedy, on 30 March 1962, selected White as his first Supreme Court nominee. He was confirmed by the Senate on 11 April. Contrary to expectations, the **New Frontier** Democrat White usually voted with the conservative bloc in cases involving civil liberties and criminal rights. He registered his first dissent in June in a case in which the court majority overturned a California law that made drug addiction a crime. He dissented in another case in which the majority placed limits on the powers of a Florida legislative committee investigating the **National Association for the Advancement of Colored People**. White remained a conservative on the issue of criminal rights during the **Lyndon B. Johnson** years—dissenting, for example, from the court's celebrated *Miranda v. Arizona* ruling in 1966. He took a more liberal and activist position in certain race discrimination cases, however, and voted consistently in favor of the "one man, one vote" rule for reapportionment of legislative districts.

White retired from the court on 28 June 1993. He died of pneumonia in Denver on 15 April 2002 at the age of 84. He was the last living justice of the Warren court.

WHITTAKER, CHARLES EVANS (1901–1973).

Charles Evans Whittaker was born on a farm in Troy, Kansas, on 22 February 1901. After his mother died when he was 16, he worked on a farm, and in 1920 he moved to Kansas City, Missouri, where he worked as an office boy for a local law firm while attending the University of Kansas City Law School at night. He was admitted to the state bar in 1923 and received his law degree the next year. Joining the firm where he had been office boy, Whittaker eventually became one of the leading corporate attorneys in the Midwest. He was a close friend of President **Dwight D. Eisenhower**'s brother Arthur and developed close ties to the **Republican Party**. He was named a federal district court judge in Kansas City in 1954 with virtually unanimous support from local political and bar leaders. Two years later, he was promoted to a judgeship on the Eighth Circuit Court of Appeals. In March 1957, President Eisenhower nominated Whittaker as an associate justice of the **Supreme Court**. The Senate confirmed his appointment the same month.

On the court, Whittaker generally aligned himself with justices such as Felix Frankfurter, who advocated judicial self-restraint and deference to the legislature. Although Whittaker sometimes voted with the court's "liberal bloc" in cases involving criminal rights, citizenship, and the rights of aliens, he usually took what was considered a conservative position, voting to deny a claimed civil liberty or right and to uphold statutes against constitutional challenges. During his five-year court tenure, he voted with conservatives in 41 five-to-four decisions involving civil liberties. Whittaker wrote the opinion for a unanimous court in a 1961 case holding that an uneducated and mentally ill defendant needed the assistance of counsel in a state prosecution for assault. He also delivered the majority opinion in a 6–3 decision the same year that overturned a federal conviction based on an illegal search by state police. Whittaker voted with the majority in a series of 5–4 decisions in 1961 involving communism.

On 16 March 1962, Whittaker entered the hospital, suffering from exhaustion. He resigned from the court on 29 March, explaining that his doctors had warned him that staying on the court would jeopardize his health. On his retirement, there was wide praise from his fellow justices and others for Whittaker's hard

work on the court and for his qualities of modesty, gentleness, and sincerity. Court experts, however, did not rate his judicial performance highly. In a 1970 survey of legal historians and scholars, Whittaker was ranked as one of eight "failures" to serve on the court since 1789. Whittaker later took a position as chief counsel of General Motors. In April 1966, he was appointed a consultant to the Senate Committee on Standards and Conduct to help work on a code of senatorial ethics. He played an important role in the subsequent investigation of Senator Thomas Dodd (D-Conn.) for improper use of campaign funds. Whittaker died at St Luke's Hospital in Kansas City of a ruptured abdominal aneurysm on 26 November 1973. *See also* WHITE, BYRON RAYMOND.

WILKINS, ROY OTTOWAY (1901–1981). Roy Ottoway Wilkins was born in St. Louis, Missouri, on 30 August 1901, and was raised by an aunt and uncle in an integrated neighborhood in St. Paul, Minnesota. He graduated from the University of Minnesota with a degree in sociology in 1923. While working his way through university, Wilkins became secretary of the local **National Association for the Advancement of Colored People** (NAACP) chapter. The NAACP, founded in 1909, aimed to achieve by peaceful and lawful means equal rights for all Americans. Wilkins left St. Paul the following year to become the editor of the *Call*, Kansas City's **African American** newspaper. His leadership in local NAACP affairs persuaded the organization's national leadership to hire Wilkins in 1931 to work as an assistant secretary in its New York headquarters. Upon the death of NAACP executive secretary Walter White in 1955, Wilkins was unanimously elected as his successor. In 1957, Wilkins publicly rebuked U.S. senator John F. Kennedy for his lack of support for a 1957 **civil rights** bill, the first major attempt to advance black equality since post–Civil War Reconstruction, accusing Kennedy of "rubbing political elbows" with southern segregationists. The following year, however, during Kennedy's 1958 reelection campaign, Wilkins provided the senator with a letter endorsing his civil rights voting record in the Senate.

In his campaign for the presidency, Kennedy pledged executive action, particularly in the field of federal housing, to end discrimination "by a stroke of the president's pen." Executive actions were taken soon after his inauguration to end discrimination in federal employment, but they fell short of what civil rights leaders believed Kennedy had promised. There was no stroke of the pen ending discrimination in federally financed housing until November 1962. Civil rights leaders believed that, although he possessed the understanding and the political skill, Kennedy lacked the "moral passion" to act. Wilkins and his colleagues were also disappointed in Kennedy's refusal to back civil rights legislation introduced by congressional liberals to fulfill the 1960 Democratic platform pledges.

By the early 1960s, with a new generation of activists trying a more confrontational approach, Wilkins remained a moderate but insistent voice for progressive action, with a direct line to the White House. In 1961, at the president's request, Wilkins submitted a 61-page memorandum urging Kennedy to sign an across-the-board executive order—to govern "the whole executive branch of government"—barring employment discrimination throughout the federal government and in all state programs receiving federal aid. Federal expenditures in excess of $1.1 billion, the civil rights leader noted, continued to "require, support or condone" discrimination in 11 southern states. Sensitive to the political repercussions of cutting off aid to state programs, President Kennedy never issued the sweeping order. Instead the administration pressed voting rights and school discrimination cases in the courts and used federal marshals to defend Freedom Riders in Alabama. Addressing the annual meeting of the NAACP in January 1962, Wilkins praised Kennedy for "his personal role in civil rights" but declared his "disappointment with Mr. Kennedy's first year" because of his failure to issue the housing order and his strategy of "no legislative action on civil rights."

The rapid spread in early 1963 of the direct-action movement and the repression it met in many southern communities forced the

administration to revise the "no legislation" strategy. By June 1963, Kennedy appeared to have found his moral passion. He sent Congress a draft civil rights act aimed at ending discrimination in public accommodations, permitting federal initiation of school desegregation suits, and eliminating racial bias in voter registration. In a nationally televised address that was largely extemporaneous, he made a heartfelt appeal to the American people: "We are confronted primarily with a moral issue," Kennedy said. He continued,

> It is as old as the Scriptures and is as clear as the American Constitution. The heart of the question is whether all Americans are to be afforded equal rights and equal opportunities. . . . One hundred years of delay have passed since President Lincoln freed the slaves, yet their heirs, their grandsons, are not fully free. They are not yet freed from the bonds of injustice. They are not yet freed from social and economic oppression. And this nation, for all its hopes and all its boasts, will not be fully free until all its citizens are free. . . . A great change is at hand, and our task, our obligation, is to make that revolution, that change, peaceful and constructive for all.

He followed his speech by asking Congress to enact his bill that, he said, removed race from consideration "in American life or law." Earlier in that month of June 1963, Wilkins had been arrested with the NAACP's Mississippi field secretary, **Medgar W. Evers**, during a demonstration in Jackson. Evers was shot to death outside his home less than two weeks later. Civil rights leaders feared that even the momentum generated by events in the South and the administration's support would prove insufficient to overcome congressional resistance. Reflecting the mood of militancy among delegates to the NAACP's Chicago convention in early July, Wilkins endorsed the idea of a peaceful mass march on Washington. Addressing the throng of more than 200,000 that assembled on 28 August at the Lincoln Memorial, he demanded not only passage of the Kennedy bill but also the inclusion of a fair employment practices provision. Wilkins's and the NAACP's long preeminence in the struggle for equality was increasingly challenged during the early 1960s by more militant leaders and organizations.

Dry and somewhat aloof in manner, Wilkins lacked the evangelical fervor of such southern leaders as **Martin Luther King Jr.** and rejected the stridency of the student leaders. Wilkins remained the leader of the nation's largest and most active civil rights organization, with some 500,000 members and 1,600 local chapters. By virtue of its size and stable leadership, the NAACP was a significant factor in the growth of the direct-action movement. Wilkins, impatient with those who disparaged the NAACP, once remarked that the more militant organizations tended to garner "the publicity while the NAACP furnishes the manpower and pays the bills." Wilkins continued to lead the NAACP during the tumultuous period of urban riots and escalating rhetoric after the **assassination of John F. Kennedy**, consistently repudiating the strategies and language of black nationalism and urging the complete integration of blacks into American society. In 1977, at the age of 76, Wilkins finally retired from the NAACP. He died of heart problems on 8 September 1981 in New York City.

WILLIAMS, G. MENNEN "SOAPY" (1911–1988). Gerhard Mennen Williams was born in Detroit, Michigan, on 23 February 1911 to Henry P. Williams and Elma Mennen. His grandfather on his mother's side was the founder of the Mennen brand of men's personal care products. Because of this, Williams acquired the popular nickname "Soapy." He graduated from Princeton University in 1933 and received a law degree from the University of Michigan Law School. While at law school, Williams became affiliated with the **Democratic Party**. During World War II, he served four years in the U.S. Navy as an air combat intelligence officer in the South Pacific. On 2 November 1948, Williams was elected governor of Michigan, subsequently serving a record six two-year terms. As governor, Williams was a strong advocate for **civil rights**, racial equality, and justice for the poor.

President John F. Kennedy selected Williams to be the assistant secretary of state for African affairs on 14 February 1961. He traveled extensively to **Africa**, where he developed an understanding of the needs of the newly independent countries and recognized their desire for American investment. Traditionalists in the State Department favored the policies of the former colonial powers, however, and were hesitant to support U.S. involvement in Africa. His remark that the Kennedy administration sought "for the Africans . . . what they want for themselves," reported in the press as "Africa for the Africans," sparked considerable controversy, especially among the white residents in South Africa, Rhodesia, and the Portuguese colonies, who interpreted his comment as a policy supporting their expulsion from the continent. Kennedy endorsed Williams's remarks, stating that "I don't know who else Africa should be for." Kennedy saved the day by saying that Williams had made it clear that he was including Africans of all colors.

Williams was unable to change the view of the State Department and received little support from Kennedy's successor, **Lyndon B. Johnson**. He resigned from his position in March 1966. Williams was elected to the Michigan Supreme Court in 1970 and was named chief justice in 1983. He left the court on 1 January 1987, and he died the following year in Detroit at the age of 76.

WOMEN AND JOHN F. KENNEDY. John F. Kennedy has entered the pantheon of American heroes, but in the reassessment of the 1960s that has taken place since his death it appears that American women have become less enamored of him. His reputation as a charming playboy is giving way to a view held by many that he was a compulsive exploiter of women.

Prior to his election as president, Kennedy had little interest in the public—or for that matter the private—status of women. Indeed some claim that his main interest in women throughout his life appeared to be to regard them as objects of sexual conquest. **Katharine Graham** in her memoir, *Personal History*, observed that Kennedy did not have a whole lot

of interest in them and didn't really know how to relate to middle-class women. She relates an incident at one party at which Kennedy complained that **Adlai Stevenson II** possessed a hold over women that he did not, and he wondered why not. Clayton Fritchley, who was Stevenson's deputy at the **United Nations**, explained to the president: "While you both love women, Adlai also likes them, and women can tell the difference." Many historians now contend that behind his otherwise charming and witty personality, Kennedy showed little respect for women and, following the example of his father, carried on promiscuously on a grand scale.

Women and Kennedy's Campaign for President

Kennedy entered the White House with no particular public agenda for women. He, like most male politicians, was aware that women voted, but he did not devote much attention to winning their votes as a bloc. During the 1950s, there was no broad-based movement for women's rights. His mother and sisters had always figured prominently in his campaign, but he had few female advisers. Marjorie Lawson, a prominent black attorney, had assisted in his 1958 senatorial race and was put in charge of the **civil rights** section of the 1960 presidential campaign. There were very few women in the higher ranks of the **Democratic Party** machine, and most women had supported Stevenson in the primary contests. Kennedy had approached Eleanor Roosevelt for her support, but she chose to keep her distance, preferring Stevenson. She also disliked Kennedy's ties to Joe McCarthy, as well as and his mediocre civil rights record. Kennedy did appoint Margaret Price, a Democratic committeewoman from Michigan, whom many Democrats regarded as the most competent woman politician in the country, as vice chairman of the Democratic National Committee and director of women's activities. However, Kennedy ignored most of her recommendations in relation to women's issues and the participation of women in the election campaign, preferring to follow the advice of his largely male

coterie, which included, of course, his brother **Robert Kennedy**. Of the more than 500 campaign stops Kennedy made, Price appeared with him at only 21.

Kennedy also tried to attract women supporters, but mainly as fund-raisers rather than as policy makers. The campaign formed two committees: the Committee of Labor Women, which included such notable reformers as Mary Anderson and **Esther Peterson** of the American Federation of Labor/Congress of Industrial Organizations (AFL-CIO), and the Women's Committee for New Frontiers, which also boasted prominent liberal women, including Frances Perkins and Eleanor Roosevelt. These committees were intended to indicate the candidate's sympathy for the causes for which these women were known. Thus, they made special efforts to call women's attention to programs regarding medical care for the aged, federal aid to education, and full employment, issues that Kennedy's staff believed concerned female voters. Kennedy himself rarely addressed proposals aimed specifically at the position of women.

After Kennedy's victory, Margaret Price encouraged the president to include women in his administration and presented him with a list of positions she thought appropriate for women, together with the names of two dozen prominent figures. Only four eventually received Senate-confirmed appointment: none were head of a department, and the one ambassadorship was a position the woman already held (Eugenie Anderson, minister to Bulgaria). Women were disappointed and disillusioned by Kennedy's initial appointments: a month after the election, of 200 appointments Kennedy had made, only eight had gone to women. The situation did not much improve during Kennedy's first year in office.

Women's Bureau

In one of his first appointments, Kennedy offered the position of assistant secretary of labor and director of the **Women's Bureau**—established in 1920 as an agency within the Department of Labor—to labor-oriented feminist **Esther Peterson**.

On the recommendation of Peterson, Kennedy created a special **President's Commission on the Status of Women** and appointed a number of prominent women, including Eleanor Roosevelt (as well as Peterson) as members of the commission. This illustrious commission investigated the working conditions of women in government, industry, and education, as well as the prevailing laws regarding women's opportunities in higher education, and it prepared a major report called *American Women*, published in 1963. In particular, the report called attention to the fact that one of the worst discriminators against women was the federal government, and Kennedy called for all federal agencies to examine their practices and procedures and eliminate all forms of discrimination.

Many women in the United States believed the election of John F. Kennedy would provide new and opportunities for equality in their economic and social lives. At that time, women were still vastly underrepresented in professional, legal, and governmental areas of American society. Most American women who worked outside the home worked in sex-segregated fields. Clerks and secretaries in offices and salespeople in shops represented the overwhelming majority of women workers. Though women were increasing their share in professional work, they were clustered in **education**, social work, and librarianship. Administrators in schools, nursing schools, and social work schools were predominantly male. Women in the private sector were slowly edging their way toward management positions. Marriage remained the expected choice for women, although many began marrying later and had fewer children. Divorce became more widespread, although in the 1960s, monogamous marriage remained a value for most Americans. Topics relating to women's sexuality occupied a great deal of the attention of women: rape, abortion, and battered women all became highly publicized issues. Reproductive freedom and the right to end a pregnancy safely if all other forms of prevention failed was also a controversial issue—as it has been for the previous century. In the 1960s, a newly developed contraceptive pill provided

the first effective and by and large safe form of contraception for women.

By the mid-1960s, the attempts by women to achieve greater equality morphed into the women's liberation movement, a phrase expropriated from the black liberation movement. Although there were many political, philosophical, and social differences among the leaders of women's groups in the 1960s, the goals for women's liberation were slowly enacted in the decade following the death of John F. Kennedy. *See also* PETERSON, ESTHER; PRESIDENT'S COMMISSION ON THE STATUS OF WOMEN; UNITED STATES WOMEN'S BUREAU.

WOMEN'S BUREAU. *See* UNITED STATES WOMEN'S BUREAU.

Y

YARBOROUGH, RALPH WEBSTER (1903–1996). Ralph Webster Yarborough was born in Chandler, Texas, on 8 June 1903. He was a schoolteacher in Henderson County for three years before moving to Germany where he was assistant secretary for the American Chamber of Commerce in Berlin. On his return, he attended the University of Texas Law School, graduating in 1927. He then practiced law in El Paso. He served in Europe and Japan during the Second World War, and on his return after the war, he became a lawyer in Austin. He joined the **Democratic Party** and became one of the leaders of the progressive wing of the party in Texas. In 1952, 1954, and 1956, he was unsuccessful in running for the governorship, but in April 1957, with the support of the trade unions, Mexican Americans, and **African Americans**, he was elected to fill a vacated U.S. Senate seat, and the following year he was elected to a full term in the Senate. Antagonistic to the powerful Texas business establishment and Texas's extremely restrictive labor laws, Yarborough was the only member of the Senate representing a former Confederate state to vote for every significant piece of **civil rights** legislation.

According to the *Congressional Quarterly*, he generally opposed the conservative coalition of Southern Democrats and Republicans; he supported major John F. Kennedy administration bills on 73 percent of the key votes in 1961 and on 69 percent of such votes in 1962 and 1963. Yarborough voted for such social welfare programs as the **Area Redevelopment Act** of 1961, the minimum-wage bill of the same year, and the Medicare program of 1962. Most striking in its contrast to the record of the majority of his fellow southerners was Yarborough's support of civil rights measures. In 1961, he supported a bill to extend the life of the Civil Rights Commission for two years. In 1963, he voted to approve an administration-supported constitutional amendment to bar the poll tax as a condition for voting in federal elections. He also voted for the Civil Rights Act of 1957 and the Civil Rights Act of 1960.

In 1962, Yarborough was caught up in the **Billie Sol Estes** scandal surrounding the illegal business practices of the Texas promoter; however, it did not have a significant impact upon the senator's political career. Most political observers believed that one of the purposes of President Kennedy's trip to Texas in November 1963, which ended with his assassination in Dallas, was to try to resolve the deep divisions between liberals and the conservatives within the Democratic Party in that state. In summer 1963, Kennedy contacted Yarborough and asked him what could be done to help his image in Texas. Yarborough apparently told Kennedy "the best thing he could do was to bring Jackie to Texas and let all those women see her." Kennedy had won Texas by only a small margin in the **presidential election of 1960**. It was believed that this victory was mainly due to the campaigning of his running mate, **Lyndon B. Johnson**, who was the dominant political figure in Texas at the time. Kennedy believed that he needed to win Texas in 1964 if he was to be reelected as president. On 22 November, Yarborough and Johnson

were traveling in the same car in the fateful procession through Dallas.

Yarborough remained a member of the Senate until he was defeated by Lloyd Bentsen, a well-financed conservative, in 1970. He then returned to work as a lawyer in Austin. He also served as a member of the State Library and Archives Commission of Texas from 1983 to 1987. Ralph Yarborough died in Austin on 27 January 1996. *See also* ASSASSINATION OF JOHN F. KENNEDY.

YARMOLINSKY, ADAM (1922–2000). Adam Yarmolinsky was born on 17 November 1922 and raised in New York City. His father, Avrahm Yarmolinsky, a distinguished scholar of Russian literature, was chief of the Slavonic division of the New York Public Library; his mother, Babette Deutsch, was a well-known poet and critic. He attended Fieldston School in Riverdale, Harvard College, and after serving in the U.S. Army Air Corps during World War II, he received a law degree from Yale Law School in 1948. In 1950, he served as a law clerk to **Supreme Court** justice Stanley F. Reed. He practiced law in Washington, served two years as secretary at the Fund for the Republic, and then was public affairs editor for Doubleday and Company.

After John F. Kennedy's election as president in 1960, Yarmolinsky joined a task force headed by **R. Sargent Shriver Jr.**, Kennedy's brother-in-law, to screen candidates for posts in the new administration. Yarmolinsky personally recommended **Robert S. McNamara** for secretary of defense, and shortly after his appointment in January 1961, McNamara named Yarmolinsky as his special assistant. In that role, as one of McNamara's "whiz kids," he was a brilliant behind-the-scenes operator who put in place modern management systems in the Pentagon. He also oversaw work on the integration of armed forces facilities.

Yarmolinsky was a political liberal among conservatives, and he was said to have been witty, brilliant, and perceptive but also impatient, blunt, and sometimes arrogant. He was known to have stepped on the toes of several high-ranking military officers as an enforcer of McNamara's directive to centralize authority. He acquired the nickname "Cardinal Richelieu of the Pentagon," and he seemed to provoke controversy easily. One such example came to public attention in April 1962 when former major general **Edwin A. Walker**, in testimony before the Special Senate Preparedness Subcommittee, charged that Yarmolinsky, whom Walker believed had connections to the communists, was in part responsible for ousting him from his command. McNamara defended Yarmolinsky, citing his record of "strong and active anti-Communism." Walker's remarks were widely dismissed as irresponsible, but they nonetheless marked the beginning of a right-wing attack on Yarmolinsky that ultimately limited his role in public life.

He was to write later:

> When I left the Pentagon in 1966 I believed that the reforms carried out by Robert McNamara in the early sixties had tightened civilian control over the American military establishment. Today I am not so sure that their purpose coincided with their effect. Perhaps the greater efficiencies we tried to build into the system in the Kennedy years had the perverse consequence of strengthening America's military options at the expense of her diplomatic and political flexibility. Theories of limited war and programs to widen the President's range of choice made military solutions to our foreign problems more available and even more attractive. Without question, they contributed to the size of the defense budget and to the deepening involvement in Vietnam.

In summer 1961, Yarmolinsky assumed temporary responsibility for the management of a $207 million national fallout shelter program. Despite its much-heralded beginnings, the fallout shelter program was abandoned by the administration within two years because of a lack of congressional funding. Early in 1964, Yarmolinsky took temporary leave from the Defense Department to aid Sargent Shriver in shaping antipoverty legislation for the **Lyndon B. Johnson** administration, but in September, he returned to the Defense Department. In

September 1966, Yarmolinsky left the Defense Department and joined the faculty of Harvard University Law School. He died on 5 January 2000, in Washington, DC.

YOUNG, WHITNEY MOORE (1921–1971). Whitney Moore Young was born on 31 July 1921, in Lincoln Ridge, Kentucky. He graduated from the historically black Kentucky State College in 1941 and trained as an electrical engineer while serving in World War II. In 1947, he received an MA in social work from the University of Minnesota. He worked for the St. Paul Urban League from 1947 to 1950 and then served as executive secretary of the Omaha (Nebraska) Urban League. In 1954, Young was appointed the first dean of the School of Social Work at Atlanta University, and he served as vice president of the **National Association for the Advancement of Colored People** in Georgia and as an adviser to the black students who organized the 1960 Atlanta sit-ins. In August 1961, at the age of 40, Young was appointed executive director of the National Urban League, then a professional social work agency that provided a variety of social services for urban blacks. Young served as president of the Urban League until his death in 1971.

The Urban League had traditionally been a cautious and moderate organization with many white members. During Young's 10-year tenure, he brought the organization to the forefront of the American **civil rights** movement. The sophisticated and articulate Young broadened the league's programs and supplied it with more aggressive and outspoken leadership. He improved the planning and coordination between local branches and the national office early in his tenure, increased the league's funding, and expanded its staff. Within four years, he expanded the organization from 38 to 1,600 employees and from an annual budget of $325,000 to one of $6,100,000. In a 1964 interview with Robert Penn Warren, Young expressed the mission of the Urban League not as ground-level activism in itself but as the supplement and complement of the activities of all other organizations. He stated:

We are the social engineers, we are the strategists, we are the planners, we are the people who work at the level of policy-making, policy implementation, the highest echelons of the corporate community, the highest echelons of the governmental community—both at the federal, state and local level—the highest echelons of the labor movement.

In line with the Urban League's traditional social work interests, Young emphasized the economic and social needs of urban blacks in the early 1960s. At a September 1962 convention of the Southern Christian Leadership Conference, Young noted that blacks had made little progress on the issue of integration and that the average black family's income was 54 percent of the average white family's income. In 1963, he launched one of the league's most successful projects, the National Skills Bank, which collected job profiles on skilled blacks and placed them in positions in government and industry. In June 1963, Young proposed a "domestic Marshall Plan." Warning that racial incidents in the South were "mild in comparison with those on the verge of taking flame in the tinderbox of racial unrest in Northern cities," Young called for a massive aid program to close the economic, social, and educational gaps between the races. He proposed that $145 billion be spent on job training and apprenticeship programs; health programs and hospital construction; capitalization of cooperative business and industrial enterprises; programs for nursery children and working mothers; and scholarships, book-buying, and tutorial programs. The plan was one of several proposals for aid to the poor that contributed to the **Lyndon B. Johnson** administration's War on Poverty legislation.

Young also was a cosponsor of the August 1963 March on Washington. After meeting with President John F. Kennedy on the day of the march, Young addressed the crowd assembled at the Lincoln Memorial, declaring, "Civil rights, which are God-given and constitutionally guaranteed, are not negotiable in 1963." Young cooperated closely with the Johnson administration in the planning and

implementation of its antipoverty program. Skeptical of "black power" when the concept first captured national attention in 1966, Young eventually gave it a qualified endorsement. Young brought about a major reorientation within the Urban League in 1968, shifting its emphasis from social services to rehabilitation and institutional change in the black ghetto. On 11 March 1971, Whitney Young drowned while swimming with friends in Lagos, Nigeria, where he was attending a conference sponsored by the African-American Institute.

Z

ZUCKERT, EUGENE M. (1911–2000). Eugene M. Zuckert was born on 9 November 1911 in New York City. He gained a BA degree at Yale before graduating with a joint degree from the Yale Law School and the Harvard University Business School in 1937. He then worked for the Securities and Exchange Commission during the late 1930s and, in 1940, joined the faculty of the Harvard Business School where he became assistant dean. Zuckert was a key statistical consultant to the U.S. Army and U.S. Navy during World War II and, from 1947 to 1952, served as assistant secretary to W. Stuart Symington, the first secretary of the recently created branch of the U.S. military, the air force. His principal duties were in the field of management, and one of his tasks was overseeing the implementation of the armed services integration program ordered by President **Harry S. Truman** in 1948. He was a member of the board of the Atomic Energy Commission from 1952 to 1954.

In January 1961, U.S. secretary of defense **Robert S. McNamara** nominated Zuckert, his former colleague at the Harvard Business School, to be secretary of the U.S. Air Force. Zuckert, who had taught statistics and other management-related courses at Harvard, meshed well with McNamara in analyzing Pentagon budget and management problems. McNamara's reorganization of the Pentagon stripped the secretaries of the army, navy, and air force of much of their authority—especially their ability to oppose his decisions—but Zuckert, along with U.S. Navy secretary John Connally, accepted the new situation, albeit reluctantly. During Zuckert's time as secretary, the United States was involved in the **Bay of Pigs** invasion and the **Cuban missile crisis** and became increasingly involved in the war in **Vietnam**. He endured a stormy and combative relationship with forceful "hawk" general Curtis LeMay, air force chief of staff from 1961 to 1965, who had little use for his civilian masters.

Zuckert sided with McNamara in the controversy surrounding the development of the controversial TFX (tactical fighter, experimental—later designated the F-111) airplane. In summer 1962, McNamara determined that the air force rather than the navy should develop the TFX as a fighter/bomber aircraft suitable for both armed services. Zuckert solicited bids for the plane, and eventually the choice was narrowed to competing designs offered by Boeing and General Dynamics. On 21 November 1962, Zuckert, McNamara, and U.S. Navy secretary Fred Korth signed a memorandum awarding the contract to General Dynamics, claiming that its aircraft would prove cheaper to manufacture and was more adaptable to the needs of both the air force and the navy. The unexpected decision—Boeing's design had been the nearly unanimous choice of military officers—angered a number of influential senators and congressmen, and in summer 1963 the Senate permanent Investigations Subcommittee, under the chairmanship of Senator John McClellan (D-Ark.), called Zuckert, Korth, McNamara, and deputy secretary of defense Roswell Gilpatric to explain their choice. Neither McNamara nor

Zuckert was able to deny Comptroller General Joseph Campbell's allegations that the two men had relied on their own "rough judgment" rather than independent analysis in estimating costs. There were also charges that the decision had been influenced by political considerations relating to the location of the home states of manufacturing plants of General Dynamics and its chief subcontractor, Grumman Aviation, favorable to the Kennedy administration (Texas and New York), as well as claims that Zuckert, along with Korth and Gilpatric, had been involved in business interests that should have disqualified them from making the TFX decision. General Dynamics eventually built the TFX, but the aircraft was plagued by mechanical problems, and its performance did not live up to expectations.

Controversy dogged Zuckert over a number of crashes of U.S. aircraft in the **Vietnam War** in 1964, and in the same year he was faced with a scandal at the Air Force Academy in which 105 students were dismissed for cheating. Zuckert resigned as air force secretary in July 1965 and later served on the boards of several corporations, including Martin Marietta, an aircraft manufacturer. He died of pneumonia at the age of 88 in Chevy Chase, Maryland, on 5 June 2000.

Appendix A

Lists of Officials, Elections, Congresses

John F. Kennedy, 35th president (1961–1963)

Lyndon B. Johnson, vice president (1961–1963)

Election of 1960

Candidate	Party	Electoral Vote	Popular Vote (%)
John F. Kennedy	Democrat	303	49.9
Richard M. Nixon	Republican	219	49.6

Cabinet

Dean Rusk, secretary of state (1961–1963)

C. Douglas Dillon, secretary of the treasury (1961–1963)

Robert S. McNamara, secretary of defense (1961–1963)

Robert F. Kennedy, attorney general (1961–1963)

J. Edward Day, postmaster general (1961–1963)

John A. Gronouski, postmaster general (1963)

Stewart L. Udall, secretary of the interior (1961–1963)

Orville L. Freeman, secretary of agriculture (1961–1963)

Luther H. Hodges, secretary of commerce (1961–1963)

Arthur J. Goldberg, secretary of labor (1961–1962)

W. Willard Wirtz, secretary of labor (1962–1963)

Abraham A. Ribicoff, secretary of health, education, and welfare (1961–1962)

Anthony J. Celebrezze, secretary of health, education, and welfare (1962–1963)

Congresses

87th Congress (1961–1963)

	Democrats	Republicans
Senate	65	35
House	263	174

Supreme Court Appointments

Byron R. White (1962–1993)

Arthur J. Goldberg (1962–1965)

Appendix B

Constitutional Amendments

TWENTY-THIRD AMENDMENT

This amendment was proposed by Congress on 17 June 1960 and ratified by the states on 29 March 1961.

Section 1

The District constituting the seat of government of the United States shall appoint in such manner as the Congress may direct: A number of electors of President and Vice President equal to the whole number of Senators and Representatives in Congress to which the District would be entitled if it were a state, but in no event more than the least populous state; they shall be in addition to those appointed by the states, but they shall be considered, for the purposes of the election of President and Vice President, to be electors appointed by a state; and they shall meet in the District and perform such duties as provided by the twelfth article of amendment.

Section 2

The Congress shall have power to enforce this article by appropriate legislation.

TWENTY-FOURTH AMENDMENT

This amendment was proposed by Congress on 27 August 1962 and ratified by the states on 4 February 1964.

Section 1

The right of citizens of the United States to vote in any primary or other election for President or Vice President, for electors for President or Vice President, or for Senator or Representative in Congress, shall not be denied or abridged by the United States or any State by reason of failure to pay any poll tax or other tax.

Section 2

Congress shall have power to enforce this article by appropriate legislation.

Appendix C

John F. Kennedy's Addresses

ADDRESS OF SENATOR
JOHN F. KENNEDY ACCEPTING
THE DEMOCRATIC PARTY
NOMINATION FOR THE PRESIDENCY
OF THE UNITED STATES

Memorial Coliseum, Los Angeles, 15 July 1960

At the Democratic National Convention meeting in Los Angeles in early July, Senator John F. Kennedy swept a first-ballot nomination and, in the process, overwhelmed his nearest rival, Senator Lyndon B. Johnson of Texas, the veteran Senate majority leader.

Governor Stevenson, Senator Johnson, Mr. Butler, Senator Symington, Senator Humphrey, Speaker Rayburn, Fellow Democrats,

I want to express my thanks to Governor Stevenson for his generous and heart-warming introduction.

It was my great honor to place his name in nomination at the 1956 Democratic Convention, and I am delighted to have his support and his counsel and his advice in the coming months ahead.

With a deep sense of duty and high resolve, I accept your nomination. I accept it with a full and grateful heart—without reservation—and with only one obligation—the obligation to devote every effort of body, mind and spirit to lead our Party back to victory and our nation back to greatness.

I am grateful, too, that you have provided me with such an eloquent statement of our party's platform. Pledges which are made so eloquently are made to be kept. "The Rights of Man"—the civil and economic rights essential to the human dignity of all men—are indeed our goal and our first principles. This is a platform on which I can run with enthusiasm and conviction.

And I am grateful, finally, that I can rely in the coming months on so many others—on a distinguished running mate who brings unity to our ticket and strength to our Platform, Lyndon Johnson; on one of the most articulate statesmen of our time, Adlai Stevenson; on a great spokesman for our needs as a Nation and a people, Stuart Symington; and on that fighting campaigner whose support I welcome, President Harry S. Truman; on my traveling companion in Wisconsin and West Virginia, Senator Hubert Humphrey; on Paul Butler, our devoted and courageous chairman.

I feel a lot safer now that they are on my side again. And I am proud of the contrast with our Republican competitors. For their ranks are apparently so thin that not one challenger has come forth with both the competence and the courage to make theirs an open convention.

I am fully aware of the fact that the Democratic Party, by nominating someone of my faith, has taken on what many regard as a new and hazardous risk—new, at least since 1928. But I look at it this way: the Democratic Party has once again placed its confidence in the American people, and in their ability to render a free, fair judgment. And you have, at the same time, placed your confidence in me, and in my ability to render a free, fair

judgment—to uphold the Constitution and my oath of office—and to reject any kind of religious pressure or obligation that might directly or indirectly interfere with my conduct of the Presidency in the national interest. My record of fourteen years supporting public education—supporting complete separation of church and state—and resisting pressure from any source on any issue should be clear by now to everyone.

I hope that no American, considering the really critical issues facing this country, will waste his franchise by voting either for me or against me solely on account of my religious affiliation. It is not relevant. I want to stress what some other political or religious leader may have said on this subject. It is not relevant what abuses may have existed in other countries or in other times. It is not relevant what pressures, if any, might conceivably be brought to bear on me. I am telling you now what you are entitled to know: that my decisions on any public policy will be my own—as an American, a Democrat, and a free man.

Under any circumstances, however, the victory we seek in November will not be easy. We all know that in our hearts. We recognize the power of the forces that will be aligned against us. We know they will invoke the name of Abraham Lincoln on behalf of their candidate—despite the fact that the political career of their candidate has often seemed to show charity toward none and malice for all.

We know that it will not be easy to campaign against a man who has spoken or voted on every known side of every known issue. Mr. Nixon may feel it is his turn now after the New Deal and the Fair Deal—but before he deals, someone had better cut the cards.

That "someone" may be the millions of Americans who voted for President Eisenhower but balk at his would-be, self-appointed successor. For just as historians tell us that Richard I was not fit to fill the shoes of bold Henry II—and that Richard Cromwell was not fit to wear the mantle of his uncle—they might add in future years that Richard M. Nixon did not measure up to the footsteps of Dwight D. Eisenhower.

Perhaps he could carry on the party policies—the policies of Nixon, Benson, Dirksen and Goldwater. But this Nation cannot afford such a luxury. Perhaps we could better afford a Coolidge following Harding. And perhaps we could afford a Pierce following Fillmore. But after Buchanan this nation needed a Lincoln; after Taft we needed a Wilson; after Hoover we needed Franklin Roosevelt. . . . And after eight years of drugged and fitful sleep, this nation needs strong, creative Democratic leadership in the White House.

But we are not merely running against Mr. Nixon. Our task is not merely one of itemizing Republican failures. Nor is that wholly necessary. For the families forced from the farm will know how to vote without our telling them. The unemployed miners and textile workers will know how to vote. The old people without medical care, the families without a decent home, the parents of children without adequate food or schools—they all know that it's time for a change.

But I think the American people expect more from us than cries of indignation and attack. The times are too grave, the challenge too urgent, and the stakes too high to permit the customary passions of political debate. We are not here to curse the darkness, but to light the candle that can guide us through that darkness to a safe and sane future. As Winston Churchill said on taking office some twenty years ago, if we open a quarrel between the present and the past, we shall be in danger of losing the future.

Today our concern must be with that future. For the world is changing. The old era is ending. The old ways will not do.

Abroad, the balance of power is shifting. There are new and more terrible weapons, new and uncertain nations, new pressures of population and deprivation. One-third of the world, it has been said, may be free—but one-third is the victim of cruel repression, and the other one-third is rocked by the pangs of poverty, hunger, and envy. More energy is released by the awakening of these new nations than by the fission of the atom itself.

Meanwhile, communist influence has penetrated further into Asia, stood astride the Middle East and now festers some ninety miles off the coast of Florida. Friends have slipped

into neutrality, and neutrals into hostility. As our keynoter reminded us, the president who began his career by going to Korea ends it by staying away from Japan.

The world has been close to war before but now man, who has survived all previous threats to his existence, has taken into his mortal hands the power to exterminate the entire species some seven times over.

Here at home, the changing face of the future is equally revolutionary. The New Deal and the Fair Deal were bold measures for their generations—but this is a new generation.

A technological revolution on the farm has led to an output explosion—but we have not yet learned to harness that explosion usefully, while protecting our farmers' right to full parity income.

An urban population explosion has overcrowded our schools, cluttered up our suburbs, and increased the squalor of our slums.

A peaceful revolution for human rights demanding an end to racial discrimination in all parts of our community life has strained at the leashes imposed by timid executive leadership.

A medical revolution has extended the life of our elder citizens without providing the dignity and security those later years deserve. And a revolution of automation finds machines replacing men in the mines and mills of America, without replacing their incomes or their training or their needs to pay the family doctor, grocer, and landlord.

There has also been a change—a slippage—in our intellectual and moral strength. Seven lean years of drought and famine have withered a field of ideas. Blight has descended on our regulatory agencies, and a dry rot, beginning in Washington, is seeping into every corner of America—in the payola mentality, the expense account way of life, the confusion between what is legal and what is right. Too many Americans have lost their way, their will, and their sense of historic purpose.

It is a time, in short, for a new generation of leadership—new men to cope with new problems and new opportunities.

All over the world, particularly in the newer nations, young men are coming to power—men who are not bound by the traditions of the past, men who are not blinded by the old fears and hates and rivalries, young men who can cast off the old slogans and delusions and suspicions.

The Republican nominee-to-be, of course, is also a young man. But his approach is as old as McKinley. His party is the party of the past. His speeches are generalities from poor Richard's Almanac. Their platform, made up of leftover Democratic planks, has the courage of our old convictions. Their pledge is a pledge to the status quo—and today there can be no status quo.

For I stand tonight facing west on what was once the last frontier. From the lands that stretch three thousand miles behind me, the pioneers of old gave up their safety, their comfort, and sometimes their lives to build a new world here in the West. They were not the captives of their own doubts, the prisoners of their own price tags. Their motto was not "Every man for himself" but "All for the common cause." They were determined to make that new world strong and free, to overcome its hazards and its hardships, to conquer the enemies that threatened from without and within.

Today some would say that those struggles are all over—that all the horizons have been explored, that all the battles have been won, that there is no longer an American frontier.

But I trust that no one in this vast assemblage will agree with those sentiments. For the problems are not all solved and the battles are not all won, and we stand today on the edge of a New Frontier—the frontier of the 1960s, a frontier of unknown opportunities and perils, a frontier of unfulfilled hopes and threats.

Woodrow Wilson's New Freedom promised our nation a new political and economic framework. Franklin Roosevelt's New Deal promised security and succor to those in need. But the New Frontier of which I speak is not a set of promises; it is a set of challenges. It sums up not what I intend to offer the American people, but what I intend to ask of them. It appeals to their pride, not to their pocketbook. It holds out the promise of more sacrifice instead of more security.

But I tell you the New Frontier is here, whether we seek it or not. Beyond that frontier are the uncharted areas of science and space, unsolved problems of peace and war, unconquered pockets of ignorance and prejudice, unanswered questions of poverty and surplus.

It would be easier to shrink back from that frontier, to look to the safe mediocrity of the past, to be lulled by good intentions and high rhetoric—and those who prefer that course should not cast their votes for me, regardless of party.

But I believe the times demand new invention, innovation, imagination, decision. I am asking each of you to be pioneers on that New Frontier. My call is to the young in heart, regardless of age—to all who respond to the scriptural call: "Be strong and of a good courage; be not afraid, neither be thou dismayed."

For courage—not complacency—is our need today; leadership, not salesmanship. And the only valid test of leadership is the ability to lead, and lead vigorously.

A tired nation, said David Lloyd George, is a Tory nation—and the United States today cannot afford to be either tired or Tory.

There may be those who wish to hear more—more promises to this group or that, more harsh rhetoric about the men in the Kremlin, more assurances of a golden future, where taxes are always low and subsidies ever high. But my promises are in the platform you have adopted. Our ends will not be won by rhetoric and we can have faith in the future only if we have faith in ourselves.

For the harsh facts of the matter are that we stand on this frontier at a turning point in history. We must prove all over again whether this nation—or any nation so conceived—can long endure; whether our society—with its freedom of choice, its breadth of opportunity, its range of alternatives—can compete with the single-minded advance of the communist system.

Can a nation organized and governed such as ours endure? That is the real question. Have we the nerve and the will? Can we carry through in an age where we will witness not only new breakthroughs in weapons of destruction, but also a race for mastery of the sky and the rain, the ocean and the tides, the far side of space and the inside of men's minds?

Are we up to the task? Are we equal to the challenge? Are we willing to match the Russian sacrifice of the present for the future, or must we sacrifice our future in order to enjoy the present?

That is the question of the New Frontier. That is the choice our nation must make—a choice that lies not merely between two men or two parties, but between the public interest and private comfort; between national greatness and national decline; between the fresh air of progress and the stale, dank atmosphere of "normalcy"; between determined dedication and creeping mediocrity.

All mankind waits upon our decision. A whole world looks to see what we will do. We cannot fail their trust, we cannot fail to try.

It has been a long road from that first snowy day in New Hampshire to this crowded convention city. Now begins another long journey, taking me into your cities and homes all over America. Give me your help, your hand, your voice, your vote. Recall with me the words of Isaiah: "They that wait upon the Lord shall renew their strength; they shall mount up with wings as eagles; they shall run and not be weary."

As we face the coming challenge, we too, shall wait upon the Lord, and ask that he renew our strength. Then shall we be equal to the test. Then we shall not be weary. And then we shall prevail.

Thank you.

Source: Kennedy, John F. "Acceptance of the Democratic Party Nomination for the Presidency of the United States." Speech. John F. Kennedy Presidential Library and Museum, Boston, Massachusetts.

ADDRESS OF SENATOR JOHN F. KENNEDY TO THE GREATER HOUSTON MINISTERIAL ASSOCIATION

Rice Hotel, Houston, Texas, 12 September 1960

Only one other Roman Catholic, Al Smith, had ever led the Democratic national ticket prior

to John F. Kennedy, and he was comprehensively defeated by Herbert Hoover in the 1928 presidential election. The "Catholic question" was raised in the West Virginia primary and remained a major issue. Senator Kennedy spoke to an influential gathering of Protestant ministers in Houston in September 1960 to resolve the matter, and in doing so, he succeeded in neutralizing the religious question.

Reverend Meza, Reverend Reck, I'm grateful for your generous invitation to speak my views.

While the so-called religious issue is necessarily and properly the chief topic here tonight, I want to emphasize from the outset that we have far more critical issues to face in the 1960 election: the spread of communist influence, until it now festers 90 miles off the coast of Florida; the humiliating treatment of our president and vice president by those who no longer respect our power; the hungry children I saw in West Virginia; the old people who cannot pay their doctor bills; the families forced to give up their farms—an America with too many slums, with too few schools, and too late to the moon and outer space.

These are the real issues which should decide this campaign. And they are not religious issues, for war and hunger and ignorance and despair know no religious barriers.

But because I am a Catholic, and no Catholic has ever been elected president, the real issues in this campaign have been obscured—perhaps deliberately in some quarters less responsible than this. So it is apparently necessary for me to state once again, not what kind of church I believe in, for that should be important only to me, but what kind of America I believe in.

I believe in an America where the separation of church and state is absolute—where no Catholic prelate would tell the president (should he be Catholic) how to act, and no Protestant minister would tell his parishioners for whom to vote; where no church or church school is granted any public funds or political preference; and where no man is denied public office merely because his religion differs from the president who might appoint him or the people who might elect him.

I believe in an America that is officially neither Catholic, Protestant, nor Jewish; where no public official either requests or accepts instructions on public policy from the Pope, the National Council of Churches, or any other ecclesiastical source; where no religious body seeks to impose its will directly or indirectly upon the general populace or the public acts of its officials; and where religious liberty is so indivisible that an act against one church is treated as an act against all.

For while this year it may be a Catholic against whom the finger of suspicion is pointed, in other years it has been, and may someday be again, a Jew, or a Quaker, or a Unitarian, or a Baptist. It was Virginia's harassment of Baptist preachers, for example, that helped lead to Jefferson's statute of religious freedom. Today I may be the victim, but tomorrow it may be you—until the whole fabric of our harmonious society is ripped at a time of great national peril.

Finally, I believe in an America where religious intolerance will someday end; where all men and all churches are treated as equal; where every man has the same right to attend or not attend the church of his choice; where there is no Catholic vote, no anti-Catholic vote, no bloc voting of any kind; and where Catholics, Protestants, and Jews, at both the lay and pastoral level, will refrain from those attitudes of disdain and division which have so often marred their works in the past, and promote instead the American ideal of brotherhood.

That is the kind of America in which I believe. And it represents the kind of presidency in which I believe—a great office that must neither be humbled by making it the instrument of any one religious group, nor tarnished by arbitrarily withholding its occupancy from the members of any one religious group. I believe in a president whose religious views are his own private affair, neither imposed by him upon the nation or imposed by the nation upon him as a condition to holding that office.

I would not look with favor upon a president working to subvert the First Amendment's guarantees of religious liberty. Nor would our system of checks and balances permit him to do so. And neither do I look with favor upon

those who would work to subvert Article VI of the Constitution by requiring a religious test—even by indirection—for it. If they disagree with that safeguard they should be out openly working to repeal it.

I want a chief executive whose public acts are responsible to all groups and obligated to none; who can attend any ceremony, service, or dinner his office may appropriately require of him; and whose fulfillment of his presidential oath is not limited or conditioned by any religious oath, ritual, or obligation.

This is the kind of America I believe in—and this is the kind I fought for in the South Pacific, and the kind my brother died for in Europe. No one suggested then that we may have a "divided loyalty," that we did "not believe in liberty," or that we belonged to a disloyal group that threatened the "freedoms for which our forefathers died."

And in fact, this is the kind of America for which our forefathers died—when they fled here to escape religious test oaths that denied office to members of less favored churches; when they fought for the Constitution, the Bill of Rights, and the Virginia Statute of Religious Freedom; and when they fought at the shrine I visited today, the Alamo. For side by side with Bowie and Crockett died McCafferty and Bailey and Carey—but no one knows whether they were Catholic or not. For there was no religious test at the Alamo.

I ask you tonight to follow in that tradition: to judge me on the basis of my record of 14 years in Congress, on my declared stands against an ambassador to the Vatican, against unconstitutional aid to parochial schools, and against any boycott of the public schools (which I have attended myself)—instead of judging me on the basis of these pamphlets and publications we all have seen that carefully select quotations out of context from the statements of Catholic church leaders, usually in other countries, frequently in other centuries, and always omitting, of course, the statement of the American Bishops in 1948 which strongly endorsed church–state separation, and which more nearly reflects the views of almost every American Catholic.

I do not consider these other quotations binding upon my public acts; why should you? But let me say, with respect to other countries, that I am wholly opposed to the state being used by any religious group, Catholic or Protestant, to compel, prohibit, or persecute the free exercise of any other religion. And I hope that you and I condemn with equal fervor those nations which deny their presidency to Protestants and those which deny it to Catholics. And rather than cite the misdeeds of those who differ, I would cite the record of the Catholic Church in such nations as Ireland and France, and the independence of such states—men such as Adenauer and de Gaulle.

But let me stress again that these are my views. For contrary to common newspaper usage, I am not the Catholic candidate for president. I am the Democratic Party's candidate for president, who happens also to be a Catholic. I do not speak for my church on public matters, and the church does not speak for me.

Whatever issue may come before me as president—on birth control, divorce, censorship, gambling, or any other subject—I will make my decision in accordance with these views, in accordance with what my conscience tells me to be the national interest, and without regard to outside religious pressures or dictates. And no power or threat of punishment could cause me to decide otherwise.

But if the time should ever come—and I do not concede any conflict to be even remotely possible—when my office would require me to either violate my conscience or violate the national interest, then I would resign the office; and I hope any conscientious public servant would do the same.

But I do not intend to apologize for these views to my critics of either Catholic or Protestant faith, nor do I intend to disavow either my views or my church in order to win this election.

If I should lose on the real issues, I shall return to my seat in the Senate, satisfied that I had tried my best and was fairly judged. But if this election is decided on the basis that 40 million Americans lost their chance of being president on the day they were baptized, then

it is the whole nation that will be the loser, in the eyes of Catholics and non-Catholics around the world, in the eyes of history and in the eyes of our own people.

But if, on the other hand, I should win the election, then I shall devote every effort of mind and spirit to fulfilling the oath of the presidency—practically identical, I might add, to the oath I have taken for 14 years in the Congress. For without reservation, I can "solemnly swear that I will faithfully execute the office of President of the United States, and will to the best of my ability preserve, protect, and defend the Constitution . . . so help me God."

Source: Kennedy, John F. "Address of Senator John F. Kennedy to the Greater Houston Ministerial Association." Speech. John F. Kennedy Presidential Library and Museum, Boston, Massachusetts.

JOHN F. KENNEDY'S INAUGURAL ADDRESS

Washington, DC, 20 January 1961

Vice President Johnson, Mr. Speaker, Mr. Chief Justice, President Eisenhower, Vice President Nixon, President Truman, reverend clergy, fellow citizens, we observe today not a victory of party, but a celebration of freedom—symbolizing an end, as well as a beginning—signifying renewal, as well as change. For I have sworn before you and Almighty God the same solemn oath our forebears prescribed nearly a century and three quarters ago. The world is very different now. For man holds in his mortal hands the power to abolish all forms of human poverty and all forms of human life. And yet the same revolutionary beliefs for which our forebears fought are still at issue around the globe—the belief that the rights of man come not from the generosity of the state, but from the hand of God. We dare not forget today that we are the heirs of that first revolution. Let the word go forth from this time and place, to friend and foe alike, that the torch has been passed to a new generation of Americans—born in this century, tempered by war, disciplined by a hard and bitter peace, proud of our ancient heritage—and unwilling to witness or permit the slow undoing of those human rights to which this Nation has always been committed, and to which we are committed today at home and around the world. Let every nation know, whether it wishes us well or ill, that we shall pay any price, bear any burden, meet any hardship, support any friend, oppose any foe, in order to assure the survival and the success of liberty. This much we pledge—and more. To those old allies whose cultural and spiritual origins we share, we pledge the loyalty of faithful friends. United, there is little we cannot do in a host of cooperative ventures. Divided, there is little we can do—for we dare not meet a powerful challenge at odds and split asunder. To those new States whom we welcome to the ranks of the free, we pledge our word that one form of colonial control shall not have passed away merely to be replaced by a far more iron tyranny. We shall not always expect to find them supporting our view. But we shall always hope to find them strongly supporting their own freedom—and to remember that, in the past, those who foolishly sought power by riding the back of the tiger ended up inside. To those peoples in the huts and villages across the globe struggling to break the bonds of mass misery, we pledge our best efforts to help them help themselves, for whatever period is required—not because the Communists may be doing it, not because we seek their votes, but because it is right. If a free society cannot help the many who are poor, it cannot save the few who are rich. To our sister republics south of our border, we offer a special pledge—to convert our good words into good deeds—in a new alliance for progress—to assist free men and free governments in casting off the chains of poverty. But this peaceful revolution of hope cannot become the prey of hostile powers. Let all our neighbors know that we shall join with them to oppose aggression or subversion anywhere in the Americas. And let every other power know that this Hemisphere intends to remain the master of its own house. To that world assembly of sovereign states, the United Nations, our last best hope in an age where the instruments of war have far outpaced the instruments of peace, we renew our

pledge of support—to prevent it from becoming merely a forum for invective—to strengthen its shield of the new and the weak—and to enlarge the area in which its writ may run. Finally, to those nations who would make themselves our adversary, we offer not a pledge but a request: that both sides begin anew the quest for peace, before the dark powers of destruction unleashed by science engulf all humanity in planned or accidental self-destruction. We dare not tempt them with weakness. For only when our arms are sufficient beyond doubt can we be certain beyond doubt that they will never be employed. But neither can two great and powerful groups of nations take comfort from our present course—both sides overburdened by the cost of modern weapons, both rightly alarmed by the steady spread of the deadly atom, yet both racing to alter that uncertain balance of terror that stays the hand of mankind's final war. So let us begin anew—remembering on both sides that civility is not a sign of weakness, and sincerity is always subject to proof. Let us never negotiate out of fear. But let us never fear to negotiate. Let both sides explore what problems unite us instead of belaboring those problems which divide us. Let both sides, for the first time, formulate serious and precise proposals for the inspection and control of arms—and bring the absolute power to destroy other nations under the absolute control of all nations. Let both sides seek to invoke the wonders of science instead of its terrors. Together let us explore the stars, conquer the deserts, eradicate disease, tap the ocean depths, and encourage the arts and commerce. Let both sides unite to heed in all corners of the earth the command of Isaiah—to "undo the heavy burdens . . . and to let the oppressed go free."

And if a beachhead of cooperation may push back the jungle of suspicion, let both sides join in creating a new endeavor, not a new balance of power, but a new world of law, where the strong are just and the weak secure and the peace preserved. All this will not be finished in the first 100 days. Nor will it be finished in the first 1,000 days, nor in the life of this Administration, nor even perhaps in our lifetime on this planet. But let us begin. In your hands, my fellow citizens, more than in mine, will rest the final success or failure of our course. Since this country was founded, each generation of Americans has been summoned to give testimony to its national loyalty. The graves of young Americans who answered the call to service surround the globe. Now the trumpet summons us again—not as a call to bear arms, though arms we need; not as a call to battle, though embattled we are—but a call to bear the burden of a long twilight struggle, year in and year out, "rejoicing in hope, patient in tribulation"—a struggle against the common enemies of man: tyranny, poverty, disease, and war itself. Can we forge against these enemies a grand and global alliance, North and South, East and West, that can assure a more fruitful life for all mankind? Will you join in that historic effort? In the long history of the world, only a few generations have been granted the role of defending freedom in its hour of maximum danger. I do not shrink from this responsibility—I welcome it. I do not believe that any of us would exchange places with any other people or any other generation. The energy, the faith, the devotion which we bring to this endeavor will light our country and all who serve it—and the glow from that fire can truly light the world. And so, my fellow Americans: ask not what your country can do for you—ask what you can do for your country. My fellow citizens of the world: ask not what America will do for you, but what together we can do for the freedom of man. Finally, whether you are citizens of America or citizens of the world, ask of us the same high standards of strength and sacrifice which we ask of you. With a good conscience our only sure reward, with history the final judge of our deeds, let us go forth to lead the land we love, asking His blessing and His help, but knowing that here on earth God's work must truly be our own.

JOHN F. KENNEDY'S "LONG TWILIGHT STRUGGLE"

University of Washington, 16 November 1961

In 1961 the world relations of this country have become tangled and complex. One of

our former allies has become our adversary—and he has his own adversaries who are not our allies. Heroes are removed from their tombs, history rewritten, the names of cities changed overnight. We increase our arms at a heavy cost, primarily to make certain that we will not have to use them. We must face up to the chance of war if we are to maintain the peace. We must work with certain countries lacking in freedom in order to strengthen the cause of freedom. We find some who call themselves neutrals who are our friends and sympathetic to us, and others who call themselves neutral who are unremittingly hostile to us. And as the most powerful defender of freedom on earth, we find ourselves unable to escape the responsibilities of freedom and yet unable to exercise it without restraints imposed by the very freedoms we seek to protect. We cannot, as a free nation, compete with our adversaries in tactics of terror, assassination, false promises, counterfeit mobs, and crises. We cannot, under the scrutiny of a free press and public, tell different stories to different audiences, foreign, domestic, friendly, and hostile. We cannot abandon the slow processes of consulting with our allies to match the swift expediencies of those who merely dictate to their satellites. We can neither abandon nor control the international organization in which we now cast less than 1 percent of the vote in the General Assembly. We possess weapons of tremendous power, but they are least effective in combating the weapons most often used by freedom's foes: subversion, infiltration, guerrilla warfare, and civil disorder. We send arms to other peoples—just as we can send them the ideals of democracy in which we believe—but we cannot send them the will to use those arms or to abide by those ideals. And while we believe not only in the force of arms but in the force of right and reason, we have learned that reason does not always appeal to unreasonable men, that it is not always true that "a soft answer turneth away wrath," and that right does not always make might. In short we must face problems which do not lend themselves to easy or quick or permanent solutions. And we must face the fact that the United States is neither omnip-

otent or omniscient, that we are only 6 percent of the world's population, that we cannot impose our will upon the other 94 percent of mankind, that we cannot right every wrong or reverse each adversity, and that therefore there cannot be an American solution to every world problem. These burdens and frustrations are accepted by most Americans with maturity and understanding. They may long for the days when war meant charging up San Juan Hill, or when our isolation was guarded by two oceans, or when the atomic bomb was ours alone, or when much of the industrialized world depended upon our resources and our aid. But they now know that those days are gone and that gone with them are the old policies and the old complacencies. And they know, too, that we must make the best of our new problems and our new opportunities, whatever the risk and the cost. But there are others who cannot bear the burden of a long twilight struggle. They lack confidence in our long-run capacity to survive and succeed. Hating communism, yet they see communism in the long run, perhaps, as the wave of the future. And they want some quick and easy and final and cheap solution—now. There are two groups of these frustrated citizens, far apart in their views yet very much alike in their approach. On the one hand are those who urge upon us what I regard to be the pathway of surrender—appeasing our enemies, compromising our commitments, purchasing peace at any price, disavowing our arms, our friends, our obligations. If their view had prevailed the world of free choice would be smaller today. On the other hand are those who urge upon us what I regard to be the pathway of war: equating negotiations with appeasement and substituting rigidity for firmness. If their view had prevailed, we would be at war today, and in more than one place. It is a curious fact that each of these extreme opposites resembles the other. Each believes that we have only two choices: appeasement or war, suicide or surrender, humiliation or holocaust, to be either Red or dead. Each side sees only "hard" and "soft" nations, hard and soft policies, hard and soft men. Each believes that any departure from its own course inevitably leads to the other: one

group believes that any peaceful solution means appeasement; the other believes that any arms buildup means war. One group regards everyone else as warmongers; the other regards everyone else as appeasers. Neither side admits its path will lead to disaster, but neither can tell us how or where to draw the line once we descend the slippery slopes of appeasement or constant intervention. In short, while both extremes profess to be the true realists of our time, neither could be more unrealistic. While both claim to be doing the nation a service, they could do it no greater disservice. For this kind of talk and easy solution to difficult problems, if believed, could inspire a lack of confidence among our people when they must all—above all else—be united in recognizing the long and difficult days that lie ahead. It could inspire uncertainty among our allies when above all else they must be confident in us. And even more dangerously, it could, if believed, inspire doubt among our adversaries when they must above all be convinced that we will defend our vital interests. The essential fact that both of these groups fail to grasp is that diplomacy and defense are not substitutes for one another. Either alone would fail. A willingness to resist force, unaccompanied by a willingness to talk, could provoke belligerence, while a willingness to talk, unaccompanied by a willingness to resist force, could invite disaster. But as long as we know what comprises our vital interests and our long-range goals, we have nothing to fear from negotiations at the appropriate time and nothing to gain by refusing to play a part in them. At a time when a single clash could escalate overnight into a holocaust of mushroom clouds, a great power does not prove its firmness by leaving the task of exploring the other's intentions to sentries or those without full responsibility. Nor can ultimate weapons rightfully be employed, or the ultimate sacrifice rightfully demanded of our citizens, until every reasonable solution has been explored. "How many wars," Winston Churchill has written, "have been averted by patience and persisting goodwill! . . . How many wars have been precipitated by firebrands!" If vital interests under duress can be preserved by peaceful means,

negotiations will find that out. If our adversary will accept nothing less than a concession of our rights, negotiations will find that out. And if negotiations are to take place, this nation cannot abdicate to its adversaries the task of choosing the forum and the framework and the time. For there are carefully defined limits within which any serious negotiations must take place. With respect to any future talks on Germany and Berlin, for example, we cannot, on the one hand, confine our proposals to a list of concessions we are willing to make, nor can we, on the other hand, advance any proposals which compromise the security of free Germans and West Berliners or endanger their ties with the West. No one should be under the illusion that negotiations for the sake of negotiations always advance the cause of peace. If for lack of preparation they break up in bitterness, the prospects of peace have been endangered. If they are made a forum for propaganda or a cover for aggression, the processes of peace have been abused. But it is a test of our national maturity to accept the fact that negotiations are not a contest spelling victory or defeat. They may succeed; they may fail. They are likely to be successful only if both sides reach an agreement which both regard as preferable to the status quo—an agreement in which each side can consider its own situation can be improved. And this is most difficult to obtain. But, while we shall negotiate freely, we shall not negotiate freedom. Our answer to the classic question of Patrick Henry is still "No." Life is not so dear and peace is not so precious ". . . as to be purchased at the price of chains and slavery." And that is our answer even though, for the first time since the ancient battles between Greek city-states, war entails the threat of total annihilation, of everything we know, of society itself. For to save mankind's future freedom we must face up to any risk that is necessary. We will always seek peace—but we will never surrender. In short, we are neither "warmongers" nor "appeasers," neither "hard" nor "soft." We are Americans, determined to defend the frontiers of freedom by an honorable peace if peace is possible, but by arms if arms are used against us. And if we are to move forward in that spirit, we shall need all

the calm and thoughtful citizens that this great university can produce, all the light they can shed, all the wisdom they can bring to bear. It is customary, both here and around the world, to regard life in the United States as easy. Our advantages are many. But more than any other people on earth, we bear burdens and accept risks unprecedented in their size and their duration, not for ourselves alone but for all who wish to be free. No other generation of free men in any country has ever faced so many and such difficult challenges—not even those who lived in the days when this university was founded in 1861. This nation was then torn by war. This territory had only the simplest elements of civilization. And this city had barely begun to function. But a university was one of their earliest thoughts, and they summed it up in the motto that they adopted: "Let there be light." What more can be said today regarding all the dark and tangled problems we face than: Let there be light.

REPORT ON THE SOVIET ARMS BUILDUP IN CUBA

White House, 22 October 1962

Good evening my fellow citizens: This Government, as promised, has maintained the closest surveillance of the Soviet military buildup on the island of Cuba. Within the past week, unmistakable evidence has established the fact that a series of offensive missile sites is now in preparation on that imprisoned island. The purpose of these bases can be none other than to provide a nuclear strike capability against the Western Hemisphere. Upon receiving the first preliminary hard information of this nature last Tuesday morning at 9 a.m., I directed that our surveillance be stepped up. And having now confirmed and completed our evaluation of the evidence and our decision on a course of action, this Government feels obliged to report this new crisis to you in fullest detail. The characteristics of these new missile sites indicate two distinct types of installations. Several of them include medium range ballistic missiles capable of carrying a nuclear warhead for a distance of more than 1,000 nautical miles.

Each of these missiles, in short, is capable of striking Washington, D.C., the Panama Canal, Cape Canaveral, Mexico City, or any other city in the south-eastern part of the United States, in Central America, or in the Caribbean area. Additional sites not yet completed appear to be designed for intermediate range ballistic missiles—capable of traveling more than twice as far—and thus capable of striking most of the major cities in the Western Hemisphere, ranging as far north as Hudson Bay, Canada, and as far south as Lima, Peru. In addition, jet bombers, capable of carrying nuclear weapons, are now being uncrated and assembled in Cuba, while the necessary air bases are being prepared. This urgent transformation of Cuba into an important strategic base—by the presence of these large, long range, and clearly offensive weapons of sudden mass destruction—constitutes an explicit threat to the peace and security of all the Americas, in flagrant and deliberate defiance of the Rio Pact of 1947, the traditions of this Nation and hemisphere, the joint resolution of the 87th Congress, the Charter of the United Nations, and my own public warnings to the Soviets on September 4 and 13. This action also contradicts the repeated assurances of Soviet spokesmen, both publicly and privately delivered, that the arms buildup in Cuba would retain its original defensive character, and that the Soviet Union had no need or desire to station strategic missiles on the territory of any other nation. The size of this undertaking makes clear that it has been planned for some months. Yet only last month, after I had made clear the distinction between any introduction of ground-to-ground missiles and the existence of defensive anti-aircraft missiles, the Soviet Government publicly stated on September 11, and I quote, "the armaments and military equipment sent to Cuba are designed exclusively for defensive purposes," that, and I quote the Soviet Government, "there is no need for the Soviet Government to shift its weapons . . . for a retaliatory blow to any other country, for instance Cuba," and that, and I quote their government, "the Soviet Union has so powerful rockets to carry these nuclear warheads that there is no need to search for sites for them

beyond the boundaries of the Soviet Union." That statement was false. Only last Thursday, as evidence of this rapid offensive buildup was already in my hand, Soviet Foreign Minister Gromyko told me in my office that he was instructed to make it clear once again, as he said his government had already done, that Soviet assistance to Cuba, and I quote, "pursued solely the purpose of contributing to the defense capabilities of Cuba," that, and I quote him, "training by Soviet specialists of Cuban nationals in handling defensive armaments was by no means offensive, and if it were otherwise," Mr. Gromyko went on, "the Soviet Government would never become involved in rendering such assistance." That statement also was false.

Neither the United States of America nor the world community of nations can tolerate deliberate deception and offensive threats on the part of any nation, large or small. We no longer live in a world where only the actual firing of weapons represents a sufficient challenge to a nation's security to constitute maximum peril. Nuclear weapons are so destructive and ballistic missiles are so swift, that any substantially increased possibility of their use or any sudden change in their deployment may well be regarded as a definite threat to peace. For many years both the Soviet Union and the United States, recognizing this fact, have deployed strategic nuclear weapons with great care, never upsetting the precarious status quo which insured that these weapons would not be used in the absence of some vital challenge. Our own strategic missiles have never been transferred to the territory of any other nation under a cloak of secrecy and deception; and our history—unlike that of the Soviets since the end of World War II—demonstrates that we have no desire to dominate or conquer any other nation or impose our system upon its people. Nevertheless, American citizens have become adjusted to living daily on the Bull's-eye of Soviet missiles located inside the U.S.S.R. or in submarines. In that sense, missiles in Cuba add to an already clear and present danger—although it should be noted the nations of Latin America have never previously been subjected to a potential nuclear threat. But this secret, swift, and extraordinary buildup of Communist missiles—in an area well known to have a special and historical relationship to the United States and the nations of the Western Hemisphere, in violation of Soviet assurances, and in defiance of American and hemispheric policy—this sudden, clandestine decision to station strategic weapons for the first time outside of Soviet soil—is a deliberately provocative and unjustified change in the status quo which cannot be accepted by this country, if our courage and our commitments are ever to be trusted again by either friend or foe. The 1930s taught us a clear lesson: aggressive conduct, if allowed to go unchecked and unchallenged ultimately leads to war. This nation is opposed to war. We are also true to our word. Our unswerving objective, therefore, must be to prevent the use of these missiles against this or any other country, and to secure their withdrawal or elimination from the Western Hemisphere. Our policy has been one of patience and restraint, as befits a peaceful and powerful nation, which leads a worldwide alliance. We have been determined not to be diverted from our central concerns by mere irritants and fanatics. But now further action is required—and it is under way; and these actions may only be the beginning. We will not prematurely or unnecessarily risk the costs of worldwide nuclear war in which even the fruits of victory would be ashes in our mouth—but neither will we shrink from that risk at any time it must be faced.

Acting, therefore, in the defense of our own security and of the entire Western Hemisphere, and under the authority entrusted to me by the Constitution as endorsed by the resolution of the Congress, I have directed that the following initial steps be taken immediately: First: To halt this offensive buildup, a strict quarantine on all offensive military equipment under shipment to Cuba is being initiated. All ships of any kind bound for Cuba from whatever nation or port will, if found to contain cargoes of offensive weapons, be turned back. This quarantine will be extended, if needed, to other types of cargo and carriers. We are not at this time, however, denying the necessities of life as the Soviets

attempted to do in their Berlin blockade of 1948. Second: I have directed the continued and increased close surveillance of Cuba and its military buildup. The foreign ministers of the OAS, in their communique of October 6, rejected secrecy in such matters in this hemisphere. Should these offensive military preparations continue, thus increasing the threat to the hemisphere, further action will be justified. I have directed the Armed Forces to prepare for any eventualities; and I trust that in the interest of both the Cuban people and the Soviet technicians at the sites, the hazards to all concerned in continuing this threat will be recognized. Third: It shall be the policy of this Nation to regard any nuclear missile launched from Cuba against any nation in the Western Hemisphere as an attack by the Soviet Union on the United States, requiring a full retaliatory response upon the Soviet Union. Fourth: As a necessary military precaution, I have reinforced our base at Guantanamo, evacuated today the dependents of our personnel there, and ordered additional military units to be on a standby alert basis. Fifth: We are calling tonight for an immediate meeting of the Organ of Consultation under the Organization of American States, to consider this threat to hemispheric security and to invoke articles 6 and 8 of the Rio Treaty in support of all necessary action. The United Nations Charter allows for regional security arrangements—and the nations of this hemisphere decided long ago against the military presence of outside powers. Our other allies around the world have also been alerted. Sixth: Under the Charter of the United Nations, we are asking tonight that an emergency meeting of the Security Council be convoked without delay to take action against this latest Soviet threat to world peace. Our resolution will call for the prompt dismantling and withdrawal of all offensive weapons in Cuba, under the supervision of U.N. observers, before the quarantine can be lifted. Seventh and finally: I call upon Chairman Khrushchev to halt and eliminate this clandestine, reckless and provocative threat to world peace and to stable relations between our two nations. I call upon him further to abandon this course of world

domination, and to join in an historic effort to end the perilous arms race and to transform the history of man. He has an opportunity now to move the world back from the abyss of destruction—by returning to his government's own words that it had no need to station missiles outside its own territory, and withdrawing these weapons from Cuba—by refraining from any action which will widen or deepen the present crisis—and then by participating in a search for peaceful and permanent solutions. This Nation is prepared to present its case against the Soviet threat to peace, and our own proposals for a peaceful world, at any time and in any forum—in the OAS, in the United Nations, or in any other meeting that could be useful—without limiting our freedom of action. We have in the past made strenuous efforts to limit the spread of nuclear weapons. We have proposed the elimination of all arms and military bases in a fair and effective disarmament treaty. We are prepared to discuss new proposals for the removal of tensions on both sides—including the possibility of a genuinely independent Cuba, free to determine its own destiny. We have no wish to war with the Soviet Union—for we are a peaceful people who desire to live in peace with all other peoples. But it is difficult to settle or even discuss these problems in an atmosphere of intimidation. That is why this latest Soviet threat—or any other threat which is made independently or in response to our actions this week—must and will be met with determination. Any hostile move anywhere in the world against the safety and freedom of peoples to whom we are committed—including in particular the brave people of West Berlin—will be met by whatever action is needed. Finally, I want to say a few words to the captive people of Cuba, to whom this speech is being directly carried by special radio facilities. I speak to you as a friend, as one who knows of your deep attachment to your fatherland, as one who shares your aspirations for liberty and justice for all. And I have watched and the American people have watched with deep sorrow how your nationalist revolution was betrayed—and how your fatherland fell under foreign domination. Now

your leaders are no longer Cuban leaders inspired by Cuban ideals. They are puppets and agents of an international conspiracy which has turned Cuba against your friends and neighbors in the Americas—and turned it into the first Latin American country to become a target for nuclear war—the first Latin American country to have these weapons on its soil. These new weapons are not in your interest. They contribute nothing to your peace and well-being. They can only undermine it. But this country has no wish to cause you to suffer or to impose any system upon you. We know that your lives and land are being used as pawns by those who deny your freedom.

Many times in the past, the Cuban people have risen to throw out tyrants who destroyed their liberty. And I have no doubt that most Cubans today look forward to the time when they will be truly free—free from foreign domination, free to choose their own leaders, free to select their own system, free to own their own land, free to speak and write and worship without fear or degradation. And then shall Cuba be welcomed back to the society of free nations and to the associations of this hemisphere. My fellow citizens: let no one doubt that this is a difficult and dangerous effort on which we have set out. No one can see precisely what course it will take or what costs or casualties will be incurred. Many months of sacrifice and self-discipline lie ahead—months in which our patience and our will will be tested—months in which many threats and denunciations will keep us aware of our dangers. But the greatest danger of all would be to do nothing. The path we have chosen for the present is full of hazards, as all paths are—but it is the one most consistent with our character and courage as a nation and our commitments around the world. The cost of freedom is always high—and Americans have always paid it. And one path we shall never choose, and that is the path of surrender or submission. Our goal is not the victory of might, but the vindication of right—not peace at the expense of freedom, but both peace and freedom, here in this hemisphere, and, we hope, around the world. God willing, that goal will be achieved. Thank you and good night.

CIVIL RIGHTS ANNOUNCEMENT

White House, 11 June 1963

This afternoon, following a series of threats and defiant statements, the presence of Alabama National Guardsmen was required on the University of Alabama to carry out the final and unequivocal order of the United States District Court of the Northern District of Alabama. This order called for the admission of two clearly qualified young Alabama residents who happen to have been born Negro. That they were admitted peacefully on the campus is due in good measure to the conduct of the students of the University of Alabama, who met their responsibilities in a constructive way. I hope that every American, regardless of where he lives, will stop and examine his conscience about this and other related incidents. This nation was founded by men of many nations and backgrounds. It was founded on the principle that all men are created equal, and that the rights of every man are diminished when the rights of one man are threatened.

Today we are committed to a worldwide struggle to promote and protect the rights of all who wish to be free. When Americans are sent to Vietnam or West Berlin, we do not ask for whites only. It ought to be possible, therefore, for American students of any color to attend any public institution they select without having to be backed up by troops. It ought to be possible for American consumers of any color to receive equal service in places of public accommodation, such as hotels and restaurants and theaters and retail stores, without being forced to resort to demonstration in the street. It ought to be possible for American citizens of any color to register and to vote in a free election without interference or fear of reprisal. It ought to be possible, in short, for every American to enjoy the privileges of being American without regard to his race or his color. In short, every American ought to have the right to be treated as he would wish to be treated, as one would wish his children to be treated. But this is not the case today. The Negro baby born in America today, regardless of the section of the nation in which he is born, has about one half as much chance of completing high school as

a white baby born in the same place on the same day, one third as much chance of completing college, one third as much chance of becoming a professional man, twice as much chance of becoming unemployed, about one seventh as much chance of earning $10,000 a year or more, a life expectancy which is seven years shorter, and the prospects of earning only half as much. This is not a sectional issue. Difficulties over segregation and discrimination exist in every city, in every state of the Union, producing in many cities a rising tide of discontent that threatens the public safety. Nor is this a partisan issue. In a time of domestic crisis men of goodwill and generosity should be able to unite regardless of party or politics. This is not even a legal or legislative issue alone. It is better to settle these methods in the courts than on the streets, and new laws are needed at every level, but law alone cannot make men see right. We are confronted primarily with a moral issue. It is as old as the Scriptures and is as clear as the American Constitution. The heart of the question is whether all Americans are to be afforded equal rights and equal opportunities, whether we are going to treat our fellow Americans as we want to be treated. If an American, because his skin is dark, cannot eat lunch in a restaurant open to the public, if he cannot send his children to the best public school available, if he cannot vote for the public officials who represent him, if, in short, he cannot enjoy the full and free life which all of us want, then who among us would be content to have the color of his skin changed and stand in his place? Who among us would be content with the counsels of patience and delay?

One hundred years have passed since President Lincoln freed the slaves, yet their heirs, their grandsons, are not fully free. They are not yet freed from the bonds of injustice. They are not yet freed from social and economic oppression. And this nation, for all its hopes and all its boasts, will not be fully free until all its citizens are free. We preach freedom around the world, and we mean it, and we cherish our freedom here at home; but are we to say to the world, and, much more importantly, for each other, that this is a land of the free except for the Negroes; that we have no second-class citizens except Negroes; that we have no class or caste system, no ghettos, no master race, except with respect to Negroes? Now the time has come for this nation to fulfill its promise. The events in Birmingham and elsewhere have so increased the cries for equality that no city or state or legislative body can prudently choose to ignore them. The fires of frustration and discord are burning in every city, North and South, where legal remedies are not at hand. Redress is sought in the streets, in demonstrations, parades, and protests which create tensions and threaten violence and threaten lives. We face, therefore, a moral crisis as a country and as a people. It cannot be met by repressive police action. It cannot be left to increased demonstrations in the streets. It cannot be quieted by token moves or talk. It is a time to act in the Congress, in your state and local legislative bodies and, above all, in all of our daily lives. It is not enough to pin the blame on others, to say this is a problem of one section of the country or another, or deplore the facts that we face. A great change is at hand, and our task, our obligation, is to make that revolution, that change, peaceful and constructive for all. Those who do nothing are inviting shame as well as violence. Those who act boldly are recognizing right as well as reality. Next week I shall ask the Congress of the United States to act, to make a commitment it has not fully made in this century to the proposition that race has no place in American life or law. The federal judiciary has upheld that proposition in the conduct of its affairs, including the employment of federal personnel, the use of federal facilities, and the sale of federally financed housing. But there are other necessary measures which only the Congress can provide, and they must be provided at this session. The old code of equity law under which we live commands for every wrong a remedy, but in too many communities, in too many parts of the country, wrongs are inflicted on Negro citizens and there are no remedies at law. Unless the Congress acts, their only remedy is in the streets. I am, therefore, asking the Congress to enact legislation giving all Americans the right to be served in

facilities which are open to the public—hotels, restaurants, theaters, retail stores, and similar establishments.

This seems to me to be an elementary right. Its denial is an arbitrary indignity that no American in 1963 should have to endure. But many do. I have recently met with scores of business leaders urging them to take voluntary action to end this discrimination, and I have been encouraged by their response. In the last two weeks over seventy-five cities have seen progress made in desegregating these kinds of facilities. But many are unwilling to act alone, and for this reason, nationwide legislation is needed if we are to move this problem from the streets to the courts. I am also asking Congress to authorize the federal government to participate more fully in lawsuits designed to end segregation in public education. We have succeeded in persuading many districts to desegregate voluntarily. Dozens have admitted Negroes without violence. Today, a negro is attending a state-supported institution in every one of our fifty states. But the pace is very slow. Too many Negro children entering segregated grade schools at the time of the Supreme Court's decision nine years ago will enter segregated high schools this fall, having suffered a loss which can never be restored. The lack of an adequate education denied the Negro a chance to get a decent job. The orderly implementation of the Supreme Court decision, therefore, cannot be left solely to those who may not have the economic resources to carry the legal action or who may be subject to harassment. Other features will also be requested, including greater protection for the right to vote. But legislation, I repeat, cannot solve this problem alone. It must be solved in the homes of every American in every community across our country. In this respect, I want to pay tribute to those citizens, North and South, who have been working in their communities to make life better for all. They are acting not out of a sense of legal duty but out of a sense of human decency. Like our soldiers and sailors in all parts of the world, they are meeting freedom's challenge on the firing line, and I salute them for their honor and courage. My fellow Americans, this is a

problem which faces us all—in every city of the North as well as the South. Today there are Negroes, unemployed—two or three times as many compared to whites—with inadequate education, moving into the large cities, unable to find work, young people particularly out of work and without hope, denied equal rights, denied the opportunity to eat at a restaurant or lunch counter or go to a movie theater, denied the right to a decent education. . . . It seems to me that these are matters which concern us all, not merely Presidents or congressmen or governors, but every citizen of the United States. This is one country. It has become one country because all the people who came here had an equal chance to develop their talents. . . . We have a right to expect that the Negro community will be responsible and will uphold the law; but they have a right to expect that the law will be fair, that the constitution will be color blind, as Justice Harlan said at the turn of the century. This is what we are talking about. This is a matter which concerns this country and what it stands for, and in meeting it I ask the support of all our citizens.

NATION'S SPACE EFFORT

Rice University, Houston, Texas, 12 September 1962

Mr. Bell, scientists, distinguished guests, and ladies and gentlemen: I appreciate your president having made me an honorary visiting professor, and I will assure you that my first lecture will be very brief. I am delighted to be here and I'm particularly delighted to be here on this occasion. We meet at a college noted for knowledge, in a city noted for progress, in a state noted for strength, and we stand in need of all three, for we meet in an hour of change and challenge, in a decade of hope and fear, in an age of both knowledge and ignorance. The greater our knowledge increases, the greater our ignorance unfolds. Despite the striking fact that most of the scientists that the world has ever known are alive and working today, despite the fact that this nation's own scientific manpower is doubling every 12 years in a rate of growth more than three times that of our

population as a whole, despite that, the vast stretches of the unknown and the unanswered and the unfinished still far outstrip our collective comprehension. No man can fully grasp how far and how fast we have come, but condense, if you will, the 50,000 years of man's recorded history in a time span of but a half-century. Stated in these terms, we know very little about the first 40 years, except at the end of them advanced man had learned to use the skins of animals to cover them. Then about 10 years ago, under this standard, man emerged from his caves to construct other kinds of shelter. Only five years ago man learned to write and use a cart with wheels. Christianity began less than two years ago. The printing press came this year, and then less than two months ago, during this whole 50-year span of human history, the steam engine provided a new source of power. Newton explored the meaning of gravity. Last month electric lights and telephones and automobiles and airplanes became available. Only last week did we develop penicillin and television and nuclear power, and now if America's new spacecraft succeeds in reaching Venus, we will have literally reached the stars before midnight tonight. This is a breathtaking pace, and such a pace cannot help but create new ills as it dispels old, new ignorance, new problems, new dangers. Surely the opening vistas of space promise high costs and hardships, as well as high reward. So it is not surprising that some would have us stay where we are a little longer to rest, to wait. But this city of Houston, this state of Texas, this country of the United States was not built by those who waited and rested and wished to look behind them. This country was conquered by those who moved forward—and so will space. William Bradford, speaking in 1630 of the founding of the Plymouth Bay Colony, said that all great and honorable actions are accompanied with great difficulties, and both must be enterprised and overcome with answerable courage. If this capsule history of our progress teaches us anything, it is that man, in his quest for knowledge and progress, is determined and cannot be deterred. The exploration of space will go ahead, whether we join in it or not, and it is one of the great

adventures of all time, and no nation which expects to be the leader of other nations can expect to stay behind in the race for space. Those who came before us made certain that this country rode the first waves of the industrial revolutions, the first waves of modern invention, and the first wave of nuclear power, and this generation does not intend to founder in the backwash of the coming age of space. We mean to be a part of it—we mean to lead it. For the eyes of the world now look into space, to the moon and to the planets beyond, and we have vowed that we shall not see it governed by a hostile flag of conquest, but by a banner of freedom and peace. We have vowed that we shall not see space filled with weapons of mass destruction, but with instruments of knowledge and understanding. Yet the vows of this Nation can only be fulfilled if we in this Nation are first, and, therefore, we intend to be first. In short, our leadership in science and in industry, our hopes for peace and security, our obligations to ourselves as well as others, all require us to make this effort, to solve these mysteries, to solve them for the good of all men, and to become the world's leading space-faring nation. We set sail on this new sea because there is new knowledge to be gained, and new rights to be won, and they must be won and used for the progress of all people. For space science, like nuclear science and all technology, has no conscience of its own. Whether it will become a force for good or ill depends on man, and only if the United States occupies a position of preeminence can we help decide whether this new ocean will be a sea of peace or a new terrifying theater of war. I do not say the we should or will go unprotected against the hostile misuse of space any more than we go unprotected against the hostile use of land or sea, but I do say that space can be explored and mastered without feeding the fires of war, without repeating the mistakes that man has made in extending his writ around this globe of ours. There is no strife, no prejudice, no national conflict in outer space as yet. Its hazards are hostile to us all. Its conquest deserves the best of all mankind, and its opportunity for peaceful cooperation may never come again. But why, some say, the moon? Why choose this as our goal?

And they may well ask, why climb the highest mountain? Why, 35 years ago, fly the Atlantic? Why does Rice play Texas? We choose to go to the moon. We choose to go to the moon in this decade and do the other things, not only because they are easy, but because they are hard, because that goal will serve to organize and measure the best of our energies and skills, because that challenge is one that we are willing to accept, one we are unwilling to postpone, and one which we intend to win, and the others, too. It is for these reasons that I regard the decision last year to shift our efforts in space from low to high gear as among the most important decisions that will be made during my incumbency in the office of the Presidency. In the last 24 hours we have seen facilities now being created for the greatest and most complex exploration in man's history. We have felt the ground shake and the air shattered by the testing of a Saturn C-1 booster rocket, many times as powerful as the Atlas which launched John Glenn, generating power equivalent to 10,000 automobiles with their accelerators on the floor. We have seen the site where the F-1 rocket engines, each one as powerful as all eight engines of the Saturn combined, will be clustered together to make the advanced Saturn missile, assembled in a new building to be built at Cape Canaveral as tall as a 48 story structure, as wide as a city block, and as long as two lengths of this field. Within these last 19 months at least 45 satellites have circled the earth. Some 40 of them were in the United States of America; and they were far more sophisticated and supplied far more knowledge to the people of the world than those of the Soviet Union. The Mariner spacecraft now on its way to Venus is the most intricate instrument in the history of space science. The accuracy of that shot is comparable to firing a missile from Cape Canaveral and dropping it in this stadium between the 40-yard lines. Transit satellites are helping our ships at sea to steer a safer course. Tiros satellites have given us unprecedented warnings of hurricanes and storms, and will do the same for forest fires and icebergs. We have had our failures, but so have others, even if they do not admit them. And they may be less public. To be sure, we are behind, and will be behind for some time in manned flight. But we do not intend to stay behind, and in this decade, we shall make up and move ahead. The growth of our science and education will be enriched by new knowledge of our universe and environment, by new techniques of learning and mapping and observation, by new tools and computers for industry, medicine, the home as well as the school. Technical institutions, such as Rice, will reap the harvest of these gains. And finally, the space effort itself, while still in its infancy, has already created a great number of new companies, and tens of thousands of new jobs. Space and related industries are generating new demands in investment and skilled personnel, and this city and this State, and this region, will share greatly in this growth. What was once the furthest outpost on the old frontier of the West will be the furthest outpost on the new frontier of science and space. Houston, your City of Houston, with its Manned Spacecraft Center, will become the heart of a large scientific and engineering community. During the next 5 years the National Aeronautics and Space Administration expects to double the number of scientists and engineers in this area, to increase its outlays for salaries and expenses to $60 million a year; to invest some $200 million in plant and laboratory facilities; and to direct or contract for new space efforts over $1 billion from this center in this city. To be sure, all this costs us all a good deal of money. This year's space budget is three times what it was in January 1961, and it is greater than the space budget of the previous eight years combined. That budget now stands at $5,400 million a year—a staggering sum, though somewhat less than we pay for cigarettes and cigars every year. Space expenditures will soon rise some more, from 40 cents per person per week to more than 50 cents a week for every man, woman and child in the United States, for we have given this program a high national priority—even though I realize that this is in some measure an act of faith and vision, for we do not now know what benefits await us. But if I were to say, my fellow citizens, that we shall send to the moon, 240,000 miles away from the control station in Houston, a giant rocket more than 300 feet tall, the length of this

football field, made of new metal alloys, some of which have not yet been invented, capable of standing heat and stresses several times more than have ever been experienced, fitted together with a precision better than the finest watch, carrying all the equipment needed for propulsion, guidance, control, communications, food, and survival, on an untried mission, to an unknown celestial body, and then return it safely to earth, re-entering the atmosphere at speeds of over 25,000 miles per hour, causing heat about half that of the temperature of the sun—almost as hot as it is here today—and do all this, and do it right, and do it first before this decade is out—then we must be bold. I'm the one who is doing all the work, so we just want you to stay cool for a minute. However, I think we're going to do it, and I think that we must pay what needs to be paid. I don't think we ought to waste any money, but I think we ought to do the job. And this will be done in the decade of the sixties. It may be done while some of you are still here at school at this college and university. It will be done during the term of office of some of the people who sit here on this platform. But it will be done. And it will be done before the end of this decade. I am delighted that this university is playing a part in putting a man on the moon as part of a great national effort of the United States of America. Many years ago the great British explorer George Mallory, who was to die on Mount Everest, was asked why did he want to climb it. He said, it is there, well, space is there, and we're going to climb it, and the moon and the planets are there, and new hopes for knowledge and peace are there. And, therefore, as we set sail we ask God's blessing on the most hazardous and dangerous and greatest adventure on which man has ever embarked. Thank you.

THE BERLIN ADDRESS—"ICH BIN EIN BERLINER" ("I AM A BERLINER")

West Berlin, 26 June 1963

I am proud to come to this city as the guest of your distinguished Mayor, who has symbolized throughout the world the fighting spirit of West Berlin. And I am proud—And I am proud to visit the Federal Republic with your distinguished Chancellor who for so many years has committed Germany to democracy and freedom and progress, and to come here in the company of my fellow American, General Clay, who—who has been in this city during its great moments of crisis and will come again if ever needed. Two thousand years ago, two thousand years ago, the proudest boast was "civis Romanus sum." Today, in the world of freedom, the proudest boast is "Ich bin ein Berliner." ("I am a Berliner.") (I appreciate my interpreter translating my German.) There are many people in the world who really don't understand, or say they don't, what is the great issue between the free world and the Communist world. Let them come to Berlin. There are some who say—There are some who say that communism is the wave of the future. Let them come to Berlin. And there are some who say, in Europe and elsewhere, we can work with the Communists. Let them come to Berlin. And there are even a few who say that it is true that communism is an evil system, but it permits us to make economic progress. Lass' sie nach Berlin kommen. Let them come to Berlin. Freedom has many difficulties and democracy is not perfect. But we have never had to put a wall up to keep our people in—to prevent them from leaving us. I want to say on behalf of my countrymen who live many miles away on the other side of the Atlantic, who are far distant from you, that they take the greatest pride, that they have been able to share with you, even from a distance, the story of the last 18 years. I know of no town, no city, that has been besieged for 18 years that still lives with the vitality and the force, and the hope, and the determination of the city of West Berlin. While the wall is the most obvious and vivid demonstration of the failures of the Communist system—for all the world to see—we take no satisfaction in it; for it is, as your Mayor has said, an offense not only against history but an offense against humanity, separating families, dividing husbands and wives and brothers and sisters, and dividing a people who wish to be joined together. What is true of this city is true of Germany: Real, lasting peace in Europe can never be assured as long as one German out of

four is denied the elementary right of free men, and that is to make a free choice. In 18 years of peace and good faith, this generation of Germans has earned the right to be free, including the right to unite their families and their nation in lasting peace, with good will to all people. You live in a defended island of freedom, but your life is part of the main. So let me ask you, as I close, to lift your eyes beyond the dangers of today, to the hopes of tomorrow, beyond the freedom merely of this city of Berlin, or your country of Germany, to the advance of freedom everywhere, beyond the wall to the day of peace with justice, beyond yourselves and ourselves to all mankind. Freedom is indivisible, and when one man is enslaved, all are not free. When all are free, then we look—can look forward to that day when this city will be joined as one and this country and this great Continent of Europe in a peaceful and hopeful globe. When that day finally comes, as it will, the people of West Berlin can take sober satisfaction in the fact that they were in the front lines for almost two decades. All—All free men, wherever they may live, are citizens of Berlin. And, therefore, as a free man, I take pride in the words "Ich bin ein Berliner."

Appendix D
Martin Luther King Jr.'s
"I Have a Dream" Speech

The Lincoln Memorial, Washington, DC, 28 August 1963

Five score years ago, a great American, in whose symbolic shadow we stand signed the Emancipation Proclamation. This momentous decree came as a great beacon light of hope to millions of Negro slaves who had been seared in the flames of withering injustice. It came as a joyous daybreak to end the long night of captivity. But one hundred years later, we must face the tragic fact that the Negro is still not free. One hundred years later, the life of the Negro is still sadly crippled by the manacles of segregation and the chains of discrimination. One hundred years later, the Negro lives on a lonely island of poverty in the midst of a vast ocean of material prosperity. One hundred years later, the Negro is still languishing in the corners of American society and finds himself an exile in his own land. So we have come here today to dramatize an appalling condition. In a sense we have come to our nation's capital to cash a check. When the architects of our republic wrote the magnificent words of the Constitution and the Declaration of Independence, they were signing a promissory note to which every American was to fall heir. This note was a promise that all men would be guaranteed the inalienable rights of life, liberty, and the pursuit of happiness. It is obvious today that America has defaulted on this promissory note insofar as her citizens of color are concerned. Instead of honoring this sacred obligation, America has given the Negro people a bad check which has come back marked "insufficient funds." But we refuse to believe that the bank of justice is bankrupt. We refuse to believe that there are insufficient funds in the great vaults of opportunity of this nation. So we have come to cash this check— a check that will give us upon demand the riches of freedom and the security of justice. We have also come to this hallowed spot to remind America of the fierce urgency of now. This is no time to engage in the luxury of cooling off or to take the tranquilizing drug of gradualism. Now is the time to rise from the dark and desolate valley of segregation to the sunlit path of racial justice. Now is the time to open the doors of opportunity to all of God's children. Now is the time to lift our nation from the quicksand of racial injustice to the solid rock of brotherhood. It would be fatal for the nation to overlook the urgency of the moment and to underestimate the determination of the Negro. This sweltering summer of the Negro's legitimate discontent will not pass until there is an invigorating autumn of freedom and equality. Nineteen sixty-three is not an end, but a beginning. Those who hope that the Negro needed to blow off steam and will now be content will have a rude awakening if the nation returns to business as usual. There will be neither rest nor tranquility in America until the Negro is granted his citizenship rights. The whirlwinds of revolt will continue to shake the foundations of our nation until the bright day of justice emerges. But there is something that I must say to my people who stand on the warm threshold which leads into the palace of justice. In the process of gaining our rightful place

we must not be guilty of wrongful deeds. Let us not seek to satisfy our thirst for freedom by drinking from the cup of bitterness and hatred. We must forever conduct our struggle on the high plane of dignity and discipline. We must not allow our creative protest to degenerate into physical violence. Again and again we must rise to the majestic heights of meeting physical force with soul force. The marvelous new militancy which has engulfed the Negro community must not lead us to distrust of all white people, for many of our white brothers, as evidenced by their presence here today, have come to realize that their destiny is tied up with our destiny and their freedom is inextricably bound to our freedom. We cannot walk alone. And as we walk, we must make the pledge that we shall march ahead. We cannot turn back. There are those who are asking the devotees of civil rights, "When will you be satisfied?" We can never be satisfied as long as our bodies, heavy with the fatigue of travel, cannot gain lodging in the motels of the highways and the hotels of the cities. We cannot be satisfied as long as the Negro's basic mobility is from a smaller ghetto to a larger one. We can never be satisfied as long as a Negro in Mississippi cannot vote and a Negro in New York believes he has nothing for which to vote. No, no, we are not satisfied, and we will not be satisfied until justice rolls down like waters and righteousness like a mighty stream. I am not unmindful that some of you have come here out of great trials and tribulations. Some of you have come fresh from narrow cells. Some of you have come from areas where your quest for freedom left you battered by the storms of persecution and staggered by the winds of police brutality. You have been the veterans of creative suffering. Continue to work with the faith that unearned suffering is redemptive. Go back to Mississippi, go back to Alabama, go back to Georgia, go back to Louisiana, go back to the slums and ghettos of our northern cities, knowing that somehow this situation can and will be changed. Let us not wallow in the valley of despair. I say to you today, my friends, that in spite of the difficulties and frustrations of the moment, I still have a dream. It is a dream deeply rooted in the American dream. I have a dream that one day this nation will rise up and live out the true meaning of its creed: "We hold these truths to be self-evident: that all men are created equal." I have a dream that one day on the red hills of Georgia the sons of former slaves and the sons of former slave owners will be able to sit down together at a table of brotherhood. I have a dream that one day even the state of Mississippi, a desert state, sweltering with the heat of injustice and oppression, will be transformed into an oasis of freedom and justice. I have a dream that my four children will one day live in a nation where they will not be judged by the color of their skin but by the content of their character. I have a dream today. I have a dream that one day the state of Alabama, whose governor's lips are presently dripping with the words of interposition and nullification, will be transformed into a situation where little black boys and black girls will be able to join hands with little white boys and white girls and walk together as sisters and brothers. I have a dream today. I have a dream that one day every valley shall be exalted, every hill and mountain shall be made low, the rough places will be made plain, and the crooked places will be made straight, and the glory of the Lord shall be revealed, and all flesh shall see it together. This is our hope. This is the faith with which I return to the South. With this faith we will be able to hew out of the mountain of despair a stone of hope. With this faith we will be able to transform the jangling discords of our nation into a beautiful symphony of brotherhood. With this faith we will be able to work together, to pray together, to struggle together, to go to jail together, to stand up for freedom together, knowing that we will be free one day. This will be the day when all of God's children will be able to sing with a new meaning, "My country, 'tis of thee, sweet land of liberty, of thee I sing. Land where my fathers died, land of the pilgrim's pride, from every mountainside, let freedom ring." And if America is to be a great nation this must become true. So let freedom ring from the prodigious hilltops of New Hampshire. Let freedom ring from the mighty mountains of New York. Let freedom ring from the heightening Alleghenies of Pennsylvania! Let

freedom ring from the snow-capped Rockies of Colorado! Let freedom ring from the curvaceous peaks of California! But not only that; let freedom ring from Stone Mountain of Georgia! Let freedom ring from Lookout Mountain of Tennessee! Let freedom ring from every hill and every molehill of Mississippi. From every mountainside, let freedom ring. When we let freedom ring, when we let it ring from every village and every hamlet, from every state and every city, we will be able to speed up that day when all of God's children, black men and white men, Jews and Gentiles, Protestants and Catholics, will be able to join hands and sing in the words of the old Negro spiritual, "Free at last! free at last! thank God Almighty, we are free at last!"

Bibliography

INTRODUCTION

Books, articles, and films focusing on the events, issues, and personalities of the Kennedy years continue to appear as questions that were thought to be resolved in the early 1960s continue to haunt the 21st century. Domestically, civil rights, racial violence, ethnic assertiveness, gender equality, and poverty and wealth distribution remain the defining key issues today as they did more than six decades ago. Internationally, the United States is faced with the challenge of restricting international terrorism, an ongoing arms buildup, and nuclear proliferation, echoing similar tensions relating to national security that characterized the Cold War years of John F. Kennedy. Kennedy's assassination remains a topic of unquenchable fascination as new documents were released for public scrutiny, and the 50-year anniversary of his death prompted new assessments of Kennedy's life, his brief presidency, and especially his assassination. For example, *Life* magazine printed a 112-page photo tribute—"The Day Kennedy Died: 50 Years Later: *Life* Remembers the Man and the Moment"—to the former president, which reflected his continuing popularity. The common thread of the many published conspiracy theories was that Oswald did not act alone.

Initially, many of the books published on John F. Kennedy were written by admiring "friends at court" and were highly laudatory, designed to create and preserve a legacy of his presidency. Later accounts were somewhat more critical and balanced, especially as participants, journalists, and historians focused on particular aspects or elements of Kennedy's life and brief administration.

Theodore White recounted Kennedy's presidential campaign in *The Making of the President* (1960). Three advisers close to the

president have written accounts of the Kennedy they knew: Arthur Schlesinger Jr.'s *A Thousand Days: John F. Kennedy in the White House*, Theodore Sorensen's *Kennedy* and *The Kennedy Legacy*, and Pierre Salinger's *With Kennedy*. James Giglio's *The Presidency of John F. Kennedy* provides a useful introduction to the study of Kennedy's presidency, while Herbert Parmet's earlier balanced account, *JFK: The Presidency of John F. Kennedy*, records the limitations of leadership despite personal popularity. A critical view of Kennedy's private life is provided in Thomas Reeves's *A Question of Character: A Life of John F. Kennedy*. Robert Dallek's *An Unfinished Life: John F. Kennedy, 1917–1963* offers a judicious and balanced account of Kennedy's life and presidency, based in part on newly opened medical files that suggest JFK suffered from far more dire health problems than was publicly known. James Swanson's 2013 study, *"The President Has Been Shot": The Assassination of John F. Kennedy*, and Larry Sabato's 2013 account, *The Kennedy Half-Century: The Presidency, Assassination, and Lasting Legacy of John F. Kennedy*, demonstrate again JFK's continuing popular appeal. Timothy Naftali's editorial team has provided a unique look into the real workings of the Kennedy White House by drawing upon his presidential recordings. *The Presidential Recordings*, dealing with both domestic and foreign policy issues, may present the most reliable record of the Kennedy presidency ever published. The section titled "Assassination of John F. Kennedy" notes some of the more recent accounts, such as Terry Collins's *The Assassination of John F. Kennedy, November 22, 1963*. Other accounts include Leroy Fletcher Prouty's *JFK: The CIA, Vietnam, and the Plot to Assassinate John F. Kennedy* and Jodie Hansen and Laura Hansen's *November 22, 1963: Ordinary and Extraordinary People Recall Their Reactions When They Heard the News*. This is far from a complete list of all the "conspiracy accounts" that have appeared over the years.

The political-economic policies of the 1960s have been studied in the essays collected by Mark White, *Kennedy: The New Frontier Revisited*; Hugh Davis Graham's *The Uncertain Triumph: Federal Education Policy in the Kennedy and Johnson Years* looks thoughtfully and critically at Kennedy's education policies.

Charles Pellegrino and Joshua Stoff review the decade's space program in *Chariots for Apollo: The Untold Story behind the Race to the Moon*, and David Greenstone examines the role of labor in *Labor in American Politics*.

The Supreme Court played an activist role in the 1960s, overturning several past practices. *The Unraveling of America: A History of Liberalism in the 1960s* by Allen Matusow focuses on what the author believes to be the shortcomings of liberal reforms. Competing pressures from various groups with often quite different agendas complicated domestic affairs in the 1960s.

The civil rights movement played a major role in disturbing the political processes of the decade. *The Origins of the Civil Rights Movement* by Aldon Morris emphasizes the economic and leadership of African American churches in launching the crusade, while Hugh Davis Graham's *The Civil Rights Era: Origins and Development of National Policy, 1960–1975* focuses on the roles of the executive and congressional branches. Reverend Martin Luther King Jr.'s participation during the critical first years has been told by Taylor Branch in *Pillar of Fire: America in the King Years, 1963–65*, and David Garrow's *Bearing the Cross: Martin Luther King, Jr. and the Southern Christian Leadership Conference* deals more generally with his life and the group that supported his efforts. Nick Bryant's *The Bystander: John F. Kennedy and the Struggle for Black Equality* and Carl M. Brauer's *John F. Kennedy and the Second Reconstruction* present well-researched accounts of the president's record on civil rights.

James Hanigan records King's moderate approach in *Martin Luther King, Jr. and the Foundations of Nonviolence*, while Herbert Haines's *Black Radicals and the Civil Rights Mainstream, 1954–1970* and Stokely Carmichael and Charles V. Hamilton's *Black Power: The Politics of Liberation in America* explain the motivations and activities of those willing to take more strenuous measures. Other

groups also pressed for official recognition of their entitlements and rights.

Accounts of the American Indian movement may be found in Vine Deloria's *Behind the Trail of Broken Treaties: An Indian Declaration of Independence* and Paul Chaat Smith and Robert Allen Warrior's *Like a Hurricane: The Indian Movement from Alcatraz to Wounded Knee*. Latino (Hispanic) protest movements involved several different groups pressing for changes. Susan Feriss and Richard Sandoval recount one of the more prominent and persistent struggles in *The Fight in the Fields: César Chávez and the Farmworkers Movement*, as do Dick Meister and Anne Loftis in *A Long Time Coming: The Struggle to Unionize America's Farm Workers*; Rufus Browning et al. examine the urban scene in *Protest Is Not Enough: The Struggle of Blacks and Hispanics for Equity in Urban Politics*. A more radical protest movement has been described by Tony Castro in *Chicano Power: The Emergence of Mexican American America*. Kennedy sought the Latino vote: see Ignacio Garcia, *Viva Kennedy: Mexican Americans in Search of Camelot*.

In a collection of essays, David Farber's wide-ranging retrospective, *The Sixties: From Memory to History*, examines the impact of liberal policies, the women's movement, the sexual revolution, television news, Vietnam, and other topics. In *From Margin to Mainstream: American Women and Politics since 1960*, Susan Hartmann provides a basic account of how individuals and groups put women's issues on the public agenda. Other works on the women's movement include F. Davis's *Moving the Mountain: The Women's Movement in America since 1960* and Cynthia Harrison, *On Account of Sex: The Politics of Women's Issues 1945–1968*. Other factors that contributed to the political and cultural turmoil of the 1960s are recounted by Todd Gitlin in *The Sixties: Years of Hope, Days of Rage*, Stewart Burns in *Social Movements of the 1960s: Searching for Democracy*, and Morris Dickstein in *Gates of Eden: American Culture in the Sixties*. The counterculture movement challenged traditional values; see Timothy Miller's *The '60s Communes: Hippies and Beyond* and Theodore Roszak's *The Making of a Counter Culture: Reflections on the Technocratic Society and Its Youthful Opposition*. Traditional politics were challenged by the New Left, which argued for widespread reforms, as reported by Wini Breines in *Community and Organization in the New Left, 1962–1968: The Great Refusal* and Maurice Isserman in *If I Had a Hammer: The Death of the Old Left and the Birth of the New Left*. The Students for a Democratic Society (SDS) saga is told by Jim Miller in *Democracy Is in the Streets: From Port Huron to the Siege of Chicago*. Critical interpretations of these events may be found in Jim Heath's *Decade of Disillusionment: The Kennedy-Johnson Years* and Roger Kimball's *The Long March: How the Cultural Revolution of the 1960s Changed America*. The antiwar movement and nascent antinuclear protest groups also expressed their concerns regarding government policies. As Milton Katz recounts in *Ban the Bomb: A History of SANE, the Committee for a Sane Nuclear Policy, 1957–1985*, SANE began as a protest group against nuclear testing. The most prominent "official" protestor was Senator J. William Fulbright; see William C. Berman's *William Fulbright and the Vietnam War: The Dissent of a Political Realist* and, especially, J. William Fulbright's *The Arrogance of Power*.

Foreign affairs also occupied a considerable amount of Kennedy's attention. A collection of essays, *The Diplomacy of the Crucial Decade: American Foreign Relations during the 1960s*, edited by Diane Kunz, examines many different dimensions of Kennedy's Cold War policies. Two enlightening accounts of the Cold War are Anatoly Dobrynin's *In Confidence: Moscow's Ambassador to America's Six Cold War Presidents* and Raymond Garthoff's *A Journey through the Cold War*. In *The Crisis Years: Kennedy and Khrushchev, 1960–1963*, Michael Beschloss provides a detailed examination of the crises faced by the young president—the Bay of Pigs, the Vienna Conference, Berlin, and the Cuban missile episode; Thomas Schoenbaum looks at these events from the standpoint of the secretary of state in *Waging Peace and War: Dean Rusk in the Truman, Kennedy and Johnson Years*. Thomas Patterson's collected essays,

Kennedy's Quest for Victory: American Foreign Policy, 1961–1963, and Richard Walton's *Cold War and Counter-revolution: The Foreign Policy of John F. Kennedy* present critical interpretations of Kennedy's and his administration's handling of foreign policy issues. Of the several accounts of the Cuban missile affair, Graham Allison and Philip Zelikow's *Essence of Decision: Explaining the Cuban Missile Crisis*, 2nd ed., is a standard read. Aleksandr Fursenko and Timothy Naftali's *"One Hell of a Gamble": Khrushchev, Castro, and Kennedy, 1958–1964: The Secret History of the Cuban Missile Crisis* had unprecedented access to former Soviet archives, while Ernest May and Philip Zelikow's *The Kennedy Tapes: Inside the White House during the Cuban Missile Crisis* provides transcripts of most audio recordings JFK secretly made during the episode.

The Vietnam War dominated America's foreign policy and domestic concerns during the 1960s. George Herring's *America's Longest War: The United States and Vietnam, 1950–1975* provides a fine overview of U.S. involvement in Vietnam; Marilyn Young's *The Vietnam Wars, 1945–1990* is more critical. John Newman argues that Kennedy secretly planned to withdraw completely from Vietnam after his reelection in *JFK and Vietnam: Deception, Intrigue and the Struggle for Power*. Larry Berman is critical in his book *Planning a Tragedy: The Americanization of the War in Vietnam*. Equally thoughtful are the accounts by Leslie H. Gelb and Richard K. Betts, *The Irony of Vietnam: The System Worked*, as well as David Halberstam's *The Best and the Brightest*. America's Cold War strategic military policies are discussed in Harland Moulton's *From Superiority to Parity: The United States and the Strategic Arms Race, 1961–1971* and Andreas Wenger's *Living with Peril: Eisenhower, Kennedy and Nuclear Weapons*. How the two administrations viewed Cold War threats is examined in John S. Duffield's essay "The Soviet Military Threat to Western Europe: US Estimates in the 1950s and 1960s." Former U.S. secretary of defense Robert McNamara emphasized that the balance in nuclear weaponry had resulted in mutual deterrence; see his *Blundering into Disaster: Surviving the First Century of the Nuclear Age* and Joseph Siracusa and David Colman's *Real World Nuclear Deterrence: The Making of International Strategy*. McNamara also sought to restrict antiballistic missiles, as they stimulated the arms race; see Donald Baucom's *The Origins of SDI, 1944–1983* and Edward Jayne's *The ABM Debate: Strategic Defense and National Security*.

Strategists and weapons experts have left insightful accounts; see Fred Kaplan's *The Wizards of Armageddon* and Lawrence Badash's *Scientists and the Development of Nuclear Weapons: From Fission to the Limited Test Ban Treaty, 1939–1963*. Critical of the nuclear arms race is Sidney Lens in *The Day before Doomsday: An Anatomy of the Nuclear Arms Race*. Arms control efforts to limit the potential threat of strategic weaponry are covered in McGeorge Bundy's *Danger and Survival: Choices about the Bomb in the First Fifty Years* and Robin Ranger's *Arms and Politics, 1958–1978: Arms Control in a Changing Political Context*.

Kennedy's creation of the Arms Control and Disarmament Agency is described by Duncan Clarke in *Politics of Arms Control: The Role and Effectiveness of the U.S. Arms Control and Disarmament Agency*. The debate over nuclear testing and negotiation of the limited test ban treaty are detailed in Robert Divine's *Blowing on the Wind: The Nuclear Test Ban Debate, 1954–1960* and Glenn Seaborg, *Kennedy, Khrushchev and the Test Ban*. The importance of the Non-Proliferation Treaty is discussed in Michael Fry et al., eds., *Nuclear Non-Proliferation and the Non-Proliferation Treaty*.

The following is a topical list of publications relating to John F. Kennedy, his administration, and his times.

JOHN F. KENNEDY AND FAMILY

Brauer, Carl M. *John F. Kennedy and the Second Reconstruction*. New York: Columbia University Press, 1979.

Brown, Thomas. *JFK: History of an Image*. Bloomington: Indiana University Press, 1988.

Burner, David. *John F. Kennedy and a New Generation*. Boston: Little, Brown, 1988.

Clarke, Thurston. *JFK's Last Hundred Days: The Transformation of a Man and the Emergence of a Great President*. New York: Penguin, 2013.

Clymer, Adam. *Edward M. Kennedy: A Biography*. New York: Morrow, 1999.

Collins, Max Allen. *Ask Not*. New York: Forge, 2013.

Dallek, Robert. *An Unfinished Life: John F. Kennedy, 1917–1963*. New York: Little, Brown, 2003.

Davis, John H. *The Kennedys: Dynasty and Disaster, 1848–1983*. New York: McGraw-Hill, 1984.

Dean, Robert D. "Masculinity as Ideology: John F. Kennedy and the Domestic Politics of Foreign Policy." *Diplomatic History* 22, no. 1 (1998).

Douglass, James W. *JFK and the Unspeakable: Why He Died and Why It Matters*. New York: Simon & Schuster, 2008.

Edison, Erin. *John F. Kennedy*. North Mankato, MN: Capstone Press, 2013.

Farris, Scott. *Kennedy and Reagan: Why Their Legacies Endure*. Guilford, CT: Lyons Press, 2013.

Freedman, Eric, and Edward Hoffman. *John F. Kennedy in His Own Words*. New York: Citadel Press, 2006.

Giglio, James N. *The Presidency of John F. Kennedy*. Lawrence: University Press of Kansas, 1991.

Harper, Paul, and Joann Krieg. *John F. Kennedy: The Promise Revisited*. New York: Greenwood, 1988.

Hersh, Seymour. *The Dark Side of Camelot*. Hammersmith, London: HarperCollins, 1997.

Heymann, C. David. *American Legacy: The Story of John and Caroline Kennedy*. New York: Atria, 2002.

Kennedy, John F. *A Nation of Immigrants*. 2nd ed. New York: Harper Torchbooks, 1964.

Leamer, Laurence. *The Kennedy Men, 1901–1963: The Laws of the Father*. New York: Morrow, 2001.

Leaming, Barbara. *The Education of a Statesman*. New York: Norton, 2006.

Maier, Thomas. *The Kennedys: America's Emerald Kings*. New York: Basic, 2003.

Naftali, Timothy, Philip Zelikow, and Ernest May, eds. *The Presidential Recordings: John F. Kennedy: The Great Crises*. 3 vols. New York: Norton, 2001.

Navasky, Victor S. *Kennedy Justice*. New York: Atheneum, 1971.

O'Brien, Michael. *John F. Kennedy: A Biography*. New York: St. Martin's, 2005.

Paper, Lewis J. *John F. Kennedy: The Promise and the Performance*. New York: Crown, 1975.

Parmet, Herbert S. *Jack: The Struggles of John F. Kennedy*. New York: Dial, 1983.

———. *JFK: The Presidency of John F. Kennedy*. New York: Dial, 1980.

Public Papers of the Presidents of the United States: John F. Kennedy. 3 vols. Washington, DC: Government Printing Office, 1962–1964.

Reeves, Thomas C. *A Question of Character: A Life of John F. Kennedy*. New York: Free Press, 1991.

Reich, Scott D. *The Power of Citizenship: Why John F. Kennedy Matters to a New Generation*. Dallas, TX: BenBella, 2013.

Riemer, Neal. "Kennedy's Grand Democratic Design." *Review of Politics* 27, no. 1 (January 1965): 3–16.

Salinger, Pierre. *With Kennedy*. Garden City, NY: Doubleday, 1966.

Schlesinger, Arthur M., Jr. *A Thousand Days: John F. Kennedy in the White House*. Boston: Houghton Mifflin, 1965.

———. *Jacqueline Kennedy: The White House Years*. Boston: Bullfinch Press / Little, Brown, 2011.

Sorenson, Theodore C. *Kennedy*. New York: Harper & Row, 1965.

———. *The Kennedy Legacy*. New York: Macmillan, 1969.

Von Hoffman, Alexander. *John F. Kennedy's Birthplace, a Presidential Home in History and Memory: A Historic Resource Study*. Washington, DC: National Park Service, U.S. Department of the Interior, 2007.

White, Theodore H. *The Making of the President, 1960*. New York: Atheneum, 1961.

Wills, Gary. *The Kennedy Imprisonment: A Meditation in Power*. Boston: Little, Brown, 1982.

OTHER PERSONALITIES

Abramson, Rudy. *Spanning the Century: The Life of W. Averell Harriman, 1891–1986*. New York: Morrow, 1992.

Ambrose, Stephen E. *Eisenhower: Soldier and President*. New York: Simon & Schuster, 1990.

Ball, George W. *The Past Has Another Pattern: Memoirs*. New York: Norton, 1982.

Bill, James A. *George Ball: Behind the Scenes in U.S. Foreign Policy*. New Haven, CT: Yale University Press, 1997.

Bird, Kai. *The Color of Truth: McGeorge Bundy and William Bundy: Brothers in Arms*. New York: Simon & Schuster, 1998.

Brinkley, David. *Brinkley's Beat*. New York: Knopf, 2003.

Brinkley, Douglas. *Dean Acheson: The Cold War Years, 1953–71*. New Haven, CT: Yale University Press, 1992.

Broadwater, Jeff. *Adlai Stevenson: The Odyssey of a Cold War Liberal*. New York: Twayne, 1994.

Byrd, Robert C. *Child of the Appalachian Coalfields*. Morgantown: West Virginia University Press, 2005.

Callahan, David. *Dangerous Capabilities: Paul Nitze and the Cold War*. New York: Harper & Row, 1990.

Clifford, Clark, with Richard C. Holbrook. *Counsel to the President: A Memoir*. New York: Random House, 1991.

Cohen, Adam, and Elizabeth Taylor. *American Pharaoh: Mayor Richard J. Daley; His Battle for Chicago and the Nation*. Boston: Little, Brown, 2000.

DiLeo, David M. *George Ball, Vietnam, and the Rethinking of Containment*. Chapel Hill: University of North Carolina Press, 1991.

Dillon, C. Douglas. *The International Monetary System: An American Perspective*. Ditchley Park, UK: Ditchley Foundation, 1966.

Dobrynin, Anatoly. *In Confidence: Moscow's Ambassador to America's Six Cold War Presidents*. New York: Times Books, 1995.

Dulles, Allen. *The Craft of Intelligence*. New York: Harper & Row, 1963.

Forte, David. *The Policies and Principles of Dean Rusk*. Toronto: University of Toronto Press, 1974.

Garthoff, Raymond L. *A Journey through the Cold War*. Washington, DC: Brookings, 2001.

Graham, Katherine. *Personal History*. New York: Knopf, 1997.

Halberstam, David. *The Best and the Brightest*. New York: Vintage, 1993.

Hayden, Tom. *Reunion: A Memoir*. New York: Times Books, 1988.

Helms, Richard. *A Look over My Shoulder: A Life in the Central Intelligence Agency*. New York: Random House, 2003.

Herken, Gregg. *The Georgetown Set: Friends and Rivals in Cold War Washington*. New York: Vintage, 2014.

Herskowitz, Mickey. *Duty, Honor, Country: The Life and Legacy of Prescott Bush*. Nashville, TN: Rutledge Hill Press, 2003.

Hilsman, Roger. *To Move a Nation*. New York: Doubleday, 1972.

Hodgson, Godfrey. *The Gentleman from New York: Daniel Patrick Moynihan*. Boston: Houghton Mifflin, 2000.

Katzmann, Robert A., ed. *Daniel Patrick Moynihan: The Intellectual in Public Life*. Washington, DC: Woodrow Wilson Center Press, 1998.

Kennan, George F. *Memoirs*. 2 vols. Boston: Little, Brown, 1967.

Kennedy, Robert. *To Seek a Newer World*. Garden City, NY: Doubleday, 1967.

Khrushchev, Nikita. *Khrushchev Remembers: The Glasnost Tapes*. Boston: Little, Brown, 1990.

Khrushchev, Sergei. *Nikita Khrushchev and the Creation of a Superpower*. Translated by Shirley Benson. University Park: Pennsylvania State University Press, 2000.

Kinzer, Stephen. *The Brothers: John Foster Dulles, Allen Dulles, and Their Secret World War*. New York: Times Books, 2013.

Martin, John Bartlow. *Adlai Stevenson and the World: The Life of Adlai Stevenson*. New York: Doubleday, 1977.

———. *Adlai Stevenson of Illinois: The Life of Adlai Stevenson*. New York: Doubleday, 1976.

McNamara, Robert. *Blundering into Disaster: Surviving the First Century of the Nuclear Age*. New York: Pantheon, 1986.

Mills, Judie. *Robert Kennedy*. Brookfield, CT: Millbrook Press, 1998.

Moynihan, Daniel Patrick. *On the Law of Nations*. Cambridge, MA: Harvard University Press, 1990.

Murray, Pauli. *The Autobiography of a Black Activist, Feminist, Lawyer, Priest and Poet*. Knoxville: University of Tennessee Press, 1989.

Nitze, Paul H., with Steven L. Rearden and Ann M. Smith. *From Hiroshima to Glasnost: At the Center of Decisions, a Memoir*. New York: Weidenfeld and Nicolson, 1898.

Oberdorfer, Don. *Senator Mansfield: The Extraordinary Life of a Great American Statesman and Diplomat*. Washington, DC: Smithsonian, 2003.

Olsen, Jack. *The Bridge at Chappaquiddick*. Boston: Little, Brown, 1970.

Prouty, Marco G. *Cesar Chavez, the Catholic Bishops, and the Farmworkers' Struggle for Social Justice*. Tucson: University of Arizona Press, 2006.

Ruddy, T. Michael. *The Cautious Diplomat: Charles E. Bohlen and the Soviet Union, 1929–1969*. Kent, OH: Kent State University Press, 1986.

Rusk, Dean, as told to Richard Rusk. *As I Saw It*. New York: Norton, 1990.

Schiesl, Martin, ed. *Responsible Liberalism: Edmund G. "Pat" Brown and Reform Government in California, 1958–1967*. Los Angeles: California State University, Los Angeles, Edmund G. "Pat" Brown Institute of Public Affairs, 2003.

Schlesinger, Arthur M., Jr. *Robert Kennedy and His Times*. New York: Random House, 1978.

Schoenbaum, Thomas J. *Waging Peace and War: Dean Rusk in the Truman, Kennedy and Johnson Years*. New York: Simon & Schuster, 1988.

Smith, Gaddis. *Dean Acheson*. New York: Cooper Square, 1972.

Smith, Jean Edward. *Lucius D. Clay: An American Life*. New York: Holt, 1990.

Srodes, James. *Allen Dulles: Master of Spies*. Washington, DC: Regnery, 1999.

Steel, Ronald. *In Love with Night: The American Romance with Robert Kennedy*. New York: Simon & Schuster, 2000.

Taubman, William. *Khrushchev: The Man and His Era*. New York: Norton, 2003.

Taylor, Maxwell D. *Swords and Ploughshares*. New York: Norton, 1972.

Valeo, Francis R. *Mike Mansfield, Majority Leader: A Different Kind of Senate, 1961–1976*. Armonk, NY: Sharpe, 1999.

Wilkins, Roy. *Standing Fast: The Autobiography of Roy Wilkins*. New York: Viking, 1982.

Zeiler, Thomas W. *Dean Rusk: Defending the American Mission Abroad*. Wilmington, DE: Scholarly Resources, 2000.

AFRICAN AMERICANS

Baldwin, James. *Nobody Knows My Name: More Notes of a Native Son*. New York: Dial Press, 1963.

Brown, H. Rap. *Die, Nigger, Die!* New York: Dial Press, 1969.

Carmichael, Stokely. *Stokely Speaks: Black Power Back to Pan-Africanism*. New York: Random House, 1971.

Carmichael, Stokely, and Charles V. Hamilton. *Black Power: The Politics of Liberation in America*. New York: Random House, 1967.

Carson, Clayborne. *In Struggle: SNCC and the Black Awakening of the 1960s*. Cambridge, MA: Harvard University Press, 1981.

Cleaver, Eldridge. *Eldridge Cleaver: Post-Prison Writings and Speeches*. New York: Random House, 1969.

———. *Soul on Ice*. New York: McGraw-Hill, 1967.

Colaiaco, James A. *Martin Luther King, Jr.: Apostle of Militant Nonviolence*. New York: St. Martin's, 1988.

Cottrell, John. *Muhammad Ali, Who Once Was Cassius Clay*. New York: Funk & Wagnalls, 1968.

Davis, Angela. *Angela Davis: An Autobiography*. New York: Random House, 1974.

——. *If They Come in the Morning: Voices of Resistance.* Foreword by Julian Bond. New York: Third Press, 1971.

de Graaf, Lawrence B., Kevin Mulroy, and Quintard Taylor, eds. *Seeking El Dorado: African Americans in California.* Los Angeles: Autry Museum of Western Heritage, in association with University of Washington Press, 2001.

Evers, Mrs. Medgar. *For Us, the Living.* Garden City, NY: Doubleday, 1967.

Fairclough, Adam. *To Redeem the Soul of America: The Southern Christian Leadership Conference and Martin Luther King, Jr.* Athens: University of Georgia Press, 1987.

Finch, Minnie. *The NAACP: Its Fight for Justice.* Metuchen, NJ: Scarecrow Press, 1981.

Foner, Philip S., ed. *The Black Panthers Speak.* Philadelphia, PA: Lippincott, 1970.

Forman, James. *Making of Black Revolutionaries: A Personal Account.* New York: Macmillan, 1972.

——. *Sammy Younge, Jr.: The First Black College Student to Die in the Black Liberation Movement.* Washington, DC: Open Hand, 1986.

Garrow, David. *Bearing the Cross: Martin Luther King, Jr. and the Southern Christian Leadership Conference.* New York: Morrow, 1986.

——, ed. *Martin Luther King Jr. and the Civil Rights Movement.* 18 vols. Brooklyn, NY: Carlson, 1985–1990.

Goudsouzian, Aram. *Down to the Crossroads: Civil Rights, Black Power, and the Meredith March against Fear.* New York: Farrar, Straus & Giroux, 2014.

Haines, Herbert. *Black Radicals and the Civil Rights Mainstream, 1954–1970.* Knoxville: University of Tennessee Press, 1988.

Hampton, Henry, and Steve Fayer, with Sarah Flynn. *Voices of Freedom: An Oral History of the Civil Rights Movement.* New York: Bantam, 1990.

Hanigan, James P. *Martin Luther King, Jr. and the Foundations of Nonviolence.* Lanham, MD: University Press of America, 1984.

Harris, Fred R., and Roger W. Wilkins. *Quiet Riots: Race and Poverty in the United States.* New York: Pantheon, 1988.

Hubert, M. "The Vietnam War and American Civil Liberties Movement." *Journal of Ethnic Studies* 16 (Winter 1989): 117–41.

King, Coretta Scott. *My Life with Martin Luther King, Jr.* New York: Holt, Rinehart & Winston, 1969.

King, Martin Luther, Jr. *A Testament of Hope: The Essential Writings of Martin Luther King, Jr.* Edited by James M. Washington. San Francisco: Harper & Row, 1986.

McCormick, Richard P. *The Black Student Protest Movement at Rutgers.* New Brunswick, NJ: Rutgers University Press, 1990.

Meier, August, and Elliott Rudwick. *CORE: A Study in the Civil Rights Movement, 1942–1968.* New York: Oxford University Press, 1973.

O'Reilly, Kenneth. *"Racial Matters": The FBI's Secret File on Black America, 1960–1972.* New York: Free Press, 1989.

Powell, Adam Clayton. *Adam by Adam: The Autobiography of Adam Clayton Powell, Jr.* New York: Dial Press, 1971.

Risen, Clay. *The Bill of the Century: The Epic Battle for the Civil Rights Act.* New York: Bloomsbury, 2014.

Rivlin, Benjamin, ed. *Ralph Bunche, the Man and His Times.* New York: Holmes & Meier, 1990.

Rudwick, Elliot, August Meier, and John Bracey Jr., eds. *Black Protest in the Sixties: Articles from the* New York Times Magazine. New York: Markus Wiener, 1990.

Rustin, Bayard. *Down the Line: The Collected Writings.* Chicago: Quadrangle, 1971.

United States Congress, House. *Civil Rights Acts of 1957, 1960, 1964.* Washington, DC: Government Printing Office, 1970.

Weiss, Nancy J. *Whitney M. Young, Jr. and the Struggle for Civil Rights.* Princeton, NJ: Princeton University Press, 1989.

Wilkins, Roger W. *A Man's Life: An Autobiography.* New York: Simon & Schuster, 1982.

Wilkins, Roy. *Standing Fast: The Autobiography of Roy Wilkins.* New York: Viking, 1982.

——. *Talking It Over with Roy Wilkins: Selected Speeches and Writings.* Compiled by Helen Solomon and Aminda Wilkins. Norwalk, CT: M & B, 1977.

X, Malcolm. *The Autobiography of Malcolm X*. With the assistance of Alex Haley. Introduction by M. S. Handler. Epilogue by Alex Haley. New York: Grove Press, 1965.

———. *The Speeches of Malcolm X at Harvard*. Edited with an introductory essay by Archie Epps. New York: Morrow, 1968.

Zinn, Howard. *SNCC: The New Abolitionists*. Westport, CT: Greenwood, 1985.

AMERICAN INDIAN MOVEMENT (FIRST AMERICANS)

Brand, Johanna. *The Life and Death of Anna Mae Aquash*. Toronto: J. Lorimer, 1978.

Brave Bird, Mary, and Richard Erdoes. *Ohitika Woman*. New York: Harper Perennial, 1994.

Cheatham, Kae. *Dennis Banks: Native American Activist*. Springfield, NJ: Enslow, 1997.

Churchill, Ward, and Jim Vander Wall. *Agents of Repression: The FBI's Secret War against the Black Panther Party and the American Indian Movement*. Boston: South End Press, 1988.

———. *Since Predator Came: Notes from the Struggle for American Indian Liberation*. Littleton, CO: Aigis, 1995.

Deloria, Vine. *Behind the Trail of Broken Treaties: An Indian Declaration of Independence*. New York: Dell, 1974.

Kelleher, Michael. "The Removal of the Southeastern Indians: Historians Respond to the 1960s and the Trail of Tears." *Chronicles of Oklahoma* 78 (Fall 2000): 346–53.

Matthiessen, Peter. *In the Spirit of Crazy Horse*. New York: Viking, 1983.

Peltier, Leonard. *Prison Writings: My Life Is My Sundance*. Edited by Harvey Arden. New York: St. Martin's, 1999.

Riggs, Christopher K. "American Indians, Economic Development, and Self-Determination in the 1960s." *Pacific Historical Review* 69 (August 2000): 431–63.

Smith, Paul Chaat, and Robert Allen Warrior. *Like a Hurricane: The Indian Movement from Alcatraz to Wounded Knee*. New York: New Press, 1997.

United States Congress, Senate. *Committee on the Judiciary. Subcommittee to Investigate the Administration of the Internal Security Act and Other Internal Security Laws. Revolutionary Activities within the United States: The American Indian Movement; Hearing before the Subcommittee to Investigate the Administration of the Internal Security Act and Other Internal Security Laws of the Committee on the Judiciary, United States Senate*. 94th Congress, 2nd session, April 6, 1976. Washington, DC: Government Printing Office, 1976.

Weyler, Rex. *Blood of the Land: The Government and Corporate War against the American Indian Movement*. New York: Everest House, 1982.

Wideman, John Edgar. "Russell Means: The Profound and Outspoken Activist Shares Some of His Most Ardent Convictions." *Modern Maturity* 38, no. 5 (September–October 1995): 68–79.

ARMS CONTROL/DISARMAMENT

Ayson, Robert. "Bargaining with Nuclear Weapons: Thomas Schelling's 'General' Concept of Stability." *Journal of Strategic Studies* (London) 23 (June 2000): 48–71.

Barton, John H. *The Politics of Peace: An Evaluation of Arms Control*. Stanford, CA: Stanford University Press, 1981.

Brown, James, ed. *Arms Control in a Multipolar World*. Amsterdam: Vu University Press, 1996.

Bundy, McGeorge. *Danger and Survival: Choices about the Bomb in the First Fifty Years*. New York: Random House, 1988.

———. "Kennedy and the Nuclear Question." In *The Kennedy Presidency*, edited by Kenneth W. Thompson. Lanham, MD: University Press of America, 1985.

Burns, Richard Dean. *The Evolution of Arms Control: From Antiquity to the Nuclear Age*. Santa Barbara, CA: Praeger, 2009.

Clarke, Duncan L. *Politics of Arms Control: The Role and Effectiveness of the U.S. Arms Control and Disarmament Agency*. New York: Free Press, 1979.

Freeman, J. P. G. *Britain's Nuclear Arms Control Policy in the Context of Anglo-American Relations, 1957–68*. New York: St. Martin's, 1986.

Fry, Michael P., N. Patrick Keatinge, and Joseph Rotblat, eds. *Nuclear Non-Proliferation and the Non-Proliferation Treaty.* New York: Springer, 1990.

Fuhrmann, Matthew. *Atomic Assistance: How "Atoms for Peace" Programs Cause Nuclear Insecurity.* Ithaca, NY: Cornell University Press, 2012.

Garfinkle, Adam M., ed. *Global Perspectives on Arms Control.* New York: Praeger, 1984.

Goldman, Ralph M. *Arms Control and Peacekeeping: Feeling Safe in This World.* New York: Random House, 1982.

Goldstein, Martin E. *Arms Control and Military Preparedness from Truman to Bush.* New York: Peter Lang, 1993.

Graham, Thomas, Jr. *Disarmament Sketches: Three Decades of Arms Control and International Law.* Seattle: University of Washington Press, 2002.

Hewlett, Richard G., and Jack M. Holl. *Atoms for Peace and War: Eisenhower and the Atomic Energy Commission.* Berkeley: University of California Press, 1989.

Horn, Sally K. "The Hotline." In *Avoiding War in the Nuclear Age: Confidence-Building Measures for Crisis Stability*, edited by John Borawski, 43–55. Boulder, CO: Westview, 1986.

Jasani, Bhupendra, ed. *Space Weapons—the Arms Control Dilemma.* London: Taylor & Francis, 1984.

Orwell, Russell B. *The International Atomic Energy Agency.* New York: Chelsea House, 2009.

Ranger, Robin. *Arms and Politics, 1958–1978: Arms Control in a Changing Political Context.* Toronto: Gage, 1979.

Winkler, David F. *Cold War at Sea: High-Seas Confrontation between the United States and the Soviet Union.* Annapolis, MD: Naval Institute Press, 2000.

ASSASSINATION OF JOHN F. KENNEDY

Collins, Terry. *The Assassination of John F. Kennedy, November 22, 1963.* Chicago: Heinemann Library, 2014.

Emmett, Dan. *Within Arm's Length: A Secret Service Agent's Definitive Inside Account of Protecting the President.* New York: St. Martin's, 2014.

George, Alice L. *The Assassination of John F. Kennedy: Political Trauma and American Memory.* New York: Routledge, 2013.

Hansen, Jodie Elliott, and Laura Hansen. *November 22, 1963: Ordinary and Extraordinary People Recall Their Reactions When They Heard the News.* New York: Dunne / St. Martin's, 2013.

Hill, Clint, and Lisa McCubbin. *Five Days in November.* New York: Gallery, 2013.

Mailer, Norman. *Oswald's Tale: An American Mystery.* New York: Random House, 1995.

McAdams, John. *JFK Assassination Logic: How to Think about Claims of Conspiracy.* Lincoln, NE: Potomac, 2014.

McClellan, Barr. *The Verdict: Justice for J.F.K., Justice for America.* Springdale, AR: Hannover House, 2014.

Nardo, Don. *Assassination and Its Aftermath: How a Photograph Reassured a Shocked Nation.* North Mankato, MN: Compass Point, 2014.

Posner, Gerald L. *Case Closed: Lee Harvey Oswald and the Assassination of JFK.* New York: Random House, 1995.

Prouty, Leroy Fletcher. *JFK: The CIA, Vietnam, and the Plot to Assassinate John F. Kennedy.* New York: Skyhorse, 2013.

Sabato, Larry J. *The Kennedy Half-Century: The Presidency, Assassination, and Lasting Legacy of John F. Kennedy.* New York: Bloomsbury, 2013.

Swanson, James L. *"The President Has Been Shot": The Assassination of John F. Kennedy.* New York: Scholastic, 2013.

Willens, Howard P. *History Will Prove Us Right: Inside the Warren Commission Report on the Assassination of John F. Kennedy.* New York: Overlook Press, 2013.

CIVIL RIGHTS MOVEMENT

Ashmore, Harry S. *Civil Rights and Wrongs: A Memoir of Race and Politics, 1944–1996.*

Columbia: University of South Carolina Press, 1997.

Blumberg, Rhoda Lois. *Civil Rights: The 1960s Freedom Struggle*. New York: Twayne, 1991.

Branch, Taylor. *Pillar of Fire: America in the King Years, 1963–65*. New York: Simon & Schuster, 1998.

Brauer, Carl M. *John F. Kennedy and the Second Reconstruction*. New York: Columbia University Press, 1977.

Brown, Jennie. *Medgar Evers*. Los Angeles: Melrose Square, 1994.

Bryant, Nick. *The Bystander: John F. Kennedy and the Struggle for Black Equality*. New York: Basic, 2006.

Burstein, Paul. "Public Opinion, Demonstrations, and the Passage of Antidiscrimination Legislation." *Public Opinion Quarterly* 43, no. 2 (Summer 1979): 157–72.

Davidson, C., and B. Grofman. *Quiet Revolution in the South: The Impact of the Voting Rights Act, 1965–1990*. Princeton, NJ: Princeton University Press, 1994.

Eldridge, Lawrence Allen. *Chronicles of a Two-Front War: Civil Rights and Vietnam in the African American Press*. Columbia: University of Missouri Press, 2011.

Ellis, Sylvia. *Freedom's Pragmatist: Lyndon Johnson and Civil Rights*. Gainesville: University Press of Florida, 2013.

Freeman, Jo. "How 'Sex' Got into Title VII: Persistent Opportunism as a Maker of Public Policy." *Law and Inequality: A Journal of Theory and Practice* 9, no. 2 (March 1991): 163–84.

Garrow, David J. *Bearing the Cross: Martin Luther King, Jr. and the Southern Christian Leadership Conference*. New York: Vintage, 1988.

Goduti, Philip A. *Robert F. Kennedy and the Shaping of Civil Rights, 1960–1964*. Jefferson, NC: McFarland, 2013.

Graham, Hugh Davis. *The Civil Rights Era: Origins and Development of National Policy, 1960–1972*. New York: Oxford University Press, 1990.

Humphrey, Hubert H. *Beyond Civil Rights: A New Day of Equality*. New York: Random House, 1968.

King, Mary. *Freedom Song: A Personal Story of the 1960s Civil Rights Movement*. New York: Morrow, 1987.

Loevy, Robert D. *To End All Segregation: The Politics and Passage of the Civil Rights Act of 1964*. Lanham, MD: University Press of America, 1990.

Matthews, Christopher. *Kennedy & Nixon: The Rivalry That Shaped Postwar America*. New York: Simon & Schuster, 1996.

Morris, Aldon D. *The Origins of the Civil Rights Movement*. New York: Free Press, 1984.

Polenberg, Richard. *One Nation Divisible: Class, Race, and Ethnicity in the United States since 1938*. New York: Penguin, 1980.

Powledge, Fred. *Free at Last? The Civil Rights Movement and the People Who Made It*. Boston: Little, Brown, 1991.

Purdum, Todd S. *An Idea Whose Time Has Come: Two Presidents, Two Parties, and the Battle for the Civil Rights Act of 1964*. New York: Holt, 2014.

Salmond, John A. *"My Mind Set on Freedom": A History of the Civil Rights Movement, 1954–1968*. Chicago: Ivan R. Dee, 1997.

Smith, Robert Charles. *John F. Kennedy, Barack Obama, and the Politics of Ethnic Incorporation and Avoidance*. Albany: State University of New York Press, 2013.

Viorst, Milton. *Fire in the Streets: America in the 1960s*. New York: Simon & Schuster, 1979.

Weisbrot, Robert. *Freedom Bound: A History of America's Civil Rights Movement*. New York: Norton, 1990.

Whalen, Charles, and Barbara Whalen. *The Longest Debate: A Legislative History of the 1964 Civil Rights Act*. Cabin John, MD: Seven Locks Press, 1985.

Williams, Juan. *Eyes on the Prize: America's Civil Rights Years, 1954–1965*. New York: Viking, 1987.

Williams, Michael V. *Medgar Evers: Mississippi Martyr*. Fayetteville: University of Arkansas Press, 2011.

Zinn, Howard. *Howard Zinn on Race*. New York: Seven Stories Press, 2011.

CUBAN MISSILE CRISIS (1962)

Absher, Kenneth Michael. *Mind-Sets and Missiles: A First Hand Account of the Cuban Missile Crisis.* Carlisle, PA: Strategic Studies Institute, U.S. Army War College, 2009.

Allison, Graham T., and Philip D. Zelikow. *Essence of Decision: Explaining the Cuban Missile Crisis.* 2nd ed. New York: Longman, 1999.

Blight, James G., and David A. Welch. *On the Brink: Americans and Soviets Reexamine the Cuban Missile Crisis.* New York: Hill & Wang, 1989.

Brugioni, Dino A. *Eyeball to Eyeball: The Inside Story of the Cuban Missile Crisis.* New York: Random House, 1991.

Brune, Lester H. *The Cuba-Caribbean Missile Crisis of October 1962.* Claremont, CA: Regina Books, 1996.

Chayes, Abram. *The Cuban Missile Crisis, International Crisis and the Role of Law.* 2nd ed. New York: Oxford University Press, 1987.

Diez Acosta, Tomás. *October 1962: The "Missile" Crisis as Seen from Cuba.* New York: Pathfinder Press, 2002.

Divine, Robert A., ed. *The Cuban Missile Crisis.* New York: M. Wiener, 1988.

Frankel, Max. *High Noon in the Cold War: Kennedy, Khrushchev, and the Cuban Missile Crisis.* New York: Ballantine, 2004.

Fursenko, Aleksandr, and Timothy Naftali. *"One Hell of a Gamble": Khrushchev, Castro, and Kennedy, 1958–1964: The Secret History of the Cuban Missile Crisis.* New York: Norton, 1997.

Gioe, David, Len Scott, and Christopher Andrew, eds. *An International History of the Cuban Missile Crisis: New Perspectives after Fifty Years.* Abingdon, Oxon: Routledge, 2014.

Kennedy, Robert. *Thirteen Days: A Memoir of the Cuban Missile Crisis.* New York: Norton, 1969.

May, Ernest R., and Philip D. Zelikow, eds. *The Kennedy Tapes: Inside the White House during the Cuban Missile Crisis.* Cambridge, MA: Belknap Press, 1997.

Nathan, James A., ed. *The Cuban Missile Crisis Revisited.* New York: St. Martin's, 1992.

Polmar, Norman, and John D. Gresham. *DEFCON–2: Standing on the Brink of Nuclear War during the Cuban Missile Crisis.* New York: Wiley, 2006.

Pope, Ronald R. *Soviet Views on the Cuban Missile Crisis: Myth and Reality in Foreign Policy Analysis.* Lanham, MD: University Press of America, 1982.

Senker, Cath. *Kennedy and the Cuban Missile Crisis.* Chicago: Heinemann Library, 2014.

Stern, Sheldon M. *Averting the Final Failure: John F. Kennedy and the Secret Cuban Missile Crisis Meetings.* Stanford, CA: Stanford University Press, 2003.

———. *The Cuban Missile Crisis in American Memory: Myths versus Reality.* Stanford, CA: Stanford University Press, 2012.

Weisbot, Robert. *Maximum Danger: Kennedy, the Missiles, and the Crisis of American Confidence.* Chicago: Ivan R. Dee, 2001.

White, Mark J. *The Cuban Missile Crisis.* Basingstoke, UK: Macmillan, 1996.

———. *The Kennedys and Cuba: The Declassified Documentary History.* Rev. ed. Chicago: Ivan R. Dee, 2003.

Zelikow, Philip D., and Ernest R. May, eds. *The Kennedy Tapes: Inside the White House during the Cuban Missile Crisis.* Concise ed. New York: Norton, 2002.

CULTURE

Baldwin, James. *Nobody Knows My Name: More Notes of a Native Son.* New York: Dial Press, 1963.

Buhle, Paul, ed. *History and the New Left: Madison Wisconsin, 1950–1970.* Philadelphia, PA: Temple University Press, 1990.

Burns, Stewart. *Social Movements of the 1960s: Searching for Democracy.* Boston: Twayne, 1990.

Dickstein, Morris. *Gates of Eden: American Culture in the Sixties.* New York: Basic, 1977.

Gitlin, Todd. *The Sixties: Years of Hope, Days of Rage.* New York: Bantam, 1987.

———. *The Whole World Is Watching: Mass Media in the Making and Unmaking of the New Left.* Berkeley: University of California Press, 1980.

Hine, Thomas. *The Rise and Fall of the American Teenager*. New York: Bard, 1999.

Kerr, Clark. *The Great Transformation in Higher Education, 1960–1980*. Albany: State University of New York Press, 1999.

Kimball, Roger. *Tenured Radicals: How Politics Has Corrupted Our Higher Education*. Scranton, PA: Harper & Row, 1990.

———. *The Long March: How the Cultural Revolution of the 1960s Changed America*. San Francisco: Encounter, 2000.

King, Richard. *The Party of Eros*. Chapel Hill: University of North Carolina Press, 1972.

Koerselman, Gary H. *The Lost Decade: A Story of America in the 1960s*. New York: Peter Lang, 1987.

Lee, Martin A., and Bruce Shlain. *Acid Dreams: The CIA, LSD, and the Sixties Rebellion*. New York: Grove Press, 1985.

Margolis, Jon. *The Last Innocent Year: America in 1964*. New York: Morrow, 1999.

Miller, Timothy. *The '60s Communes: Hippies and Beyond*. Syracuse, NY: Syracuse University Press, 1999.

Murray, Charles. *Losing Ground: American Social Policy, 1950–1980*. New York: Basic, 1995.

Peck, Abe. *Dancing Madness*. New York: Anchor Press, 1976.

———. *Uncovering the Sixties: The Life and Times of the Underground Press*. New York: Pantheon, 1985.

Penkower, Monty Noam. *Twentieth-Century Jews: Forging Identities in the Land of Promise and the Promised Land*. Boston: Academic Studies Press, 2010.

Rorabaugh, W. J. *Berkeley at War: The 1960s*. New York: Oxford University Press, 1989.

Roszak, Theodore. *The Making of a Counter Culture: Reflections on the Technocratic Society and Its Youthful Opposition*. Garden City, NY: Doubleday, 1969.

Spring, Joel. *Conflicts of Interest: The Politics of American Education*. New York: Longman, 1993.

Sulzberger, C. L. *Fathers and Children*. New York: Arbor House, 1987.

Wouters, Cas. "Balancing Sex and Love since the 1960s Sexual Revolution." *Theory, Culture, and Society* 15 (August–November 1998): 187–214.

Yinger, John Milton. *Countercultures: The Promise and the Peril of a World Turned Upside Down*. New York: Free Press, 1982.

DOMESTIC AFFAIRS

Albert, Judith Clavir, and Stewart Edward Albert, eds. *The Sixties Papers: Documents of a Rebellious Decade*. New York: Praeger, 1984.

Anderson, Terry H. *The Movement and the Sixties*. New York: Oxford University Press, 1995.

———. *The Pursuit of Fairness: A History of Affirmative Action*. New York: Oxford University Press, 2004.

———. *The Sixties*. New York: Oxford University Press, 1996.

Bennett, Marion T. "The Immigration and Nationality (McCarran-Walter) Act of 1952, as Amended to 1965." *Annals of the American Academy of Political and Social Science* 367 (September 1966): 127–36.

Berman, Ronald. *America in the Sixties: An Intellectual History*. New York: Free Press, 1968.

Bok, Derek C., and John T. Dunlap. *Labor and the American Community*. New York: Simon & Schuster, 1970.

Brauer, Carl M. *John F. Kennedy and the Second Reconstruction*. New York: Columbia University Press, 1977.

Cherny, Robert W., William Issel, and Kieran Walsh Taylor. *American Labor and the Cold War*. New Brunswick, NJ: Rutgers University Press, 2004.

Churchill, Ward, and Jim Vander Wall. *The COINTELPRO Papers: Documents from the FBI's Secret Wars against Domestic Dissent*. Boston: South End Press, 1990.

Cluster, Dick, ed. *They Should Have Served That Cup of Coffee: Seven Radicals Remember the '60s*. Boston: South End Press, 1979.

Collier, Peter, and David Horowitz. *Destructive Generation: Second Thoughts about the Sixties*. New York: Summit, 1989.

Ehrlich, Paul. *The Population Bomb*. New York: Ballantine, 1968.

Farber, David. *The Age of Great Dreams: America in the 1960s*. New York: Hill & Wang, 1994.

———, ed. *The Sixties: From Memory to History*. Chapel Hill: University of North Carolina Press, 1994.

Foner, Philip S. *Organized Labor and the Black Worker, 1619–1973*. New York: International, 1976.

Gagliardi, Robert M. *Satellite Communications*. New York: Van Nostrand Reinhold, 1984.

Greenstone, J. David. *Labor in American Politics*. New York: Knopf, 1969.

Hasmath, Reza, ed. *Managing Ethnic Diversity: Meanings and Practices from an International Perspective*. Burlington, VT: Ashgate, 2011.

Heath, Jim F. *Decade of Disillusionment: The Kennedy-Johnson Years*. Bloomington: Indiana University Press, 1975.

———. *John F. Kennedy and the Business Community*. Chicago: University of Chicago Press, 1969.

Higgins, George G. *Organized Labor and the Church: Reflections of a "Labor Priest."* New York: Paulist Press, 1993.

Hoffman, Pat. *Ministry of the Dispossessed: Learning from the Farm Worker Movement*. Los Angeles: Wallace Press, 1987.

Kay, W. D. "Problem Definitions and Policy Contradictions: John F. Kennedy and the 'Space Race.'" *Policy Studies Journal* 31, no. 1 (2003): 53–69.

Latham, Michael E. *Modernization as Ideology: American Social Science and "Nation-Building" in the Kennedy Era*. Chapel Hill: University of North Carolina Press, 2000.

Martin, Donald H. *Communication Satellites 1958–1992*. El Segundo, CA: Aerospace Corporation, 1991.

Morrison, Joan, and Robert M. Morrison. *From Camelot to Kent State: The Sixties Experience in the Words of Those Who Lived It*. New York: Times Books, 1987.

Murray, Charles. *Losing Ground: American Social Policy, 1950–1980*. New York: Basic, 1995.

Murray, Charles, and Catherine B. Cox. *Apollo: The Race to the Moon*. New York: Simon & Schuster, 1968.

Patterson, James T. *Grand Expectations: The United States, 1945–1974*. New York: Oxford University Press, 1996.

Pellegrino, Charles R., and Joshua Stoff. *Chariots for Apollo: The Untold Story behind the Race to the Moon*. New York: Atheneum, 1985.

Reavill, Gil. *Mafia Summit: J. Edgar Hoover, the Kennedy Brothers, and the Meeting That Unmasked the Mob*. New York: Dunne / St. Martin's, 2013.

Sayres, Sohnya, Anders Stephanson, Stanley Aronowitz, and Fredric Jameson, eds. *The '60s: Without Apology*. Minneapolis: University of Minnesota Press, 1984.

Schell, Jonathan. *The Time of Illusion*. New York: Knopf, 1976.

Thompson, Neal. *Light This Candle: The Life & Times of Alan Shepard—America's First Spaceman*. New York: Three Rivers Press, 2004.

Utley, Jonathan. *The Movement: A History of the American New Left*. New York: Dodd, Mead, 1974.

White, Theodore H. *America in Search of Itself: The Making of a President, 1956–1980*. New York: Harper & Row, 1982.

FOREIGN AFFAIRS

Cobbs Hoffman, Elizabeth. *All You Need Is Love: The Peace Corps and the Spirit of the 1960s*. Cambridge, MA: Harvard University Press, 1998.

Duncan, Jason K. *John F. Kennedy: The Spirit of Cold War Liberalism*. New York: Routledge, 2013.

Fischer, Fritz. *Making Them Like Us: Peace Corps Volunteers in the 1960s*. Washington, DC: Smithsonian, 2000.

Grasso, June. "The Politics of Food Aid: John F. Kennedy and Famine in China." *Diplomacy and Statecraft* 14, no. 4 (December 2003): 153–78.

Haefele, Mark. "John F. Kennedy, USIA, and World Public Opinion." *Diplomatic History* 25 (Winter 2001): 63–84.

Hybel, Alex Roberto. *U.S. Foreign Policy Decision-Making from Truman to Kennedy: Responses to International Challenges.* New York: Palgrave Macmillan, 2014.

Kunz, Diane, ed. *The Diplomacy of the Crucial Decade: American Foreign Relations during the 1960s.* New York: Columbia University Press, 1994.

Latell, Brian. *Castro's Secrets: The CIA and Cuba's Intelligence Machine.* New York: Palgrave Macmillan, 2012.

Matthias, Willard C. *America's Strategic Blunders: Intelligence Analysis and National Security Policy, 1936–1991.* University Park: Pennsylvania State University Press, 2001.

Moore, John Allpkin, Jr., and Jerry Pubantz. *To Create a New World? American Presidents and the United Nations.* New York: Lang, 1999.

Patterson, Thomas G. "Bearing the Burden: A Critical Look at JFK's Foreign Policy." *Virginia Quarterly Review* 54 (Spring 1978): 193–212.

———, ed. *Kennedy's Quest for Victory: American Foreign Policy, 1961–1963.* New York: Oxford University Press, 1989.

Rakove, Robert B. *Kennedy, Johnson, and the Nonaligned World.* Cambridge: Cambridge University Press, 2013.

Rice, Gerard. *The Bold Experiment: JFK's Peace Corps.* Notre Dame, IN: University of Notre Dame Press, 1985.

Sachs, Jeffrey. *To Move the World: JFK's Quest for Peace.* New York: Random House, 2013.

Walton, Richard J. *Cold War and Counter-Revolution: The Foreign Policy of John F. Kennedy.* New York: Viking, 1973.

Africa/Asia

Chang, Gordon H. *Friends and Enemies: The United States, China, and the Soviet Union, 1948 to 1972.* Stanford, CA: Stanford University Press, 1990.

Kusmitz, Leonard A. *Public Opinion and Foreign Policy: America's China Policy, 1949–1979.* Westport, CT: Greenwood, 1984.

Lefebvre, Jeffrey A. *Arms for the Horn: U.S. Policy in Ethiopia and Somalia, 1953–1991.* Pittsburgh, PA: University of Pittsburgh Press, 1993.

Maga, Timothy P. *John F. Kennedy and the New Pacific Community, 1961–1963.* New York: St. Martin's, 1990.

———. "The New Frontier vs. Guided Democracy: JFK, Sukarno, and Indonesia." *Presidential Studies Quarterly* 20 (Winter 1989): 1–22.

Mahoney, Richard D. *JFK: Ordeal in Africa.* New York: Oxford University Press, 1983.

Muehlenbeck, Philip E. *Betting on Africa: John F. Kennedy's Courting of African Nationalist Leaders.* New York: Oxford University Press, 2012.

Pant, Harsh V. *The U.S.-India Nuclear Pact: Policy, Process, and Great Power Politics.* New York: Oxford University Press, 2011.

Romano, Renee. "No Diplomatic Immunity: African Diplomats, the State Department, and Civil Rights, 1961–1964." *Journal of American History* 87 (September 2000): 546–79.

Tucker, Nancy Bernkopf. *China Confidential: American Diplomats and Sino-American Relations, 1945–1996.* New York: Columbia University Press, 2001.

Caribbean/Central and South America

Bissell, Richard M. *Reflections of a Cold Warrior: From Yalta to the Bay of Pigs.* New Haven, CT: Yale University Press, 1996.

Bonsal, Philip Wilson. *Cuba, Castro and the United States.* Pittsburgh, PA: University of Pittsburgh Press, 1971.

Higgins, Trumbull. *The Perfect Failure: Kennedy, Eisenhower, and the CIA at the Bay of Pigs.* New York: Norton, 1987.

Kornbluh, Peter, ed. *Bay of Pigs Declassified: The Secret CIA Report on the Invasion of Cuba.* New York: New Press, 1998.

Lynch, Grayston L. *Decision for Disaster: Betrayal at the Bay of Pigs.* Washington, DC: Potomac, 2000.

Martz, John D. *United States Policy in Latin America: A Quarter Century of Crisis and Challenge, 1961–1986.* Lincoln: University of Nebraska Press, 1988.

Perez, Louis A., Jr. *Cuba and the United States: Ties of Singular Intimacy.* Athens: University of Georgia Press, 1990.

Rodriguez, Juan Carlos. *The Bay of Pigs and the CIA: Cuban Secret Files on the 1961 Invasion.* Melbourne, Australia: Ocean Press, 1999.

Rogers, W. D. *The Twilight Struggle: The Alliance for Progress and the Politics of Development in Latin America.* New York: Random House, 1967.

Scheman, L. Ronald, ed. *The Alliance for Progress: A Retrospective.* New York: Praeger, 1988.

Smith, Tony. "The Alliance for Progress: The 1960s." In *Exporting Democracy: The United States and Latin America,* edited by Abraham F. Lowenthal. Baltimore, MD: Johns Hopkins University Press, 1991.

Wyden, Peter. *The Bay of Pigs: The Untold Story.* New York: Simon & Schuster, 1979.

Europe

Brinkley, Douglas, and Richard T. Griffiths, eds. *John F. Kennedy and Europe.* Baton Rouge: Louisiana State University Press, 1999.

Burr, William. "New Sources on the Berlin Crisis, 1958–1962." *Cold War International History Project Bulletin* 2 (Fall 1992): 21–24, 32.

Gavin, Francis J. "The Gold Battles within the Cold War: American Monetary Policy and the Defense of Europe, 1960–1963." *Diplomatic History* 26 (Winter 2002): 61–94.

Hofmann, Arne. "Small Steps towards New Frontiers? Ideas, Concepts and the Emergence of a Détente Strategy in the Thinking of Willy Brandt and John F. Kennedy." *Historical Research* 79, no. 205 (August 2006): 429–49.

Mackby, Jenifer, and Walter B. Slocombe. "Germany: The Model Case, a Historical Imperative." In *The Nuclear Tipping Point: Why States Reconsider Their Nuclear Choices,* edited by Kurt M. Campbell, Robert J. Einhorn, and Mitchell B. Reiss, 175–217. Washington, DC: Brookings, 2004.

Mayer, Frank A. "Adenauer and Kennedy: An Era of Distrust in German-American Relations?" *German Studies Review* 17, no. 1 (February 1994): 83–104.

Morgan, Roger. *The United States and West Germany, 1945–1973: A Study in Alliance Politics.* London: Oxford University Press, 1974.

Schick, Jack M. *The Berlin Crisis, 1958–1962.* Philadelphia: University of Pennsylvania Press, 1971.

Smith, Jean Edward. *Lucius D. Clay: An American Life.* New York: Holt, 1990.

Middle East

Bass, Warren. *Support Any Friend: Kennedy's Middle East and the Making of the U.S.-Israel Alliance.* New York: Oxford University Press, 2003.

Bickerton, Ian J. "Kennedy, the Jewish Community and Israel." In *John F. Kennedy: Person, Policy, Presidency,* edited by J. Richard Snyder. Wilmington, DE: Scholarly Resources, 1988.

Brands, H. W. *Into the Labyrinth: The United States and the Middle East, 1945–1993.* New York: McGraw-Hill, 1994.

Crosbie, Sylvia K. *A Tacit Alliance: France and Israel from Suez to the Six Day War.* Princeton, NJ: Princeton University Press, 1974.

Druks, Herbert. *The Uncertain Friendship: The U.S. and Israel from Roosevelt to Kennedy.* Contributions to the Study of World History 80. Westport, CT: Greenwood, 2001.

Gazit, Mordechai. *President Kennedy's Policy toward the Arab States and Israel.* Tel Aviv: Shiloah Center for Middle Eastern and African Studies, Tel Aviv University, 1983.

Gerges, Fawaz A. *Superpowers and the Middle East: Regional and International Politics, 1955–1967.* Boulder, CO: Westview, 1994.

Glassman, John D. *Arms for the Arabs: The Soviet Union and War in the Middle East.* Baltimore, MD: Johns Hopkins University Press, 1975.

Lendowsky, George. *American Presidents and the Middle East.* Durham, NC: Duke University Press, 1990.

Southeast Asia

Fifield, Russell H. *Americans in Southeast Asia: The Roots of Commitment*. New York: Crowell, 1973.

Garrett, Banning. *The China Card and Its Origins: U.S. Bureaucratic Politics and the Strategic Triangle*. Berkeley: University of California Press, 1991.

Kail, E. M. "The Domino Principle." In *What Washington Said: Administration Rhetoric and the Vietnam War, 1949–1969*, 84–95. New York: Harper & Row, 1973.

Levine, Alan J. *The United States and the Struggle for Southeast Asia, 1945–1975*. Westport, CT: Praeger, 1995.

McCoy, Alfred W., with Cathleen Reed and Leonard Adams III. *The Politics of Heroin in Southeast Asia*. New York: Harper & Row, 1972.

McGlinchey, Stephen Thomas. *U.S. Arms Policies towards the Shah's Iran*. Abingdon, Oxfordshire: Routledge, 2014.

McMahon, Robert. *The Limits of Empire: The United States and Southeast Asia since World War II*. New York: Columbia University Press, 1999.

Rostow, W. W. *The United States and the Regional Organization of Asia and the Pacific, 1965–1985*. Austin: University of Texas Press, 1986.

Roth, David F. "Political Changes in Asia after Vietnam: Some Thoughts and Alternatives to Dominoes." *Asia Quarterly* 1 (1977): 3–16.

Rust, William J. *So Much to Lose: John F. Kennedy and American Policy in Laos*. Lexington: University Press of Kentucky, 2014.

Silverman, Jerry Mark. "The Domino Theory: Alternatives to a Self-Fulfilling Prophecy." *Asian Survey* 15, no. 11 (1975): 915–39.

The Cold War

Beschloss, Michael R. *The Crisis Years: Kennedy and Khrushchev, 1960–1963*. New York: HarperCollins, 1991.

Bowie, Robert R., and Richard H. Immerman. *Waging Peace: How Eisenhower Shaped an Enduring Cold War Strategy*. New York: Oxford University Press, 1998.

Boyle, Peter G. *American-Soviet Relations: From the Russian Revolution to the Fall of Communism*. New York: Routledge, 1993.

Brands, H. W. *The Devil We Knew: Americans and the Cold War*. New York: Oxford University Press, 1993.

Caldwell, Dan. *American-Soviet Relations: From 1947 to the Nixon-Kissinger Grand Design*. Westport, CT: Greenwood, 1981.

Chang, Gordon H. *Friends and Enemies: The United States, China and the Soviet Union, 1948–1972*. Stanford, CA: Stanford University Press, 1990.

Cohen, Warren I. *America in the Age of Soviet Power, 1945–1991*. Vol. 4 of *The Cambridge History of American Foreign Relations*, edited by Warren I. Cohen. New York: Cambridge University Press, 1993.

Cohen, Warren I., and Nancy Bernkopf Tucker, eds. *Lyndon Johnson Confronts the World: American Foreign Policy, 1963–1968*. New York: Cambridge University Press, 1994.

Dubziak, Mary L. *Cold War Civil Rights: Race and Image of American Diplomacy*. Princeton, NJ: Princeton University Press, 2000.

Freedman, Lawrence. *Kennedy's Wars: Berlin, Cuba, Laos and Vietnam*. New York: Oxford University Press, 2000.

Gaddis, John Lewis. *The Long Peace: Inquiries into the History of the Cold War*. New York: Oxford University Press, 1987.

Gorodetsky, Gabriel, ed. *Soviet Foreign Policy, 1917–1991: A Retrospective*. Portland, OR: Cass, 1994.

Kaplan, Lawrence S. *NATO and the United States: The Enduring Alliance*. Updated ed. New York: Twayne, 1994.

LaFeber, Walter. *America, Russia, and the Cold War, 1945–1996*. 8th ed. New York: McGraw-Hill, 1997.

Larson, Deborah Welch. *Anatomy of Mistrust: U.S.-Soviet Relations during the Cold War*. Ithaca, NY: Cornell University Press, 1997.

Lerner, Mitchell B. *The Pueblo Incident: A Spy Ship and the Failure of American Foreign Policy*. Lawrence: University Press of Kansas, 2002.

MacDonald, J. Fred. *Television and the Red Menace: The Video Road to Vietnam*. New York: Praeger, 1985.

Paterson, Thomas B., ed. *Kennedy's Quest for Victory: American Foreign Policy, 1961–1963*. New York: Oxford University Press, 1989.

Sakwa, Richard. *The Rise and Fall of the Soviet Union, 1917–1991*. New York: Routledge, 1999.

See, J. "An Uneasy Truce: John F. Kennedy and Soviet-American Détente, 1963." *Cold War History* 2, no. 2 (January 2002): 161–94.

Siracusa, Joseph M., and David G. Coleman. *Depression to Cold War: A History of America from Depression to Cold War*. Westport, CT: Praeger, 2002.

Walton, Richard J. *Cold War and Counter-Revolution: The Foreign Policy of John F. Kennedy*. New York: Viking, 1972.

Weihmiller, Gordon R. *U.S.-Soviet Summits: An Account of East-West Diplomacy at the Top, 1955–1985*. Lanham, MD: University Press of America, 1986.

JUDICIAL SYSTEM

Belknap, Michal R. *The Supreme Court under Earl Warren, 1953–1969*. Columbia: University of South Carolina Press, 2004.

Cox, Archibald. *The Warren Court: Constitutional Decision as an Instrument of Reform*. Cambridge, MA: Harvard University Press, 1968.

Cray, Ed. *Chief Justice: A Biography of Earl Warren*. New York: Simon & Schuster, 1997.

Newton, Jim. *Justice for All: Earl Warren and the Nation He Made*. New York: Riverhead, 2006.

Powe, Lucas A., Jr. *The Warren Court and American Politics*. Cambridge, MA: Harvard University Press, 2000.

Schwartz, Bernard, ed. *The Warren Court: A Retrospective*. New York: Oxford University Press, 1996.

Schwartz, Bernard, with Stephan Lesher. *Inside the Warren Court*. Garden City, NY: Doubleday, 1983.

Urofsky, Melvin I. *The Warren Court: Justices, Rulings, and Legacy*. Santa Barbara, CA: ABC-CLIO, 2001.

Warren, Earl. *The Memoirs of Earl Warren*. Edited by Jon Wiener. Garden City, NY: Doubleday, 1977.

LIMITED NUCLEAR TEST BAN

Badash, Lawrence. *Scientists and the Development of Nuclear Weapons: From Fission to the Limited Test Ban Treaty, 1939–1963*. Atlantic Highlands, NJ: Humanities Press, 1995.

Divine, Robert A. *Blowing on the Wind: The Nuclear Test Ban Debate, 1954–1960*. New York: Oxford University Press, 1978.

Greene, Benjamin. *Eisenhower, Science Advice, and the Nuclear Test Ban Debate, 1945–1963*. Stanford, CA: Stanford University Press, 2007.

Hacker, Barton C. *Elements of Controversy: The Atomic Energy Commission and Radiation Safety in Nuclear Weapons Testing, 1947–1974*. Berkeley: University of California Press, 1994.

Jacobson, Harold, and Eric Stein. *Diplomats, Scientists and Politicians: The United States and the Test Ban Negotiations*. Ann Arbor: University of Michigan Press, 1966.

Jönsson, Christer. *Soviet Bargaining Behavior: The Nuclear Test Ban*. New York: Columbia University Press, 1979.

Kleidman, Robert. *Organizing for Peace: Neutrality, the Test Ban, and the Freeze*. Syracuse, NY: Syracuse University Press, 1993.

Miller, Richard L. *Under the Cloud: The Decades of Nuclear Testing*. New York: Free Press, 1986.

Oliver, Kendrick. *Kennedy, Macmillan, and the Nuclear Test-Ban Debate, 1961–63*. New York: St. Martin's, 1998.

Rubinson, Paul. "'Crucified on a Cross of Atoms': Scientists, Politics, and the Test Ban Treaty." *Diplomatic History* 35 (April 2011): 283–319.

Seaborg, Glenn T. *Kennedy, Khrushchev and the Test Ban*. Berkeley: University of California Press, 1981.

Van Cleave, William R., and S. T. Cohen. *Nuclear Weapons, Policies, and the Test Ban Issues*. New York: Praeger, 1987.

Wenger, Andreas, and Marcel Gerber. "John F. Kennedy and the Limited Test Ban Treaty: A Case Study of Presidential Leadership." *Presidential Studies Quarterly* 29, no. 2 (1999): 460–87.

MEXICAN AMERICANS

Acuña, Rodolfo F. *Occupied America: A History of Chicanos*. 4th ed. New York: Longman, 2000.

Banfield, Edward C. *Big City Politics: A Comparative Guide to the Political Systems of Atlanta, Boston, Detroit, El Paso, Los Angeles, Miami, Philadelphia, St. Louis, Seattle*. New York: Random House, 1965.

Browning, Rufus P., Dale Rogers Marshall, and David H. Tabb. *Protest Is Not Enough: The Struggle of Blacks and Hispanics for Equity in Urban Politics*. Berkeley: University of California Press, 1984.

Castro, Tony. *Chicano Power: The Emergence of Mexican American America*. New York: Saturday Review Press / Dutton, 1974.

de la Isla, José. *The Rise of Hispanic Political Power*. Los Angeles: Archer, 2003.

DeSipio, Louis. *Counting on the Latino Vote: Latinos as a New Electorate*. Charlottesville: University Press of Virginia, 1996.

Dolan, Jay P., and Gilberto M. Hinojosa. *Mexican Americans and the Catholic Church, 1900–1965*. Notre Dame, IN: University of Notre Dame Press, 1994.

Feriss, Susan, and Richard Sandoval. *The Fight in the Fields: César Chávez and the Farmworkers Movement*. San Diego, CA: Harcourt Brace, 1997.

Galarza, Ernesto. *Merchants of Labor: The Mexican Bracero Story*. Santa Barbara, CA: McNally & Loftin, 1964.

Garcia, Ignacio M. *Chicanismo: The Forging of a Militant Ethos among Mexican Americans*. Tucson: University of Arizona Press, 1998.

———. *Viva Kennedy: Mexican Americans in Search of Camelot*. College Station: Texas A&M University Press, 2000.

Garcia, Mario T. *Memories of Chicano History: The Life and Narrative of Bert Corona*. Berkeley: University of California Press, 1984.

Gómez-Quiñones, Juan. *Chicano Politics: Reality & Promise, 1940–1990*. Albuquerque: University of New Mexico Press, 1990.

Gutiérrez, David G. *Walls and Mirrors: Mexican Americans, Mexican Immigrants, and the Politics of Ethnicity*. Berkeley: University of California Press, 1995.

Guzman, Ralph C. *The Political Socialization of the Mexican American People*. New York: Arno Press, 1976.

Kaplowitz, Craig Allan. *LULAC: Mexican Americans and National Policy*. College Station: Texas A&M University Press, 2005.

Levy, Jacques. *Cesar Chavez: Autobiography of La Causa*. New York: Norton, 1975.

Levy, Mark R., and Michael S. Kramer. *The Ethnic Factor: How Minorities Decide Elections*. New York: Simon & Schuster, 1973.

Meier, Matt S., and Feliciano Rivera. *The Chicanos: A History of Mexican-Americans*. New York: Hill & Wang, 1972.

Meister, Dick, and Anne Loftis. *A Long Time Coming: The Struggle to Unionize America's Farm Workers*. New York: Macmillan, 1977.

Ramos, Henry A. J. *The American GI Forum: In Pursuit of the Dream, 1948–1983*. Houston, TX: Arte Público Press, 1998.

Ross, Fred. *Conquering Goliath: Cesar Chavez at the Beginning*. Keene, CA: El Taller Grafico Press, 1989.

Vargas, Zaragosa. *Labor Rights Are Civil Rights: Mexican American Workers in Twentieth-Century America*. Berkeley: University of California Press, 2005.

MILITARY AFFAIRS

Adams, Benson D. *Ballistic Missile Defense*. New York: American Elsevier, 1971.

Aldridge, Robert C. *The Counterforce Syndrome: A Guide to U.S. Nuclear Weapons and Strategic Doctrine*. Rev. ed. Washington, DC: Institute for Policy Studies, 1978.

Aliano, Richard. *American Defense Policy from Eisenhower to Kennedy: The Politics*

of Changing Military Requirements, 1957–1961. Athens: Ohio University Press, 1975.

Baucom, Donald R. The Origins of SDI, 1944–1983. Lawrence: University Press of Kansas, 1992.

Bundy, McGeorge. Danger and Survival: Choices about the Bomb in the First Fifty Years. New York: Random House, 1988.

Chang, Gordon H. "JFK, China, and the Bomb." Journal of American History 74 (March 1988): 1287–1310.

Chayes, Abram, and Jerome B. Wiesner, eds. ABM. New York: Harper & Row, 1969.

Duffield, John S. "The Soviet Military Threat to Western Europe: US Estimates in the 1950s and 1960s." Journal of Strategic Studies 15 (June 1992): 208–27.

Dyson, Freeman. Weapons and Hope. New York: Harper Colophon, 1984.

Gaddis, John Lewis, Philip Gordon, Ernest May, and Jonathan Rosenberg, eds. Cold War Statesman Confront the Bomb: Nuclear Diplomacy since 1945. New York: Oxford University Press, 1999.

Gagliardi, Robert M. Satellite Communications. New York: Van Nostrand Reinhold, 1991.

Garthoff, Raymond L. Deterrence and the Revolution in Soviet Military Doctrine. Washington, DC: Brookings, 1990.

Gavin, Francis J. "The Myth of Flexible Response: United States Strategy in Europe during the 1960s." International History Review 23 (December 2001): 847–75.

Jayne, Edward R. The ABM Debate: Strategic Defense and National Security. Cambridge, MA: MIT, Center for Strategic Studies, 1969.

Kaplan, Fred. The Wizards of Armageddon. Stanford, CA: Stanford University Press, 1983.

Lens, Sidney. The Day before Doomsday: An Anatomy of the Nuclear Arms Race. Boston: Beacon, 1977.

Martin, Donald H. Communications Satellites, 1958–1992. El Segundo, CA: Aerospace Corporation, 1991.

McNamara, Robert. Blundering into Disaster: Surviving the First Century of the Nuclear Age. New York: Pantheon, 1986.

Moulton, Harland B. From Superiority to Parity: The United States and the Strategic Arms Race, 1961–1971. Westport, CT: Greenwood, 1973.

Oakes, Guy. The Imaginary War: Civil Defense and American Cold War Culture. New York: Oxford University Press, 1994.

Preble, Christopher A. "Who Ever Believed in the 'Missile Gap'? John F. Kennedy and the Politics of National Security." Presidential Studies Quarterly 33, no. 4 (2003): 803–26.

Siracusa, Joseph, and David Colman. Real-World Nuclear Deterrence: The Making of International Strategy. Westfield, CT: Praeger, 2006.

Twigge, Stephen, and Len Scott. Planning Armageddon: Britain, the United States and the Command of Western Nuclear Forces, 1945–1964. Amsterdam: Harwood, 2000.

Wenger, Andreas. Living with Peril: Eisenhower, Kennedy and Nuclear Weapons. Lanham, MD: Rowman & Littlefield, 1997.

York, Herbert F. Race to Oblivion: A Participant's View of the Arms Race. New York: Simon & Schuster, 1970.

Zaloga, Stephen J. Target America: The Soviet Union and the Strategic Arms Race, 1945–1964. Novato, CA: Presidio, 1993.

——. The Kremlin's Nuclear Sword: The Rise and Fall of Russia's Strategic Nuclear Forces, 1945–2000. Washington, DC: Smithsonian, 2002.

Zuckerman, Solly. Nuclear Illusion and Reality. New York: Viking, 1982.

NEW FRONTIER

Burstein, Paul. Discrimination, Jobs and Politics: The Struggle for Equal Employment Opportunity in the United States since the New Deal. Chicago: University of Chicago Press, 1985.

Chay, Kenneth Y., and Michael Greenstone. "The Convergence in Black-White Infant Mortality Rates during the 1960s." American Economic Review 90, no. 2 (May 2000): 326–32.

Collins, William J. "The Political Economy of State-Level Fair Employment Laws, 1940–

1964." *Explorations in Economic History* 40 (January 2003): 24–51.

Graham, Hugh Davis. *The Uncertain Triumph: Federal Education Policy in the Kennedy and Johnson Years.* Chapel Hill: University of North Carolina Press, 1984.

Kamin, Ben. *Dangerous Friendship: Stanley Levison, Martin Luther King Jr., and the Kennedy Brothers.* East Lansing: Michigan State University Press, 2014.

Matusow, Allen J. *The Unraveling of America: A History of Liberalism in the 1960s.* New York: Harper & Row, 1984.

Sandford, Christopher. *Harold and Jack: The Remarkable Friendship of Prime Minister Macmillan and President Kennedy.* Washington, DC: National Park Service, U.S. Department of the Interior, 2007.

Spring, Joel. *Conflicts of Interests: The Politics of American Education.* New York: Longman, 1993.

Unger, Irwin. *The Best of Intentions: The Triumphs and Failures of the Great Society under Kennedy, Johnson, and Nixon.* New York: Doubleday, 1996.

White, Mark J., ed. *Kennedy: The New Frontier Revisited.* New York: Palgrave Macmillan, 1998.

POLITICS

Bacciocio, Edward J., Jr. *The New Left in America: Reform to Revolution, 1950–1970.* Stanford, CA: Stanford University Press, 1974.

Breines, Wini. *Community and Organization in the New Left, 1962–1968: The Great Refusal.* New York: Praeger, 1982.

Druckman, James N. "The Power of Television Images: The First Kennedy-Nixon Debate Revisited." *Journal of Politics* 65 (May 2003): 559–71.

Gillon, Steven M. *Politics and Vision: The ADA and American Liberalism, 1947–1985.* New York: Oxford University Press, 1987.

Hulsey, Byron C. "'He Is My President': Everett Dirksen, John Kennedy, and the Politics of Consensus." *Journal of Illinois History* 2 (Autumn 1999): 183–204.

Isserman, Maurice. *If I Had a Hammer: The Death of the Old Left and the Birth of the New Left.* Urbana: University of Illinois Press, 1993.

Isserman, Maurice, and Michael Kazin. *America Divided: The Civil War of the 1960s.* New York: Oxford University Press, 2000.

Jacobs, Paul, and Saul Landau, eds. *The New Radicals: A Report with Documents.* New York: Random House, 1966.

Katz, Milton S. *Ban the Bomb: A History of SANE, the Committee for a Sane Nuclear Policy, 1957–1985.* Westport, CT: Greenwood, 1986.

Kessler, Lauren. *After All These Years: '60s Ideals in a Different World.* New York: Thunder's Mouth Press, 1990.

Langston, Thomas S. *Ideologues and Presidents.* New Brunswick, NJ: Transaction, 2014.

Mendel-Reyes, Meta. *Reclaiming Democracy: The Sixties in Politics and Memory.* New York: Routledge, 1996.

Miller, Jim. *Democracy Is in the Streets: From Port Huron to the Siege of Chicago.* New York: Simon & Schuster, 1970.

Myers, R. David, ed. *Toward a History of the New Left: Essays from within the Movement.* Brooklyn, NY: Carlson, 1990

Pearson, Drew. *The President.* Garden City, NY: Doubleday, 1970.

Sale, Kirkpatrick. *SDS.* New York: Random House, 1973.

Whalen, Jack, and Richard Flacks. *Beyond the Barricades: The Sixties Generation Grows Up.* Philadelphia, PA: Temple University Press, 1989.

SPORTS

Arlott, John, ed. *The Oxford Companion to Sports and Games.* London: Oxford University Press, 1975.

Baker, William J., and John M. Carroll, eds. *Sports in Modern America.* St. Louis, MO: River City, 1981.

Feinstein, John, and Red Auerbach. *Let Me Tell You a Story: A Lifetime in the Game.* Boston: Little, Brown, 2004.

Guttmann, Allen. *From Ritual to Record: The Nature of Modern Sports.* New York: Columbia University Press, 1978.

——. *A Whole New Ballgame: An Interpretation of American Sports.* Chapel Hill: University of North Carolina Press, 1988.

Hickok, Ralph. *The Encyclopedia of North American Sports History.* 2nd ed. New York: Facts on File, 2002.

Krzyewski, Mike, and Donald T. Phillips. *Leading with the Heart: Coach K's Successful Strategies for Basketball, Business and Life.* New York: Warner, 2000.

Maraniss, David. *When Pride Still Mattered: A Life of Vince Lombardi.* New York: Simon & Schuster, 1999.

Riley, Pat. *The Winner Within: A Life Plan for Team Players.* East Rutherford, NJ: Putnam, 1993.

Will, George F. *Men at Work: The Craft of Baseball.* New York: Macmillan, 1990.

VIETNAM WAR

Adamson, Michael R. "Ambassadorial Roles and Foreign Policy: Elbridge Durbrow, Frederick Nolting, and the U.S. Commitment to Diem's Vietnam, 1957–61." *Presidential Studies Quarterly* 32 (June 2002): 229–55.

Anderson, David L., ed. *The Columbia History of the Vietnam War.* New York: Columbia University Press, 2011.

Barclay, Glen St. John. *A Very Small Insurance Policy: The Politics of Australian Involvement in Vietnam, 1954–1967.* St. Lucia, Australia: University of Queensland Press, 1988.

Berman, Larry. *Planning a Tragedy: The Americanization of the War in Vietnam.* New York: Norton, 1983.

Berman, William C. *William Fulbright and the Vietnam War: The Dissent of a Political Realist.* Kent, OH: Kent State University Press, 1988.

Bird, Kai. *The Color of Truth: McGeorge Bundy and William Bundy: Brothers in Arms.* New York: Simon & Schuster, 1998.

Blair, Anne E. *Lodge in Vietnam: A Patriot Abroad.* New Haven, CT: Yale University Press, 1995.

Blang, Eugenie M. *Allies at Odds: America, Europe, and Vietnam, 1961–1968.* Lanham, MD: Rowman & Littlefield, 2011.

Brown, Eugene. *J. William Fulbright: Advice and Dissent.* Iowa City: University of Iowa Press, 1985.

Combs, Arthur. "The Path Not Taken: British Alternatives to U.S. Policy in Vietnam, 1954–1956." *Diplomatic History* 19, no. 1 (1995): 33–57.

Dittmar, Linda, and Gene Michaud, eds. *From Hanoi to Hollywood: The Vietnam War in American Film.* New Brunswick, NJ: Rutgers University Press, 1990.

Duiker, William J. *U.S. Containment Policy and the Conflict in Indochina.* Stanford, CA: Stanford University Press, 1994.

Dumbrell, John. *Rethinking the Vietnam War.* New York: Palgrave Macmillan, 2012.

Franklin, H. Bruce, ed. *The Vietnam War in American Stories, Songs, and Poems.* Boston: Bedford, 1996.

Fulbright, J. William. *The Arrogance of Power.* New York: Random House, 1967.

——, ed. *The Vietnam Hearings.* New York: Random House / Vintage, 1966.

Galloway, John. *The Gulf of Tonkin Resolution.* Rutherford, NJ: Fairleigh Dickinson University Press, 1970.

Gardner, Lloyd C., and Ted Gittinger, eds. *Vietnam: The Early Decisions.* Austin: University of Texas Press, 1997.

Gelb, Leslie H., and Richard K. Betts. *The Irony of Vietnam: The System Worked.* Washington, DC: Brookings, 1979.

Gibson, James William. *The Perfect War: Techno-War in Vietnam.* New York: Atlantic Monthly, 1987.

Guan, Ang Cheng. "The Vietnam War, 1962–64: The Vietnamese Communist Perspective." *Journal of Contemporary History* (London) 35 (October 2000): 601–18.

Halberstam, David. *The Best and the Brightest.* New York: Random House, 1972.

Herring, George C. *America's Longest War: The United States and Vietnam, 1950–1975.* 3rd ed. New York: Wiley, 1996.

Jacobs, Seth. *America's Miracle Man in Vietnam: Ngo Dinh Diem, Religion, Race, and*

U.S. Intervention in Southeast Asia. Durham, NC: Duke University Press, 2004.

Jones, Matthew. "U.S. Relations with Indonesia, the Kennedy-Johnson Transition, and the Vietnam Connection, 1963–1965." *Diplomatic History* 26, no. 2 (Spring 2002): 249–81.

Kaiser, David. *American Tragedy: Kennedy, Johnson and the Origins of the Vietnam War.* Cambridge, MA: Harvard University Press, 2000.

Langguth, A. J. *Our Vietnam: The War, 1954–1975.* New York: Simon & Schuster, 2001.

Lewy, Guenter. *America in Vietnam.* New York: Oxford University Press, 1978.

Logevall, Fredrik. *Choosing War: The Lost Chance for Peace and the Escalation of War in Vietnam.* Berkeley: University of California Press, 1999.

———. "De Gaulle, Neutralization, and American Involvement in Vietnam, 1963–1964." *Pacific Historical Review* 41 (February 1992): 62–102.

Mangold, Tom, and John Penycate. *The Tunnels of Cu Chi: The Untold Story of Vietnam.* New York: Random House, 1985.

Matsuoka, Hiroshi. "Cold War Perspectives on U.S. Commitment in Vietnam." *Japanese Journal of American Studies* (Tokyo) 11 (2000): 49–69.

McNamara, Robert S., James G. Blight, and Robert K. Brigham. *Argument without End: In Search of Answers to the Vietnam Tragedy.* New York: PublicAffairs, 2000.

McNamara, Robert S., with Brian Van De-Mark. *In Retrospect: The Tragedy and Lessons of Vietnam.* New York: Times Books, 1995.

Newman, John M. *JFK and Vietnam: Deception, Intrigue and the Struggle for Power.* New York: Warner, 1992.

Palmer, Gregory. *The McNamara Strategy and the Vietnam War: Program Budgeting in the Pentagon, 1960–1968.* Westport, CT: Greenwood, 1978.

Preston, Andrew. "Balancing War and Peace: Canadian Foreign Policy and the Vietnam War, 1961–1965." *Diplomatic History* 27, no. 1 (January 2003): 73–112.

Qiang Zhai. *China and the Vietnam Wars, 1950–1975.* Chapel Hill: University of North Carolina Press, 2000.

Rust, William J. *Kennedy in Vietnam: American Vietnam Policy, 1960–63.* New York: Scribner, 1985.

Saunders, Elizabeth Nathan. *Leaders at War: How Presidents Shape Military Interventions.* Ithaca, NY: Cornell University Press, 2011.

Shultz, Richard H., Jr. *The Secret War against Hanoi: Kennedy's and Johnson's Use of Spies, Saboteurs, and Covert Warriors in North Vietnam.* New York: HarperCollins, 1999.

United States Department of Defense. *The Pentagon Papers: The Defense Department History of United States Decision Making on Vietnam; the Senator Gravel Edition.* 5 vols. Boston: Beacon, 1971–1972.

Warner, Geoffrey. "The United States and Vietnam: From Kennedy to Johnson." *International Affairs* 73 (April 1997): 333–49.

Young, Marilyn. *The Vietnam Wars, 1945–1990.* New York: HarperCollins, 1991.

WOMEN

Brauer, Carl M. "Women Activists, Southern Conservatives, and the Prohibition of Sex Discrimination in Title VII of the 1964 Civil Rights Act." *Journal of Southern History* 49, no. 1 (February 1983): 37–56.

Davis, F. *Moving the Mountain: The Women's Movement in America since 1960.* Chicago: University of Illinois Press, 1999.

Echols, Alice. *Daring to Be Bad: Radical Feminism in America, 1967–1975.* Minneapolis: University of Minnesota Press, 1989.

Evans, Sara. *Personal Politics: The Roots of Women's Liberation in the Movement and the New Left.* New York: Random House, 1979.

Freeman, Jo. "How 'Sex' Got into Title VII: Persistent Opportunism as a Maker of Public Policy." *Law and Inequality: A Journal of Theory and Practice* 9, no. 2 (March 1991): 163–84.

Gartner, Rosemary, and Candace Kruttschnitt. "A Brief History of Doing Time: The Cali-

fornia Institution for Women in the 1960s and the 1990s." *Law & Society Review* 38 (June 2004): 267–300.

Gould, Lewis L. *Lady Bird Johnson: Our Environmental First Lady.* Lawrence: University Press of Kansas, 1999.

Harrison, Cynthia. *On Account of Sex: The Politics of Women's Issues 1945–1968.* Berkeley: University of California Press, 1988.

Hartmann, Susan M. *From Margin to Mainstream: American Women and Politics since 1960.* New York: Knopf, 1989.

Martin, J. M. *The Presidency and Women: Promise, Performance, and Illusion.* College Station: Texas A&M University Press, 2003.

Parry, Janine A. "Putting Feminism to a Vote: The Washington State Women's Council, 1963–78." *Pacific Northwest Quarterly* 91 (Fall 2000): 171–82.

Peterson, Esther. *Restless: The Memoirs of Labor and Consumer Activist Esther Peterson.* Washington, DC: Caring Publishing, 1997.

Zolotow, Maurice. *Marilyn Monroe.* New York: Perennial Library, 1990.

REFERENCE WORKS

Brune, Lester H., comp. *America and the Indochina Wars, 1945–1990: A Bibliographical Guide.* Edited by Richard Dean Burns. Claremont, CA: Regina Books, 1992.

———. *Chronology of the Cold War, 1917–1992.* New York: Routledge, 2005.

Burns, Richard Dean, ed. *Encyclopedia of Arms Control and Disarmament.* 3 vols. New York: Scribner, 1992.

Burns, Richard Dean, and Joseph M. Siracusa. *A Global History of the Nuclear Arm Race: Weapons, Strategy, and Politics.* 2 vols. Santa Barbara, CA: Praeger, 2013.

DeConde, Alexander, Richard Dean Burns, and Fredrik Logevall, eds. *Encyclopedia of American Foreign Policy.* 2nd ed. 3 vols. New York: Scribner, 2002.

Fomerand, Jacques. *Historical Dictionary of the United Nations.* Lanham, MD: Scarecrow Press, 2007.

Garrett, Benjamin C., and John Hart. *Historical Dictionary of Nuclear, Biological and Chemical Warfare.* Lanham, MD: Scarecrow Press, 2007.

Hahn, Peter L. *Historical Dictionary of United States–Middle East Relations.* Lanham, MD: Scarecrow Press, 2007.

Janousek, Kelly S. *United States Supreme Court Decisions, 1778–1996.* Lanham, MD: Scarecrow Press, 2002.

Jessup, John E., and Louise B. Ketz, eds. *Encyclopedia of the American Military.* 3 vols. New York: Scribner, 1994.

John F. Kennedy Presidential Library and Museum. https://www.jfklibrary.org/.

Kaufman, Burton I., and Diane Kaufman. *Historical Dictionary of the Eisenhower Era.* Lanham, MD: Scarecrow Press, 2008.

Kumaraswamy, P. R. *Historical Dictionary of the Arab-Israeli Conflict.* Lanham, MD: Scarecrow Press, 2006.

Kutler, Stanley I., ed. *Encyclopedia of the Vietnam War.* New York: Scribner, 1996.

Larsen, Jeffrey A., and James M. Smith. *Historical Dictionary of Arms Control and Disarmament.* Lanham, MD: Scarecrow Press, 2005.

Moïse, Edwin E. *Historical Dictionary of the Vietnam War.* Lanham, MD: Scarecrow Press, 2002.

Olson, James S., ed. *Dictionary of the Vietnam War.* Westport, CT: Greenwood, 1988.

Pringle, Robert W. *Historical Dictionary of Russian and Soviet Intelligence.* Lanham, MD: Scarecrow Press, 2006.

Smith, Joseph. *Historical Dictionary of United States–Latin American Relations.* Lanham, MD: Scarecrow Press, 2006.

Smith, Joseph, and Simon Davis. *Historical Dictionary of the Cold War.* Lanham, MD: Scarecrow Press, 2000.

Sutter, Robert. *Historical Dictionary of United States–China Relations.* Lanham, MD: Scarecrow Press, 2005.

Van Sant, John, et al. *Historical Dictionary of United States–Japan Relations.* Lanham, MD: Scarecrow Press, 2007.

West, Nigel. *Historical Dictionary of Cold War Counterintelligence.* Lanham, MD: Scarecrow Press, 2007.

About the Author

Ian James Bickerton is an honorary associate professor and former member of the School of History at the University of New South Wales, Sydney, Australia. He received a BA (Honors) in 1961 from the University of Adelaide, an MA in 1965 from Kansas State University, and a PhD in 1974 from the Claremont Graduate School in California. He has authored and edited nine books and several in-depth articles covering United States diplomatic history, the Arab-Israeli conflict, and the futility of war. He is internationally known for his writings on the Arab-Israeli conflict, and his *History of the Arab-Israeli Conflict* (coauthored with Carla Klausner), widely regarded as the most balanced text on the subject, is now in its eighth edition. He has twice been a visiting fellow at the Oxford Centre for Hebrew and Jewish Studies in the United Kingdom and twice at the Johns Hopkins School of International Affairs in Washington, DC. Professor Bickerton is also frequently called upon as a commentator on the United States and the Middle East for the Australian media, including the Australian Broadcasting Commission (ABC).

SEARCH THOUSANDS OF BOOKS FROM LEADING PUBLISHERS

Safari® Bookshelf is a searchable electronic reference library for IT professionals that features more than 2,000 titles from technical publishers, including Cisco Press.

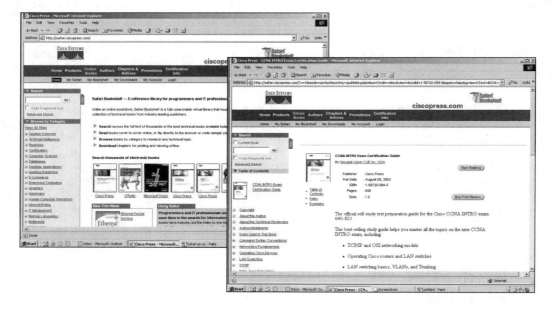

With Safari Bookshelf you can

- **Search** the full text of thousands of technical books, including more than 70 Cisco Press titles from authors such as Wendell Odom, Jeff Doyle, Bill Parkhurst, Sam Halabi, and Karl Solie.

- **Read** the books on My Bookshelf from cover to cover, or just flip to the information you need.

- **Browse** books by category to research any technical topic.

- **Download** chapters for printing and viewing offline.

With a customized library, you'll have access to your books when and where you need them—and all you need is a user name and password.

TRY SAFARI BOOKSHELF FREE FOR 14 DAYS!

You can sign up to get a 10-slot Bookshelf free for the first 14 days.
Visit **http://safari.ciscopress.com** to register.

THIS BOOK IS SAFARI ENABLED

INCLUDES FREE 45-DAY ACCESS TO THE ONLINE EDITION

The Safari® Enabled icon on the cover of your favorite technology book means the book is available through Safari Bookshelf. When you buy this book, you get free access to the online edition for 45 days.

Safari Bookshelf is an electronic reference library that lets you easily search thousands of technical books, find code samples, download chapters, and access technical information whenever and wherever you need it.

TO GAIN 45-DAY SAFARI ENABLED ACCESS TO THIS BOOK:

- Go to **http://www.ciscopress.com/safarienabled**
- Complete the brief registration form
- Enter the coupon code found in the front of this book before the "Contents at a Glance" page

If you have difficulty registering on Safari Bookshelf or accessing the online edition, please e-mail customer-service@safaribooksonline.com.

CISCO SYSTEMS

Cisco Press

SAVE UP TO 30%

Become a member and save at **ciscopress.com**!

Complete a **user profile** at ciscopress.com today to become a member and benefit from **discounts up to 30% on every purchase** at ciscopress.com, as well as a more customized user experience. Your membership will also allow you access to the entire Informit network of sites.

Don't forget to subscribe to the monthly Cisco Press newsletter to be the first to learn about new releases and special promotions. You can also sign up to get your first **30 days FREE on Safari Bookshelf** and preview Cisco Press content. Safari Bookshelf lets you access Cisco Press books online and build your own customized, searchable electronic reference library.

Visit **www.ciscopress.com/register** to sign up and start saving today!

The profile information we collect is used in aggregate to provide us with better insight into your technology interests and to create a better user experience for you. You must be logged into ciscopress.com to receive your discount. Discount is on Cisco Press products only; shipping and handling are not included.

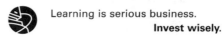

Learning is serious business.
Invest wisely.

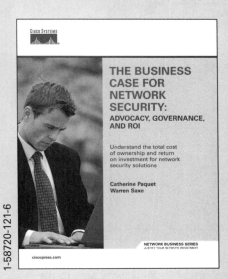

Cisco Press

Learning is serious business.

Invest wisely.